Encyclopedia of Community Planning and Environmental Management

Encyclopedia of
Community Planning
and
Environmental Management

Marilyn Spigel Schultz, AICP
Vivian Loeb Kasen, AICP

Illustrations by Diane Callahan Caro

66816

Facts On File Publications
New York, New York ● Bicester, England

Encyclopedia of Community Planning and Environmental Management

Copyright © 1984 by Facts On File, Inc.

Library of Congress Cataloging in Publication Data

Schultz, Marilyn Spigel.
  Encyclopedia of community planning and environmental management.

  Includes index.
  1. Land use—Planning—Dictionaries.   2. Environmental protection—Dictionaries.   3. Municipal engineering—Dictionaries.   4. Regional planning—Dictionaries.
I. Kasen, Vivian Loeb.   II. Title.
HD108.6.S38   307′.12′0321   82-7366
ISBN 0-87196-447-3   AACR2

Printed in the United States of America
10   9   8   7   6   5   4   3   2   1

To Stephen M. Schultz and Allison Rachel Schultz
Leonard Kasen, Raphael Jacob Kasen and Ella Loeb

Contents

Preface

Few fields encompass as many areas of concern as community planning and environmental management. Land use coordination and control, economic development, transportation, flood control, housing, air and water pollution and historic preservation are but a few of the important issues with which planners must be involved. At the same time, planning and environmental management are characterized by continual evolution. Research points the way to improved techniques and tools, legislation ends programs that have become important parts of planning practice and establishes new programs in their place, and our society changes, bringing about new needs and demanding new approaches.

The *Encyclopedia of Community Planning and Environmental Management* is our attempt to incorporate the diverse aspects of these complex fields into one easy-to-use, comprehensive and current desk-top reference volume. Among the topics related to community planning that are prominently featured are land use regulation, community facility planning, economic development, transportation planning, urban design, analytic techniques and tools, housing, social planning, historic preservation, and recreation and open space management. Environmental management topics that are featured include energy conservation, air and water quality management, solid waste management, land and soil management and flood control. Current practice and specific applications found in the United States, Canada and Europe are cited throughout the discussions of these issues.

Several aspects of the book are worthy of special attention. A descriptive entry is provided for important legislation enacted in the field, particularly if the legislation is of current relevance or played an important role in the development of planning practice. This enables the user to rapidly survey legislation relevant to a particular topic. Articles and legal citations for many significant court cases relevant to the history and development of planning are also included.

In addition, the encyclopedia contains articles describing federal agencies that have a relationship to community planning or environmental management. Similarly, there are entries found describing many of the membership and research organizations in these fields.

Many of the diverse terms and concepts used in or introduced by the 1980 census are included and described, so that the reader can use census material more easily and more knowledgeably. Finally, entries related to the history of planning and those individuals that influenced its development are

included. Illustrations, photographs and maps of key terms and concepts are placed throughout the book to aid the reader in gaining a clear understanding of the issues.

The *Encyclopedia of Community Planning and Environmental Management* contains more than 2,000 articles and 300,000 words on the many aspects of planning practice and environmental management in a convenient word-by-word alphabetical format, enabling a discrete topic to be found rapidly. In addition, cross-references will send the reader to selected entries that discuss that topic or related topics.

An index is also provided so that the reader may look up a subject and find a comprehensive list of the articles appearing in the *Encyclopedia* that discuss some aspect of the subject.

We intended the *Encyclopedia of Community Planning and Environmental Management* to be responsive to the needs of planners, professionals in related fields, government officials and staff, librarians and researchers, interested laymen and students. Because of the increasing specialization of planners in response to the breadth of the field, planning practitioners should find it especially useful when their work takes them into subject areas that they do not encounter on a daily basis. Similarly, professionals in related fields, such as architecture, engineering, law and real estate, should find it helpful to be able to quickly review a planning–related aspect of their work that they may not have previously encountered. Government officials at all levels can rapidly obtain background on the development and management of land and environmental resources by using this book as a reference source.

The layman often has need of planning and environmental information, as when he is named to a citizen board, wants to expand his home, is experiencing flooding or seeks historic designation for a building he owns. This book also attempts to respond to those needs and to provide the interested reader with sufficient background information to determine the necessary steps that should be taken. Reference librarians, researchers and students should find their work made easier by this book, as the *Encyclopedia of Community Planning and Environmental Management* specifically answers questions and addresses issues that could previously be answered only by consulting numerous reference sources.

For convenience and ease of international usage, metric equivalents are provided for measurements throughout the book.

Subject listings were selected for the *Encyclopedia* on the basis of their relevance to the current practice of community planning and environmental management, their importance to the broad development of these fields or their value in illustrating major issues.

We have made every effort to include all important topics and hope no significant omissions have been made. Similarly, great care has been exercised in the preparation of this manuscript to minimize the errors that may occur in books of this scope. We would, however, appreciate having inadvertent errors or omissions brought to our attention.

A number of products or services described in this book are trademarked. Whenever you see a product or service named, you should assume it is the trade name of a company.

Development and preparation of the *Encyclopedia* were made possible by the help of many other individuals. Gene R. Hawes and David M. Brownstone were both extremely generous with their time as well as unfailingly patient in answering questions and providing advice on the numerous aspects of researching and writing a reference work of this type. Thanks are also owed to the Hudson Group for its assistance.

Research and preparation of draft manuscript for selected entries was ably and carefully performed by Roy Bateman, AICP; Carol L. Bogin; Lisa Davis; Barry F. Hersh, AICP; Jerry Mulligan, AICP; Davida Scher; Stephen M. Schultz, Esq. and John A. Yoegel, AICP. Carol L. Bogin, Willa Kay Wiener Ehrlich, James Cropper and Stephen M. Schultz each generously reviewed certain entries and helped to verify their accuracy.

A number of photographs and illustrations were graciously provided by various governmental organizations and individuals. Their names appear adjacent to each illustration for which they are responsible. All other artwork consists of original illustrations prepared by Diane Callahan Caro.

Competent and cheerful typing of the final manuscript was performed primarily by Laurie Sterlacci and Ann Mancini. Lorraine Petro also provided able assistance in typing final manuscript for a number of articles.

Many government agencies, professional organizations, practicing planners and local libraries and librarians too numerous to list were extremely helpful and giving of their time. In particular, however, we should like to thank the staffs of the Westchester County Department of Planning and the American Planning Association as well as the librarians of the State University of New York College at Purchase, Ossining Public Library, Manhattan College Engineering Library and Yonkers Public Library (Broadway-Main branch).

Above all, we are indebted to our families for all the support and assistance they gave us during preparation of the book.

Marilyn Spigel Schultz, AICP
Vivian Loeb Kasen, AICP

A

Abandonment

1. The voluntary relinquishment of property or a right in property, with the intention by the former property owner of terminating his ownership. The legal consequence of an abandonment is the permanent loss of the property abandoned.

To constitute a legal abandonment of property, there must be a combination of two factors: (1) an intent to abandon the property and (2) some overt act or acts, or a failure to act when action is normally called for, that supports a conclusion that the owner no longer claims or retains any interest in the property abandoned. Since subjective intent is often unknowable except as manifested by objective acts, frequently the same overt acts or failure to act must also support a finding of intent.

Abandonment may differ from a surrender or forfeiture of property. Surrender of property or an interest in property often connotes an intent to convey the property or interest surrendered to another and may require the affirmative acceptance of the surrender by the other person. Forfeiture may involve a transfer of property or property rights against the wishes of the owner. For example, in the case of a lease of property, if the tenant abandons the property, he may remain liable to his landlord for his lease obligations, while if he surrenders his leasehold interest to the landlord and the landlord accepts the surrender, he may be excused from further performance under his lease. Finally, a failure by a tenant to perform his lease obligations may result in his forfeiture of his rights as a tenant.

2. Also used in connection with a property owner's right to the continued enjoyment of a nonconforming use. If an abandonment of the use is found, the right to resume the nonconforming use may be permanently lost.
See: ADVERSE POSSESSION; NONCONFORMING USE

Abercrombie, Sir Leslie Patrick (1879–1957)

A British architect and town planner who is most famous for the County of London Plan (1943) and for the Greater London Plan (1944), which were written to guide the post–World War II redevelopment of the area. In addition, his proposals for the creation of new towns on specific sites helped serve as a basis for Britain's New Towns Act of 1946. He was also responsible for the preparation of plans for many other regions and communities throughout the British Isles, including Dublin, Duncaster, Edinburgh and Plymouth, as well as abroad in Hong Kong and Cyprus.

A professor of civic design at Liverpool University from 1915 to 1935, Abercrombie was also author of *Town and Country Planning*. He received the gold medal of the Royal Institute of British Architects in 1948, the gold medal of the American Institute of Architects in 1949 and was knighted in 1946.
See: COUNTY OF LONDON PLAN; NEW TOWNS ACT, 1946

Abortive or Premature Subdivision

Subdivisions, generally speculative in nature, in which development has not occurred and for which there is no likely date on which development will begin. Abortive subdivisions are those that should not have been started because construction is unlikely to occur. Premature subdivisions are those in which development may still occur but that have been laid out far ahead of the actual development.

It is not uncommon for abortive or premature subdivisions to revert to public ownership as a result of nonpayment of taxes. This occurred extensively throughout Florida during the land development boom of the 1920s and during the Depression years. In abortive or premature subdivisions, it may also be difficult to reassemble the land for future development if some individual lots have been sold.
See: SUBDIVISION

Absentee Owner

An owner of real property (normally income-producing) who does not live at the premises. Often in such cases the property is managed by a real estate management company under a management agreement.

Absorption Rate

The rate at which it is possible to sell or lease a specific type of development, such as industrial space, housing or

office space. An estimate of this rate is often used as an aid in determining project feasibility and in securing financing.
See: MARKET DEMAND; MARKET STUDY

Abutment

1. A part of a structure that supports or buttresses the rest of the structure by directly receiving pressure or thrust, as in an arch or vault.

2. The supporting structure of a bridge that is adjacent to the land at either side of the body of water spanned by the bridge and that serves as a retaining wall for the earth as well as a support for the bridge. It is similar in function to a pier but must also resist the pressure of the earth behind it.
See: FOUNDATION; PIER; RETAINING WALL

Abutting Property

Property that is contiguous to another property along a common boundary line. The term may also be defined in certain zoning ordinances to include properties located on opposite sides of an alley.
See: ZONING

Accelerated Depreciation

The ability to depreciate the value of income-producing real property for federal tax purposes at a faster rate in the early years of its useful life rather than at a constant rate. This tax provision allows the owner to receive a more rapid return of his investment than does straight-line depreciation.

The purpose of this incentive is to stimulate new construction, encourage additions to the housing stock and preserve the existing supply of housing. Accelerated depreciation is also available for rehabilitation of certain historic buildings.

The type of property invested in and the specific program involved determine the type of accelerated depreciation available. Common methods for calculating accelerated depreciation include the declining-balance method (also known as the diminishing-balance method) and the sum-of-the-years'-digits method.
See: HISTORIC PRESERVATION TAX INCENTIVES; STRAIGHT- LINE DEPRECIATION

Accelerating Walkway

A pedestrian-assistance device that is capable of moving large numbers of people over short distances—e.g., up to 500 feet (152 meters). An accelerating walkway, or moving walkway, is a mechanical device that looks like a flat escalator or conveyor belt. It typically moves at more than twice the normal walking speed but slows at its entrance and exit points. Now used at some airports to carry passengers over long walking distances, it has application possibilities for all large complexes of buildings, where it can shorten the time necessary to traverse a given area and can also reduce congestion.
See: PEDESTRIANIZATION

Access

A means of entering or exiting a property. Zoning and subdivision regulations generally require a lot to directly abut a public street or highway or a private road constructed to specified public standards. This requirement not only ensures the ability of the property owner to make use of his property but provides for the ingress and egress of emergency vehicles, such as ambulances and fire trucks.

In the case of property abutting a limited-access highway, it is permissible for a government agency to deny access to abutting landowners in the interest of facilitating highway traffic flow. In such cases, a landowner may secure access to his property by means of another street or by an easement across land owned by others.
See: LANDLOCKED

Accessory Building

A detached building whose purpose is related to, but subordinate to, that of the principal building on a given parcel of land. Detached garages, tool sheds and barns are all examples of accessory buildings.
See: ACCESSORY USE; ZONING

Accessory Use

A land use whose purpose is related and incidental to the permitted principal use. An accessory use must in some way serve the principal use, and must usually be located on the same building lot. Exceptions are often made, however, so that necessary off-street parking may sometimes be located nearby rather than on the same lot.
See: ACCESSORY BUILDING; ZONING

Accident Rates

The calculation of the number of vehicular accidents that occur at particular locations. Records of accidents are maintained by most municipal and state law enforcement agencies and highway departments. Accident records and rates are a useful tool in analyzing and correcting hazardous road conditions or traffic situations.

Accretion

The process by which land area is slowly increased due to natural forces, such as the deposit of sediment by a stream or by wave action. When this occurs, the owner of the land fronting on the water, called the riparian or littoral owner, gains title to the added land.
See: AVULSION

Acid Rain

Precipitation that is made much more acidic than usual when water vapor in the atmosphere combines with sulfur oxides and nitrogen oxides to form sulfuric and nitric acids, which are carried to the Earth's surface. It is generally believed that most sulfur and nitrogen oxides are produced by coal-burning power plants, industry, smelters, home heating and automobile emissions, although some acidity derives from natural causes, such as lightning and volcanic eruptions.

The normal pH of rain is about 5.6 on a 0 to 14 scale on which the low numbers are very acidic, the high numbers very alkaline, and a pH of 7 is neutral. Recently, a federal Interagency Task Force on Acid Precipitation reported that typical precipitation in the northeastern United States and Canada was approximately 10 times more acidic than the norm of pH 5.6. Another study indicated that approximately 3,000 lakes and 25,000 miles of streams in the northeastern United States were acidic.

Acid rain has become a controversial topic for a number of reasons. One aspect of the controversy concerns the scope of effects it can cause. In Scandinavia, Canada and the northeastern United States, where it is prevalent, fish kills have taken place, and sometimes the entire fish populations of particular lakes or estuaries have been destroyed. Other problems that may be caused by acid rain include diminished crop productivity and timber yields, damage to buildings and structures made of stone or steel, and increased concentrations of trace metals in drinking water. It is not currently known to what extent, if any, acid rain can affect human health.

Another controversial aspect of acid rain concerns the point of origin of the pollutants that contribute to the formation of acid precipitation. Many of the northeastern states have charged the industrial Midwest with being responsible for much of their acid rain. Similarly, Canada asserts that the United States is responsible for causing much of its acid rain, while Sweden and Norway charge that Britain, France and West Germany have helped to cause their acid rain problems. A trend toward the use of much taller smokestacks than were used in the past can, with the aid of prevailing winds, help to transport pollutants, such as sulfur oxides, over long distances, lending support to these accusations.

The Interagency Task Force on Acid Precipitation was created by the Acid Precipitation Act of 1980 (Title VII of PL 96-294) to conduct research into the phenomenon of acid rain and its causes and effects. The task force is chaired by the heads of the Department of Agriculture, the Environmental Protection Agency and the National Oceanic and Atmospheric Administration and has representatives of a number of other federal agencies and offices.
See: AIR POLLUTION; WATER POLLUTION

Acre

A unit of land area equal to 43,560 square feet or 160 square rods. There are 640 acres to a square mile. The acre's metric equivalent is 0.405 hectares (4,047 square meters). The acre and fractions of an acre are frequently used as the basis for determining the minimum lot size of various residential zoning districts.
See: HECTARE

Activated Sludge Process

A widely used biological sewage treatment process, developed in England in 1914, in which the content of organic matter in sewage effluent (usually domestic) is reduced. The activated sludge process can remove 85 percent to 95 percent of the biochemical oxygen demand (BOD).

This technique duplicates natural processes of organic decomposition by using the bacteria present in sewage to feed on organic matter and produce more bacteria, but it takes place more rapidly than decomposition would occur in nature. The activated sludge process takes place while wastewater is continuously aerated and mixed in aeration tanks and then allowed to settle in sedimentation tanks. As the microorganisms grow in number, they become heavier and form flocs (masses), which then settle to the bottom of the tank. After sedimentation, the settled material, which is now referred to as sludge, is separated from the remaining liquid. Part of the sludge is disposed of, and part is recycled to the aeration tank so that the biological mass that has formed can be used as the organic matter that speeds the decomposition process.
See: AERATION; BIOCHEMICAL OXYGEN DEMAND (BOD); OXIDATION PROCESSES; SETTLING TANK; SEWAGE TREATMENT

Active Recreation

Recreational activities that require physical participation. Sports (such as baseball, tennis and golf) are typical of active recreation, although hobbies (such as woodworking and gardening) are also included in this category.

Active recreation often requires far more extensive facilities and equipment than does passive recreation, as well as sometimes requiring the participation of other people. In addition, administrative support and instruction are generally necessary for extensive and successful active recreation programs.

Planning for active recreation requires assessment of the use of existing facilities and of latent demand for more facilities or for new types of facilities. Because many forms of active recreation are also offered by commercial enterprises, the need for municipal involvement should also be studied.
See: COMMERCIAL INDOOR RECREATION FACILITIES; PASSIVE RECREATION; RECREATION FACILITIES

Active Solar Energy System

Active solar energy systems use solar collectors to gather solar energy. They then apply mechanical devices, such as pumps or fans, to circulate the air or fluid that has been heated by the sun and transfer it to a storage component or to the area where it will be used. Also known as an indirect solar energy system, this type of system may be used for space heating, hot water heating or space cooling.

The required collectors for an active solar energy system are most often located on the rooftop of a building but may also be placed on the building's wall, on the ground or on the roof of an accessory structure. In general, rooftop placement offers good access to sunlight and a favorable surface for mounting of the equipment, and also allows required ductwork or piping to be placed inside the building, where it will be less subject to heat loss. However, rooftop collectors can be highly visible, particularly when many solar collectors are necessary, as is often the case when they are being used for space heating in a cold climate. Pitched roofs that do not have a south-facing slope make it difficult to place a collector without significantly affecting building appearance, but when a roof is flat, it is usually a simple matter to mount the collectors in an unobtrusive manner.

See: DETACHED SOLAR COLLECTOR; PASSIVE SOLAR ENERGY SYSTEM; SOLAR ACCESS; SOLAR ACCESS DESIGN TECHNIQUES; SOLAR COLLECTOR; SOLAR EASEMENTS AND COVENANTS; SOLAR ENERGY

Acute Care Hospital

A facility designed to provide diagnostic and short-term care (generally under 30 days) to patients who are in an acute phase of an illness. Acute care hospitals vary widely in size and level of service, but the majority of such facilities contain basic medical/surgical services, including general surgery, internal medicine, obstetrics and gynecology, pediatrics, pathology and radiology. Larger hospitals may contain more specialized services, including intensive care and coronary care units, organized emergency and outpatient services, and diagnostic and in-patient facilities for short-term psychiatric patients. Although the majority of acute care facilities are sponsored by voluntary, nonprofit groups, sponsorships may also be proprietary or public.

By virtue of the variety of services offered, acute care facilities are distinct from facilities designed for one type of patient (such as psychiatric) or one category of patient (such as children) and, by nature, also differ from long-term care facilities. Extended care facilities, such as rehabilitative institutes and convalescent homes, are relied on to serve patients who need care after leaving the hospital. Many voluntary acute care hospitals operate their own extended care facilities or have arrangements with private facilities that enable expedient patient transfers.

See: HEALTH CARE SYSTEM; INTERMEDIATE CARE FACILITIES (ICF); LONG-TERM CARE FACILITIES; SKILLED NURSING FACILITY (SNF)

Adaptive Use

The process of converting older buildings to new uses or performing necessary modifications so they can continue in their traditional use. It can provide an opportunity by which historically significant buildings as well as other sound older buildings may be saved from demolition and still be economically viable.

Because adaptive use offers a wide range of benefits, it is becoming increasingly popular. Through this technique it is possible to save on land acquisition, demolition, construction and energy costs, and projects may be completed more quickly than new construction. In addition, adaptive use often provides a distinctive architectural and aesthetic environment either unobtainable in new construction or obtainable only at very high cost.

The recycling of buildings has attracted keen interest as a method of stabilizing and revitalizing communities. As an example, many tourist dollars are being spent in such recycled developments as Ghiradelli Square in San Francisco, Faneuil Hall Marketplace in Boston, Trolley Square in Salt Lake City and Harborplace in Baltimore. Smaller-scale projects have also proved successful in halting urban decline and attracting private investment. A wide range of adaptive use projects is possible, such as the conversion of industrial or commercial space to residential use or the adaptation of large old homes for commercial uses.

Recent federal tax incentives support the rehabilitation of older structures and make it even more feasible economically to undertake adaptive use projects.

See: ECONOMIC DEVELOPMENT; ECONOMIC RECOVERY TAX ACT OF 1981; FANEUIL HALL MARKETPLACE; GHIRADELLI SQUARE; HISTORIC PRESERVATION; HISTORIC PRESERVATION TAX INCENTIVES; PUBLIC BUILDINGS; SURPLUS SCHOOLS; TOURISM

Adequate Public Facilities Ordinance

An ordinance that requires the existence or planned provision of public facilities, such as utilities and roads, prior to the granting of permission for new development. Used by some communities attempting to control their rate of growth, these types of ordinances have been upheld in court where the community is actively attempting to provide additional public facilities that can accommodate future growth.

Ramapo, New York was one municipality that successfully implemented a permit approach linked to the provision of adequate public facilities. In Ramapo a certain number of "points" were required, awarded on the basis of availability of and proximity to sewers, roads, firehouses, etc., before a development could begin. This permit system was instituted to synchronize development during an 18-year period in which an officially adopted capital improvement program specified the order in which public facilities would be systematically extended throughout town. Developers also had the option of providing the improvements ahead of schedule at their own expense.

In 1983, however, Ramapo discontinued the use of its point system (which had been instituted in 1969). Among the factors that contributed to its discontinuance were a substantially reduced growth rate, concerns over increased housing costs and insufficient economic development. One problem encountered in maintaining the system was the lessened availability of federal funds for infrastructure, such as sewers, greatly diminishing the town's ability to make capital improvements in accordance with the 18-year schedule it had adopted.

See: GOLDEN v. *PLANNING BOARD OF THE TOWN OF RAMAPO;* GROWTH MANAGEMENT; PHASED DEVELOPMENT CONTROLS; ZONING

Adult Entertainment Zone

A zoning district in which sexually oriented businesses—such as adult bookstores, adult motion picture theaters and adult cabarets—are permitted, while they are prohibited elsewhere throughout the community. This is one of the types of techniques used by communities to contain the spread of sex-related businesses and the adverse effects such businesses can have upon residential neighborhoods and other land uses. Boston and Seattle both limit adult uses to a concentrated area. In Boston's so-called combat zone, the problem of distinguishing pornographic from nonpornographic uses is avoided by defining adult uses as those that exclude minors.

Detroit and New Orleans both take the opposite tack—requiring that adult entertainment be dispersed throughout the appropriate zones in the community. In Detroit a minimum distance of 1,000 feet (300 meters) between certain types of adult uses is required; these uses must also be sited at least 500 feet from a dwelling unit. The Detroit ordinance was upheld in 1976 by the Supreme Court in *Young* v. *American Mini Theatres.*

Other practices in use include special permits (employed in Oakland and Indianapolis), mandatory spacing from civic-type uses and special sign controls.
See: SCHAD v. BOROUGH OF MOUNT EPHRAIM; SPECIAL ZONING DISTRICT; *YOUNG* v. *AMERICAN MINI THEATRES;* ZONING

Adventure Playground

1. A play area at which children construct their own play equipment, usually from scrap materials, such as poles, boards, tires, bricks, ropes and barrels. Popular in northern Europe and Britain, the adventure playground requires good adult supervision to advise and protect the children, controlled access and scheduled hours.

The concept of the adventure playground is based on the recognition that children most enjoy activities that enable them to test, construct and tear down. This form of playground also encourages group play, since assistance is inevitably needed. Adventure playgrounds are often unsightly, however, looking somewhat like a construction site or garbage dump. In addition, since most public parks are unsupervised, the adventure playground format is used less frequently than the more structurally sound, attractive and permanent creative play area format, which does not require the same degree of supervision.

2. A term used to describe a playground with unconventional play equipment that is more accurately termed a creative play area.
See: CREATIVE PLAY AREAS

Adverse Possession

The acquisition of title to property by means of occupying the property under certain conditions for a continuous period of time (usually 10 to 20 years) prescribed by statute.

For the rights of an owner to be acquired, the occupa-

tion or possession must generally be under a claim of rightful use, hostile to the claims of others, unconcealed and exclusive of the use by others.

The quality of title one may acquire by adverse possession is equivalent to that obtainable by deed. However, title acquired by adverse possession is not considered marketable (i.e., saleable in the ordinary course to a normally prudent purchaser) until it is either confirmed by judicial decree in an "action to quiet title" or supported by a quit claim deed from the prior record owner of the property.

Under normal circumstances one may not acquire title by adverse possession to land owned by a governmental authority (e.g., the federal government or a state government). Thus, for example, a property owner generally will not be able to acquire title within a public right-of-way by fencing in a portion of the right-of-way and cultivating it.
See: PRESCRIPTIVE EASEMENT; SQUATTER SETTLEMENTS

Advertising Signs

A means of conveying information or directing attention to a business, product, service or other commodity. Business signs, one form of advertising sign, are generally attached to or on the same site as the service offered, while billboards are generally off-site and refer to a service or commodity in a different location.

Signs can vary in size from sandwich board to billboard, and in the type of materials used from paper to masonry walls. Displays may be painted, printed or have raised lettering, while lighting or illumination options include neon tubes, reflective lettering and indirect lighting. The style or character of signs also ranges from the artistic to the mundane and from simple to elaborate. With proper design, placement and lighting, it is possible for signage to enhance community appearance while still serving its primary purpose of advertising a service or product. In the absence of adequate sign regulation, however, advertising signs can present a series of jarring visual images that can unpleasantly dominate the character of an area.
See: BILLBOARD; DESIGN STANDARDS; SIGN REGULATION; STREET GRAPHICS

Advisory Commission on Intergovernmental Relations (ACIR)

A permanent, bipartisan independent agency created by the United States Congress in 1959 to study and recommend reform on intergovernmental issues. ACIR provides a forum for discussion of problems common to federal, state and local government, such as federal grant administration and fiscal relationships among governments, and provides technical assistance to the executive and legislative branches of the federal government in the review of proposed legislation to determine its effect on intergovernmental relations.

ACIR undertakes polls and other research and develops policy recommendations in many areas, which are published in reports available through its Washington, D.C.

offices or through the United States Government Printing Office. Annual publications include *Significant Features of Fiscal Federalism*, a compendium of statistical information on state and local revenues and expenditures, and *Changing Public Attitudes on Governments and Taxes,* a poll. The *Catalog of Federal Grant-in-Aid Programs to State and Local Governments* is published periodically, while a quarterly periodical, *Intergovernmental Perspective,* discusses issues in intergovernmental matters, such as grant program administration and grant availability. Other areas of ACIR's work are reflected in its 11-volume series on a state legislative reform program, including volumes on *Local Government Modernization, Environment, Land Use and Growth Policy* and *Housing and Community Development*.

ACIR is also working with individual states on the establishment of state ACIRs to become state-local advisory bodies and maintains a working relationship with similar agencies in nearly half of the 50 states.

Advisory Council on Historic Preservation

A United States federal agency, established by the National Historic Preservation Act of 1966, that serves as adviser to the president and Congress on matters related to historic preservation. A major function of the council, under Section 106 of the National Historic Preservation Act, is the review of federal, federally assisted or federally licensed projects that can have an effect upon properties that are eligible for or listed on the National Register of Historic Places. The council also prepares special reports and studies, provides legislative assistance to Congress, and reviews the programs of other federal agencies and consults with those agencies. In addition, it disseminates information and coordinates the historic preservation activities of various levels of government. The Advisory Council is responsible, as well, for coordination of United States membership in the International Center for the Study of the Preservation and Restoration of Cultural Property, in Rome, Italy.

The 19-member council is appointed by the president and is required to include members of the general public, certain designated federal agency heads, a governor and a mayor, the chairman of the National Trust for Historic Preservation, preservation experts and the president of the National Conference of State Historic Preservation Officers.
See: HISTORIC PRESERVATION; NATIONAL HISTORIC PRESERVATION ACT OF 1966; NATIONAL REGISTER OF HISTORIC PLACES

Advocacy Planning

The use of professional planners to develop plans on behalf of a community group or organization that are an alternative to plans offered by an official government agency. The advocacy of these plans before decision-making bodies is an integral component of the process.

The theory behind advocacy planning assumes that the diverse interest groups in society deserve the official representation of professional planners, similar to the way in which clients are represented by lawyers. Proposals have also been made to employ an advocacy planner in government agencies as a representative of the groups affected by government plans, but this is a less workable arrangement, since the planner cannot adequately represent both the government and the special-interest groups.

An outgrowth of the Economic Opportunity Act of 1964, which required maximum feasible participation of the poor, and the Model Cities legislation, which required widespread citizen participation, the initial thrust of advocacy planning was to meet the needs of disadvantaged inner city groups.
See: CITIZEN PARTICIPATION TECHNIQUES

Aeration

The mixture of air into water to permit the oxidation of organic matter. In sewage treatment, aeration (which takes place in tanks) is accomplished by diffusing effluent from primary treatment with compressed air, mixing it with microorganisms from sludge and then permitting the effluent to settle for a few days. This creates a suitable environment for the growth of biological masses that will settle on tank elements provided for their collection, thereby removing a significant amount of the remaining organic matter. Aeration methods used for sewage treatment are contact aeration, mechanical aeration and the activated sludge process. Preaeration (aeration of raw sewage) may be undertaken before sedimentation to decrease odors and increase treatability.

In water treatment, aeration is sometimes used to reduce unpleasant tastes, odors and corrosivity, as well as to remove carbon dioxide and hydrogen sulfide and to oxidize dissolved substances. It is accomplished by exposing water to the atmosphere in open aqueducts or reservoirs, permitting it to flow over cascades or through trickling devices, spraying it into the air, forcing compressed air through it or by using a combination of these methods. Although effective, aeration is used less extensively now because other methods are more economical.
See: ACTIVATED SLUDGE PROCESS; OXIDATION PROCESSES; PRETREATMENT; SEDIMENTATION TANK; WATER TREATMENT

Aerial Photo Interpretation

The examination of patterns or features disclosed on aerial photographs to make inferences about the natural and man-made environment. Characteristics such as size, shape, shadow, tone and color, texture, pattern and association are of significant assistance in the interpretation of aerial photographs.

Size can usually be determined relative to other objects in the photograph, while shape provides important information on types of uses. Shadow helps to indicate size and shape but may not usually be used for height measurement. Tones are often indicative of surface conditions, such as moisture; tone variation as well as the boundary between tones is important. Association describes the process of identifying the context within which an object is viewed; for example, a cleared and sloping area covered with snow might be a firebreak, a ski slope or agricultural land. Pattern is constantly used in photo interpretation. Planners can usually identify new subdivisions immediately by typical spatial arrangements that may be accompanied by a lack of vegetation. Pattern can also describe the nature of drainage in an area, including the major channels and tributaries.

As reconnaissance satellites supply increasingly large volumes of information, automated image interpretation is being developed. In this process, basic features such as water, trees, cultivated land or urban areas are differentiated and recorded. The output may be in map or printout form, and the data are stored digitally.
See: AERIAL PHOTOGRAPHIC APPLICATIONS; AERIAL PHOTOGRAPHY

Aerial Photo Mosaic

An assembly of overlapping aerial photographs that make one composite picture. They may be compiled for index purposes or to create the appearance of one large photograph.

In an index mosaic the overlap of the photographs and their indexing numbers are purposely allowed to remain so that particular views may be selected and requested by code number. If a single-picture appearance is desired, the code numbers and overlapping areas are cut away, and the photos are pieced together.

This second type of mosaic may be controlled or uncontrolled. In an uncontrolled mosaic, the photographs have been matched without ground control that allows correct scale and orientation to be maintained. The photographs will not match exactly, and they may not be used to take measurements. In a controlled mosaic, the match will be accurate, and approximate measurements may be made. The process required to rectify (convert to true vertical) aerial photographs is expensive and precise, so many aerial photograph users piece together the best uncontrolled mosaic they can.
See: AERIAL PHOTOGRAPHY

Aerial Photographic Applications

There are numerous ways in which aerial photography can aid in planning and related activities, ranging from land mapping to archaeology.

In analyzing land use patterns, for example, two aerial photographs of the same location taken a number of years apart can provide an immediate visual image of the changes that have taken place. Specific types of land use and land cover interpretation are also possible with aerial photos and data resulting from remote sensing.

Archaeological artifacts can be systematically searched for with aerial photography, since clues that may be invisible from the ground become apparent from the air.

Shadow marks, for example, caused by the way in which rays of the sun strike irregularities in the ground, help to identify buried mounds and old earthworks. Soil marks (soil variations such as color) and crop or plant marks (differences in factors such as color or density) may also be a sign of past development. These indicators have helped to locate ancient Roman developments and military encampments in Britain.

Land managers and foresters often use aerial photography to classify vegetation, make estimates of the number of trees by type and conduct recreational surveys. Engineers routinely use aerial photography for the routing or location of highways, pipelines, railroads and dams. Other aerial photo applications include wetlands mapping and surveying, and water pollution monitoring.
See: AERIAL PHOTOGRAPHY; INFRARED PHOTOGRAPHY; PHOTOGRAMMETRY; REMOTE SENSING

Aerial Photography

The use of aircraft to take photographs of terrain. Generally the photos are taken in parallel flight lines with some degree of overlap, so that complete photo coverage is obtained. It is possible to obtain existing aerial photographs from many government agencies. The Geological Survey, Soil Conservation Service, Forest Service, Corps of Engineers and, in Canada, the National Air Photo Library all maintain files of aerial photographs. There are also many commercial aerial survey companies that will sell prints.

If existing photographic surveys do not meet the requirements of a particular project, however, it may be necessary to contract for aerial coverage. In order to justify the expense of custom coverage, it is necessary to know precisely what the desired end product should be and to communicate this effectively. Many factors affect the results of an aerial photo mission and determine the type of photograph that is produced. Among these variables are the required scale, season and time of day.

The focal length of the camera divided by the flight altitude is a general formula for calculating the scale of an aerial photograph. Scale selection will greatly influence project cost as well as project efficiency. It is generally considered prudent to select the smallest scale that will satisfy the requirements of a particular project, since fewer photographs will be necessary.

The season selected also depends upon project objectives. Planners, engineers, surveyors, site designers and geologists are usually most interested in terrain detail and avoid the seasons of maximum tree foliage. Foresters or wildlife managers would probably be more interested in vegetative cover; infrared coverage may also be used to aid in vegetative differentiation. Snow cover, or lack of it, is another factor that would influence seasonal choice.

The time of day that the photographs are taken influences color or tone, amount of light, and shadow length. Other factors that must be considered in negotiating a contract are the maximum acceptable cloud cover and quality of the final product. The desired degree of overlap between the photographs, consisting of endlap (overlap in a particular flight line) and sidelap (overlap in adjoining parallel lines), must also be considered. (See Fig. 1)

See: AERIAL PHOTO INTERPRETATION; AERIAL PHOTO MOSAIC; AERIAL PHOTOGRAPHIC APPLICATIONS; INFRARED PHOTOGRAPHY; PHOTOGRAMMETRY; REMOTE SENSING; STEREO VIEWING OF AERIAL PHOTOGRAPHS

Aesthetic Zoning

The use of zoning regulations expressly to control the aesthetic appearance of buildings or to preserve views. Height, bulk and setback regulations, which affect aesthetics, are standard elements of zoning regulations, but their use has traditionally been related primarily to the provision of light and air. In aesthetic zoning they are used to control such design elements as skylines and neighborhood appearance.

Fig. 1.   Aerial photograph of part of Sioux Falls, South Dakota. An airport is in the upper middle of the photo (north), an industrial park immediately below it. The large rectangular areas are farmland and the smaller rectangular areas with white specks are residential areas. Freeways and rivers can be easily recognized. The downtown commercial center is in the lower middle of the photo adjacent to the river and a strip commercial area extends straight to the west.
Credit: U.S. Geological Survey, EROS Data Center

Height limitations in aesthetic zoning are imposed to prevent buildings from changing a skyline by virtue of height and to keep buildings in the sight lines of major views from blocking the views of buildings farther away. Bulk and setback regulations are used to vary a skyline as well as to set a pattern of development at street level that will yield a selected neighborhood ambience.

See: ARCHITECTURAL CONTROLS; SKYLINE; VIEW PROTECTION REGULATIONS; ZONING

Aesthetics

A design term that describes the visual quality of buildings and spaces within a townscape. Designers usually indicate a desired aesthetic result in their plans, and communities dictate site development and/or architectural controls to produce a development that has a desired aesthetic appearance.

See: AESTHETIC ZONING; AMBIENCE; AMENITY; ARCHITECTURAL CONTROLS; COLOR; COMMUNITY CHARACTER; DESIGN CONTINUITY; DESIGN REVIEW; EDGE; LANDSCAPING; PUBLIC ART; SCALE OF DEVELOPMENT; SENSE OF PLACE; SIGN REGULATION; SKYLINE; STREET BEAUTIFICATION; SUBDIVISION REGULATIONS; VISTA

Affirmative Easement

An easement in which one party has the right to use or perform some activity upon another's property. In an affirmative easement the owner of the easement (in the case of an easement in gross) or the owner of the dominant estate (in the case of an appurtenant easement) has the right to affirmatively use or take some action upon the servient estate that would otherwise be unlawful.

Examples of affirmative easements include rights-of-way and easements permitting an upland property owner to discharge water upon the land of his neighbor.

See: EASEMENT; NEGATIVE EASEMENT

Affirmative Fair Housing Marketing

A program intended to promote equal housing opportunity for individuals of similar income, regardless of race, religion, sex or national origin. All participants (e.g., those that develop or rehabilitate housing) in Department of Housing and Urban Development (HUD) subsidized or unsubsidized housing programs that involve either subdivisions, multifamily housing or mobile home parks of at least five units, lots or spaces, or individual applications for a total of five dwelling units during the course of a year, are required to participate in the program.

Affirmative fair housing marketing provisions, which are required by Title VIII of the Civil Rights Act of 1968 as amended (PL 90-284), revolve around preparation of an affirmative fair housing marketing (AFHM) plan. Such a plan, which is made available to the public at the participant's sales or rental offices, must contain the following: an affirmative program to attract buyers or tenants regardless of sex or minority group to which they may belong; maintenance of a nondiscriminatory hiring policy for staff engaged in sales or rentals; and instruction of staff in the policy of nondiscrimination and fair housing. In addition, there must be an effort to specifically solicit eligible tenants or buyers who are referred by HUD, the HUD fair housing poster must be prominently displayed, and the HUD equal housing opportunity logo, slogan or statement must be used on printed materials and at the project site.

See: FAIR HOUSING LEGISLATION

Age-Oriented Community

A housing development designed for a population whose age is specified. Typically an age-oriented community is one that is built for adults who are 50 years old or older and does not permit children under 18. Residential units, often built as townhouses, are usually tastefully designed, but small, and community facilities and recreational complexes are often provided.

An age-oriented community is designed to appeal to empty nesters, who may want to exchange a large house for a compact and efficient living space with numerous social and recreative amenities. Municipalities are usually pleased to have this form of development, since it makes few demands on municipal facilities, but its legality is continually being tested in the courts.

See: EMPTY NESTERS; RETIREMENT COMMUNITY

Age Structure

The number and percentage of people in each age group of a population. This information is important in many types of planning studies, including the planning of educational and recreational facilities, services for the aging, transportation planning and health planning. Data on age composition are useful for analyzing the potential labor force, future housing requirements and community facility needs. Age is also a critical variable in analyses or projections concerning birthrate and mortality.

The census is a primary source for detailed information concerning age distribution. In population projection the cohort survival method is useful, as it provides information on future population by age group. It is also possible to roughly approximate age distribution using other projection methods by applying the same age ratios that existed in the most recent census to the total population estimate obtained.

See: COHORT SURVIVAL METHOD; POPULATION CHARACTERISTICS

Agglomeration

1. The unplanned, incremental growth of a city over time. The most typical form of urban growth, agglomeration often results in the juxtaposition of incompatible land uses, lack of necessary public utilities and infrastructure, and inappropriate use of resources.

2. The clustering of firms, their suppliers and major customers to enable them to reduce transfer costs. It is

thought that this clustering, which can create a highly dependent network of firms, discourages independent firms from moving away.
See: CONURBATION; GROWTH MANAGEMENT; MEGALOPOLIS; PLANNED COMMUNITY; SPRAWL

Aggradation

The process by which a grade or slope is built up through deposition. The term applies particularly to the raising in elevation of a streambed—through deposits of gravel, soil or other materials—so that it can establish or maintain equilibrium.

Aggregate

An inert material used as a component of concrete, mastic (a pastelike cement), mortar, plaster and bituminous pavements. Sand, gravel or crushed stone are the most common aggregates, but certain lightweight materials such as slag, vermiculite, pumice and lava are used to create lightweight concrete. Asbestos fiber, sawdust and cinders are used as aggregates in making concrete into which nails can be driven.

Aggregates are divided into two classes: coarse aggregates, such as crushed stone or gravel; and fine aggregates, such as sand. These classes are determined by sieving the material through a set of nine sieves and classifying those aggregates that cannot pass through a number 4 sieve (.25-inch or .635-centimeter openings) as coarse, and those that can, as fine.
See: CONCRETE; PAVEMENT

Agins v. *City of Tiburon* (447 U.S. 255, 100 S.Ct. 2138, 65 L.Ed.2d 106 [1980])

A decision by the United States Supreme Court, on appeal from the California Supreme Court, sustaining the principle that even where a zoning ordinance has the potential of substantially diminishing the value of a landowner's property, a taking will not be found to occur unless the ordinance does not substantially advance legitimate state interests or denies the owner economically viable use of his land.

The ordinance at issue rezoned land considered to be environmentally sensitive from 1-acre zoning to zoning permitting as little as 0.2 house per acre.

The California Supreme Court had ruled in this case that, even if the rezoning had constituted a taking, the landowner's only remedy was invalidation of the ordinance and not a monetary damage award based upon inverse condemnation. The United States Supreme Court, having found that no taking had occurred, declined to rule on this aspect of the California court's decision, thus leaving as an open issue the question of whether a landowner could recover inverse condemnation damages for an unduly restrictive zoning ordinance.
See: CONFISCATORY REGULATION; INVERSE CONDEMNATION; TAKING

Agricultural District

1.   A designated agricultural area eligible for property tax relief. Agricultural districts are usually quite large, ranging from a portion of a county sufficient to include several farms to several counties. To qualify for inclusion in a district, farmlands must generally meet criteria of minimum agricultural production and income.

Agricultural district designation is sought by farmers, conservationists and planners so that assessments will be based on the land's agricultural value rather than its prevailing real estate value. The lower assessments offer an inducement to property owners to continue farming their lands.

2.   A zoning classification in which agricultural uses as well as single-family residential development on large parcels are permitted.
See: FARMLAND PROTECTION; FULL-VALUE ASSESSMENT; ZONING

Agricultural Extension Agent

A county-level official who is responsible for disseminating information on current farm and conservation technology. The agricultural extension agent works under the direction of the state agricultural college's extension service or a division of the state's land grant college, but in many states he is appointed by the county legislative body or a county cooperative extension board.

The agent typically works directly with farmers, land owners and nurserymen on methods of soil conservation, cultivation, cooperative marketing and the use of improved seeds and breeds of livestock; he also cooperates closely with the local soil and water board and with representatives of other agricultural agencies. In recent years agricultural extension agents have undertaken programs in urban areas, such as nutrition education and city gardening.
See: SOIL CONSERVATION DISTRICT; SOIL CONSERVATION SERVICE (SCS)

Agricultural Land Use

The use of land primarily for farming, ranching, horse breeding, dairy farming and other forms of food and crop production. From a planning perspective, agricultural land use connotes primary economic use of the property.

The term "prime agricultural land" is used to describe property with superior soils, topography and drainage for the region. Farmland protection measures are aimed at preventing development of the most productive prime agricultural land while conservation measures are aimed at preserving its productive capacity.
See: FARMLAND PROTECTION

Agricultural Pollution

Pollution caused by activities related to the raising of crops and livestock.

A significant amount of water pollution in various forms

is caused by agriculture, which is considered to be one of the prime causes of nonpoint-source water pollution. It has been estimated by the U.S. Environmental Protection Agency that 68 percent of all United States river basins are affected by agricultural activities. Croplands are a major source of the sediment that enters bodies of water as a result of soil erosion. Agricultural runoff, which is rich in nutrients from fertilizers and animal wastes, can help cause accelerated eutrophication in lakes and other water bodies. Other pollution sources are the use of water for irrigation, which can lead to increased salinity, and the use of pesticides, which can pollute the air as well as water.

There are, however, potentially successful means of controlling these pollution problems. Sediment can be greatly reduced through soil erosion control techniques, which also enable the farmer to maintain the productive capacity of his land. Eutrophication can be lessened through soil conservation practices and minimization of runoff. Integrated pest management is an approach to reducing the use of chemical pesticides that has proved successful in many instances.

See: EUTROPHICATION; IRRIGATION; NONPOINT SOURCE; PESTICIDES; RUNOFF; SOIL EROSION CONTROL TECHNIQUES; WATER POLLUTION

Air Pollution

Introduction into the atmosphere of contaminants—such as smoke, fumes or odors—that are of sufficient quantity, concentration or duration as to have a negative effect on human, animal or plant life or on human activities. Air pollution may be classified by physical form (e.g., gases or particles), by pollution source (e.g., mobile source, stationary source, indirect source) or by some other useful characteristic, such as degree of severity.

Air pollution derives from diverse sources, both man-made and natural. In industrialized countries principal pollution problems are generally traceable to such prime sources as motor vehicle exhausts, industrial and power plant emissions, space heating and incineration. Forest fires, volcanic eruptions and windblown dust can also contribute significantly to pollution levels. Agricultural practices, such as applications of pesticides, and construction activities are other sources of air contaminants.

Efforts to control air pollution date to the 19th century. In the United States smoke control laws were passed in Chicago and Cincinnati in 1881, and most other major cities had such laws by 1912. Britain took national steps to control air pollution as early as 1863 and passed the Alkali Act in 1906 to attempt to control industrial pollution and the escape of contaminants. The first federal legislation in the United States aimed exclusively at controlling air pollution was enacted in 1955.

The pollutants to which chief regulatory attention has been directed in the United States are total suspended particulates, sulfur dioxide, photochemical oxidants, hydrocarbons and lead. The enactment of more stringent air pollution control legislation in 1970 and 1977 has helped to reduce levels of these pollutants to varying degrees. A steady decline has been evident in the average number of days for which urban areas have recorded pollution in the ranges considered to be unhealthful, very unhealthful or hazardous. Significant pollution problems still exist, however, in a number of urban areas.

See: ACID RAIN; AIR POLLUTION CONTROL; AIR POLLUTION EPISODE; AIR POLLUTION FILTER; AIR QUALITY CONTROL REGION (AQCR); AIR QUALITY CRITERIA; AMBIENT AIR; AREA SOURCE; ATTAINMENT AREA; CLEAN AIR AMENDMENTS OF 1970; CYCLONE COLLECTOR; DUST; ELECTROSTATIC PRECIPITATOR (ESP); EMISSION INVENTORY; EMISSION STANDARD; EMISSIONS TRADING SYSTEMS; HEAT ISLAND; INDIRECT SOURCE; INVERSION; LINE SOURCE; MOBILE SOURCE; NATIONAL AMBIENT AIR QUALITY STANDARDS (NAAQS); NEW SOURCE PERFORMANCE STANDARDS (NSPS); NONATTAINMENT AREA; NONDEGRADATION CLAUSE; PARTICULATES; PLUME; POLLUTANT STANDARD INDEX (PSI); RINGELMANN CHART; SMOG; SMOKE; STACK; STATE IMPLEMENTATION PLAN (SIP); STATIONARY SOURCE; WET SCRUBBER

Air Pollution Control

The process of reducing and controlling the emission of pollutants into the air. Air pollution control is approached from two basic directions. At the regulatory level, federal and state programs are directed at developing air quality criteria, setting air quality standards, and imposing emission standards upon various mobile and stationary sources. Air quality monitoring is conducted on a comprehensive basis to record pollution levels and note particular problems or progress being made. Major and complex air pollution control legislation is in effect in the United States and is directed at many aspects of pollution control. Air pollution legislation has also been enacted in many other countries, including the Netherlands, Britain, France, Germany and Norway.

Another major aspect of controlling air pollution is the use of various technical practices and procedures to reduce or remove air pollution. Included in this group are changes in manufacturing processes or types of fuel to help prevent or reduce pollution, and the development of a wide variety of collection and removal equipment to remove pollution at its source. Another common procedure is the dispersion of air pollution into the atmosphere to reduce and dilute contaminants to acceptable limits at ground level.

Air pollution control devices are generally categorized by whether they are intended to control pollution resulting from mobile sources or stationary sources. Further distinctions may also be made as to whether the device is intended to remove particulates or gaseous pollutants. Filters, settling chambers, inertial collectors, wet scrubbers and electrostatic precipitators are common methods of removing particulates. Gaseous contaminants may be removed by such techniques as the use of adsorbers, which are porous materials to which the pollutant gases adhere, or through chemical processes that convert pollutants into non-polluting forms.

See: AIR POLLUTION; AIR POLLUTION FILTER; CYCLONE COLLECTOR; ELECTROSTATIC PRECIPITATOR (ESP); NATIONAL AMBIENT AIR QUALITY STANDARDS (NAAQS); PARTICULATES; STACK; WET SCRUBBER

Air Pollution Control Association (APCA)

A nonprofit organization whose members include professional engineers, planners, government officials and scientists active in air pollution control, as well as manufacturers of control equipment and educational and scientific institutions from throughout the United States and Canada. Founded in 1907, APCA maintains its staff headquarters in Pittsburgh. It offers continuing education courses, meetings and conferences, and a wide variety of publications, including the monthly *Journal of the Air Pollution Control Association* and five different newsletters. APCA maintains a large number of technical committees organized into five divisions: Effects, Control Technology, Basic Science and Technology, Control Program Administration, and Sources.

Air Pollution Episode

An acute air pollution epidemic lasting for a number of days. Episodes are thought to be caused by a combination of a high concentration of pollution generators and specific adverse meteorological and topographical conditions. The phenomenon was first observed in the United States in Donora, Pennsylvania in 1948, when 43 percent of the population became ill and 20 individuals died over a five-day period.

See: AIR POLLUTION; INVERSION; POLLUTANT STANDARD INDEX (PSI)

Air Pollution Filter

A device designed to remove particulates from an air stream. Filters, which may be made of such materials as cloth, sand, coarse gravel, felt, or vegetable fibers, are considered an effective means of collecting particles by allowing particles to adhere.

See: AIR POLLUTION; AIR POLLUTION CONTROL

Air Quality Control Region (AQCR)

One of the basic geographic areas that the Clean Air Act created in which air pollution control measures are to be taken. An AQCR is comprised of areas of similar climate, topography and degree of urbanization so that similar air pollution problems are found. Consequently, an AQCR may cover an entire state, cross state boundaries, or consist of a portion of a state.

Each state is responsible for adopting a plan that shows how national primary ambient air quality standards will be attained and maintained in each air quality control region or portion of a region within that state.

See: AIR POLLUTION; NATIONAL AMBIENT AIR QUALITY STANDARDS (NAAQS); STATE IMPLEMENTATION PLAN (SIP)

Air Quality Criteria

Descriptive scientific statements concerning the observed or probable effects of exposure to various levels of specified air pollutants.

See: AIR POLLUTION; NATIONAL AMBIENT AIR QUALITY STANDARDS (NAAQS)

Air Rights

The right to use the air space above the surface of real estate.

Traditionally, the owner of real estate owned all of the air rights above his property. However, with the advent of the airplane, it was determined that airplane flight over another's land did not violate the landowner's air rights, so long as the flight did not interfere with the owner's use of his property.

Like real estate itself, air rights may be purchased in fee or leased from the underlying landowner. In densely developed urban areas, air rights comprise a valuable and heretofore largely untapped resource, affording potential development opportunities in the air space over such low-profile structures as railroad rights-of-way, highways, schools and municipal buildings. For example, in New York City major development has occurred utilizing the

Fig. 2. Development on air rights over the approach to the George Washington Bridge in New York City. Four 32-story apartment buildings and a bus station are located over the twelve lanes of I-95.
Credit: Courtesy of the Port Authority of New York and New Jersey

air space over Pennsylvania Railroad Station, Grand Central Terminal, railroad tracks and highway approaches to the George Washington Bridge. Prospective air space developers must also acquire sufficient rights on the surface property to permit the establishment of building foundations and maintenance of the overlying structure.

A more typical example of the treatment of air rights as independent real property is the purchase of a condominium apartment in a high-rise apartment building, in which part of what is being acquired is a fee interest in a three-dimensional air space in relation to specified surface property. In some jurisdictions it has been determined that where air rights and surface real estate are separately owned, each may be separately assessed and subjected to real property tax.

Easements (both negative and affirmative) may be acquired over air space, just as with surface real estate. Examples include the easement of light and air that one landowner may acquire over the land of his neighbor and easements (referred to as aviation or navigation easements) acquired over land adjoining airports to accommodate flight patterns. (See Fig. 2)
See: EASEMENT

Aircraft Navigational Aids

Devices located both on planes and on the ground. The latter are divided between aircraft navigational aids categorized as en route aids (used while in flight) and those categorized as terminal aids (used in approaches to airfields).

En route aids are contained in small buildings that pose few location problems, while terminal aids require complex, and often elaborate, lighting systems. From the planning standpoint the most critical problem is in locating the heavier concentration of these lights and instruments close to the airport so that they do not interfere with surrounding development.

One type of system that requires equipment outside the airport is the Instrument Landing System (ILS), to help pilots in their approach; it involves the installation of two markers (radio equipment enclosed in a small radio shack, usually surrounded by a barbed wire fence), located up to 5 miles (8 kilometers) from the airport. Another system, approach lights, can extend 3,000 feet (914 meters) from the runway and may be very high intensity and/or flashing. Several other forms of navigational aids are widely used but are located within the airport boundaries and generally do not cause land use conflicts.
See: AIRPORT PLANNING

Airfield Clearances

Areas surrounding an airport that must be kept free of obstructions to aircraft takeoff and landing. They are defined as imaginary planes, of a size based on the functions of the airport and the lengths of its runways. They are located over, and extend upward and outward from runways. Airfield clearance requirements for a particular air-

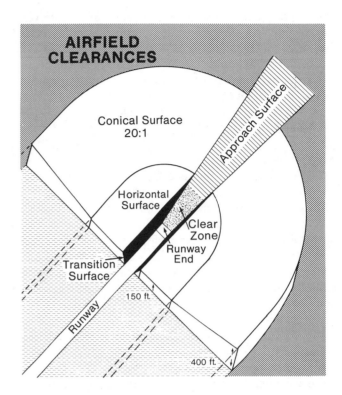

Fig. 3. Imaginary surfaces extending over and outward from airfield runways.

port can be obtained from the Federal Aviation Administration (FAA) and incorporated into municipal zoning and building regulations. (See Fig. 3)
See: AIRPORT ZONING; BUILDING RESTRICTION LINE (BRL); CLEAR ZONE

Airport Classification

Airports are classified into categories by the Federal Aviation Administration (FAA), the National Airport System Plan, and the International Civil Aviation Organization (ICAO). These categories describe either their functions (e.g., air carrier or general aviation), their traffic volume, the lengths of their runways or the widths of their taxiways. Design standards are generally established for each class. Since these classification systems change frequently, it is necessary to contact these organizations for current specifications.
See: AIRPORT PLANNING; NATIONAL SYSTEM OF AIRPORTS

Airport Industrial Park

An industrial park located near or adjacent to an airport that accommodates industries either serving the airport and airlines or requiring ready access for air freight purposes. Airport industrial parks are usually attractive, well-landscaped facilities that principally contain light industry.

Often 50 acres (20 hectares) in size or larger, these industrial parks should have their own access from major arterial routes and be physically separate from airport ter-

minal approaches. This separates truck traffic from vehicles destined for the airport and permits terminal-related use—e.g., car rental services— to locate on land closer to the terminal. When adjacent to the airport, an airport industrial park may have a taxiway or aircraft apron that serves some or all of its building sites.
See: AIRPORT PLANNING; INDUSTRIAL PARK; LIGHT INDUSTRY

Airport Noise

The predominant nuisance factor associated with airports that are located near populated areas. Noise that spills over airport boundaries and interferes with sleep, speech, recreation and other activities is a major problem in the siting and expansion of airport and heliport facilities. Where land surrounding an airport is undeveloped, zoning controls that require that land use be airport-related or industrial can be effective in creating compatible neighbors. In fully developed areas it may be necessary to purchase land under a critical flight path or to obtain avigation easements (the right of planes to fly over a particular property) to compensate those who are particularly inconvenienced by the noise. Building regulations that require substantial sound insulation are useful in areas near airports.

When airport master plans are undertaken, the Federal Aviation Administration (FAA) requires that noise studies be made of expected future air traffic levels. The studies known as composite noise rating (CNR) and noise exposure forecast (NEF), produce noise contour maps, which indicate noise concentrations at the airport and in the surrounding area. The noise and number index (NNI) is used in Britain, and the total noise load (TNL) is used in the Netherlands for the same purpose; they differ only in the unit of measure of sound level.
See: AIRPORT PLANNING; AIRPORT ZONING; NOISE POLLUTION; SONIC BOOM

Airport Planning

Planning for airport facilities is undertaken on a macroscale at the federal, state and municipal levels and on a microscale at the single-facility level. Plans at all levels propose airport improvements to meet immediate and future aviation needs; they illustrate general or specific locations of proposed facilities—such as new airports, new runways and additional runway lighting—and the estimated timing and cost of improvements. Airport plans must also analyze problems of land development adjacent to the airport, requirements for airport access and the financial feasibility of proposed improvements. Environmental impact of all proposals, and the mitigation of potentially negative environmental impacts, must be studied and incorporated into the analysis. Citizen participation must also be sought in the development of plans. Airport plans are generally made for short-range (5 years), intermediate-range (10 years) and long-range (20 years) time periods because of the extended length of time required to obtain approval for and build airport facilities.

Planning on the macroscale is undertaken to establish criteria, locations, functions and sizes for airports and heliports throughout an area. This ensures proper allocation of federal funding to provide the correct mix of facilities to meet the needs of air carrier traffic (commercial airlines and scheduled commuter airlines) and general aviation (all other nonmilitary aircraft movements).

Planning for the single airport is extremely complex, requiring the integration of many airport functions. The location of each of the facilities and their relationship to each other constitute the physical airport plan. All airports have runways, which are takeoff and landing areas. Other facilities common to airports are aprons for aircraft parking and fueling; taxiways (roads that permit aircraft to move between runways and aprons); and holding aprons, also called run-up pads or warm-up pads, at the ends of runways where aircraft must wait for takeoff clearance. Holding bays (small aprons used for the temporary storage of aircraft until a terminal gate is available), aircraft hangars, passenger terminal facilities, and automobile parking and loading areas are also provided.

Of concern to planners is the provision of adequate roads, parking and mass transit to provide sufficient access to meet peak demand. Peak hours at large airports have been found to be the same as those of business districts and are more closely related to airport employee peaks than to passenger use.
See: AIRCRAFT NAVIGATIONAL AIDS; AIRFIELD CLEARANCES; AIRPORT CLASSIFICATION; AIRPORT NOISE; AIRPORT ZONING; BUILDING RESTRICTION LINE (BRL); CLEAR ZONE; HELIPORT; LANDING STRIP; NATIONAL SYSTEM OF AIRPORTS; OFFSHORE AIRPORTS; SONIC BOOM

Airport Zoning

A type of zoning control, often used as an overlay to existing zoning, aimed at allowing an airport to operate efficiently and safely. The primary focus of airport zoning is control of the height of structures within specified distances from the airport. Height restrictions are established as a function of distance from the runway, with greater heights permitted at greater distances.

Another aspect of airport zoning is the use to which land surrounding the airport is put. A community may choose to establish a policy of zoning nearby land for uses unlikely to conflict with or be affected by the airport, such as agriculture, industry, or airport-related services and facilities. Places of public assembly (such as schools and hospitals) and residential uses (which are likely to be chronically bothered by noise) are often not permitted to be developed.

The Federal Aviation Administration (FAA) has made available a set of Model Airport Zoning Regulations, which are used by many communities.
See: AIRPORT PLANNING; HEIGHT CONTROLS; OVERLAY DISTRICT; ZONING

Algal Bloom

Large concentrations of algae that can develop in lakes as a result of eutrophication. The algae may be of the green variety, but the generally more noxious blue-green algae are also often found in eutrophic lakes.

Algal bloom significantly lessens the aesthetic quality and recreational potential of a lake, making it difficult and unpleasant to swim, fish or boat. The bloom can impart a displeasing taste to the water, lessening its suitability as a water supply, and may have an offensive odor. Some blue-green algae can also emit toxic materials that can affect fish, wildlife and humans. Finally, algal blooms can deplete the oxygen stores of a lake and be harmful to aquatic life.
See: EUTROPHICATION

Alley

A generally narrow vehicular or pedestrian right-of-way that permits access to a rear yard, parking lot or other area behind a row of buildings. Traditionally, an alley was considered to be strictly a service road for deliveries, refuse collection or other support functions and was the principal means of accommodating such needs. With the advent of underground service drives for large building complexes, off-street parking and loading, and related design solutions, however, the alley has been rendered somewhat anachronistic. Instead, alleys behind or between existing buildings are now often perceived as a design opportunity for the development of shops, walkways and open spaces. Narrow, alleylike walkways are also being used in new low-rise and townhouse developments to provide access to parking areas and building entrances in an attempt to create an intimate and quaint environment conducive to social mingling.

Alteration

1. In planning practice, changes made to a building or structure, including the construction of additions. Alterations may involve relatively small physical changes, such as the creation of additional windows, or more extensive work. Normal maintenance and repairs are not considered to be alterations. Zoning ordinances often contain provisions prohibiting alterations on nonconforming structures or uses.

2. In real estate the term usually refers to a change that is made to a building or structure that is relatively substantial but that leaves its exterior dimensions unaltered. Leases often contain provisions that prohibit alterations without landlord consent or restrict the types of alterations a tenant may make without consent.
See: RECONSTRUCTION; REHABILITATION; RESTORATION

Alternative Plans

Various approaches to solving the same problem. Alternatives are offered because there is seldom one right answer in planning—instead, there is a series of potentially acceptable answers, which may vary widely in approach, analysis and conclusion.

Planners develop alternative plans because this practice allows them to explore a variety of ways in which the expressed community goals and objectives can be met. The consequences of each scenario are then followed through to a logical outcome and the advantages and disadvantages of each approach weighed and compared. These alternatives are then presented to elected officials and to the community at large for reaction and comment so that, ultimately, one alternative may be chosen.

Similarly, developers may prepare alternative plans at an early stage in the preparation of their development proposals. Based on reactions and comments they receive from planning staff, the planning commission and other appropriate officials, they will concentrate on the refinement of one of the alternatives.
See: COMPREHENSIVE PLAN; COST-BENEFIT ANALYSIS

Ambience

The atmosphere or tone of an environment, as determined largely by style of architecture, amount of activity, density of use and related factors influencing the quality of the environment. In planning, the establishment of a particular ambience is achieved by selection of land uses and design standards that will produce the desired effect. Generally associated with the design of ambience is the consistent use of design elements, such as the type and style of lighting; use of selected materials or colors; selection of paving; graphics and landscaping; and the coordination of all aspects to achieve a desired effect.

Frequently, ambience is the quality of a space, and a principal concern is preservation of those factors responsible for this unique quality. This might be the case with a European piazza or town square, where the introduction of an architectural element that is out of character with the existing space will disrupt if not destroy its ambience.
See: DESIGN STANDARDS; SCALE OF DEVELOPMENT; SENSE OF PLACE

Ambient Air

The outdoor air, in which pollution is influenced by natural forces, such as diffusion by the wind. The term is used to distinguish air quality found in outdoor air (which is affected by air pollution released into the atmosphere) from air quality found in indoor spaces.
See: AIR POLLUTION; NATIONAL AMBIENT AIR QUALITY STANDARDS (NAAQS)

Ambient Noise

Background noise or noise that cannot be identified as coming from any particular source.
See: NOISE POLLUTION

Amenity

In urban design, an element of the landscape or cityscape that contributes to the aesthetic quality and appeal of a place, such as plazas, fountains, street furniture or vistas. Generally speaking, such elements are included in a design to enhance the quality of a space for the user and are not necessarily integral to the function or structure of a project. In zoning ordinances the provision of amenities as part of housing, commercial or office developments is often encouraged by giving bonuses to a developer, such as increases in floor area ratio or a lessening of other zoning requirements.

In a broader sense, *amenity* can also refer to major components of a community plan, such as a large boulevard or an open space. Traditionally these types of design elements are, if well integrated into the fabric of a community, considered to be major urban amenities.
See: FOUNTAINS; INCENTIVE ZONING; PEDESTRIAN IMPROVEMENTS; PLAZA; VISTA

American City Planning Institute (ACPI)

A professional planning organization formed in 1917 that subsequently became the American Institute of Planners (AIP). It was started in Kansas City, Missouri, at the ninth national planning conference, to provide opportunities for professionals to discuss the technical aspects of planning.

There were 52 charter members in the organization, representing fields such as landscape architecture, engineering, law, architecture, real estate and housing. Among the best known of the charter members were Thomas Adams, Edward Bassett, Alfred Bettman and Frederick Law Olmsted Jr., who was ACPI's first president.
See: AMERICAN INSTITUTE OF PLANNERS (AIP); AMERICAN PLANNING ASSOCIATION (APA)

American Economic Development Council (AEDC)

An organization, founded in 1926, concerned with encouraging high standards for industrial and economic development. AEDC members consist of economic development organizations and agencies, chambers of commerce, financial institutions, utilities, land developers, attorneys, realtors and others involved in the field of economic development from the United States, Canada and Mexico.

AEDC, which until 1980 was known as the American Industrial Development Council, offers basic economic development courses at universities throughout the United States, an annual Economic Development Institute, and periodic seminars and workshops. A designation of Certified Industrial Developer (CID) or Certified Economic Developer (CED) is also established and administered by AEDC for professionals qualified by work experience who are able to pass an examination. AEDC publications include a monthly legislative report, a monthly *FORUM Newsletter* and an annual membership directory. AEDC headquarters are in Schiller Park, Illinois.

American Health Planning Association (AHPA)

A national nonprofit organization, founded in 1970, whose principal goal is to maximize the contribution of health planning to the development of a health care system in which high quality care is available to all who require it at reasonable cost. Its membership consists of individuals as well as local health systems agencies, state health planning and development agencies, health insurance plans, and corporations.

AHPA carries out a variety of activities including research, liaison with various levels of the public and private health care sectors, and dissemination of information. The organization, which is based in Washington, D.C., conducts a variety of conferences, seminars and meetings on aspects of health planning, including an annual health planning and the law conference, and publishes a weekly newsletter, *Today in Health Planning*.

American Institute of Architects (AIA)

An organization of professional architects in the United States. Membership categories are available for registered architects, for those working towards registration, and for students and those in related professions. Founded in 1857, AIA's goals include the improvement of the profession of architecture and the fostering of public interest in good design.

AIA maintains a reference library, sponsors design competitions and awards programs, operates a speakers bureau, and provides a number of community services, such as the Regional/Urban Design Assistance Teams, which are a program of the AIA's National Urban Planning and Design Committee. Services provided by AIA to its 37,000 members include assistance in preparing for state licensing exams, professional practice aids and documents, continuing education programs, conferences and an employment referral service.

AIA publications include *MEMO,* published twice a month; the *AIA Journal,* published monthly; and *In Brief,* published monthly. AIA national headquarters are in Washington, D.C., but each state has an AIA unit and there are numerous local groups.
See: REGIONAL/URBAN DESIGN ASSISTANCE TEAM (R/UDAT)

American Institute of Certified Planners (AICP)

An institute of the American Planning Association (APA) for APA members able to demonstrate a specified level of achievement and competence in professional planning. In order to become an AICP member, a planner must first possess a required combination of education and experience. As an example, an individual with a graduate planning degree from an APA-recognized planning program must also have two years of professional planning experience meeting specified criteria.

Once these requirements are met, a prospective AICP member must be able to pass a written examination designed to test both planning knowledge and skills. The examination tests familiarity with subjects such as history and theory, the urbanization process and the planning profession. It also contains questions designed to assess ability to develop strategies, meet goals and needs, and carry out plans; logical abilities; ability to research, analyze and interpret data; management skills; and sensitivity to political and social constraints. Those who pass the exam are certified as members and are entitled to place the initials *AICP* after their names. Since state licensing is rarely used for planners, AICP membership serves as a nationally standardized means of designating and identifying qualified planners.

AICP promulgates a Code of Ethics and Professional Conduct for its membership and also develops criteria for APA to use in recognizing the planning programs found at colleges and universities. A lesser category of membership, that of associate, is available to those planners who will complete their professional planning experience necessary to become a member within two years.
See: AMERICAN PLANNING ASSOCIATION (APA); CODE OF ETHICS AND PROFESSIONAL CONDUCT

American Institute of Planners (AIP)

A professional planning organization formed in 1917 as the American City Planning Institute (ACPI) and renamed the American Institute of Planners (AIP) in 1939. In 1978 AIP consolidated with the American Society of Planning Officials (ASPO) to form the American Planning Association (APA). AIP was concerned with recognizing and designating professional competency and only granted full membership to those who qualified because of technical training or professional work experience and performance on a competency examination. Associate memberships were, however, made more widely available.

Among AIP's accomplishments were the establishment of standards for planning schools in order to achieve AIP recognition and the development of a code of professional conduct. Through its *Journal of the American Institute of Planners,* it helped to explore the theoretical bases of planning and reported on the results of research in the field.
See: AMERICAN PLANNING ASSOCIATION (APA); AMERICAN SOCIETY OF PLANNING OFFICIALS (ASPO)

American Institute of Real Estate Appraisers (AIREA)

A professional organization for real estate appraisers located in Chicago. AIREA, which was founded in 1932, awards the designations of MAI (Member, Appraisal Institute) and RM (Residential Member) to those individuals able to qualify through education, successful completion of a series of courses, appropriate work experience, and preparation of demonstration appraisal reports. All members must agree to comply with the Institute's Code of Ethics and Standards of Professional Conduct.

AIREA offers a comprehensive training program for appraisers in locations throughout the United States as well as continuing education courses of interest to appraisers and those in allied professions. It also offers a series of books, primarily related to real estate valuation, including the standard textbook *The Appraisal of Real Estate,* a recognized guide to proper appraisal techniques. Regular publications are *The Appraisal Journal,* issued quarterly, and *The Appraiser,* a monthly news bulletin.

American Law Institute Model Land Development Code

A model enabling act governing the development of land, adopted by the American Law Institute in 1975. The first significant model code since the Department of Commerce issued its Standard Enabling Acts for city planning and zoning in the 1920s, it is expected to have considerable influence on land use legislation and development practice in the future.

Among the features of the code are an emphasis upon production and adoption of a local land development plan that contains not only long-term goals but short-term courses of action, and the adoption of local land development regulations that combine provisions commonly found in both zoning ordinances and subdivision regulations. Other sections set forth a way by which incompatible or deleterious land uses can be discontinued in a given district, provide for a state land banking agency and establish a means by which the states can intervene in local land use regulatory matters where an important state or regional interest is involved. In addition, it creates a state land planning agency within the governor's office and establishes a state land adjudicatory board that would hear appeals on land use matters.
See: STANDARD CITY PLANNING ENABLING ACT; STANDARD STATE ZONING ENABLING ACT

American Planning Association (APA)

A national organization for professional planners from all branches of planning, citizen members of planning commissions, elected officials, students, educators, and any other individuals interested in public planning. A separate affiliate of APA, the American Institute of Certified Planners (AICP), is reserved for APA members meeting a specified combination of work experience and professional training who are able to pass a comprehensive examination.

APA serves as a central source of information on planning, conducts research, develops policy statements on important planning-related issues, accredits planning degree programs, and presents awards for achievements in planning. APA also offers a wide range of services and programs to its more than 21,000 members. Among these are a planners training service, a computerized system for matching employers with planners seeking employment and an annual national conference. APA members are also able to join special topic divisions focusing on subjects as diverse as planning and law, information systems, economic development, historic preservation and international planning.

The Planning Advisory Service (PAS) is a research and information service, available by special subscription, that provides a series of PAS reports and a monthly *PAS Memo*, and is available to answer inquiries on topics of concern to subscribers. In addition to Planning Advisory Service publications, APA publishes *Planning,* a magazine, and *APA News,* a newsletter, each issued eleven times per year. Available by subscription are the *Land Use Law and Zoning Digest,* a monthly, and the *Journal of the American Planning Association,* issued quarterly.

All members of APA are automatically members of a local chapter that offers additional activities, conferences and publications. APA, which was formed by the merger of the American Society of Planning Officials (ASPO) and the American Institute of Planners (AIP), has offices in Chicago and Washington, D.C.
See: AMERICAN CITY PLANNING INSTITUTE (ACPI); AMERICAN INSTITUTE OF CERTIFIED PLANNERS (AICP); AMERICAN INSTITUTE OF PLANNERS (AIP); AMERICAN SOCIETY OF PLANNING OFFICIALS (ASPO)

American Society for Public Administration (ASPA)

A 17,000-member organization concerned with improving the quality of public service. Membership consists primarily of administrators at all levels of government, business and community leaders, academicians and others concerned with public management. Established in 1939, ASPA maintains chapters throughout the United States and includes sections on various specialized topics, such as management sciences or natural resources and environmental administration. A national conference and regional conferences are held each year, and workshops are offered to help members improve their skills. Publications of ASPA are *Public Administration Review,* a bimonthly journal, and *Public Administration Times,* published twice a month. ASPA headquarters are located in Washington, D.C.

American Society of Agricultural Engineers (ASAE)

A professional organization comprised of agricultural engineers and others concerned with improving agriculture with the aid of engineering techniques. ASAE, located in St. Joseph, Michigan, develops standards for the agriculture industry; conducts a variety of conferences, meetings and continuing education programs; and produces a number of publications. The organization maintains five technical divisions, each of which contains numerous committees. Of particular interest to planners is the Soil and Water Division, which has major committees on groundwater, land use, precipitation and runoff, erosion control, drainage and water resources. The Structures

and Environment Division is also of interest with committees on solar energy, and agricultural sanitation and waste management.

American Society of Civil Engineers (ASCE)

An organization of professional civil engineers and those in related professions, located in New York City. Among the concerns of ASCE are the advancement of the field, the support of research on new civil engineering techniques, ethical conduct in civil engineering practice, and an improved public understanding of the profession.

ASCE conducts national conventions, specialty conferences and continuing education courses designed to aid the professional engineer, and maintains a technical information service. The society has received accreditation by the American National Standards Institute to write civil engineering standards. It publishes a wide variety of manuals, reports and special publications as well as 15 technical journals. In addition, regular publications are a monthly magazine, *Civil Engineering,* and a monthly tabloid, *ASCE News.* ASCE also presents Outstanding Civil Engineering Awards for projects of special merit.

American Society of Consulting Planners (ASCP)

An organization for firms engaged in the professional practice of planning. Established in 1966, ASCP promulgates a code of professional conduct for member firms, distributes information related to private planning practice, conducts research, and operates a legislative program. Other activities include a continuing education program and an annual meeting. Publications include a quarterly *ASCP Newsletter* and an annual membership directory. ASCP also produces a variety of booklets and brochures on topics such as the selection of a professional planning consultant. The offices of ASCP are in Washington, D.C.

American Society of Landscape Architects (ASLA)

A nonprofit professional organization devoted to the advancement of landscape architecture. Established in 1899, this Washington, D.C.-based organization provides a wide variety of services to its members including continuing education seminars, a professional practice institute, a professional placement service, and an awards program. ASLA also offers current information on legislation, regulations and other government matters, as well as data on new products of use to those involved in landscape and site design.

Publications of ASLA include *LAND* (Landscape Architecture News Digest), a monthly; *Landscape Architecture,* a bimonthly magazine and *LATIS* (Landscape Architecture Technical Information Series), a series of reports on various technical subject areas. ASLA also publishes a *Uniform National Exam Study Guide for Landscape Architects.*

American Society of Planning Officials (ASPO)

An organization formed in 1934 dedicated to exchanging planning information and increasing communication about planning. ASPO was a service-oriented organization: Planners, elected and appointed officials, and interested citizens could all gain membership.

A particular emphasis of ASPO was on the "how to" aspects of planning. Its *Planning Advisory Service (PAS)*, instituted in 1949 and circulated on a subscription basis, stressed particular technical topics that planners and officials would encounter in their daily practice. Many of the *PAS* reports helped to set standards for the field. In 1978 ASPO consolidated with the American Institute of Planners (AIP) to form the American Planning Association (APA). APA continues to issue many of the publications begun by ASPO, including the *PAS* series.
See: AMERICAN INSTITUTE OF PLANNERS (AIP); AMERICAN PLANNING ASSOCIATION (APA)

Amicus Curiae

Literally, friend of the court. A person who is not a party to a judicial proceeding but who has strong views as to how a legal issue before a court should be decided may petition the court for permission to file a brief. The brief (commonly referred to as an "amicus brief") would suggest a resolution of the issue, accompanied by supporting rationale.

Amicus briefs are most commonly filed in proceedings involving issues of broad public interest—for example, cases dealing with conservation of public lands. They may be filed either by governmental authorities or by private individuals.

Amortization

1. The process by which debt is gradually retired through periodic payments of interest and principal. Typically, residential mortgages in the United States have been fully amortized or self-liquidating; that is, the mortgage loan is repaid in equal periodic payments sufficient to retire the debt at maturity. A balloon loan, on the other hand, is only partially amortized, since an outstanding balance remains at the end of the loan term and is due at that time. A standing loan is not amortized at all; rather, the entire principal falls due at the end of the loan period.

2. The writing off of the cost of an asset over a period of time.
See: BALLOON MORTGAGE; DEBT SERVICE

Amortization of Nonconforming Uses

A term that describes the requirement found in zoning ordinances that a nonconforming use either be discontinued or be made to adhere to ordinance provisions after a specified length of time prescribed by the ordinance. The process developed as a means of causing nonconforming uses to conform to an ordinance without imposing the undue economic hardship to the nonconforming user that could occur as a result of requiring immediate conformance to a new ordinance. The amortization period responded to arguments that causing immediate cessation of a prior nonconforming use could constitute an unconstitutional taking of property.
See: NONCONFORMING LOT; NONCONFORMING STRUCTURE; NONCONFORMING USE

Amphitheater

An outdoor theater that may take any of several forms. It may be a permanent structure constructed for theatrical purposes or a movable stage set in a clearing. A plateau that serves as a stage and that is partially surrounded by hills on which seating can be located is a more natural form, while a covered but not enclosed structure that permits seating within it offers the best acoustical qualities. On many college campuses, new buildings are being designed so that areas outside may serve as small amphitheaters for theatrical or educational purposes.

Amphitheaters require settings with good natural acoustics that are not compromised by noise from traffic, airplanes or surrounding development. Depending upon the size, purpose and design of the amphitheater, the stage may be a permanent structure, a temporary one that can be collapsed for storage or even a grassed area with tall plantings as a backdrop. A design that incorporates a high rear wall and inclined ceiling is often used, while a band shell, which may be smaller than an amphitheater stage, is another option. Some municipalities maintain movable stages, constructed from trailer trucks or mobile homes, that can be taken to neighborhood parks.

Seating may be on the grass, on folding chairs, benches or bleachers, or it may be permanently installed. Sufficient parking should be available, but if the amphitheater is used only occasionally, temporary facilities, such as adjoining grassed areas, may suffice.
See: THEATERS

Amusement Facility

An outdoor recreational area at which amusement rides, thrill rides, games of chance and other forms of entertainment are offered, often in conjunction with beach or pool facilities. Amusement facilities vary in size from less than one acre to hundreds of acres and vary also in the quality and quantity of facilities. They are usually privately owned, commercial operations, but a few are municipally owned.

Modern amusement facilities are generally very large theme parks, which often integrate the natural environment into their planning, preserving major open-space areas. Tivoli Gardens, in the center of Copenhagen, serves as both an urban park and an amusement area and is the model for many modern theme parks, as is Disneyland in Anaheim, California.

Amusement facilities, which usually draw regional attendance, often attract large crowds on holidays and in

favorable weather. Good road access must be provided, and parking, public transit, public facilities and food services should be sufficient for demand.
See: DISNEY WORLD

Anchor Lease

The lease offered by a shopping center developer to the anchor tenant.

A strong anchor tenant is generally thought to be essential to the success of a shopping center. Frequently, obtaining the commitment of an acceptable anchor tenant is a precondition to the developer's obtaining the financing he needs to proceed. In addition, since shopping center leases typically have percentage rent clauses, the developer's rental income will be directly related to the anchor tenant's ability to generate shopping traffic to satellite stores in the center.

Because of its importance to the success of the shopping center, the anchor tenant is frequently offered lease terms that are more favorable than those offered to satellite stores, which may include some degree of control over the nature of other retailers who may be offered leases in the center.
See: ANCHOR STORE

Anchor Store

A department store at a regional shopping center, a junior department store or discount store at a community shopping center, or a supermarket at a neighborhood shopping center. Shopping center design is usually based on the number of anchor stores and their particular requirements, since they occupy the most floor area, are frequently the first to rent space or are the developers of the shopping center and usually dictate the nature of the other tenants.

In shopping center design the primary function of anchor stores, which may also be called magnet stores, is to draw people to the shopping center. When two or more are placed at opposite ends of a shopping mall, they serve to draw shoppers past the smaller shops.
See: SHOPPING CENTER DESIGN; SHOPPING MALL

Angle of Incidence

The angle of direct sunlight meeting a surface, which is one factor that determines how effectively a solar collector can operate. The more perpendicular the sunlight is to the surface, the more likely it is to be absorbed, while sunlight striking a surface at an angle well below 90 degrees is often reflected. Sunlight strikes the Earth at a more oblique angle in the early morning and late afternoon, in the winter and at higher latitudes. This should be taken into account in designing systems using solar energy. (See Fig. 4)
See: SHADOW PATTERN; SKYSPACE; SOLAR ACCESS DESIGN TECHNIQUES; SOLAR COLLECTOR; SOLAR ENERGY

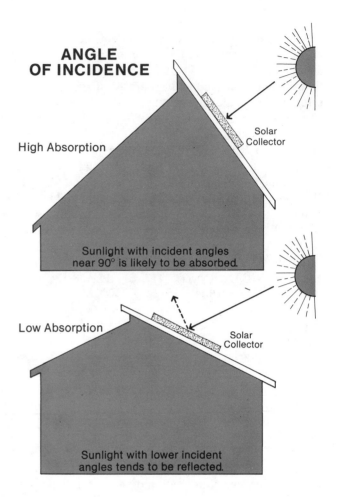

Fig. 4. The angle at which a solar collector is placed can affect its efficiency.

A-95 Review

The review of applications for federal grants-in-aid by areawide and state planning and development clearinghouses, as established in 1968 by the Office of Management and Budget in OMB circular No. A-95, "Evaluation, Review, and Coordination of Federal and Federally Assisted Programs and Projects." The A-95 review procedure, which was replaced in 1983 by Executive Order 12372, was designed to facilitate coordinated planning on an intergovernmental basis for certain programs and to promote efficient government spending.

The review procedure involved an analysis of a proposal as it related to regional plans as well as an active attempt by the reviewing clearinghouse to obtain comments from state and local government agencies and citizens' groups whose programs might be affected by the proposed project. After completion of the review process, the proposal and all comments were forwarded to the federal funding agency responsible for making the grant.
See: AREAWIDE CLEARINGHOUSE; EXECUTIVE ORDER 12372

Annexation

The process by which one municipality acquires surrounding land and incorporates it into its jurisdiction.

Historically, this constituted a primary means by which major cities grew to their current land area and boundary configuration. However, annexation has also occurred in suburban areas, where one suburban municipality grows by acquiring surrounding unincorporated territory or, less commonly, a neighboring municipality. More recently, suburban municipalities adjoining large urban areas have resisted incorporation into the city in order to maintain local control over schools and other municipal services and avoid being forced to share in problems currently confronted by large cities.

Consolidation, a variant of annexation, refers to the process by which two incorporated municipalities merge to create a single new governmental unit. Currently, this process is used most frequently in connection with school districts, as a reaction in part to rising costs of education and declining numbers of school-age children.

Annual Implementation Plan (AIP)

A document containing the detailed short-range objectives and priorities of a Health Systems Agency (HSA). It presents those actions or changes in health resources that should be carried out over a period of one year in order to achieve long-range objectives of the Health Systems Plan, and is intended to provide a basis for project review.
See: HEALTH SYSTEMS AGENCY (HSA); HEALTH SYSTEMS PLAN (HSP)

Apartment

A room or group of rooms that is designed to function as a single, complete dwelling unit and is located in a multi-family dwelling. Apartments, which are called flats in Britain, may be leased, or they may be purchased as condominium or cooperative housing. As of the 1980 census there were 15,337,731 renter-occupied housing units in the United States in buildings containing two or more housing units. This represented 17.3 percent of total housing units.
See: CONDOMINIUM HOUSING; COOPERATIVE HOUSING; GARDEN APARTMENT; HOUSING TYPE

Appeal of *Girsh* (437 Pa. 237, 263 A.2d 395 [1970])

A decision by the Supreme Court of Pennsylvania holding that the failure of a municipality's zoning ordinance to provide for multifamily development anywhere within the municipal boundaries was unconstitutional.

The court found that when there was a demand for multifamily housing in an area (even a demand generated from outside a municipality), a municipality must include provision for apartment house development in its plans for future growth; the desire to preserve the character of the community could not justify the total exclusion of apartment uses.
See: EXCLUSIONARY ZONING

Appraisal

An estimate of the value of property, prepared by a person qualified to evaluate that type of property.

There are three primary approaches to valuing real estate. In one approach, the market data approach, value is established based on recent sales of comparable property after such sales have been adjusted to reflect differences between the property being appraised (often referred to as the "subject property") and the comparable sales. In a second approach, the replacement cost approach, value is estimated by evaluating the cost to replace or reproduce new an existing improvement to real property, then adjusting for existing depreciation to the subject property. In this approach the underlying land is valued as if it were vacant. In a third approach, the income approach, income generated by a property is capitalized to arrive at a value for the property.

The appraisal process consists of a series of steps. First, the real estate and the interest to be valued (e.g., fee, life estate, lease) must be identified. Next, the reason for the appraisal is determined, as it can affect the approach to be taken by the appraiser. Data are collected about the subject property, the area in which it is located and comparable properties, and the three approaches to value described above are applied. Finally, the indications of value derived from the three approaches are reconciled in light of the type of property being appraised and the objective of the appraisal, to arrive at a final estimate of value.

When a real estate appraisal is required, it is often specified that the appraiser must be a member of a recognized organization of appraisers, such as the American Institute of Real Estate Appraisers.
See: APPRAISED VALUE; CAPITALIZATION; COST APPROACH APPRAISAL; INCOME APPROACH APPRAISAL; MARKET DATA APPROACH APPRAISAL; MARKET VALUE

Appraised Value

The value of property as estimated by an individual qualified to appraise that type of property.

Appraised value of real estate is required for a variety of purposes, such as in connection with mortgage financing, sales, a condemnation of the property, for tax assessment and estate tax purposes, and in order to determine the value of donated property.
See: APPRAISAL; MARKET VALUE

Aquaculture

The commercial cultivation of aquatic life such as fish, shellfish and seaweed. When limited solely to the production of fish, the term "fish farming" is often used while the term "mariculture" is frequently used to describe the cultivation of marine rather than freshwater species. Aquaculture has been growing steadily in importance in terms of total fish and shellfish production.

Commercial fish production is an ancient practice dating

back thousands of years to India and China. Today it is employed on a worldwide basis although types of aquatic life cultivated vary widely according to local food preferences and environmental conditions. As an example, catfish, trout, salmon, oysters and shrimp are popular in North America while sturgeon and carp aquaculture facilities are common in the Soviet Union. Plant aquaculture is practiced in Japan, Korea and China to provide macroalgae (seaweed) as a basic food source.

Aquaculture may be operated simply and on a small scale, or it may be operated on a high technology basis employing sophisticated management techniques. At its simplest levels, which generally produce low yields, natural water bodies are used and stock is periodically replenished. A more intensive technique is employed in catfish farming in the United States, where large ponds are used and the fish are fed special feed mixtures. There is little dependence on the natural environment in the most sophisticated methods in which marine life, such as shrimp, are raised in raceways or tanks in buildings covered by inflatable domes. Waterflow and feed are carefully controlled.

Recently, experiments have been conducted in which the heated water discharged by power plants and industrial plants is used for aquaculture. As an example, the warm water discharged by a generating station in Dorset, England has been used to raise quahog clams.
See: AGRICULTURAL LAND USE; THERMAL POLLUTION

Aqueduct

A man-made structure built to carry water, which may include canals, viaducts, tunnels, pipes and ditches. Generally aqueducts are used to carry water from reservoirs to distribution systems to allow urban areas to obtain their water supply from distant sources as local supplies become inadequate.

An extensive aqueduct system provided ancient Rome with its water. Today modern cities throughout the world—including Glasgow, Manchester, Vienna, Los Angeles and San Francisco—depend on aqueduct systems.

Aqueducts may rely upon gravity flow (grade-line aqueducts) or pressure. Gravity-flow aqueducts follow a hydraulic gradeline and are usually built through cut and fill construction. They are most often used where the terrain is fairly level. In pressure aqueducts the aqueduct is completely enclosed and filled with water flowing under pressure. They are often found in hilly and mountainous areas because pressure aqueducts can follow rugged terrain. In modern water distribution systems, these two aqueduct types can be combined, depending upon topography.

A good example of modern aqueduct use may be seen in New York City, where three aqueduct systems—the Croton, Catskill and Delaware—deliver water from upstate to provide most of the city's supply.
See: GRAVITY FLOW; RESERVOIR; WATER SUPPLY ENGINEERING; WATER SUPPLY SYSTEM

Aquifer

Subsurface rock or other materials capable of holding a significant amount of water in their interstices. Aquifers can exist for hundreds or thousands of connected square miles and may be several hundred feet thick. Certain types of material—such as coarse sands, gravel and limestone—are more likely to be productive aquifers. The quality of water in an aquifer varies with the type of surface rock and any nearby sources of pollution.

Aquifers are of special importance as a water source in areas of low rainfall and scant surface water.
See: ARTESIAN WELL; GROUNDWATER; INFILTRATION; RECHARGE; WATER TABLE

Arable Land

Land that can be used for the cultivation of crops.
See: DESERT; FARMLAND PROTECTION

Archaeological Site

A site that contains evidence or artifacts of human activities, usually of the distant past or of periods from which little else remains. Properties may be nominated to the National Register of Historic Places for their archaeological value, providing they are relevant to significant past cultural patterns, activities, persons or events.
See: AERIAL PHOTOGRAPHIC APPLICATIONS; HISTORIC PRESERVATION; HUMAN SETTLEMENTS; NATIONAL REGISTER OF HISTORIC PLACES

Architectural and Transportation Barriers

Structural elements in the man-made environment that prevent access to persons with physical handicaps. Walks, seats, steps, railings, drinking fountains, lighting fixture switches, playground equipment, signs, telephones, toilet facilities, doorways and interior circulation can all be difficult or impossible to negotiate for persons who are in wheelchairs, on crutches or blind.

The Architectural Barrier Act of 1968 and its amendments mandates that all federal buildings and installations that are accessible to the public as well as projects that receive federal aid—e.g., municipal buses—be built with barrier-free design. Most state governments and many municipal governments have adopted similar requirements for facilities under their jurisdiction. Some states and municipalities also have included barrier-free requirements in their building codes, which are applicable to private multifamily residential, commercial and industrial construction.

In federal language removal of an architectural barrier is referred to as a 504 improvement, named after Section 504 of Title V of the Rehabilitation Act of 1973, which states that handicapped people cannot be discriminated against solely by reason of their handicap under any program or activity receiving federal financial assistance.

The removal of architectural barriers usually involves lowering fixtures that are normally placed for the convenience of a standing person—e.g., water fountains and

signs; adding ramps and elevators where once only steps were provided; providing extra-wide doors, hallways and toilet booths to accommodate wheelchairs; providing handrails and curb cuts; equipping buses with steps that lower to the ground to accommodate persons who cannot step up (called kneeling busses); and developing recreational facilities, such as braille trails and fragrance gardens.
See: BRAILLE TRAIL; BUILDING CODE; PLANNING FOR THE DISABLED; PLANNING FOR THE ELDERLY

Architectural Concrete Construction

The use of textured or patterned concrete as an exterior building material to provide interesting effects and an enhanced appearance. Numerous patterns are available for either poured-in-place concrete (where the texture is supplied by the formwork) or precast elements. In the manufacture of precast panels, which are cast horizontally (in contrast to poured-in-place panels, which are cast vertically), an aggregate can be placed in the form first and the concrete poured on top, yielding a panel with an aggregate that is exposed.
See: AGGREGATE; CONCRETE

Architectural Controls

Regulations, designed to be used in conjunction with zoning, that control the architectural design of buildings or structures. They are generally administered by architectural review boards and may be applicable to entire municipalities or to particular areas. Architectural controls are intended to produce buildings that are aesthetically acceptable to a community. They are used principally for new development in suburban areas and to preserve architecturally significant areas by ensuring that new or renovated structures are harmonious with the environment in which they are to be located. Some communities have adopted ordinances that prohibit "look-alike" design to encourage architectural diversity, while other municipalities require a certain degree of architectural conformity.

Architectural controls regulate such building elements as facades, rooflines, door and window locations, and massing of building components and may even allow reviewing agencies to make judgments regarding good or bad design. Although criticized by some as preventing innovative design, such controls have tended in many cases to prevent development that is damaging to the community.
See: AESTHETIC ZONING; ARCHITECTURAL REVIEW BOARD; DESIGN STANDARDS; HISTORIC DISTRICT ORDINANCE; LOCAL AUTHORITY; SIGN REGULATION

Architectural Design for Energy Conservation

The use of energy-conserving design principles and concepts is gaining increased attention as fuel prices rise. Prior to the advent of the era of readily available and inexpensive fuel, design and construction methods were oriented to climate, resulting in distinctive regional architectural styles best suited to local requirements. Cape Cod houses were deliberately constructed with long north-facing roofs and small windows to afford protection against cold temperatures and north winds, while southern houses in humid areas featured high ceilings, tall windows and shaded porches. The era of cheap energy resulted in a blurring of regional styles, as unlimited fuel oil and air conditioning were used to compensate for whatever architectural style an individual chose for his house, even if unsuited to the climate. Now, with high energy costs, architectural styles that suit the climate are once again being emphasized, as well as fuel-saving techniques such as vestibules that can act as air locks, triple-glazed windows and additional space for insulation.

A set of specific design principles has also developed around the use of solar heating and cooling. Features such as increased south-facing windows and walls, fewer north windows in cold climates, skylights, greenhouses that can be covered by insulating panels at night and construction materials that can store heat at night are all being used to maximize winter heat gain. A model energy-saving house recently constructed at the Brookhaven National Laboratory on Long Island, New York with Department of Energy funding uses solar and conventional energy-saving design techniques and is expected to use roughly 15 percent of the fuel oil a conventional house might require.
See: EARTH-COVERED BUILDING; ENERGY CONSERVATION PLANNING; ENERGY-EFFICIENT LAND USE PRACTICES; HOME WEATHERIZATION; NATURAL COOLING; SOLAR ENERGY; THERMAL WINDOWS

Architectural Illustration

A method of design presentation employed in architecture, civil engineering and urban design. Three-dimensional views—presented in perspective renderings, sketches or paintings of proposed projects—are prepared for information and promotional purposes.
See: PERSPECTIVE RENDERING

Architectural Model

A three-dimensional construction of a proposed building or complex of buildings at a reduced scale. Models are made to aid in site analysis and in the siting of buildings, as well as for presentation to clients or the public.

Working models, usually crude in comparison with presentation models, are often constructed of cardboard or styrofoam on which simple cardboard buildings are placed. Presentation models may be made of masonite, with richly detailed building facades and ground areas, and may have people, trees, cars, etc., to illustrate size relationships and animate the setting. In order to enable detail to be shown and to make the model easier to understand, it is customary to exaggerate the heights of contours and buildings in architectural models by constructing them at double or triple the scale of the map beneath them.

Architectural Review Board

A jury or board of local citizens who are charged by local ordinance with the review of building plans and other stipulated documents, usually for the purpose of controlling inappropriate design throughout a municipality. The general purpose of an architectural review board is to guard against development that will have a negative effect on property values or damage the community's appearance. Members of the board, who are generally appointed for three-year terms, are usually architects, planners, developers or experts in art or aesthetics.

The scope of work assigned to these boards varies from municipality to municipality. It generally includes review of the plans of all building permit applications referred to it by the building inspector or other agencies for compliance with architectural standards. In some communities, plans are referred to the architectural review board only if they fall within certain categories, such as commercial or industrial development. The board's activities may also involve review of planning documents, such as a comprehensive plan, and of other land use activities—such as a proposed rezoning, subdivision, site plan or erection of a sign—so that community design standards may be maintained.

Architectural review boards generally evaluate projects on the basis of excessive similarity, excessive dissimilarity and design that is otherwise considered to be unsuitable. Excessive similarity—such as identical facades, doors, windows, porticos or other elements—or excessive dissimilarity in the form of size, gross floor area, building height, building materials or design quality may have equally undesirable effects on areas that surround them. Similarly, poor design, poorly placed entrances or other building elements, or the use of building materials that may have adverse effects on surrounding areas, such as a glass facade that might cause excessive glare from sunlight, are subject to potential prohibition. In some cases the board may be permitted to deny a building permit to proposals found to be potentially undesirable, while in other cases it may recommend denial to another body having this authority. In practice, the board will negotiate with the developer to obtain design changes that avoid the need for permit disapproval. In cases where permits are denied, the developer may be allowed to appeal to the zoning board of appeals or municipal legislative body, but if an appeal mechanism is not specified in legislation pertaining to the architectural board of review, legal action may be necessary.

Two other boards that have similar forms of authority are the historic review board and the landmarks commission. The historic review board has architectural review authority within an officially designated historic district, while the landmarks commission generally has citywide jurisdiction over landmark structures. In some municipalities, an architectural design ordinance that controls certain design elements may be used to ensure adherence to design principles.

See: ARCHITECTURAL CONTROLS; HISTORIC REVIEW BOARD; LANDMARKS COMMISSION ORDINANCE

Architecture

1. The art and science of designing and constructing buildings that fulfill the practical and aesthetic requirements of civilized societies.
2. The buildings produced by architectural design.
See: ARCHITECTURAL CONTROLS; ARCHITECTURAL REVIEW BOARD; BUILT ENVIRONMENT; COMMUNITY CHARACTER; LANDSCAPE ARCHITECTURE; SCALE OF DEVELOPMENT; STREETSCAPE; URBAN DESIGN

Area Source

An air pollution term found in federal regulations promulgated to implement the Clean Air Act and used to describe a small fuel combustion source. In this context, examples of area sources are on-site solid waste disposal facilities, motor vehicles or aircraft.
See: AIR POLLUTION

Area Variance

A zoning variance that is granted concerning the size and shape of a building lot and the size, shape and location of the physical structure to be erected on the lot. This type of variance concerns such zoning requirements as density, required yards, number of parking or loading spaces, frontage, lot size or height. In some states additional distinctions are made between variances that concern the lot area and its dimensions and those that increase the density of the development (density variance) or the size of the structure (bulk variance).

The traditional requirement for the granting of an area variance is a showing of practical difficulty, which is usually considered to be the inability of the property owner to comply with the requirements of the zoning ordinance because of the physical features of the property. The judicial standard that must be met in order to obtain an area variance is normally easier to satisfy than the standard for obtaining a use variance. The rationale for this concerns the difference between granting a change in measurement or scale as opposed to permitting a use that the zoning ordinance does not allow, usually a more drastic change in terms of neighborhood impact. In some states, however, no distinction is made between use and area variances, and all requests for a variance must be able to meet the test of unnecessary hardship.
See: USE VARIANCE; ZONING VARIANCE

Areawide Clearinghouse

A state or regional agency designated, under the now defunct A-95 review procedure, to review applications for federal funds made by lower levels of government within its jurisdiction. Regional planning agencies and councils of government were frequently designated as the areawide clearinghouse for an extended area but were permitted to delegate some of their review authority to a lower level of government that was more directly affected by a proposed project.

See: A-95 REVIEW

Areawide Waste Treatment Management Planning (Section 208)

A process of water pollution control planning required by Section 208 of the Federal Water Pollution Control Act Amendments of 1972. Section 208 covers both point sources (such as factories and sewage treatment plants) and nonpoint sources (such as agricultural and mining activities and urban runoff).

Under Section 208, states must identify planning areas, designate regional planning agencies to prepare areawide waste treatment management plans and then designate management agencies to implement these plans. The 208 plan must include a plan for sewage treatment plant construction or upgrading suitable for the next 25 years; improvements to the system; regulations to control the development of point sources; regulatory controls and nonregulatory measures on nonpoint sources, including best management practices that reduce nonpoint source pollution; and an implementation strategy. Federal grants covering up to 100 percent of the planning process are made available.

After state and federal approval of the 208 plan, federal sewage treatment construction grants are channeled to the designated implementation agency and are restricted to projects that comply with the plan. In addition, National Pollutant Discharge Elimination System permits may not be issued to projects that conflict with the 208 plan.

See: BEST MANAGEMENT PRACTICES (BMPs); FEDERAL WATER POLLUTION CONTROL ACT AMENDMENTS OF 1972; NATIONAL POLLUTANT DISCHARGE ELIMINATION SYSTEM (NPDES)

Arm's-Length Transaction

A commercial or business transaction entered into by unrelated parties as strangers, each independent of the other and each insisting that he receive the maximum benefit of the bargain to be reached.

The terms agreed upon by parties negotiating an arms-length transaction are typically looked to as evidence of value. For example, real estate appraisers and tax assessors will attempt to measure the fair market value of a parcel of real estate by comparing it to parcels that have been sold for a known price in an arm's-length transaction.

Army Corps of Engineers

A command of the United States Army that is responsible for the Civil Works Program, a water resources development activity dating to 1824. The corps is analogous to a major construction and development company, with its engineering works including major dams, reservoirs, harbors, navigation channels and related structures. Its functions also include planning and implementation of flood-management and control measures, beach and streambank erosion control, and provision of hydroelectric power and recreational facilities as additional benefits of navigation and flood-control projects. In addition, the corps has regulatory powers concerning construction and dredging in navigable waters and disposal of dredged materials.

Navigation, the original jurisdiction of the corps, is one of its primary activities. Navigation improvements extend to providing waterway channels, anchorages, turning basins, locks, dams, harbor areas, protective jetties and breakwaters for inland waterways, deep-draft harbors and small boat harbors. Through the Floodplain Management Services Program, the corps provides technical planning assistance in identifying flood hazard areas and planning use of floodplains. Floodway delineation and assistance in writing floodplain zoning, subdivision regulations and building codes are among the services that aid jurisdictions in participating in the national flood insurance program. The corps also constructs flood-protection facilities—such as dams, reservoirs, levees, dikes and diversion channels—and operates programs such as flood forecasting and warning systems to help limit flood damage. Other activities are assistance in temporary or permanent evacuation and relocation, and operation of an elaborate disaster-assistance program.

Beach erosion control, an ongoing program, is available for continued restoration of the historic shorelines of coastal areas, the Great Lakes and lakes, estuaries and bays directly connected with them, providing the areas are open to public use. Solutions may be structural or require periodic beach nourishment (sand replacement). Cost sharing is usually on a 50 percent federal, 50 percent local government basis, with certain public park and conservation areas eligible for a 70 percent federal share. Streambank erosion control, however, is a smaller program. Construction or modification of emergency streambank and shoreline protection works is permitted only to prevent damage to primary highways, bridge approaches, public works, churches, hospitals, schools and other buildings housing nonprofit public services.

As part of other projects, or by special legislation, the corps also undertakes development of water storage reservoirs and hydroelectric power facilities. Storage reservoirs may be for water supply, stream flow regulation or agricultural purposes. Hydroelectric power is marketed by one of the Power Administrations of the Department of Energy, and the investment in the facility is repaid by its users via user taxes.

Other activities of the corps include development of recreation areas in conjunction with corps projects (for which the local cost share is generally 50 percent), fish and wildlife protection, and wetlands conservation in connection with its projects. Wetlands establishment (the creation of new wetlands by filling submerged areas with dredged material and appropriate planting) is also authorized for certain water resources development projects.

Regulatory functions to protect and preserve navigable waters and aquatic environments are also administered by the corps. Construction of dams or dikes in navigable waters as well as any alteration or modification of the course, condition, location or physical capacity of these waters requires approval of the Secretary of the Army and/or the Congress. Construction of fixed structures and artificial islands on the outer continental shelf is also subject to this approval. Discharge of dredged or fill material into navigable waters and the transportation of dredged material for dumping in ocean waters are regulated by permit.
See: ARMY CORPS OF ENGINEERS' PERMIT PROGRAM; NATIONAL FLOOD INSURANCE PROGRAM

Army Corps of Engineers' Permit Program

A program administered by the Army Corps of Engineers in which permits are required for a range of activities related to protection and maintenance of water quality and navigability. Typical marine activities for which permits are required are dredging, filling, discharge of materials and construction of facilities such as boat ramps, piers, wharves, dams or bulkheads.

The program began in 1899 with the River and Harbor Act of that year, with an emphasis upon preventing obstructions in navigable waters. As a result of increasing concern about water quality, the Federal Water Pollution Control Act Amendments of 1972 expanded the corps' responsibility to include provisions protecting fish, shellfish and wildlife habitats, and recreational areas.

Although the Corps of Engineers has authority only over navigable waters, this term has been defined in its broadest sense to include coastal waters; coastal wetlands; navigable rivers, lakes, streams and artificial water bodies; tributaries of navigable waters; interstate waters; intrastate waters with a relationship to interstate commerce; and many freshwater wetlands.

Generally, federal policy is to deny permits in wetlands unless the proposed project is necessary to promote the public interest. In determining the necessity of the project, the corps is primarily required to examine whether the project is dependent upon the wetlands and whether realistic alternatives to that site are available.
See: ARMY CORPS OF ENGINEERS; DREDGING; FEDERAL WATER POLLUTION CONTROL ACT AMENDMENTS OF 1972; LAND RECLAMATION; WETLANDS

Arterial Road

A vehicular right-of-way whose primary function is to carry through traffic in a continuous route across an urban area while also providing some access to abutting land. Arterial roads take traffic from collector streets that serve neighborhoods and often connect to freeways, expressways and/or parkways. Arterials are typically a principal part of the road network for through-traffic flow and constitute 20 percent to 40 percent of the total mileage of a road system. They carry the major portion of trips entering or leaving an urban area and normally carry important intraurban and intercity bus routes. In some areas arterial roads are further classified as principal arterials and minor arterials; they are usually found 1 to 3 miles (1.6 to 4.8 kilometers) apart.

Cross sections of typical minor arterials provide an 80-foot (24.4-meter) right-of-way, consisting of 60 to 68 feet (18.3 to 20.7 meters) of paved road surface and 12 to 20 feet (3.7 to 6.1 meters) of sidewalk and planting areas. The roadway includes four moving lanes 11 to 12 feet (3.4 to 3.7 meters) in width and two parking lanes 8 to 10 feet (2.4 to 3.0 meters) in width. It should have a maximum grade of 5 percent and a design speed of 35 to 40 mph (56 to 64 kph) and should be expected to carry 10,000 to 25,000 trips per day.

Major arterial cross sections provide a right-of-way of 120 to 150 feet (36.6 to 45.7 meters) and a pavement width of 84 to 116 feet (25.6 to 35.4 meters) which includes a median, four to six 12-foot (3.7-meter) moving lanes and two 12-foot (3.7-meter) parking lanes. A maximum grade of 4 percent and a design speed of 35 to 50 mph (56 to 80 kph) should be provided. Major arterials should be expected to carry 25,000 to 40,000 trips per day. The design of all urban arterials should also include sidewalks at least 5 feet (1.5 meters) in width, with planting strips between the sidewalk and street surface at least 5 to 10 feet (1.5 to 3.0 meters) in width. Minimum building setback lines should be 30 feet (9.1 meters) from the right-of-way line for those fronting on the arterial and 60 feet (18.2 meters) for those backing on the arterial.

Arterials are placed as, or become, dividing lines between neighborhoods and are also used to separate incompatible land uses. (See Fig. 43)

Artesian Well

A well that taps water located between layers of impermeable rock. When a well is drilled through this rock and reaches an aquifer, the water will surge upward under natural pressure in a manner similar to an oil well. The flow can, however, be affected by other wells drawing on the same aquifer.

Artesian wells are an important water source in portions of central and western Canada and the United States, as well as in Argentina and Australia.
See: AQUIFER; GROUNDWATER; INFILTRATION; WATER RESOURCES MANAGEMENT; WATER TABLE; WELL

Artificial Water Bodies

Man-made water resources created for such purposes as irrigation, recreation, drainage, water supply or livestock watering. Man-made water bodies include such diverse water resources as reservoirs, which are an integral part of water supply systems; farm ponds, which are created for personal or farm use; and man-made lakes, which can help

to hold stormwater runoff, serve as focal points in site plan design and provide recreational resources.
See: DAM; DETENTION BASIN; EMBANKMENT POND; EXCAVATED POND; FARM POND; RESERVOIR; RETENTION BASIN

As-of-Right Zoning

Zoning in which all standards are explicitly set forth and predetermined. In as-of-right zoning, also known as self-executing zoning, the types of uses permitted in each district, maximum height, minimum yard setbacks, lot width and all other criteria for development are predetermined and clearly set forth. Assuming an applicant meets these site development standards for a permitted use, permission for development would be granted.

As-of-right zoning may be contrasted with the newer types of flexible zones and regulations that are coming into widespread use. Techniques such as planned unit development and incentive zoning provide for significant leeway in the design of a project and give a developer many more options. With these techniques, the final version of an application that is approved is the result of a negotiation process, the application and enforcement of flexible standards that are often based upon performance criteria, and the discretion of the decision-making body.
See: EUCLIDEAN ZONING; FLEXIBLE REGULATIONS; INCENTIVE ZONING; NEGOTIATION; PLANNED UNIT DEVELOPMENT (PUD); ZONING

Assessed Valuation

A percentage of the total value of a property (land, buildings and other improvements) determined for the purpose of property taxation on the basis of locally accepted methodology. Assessed valuations (or assessments, as they are often called) are calculated by the municipal or county assessor by determining current property value and applying an assessment ratio, which yields a fractional assessment. In some states, however, the assessed value is the full or market value of the property. The current property value is determined by examining recent sales of comparable property, available data on property improvements and property income yield or by other accepted appraisal methodology.

Fractional assessment of property has been practiced since the middle of the 19th century. It was first used to undervalue properties so that they would pay a smaller percentage of the state tax burden; later it served to disguise assessment errors, often made by untrained assessors who may have been elected to their posts, that gave tax breaks to individual properties or classes of properties. Even today, most communities reassess properties very infrequently, and records of improvements are sometimes not obtained, causing more properties to be undervalued for tax purposes. Undervaluation of a municipality's tax base is a problem for some communities because it limits their borrowing power, which is usually established by the state as a percentage of the municipality's total assessed value.

The use of computers in the maintenance of assessment records has enabled annual reassessment, which is required by a few states. This permits older properties to be taxed on their current value and makes the distribution of the municipal tax burden more equitable. There is also a growing trend in support of better training for assessors, the appointment of professional assessors and the hiring of consultants, when necessary, and states now supervise local assessment activities more closely.
See: ASSESSMENT RATIO; ASSESSOR; TAX RATE; UNIFORM ASSESSMENT PROCEDURES

Assessment Ratio

A ratio of taxable property value to full value, established by the local tax assessor on the basis of the average assessed valuation of various classes of property in the municipality.

When the assessor assesses property, he determines its market value and informally applies an assessment ratio to it, unless assessment at full value or a classified tax system is mandated. The ratio applied is developed by the assessor on the basis of his experience and, depending on local custom, generally is skewed so that certain classes of property will carry a higher tax burden than others. As a result, commercial property is frequently taxed higher than residential property, and apartment houses are usually taxed higher than single-family houses.

Individual assessments within a municipality are generally inequitable, unless the entire municipality has recently been reassessed. In most cases, properties are rarely reassessed and retain assessments made decades earlier. Unless mandated by state law, reassessment generally occurs only when major improvements are added or other significant change takes place, such as conversion of a rental building to cooperative status. The perpetuation of a system in which properties are not reassessed causes the municipality's average assessment ratio to decline annually as the values of properties rise. As this assessment ratio declines, moreover, the assessor gains more leeway in the use of discretion in applying a ratio, since assessment at a small fraction of full value is generally uncontested, and comparison with other property assessments is difficult. In order to gain equity within an otherwise inequitable system, the assessor is required to assign values that he considers to be comparable to similar properties.
See: ASSESSED VALUATION; FULL-VALUE ASSESSMENT; PROPERTY TAX; UNIFORM ASSESSMENT PROCEDURES

Assessor

The official in municipal government responsible for establishing property values for tax purposes in accordance with state and local laws. The assessor's duties involve the valuation of property and the application of the overall budget to the total assessed value of the community to determine the tax rate. The assessor is also responsible for filing updated tax rolls and other reports that may be required by law.

An assessor may be appointed by the mayor, the mayor and the council, or the city manager, or he may be elected, although this practice is much less common. He may be appointed for a fixed term or serve at the pleasure of the appointing authority. Appointed assessors must generally meet certain qualifications of education and experience established by state and local law, although this education often can be obtained after appointment to the position. Assessors may also be appointed or elected to serve singly, or on boards or commissions.

See: ASSESSED VALUATION; ASSESSMENT RATIO; PROPERTY TAX; TAX ASSESSMENT ROLL; TAX RATE

Associated Home Builders of Greater East Bay, Inc. v. *City of Walnut Creek (4 Cal.3d 633, 484 P.2d 606 [1971])*

A decision of the California Supreme Court upholding the constitutionality of state legislation authorizing local governments to require landowners seeking to subdivide their property to dedicate land for park or recreational purposes. Payment of fees in lieu of dedicating the land was also found to be acceptable as a condition to the approval of subdivision plat maps.

The court determined the legislation to be proper exercise of the state's police power based upon the relationship of the need for recreational facilities caused by present and future subdivisions to the maintenance of public health, safety and general welfare.

In reaching its decision the court touched upon and discussed two issues of particular significance for planners. First, the court held that the requirement of dedicating land for recreational use (or paying a fee in lieu of dedication) did not have to be justified by the need for recreational space caused by the subdivision. In effect, the needs of the entire community for recreation facilities could be considered.

Second, the court went beyond the specific holding of the case, since the statute it was then reviewing required that there be a reasonable relationship between the amount of required land dedication and the potential use of the recreational facility by present and future subdivision residents. The court stated that a fee in lieu of dedication requirement for subdivision approval could be justified based merely on the general need of a municipality for more recreational space, even if the land acquired with the fee was not conveniently accessible to occupants of the subdivision.

See: FEE IN LIEU OF DEDICATION; POLICE POWER; TAKING

At-Grade Intersection

An intersection of two or more connecting roadways that join in such a way that traffic on the roads might come into conflict. Their design is classified as plain, flared or channelized. Plain intersections are those at which the cross sections of the intersecting roads are the same width at the intersection as along the length of the road. Flared intersections provide extra lanes for use by through and turning vehicles to achieve greater safety and capacity. Channelization, which is the provision of separated turning lanes and medians, is the most sophisticated form of intersection design. The predominant forms of at-grade intersections are the grade crossing, the T-intersection and the Y-intersection.

Intersections are a limiting factor in roadway capacity. The number of intersections on a road, their spacing and geometric design will affect capacity, operating speed and safety. Intersections that have traffic volumes approaching their capacities are usually controlled by traffic signals.

Design of at-grade intersections should provide for minimum safe-stopping sight distances, grades that do not exceed 5 percent in regions subject to ice and snow, and right-angle turns. Jogged intersections (opposing T-intersections that are separated but closely spaced) should be avoided; they complicate traffic weaving and turning movements, require greater traffic control, and consequently reduce intersection capacity and increase hazards. (See Fig. 5)

See: CAPACITY; GEOMETRIC DESIGN; GRADE CROSSING; JUG-HANDLE TURN; ROTARY; SIGHT DISTANCE; T-INTERSECTION; Y-INTERSECTION

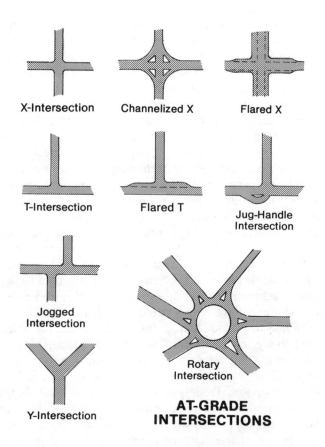

AT-GRADE INTERSECTIONS

X-Intersection   Channelized X   Flared X

T-Intersection   Flared T   Jug-Handle Intersection

Jogged Intersection

Y-Intersection

Rotary Intersection

Fig. 5.

Athletic Courts

Areas of specified dimensions and fixtures that are provided in public and private recreation areas to accommodate such active sports as tennis, squash, basketball, handball and volleyball, and more passive games such as boccie or shuffleboard. Horseshoes and croquet, although frequently played as lawn games, also require courts when played as official competitions. Athletic courts, in general, may be placed in either indoor or outdoor settings.

A basketball court, for which a paved surface and permanently placed baskets are necessary, requires a minimum area of 42×74 feet (12.8×22.6 meters) plus surrounding space, while a volleyball court needs a minimum area of 30×60 feet (9.1×18.2 meters) plus surrounding space and may have permanent or temporary poles that support the net. A volleyball court may have either a paved or turfed surface. A handball court requires a minimum size of 20×37 feet (6.1×11.3 meters) for play on one side, with a 16-foot (4.9-meter) high concrete wall at one end that may have an additional 4-foot (1.2-meter) high chain link fence on top of it. The surface is usually concrete or bituminous material.

Boccie and shuffleboard courts are generally provided in groups, with each boccie court needing 18×62 feet (5.5×18.9 meters) plus surrounding space and each shuffleboard court using 6×52 feet (1.8×15.8 meters) plus surrounding space. Shuffleboard courts must have paved surfaces. A horseshoe pit requires a minimum of 10×50 feet (3.0×15.2 meters), while a croquet court is 30×60 feet (9.1×18.3 meters). These have grass surfaces. Other games, such as lawn bowling and quoits, also require courts.
See: ATHLETIC FIELDS; RACKET SPORTS

Athletic Fields

Play areas for such sports as baseball, softball, soccer, football and field hockey that are provided at most public recreation areas. Limited space in public parks often requires that one area be used for different sports at different times of the year or within the same season. With careful planning, it is possible to site these fields so that they overlap, allowing the same areas to serve for alternative games.

Playfields should be located on well-drained land that is fairly level, ideally with a grade of between 1 percent and 2.5 percent. Equipment, such as backstops, should be permanently placed, and it is desirable for playfields to be lighted. Banking of the land at the sides of fields is useful for providing seating areas for observers, while bleachers may be built where games are played on a regular basis. Since football is played in the fall, the best orientation is northwest to southeast. For baseball, the orientation of home base varies, but a north or south position is sometimes preferred. The extent to which the sun at low altitude is obscured by surrounding development may also affect the siting.

Sizes of playfields are generally prescribed within ranges for each sport, and space should also be provided outside the required minimum areas. The minimum area required for a baseball field is 300×300 feet (91×91 meters), while a softball field may be as small as 250×250 feet (76×76 meters). A football field needs 195×360 feet (59×110 meters), while a soccer field requires a minimum of 200×320 feet (61×98 meters) and field hockey a minimum of 150×270 feet (46×82 meters). A polo field should be at least 480×900 feet (146×274 meters).
See: ATHLETIC COURTS

Atrium

A courtyard located in an interior area of a building, which is either open to the sky or covered with a roof, often made of glass. Originally a part of ancient Roman houses, where it contained a shallow pool of water and was surrounded by a covered walk supported by columns, it has been transposed into modern architecture as a central courtyard. Atriums are often used in office buildings and enclosed shopping malls, where they frequently are richly landscaped and climate-controlled.

Attached Housing

Housing that shares common, or party, walls with at least one other residence.
See: HOUSING TYPE; ROWHOUSE; TOWNHOUSE

Attainment Area

An air quality control region that is not in violation of the national ambient air quality standards with respect to one or more criteria pollutants. An area may, however, be an attainment area with respect to certain criteria pollutants and a nonattainment area for other criteria pollutants, for which standards are not met.

According to the Clean Air Act Amendments of 1977, attainment areas become subject to requirements, referred to as "prevention of significant deterioration (PSD) rules," aimed at preserving those air quality levels that have been attained.
See: AIR POLLUTION; NATIONAL AMBIENT AIR QUALITY STANDARDS (NAAQS); NONATTAINMENT AREA; NONDEGRADATION CLAUSE

Audiovisual Techniques

Various means of using equipment—such as cameras, projectors and tape recorders—to provide a clear image of a place, a concept or a design. Audiovisual aids are used in planning practice for citizen participation, public hearings, lectures, instructional seminars and exhibits. The material used may be prepared specifically for that event—e.g., a presentation of a development proposal—or it may be a canned program that has been produced for more general use.

In addition to the standard slide or movie projector, more specialized equipment is becoming popular. One type of device, which resembles a small television, allows electronic signals to be recorded on a cassette tape; these

signals cue a projector to change slides while the tape simultaneously provides accompanying narration. Cable television, with its public access channels, provides additional opportunities for the taping and broadcasting of public hearings and educational seminars.
See: CABLE TELEVISION

Auto Disincentives

Employment of transportation policy and municipal regulation to discourage the use of private automobiles in heavily congested areas. Numerous approaches are utilized to deter people from driving their cars into the central business district during peak travel periods. Disincentives may focus either upon making use of the automobile difficult or upon making its use more expensive. Policies relating to financial charges are known as pricing disincentives.

The two principal transportation elements that are targets of control are parking and highways. Control of parking includes eliminating parking from streets that carry high traffic volumes; imposing high parking taxes on parking lot use; raising parking meter charges; actively enforcing parking laws; and, as in London, regulating the number of off-street parking spaces. Controls that deal with highways include imposing tolls where none previously existed and raising them where they do exist; providing preferential lanes and rates for high-occupancy vehicles; providing automobile restricted zones; and requiring supplementary cordon licensing. A notable example of cordon licensing was instituted in Singapore, which requires that any vehicle that enters downtown Singapore during the business week have a prepurchased sticker on its windshield, costing in excess of $30 per month. Corporate vehicles pay twice as much, but buses, some delivery trucks and carpooling vehicles with four or more passengers are exempt from the charge. The Singapore system is known as road pricing.

Other approaches to luring drivers from their cars that are often used in conjunction with auto disincentives include development of park-and-ride facilities and express bus service; improvements in bus fares, routes and schedules; and promotion of ridepooling.
See: AUTOMOBILE RESTRICTED ZONE (ARZ); PARK-AND-RIDE FACILITIES; RESERVED LANES; RIDE-POOLING

Automobile Restricted Zone (ARZ)

An area of a municipality within which private automobile use is either prohibited or permitted on a controlled basis. In Europe, where this concept originated, an ARZ is an area in which traffic is markedly restricted; it is banned entirely in certain town squares and shopping streets. In North America the term is generally taken to mean a shopping mall created from a city street that now permits use only by pedestrians and certain types of mass transit. Experience with existing traffic-free zones has shown that street-level air and noise pollution levels are

markedly reduced. Since most proposals for traffic-free zones are met by local business opposition, it is noteworthy that all European projects developed have led to increased business or to volumes comparable to pre-ARZ levels in the least successful cases. In Germany the ARZ is so popular that by 1979, 500 cities reported that they had instituted an ARZ in one form or another. In the United States, however, businesses adjacent to pedestrian or transit malls have not done as well. Problems related to width of malls (they are often too wide), declining use of central business districts and dependence on auto access make application of such malls difficult except in areas with very high pedestrian use, e.g., university towns and successful central business districts. Projects in Philadelphia, Boston, Madison, Wisconsin, and Boulder, Colorado are among mall developments that are heavily used.

In the European model a new town center plan has evolved in several cities that prevents through traffic from going through the center by directing it to an inner-ring or outer-ring road. Traffic destined for the central business district (CBD) can only reach it via the inner-ring road at entry points along it into specific traffic cells or precincts. These traffic cells are wedges of the CBD that have vehicular access only from the ring road. There is no vehicular connection between them. As a result, traffic into these cells can be controlled at each entry point. Pedestrian zones, high-occupancy vehicle priority and parking restrictions are often used in conjunction with this system. The traffic cell system has been employed successfully in Nottingham, England; Gothenburg, Sweden; and Groningen, the Netherlands.

A variation on this, known as a zone and collar plan, is the establishment of zones throughout an urbanized area, all of which have access only to a ring road and not to each other. The ring road, or collar, then acts as a valve, which permits flow into and out of each zone on the basis of space availability on the ring road and in other zones. Except for high-occupancy vehicles, zones that are filled to a prescribed level will not take any more traffic. This is still in the very early stages of trial and development in Europe.
See: AUTO DISINCENTIVES; CIRCUMFERENTIAL HIGHWAY; PEDESTRIANIZATION; TRANSIT MALL

Auxiliary Lanes

Those lanes of a road adjacent to the through-traffic lanes and provided for specialized purposes. These functions include parking, acceleration or deceleration; turning; storage for turning; additional lanes for weaving; or truck climbing. They are provided to maintain movement at capacity on through-travel lanes.

Parking lanes should be 10 to 12 feet (3.0 to 3.7 meters) in width on all but local streets, but road markings should be at the 8-foot (2.4 meter) mark to keep cars close to the curb. When not used for parking, such lanes can be used for through traffic or as storage or turning lanes.

Speed-change lanes, for acceleration or deceleration to

or from through lanes, are provided to increase safety for vehicles merging or leaving through lanes, by permitting them to increase or decrease speed gradually. This permits the stream of traffic in through lanes to make necessary time and distance adjustments. A tapered area should be provided at the beginning or end of such lanes for smooth transition.

Turning lanes and storage lanes for turning provide safe resting areas out of the flow of traffic for cars waiting to make turns.

Weaving lanes are additional through-traffic lanes provided in areas of a roadway that exhibit high amounts of weaving movements, usually leaving or approaching interchanges.

Climbing lanes are auxiliary lanes provided for slow-moving trucks in areas with steep sustained grades. They should be 12 feet (3.7 meters) wide, but full road shoulders need not be provided, since the climbing lane will serve the functions of a shoulder. Climbing lanes should be provided when the speed of a large truck would be reduced to 30 mph (48 kph) and should end beyond the crest of the hill where such a truck could again exceed this speed. A tapered area should be provided approaching and leaving the climbing lane.
See: HIGHWAY CAPACITY DETERMINANTS; LANE WIDTH

Average Annual Daily Traffic (AADT)

An expression of traffic volume, AADT means the average number of cars per day that pass over a given point in a given year. It is calculated by taking daily traffic counts, to determine the total number of cars that passed over a particular point within the year, then dividing the total by the number of days in the year. Counts can be taken as directional (separate counts for opposing lanes) or nondirectional (combined for both directions), depending on the type of roadway (divided highways are usually taken as directional counts). Maps or tabular sheets that show these counts usually specify whether they are separate or combined. Similarly, average annual weekday traffic (AAWT) is the total weekday traffic in a year divided by the number of weekdays. It is a traffic count that is particularly useful for business areas that have little weekend traffic and would show lower averages if weekend counts were included.

Counting stations on roads representative of each type of road in the classification system are often established, and generalizations are then made about relative traffic volume. Counts are taken for shorter periods of time at minor stations than at key stations, but a factor is developed to represent the ratio between the key stations and the minor stations to allow an AADT to be derived.

When studying specific local roads or intersections for possible improvement, counts are often taken for short time periods. These counts are expressed as average daily traffic (ADT), the average daily flow for the time period studied or average weekday traffic (AWT).
See: DESIGN HOUR VOLUME (DHV); PEAK-HOUR TRAFFIC VOLUME

Avulsion

A measurable and sudden shift of land area caused by the changing configurations of a body of water, such as a river changing its course. Generally, property line boundaries between adjoining riparian landowners (owners of the land fronting on the water) remain the same when this occurs—i.e., they are not shifted to reflect the change in land configuration.
See: ACCRETION

A-Weighted Sound Level

A scale of sound measurement or a method of weighing sound pressure levels that gives more weight to the frequencies that the human ear hears more easily, which are those of medium frequency. Sound levels measured in the A scale may be written as dB(A).

A-weighting in the measurement of environmental noise is widely used throughout the world because of its accuracy and convenience. Maximum permissible sound levels in municipal noise control and zoning ordinances are often expressed in this manner.
See: DECIBEL; NOISE POLLUTION; SOUND-LEVEL METER

Axial Growth

City development along one or more straight roads. Axial growth is a basic organizing mechanism of urban design, with buildings relating to the linear elements.

Axiality is one of the most ancient planning approaches to urban design. The buildings of the Roman Forum were related to each other along a major road, called the Sacred Way, and Michaelangelo utilized axiality as an element of the geometric design of St. Peter's Square. It is still used today in the design of new town centers and other formal urban spaces and is the basis of shopping mall design. Axial growth also forms the basic design of many municipal plans, where two or more intersecting streets (axes) to which all other streets relate attract the greatest density of development and traffic. (See Fig. 24)
See: CEREMONIAL AXIS PLAN; LINEAR CITY; SECTOR THEORY

B

Backfill

1.   Material such as earth and broken stone used to fill that part of an excavation between the outside foundation wall of a structure and a desired grade level or to cover a trench in order to restore the grade over it.

2.   The process of refilling an excavation to restore it to a desired level.

See: EXCAVATION; FILL; GRADE

Baling

A process by which loose refuse is formed into high-density blocks of a uniform size through compaction. Used for many years in industry, baling of municipal refuse allows a community to operate a landfill for a longer period of time, minimizing the difficulties associated with finding new landfill sites.

Not only does baling decrease the amount of space a given volume of refuse must occupy in a municipal landfill; it also makes shipping the refuse easier. In addition, there are reduced cover requirements, and the landfill site may be reused at an earlier date after the landfill is closed because baling improves stability and reduces settling. Baled refuse may also be used as fill at locations considered too small to be conventional sanitary landfill sites.

See: SANITARY LANDFILL; SHREDDING; SOLID WASTE MANAGEMENT; WASTE REDUCTION

Balloon Mortgage

A mortgage in which the monthly payment schedule leaves a substantial portion of the original principal amount outstanding at the end of the loan period. The final principal payment, which is called the balloon and is larger than any previous monthly payment, retires the mortgage. Although commercial balloon mortgages have been fairly common in the past, they are now also seen in residential financing.

Bank Protection

The protection of the banks of rivers or streams is often necessary to minimize soil erosion, reduce sedimentation that pollutes the water body and ensure the safety of nearby roads, bridges and developments. The main causes of bank erosion are the scouring due to water flow and, particularly in the case of smaller streams, the surface runoff that falls over the bank edges into the river or stream. This is worsened by the removal of vegetation at these edges.

It is possible to reduce stream bank erosion either by controlling the flow of water so as to reduce its effect upon the bank or by strengthening the bank. In the first approach water may be deflected from the weak points of the bank or slowed to reduce its scouring effect. Stream de-flectors built of piled rock, timber piling or gabions (wire baskets filled loosely with stone) project from the bank at a right angle or with a downstream tilt. Stream flow may be slowed by using a device called a retard or permeable spur, which projects into the water.

Bank strengthening may be conducted alone or in conjunction with stream control projects. A simple method of bank strengthening is covering the bank with woven mats made of willow or other flexible plant materials, using stakes to fix the mats to the bank. In addition to providing some support, the willows may send out shoots, which help to hold the bank together and slow flood waters. Riprap (stone facing material) lining the bank is also effective. Gabions may be used to build walls as well as to deflect water flow, as can the reno mattress, another type of wire mesh basket that is wider and thinner and used on sloping banks. In emergency situations sandbags can shore up an eroding bank.

See: CHANNELIZATION; RIPRAP

Base Flood

A one hundred year flood, which is a flood with a 1 percent chance of occurring in any given year. This is the minimum level of flooding that the National Flood Insurance Program requires a community to protect itself against in floodplain management regulations. (See Fig. 15)

See: HUNDRED-YEAR STORM; NATIONAL FLOOD INSURANCE PROGRAM

Base Map

1.   A map that contains basic background information necessary for a variety of purposes. A base map is designed to be colored, annotated or used as a base for overlays; because it already contains standard features, such as municipal boundaries, these need not be redrawn each time a map is required. A base map may be prepared for a specific purpose, or existing maps may be adapted for base map use.

Planning agencies may often prepare three types of base maps, depending upon their needs and their budgets. The first type shows only the most basic features, such as transportation rights-of-way, water bodies and political boundaries. The second map adds detail, such as property boundaries and easement lines, and is helpful in conducting neighborhood studies and in monitoring land ownership and development trends. The third adds individual structures and may be employed for recording changes in land uses and for other detailed record keeping.

Because of the effort that is required to develop base maps, it is most efficient to establish procedures for continual updating as changes occur. This may be accomplished through a cooperative arrangement with the building inspector, or in larger areas a computerized data bank may be involved.

2. Maps of a variety of sizes that show street names and community highlights and are mass-produced for public distribution. (See Fig. 33)
See: REFERENCE MAPS

Beach Erosion

A recession of the shoreline that occurs when sand loss is taking place faster than sand is being replaced. Beaches are in a state of constant change and are continually affected by a wide variety of powerful natural forces, such as wind and the force of breaking waves, which can alter their profile. Normally, however, they remain in equilibrium; that is, sand is retained by various elements of the beach system, such as the dune, berm or offshore sand bar. If sand is swept away from one element of the system (e.g., the berms), it will be trapped by another (e.g., the dunes). Each component of the system can receive sand, donate sand or store sand. If something occurs that destroys this natural equilibrium, the beach system becomes unstable, and the beach can recede dramatically.

Equilibrium can be affected by a number of natural or man-made causes. Natural events that can have a significant impact upon a beach are storms and seasonal or long-term variation in wave structure or sea level. Among the human activities that can have a detrimental effect are: dredging; the development of channels or canals; the construction of offshore structures, such as docks or breakwaters, or those connected to the beach, such as jetties or boat launch ramps; and the alteration of the natural sand storage system by removing, or building on, the dunes.

The primary emphasis in stabilizing beaches for many years was on the construction of shoreline protection structures, such as bulkheads, seawalls, groins and jetties. It is now thought that a combination of proper planning and new coastal engineering techniques, combined with the construction of selected shoreline protection projects, produces the best results.

Planning for prevention of beach erosion should stress the complete preservation of the frontal dune system and its protection from construction of roads or structures, from passage of vehicular traffic or from being mined for sand. Paths across dune areas should be simple board walkways that do not obstruct sand flow or destroy natural vegetation. Federal flood disaster regulations for coastal erosion areas stress proper setback from the beach for any structures. A number of states and communities also have regulations specifying the proper setback from dunes. It has been recommended, in addition, that a setback line be established for the construction of new buildings that allows for the predictable recession of the beach for a period of 50 years. In the Netherlands successful coastal protection measures depend partially upon a strict policy prohibiting passage through or breaching of the dunes, as well as construction on them.

Engineering techniques currently stress the stabilization of existing dunes and the reestablishment of dunes that have been destroyed in order to provide protection to development that takes place behind the dune area and to help maintain the beach. Measures often used to stabilize existing dunes or construct replacement dunes include snow fencing, which helps to collect windblown sand, and vegetation, such as wetgrass, which helps protect the dunes against erosion. Beach nourishment, the practice of supplying sand to replace lost sand, is also considered useful in preventing the deterioration of the beachfront, particularly if sand is readily available nearby. (See Fig. 9)
See: BERM; BREAKWATER; BULKHEAD; COASTAL AREA PLANNING; GROIN; JETTY; SEAWALL

Beach Facilities

Improvements to shore areas to enhance their aesthetic appeal for swimming and to accommodate large numbers of people. Beaches may be natural or man-made and are provided on most water bodies.

Beachfront areas require a gradual slope of about 10 percent in the beach area and 6 percent in the bathing area. The water quality must be suitable for bathing and the water bottom unobstructed; cleared of debris, rocks, seaweed and mud; and ideally, covered with sand or gravel. A site that will be able to retain most of its sand during heavy storms should be selected, while areas where silt is deposited should be avoided. A minimum width of 100 feet (30 meters) is desirable for a beach, while on beaches that extend for great distances, units of a maximum of 600 feet (183 meters) are desirable for lifeguard supervision and user orientation.

For purposes of estimating beach capacity, a ratio of 2 to 1 of beach area to swimming area is often used, with swimming area computed at a range of 50 to 150 square feet (4.6 to 14 square meters) per swimmer. Supporting areas at a ratio of approximately 3 to 4 acres (1.2 to 1.6 hectares) per acre of beach are needed for buffer zones, picnic areas, parking and bathhouses.

Where swimming must be provided at an artificial beach (either on a natural or artificial water body) where a gradual slope is not possible, it may be necessary to construct docks that are built on foundations. These should be 6 to 10 feet (1.8 to 3.0 meters) wide and may be constructed so that swimmers are directed to areas of measured water depth or to locations where the bottom has been cleared of plant materials. Small floats may be used to mark confined areas, and rafts may be placed in deep water.
See: BEACH EROSION; COASTAL AREA PLANNING; SWIMMING POOLS

Bearing Wall

A wall that supports vertical loads as well as its own weight. In bearing wall construction, an early form of building construction, exterior and interior walls support floor and roof beams and transmit the loads to the building foundations. Because walls must be of sufficient thickness

to carry these loads, the thick walls become impractical and weights become excessive as the height of a building increases.
See: SKELETON FRAME CONSTRUCTION

Bedrock

The solid rock that underlies the soil or other unconsolidated materials such as loose rock or sand. Underlying geological conditions can play a major role in the pattern of development that takes place. For example, the schist that underlies much of Manhattan at or near the surface enabled large-scale development of massive skyscrapers to take place safely early in the 20th century. Conversely, the clay that prevails beneath London kept development low-profile until modern foundation engineering techniques were developed. In many areas of the Great Plains in the United States, and in the prairies of Canada, bedrock lies so far below the surface that it is expensive and very difficult to transmit building loads to it; the soil must be relied upon for foundation support.

When excavation of bedrock is required, investigation is conducted to determine whether it can be removed with power equipment or is hard enough to require blasting; blasting can cause land development and site preparation costs to increase sharply.
See: FOUNDATION

Bedroom Community

A predominantly residential suburb from which many residents commute daily to employment in commercial areas, frequently the region's central business district. Due to their homogeneously residential character, bedroom communities are often attractive but may suffer financial problems because of a lack of business and industry to share the tax burden.
See: COMMUTATION; SUBURB

Behavioral Design

The control of the physical environment to encourage and support specific types of human behavior. In psychological terms behavioral design, also referred to as environmental design, considers the built environment as a stimulus intended to elicit specific human responses.

There are many demonstrated examples of behavioral design, such as office work places designed to improve productivity or retail spaces in malls intended to encourage purchasing. Children's playgrounds are another specialized environment analyzed to determine behavior patterns and modified by creative play equipment to encourage more imaginative play. Defensible space is a behavioral design concept intended to reduce crime. In each case the design intent is not only to be functional and attractive but to evoke particular behavior as well.
See: CREATIVE PLAY AREAS; DEFENSIBLE SPACE; ENVIRONMENTAL PSYCHOLOGY; PERSONAL SPACE; TERRITORIALITY

Bench Mark

A permanent marker that serves as a reference point for an elevation, usually elevation above sea level. A bench mark may be carved into stone or metal and is designated by the initials *B.M.* or *P.B.M.* (permanent bench mark).

Berenson v. *Town of New Castle* (38 N.Y.S.2d. 102, 377 N.Y.S.2d 448, 339 N.E.2d 863 [1975])

A decision by the New York Court of Appeals (the highest court in New York) that set forth principles against which zoning ordinances claimed to be exclusionary were to be measured.

The test established by the court required that in order to overturn an ordinance as exclusionary, a plaintiff must show either that the ordinance was intended to be exclusionary when it was adopted or that the effect of the ordinance was exclusionary and it was adopted without considering regional housing needs.

The court applied the principles announced in this case shortly thereafter in *Robert E. Kurzius, Inc.* v. *Incorporated Village of Upper Brookville* (51 N.Y.2d 338, 434 N.Y.S.2d 180, 414 N.E.2d 680 [1980]). This latter case involved a claim by a land developer seeking to subdivide land subject to minimum five-acre zoning into two-acre residential lots. The developer claimed that the five-acre zoning was exclusionary. The Court of Appeals upheld the five-acre zoning, relying in part on its finding that a desire to preserve a village's character was not per se attributable to exclusionary motives.
See: EXCLUSIONARY ZONING

Berm

1.   A shelf, ledge or bench that is approximately horizontal, cut into an embankment partway up a slope. One or more berms may be constructed at critical points along a slope to help to stabilize it, collect any material or debris that may fall from a higher point up the slope and control drainage.

2.   An earth mound that is designed to divert and control surface runoff or to serve as a visual buffer.

3.   A relatively flat ledge or shelf, found above the mean high-water level of a beach, that is made of material cast ashore by storm waves.

4.   A terrace that is a remnant of an earlier valley floor.

Berman v. *Parker* (348 U.S. 26, 75 S.Ct. 98, 99 L.Ed. 26 [1954])

A decision by the United States Supreme Court involving the exercise by the District of Columbia of its eminent domain power in furtherance of an urban renewal project. The Court held that the legislature should be afforded broad latitude in determining what are appropriate public ends that justify the taking of property. These public ends could include, in the urban renewal context, the taking of property from one private owner to make the property available for use and development by another private owner.

The case is also significant for planning purposes because, in reaching its decision, the Supreme Court expressly acknowledged that aesthetics fall within the concept of the public welfare and could alone justify the exercise of the police power.

See: AESTHETICS; EMINENT DOMAIN; POLICE POWER; URBAN RENEWAL

Best Management Practices (BMPs)

Practices that aid in controlling water pollution that derives from nonpoint sources. BMPs—which can include structural controls, nonstructural controls and procedures for the operation and maintenance of land uses—are required pursuant to Section 208 of the Clean Water Act and may also be required for Section 303 (e) plans and permit applications under the National Pollutant Discharge Elimination System.

Section 208 requires a description of those practices chosen by an areawide water quality planning agency as a means of controlling nonpoint source pollution, where necessary, to protect or achieve approved water uses. Economic, institutional and technical factors are considered as part of a continuing process in which needed controls are identified and BMPs are evaluated and modified.

Nonpoint sources for which BMPs must be considered include agriculture and silviculture, mining, construction, saltwater intrusion and urban runoff. Examples of how BMPs might be applied include requirements that soil erosion be minimized at a construction site by measures that protect excavated soil materials, as by covering or seeding it; a highway maintenance manual that prescribes when and how much sand and salt should be used for roadway deicing purposes; or recommendations that land use regulations require that a flood-retention basin be constructed for all new parking lots over a certain size.

Under Section 304 (e) of the Clean Water Act, the Environmental Protection Agency has stronger control powers in the form of permit review authority for the control of toxic or hazardous nonpoint source pollution from industry. For activities likely to contribute significant amounts of pollutants to navigable waters—such as sludge or waste disposal, or drainage from raw material storage—permits must be obtained.

See: AREAWIDE WASTE TREATMENT MANAGEMENT PLANNING (SECTION 208); CLEAN WATER ACT OF 1977; NATIONAL POLLUTANT DISCHARGE ELIMINATION SYSTEM (NPDES); NONPOINT SOURCE; STATE WATER QUALITY MANAGEMENT PLAN (SECTION 303 [e])

Best Practicable Technology (BPT)

A requirement imposed by the Federal Water Pollution Control Act Amendments of 1972 that applies to point sources of water pollution other than publicly owned treat-

ment works (POTW). The 1972 law mandated that best practicable technology currently available (BPT) be in place by July 1, 1977 to aid in reducing water pollution.

The administrator of EPA was charged with promulgating definitions, regulations and guidelines for effluent limitations (and revising them as often as necessary). The regulations were required to identify the characteristics of pollutants (e.g., biological, chemical, physical), the extent to which BPT could be expected to reduce effluents and the various categories of point sources other than POTWs. In addition, EPA was charged with enumerating the factors that were to be taken into account in determining control measures and practices that were to be applied to point sources for each of these categories. Among the factors that were to be considered for each category were total costs and benefits, the age of equipment and facilities, the process employed and environmental impacts unrelated to water quality.

A second more stringent standard, best available technology economically achievable (BAT), was to be met by July 1, 1983. In developing regulations for BAT, EPA was to consider the extent to which effluent could be reduced by using various techniques, including those that employed innovations in process and procedure. In addition, BAT was to consider many of the same factors required for development of BPT guidelines as well as take into account the cost of achieving effluent reduction.

Because of the time needed by EPA to produce these guidelines and standards, lawsuits were initiated by citizen groups that led to a consent decree in 1976 and eventual modifications in federal policy that were incorporated in the Clean Water Act Amendments of 1977. The 1977 law established three pollutant categories: conventional pollutants, toxic pollutants and nonconventional pollutants. Conventional pollutants are those usually treated by standard wastewater treatment plants, such as oil and grease or suspended solids. Toxic pollutants are those that fall into categories named in the consent decree and that are included in the act, such as heavy metals and PCBs. Nonconventional pollutants are those that do not fall into the other two categories, such as ammonia and phosphorus.

A new treatment standard, best conventional technology (BCT), was created to control conventional pollutants, and a deadline of July 1, 1984 was set for achieving BCT. In developing regulations for BCT, EPA was charged, among other things, with considering the relative costs and benefits of achieving reductions in effluents. In addition, new schedules were established for attaining BAT (for toxic pollutants—July 1, 1984; for nonconventional pollutants—July 1, 1987).

As of 1982, BPT effluent requirements had been met by 96 percent of all industries. EPA has had great difficulty, however, in developing the effluent guidelines necessary to implementation of BAT and BCT because of the numerous and complicated engineering studies and economic evaluations that must be made for each type of industry. The agency is now attempting to comply with a revised rule-making schedule (originally established in the consent decree) that has been agreed to by the court. As of the end of 1982, effluent guidelines had been issued for 12 classes of industry.

See: CLEAN WATER ACT OF 1977; FEDERAL WATER POLLUTION CONTROL ACT AMENDMENTS OF 1972; INDUSTRIAL SEWAGE; WATER POLLUTION

Betterment Tax

A tax, used in Britain, that is imposed on an increase in the value of land. The theory is that the tax recaptures for the community increased property values that are conferred by the community by virtue of improving the infrastructure—e.g., by building a road or by permitting the construction of another development that enhances the value of land around it. As an example, if a property increases in value because of construction on it, inflation or improvements in its vicinity, at the time of its sale, the owner must relinquish part of his profit (excess returns over expenditures) to the government.

The tax rate in Britain in 1980 was 60 percent of the increased value of the land above the first £50,000 of increase, but private homes, development in enterprise zones and certain other categories of development are exempted from the tax, currently known as the development land tax (DLT).

See: LAND VALUE TAX; URBAN ENTERPRISE ZONES; WINDFALLS AND WIPEOUTS

Bettman, Alfred (1873–1945)

A Cincinnati lawyer and city planner who helped to shape the foundations of 20th-century American city planning. He consistently championed the cause of comprehensive planning as a basis for zoning and, through his involvement in numerous activities and organizations, helped to promote this concept.

His interest in planning developed as a result of his legal work and led to his involvement with the United City Planning Committee of Cincinnati. Bettman drafted a state enabling act to permit the creation of city planning boards in Ohio, and the committee helped to secure passage of this act in 1917. A major force behind the development and official adoption of a comprehensive plan for the city of Cincinnati in 1925, Bettman filed an amicus brief in 1926 in support of comprehensive zoning in the case of *Village of Euclid* v. *Ambler Realty Company*. His arguments are thought to have had a major role in securing the ruling in favor of the village.

As a member of the United States Department of Commerce's advisory committee on housing and zoning, Bettman helped to draft the Standard State Zoning Enabling Act and the Standard City Planning Enabling Act. Among his many other activities, he was a charter member of the American City Planning Institute, president of the National Conference on City Planning (1932) and served as the first president of the American Society of Planning Officials.

See: CINCINNATI COMPREHENSIVE PLAN; *VILLAGE OF EUCLID* V. *AMBLER REALTY COMPANY;* STANDARD CITY PLANNING ENABLING ACT; STANDARD STATE ZONING ENABLING ACT

Bid

1. A formal offer presented to a potential buyer to supply specific goods or services at a stated price in response to request for bids. Normally included in the request are highly detailed specifications and the time frame in which the service must be completed or the product delivered. The request for bids may be publicly advertised in an announcement, in which case it is a competitive bid, or specific contractors may be asked to participate.

It is common for government agencies to require that bids be submitted at a particular time, and often they must be sealed; that is, their contents are not made public until all other bids are received, to encourage the lowest offering prices. The lowest of the price offers is the low bid. In some competitions the best bid—which may not be the lowest bid, but which offers the most appealing features to the buyer when all factors are considered—may be selected.

2. An offer to purchase real estate or other property, usually in competition with other potential buyers.

Bikeway

A bicycle path designed for exclusive use by bicyclists or the lane of roadway that is designed to be shared by bicyclists and motor vehicles. Once thought of as recreational facilities, bikeways are now an integral part of transportation planning as well. Three classifications of bikeways have been widely adopted on the basis of standards developed in Germany and subsequently modified by the California Department of Transportation.

- *Class I—Bike Paths:* A completely separate right-of-way designed for the exclusive use of bicycles. They are found primarily in recreation areas, rural areas and new developments.
- *Class II—Bike Lanes:* A restricted right-of-way designated for the exclusive or semiexclusive use of bicycles. They are usually provided on an existing roadway, permitting cross traffic or parking but separated from through traffic by a curb or barrier.
- *Class III—Bike Routes:* A shared right-of-way designated by signs or pavement markings. They are provided on an existing roadway, permitting use by all types of vehicles.

The design of a bikeway depends on available right-of-way and desired capacity and level of service. A design speed of 20 mph (32 kph) is considered adequate in most cases. Minimum lane width guidelines established in California allow for lateral clearance and maneuvering. A one-way width should be no less than 6 feet (1.8 meters) [5 feet

BIKEWAY

Class I - Bike Path

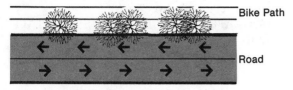

Class II-Bike Lane

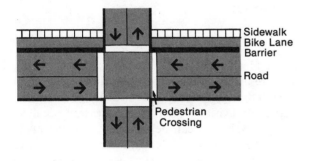

Class III-Bike Route

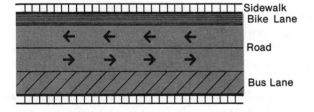

Fig. 6.

(1.5 meters) where a bike lane is adjacent to a parking lane] and the minimum two-way width should be 10 feet (3 meters). In addition, a minimum of a 4-foot-wide (1.2 meter) graded area should be provided on either side of a Class I bikeway, and it should be no closer than 12 feet (3.7 meters) to the edge of a highway. Grades should be no steeper than 5 percent, and sustained grades of 2 percent or less are desirable. Two-way bike lanes may be dangerous where vehicular traffic flow is one-way. In Britain bikeways are called cycleways and cycle routes. (See Fig. 6)
See: BIKING FACILITIES

Biking Facilities

Biking facilities are specialized structural improvements and equipment that encourage bicycle use by increasing its safety and convenience. Such facilities should be consid-

ered wherever bikeways are designated or where bicycling is a prominent mode of transportation. Examples are:

1. Bicycle parking racks for bicycle parking at public facilities of all types, parking lots, garages and transportation terminals. These can be bought commercially or designed as part of a building or complex. They should provide for secure locking and should be screened, where possible, to reduce casual theft.

2. Elimination of curbs, catch basins, ditches and poor roadway surfaces, or the placement of the bikelane away from such obstructions.

3. Official designation of bikeways by placement of signs or pavement markings.

4. Provision of bike racks on the backs of buses to transport bikes over routes where bike riding is prohibited—e.g., bridges.

5. Encouragement of the use of devices that add to the visibility of the bicycle—e.g., reflectors, bike flags or riding pennants (long, flexible plastic rods that extend from both sides of a bicycle to keep overtaking cars at a safe distance), which are used extensively in northern Europe.
See: BIKEWAY

Billboard

A large flat surface or board, normally mounted on a frame, that is designed to carry outdoor advertising. Billboards are generally used along roads to draw attention to a product or service that is offered elsewhere. They may be freestanding or attached to a building and range in size frometers 5 feet × 9 feet (1.5 meters × 2.7 meters) to 14 feet × 48 feet (4.3 meters × 14.6 meters).

Billboards differ from business signs in that they are usually not on the premises of the business or service being advertised and are larger than signs. They are often prohibited by zoning ordinances and sign regulations because they are regarded by many as unattractive additions to the environment and may also distract drivers and obscure views of official signs and approaching traffic.

Billboard control legislation first appeared in the 1958 Highway Act, which provided bonuses in federal highway funds to states protecting the interstate highway system from the visual intrusion of billboards. In the 1965 Highway Act, it was required that, subject to state concurrence, all billboards be removed in noncommercial and nonindustrial areas through which interstate and federal-aid primary highways pass. This provision was substantially weakened by an amendment requiring full remuneration to owners for billboard removal. The state of Vermont, a leader in the area of billboard control, resolved the problem of the cost of removal by requiring remuneration only if federal funds are available. In that state, billboards are prohibited anywhere adjacent to interstate and federal-aid primary highways. Billboards are also prohibited in most state and national parks.
See: ADVERTISING SIGNS; HIGHWAY BEAUTIFICATION ACT OF 1965; SIGN REGULATION

Biochemical Oxygen Demand (BOD)

The most widely used measure of organic pollution, biochemical oxygen demand indicates the organic content of wastewater and surface water.

The oxygen that organic matter requires to enable its biochemical oxidation (decomposition) is measured to determine BOD. The depletion of dissolved oxygen can change the balance of an ecosystem, causing existing animal and plant life to die and often permitting undesirable and pathogenic forms to grow.

In sewage treatment BOD data are used to establish the size of sewage treatment facilities and to measure the effectiveness of treatment processes. BOD levels in water sources and at recreational facilities are regularly monitored by health departments to determine whether the water is safe for drinking and swimming. The BOD is usually measured in the laboratory for a 5-day period (BOD$_5$) at 20 degrees Celsius (68 F).
See: WATER SAMPLING

Biodegradable

Substances, such as paper and organic wastes, that are capable of decomposing and being broken down rapidly by the action of microorganisms. Detergents that are nonbiodegradable can present a particular problem by causing water bodies to foam and by inhibiting necessary bacterial action in sewage treatment plants and septic tanks.
See: BIOCHEMICAL OXYGEN DEMAND (BOD); OXIDATION PROCESSES

Biomass Energy

Energy that is produced by burning or processing organic materials such as wood, plants or organic wastes. One way of generating biomass energy is by direct burning of wood, crops grown for their energy value or water-growing plants such as water hyacinths or algae. Agricultural crops may also be fermented to produce alcohol, which may be blended with gasoline to result in gasohol. The use of organic wastes to generate electricity through resource recovery is also gaining rapidly in popularity, since these wastes would require costly disposal if not used to produce electricity.

Among the most attractive features of biomass fuels are their ready availability and their abundance. They can also be produced in gas, liquid or solid form, facilitating compatibility with a variety of energy production systems.
See: RENEWABLE ENERGY SOURCES; RESOURCE RECOVERY; WOOD FUEL

Biomonitoring

The practice of using living organisms to assess water quality.
See: INDICATOR SPECIES

Birthrate

There are a number of ways in which this figure, representing the number of births for a given population, may be calculated. The crude birthrate, used most commonly, is the number of births that occur in a particular year per 1,000 people. The rate may sometimes be calculated based on annual average data obtained over several years to increase its accuracy. The population may also be subdivided to obtain a crude rate for a particular segment of the population—e.g., city dwellers.
See: DEMOGRAPHY; FERTILITY RATE; MORTALITY RATE; REPRODUCTION RATE

Blacktop

1. A term used by engineers to describe asphalt concrete. It is used colloquially, however, to describe any surface that is paved with bituminous materials.

2. To pave a surface with a bituminous material.
See: PAVEMENT

Blanket Mortgage

A single mortgage in which a number of pieces of real property are involved as collateral for the debt. It is common to find this type of mortgage used in the financing of residential subdivisions. Generally, the individual sites within the subdivision can be released from the blanket mortgage when they are sold and the proceeds given to the mortgagee. Some blanket mortgages, however, carry no provisions for the release of individual parcels from the mortgage terms until the full mortgage debt is satisfied.
See: MORTGAGE

Blighted Area

A neighborhood with a substantial portion of its building stock dilapidated, deteriorated or in need or repair. The evaluation of existing structures to determine blight was a basis for selection of urban renewal sites. Designation of an area as blighted meant a significant chance of eventual clearance, thereby discouraging maintenance and reinvestment. The term is now sometimes avoided because of that connotation and has also come to include any aspect of neighborhood decline.
See: DEPRESSED AREA; SLUM CLEARANCE; URBAN RENEWAL

Block Grant

A grant distributed by the federal government according to a formula; subject to general legislative and administrative guidelines, it may be used for a fairly wide range of purposes. The grants may be made to state governments or to municipalities; in recent years there has been a trend toward the more flexible block grant program rather than categorical aid programs. In Britain block grants or general grants are made to local authorities to be spent at their discretion. As in the United States, this practice was instituted to replace one in which grants were made only for specific purposes.
See: CATEGORICAL GRANT; FORMULA GRANT

Blockbusting

A tactic employed by real estate agents, generally in urban areas, to convince individuals to sell property in response to a fear of racial change. In blockbusting, also referred to as panic peddling, residents are pressured to sell their homes, often at reduced prices, by being told that a large minority population is or will be moving into the community, thereby destroying the neighborhood and devaluing property. An associated strategy, which frequently accompanies this tactic, is the practice of racial steering, whereby real estate agents consciously direct individuals looking for homes to certain neighborhoods based on the race of the individual and the racial composition of the area.

Such actions are prohibited by the Fair Housing Act on the federal level and by a number of state acts generally relating to antidiscrimination in housing.

See: FAIR HOUSING LEGISLATION; NEIGHBORHOOD CHANGE; REDLINING; TIPPING POINT

Blueprint

1. A detailed architectural or engineering drawing or plan often used at the work site during construction or production.

2. A print with white lines on a blue background resulting from a reproduction process in which a positive original is placed next to paper that has been iron-sensitized and is then exposed to ultraviolet light. The blueprint is a reverse image, or negative, of the original. Modern blueprint machines develop, wash and dry the print; because of the wetting, the scale may be inexact due to possible warping and shrinking, but blueprints are sturdy, durable and economical.

Because no lens is involved, all blueprints are of the same size as the original. It is also possible to create a negative from the original, which will then produce a positive print (blue lines on a white background), known as a blueline print.

See: GRAPHIC REPRODUCTION PROCESSES; WORKING DRAWINGS

Blue-Ribbon Commission

A group of persons who are charged with the responsibility of studying a particular problem and reporting or recommending action on it. Members of such a commission, board or panel are usually appointed by the chief elected official on the basis of their expertise or interest in the matter, their prestige in the community and/or their impartiality.

See: CITIZEN ADVISORY ORGANIZATIONS; CITIZEN BOARD; CITIZEN PARTICIPATION; TASK FORCE

Boat Launch Ramp

A ramp of an approximate width of 15 feet (4.6 meters) that extends from a shorefront into a body of water to permit the launching of a boat transported by trailer. Pro-vided at marinas, public parks and other municipal sites where boating is popular, it enables access to a water body for the boater who stores his boat at home.

Often constructed so that two or more boats may be launched simultaneously, the ramp may be a permanent placement of concrete, asphalt or gravel, or a floating design, in which part is anchored to the shore while the portion extending into the water is hinged and floats. A site that is protected from waves and high winds should be selected, and a dock or catwalk is desirable in connection with the ramp so that passengers may board without entering the water. Parking lots of an approximate size of 1 acre (0.4 hectare) per ramp are necessary to accommodate trailers and cars while boaters are on the water. In addition to spaces for parking, lots should contain sufficient turnaround space for cars with trailers so that they can back into the water and wide roads for maneuvering.

See: MARINA; MOORING FACILITIES

Bog

A wet, spongy area filled with partially decayed vegetation. Very common throughout North America and Europe, bogs often form in stagnant shallow lakes or ponds, where in cold climates plant matter decays slowly. Eventually, sphagnum moss (peat moss), which thrives in the acidic water of bogs, completely covers the water surface and fills the water body. At a later stage, peat, sometimes used as fuel, may develop from the organic remains of the moss. Shrubs such as cranberry and blueberry and acid-tolerant trees, such as spruce and larch, may also begin to develop.

See: FRESHWATER MARSH; SALT MARSH; SWAMP; WETLANDS

Bond

1. A legal certificate of indebtedness that serves as a promise by the borrower to repay the lender a particular amount of money plus interest on specified dates. Bonds may be issued by federal, state or local government agencies or by corporations and are generally issued for periods of five years or more. If the maturity date is less than five years distant, it is generally called a note.

2. A form of insurance required of an individual to secure the performance of an obligation; often used in construction—for example, as in a performance bond.

3. A type of pattern in which brick or stone is laid either in walkways or in walls—e.g., American bond, English bond, Flemish bond.

4. The adhesive element used to connect building materials, such as brick, plywood or concrete.

See: BOND RATINGS; GENERAL OBLIGATION BOND; MUNICIPAL BOND; PERFORMANCE BOND; REVENUE BOND

Bond Ratings

Indicators of the investment quality or level of risk associated with certain bonds, these ratings are published by a

number of organizations. The two best known, Standard & Poor's and Moody's, each have their own rating code for both corporate bonds and municipal bonds. The highest municipal ratings by Moody's (Aaa) or Standard & Poor's (AAA) can make it far easier and less expensive for a municipality to market a bond issue. High ratings are intended to indicate a low probability of default, reasonable debt burdens, good management, etc.
See: BOND

Boomer v. Atlantic Cement Company (26 N.Y.2d 219, 309 N.Y.S.2d 312, 257 N.E.2d 870 [1970])

A decision by the Court of Appeals of New York (the highest court of the state) involving an action by one property owner to enjoin another property owner, who was operating a cement plant on his property, from continuing to engage in conduct constituting a nuisance. The nuisance consisted of the emission of dirt, smoke and vibration from the cement plant onto the plaintiff's property.

The court held that the cement plant owner would not be enjoined from creating the nuisance as long as he paid an amount to be determined as permanent damages. In effect, the court's decision permitted one private property owner to acquire an easement by inverse condemnation over the land of another, against the will of the second landowner, merely by agreeing to pay damages for the taking. The court acknowledged that the decision was in conflict with established law, which required that a nuisance be enjoined as long as a complaining property owner could show any substantial damage.

The rationale for the court's decision was the disparity in economic consequences between the effect of the nuisance and the likely effect of issuing the injunction. The court felt that the cement plant would not be able to continue operation on economically feasible terms if it were required to abate the nuisance.
See: INVERSE CONDEMNATION

Boomtown

A community undergoing a sudden and dramatic growth. Boomtowns are categorized by a virtual explosion of population and development, in contrast to the long-term, gradual growth of most cities. Among the most common reasons for the development of boomtowns are government action, such as the establishment of military posts, or a location near valuable natural resources. The American West was particularly fertile ground for boomtowns. Some mining and trade communities eventually withered and became ghost towns, while others, such as Denver and San Francisco, continued to prosper and became permanent centers of commerce and industry.

While there is an opportunity to mold an enormous amount of energy and financial growth in booming communities, rational planning and rural qualities often get lost in the momentum of industrial development and the need to expeditiously accommodate massive population increases. The protection of environmentally sensitive land, controls on nuisances caused by industry, housing development and the ability to ease social dislocations, such as that associated with a disproportionate influx of unattached male workers, determine the ability to convert the boomtown into a stable community.
See: COMPANY TOWN

Borings

Holes made in the ground to obtain soil or rock samples so that subsurface conditions may be accurately evaluated. They may be used for a number of purposes, including the investigation of a construction site, the identification of mineral resources or the evaluation of groundwater resources. Depending upon the purpose of the test, the soil layers may be the prime concern, or the bedrock may be the target, as in mineral investigation.

The number of borings to be made, their location, the method to be used and their depth are selected based upon preliminary information provided by site inspection, research on the area, and geologic maps and surveys. Dry sampling, in which a complete core of natural soil is obtained, generally provides the best results. Rock cores may also be obtained with the use of special drill bits.

Borrow

Material that is excavated so that it can be used as fill for another location. The area that the material is removed from is called a borrow pit and often requires clearing of vegetation or debris before excavation can begin. Generally borrow is not obtained until it is certain that an adequate quantity of fill will not be available on-site. It is sometimes necessary to obtain borrow because a particular material is needed for the fill.
See: CUT; EXCAVATION; FILL

Botanical Garden

A garden where plants are collected and cultivated for purposes of scientific study and display. Botanical gardens usually have large varieties of plants, trees and flowers, some of which are displayed in large greenhouses. An arboretum, another form of botanical garden with only trees and shrubs, may be more specialized in its collection.

Botanical gardens are generally regional facilities because of their unique collections and may draw substantial attendance on peak days, such as when large flower displays are in bloom. Some botanical gardens also incorporate restaurants or other recreational facilities that make them attractive to tourists. Sufficient parking and access to public transportation are the principal planning concerns.
See: COMMUNITY GARDEN; NATURE PRESERVE

Bottle Bill

Legislation requiring that mandatory deposits on beverage containers be collected as part of the purchase price when beer and soft drinks are bought. The phrase *bottle bill* came into use because beverage container deposit legislation tended to increase the use of refillable glass bottles and decrease the use of cans.

The purpose of these laws is to encourage the return of the container so that it may either be refilled or recycled. In addition to reducing the volume of solid waste requiring disposal, bottle bills have been shown to reduce the volume of roadside litter and the amount of energy expended in beverage container production. A federal Resource Conservation Committee, studying the possibility of a national mandatory deposit system, also concluded in a 1979 report that there would be savings in steel and aluminum consumption, reduced air and water pollution, and reduced retail prices of beverages. Although jobs would be lost in the container production industries, it was expected that there would be job gains in beverage distribution. Connecticut, Delaware, Iowa, Maine, Michigan, New York, Oregon and Vermont have all passed various forms of bottle bills.
See: RECYCLING; SOLID WASTE MANAGEMENT

Boundary Waters Treaty of 1909

An agreement between the United States and Great Britain regarding the use of water bodies that border the United States and Canada. It also established the International Joint Commission.

The treaty set the limits of water bodies that would be considered international and prohibited pollution by either party that would adversely affect the other party. It also specified uses for which diversion of waters would be permitted and required mitigating measures to prevent damage to the other country because of such diversions.
See: INTERNATIONAL JOINT COMMISSION

Braille Trail

A walking trail in a scenic area designed to enable blind visitors to more fully experience the area. Part of the effort to make parks more accessible to the handicapped, braille trails not only include braille descriptions of the particular features of a trail; they also have demonstrations along the route. Signs might ask the visitor, for example, to touch adjacent evergreens to feel the difference in needle shape, or describe the types of birds and animals whose sounds might be heard. Contour models of the terrain are often provided at parks with large canyons or mountainous areas.

The first braille trail on federal parkland in the United States was opened in 1967 in the White River National Forest in Colorado. The concept has rapidly spread to many other federally owned recreation facilities as well as to other recreation areas.
See: PLANNING FOR THE DISABLED

Breakwater

A structure designed to protect a harbor by breaking the force of waves. A breakwater may be designed so that it is completely detached from land and runs parallel to shore,

or it may project from shore, possibly angling toward another breakwater. Breakwaters may even partially surround a harbor.

Because they are subjected to direct wave force and may be located in quite deep water, breakwaters are larger and stronger than groins or jetties and are constructed with an armored outer layer. Like groins and jetties, they are usually built either of rubble (primarily stones), steel or concrete. (See Fig. 9)
See: GROIN; JETTY

Bridge

A structure that spans a low-lying area and is designed to accommodate vehicles, trains, pedestrians or pipelines. Bridges are used to cross bodies of water and areas separated by grade differences. The predominant types of bridges are the rigid beam, cantilever, suspension and arch, which are fixed in place, and the bascule, swing, vertical lift and pontoon, which are movable. Modern day bridges are usually constructed of steel girders, reinforced concrete or prestressed concrete, depending upon the length of the bridge, its purpose and its desired appearance.

The rigid beam bridge is a flat bridge supported at both ends by piers or abutments and supported at intermediate points where necessary. It may be constructed of wood, steel girders or concrete and may have elaborate truss work or be covered.

The cantilever is a bridge type in which the rigid beam is firmly anchored at only one end. It is used where it is difficult or impractical to build supporting piers, such as in deep rivers. In a cantilever bridge a beam is anchored at each shore, and the unsupported sections of each of the beams meet at the middle of the water body. For larger spans, each of the cantilevered sections supports one end of a rigid beam that serves to extend the bridge span.

The suspension bridge, like the cantilever, is also used where intermediate piers are impractical, but it can span even greater areas using continuous flexible steel cable to support the flat roadway.

The steel arch bridge curves upward from abutments or piers, providing a roadway that is either suspended from steel cables supported by the arch or located above the arch and supported by piers and girders.

Movable bridges are used where it is necessary to provide passage for ships but where it is uneconomical to build a fixed bridge of sufficient clearance. The bascule bridge is analagous to a drawbridge, providing one or two platforms that open. The swing bridge pivots horizontally around an axis at its middle, providing unlimited clearance for ships. The vertical lift bridge has two towers, one on each side of the channel, connected by a flat bridge section that can be moved up and down by counterweights in the towers. Pontoon bridges have a series of floating sections that support a bridge deck and, usually, a movable section to permit passage for ships. Pontoon bridges are often used as temporary bridges, particularly by the military.

Bridge Financing

Short-term financing intended to cover a temporary illiquid position, such as the period in which one loan expires while another has not begun. A common use of bridge financing is the financing of a portion of the cost of a new home before the old one is sold.

Bridle Path

A trail designed for or passable by saddle horses or pack horses. Bridle path development is usually undertaken in larger parks where stable and corral facilities are provided as well. Paths should be about 10 feet (3 meters) wide to permit riders to pass each other, have a maximum sustained grade of 5 percent, and be cleared and leveled. Large rocks and low-hanging tree limbs should also be removed. While bridle paths may also serve as pedestrian paths, they should not be intended for use by bicycles, which can frighten horses in close proximity. In areas where overnight trips may be expected, campsites should be developed at points about 20 miles (32 kilometers) apart, and trails may be narrower, with passing areas provided. For planning purposes, a ratio of 1 trail mile per horse (0.6 horses to 1 kilometer) is often used, but in practice many more horses may be accommodated.
See: HIKING TRAIL

Budget

A financial plan that correlates anticipated revenues and expenditures and serves as a basis for decisions on future expenditures. Budgets, which are generally adopted annually, usually present the previous fiscal year's financial data, estimates of revenue and expenditures for the current year and recommendations for the coming year.

Most states require that local governments prepare budgets, and more than half of the states require that budget preparation follow specific procedures established by that state. These procedures generally require that estimates of expenditures be made prior to establishing the tax rates and prescribe procedures to be used regarding supluses or deficits, tax yields, tax delinquencies, emergency appropriations and other fundamental budgeting techniques. The purpose of these laws is to prevent local deficits and extravagance. Planning departments are regularly employed in budget development and/or evaluation.
See: BUDGETARY PROCESS; CAPITAL BUDGET; CAPITAL IMPROVEMENT PROGRAM (CIP); DEFICIT SPENDING; LINE-ITEM BUDGET; OPERATING BUDGET; PERFORMANCE BUDGET; PLANNING-PROGRAMMING-BUDGETING SYSTEM (PPBS); PROGRAM BUDGET; ZERO-BASE BUDGET (ZBB)

Budget Director

The municipal official appointed by the chief executive or chief administrator to develop the executive budget. With the assistance of a staff, the budget director receives and evaluates budget estimates for each municipal department and agency for the coming year or years as required locally. Through negotiation with department heads, the budget director reduces requested estimates to meet expected revenue levels. He transmits the revised estimates in the form of a proposed executive budget to the chief executive, who may further alter the departmental estimates prior to submission for legislative action. The budget director is usually responsible for developing both the operating and the capital budget.
See: BUDGETARY PROCESS; CAPITAL BUDGET; MUNICIPAL TREASURER; OPERATING BUDGET

Budgetary Process

The stages of development of a municipal budget that are usually undertaken annually in either a formally established procedure, necessary in large municipalities, or a less formal procedure, common to small localities. During the budgetary cycle, choices are made about the allocation of limited resources to competing projects. Current practice emphasizes policy development and planning for each municipal agency as a basis for establishing the agency's program goals and priorities prior to development of budgetary requests. Often conducted by or in conjunction with the planning department, this practice enables choices to be made between programs of equal priority.

An initial step is the development of policy and fiscal planning for a period several years into the future to provide a priority framework for current requests. This is followed by development of agency program and project estimates or requests for the forthcoming budget; estimation of revenues for the proposed budgetary period to determine expenditure limits; and review of the estimates by the budget department and other reviewing agencies to determine compliance with government policy and with expenditure limitations. Next, the administrative head of the unit of government prepares and issues his executive or proposed budget, in which major policy decisions on programs and expenditure levels have been made. The legislative body reviews this budget, adding programs it feels should be funded and deleting other activities. Public hearings are then held, and after additional changes that may be made as a result of public comment, the budget is adopted.
See: BUDGET; BUDGET DIRECTOR

Buffer Zone

1. A zone in the form of a strip of land, usually a landscaped open area, designed to separate incompatible land uses. A zoning ordinance will identify buffer zones, either on the zoning map or in the zoning ordinance text, and impose appropriate conditions.

2. A loosely used term that describes any zone used to separate and provide transition between two other zones that are incompatible. An example of this would be the placement of a multifamily zone between a single-family district and a retail district.
See: SCREENING; TRANSITIONAL LOT

Buildable Area

The land area of a given lot that is potentially available for construction after all zoning and other municipal requirements have been fulfilled. Buildable area would exclude required yards and areas on which construction may be prohibited, such as floodplains. (See Fig. 50)
See: NET ACRE

Building

A structure that is permanently affixed to the ground, has a roof and is used for the shelter of humans, animals, property or goods.
See: STRUCTURE

Building Code

An ordinance adopted by a municipality that prescribes minimum standards for the construction of buildings within its boundaries. The building code specifies many types of standards, including permissible types of construction; quality of building materials; minimum loads that floors and roofs must be able to tolerate; minimum tolerable wind loads; stresses that buildings must be capable of withstanding; health and safety requirements—e.g., water pressure and fire ratings; and types of permissible electrical and mechanical equipment.

Most municipalities have adopted a building code or have elected to use a state building code if one is promulgated by the state. Four model codes, which are used as a basis for many municipal and state codes, are: the *National Code* of the American Insurance Association; the *Uniform Building Code* of the International Conference of Building Officials (ICBO); the *Southern Standard Building Code* of the Southern Building Code Conference; and the *Basic Building Code* of the Building Officials and Code Administrators International Inc. (BOCA). These codes are revised periodically as a result of new technology and to incorporate new standards. Separate codes for specialized building equipment are also adopted in certain municipalities.

Today most building codes are of the performance type, in which minimum requirements are established for materials, systems, designs and construction methods, without specifying which materials or system should be used. Performance standards encourage innovative solutions to design problems by giving architects and engineers the opportunity to employ new methods and equipment. The test of a material or technique's performance is provided by scientific testing, measurement and analysis undertaken by national testing agencies. The evaluations of these agencies, called reference standards, are used by building departments to evaluate plans.
See: FIRE RATINGS

Building Codes for Historic Buildings

Building codes that contain provisions allowing for adequate public safety in historic buildings without destruction of their historic qualities. Strict letter-of-the-law compliance is often difficult or impossible in historic properties, yet buildings that predate building codes often become subject to code when a change of use is involved or alteration costs exceed a certain percentage of the property's value.

To resolve this difficulty, several of the national model codes have included provisions by which certain standards can be waived for recognized historic properties if it can be demonstrated that public safety may be protected by using other methods. A number of states and cities have also adopted this approach.
See: BUILDING CODE; HISTORIC PRESERVATION

Building Department

The government department with responsibility for the administration and enforcement of laws regulating construction. The laws that generally come under its authority are the building code; housing code; electrical, plumbing and fire prevention codes, if separate from the building code; health code; and zoning ordinance. Building departments usually make building inspections to determine compliance with municipal codes, propose changes in codes when necessary and sometimes undertake laboratory testing and research.

Building departments vary in size from one employee (the building inspector) to more than a hundred employees, depending on the size of the municipality and the complexity of the department's duties. Building department functions in some municipalities, however, are combined with the public works, engineering, or housing and development department.
See: ARCHITECTURAL REVIEW BOARD; BUILDING INSPECTOR; ZONING ADMINISTRATION; ZONING BOARD OF APPEALS

Building Inspector

The municipal official responsible for reviewing building plans to ascertain compliance with all local codes, such as the building code and the zoning ordinance, for the purpose of issuing building permits. The building inspector, usually a civil engineer, is also responsible for the inspection of premises to determine ongoing compliance.
See: BUILDING DEPARTMENT; BUILDING PERMIT; ZONING ADMINISTRATION; ZONING BOARD OF APPEALS

Building Line

A line, established by zoning ordinance requirements, that delineates the boundary beyond which there may be no construction and buildings may not extend.
See: BUILDING RESTRICTION LINE (BRL); SETBACK; YARD; ZONING

Building Officials and Code Administrators International (BOCA)

A nonprofit organization, founded in 1915, concerned with the professional administration of construction codes and with their enforcement. BOCA's active membership consists primarily of units of government and their employees concerned with administering, formulating or enforcing ordinances or regulations related to building, housing, city planning or zoning. Other membership categories are available for engineers, architects, organizations, trade associations, builders and others concerned with building and construction.

BOCA, which is located in Homewood, Illinois, promulgates a set of model regulatory codes designed to address many aspects of construction. They are: *Basic Building Code; Basic Fire Prevention Code; Basic Plumbing Code; Basic Mechanical Code; Basic Property Maintenance Code* and *Basic Energy Conservation Code.* New editions of the codes are published every three years, and annual supplements are released. Other BOCA publications include the magazine *Building Official and Code Administrator; the BOCA Bulletin;* and a variety of handbooks, textbooks, and preprinted forms and permits. Services available include seminars and other educational programs, and code interpretation and plan review assistance.

Building Orientation

The position or arrangement of a building or other structure on a piece of property. In planning for residential development and certain office development, primary emphasis is placed upon the relationship of buildings and their various functional areas to sunlight, prevailing winds and views. The resurgence of energy consumption as a major concern, however, has led to a much greater emphasis being placed on orientation as an energy conserving technique. In cooler climates, buildings should be sited to take full advantage of sunlight and warm breezes and to minimize the impact of cold winter winds, whereas in warmer climates the reverse should hold true. The increased use of solar energy for various applications has also focused additional attention upon building orientation.

In the context of larger-scale development, as with a skyscraper in an urban setting, orientation concerns will be chiefly related to the availability of light and air, both for the new building and for adjoining development that will be affected by the position of the new building.
See: SITE ORIENTATION; SOLAR ACCESS

Building Permit

A permit that a municipal government must issue before such activities as construction, substantial rehabilitation or alteration, or installation of manufactured housing can legally take place. Building permits are also issued for demolition, although some communities issue separate demolition permits.

When a building permit application is received, proposed plans are reviewed for compliance with municipal building and zoning regulations. The reviewer—usually the building inspector, municipal engineer or staff from those departments—will compare the proposal to the zoning ordinance, which may include requirements for use, setback, height, parking, proposed land coverage and the use of signs. It is through this procedure that zoning is enforced on a daily basis. If the plans differ from permitted zoning standards, a permit will not be issued at that time; the applicant can, however, have the determination to deny a building permit reviewed by the zoning board of appeals.
See: BUILDING CODE; BUILDING PERMIT DATA; CERTIFICATE OF OCCUPANCY (CO)

Building Permit Data

Data obtained from permits issued for new construction. Building permits provide reasonably accurate and current information concerning the building inventory of a community. Such data are not a substitute, however, for an actual field survey, because a permit may be issued and the structure never built. It is also not uncommon for construction to take place, particularly alterations or conversions, without the benefit of a permit. Within these limitations, however, permits can be a useful data source.

Residential permits provide current information on the total housing stock and the rate at which it is growing. In addition, building permit data can be used as a check against the accuracy of the national census, and housing unit data can become the basis for municipal population estimates.

Building permits also provide information on nonresidential construction trends that is useful for such purposes as economic planning or tax base studies.
See: BUILDING PERMIT; CURRENT POPULATION ESTIMATES

Building Restriction Line (BRL)

An imaginary line drawn at a prescribed distance parallel or perpendicular to airport runways, aprons, taxiways and approach zones. Within the line no building or other obstruction to airspace can be constructed.
See: AIRPORT PLANNING

Built Environment

All elements of the man-made environment (including buildings, streets and transit systems) that, by definition, involve some application of human effort and technology toward their design, construction or manufacture. From a planning perspective, the term most commonly refers to architectural elements, such as buildings, plazas and other components associated with the design process or subject to some form of municipal regulation. From an engineering standpoint, the term is more commonly used to describe the mechanical, electrical and other systems that are associated with the infrastructure of an area, such as sewer and water lines and electrical transmission systems.

Bulk Envelope

The three-dimensional area that defines the limits within which an improvement may be built on a building

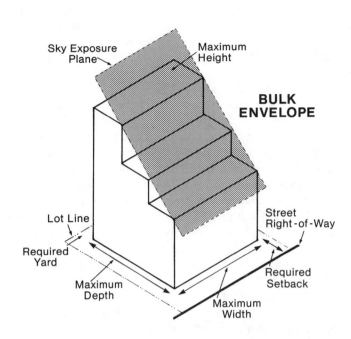

Fig. 7.   The three-dimensional space in which a building may be enclosed.

lot. This envelope is delineated by bulk regulations pertaining to such matters as permitted maximum height, required yards, permitted floor area ratio, maximum lot coverage and required bulk plane. (See Fig. 7)
See: BULK PLANE; BULK REGULATIONS; FLOOR AREA RATIO (FAR); HEIGHT CONTROLS; LOT COVERAGE

Bulk Plane

A theoretical inclined plane that rises at an angle over a lot beginning at a lot line or at a defined point above the lot line. The required bulk plane angle, which is established by the zoning ordinance, helps to delineate the total bulk of a building.

When bulk plane requirements are in effect, the upper floors of a building must have a greater setback from the street or lot lines than the lower floors, creating a distinctive architectural effect, such as the wedding cake architecture found in New York City. Floor area ratio requirements are increasingly being used to replace or supplement the bulk plane, which is also known as a sky exposure plane, light plane or setback plane. Bulk plane requirements are, however, being employed as a means of improving solar access. (See Fig. 7)
See: BULK ENVELOPE; BULK REGULATIONS; FLOOR AREA RATIO (FAR); SOLAR ACCESS

Bulk Regulations

Those regulations that determine the maximum permitted size of a building and its placement on a building lot. Aimed at ensuring an adequate amount of light, air and open space, as well as encouraging attractive and com-

patible development, these regulations govern the height and size of a building, coverage, floor area ratio, open space and yard requirements. They also govern the placement of exterior walls throughout the height of the building as these walls relate to property lines and to adjacent streets and development.
See: BULK ENVELOPE; BULK PLANE; FLOOR AREA RATIO (FAR); HEIGHT CONTROLS; LOT COVERAGE; ZONING

Bulkhead

1.   A retaining wall, often located at the high-tide line, made of wood, steel, concrete, plastic or fiberglass, that protects waterfront property. As beach erosion becomes more severe, oceanfront bulkheads often are replaced by much larger seawalls.

2.   A small structure found on a roof that covers an elevator shaft or stairway.
See: BEACH EROSION; SEAWALL

Bundle of Rights

Most often used in connection with real property, the term refers to the aggregate of rights inherent in the ownership of real estate. These rights include the right to occupy; to pass through, over or under; to farm, mine or develop; to transfer during one's life (inter vivos transfer) or at death (testamentary transfer); to lease, grant easements or life estates, or create remainder interests (future interests in land); and many other rights.

An owner of real property may normally transfer all, or any portion, of his bundle or rights. Unless otherwise specified, a transfer of real estate normally transfers all (but not more than) the bundle of rights that the transferrer had in the property.

Bureau of Labor Statistics (BLS)

An agency within the Department of Labor with responsibility for statistical research and analysis of matters related to labor economics. The agency studies topics such as labor force, unemployment, wages, prices, productivity, technological developments, structure and condition of the economy, and urban and related socioeconomic matters. Data are supplied voluntarily by government agencies, businesses and workers, often based on their need for the resulting reports.

BLS publishes the *Monthly Labor Review, Consumer Price Index, Occupational Outlook Handbook* and other major periodicals. Regional and local detail can often be obtained from BLS regional offices.
See: DEPARTMENT OF LABOR

Bureau of Land Management (BLM)

An agency within the Department of the Interior that is responsible for the management of 341 million acres (138 million hectares) of federal lands, located predominantly in the far West and Alaska. It also has responsibility for managing mineral resources on the outer continental shelf and subsurface resources on an additional 169 million acres (68.4 million hectares) on which the federal government has mineral rights.

The bureau manages a wide variety of natural resources on the federal lands, ranging from minerals, oil, gas and timber to wild and scenic rivers, conservation and wilderness areas, and endangered plants and animals. It operates under a policy of multiple use and sustained yield for use of public lands and consults with a system of advisory councils in the development of management plans and policies. The agency also leases certain lands to state and local governments and nonprofit organizations and sells land, under certain conditions, to individuals, organizations, local governments and other federal agencies.

Other responsibilities include the issuance of rights-of-way across certain federal lands, the maintenance of public land records and mining claims, and the surveying of federal lands. The BLM also makes payments in lieu of taxes to local governments for all federal lands (except defense installations) located within their jurisdictions.
See: DEPARTMENT OF THE INTERIOR

Bureau of Reclamation

An agency of the Department of the Interior that is responsible for development and management of water resources projects in the 17 western states. Its purpose, as stipulated in the Reclamation Act of 1902, is to reclaim arid and semiarid lands in the West.

The Bureau of Reclamation operates 50 water and sewer projects, such as the Hoover and Grand Coulee Dams, which are a source of municipal and industrial water supplies and hydroelectric power. It is also involved in irrigation, over 280 outdoor recreation facilities, research in wind and solar power and cloud seeding, river control projects, and fish and wildlife management. Other major bureau functions include development of plans for the conservation and utilization of water, such as basinwide water studies, and loans for the construction or rehabilitation of irrigation systems. Approximately 84 percent of the construction cost of water and power projects is reimbursed by their direct beneficiaries through additional tax payments. Marketing of power produced by the hydroelectric plants is conducted by the Department of Energy through its power administrations. For a period in 1979 to 1981, the bureau was called the Water and Power Resources Service.
See: DEPARTMENT OF ENERGY (DOE)

Bureau of the Census

A United States federal agency within the Department of Commerce that collects, tabulates and publishes statistical data about the population and economy of the country. In addition to publishing the decennial censuses of population and housing, it also produces censuses of agriculture, government and economic conditions, as well as special censuses at the request of state and local governments.

Other reports of the agency relate to population estimates and projections, and current surveys on many of the subjects on which it undertakes censuses.
See: CENSUS

Burnham, Daniel (1846–1912)

An American architect and city planner, best known for his work associated with the city of Chicago. He established an architectural practice in that city with John Root and helped to pioneer the use of steel frame construction. Placed in charge of construction for the World's Columbian Exposition of 1893 to be held in Chicago, Burnham also became chief consulting architect for the exposition upon Root's death in 1891. His talents in achieving a unified visual image helped to bring him to national prominence and to publicize to the millions who attended the fair the benefits of an attractive, graceful, planned environment. Many consider this the beginning of the "city beautiful" movement.

Elected president of the American Institute of Architects in 1894, Burnham was appointed by Congress to head the McMillan Committee for the purpose of creating a plan to restore portions of Washington, D.C. Other cities for which he subsequently developed plans included Cleveland, San Francisco and Baltimore. In 1909 his *Plan for Chicago,* the country's first regional plan for a metropolitan area, was released. In this plan, which came to be known as the Burnham plan, planning principles were established that are still followed today.

In his role as an architect, Burnham also designed a number of well-known buildings, including the Monadnock Building in Chicago (1891), the Flatiron Building in New York (1901) and Union Station in Washington, D.C. (1909).
See: CHICAGO PLAN (1909); CITY BEAUTIFUL MOVEMENT; SAN FRANCISCO PLAN; WORLD'S COLUMBIAN EXPOSITION

Bus Loading Area

A term used to refer to locations, commonly known as bus stops, where buses receive and discharge passengers.

Bus loading areas are usually located along streets at the curb. On very highly trafficked arterials and freeways, bus turnout areas are often provided, where space exists, to permit the bus to get out of the through-traffic lanes. The turnout can take the form of an extra traffic lane that might be two or three bus lengths in size, or diagonal or sawtooth parking can be provided for the buses, requiring a deeper turnout area. These latter forms are particularly useful in busway design and at bus terminals.
See: BUS TERMINAL; RESERVED LANES

Bus Route Planning

The selection of roads over which a bus will run on a regularly scheduled basis, so as to maximize potential access to public transit and serve the travel corridors that have been shown to warrant bus service. The selection of bus routes is based on origin-destination studies, which indicate travel route needs of current and potential passengers, and on analysis of existing routes. In comprehensive metropolitan studies, network assignment models may be employed to analyze potential bus route volumes and the effect of the new routes on the entire transportation system.

In heavily urbanized areas bus routes are generally located on arterial and collector streets in interconnecting patterns that permit transfers. Routes to outlying areas frequently form a radial pattern, with the central business district at the center. In these areas routes are planned so that they either end at the city center or continue through it to the end of another spoke, in an attempt to link outlying areas.

The success or failure of particular bus routes is related to need for the route, fares, frequency and reliability of service, relative comfort, travel time and prevailing attitudes toward bus transit.
See: BUS TERMINAL; HEADWAY; NETWORK ASSIGNMENT; ORIGIN-DESTINATION (O-D) STUDY

Bus Shelter

A covered area, located at a bus stop, designed to protect waiting passengers from severe weather conditions. Bus shelters have a roof and frequently one or more side walls, which provide shelter from wind and rain. Seating and trash baskets are also provided under or near many bus shelters. Lighting under the shelter, or adjacent to it, is useful for nighttime comfort and crime deterrence. Bus shelters that have overhead heating elements and heated sidewalks beneath them have been used in cold climates.

Bus Terminal

A bus loading and unloading station, located at the end of a bus route, that is designed to accommodate one or more buses. Tickets may also be sold and passenger waiting rooms provided. In current practice bus terminals are located in central business districts where a majority of bus routes cross, providing a convenient transfer point for passengers. Usually, a retail component is also included, which provides services to passengers and adds revenue to the terminal facility. Intercity bus terminals should be lo-

cated as close as possible to interstate highway entrances to facilitate bus movement into and out of the city and reduce running time.

Off-street local service bus terminals can be provided for single bus routes by creating a loop that takes the bus out of the street system (similar to a jug-handle turn) and can be designed to accommodate several buses. Most local bus routes, however, simply circle around a block at the end of a run to begin the next run.

Design and siting of bus terminals should take into consideration environmental effects of bus noise and fumes.
See: INTERMODAL TERMINAL

Bylaws

A set of rules that provide for the organization and ongoing operations of a legal body or entity, such as a corporation, a condominium owners' association or a planning commission. Bylaws stand midway between the document that creates the entity (referred to in some instances as a certificate or charter) and minutes, which record individual actions of the entity.

Historically, the term *bylaws* was used to refer to laws adopted by local municipalities; while this usage continues in Canada, it has for the most part been superseded in the United States in favor of the term *ordinance.*

Bypass

1. A road that circumvents a congested area, providing an alternate route for through traffic.

2. A channel that provides an additional outlet for flood water, diverting it to another body of water.

3. A diversion to a sewer line that provides an outlet during high or peak flows. Bypasses are used frequently in combined sewer systems, to permit excess storm sewage flows caused by heavy rains to bypass a sewage treatment plant and flow directly into the receiving body of water. This is necessary, if the sewage volumes exceed the capacity of the sewage treatment plant, to prevent backups that might cause damage to the sewerage system or cause a health hazard by allowing sewage to back up into the street catch basins.
See: CIRCUMFERENTIAL HIGHWAY; COMBINED SEWER

C

Cable Television

Television transmission by coaxial cable, similar to telephone lines, which is capable of transmitting up to 80 simultaneous signals. Cable television, also called community antenna television (CATV), is operated by over 2,500 companies in the United States and is expected to serve

one-third of the nation's households by the mid-1980s.

The proliferation of cable television networks in addition to instructional television fixed service (ITFS), which uses a 28-channel microwave frequency, and communications satellites is expected to change and vastly increase opportunities for communication in the next decade.

Use of cable television for planning and other municipal purposes is already well established. United States congressional hearings are regularly broadcast, and some cities use cable TV to communicate on a regular basis or for special purposes with decentralized departments, council members' offices or neighborhood planning boards. A municipal cable channel may be arranged to reach private homes, as in New York City, where Channel L reaches about 220,000 private television sets. Columbus, Ohio's QUBE is a two-way system in which viewers can press a response button to answer questions, while the Miami Valley system in Ohio connects 10 municipalities. It is expected that municipal systems will be developed more widely in the future for purposes such as the broadcast of public hearings and meetings and may become a common means of communication between municipal governments and the public.

See: CITIZEN PARTICIPATION

Caliper

1.   An instrument consisting of a movable and a fixed leg, and a calibrated beam, that is used to measure the diameter of trees and logs.

2.   The term is also used to indicate tree trunk diameter; breast-height caliper refers to the diameter of a trunk at a height of approximately 5 feet (1.5 meters) above the ground. Trees of a particular caliper are often specified for street tree planting or on site plans.

Campground

A public or private open area divided into campsites that, at a minimum, provides a potable water supply and some form of toilet facilities. While traditional camping involves only tenting in remote areas or bedding down in lean-tos, many modern campers prefer proximity to other campers and to sanitary and recreational facilities. Campgrounds are designed to accommodate such individuals, families and groups by allowing them to park their cars near their tents or to locate in compact arrangements where recreational vehicles (RVs) can hook up to sanitary, water and electrical connections. Campgrounds usually have outdoor grills and picnic tables and often have such amenities as shower and laundry facilities. At "destination" parks—those at which campers stay for an extended period—recreational facilities, such as a swimming pool or recreation building, may also be provided, as may a grocery.

Campsite arrangements vary as to alloted space per family and overall density, topography, numbers of RVs permitted or considered desirable, and degree of attractiveness. They may be as compact as 30 per acre (74 per hectare) or as separate as 10 or less per acre (25 per hectare) but should, as far as possible, be surrounded by trees and shrubbery for maximum privacy.

Regional, state and national parks have been adding campsites steadily for many years to accommodate growing numbers of campers, due in part to increased recrea-

tion time and rising costs of hotel accommodations. In some national parks it has been found that the large increase in people in these developed areas is threatening the ecological balance of the park, requiring that protective measures be taken.

See: PRIMITIVE RECREATION AREA; RECREATIONAL VEHICLES (RV)

Campus Office Park

One or more office buildings in a parklike setting with large parking lots or parking structures. Usually located in a suburban area, campus office parks, which are generally well maintained, may permit certain types of light industry that are considered compatible with office development. Communities generally find these parks desirable from both an aesthetic and an economic standpoint, but corporations can sometimes find clerical help difficult to obtain because of a lack of proximity to housing and public transportation.

When compared to strip development, campus development provides more controlled traffic patterns because several buildings have access to one interior road rather than to the public street. The office park also provides an opportunity for more creative site design and is often more visually attractive. In some cases, these parks are of such a low density that they have the effect of providing open space for a community.

See: INDUSTRIAL PARK; OFFICE BUILDING LOCATION; OFFICE DEVELOPMENT; OPEN-SPACE PLANNING; RATABLES

Canadian Institute of Planners (CIP)

A professional planning organization founded in 1923 as the Town Planning Institute of Canada. Oriented toward developing and maintaining high standards of professional planning practice, the organization was given its current name in 1974. Among the other functions of CIP are the dissemination of planning information and the setting of professional standards necessary for membership. The CIP also holds planning conferences and publishes a newsletter and a journal.

The CIP, whose national office is in Ottawa, Ontario, formally recognizes planning programs at Canadian universities and colleges meeting designated standards.

Canal

1.   An artificial body of water designed to connect natural water bodies for navigational purposes.

The shipment of goods by water is still considered the cheapest means of transport. Canals provide the necessary link to inland areas otherwise not accessible by this mode of transportation, and are therefore thought to be an important capital investment to support economic growth. Narrow inland canals are used extensively for recreational boating.

2.   A man-made waterway designed for the drainage or irrigation of land. Depending on the size of the canal and

its purpose it may also be called a channel, aqueduct or bayou.
See: FINGER FILL CANALS

Capacity

1. The maximum number of vehicles that can reasonably be expected to pass over a given roadway in a given time period under the prevailing roadway and traffic conditions as defined. This term was once called "possible capacity." Capacity is expressed as an hourly volume either per lane, per direction or for both directions, stating the roadway and traffic conditions under which the capacity figure is applicable.

The *Highway Capacity Manual* is a useful standard reference source for traffic engineering information.

2. The maximum number of people who may use a room or building intended for assembly occupancy, e.g., an auditorium or school, as established by the local building or fire department.

3. The maximum number of people or things that can comfortably or safely use any facility, e.g., boats at a marina, people on buses, etc.
See: CAPACITY UNDER IDEAL CONDITIONS; CARRYING CAPACITY; HIGHWAY CAPACITY DETERMINANTS

Capacity Under Ideal Conditions

Capacity under ideal conditions, or maximum roadway capacity, is found on roads that have design features permitting fast driving speeds and ease of vehicular movement greater than most roadways. The Transportation Research Board describes the basic conditions that will yield such capacity as: (1) uninterrupted flow, free from side interferences of vehicles and pedestrians; (2) passenger cars only in the traffic stream; (3) traffic lanes 12 feet (3.7 meters) wide with adequate shoulders and no obstructions within 6 feet (1.8 meters) of the edge of the pavement; and (4) horizontal and vertical alignment satisfactory for average highway speeds of 70 mph (113 kph), with no restricted passing sight distance on two- and three-lane highways. This concept was formerly called *basic capacity*.
See: CAPACITY; GEOMETRIC DESIGN; HIGHWAY CAPACITY DETERMINANTS

Capital

1. In economic theory, capital is considered, along with land and labor, to be one of the major factors of production. It is one of the elements necessary for the production of additional goods. Factories, machinery and other equipment, transportation facilities and raw materials are all examples of capital goods.

2. In accounting, capital is essentially net worth—i.e., the difference between the assets and the liabilities of a business enterprise.

3. In business, capital consists of all the assets that a firm holds, generally divided into working capital and fixed capital. Working capital consists of such items as cash and other assets that are, or will be, convertible into cash in the ordinary course of business (e.g., accounts receivable) and is also known by the term *liquid assets*. Fixed capital consists of those assets that are held for use in connection with the daily operations of the business but are not ordinarily converted into cash. Examples of fixed capital include real estate, buildings and machinery.
See: CAPITAL BUDGET; CAPITAL IMPROVEMENTS

Capital Budget

A budget, used by most municipal and state governments, that proposes expenditures for capital improvements for the coming fiscal year.

Since capital improvements usually take several years to become operational and often have a life span of one or more decades, governments usually regard them as appropriate items for future payment by bond issue or other borrowing technique. The tradition of budget balance is usually not applied to these expenditures, since it is reasoned that they will benefit future generations and should therefore be paid for in the future. Another reason for borrowing is that the high cost of capital project development usually precludes payment from general revenues without an increase in the tax rate.

The capital budget customarily lists the capital projects and their costs but usually does not show details of the materials needed to undertake each project. Financing sources—e.g., bonds or federal grants—may also be indicated.
See: BUDGET; CAPITAL IMPROVEMENT PROGRAM (CIP); CAPITAL IMPROVEMENTS

Capital Improvement Program (CIP)

A multiyear program of proposed capital expenditures used as a programming guide for public improvements, of which the first year of the program is the capital budget. CIPs generally project capital spending three to six years into the future but rarely constitute a binding commitment for future spending; in contrast, the capital budget represents a formal commitment to expend funds. CIPs are developed or redeveloped annually, usually by the planning department working alone or in conjuction with the budget department.

Capital improvement programs become important when the volume of capital projects requires spacing over a period of years to enable a municipality to stay within its debt limit. They are also necessary when funding is scarce and essential projects must be carefully staged, and when capital projects require more than one year to be designed and constructed. Use of the capital program is now regarded by most municipalities as an essential tool in determining which capital projects should receive funding each year, and many planning departments devote a substantial amount of time to their preparation. CIPs that project community facility needs well into the future—e.g., 20 years—may also be undertaken as a guide to setting priorities for the more standard short-term program. In general, each municipal department will develop a list of its own long-term needs to be used as the basis of CIP preparation.

In recent years the capital program has also been used to control the rate of community growth by requiring that necessary public facilities be in place prior to granting approval to proposed developments, and development timing has been keyed to the provision of these facilities.
See: CAPITAL BUDGET; GROWTH MANAGEMENT

Capital Improvements

Physical facilities or other fixed assets with relatively long-term usefulness, such as buildings, land, parks or roads. Rolling stock—such as buses or subway cars, garbage trucks or fire engines, and major construction equipment—are also considered to be capital improvements.

Expenditures for capital improvements are differentiated from maintenance and operating expenditures by the longer life span of the improvement and because these expenditures are required relatively infrequently. For example, the addition of new lanes to a road would generally be considered a capital improvement, while road resurfacing might not. As a rule, municipalities develop their own definitions of what is properly a capital improvement.
See: CAPITAL BUDGET; CAPITAL IMPROVEMENT PROGRAM (CIP)

Capitalization

The process of converting an anticipated future income stream into an estimate of the present value of property.

A capitalization rate must be chosen that represents an estimate or opinion of the rate of return that an investor would demand for an investment carrying comparable risk, liquidity and other factors. Where improved real estate is being valued by this approach (referred to as the income approach to value), the capitalization rate must also reflect an additional rate of return needed to enable the investor to recapture that portion of his investment, allocable to the improvement, which is subject to loss through depreciation.

The anticipated annual net income is then divided by the chosen capitalization rate to arrive at the estimate of value. For example, if estimated future net income of $18,000 per year is anticipated, and a capitalization rate of 9 percent is chosen as reasonable, the capitalization of the income stream would indicate a present value of $200,000. Of course, the estimate of value varies inversely with the chosen capitalization rate.
See: APPRAISAL; INCOME APPROACH APPRAISAL

Carrying Capacity

The capability of a system to absorb any, or increased, population and development within the parameters of an acceptable environment. It is derived from the ecological concept of the maximum animal population that a given land area can support through all seasons of the year.

Carrying capacity studies are often referred to as land capability studies.

Cartography

The practice of making maps and models, requiring an unusual combination of scientific and artistic skills. In working with cartographers and graphic designers, it is important for planners to be familiar with the basic aspects of cartographic design. Decisions must be made in map preparation concerning scale, data sources that will be used, features that will be shown, types of symbols to be used and information that will be shown in the map legend. If many types of information will be presented, black-and-white patterns or appropriate colors must be selected that will allow the categories to be clearly differentiated. If the map is to be reduced, it must also be readable after reduction occurs.

In using maps, basic features that should be noted include the map orientation, which is indicated by a north arrow; the map scale; the contour interval; and the date of the map. If several overlays are employed, they are matched with the use of register marks, which usually appear as crosses on the map's four corners.
See: GRAPHIC REPRODUCTION PROCESSES; REFERENCE MAPS

Cash Flow

The proceeds available from an investment after both fixed and operating expenditures and allocated overhead are deducted from the gross receipts derived from the investment.

Catalog of Federal Domestic Assistance (CFDA)

An annual publication of the U.S. Office of Management and Budget (OMB) that lists all federal programs, projects, services and activities that provide assistance to the public. Published since 1965, it includes programs of all agencies that offer financial, technical or other forms of assistance.

The Federal Assistance Program Retrieval System (FAPRS), essentially a computerized form of the catalog, is also maintained by OMB. Access may be obtained through designated state access points, through certain time-sharing companies or by direct access for agencies with proper hardware.

Catch Basin

A chamber located beneath a street that collects storm water runoff entering through an inlet located at street level. The catch basin serves to intercept refuse and sediment to prevent it from being flushed through the sewer. Catch basins are frequently used for combined sewers; modern storm sewer systems, with better self-cleaning capability, generally use drop inlets connecting directly to the sewer.
See: COMBINED SEWER; STORM SEWER

Catchment Area

The geographic area from which a program, facility or institution draws the majority of its users. Also referred to as a service area, the term may range in definition from a special planning area designated by law to a community within which the bulk of an institution's clientele resides.

In planning for delivery of human services, the concept is most commonly viewed as a means of defining a market area for determining the location of a facility and the distribution of satellite clinics. One field in which catchment area analysis has been widely applied has been in the study of service areas for the location of community mental health care centers.

Catchment Basin

The entire area from which a body of water receives replenishment. A drainage basin may have numerous catchment basins.
See: DRAINAGE BASIN; WATERSHED

Categorical Grant

A grant that is intended to finance a highly specific activity. In contrast to a block grant, there are many more legislative requirements as to how the money may be spent.
See: BLOCK GRANT; GRANT-IN-AID

Cement

A variety of inorganic materials that may be mixed with a controlled amount of water to form a paste that later hardens into a rigid mass. The hardening process, called curing, takes an extended period of time to attain maximum strength. The most commonly used cements are described below:

- *Portland cement*: a product obtained by mixing and then burning two ground-up raw materials—one composed largely of lime and the other of a claylike material containing silica, alumina and iron—so that they fuse. The raw materials are ground before burning. The product that results, called clinker, is finely pulverized, and a small amount of gypsum is added to retard setting. Portland cement reaches its maximum strength in about 28 days.
- *Air-entraining portland cement:* Materials are added to portland cement that trap air in tiny bubbles when the cement is mixed with water and an aggregate to form concrete. The result reduces deterioration from frost and increases the cement's resistance to scaling from salt that has been applied to melt snow and ice on roads and sidewalks. It also increases concrete strength.
- *High early strength cement:* a cement that attains a high strength in three to seven days. This is particularly useful in concrete road construction, emergency repairs and concrete building projects undertaken in freezing weather, since concrete must be set at a minimum of 40 degrees Fahrenheit (4 degrees Celsius) to

ensure strength. This temperature must be supplied artificially in freezing weather by heating and covering the area under construction.

The numerous types of cement also include natural cement, pozzuolan cement, masonry cement, nonstaining cement and low-heat cement.
See: CONCRETE

Cemetery

Land reserved and/or used for gravesites. Cemeteries usually require a special use permit and are not allowed in many municipalities. Sometimes very small, such as graveyards found on church property, they may also extend for hundreds of acres. Large cemeteries are usually established in urban fringe areas because central cities often prohibit them—a practice that dates from ancient times.

Cemeteries are provided by all levels of government and by churches and religious organizations. They are also frequently in private, cooperative or mutual ownership. Often constituted as nonprofit corporations, they are usually exempt from property taxes. In private and religious cemeteries, gravesites are usually sold, thereby permanently dividing the property among many owners and making land resassembly possible only by lengthy legal procedures. For this reason, cemetery land is generally acquired only for essential public improvements.

Use of land for cemeteries where population density is high can preclude the development of that land for other more important urban land uses. Cities in Switzerland have therefore limited the amount of cemetery land and the number of years that one may use a gravesite so that these sites can be reused. After 25 years the deceased's family may remove the remains to a rural cemetery, or the city places them in a common grave. Other municipalities have turned some older graveyards into parks and playgrounds, while still others have capitalized on notable or scenic cemeteries as tourist attractions. The use of ground-level plaques instead of gravestones is a growing trend (these cemeteries are called memorial parks), while the use of multifamily and high-rise mausoleums is popular in countries where aboveground interment is preferred.
See: OPEN SPACE

Census

A periodic enumeration of the entire population, selected subpopulations or other specialized items, such as businesses or farms, to produce a data base. Census data are used extensively by government for planning and fiscal disbursement purposes.

In the United States a census of population and housing is taken every 10 years, although authorized to occur every 5 years if sufficient funding is available, while certain business censuses are routinely taken every 5 years. Sample surveys, which question a much smaller population, are taken at frequent intervals to update the data. Similar censuses and surveys are taken by many other countries;

some of these reports are published in aggregated form by the United Nations and the U.S. Bureau of the Census.

In the United States the Bureau of the Census publishes census data in printed reports, on microfiche and on computer tapes. Various levels of data are available for the nation, regional areas, metropolitan areas, cities, counties and smaller areas, with the most data available for the larger geographic divisions. Availability of information depends upon the nature of the data, the frequency of data collection and the ability of the Census Bureau to present statistics without revealing confidential information. Since response to census questionnaires is mandatory in most cases, and statistical techniques are highly refined, U.S. census data are considered to be quite reliable.

See: CENSUS BLOCK; CENSUS DISPLAY MAPS; CENSUS GEOGRAPHIC CODE SCHEMES; CENSUS HISTORICAL COMPARABILITY; CENSUS MICRODATA FILES; *CENSUS OF AGRICULTURE; CENSUS OF GOVERNMENTS; CENSUS OF HOUSING; CENSUS OF POPULATION:* CENSUS OUTLINE MAPS; CENSUS REPORTS; CENSUS SURVEYS; CENSUS TRACT (CT); ECONOMIC CENSUSES; ENUMERATION DISTRICT (ED); GBF/DIME FILES; METROPOLITAN STATISTICAL AREA (MSA); MINOR CIVIL DIVISION (MCD); NEIGHBORHOOD STATISTICS PROGRAM; POLITICAL SUBDIVISION; PRIVACY; STANDARD CONSOLIDATED STATISTICAL AREA (SCSA); STANDARD METROPOLITAN STATISTICAL AREA (SMSA): SUMMARY TAPE FILES (STF); URBANIZED AREA (UA)

Census Block

The smallest census data collection area, containing an average of about 100 people. They are most commonly small rectangular areas bounded by four streets, but they may be irregularly shaped and bounded by railroad tracks or by a feature of the topography. Census block boundaries may change from one census to another, making comparison difficult. Block statistics are published for all urbanized areas and all incorporated municipalities with populations of 10,000 or more, as well as for the entire states of Georgia, Mississippi, New York, Rhode Island and Virginia, which contracted for this coverage.

Where census block statistics are prepared, data are first presented for block groups (BGs), which are aggregated blocks averaging approximately 1,000 people; BGs have replaced enumeration districts for these areas. Several block groups comprise a census tract. In places that have no census tracts, block numbering areas (BNAs) are used for aggregated block statistics.
See: CENSUS; CENSUS TRACT (CT); ENUMERATION DISTRICT (ED)

Census Display Maps

Maps available from the Bureau of the Census that illustrate, at various scales, statistical information gathered in the census. Net migration, numbers of persons of Spanish origin, families below the poverty level, and number of renter-occupied housing units, all by county, are examples

of multicolored statistical maps that can be obtained. Shaded maps giving data by census tract are available for Standard Metropolitan Statistical Areas.
See: CENSUS; CENSUS OUTLINE MAPS

Census Geographic Code Schemes

Code numbers used for identification of geographic areas by the Bureau of the Census and other federal agencies. Knowledge of code numbers is necessary for identification of data on specific locations.

Census codes are published in several forms in addition to the census reports and tapes. The *Geographic Identification Code Scheme* (GICS) is a set of tables, organized by state, that show codes for all areas for which census data are tabulated. The *Master Area Reference File* (MARF) is a machine-readable file that gives code numbers down to the enumeration district and block group level along with population and housing data for decennial census questions. The *Federal Information Processing Standards* publications (FIPS), published by the Bureau of Standards, indicate codes used by all federal agencies, some of which are used by the Census Bureau.
See: CENSUS

Census Historical Comparability

The ability to compare data from one census to another for determination of trends. One of the important uses of census data is determination of growth, decline or stability in selected data categories, such as population by municipality or housing units lacking complete plumbing facilities. The ability to make comparisons depends upon the consistency of census definitions and the boundaries of data tabulation areas.

Certain basic questions remain on census questionnaires for many years, particularly those related to total population counts, income, education and housing units. Over time some subject areas are expanded while others are deleted because some important information needs emerge. Many geographic area definitions also change, but some, such as counties and census tracts, are less likely to change than others.

As a result of these changes, it is necessary for the data user to compare maps of the decennial census geographic boundaries as well as definitions if there is an indication that they might be different. Where differences occur, it may be possible to derive comparable data by aggregating data from other districts or questions.
See: CENSUS

Census Microdata Files

Computer tapes that contain census data, for a sample of housing units, on the characteristics of each unit and the people who live in it. This information differs dramatically from most other census tabulations, which are given as counts for each census question for specific geographic areas. Census microdata files consist of confidential microdata, which are not available for other than Census Bureau use, and public-use microdata, which are extracts from the confidential microdata that avoid disclosure of information about identifiable households or individuals.

Census microdata files are available for areas of 100,000 population or greater and contain data for households that received the long form of the census questionnaire covering the full range of questions in the census. They make possible cross tabulations of any items in the census and are useful in the study of trends on specialized subject areas or population subgroups.

See: CENSUS

Census of Agriculture

A census of farming, ranching and related activities taken every five years by the Bureau of the Census in years ending in 2 and 7. This census reports data on agricultural production, resources and inventory for counties, states and regions. Once in each decade data are also collected on irrigation, drainage and horticultural specialities.

Data on subjects such as acreage, crops, value of sales, use of fertilizers and market value of land and buildings are used primarily for planning purposes by farm cooperatives, local governments in rural areas and the Department of Agriculture.

See: CENSUS; CENSUS SURVEYS

Census of Construction Industries

A census of general contractors, operative builders (speculative builders), special trade contractors, and land subdividers and developers. The census collects data on employees, payrolls, receipts, expenditures, assets, depreciation, project locations, ownership and class of construction (new or maintenance). Data are tabulated for the entire country, for regions and for each state.

Construction industry data are used by planners in evaluating building rates, costs and production. They are also used for information on employment in construction trades and for determination of future needs for supplies and natural resources.

See: CENSUS; CENSUS SURVEYS; CONSTRUCTION COST DATA; ECONOMIC CENSUSES

Census of Governments

A census of government administrations conducted by the Bureau of the Census every five years in years ending in 2 and 7. The principal governments queried are federal, state, county, municipal, township, school district and special district, but response to this census is voluntary, unlike other censuses.

The subjects covered relate to governmental organization, taxable property values (assessed valuation), measurable sales and the ratio of assessments to sales, and nominal and effective tax rates. This census also collects data on governmental employment and governmental finances (revenues, expenditures, indebtedness, and cash and security holdings).

The *Census of Governments* is useful for fiscal planning, for the study of revenue distribution and for analysis of comparative statistics.

See: CENSUS; CENSUS SURVEYS

Census of Housing

The portion of the decennial census in the United States that presents data on housing. Housing data are a basic tool for evaluation of housing conditions as well as for determination of the age of housing units, their size, value and the vacancy rate. They are also useful as social indicators and for analysis of density patterns. Housing data are used for planning purposes by the construction industry, banks, insurance companies and utility companies as well as by government.

See: CENSUS; CENSUS OF POPULATION; CENSUS 100 PERCENT ITEMS; CENSUS SAMPLE ITEMS; CENSUS SURVEYS

Census of Manufactures

A census of manufacturing industries. Data collected relate to employment, inventories, assets, capital expenditures and costs of materials, fuels and contract work. Information is also gathered on materials and supplies used and products made and shipped, and plant characteristics are obtained for some industries. Data are presented for Standard Metropolitan Statistical Areas (SMSAs), counties and cities.

The Census of Manufactures and the monthly surveys are used extensively by the federal government in compiling the gross national product (GNP) and in deriving monthly indexes. Lower levels of government evaluate local economic changes with the data and can study statistics on individual plants, while manufacturers and distributors use the data for sales analysis and forecasting purposes.

See: CENSUS; CENSUS SURVEYS; ECONOMIC CENSUSES

Census of Mineral Industries

A census of mines and mining industries. This census collects data on five major mining categories: metal, anthracite, bituminous coal and lignite, oil and gas, and nonmetallic minerals. Further detail is also available by 42 standard industrial classification (SIC) codes. Data are presented for the entire country, census regions and states.

Mineral industry data are used by the federal government to calculate the gross national product and mineral reserves, in planning legislation on conservation and energy-related matters and in determining mineral policies and development programs.

See: CENSUS SURVEYS; ECONOMIC CENSUSES

Census of Population

A census of the entire population of the country taken in years ending in 0 in the United States and in years ending in 1 and 6 in Canada. In the United States the population census has been taken every 10 years since 1790, while more recently special censuses of selected areas have also been taken at the 5-year point between censuses, particularly in areas with considerable population change. In 1976 the U.S. Congress authorized mid-decade censuses to begin in 1985 but ultimately did not fund one for that year.

The Census of Population is the most important of the censuses taken, since it is used to compute the number of congressional representatives allocated to each state and to align the congressional district boundaries so that each member of Congress represents approximately the same number of people. It is used for similar purposes by state and local governments. Most grant-in-aid and revenue-sharing programs are also based by law on census statistics for population, per capita income or population density.

The 1980 Census, however, was attacked by some municipalities that claimed they had been undercounted in areas with largely black populations or substantial numbers of illegal aliens. As this could potentially affect their congressional representation and federal funding levels, they took the matter to court. The courts upheld the confidentiality of the census data by denying cities the right to examine census returns. Results of the 1980 Census showed an 11.4 percent rise in population nationwide and a shift of 17 seats in the House of Representatives from the northeastern and midwestern states to those in the South and Southwest.

See: CENSUS; CENSUS OF HOUSING; CENSUS 100 PERCENT ITEMS; CENSUS SAMPLE ITEMS; CURRENT POPULATION REPORTS; NONWHITE; SUNBELT

Census of Retail Trade

A census of retail establishments that produces data on such items as sales receipts, employment, establishment size and floor space for each type of retail business. Statistics are available for states, Standard Metropolitan Statistical Areas (SMSAs), counties, places of 2,500 or more inhabitants, and 386 central business districts (CBDs) and 1,450 major retail centers (MRCs).

Retail trade data from the census are important for municipal economic forecasting and for economic planning. The census is also used by manufacturers, importers and distributors for such purposes as forecasting sales and planning new plants and warehouses.

See: CENSUS SURVEYS; ECONOMIC CENSUSES

Census of Service Industries

A census of businesses that provide services to the public. Personal and business services are included, as are travel-related services and those offered for entertainment and recreation. Health, legal, educational and social services are listed, as are membership and research organizations. Data are also given for engineering, architectural, planning and surveying services. Data are available for Standard Metropolitan Statistical Areas (SMSAs), counties and cities of 2,500 or more inhabitants.

The data produced, particularly those on employment and receipts, are useful in municipal economic analysis

and for planning government services. They are also used by the industries for their planning and marketing purposes.

See: CENSUS; CENSUS SURVEYS; ECONOMIC CENSUSES

Census of Transportation

A census that presents data by state concerning the amount of travel of persons, trucks and commodities. The Census of Transportation differs from other censuses in that it is comprised of four census surveys rather than being a single, complete census.

Volume I, National Travel Survey, provides data on the volume and characteristics of travel for trips over 100 miles (160.9 kilometers) by United States civilians. Taken from a sample of 24,000 households, it gives data on such items as means of transportation; distance traveled; trip purpose; weekend, spring and summer travel; and destinations. Volume II, Truck Inventory and Use Survey, reports data on the characteristics and use of trucks, other than government vehicles, and includes items on truck mileage and products carried. The Commodity Transportation Survey provides data on the volume and characteristics of intercity shipments originated by manufacturers in the 50 states. The Motor Carrier Survey reports on public carriers not subject to federal regulation.

Transportation data are used extensively by the travel and trucking industries but are also useful to highway departments and resort areas for planning purposes.

See: CENSUS; CENSUS SURVEYS; ECONOMIC CENSUSES

Census of Wholesale Trade

A census of businesses that primarily sell to retailers and repair shops; to industrial, commercial, institutional or professional business users; to farms; or to other wholesalers. Data are available on items such as sales, employment, warehouse space and storage capacity of petroleum terminals. The data are presented for states, Standard Metropolitan Statistical Areas (SMSAs), counties and places with 2,500 or more inhabitants.

Wholesale trade statistics are used by government for economic forecasting purposes; data on employment and plant size are particularly useful for planning purposes.

See: CENSUS; CENSUS SURVEYS; ECONOMIC CENSUSES

Census 100 Percent Items

Questions asked on all census questionnaires. The 1980 Census of Population and Housing was administered in two forms: a short form, given to approximately 81 percent of the population, and a long form, given to the remaining 19 percent. Both forms contained seven questions about each household member, nine questions about the housing unit and three questions to ensure that all household members were included. Data derived from these questions are referred to as complete-count, or 100 percent, data.

Since these questions were answered by all respondents, the data are considered to be more accurate than those for the sample items on the long form and are made available for areas as small as blocks. Complete-count population items related to household relationship, sex, race, age, marital status and Spanish/Hispanic origin or descent. Housing items asked the number of housing units at the address, whether the unit had complete plumbing facilities and a private entrance, the number of rooms in the unit, housing tenure, condominium identification, value of the home, rent, vacancy status and whether the unit was on a property of 10 or more acres or contained a medical or commercial establishment.
See: CENSUS; CENSUS OF HOUSING; CENSUS OF POPULATION; CENSUS SAMPLE ITEMS

Census Outline Maps

Bureau of the Census base map series that show boundaries of data collection and aggregation areas, such as Standard Metropolitan Statistical Areas (SMSAs), census tracts and enumeration districts. Those map series used for the 1980 Census are available for purchase and are published for areas of different sizes.

Census Tract Maps are available for SMSAs and tracted nonmetropolitan counties, and Urban Area Outline Maps show counties, minor civil divisions (MCDs) and places. The Metropolitan Map Series (MMS) shows urbanized areas within SMSAs and adjacent non-SMSA counties, while the Vicinity Map Series (VMS) shows selected urban concentrations outside of SMSAs. Place Maps depict incorporated and census-designated places outside of MMS/VMS areas; County Maps illustrate counties outside all of the above areas; and County Subdivision Maps of States show the boundaries of counties, MCDs and Indian reservations. A single map or a series is also available showing Standard Consolidated Statistical Areas, SMSAs and counties.
See: CENSUS; CENSUS DISPLAY MAPS; GBF/DIME FILES

Census Reports

Published data resulting from censuses conducted by the Bureau of the Census. Reports are produced for all regularly scheduled censuses, for special censuses and for special subjects on which data are culled from several censuses or from special survey data.

Among the special reports are those on residential energy uses, statistics on women in the United States, social indicators, international population statistics and foreign economic reports. *The County and City Data Book* and *Historical Statistics of the United States* are two special reports that are frequently used by planners.
See: CENSUS; CENSUS SURVEYS; CURRENT POPULATION REPORTS

Census Sample Items

Questions asked of a statistical sample of the population in the Census of Population and Housing. In the 1980 Census households that received the long form completed 26 questions on population and 20 more on housing subjects in addition to the 100 percent questions completed by all households.

Long forms were administered to approximately 19 percent of the population, as follows: a 50 percent sample in governmental jurisdictions with fewer than 2,500 people as estimated by the Bureau of the Census for July 1, 1977 and a 17 percent sample in the remainder of the country. The higher rate in small municipalities was used to ensure the collection of accurate income data, since statistical samples of small populations are subject to greater inaccuracy.

Sample questions on population related to education, birthplace, citizenship, English proficiency and ancestry. Questions were also asked regarding place of residence and activity five years ago, veteran status and presence of a disability. Other questions pertained to numbers of children, marital history, employment status, place of work, travel time and means of transportation to work, and the number of persons in one's carpool. Questions on occupation included the year last worked, the industry and the class of worker, as well as the amount of income by source in 1979 and total income in 1979.

Housing questions included the number of units in the structure, the number of stories in the building, the presence of an elevator, the age of the structure and the year that the respondent moved into the house. Questions were also asked concerning sewage disposal; heating equipment; fuels used for house heating, water heating and cooking; and costs of utilities and fuels. Other questions related to the presence of certain types of facilities, such as kitchens, bedrooms, bathrooms, telephones and air conditioning; ownership of motor vehicles, including automobiles, light trucks and vans; and homeowner shelter costs for mortgage, real estate taxes and hazard insurance.
See: CENSUS; CENSUS OF HOUSING; CENSUS OF POPULATION; CENSUS 100 PERCENT ITEMS

Census Surveys

Periodic surveys, conducted at regular and irregular intervals by the Bureau of the Census, that are designed to give current estimates about selected data areas. The bureau conducts more than 250 surveys annually on a wide range of topics. Surveys are taken by sampling relatively small populations, making the surveys less accurate than the periodic censuses on the same subjects; however, they are useful in determining trends and form the basis of some federal indexes, such as the Consumer Price Index (CPI).

The *Current Population Survey* (CPS) is a monthly survey of 65,000 households that gives data on education, migration, occupation, family size and composition, birthrates, income and housing vacancies. The *Quarterly*

Household Survey (QHS) queries 6,000 households on alterations, additions and repairs. The *Annual Housing Survey* (AHS) measures the housing inventory and housing conditions in two separate surveys: One consists of 82,000 housing units nationally and the other of 435,000 units in 60 Standard Metropolitan Statistical Areas (SMSAs).

Business surveys are conducted monthly on retail, wholesale and service trade, while the monthly *Survey of Construction* (SOC) produces reports on such areas as housing starts, housing completions, new residential construction, characteristics of new housing and value of new construction.

Other surveys useful to planners relate to government finance and state and local tax revenue, while health and social planners may use the health and medicare surveys or the national crime and commercial victimization surveys.
See: CENSUS; CENSUS OF TRANSPORTATION; CURRENT POPULATION REPORTS

Census Tract (CT)

An area used for census data presentation that contains an average of 4,000 people. A subdivision of a county, census tracts are delineated for all Standard Metropolitan Statistical Areas (SMSAs) and for certain counties outside SMSAs that have defined them. The states of Connecticut, Delaware, Hawaii, New Jersey and Rhode Island have been entirely divided into census tracts.

Census tract boundaries are chosen on the basis of relatively permanent features, such as county lines and rivers, and are generally not changed between censuses so that comparability is preserved (adjustments may be made for a new freeway or major development). Where population increases require tract subdivision, the new tracts usually can be combined to compare similar areas. In a few locations, where population has decreased, census tracts have been combined, while in rare situations local Census Statistical Area Committees undertake a wholesale revision of census tract boundaries.

Central Business District (CBD)

The traditional business core of a community, characterized by a high concentration of activity within a relatively small area. The CBD is usually the office, financial, retail and service center of a city, providing both employment opportunities for a large number of people and a significant share of the tax base.

The compactness and concentrated development of a CBD encourages pedestrian traffic, creating a favorable shopping environment, and facilitates the activities of businesses needing to be in close proximity to each other. An effort is usually made to preserve a continuous retail store frontage in CBD shopping areas and to avoid types of development and overly long blocks that can interfere with pedestrian movement.

Most cities have a central business district, although they vary greatly in size and character, and some large cities may have more than one CBD. In recent years,

however, many central business districts have been in decline to varying degrees, faced with increasing competition from outlying retail areas and shopping centers. Office and industrial development has also been attracted to suburban areas by factors such as sufficient land to build modern plants and the ease of automobile and truck access and parking. To combat this trend, cities have adopted a variety of strategies, ranging from improved access and parking and beautification projects to the construction of major shopping malls and mixed-use developments, such as Atlanta's Peachtree Center.
See: CENTRAL BUSINESS DISTRICT PLAN; DOWNTOWN REVITALIZATION; ECONOMIC DEVELOPMENT; PEDESTRIANIZATION

Central Business District Plan

A plan that provides a framework for guiding expansion or revitalization within the downtown. It is a long-range guide for policy decisions and future development that, ideally, is officially adopted by the municipality. Zoning controls, building codes and environmental controls, as well as scheduled capital expenditures and transportation improvements, should all be consistent with the plan.

Most central business district (CBD) plans begin with a generalized statement of objectives and goals, usually followed by a history of the CBD, including an analysis of past, present and projected future trends. Surveys are also taken to quantify and evaluate such features of the CBD as current building condition, traffic volume and circulation patterns, and availability of parking. This information is used to develop a series of concept plans and a general development plan for the CBD. Policy recommendations are also made regarding specific activities and programs that should be undertaken in order to achieve this desired pattern of development. The policy recommendations may also include a discussion of funding sources and the organizational structure needed to implement these activities and programs.
See: CENTRAL BUSINESS DISTRICT (CBD); COMPREHENSIVE PLAN

Central Park

A public park in New York City designed by Frederick Law Olmsted and Calvert Vaux. The park, which is rectangular in shape and located in the middle of Manhattan, consists of 843 acres (341 hectares), of which 150 acres (61 hectares) are water bodies. The site that Central Park occupies was purchased between 1853 and 1859, and Olmsted and Vaux won the nationwide competition to design it in 1857. The park was named to the National Register of Historic Places in 1965.

The first urban park in the United States, its design is notable for its use of innovative methods of separating pedestrian and vehicular paths, its varied environments—some formal, others pastoral—and its numerous specimen plantings. The site—which was originally scrubland, foul swamps and stone quarries—was transformed according to

the Olmsted and Vaux plan by massive earth moving, dynamiting and topsoil placement operations. A large restoration project that is currently underway, necessitated by damage caused by attendance well beyond the parks environmental capacity and aging of its structures, is rehabilitating park buildings, bridges and outdoor furniture and replenishing its plantings.
See: OLMSTED, FREDERICK LAW

Central Place Theory

A theory that seeks to explain the distribution of urban areas within a region and their relative differences in size. According to this theory, the basic function of a city is the provision of goods and services to the surrounding area, called the hinterland.

The most important central places are not necessarily the largest in population, but those that are located at key points in a transportation network and are able to provide such amenities as a wide range of goods and services, and banking and other commercial facilities. Other factors considered important in creating major central places are resort facilities, government, and educational and cultural institutions. The theory also asserts that a hierarchy of urban settlements will emerge, with the larger urban areas providing goods and services that cannot be found in smaller towns.
See: GROWTH THEORY

Ceremonial Axis Plan

A land pattern in which boulevards of exceedingly wide dimension serve as axes between monumental buildings or other important sites. In the ceremonial axis plan, these boulevards often connect government buildings, major public instituions, palaces or cathedrals and are designed to permit formal processions and pilgrimages. Washington, D.C., New Delhi and Brazilia are examples of cities planned on this basis, while parts of Paris, London and Rome also have famous ceremonial boulevards. The processional way, a wide road that leads to an important building, dates to ancient Egypt, where streets up to 180 feet (55 meters) wide led to major palaces. (See Fig. 24)
See: AXIAL GROWTH; RADIAL PATTERN

Certificate of Need (CON)

A process established under the National Health Planning and Resources Development Act of 1974 whereby a proposal to establish a new program, to add, delete or replace equipment, or to construct or renovate a facility is reviewed by an approved agency. The approved organization, usually the local health systems agency, determines whether existing facilities are capable of meeting community needs. The procedure, which also takes into consideration financial feasibility and the character and competence of the facility making the proposal, results in a document issued by the state health department that confirms whether or not the proposed change is required to satisfy an unmet need. The process is intended to provide

a mechanism for coordinating plans of various community health facilities without unnecessary, and often costly, duplication of services.
See: ANNUAL IMPLEMENTATION PLAN (AIP); HEALTH SYSTEMS AGENCY (HSA); HEALTH SYSTEMS PLAN (HSP); NATIONAL HEALTH PLANNING AND RESOURCES DEVELOPMENT ACT OF 1974

Certificate of Occupancy (CO)

A document that is issued by a municipal government upon completion of a structure to indicate that it is ready for occupancy and in compliance with municipal building codes.
See: BUILDING CODE

Certified Development Company

A private nonprofit corporation or a for-profit stock corporation incorporated under state law and certified by the Small Business Administration (SBA) to make long-term loans to small businesses. Authorized by Section 503 of the Small Business Investment Act, as amended in 1980, the intent of the program is to aid communities in encouraging the development and expansion of small business in that area through joint participation of both the federal government and the private sector. This differs from the goal of many other SBA programs in which SBA serves as a "last resort" source of financing.

To be certified by the SBA, a development company must meet certain organizational criteria, such as having a minimum of 25 members or stockholders and a professional staff capable of packaging and servicing its loans. The company must operate within a defined target area that can be no larger than statewide and must have representation from a minimum of two of the following: local government, a private lending institution, a community organization or a business organization.

SBA obtains funding for certified development company projects by the sale of 100 percent SBA-guaranteed debentures to the Federal Financing Bank (FFB), a federal entity created by the Federal Financing Bank Act of 1973 (PL 93-224) to coordinate federal agency borrowing and to purchase and sell those obligations that are guaranteed or issued by federal agencies. The debenture guaranteed by SBA may be for up to $500,000, for a term of no more than 25 years and may not represent more than 50 percent of the cost of completing a project that a particular small business will undertake. (The remaining 50 percent of the project cost may not be federally financed.) The debenture is generally secured by collateral, such as by a mortgage on the land and buildings that are being financed. The development company is required to provide 10 percent of the total project funding, which it may obtain from the small business that it will be assisting or other sources.

A development company may assist small business concerns in one of two ways. In the relend plan the development company may serve as a means through which the debentures and nonfederal funds are channeled to the small business. Alternatively, the development company may own the property and lease it to the business, using the borrowed funds to make the purchase and undertake improvements.

Activities eligible for financing include land acquisition; plant acquisition, expansion, construction and renovation; and the purchase of equipment and machinery. The small business concern must conform to SBA standards for the program that are used to define a small business.
See: COMMUNITY DEVELOPMENT CORPORATION (CDC); ECONOMIC DEVELOPMENT; SMALL BUSINESS ADMINISTRATION (SBA); SMALL BUSINESS INVESTMENT COMPANY (SBIC)

Certiorari

Used generally to refer to a legal writ issued by a higher court or appellate body to an inferior court, ordering the lower court to produce a certified record of proceedings for the purpose of allowing the appellate body to review the controversy or appeal.

The term *tax certiorari* is often used to refer to proceedings initiated by a property owner for the purpose of obtaining judicial review of a real estate tax assessment affecting his property, in order to obtain a lower tax assessment. Property owners challenge assessments on a variety of grounds, including that their property was assessed at too high a value and that their property was assessed unfairly when compared to comparable neighboring properties.

The granting and denial of writs of certiorari to lower courts is the mechanism used by the United States Supreme Court to choose cases it wishes to review in the exercise of its discretionary jurisdiction.

Chamber of Commerce

A voluntary association of businessmen whose objective is to promote the interests of the commercial and industrial sectors of a community. Found in many communities and often affiliated with regional or national organizations, local chamber of commerce chapters disseminate information about their communities' businesses and industries and assist businesses in becoming established. Promotion of tourism may also be a chamber of commerce function.

A chamber of commerce often works closely with local economic development agencies to promote economic expansion and may assist community development corporations, develop programs to attract new businesses and serve as a lobbying group on behalf of the business community.
See: ECONOMIC DEVELOPMENT; TOURISM

Channelization

1. The process of altering stream channels by such methods as straightening, widening, deepening them, or lining them with concrete to reduce resistance to flow. Channelization, which allows larger volumes of water to be conveyed by a water body without dangerously raising the water level, is usually undertaken to minimize flooding problems or to improve agricultural land by facilitating drainage.

Large numbers of channelization projects have been undertaken in the United States, many supported by federal programs. In numerous cases they have successfully accomplished their goals. There are, however, certain potential undesirable effects associated with channelization, including channel instability; increased downstream bank erosion; disturbance of fish breeding and a lowering of aesthetic quality. For this reason, it is recommended that modern stream improvement projects attempt to preserve the general gradients and natural curving pattern of the stream, and to keep the channel as close as possible to its natural depth and width.

2. The process of placing fixed or movable barriers or painted lines between lanes of a roadway to control traffic and increase the road's capacity. Channelization is also used to add extra lanes at intersections and to create reserved lanes for such purposes as the operation of express buses.
See: AT-GRADE INTERSECTION; FLOOD CONTROL; RESERVED LANES

Charitable Contribution of Real Estate

The donation of real property to a government agency, a public charity or a private foundation. An interest in land—such as air rights, development rights or a facade easement—may also be donated. In general, donations of real property that qualify as capital gain property entitle the donor to an income tax deduction equal to the property's market value.

Contributions of real estate are a principal means by which open space is preserved and have also been responsible for the establishment of numerous wildlife sanctuaries and parks. Donations of estates with large buildings have provided locations for schools, conference centers and government buildings, while donations of partial real estate interests, such as easements or development rights, have helped to preserve existing land use and density.

Use of a charitable contribution is often beneficial to all parties, since the preservation of the property is a public benefit and the owner obtains partial reimbursement via tax savings. However, not all land that is offered as a contribution is worth accepting. Acceptance of land implies loss of future real estate taxes as well as ongoing costs for maintenance, insurance, programs and development. If the recipient agency is financially unprepared for this burden, the property will become a physical and financial problem.
See: LAND ENDOWMENT; PROPERTY ACQUISITION; STEWARDSHIP; VACANT LAND

Charrette

An intensive meeting at which community members participate with government officials to develop a proposal or to resolve areas of contention related to a pro-

posed plan or program. The term derives from architectural training in which students are required to develop solutions to an architectural problem within a specified time period. Charrettes have been used as a form of citizen participation.
See: CITIZEN PARTICIPATION

Cheney v. Village 2 at New Hope, Inc. (429 Pa. 626, 241 A.2d 81 [1968])

A decision by the Supreme Court of Pennsylvania holding that under the state zoning enabling act then in effect, a municipality's legislative body could confer authority upon the planning commission to approve plans submitted by a private developer for the development of a planned unit development (PUD) district. The court found that this action did not constitute either spot zoning or an unlawful delegation of legislative authority to the planning commission in violation of the zoning enabling legislation. Thus, the decision adds flexibility to the ways in which a municipality can respond to changing land use needs and demands, by eliminating the requirement that the legislative body expressly authorize each new land use.

Applicability of the case to other similar cases is limited, however, by the fact that the legislative body had specifically rezoned the tract in question to a PUD district and that the PUD ordinance was quite specific in describing permitted uses, densities and spacing requirements.
See: PLANNED UNIT DEVELOPMENT (PUD)

Chicago Plan (1909)

Also know as the Burnham plan, after Daniel Burnham, who considered it his greatest achievement, the *Plan of Chicago* (1909) contained many wide-ranging and innovative features, which made it a milestone in American planning.

The first regional plan for a major United States metropolitan area, the plan encompassed an area of approximately 4,000 square miles (10,360 square kilometers) and proposed significant changes to Chicago's transportation network and open space system. It recommended a series of concentric highways that would cross the region at varying distances from downtown Chicago, as well as an extensive greenbelt near the city's lakefront and its periphery and many parks in the city itself. It also suggested an altered city road system featuring landscaped and widened roadways as well as a large-scale civic center complex.

Although in many ways the plan adhered to "city beautiful" principles, it also discussed subjects usually missing from plans of that era, such as freight handling, railroad facilities, suburban growth and subdivision control. Burnham also discussed the possibility of the need for a public housing program for Chicago at some future time, although no programs of that type currently existed in the United States. Eventually, the Chicago plan led to extensive changes in the Chicago area and influenced the way plans were developed throughout the United States.
See: BURNHAM, DANIEL; CITY BEAUTIFUL MOVEMENT; WORLD'S COLUMBIAN EXPOSITION

Chlorination

1. The addition of chlorine to a water supply for purposes of disinfection. Chlorine is used in most public water supplies to kill pathogenic organisms that can carry waterborne diseases, but other forms of disinfection are available, such as the addition of ozone, lime or bromine; exposure to ultraviolet rays; or heating. Chlorine, which is placed in a water supply at the water treatment plant, can cause an undesirable odor and taste if too much is added.

2. The addition of chlorine and its compounds to wastewater. Used principally for disinfection of treatment plant effluent, it is also used for grease removal, oxidation of liquid removed from digester tanks, foam control in digesters and Imhoff tanks, nitrate reduction and bacterial reduction in storm water and treatment plant overflows. In the sewage collection system, it is used to control the growth of slime and to reduce corrosion and odor.
See: IMHOFF TANK; SEWERAGE SYSTEM; SLUDGE DIGESTION; WATER TREATMENT

Church Uses

Churches, synagogues, mosques, church schools, church residences and church-owned land—all of which are generally exempt from property taxes. Church-owned buildings used or rented for other than church-related purposes may be fully or partially taxable.

Once considered to be one of the most important buildings in a town, churches were located at its center and were generally permitted to be taller than other buildings. Today churches and church-related buildings are generally built where their constituents have been able to raise funds to purchase land and undertake construction; their size is most often predicated upon available funds and estimates of the future size of their congregations. Sites are selected to permit later expansion and may be located to attract regional attendance. Often the church may become a form of community center or neighborhood focal point at which large numbers of people may gather.

Depending upon the size of a church, a desirable location is on a collector or arterial street that will provide adequate access but be relatively quiet. Zoning ordinances generally permit churches and other church uses to locate in most zoning districts either by right or by special permit. The Urban Land Institute has suggested that the location of churches adjacent to shopping centers is optimal, particularly where everyone arrives by car, because the parking facilities at the shopping center are generally little-used when church functions normally take place.
See: MULTISERVICE CENTER; OFF-STREET PARKING REQUIREMENTS; TAX-EXEMPT PROPERTY

Cincinnati Comprehensive Plan

Cincinnati became the first major city in the United States to officially adopt a comprehensive plan in 1925. Because of the city planning commission's official adoption of the plan, all proposed deviations from the plan required approval of the commission or a two-thirds vote of approval by the city council.

It was of a much broader scope than was typical of plans of this era, containing such features as sections on housing, waste disposal and methods of financing proposed improvements. The plan was prepared over a three-year period, with its long-range development policies intended to serve as a guide for all other municipal land use activities, including the establishment of a comprehensive zoning ordinance. This process may be compared to the New York City approach of the time, in which a zoning code was adopted independent of a comprehensive and long-range development plan.

See: BETTMAN, ALFRED; NEW YORK CITY ZONING CODE

Circuit Breaker Taxes

Property tax reductions or limited tax exemptions granted to elderly homeowners and to other specified classes of homeowners, such as those who have income below a stated minimum or who are disabled, to permit them to remain in their homes. These tax reductions are primarily intended to give relief to elderly persons whose property has escalated in value, often through inflation, and whose property taxes, as a result, have risen beyond the means of a declining income. The Office of Policy Development and Research of the U.S. Department of Housing and Urban Development has suggested that circuit breaker taxes are analogous in impact to a very low benefit percentage-of-rent housing allowance.

See: FULL-VALUE ASSESSMENT

Circulation Pattern

The repetitive movement of pedestrians and vehicles through a city, a development or a building. Circulation patterns are a basic element in the design of new buildings, subdivisions, urban revitalization plans, new towns and parks. They are also a tool for the analysis of traffic problems or pedestrian congestion.

In the design of new development, traffic volumes at key entry points can be studied to determine the impact of additional proposed traffic loads on adjoining streets. Provision of adequate road capacity and appropriate support facilities—e.g., parking structures or bus loading areas—based on these estimates will enable a particular circulation plan to direct traffic in a desired direction. Failure to make these provisions may cause congestion or undesirable traffic volume in another location. The use of a particular route is related to a variety of factors, which include a desired origin and destination, speed and convenience, and desirable amenities of the route. If these can be duplicated in another location or by another travel mode, the traffic pattern can be altered.

Circumferential Highway

A road that surrounds an urban area, providing access to all major expressways and arterials that radiate from the urban center and that cross it. A circumferential road, ring road or orbital road is a form of bypass that permits traffic not intended for the urban center to circumvent it.

The concept was proposed in the 19th century by Ebenezer Howard to connect garden cities, which would form a ring around a central city. It was first employed in the United States in the interstate highway system in an attempt to increase the speed of vehicles through urbanized areas by enabling them to avoid the congested inner city, as well as to lighten traffic congestion on inner city streets. Several highly automobile-oriented cities now have multiple concentric ring roads to serve the development spreading outward from the center.

The concept of the circumferential highway is now being studied, particularly in Europe, as a means of controlling the numbers and types of vehicles that are permitted to enter a town center. (See Fig. 33)

See: AUTOMOBILE RESTRICTED ZONE (ARZ); HOWARD, SIR EBENEZER

Circumferential Plan

A form of urban growth in which development is focused on a band surrounding the city. A circumferential highway is often the key element of the plan, with subcenters along the circumference, usually at highway interchanges. (See Fig. 24)

See: CONCENTRIC ZONE THEORY; RING PATTERN

Cistern

1. A man-made water-storage facility, usually located underground. Typically, rainwater is collected as it drains off roofs and then channeled into these storage areas, which are usually lined to protect the water supply and covered to minimize evaporation. Cisterns are an important means of storing water in arid climates, in which open reservoir storage is subject to intense evaporation.

2. A natural depression that holds water.

See: RESERVOIR; WATER SUPPLY SYSTEM; WELL

Citizen Advisory Organizations

Groups formed for the purpose of presenting, discussing or studying particular planning issues and advising public officials of their views. A common form of citizen participation, advisory organizations may be composed of officially appointed members or may comprise an informal association of anyone interested in a particular topic or in obtaining membership.

Citizen advisory committees were often established in connection with the urban renewal program, which required that citizen groups be formed to encourage public participation in the renewal process. The term now applies mainly to groups whose principal role is discussion or presentation of programs.

Citizen planning committees offer an opportunity to involve a wider segment of the community in the creation of plans and the study of planning issues than just the planning commission. This type of advisory group provides community officials with a broader cross section of the community's views. The large numbers of citizens that may participate may be organized into subcommittees so that many aspects of an issue can be studied. A frequent role of citizen planning committees is the development of statements on community goals and objectives.

Communitywide housing and planning councils are generally comprised of professionals and civic leaders and are usually found in larger metropolitan areas. The chief role of this type of organization is public education, legislative reform and informed support for new programs.

Associations that form around a relatively narrow issue, geographic area or idea that they are devoted to promoting are referred to as special-purpose planning groups. Local businessmen, for example, may form a group to support improvements in the downtown business district.

Finally, advisory organizations may exist at the regional, state or national level and may conduct research, disseminate information, set standards and engage in political activity.

See: BLUE-RIBBON COMMISSION; CITIZEN BOARD; CITIZEN PARTICIPATION; CITIZEN PARTICIPATION TECHNIQUES; PLANNING COMMISSION; TASK FORCE

Citizen Board

A standing committee of residents living under the jurisdiction of a local or state government who are appointed for fixed terms to offer their opinions on matters related to the work or policy of an agency or department of that government. Citizen boards are used both to act as a local sounding board for programs and ideas that the professional staff may formulate and to guide the range of matters or programs that a particular department undertakes.

Members of these boards, who are usually appointed by the chief executive or administrative head of the local government because of their particular expertise in matters related to the department's work, most often are unpaid or receive token salaries.

See: BLUE-RIBBON COMMISSION; CITIZEN ADVISORY ORGANIZATIONS; PLANNING COMMISSION

Citizen Participation

The involvement of individuals and community groups in the development and evaluation of government proposals and in decision making. Citizen participation is required for government funding for certain development programs in the United States, Canada and Britain and, in many cities, has become the means by which neighborhood groups influence planning and development activities. While planning was, at one time, performed largely without citizen involvement, planners have recognized that citizen input frequently results in projects that are sensitive to community needs and developments that receive community support. The development of active citizen groups through citizen participation techniques has also produced a large body of civic-minded individuals.

In the United States, citizen participation in planning began in the 1920s with the appointment of citizens to planning and zoning boards. In the 1960s citywide or neighborhood participation in the form of citizen advisory boards became a requirement of the Community Action program, the Model Cities program and the urban renewal program. Other acts, such as the Freedom of Information Act of 1966 and the Government in the Sunshine Act of 1976, have made information on government actions more accessible to the citizen.

Although governments have found that citizen involvement is not always forthcoming and that it is often costly and time-consuming to operate programs to gain such involvement, community support often prevents projects in late design stages from being abandoned because of sudden citizen opposition. The success of citizen participation, however, may be dependent on the ground rules established for citizen input and the ability of both sides to adhere to them.

Experiments have also taken place in extending the concept of citizen participation to private industry in order to moderate adversary relationships that can evolve, such as in siting major plants.

See: ADVOCACY PLANNING; CITIZEN PARTICIPATION TECHNIQUES; COMMUNITY CONTROL; LADDER OF CITIZEN PARTICIPATION; NEIGHBORHOOD PLANNING

Citizen Participation Techniques

Approaches to involving the public in planning and decision making. Techniques range from eliciting opinions to development of policy and programs. The wide range of options found in the delegation of decision-making power to citizens relate to the matter under consideration, the local political milieu, time constraints and legislative requirements.

By far the most common approach is the public hearing, which is usually mandated by law, at which opinions on a formal proposal are obtained. The hearing, however, often involves citizens only late in the planning or development process, when it is more difficult to modify proposals or formulate alternative courses of action. A referendum on a particular project is another means of assessing opinion but is also often used well into the planning process. Other forms that obtain input at an earlier point include information and neighborhood meetings, and public information programs that invite public feedback; citizen advisory committees or neighborhood planning boards; and the use of charrettes, group dynamics and the delphi process, which involve citizens in problem solving.

Little city halls, multiservice centers and community hot lines are used for fast response to local issues, while cable television networks have been employed by government to broadcast information and in some cases receive immediate input.

Approaches used in choosing between alternatives include games and simulations, in which participants may play various roles; design-ins, in which participants learn to use planning materials, such as maps and plans; and fishbowl techniques, in which participants express their support or opposition to alternative proposals thereby constructing an acceptable revised plan. The technique of delegating decision-making powers to neighborhood groups that must then take responsiblity for their decisions is also used.

See: CABLE TELEVISION; CHARRETTE; CITIZEN ADVISORY ORGANIZATIONS; CITIZEN PARTICIPATION; COMMUNITY CONTROL; DELPHI PROCESS; FEEDBACK; HOT LINE; LITTLE CITY HALLS; NEIGHBORHOOD PLANNING; PUBLIC HEARING; PUBLIC INFORMATION; REFERENDUM; SIMULATION GAMES

Citizens Forum on Self-Government/National Municipal League

A national nonpartisan civic organization founded in 1894 as the National Municipal League. Headquartered in New York City, the organization's membership consists primarily of educators, civic leaders and organizations, public officials, libraries, and businesses concerned with sound government at all levels and in the informed participation of citizens in state and local government.

Citizens Forum/NML functions as an information clearing house concerning issues such as legislative apportionment and districting, local charters and state constitutions, intergovernmental relationships, the organization of government, and citizen participation. It maintains a reference library, conducts research, holds seminars and workshops, and conducts an annual National Conference on Government in which officials and citizens participate. In addition, it publishes a substantial number of model laws, research reports, and guides on topics ranging from creative localism to court decisions on reapportinment.

It operates a national recognition program for citizen achievement, known as the All-America Cities Awards, and publishes a monthly journal, the *National Civic Review.* The organization has recently begun operating a new information system, Partnerships Dataline, USA, in cooperation with Partners for Livable Places. The system provides practical information, via a computerized data base, on ways in which major physical, social and economic problems are being managed in communities throughout the United States. The system, which is an outgrowth of the President's Task Force on Private Sector Initiatives, places an emphasis on solutions using local partnerships among corporate leaders, citizens, and public officials, and other self-help strategies.

City Beautiful Movement

An urban planning trend that developed in the United States after the World's Columbian Exposition in 1893. Influenced by the beauty and grandeur evident at the fair, American cities began incorporating wide boulevards, civic centers, open space, and public sculpture and fountains into their plans. Municipal art societies also came into being at this time. The first was organized in New York in 1893, and by 1899 a national conference was held concerning the aesthetic aspects of the city environment.

The Burnham plan for Chicago in 1909 is thought of as a major example of the effect that this movement had upon American planning. But the city beautiful influence was also felt in numerous other cities, as plans were prepared and parks commissions and other civic organizations were formed. Planning commissions were established, as well, in many of these municipalites, as communities began expanding the scope of their concern resulting from this early involvement in beautification.

The movement eventually declined, as increased attention was focused upon pressing civic and social concerns and the need for more practical planning. However, it left behind a legacy of the importance of undertaking planning and the need for planning commissions.

See: BURNHAM, DANIEL; CHICAGO PLAN (1909); SAN FRANCISCO PLAN; WORLD'S COLUMBIAN EXPOSITION

City Council

A legislative body composed of members elected at large, by wards or by proportional representation. Each member has one vote on the council. The city council enacts ordinances, imposes taxes, makes appropriations and has the power to investigate the administrative branch. It is the principal policymaking body in the commission form of municipal government, which has no administrator, and in the weak mayor form of muncipal government, which has an administrator who functions predominantly as a figurehead. The parallel legislative body in towns is often known as a town board or board of selectmen; in a village it is often called the board of trustees or village board.

The city council in Canada and Britain is a direct parallel to the commission form of American government. The council forms committees to undertake various administrative activities and elects a chairman, who is known by a variety of names such as warden, mayor, overseer or convenor.

See: COMMISSION FORM OF GOVERNMENT; COUNCIL-MANAGER FORM OF GOVERNMENT; MAYOR-COUNCIL FORM OF GOVERNMENT

City Manager

The appointed professional administrator of a city (or a village, town or county—e.g., village manager) who operates as the chief executive of the community. The manager, who has usually received advanced academic training in public administration, provides the city council with information and advice to allow council members to make informed decisions on policy matters. The manager is then charged with implementation of those policies. Although the council is responsible for all decisions on appropriations, the manager formulates and administers the community's budget.

The relationship of the manager to the council is one of administrator to policymaker, but the manager may often be involved in policy decisions as well. City managers usually are not political figures, although manager appointments are frequently influenced by politics; as a result managers often serve several different communities through their careers. They are prohibited from political activity in their communities by the International City Management Association's Code of Ethics.

See: CITY COUNCIL; COUNCIL-MANAGER FORM OF GOVERNMENT; INTERNATIONAL CITY MANAGEMENT ASSOCIATION (ICMA); MAYOR-COUNCIL FORM OF GOVERNMENT

City of Eastlake v. *Forest City Enterprises, Inc.* (426 U.S. 668, 96 S.Ct. 2358, 49 L.Ed. 132 [1976])

A decision by the United States Supreme Court upholding the right of a municipality to require that changes in legally permitted land uses be subject to ratification by popular referendum.

The city charter amendment that was sustained by the Supreme Court required that any zoning or land use change approved by the city council be submitted to a citywide vote and that the change not take effect unless approved by 55 percent of those voting.

See: JAMES v. *VALTIERRA*

City of Lafayette v. *Louisiana Power & Light Co.* (435 U.S. 389 [1978])

A decision by the United States Supreme Court holding that the blanket exemption from federal antitrust laws usually accorded state action does not apply to action by municipalities. The decision leads to the possibility that local governments may be held accountable for land use ordinances and acts that are found to violate federal antitrust law.

For example, the dissenting opinion in this case raised the specter of a municipality having to be concerned about potential antitrust violations every time it granted an exclusive franchise, chose to provide a service by itself on a monopoly basis or refused to grant a zoning variance to a business.

City of Memphis et al. v. *N.T. Greene et al.* (451 U.S. 100, 101 S.Ct. 1584, 67 L.Ed.2d 769 [1981])

A decision by the United States Supreme Court holding that the closing of a street traversing a white neighborhood, at the point where the street entered a predominantly black neighborhood, did not violate civil rights law or the constitution.

The City of Memphis, Tennessee decided to close the north end of a street that traverses a white residential community, the area to the north being largely black. The stated reasons were the reduction of traffic flow and increased pedestrian safety. Although it was acknowledged that the street closing would have a disproportionate impact on blacks and whites, the Court declined to hold that

this impact required a finding of unlawful discrimination in the absence of proof of discriminatory intent.

The Court further reiterated its general preference for relying upon the judgment of local governments with respect to municipal affairs, in the absence of proof that the municipality was motivated by a racially discriminatory intent. The court restated its position that protecting and preserving the character of a residential community, including its relative tranquility and privacy, is a legitimate foundation for municipal action.

See: EXCLUSIONARY ZONING; *VILLAGE OF ARLINGTON HEIGHTS* v. *METROPOLITAN HOUSING DEVELOPMENT CORPORATION*

Citywide Park

An automobile- or mass transit-oriented park containing approximately 50 to 100 acres (20 to 40 hectares) generally designed for a minimum population of 100,000. It encompasses a wide variety of recreational facilities and usually serves a population radius of 3 or more miles (4.8 kilometers).

While citywide parks contain extensive natural areas, these parks will also often have all of the facilities provided in community parks but may have more of them, larger installations or other specialized facilities. The most capital-intensive recreational facilities—such as swimming pools, skating rinks, zoos and outdoor theaters—are usually placed in citywide parks so that they can serve the largest possible population.

See: COMMUNITY PARK; REGIONAL PARK

Civic Center

The section of a municipality located around major government buildings, such as the city hall and courthouse, that functions as the municipal administrative center. In small towns this area may be limited to the town hall and perhaps a library, while in large cities the civic center may spread for many blocks and contain offices of the state and federal governments as well.

Civic center planning generally involves provision for parking, improvements to traffic flow, adequate public transit and eventual expansion of facilities if additional space is required at a later date. Expansion of civic centers is usually accomplished either by a comprehensive rebuilding of all facilities into one unified complex, such as the Toronto City Hall, or the piecemeal addition of new space by new construction or renovation of existing space. Municipalities often use the need for new space as an opportunity to preserve an architecturally or historically significant building by converting it to government use.

See: COUNTY SEAT; PUBLIC BUILDINGS

Civic Groups

Associations of individuals interested in the general welfare and betterment of the community or with a particular aspect of community enhancement. Civic groups form the foundation of citizen participation in government and serve as an intermediary between official agencies and the individual constituents of the groups.

Civic group are formed for a variety of reasons generally related to neighborhood preservation or to improvement of a segment of community life. They can be influential in directing municipal policy and providing advice concerning community needs or problems, and have often been instrumental in raising funds for specific development projects or community services. They form the basis of neighborhood planning and urban beautification efforts.
See: CITIZEN PARTICIPATION; NEIGHBORHOOD PLANNING

Civil Engineering

The field of engineering concerned with the design and construction of projects that are usually closely related to the health, safety and convenience of the general public. Major divisions of the field are hydraulic engineering (e.g., design of dams), sanitary engineering (e.g., water supply and sewerage systems), transportation engineering (e.g., highways, railroads, airports, terminals), structural engineering (e.g., bridges and tunnels), architectural engineering (e.g., engineering aspects of architectural projects) and surveying.
See: ENVIRONMENTAL ENGINEERING; SANITARY ENGINEERING; SURVEY; TRANSPORTATION ENGINEERING; WATER SUPPLY ENGINEERING

Class Action

A form of judicial proceeding in which numerous persons who comprise a "class" may sue or be sued through the mechanism of naming a relatively small number of persons as representatives of the class.

The class action device is often used in civil rights and civil liberties litigation and in other types of lawsuits brought to advocate a particular viewpoint or an issue. For example, in lawsuits brought to challenge exclusionary zoning practices, the plaintiffs are often defined as a class of low-or moderate-income persons in need of housing, and the defendants are sometimes defined as a class of municipalities within a certain region that have adopted particular zoning restrictions.

The class action procedure is available in federal court and in most states. To qualify as class action, certain prerequisites must normally be satisfied. These prerequisites include the following: The class members must be too numerous to permit all to participate directly; there must be legal or factual questions common to all members of the class; the claims or defenses of the named class representatives must be typical of those of the class at large; and the named representatives must be able to protect the interests of the class.

Clean Air Act Amendments of 1977

Federal legislation (PL 95-95) that strengthens the requirements for adoption of and compliance with state implementation plans to enable achievement of national air quality standards. For areas not yet meeting the national standards, the amendments set a sequence of deadlines that states had to meet in implementing procedures to improve compliance. For areas already meeting the standards, the state plan must make provisions to prevent the deterioration of air quality.

In "nonattainment" areas (places that do not comply with standards) and "nondegradation" areas (places that meet or exceed standards and that are not permitted to degrade existing air quality—e.g., locations near national parks), the amendments also require permits for the construction or modification of major stationary pollution sources. New stationary sources are allowed, however, if they are offset by a reduction in emissions from existing sources.

This legislation also links air quality planning with comprehensive transportation planning required under other programs, stipulating that it is desirable to have the same metropolitan planning agency undertake both. It also authorizes air quality monitoring by the federal government and establishes a National Commission on Air Quality.
See: AIR POLLUTION; CLEAN AIR AMENDMENTS OF 1970; EMISSIONS TRADING SYSTEMS; STATE IMPLEMENTATION (SIP)

Clean Air Amendments of 1970

The most comprehensive legislation on the control of air pollution to that date, this law (PL 91-604) vastly strengthened federal regulation of air quality. The 1970 amendments to the Clean Air Act of 1963 (PL 88-206) gave the Environmental Protection Agency (EPA) the authority to set national ambient air quality standards (NAAQS) and required states to develop state implementation plans (SIP) to achieve these standards within a reasonable period. States are required to adopt the implementation plans and maintain and enforce the standards for each air quality control region (AQCR) within the state. If a state's program is inadequate, EPA may assume direct jurisdiction. The act also authorized grants to air pollution control agencies for their programs. Grants in the amount of two-thirds of planning costs and up to 50 percent of operating costs were made available to single municipalities, while two or more municipalities forming a joint program could obtain up to 75 percent of planning costs and 60 percent of operating costs. Interstate air quality control regions were eligible for 100 percent of costs for the first two years and 75 percent thereafter.

Other provisions of the act authorized EPA to set emission control standards for new stationary pollution sources (new source performance standards [NSPS]) as well as for hazardous air pollutants (national emissions standards for hazardous air pollutants [NESHAP]). The legislation also required automobile emissions of carbon monoxide and hydrocarbons to be reduced by 90 percent beginning with 1975 models, imposed additional requirements for 1976 models and required that automobile manufacturers guar-

antee that their vehicles meet these standards. Studies on aviation emissions and aviation fuel standards were authorized, as was a study on aviation noise pollution, including an analysis of the effects of sonic booms.
See: AIR POLLUTION; CLEAN AIR ACT AMENDMENTS OF 1977; NOISE CONTROL ACT OF 1972

Clean Water Act of 1977

Federal legislation that modifies certain provisions of the Federal Water Pollution Control Act Amendments of 1972. Generally, the act (PL 95-217) eases deadlines for compliance with discharge treatment standards and continues funding for many programs begun under the 1972 act, such as areawide waste treatment management planning and pollution control in lakes.

The 1977 act continues the program of federal grants for construction of sewage treatment plants but places an increased emphasis on recycling and nonconventional technology and increases grants to 85 percent for alternative treatment methodologies. If the state lists such projects as sewer system rehabilitation, new collectors and interceptors, and prevention of overflows from combined sewer systems as having a priority for a particular year, the act requires that municipalities use a minimum of 25 percent of their construction funds for these projects. Municipalities must also take into account potential open space and recreational opportunities in connection with construction of treatment plants. For municipal sewage systems that had not been upgraded because of delays in receiving federal grants, compliance deadlines are extended from 1977 to 1983.

The act strengthens controls over toxic pollutants, setting a 1984 deadline for industry to meet "best available technology" (BAT) standards. The BAT treatment standard for conventional industrial pollutants is replaced by a new "best conventional technology" (BCT) standard, and the compliance deadline is changed from 1983 to 1984. For industrial pollutants that are not classified as either toxic or conventional, the BAT standard is retained, but with the deadline extended from 1983 to 1987. At least 80 percent of all industrial facilities had met the 1977 deadline for "best practicable technology" (BPT) treatment systems. For those acting in good faith to meet the standard, the deadline was extended from 1977 to 1979.

Other provisions of the act authorize funding to aid farmers in soil conservation practices, require that the Environmental Protection Agency (EPA) set national standards for pretreatment of industrial discharges into public treatment systems and give EPA authority to delegate dredge and fill permit activity to states for nonnavigable waterways. Requirements for the cleanup of spills of oil and hazardous substances are extended from 12 miles to 200 miles from shore, and fines are increased. In addition, a national clearinghouse on water pollution control technology is established in EPA, and states having a large rural population are permitted to reserve 4 percent of their allotments for alternative methods of sewage treatment

(other than conventional sewage treatment plants) for areas with populations of 3,500 or less.
See: BEST MANAGEMENT PRACTICES (BMPs); BEST PRACTICABLE TECHNOLOGY (BPT); FEDERAL WATER POLLUTION CONTROL ACT AMENDMENTS OF 1972; MUNICIPAL WASTEWATER TREATMENT CONSTRUCTION GRANT AMENDMENTS OF 1981; PRETREATMENT STANDARDS

Clear Zone

The innermost area of a runway approach, either within the airport or under control of airport authorities. It is kept clear of man-made improvements and natural obstructions, including vegetation and terrain, that have an elevation that could protrude beyond the approach plane. The clear zone begins 200 feet (61 meters) beyond a runway, is centered on it and extends outward from it. Clear zone dimensions are based on the types of aircraft that use the airport and the airport classification. (See Fig. 3)
See: AIRFIELD CLEARANCES; AIRPORT CLASSIFICATION

Clearcutting

Clearcutting is the practice of removing an entire stand of trees at once rather than selectively cutting individual trees. It is generally followed by reseeding and replanting so that all the new trees that develop are of an equivalent age, producing what is known as an even-aged stand.

Clearcutting has been the subject of considerable controversy, in part because of the unsightly appearance that can be presented by an area that has been clear-cut. This practice, carried out on a substantial scale, can scar scenic and recreation areas, accelerate soil erosion and adversely affect watersheds. Wildlife habitats are sometimes destroyed by clearcutting, and the even-aged trees can be more prone to disease and wind damage. Clearcutting does, however, have several good features: It requires fewer roads than selective cutting, is economical, encourages fast timber growth, and allows the desired tree species to be planted. Certain species, such as Douglas fir, also thrive in these conditions; they could not regenerate in shade.

The manner in which a harvesting technique is carried out can sometimes have greater environmental impact than the technique selected. Thus, the alternative to clearcutting, selective cutting, can also be extremely damaging if all trees of any commercial value are taken, leaving only diseased or deformed trees. Similarly, clearcutting can be conducted in a less destructive manner by limiting the size, location and distribution of clear-cut areas. For example, small areas, known as patch or group cuttings, which can be blended in with the landscape, may be less obtrusive and less environmentally objectionable.

Approximately 50 percent of the wood that is harvested on national forest lands is clear-cut. Land and resource planning regulations were issued in 1979 in connection with the National Forest Management Act to direct the

Forest Service in its preparation of forest management plans. These regulations specifically addressed the issue of clearcutting, by establishing a policy that limits the size of contiguous clear-cut areas on federal lands.
See: FORESTRY

Climatic Conditions

The set of characteristics—such as temperature, wind velocity and direction, humidity, precipitation and sun—associated with natural forces or meteorological elements. In planning, knowledge of climatic conditions is critical to the siting and design of any type of development. This is particularly true in the context of microclimatic conditions, which will have a direct impact on a structure and its users.

A proposed development can also have a significant potential impact upon climatic conditions. This is often true in an urban area, where construction of a skyscraper may have dramatic consequences with respect to airflows and light for adjoining properties.
See: MICROCLIMATE; WIND CONTROL; WIND TUNNEL EFFECT

Cloverleaf Interchange

A grade-separated interchange that has four legs and loop ramps to provide for some or all of the left-turn movements. It provides a separate one-way ramp for each turning movement—i.e., two ramps in each quadrant. The loop design requires that all vehicles must exit to the right before they can turn to the left. A partial cloverleaf is an interchange that uses the loop configuration but provides fewer than two ramps per quadrant.

Cloverleaf interchanges are usually unsignalized. Their capacities are determined by the geometric design of their ramps. The primary disadvantage in their design is that they require vehicles exiting and entering to weave with each other to or from the exit or entrance. Large traffic volumes may require the presence of a service road to accommodate the weaving in order to prevent a decrease in the capacity of the through lanes. (See Fig. 18)
See: DIRECTIONAL INTERCHANGE; GRADE-SEPARATED INTERCHANGE

Cluster Development

A development approach in which building lots may be reduced in size and buildings sited closer together, usually in groups or clusters, provided that the total development density does not exceed that which could be constructed on the site under conventional zoning and subdivision regulations. The additional land that remains undeveloped is then preserved as open space and recreational land.

Cluster developments have become popular because, in addition to preserving more open space than if the building units were evenly spread across the property, they allow the preservation of fragile environmental areas such as wetlands and steep hillsides. As this land, which in many cases would not have been buildable anyway, can be

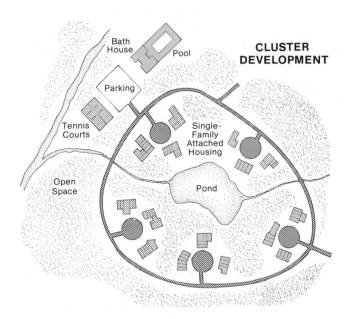

Fig. 8.   Clustering permits preservation of open space.

preserved at no additonal cost to the developer, it is possible to keep development costs lower. Other cost-saving factors are the shorter street and utility lines that are possible with clustering. Open space that is preserved through clustering is often maintained by a homeowners' association, or it may be dedicated as public land. (See Fig. 8)
See: DENSITY TRANSFER; PERFORMANCE ZONING; PLANNED UNIT DEVELOPMENT (PUD); SUBDIVISION REGULATIONS

Cluster Sample

A sampling technique in which the population is divided into groups, know as clusters. Certain clusters are then selected by random methods, and then particular individuals are selected at random from these clusters. This technique is considered particularly useful when cost savings are important or accurate population lists are unavailable.
See: SAMPLING

Coastal Area Planning

The regulation and management of development in coastal areas, including the safe and environmentally sound location of various types of land use, structures and roads; the protection of coastal resources; and the provision of public access to beaches.

Coastal areas require special planning consideration because they are a relatively scarce resource in comparison to total land area yet are aggressively sought after for development and recreational use. In addition, they are subject to high-intensity seasonal use, as well as flooding and storm damage, and are part of a fragile environmental system.

To some extent many of the same measures that can minimize such hazards of coastal development as flooding can also minimize destruction to the coastal environment. Proper setback from fragile dune areas, for example, helps to protect both the dunes and the development by allowing the dunes to fulfill their natural protective and sand replenishment functions. Zoning, subdivision regulations and building codes may all be used to help provide proper regulation in the coastal area. In addition to standard features, however, it may be necessary to incorporate special provisions or create separate ordinances. Additional regulations may relate to the alteration of land surfaces, e.g., through grading or excavation standards; the protection of views and critical environmental areas; waterfront development; and construction and design practices.

Certain design principles are particularly appropriate to coastal areas to encourage an aesthetically pleasing result. Tall structures or those located close to the shore in visually prominent positions can result in an appearance that detracts from the natural environment. Roof type and the choice of exterior color and building materials can also have a decided impact upon the compatibility of a project with a coastal setting.

Providing access to beach areas for recreational use is a particular problem of the coastal area. Only a small fraction of the coastal shoreline in the United States is publicly owned, with lesser amounts available for public use on the Atlantic coast than along the Pacific coast. Yet the demand for access to oceanfront areas continues to grow, particularly near urban areas. This has resulted in a variety of strategies to secure public access without outright government purchase.

One method that may be used in communities with remaining undeveloped beach area is the mandatory dedication of public access by the prospective developer of beachfront property. Payments in lieu of providing access might also be used to purchase easements or other beach rights. Another way in which public access may be continued is through the exercise of certain common-law doctrines. For example, by virtue of a long historical use by

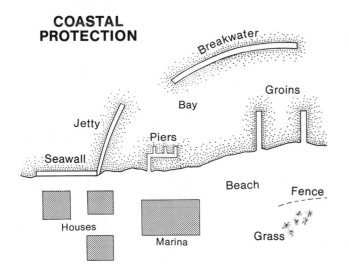

Fig. 9. The variety of structures used to protect shore areas, harbors and channels.

the public of a stretch of beach, the public may acquire rights to the continued use of the beach.
See: BEACH EROSION; COASTAL AREA; COASTAL BARRIER RESOURCES ACT; COASTAL ZONE MANAGEMENT IMPROVEMENT ACT OF 1980; OFFSHORE DRILLING

Coastal Barrier Resources Act

A law (PL 97-348) enacted in 1982 that withdraws authorization for federal funding, assistance or insurance for new construction on coastal barrier islands and other coastal geologic features. These islands act as barriers to storms, wind and heavy waves, helping to protect coastal areas from damage, but are themselves subject to frequent storm damage, flooding and other natural hazards. The purpose of the act is to prevent the waste of federal funds that results both from assistance to or investment in development that is washed away by storms and wave action as well as from necessary disaster assistance after catastrophes. It is also intended to protect the ecologically significant habitats on the barriers and in the intervening waters that are damaged by development.

The act establishes a Coastal Barrier Resources System for the Atlantic and Gulf Coasts that includes all undeveloped coastal barrier areas, making them subject to restrictions on expenditures of federal funding. However, federal assistance for certain activities—including scientific research, wildlife management, exploration and extraction of energy resources, and maintenance of essential structures—is permissible in these locations. Maps of all coastal barrier areas subject to these restrictions are included in the legislation and must be reviewed every five years for revisions that reflect changes caused by natural phenomena.
See: COASTAL AREA PLANNING

Coastal Waters

The term is usually used by planners in connection with the Coastal Zone Management Act of 1972, which defined coastal waters as "those waters, adjacent to the shorelines, which contain a measurable quantity or percentage of sea water, including, but not limited to, sounds, bays, lagoons, bayous, ponds and estuaries." The act also defined this term to include the Great Lakes and their connecting waters, harbors and estuary-type areas such as bays.
See: COASTAL ZONE; COASTAL ZONE MANAGEMENT ACT OF 1972 (CZMA)

Coastal Watershed

A land area that drains directly into coastal waters— i.e., those waters containing a measurable quantity of seawater. Coastal watersheds act as water control systems by storing heavy rainflow and then slowly releasing it. As the water passes through tidal wetlands and marshes, it is filtered; sediments are removed; and it is finally released into the water body at a controlled rate of flow.
See: ESTUARY

Coastal Zone

Zone that includes the coastal waters and those land areas near the coastal waters that influence and affect each other. The Coastal Zone Management Act of 1972 defined the coastal zone as the coastal waters and adjacent shorelands "strongly influenced by each other and in proximity to the shorelines of the several coastal states, and includes islands, transitional and intertidal areas, salt marshes, wetlands and beaches." The landward portion of the coastal zone is further defined as extending "inland from the shorelines only to the extent necessary to control shorelands, the uses of which have a direct and significant impact on the coastal waters."

Each coastal state is required to develop and apply a procedure for identifying the coastal zone boundaries of the state that takes into account the inland boundary necessary to control shorelands with direct impacts upon coastal waters; the extent of the territorial sea; and transitional areas, wetlands, intertidal areas and beaches. As a result of this required procedure, boundaries of the coastal zone vary from state to state.

See: COASTAL WATERS; COASTAL ZONE MANAGEMENT ACT OF 1972 (CZMA)

Coastal Zone Management Act of 1972 (CZMA)

Legislation that established federal policy on coastal zone management and authorized a program designed to encourage states to plan and undertake land and water resource management programs for coastal areas. The act (PL 92-582) and its subsequent amendments provide funding to state governments for the development and implementation of coastal management programs through the National Oceanic and Atmospheric Administration in the Department of Commerce. States with shore areas on the Atlantic or Pacific Oceans, the Gulf of Mexico or the Great Lakes are eligible for funding.

Each state coastal management plan must define the geographic area and uses that are subject to the management program, identify coastal resources that require state management or protection and set policies for coastal resource management. It is required that the management program be backed by the legal authority and administrative arrangements necessary for implementation and enforcement.

A state may receive up to four annual grants to plan its coastal management program. Once the program is approved by the Secretary of Commerce, the state becomes eligible for annual grants to implement its program.

See: COASTAL ZONE MANAGEMENT IMPROVEMENT ACT OF 1980

Coastal Zone Management Improvement Act of 1980

Legislation that reauthorizes the coastal zone management program and provides funding for another five-year period. This act (PL 96-464) also expands federal policy with respect to coastal zone management and creates an additional grant program for waterfront and port redevelopment and for obtaining increased public access to beaches and other coastal areas. Redevelopment projects, however, are intended to be small-scale, such as development of walkways or historic building rehabilitation.

Federal grants to the 25 coastal states that had previously participated in the program are allowed on the basis of 80 percent of project cost for both the coastal zone management program and the waterfront development/access program. Also authorized are interstate coastal zone compacts and up to 90 percent funding for activities related to interstate coastal zone planning, policy development and implementation.

The act also establishes a coastal energy impact program (CEIP) of grants for the study of problems related to energy production or transportation that affect the coastal zone, such as offshore oil drilling, and authorizes grants and loans for mitigation of problems related to these facilities. Grants for public facility development for expanded or new energy-related facilities are also provided.

See: COASTAL ZONE MANAGEMENT ACT OF 1972 (CZMA)

Code Enforcement

The power of a municipality to inspect privately owned buildings; determine whether such buildings meet the minimum safety and health standards of the community's building, housing or other municipal code; and if not, require compliance with these standards.

Housing code enforcement is a particular problem. Although the primary goal of such enforcement is the conservation of housing stock, a landlord with a marginally profitable building or with limited financial resources may abandon the building rather than correct expensive code violations. For this reason, code enforcement is most appropriately combined with and supported by other government programs that can assist in the correction of violations. Landlords may, for example, be given tax incentives and low-interest rehabilitation loans for upgrading their buildings.

Housing code enforcement may be conducted primarily in response to complaints or on a more systematic basis in areas selected, with the aid of the municipal planning department, for their need for a code enforcement program.

See: BUILDING CODE; HOUSING CODE; SUBSTANDARD HOUSING

Code of Ethics and Professional Conduct

A guide to the proper behavior and professional conduct required of planners who are certified by the American Institute of Certified Planners (AICP).

The code, adopted by AICP in 1981, establishes minimum standards of acceptable behavior as well as standards that planners should attempt to meet. It also contains a range of guidelines related to the planner's public responsibility, responsibility to clients and employers, responsibility to the profession and to colleagues, and self-responsibility. In addition, the code contains formal procedures for filing complaints and resolving violations. In some cases, violation of the code may lead to expulsion from AICP.

See: AMERICAN INSTITUTE OF CERTIFIED PLANNERS (AICP)

Codisposal

A method by which sewage sludge and solid waste may be disposed of through an integrated process that usually involves combustion. Pioneered in Europe, where plants are in operation in several countries, including France and West Germany, codisposal allows a community to solve its solid waste and sludge processing problems by building one facility or by converting an existing sewage sludge or solid waste incinerator.

Codisposal works by using energy generated in the incineration of solid waste to dewater sludge. Eventually, the sludge reaches a ratio of moisture to solids sufficient to permit it to burn independently.

The Harrisburg, Pennsylvania Resource Recovery System, which was completed in 1979, is a good example of the versatility of codisposal technology. The city's solid waste incineration plant was modified to allow sludge (pumped directly from the sewage treatment plant) to be dried and then burned along with other waste. The steam generated in this process is used both for sludge drying and for heating and cooling other buildings. Ferrous metals are also recovered and sold.

The possibility of codisposing solid waste and sludge through nonthermal processes, such as composting or making bricks that can serve as a fuel, is also being explored.

See: INCINERATION; RESOURCE RECOVERY; SLUDGE DISPOSAL; SOLID WASTE MANAGEMENT

Cogeneration

The practice of capturing waste heat generated during the production of electricity and then using this heat for space heating, cooling, heating water and wastewater treatment. Among the advantages of cogeneration, which is accomplished by the use of steam or gas turbine systems or diesel engines, are efficient use of energy and fuel as well as reduced costs. Cogeneration may be used by industry, institutions, large residential developments, commercial developments and public utilities. In some cases, arrangements are made by the management of the cogeneration facility to sell excess electricity to a utility or to purchase supplemental electricity from a utility when needed to ensure an adequate supply of power and keep costs to a minimum.

Cogeneration is a long-established practice, particularly for industrial use; during the 1920s roughly 25 percent of the energy produced by on-site power generation was cogenerated. As cheap and reliable energy became available, however, interest in cogeneration declined in the United States, to return only relatively recently. On the other hand, cogeneration has been consistently popular in Europe, particularly with industry and utilities. Among the large cogeneration projects currently in operation in the United States are the Regency Square Shopping Center in Jacksonville, Florida, which produces all of its own power and uses its waste heat for space heating and cooling, and Starrett City, a 20,000-resident apartment complex in Brooklyn, New York.

See: ELECTRIC POWER GENERATION AND TRANSMISSION; RENEWABLE ENERGY SOURCES

Cohort Survival Method

A means of population projection in which population cohorts, consisting of groups divided by age and sex, are aged to a future date based upon probable age- and sex-specific survival rates, fertility rates and net migration.

The method uses a total of 36 age cohorts (18 each for males and females); the cohorts are in five-year age groupings ranging from 0 to 4 years to 85 years and over. Generally, the cohorts are aged forward in five-year intervals after mortality rates are applied. For example, the 50-year-olds in 1980 who survive to 1985 will then be part of the 55-year-old age group. New births for the youngest age group are based upon the probable number of births that women aged 15 to 44 years old can be expected to have, based on studies of past local and national trends. Net migration may be determined based upon studies of past census figures for the area and the planner's assessment of future community trends.

Each appropriate variable, such as mortality and fertility, is calculated separately by age group and sex. In addition, more than one projection may be made based upon varying assumptions concerning the fertility rate and the net migration rate (the death rate is less variable, barring unusual circumstances).

Since this method takes into account natural increase as well as net migration, and employs an analytic and detailed approach, it is a commonly used means of projection. It can be cumbersome and time-consuming to perform with the use of hand calculators, but the wider availability of computers and specialized programming packages has increased its popularity. It also provides projections by age group and sex, which can be extremely useful in certain types of population studies, such as those in which future school enrollment would be important.

See: DEMOGRAPHY; FERTILITY RATE; MORTALITY RATE; NATURAL INCREASE; NET MIGRATION; POPULATION PROJECTION; POPULATION PROJECTION METHODS

Coliform Bacteria

A group of bacteria found in the large intestine of warm-blooded animals and humans that are used as an indicator of the extent to which water has been polluted with fecal waste. Sources of coliform bacteria pollution are improperly treated or untreated sewage, sewer overflows when sanitary and storm sewers are combined, wildlife, and runoff from both urban streets and agricultural lands.

Counts of the prevalence of this bacteria have been conducted routinely for many years as a sanitary engineering measure. The recommended U.S. Environmental Protection Agency fecal coliform bacteria level for bathing waters is 200 cells per 100 milliliters of water, although actual standards vary by state.

See: INDICATOR SPECIES; WATER POLLUTION; WATER SAMPLING

Collector Street

A street that carries traffic between urban arterials and local streets and provides access to abutting property. Collector streets serve as through streets within neighborhoods, are often local shopping streets and frequently carry local bus routes. Collectors are generally spaced from .25 to 1 mile (.4 to 1.6 kilometers) apart in the urban network and constitute approximately 20 percent to 40 percent of the mileage of the total street system.

Typical cross sections provide a right-of-way of 64 feet (19.5 meters); pavement width of 40 to 44 feet (12.2 to 13.4 meters), which would include two 10- to 12-foot (3.0- to 3.7-meter) moving lanes and two parking lanes of 8 to 10 feet (2.4 to 3.0 meters); and sidewalks at least 4 feet (1.2 meters) wide with vertical curbs and planting strips where possible. Building setback lines should be 30 feet (9.1 meters) from the right-of-way line. A maximum grade of 5 percent and a design speed of 30 to 35 mph (48 to 56 kph) should be provided. A collector should be designed to carry 1,500 to 10,000 trips per day. (See Fig. 43)

College Town

A community in which a major college or university is the principal employer and social force. Institutions of higher learning often choose sites in rural areas because of available land or a desire for seclusion and grow to become important economic factors in those small communities. Cambridge, England and Perugia, Italy could be classified as early European college towns, but the term originated with small American towns in which a major university, often a land grant or state institution, has located. State College, Pennsylvania; Ann Arbor, Michigan; and Norman, Oklahoma are examples.

The campus is usually the focus of college town development, with pedestrian and bicycle access more important than in most locations. While the college often provides on-campus housing for students and perhaps some faculty, there is great demand for private apartments, boarding houses and house rentals by staff, faculty and students choosing to live off-campus. "Town-gown" conflict is also common between town residents and college-affiliated persons, involving such issues as campus expansion, housing rent levels, differences in life-style and use of municipal and college recreation facilities.

See: COMPANY TOWN

Color

A design element commonly used to introduce visual excitement or vitality to a space. Color may be used in graphics, signage or art in the streetscape or other urban setting, and it may be employed as a coordinating element or as a means of providing a degree of continuity to an otherwise unrelated series of spaces. Color is also used extensively in planning practice for land use mapping or to depict concepts in plans.

In architecture, colors are associated with particular styles of buildings, as in the case of the pastel hues of a hillside village in the Mediterranean, the darker, more somber tones of a community in a northern climate or the white clapboard of a New England town. As in nature, colors suggest a particular ambience and are used to instill a certain character in a development. Earth tones or shades of green and brown are suggestive of a country setting and encourage buildings to blend into the environment, while brighter, bolder colors, such as reds or yellows, are more exciting and are frequently used in an urban setting.

Color is an important element used by landscape architects to bring life to an outdoor space, and its use may be seen in a downtown with bright awnings or a plaza with a bold color pattern in the paving. The diverse coloring of various plant materials is another tool used to add distinction or character to a design scheme.

See: COLOR CODE; DESIGN CONTINUITY

Color Code

A code in which colors are used to present information. Several color systems are available for designating types of uses on land use maps. In one common system, residential uses are shown in yellow, orange and brown, representing low-density, medium-density and high-density uses. Retail business is shown in red, transportation and utilities in ultramarine and industrial uses in indigo. Wholesale uses are in purple, public buildings and open space in green and institutional uses in gray. Vacant land is left uncolored. Other systems may alter these colors somewhat or divide them into fine gradations so that, for example, offices and banks are differentiated from general business.

Color is used in many other ways to convey information on maps and charts. On maps, for example, different-colored roadways can represent road jurisdiction—e.g., state, county; traffic volume; or type of roadway—e.g., parkway or expressway. On maps in which housing is described, color could be used to represent the age of the structures, their value or the number of units per structure.

See: REFERENCE MAPS

Columbia, Maryland

A new city located in Howard County, Maryland approximately 18 miles (29 kilometers) from Baltimore's downtown and 26 miles (42 kilometers) from downtown Washington, D.C. Situated on 14,047 acres (5,675 hectares), Columbia was built on land acquired parcel by parcel by the Rouse Company in 1963 amid great secrecy. After a period of intensive planning, construction was begun in 1966 by the Howard Research and Development Corporation, a joint venture formed for this purpose. The first residents moved into Columbia in 1967, and by 1982 the population of this city was about 60,000, with an ultimate projected population of 100,000 when all development is completed.

Columbia has eight villages, each designed to contain approximately three to five neighborhoods of about 2,000 to 5,000 people. A town center containing a variety of additional commercial and public facilities is located in the central portion of Columbia. As of 1982 there were almost 30,000 jobs in Columbia and approximately 8.4 million square feet (780,360 square meters) of industrial floor area as well as additional space devoted to commercial use.

Columbia contains a wide variety of owner- and renter-occupied housing and has extensive amounts of open space, of which 1,500 acres (607 hectares) are maintained by the Columbia Association (CA), a nonprofit corporation whose directors are elected by Columbia residents. The CA is also responsible for the operation of a citywide bus system that connects the various parts of Columbia.
See: NEW TOWN; PLANNED COMMUNITY; RESTON, VIRGINIA

Combined Sewer

A sewerage system in which both sanitary wastewater and storm water runoff are collected. Combined sewers are found predominantly in older urban areas with commensurately aged sewerage systems; in some localities they are gradually being converted to separate sanitary and storm systems. Combined systems have pipe sizes similar to those of storm sewers but are located deeper in the ground to enable collection of sanitary sewage from basements.

The problem with the combined system lies largely at the treatment plant. Treatment plants are generally sized to handle sanitary sewage flows on the basis of an average number of gallons per capita per day (gcd) for the population they serve. When storm water is added to the sanitary flow, the capacity of the treatment plant may be exceeded, requiring that some of the combined flow be released untreated into the receiving waters. It is not considered practical or cost-effective to build treatment plants of a sufficient capacity to treat high volumes of combined sewage flow. Instead, some treatment plants employ retention basins or tanks to contain the overflow until the plant can adequately handle its volume. New York City is planning to begin a demonstration project in 1984 in which a new low-cost method, pioneered in Sweden, will be used. Known as the Donkers procedure, it is a flow-balance method that holds the combined sewer overflow (CSO) in compartments in a water body created by floating plastic curtains anchored to the bottom and fastened to fixed pontoons. When there is no longer an overflow, the CSO is allowed to enter the treatment plant.
See: SANITARY SEWER; SEDIMENTATION TANK; SEWAGE TREATMENT PLANT; STORM SEWER

Commercial Area

Any area of a municipality that is developed with or zoned for businesses, such as offices, stores, theaters, restaurants, hotels, medical buildings and service stations.

Commercial areas take several forms within any municipality, related in part to municipal zoning requirements and in part to the nature of businesses. A hierarchy of shopping areas exists that includes central business districts (CBDs), suburban shopping centers, strip development and neighborhood business streets, as well as specialized areas such as mixed-use developments and renewed waterfronts. Office uses follow a similar pattern, with high densities in CBD locations, low-density office parks in suburban areas, and strip development and neighborhood office buildings in areas with low- and moderate-density residential development.

Zoning ordinances usually divide commercial areas by types of permitted uses and maximum densities, and will usually include off-street parking and loading requirements. Sign regulations may also be specified.
See: AMUSEMENT FACILITY; CENTRAL BUSINESS DISTRICT (CBD); COMMERCIAL PARKING FACILITIES; DRIVE-IN FACILITIES; HOTEL; MIXED-USE DEVELOPMENT (MXD); MUNICIPAL PARKING FACILITIES; NEIGHBORHOOD BUSINESS STREET; OFFICE DEVELOPMENT; SERVICE STATIONS; SHOPPING CENTER DESIGN; STRIP DEVELOPMENT; THEATERS; WATERFRONT REVITALIZATION

Commercial Indoor Recreation Facilities

Part of a community's recreation system that includes bowling alleys, health spas, tennis clubs, squash courts, ice- and roller-skating rinks, electronic game arcades and other privately owned establishments offering recreational opportunities. In general, these facilities are restricted to commercially or industrially zoned areas. Many have nuisance characteristics associated with attendance by large numbers of children.

Most commercial recreation facilities require substantial off-street parking for peak periods and may also have passenger drop-off areas for safety reasons. Public transit access to facilities that draw children and teen-agers is also important.
See: INDOOR RECREATION CENTER; RECREATION FACILITIES; RECREATION PLANNING; RECREATION SYSTEM

Commercial Outdoor Recreation Facilities

Private enterprises such as miniature golf courses, golf driving ranges, marinas, swimming pools and amusement parks that offer recreational opportunities to the public. These facilities provide an important component of the total recreational system and help to preserve open space without removing it from the tax rolls.

Principal planning concerns are the provision of adequate off-street parking and screening of parking lots and

heavily used or night-lighted facilities from residential areas.
See: COUNTRY CLUB; OPEN SPACE; RECREATION FACILITIES; RECREATION PLANNING; RECREATION SYSTEM

Commercial Parking Facilities

Parking lots and structures, operated for profit by private entrepreneurs, that are usually located in densely developed urban areas or at transportation nodes. The fees charged by these facilities are often increased by municipal parking taxes or parking surcharges, imposed to provide municipal revenue and to reduce automobile use. In cities that limit vehicular traffic, the number of spaces that commercial parking facilities may provide may also be controlled.
See: AUTO DISINCENTIVES

Comminution

A process used in wastewater treatment in which coarse solids are reduced in size by cutting mechanisms so that they can be processed with the remainder of the sewage without removal from the wastewater. Comminuters—devices that have cutting teeth mounted on moving bars or drums—cut or grind the solids that have been caught on intercepting screens. Comminution is also used in solid waste management to reduce waste to smaller-sized particles.
See: SCREENING; SHREDDING

Commission Form of Government

A form of municipal government in which individuals are elected to a commission that performs both legislative and administrative functions. The commission usually consists of five, seven or nine members, including a mayor, independently elected at large. Although the mayor acts as chairman of the commission, he has no veto power over commission decisions.

In its legislative role the commission exercises all normal powers of municipal councils. In their administrative capacities, commissioners act as department heads; in some communities commissioners are directly elected to run specific departments. The success of the system is contingent on the ability of the elected commissioners to be both legislators and administrators. As the technical aspects of running a community become more complex, this form of government becomes less adequate.
See: CITY COUNCIL; COUNCIL-MANAGER FORM OF GOVERNMENT; MAYOR-COUNCIL FORM OF GOVERNMENT

Common Areas

Land, facilities and other improvements that are used jointly by groups of property owners or renters. Common areas may include swimming pools, clubhouses, playgrounds, tennis courts and other recreational facilities, as well as elevators, laundry rooms, common corridors and parking areas. In renter-occupied developments, the landlord is required to maintain common areas. In cooperative and condominum developments, the homeowners' association maintains common areas, and the cost of such maintenance is allocated among owners as part of their monthly maintenance fees. The grouping of housing units around common areas conserves land and reduces construction costs.
See: CONDOMINIUM HOUSING; COOPERATIVE HOUSING; HOMEOWNERS' ASSOCIATION

Common Law

The body of legal principles that derives its authority from judicial pronouncements based on custom, prior usage and accepted principles, as opposed to statutes enacted by legislation.

In the United States, this term often refers to the body of case law, rules and principles that existed in England at the time of the American Revolution.

Common Wall

A wall shared by two buildings or used to separate units within a building.
See: PARTY WALL

Commons

In the United States this term refers to a public square or park owned by a municipality that is open to the public for recreational purposes.

In England, commons, or common land, refers to land that is usually privately owned but over which others (the citizens of the district where the land is located) have various rights. Historically, these included such important economic rights as the right to graze animals on the land, the right to fish from waters running through the land, the right to gather wood or dig turf on the land for use as fuel, as well as the right to use the land for recreation. Common land could not be enclosed or developed without governmental consent. The 1965 Commons Registration Act provided for the registration of all commons and village greens in England, with a view toward developing the most desirable policy for use of these open spaces.

Community

1. A group of individuals who interact socially and have common ties and who are located in a defined geographic area, as in a neighborhood or a municipality. Alternatively, the term may define the physical area within which the defined population exists. In urban planning, community often refers to the geographic location, while in social planning it usually refers to the inhabitants.

2. A group that possesses a measurable set of social, cultural and/or economic characteristics that may be used to describe it. An ethnic group or a business group are examples.

Community Action Program (CAP)

An antipoverty program established by the Economic Opportunity Act of 1964 in which Community Action Agencies (CAAs) were authorized to attempt to better living conditions in communities and to assist their residents in finding employment, receiving job training and obtaining other support. Full or partial funding was provided for programs related to such activities as health, housing, home management, job training and remedial education. Examples of eligible programs included new employment or volunteer services for the elderly and environmental action programs for youths, where they would engage in conservation or beautification activities or reclamation of environmentally damaged areas. Public and private nonprofit agencies in urban and rural areas with high levels of unemployment and large numbers of persons on public assistance and school dropouts, among other criteria, were eligible to become CAAs, with the requirement that there be maximum participation of local residents.

In 1981 categorical funding for CAAs ended when Congress established the Community Services Block Grant, to be administered by the Office of Community Services. The legislation establishing the block grant, however, required that beginning in fiscal year 1983, the states give at least 90 percent of their allocation to local governments. Local governments would either use the funds directly (for programs with a measurable effect on the causes of poverty and related problems of employment, housing and education) or give them to CAAs.

See: COMMUNITY SERVICES BLOCK GRANT; ECONOMIC OPPORTUNITY ACT OF 1964; OFFICE OF COMMUNITY SERVICES (OCS)

Community Arts Councils

Public or private not-for-profit agencies that coordinate and support local arts projects. Found at a variety of municipal levels, community arts councils may function administratively as commissions, cultural affairs offices, municipal departments, independent authorities or advisory boards. They provide information on activities in the arts, provide or sponsor arts programs, assist in finding space for programs, raise funds for arts activities and, in some cases, make grants to local applicants. Research, analysis and planning for the arts may also be undertaken by the community arts council, often in conjunction with the municipal planning department, to enable policy development. The programs that a community arts council sponsors are often closely related to certain planning department goals and activities, such as stimulating economic development or improving community appearance.

See: NATIONAL ENDOWMENT ON THE ARTS AND HUMANITIES; STATE ARTS AGENCIES

Community Center

A building or set of rooms provided for people to gather for purposes of recreation, education or other communal activity. Frequently sponsored by municipal, social or recreation agencies and religious organizations, community centers may be large facilities with programs available to a broad age range or small facilities, possibly in rented space, available to one selected age group, such as a "senior center."

New towns and planned communities in Britain and the United States have traditionally provided a large community center building as both a community focus and a location for recreation and socialization.

See: COMMUNITY FACILITY PLANNING; INDOOR RECREATION CENTER; MULTISERVICE CENTER

Community Character

The image or tone of a community as reflected in its size, the type and density of its development, and the general pattern of land use. Along with natural features and open-space elements, the character of a community is defined largely by man-made or architectural improvements, such as the types of housing and predominant architectural styles. The types and quality of public facilities, urban infrastructure and the nature of services and resources available to residents (including cultural, educational and recreational amenities) also define community character.

Used as an index to the quality of life in a particular area, community character has, in recent years, become an important factor in decisions relating to corporate relocation, particularly with regard to the choice between city or suburban locations.

See: AMBIENCE; NEIGHBORHOOD IDENTITY; SENSE OF PLACE

Community Control

The decentralization of certain municipal functions and the transfer of selected powers to the community level. Community control is an attempt by municipal governments, often in larger cities, to involve community leaders in decision making about programs and services affecting them, generally in response to community demand for increased involvement.

Community control stems from mechanisms for federal disbursement of funds established in the 1960s, when it was expected that a large influx of funds, designed to help solve the problems of the disadvantaged, could be used to provide local control over a pool of money and jobs. Currently, local control is seen more as a mechanism by which community groups may influence and operate programs directly affecting them. As examples, the powers to hire and fire school personnel and to select certain program areas in public schools have been delegated to community school boards in some cities with centralized school boards. In New York City, under its Uniform Land Use Review Procedure (ULURP), community planning boards are required to participate in the early stages of review of planning matters, such as decisions related to local zoning, subdivisions, site selection for capital proj-

ects, budget development and monitoring of delivery of city services to the community.
See: CITIZEN PARTICIPATION; DECENTRALIZATION; LITTLE CITY HALLS; NEIGHBORHOOD ZONING PARTICIPATION

Community Development Block Grant (CDBG)

A flexible federal aid program for neighborhood revitalization and community improvement, established by Title I of the Housing and Community Development Act of 1974. The first of the federal block grant programs, CDBG replaced numerous separate categorical grant programs of the Department of Housing and Urban Development, including urban renewal, neighborhood development, model cities, neighborhood facilities grants, public facilities loans, housing rehabilitation, open space, urban beautification, and water and sewer programs.

Large metropolitan cities and urban counties receive entitlement funding amounting to 70 percent of the annual CDBG allocation distributed by formula; rural localities and small communities in metropolitan areas compete for funding in the Small Cities program. Outlying areas, such as American Samoa, receive funding via the Secretary's Discretionary Fund. Local governments may select from a broad range of eligible activities, including property acquisition, construction of public facilities, code enforcement, demolition, rehabilitation, removal of architectural barriers, provision of public services, economic development, neighborhood revitalization, historic preservation, relocation assistance, planning and provision of the local matching funds for other federal programs. Program activities must benefit low- and moderate-income residents, prevent or eliminate slums or blight, or meet an urgent community need. A housing assistance plan (HAP) is required as part of an entitlement community's application for funds. Recently, the Housing and Urban-Rural Recovery Act of 1983 modified CDBG requirements with respect to statements of program objectives and certification concerning use of funds for low and moderate income individuals.
See: HOUSING ASSISTANCE PLAN (HAP); NEIGHBORHOOD STRATEGY AREA (NSA); SECRETARY'S DISCRETIONARY FUND; SMALL CITIES PROGRAM; URBAN COUNTY; URBAN DEVELOPMENT ACTION GRANT (UDAG)

Community Development Corporation (CDC)

An organization formed to promote employment opportunities and private-sector investment within a community, often an area of low income or high unemployment, through coordinated economic development activities. CDCs, which are usually nonprofit and governed by representatives of the community they serve, have been successful in improving the local economy and the quality of life of area residents in both urban and rural areas.

Community development corporations, sometimes called local development corporations or local economic development corporations, vary greatly in design and objective to best meet community needs. Some are formed to pursue one specific goal, while others engage in a wide variety of economic development activities. Urban CDCs have often participated in projects related to real estate, commercial ventures, manufacturing and finance, while rural CDC projects may involve some of the same areas as urban development corporations as well as such ventures as food processing, agriculture or aquaculture. CDCs—which are usually formed either by community or church groups, chambers of commerce or governmental agencies—may be publicly and/or privately funded and may have a professional staff or be staffed by governmental agencies.

CDCs typically operate by obtaining funding from government programs, grants from foundations, private capital and bank loans or a combination of these sources. Among the activities these funds typically support are stock purchases in, or the making of loans to, subsidiary organizations intended to be profit-making. CDCs sometimes also organize businesses within the internal structure of the CDC.

A CDC may sometimes qualify as a certified development company under Small Business Administration certification procedures, and other federal programs, such as those established pursuant to the Community Economic Development Act of 1981, have made provisions for funding to CDCs. There is also a significant history of corporate participation in community development corporation enterprises, particularly when corporate headquarters are located in or near a community in which a CDC operates or is being established.
See: CERTIFIED DEVELOPMENT COMPANY; COMMUNITY ECONOMIC DEVELOPMENT ACT OF 1981; ECONOMIC DEVELOPMENT

Community Development Department

A relatively new municipal agency, found in some municipalities, that serves as an umbrella agency for a number of functions related to community planning, such as public housing, economic development, urban redevelopment and code enforcement. Each of these functions may be undertaken by an established subagency; the planning department may also be included within this department.

This form of superagency, usually funded by government grants, can be effective in coordinating the activities of the several departments that perform related work but tends to relegate planning to a diminished position in the governmental structure.
See: PLANNING DEPARTMENT

Community Economic Development Act of 1981

Legislation that authorizes the establishment of programs to aid residents of urban and rural low-income areas, to be operated by private, locally initiated community development corporations (CDCs) or self-help cooperatives. Many of these programs had previously been authorized by the Economic Opportunity Act of 1964. Part of the Omnibus Budget Reconciliation Act of 1981 (Title VI, Chapter 8, Subchapter A of PL 97-35), the Community Economic Development Act authorizes the creation of a National Advisory Community Investment Board to promote cooperation among private investors, businesses and community development corporations. It also directs the Office of Community Services in the Department of Health and Human Services to administer a variety of programs that offer financial assistance to CDCs, self-help cooperatives, local cooperative associations, or local public or private nonprofit organizations or agencies. Funds for these programs are to be provided by up to 9 percent of community services block grant funds and by the Rural Development Loan Fund and the Community Development Credit Union Revolving Loan Fund, both of which are established by this act.

Urban and rural special-impact programs consist of grants for economic development programs to nonprofit and for-profit CDCs. The programs may consist of community business and commercial development programs; community physical development programs, including industrial parks and housing; training and public service employment programs; and social service programs. Grants of up to 90 percent of program costs are authorized, and the programs must be appropriately coordinated with local planning, housing, community development, and employment and training programs.

Another provision of the act authorizes direct and guaranteed loans to CDCs, families and local cooperatives, and public and private nonprofit organizations and agencies, for business facilities and community development projects. Loans, which may be granted for up to 30 years, are provided at below-market interest rates for the first 5 years. Financial assistance is also provided for planning of community economic development programs and cooperative programs.

Other provisions of this act authorize additional activities associated with funding of community development corporations. These include the development of a Model Community Economic Development Finance Corporation to provide financial support to CDCs, the provision of training and technical assistance to CDCs and local cooperative organizations, and their inclusion as eligible recipients of Small Business Administration and Economic Development Administration programs. CDCs and local cooperative associations are also to be eligible for Department of Housing and Urban Development and Department of Agriculture grants.
See: COMMUNITY DEVELOPMENT CORPORATION (CDC); ECONOMIC DEVELOPMENT; OFFICE OF COMMUNITY SERVICES (OCS)

Community Facilities Plan

A guide to public policy that identifies present deficiencies in community facilities and projects future needs

consistent with land use and transportation plans. Community facilities are those facilities used in common by a large number of people, generally owned by a public agency or a nonprofit organization, such as schools, libraries, hospitals and fire stations.

Most community facilities plans contain an inventory of existing facilities indicated on a map or a series of maps. These facilities are then analyzed to determine whether they satisfy existing needs by comparing the present facilities with standards for the types and sizes of facilities needed to serve different populations. The analysis may also contain a qualitative description of the level of services delivered by these facilities.

The final section of the plan usually projects future needs for both the short term and the long term based on current and projected economic and demographic trends.
See: COMMUNITY FACILITY PLANNING; COMPREHENSIVE PLAN

Community Facility Loan

A program of guaranteed or insured loans for construction or improvement of community facilities that are made available to states, municipalities or nonprofit corporations by the Farmers Home Administration. Loans are limited to facilities that provide essential services, such as those related to safety or health, to rural residents in municipalities with a maximum population of 20,000. They are intended for use when a proposed project cannot be funded by a community's own resources or when commercial financing is not available at reasonable rates and terms. Examples of projects funded through this program are improvements to hospitals for life/safety code compliance, acquisition of fire-fighting equipment and new school construction.
See: FARMERS HOME ADMINISTRATION (FmHA)

Community Facility Planning

The analysis of existing community facilities and the development of a plan for new facilities and improvements to existing structures and programs. Community facilities generally include schools, hospitals, parks, libraries, churches, cultural facilities, community centers, day-care centers, senior citizen centers and public buildings.

Community facility planning may be undertaken by a planning department on a citywide or localized basis. Because of their diverse requirements, however, planning for these facilities may be undertaken by the agencies responsible for them. As a result, a common approach is to study only one type of facility or one specific site. School planning is therefore generally undertaken by the school board; park planning, by the municipal parks and planning departments; and hospital planning, by hospitals in conjunction with the health systems agency. All of these plans are best coordinated with the municipal comprehensive plan, in which policies on the siting and locations of these facilities may be recommended. Community facility planning, when undertaken by a planning department, may involve an inventory of community facilities and suggestions to pertinent agencies concerning deficiencies and recommended improvements.

See: CHURCH USES; COMMUNITY CENTER; COMMUNITY FACILITIES PLAN; CULTURAL RESOURCES PLANNING; DAY-CARE CENTER; FIRE STATION; HEALTH PLANNING; LIBRARY; OPEN-SPACE PLANNING; PUBLIC BUILDINGS; PUBLIC SAFETY BUILDINGS; PUBLIC UTILITIES PLAN; SCHOOL PLANNING; TRANSPORTATION PLANNING

Community Garden

Also called a community or city farm, a community garden is a public park, abandoned property or vacant parcel that is cultivated and maintained by community residents. The community garden may be a lot divided into planting beds that are distributed to community residents for farming purposes, or it may have an overall plan—such as a lawn area for trees, flowers and seating—that is designed and executed by community effort. Such gardens are generally planned and undertaken by a community group or other urban "greening" organization, with participants often receiving financial and technical assistance from the municipal or state government or from agricultural agencies or clubs. Since many community gardens are developed on sites recently cleared of buildings, they often require removal of about the top 3 feet (0.9 meter) of soil and rubble and replacement with clean sand and new topsoil.

Community gardens have frequently been successful in stimulating community involvement and pride in inner city areas and have also enabled community residents to raise produce for their families. Municipalities sometimes allow community gardens as a long-term temporary use on undeveloped public property that will eventually be developed.

Community Park

A park containing approximately 10 to 50 acres (4 to 20 hectares) designed to serve the recreation needs of 20,000 to 30,000 or more people. The community park contains a large diversity of facilities, including extensive landscaped areas, shaded areas, athletic courts and playfields, a running track, playgrounds and playlots, a community recreation center, walks and parking areas. It may also have such other facilities as a band shell, an ice-skating rink or a lake and may be pedestrian-, auto-or mass transit-oriented.

In lower-density areas this type of park may be provided adjacent to a junior or senior high school, where it would serve a radius of 0.5 mile to 1.5 miles (0.8 kilometer to 2.4 kilometers). In denser areas, such parks have often been provided at the convergence of several neighborhoods and are intended to serve a larger population.

See: CITYWIDE PARK; NEIGHBORHOOD PARK

Community Reinvestment Act of 1977 (CRA)

A federal law requiring that financial institutions meet the credit needs of their local communities, including low-and moderate-income neighborhoods, particularly for mortgages and home-improvement loans. Authorized by Title VIII of the Housing and Community Development Act of 1977, CRA covers every depository institution that is either federally chartered or federally insured, except credit unions. Regulations implementing the CRA require a lender to display a CRA notice, adopt a CRA statement specifying the institution's lending area and the types of loans it will make, and maintain a public CRA file. The lender may also describe special efforts to meet community credit needs in its CRA statement.

Under the CRA the federal agency that supervises a financial institution must, as part of its examination procedures, assess the institution's record of meeting its CRA obligations. It must also consider this record when the institution applies to open a new branch, relocate an office or merge with another institution. Community groups have used this last provision to file challenges and negotiate affirmative lending agreements that commit the institution to modify management and lending policies in order to be more responsive to community needs. In some cases, lenders have agreed to target advertising to minority or low-income neighborhoods, provide home ownership counseling, establish citizen advisory boards or provide technical assistance to community organizations.

The Home Mortgage Disclosure Act (PL 94-200), which requires lenders to release statistics showing the location of their mortgage and home-improvement loans, is an important tool for measuring CRA compliance.

See: REDLINING

Community Services Administration (CSA)

A federal agency that administered antipoverty programs in the United States between 1974 and 1981. Its programs were terminated in 1981 by repeal of most of the provisions of the Economic Opportunity Act of 1964, although some programs later received reauthorization in other legislation and are administered by other agencies. The Office of Community Services is completing the closeout of CSA programs. The CSA was the successor to the Office of Economic Opportunity (OEO).

See: ECONOMIC OPPORTUNITY ACT OF 1964; OFFICE OF COMMUNITY SERVICES (OCS)

Community Services Block Grant

A federal block grant provided to states on a formula basis by the Office of Community Services for programs designed to reduce the causes of poverty in a community. Programs in job training, locating employment or housing, income management, health services, emergency food supply and nutrition are among a broad range of activities that may be undertaken. The community services block grant, authorized by the Omnibus Budget Reconciliation Act of 1981 (PL 97-35), replaced several categorical antipoverty grant programs initiated in the 1960s.

See: COMMUNITY ACTION PROGRAM (CAP); OFFICE OF COMMUNITY SERVICES (OCS)

Community Shopping Center

A unified development of retail stores located on a 10- to 30-acre (4- to 12-hectare) tract of land and containing 15 or more shops. Community shopping centers contain a range of from 100,000 to 400,000 square feet (9,290 to 37,160 square meters) of leasable floor space. Designed to serve a population of 40,000 to 150,000, they usually have a service radius of 2 to 8 miles (3 to 13 kilometers) and will therefore contain a combination of stores that feature convenience goods and specialty merchandise. A junior department store may be the prime tenant.

Community shopping centers generally locate at freeway interchanges and on arterial streets, and are usually planned to look like small regional shopping centers. Newer centers may be enclosed and called minimalls.
See: SHOPPING CENTER DESIGN

Commutation

The repeated act of traveling to and from work. Commutation is the chief cause of peak-hour traffic generation and accounts for the majority of the demand for an efficient transportation system.
See: FLEX-TIME; JOURNEY TO WORK; PEAK-HOUR TRAFFIC VOLUME; RIDEPOOLING; STAGGERED WORK HOURS

Compact Car Parking

Parking spaces, in parking lots and parking structures, of smaller dimensions than those provided for standard American cars. The growing use of compact and subcompact cars in North America has prompted the provision of reduced-size parking stalls in lots and garages. These permit 15 percent to 30 percent more parking spaces to be provided in a facility than would be possible with only conventional-size spaces.

Zoning ordinances that permit compact car spaces often specify the size of spaces and the percentage of spaces that may be devoted to the smaller stalls. The size recommended for compact car spaces is 15 feet (4.6 meters) by 7.5 feet (2.3 meters). They should be placed in an optimal location to encourage their use—e.g., grouped near an entrance to a building for long-term parking or scattered through a shopping center for short-term parking. The municipalities that have compact car parking provisions in their zoning ordinances generally permit 20 percent to 30 percent of the spaces in a large parking lot to be devoted to this use. Small lots usually have lower percentage allowances or none because of the smaller probability of use by a compact car. As the number of small cars increases, municipalities may find it advantageous to increase the percentage of permitted compact car spaces.
See: PARKING LOT DESIGN

Company Town

A community whose existence is due primarily to one company and that is often planned, built and occupied primarily by the employees of that company. Company towns most often occur when a relatively isolated site for a major facility is selected because of proximity to natural resources, ports or markets; the necessity of housing workers creates the need for the town. This pattern occurred when U.S. Steel located in Gary, Indiana and the Aluminum Company of Canada located in Kitimat, British Columbia. More recent communities have been created near petrochemical facilities, such as El Tablazo, Venezuela and Aliaga, Turkey. In some cases the company has actively planned, constructed and even retained ownership of residential portions of a community in order to provide or control the labor market, provide a source of income or for philanthropic reasons.

The term *company town* has a pejorative connotation in the United States because some firms used ownership of housing (historically called tied housing) and shops to manipulate their labor force. The concept of communities built around industrial facilities has, however, been used in many nations. It was described as early as 1917 by Frenchman Tony Garnier as the *cité industrielle*; in Britain such communities are called industrial housing estates. The Soviet Union has built several communities around individual industrial facilities, which, while state-owned, could be considered company towns, as is Jubail, Saudi Arabia. It has also been suggested that some new towns, such as Brasilia, Brazil and Chandigarh, India, whose major employers are the government, are a form of company town.
See: COLLEGE TOWN; NEW TOWN; PLANNED COMMUNITY

Compensable Regulations

Regulations adopted pursuant to a state's police power that severely restrict or limit the use or development of land; they are intended to chart a middle course between ordinary police power regulation (for which no compensation is necessary) and the exercise of the power of eminent domain (for which just compensation is constitutionally required).

Absent the use of compensable regulations, a municipality wishing to limit development in an area has two options—it may adopt restrictive police power regulations, which prohibit undesired development, or it may acquire the property or an easement over the property via the exercise of the eminent domain power. The latter choice may be prohibitively expensive and allows for little flexibility in the amount or nature of compensation that is constitutionally required. If the former alternative is chosen and the regulation is challenged, a court normally will only be able to either uphold the regulation as valid or declare it to be confiscatory and therefore invalid as an unconstitutional taking of property. Other than in circumstances where a decree of inverse condemnation is appropriate, a court will ordinarily not be empowered to uphold a regulation but will require that compensation be paid. If a regulation is invalidated, undesirable development may result.

A compensable regulation may address this issue by expressly permitting a municipality to compensate a landowner to the extent that the regulation results in a taking of his property. The regulation may also authorize the payment of compensation in forms other than cash—e.g., by transferring development rights to other parcels owned by the affected landowner. Compensable regulations have yet to be widely employed in practice.

See: CONDEMNATION; CONFISCATORY REGULATION; EMINENT DOMAIN; INVERSE CONDEMNATION; JUST COMPENSATION; POLICE POWER; TAKING; TRANSFER OF DEVELOPMENT RIGHTS (TDR)

Composting

A means of converting organic materials, such as solid waste and sludge, into an odor-free and sanitary soil conditioner. This is accomplished by the action of microorganisms in a process known as aerobic digestion.

Used more extensively in Europe than in the United States, composting has appeal because of its ability to convert waste, which must be disposed of, into a useful product. It is accomplished through a number of different methods in which the refuse is either piled in open stacks or ventilated bins, tilled into soil along with mature compost or processed in mechanical composting plants that mechanically mix and aerate the material. The organic waste material must, however, first be separated from inert materials to some extent and the waste particles reduced in size.

Composting on a large-scale basis has met with limited success in the United States. An insufficient market has existed for the compost that is produced due to a number of factors, such as the ready availability of chemical fertilizers. In addition, compost processing has similarities to the procedure for producing the potentially more marketable refuse-derived fuel, which is able to supplement fossil fuel supplies. Community garden projects and individual gardeners often produce their own compost, however, from food waste and other organic material, helping to reduce the amount of waste requiring disposal, while improving their gardens.

See: RECYCLING; REFUSE-DERIVED FUEL (RDF); RESOURCE RECOVERY; SHREDDING; SLUDGE DISPOSAL; SOLID WASTE MANAGEMENT

Comprehensive Economic Development Strategy (CEDS)

A detailed plan and implementation program for economic development. The CEDS approach, first used in 1978, was designed to supplement the then-required Overall Economic Development Plan (OEDP) mandated by the Economic Development Administration (EDA) as the basis for funding of its programs. CEDS requirements, which are more rigorous than those for an OEDP, call for a detailed analysis of an area's economy; a closer link to implementation, such as proposed investments and strategies utilizing available personnel, infrastructure and financing; and the setting of specific project priorities. The CEDS concept was not widely implemented and is now a discretionary submission to the EDA for its use in evaluating applications for grants, loans or loan guarantees for specified types of projects in redevelopment areas and economic development centers.

See: ECONOMIC DEVELOPMENT ADMINISTRATION (EDA); OVERALL ECONOMIC DEVELOPMENT PROGRAM (OEDP)

Comprehensive Employment and Training Act of 1973 (CETA)

An act (PL 93-203) and its amendments that authorized federal assistance to states and localities for job training and employment assistance for economically disadvantaged unemployed and underemployed individuals. Assistance was provided by the federal Department of Labor through a local nonprofit CETA agency (usually a city or county), officially referred to as a Prime Sponsor. The Prime Sponsor was supervised by a locally established planning council, which was required to submit an annual comprehensive manpower program to qualify for funding. A variety of programs were offered in each locality, such as apprenticeships, training courses, on-the-job training and employer incentives. CETA requirements included a special emphasis upon improved employment opportunities and career development for minorities, youths and other economically disadvantaged persons, and programs were often used in conjunction with local economic development and revitalization efforts. The Job Corps, originally authorized by the Economic Opportunity Act of 1964, was also consolidated with this program.

The 1973 CETA act provided funding for both public and private sector jobs, but public sector employment was eliminated in 1981. The remainder of the act was superseded by the Job Training Partnership Act of 1982, which permits the funding of many of the programs begun under CETA.

See: ECONOMIC DEVELOPMENT; EMPLOYMENT AND TRAINING ADMINISTRATION (ETA); JOB TRAINING PARTNERSHIP ACT OF 1982.

Comprehensive Environmental Response, Compensation and Liability Act of 1980 (CERCLA)

A law that establishes a $1.6 billion emergency "superfund" to assist in the removal or control of hazardous wastes and substances that endanger public health. CERCLA is intended both to address the problems of emergency cleanup of major spills of hazardous substances and as long-term remedial action at abandoned hazardous waste-disposal sites. Specifically exempted from provisions of the act, however, are petroleum, natural gas or synthetic fuel spills or releases and releases of nuclear materials.

CERCLA was passed in reaction to the discovery of the

volume of dangerous chemical wastes that had been dumped and then abandoned in numerous sites across the country. A number of these sites had subsequently been developed for such uses as residences (as occurred at the Love Canal), farms, pastureland or recreational facilities, posing serious risks to users and residents. Prior to enactment of this legislation a variety of federal laws, including the Clean Water Act and the Resource Conservation and Recovery Act, addressed the issue of hazardous waste in a piecemeal fashion at significantly smaller funding levels.

The act creates a superfund, formally known as the Hazardous Substances Response Trust Fund, of which 86 percent is provided by taxes on the import or manufacture of a variety of chemical and petroleum products. The remaining portion of the fund will come from general revenue appropriations during fiscal years 1981 to 1985. The fund may be used to pay for the cost of action at the site of a release or spill and for damage to natural resources.

A key aspect of the legislation is that it grants broad powers to the president to respond to releases (or threats of releases) of hazardous substances that may endanger the public health and welfare. Options available include ordering removal or control of the hazardous substance or mandating long-term cleanup of a site by either the responsible party or the government. Procedures that are used in investigating, assessing and removing dangerous substances are contained in the National Contingency Plan. Providing that actions taken by the government are consistent with the National Contingency Plan, liability is imposed on parties responsible for the hazardous substance release for removal costs, remedial action and damage to natural resources. CERCLA requires those operating a facility to notify the federal government of releases of hazardous substances on penalty of fine or criminal action. In addition, owners or operators of disposal facilities must notify the Environmental Protection Agency (EPA) of the existence of their facility. One further provision of the act requires that deeds for sites on which hazardous wastes have been disposed specify the location of any such wastes on the site.

For purposes of the act, hazardous substances are defined as including those substances specifically identified in the Clean Water Act, the Solid Waste Disposal Act, the Clean Air Act and the Toxic Substances Control Act. EPA may, however, expand the list. EPA is also responsible for developing a comprehensive list of sites of known or threatened hazardous substance releases. From this list the National Priorities List is to be prepared, with input from the states, of at least 400 sites most urgently requiring priority action. As of March 1983, the proposed list contained 419 hazardous waste sites, heavily concentrated in industrialized portions of the East, Midwest and South.

Emergency responses are coordinated via the National Response Center (initially formed under authority of the Clean Water Act), which is run by the U.S. Coast Guard. EPA also maintains an environmental response team and emergency response specialists. Remedial responses for abandoned disposal sites are carried out with state and local support. The state may either sign a cooperative agreement and coordinate the project with the aid of federal funding, or enter into a superfund state contract, in which case EPA directs the cleanup.

See: HAZARDOUS WASTE; LOVE CANAL; TOXIC SUBSTANCES

Comprehensive Plan

An official document that serves as a guide to the long-range physical development of a city or planning area. Typically, comprehensive plans are concerned with a time frame of at least five years and are primarily oriented to the various aspects of the physical development of an area.

A comprehensive plan performs a number of important community functions. First, it is a written policy statement of community values that expresses the form and character the community hopes to achieve. Second, it serves as a coordinative framework upon which all other administrative and regulatory documents relating to land development should be based. The zoning ordinance, subdivision regulations, official map, capital improvements program and budget, and community development activities should all be in accord with the policies set forth in the plan. Third, plans are increasingly attaining status as legal documents governing the content of land use controls, and a number of states now require local governments to adopt plans and to make all land use regulations consistent with the provisions of these plans.

Typically, a plan is comprehensive in that it covers the entire geographic area of the community and considers all of the components necessary to allow the community to function. A comprehensive plan, generally consisting of a mixture of text and graphic materials, usually includes a description of past trends, current conditions, community goals and objectives, recommendations for each substantive subject area the plan discusses and assumptions on which the plan is based.

It also should generally contain recommendations for implementing the plan, coordinating its various elements, and coordinating the plan with the plans of neighboring communities and larger political jurisdictions of which the community is a part.

Specific plan elements ar prepared for those topics of greatest concern to the community. Elements are commonly included on land use, housing, transportation, public utilities (including sanitary sewer, water supply, solid waste, drainage and electricity), environmental quality, and recreation and open space. Each element would address existing and future needs, and include various proposals and plans for meeting these needs. Additional elements may also be prepared on such topics as historic or scenic preservation, mass transit, economic development, community facilities, public safety, downtown redevelopment and waterfront development, depending upon community needs.

See: COMMUNITY FACILITIES PLAN; HOUSING PLAN; IN ACCORDANCE WITH A COMPREHENSIVE PLAN; OPEN SPACE PLAN; PARKS AND RECREATION PLAN; PLAN IMPLEMENTATION; PLAN PREPARATION; PUBLIC UTILITIES PLAN; TRANSPORTATION PLAN

Comprehensive Planning Grants (Section 701)

A federal program that provided grants to support comprehensive planning by state, regional and local public agencies as authorized by Section 701 of the Housing Act of 1954. Initially aimed at stimulating urban renewal proposals, Section 701 funds were used to assess needs, formulate goals, prepare comprehensive plans, upgrade administrative capacity for implementation, and plan and evaluate programs.

In the 1960s Section 701 funded many municipal comprehensive plans, while in the 1970s the focus of the program shifted to state, metropolitan and regional planning. In 1974 the original legislation was amended to require that all plans prepared with Section 701 assistance include housing and land use elements.

Although this program was terminated in 1982, it is significant because it was the single most influential legislation supporting comprehensive municipal planning. Because of the availability of 701 funding, the planning consulting industry developed to serve small municipalities that could not support a planning staff. The requirement that comprehensive plans be developed to qualify for urban renewal funds also increased the demand for planners at the municipal, county and state levels.

See: HOUSING AND COMMUNITY DEVELOPMENT AMENDMENTS OF 1981

Computer Graphics

The use of computers to receive and generate pictorial materials. Computers may be used to produce a wide variety of graphic displays, ranging from charts, graphs and maps to complex designs for buildings or machines. Input to the computer can take place in numeric form, or it may be introduced in graphic form, as when sketches are made on the face of a cathode-ray tube (CRT) with an electronic light pen.

Among the characteristics of computer graphics that make it highly desirable in planning, engineering, architecture and other design-related fields is the ability of a computer to alter a design and produce many variations. CRTs may be used to display a design that may readily be enlarged, reduced, manipulated or rotated to allow it to be viewed from different perspectives. In this manner, a variety of alternatives may rapidly be produced and scrutinized and the best alternatives selected. Computers may also be used to produce fast and extremely accurate drawings. (See Fig. 10)

See: DIGITAL CARTOGRAPHY

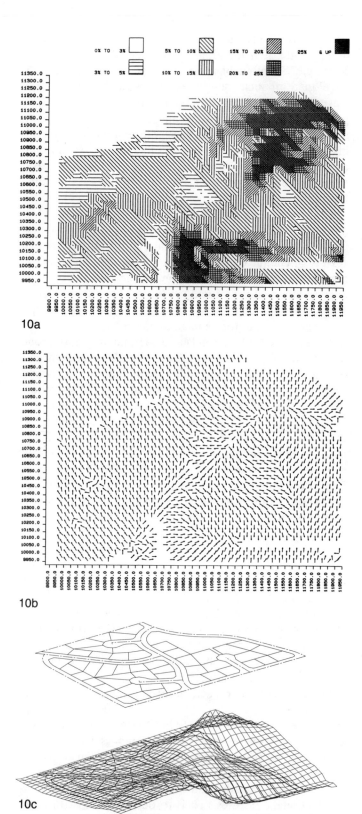

10a

10b

10c

Fig. 10.   Examples of computer graphics. This series of programs by PacSoft of Kirkland, Washington, designed for personal computers, illustrates the configuration of the land area being analyzed and shows: (a) the steepness of land surfaces, (b) the direction of drainage flow, and (c) overlays a subdivision plat upon a three-dimensional depiction of terrain. Other programs in this series enable display of cross sections, calculations for cut and fill and contour mapping.
Credit: Courtesy of PacSoft

Concentration of Activity

1. The convergence or intensification of activities within an urban area. Concentration of activity can include increased population and density as well as centralization of different functions, as frequently occurs in major cities. The term can also apply to an intensification of land use within a city, such as infill of additional houses or development of a district with many specialists in the same field, such as a jewelry district or Silicon Valley for the computer chip industry. Concentration of activity is often an asset within an urban area. For example, the density of stores and shoppers that can be found in a concentrated urban environment can help to create an exciting and successful shopping area.

2. An economic concept for analyzing the locational patterns of specific industries. Concentration of activity refers to the tendency of certain businesses or industries to locate in specific geographic areas, as opposed to being dispersed in a pattern similar to the population. A coefficient of concentration can be calculated, measuring this relationship between industry and population patterns. As examples, the food industry is dispersed in a manner very similar to the population, while high-technology industries have tended to cluster in certain locations.
See: DECENTRALIZATION; INFILL DEVELOPMENT

Concentric Zone Theory

A theory of urban land use growth, based on a pattern of several concentric zones, that served as a basis for theoretical analysis and modeling of urban growth patterns. Conceived by Ernest W. Burgess in 1925, the concentric zone theory was an explanation of an urban growth pattern that occurred as a result of market forces, such as the intrusion of commercial uses into previously residential areas.

Burgess described the core of the city as the central business district (CBD), which was the Loop in his Chicago model. The next zone, called a zone of transition, contained warehouses and CBD support activities, the remnants of early neighborhoods and marginal businesses. The next zone contained workingmen's homes and, beyond that, better residences. The fifth zone was described as the commuter's zone, consisting of suburbs. Burgess noted that each zone tended to invade the next outer zone more quickly in rapidly growing communities.

The concentric zone theory, while somewhat simplistic, is a general description of many American cities. As Burgess himself noted, however, the diagram was only a technique to explain observable tendencies rather than a detailed analysis. (See Fig. 20)
See: GROWTH THEORY

Concessionaire

A private individual, group or corporation that is granted the privilege of operating facilities or selling services or commodities in a given location. The operation of such a privilege, known as a concession, is usually governed by a written agreement between the property owner and the concessionaire that includes the time period within which the contract is valid, details with respect to the relationship of the parties and performance requirements of the concessionaire.

The practice of granting concessions has become common in government for a variety of services, particularly for management of parking facilities and for specialized services in parks. It is usually designed to increase revenues from the facilities as well as to enable provision of services for which the government body has insufficient staff or management ability.
See: PARKLAND LEASING

Concrete

An artificial stone made by mixing cement and water and adding a fine aggregate, such as sand, a coarse aggregate, such as gravel, and often an admixture (an additive) to obtain special effects—e.g., color or bonding strength. Concrete is temporarily fluid and capable of being poured but later sets and hardens (hydrates) to form a solid, stonelike mass. Concrete has great compressive strength (it can hold weight) but little tensile strength (it cannot stretch). For this reason concrete is reinforced, when necessary, with steel rods or steel mesh to increase its tensile strength.

Plain concrete, also called mass concrete, is used where weight or bulk is required and where compressive stresses predominate, such as in basement floor slabs. Concrete also has very good acoustic and thermal insulation properties and an extremely high fire resistance, which makes it particularly useful in protecting other materials such as steel. Because it can easily be poured into complex shapes, such as curved walls and shell roofs, and can be provided with an almost infinite variety of textures, it is a versatile structural material.

Concrete can be varied in composition, in terms of the amounts of each of its components, to produce a product of differing workability and weight. Most concrete is poured into formwork to give it shape and must be set under controlled heat conditions—i.e., 40 to 90 degrees Fahrenheit (4 to 33 degrees Celsius) to ensure its strength. Many products used in building construction are manufactured from plain concrete or from a lightweight mixture. These include such items as concrete brick, concrete block or tile, and concrete floor and roof slabs.
See: AGGREGATE; ARCHITECTURAL CONCRETE CONSTRUCTION; CEMENT: PRECAST CONCRETE; PRESTRESSED CONCRETE; REINFORCED CONCRETE

Condemnation

1. The process by which property or an interest in property is acquired through the exercise of the power of eminent domain. States, municipalities and, to a more limited degree, certain public utilities, authorities and common carriers, such as railroads, all possess the power to acquire property via condemnation.

The 5th and 14th Amendments to the United States Constitution, as well as the constitutions of many states, prescribe that property may be taken only for a public use, and then only upon payment of just compensation.

In many cases, a governmental authority may tailor a condemnation so that it acquires (and need pay for) only that interest in the property which is required. For example, condemnation may involve a partial or total taking of a fee simple interest in property or one of a variety of types of permanent or temporary easements.

2.   The process by which a determination is reached to destroy a building or other structure for health or safety reasons.

See: COMPENSABLE REGULATIONS; EMINENT DO-MAIN; EXCESS CONDEMNATION; INVERSE CONDEM-NATION; JUST COMPENSATION; PUBLIC USE

Condominium Housing

A form of housing ownership by which a person may purchase and own one dwelling unit in a multiunit building or development.

The ownership of a condominium home generally entails the fee ownership of the interior walls, floors and ceilings surrounding the dwelling unit and the air space within. In addition, together with other condominium owner owns a proportionate interest, together with other condominium owners, in the common elements of the housing development. Depending upon the type of housing development involved, common elements could include the land underlying the development, common walls, stairwells, elevators, lobbies, laundry rooms and recreation areas. Condominium owners pay a monthly fee, called a maintenance or common charge, representing their proportionate share of the cost of administering the condominium and maintaining the common elements. The fee may also include a proportionate share of the utility bill for the development, if utilities are not separately metered and billed for each unit.

In many ways, condominium ownership is similar to single-family home ownership. The condominium owner receives a deed for his unit, which is recorded with all other legal instruments affecting title to real property. He may mortgage his unit and may sell his unit, generally without the consent of other condominium unit owners (but sometimes he must first offer the condominium a right of first refusal to purchase his unit at the same price that a third-party purchaser is willing to pay). Each condominium unit is generally treated as a separate parcel for real estate tax assessment purposes, and the unit owner is responsible for paying the real estate tax assessed against his unit.

A condominium unit owner is generally treated like a homeowner for federal income tax purposes. He may deduct the real estate tax and mortgage interest that he pays; he may defer recognition of gain on a sale of a condominium home (assuming certain other conditions are also satisfied) if he purchases a new home within the time limits provided in the tax law; and if he is a senior citizen, he may qualify for a one-time permanent exclusion for tax on the gain resulting from the sale of his condominium unit.

In the United States condominium ownership is governed by statutes adopted by the states. A building or housing development in single ownership is converted to condominium ownership by the filing of a declaration of condominium with the real estate records in the county where the property is located. The declaration and exhibits that accompany it describe the property as a whole, each dwelling unit within the property and the common elements. Bylaws that are recorded with the declaration govern how the condominium association, which is formed by the declaration, will be organized and administered. States also have rules that govern how condominium units may be sold to the public, including to persons already residing in the housing development as tenants.

Condominium ownership in the United States has primarily been limited to residential uses. Recently, however, it has begun to be employed for a much wider range of land uses, including offices, mobile home parks, commercial and industrial development, recreational facilities and parking structures.

Cooperative housing ownership differs from condominium ownership in that the owner of a cooperative apartment does not own his dwelling unit. Rather, he owns an interest in a corporation that owns the entire building or housing development, has a proprietary lease on his apartment and pays real estate taxes via his maintenance charge.

As of the 1980 census, there were 1,224,558 owner-occupied condominium units in the United States. An additional 483,249 condominium units were occupied by renters.

See: COMMON AREAS; COOPERATIVE HOUSING

Conference Center

A building, usually located in an estate environment, in which meeting rooms, conference areas and dining facilities are provided and that may also have hotel accommodations. Conference centers may be commercial ventures providing space for corporate, government, social or other types of meetings, or they may be maintained by large institutions, such as universities or corporations, for their own use.

While many large estates are offered for sale for this purpose, most university conference centers evolved as a result of donations of estate properties, thereby enabling the preservation of many large, historic houses that might otherwise have been demolished.

See: ADAPTIVE USE; CORPORATE TRAINING CEN-TER

Confidence Limits

Two numbers marking the boundaries of a numerical range within which there is a specified degree of certainty that a particular value or population parameter will be found.

If, for example, a random sample of current values of three-bedroom homes in a community showed a particular mean value, it is unlikely that this figure is the exact mean value of all three-bedroom homes in the community. It is possible, however, to use statistical tests to assign confidence limits (in this case, house values) that define the range in which the mean is likely to fall. By expanding or contracting this range of values, it is possible to increase or decrease the degree of confidence that the range selected includes the true value of the mean.
See: INFERENTIAL STATISTICS

Confiscatory Regulation

Restrictions or limitations placed upon the use of property that prevent a landowner from making any economically reasonable use or deriving any economically reasonable return from his property and that amount, in effect, to a taking of the property.

A finding that a regulation is confiscatory may support a property owner's claim that the regulation should be stricken as unconstitutional or that he is constitutionally entitled to a variance. It may also support his request for a judicial decree of inverse condemnation, with the court requiring that the regulating government either pay damages or purchase the property.
See: AGINS v. *CITY OF TIBURON;* COMPENSABLE REGULATIONS; INVERSE CONDEMNATION; TAKING; ZONING VARIANCE

Conflict Resolution

The satisfactory settling of disputes that can occur among groups of constituents or other parties in order to attain a particular end result. Conflict resolution requires that the planner understand the diverse viewpoints of conflicting interest groups, including those subtle issues that may not be expressed, and that he work with the constituencies, separately and together, to resolve them. A variety of citizen participation techniques, involving negotiation and consensus building, are often used for this purpose.
See: CITIZEN PARTICIPATION TECHNIQUES

Congregate Housing

A residential development designed to accommodate individuals, most often elderly, who are unable or do not wish to provide living arragements for themselves. Services most commonly associated with congregate housing include food preparation, dining and housekeeping but may also include medical, social, recreational and educational services.

Congregate housing is intended to accommodate those unable to maintain a completely independent life-style but for whom more intensive care is not considered necessary or desirable. Considered socially beneficial, this type of housing is also economically desirable, in that it reduces the demand for more costly forms of care in institutions.

The physical setting for congregate housing may vary from a low-rise development with a communal center to a high-rise building with decentralized facilities throughout.
See: GROUP HOME; HOUSING FOR THE ELDERLY; INTERMEDIATE CARE FACILITIES (ICF); PLANNING FOR THE ELDERLY

Conservation

Preservation and management of the natural environment and its resources. The term may also be applied to the man-made environment, as in conservation of historic buildings.

Many factors have contributed to the increased importance and use of conservation techniques in recent years. A heightened environmental awareness has meant that many more individuals and units of government are cognizant of the environmental consequences of their actions, and more environmental professionals are available to assist in applying conservation methods. In addition, increased costs—such as for energy, materials and labor—have made it more economical to conserve.

Conservation Advisory Council (CAC)

Also called an environmental advisory board, council or commission, it is an appointed body in a municipality with the responsibility of advising the legislative body, executive or planning board on environmental issues in the community. Council members are normally appointed for specific terms and are often selected because of special skills or interests.

State enabling legislation generally authorizes communities to appoint such councils and delimits their powers. Common responsibilities of the councils are the review of development plans, preparation of environmental analyses and promotion of environmental concerns in the community. In some municipalities councils are empowered to receive and hold land for environmental purposes.

Conservation and Renewable Energy Inquiry and Referral Service

An energy information service operated under the auspices of the U.S. Department of Energy. Information may be obtained from this service, which maintains a toll-free telephone number, on a broad range of topics related to renewable energy technologies and the conservation of energy. The service—whose mailing address is in Silver Spring, Maryland—was formerly known as the National Solar Heating and Cooling Information Center.

Conservation Easement

An easement, generally granted by the owner of property to the public, that is designed to limit or preclude future development of the property or otherwise conserve the property for the benefit of the public.

Conservation easements are usually negative easements. Examples include restricting development of open land (an open-space easement), restricting interference with a scenic view (scenic easement), restricting development in flood-prone areas and restricting the alteration of a building facade. Less commonly, conservation easements may take the form of affirmative easements, such as an easement preserving public rights to continue using hiking trails.

Conservation easements may be acquired by the public by eminent domain, which requires that the landowner be compensated. Alternatively, in circumstances where the conservation easement would not be inconsistent with the intended use of the property by its owner, the owner may be induced to donate the easement to the public with a view toward obtaining a charitable contribution tax deduction and at the same time reducing his property tax assessment.

See: EASEMENT; OPEN-SPACE PRESERVATION

Conservation Foundation

A nonprofit organization whose principal goals are improved environmental quality and sound management of the natural resources of the planet. The Foundation, which was established in 1948, conducts interdisciplinary research on a range of topics, and then communicates its findings to the general public and to policy makers through an active publications program, films, conferences and citizen training institutes.

Among the topics currently of concern to the Foundation are land use, including land conservation and development, management of public lands, and conservation of urban and rural land; economics and the environment; coastal and water resources; pollution and toxic substances control; and energy. The Conservation Foundation, which is located in Washington, D.C., also engages in environmental mediation, assists in the establishment of new organizations, and maintains a reference library.

Publications recently issued by the organization include *The Social Life of Small Urban Spaces; Land Development in Crowded Places: Lessons From Abroad;* and *Public Policy for Chemicals: National and International Issues.* Among the films of interest to planners are *Growing Pains: Rural America in the 1980s; Onshore Planning for Offshore Oil: Voices From Scotland;* and *Neighbors: Conservation in a Changing Community.* A monthly newsletter, the *Conservation Foundation Letter,* is also available by subscription. The Conservation Foundation is a nonmember organization.

Construction Cost

The total amount of money necessary to construct an engineering or building project. This cost includes preliminary planning, design, development of detailed drawings, cost estimation by consultants and supervision of work, as well as the actual costs of materials and labor, but excludes land acquisition cost. For purposes of cost estimation by contractors, the construction cost would consist only of materials and labor based on the supplied plans and speci-

fications, and cost increases if the project is delayed or changed.

See: CONSTRUCTION COST DATA; WORKING DRAWINGS

Construction Cost Data

Data published by a variety of sources on the cost of construction of different project types in various parts of the country. These data, generally given as average costs, are used for cost estimation of proposed projects. Among the better-known sources are *Building Construction Cost Data,* published in annual editions by Robert Snow Means Company Inc., and the *Dodge Construction Systems Costs,* published annually by McGraw-Hill Information Systems Company. Special reports, such as the *Dodge Guide to Public Works and Heavy Construction Costs,* may be particularly useful to planners.

In addition, a number of publications issued periodically throughout the year contain cost indexes that may be used to supplement annual reports. These include the *Means Construction Cost Indexes,* with statistics for 209 cities (issued quarterly by the R.S. Means Company), *Engineering News-Record* (a weekly publication) and *Architectural Record* (a monthly publication), which periodically publish data on regional construction activity and specific projects, giving information on materials and labor costs. Data published by the Bureau of the Census, such as the monthly C-30 series "Value of New Construction Put in Place," may also be helpful, as can *Construction Review,* a bimonthly publication of the Department of Commerce. Particular product cost information can also be obtained from manufacturers.

See: CENSUS SURVEYS; CONSTRUCTION COST; DEPARTMENT OF COMMERCE

Construction Industry Ass'n of Sonoma County v. *City of Petaluma* (522 F.2d 897 [9th Cir. 1975], cert. denied 424 U.S. 934 [1976]

A decision by the federal Court of Appeals for the ninth circuit upholding the adoption by the City of Petaluma, California of a plan to limit the housing development growth rate over a five-year period.

The plan imposed a 500-unit per year limitation for the period 1972 to 1977 on all housing units that were part of projects involving 5 or more units (and thus did not apply at all to housing growth resulting from construction of single-family homes not part of a larger project). The stated purpose of the plan was to ensure orderly growth and to protect the "small town character" of Petaluma.

The court found that even if it were demonstrated that the plan had an exclusionary purpose and effect, it was entitled to be upheld so long as it bore a rational relationship to a legitimate state interest. The court went on to hold that Petaluma's interest in preserving its small town character and avoiding uncontrolled and rapid growth were within the broad police power concept of "general welfare" and were therefore a proper object of zoning regulation.

The court noted that although the plan could have the effect of frustrating legitimate regional housing needs, it offered more housing opportunities for low- and moderate-income persons than had existed prior to adoption of the plan. Therefore, the court was able to distinguish this case from other cases in which zoning regulations that had an exclusionary impact were invalidated.

Subsequent to this ruling Petaluma raised its annual limit on new dwelling units to 625 and also exempted all projects with less than 15 units from this limit. In recent years, however, Petaluma's growth rate has slowed sufficiently so that applications for new development do not generally reach the development ceiling.
See: EXCLUSIONARY ZONING; GROWTH MANAGEMENT; PHASED DEVELOPMENT CONTROLS; POLICE POWER

Construction Loan

A short-term loan to enable the construction of real estate improvements. Generally, the funding is distributed to a builder in phases as costs are incurred. The construction loan is later replaced by the permanent financing, which is secured either from the original lender or from a new lender. Most commonly, a lender of construction money will require that the builder secure a written commitment for permanent financing, known as a takeout commitment, to assure that the construction loan will be repaid upon completion of the structure.

Construction Technology

New methods of on-site construction, many of which use poured concrete, that are increasing in popularity in Europe and North America. In general, these methods permit quicker construction by using special machinery that helps to mechanize a trade that otherwise relies on hand craft.

Three different prefabricated systems proving to be effective are lift-slab, tilt-up and push-up construction. In the lift-slab method slabs are cast at grade with sleeves for connection to columns and lifted into position by sophisticated lifting mechanisms, while in tilt-up construction walls are cast horizontally on top of floor slabs and then tilted into position by cranes. In push-up construction the entire top floor slab is cast on the ground and raised into place; lower floors are similarly cast and raised in turn.

Tunnelforms are used to quickly produce an entire building floor with all of its partitions and walls in place. U-shaped forms, in one- or two-room widths, are placed adjacent to one another and, when the concrete has cured, are removed by crane and used for the next story.

Other forms of construction use new or unconventional materials to speed the building process. All dry construction, as an example, consists of the use of lightweight steel joists and studs, gypsum board and prefabricated panels assembled without concrete or plaster. High-strength mor-

tars and epoxy adhesives are now being used to bond brick and concrete block more strongly than conventional mortars. These bonding materials enable the use of single-thickness walls instead of the normal double-thickness and permit bricks to be prelayed and lifted into place by crane.
See: BEARING WALL; CONCRETE; INDUSTRIALIZED HOUSING; SKELETON FRAME CONSTRUCTION

Consultants

Consultants are often used by planning agencies to obtain special skills not available among staff members or to undertake a specific project for which the agency has insufficient staff.

Planning consultants are also used by communities that have no professional planning staff. The role the consultant fills in that situation will depend upon the needs of the community; however, in these circumstances the consultant's scope of responsibility is typically broader than that of a consultant retained for a specific project or to provide a specific service.

Consumer of Services

A member of a board of directors of a Health Systems Agency (HSA) who is a layperson in the health field as defined in the National Health Planning and Resources Development Act of 1974 and its amendments. This act requires that HSA boards be composed of a majority of consumers of services, but not more than 60 percent. Providers of services comprise the remainder of the board.
See: CITIZEN PARTICIPATION; HEALTH SYSTEMS AGENCY (HSA); PROVIDER OF SERVICES

Contaminant

A substance that causes pollution or diminished quality when brought into contact with air, water, soil or other aspects of the environment.
See: POLLUTION

Contour Lines

Lines that appear on topographic maps and link points that are of an equal elevation above sea level. They appear at set intervals (for example, every 10 feet) based on the scale of the map and the relief of the area. The difference in elevation between each line is known as the contour interval. Typically, the elevation will be printed on every fifth contour line, and this line will be heavier than the preceeding four.

Contour lines enable the map users to gain a clear picture of the slope configuration and the terrain in the area that they are studying. If the contour lines are spaced uniformly, the slope is ascending or descending uniformly. An area in which contour lines are spaced very closely indicates a steeply sloped area, while lines that are widely spaced indicate gradual slopes. Jagged or uneven patterns indicate a rough rather than a rolling terrain.
See: TOPOGRAPHIC MAP

Contract Rent

Contract rent, also known as shelter rent, is the rent listed on the lease agreement signed by the tenant and the landlord.
See: GROSS RENT

Contract Zoning

A type of rezoning in which conditions are imposed that are not usually applied to land in that zoning district or in which a contract is made between the municipality and the landowner. Distinctions are sometimes made between contract zoning and conditional zoning, but they are essentially alike.

There are a number of forms of contract zoning. In one common type, the applicant for a rezoning will agree to limit development to a particular agreed-upon land use even though the zone actually permits numerous other uses, some of which might be undesirable at that location. This may be accomplished by the applicant's registering a deed restriction or by an agreement that in exchange for receiving a zoning reclassification, the applicant will agree to a particular use. Contract zoning may also involve an agreement that rezoning will be granted if certain site improvements are undertaken first or if certain land is dedicated to the municipality.

There is wide variation as to whether this practice is considered legal. A key factor is thought to be the extent to which the municipality makes binding promises that are equivalent to a surrender of its police power, as well as the purpose for which the contract zoning is used.
See: RESTRICTIVE COVENANT; ZONING

Control of Access

The imposition of restrictions on ingress to public thoroughfares so that abutting property owners or occupants are denied direct access to the thoroughfares. Access may be fully controlled, partially controlled or uncontrolled and is determined in the roadway design or redesign phase.

Full control of access permits access to a stream of traffic only at interchanges with selected public roads, thereby giving preference to through traffic. It eliminates grade crossings and driveway entrances. Roads with full control of access are called limited-access highways.

Partial control of access permits some at-grade interchanges and driveways, as well as fully controlled grade-separated interchanges.

Uncontrolled access permits unlimited interconnections of roads and driveways, as authorized by local authorities according to municipal master plans, subdivision ordinances and various codes that control curb cuts. Uncontrolled access gives preference to land use-related traffic.
See: AT-GRADE INTERSECTION; GRADE CROSSING; GRADE-SEPARATED INTERCHANGE

Conurbation

A polynucleated metropolitan area that includes a number of identifiable municipalities that have merged. A classic example of this phenomenon is the Minneapolis-St. Paul area. The term *conurbation* was coined by Patrick Geddes, who earlier had suggested the word *conglomeration*.

Unlike agglomeration, which is any unplanned incremental growth, the term *conurbation* implies two or more communities that have grown together. The term *megalopolis* is now used when entire metropolitan areas, not just communities, have grown together. Conurbations have occurred throughout the world as major cities grew and existing communities became part of the metropolitan area.
See: AGGLOMERATION; GEDDES, SIR PATRICK; MEGALOPOLIS; METROPOLITAN AREA

Conventional Mortgage

A mortgage granted by an institutional lender, such as a bank or a savings and loan association, that is secured by real estate rather than guaranteed or insured by a government agency.

Convention Center

A large indoor facility used for business conferences and conventions, trade shows, expositions and other public functions. A convention center generally has the capacity to accommodate at least 300 persons. As the number of conventions held increases, many cities have built convention centers on vacant or cleared land within the downtown, usually with public funds.

Because of the potential economic benefits that can result from convention centers, they are often a major component of a city's economic development strategy. Convention centers can attract visitors who generate income and tax revenue through their spending as well as increased employment, primarily in the service industries. A convention center may also be part of an overall plan to revitalize the downtown, since the visitors to the center also support hotels, restaurants, and retail and service establishments that are often situated in the downtown. An additional benefit is the creation of temporary employment for the construction trades.

While the economic benefits from a convention center can be significant, however, the costs associated with the center are also high. Most convention centers are extremely expensive to build, and many operate at a deficit. Smaller communities may also find it difficult to compete with larger cities for conventions. As a result, the costs of the convention center may outweigh the benefits.
See: DOWNTOWN REVITALIZATION; ECONOMIC DEVELOPMENT; TOURISM

Conversion

1.   A change in the use of an existing building. A residence, for example, may be converted into apartments or into a nonresidential use.

2.   The change in the ownership arrangement of prop-

erty when rental units are converted into condominium or cooperative units.
See: ADAPTIVE USE; CONDOMINIUM HOUSING; CO-OPERATIVE HOUSING; ILLEGAL CONVERSION

Conveyance

A transfer of title to property or an interest in property, from one person or legal entity to another, by means of a legal instrument. The term is most often used in connection with real estate and may include transfer of fee simple title, a life estate, a leasehold estate, an easement or a mortgage. Conveyancing instruments include deeds, leases, mortgages and indentures.
See: DEED; EASEMENT; FEE SIMPLE; MORTGAGE

Cooling Tower

A towerlike structure used to lower the temperature of water that has been used as a power plant coolant before it is discharged back into a body of water. If the water is not cooled before release, it can disrupt the ecology of the receiving water body and result in the killing of a wide variety of aquatic organisms.

Towers are usually either evaporative (or wet cooling) towers, which cool water through evaporation, or the non-evaporative (or dry cooling) tower type, which uses air-cooled condensers or heat exchangers in the cooling process. Evaporative towers are most effective at cooling but emit large vapor plumes and can also create increased fog, cloudiness, humidity and icing, contributing to potential driving hazards and crop damage. Dry cooling towers have no vapor plume but are less effective, more expensive and consume more energy. Cooling towers may rise hundreds of feet in height and be visible for great distances.
See: ELECTRIC POWER GENERATION AND TRANSMISSION; NUCLEAR ENERGY; THERMAL POLLUTION

Cooperative Housing

A form of residential ownership in which one may acquire a proprietary interest akin to ownership in one dwelling unit of a multiunit building or development.

The owner of a cooperative apartment does not actually own a direct interest in the real estate comprising the apartment. Rather, he owns shares of stock in a corporation that owns the entire building or housing development, including his apartment. The corporation, as landlord, issues to the stockholder a proprietary lease for his apartment. The lease is referred to as a proprietary lease because it may only be issued to the person owning the shares of stock allocated to that apartment.

A cooperative owner pays a monthly rent, or maintenance charge, to the corporation. This charge covers his proportionate share of the cost of maintaining the common areas of the building, the cost of administering the cooperative, real estate taxes and amortization of the mortgage, if any, on the real estate owned by the corporation. It may also include a share of the utility bill for the entire building or development if utilities are not separately metered and billed for each unit.

A cooperative apartment owner may sell his apartment (i.e., sell the shares allocated to his apartment and assign his proprietary lease); however, he often must obtain the consent of the board of directors of the corporation to any sale. He may pledge his stock and his lease as security for a loan (similar to a mortgage) when buying his apartment.

A cooperative apartment owner is treated like a homeowner for purposes of the tax rules permitting deferral of income tax on the sale of a home when another home is purchased within a specified period and for purposes of the tax rules affording senior citizens a one-time exemption from tax on the gain from the sale of a house. In addition, if certain specified tax rules contained in the Internal Revenue Code, Section 216, are met, tenant shareholders of a cooperative apartment may deduct their proportionate share of the real estate tax and mortgage interest paid by the corporation on the entire building or housing development.

As with condominium ownership, states have rules governing how cooperative housing interests may be marketed and sold to the public, including to persons already residing in the building being converted.

Because the cooperative form of ownership does not afford apartment owners the same degree of flexibility and independence as that enjoyed by condominium unit owners, and because cooperative ownership does not provide the security of owning an interest in real estate that is provided by condominium ownership, the cooperative form of home ownership is less common nationally than condominium ownership. However, in certain regions of the United States—in particular, portions of the Northeast—the cooperative form of home ownership predominates.
See: CONDOMINIUM HOUSING

Cordon and Screenline Counts

A count of the number of vehicles, pedestrians, trucks or transit passengers that cross boundary lines designated for the purpose of counting traffic movements.

A cordon line is a line that circumscribes an area along which counting stations are established to record counts. These can be placed at every intersection of the cordon line with a road or rail line but more frequently are located at principal highways at the edge of the area; at bridge and tunnel entrances; and at bus, rail and air terminals for intercity passenger movements. Counts are often taken by sampling procedure and are recorded in half-hour intervals to show changes in volume over the course of a day. The cordon count was the direct predecessor of the origin-destination study.

A screenline is a line drawn between two points of a cordon line, often along a natural divide such as a river or valley, where relatively few crossings exist. It usually intercepts all streets extending in one general direction. Counts are taken at stations along the line to determine the

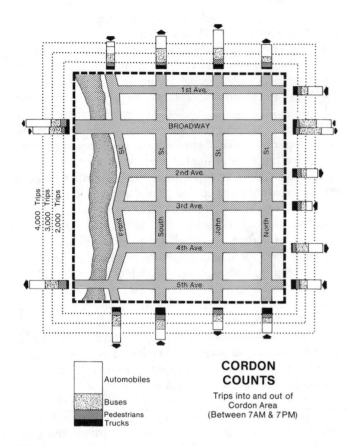

CORDON COUNTS

Trips into and out of
Cordon Area
(Between 7AM & 7PM)

Automobiles

Buses

Pedestrians

Trucks

Fig. 11.

amount of traffic that crosses the line. Screenlines can be drawn at several locations to count the volume of traffic moving between two points across screenlines, adjusting for traffic originating and terminating between the two screenlines. (See Fig. 11)
See: ORIGIN-DESTINATION (O-D) STUDY

Corner Lot

A lot that is situated at the junction of at least two streets, at which the angle of intersection is no greater than 135 degrees. Some zoning ordinances may specify that corner lots are considered to have two front yards and two side yards, and to lack a rear yard. (See Fig. 26)
See: LOT; YARD; ZONING

Corporate Training Center

A building located in an estate or parklike setting, with office space, conference rooms, dining facilities and hotel accommodations, and used for the training of corporate personnel. Large estates are frequently marketed for this function.

Corporate training centers are built or purchased by corporations that must train large numbers of employees for extended periods of time. These employees are often brought to the training centers from diverse locations for a training period of a week or more.
See: ADAPTIVE USE; CONFERENCE CENTER

Corporation Counsel

The appointed municipal official responsible for acting as the municipality's legal representative and for issuing legal opinions on the municipality's authority in the many areas in which the government undertakes actions. The corporation counsel advises the mayor, council and other officials on legal matters; represents the municipality in court actions; drafts ordinances; administers contracts; and in some municipalities, prosecutes violators of local ordinances. The corporation counsel also, to a considerable extent, decides upon levels of enforcement of city ordinances and state laws and may be able to alter the intent of these laws through his opinions.

The title "corporation counsel" is used only in incorporated municipalities, but various other titles such as city, village, town or county attorney are also used. The corporation counsel usually has a legal staff; some small communities may, however, choose to hire a law firm to perform their legal work rather than appoint a corporation counsel.

Correlation

The degree to which two or more variables are related. It is measured by the calculation of a correlation coefficient, which is a figure ranging from +1.00 to −1.00. A coefficient of +1.00 would represent a perfect positive relationship between the variables, while −1.00 would signify a perfect negative relationship. A zero correlation coefficient would mean that no discernible relationship exists.

Positive correlation coefficients mean that high measurements or readings on one variable would mean high scores on the other. Similarly, low readings would be related. As an example, a positive correlation would be found between the value of housing and the income of its occupants. Negative correlation works in the opposite way—a high reading on one variable would elicit a low reading on the other. In both positive and negative correlation coefficients, the closer the number is to +1.00 or −1.00, the higher the degree of association.

Corridor Study

An analysis of alternative routes for a proposed highway, rail line, mass transit line or fixed guideway system. The corridor includes the width of the right-of-way as well as land in the vicinity that is affected by the right-of-way. In the United States and Britain, it is now customary to present corridor studies for public scrutiny prior to selection of the route and design of the facility, since transportation corridors undergo changes in land use, density and environmental quality. In the United States a public hearing on the corridor is a prerequisite for federal assistance for design and construction. Studies are also undertaken of corridors around proposed utility rights-of-way.

Cost Approach Appraisal

Together with the income and market data approaches, one of three basic approaches to estimating the value of real estate.

In the cost approach the land is valued separately from the improvements on the property, as if it were vacant, generally by means of either the income or market data approaches to value. The improvements are valued by estimating the cost to replace or reproduce the improvements, as if they were new, and then subtracting the depreciation to which the existing building has been subject to reflect the fact that the building is not new. Depreciation consists of three components: physical depreciation the deterioration of the property; functional obsolescence—the reduction of value because of dysfunctional layout or design as compared with a building newly constructed for the same purpose; and economic obsolescence—the reduction of value because of changes in the economy and the surrounding area from the time the building was first constructed. The estimated land and building values are then added to arrive at the estimated value for the improved parcel.

The cost approach is accorded greatest weight for specialty properties—parcels that have been improved with non–income producing buildings with special functions, which are therefore of limited marketability. Examples include churches, certain types of government buildings and certain types of manufacturing facilities. For other types of improved properties, the cost approach is generally used in conjunction with the income and market data approaches to value and represents the upper limit on the estimated value of the property.

See: APPRAISAL; APPRAISED VALUE; ECONOMIC OBSOLESCENCE; FUNCTIONAL OBSOLESCENCE; PHYSICAL DETERIORATION; REPLACEMENT COST; REPRODUCTION COST

Cost-Benefit Analysis

The examination of a variety of potential program goals, or alternatives to achieving a single goal, to determine which are preferred or optimum on the basis of their financial value. Cost-benefit analysis, unlike other cost studies, considers both short-term and long-term costs and benefits as well as direct and indirect costs and benefits. It is an attempt to objectify decision making by substituting dollar values for all elements under consideration. Value judgments are still necessary, however, in establishing desirable goals and in evaluating intangible effects.

A cost-benefit analysis involves a number of major steps:

- *Statement of goals and alternatives.* The results that the program seeks to obtain must be defined as narrowly as possible, stating short-and long-term expectations if appropriate. Since cost-benefit analysis can be expensive, alternatives to achieving the goal should be restricted to those deserving serious consideration.

- *Statement and analysis of benefits.* All direct and indirect benefits should be listed, but it is the determination of the financial value of these benefits that is the most difficult aspect of the study. Where possible, a benefit can be calculated as units of output of the activity—e.g., installation of sewers will generate sewer tax revenues and permit additional construction that will yield an increase in property taxes. Many benefits, however, have no calculable monetary value or are extremely difficult to quantify, such as the increase in water quality of a water body adjacent to a newly sewered area. Development of shadow costs (those that can be found for a somewhat comparable product or program) is a useful approach to estimating the value of these types of benefits. Where the financial value of benefits cannot be determined, it is more appropriate to conduct a cost-effectiveness analysis.

- *Cost development.* All direct and indirect costs must be ascertained. An important component of this phase is the determination of the negative effects of the program and their costs.

- *Determination of the interest rate.* Projects that will have future benefits or current and future costs must be discounted to present value via a discount rate for cost comparisons to be made.

- *Selection of alternative.* To show program viability in a cost-benefit analysis, the costs of the program should be lower than, or equal to, the financial value of the benefits. In evaluating various programs with equally important goals, those with a majority of benefits as compared to costs should receive priority.

Cost-benefit analysis has been in use since the 1930s, principally for the purpose of deciding how scarce resources should be allocated. It can also be employed to determine preferable program alternatives, to develop other alternatives worthy of study, to assess the optimal scale of a program and to determine where further research may enable cost reduction. It is not particularly useful, however, in evaluating programs that are vaguely defined or in comparing programs with different objectives.

See: COST-EFFECTIVENESS ANALYSIS; COST-REVENUE ANALYSIS; DIRECT AND INDIRECT BENEFITS; DIRECT AND INDIRECT COSTS

Cost-Effectiveness Analysis

A comparison of the costs of different alternatives for achieving a stated goal, which may be conducted as part of a cost-benefit analysis.

In a cost-effectiveness analysis, all of the costs (direct and indirect) of each alternative are compared, with the aim of selecting the alternative that reaches the goal or achieves an established effectiveness level for the least cost. Programs that must be deleted to permit a particular alternative to be undertaken can be included as cost savings for the alternative or as a negative effectiveness level, if appropriate.

The steps taken in a cost-effectiveness analysis are: statement of the goal, identification of alternatives, selection of measures of effectiveness for each alternative and development of cost estimates. In complex studies it may also be necessary to choose a range of criteria that can be used to select the best alternatives, as well as to formulate models.

See: COST-BENEFIT ANALYSIS; COST-REVENUE ANALYSIS; DIRECT AND INDIRECT BENEFITS; DIRECT AND INDIRECT COSTS

Cost-Revenue Analysis

A comparison of the costs of undertaking a program or project and the revenues that will be generated when the project is operational, often used to determine project feasibility.

While operating costs of a program or facility are usually compared with revenues, capital costs may or may not be included. As an example, a municipality may be willing to absorb the costs of open-space acquisition to preserve an open area and, thus, would not include the costs of land acquisition in a cost-revenue analysis. The same municipality, however, may require that certain park improvements within the site pay for themselves through revenue they generate and would therefore include the cost of facility development in such an analysis.

Cost-revenue analysis is also used to compare the financial balance of program costs and tax revenues before and after a declining area of a municipality is redeveloped.

See: COST-BENEFIT ANALYSIS; FEASIBILITY STUDY; FISCAL IMPACT ANALYSIS

Council for International Urban Liaison (CIUL)

A Washington, D.C.-based organization, founded in 1976, that serves as a clearinghouse for innovative solutions to urban problems throughout the world. It is aimed at assisting urban practitioners in North America and Europe and also serves as a means for international urban organizations to communicate with each other. Among the subject areas it collects information on are transportation, finance, conservation, waste management and the operations of government.

Regular publications of CIUL are *Urban Innovation Abroad,* a monthly newsletter; *Urban Transportation Abroad,* a quarterly newsletter; and *The Urban Edge,* which concentrates on Third World urban development. CIUL also publishes a variety of special reports.

Council-Manager Form of Government

The form of municipal government in which the elected council appoints an executive to administer the government and carry out the council's policies. The council-manager form of government, also called the city manager form, is generally authorized by state enabling legislation. It permits a local government to adopt specific legislation in which it selects this system and specifies duties and responsibilities. The duties of the city manager normally include budget preparation and administration, and appointment of all department heads, although occasionally the council retains this right for certain departments. The city manager plan grew out of the reform and scientific management movements of the early 20th century; the first city to actually put the system into effect was Sumter, South Carolina in 1912.

The city manager form of government has gained some acceptance in Canada and Britain, where a chief executive or a board of commissioners (who collectively perform the functions of a city manager) have been appointed in some municipalities to perform overall planning coordination and administer the activities of local departments.

See: CITY COUNCIL; CITY MANAGER; COMMISSION FORM OF GOVERNMENT; MAYOR-COUNCIL FORM OF GOVERNMENT

Council of Government (COG)

A voluntary association of municipal governments or regional agencies formed to study and discuss areawide problems and to recommend remedial actions to the member governments. Such councils are usually composed of the elected officials of the participating governments and agencies or their representatives. COGs undertake a variety of functions under authority granted by their members, such as regional planning, community development, pollution control, water system development and airport construction.

Approximately 200 COGs have been established (mostly since 1966), often under incentives provided by federal programs to support COGs and in response to federal requirements that a regional agency review applications for funds for certain types of federal grants. The establishment of so many regional councils is also an indication of the number of problems transcending artificial geographic boundaries that require regional cooperation and coordination.

See: REGIONAL PLANNING; REGIONAL PLANNING COMMISION; REGIONAL TAX BASE SHARING (TBS)

Council of Planning Librarians (CPL)

An international organization concerned with making information available on all aspects of urban and regional planning, and with organizing and maintaining collections of planning materials. CPL members include librarians and libraries; planning agencies; planners; researchers; colleges and universities; developers; and consultants.

The organization, which was founded in 1957, publishes a large number of bibliographies related to specific topics in the field of planning. Recent examples include bibliographies on urban enterprise zones, regulation of manufactured housing, and hazardous substances in Canada.

The organization, which is located in Chicago, also publishes a quarterly *CPL Newsletter,* and the *CPL Planning and Urban Affairs Manual,* which discusses the organization and operation of a planning library for a small office or agency.

Council of State Planning Agencies (CSPA)

An organization whose membership consists of the planning staffs and policy analysts of the various governors of the United States. CSPA, which is based in Washington, D.C. and affiliated with the National Governors' Association, is concerned with conducting research and developing programs and policies of use to the states on a broad variety of subject areas, particularly as related to the economy. The current program of the Council addresses issues related to governance, economic development, human development, human resources management and renewable resources.

The Council, which was founded in 1965, provides direct assistance to the states through a variety of mechanisms, and conducts conferences and seminars on a range of issues. It is currently assisting in the development of a State Institute for Executive Management, and is developing a subscription service for information on state government. It also operates an active publications program that has produced books and papers on such topics as *Venture Capital and Urban Development,* and *Environmental Quality and Economic Growth.*

Council on Environmental Quality (CEQ)

An agency within the Executive Office of the president that develops and recommends policies that promote the improvement of environmental quality. The CEQ also continually analyzes trends in the national environment, conducts studies related to ecological systems and environmental quality, advises federal agencies and appraises their programs with respect to support of environmental policy.

The CEQ developed the requirements for environmental impact statements (EISs) and reviews these statements on matters that may have a national impact and for projects where there is disagreement between federal agencies. It also prepares the annual report to Congress on environmental quality, which contains a summary of current environmental concerns and legislative activity and is a useful document for planners.

The Office of Environmental Quality provides professional and administrative staff for the CEQ, and the chairman of the CEQ is also the director of the Office of Environmental Quality.
See: ENVIRONMENTAL IMPACT STATEMENT (EIS); NATIONAL ENVIRONMENTAL POLICY ACT OF 1969 (NEPA)

Country Club

A large tract of land owned by a private club, intended for the use of its members, on which a club building and a variety of recreational facilities are usually provided. Recreational facilities may include one or more golf courses, tennis courts, swimming pools and other court games. The clubhouse generally contains a restaurant and locker rooms and may also have hotel accommodations.

Country clubs offer recreational facilities to middle- and upper-income population segments and preserve scenic open space within the community. Because of development pressures, and the fact that they rely on membership dues for support, leading to insolvency at times, many clubs have sold their land for development. Municipalities often consider the purchase of all or a portion of these clubs to provide public parks with built-in amenities or to preserve the open space. Some communities have entered into first-refusal agreements with clubs that provide important open space attributes to obtain the right to purchase the club, if so desired, at the time that it may be offered for sale.
See: FIRST REFUSAL; OPEN-SPACE PRESERVATION; RECREATION PLANNING

County Board

The principal governing authority of a county, generally having both policymaking and administrative functions. County boards are known by over 30 different titles, among which are board of commissioners, board of supervisors and county court. Two-thirds of the boards are composed of 3 to 5 elected members, but many have 30 or more. In states with township government, the county board has often been composed of township supervisors and representatives of cities within the county, but this is changing because of the Supreme Court ruling that counties must have one-man, one-vote representation.

The responsibilities of the board are to administer state law, levy taxes, approve the budget and supervise affairs of the county. In counties where the county executive plan has been adopted, county boards do not have administrative functions. The county executive performs these functions as the head of the executive branch of county government. In counties that have adopted the county manager plan, the county board delegates its administrative functions to the county manager, who is analagous to a city manager. County boards, which have historically been strongholds of political power, appear to be gaining more power because of the increasing urbanization of counties throughout the United States.
See: CITY MANAGER; LOCAL GOVERNMENT

County Executive

The elected chief executive of a county that has adopted the county executive form of government. The county executive is the administrative head of the government, with power to appoint and discharge department heads and with other executive powers similar to those of a strong mayor. By contrast, other forms of county government that have administrators include the county manager form, analogous to a city manager, and the chief administrative officer (CAO) form. The CAO is a restricted version of the county manager and has only those powers specifically delegated by the governing board. Most counties, however, have only a county board, which performs both legislative and administrative duties.

Other elective county positions that still prevail in many states are county clerk, clerk of the court, treasurer, sheriff, register of deeds, superintendent of schools, assessor, county attorney, and county surveyor or engineer. In counties that have executive or administrative forms of government, however, many or all of these positions are appointed and are under the authority of the administrator.

See: CITY MANAGER; COUNTY BOARD; MAYOR

County of London Plan

A plan prepared in 1943 for the 117-square mile (303-square kilometer) area of the County of London following the damages it suffered during World War II. In this plan Patrick Abercrombie and F.J. Forshaw recommended that between 500,000 and 600,000 people (the 1944 population of the County of London was about 4 million) be relocated in order to facilitate the rebuilding of heavily damaged London, reduce overcrowding and introduce more open space to this area.

As a result of this plan, Abercrombie was commissioned to prepare a Greater London Plan, which was released in 1944. Covering an area of about 2,600 square miles (6,734 square kilometers), the plan recommended a system for relocating the above-mentioned population. It covered a 50-year time span and proposed a series of four rings around the County of London: an inner ring, in which population would be lessened; a suburban ring; a greenbelt; and an outer ring. The Greater London Plan also called for the creation of new towns and suggested possible sites for these communities. These recommendations led to the passage of the New Towns Act of 1946.

See: ABERCROMBIE, SIR LESLIE PATRICK; NEW TOWN; NEW TOWNS ACT, 1946

County Planning

Planning programs conducted by county planning agencies. Depending upon state enabling legislation, county planning may include preparation of plans for county-owned facilities or for the development of the county as a whole; review of major developments, subdivisions and municipal ordinances; development and analysis of capital budgets; or detailed planning and zoning for communities in lieu of these activities' being conducted by the individual municipalities.

Typically, county planning is concerned with the provision of major infrastructure that may not be provided by municipalities, such as water supply or sewerage systems, county roads, solid waste disposal facilities and regional parks. Other facilities, such as a county court and jail and facilities for the county coroner, may be mandated by the state. Health facilities, a community college or an airport might be other regional facilities managed at the county level. A county may also be involved in housing, such as through participation in the Urban County Program, under which it may manage community development block grant funds for its constituent municipalities.

Environmental planning—such as drainage basin analyses, air pollution management and coastal zone planning—are other typical areas of county-level involvement, while counties are often involved in various aspects of open-space planning, including farmland preservation. Economic development activities of a diverse nature are other aspects of county planning, as is historic preservation.

Other functions that may be undertaken by planning agencies are the acquisition and dissemination of data that are often too expensive or complicated for communities to obtain; technical liaison with the Bureau of the Census in preparation for the decennial census and in data handling once the results are released; maintenance of a planning library and computer facilities; and preparation of grant applications and administration of programs.

In many states, including Michigan and Illinois, counties regularly undertake local planning and zoning matters as well as the other aspects of county planning, or they may supervise a planning consultant hired to handle local planning matters. This function is performed for unincorporated municipalities, either as a matter of general policy or in rural areas where municipalities do not wish to engage in these functions. Joint county-city planning is also undertaken where large metropolitan cities constitute most of a county, or where the boundaries are coterminous.

See: REGIONAL PLANNING; RURAL PLANNING; STATE PLANNING; URBAN PLANNING

County Records

1. Records of legal documents—usually related to real estate ownership, transfers and mortgages—that are kept by a recorder of deeds or land records department.

County real estate records are maintained for the purpose of creating a system by which interests in real estate may be transferred or verified. Since most land transfers are recorded, they are useful to planners in determining current property ownership in studies relating to potential land acquisition. A property's monetary value at the time of its transfer can also be determined in many states by calculating the value of the documentary tax stamps that are affixed to the deed in payment of the property transfer tax. The stamps are usually issued on the basis of the price paid for the property.

2. Official records maintained by the county that may include marriage certificates, wills submitted for probate, notices of business formations and other legal documents, as well as official records of the county board. These records are often retained by a county clerk.

See: PUBLIC RECORD

County Seat

The municipality that is selected to become the county administrative headquarters, where a courthouse, jail and county office building are usually provided. The selection of a county seat has often determined the community that would become the principal, most prosperous or most populous in the county.

Cover Material

The soil that is used at sanitary landfills to cover the solid waste that has been deposited there. The use of cover material helps to control odor, prevents scattering of the waste by wind, is a deterrent to insects and rodents, and decreases the likelihood of spreading internal fires.

Many kinds of soil can be used for cover materials, but each soil will perform somewhat differently, and this will affect the procedures that are followed at the landfill. Some soils will, for example, be better for establishing vegetation growth, which improves the appearance of a landfill, but will not be as resistant to burrowing rodents.

In selecting the site for a sanitary landfill, the amount of soil available for use as cover material, and its characteristics, must be assessed. The need to import soil can add greatly to the costs of operating a landfill. (See Fig. 38)
See: DAILY COVER; FINAL COVER; SANITARY LAND-FILL

Creative Play Areas

Places for children's play that are designed to stimulate imaginative activities and physical exercise. Creative play areas are becoming an increasingly popular aspect of playground design.

In the United States the permanently constructed playground made from unconventional play equipment is often used. Frequently constructed from such materials as wood posts, rubber tires, or concrete blocks and tubes, they permit active and passive play and are usually designed to accommodate children of varying degrees of physical ability and skill. The more successful designs employ a linked system, so that children proceed from one

Fig. 12.   A playground with creative play equipment in Washington, D.C., designed by M. Paul Friedberg & Partners. This is part of a 73-acre (29.5-hectare) area in the Fort Lincoln new-town-in-town for which the firm is preparing a comprehensive open-space plan.
Credit: Courtesy of M. Paul Friedberg & Partners

activity to another, while escape routes are provided so that they can find exits when necessary. In Europe extensive use is also made of the adventure playground, in which children may construct their own play equipment, under adult supervision, from materials that are provided. The adventure park, operated as a commercial enterprise, is an expansion of both of these concepts and offers unusual play environments, such as swimming pools filled with plastic balls, rope-net ladders and tunnels, or water-filled mattresses. (See Fig. 12)
See: ADVENTURE PLAYGROUND; PLAYGROUND DESIGN

Criminal Justice Planning

The coordination of expenditures for all elements of the criminal justice system by development and implementation of comprehensive short-term and long-term plans. After development and review of alternative actions and scenarios, plans are formulated that are designed to effect improvements in various crime-related areas, such as crime control or prevention.

Criminal justice planning is an attempt to increase the effectiveness of the entire criminal justice system rather than of individual components that may outwardly appear to require increased funding. As an example, the need for more arrests of drug dealers may require more police officers, more judges, more courtrooms, more jails and more parole officers, so that an improvement in any one area may not solve the problem. In the planning process, goals are set, the data are collected and evaluated, and alternative actions and expenditures necessary to accomplish the goals are proposed and studied. The process involves all elements of the system, including the police, courts, public defenders, prosecutors, parole and probation authorities, and corrections departments, as well as political and citizen input.

Federal funding for criminal justice planning, in the form of block grants to states made available as the result of the Omnibus Crime Control and Safe Streets Act of 1968, stimulated the growth of the field. The same act also established the Law Enforcement Assistance Administration (LEAA) in the Department of Justice to administer the funds. To be eligible for funding, states had to establish a state criminal justice planning agency (SPA) and an annual comprehensive plan; the states, in turn, were permitted to establish local and regional planning agencies and Criminal Justice Coordinating Councils (CJCCs). Later amendments required development of three-year master plans and annual implementation plans, program budgeting and development of minimum standards for various activities. To undertake these studies, each agency needed a technical staff of criminal justice planners. The Justice System Improvement Act of 1979 authorized the transfer of some of the significant programs funded by the LEAA to three new federal agencies in the Department of Justice: the Office of Justice Assistance, Research and Statistics (OJARS); the National Institute of Justice

(NIJ); and the Bureau of Justice Statistics (BJS). The LEAA was terminated in 1982. Federal funding for certain activities is still available, but comprehensive plans are no longer required. Without federal funding for planning or requirements that it be undertaken, many states have found it necessary to eliminate SPAs and local agencies.
See: CENSUS SURVEYS; UNIFORM CRIME REPORTS

Critical Areas

Environmentally sensitive areas, such as wetlands, and hazardous areas, such as floodplains, upon which development should be prevented or strictly controlled. When critical areas are routinely developed, their unique environmental properties are often destroyed, as when wetlands are filled. In other cases, as when floodplains are developed without special regulation, the damage that is sustained can extend over large areas in the form of flooding. Critical areas may be conserved through such means as government acquisition for conservation or park purposes, or they may be protected by stringent development regulations that can assure their continued ability to function. An example of this might be development permitted only at a very low density, with required retention of natural flora. Regulation of development, however, may not be sufficient to protect some of these areas, requiring that development be prevented. In some recent land use regulations, prime farmland, recreational open space, and historic and archeological sites are also considered to be critical areas because of their rare and unique qualities.

In recent years states and localities have begun to protect critical areas (defined differently in each state) through a variety of means. Some states, including Minnesota and Nevada, and the Canadian provinces of Alberta and Ontario have enacted legislation that allows the state (or province) or its municipalities to set aside areas considered to be critical, although other terms may be used to describe these areas. In Minnesota, as an example, the state may designate critical areas, while local governments may adopt land use regulations for them. These regulations are subject to state review and enforcement. Similarly, in Maine critical area designation is a state function, but localities must develop plans to protect areas. In Nevada the entire process is handled by the state. In Hawaii, where zoning is undertaken at the state level, conservation districts (zones) include environmentally fragile areas, areas subject to landslides and volcanic activity, terrain with slopes above 20 percent, and a band of shoreline 40 feet (12.2 meters) wide extending around the Hawaiian coastline. The American Law Institute (ALI) Model Land Development Code also encourages the placement of "areas of critical state concern" under state jurisdiction. The ALI Code recommends including in critical areas such locations as environmentally significant sites, inland wetlands, agricultural lands, areas having major public facilities or investments, and developments that have an effect on, or benefit, a regional area.

Many jurisdictions have taken inventories of critical

areas as a basis for future development control and to create public awareness of the existence of these sites. Special controls have also been instituted in local areas via zoning and special area protection ordinances, such as for hillsides and wetlands, and many jurisdictions and private nonprofit organizations have undertaken programs to purchase critical areas to protect them for the future.

See: CARRYING CAPACITY; ENVIRONMENTALLY SENSITIVE LANDS; HAZARDOUS AREAS; NATURE PRESERVE; RESTRICTED DEVELOPMENT AREAS (RDA)

Critical Path Method (CPM)

A planning and scheduling technique developed by industry in the 1950s that permits a project to be undertaken so that costs and timing are reduced to the most cost-effective level. It is used extensively in construction and development projects.

A CPM diagram is similar to a PERT chart, in that it indicates events (completed activities) as circles and on-going activities as arrows. It will, however, also show the time and cost of each activity in "normal time" (the longest time and lowest cost) and in "crash time" (the minimum time and maximum cost). The diagram will also indicate the critical path, which is the sequence of activities that will take the longest normal time to accomplish, shown by a double line.

Optimization of a project's time schedule and costs is achieved by scheduling the parts of the project that will take the longest so that they can be started the earliest, and by determining where it is most effective to increase costs in order to save time. The computation of the time frame and costs in a CPM study is based on practical experience rather than on the theoretical estimates used in PERT studies.

See: PROGRAM EVALUATION AND REVIEW TECHNIQUE (PERT)

Cross Section

1. Usually referred to as a section, it is a representation of a slice through a structure taken at a point that illustrates as many elements of interior construction, engineering or architectural treatment as possible. Cross sections are often necessary to clarify construction details, since they show the interiors of walls, floors, mechanical equipment or any other structure that has been cut through. Architectural treatment of interior walls and built-in equipment is also shown. A cross section of an area of land may be made to illustrate the soil profile as well as the locations of structures that may be present, e.g., utility pipes.

2. The composition of something—e.g., a cross section of the population. (See Fig. 15)

Crosswalk

A specially marked area of a road for use by pedestrians crossing the road. Crosswalks should be provided wher-

ever studies indicate that there are substantial conflicts between pedestrian and vehicular movements, at points of pedestrian concentration and where pedestrians cannot recognize the safest crossing path.

Crosswalk markings frequently take the form of painted white lines with diagonal or perpendicular markings for emphasis. Downtown improvement projects in some cities have instituted use of contrasting pavement or paving stones to delineate the pedestrian path.

Pedestrian underpasses and overpasses are grade-separated forms of crosswalks, provided where traffic capacity would be severely altered by provision of a pedestrian crossing or where it is too dangerous for pedestrians to cross. Overpasses and underpasses should be built with ramps for bicycles, baby carriages and wheelchairs. Underpasses must be well lighted, cleaned and patrolled.

See: PEDESTRIANIZATION

Cul-de-Sac

A local street with an outlet at only one end and a turnaround area at the other end. Also called a close, or a blind alley, culs-de-sac are used extensively in the design of residential subdivisions because through traffic is excluded by design, permitting them to be quiet and relatively safe for children. The street therefore serves a land-access function solely.

A cul-de-sac should be no longer than 500 feet (152.4 meters) and serve no more than 25 dwelling units. Typical cross sections provide a 50-foot (15.2-meter) right-of-way and 30- to 36-foot (9.1- to 11.0-meter) pavement width for the length of the road, and a 90-foot (27.4-meter) diameter right-of-way and 75-foot (22.9-meter) diameter pavement for the turnaround. The grade of the road should be no greater than 5 percent, and a design speed of 25 mph (40 kph) is considered adequate.

Culs-de-sac are used in subdivision design in a more or less standard elongated shape with a circular turnaround at the end because of the expedience of this design and its relatively minimal use of land for roads. In the design of cluster housing, row housing and multifamily developments, however, culs-de-sac have turnarounds of a variety of other shapes and may have gardens or other plantings in the center that are used as a focal point for development. Such designs have been employed extensively in the British new towns. (See Fig. 43)

See: LOCAL STREET

Cullet

Pieces of recycled glass that are used in the production of new glass. Although most new glass is comprised of 15 percent to 20 percent cullet, new glass may be made of as much as 50 percent recycled glass. The benefits of increased use of cullet include greater energy efficiency as well as resource conservation.

See: BOTTLE BILL; GLASPHALT; RECYCLING

Cultural Resources Planning

Analysis of existing cultural resources and recommendations for improvements to facilities and programs. Cultural resources may include theaters, museums, libraries, exhibition halls, historic sites, architecturally significant buildings, universities, public parks or zoos. School auditoriums may also be included.

In general, planning involves gathering data on facility locations, characteristics, plans for expansion, and existing and proposed programs. When analyzed in connection with population projections and community policies related to the provision and support of cultural resources, plans can be suggested for these facilities. In many cases, cultural facility development relies on government or foundation aid, which determines the nature of possible expansion. It is also important that selection of facility locations or program expansions be undertaken in coordination with transportation planning.

See: COMMUNITY FACILITY PLANNING; COMPREHENSIVE PLAN, LIBRARY; RECREATION PLANNING; THEATERS; TRANSPORTATION PLANNING; UNIVERSITIES

Cultural Tithing

Programs undertaken by universities and municipal arts councils in which they share certain arts resources with the community at large. Examples of these programs, which are often supported by grants from foundations and the federal government, include the provision of space for community arts projects, the circulation of art exhibits to public libraries or the establishment of a reduced-price theater ticket policy for the elderly.

See: COMMUNITY ARTS COUNCILS; UNIVERSITIES

Culvert

A structure designed to carry drainage water or small streams below barriers such as railway embankments, roads or driveways. A culvert may consist of a pipe, ditch or covered channel

See: STORM DRAINAGE SYSTEM; SURFACE WATER

Cumulative Zoning

Also known as pyramidal zoning, this type of zoning practice is oriented to the protection of the single-family residential district, which is viewed as being at the top of a pyramid of zoning districts. Below the single-family district are the multifamily residential district, the commercial districts and, at the bottom of the triangle, the industrial districts. Anything permitted in a single-family residential district may be built in any of the "lower" districts. Similarly, anything permitted in a multifamily district may be built in a commercial or an industrial district. The district at the bottom of the pyramid must accept the cumulative permitted land uses of all other zoning districts.

A variant of this system may permit cumulative zoning within land use categories but not among totally different land uses. Single-family residences, for example, would be permitted in multifamily districts but not in commercial districts.

Cumulative zoning is no longer commonly found in modern zoning ordinances. The concept of "lower" and "higher" districts is now usually considered invalid, in the sense that single-family homes are often as inappropriate in areas of office or industrial development as the opposite case would be. Commercial and industrial uses are also thought to be entitled to municipal regulation that helps to foster their development and allows them to prosper and thrive. Because of this, exclusive-use zoning, which only allows a limited range of land uses within a district that are thought to be compatible, has gradually replaced cumulative zoning.

It, in turn, is already being supplemented or replaced by other zoning variations, such as mixed-use zoning or vertical zoning, in which compatible land uses are combined in a development or found on different floors of a building. A large downtown building might, for example, successfully combine retail stores at the ground level with a health club at the next level followed by apartments.

See: EUCLIDEAN ZONING; EXCLUSIVE-USE ZONING; MIXED-USE ZONING; VERTICAL ZONING; ZONING

Curb

A vertical or sloping edge of a roadway. Curbs are used for purposes of drainage control, delineation of roadway edges and to deter vehicles from encroaching on specific areas—e.g., those designed for pedestrian or bicycle use. They are used most often in urbanized areas and along highways. The two most common types of curbs are the mountable curb and the barrier, or vertical, curb.

Mountable curbs are designed so they can be crossed easily without discomfort, even at relatively high speeds. They are generally low, under 6 inches (15.2 centimeters) in height and have a flat slope, preferably 2:1 or flatter. They are used along sections of expressways and parkways, or where drainage and edge marking is the primary purpose.

Barrier curbs are intended to prevent encroachments. They are steep-faced and range in height from 6 inches (15.2 centimeters) to 24 inches (61.0 centimeters), depending upon the nature of encroachment they are designed to prevent and the speed of traffic. Barrier curbs, when used at sidewalks, should be low in height for pedestrian convenience and to permit clearance of car doors; when used along sections of expressways, where they act as guardrails, they may be higher. Curb cuts that provide a short ramp for baby carriages and wheel chairs should be made available at crosswalks.

See: GUARDRAIL; PEDESTRIANIZATION

Current Population Estimates

Population size is frequently estimated to provide data necessary for planning studies and for monitoring population trends. The most accurate way of making an estimate is through a local census or carefully controlled sample survey. As this is both expensive and time-consuming, most population estimates are based instead upon a variety of analytic techniques.

The component method takes the population figure at the last census and adjusts it to reflect subsequent births, deaths and migration, as well as loss of population to the armed forces. Armed forces personnel stationed in the area are then added to the total civilian population figure.

Censal ratio methods rely upon establishing mathematical ratios between groups of figures. In the apportionment approach a current estimate is obtained for a larger area, such as a state, from a census report series. The loss or gain in population is then allocated among the communities in the larger area on a proportional basis derived from intercensal data.

Symptomatic data—such as school enrollments, utility installations and building permits—may also be used to estimate population. Planners often use dwelling units as a basis for making estimates, on the assumption that changes in dwelling units reflect population change. A ratio is developed between housing units and population, based on the last census, and is then applied to the current housing inventory. For increased accuracy, complete building permit data should be available, and adjustments should also be made to reflect probable changes in household size.

See: CURRENT POPULATION REPORTS; DEMOGRAPHY; POPULATION PROJECTION; POPULATION PROJECTION METHODS

Current Population Reports

A series of reports of population estimates made by the Bureau of the Census that are derived from periodic surveys, such as the *Current Population Survey* (CPS), special censuses of local areas and other cooperative estimation projects in which the Bureau is involved.

Population Characteristics (P-20) appears 15 times annually, presenting data on recurring topics for the national population. *Special Studies* (P-23) appears several times a year on selected subjects, such as youth and aging. *Population Estimates and Projections* (P-25) consists of monthly and annual reports for states, Standard Metropolitan Statistical Areas (SMSAs) and counties. *The Federal-State Cooperative Program for Population Estimates* (P-26) is published as a series of reports presenting data for SMSAs and counties. Other reports in the series are *Farm Population* (P-27), *Special Censuses* (P-28) and *Consumer Income* (P-60).

See: CENSUS; CENSUS SURVEYS

Curvilinear Pattern

A land development pattern in which streets are placed to minimize the amount of cut and fill that will be neces-

sary, generally resulting in winding streets of differing lengths that create an irregular pattern. The predominant style used in single-family subdivision development because it is generally more visually interesting than the once-common gridiron pattern and tends to slow traffic, curvilinear streets are now used in many other types of development because they are more economical to construct. While lots within curvilinear subdivisions may have odd shapes because of road curvature, problems of topography, such as an excessively steep driveway, may also be avoided. (See Fig. 24)

See: GRIDIRON PATTERN; LAND USE PATTERN

Cut

1. In grading, cut is the amount of material that must be removed to achieve the contours that are specified in a grading plan. The material is then generally used as fill on another portion of the site to elevate that area. This process is known as cut and fill.

It is most economical if cut and fill are balanced so that additional materials do not need to be hauled in or out of the site. To aid in achieving this balance, a number of techniques are available for arriving at the volume of earth that must be moved on-site. Frequently used are the contour-area method, the end-area method and a calculation technique based upon the elevation of grid corners. Any attempt to balance cut and fill must also take into account the kind of materials involved and the way they will be handled, as materials tend to expand in volume when removed from the ground.

2. A depression in the ground left after material is excavated. The term may also refer to a depression created for some development purpose, such as railroad tracks in a right-of-way, that is substantially below grade and uncovered.

3. The yield of timber or another crop product that is harvested within a given period of time—e.g., the annual cut of timber. (See Fig. 19)

See: BORROW; EXCAVATION; FILL; GRADING

Cyclone Collector

A common air pollution control device best used for the removal of larger particles. A cyclone collector is a type of inertial collector in that it relies on the fact that particles in a gas stream have a greater inertia than does the gas. In a cyclone collector, polluted air is passed through a cylindrical chamber and induced to spin around so that a centrifugal force is produced that sends the heavier particles outwards. The particles are then collected and the cleaned gas is permitted to exit.

See: AIR POLLUTION; AIR POLLUTION CONTROL

D

Daily Cover

The soil that is applied on a daily (or more frequent) basis to cover the solid waste that has been deposited at a sanitary landfill on that day.

Daily cover should be at least 6 inches (15.2 centimeters) thick and compacted to resist erosion and prevent the ponding of water. Intermediate cover is applied when the daily cover would be exposed for in excess of seven days. The recommended minimum thickness for intermediate cover, which often serves as a road base for landfill vehicles, is 1 foot (30.5 centimeters). (See Fig. 38)
See: COVER MATERIAL; FINAL COVER; SANITARY LANDFILL

Dam

A structure designed to control the course of a river or stream by creating a barrier to the natural flow of water.

Dams may be categorized according to the purpose they serve and the material used to construct them. The most common dam types are power dams, used in the generation of hydroelectric power; storage dams, which impound water for a variety of uses, such as public water supply systems, irrigation and flood control; diversion dams, which alter the course of rivers or streams; and navigation dams, which increase water depth to aid navigation. When dams serve more than one purpose, they are known as multiple-purpose dams. As an example, a common by-product of dam construction is the creation of lakes suitable for recreational use.

Dams are most often constructed of earth, rock or concrete. Earthfill dams are most commonly used because of their low construction cost when suitable materials are available on-site. Rockfill dams are sometimes constructed when insufficient soil is available but suitable rock is located near the dam site. Both types, known as embankment dams, are susceptible to water seepage, so they are usually built with a watertight upstream face or with a core constructed of impervious materials. Concrete dams—which are usually of the gravity, arch or buttress type—are designed to take advantage of the compressive strength of concrete and to minimize tensile forces. Materials and construction type are selected based upon topography, availability of materials, purpose of the dam, climate and geologic conditions.

A variety of auxiliary structures are also associated with dam construction. Spillways automatically permit discharge of water before the capacity of the dam can be exceeded. A variety of gates and outlets are also used to control water release for diverse purposes. Fish passes are often provided at hydroelectric dams to allow migratory fish, such as salmon, to continue on their journey.

The desired use will contribute significantly to the selection of a dam site. For example, special site requirements are necessary for dams being developed primarily for hydroelectric power so that adequate power can be generated. Other important requirements relate to topography, such as floodplain width; geology, such as the location of faults; hydrology; land costs; and land uses or population that may require relocation.
See: DIKE; FLOOD CONTROL; FLOODWALL; HYDRO-ELECTRIC POWER; RESERVOIR; RIVER ENGINEERING; WATER RESOURCES MANAGEMENT

Data

Known or collected facts that can be analyzed and interpreted so that conclusions may be drawn. The singular form of *data* is *datum.* Data are generally classified as being either primary or secondary. Primary data are obtained from the original source materials or direct observation. Secondary data have been collected elsewhere but are made available for public use.

Reliable data allow planners to gain an accurate understanding of the nature of a community or a problem and provide indicators of scale or direction. In addition, professional planners can use data to identify trends, develop plans, construct models and formulate ideas.
See: DATA COLLECTION; DATA PROCESSING

Data Collection

Planners need to rely, to a certain extent, upon finding data that are already available rather than upon being data collectors. One key source is the federal government, which collects and disseminates enormous quantities of data and makes them widely available. The Bureau of the Census provides extensive information on topics such as population, housing, agriculture, business trends and economic characteristics. In addition, most federal agencies publish numerous detailed reports, and maps and aerial photographs are available from selected agencies.

State and local agencies are also sources of data, such as vital statistics, housing starts and traffic counts. Still other data sources are publications, such as city directories and construction cost reports; information may also be obtained from utility companies, universities and special-interest groups.

When it is necessary for planning agencies to collect primary data, they may rely upon systematic field investigation and direct observation for certain types of projects. Other projects, where public response must be solicited, may require techniques such as telephone interviews, mail questionnaires or personal interviews.
See: BUREAU OF THE CENSUS; DATA; INFORMATION SYSTEM; SURVEY RESEARCH

Data Processing

A systematic series of procedures and operations performed on data to produce a desired type of information. The term usually refers to the use of computers in conducting these operations.
See: DATA; HARDWARE; INPUT; SOFTWARE

Day-Care Center

A facility for the care of preschool children while parents are at work. They usually are maintained for three or more children.

Day-care centers are generally operated by quasi-public agencies, often with public financial assistance, but some corporations and universities now also operate their own centers. They may be housed in free-standing buildings or rented space like nursery schools, be located in a community center or public housing project, or operate in facilities provided at a parent's place of work. Their physical requirements are comparable to those of a nursery school, but their hours of operation are generally longer to span the normal workday as well as commuting hours. The provision of day-care centers is considered to be a necessary component of community facility planning and economic development, enabling parents to leave young children and work.
See: DAY HEALTH CARE FACILITIES; NURSERY SCHOOL

Day Health Care Facilities

Facilities designed to provide ambulatory services—such as physical therapy, occupational therapy, speech therapy, and nutritional and recreational services—to individuals outside of their homes, under the auspices of an agency that may be private or public. Although commonly associated with provision of services to the elderly or emotionally disturbed, facilities of this type are not restricted to specific areas of care and, for example, are in use in the treatment of alcoholism and drug addiction.

A day-care facility, along with home health care, provides an opportunity to maintain a prolonged relationship with a patient without requiring the intensive care associated with an inpatient facility or the expense associated with a residential setting in an institution. Day care is also socially and psychologically beneficial to patients in allowing them to remain in a familiar home environment. Services can be delivered in a variety of settings, including a community center, a hospital or a neighborhood storefront.
See: LONG-TERM CARE FACILITIES

Dead-End Street

A public way that has only one outlet. Dead-end streets usually exist because plans to extend them to a second outlet never materialized. This often happens when a builder has difficulty selling parcels of property along the length of the road, or when neighboring builders do not

build the extension of the road on their property. Streets are occasionally dead-ended when a new limited-access highway is built so that it bisects them. A dead-end street, unlike a cul-de-sac, generally has no turnaround area at its end.

Modern subdivision ordinances generally require that where a road is to be temporarily dead-ended a turnaround area be provided at its terminus until the next section is built. This turnaround can be removed when the road is continued. (See Fig. 43)
See: CUL-DE-SAC

Debt Limit

A legal limit on the amount of money that a municipal government may borrow, as expressed in such documents as state constitutions, state statutes or government charters. In addition to imposing a limit on the amount of borrowing, regulations are also imposed concerning how, and for what purpose, the money may be borrowed.

The most common means of limiting local borrowing is based upon the municipal property tax base and had its origins in the 1850s. A ceiling is set on the amount of tax-supported debt that may be incurred as a proportion of the assessed value of real property in the community. A frequently mentioned flaw in this system is the often arbitrary nature of the percentage as it relates to the actual needs and resources of particular municipalities. Communities may also have more or less financial capability than their total assessed value in a particular year may show.

Another type of limit that may be imposed is based upon the tax rates that may be levied to pay for debt service. The local referendum is a third way in which a ceiling may be placed upon municipal debt. Most states require that at least some types of debt be authorized by referendum, but there is a wide range of requirements among states, depending upon types of borrowing, which units of government need the funds and how much money is involved.
See: GENERAL OBLIGATION BOND; MUNICIPAL BOND; REFERENDUM; REVENUE BOND

Debt Service

Periodic payments, consisting of interest plus a portion of the principal that is owed, necessary to amortize a debt.
See: AMORTIZATION

Decentralization

1. The flow of people and activities from an urban center to outlying areas. The growth of suburbs and the decline of central cities is an example of decentralization in the United States. In Great Britain the New Towns Act of 1946 and the Town and Country Planning Act of 1947 included a specific policy of decentralization, calling for lower population densities in central cities, particularly London; development of satellite new towns; and the preservation of greenbelts.

Whether a planned policy or unplanned sprawl, decentralization represents a kind of centrifugal force spreading out of a city. Hans Blumenfeld has noted that this is somewhat reciprocal to the urbanizing centripetal flow in developing nations, where people and activities from a whole nation or a large region flow to the central city. Decentralization is a later, postindustrialization characteristic of city development.

2.   The flow of authority and activities from a central government agency out to branch locations, sometimes within the city. As an example, New York City has decentralized, to some degree, both its school administration and its planning functions, setting up outlying districts with their own administrative offices and a set of delegated responsibilities.

See: COMMUNITY CONTROL; CONCENTRATION OF ACTIVITY; NEW TOWNS ACT, 1946; SPRAWL; SUBURB; URBANIZATION

Decibel

A unit of measurement for sound pressure or the relative loudness of sound, which is abbreviated as dB.

The decibel scale is logarithmic rather than linear, because the range of sound intensities is so large that it is easier to compress the scale in order to encompass the full range of sounds. Accordingly, an increase of a few decibels can represent a large change in sound intensity. As an example, 10 decibels is 10 times as loud as 1 decibel, while 20 decibels is 100 times as loud. It is important to note that the sound levels of two sounds are not directly additive. Thus, if a sound of 70 dB is added to an existing sound of 70 dB, the total is 73 dB rather than the expected figure of 140 dB.

A human being with normal hearing can detect a change in the sound level of plus or minus 1 decibel only if he pays close attention. A quiet library would have a noise level of about 30 dB, while 70 dB is the point at which noise begins to harm hearing if it is heard for long periods of time. Painfully loud sounds, such as air raid sirens, would measure about 140 decibels.

See: A-WEIGHTED SOUND LEVEL; NOISE POLLUTION; SOUND-LEVEL METER

Deciduous Trees

Trees that drop their leaves each year at a particular time. In the temperate deciduous forest—found mainly in eastern North America, western Europe and eastern Asia—trees shed their leaves in the autumn as a protection against cold and frost. Typical trees found in this type of forest are oak, maple, chestnut, beech, ash and hickory. In the tropical deciduous forest, also known as a monsoon forest, trees such as teak drop their leaves when the long dry season arrives in order to protect themselves against an excessive moisture loss. West Africa and Malaysia have the largest areas of monsoon forest.

Deciduous trees may be used to special advantage in site planning when additional sunlight is sought in winter months but protection from the sun is desired in the summer.

See: EVERGREENS; LANDSCAPING

Decision Support Systems (DSS)

A relatively new and widely used term describing a body of computer simulation and cost-benefit analysis techniques for computer analysis of financial decision making. DSS techniques include microcomputer-based spreadsheet analysis tools in which equations containing two or more variables are used to derive matrices of numerical rows and columns. The impact of changing one or more assumptions or mathematical relationships in the calculations can quickly be shown in the cells of the matrix. Some decision support systems use computer graphics to display the results of analyses in pictorial form.

Decision theory techniques assist in answering "what if" questions for the analysis of several alternatives with varying levels of uncertainty or financial risk. Typically, DSS models are most useful in the case of semistructured decision making—when some statistics or relationships are known and are considered structured, while other variables are uncertain or unstructured. For example, municipal data, such as population or land area available for development, can be assumptions against which alternative levels and types of private and public investment are calculated. Various alternative strategies for development can then be run against the DSS model to predict resulting costs and benefits over time in terms of required public investment, tax revenue, school population, etc.

DSS is a relatively sophisticated type of analytic tool used to support modeling activities. Computerized financial techniques have evolved over time according to a classification: (1) transaction processing systems for routine data gathering and posting tasks in daily operations—e.g., property tax payment; (2) management information systems, which build on transaction data—e.g., property tax records used for land use analysis; and (3) decision support systems, which provide support to management judgment by supporting ad hoc data analysis and "what if" scenario testing.

See: COST-BENEFIT ANALYSIS; INFORMATION SYSTEM; MODEL; SIMULATION; SYSTEMS ANALYSIS

Dedication

The transfer of land or an interest in land (e.g., an easement) by its owner to public ownership, to be used for a public purpose. Dedication of property is distinguished from abandonment in that the former requires an acceptance of the property by the public.

An express dedication is one in which property is conveyed to a public authority by deed. This may be contrasted with an implied dedication, where, for example, by virtue of continuous usage, the public acquires a right-of-way or prescriptive easement through property.

The term *statutory dedication* is sometimes used to refer to the dedication of land for open space and streets, and easements for utility lines, often required by subdivision ordinances as a condition to acceptance of a subdivision plat for filing. In some cases, ordinances permit a developer to pay a fee in lieu of dedicating land in order to obtain subdivision approval.
See: ABANDONMENT; FEE IN LIEU OF DEDICATION; PRESCRIPTIVE EASEMENT; SUBDIVISION

Deed

A written instrument by which the owner of real estate (grantor) conveys his land, or an interest in his land, to another (grantee). A deed must identify the grantor and grantee, contain a legal description of the property being conveyed (either a metes and bounds description or some other acceptable substitute), identify the estate being granted (fee simple, life estate, easement, etc.) and be signed by the grantor. To effectively convey title to property, the deed must be delivered from the grantor to the grantee.

It is common for deeds to be recorded in local land records offices as a means of protecting a grantee's title against adverse claims of others. State statutes or local ordinances often specify the form of a deed and the manner of its execution (usually before a notary public) in order for it to be accepted for filing and recording.

Many different types of deeds exist. Those most commonly encountered where fee simple title to real estate is being conveyed are a warranty deed, where the grantor warrants to the grantee that he is transferring the title stated in the deed; a quitclaim deed, where the grantor warrants nothing but transfers whatever title he happens to have in the property; and a bargain and sale deed with covenants against the grantor's acts, a middle ground in which the grantor warrants merely that he has done nothing to mar the title he is conveying.
See: CONVEYANCE; COUNTY RECORDS; EASEMENT; FEE SIMPLE; RESTRICTIVE COVENANT

Deep Lot

A lot with disproportionate depth as compared to frontage. Also called a "stringbean" lot, a deep lot can present problems because its shape can make it difficult to properly lay out proposed buildings. A series of deep and narrow lots along a road can also result in an excessive number of driveways in that span of roadway, reducing safety and traffic-carrying ability.

A number of design alternatives to a series of deep lots are available and may be explored at the time of subdivision or at a later date when redevelopment is under consideration. One option is the creation of one or more culs-de-sac from which the lots may radiate, while the construction of a new public street running laterally through the property is another alternative. (See Fig. 26)
See: LOT; LOT DEPTH

Defensible Space

An architectural and site design approach to reducing crime by improving opportunities for resident supervision of space. A hierarchy of territorial spaces—public (e.g., sidewalks), semipublic (e.g., lobbies) and private (e.g., apartments)—are each made defensible from crime by

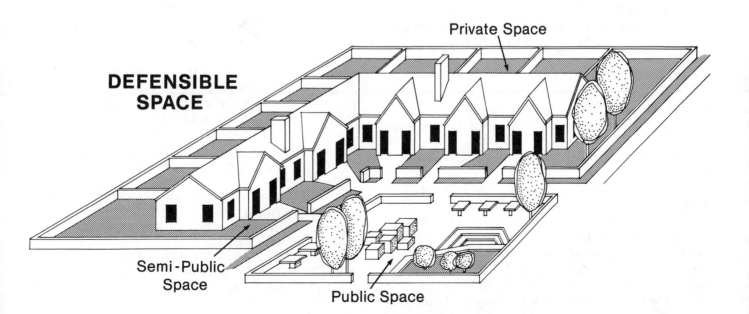

Fig. 13.   Defensible space requires a hierarchy of public to semiprivate to private spaces. Public space is provided by the play area and wide walks, semi-public by the narrow walks and common lawns in front of houses, and private space by the fenced gardens behind the houses. Public spaces are visible from the private housing units.

clear identification of appropriate use and ease of informal surveillance, thereby decreasing opportunity for criminal activities. The defensible space concepts of territoriality and ready recognition involve such design features as reducing building height, size and the number of units served by an elevator; directness and visual accessibility of entrances and corridors; and site characteristics such as visibility and fencing of yards, paths and parking areas.

Design for defensible space, suggested by architect Oscar Newman in a series of works in the 1970s, is now incorporated into many residential project plans, particularly in high-crime areas. The term has come to include the provision of hardware, lighting and electronic systems that improve security. (See Fig. 13)
See: BEHAVIORAL DESIGN; OUTDOOR LIGHTING; TERRITORIALITY

Deficit Spending

Expenditures in excess of revenues, usually by government, which are financed by borrowed funds rather than from reserves or surpluses.

Deficit spending is used by most local and state governments to enable the construction of major public works projects or for other capital spending. Growing demands for government expenditures and a shrinking tax base or a tax base that is growing at a slower rate than government spending have also encouraged deficit spending.
See: BOND; CAPITAL IMPROVEMENTS; DEBT LIMIT

Definitions

Clear descriptions of the meanings of technical words, terms or phrases, which should appear in any municipal ordinance or set of regulations. In the absence of definitions or an adequate number of definitions, the interpretation, administration and enforcement of an ordinance are open to unnecessary question. Any definition change that is made should also be considered carefully for all of its implications.
See: SUBDIVISION REGULATIONS; ZONING

Delphi Process

A qualitative survey technique, developed by the Rand Corporation in the 1950s, used to establish a consensus of expert opinion about the future that may serve as a basis for forecasting.

Delphi questionnaires are administered sequentially to several groups of experts, whose anonymous responses are processed with those within their group. The questionnaire responses are used to prepare summaries that are submitted to participants to allow them to revise their thinking. The number of groups to be used, as well as the size and composition of the group, vary from study to study. The delphi technique has been shown to be useful in a wide range of areas related to futures forecasting, such as research and development, economic and social projections, urban planning and budgeting.

Nominal group techniques (NGT) is a variation of the delphi process that does not use a questionnaire but in which all participants meet to discuss and clarify issues, evaluate alternatives and vote to establish a sequential order of preferred action. This technique is particularly useful in generating input from experts in a variety of fields and in eliciting citizen response to aid in decision making.
See: SURVEY RESEARCH

Demand-Responsive Transportation (DRT)

Public or private transport vehicles available for public hire that are not on a fixed route or schedule and are designed to meet individual needs. The two principal forms of demand-responsive service are taxicabs and dial-a-ride systems.

Taxicabs have historically been the major source of transportation for individuals wishing door-to-door service or those unable to use public transport because of physical handicaps. The high cost of taxi service puts this mode out of reach of many people in the two groups that require such service—the elderly and the handicapped. The dial-a-ride system has been implemented in some locations to service this population.

Shared-ride taxis (SRT) are being encouraged by the Urban Mass Transportation Administration (UMTA) to supplement fixed-route service. Shared-ride service has operational and cost advantages over exclusive-ride service because more people can be transported at lower cost but is prohibited by local ordinance in most cities.
See: DIAL-A-RIDE

Demography

The study of population and its characteristics, including its age structure, spatial distribution, growth patterns, social and economic characteristics, and ethnic composition. This information provides a capsule description of the community and is necessary to almost all types of planning decisions.

Among the many types of activities that require demographic information are school planning, recreational planning, economic planning and health planning. Standard sources of demographic data are the decennial census; national, state and local population surveys and estimates; vital statistics records, such as birth and death certificates; and registration figures for programs or licenses.
See: AGE STRUCTURE; BIRTHRATE; CURRENT POPULATION ESTIMATES; FERTILITY RATE; INMIGRATION; MORBIDITY RATE; MORTALITY RATE; NATURAL INCREASE; NET MIGRATION; OUT-MIGRATION; POPULATION CHARACTERISTICS; POPULATION DISTRIBUTION; POPULATION PROJECTION; POPULATION PROJECTION METHODS

Demolition

The razing of a building through public or private action. Housing units and other structures are demolished through clearance for various public works projects, for

urban development or other new construction, or because they are found to be unsafe. Demolished units represent approximately 50 percent of all housing units lost. Housing units are also removed from the housing stock through conversion to nonresidential use and through disasters such as fire and flooding.
See: CODE ENFORCEMENT; HOUSING STOCK; SUBSTANDARD HOUSING

Demolition by Neglect

The deterioration of a structure, often through deliberate neglect, to a point at which it becomes a public safety hazard and must be razed. This may occur when an owner of historic property deliberately allows a building to deteriorate to circumvent a landmark designation. Eventually, if the municipal ordinance contains no minimum maintenance standards, the historic building can become a hazard that must be demolished, leaving the landowner free to build on the property.
See: EMERGENCY REPAIR AND STABILIZATION; HISTORIC DISTRICT ORDINANCE; HISTORIC PRESERVATION; MINIMUM MAINTENANCE STANDARDS

Demonstration Cities and Metropolitan Development Act of 1966

Legislation that created the Model Cities program, which was designed to arrest blight and decay in entire neighborhoods by making a substantial impact on their physical and social problems. This act (PL 89-754) also authorized grants for development of schools, hospitals, sewers and other community facilities; expenditure of Urban Renewal and Section 701 planning assistance funds for activities related to preservation of historic structures; and Federal Housing Administration (FHA) mortgage insurance for group practice medical facilities. Experimental programs were also included in the legislation, such as mortgage insurance for new town construction and application of technological advances to housing and urban development.
See: HOUSING AND URBAN DEVELOPMENT ACT OF 1968; MODEL CITIES PROGRAM; NATIONAL HOUSING ACT; NEW COMMUNITIES ACT OF 1968

Demonstration Projects

Projects in which government or nonprofit agencies demonstrate ways in which a community may be improved and help to create a climate that will encourage private investment. Demonstration projects may range from acquisition and rehabilitation of homes in target residential areas, to illustrate how a typical home in the community might be upgraded, to testing and developing new techniques that can be applied to solve community problems.

Density

A ratio of population, residential units or floor area of development to a unit of land area, such as a square mile, hectare or acre. Density is a primary planning tool for the analysis of comparative areas and for determining desired population levels. Calculation of population density is also a necessity when planning public infrastructure, such as water supply and sewerage systems, public transportation facilities, schools and parks. Knowledge of residential or floor area density is particularly necessary for placement of fire stations.

Determination of desirable density levels is based on local public policy and varies from country to country. Zoning ordinances generally establish maximum residential densities—i.e., numbers of residences per acre—as well as maximum floor area ratios for other forms of development. In doing so they significantly affect population levels and help to determine community character.
See: FLOOR AREA RATIO (FAR); LAND-USE-INTENSITY STANDARDS (LUI); OVERCROWDING

Density Transfer

The transfer of unused development potential, either internally within a development or externally from one site to another. An example of internal density transfer is cluster development, where total average density remains unchanged but in which portions of the site are developed more intensively while other areas remain undeveloped. In transfer of development rights, unused allowable density, such as may be found on the site of a historic building, may be sold or transferred elsewhere.
See: CLUSTER DEVELOPMENT; TRANSFER OF DEVELOPMENT RIGHTS (TDR); ZONING

Department of Commerce

A cabinet-level United States department with responsibilities related to domestic and international commerce, economic growth, technological development, tourism, the oceans and the atmosphere. It functions via 12 operating agencies concerned with different matters.

Agencies of the Department of Commerce that conduct activities most pertinent to planning are the Economic Development Administration (EDA), which administers grants to municipalities for long-range economic development, and the Bureau of the Census, which produces statistical data on a wide variety of subjects. The Bureau of Economic Analysis (BEA) prepares economic analyses concerning such subjects as the gross national product that are published in its monthly publications, the *Survey of Current Business* and the *Business Conditions Digest*. The Bureau of Industrial Economics publishes reports such as the bimonthly *Construction Review,* which gives statistics on building permits and construction activity.

The National Oceanic and Atmospheric Administration (NOAA), another Commerce agency, has responsibility for exploration and mapping of the oceans of the world, management of their resources and monitoring of atmospheric conditions. As part of its functions, it administers grants for coastal zone management. Other agencies of the Department of Commerce are the International Trade Administration, the Minority Business Development

Agency, the National Bureau of Standards, the National Technical Information Service, the Patent and Trademark Office, the National Telecommunications and Information Administration, and the United States Travel and Tourism Administration.

See: BUREAU OF THE CENSUS; ECONOMIC DEVELOPMENT ADMINISTRATION (EDA); NATIONAL OCEANIC AND ATMOSPHERIC ADMINISTRATION (NOAA)

Department of Energy (DOE)

A cabinet-level department whose areas of jurisdiction include development of federal energy policy and programs, energy research, development of energy technology, and energy regulatory and conservation programs.

Through contractor operated laboratories and field installations, university contracts and other contractors, DOE conducts largely high-risk and high-payoff experimental programs in the use of fossil energy, nuclear energy, and the production of renewable energy, and studies means of improving efficiency in transportation, buildings, and communities. Administration of assistance programs for state energy planning, weatherization of housing owned by low income persons, and energy conservation implementation by public institutions are other DOE programs.

The Energy Information Administration, a subsidiary agency, collects, processes and publishes data on energy matters, such as energy production and consumption, and produces special studies, such as the impact of energy trends on regional areas. The five power administrations under DOE's jurisdiction, i.e., the Bonneville, Southeastern, Alaska, Southwestern and Western Area Power Administrations, market electric power and energy generated largely by federal hydroelectric projects.

See: CONSERVATION AND RENEWABLE ENERGY INQUIRY AND REFERRAL SERVICE; ENERGY CONSERVATION AND PRODUCTION ACT; ENERGY SECURITY ACT; NATIONAL ENERGY ACT OF 1978; NUCLEAR WASTE POLICY ACT OF 1982; SOLAR ENERGY RESEARCH INSTITUTE (SERI)

Department of Health and Human Services (HHS)

A cabinet-level United States department, formerly known as the Department of Health, Education and Welfare (HEW), that is responsible for a wide range of matters related to health and social welfare. It operates programs and provides services through its diverse agencies.

The Office of Human Development Services (HDS) administers programs for the elderly, children, Native Americans, persons with physical disabilities and those who receive public financial assistance. The Public Health Service contains the National Center for Health Statistics, the National Center for Health Services Research and the National Center for Health Care Technology, all of which collect, analyze and disseminate data and the results of research. The Public Health Service also contains six operating agencies, among which are the Alcohol, Drug Abuse

and Mental Health Administration; the Centers for Disease Control; the Food and Drug Administration; and the National Institutes of Health. The fifth Public Health Service operating agency, the Health Resources Administration, contains the Bureau of Health Facilities and the Bureau of Health Planning, both of which develop federal policy on community health care, its costs and the manner in which health care should be offered, while the Health Services Administration, the sixth agency, administers the Primary Health Care block grant and Maternal and Child Health Services block grant programs, which offer aid to states for primary health care for underserved populations.

The Health Care Financing Administration (HCFA) is responsible for the Medicare and Medicaid programs, for administration of contracts with Provider Reimbursement Review Boards and for policy related to long-term care. The Social Security Administration, the Office of Child Support Enforcement and the Office of Community Services, which is responsible for the Community Services block grant and discretionary grant programs, are also located within HHS.

See: OFFICE OF COMMUNITY SERVICES (OCS); OFFICE OF HUMAN DEVELOPMENT SERVICES (HDS)

Department of Housing and Urban Development (HUD)

A cabinet-level department that is responsible for the majority of United States housing and community development programs. Established in 1965, it is the successor agency to the Housing and Home Finance Agency.

HUD, as it is commonly known, administers the Community Development Block Grant and Urban Development Action Grant programs, the Secretary's Discretionary Fund, the Urban Homesteading program, the New Communities program (which is being phased out) and the Section 312 rehabilitation loan program. It also makes technical assistance available to localities for energy-related projects, such as weatherization, solar equipment installation, studies of renewable resources and resource recovery, and comprehensive energy use strategies.

HUD administers the Federal Housing Administration (FHA) mortgage insurance and loan programs for purchase and rehabilitation of housing and medical facilities, low-income public housing and the Section 8 programs, the Section 202 housing program for the elderly and a housing program for Native Americans. Regulatory programs, such as Interstate Land Sales Registration and Manufactured Housing Construction and Safety Standards, are other areas of concern. For purposes of increasing the money supply available for housing, the Government National Mortgage Association (GNMA) is under the authority of HUD, and the Federal National Mortgage Association (FNMA) is regulated by this department.

HUD is also responsible for formulating policy in the areas of housing and community development and advising the president on these matters. The secretary of HUD serves as chairperson of the boards of directors of the New Community Development Corporation and the Solar Energy and Energy Conservation Bank and is a member of the board of the Neighborhood Reinvestment Corporation. Ten regional HUD offices are responsible for program administration, while several area and service offices manage details within each region.

See: AFFIRMATIVE FAIR HOUSING MARKETING; COMMUNITY DEVELOPMENT BLOCK GRANT (CDBG); FEDERAL HOUSING ADMINISTRATION (FHA) MORTGAGE INSURANCE; FEDERAL NATIONAL MORTGAGE ASSOCIATION (FNMA); GOVERNMENT NATIONAL MORTGAGE ASSOCIATION (GNMA); HOUSING COUNSELING; HOUSING PROGRAMS FOR NATIVE AMERICANS; INDEPENDENT LIVING FOR THE DISABLED; PUBLIC HOUSING; SECRETARY'S DISCRETIONARY FUND; SECTION 8 HOUSING PROGRAM; SECTION 202 HOUSING PROGRAM; SECTION 312 HOUSING PROGRAM; URBAN DEVELOPMENT ACTION GRANT (UDAG); URBAN GROWTH AND NEW COMMUNITY DEVELOPMENT ACT OF 1970; URBAN HOMESTEADING

Department of the Interior

A cabinet-level United States department responsible for diverse programs, largely related to protection and management of natural resources and public land. Through eight bureaus, the Department of the Interior is involved in activities as varied as programs for Native Americans, mining and topographic mapping.

The United States Fish and Wildlife Service, one of the bureaus, manages wildlife refuges, undertakes biological monitoring, studies and preserves habitats, undertakes animal damage control projects and maintains programs related to endangered species, among other activities. The National Park Service manages the National Park System and programs of grants to states and municipalities for local park planning and development. Another agency, the Bureau of Land Management, manages federal lands other than the national parks, and lands on which the government owns mineral rights.

The Bureau of Reclamation is a water resource development agency that operates in the 17 contiguous western states, while the Geological Survey is the major surveyor and mapping agency of the United States. Mining activities and studies are managed by two agencies, the Bureau of Mines and the Office of Surface Mining Reclamation and Enforcement. The Bureau of Mines is largely a research agency, concerned with such matters as mining technology, mineral resource development, resource availability and the use of low-grade ore as an alternative to importing other minerals. The Office of Surface Mining Reclamation and Enforcement oversees state programs designed to reclaim land used for the surface mining of coal, to reclaim abandoned mines and to designate lands determined to be environmentally unsuitable for mining. In states not wishing to assume primary responsibility for

these activities, the federal office oversees regulatory and reclamation activities.

The Bureau of Indian Affairs, the oldest agency within the department, provides educational and social services programs as well as those connected with the management of lands and resources. In addition, this bureau undertakes programs in economic and community development for Indian and Alaska Native people.

See: BUREAU OF LAND MANAGEMENT (BLM); BUREAU OF RECLAMATION; GEOLOGICAL SURVEY (USGS); NATIONAL PARK SERVICE; SURFACE MINING CONTROL AND RECLAMATION ACT OF 1977

Department of Labor

A cabinet-level United States department with responsibility for administering federal labor laws and programs related to employment, unemployment, collective bargaining, job training, working conditions and wages. The department is composed of seven operating agencies, of which two, the Employment and Training Administration and the Bureau of Labor Statistics, are most pertinent to planning.

See: BUREAU OF LABOR STATISTICS (BLS); EMPLOYMENT AND TRAINING ADMINISTRATION (ETA)

Department of Transportation (DOT)

A cabinet-level department that establishes transportation policy for all modes of transportation and, through its eight operating administrations, conducts research and grant programs and operates transportation safety activities.

The Federal Highway Administration (FHWA) has jurisdiction over highway planning, construction and rehabilitation for which federal funds are used, including development of bikeways and fringe parking facilities, while the National Highway Traffic Safety Administration carries out programs related to motor vehicle safety and administers grants to states for driver, pedestrian and motor vehicle safety programs. The Federal Railroad Administration (FRA) conducts research and develops policy with respect to intercity rail transportation. The Urban Mass Transportation Administration (UMTA) conducts assistance programs that aid urban public transportation, including buses, trolleys, rapid transit systems and paratransit programs.

The Federal Aviation Administration (FAA) regulates air commerce and safety, operates air traffic control towers and funds airport development. The United States Coast Guard, a division of DOT that is also a branch of the United States Navy, enforces the law as it relates to maritime activities and provides services such as maintenance of navigational aids, administration of matters relating to bridges that cross navigable waters, and construction and operation of deep-water ports on the high seas where oil is transferred from tankers. It also has responsibilities related to protection of the quality of the marine environment, particularly concerning discharge of pollutants. Two other divisions with responsibility involving shipping are the Maritime Administration, which has programs related to the merchant marine and development of ports and domestic shipping, and the Saint Lawrence Seaway Development Corporation, with jurisdiction over the seaway from Montreal to Lake Erie within United States territorial boundaries. As part of its activities, the Seaway Development Corporation is involved in the comprehensive economic and environmental development of the region. Regulations regarding transportation of hazardous materials and pipeline safety, as well as analysis of multimodal transportation systems and transportation data collection and dissemination are conducted by the Research and Special Programs Administration.

See: FEDERAL AVIATION ADMINISTRATION (FAA); FEDERAL HIGHWAY ADMINISTRATION (FHWA); FEDERAL RAILROAD ADMINISTRATION (FRA); URBAN MASS TRANSPORTATION ADMINISTRATION (UMTA)

Depreciation

1.   For income tax purposes depreciation is the writing off of the cost of a depreciable asset over a period of time. It allows the owner of an asset to recover its cost, as an expense, over a period of years roughly equivalent to its useful life. Depreciation deductions are permissible even if the value of the asset or property increases.

2.   For real estate appraisal purposes, depreciation is a loss in the value of real property due to any one of a number of causes.

3.   For accounting purposes it is a charge against current income to reflect the fact that the property's useful life is being exhausted over time.

See: ACCELERATED DEPRECIATION; ECONOMIC OBSOLESCENCE; FUNCTIONAL OBSOLESCENCE; PHYSICAL DETERIORATION; STRAIGHT-LINE DEPRECIATION

Depressed Area

An area, also called an economically depressed area, that exhibits physical and economic deterioriation, a stagnating or declining tax base, and a high rate of unemployment. Ranging in size from a neighborhood to a region, it may also be experiencing a high rate of out-migration, housing deterioriation or building abandonment. Community development programs begun in the 1970s—such as the Community Development Block Grant, the Urban Development Action Grant and the Urban Parks and Recreation Recovery Program—were specifically directed at depressed areas.

See: BLIGHTED AREA; SLUM

Depressed Roadway

A highway built at a grade lower than surrounding streets and land use, for purposes of grade separation and noise control in urban areas. A depressed roadway separates traffic by permitting local traffic and pedestrians to move at grade over the depressed road via bridges. Noise and fumes from the depressed road are contained to some extent within its walls. Where frontage or service roads are supplied, trees can be planted to detract from the visual cut in the environment. In certain circumstances, a depressed road can be tunneled under existing streets, essentially permitting the use of one right-of-way for two streets.

Depressed roads also provide an opportunity for construction of municipal facilities, such as parks and parking lots, or commercial development on the roadway's air rights, maximizing use of scarce urban land.

See: AIR RIGHTS; GRADE SEPARATION; JOINT DEVELOPMENT

Desalination

The process by which dissolved salts are removed from seawater or brackish water (water containing at least 1,000 parts dissolved minerals to 1,000,000 parts of water) to make this water usable for human and animal consumption, industrial uses or irrigation. This technique can provide a valuable additional source of potable water to help meet increasing water consumption needs and to supplement conventional sources that are being depleted or polluted. Desalination is particularly applicable in rapidly growing areas with limited fresh water supplies but with proximity to salt water. To determine feasibility for this purpose, an analysis of the cost of a desalination project must be made and compared to the cost of piping fresh water to a particular area.

The concept of desalination has been understood for many years; a patent for a process was granted as early as 1869 in England. Today desalination projects are in operation or under construction in such diverse locations as Roswell, New Mexico; Aruba; the Soviet Union; Israel; Italy; and Spain.

Various procedures are available for reclaiming salt water, including distillation, vertical tube evaporation, vapor compression, solar distillation, freezing methods, electrodialysis, solvent extraction and reverse osmosis. No process works best in all applications; a method must be chosen to meet the particular requirements of the situation. Factors that must be evaluated in system selection include the water source to be used and the quality of the desired final product, cost and plant capacity.

Vapor compression plants, for example, are most commonly used when small, portable plants are required. Large plants are usually of the flash distillation or vertical tube evaporation type. The lowest costs are obtained in combination plants where distillation and power generation are merged, often found where desalination is conducted for industrial use. Electrodialysis and freezing methods have not proved cost-effective thus far, but solar distillation works well for small plants located in remote areas.

See: WATER SUPPLY SYSTEM

Descriptive Statistics

Statistical methods by which masses of data may be summarized and condensed so that they become more meaningful. The data may then be presented in tabular or graphic form. Common descriptive statistics techniques are frequency distributions, measures of central tendency, measures of dispersion and correlation coefficients.
See: CORRELATION; FREQUENCY DISTRIBUTION; INFERENTIAL STATISTICS; MEASURES OF CENTRAL TENDENCY; MEASURES OF DISPERSION

Desert

Arid areas characterized by scant rainfall, sparse vegetation and few human settlements. Three types of desert are often recognized: the hot, or tropical desert; the polar, or cold, desert; and the edaphic, or midlatitude, desert.

The hot desert, the type most often thought of in connection with the term, has very low levels of precipitation; the Sahara, Kalahari, Australian and Sonoran deserts are examples of this category. The edaphic, or midlatitude, desert receives more rainfall than the hot deserts, but because of the physical makeup of its surface materials, remains unable to support much vegetation. Examples of this type are the Gobi, portions of the Great Basin and Colorado Plateau areas of the United States, and parts of Iceland. The polar, or cold, deserts may be found bordering the Arctic Ocean in Europe, Asia and North America. They share with the other desert types an inability to support substantial vegetation; they also have little available atmospheric water vapor because of the low temperature.

Deserts or areas considered likely to become deserts occupy approximately 9 million square miles (23.3 million square kilometers) of the Earth's surface. A serious problem, with major implications for the long-term world food supply, is the continuing desertification (conversion to desert) of additional dry land area through overgrazing, extensive deforestation and improper agricultural or irrigation practices.
See: LAND MANAGEMENT

Design Competition

A contest, generally sponsored by a governmental agency, in which architects and/or planners compete for the award to design a specified government structure, complex, park or other public facility. Used as a means by which government agencies can obtain the best possible design for a facility, the competition enables talented but unknown professionals to compete with larger, more established firms. The American Institute of Architects and local chapters of other professional organizations publish guidelines for running and participating in design competitions.

Design Continuity

A principle of design wherein one or more elements within the natural or man-made environment provide a unifying or connecting force for a particular setting. In urban areas continuity may be provided by an element such as a road system, while in rural areas the quality may be present as a sequence of open spaces or in the form of a common natural element such as a river, ridge or type of vegetation.

As a principle of architectural design, continuity is frequently achieved through repetition of structural elements that, in the case of a row of townhouses or storefronts, may impart a visual sense of movement or flow along a streetscape. Within the larger context of urban design, similar scale or relationships among building styles may provide a thread of continuity, while in a suburban landscape this quality may exist in the form of rows of housing and street trees.

As a design principle, continuity is considered desirable as a means of linking components of the built environment, thereby establishing a sense of order and organization to what otherwise can be perceived as disjointed and haphazard development.
See: ARCHITECTURAL REVIEW BOARD; DESIGN STANDARDS; SCALE OF DEVELOPMENT; STREETSCAPE; URBAN DESIGN

Design Fit

An urban design concept that refers to the need to maintain a balance between new development and the existing natural or man-made environment.

As a guideline for development in the built environment, it can help to establish a degree of harmony and consistency in scale, quality or character between new and existing development. This can be especially critical where the potential for architectural incompatibility is high, as in the case of a new building in a historic district or a multifamily complex in a single-family residential area.

As a design parameter for development of areas that have previously remained undeveloped, it can preserve natural resources or ensure a maximum degree of compatibility between the natural and built environment. A good example of this type of design fit can be found in many recent planned unit development complexes where careful selection of materials and the scale of structures are combined with proper siting and landscaping.
See: COMMUNITY CHARACTER; DESIGN REVIEW; DESIGN STANDARDS; SCALE OF DEVELOPMENT

Design Hour Volume (DHV)

The number of vehicles expected to use a roadway in a peak hour in both directions and in all lanes. It is sometimes expressed as a percentage of average daily traffic (ADT).

Roadway design is based on estimates of the amounts of traffic expected for its various links (sections between interchanges or intersections) at a future date. The design is usually based on selection of a volume below the expected absolute peak volume. Use of the 30th highest hour occur-

ring in one year has been shown to have a nearly optimal ratio of benefit to expenditure and is therefore used most often, but this is not a rule or requirement. Design hour volume (DHV), then, is the estimated 30th highest (or other) hour of the design year—the year, perhaps 10 to 20 years in the future, in which the road is expected to be serving all the traffic that it would be built to serve.
See: GEOMETRIC DESIGN

Design Population

The number of persons that a proposed project, such as a sewage treatment plant, is designed to serve.

Design Review

The mandatory submission of a site or building design for review by a design review body constituted to comment or make recommendations on the design or to grant approval. Design review is intended to protect areas from new construction, building alterations or site design that could be incompatible with or adversely affect the quality of an area. Entire municipalities may be subject to design review for certain types of development, or review requirements may apply only to specified areas, such as historic districts. Large private developments, such as new towns, may also impose their own design standards.
See: ARCHITECTURAL REVIEW BOARD; DESIGN STANDARDS; HISTORIC REVIEW BOARD; SITE PLAN REVIEW

Design Standards

A set of guidelines defining parameters to be followed in the design of a building or development. Generally, standards consist of a range of options that may be selected in the use of certain materials, choice of colors or placement of appurtenant structures. They are intended to serve as a means of obtaining or maintaining a particular style or character of architecture and are often adopted as a means of enforcing design conformance.

Examples of successful use of such standards are prevalent among residential developments in "new towns" constructed during the 1960s and 1970s in the United States and Britain, where they were used to encourage a degree of architectural uniformity. Although the imposition of standards has been criticized as an infringement upon an owner's traditional ability to personalize a dwelling, standards are generally recognized as a means of enhancing the overall visual and aesthetic quality of an environment because of the design compatibility they help to achieve.

Other areas where design standards have been used include downtown redevelopment plans, historic districts and office parks. In each case, standards relating to such areas as facade treatment, use of graphics or landscaping allow for a degree of design continuity that contributes to architectural quality and very often to commercial viability and an increase in real estate values.
See: ARCHITECTURAL REVIEW BOARD; COLOR; DESIGN CONTINUITY

Desire Line

A technique used in transportation planning to visually portray the volume of persons wishing to travel between two points within a given area, regardless of the mode of transportation they wish to use. A desire line diagram or map will have straight lines of various widths representing the expected traffic volumes between all points studied or between all points that show travel demand in excess of a minimum number of trips per day. Desire lines may be superimposed on a map of the municipality, or they may be charted in a grid pattern. (See Fig. 29)
See: MODAL SPLIT; NETWORK ASSIGNMENT; ORIGIN-DESTINATION (O-D) STUDY

Detached Housing

Housing that does not share a common wall, roof, floor or any other structural component with another dwelling unit.
See: ATTACHED HOUSING; HOUSING TYPE; SINGLE-FAMILY HOUSING

Detached Solar Collector

A solar energy collector that is not attached to the building or buildings for which it is providing energy. Detached collectors are used when it is not feasible or desirable to mount solar collectors on a building's rooftop or on its south wall. This may occur because there is insufficient room on the roof for the necessary number of collectors, because the collectors would be too visually prominent, where vegetation that is shading the collector area must be preserved or where existing development has been laid out in such a way as to significantly hinder solar access.

Detached collectors may be located on an adjoining structure or on the ground (either on the same lot or in an open common area). Collectors mounted on the ground must, like rooftop collectors, be properly oriented south and at an appropriate angle for absorbing sunlight.
See: ENERGY SHARING; SOLAR ACCESS; SOLAR COLLECTOR; SOLAR ENERGY

Detention Basin

A pond or reservoir designed to hold storm water during the period of onset of a storm and up to 24 hours after a storm in order to prevent flooding. Detention basins serve to reduce peak discharge levels to roughly those levels that existed before development occurred by releasing water slowly.

Detention basins—which may be created in natural water bodies, in natural depressions or through excavation and the construction of dikes—typically range in size from about 0.1 acre (0.04 hectare) to 20 acres (8 hectares). It can often cost less to construct such basins than to enlarge storm sewers or take other flood prevention measures. Detention basins frequently serve a dual function in developments and are used as open space suitable for recreation during dry periods.
See: FLOOD CONTROL; RETENTION BASIN; RUNOFF; STORM DRAINAGE SYSTEM

Development

1. A planning or construction project involving substantial property improvement and, usually, change of land use character within the site, such as low-density to high-density or residential to commercial.

2. The act of using land for building or extractive purposes. Land development is undertaken to erect buildings or structures; to provide recreational facilities, agricultural irrigation and public utilities; and to provide access to natural resources. Numerous regulations at all government levels control the manner in which development may take place, as well as whether it shall be permitted.

See: ARCHITECTURAL CONTROLS; DESIGN REVIEW; ENVIRONMENTAL IMPACT STATEMENT (EIS); SIGN REGULATION; SUBDIVISION REGULATIONS; ZONING

Development Focus

A design term referring to the establishment of a central point or area that provides a sense of organization and a means of orientation within a physical setting. As an element of urban design, the focus is viewed as a means of developing an image or identity for a locale. Although usually a space or architectural landmark, a development focus may also be a natural feature or landform, such as a hill, that physically and visually lends a sense of organization to a place.

In town planning, a development focus has historically been a center of activity, such as a town square or, in earlier times, a piazza or forum. In the context of neighborhood planning, a development focus might be a community center or school or, on a larger scale, a downtown area.

See: NEIGHBORHOOD IDENTITY; SENSE OF PLACE

Development Ordinance

A unified and integrated code that contains all provisions related to the development of land normally found independently in zoning and subdivision regulations. One advantage of a development ordinance is that it can simplify and combine procedural and hearing requirements that formerly appeared in a variety of municipal documents, making it simpler for developers and members of the public to understand what requirements they must meet.

Recommended in the American Law Institute's *A Model Land Development Code,* development ordinances are gradually becoming more common. This is particularly true in California, where communities may also include the municipal comprehensive plan in the document as evidence of compliance with state of California requirements for comprehensive planning.

See: AMERICAN LAW INSTITUTE MODEL LAND DEVELOPMENT CODE; COMPREHENSIVE PLAN; SUBDIVISION REGULATIONS; ZONING; ZONING ORDINANCE

Development Rights

The rights to develop property, which the owner of the fee simple interest in real estate may transfer to another. Development rights may be transferred either in the form of an easement or a ground lease (a lease of undeveloped land, with development rights), with the landowner in either case retaining title to the remaining interests in the land.

In some cases, development rights are acquired by a municipality in order to preserve open space, as a somewhat less expensive alternative to acquisition of a fee simple interest.

See: FEE SIMPLE; SCENIC EASEMENT; TRANSFER OF DEVELOPMENT RIGHTS (TDR)

Dewatered Sludge

Sewage sludge that has been treated to decrease its liquid content to enable handling and processing as a semisolid rather than as a liquid. This is necessary to produce a consistency that is amenable to incineration and that will serve other purposes, such as use for fertilizer.

Vacuum filtration, drying beds or lagoons, centrifugation and pressure filtration (used extensively in England and other European countries) can yield a solids content of 20 percent to 45 percent. Heat-drying is capable of increasing the proportion of solids to 90 percent but can create problems in the collection of fly ash and in odor control.

See: LAGOON; SLUDGE; SLUDGE DISPOSAL; SLUDGE INCINERATION; ZIMMERMAN PROCESS (ZIMPRO)

Dial-A-Ride

A form of demand-responsive transportation that provides door-to-door service on the basis of telephone requests. Vehicles that seat from 5 to 15 people are used to transport passengers from their homes to specific destinations or to central locations—e.g., shopping center, transit terminal. Routing is arranged by a central dispatcher to combine as many passenger trips as possible.

Dial-a-ride systems have been successfully employed in low-density areas, where fixed-route bus service is not economical. They are also provided by communities and medical centers to furnish transportation for the elderly and handicapped on a scheduled and/or demand basis. In current practice, service areas vary in extent up to about 10 square miles (approximately 26 square kilometers) and provide service to populations from 10,000 to 45,000 in size. Fleet size varies from 1 to 20 vehicles. Passenger costs are higher than for fixed-route bus service but lower than for taxi service.

See: DEMAND RESPONSIVE TRANSPORTATION (DRT)

Diamond Interchange

A four-legged, grade-separated interchange with a single one-way ramp in each quadrant. Particularly suited to interchanges of a major and minor road, it requires that left turns to and from the minor road be made on the

minor road. Diamond interchanges always have traffic signals in urban areas and usually have other forms of traffic controls elsewhere. (See Fig. 18)
See: GRADE-SEPARATED INTERCHANGE

Diazo Reproduction

A reproduction process in which positive prints can be made directly from positive originals or intermediates. The diazo process may be used on a number of materials—such as translucent paper, film or opaque stock—but the originals must be transparent or translucent. It provides an inexpensive and fast means of obtaining same-size duplications of plans and drawings.

Diazo reproduction works because of the interaction of diazo compounds with light; prints may be made through dry development, semiwet development or pressure development. Blackline prints are most common, but diazo reproductions are also possible in blue, red, brown, yellow, green and violet. An Ozalid print is a trade name for the dry-development diazo process in which diazo-sensitized printing paper is exposed and then developed with ammonia fumes.
See: GRAPHIC REPRODUCTION PROCESSES

Digital Cartography

The process by which computers are used to collect, store, analyze, manipulate and display spatial data.

The U.S. Geological Survey operates a program in which certain data derived from various USGS map series are gradually being digitized and made part of a national data base. As an example, digital tapes of terrain elevations are available that may be used to graphically display slopes, and land use and land cover maps are also in the process of being digitized.
See: COMPUTER GRAPHICS

Dike

1. An embankment, consisting of earth or other materials, designed to separate water bodies from land or to protect land from flooding during high-water periods. Dikes are used extensively in the Netherlands to protect reclaimed land from inundation by the sea.
2. A structure intended to rechannel river movements. By deflecting currents and trapping sand, dikes are able to realign and deepen water channels and to reduce erosion. They are often constructed of timber piles, rock or rubble, or steel frame.
See: BANK PROTECTION; DAM; FLOOD CONTROL; FLOODWALL; LAND RECLAMATION; RIVER ENGINEERING

Direct and Indirect Benefits

Benefits gained as a result of undertaking a new program or project. Direct benefits are those the program or project was designed to achieve, while indirect benefits are other beneficial effects resulting from the program that

would not of themselves have been reasons for undertaking the program.

The term *negative benefits,* sometimes used in a cost benefit analysis, refers to the negative aspects of a proposed program. These are essentially indirect costs that have been moved to the benefit column.
See: COST-BENEFIT ANALYSIS; DIRECT AND INDIRECT COSTS

Direct and Indirect Costs

Direct costs are those funds that must be expended to enable a project to be undertaken, including all costs of development, planning, demolition and relocation, if necessary.

Indirect costs are undesirable results, anticipated or unanticipated, of undertaking a new program or project. They may comprise cost savings generated by other programs that must be eliminated in order to permit this project to be undertaken or cost increases related directly to the project, although these costs may not be borne by those responsible for the project. As an example, in evaluating sites for urban redevelopment, the inconvenience and discomfort caused to businesses and residents that must be relocated, and the likelihood that they will leave the community, can be considered to be indirect costs. In a cost benefit analysis, indirect costs might be classified as "negative benefits" in order to directly relate cost to project development.
See: COST-BENEFIT ANALYSIS; COST-EFFECTIVENESS ANALYSIS; DIRECT AND INDIRECT BENEFITS; EXTERNALITIES

Directional Growth

Municipal or regional growth in one or more directions rather than evenly in all directions. Directional growth usually occurs because of topographic constraints, such as steep terrain, that limit growth in certain directions and/or because of municipal facilities, such as sewer lines, that encourage growth in particular areas. (See Fig. 24)
See: AXIAL GROWTH; FINGER PATTERN; SECTOR THEORY

Directional Interchange

A grade-separated interchange between two major roads that provides for left-turn exits with ramps that follow the natural direction of traffic movement. This is in contrast to a cloverleaf pattern, which requires a left-turning vehicle to make a loop to the right before actually moving in the desired direction. Directional interchanges also eliminate the weaving of entering and exiting vehicles common to cloverleaf design. They frequently require bridge structures of two or more levels, as well as more ramps than other forms of interchanges, making them extremely costly. (See Fig. 18)
See: CLOVERLEAF INTERCHANGE; GRADE-SEPARATED INTERCHANGE

Disaster Housing

Financial assistance for housing of persons who have experienced a disaster—such as a flood, tornado, earthquake or riot—of sufficient magnitude to be declared a federal disaster area by the president under the Disaster Relief Act of 1974.

Department of Housing and Urban Development (HUD) disaster assistance for housing consists of the direct channeling of funds from its many programs. In addition, a special program, Section 203 (h) of the National Housing Act as added by Section 110 of the Housing Act of 1954, provides Federal Housing Administration (FHA) insurance of up to 100 percent on mortgages for inexpensive new homes to persons whose homes were damaged too extensively for reconstruction. In rural areas the Farmers Home Administration can also make special very low interest disaster loans available under the FmHA Section 502 program.

The Disaster Relief Act also provides that temporary emergency housing may be furnished at no cost to victims. Administered by HUD, such housing has included mobile homes made available through the Title I program, placement of displaced families in existing vacant housing, and temporary mortgage and rent payments to persons experiencing financial hardship resulting from the disaster.

See: DISASTER RELIEF ACTS OF 1970 AND 1974; FLOOD DISASTER PROTECTION ACT OF 1973; SECTION 502 FmHA HOUSING PROGRAM

Disaster Preparedness Improvement Grants

A program of grants to states for improvement, maintenance and updating of state disaster-assistance plans. Disaster-assistance plans were prepared by all states and territories, except the Canal Zone, under a program of plan development authorized by the Disaster Relief Act of 1974. The current program, administered by the Federal Emergency Management Agency (FEMA), encourages annual updating of plans.

Grants of up to 50 percent of the cost of program updating, not to exceed $25,000 in one year, are available for a wide variety of planning activities necessary for plan preparation. Examples of subjects that may be studied with these grants include planning for disaster response, long-range recovery, and disaster mitigation and hazard reduction; vulnerability analysis; revision of state legislation or other authority relevant to disaster preparedness and assistance; design of disaster-related emergency systems; and public information and education programs.

See: DISASTER RELIEF ACTS OF 1970 AND 1974; EARTHQUAKE AND HURRICANE PREPAREDNESS PLANS; FEDERAL EMERGENCY MANAGEMENT AGENCY (FEMA)

Disaster Relief Acts of 1970 and 1974

Two acts intended to coordinate the federal response to natural disasters such as floods, earthquakes or tornadoes. Although not specifically authorized by the acts, applications for funding in response to major accidents, such as oil spills and pollution by toxic substances, have also been approved.

The 1970 act (PL 91-606) includes guidelines for providing temporary housing, authorizes grants to repair public buildings and makes business and farm loans available. It also authorized one-time grants to states of up to $250,000 and annual grants of up to $25,000, both on a 50 percent matching basis, for development and updating of comprehensive plans for disaster mitigation, assistance and relief, and long-range recovery and reconstruction. Other provisions include extension of unemployment insurance from 26 weeks to one year for those employed in the disaster area and grants to municipalities that have suffered substantial tax losses as a result of a disaster.

The 1974 act (PL 93-288) reauthorized the planning grant program, now called the Disaster Preparedness Assistance Program, as well as grants for public building repair. Economic recovery for disaster areas was initiated by the 1974 act via Recovery Planning Councils designated by state governors for affected areas. These councils prepare recovery investment plans for the following five-year period and make recommendations on proposed federal-aid projects and programs. The councils, which are authorized to receive federal funds for the implementation of a recovery investment plan, may use the funds for purposes of granting loans to state and local governments or to private or public nonprofit organizations. The funds may be spent for the acquisition or development of land for public works projects, public services or public facilities, including parks and open space. Supplementary grants to bring the federal share of costs to a maximum of 90 percent are also authorized by this act, and private loans, such as for building repair, are guaranteed to 90 percent of their value.

See: DISASTER HOUSING; DISASTER PREPAREDNESS IMPROVEMENT GRANTS

Disney World

A vast amusement park complex located in Orlando, Florida that opened in 1971 and spans 27,400 acres (11,088 hectares). Disney World, which accommodates approximately 10 million visitors a year, has a number of facilities that are of special interest to planners.

A monorail circles Disney World and connects the parking area, hotels and entertainment complexes, thus helping to minimize automobile traffic. The monorail system, which carries almost 10,000 passengers per hour, uses both local and express trains and contains front and rear guidance systems that allow them to move in either direction. The first daily operating monorail system in North America was introduced at Disneyland (Disney World's California counterpart) in 1959 but was of a smaller scale.

A waste disposal system was also introduced at Disney World that allows refuse to be disposed of without requiring truck pickup in or near guest areas. Known as AVAC (Automated Vacuum-Activating Collection), it involves a 6,000-foot (1,830-meter) underground network of 20-inch (50.8-centimeter) piping and 15 AVAC stations at appropriately selected locations. Designed in Sweden, AVAC transports refuse by a high-velocity airstream to a building where it is compacted and baled for final disposal. When completed in 1970, it was the first system of its type in the United States and the largest in the world.

Other aspects of Disney World incorporate the most modern technology. Examples are the telephone system, the first in the United States to use completely electronic equipment, and the use of water hyacinths for purification of wastewater at its treatment facility. In addition, Disney World contains an extensive water-control system consisting of networks of levees, canals and dams, intended to be able to accommodate the most severe storms. Still another feature is a system that recycles waste heat and uses it for space heating, hot water and air conditioning.

In October 1982 the Epcot Center, an acronym for Experimental Prototype Community of Tomorrow, opened at Disney World. Intended to depict aspects of future life, Epcot features such innovations as what is thought to be the world's largest privately built solar energy collector.
See: AMUSEMENT FACILITY; PLANNED COMMUNITY

Dispersion Pattern

A pattern of land use development in which the population is scattered, at regular or irregular intervals, throughout the land. The dispersion pattern is the common form of development in rural and most suburban development. It was recommended by Frank Lloyd Wright in his Broadacre City plan in the 1930s, in which an even dispersal (he called it decentralization) of population on 1-acre (0.4-hectare) lots was proposed.

More recently the concept of dispersal has been extended to suggest that rather than focus resources on economic revitalization of inner cities, it might be more economical to encourage dispersion of persons to suburbs, where newer infrastructure and jobs are located, or even to the growing sunbelt. A relevant issue to all dispersion concepts is the cost of constructing necessary public facilities, such as water supply and sewer systems. (See Fig. 24)
See: DECENTRALIZATION; LAND USE PATTERN; SPRAWL; SUBURBAN DEVELOPMENT

Distressed Property

1. Existing property for which fixed costs—such as debt service, property tax and operating expenses—almost equal or exceed the income to the owner. In an apartment building such cash flow problems often exist due to a high vacancy rate or an inability to raise rents because of rent control regulations, resulting in poor building maintenance, lowered services and a decline in the reputation of a building. These problems are considered to be prime indicators of a distressed property.

In a distress situation, owners are generally unable to improve their cash flow position without a substantial capital investment in the property. As a result of sustaining a limited return or loss over an extended period, an owner may be forced to sell the property.

2. New construction where cost overruns prevent completion.

3. Property that must be sold due to imminent foreclosure or to administer an insolvent estate.
See: DEPRESSED AREA; NEIGHBORHOOD PRESERVATION

Domestic Sewage

All the wastewater produced by homes and businesses in a municipality, including sewage that is produced by factories but is not of manufacturing origin but excluding all industrial sewage. Domestic sewage is a combination of water and waterborne contaminants that are either suspended, dissolved or colloidal (0.1 to 1 micron in size). It usually contains bacteria and viruses that may sometimes be pathogenic.

The composition and quantity of domestic sewage varies from location to location and by time of day and season, but it is usually proportional to water consumption. Water conservation and water metering will yield fewer gallons of wastewater per capita per day. Introduction of new domestic or business equipment, such as the use of food waste disposal systems, will also alter the amount of sewage produced.
See: BIOCHEMICAL OXYGEN DEMAND (BOD); DOMESTIC WASTE; INDUSTRIAL SEWAGE; WASTEWATER

Domestic Waste

The solid waste that is generated by residential use.
See: SOLID WASTE

Downtown Revitalization

The physical and economic renewal of the central business district (CBD) of a community. Downtown revitalization is often stimulated by a variety of government investment programs and incentives aimed at halting central city decline, but it may be initiated by the private sector when economic forces make it advantageous to invest in the downtown.

Many downtown revitalization projects fall into one of two types. In the first type, amenities—such as pedestrian malls, off-street parking and street beautification—are used to improve the physical and aesthetic environment and to spark investment. In conjunction with these amenities, the local government often provides incentives to encourage the development of underutilized or vacant land within or adjacent to the CBD.

In the second type of project, major clearance of an area within the CBD takes place, followed by reconstruction of land uses thought unlikely to compete with those established uses in the other portions of the CBD but likely instead to attract new business. Typically, office space is the major use in these projects, while hotel and convention centers are often found as well. A wide variety of other land uses may be represented in downtown revitalization projects of this sort, however, including high-rise housing, cultural facilities and public buildings.

Many more specialized downtown revitalization strategies have been used successfully. As an example, the historic resources of a downtown area may be emphasized and rehabilitated, when necessary, to provide an attractive downtown that stresses the heritage of that city. This technique has been used successfully in such cities as Denver (Larimer Square), Boston (Faneuil Hall Marketplace) and Seattle (Pioneer Square). The development of mixed-use projects, such as Atlanta's Peachtree Center, has also been used successfully in downtown renewal.

See: CENTRAL BUSINESS DISTRICT (CBD); ECONOMIC DEVELOPMENT; ECONOMIC DEVELOPMENT INCENTIVES; HISTORIC PRESERVATION; MIXED-USE DEVELOPMENT (MXD); PEDESTRIAN IMPROVEMENTS; STREET BEAUTIFICATION; URBAN CULTURAL PARK; URBAN ENTERPRISE ZONES

Downzoning

1. A zoning classification change for a parcel of land to a category that permits less intensive development. Examples of downzoning are a change from multifamily to single-family residential use or a change from industrial to residential use.

2. A zoning classification change for a parcel of land to a zoning category permitting more intensive development. Although not the accepted meaning of the term as evolved from usage by the courts and professional planners, it is nevertheless often used by the general public and the news media.

See: HIGHEST AND BEST USE; UPZONING; ZONING

Drainage Basin

The land area within which it is theoretically possible to place a drop of water and observe it take a continuously downhill surface route to an established outlet. Drainage basins are divided by ridges; water that lands at the top of the ridge will have an equally likely chance of flowing into one of two drainage basins. The bottom of the basin is formed by outlets—such as streams, rivers or valleys—that are capable of holding the accumulated runoff as it flows toward larger water bodies.

Drainage basins are used as the basis for planning sewerage systems and watershed areas and for studying the potential effects of development-generated runoff to mitigate against flooding in lowland areas.

See: CATCHMENT BASIN; RIVER BASIN; RUNOFF; SEWERAGE SYSTEM; WATERSHED

Dredging

The process of conducting marine excavation with the use of a machine known as a dredge. Most commonly, dredging is performed for one of the following reasons: to construct, deepen or maintain navigation channels, canals, harbors and marinas; to mine underwater resources, rang-

ing from sand, gravel and shell to coral, sponges, platinum or gold; to obtain fill for land reclamation and other projects; to lay pipeline for oil; or to build dams and dikes. Dredges, which are floating excavators, are classified as being of either the mechanical or the hydraulic type.

A number of types of environmental degradation are associated with dredging, including increased turbidity, which can reduce light penetration; sediment redistribution; decreased oxygen; and disturbance of the estuarine bottom and estuarine circulation. The disposal of the spoil often results in additional environmental problems. It is possible, however, to offset many of the negative effects of dredging by dredging only when necessary and by planning and carrying out the operation carefully. Techniques that can be used include the proper selection of the area to be dredged, the type of dredge (hydraulic dredges are thought to be less harmful), the project design and the timing of the dredging operation to avoid important fish migration and breeding periods.

The Army Corps of Engineers regulates dredging and filling operations in a variety of water bodies including estuarine waters, oceans, rivers, and most wetlands. Its own large-scale dredging projects must be authorized by Congress.

See: ARMY CORPS OF ENGINEERS' PERMIT PROGRAM; FILL; SPOIL; WETLANDS

Drive-In Facilities

Commercial enterprises that permit the consumer to do business or be entertained without leaving his car. Predominantly connected with car washes, fast-food restaurants, movie theaters and banks, drive-in facilities have also been provided for many other types of enterprises.

Drive-ins are popular in moderate-density areas with high volumes of vehicular traffic. They are generally restricted by zoning to arterial roads where traffic will not impose a nuisance or hazard. Like gas stations, they must be provided with adequate curb cuts for ingress and egress that are placed to permit sufficient sight distance. Site layout should have ample parking space per square foot of floor area or per seat, plus additional space for temporary vehicle storage when roadway traffic is heavy.

See: FAST-FOOD RESTAURANTS; OFF-STREET PARKING REQUIREMENTS; SERVICE STATIONS; SIGHT DISTANCE; STRIP DEVELOPMENT

Driveway

A private road that gives access to property abutting a public thoroughfare. Driveways may be paved, gravel or dirt roads of any width and may give access to all types of land use. When new driveways are constructed, permission for a curb cut may depend on the requirement that the driveway be built to municipal standards as expressed by subdivision or other land development regulations.

The Institute of Transportation Engineers has established guidelines for driveway widths and turning areas that are widely used. For residential driveways, recommended widths range from a minimum of 10 feet (3 meters) to a maximum of 30 feet (9 meters), and for industrial areas the recommended minimum is 20 feet (6 meters) and the maximum 40 feet (12 meters). Where pedestrian activity is high, narrower driveways are required to slow vehicular movement. It is further recommended that the driveway be flared from the street right-of-way line to the street pavement so that it is wider where it enters the street, to permit ease in making turns to and from the driveway and to improve sight distance.

Dual Market Theory

A framework for analyzing the economic base of a geographic area based upon the theory that every region is composed of two distinct economies. Although originally used to define the economies of developing nations, where there usually exists a well-defined two-tier economy, the existence of a dual economy is evident in many central cities in the United States. The primary economy is modern, market-oriented and efficient, while the secondary economy is traditional and inefficient. These two economies may be competitive, interrelated or parallel.

Dual economies are characterized by an imbalanced development in the labor, capital and housing markets as well as in other significant economic sectors. As an example, in the primary economy labor is comprised of highly skilled technicians or professionals living in sound housing, while in the secondary economy labor tends to be unskilled and may live in relatively poor housing.
See: ECONOMIC BASE THEORY

Dump

A disposal site on which solid wastes are indiscriminately placed and left uncovered. Although dumps are extremely unsightly and cause health hazards through air pollution, water pollution, and rodent and insect infestation, many dumps still exist in the United States.

Dumps are required to be phased out or upgraded to acceptable standards under the provisions of the Resource Conservation and Recovery Act of 1976. The act requires that all states develop statewide solid waste disposal plans in which unacceptable disposal facilities are identified and the conditions remedied within five years. Criteria that address acceptability include the effect the facility has on water quality, air quality and public safety, and whether or not a cover material is employed at the site.
See: COVER MATERIAL; OPEN BURNING; RESOURCE CONSERVATION AND RECOVERY ACT OF 1976 (RCRA); SANITARY LANDFILL; SOLID WASTE MANAGEMENT

Duplex Housing

1. A building containing separate housing accommodations for two households. Each dwelling unit of a duplex, also known as a two-family house, contains its own cooking, sleeping and sanitary facilities, as well as its own entrance. The two units may be located either adjacent to each other or one unit on the lower floor with the other above it.

2. An apartment with an upper and a lower floor.
See: HOUSING TYPE

Dust

Solid particles capable of being suspended in the air. Dust generally consists of larger particles than those that comprise smoke or mist.
See: AIR POLLUTION; PARTICULATES

Dwelling Unit

A room or group of rooms—including sleeping, cooking and sanitary facilities—that are designed for the use of a single family or household. Dwelling units are intended to provide permanent living quarters, as opposed to hotels or other facilities providing temporary accommodations.
See: HOUSING TYPE

Dystrophic Lake

A lake that stands midway in the biological aging process between a eutrophic lake and a swamp. In a dystrophic lake, the waters are shallow and brown and there is a substantial content of humus and organic matter.
See: EUTROPHICATION

E

Each Community Helps Others (ECHO)

A program established by the U.S. Environmental Protection Agency (EPA) in 1976 in which cities, counties and states that had noise-abatement programs provided technical assistance to other units of governments with similar problems. This technical assistance usually involved lending the services of a local noise expert, called a community noise adviser (CNA), to another community, known as the recipient community. EPA was responsible for matching communities and for paying for the CNA's out-of-pocket expenses, such as travel. Assistance was offered in such areas as preparing attitudinal and noise measurement surveys, designing a local noise control ordinance, setting up public information programs and training in noise measurement and enforcement techniques.

EPA's noise office was closed on September 30, 1982 and EPA involvement in ECHO ended in March 1983 when a grant expired that had been given to the National

League of Cities to administer the ECHO program and pay for its costs. Despite this, some ECHO-type programs continue to operate under state sponsorship or on an informal regional basis according to which communities loan staff to each other.
See: NOISE POLLUTION

Earth Resources Observation Systems (EROS) Program

A program of the U.S. Geological Survey aimed at developing improved techniques for the use and analysis of data that have been provided by satellites and aircraft through remote sensing. The EROS Data Center in Sioux Falls, South Dakota is also a central public distribution center for remotely sensed data, including LANDSAT imagery, which may be purchased as prints or computer-compatible tape. Training programs and technical assistance are also provided.
See: EARTH RESOURCES TECHNOLOGY SATELLITE (ERTS); GEOLOGICAL SURVEY (USGS); LANDSAT; REMOTE SENSING

Earth Resources Technology Satellite (ERTS)

An unmanned National Aeronautics and Space Administration satellite program begun in 1972, designed to collect information on Earth's natural resources. ERTS, which transmitted information concerning such topics as land development, hydrology, geology, air pollution and agriculture, was subsequently renamed LANDSAT after the launching of two satellites.
See: EARTH RESOURCES OBSERVATION SYSTEMS (EROS) PROGRAM; LANDSAT; REMOTE SENSING

Earth-Covered Building

A building that is constructed largely below grade and covered with earth to take advantage of the earth's natural insulating qualities. The structure, which must conform to local building codes, is generally built of poured concrete or concrete block, with a roof of reinforced concrete to support the weight of the earth above it. Often as many as three sides of the structure are covered with earth, while interior areas are usually supplied with skylights for light and ventilation.

Earth-covered buildings are being used increasingly as a means of reducing heating and cooling costs for both solar buildings and those with conventional systems. They permit the majority of a building lot to be landscaped, creating a parklike setting.
See: NATURAL COOLING; PASSIVE SOLAR ENERGY SYSTEM

Earthquake and Hurricane Preparedness Plans

Plans that delineate areas subject to hazards in the event of an earthquake or hurricane and that describe means of averting loss of life and property damage. Grants to states and local governments to develop studies for either determination of vulnerability to earthquakes or hurricanes,

such as definition of the hazard area, or for contingency planning, such as response to warnings and actual events, are administered by the Federal Emergency Management Agency. Governments serving densely populated areas that are designated as being highly vulnerable to earthquakes and hurricanes are eligible.
See: EARTHQUAKE HAZARD MITIGATION; EARTHQUAKE HAZARDS REDUCTION ACT OF 1977

Earthquake Hazard Mitigation

Methods by which damage to human life and property caused by earthquakes can be minimized. Earthquakes of minor significance occur continually throughout the world; every few years, however, somewhere on Earth a major earthquake strikes, capable of leveling cities and claiming many lives. Although San Francisco comes to mind, many other major metropolitan areas such as Boston, Montreal, Seattle, Quebec, Charleston and Los Angeles are also earthquake-prone. In these metropolitan regions development pressures have often led to construction on unstable slopes, on reclaimed land and on loosely compacted fill, increasing the hazards if an earthquake should strike.

The current focus in reducing earthquake risk is upon earthquake forecasting and warning systems and upon earthquake-resistant construction. Although earthquakes cannot be prevented, there are certain precursors of earthquakes that have been discovered, such as a rise in minor seismic activity, which sometimes allow reliable predictions to be made and warnings to be issued. Many earthquake predictions have been made, however, without a subsequent earthquake. Incorrect earthquake predictions can lead to severe social and economic consequences in a community and reduce the likelihood that subsequent warnings will be heeded. Planners may sometimes be involved in developing emergency evacuation procedures.

It is both desirable and possible to construct buildings that will sustain little damage if struck by a "design" earthquake—an earthquake of the magnitude that can most reasonably be expected in that area given the site conditions. This is done by designing buildings to be both flexible and energy-absorbing. To aid in the construction of safe buildings, the Canadian government has prepared a national seismic map, based upon a record of all earthquakes that have taken place in Canada, for use with building codes, and special construction considerations for building on earthquake-prone sites.

Building codes, such as California's construction code, can help to minimize earthquake damage. It introduced special standards for school buildings in 1933 and subsequently broadened the standards to include other building categories. Parapet and cornice reinforcement ordinances are in effect in cities such as San Francisco and Los Angeles because such building components can be shaken loose in earthquakes or help to pull down the wall of a building.

Another way in which earthquake damage can be min·

imized is through the prevention of disasters that have often accompanied earthquakes, such as fires caused by damaged gas and electrical lines or flooding caused by ruptured dams. Land use management and planning can play an important role in this area. Siting of high-risk structures such as dams or power plants should be dependent upon the results of extensive geologic study. In general, in each land use decision, the seismic patterns of the area and the degrees and kinds of stress that can be expected must be taken into account when development type and intensity and construction methods are being considered.

See: EARTHQUAKE HAZARDS REDUCTION ACT OF 1977; FAULT; GEOLOGIC HAZARDS

Earthquake Hazards Reduction Act of 1977

Legislation (PL 95-124) that initiated a program to promote reduction of loss of life and property due to earthquakes. The act specifically authorized development and dissemination of model structural design standards and land use codes for earthquake-prone areas and the establishment of coordinated warning and implementation programs. Other research programs, such as in earthquake prediction, are also authorized.

See: EARTHQUAKE AND HURRICANE PREPAREDNESS PLANS

Earthwatch

A term used to describe the global environment assessment program developed as a result of the United Nations Conference on the Human Environment that took place in Stockholm in 1972. The function of Earthwatch, a part of the United Nations Environment Program, is to identify significant environmental trends, study the interactions of the environment and human activities, give early warning of potential environmental hazards and monitor certain natural resources.

The program is intended to encompass four closely related components: evaluation and review, research, monitoring (to gather necessary environmental data) and information exchange (to ensure that the information gathered is made widely available).

See: GLOBAL ENVIRONMENTAL MONITORING SYSTEM (GEMS)

Easement

An interest in or right over the land of another. The rights of an easement holder are typically nonpossessory—i.e., they are defined so as not to be inconsistent with rights of the holder of the primary possessory interest in the land. The parcel of land burdened by an easement is referred to as the servient estate. The easement rights may attach to and run in favor of another parcel of land—the dominant estate—and pass automatically with passage of title to that estate. This is referred to as an appurtenant easement. In contrast, an easement in gross does not run in favor of any estate but rather is a personal right of the

one holding the easement. Typically, public utility easements are easements in gross.

Easements may be created by agreement (e.g., by separate deed or by reservation in a deed); by continuous use, as in the case of a prescriptive easement; or by operation of law (e.g., to provide access to an otherwise landlocked parcel). Since an easement constitutes an interest in real property, its formation must be accompanied by the same formalities that are used in transferring the fee interest in property.

Easements may be broadly categorized into three classes. Affirmative easements are those where the servient estate must permit some act or activity to be done upon it. In a negative easement the owner of the servient estate is prohibited from engaging in otherwise permitted conduct. The profit a prende is a form of easement in which the holder may enter the servient estate and remove something of value.

Easements constitute a useful planning tool. Because the rights covered by an easement may be precisely defined as narrowly or broadly as desired, a governmental authority may acquire (by purchase or eminent domain) only as much interest in a property as is needed to accomplish the desired public purpose. Examples of easements used for public purposes include rights-of-way and scenic easements.

See: AFFIRMATIVE EASEMENT; CONSERVATION EASEMENT; FACADE EASEMENT; NEGATIVE EASEMENT; PRESCRIPTIVE EASEMENT; PUBLIC EASEMENT; SCENIC EASEMENT; SOLAR EASEMENTS AND COVENANTS; UTILITY EASEMENT

Ecology

The study of the relationships of organisms to each other and with their environment. Ecology, a multidisciplinary science, is sometimes called environmental biology, bio-ecology, or bionomics. It encompasses numerous fields, including biology, genetics, geology, sociology, physics and behavioral science.

See: ECOSYSTEM

Economic Base Analysis

A technique used to assess and measure a community's economic base. The purpose of conducting this analysis is to determine the strengths and weaknesses of a local economy, to determine its development potential and to serve as a guide to public decision making.

The first step in conducting an economic base analysis is the classification of activities as either basic or nonbasic. This is not always easily accomplished, since some activities may serve both functions. For example, doctors are usually classified as nonbasic; however, a reknowned specialist may have patients from outside the metropolitan area. Following classification, the geographic area is selected within which the study will be conducted. Very different results can be obtained depending upon the size of the economic study area.

The next step is the measurement of the basic and nonbasic sectors. Several indices, such as payrolls or physical production, may be used; employment is, however, the most commonly selected measurement. Employment may be allocated to basic and nonbasic activities by using statistical sampling techniques to survey industry and determine where its products were sent. Survey data may also be collected for other basic sectors of the economy. A ratio is ultimately obtained of basic to nonbasic employment.

Alternatively, secondary data may be used. As an example, in the location quotient method, the number of individuals employed in a particular industry nationwide may be compared to the number employed in all economic sectors. The ratio of these two figures is used with local employment figures for that industry to assess the degree to which the local area is probably importing, exporting or is self-sufficient in that industry. Refinements of the location quotient method have also been developed.

Other information sources that are useful in conducting an economic base analysis include various Bureau of the Census publications, state unemployment insurance files and information sources such as Dun & Bradstreet.
See: ECONOMIC BASE MULTIPLIER; ECONOMIC BASE THEORY; ECONOMIC FORECASTING TECHNIQUES; URBAN ECONOMICS

Economic Base Multiplier

A fixed ratio that is assumed to exist between basic and nonbasic employment for a particular community at a given time. According to this concept, once a locality's economic base multiplier is determined, it is possible to estimate changes in nonbasic employment that will result from changes in basic employment by application of the multiplier.

The multiplier is considered an index of a community's level of self-sufficiency, with a high multiplier indicating that more money made within the community is spent within that community and a low multiplier indicating the opposite case. Generally, young or small communities have lower multipliers than large cities.
See: ECONOMIC BASE ANALYSIS; ECONOMIC BASE THEORY; ECONOMIC FORECASTING TECHNIQUES; URBAN ECONOMICS

Economic Base Theory

A theory concerned with explaining economic growth within a defined area. The fundamental assumption underlying base theory is that every nation, region or city is an open economy made up of basic (export) and nonbasic (nonexport) activities. Basic activities are goods and services produced for consumption outside the community, while nonbasic activities are goods and services intended for community consumption or benefit.

According to base theory, basic activities, which bring new money into the community, are the backbone of the local economy. This flow of money generates increased economic activity, leading to an increase in nonbasic activ-

ities. Nonbasic activities, on the other hand, only recirculate existing money through the economy.

In many ways, base theory parallels international trade theory, in which rising export balances are considered to be a positive national trend. Similarly, base theory considers an increase in basic or export activities as a positive trend for a city.

Despite a widespread use of economic base theory, a number of criticisms have been made of the theory. The relationship of basic industry to long-term community growth, for example, may not always be clear without taking other variables into account. Others have noted that this concept may not be as useful in larger urban areas or in areas with larger flows of nonwage income.
See: ECONOMIC BASE ANALYSIS; ECONOMIC BASE MULTIPLIER; URBAN ECONOMICS

Economic Censuses

National censuses of industrial and business activity taken every five years by the Bureau of the Census during years ending in 2 and 7. Industries are categorized by their standard industrial classification (SIC) code, and data are collected and summarized in the censuses in terms of the establishment. An establishment is defined as a business or industrial unit at a single geographic location that produces or distributes goods or performs services.

In addition to the basic categories of manufacturing, retail and wholesale trade, construction, mining, service industries and transportation, the Census Bureau aggregates data for several other categories. *Economic Censuses for Outlying Areas* reports data for Puerto Rico, the Virgin Islands and Guam, and *Enterprise Statistics* regroups data on establishments under one ownership to show economic characteristics of controlling firms. The *Survey of Minority-Owned Business Enterprises* and the *Survey of Women-Owned Businesses* are two relatively new censuses that are a part of this series.
See: CENSUS; CENSUS OF CONSTRUCTION INDUSTRIES; CENSUS OF MANUFACTURES; CENSUS OF MINERAL INDUSTRIES; CENSUS OF RETAIL TRADE; CENSUS OF SERVICE INDUSTRIES; CENSUS OF TRANSPORTATION; CENSUS OF WHOLESALE TRADE; CENSUS SURVEYS

Economic Development

The process of intervening in the normal economic cycle in order to achieve a specific goal. Although the goal may vary, it is usually aimed at stimulating private investment within a specific area in order to generate employment, increase the tax base or increase the commercial viability of the area.

There is a growing trend toward local government involvement in economic development so that government may influence the magnitude, type and mix of industry and business that is attracted to that locale and the extent to which existing employers remain in their present locations or expand rather than move to another municipality or geographic area.

Typical planning agency activities related to economic development may include the collection of data, the preparation of various economic analyses and reports, and the provision of technical assistance to businesses considering locating or expanding. Other activities include the coordination of the functions of diverse government departments and the coordination of various ongoing grant programs such as community development and manpower. Planning agencies also help to develop programs and incentives that will further economic development, such as the strategic use of public funds to leverage substantial private investment.

See: DOWNTOWN REVITALIZATION; ECONOMIC DEVELOPMENT DEPARTMENT; ECONOMIC DEVELOPMENT INCENTIVES; WATERFRONT REVITALIZATION

Economic Development Administration (EDA)

A federal agency within the United States Department of Commerce established to carry out the provisions of the Public Works and Economic Development Act of 1965. Its primary function is to stimulate long-range economic development in areas having high unemployment and numerous low-income families by development of public facilities and private enterprises that create new jobs. Another of its primary missions is to foster the capacity to plan and conduct economic development programs at the state, community, county and multicounty levels.

Under EDA's Public Works and Development Facilities Program, public works grants and loans are made available. Loans and working capital for industrial and commercial facilities, and guarantees of leases and loans for private industry, are funded under the Business Loans Program. EDA also provides technical, planning and research assistance for locations designated as redevelopment areas and bonus grants for public works projects in certain of these locations. Areas that provide employment opportunities for residents of redevelopment areas are also eligible for assistance.

Another program, Sudden and Severe Economic Dislocation (SSED), provides economic development assistance to states and local areas for abrupt and serious economic losses, such as those caused by major industrial plant closings. The Long-Term Economic Deterioration (LTED) program provides funds to communities that are usually used to establish locally controlled revolving loan funds that serve as a source of capital not otherwise available from local financial markets.

See: COMPREHENSIVE ECONOMIC DEVELOPMENT STRATEGY (CEDS); ECONOMIC DEVELOPMENT DISTRICT (EDD); OVERALL ECONOMIC DEVELOPMENT PROGRAM (OEDP); PUBLIC WORKS AND DEVELOPMENT FACILITIES PROGRAM; PUBLIC WORKS AND ECONOMIC DEVELOPMENT ACT OF 1965

Economic Development Department

A local government agency generally established to formulate economic development plans and manage economic development programs. In many municipalities the economic development department also coordinates all local economic development, manpower and training activities and acts as an advocate of economic development in planning matters. In some cases, community economic development activities are managed by larger umbrella agencies such as a community development agency.

See: ECONOMIC DEVELOPMENT; ECONOMIC DEVELOPMENT INCENTIVES; OVERALL ECONOMIC DEVELOPMENT PROGRAM (OEDP)

Economic Development District (EDD)

A planning area designated by the Economic Development Administration (EDA), generally composed of 5 to 15 adjacent counties that are usually rural. The major city or center of economic activity must have a population of less than 250,000 and at least one county must be an EDA-designated redevelopment area (RA). During periods when Economic Development Administration funding is available, economic development districts are created to foster economic development planning on a large scale by grouping together economically distressed and economically healthy areas.

See: ECONOMIC DEVELOPMENT ADMINISTRATION (EDA)

Economic Development Incentives

Inducements offered by a government or a public agency to businesses to encourage investment in order to stimulate other private investment and generate employment. Used by many countries to foster economic growth, economic development incentives of varying types are provided by all levels of government.

At the federal level various tax incentives, such as the investment tax credit and depreciation deduction, are provided. At the state and local levels, competition for investments has caused a surge in the number and types of incentives offered. For example, most states offer tax incentives similar to those available from the federal government. In addition, many localities offer reductions or abatements in the local property tax.

A variety of other incentives are provided by state and local government. One prevalent form of assistance is the establishment of offices whose function is to attract and expedite the opening or expansion of businesses in that jurisdiction. At a more sophisticated level, industrial development agencies may be formed to help market industrial revenue bonds, which enable a business to finance a plant or equipment at below-market interest rates through tax-exempt bonds. Some states and localities also make low-interest loans to finance new construction, expansion or rehabilitation. Interest subsidies, subsidized energy and land write-downs are additional financial incentives used. Land banks may also be established, in which land is acquired by government and held until appropriate development proposals are received.

In conjunction with these incentives, many states and units of government assist businesses in complying with regulations and in preparing license and permit applications. Some communities provide indirect incentives that benefit the community as well as the investor, such as transportation and infrastructure improvements.

Considerable controversy surrounds the granting of incentives, particularly with respect to their effectiveness in influencing business location decisions and their cost as it relates to potential benefit. It has been pointed out that the widespread use of incentives may make them less effective. Instead of acting as a special lure to business development, they become a commonplace minimum requirement, forcing all units of government to spend more to attract business and industry. Others argue that they are necessary to offset an unfavorable business climate and to keep a community competitive. While it is difficult to measure the true costs and benefits of incentives, most feel that they can affect business location decisions when a business is deciding between two or three locations. There is also significant agreement concerning the necessity of minimizing unnecessary government-created barriers to development and to continuing public investment in essential infrastructure to enable existing businesses to remain and expand.
See: ECONOMIC DEVELOPMENT; FOREIGN TRADE ZONES; INDUSTRIAL DEVELOPMENT AGENCY (IDA); INDUSTRIAL REVENUE BONDS; INVESTMENT TAX CREDIT; LAND BANK; LAND WRITE-DOWN; LEVERAGE; TAX ABATEMENT; TAX-INCREMENT FINANCING; URBAN ENTERPRISE ZONES

Economic Forecasting Techniques

Models or modes of analysis used to predict future economic performance. These predictions are used as a basis for public and private decision making and are generally a component of most economic base analyses.

Although there are many forecasting techniques, most can be classified into two categories. The first group, known as time-series methods, uses past trends and historical data and extrapolates them into the future. Trend-line analysis is the simplest of this type, while shift-share analysis and input-output analysis are more sophisticated examples. The major problem with time-series analysis is its inability to predict turning points in the economy, often the most important part of a forecast.

The second group of forecasting techniques, econometric models, are highly sophisticated computer models that construct new data about the future. The data are obtained by examining sets of variables and statistically estimating their relationship in the future. Econometric models are being used with increasing frequency, particularly by businesses interested in future demand levels. As a tool for predicting the economic performance of a city, however, their use is hindered by the difficulty in obtaining data that are both current and reliable.
See: ECONOMIC BASE ANALYSIS; ECONOMIC BASE MULTIPLIER; ECONOMIC MODELS; INPUT-OUTPUT ANALYSIS; SECTOR ANALYSIS; SHIFT-SHARE ANALYSIS

Economic Models

Tools used to test economic theories by simulating realistic conditions as closely as possible. By examining the relationship among sets of economic variables, economic models can be used to explain present economic patterns as well as to predict future economic activity. Economic models may be expressed in narrative or mathematical form and may be quite simple, consisting of only two variables, or highly complex, examining the relationship between hundreds of variables.

Economic models expressed in mathematical form are known as econometric models. These models measure the relationship among variables in precise mathematical terms and are subject to statistical testing. Econometric models are often used in transportation planning in determining routes and schedules.
See: ECONOMIC FORECASTING TECHNIQUES; MODEL; URBAN ECONOMICS

Economic Obsolescence

One of the three forms of depreciation, together with physical depreciation and functional obsolescence, which must be considered in applying the cost approach to valuing improvements to real estate.

Economic obsolescence results from factors that are external to the property being valued, such as rezoning of the parcel or neighboring parcels, conflicting or nuisance generating neighboring uses, a change in the character of the community in which the parcel is located, or economic trends. Since the causes for economic obsolescence are outside of the control of the property owner, they are generally not curable,
See: ADAPTIVE USE; APPRAISAL; COST APPROACH APPRAISAL; WHITE ELEPHANT

Economic Opportunity Act of 1964

Omnibus legislation, unofficially called the "war on poverty" that provided a variety of programs intended to improve opportunities for the economically disadvantaged. The Economic Opportunity Act (PL 88-452) included provisions for manpower programs such as a Job Corps (a residential retraining program for youths), a work training program for youths aged 16 to 21, a work-study program for college students, adult education (especially to combat illiteracy) and Community Action Agencies.

The act also authorized loans to poor rural families and programs for migrant farm workers and small businesses. It established the federal Office of Economic Opportunity (OEO), to coordinate all programs and administer certain programs, and Volunteers in Service to America (VISTA), which paid volunteers subsistence wages to assist local projects. Later amendments created the Headstart Program for preschool children; a program of grants and loans to community development corporations for programs related to business and commercial development or expansion, community physical development (including housing, training and public service employment) and social services; the Legal Services Corporation, to provide noncriminal legal services for the indigent; and a program of grants to promote the economic and social self-sufficiency of American Indians and Hawaiian and Alaskan natives, known as the Native American Programs. These amendments also transferred the functions of the OEO to a new Community Services Administration.

The Economic Opportunity Act was repealed in 1981, except for programs for Native Americans and the Legal Services Corporation. Many of the programs that it began, however, are eligible for funding under other authority.
See: COMMUNITY ACTION PROGRAM (CAP); ECONOMIC DEVELOPMENT ADMINISTRATION (EDA); OFFICE OF COMMUNITY SERVICES (OCS)

Economic Recovery Tax Act of 1981

This act (PL 97-34) included a number of provisions of relevance to planning practice, particularly concerning the rehabilitation of buildings. It replaced existing rehabilitation incentives in the Internal Revenue Code with an investment tax credit (ITC) that varies with age of the structure and whether it is certified as historic. It also introduced a new accelerated cost recovery system.

Effective January 1, 1982 an ITC of 15 percent is available for qualified rehabilitation of industrial and commercial buildings at least 30 years old; if the building is at least 40 years old, a 20 percent credit is given. For certified historic structures (i.e., those in the National Register of Historic Places or of significance to a National Register historic district or a state or locally designated historic district), a 25 percent ITC is available, including for buildings used as rental housing. The rehabilitation must, however, be able to meet Department of Interior rehabilitation standards that help to preserve the special qualities of the structure.

The law also permits property owners to depreciate their property over a 15-year period (or over a 35- or 45-year extended period if they so choose) using either straight-line or accelerated methods. The straight-line method must be used, however, if the owner chooses to take an ITC. The benefits of depreciation for certified historic structures were reduced somewhat by provisions of the Tax Equity and Fiscal Responsibility act of 1982.

Other planning-related provisions of the act partially repeal disincentives to the demolition of historic properties that had been instituted in 1976 and offer incentives for the rehabilitation of low-income rental housing.
See: HISTORIC PRESERVATION; HISTORIC PRESERVATION TAX INCENTIVES; INVESTMENT TAX CREDIT; TAX EQUITY AND FISCAL RESPONSIBILITY ACT OF 1982 (TEFRA)

Ecosystem

A term that describes the system comprised of all living organisms in a given geographic area, and the physical environment with which and in which they interact. Ecosystem is derived from the phrase "ecological system."
See: ECOLOGY

Edge

A border or line of delineation between surfaces, as in the interface between a paved surface and a row of buildings or between a forest and a meadow. In physical planning, the establishment of an edge is an important means of defining a separation between spaces or of highlighting a change from the quality or character of one area to another. An edge may be hard or clean and very distinct, or it may be weak and unnoticeable, with little or no variation between surfaces.
See: SENSE OF PLACE

Educational Park

A large site on which a full range of public schools and their associated facilities are located. An educational park, which requires about 50 centrally located acres (20 hectares), is generally designed to accommodate an elementary school, a middle school and a high school that are grouped for the economy of shared facility use. A park of this nature is also expected to operate as a community center, since it has significant open space and recreational facilities, as well as community resources such as auditoriums and libraries. In addition, the relationship of the buildings to each other and their interior arrangements may be designed to encourage the mixing of people of various ages and to further unusual educational arrangements. Although relatively rare, educational parks have been constructed in such locations as New Orleans and Broward County, Florida.
See: SCHOOL PLANNING

Effluent

The liquid waste resulting from sewage treatment or other industrial process, such as water used for power plant cooling purposes. Depending upon the degree of treatment to which it has been subjected, effluent may be highly or slightly organic or toxic in nature, or it may be thoroughly cleaned of these impurities.

Effluent is most often disposed of by discharging it into a body of water, where it becomes diluted. Other methods of disposal include spraying the effluent onto irrigable land and wooded areas or placing it into evaporation ponds in arid regions. Municipal reuse of effluent that has been subjected to tertiary treatment is being considered as an auxiliary water source in many countries lacking an adequate water supply. Industrial reuse for cooling purposes is common, as is recreational reuse, such as golf course watering and creation of ponds for boating, fishing and swimming. Use of effluent for groundwater recharge to stop saltwater intrusion and for recharge of oil-bearing

strata to increase their yield is effective, and use of treated effluent for crop watering is practiced in several countries.
See: EVAPORATION POND; NATIONAL POLLUTANT DISCHARGE ELIMINATION SYSTEM (NPDES); OUTFALL; RECEIVING WATERS; SALTWATER INTRUSION; SEWAGE TREATMENT; THERMAL POLLUTION

Ekistics

The science of human settlements. Developed by Constantinos A. Doxiadis, a Greek architect and planner, and publicized in his book of that name, ekistics is a discipline that stresses the importance of the manner in which humans function in all of their environments to enable better planning to take place. Published in 1968, the theory was Doxiadis's reaction to the piecemeal planning he perceived as being prevalent and to the large urban renewal projects that were uprooting thousands of people and changing community structures in ways that often were not foreseen.

In ekistics a classification of human settlements is enumerated related to their population and physical size, and within this hierarchy the relationships between neighborhoods, towns, cities, metropolises, conurbations, megalopolises and urban regions are explained. Two settlement forms not yet in existence, the urban continent and ecumenopolis, the universal city, consisting of interconnected megalopolises that will house a vastly expanded world population, were also hypothesized.
See: CONURBATION; HUMAN SETTLEMENTS; MEGALOPOLIS; NEIGHBORHOOD; SOCIAL PLANNING; URBAN DESIGN

Electric Power Generation and Transmission

Although electric power may be produced by a wide variety of means, large-scale production of energy usually takes place in generating stations, known as power plants. Power plants usually use either hydraulic turbines driven by hydroelectric power or steam turbines powered by fossil fuels or nuclear energy. Approximately 89 percent of the electric energy produced in the United States in 1978 was generated by steam turbines (51 percent of which used coal, 16 percent natural gas, 19 percent oil and 14 percent nuclear power), while water power accounted for about another 10 percent.

Energy produced in these plants is transmitted, sometimes over long distances, by transmission systems that are also used to interconnect power systems. Because electric power is normally transmitted at high voltage levels, it must be stepped down to lower voltages, through the use of substations, when it arrives at its destination. It is then distributed to users of electricity.

A wide variety of planning issues and problems are associated with electric power generation and transmission. Among these are the provision of adequate power to and its distribution within a community; the siting of power plants and the environmental effects of different types of power plants; the routing and design of transmission lines; the siting of substations; and the development of emergency evacuation plans for areas in proximity to nuclear plants.
See: COGENERATION; COOLING TOWER; ELECTRIC TRANSMISSION LINE; ENERGY CONSERVATION PLANNING; FOSSIL FUELS; HYDROELECTRIC POWER; INTERCONNECTED POWER NETWORK; NUCLEAR ENERGY; PEAK-DEMAND PERIOD; RENEWABLE ENERGY SOURCES; UNDERGROUNDING OF UTILITIES

Electric Transmission Line

A cable designed to transmit electric power from a power plant to a designated destination, usually over a long distance. Power was first transmitted on a 2-kilovolt line in Italy in 1886; today power is transmitted at up to 765 kilovolts. Two new types of electrical transmission currently under development are the ultra-high-voltage line, which can carry loads of well over 1,000 kilovolts and the high-voltage direct-current (HVDC) line, first used in Sweden in 1965, which eliminates some of the problems that alternating-current systems face.

Higher-power lines (those of 500 kilovolts and 765 kilovolts) generally require larger rights-of-way and buffer zones, are more visually obtrusive and generate more noise, particularly in wet weather. One of the techniques planners use in routing lines to minimize their visual impact is locating the line parallel to but below the ridge line rather than on a ridge. Lower-voltage lines are also used by utility companies to carry electricity over shorter distances; these lines are often placed underground in dense urban areas or in communities with legislation requiring this action.
See: ELECTRIC POWER GENERATION AND TRANSMISSION; UNDERGROUNDING OF UTILITIES

Electrostatic Precipitator (ESP)

An air pollution control device that removes particulates from a gas stream by passing the stream through a high voltage electrical field. The particles become charged and are drawn from the gas and ultimately collected at collection plates of the opposite charge. ESPs are considered to be quite effective in controlling particulate emissions and are capable of being used with high temperature gases, but are large and relatively expensive. They are often used to remove particulates from the emissions of power plants and other large installations.
See: AIR POLLUTION; AIR POLLUTION CONTROL

Eleemosynary Uses

Those land uses that are operated on a nonprofit basis. Eleemosynary uses may be small and self-contained and present few special planning problems, or they may occupy hundreds of acres and have a major impact upon a community. A large university or medical center, for example, has the potential of generating at least as much traffic as a major commercial or industrial use and of placing heavy demands upon the municipal housing supply. Conversely, they can also provide extensive employment opportunity and attract many satellite businesses, encouraging economic growth.

A common problem communities face in planning for eleemosynary uses is that they are frequently exempt from property taxes. This becomes of special concern when a substantial proportion of a community's acreage is tax-exempt.

See: CHURCH USES; DAY-CARE CENTER; FIRE STATION; HOSPITAL PLANNING; LIBRARY; SCHOOL LAND REQUIREMENTS; TAX-EXEMPT PROPERTY; UNIVERSITIES

Elevated Roadway

A road built on a structure that raises it above the surrounding street level for the purpose of grade separation. Roads are elevated where it is necessary to have them cross local streets without causing traffic conflicts on either road or to bring a road to an elevation permitting adequate geometric design of a multilevel interchange.

Where elevated structures are used, the area beneath the roadway is frequently developed for parking or commercial purposes. It is less costly to build an elevated roadway in heavily urbanized areas than to build a depressed highway or expand an at-grade highway because of the costs of right-of-way acquisition and relocation of existing residences and businesses. Provision of drainage for elevated roads is easy, and extensive relocation of existing utilities, which would be required for a depressed road, is unnecessary. The disadvantage of elevated roadways is that they are unsightly and reduce available light and air for surrounding development.

See: GRADE SEPARATION

Elevation

1. A scale drawing of the view of one side of a building or structure that indicates location and dimensions of doors and windows, floor-to-floor heights and the final grade level of the ground adjacent to the building in relation to the floor level. Elevations generally show the types of wall finishes—such as wood, stone, brick, metal and glass—and architectural details, such as decoration and style of doors, windows and exterior stairs. The outside of the building below the grade line may also be shown. A set of working drawings will generally show a separate elevation for each side of the building or structure.

An elevation may also be used to show the relationship among buildings, as along a street, or the relationship of one site to another along the same plane, as when showing the distance between two separated sites on the same block. (See Fig. 22)

2. The altitude above sea level.

See: SCHEMATIC DRAWING; WORKING DRAWINGS

Embankment Pond

A small, man-made water resource constructed by damming a stream. Embankment ponds are usually located in a depression in a stream valley deep enough to hold at least 6 feet (1.8 meters) of water. A suitable location for such a pond requires soils, such as clays or silty clays, capable of holding water and preventing seepage.

See: ARTIFICIAL WATER BODIES; EXCAVATED POND; FARM POND

Emergency Repair and Stabilization

Work necessary to ensure the structural integrity of a building or structure. Often required to avoid the demolition of historic properties, it is important that temporary repairs be performed in such a way as to be reversible so that eventual permanent repairs may be appropriate to the building's appearance. As an example, it may be necessary to install a temporary paper roof or to block window openings with plywood for immediate weather protection, but these measures may then later be removed and permanent repairs made.

See: ALTERATION; DEMOLITION BY NEGLECT; HISTORIC PRESERVATION; PRESERVATION; REHABILITATION

Eminent Domain

The power inherent in a sovereign body (in the United States this includes each state as well as the federal government) to acquire property in private ownership. The acquisition process is sometimes referred to as appropriation, condemnation or expropriation.

The 5th and 14th Amendments to the United States Constitution, as well as the constitutions of many states, prohibit the exercise of the eminent domain power except for a public use, and then only upon condition that just compensation is paid to the former owner of the property. The power of eminent domain has been conferred by statute upon municipalities and, in more limited circumstances, upon public utilities, other public authorities and common carriers such as railroads.

Acquisition of property by eminent domain may occur in a number of ways. In some cases, the mere filing of a map or legal description of property to be acquired may be sufficient to transfer title to the acquiring authority. In other cases, a formal legal proceeding must be commenced for the purpose of seeking a judicial decree awarding title. In still other cases, formal exercise of eminent domain by inverse condemnation follows after a de facto taking has already occurred.

See: CONDEMNATION; INVERSE CONDEMNATION; JUST COMPENSATION; PUBLIC USE; TAKING

Emission Inventory

A listing of the principal air pollutants that are being released into the air of a particular geographic area, usually expressed in tons per day and listed by source. Such inventories are useful in pinpointing the major sources of

air pollution in an area, and devising the most efficient means of reducing overall air pollution in that region.
See: AIR POLLUTION; EMISSION STANDARD

Emission Standard

The maximum amount of a particular pollutant that a specified source of pollution is legally permitted to discharge or restrictions on the conditions under which discharge may take place. Each state is required to include in its state implementation plan emission limitations and measures for enforcing them that may be necessary to achieve or maintain national ambient air quality standards.

In addition, the federal government is charged with the responsibility of setting emission standards for new sources of pollution, such as new factories, known as new-source performance standards (NSPS). These standards are developed on an industrywide basis and are intended to be used by the states in setting their own emission standards, which must be at least as restrictive as the federally promulgated standards. The U.S. Environmental Protection Agency (EPA) is also charged with setting emission standards for motor vehicles with respect to carbon monoxide, hydrocarbons, nitrogen oxides and any other pollutant deriving from new motor vehicles that represents a potential danger.

An additional category of pollutants for which national emission standards are in effect is hazardous air pollutants, which are those pollutants not covered by ambient air quality standards but thought likely to be related to increased incidences of death or serious illness. The administrator of EPA is required to establish standards for such pollutants, (National Emissions Standards for Hazardous Air Pollutants [NESHAP]) that are sufficient for the protection of public health with an adequate safety margin. Currently, standards are in effect for beryllium, mercury, asbestos and vinyl chloride. Arsenic, benzene and radionuclides have been listed as hazardous, but standards for these substances have not yet been set.
See: AIR POLLUTION; EMISSION INVENTORY; NATIONAL AMBIENT AIR QUALITY STANDARDS (NAAQS); NEW SOURCE PERFORMANCE STANDARDS (NSPS); STATE IMPLEMENTATION PLAN (SIP)

Emissions Trading Systems

A group of techniques promoted by the U.S. Environmental Protection Agency (EPA) to provide incentives to industry to curb and minimize air pollution.

In the bubble concept, first introduced in December 1979, an industrial plant is permitted to emit increased air pollution from certain sources in exchange for reducing emission levels by the same amount from other sources at the plant. The term derives from a consideration of a plant as if it existed under a bubble and all of its pollution issued from one opening in the bubble. The intent of the bubble concept is to aid plants in reducing the cost of industrial pollution control by allowing them to control those emission sources that are most cost-effective to treat. As of the end of 1982, 179 bubbles had either been approved or were at the developmental or proposal stage.

Related market-based approaches subsequently introduced by EPA are the netting policy, the emissions offset policy and the emissions banking policy, which are designed to encourage a firm to reduce emissions below minimum compliance levels rather than to merely meet legal requirements.

In "netting," plants are not made to comply with new-source review procedures when they expand or modernize if there are only very small increases in emissions on a plantwide basis. "Offsetting" and "emissions banking" are both related to the practice by which firms that reduce pollution below required levels can accumulate "emissions reduction credits" (ERCs). In offsetting, the firm may use the ERCs to enable new or modified sources to expand in nonattainment areas. These credits may be traded within a firm among plant sites or to another firm but must result in some overall improvement in air quality—i.e., more ERCs are needed to compensate for any pollution increases. In emissions banking a firm may store its ERCs so that they are available for use or sale at a later date, either for bubble, netting or offsetting purposes. As of 1982 one statewide banking and trading system was operating in Oregon. In addition, banking systems were in effect in San Francisco; Seattle-Tacoma; Louisville, Kentucky; and Allegheny County, Pennsylvania. Others were in the proposal stages.

In August 1982 a decision was rendered in *Natural Resources Defense Council, Inc.* v. *Gorsuch* (685 F. 2d 718) by the U.S. Court of Appeals, D.C. Circuit, that could have a significant effect upon the entire concept of emissions trading. In this case, now under appeal, the Natural Resources Defense Council (NRDC) argued that the bubble concept made it overly simple for industries to bypass EPA's new-source review requirements by merely expanding an existing plant rather than constructing a new plant elsewhere. NRDC charged that it was not proper to bypass these requirements and further degrade air quality in areas unable to meet national ambient air quality standards (NAAQS). The court agreed, stating that EPA-promulgated regulations did not aid in bringing nonattainment areas up to standard. As a result, many aspects of the emissions trading system as it applies to nonattainment areas are currently in question.
See: AIR POLLUTION; NATIONAL AMBIENT AIR QUALITY STANDARDS (NAAQS); NONATTAINMENT AREA

Employment and Training Administration (ETA)

An agency within the Department of Labor that oversees the operation of programs related to unemployment insurance, employment services, job training, comprehensive employment and training programs, and work programs for older Americans. ETA also publishes books, reports and periodicals on topics such as job training, unemployment insurance and local trends in employment.

There are five component ETA divisions. The Office of Comprehensive Employment and Training (OCET), whose activities are most closely related to planning, administers programs authorized by the Job Training Partnership Act of 1982. Another work program under OCET jurisdiction, the Senior Community Service Employment Program (SCSEP), authorized by Title V of the Older Americans Act, consists of grants to nonprofit agencies and state governments for subsidized, part-time employment for low-income individuals aged 55 and above. OCET also contains the Bureau of Apprenticeship and Training, which promotes apprenticeship and other industrial training programs and develops appropriate labor standards.

The Office of Strategic Planning and Policy Development (OSPP), another division of ETA, formulates ETA policies, recommends allocation of resources, and develops and reviews legislative proposals relating to employment and training. The Office of Employment Security (OES) manages programs operated by state and local governments offering unemployment insurance to unemployed workers. OES also administers public employment offices of the United States Employment Service and an assistance program for workers adversely affected by foreign imports, and reviews certification applications for rural industrialization loans and grants.

See: DEPARTMENT OF LABOR; JOB TRAINING PARTNERSHIP ACT OF 1982; OLDER AMERICANS ACT OF 1965

Employment Studies

A basic element in most comprehensive planning studies, an employment study is designed to quantify the nature of the local economy and to identify its strengths, weaknesses and future potential, using employment as the basic unit of measurement. Most employment studies contain a discussion of past levels of employment by sectors of the economy and a forecast of expected future levels of employment. These are important to the planner as a basis for predicting future space requirements for industrial, commercial and residential purposes.

Two methods for predicting future employment levels are commonly used. Analytic methods estimate employment levels by analyzing the major variables that determine employment. Because it may be difficult to obtain necessary data on these variables, analytic methods can be difficult to use. Shortcut methods, on the other hand, are simpler to apply and use readily available data, such as information released by the Bureau of the Census and the Bureau of Labor Statistics. These methods rely on one or more series of employment statistics and generally involve stepping down data collected for the nation and region to a local level.

See: ECONOMIC CENSUSES; ECONOMIC FORECASTING TECHNIQUES; URBAN ECONOMICS

Empty Nesters

Individuals, normally middle-aged or older, who have raised a family and whose children have—as a result of college, job, marriage, etc.—left the home, or nest.

From a social planning standpoint, the term represents a generation of individuals who must redefine their roles apart from the lives of their children and who, as a result, may be added to the work force or require additional municipal services.

From a housing standpoint, empty nesters represent a group of older citizens often living in residences designed to accommodate larger family units. Continued occupancy of a larger home can be a major financial or physical problem for the older resident, and in a tight housing market, it can restrict the availability of these homes to younger, larger families. Some communities are taking steps to make more productive use of their housing stock and to ease the financial burden of empty nesters by legalizing the creation of certain accessory apartments.

See: AGE-ORIENTED COMMUNITY; CIRCUIT BREAKER TAXES; HOUSING FOR FAMILIES; HOUSING FOR THE ELDERLY; ILLEGAL CONVERSION

Enabling Act

Legislation that authorizes activity or conduct that was previously not permitted.

In planning, perhaps the most common type of enabling legislation encountered is legislation authorizing local governments to regulate land use and development by adopting zoning ordinances. Each state has adopted some form of zoning enabling legislation. Most such legislation enacted after 1923 has been modeled on the Standard State Zoning Enabling Act, first published under the aegis of the United States Department of Commerce in 1922.

See: AMERICAN LAW INSTITUTE MODEL LAND DEVELOPMENT CODE; STANDARD STATE ZONING ENABLING ACT

Encroachment

An illegal or unauthorized intrusion upon an adjoining public street or highway or upon adjoining private property, reducing the size of the invaded property. The encroachment may take the form of a fixture, such as a wall or fence, or a part of the real estate, such as an overhanging roof that extends beyond the property line.

The existence of an encroachment could render title to the invaded parcel unmarketable; therefore, when the existence of an encroachment is known, a contract to sell the property should be made subject to the encroachment. Mortgage lenders and purchasers of property frequently require that a survey of the property be available, which would normally reveal the existence of any encroachments. If the survey discloses any encroachments not provided for in the contract of sale, the seller must either remove the encroachment or allow the purchaser to terminate the contract and get his down payment back.

If one property owner encroaches upon the land of another, a court will ordinarily require the intruding owner to remove the encroachment at his expense. However, if the encroachment was created unintentionally, and the encroachment is insubstantial in relation to the cost of removing it, then a court may permit it to remain but require the intruding owner to pay monetary damages.

If an encroachment remains unchallenged for a period of time prescribed by law (normally 10 to 20 years), then the intruding landowner may acquire legal title to the encroached area by adverse possession.

See: ADVERSE POSSESSION; *BOOMER* v. *ATLANTIC CEMENT COMPANY*

Endangered Species

Those species of fish, wildlife, insects and plants in danger of becoming extinct throughout all or a significant part of their natural range. Endangered species are of great concern because a lessening of biological diversity limits the potential resources upon which mankind may draw for such basic necessities as oxygen, food, building materials, clothing, energy, medicines, industrial chemicals and clean water.

Human activities continue to pose distinct threats to biological diversity by modifying natural habitats through necessary activities such as construction of human settlements and transportation systems, alteration of land for agriculture, and forestry. Methods have, however, been developed to attempt to slow the rate at which plants, wildlife and aquatic life are becoming extinct while accommodating the essential needs of mankind. Construction of housing complexes can, for example, be undertaken in ways that minimize destruction of natural habitats. Cluster development, conservation easements, land acquisition and local ordinances that regulate critical environmental areas, such as wetlands, can all help to protect the most sensitive ecosystems and to direct development toward more suitable locations.

Attempts can also be made to route roads, pipelines and canals in such a way as to avoid disrupting critical natural habitats. When they do cross these habitats, they can be designed to accommodate local species, in the way that the Alaska Pipeline was designed to permit migrating caribou to pass at certain points. Off-road vehicles, snowmobiles and power boats can also be confined to suitable areas in which they are less likely to cause environmental damage. Similarly, forest management practices are available in which commercial forestry is possible while biological diversity is maintained. Among these practices are the provision of corridors that permit movement of wildlife; the use of integrated pest management, in which pesticide use is limited; letting trees stand along streambanks; the provision of food and cover for wildlife and the reduction of erosion by planting desirable vegetative species; and limiting clearcutting to small areas.

Specific conservation practices have also been devel-

oped to protect endangered species. In one approach gene banks, zoos, aquariums and botanical gardens are used to preserve seeds, sperm, tissue and living plants and animals that are extinct in the wild or would otherwise become extinct. Another method, the species approach, selects particular species as worthy of conservation and concentrates efforts on these species. They may be selected because of their commercial value (e.g., wild rice), because they are valued for sport (e.g., largemouth bass) or because they have generated special interest (e.g., polar bears, California condors). A third tactic, the ecosystem approach, stresses the protection of whole undisturbed ecosystems as ecological preserves.

A variety of federal and state legislation aimed at protection of endangered species is also available. In addition, many international agreements have been enacted for this purpose. Among them is the Convention on International Trade in Endangered Species of Wild Fauna and Flora (CITES), in which 58 nations were participating as of 1980. CITES requires the issuance of permits or certificates when protected species are being traded. Many additional agreements are in effect concerning specific species, such as polar bears, whales, fur seals and marine mammals.

See: BOTANICAL GARDEN; CRITICAL AREAS; ENDANGERED SPECIES ACT OF 1973; ENDANGERED SPECIES ACT AMENDMENTS OF 1978; ENDANGERED SPECIES ACT AMENDMENTS OF 1982; FORESTRY; WILDLIFE MANAGEMENT; ZOO

Endangered Species Act of 1973

A law (PL 93-205) that extends federal protection to threatened plant and animal species that are in jeopardy of becoming endangered as well as those already in danger of extinction. It prohibits all trading in endangered and threatened species and products derived from them, establishes fines for violations of these provisions and directs the secretaries of Commerce and the Interior to identify threatened or endangered species, designate vital habitats and create programs aimed at protecting these species from extinction. The secretaries are also authorized to acquire lands and water necessary to carry out these activities. In addition, federal agencies are prohibited from funding, undertaking or authorizing activities that could be hazardous to these species.

See: ENDANGERED SPECIES; ENDANGERED SPECIES ACT AMENDMENTS OF 1978; ENDANGERED SPECIES ACT AMENDMENTS OF 1982

Endangered Species Act Amendments of 1978

A law (PL 95-632) that was passed in reaction to a 1978 U.S. Supreme Court decision holding that the nearly complete Tellico dam in Tennessee could not be put into operation because it would destroy the habitat of the snail darter, a rare fish protected by the Endangered Species Act.

The 1978 act establishes an Endangered Species Committee with the power to exempt projects from its provisions, sets standards for granting exemptions and mandates that if an exemption is granted, methods be undertaken to attempt to save the species. It also requires that the endangered species list be scrutinized every five years by the Secretary of the Interior to determine if certain species could be deleted from the list or whether additional species should be added.

The newly created board ruled against exempting the Tellico dam. It was, however, ultimately completed as a result of a rider to the 1980 fiscal year energy and water development appropriations bill (PL 96-69), which specifically exempted the dam from Endangered Species Act provisions.

See: ENDANGERED SPECIES; ENDANGERED SPECIES ACT OF 1973; ENDANGERED SPECIES ACT AMENDMENTS OF 1982

Endangered Species Act Amendments of 1982

A law that reauthorizes many of the provisions of the Endangered Species Act of 1973, which is intended to protect plants and animals facing the threat of extinction. In addition, the act provides funding for endangered species programs for fiscal years 1983 through 1985.

A key new provision of the act is the imposition of a time limit of one year (instead of the previous two-year limit) on Department of Interior deliberations concerning the placing of species on (or removal of species from) the endangered species list. In addition, the act requires that such decisions be based on whether or not the species was being threatened or endangered from a biological viewpoint rather than on the economic implications of listing the species, although economic considerations may be weighed in deciding whether or not to designate a critical habitat.

Another provision of the act allows those engaged in projects that come under federal authority to meet with Department of Interior representatives at an early stage of project planning to receive informal notification concerning the impact the project might have on any endangered species. The act also contains the provision that endangered species that have been bred in captivity may be released into the wild without their new habitat becoming listed as a critical habitat.

See: ENDANGERED SPECIES; ENDANGERED SPECIES ACT AMENDMENTS OF 1978; ENDANGERED SPECIES ACT OF 1973

Energy Audit

A comprehensive inspection of a building to determine its level of energy efficiency. Among the areas examined in an energy audit are the portions of the structure through which heat may be escaping, such as the doors and windows, as well as the adequacy of existing insulation. Use patterns that may result in wasted energy are also examined. As a result of an audit, a property owner usually receives a list of recommended improvements, an estimate of their cost and an indication of the amount of time it would take for the cost of these improvements to be repaid in energy savings.

Energy audits are conducted by utility companies, government agencies and private consultants. Utility companies or units of government may further assist the property owner in having the necessary work completed by providing lists of recommended contractors, making low-interest loans or making grants.

See: ENERGY CONSERVATION PLANNING; HOME WEATHERIZATION

Energy Conservation and Production Act

Legislation (PL 94-385) enacted in 1976 that authorized various measures to encourage energy conservation in buildings. Under Title III, the Energy Conservation Standards for New Buildings Act of 1976, it required the development of performance standards within three years for energy conservation in new commercial and residential buildings. The act stipulated that once the performance standards are issued, no federal financial assistance would be made available for the construction of any such new building unless the municipality or state in which it is located had incorporated the energy-conserving measures into its building laws and the building would be in compliance with the laws. In 1981 the law was amended to make this a voluntary rather than a mandatory program, and voluntary performance standards are directed to be developed by April 1, 1984 to be used as guidelines in the design and construction of energy-efficient buildings. Federal building design, however, must conform to the performance standards.

Title IV, the Energy Conservation in Existing Buildings Act of 1976, provides for a weatherization program that includes grants to states and Indian tribes, or to municipal governments or community action agencies in states not participating in the program, for improvements to dwelling units housing low-income and elderly residents. Grants of up to $400 per dwelling unit are authorized for materials to improve insulation, among other activities. This act authorized the development of guidelines for state energy conservation plans and makes grants available to states for their implementation. Other provisions directed the Department of Housing and Urban Development to undertake a study of measures needed to improve energy conservation in existing buildings, the results of which are now being applied to federal buildings, and authorized a demonstration project of grants to encourage the use of renewable resource technology.

See: ENERGY CONSERVATION PLANNING; NATIONAL ENERGY ACT OF 1978

Energy Conservation Planning

An approach toward reducing energy use by addressing the many components of energy consumption in a comprehensive manner. Among the areas that can be examined are existing energy policy and use, building codes, land use regulations and other municipal ordinances, transportation policy and use of solar energy and other alternative energy sources.

The City of Davis, California has successfully reduced energy consumption in that community through a variety of municipal regulations and policy decisions. An energy conservation building code aimed at preventing excessive summer heat gain and winter heat loss is in effect in Davis. Among the areas considered in evaluating thermal efficiency are the building's insulation, proportion of glazed areas and shading of all glazed surfaces, and roof color. Builders may meet either a set of specification standards or optional performance standards. In addition, all homes that are to be resold must be checked for compliance with the code and certain improvements made, when necessary, to improve their energy efficiency. Other activities aimed at energy conservation include a comprehensive municipal tree planting program, the development of a substantial system of bicycle lanes through the community and the provision of a bicycle fleet for the use of municipal employees during the workday. It is also required that solar energy be the only means by which swimming pools for apartment houses and motels be heated.

San Diego County has taken another path, by adopting, in 1979, the first law in the United States that requires the use of solar energy. All new homes that are served only by electricity or natural gas must include solar hot water heating equipment. In addition, each lot within a new subdivision must provide adequate solar access. Similar legislation is in effect in Sacramento and Santa Clara Counties in California and in Soldiers Grove, Wisconsin.
See: ARCHITECTURAL DESIGN FOR ENERGY CONSERVATION; ENERGY-EFFICIENT LAND USE PRACTICES; RENEWABLE ENERGY SOURCES; SOLAR ACCESS; SOLAR ENERGY

Energy-Efficient Land Use Practices

Means of reducing energy consumption through such methods as the placement of various types of land uses, the design of pedestrian and traffic circulation systems and transportation facilities, and the design and siting of housing and other buildings.

On a communitywide basis the location of places of work and residential areas at substantial distances from each other results in large energy expenditures for commuting. This is particularly true when residential development is at a lower density level than is economical for public transit. Mixed-use development, infill development of vacant urban land and a closer relationship between the locations of facilities and the locations of primary users can help to effect energy savings.

Attractive and efficient circulation systems within a community—including sidewalks, footpaths and bikeways—encourage walking and the use of bicycles for short trips. Energy savings may also be accomplished through

provision of adequate public transportation alternatives linked with automobile disincentives.

Clustering of housing, because of its altered street pattern, reduces energy required for road construction, road maintenance and provision of utilities and services. Common wall construction also reduces energy needs by exposing less surface area per dwelling unit to the outdoors, thus reducing heating and cooling requirements. Higher-density residential construction can result in energy savings from a variety of perspectives because of the number of common walls, more efficient large-scale heating and cooling systems, and greater feasibility of public transit. Extensive need for elevators and other services in high-rise buildings can, however, eliminate some of these savings.
See: ARCHITECTURAL DESIGN FOR ENERGY CONSERVATION; AUTO DISINCENTIVES; ENERGY CONSERVATION PLANNING; SOLAR ACCESS DESIGN TECHNIQUES

Energy Security Act

Legislation (PL 96-294) passed in 1980 that authorizes substantial funding for development of alternative energy supplies. Containing eight titles on different forms of energy and their economic and environmental impact, the act is intended to stimulate development of sufficient energy sources to reduce the country's dependence on foreign oil imports.

In Title I, part of which is called the United States Synthetic Fuels Corporation Act of 1980, a United States Synthetic Fuels Corporation is established to promote production of these fuels by private industry. The corporation, which is authorized to spend $20 billion by 1997, may offer financial assistance for construction of facilities, land and mineral rights, equipment and transportation facilities in connection with production projects. If its various guarantees and loans are not sufficient to encourage private industry production, the corporation may build up to three government-owned synthetic fuel plants and may offer aid for two others located in other countries in the Western Hemisphere, for forms of synthetic fuel that cannot be economically produced in this country. The latter provision is to assure United States rights to the new technology. A goal of at least 500,000 barrels per day of synthetic crude oil from domestic sources is set for the corporation for 1987, with a goal of at least 2,000,000 barrels per day by 1992.

Title II, the Biomass Energy and Alcohol Fuels Act of 1980, authorizes the departments of Agriculture and Energy to encourage production of alcohol and other fuels from biomass—e.g., crops and crop residues, timber and timber residues, and animal wastes. The two departments are to submit a plan for the development of biomass fuels that is designed to achieve a level of alcohol production in the United States equal to at least 10 percent of the level of gasoline consumption estimated for 1990. Another program that uses municipal biomass wastes, such as sewage sludge or industrial or commercial waste, is also created.

Loans, loan guarantees and price-support guarantees are offered for all biomass programs; demonstration projects are authorized; and an Office of Energy from Municipal Waste is established in the Department of Energy.

Title III of the act establishes a requirement that the president of the United States submit biennial reports to Congress on energy targets for specified years. The energy target reports are to discuss the amounts of foreign oil that will be necessary for the specified target years and accomplishments in energy conservation and anticipated energy production from new sources that are expected to decrease dependence on foreign sources.

The Renewable Energy Resources Act of 1980, which is Title IV of the Energy Security Act, authorizes the secretary of energy to establish, in one or more states, a plan for a three-year pilot energy self-sufficiency program through the use of renewable energy resources. Another provision makes loans available for certain small hydroelectric power plants that had not been eligible under other legislation.

Title V, the Solar Energy and Energy Conservation Act of 1980, establishes a Solar Energy and Energy Conservation Bank within the Department of Housing and Urban Development. The bank is to provide subsidized loans for energy conservation improvements or solar equipment installation in residential or commercial buildings and to create a secondary market in these loans. Another provision of this title authorizes a demonstration residential energy efficiency program in which utility companies would pay for home energy conservation measures that would reduce customer energy requirements, thereby lessening the need for expensive new power plants.

Title VI, the Geothermal Energy Act of 1980, provides funding in the form of loans and loan guarantees for feasibility studies and the search for and verification of geothermal reservoirs. Loans are also authorized for the study of the use of geothermal energy for nonelectric purposes by geothermal utility districts and geothermal industrial development districts.

Title VII, which contains the Acid Precipitation Act of 1980, establishes an Acid Precipitation Task Force to be chaired jointly by the secretary of agriculture, the administrator of the Environmental Protection Agency and the administrator of the National Oceanic and Atmospheric Administration. The task force is directed to prepare a 10-year comprehensive research plan to identify the causes and effects of acid precipitation and to suggest actions to limit or ameliorate the harmful effects of such precipitation. Another study mandated by Title VII is of the projected impact of the level of carbon dioxide in the atmosphere resulting from fossil fuel combustion, coal conversion, synthetic fuels activities authorized by this act, and other sources. The Office of Science and Technology Policy (which is in the executive branch), in cooperation with the National Academy of Sciences, is to present to Congress the results of the study within three years.

Under Title VIII of the act, the president is directed to assure the preservation of United States oil reserves by increasing the reserves in the strategic petroleum reserve (SPR), located in sites in Texas and Louisiana, by an average of 100,000 barrels per day. If the president does not comply, the government is prohibited from selling oil from certain government-owned oil fields and must instead deposit it in the SPR.

Other energy acts passed by Congress in 1980 are concerned with research and demonstration programs for other alternative energy sources. These are the Magnetic Fusion Energy Engineering Act of 1980 (PL 96-386), concerned with nuclear fusion; the Wind Energy Systems Act of 1980 (PL 96-345), directed at energy derived from windmills; the Ocean Thermal Energy Conversion Research, Development and Demonstration Act (PL 96-310), on the use of temperature differences in the oceans; and the Methane Transportation Research, Development and Demonstration Act of 1980 (PL 96-512), on the use of methane as a motor vehicle fuel.

See: ACID RAIN; BIOMASS ENERGY; GEOTHERMAL ENERGY; OCEAN THERMAL ENERGY CONVERSION (OTEC); RENEWABLE ENERGY SOURCES; SOLAR ENERGY AND ENERGY CONSERVATION BANK; SYNTHETIC FUELS; WIND POWER

Energy Sharing

The use of a building or area with good solar access for the collection of solar energy that can then be transmitted to another building or area lacking adequate solar access. A central collector system can, for example, be located in an open common area with good sunlight, and the heat that is collected can be transferred to nearby buildings. The open area should be far enough from the buildings it would serve to be outside of any shadows they would cast but still be near enough to the buildings so that heat loss during transmission is minimized.

See: DETACHED SOLAR COLLECTOR; SOLAR ACCESS; SOLAR COLLECTOR; SOLAR ENERGY

Energy Supply and Environmental Coordination Act of 1974

Legislation that was intended to increase available energy supplies and promote energy efficiency in response to oil shortages at the time. Provisions of this act (PL 93-319) delayed implementation of the Clean Air Act to allow the burning of coal, which had been restricted because of air quality concerns. These provisions were later revised by the Clean Air Act Amendments of 1977, which established a new approach to air pollution reduction. The Energy Supply Act also mandated that the Department of Transportation develop an Emergency Mass Transportation Assistance Plan to expand mass transit systems and encourage their use. It was specified that the Transportation Plan make recommendations on additional assistance for capital and operating grants for mass transit and the use of fare-free and low-fare urban mass transit systems and fringe and transportation corridor parking facilities. A study was also mandated to determine the feasibility of requiring improved gas mileage for new cars and trucks constructed after 1979.

See: CLEAN AIR AMENDMENTS OF 1970; NATIONAL MASS TRANSPORTATION ACT OF 1974

Entitlement Grant

A term used in federal grant programs for an intergovernmental grant that is allocated on the basis of a formula related to population and other characteristics but that is technically not a formula grant.

Entitlement grants, which are noncompetitive, are allocated in the Community Development Block Grant Program to entitlement cities and urban counties on the basis of their formula ratings. Funds in this case are not allocated by state, as they would be in a formula grant. In the revenue sharing program, however, each state receives an entitlement amount, one-third of which is retained by the state, while the rest is distributed to its local governments.

See: FORMULA GRANT

Enumeration District (ED)

An area used for census data collection and statistical tabulation that generally contains a maximum of 1,600 people where the census is taken by mail and 1,000 where there is conventional canvassing. In the 1980 Census enumeration districts were used as the basic data collection level where census blocks and census tracts were not defined. They are also used as administrative units for field operations, tabulation control and statistical reporting. The boundaries of EDs are often changed from one decennial census to the next, both for population count and for administrative reasons, thereby preventing comparisons between censuses.

See: CENSUS; CENSUS HISTORICAL COMPARABILITY

Environmental Analysis

The process of conducting a comprehensive study and review of a broad range of environmental features, such as topography, hydrology, geology and cultural features, for a specified land area.

Environmental analysis serves many valuable planning-related purposes. In regional and municipal planning, it can aid in selecting those land areas most suitable for certain types of land use, such as prime recreational land suited for park use or valuable agricultural land. It can also be used to identify areas that would be hazardous to develop, such as floodplains and unstable slopes. This type of analysis can serve as one basis for the development of comprehensive plans; specialized regulation, such as floodplain zoning and hillside protection ordinances; and decisions concerning the purchase of public lands. On a more site-specific level, environmental analysis can aid a developer in selecting an appropriate site to purchase and then in developing a cost-effective and environmentally sound site plan.

On a formalized basis, the environmental assessments and environmental impact statements required for many federal, state and local projects are a type of environmental analysis in which the focus is the probable environmental consequences of various courses of action.

See: ENVIRONMENTAL ASSESSMENT; ENVIRONMENTAL IMPACT STATEMENT (EIS)

Environmental Assessment

A review process required, pursuant to regulations established to implement provisions of the National Environmental Policy Act of 1969, for proposed federal, federally funded, or federally licensed or sponsored projects or actions. The purpose of an environmental assessment is to determine whether an action or project is environmentally significant and whether an environmental impact statement (EIS) must be prepared.

A federal agency may allow an applicant to prepare an environmental assessment but must independently evaluate the information submitted and take responsibility for the scope and content of the assessment. An environmental assessment must discuss the need for the action or project, alternatives to the action or project, and probable environmental impacts. It must also include a listing of those agencies and individuals that were consulted in the course of preparing the assessment.

If the potential effects are determined to be significant, an EIS is required. If the potential impacts are not considered to be significant, a finding of no significant impact (FONSI) is made. If an agency will be preparing an EIS, it need not first prepare an environmental assessment.

See: ENVIRONMENTAL IMPACT STATEMENT (EIS); FINDING OF NO SIGNIFICANT IMPACT (FONSI)

Environmental Engineering

1. The study of environmental processes and the design of systems and technology to reduce or prevent pollution. The term is most often applied to air and water pollution control, but it also pertains to solid waste management and land management.

2. In the design of buildings, environmental engineering concerns the design and provision of mechanical systems that regulate the interior environment. It generally includes the areas of heating, ventilation and air conditioning, which are commonly referred to as HVAC.

See: AIR POLLUTION CONTROL; LAND MANAGEMENT; SANITARY ENGINEERING; SOLID WASTE MANAGEMENT; WASTEWATER MANAGEMENT; WATER RESOURCES MANAGEMENT

Environmental Impact Statement (EIS)

A detailed written document that provides an analysis of the possible impacts that a proposed federal, federally funded, federally licensed or federally sponsored project or action might have on the environment. The primary purposes of an EIS are to ensure that the goals and objectives of the National Environmental Policy Act of 1969 (NEPA) are incorporated into all federal actions, including planning and decision making, and that both the public and decision makers are provided with a full disclosure of the potential environmental risks (and benefits) of a proposed project. Unlike environmental assessments, which are prepared for most proposed federal actions, environmental impact statements are prepared for those likely to significantly affect the quality of the human environment.

Federal agencies are required to adopt procedures (supplementary to regulations issued by the Council on Environmental Quality) that aid in complying with NEPA. These procedures must include specific criteria that aid in identifying those typical classes of action: (1) that normally do require environmental impact statements, (2) that normally do not require either an environmental impact statement or an environmental assessment (i.e., that receive a "categorical exclusion"—an exemption from the process) or (3) that normally require environmental assessments but not necessarily environmental impact statements.

The format and content of an environmental impact statement follow regulations set forth by the Council on Environmental Quality for implementing the procedural provisions of NEPA. These regulations (40 CFR, Parts 1,500–8) became effective on July 30, 1979 and replace advisory guidelines issued in 1970. They are intended to streamline the EIS process by generally reducing the length of impact statements to a maximum of 150 pages (except in unusual circumstances), requiring that statements be "analytic rather than encyclopedic," that minor issues be discussed only briefly and that plain language be used. The use of "scoping," in which significant issues are identified at an early stage in the EIS process, is encouraged. In addition, to avoid repetition, the use of "tiering" is urged, in which general issues (such as a national program) are covered in a broad EIS, with shorter, more narrowly defined statements prepared for particular aspects of the program (e.g., a regional program or a site-specific project), incorporating by reference the general discussion from the earlier EIS.

In the past it was standard practice to organize an EIS according to the five subsections of Section 102 (2) (C) of NEPA. Instead, the new regulations recommend that the following format be used for all environmental impact statements, unless there is a compelling reason for not using it:

(a) A cover sheet, for which there are standard requirements.

(b) A summary, usually no longer than 15 pages, that completely and accurately summarizes all issues and findings.

(c) A table of contents.

(d) The purpose of and need for the action.

(e) Alternatives, including the proposed action and the possibility of taking no action, which should set forth, in comparative form, the environmental impacts that can be expected from the proposal as well as from each alternative. In addition, this section should include a discussion of the agency's preferred alternative(s) and appropriate mitigation measures.

(f) The environment that will be affected or created by the various alternatives.

(g) The environmental consequences of the alternative actions. This section contains the scientific and analytic materials that provide the basis for the comparisons found in (e), "alternatives." In addition, it is expected to address the elements of Section 102 (2) (C) of NEPA, including environmental impacts of the alternatives as well as the proposed action, any adverse environmental effects that are unavoidable if the proposal is implemented, the relationship between short-term uses of man's environment and the maintenance and enhancement of long-term productivity, and any irreversible or irretrievable commitments of resources that would be involved. Other significant components of this section include a discussion of the possible conflicts of the proposed action with the land use plans, policies and controls that are in effect for the area involved and a discussion of the urban quality, historic and cultural resources, and design of the built environment of the area, including the reuse and conservation potential of various alternatives and mitigation measures.

(h) A list of preparers, along with their qualifications.

(i) A list of the agencies, organizations and persons to whom copies of the statement are sent.

(j) An index.

(k) Any appendices that may be included.

Environmental impact statements are initially prepared in draft form and circulated to involved federal, state and local agencies; the applicant; and any other person, organization or agency requesting a statement. The new regulations specifically address the issue of conflict of interest in the preparation of an EIS, as can occur when those applying for federal funding or permits perform the required project analyses. The regulations limit preparation of an EIS to a lead federal agency (one or more federal agencies may join with one or more state or local agencies to be joint lead agencies) or an independent contractor, usually selected by the lead agency. Any individual or organization may submit information of relevance to the EIS, but the federal official in charge of that EIS is expected to evaluate this information, as well as materials prepared by the contractor, independently.

After an appropriate comment period, a final environmental impact statement is prepared. In the final statement substantive comments raised during review of the draft EIS must be addressed by measures such as the discussion of new alternatives, improved analyses, factual corrections or rebuttal. Procedures are available by which federal interagency disagreements concerning the acceptability of potential environmental impacts may be referred to the Council on Environmental Quality (CEQ).

Many states and some municipalities have also adopted environmental policy acts that require the preparation of EISs for certain state and locally funded projects. As of June 1, 1979, 14 states plus Puerto Rico had comprehensive statutory requirements for environmental impact statements, and 4 states had comprehensive executive or administrative orders. Other states have special or limited EIS requirements. In order to avoid duplication between state and federal requirements for such statements, the

CEQ drafted a model law for states to use that complements provisions of CEQ's regulations (Section 1506.2) for implementing NEPA. The federal regulations urge to the fullest extent possible that a single document be prepared that meets federal, state and local requirements for an environmental impact statement.

See: COUNCIL ON ENVIRONMENTAL QUALITY (CEQ); ENVIRONMENTAL ASSESSMENT; FINDING OF NO SIGNIFICANT IMPACT (FONSI); NATIONAL ENVIRONMENTAL POLICY ACT OF 1969 (NEPA); SCOPING

Environmental Management

The use and protection of natural resources through the application of environmentally sound practices. Environmental management encompasses a wide range of subject areas that are of concern to planners, including the management of land, water and air.

See: AIR POLLUTION; COASTAL AREA PLANNING; CRITICAL AREAS; EARTHQUAKE HAZARD MITIGATION; ENDANGERED SPECIES; ENERGY CONSERVATION PLANNING; ENVIRONMENTAL ANALYSIS; ENVIRONMENTAL ENGINEERING; ENVIRONMENTAL IMPACT STATEMENT (EIS); ENVIRONMENTAL MEDIATION; ENVIRONMENTALLY SENSITIVE LANDS; FLOOD CONTROL; FLOODPLAIN MANAGEMENT; FOREST FIRE CONTROL; INTEGRATED PEST MANAGEMENT (IPM); LAND MANAGEMENT; OPEN-SPACE PLANNING; RENEWABLE ENERGY SOURCES; RIVER ENGINEERING; SOLID WASTE MANAGEMENT; WASTEWATER MANAGEMENT; WATER RESOURCES MANAGEMENT

Environmental Mediation

An extension of the application of negotiation techniques, such as those traditionally used to settle labor disputes, to resolve environmental controversies. Environmental mediation often takes place with the aid of an impartial mediator, whose role is to aid the participants to the dispute in reaching a satisfactory solution. Alternatively, direct negotiation may take place between the concerned parties. These techniques are being used with increasing frequency in situations where the various parties to the conflict are willing to voluntarily explore their differences and attempt to find a reasonable compromise.

Mediation and negotiation are considered particularly appropriate in situations in which relevant government agencies or other bodies with decision-making powers are willing to cooperate so that the ultimate agreement may be implemented or in disputes in which there is disagreement or confusion concerning the basic facts of the issue.

Environmental Protection Agency (EPA)

An independent agency within the executive branch of the United States government, created in 1970 to control and abate environmental pollution. The agency undertakes research, monitoring, standard setting, regulation and enforcement activities in the areas of air, water, noise and radiation pollution; disposal of solid waste and toxic substances; and pesticide use. It also works with or supports state and local government environmental protection programs and research projects. The various technical sections of the agency provide technical assistance and guidelines and disseminate the results of research projects. The 10 regional offices of EPA administer the agency's programs and are mandated to develop and implement a comprehensive and integrated regional environmental protection program. EPA also has 14 laboratories to carry out its in-house research, provides grants, enters into cooperative agreements with universities and contracts with industrial laboratories and private institutions for other research projects. EPA also relies on the Science Advisory Board (a panel of non-EPA scientists established to advise EPA on scientific issues) for technical advice.

EPA administers major environmental control programs authorized by legislation passed in the 1970s and 1980s. The Clean Water Act and the Safe Drinking Water Act of 1974 provide authority for water pollution control programs. Under the Clean Water Act (Federal Water Pollution Control Act Amendments of 1972 as amended), EPA requires state and regional planning for control of pollution, provides a grant program for construction of sewerage systems and sewage treatment facilities, and establishes effluent limitations for municipal and industrial sources of pollution. It also operates a permit program to ensure that municipal and industrial discharges comply with effluent limitations and oversees certain aspects of the dredge and fill permit program. Under the Safe Drinking Water Act, EPA issues regulations that set national drinking water standards, requires state enforcement of the standards (or assumes this responsibility if states fail to do so) and issues rules to protect underground sources of drinking water from contamination by certain groundwater injection practices. The Marine Protection, Research and Sanctuaries Act of 1972 authorizes EPA to regulate certain aspects of ocean dumping.

The Clean Air Act of 1970 as amended gives EPA authority in air pollution matters. Under this act EPA sets primary and secondary national ambient air quality standards for specific air pollutants, requires and reviews state implementation plans that stipulate measures to be taken to achieve satisfactory air quality and sets emissions limitations for new or modified stationary air pollution sources (new source performance standards) and standards for emission of hazardous air pollutants.

EPA's waste disposal control activities are authorized by the Resource Conservation and Recovery Act of 1976 (RCRA) and the Comprehensive Environmental Response, Compensation and Liability Act of 1980 (CERCLA). Under RCRA, EPA provides grants to states for solid waste plans, inventories of municipal waste disposal sites, resource-recovery programs and demonstration programs. EPA also monitors disposal activities for solid waste and hazardous waste. For hazardous wastes all treatment, storage and disposal sites must have permits to operate, and their design must prevent the waste from reaching water sources. Over 10,000 of these sites are currently regulated by EPA, while an EPA manifest tracking system traces hazardous wastes from their source to their disposal site. Under CERCLA, EPA is involved in emergency cleanup of major spills of hazardous substances as well as in long-term remedial action at abandoned hazardous waste disposal sites.

Other EPA activities are authorized by the Toxic Substances Control Act (TSCA)—use of chemicals and disposal of toxic substances such as PCBs; the Federal Insecticide, Fungicide and Rodenticide Act (FIFRA)—control of pesticide use; the Noise Control Act of 1972 and Quiet Communities Act of 1978—noise reduction programs; and several acts that allow the agency to control emission of radiation and permit environmental radiation monitoring.

See: AREAWIDE WASTE TREATMENT MANAGEMENT PLANNING (SECTION 208); ARMY CORPS OF ENGINEERS' PERMIT PROGRAM; COUNCIL ON ENVIRONMENTAL QUALITY (CEQ); NATIONAL AMBIENT AIR QUALITY STANDARDS (NAAQS); NATIONAL POLLUTANT DISCHARGE ELIMINATION SYSTEM (NPDES); NEW SOURCE PERFORMANCE STANDARDS (NSPS); STATE IMPLEMENTATION PLAN (SIP); STATE WATER QUALITY MANAGEMENT PLAN (SECTION 303 [e])

Environmental Psychology

The study of the relationships between physical setting and human behavior. Psychologists have utilized scientific techniques to determine how people react to a wide variety of environmental features, ranging from color, furniture and room size, to open spaces and public plazas. Environmental psychology can provide useful information to architects and planners concerning the way people use space and design characteristics that assist them to function more effectively.

See: BEHAVIORAL DESIGN; DEFENSIBLE SPACE; PERSONAL SPACE; TERRITORIALITY

Environmentally Sensitive Lands

Those areas in which disturbance of characteristic features or functions can result in serious environmental, economic or safety consequences for a community. The effects of disturbing many hillsides, aquifers, streams and wetlands can range from safety hazards, such as flooding or landslides, to drought, poor water quality and the shortage of other valuable natural resources. Economic consequences include the cost of providing additional public facilities, such as flood-prevention devices or new water sources, and the loss of value in real estate, such as in slide-prone areas.

The regulation of environmentally sensitive areas can be accomplished through land use controls, such as zoning ordinances, which enumerate districts subject to special land use regulations, or through special ordinances that are supplementary to zoning or subdivision regulations. Examples of these types of controls are the wetlands ordinance, tree preservation ordinance, hillside protection ordinance, erosion and sedimentation control ordinance or water recharge ordinance.

An increasing trend is toward the use of performance controls, now frequently seen in building codes or industrial zoning, as a supplement to the specification standards usually encountered in zoning. While a specification standard will permit or prohibit specific uses or applications, a performance control will require that a specific result be attained, encouraging flexibility and experimentation. An example of a performance approach would be a requirement that surface runoff not exceed the rate that existed before development. Communities sometimes permit a land use not specified in the zoning ordinance if certain performance standards can be met. Performance controls also encourage a comprehensive approach to protecting environmentally sensitive land by separating the environmental concerns from the types of uses permitted by zoning districts.

See: BEACH EROSION; COASTAL AREA PLANNING; CRITICAL AREAS; EARTHQUAKE HAZARD MITIGATION; FLOODPLAIN; HAZARDOUS AREAS; HILLSIDE PROTECTION ORDINANCES; MASS WASTING; TREE PRESERVATION ORDINANCE; WATER RESOURCES MANAGEMENT; WETLANDS

Equalization Rate

The average percentage of the full value at which the local assessor is assessing all taxable properties in a municipality, as determined by a state or county equalization board. When a municipality's total assessed valuation is divided by the equalization rate, the full valuation of real property in that municipality is obtained. Equalization rates are used to equitably apportion the tax burden throughout a county, or throughout a school district or special district that crosses municipal boundaries. Other uses include the equitable distribution of state aid to localities, the determination of constitutional limitations on local taxing and borrowing powers, and the determination of assessments on agricultural land in agricultural districts.

To determine the equalization rate, the state board of equalization must regularly make its own sample assessments within each municipality. It then compares its findings to the local assessed valuation to determine the average percentage of full value at which the local assessor is assessing property.

See: ASSESSED VALUATION; ASSESSMENT RATIO; UNIFORM ASSESSMENT PROCEDURES

Equity

The extent of the interest of a property owner in his property, net of all mortgages, liens or other claims against the property. A property owner's equity is equal to the excess of the value of the property as if unencumbered over the dollar amount of all mortgages, liens or other claims against the property.

An owner's equity can increase either by an increase in the value of his property or by elimination of encumbrances against the property by payment or other means. Thus, assuming property values remained stable, the making of principal and interest payments on a mortgage increase the owner's equity by an amount equal to the amount of each payment that is allocable to repayment of the principal of the mortgage.

Estuary

A coastal water body that is partially enclosed but allows seawater to enter with the tide and mix with fresh water. Estuaries may be found at coastal bays, fiords, river mouths, tidal marshes, lagoons and the like; major rivers such as the Hudson, Mississippi, Rhine, Thames and Seine end as coastal plains estuaries.

Estuaries perform a key role in the food chain and provide a sheltered environment for the spawning of many types of fish and the development of plant life. They are also storehouses of plant nutrients that originate on land and are transmitted to ocean waters, where they settle and become available as food. The same capacity that allows an estuary to trap nutrients also enables it to trap pollutants such as pesticides and heavy metals.

Estuaries function efficiently as resource producers because they are protected from wave action, allowing plants and shellfish larvae to become established; at the same time, the mixture of fresh water and saltwater creates a varied and rich environment. In addition, the shallow depth discourages predators and encourages plant growth because light penetration is greater than in deeper waters.

The gradual decline of shellfish production in the United States is considered to be caused partially by the altering of estuarine habitats through such activities as dredging, filling and draining. Estuaries have been used for activities ranging from sanitary landfill to airport construction as pressure for vacant land has increased. The Coastal Zone Management Act provides some mechanisms for protection of estuaries and has encouraged states to develop protective regulations.

See: COASTAL WATERSHED; COASTAL ZONE MANAGEMENT ACT OF 1972 (CZMA); WETLANDS

Eubank v. *City of Richmond* (226 U.S. 137, 33 S. Ct. 76, 57 L.Ed. 156 [1912])

A decision by the United States Supreme Court that declined to sustain a Richmond, Virginia ordinance allowing the owners of two-thirds of the property abutting any street to determine the minimum setback line for the street.

The decision represents the only instance in the era preceding the case of *Village of Euclid* v. *Ambler Realty Co.* in which the Supreme Court refused to sustain a local land control measure. However, the Court upheld in principle the constitutionality of municipal control of building setback requirements.

See: VILLAGE OF EUCLID v. AMBLER REALTY CO.

Euclidean Zoning

A shorthand way of referring to a zoning ordinance of the type approved by the United States Supreme Court in 1926 in the landmark case *Village of Euclid* v. *Ambler Realty Co.*

The term refers to a comprehensive zoning ordinance in which uses are divided among use districts of increasing intensity (for example, ranging from single family residential to heavy industrial). The uses permitted in each district are cumulative, so that in the heavy industrial district all less intensive land uses would be permitted. Euclidean zoning is sometimes depicted physically as a pyramid or triangle, with the least intensive use at the top and each layer representing an increasingly more intensive use district.

See: CUMULATIVE ZONING; EXCLUSIVE USE ZONING; *VILLAGE OF EUCLID* v. *AMBLER REALTY CO.*

Eutrophication

The process by which nutrients stimulate aquatic plant growth and lead to the aging of a lake. Normally this process occurs gradually. Plant debris settles to the lake's bottom to decay, slowly filling in the lake and depleting dissolved oxygen stores. The lake grows shallower, and vegetation at the lake's edge advances until the lake is gone.

The rate at which eutrophication occurs can, however, be greatly accelerated through human activities that introduce large amounts of nutrients, particularly nitrates and phosphates. Discharge of domestic and industrial sewage, runoff from agricultural lands to which fertilizers have been applied and pollution by detergents or rain containing nitrogen derived from smokestacks and engines can all stimulate eutrophication. This type of eutrophication, known as cultural eutrophication, can cause the death of a lake to occur in a drastically shortened time period, representing a major problem resulting from pollution.

A National Eutrophication Survey conducted between 1972 and 1977 by the U.S. Environmental Protection Agency classified 68 percent of the lakes sampled as eutrophic, meaning their waters were generally murky with high levels of algal growth and plant decay, and abundant plankton. A eutrophic lake is also characterized by a muddy bottom and warm water, so it cannot support desirable cold-water fish species. Aesthetic quality, swimming, fishing and boating are often affected by eutrophication, and property values may decline when a recreational water body becomes eutrophic.

Among the measures that may be taken to reduce cultural eutrophication are reducing the existing levels of nutrients in water bodies and minimizing the flow of additional nutrients. Various methods proposed for reducing existing levels of nutrients are dredging, harvesting of plants and algae, and the addition of aluminum and iron salts to the water (which will combine with phosphorous and form a compound that will settle to the lake bottom). The elimination of sewage discharge to lakes, removal of phosphates from sewage and improved farming practices concerning fertilizer application, animal waste disposal and the minimization of runoff and soil erosion can help to

lessen the nutrient flow reaching lakes and other bodies of water.
See: ALGAL BLOOM; BIOCHEMICAL OXYGEN DEMAND (BOD); DYSTROPHIC LAKE; MESOTROPHIC LAKE; OLIGOTROPHIC LAKE

Evaporation Pond

A method of sewage disposal in which treated effluent is sprayed over large land areas to permit it to evaporate. A portion of the effluent will seep into the soil, where it will be further refined through natural biological processes. However, the residue that will remain in the soil may be a contaminant if the effluent is toxic.
See: EFFLUENT

Evergreens

A plant in which the leaves remain green throughout the year. Although evergreens do shed their leaves, they do not all drop at a particular time of year. Instead they remain, often more than a year, until the plant has developed a replacement.

A number of types of evergreens are found in different climatic areas. In the tropical or subtropical areas, such as Florida, broad-leaved evergreens, such as palms, may be found. Narrow-leaved evergreens, such as longleaf or loblolly pine, are common in the southern pine forests, as are broad-leaved evergreens, such as live oak, holly or magnolia. A vast belt of evergreens—mainly of the coniferous, or cone-bearing, type—extends across the temperate and colder climates of the United States, Canada, Europe and Asia. These trees—such as spruce, fir, hemlock or pine—are characterized by stiff, hard foliage well suited to resist cold and drought.

Because they bear leaves year round, evergreen trees and shrubs are widely used in landscaping to screen development from undesirable uses or views. It is often required that a certain proportion of the landscaping or screening for a new development be of the evergreen type to prevent an unsightly winter view or appearance.
See: DECIDUOUS TREES; LANDSCAPING; SCREENING

Ex Officio

The membership of a person on a board of directors of an agency by virtue of his holding another position that is related to the work of that agency. As an example, the planning director often is an ex officio member of the transportation, parks and health boards as well as other boards and commissions with responsibility for areas in which he is involved. In many cases ex officio members are not given a vote on the board. The term is Latin for "by virtue of office."

Exaction

A fee or contribution of cash or property required of a developer as a condition of receiving development approval. Most often associated with subdivision regula-

tions, an exaction may take many forms, including required parkland donation, payment of a fee in lieu of parkland donation or financing of improvements to existing public roads that are not located within the subdivision. Another type of exaction is the development impact fee, in which developers are required to pay a tax or user fee to cover the costs of municipal services to the new development.

Factors affecting the legality of exactions include the extent to which the exaction is required because of demand generated by the new development, the nature of state enabling legislation, the language of the subdivision regulation and the existence of municipal policies and plans that support the need for the exaction.
See: DEDICATION; FEE IN LIEU OF DEDICATION; OFF-SITE IMPROVEMENTS; SUBDIVISION REGULATIONS

Excavated Pond

A man-made water resource with limited storage capacity that is constructed by digging pits in areas of level terrain. An excavated pond is usually sited where either good natural drainage, sufficient groundwater resources or a combination of these sources is a available to maintain the water supply.
See: ARTIFICIAL WATER BODIES; EMBANKMENT POND; FARM POND

Excavation

1. The process of removing materials, such as soil or rock, from the ground to create a depression. Excavation may be required for numerous reasons, including the construction of buildings, tunnels, pipeline, bridges or roadway; mining; or to obtain fill. The type of excavation may be classified according to the nature of the material being removed—for example, topsoil, earth, rock, muck or a combination of these.

Excavation is often performed with a bulldozer, which can both excavate and move materials. Other types of excavating machines—such as the power shovel, backhoe or trenching machine—generally dig and then load the materials so that they can be transported by other machinery. The type of machinery selected depends upon the kind and volume of material being excavated, the distance the material must be hauled, the kind of terrain over which it must be transported and the ability of the ground to support the weight of the machinery.

2. The depression left in the ground after materials have been removed from it.

3. The specialized digging necessary to uncover archaeological artifacts. It is accomplished by careful and gradual removal and analysis of individual layers or soil. Rescue excavation is a more rapid emergency process that is employed when an archaeological site is scheduled to be used for construction.
See: CUT; GRADING

Excess Condemnation

The taking of more property than is strictly needed for the primary or principal goal of the condemnation. If the taking of the excess land can be justified for a public purpose, however, the excess condemnation may be permitted. An example of this might be a situation in which a condemnation of additional land enables the condemning authority to prepare for future contingencies related to the development of the principal improvement or in which more comprehensive planning of the surrounding areas can take place in connection with the improvements.
See: CONDEMNATION; PUBLIC USE

Exclusionary Zoning

Zoning that has the effect of precluding residential opportunities for racial minorities and persons of low and moderate income. Zoning techniques that achieve this result, whether intentional or not, include large minimum lot size and minimum floor area requirements, and prohibition or restriction on the development of multifamily housing.

Suburban communities have been accused of employing exclusionary zoning as a means of maintaining a homogeneous character. Ordinances have been challenged, in some cases successfully, on the grounds that they are employed with the intent of discriminating against racial minorities or the poor or that they are not reasonably related to the police power goals of furthering public health, safety and general welfare, which underlie zoning enabling legislation. In some cases, those challenging zoning ordinances as exclusionary have argued that each community is obligated to provide housing opportunities satisfying its fair share of regional housing needs and that a community's zoning ordinance must be consistent with this obligation.

Communities have countered these challenges by maintaining that their zoning ordinances do not intentionally discriminate. Rather, the intent of the ordinance was to preserve the suburban character of the community and prevent growth that the community was not then ready to absorb.
See: APPEAL *OF GIRSH;* BERENSON v. *TOWN OF NEW CASTLE; CONSTRUCTION INDUSTRY ASS'N OF SONOMA COUNTY* v. *CITY OF PETALUMA;* FAIR SHARE; *GOLDEN* v. *PLANNING BOARD OF THE TOWN OF RAMAPO;* GROWTH MANAGEMENT; *JAMES* v. *VALTIERRA;* LARGE-LOT ZONING; MINIMUM LOT SIZE; MINIMUM RESIDENTIAL FLOOR AREA REQUIREMENTS; *SOUTHERN BURLINGTON COUNTY NAACP* v. *TOWNSHIP OF MT. LAUREL; VILLAGE OF ARLINGTON HEIGHTS* v. *METROPOLITAN HOUSING DEVELOPMENT CORPORATION; VILLAGE OF BELLE TERRE* v. *BORAAS*

Exclusive-Use Zoning

The practice of creating zoning districts in which only one type of use or a narrow range of uses is permitted. Exclusive-use zoning was developed in response to the problems encountered in cumulative zoning, where all "higher" uses, such as residential development, are permitted in zones for "lower" uses, such as industrial development. Exclusive-use zoning attempts to eliminate this problem by permitting in any given zone only specifically enumerated uses thought to be clearly compatible.
See: CUMULATIVE ZONING; MIXED-USE ZONING; ZONING

Executive Headquarters

Office buildings built by businesses in which they house their principal offices. Executive headquarters may be wholly or partially occupied by the company, but the building bears the company's name and is designed to offer a desired corporate image. In most cases these are well-designed buildings that municipalities usually perceive as adding prestige to the community. In some cases, however, the corporation will seek to use the building's architecture to dominate the skyline or the area as a form of advertisement that may be inconsistent with municipal plans.

As with other office development, corporations today are frequently locating executive headquarters in suburban areas, where they may have campus settings and attractive landscaping. Proximity to airports and to the residences of corporate executives can be important considerations in the selection of a suburban location.
See: CAMPUS OFFICE PARK; CORPORATE TRAINING CENTER; OFFICE DEVELOPMENT

Executive Order 12372

An order signed by the president of the United States, effective September 30, 1983, that directs federal departments and agencies to promulgate new regulations for intergovernmental coordination for projects and programs receiving federal funding. A replacement for the A-95 process, which used regional and state clearinghouses to review and coordinate comments that would be forwarded to the pertinent federal agency, Executive Order 12372 allows each state to establish its own course of action, including the abandonment of an official coordination system. Federal agencies must consult with each state according to its adopted procedure, if it has one, on any project or program for which the state supplies part of the funding or that will have an effect on state or local areas.

Under the new intergovernmental coordination process, state governments may take a wide variety of actions, including maintenance of the traditional A-95 consultation process and improvements in or variations of that process. As an example, states can abolish the state clearinghouse and permit only the areawide clearinghouses to perform as the single contact point in the state for each project, as mandated by the executive order, or they may decide to have the next higher level of government coordinate comments. An interstate consultation system may also be designated by the states. Another provision of the executive order allows states to select those programs that will be subject to the state review system (from a list of programs subject to intergovernmental coordination put forth by each federal department and agency), eliminating some from the state review process. A major requirement of the executive order is that where a state has established a review system, the federal agencies are required to accommodate state and local views or provide a written explanation for rejecting the recommendation and failing to reach a mutually agreeable solution.

In states without an official system, federal agencies are required to use their discretion in acting upon public comments but must act in accordance with Section 401 of the Intergovernmental Cooperation Act of 1968 (PL 90-577), which emphasizes that federal actions should be as consistent as possible with planning activities and decisions at state, regional and local levels. They must also provide state and local governments with opportunities for consultation in matters related to federally assisted or federally developed projects.

The executive order discourages the continuation or creation of any planning agency that is established for a limited purpose—e.g., solely to review proposed projects—and that is not adequately representative of or accountable to state or local elected officials. Since a formal intergovernmental coordination process is no longer required, it is expected that many states will discard coordinative programs.
See: A-95 REVIEW

Expansion Joint

Spaces between relatively long expanses (often 200 feet or greater, or 61 meters or more) of concrete components in buildings and roads. These spaces are provided to relieve compressive stresses that would otherwise result from a rise in temperature, causing cracking or buckling of the concrete.

Expansion joints are provided in large buildings as straight horizontal or vertical lines on walls, roofs and at junctions of these elements. They are placed on roads both perpendicular and parallel to the length of the road. A filler, often made of rubber or copper, is usually provided to act as a waterstop between the concrete sections. Waterstops are necessary to prevent water seepage behind concrete walls, panels and slabs, which can freeze and expand, causing the concrete to buckle, and to prevent water damage to internal structural elements. Fillers may also be necessary in building interiors for aesthetic purposes.

Contraction joints are control joints used during concrete construction that permit the concrete to shrink during curing without causing uncontrolled cracking in random locations. A common construction method permits a space of several feet to be left in a concrete wall for subsequent concreting after the abutting wall sections dry and shrink.
See: CONCRETE

Expressway

A divided arterial highway for through traffic with full or partial control of access and, generally, with grade-separated intersections. It is a high-volume highway with high design speed providing no direct access to abutting land uses. Expressways are spaced from 1 to 10 miles (1.6 to 16.1 kilometers) apart in the urban framework, depending upon urban density, and provide up to 10 percent of the mileage of the total road system. Systems of expressways have been provided for urban areas in radial, circumferential and gridiron patterns, generally placed to compensate for deficiencies and relieve congestion on arterial roads, which constitute the primary through-traffic carrying system.

A typical expressway cross section would provide a right-of-way of 150 to 250 feet (45.7 to 76.2 meters); four to eight 12-foot (3.7-meter) moving lanes; shoulders at least 8 to 10 feet (2.4 to 3.0 meters) in width; and an 8- to 30-foot (2.4- to 9.1-meter) median strip. A maximum grade of 4 percent and a design speed of 50 mph (80 kph) should be provided. Expressways carry traffic volumes in excess of 40,000 trips per day. They are usually built at grade and have parallel service or frontage roads or substantial rear lot setbacks of 75 feet (22.9 meters) or more from the right-of-way. Landscaping is provided where sufficient space exists. Some older expressways have a few intersections at grade, which are channelized and signalized. (See Fig. 43)
See: ARTERIAL ROAD; CIRCUMFERENTIAL PLAN; CONTROL OF ACCESS; FREEWAY; GRIDIRON PATTERN; RADIAL PATTERN; TRAFFIC CONTROL DEVICES

Externalities

The social costs that a group must pay or the social benefits that a group receives as a result of the actions of others. They are the often unintended and unexpected results of a development or activity that are not directly associated with that activity and may result from both public and private-sector investment.

An example of an external diseconomy or negative externality is the generation of air or water pollution by an industry, since the costs and effects of the pollution are borne by the public at large. An external economy or positive externality might be the recreational lake that is created for public use during the course of dam construction for another purpose.
See: DIRECT AND INDIRECT BENEFITS; DIRECT AND INDIRECT COSTS

Extraterritorial Zoning

The power given to a municipality to impose zoning controls upon areas outside of the municipal boundary, albeit generally in close proximity to that boundary. Most often, extraterritorial zoning powers are granted to allow incorporated areas to extend zoning control to adjacent unincorporated areas.

The rationale for granting this authority is the promotion of orderly and compatible development on the perimeters of a locality. It is also argued that an incorporated area, such as a city, generally has an administrative structure and staff that allow it to efficiently administer zoning regulations; it also has a strong incentive to encourage proper development so close to its boundaries. The major objection that is raised to extraterritorial zoning is the imposition of zoning regulations upon areas whose citizens are not represented by the legislative body imposing the zoning. A partial solution to this problem is the appointment of citizen representatives of that area to the planning commission and the zoning board of appeals of the incorporated area.

Extraterritorial zoning is permitted only in those states with appropriate enabling legislation authorizing this activity. Extraterritorial control of subdivisions is also permitted in many states.
See: ZONING

Exurbia

The rural-urban fringe located beyond most suburbs, where low-density suburban development meets rural areas. Exurbia often contains a mixture of land uses, including large-lot suburban residences, country estates, low-density commercial development, and the remaining agricultural and rural land uses.

From 1970 to 1979 nonmetropolitan areas in the United States saw a net population increase of 3.5 million, a reversal of a 160-year-old pattern of movement to urban areas. These moves were often to exurbia. A recent study of development at the urban fringe, moreover, suggests that land speculation starts at least 20 years prior to actual urbanization, indicating that growth management must begin well before the urbanization process starts.
See: ABORTIVE OR PREMATURE SUBDIVISION; AGRICULTURAL LAND USE; GROWTH MANAGEMENT; LAND USE PATTERN; RURAL PLANNING; SUBURB; URBANIZATION

F

Facade

1.   A building's front or any of its exterior walls.
2.   A prominent side of a building or structure that has been given special architectural or design treatment to make it more attractive.
See: COMMUNITY CHARACTER; DESIGN CONTINUITY; SCALE OF DEVELOPMENT; STREETSCAPE; WALL ART

Facade Easement

A type of easement used to preserve the exterior appearance of a building, most often employed to protect historic or architecturally significant properties. The holder of a facade easement may prohibit changes or alterations to the outside of a building, although the property owner may make interior changes. A facade easement can also require preventive maintenance, such as cleaning or painting.

In one application of this device, a government agency may acquire a facade easement to a privately held building to protect government funds being spent on facade improvements. Generally, once these improvements have been made, they may not be undone for a specified period of time. Preservation groups also sometimes purchase facade easements to ensure that significant building exteriors are protected.

Tax advantages are often available, in the form of reduced local property taxes and federal income tax deductions, to the fee owner of property who donates a facade easement.
See: EASEMENT; HISTORIC PRESERVATION; HISTORIC PRESERVATION TAX INCENTIVES

Factory

A building in which goods are manufactured, either from raw materials or from component pieces. Depending upon the specific nature of the factory, it may be classified as light or heavy industry.
See: INDUSTRIAL AREA; INDUSTRIAL PARK; OFF-STREET LOADING; OFF-STREET PARKING REQUIREMENTS

Fair Housing Legislation

Legislation that prohibits discrimination in housing. Major pieces of United States housing legislation and other legal authority are: Executive Order 11063 (1962), which directs federal agencies to prevent discrimination in housing that receives federal funds, loans, guarantees or insurance; Title VI of the Civil Rights Act of 1964 (PL 88-352), which prohibits discrimination in federally supported programs; and Title VIII of the Civil Rights Act of 1968 (PL 90-284), which prohibits discrimination in many real estate transactions, including home purchase and rental. Title VIII is the most sweeping, including specific prohibition against blockbusting, redlining and discrimination. The 5th, 13th and 14th Amendments to the Constitution and the Civil Rights Act of 1866 form the legal basis for fair housing actions.

Fair housing legislation in the 1960s prohibited discrimination in housing based upon race, color, religion (creed) or national origin. Later legislation added prohibitions against discrimination on the basis of sex (Section 527 of Title V of the National Housing Act as added by Section 808 [a] and Section 109 of the Housing and Community Development Act of 1974 [PL 95-383]), age (Age Discrimination Act of 1975 [PL 94-135]) and handicap (Section 504 of the Rehabilitation Act of 1973 [PL 93-112]).

Fair housing legislation generally includes specific enforcement procedures, and the courts have often been called upon to adjudicate violations. Many states and localities have adopted their own fair housing legislation, usually administered through an Equal Rights Commission or its equivalent. All Department of Housing and Urban Development (HUD) programs are monitored to ensure affirmative action to prevent discrimination, with penalties for noncompliance. HUD also aids Community Housing Resource Boards, whose purpose is to monitor and support fair housing activity; operates the Fair Housing Assistance Program (FHAP), which supports local fair housing agencies; and promotes the Voluntary Compliance program, in which affirmative marketing agreements are negotiated with the private sector, such as with housing industry groups, and comprehensive fair housing plans are developed with local governments.

See: AFFIRMATIVE FAIR HOUSING MARKETING; BLOCKBUSTING; FAIR SHARE; *JONES* v. *ALFRED H. MAYER*; REDLINING

Fair Share

The distribution of low- and moderate-income housing among the various municipalities in a metropolitan region. The fair share concept calls for each locality to provide for a proportionate amount of housing for current and expected lower-income residents of the region, usually by addressing land use policies that prevent or restrict the development of multifamily or relatively higher density housing. The concept developed in the 1970s as a response to increasing concentrations in central cities of the poor and of minority groups, who were unable to find housing in suburban areas. Fair share approaches seek to include some proportionate amount of lower-cost housing in each community, often by rezoning of some areas or by other methods that permit higher densities.

Fair share has been utilized on both a court-ordered and voluntary basis. The landmark 1975 New Jersey case of *Southern Burlington County NAACP* v. *Township of Mt. Laurel* held that every developing municipality (now every municipality in a growth area) in that state must have a land use policy permitting a fair share of regional housing suitable for low- and moderate-income residents. Similar cases in other states, such as *Berenson* v. *Town of New Castle* in New York, also established the principle of provision for regional housing needs. Some regional planning

agencies, such as the Miami Valley (Dayton) Regional Planning Commission, had earlier prepared fair share housing distribution plans and achieved a level of voluntary acceptance.

The Housing and Community Development Act of 1974 specified that its purpose was to increase "the diversity and vitality of neighborhoods through the spatial deconcentration of housing opportunities for persons of lower income" and imposed a requirement that Housing Assistance Plans (HAPs) provide for regional distribution of low- and moderate-income housing. Although this requirement only began being enforced in 1976 as a result of a suit brought against HUD *(City of Hartford et al.* v. *Carla A. Hills et al.),* it is currently required that HAPs contain such policies as a basis for receiving Community Development Block Grants.

See: BERENSON v. *TOWN OF NEW CASTLE;* EXCLUSIONARY ZONING; FAIR HOUSING LEGISLATION; HOUSING ASSISTANCE PLAN (HAP); *SOUTHERN BURLINGTON COUNTY NAACP* v. *TOWNSHIP OF MT. LAUREL*

Family

Typically, for the purposes of zoning, a family is defined to include those sharing a dwelling unit who are related by blood, marriage or adoption. Some ordinances will specifically define which blood relatives can be considered to be part of a family, while certain other ordinances may also permit up to five unrelated individuals who are sharing one housing unit to be considered one family. Domestic servants employed by the family are usually also permitted. This definition is important in those municipalities that limit occupancy of some housing units to families.

Restrictions concerning family use are frequently included in zoning ordinances for the purpose of protecting the single-family residential neighborhood. Depending upon the precise wording of the definition, it may exclude college students or the elderly from jointly renting a house, members of a religious order from sharing housing space, or group homes for foster children or handicapped children, or it may prevent two unmarried adults from living together.

The question of how a family should be defined has been the subject of much controversy, both legal and social. In the early 1970s state and lower federal courts often struck down zoning ordinances that sought to exclude all unrelated individuals from the definition of family. Later in the 1970s, however, the Supreme Court reaffirmed the right of municipalities to limit single-family districts largely to traditional families in the case of *Village of Belle Terre* v. *Boraas* in 1974.

Definitions of family have also been of great concern to those agencies operating group homes for disabled or retarded children or adults, or for foster children, as well as for the communities in which the homes are proposed to be located. In some states courts have ruled that these types of homes function as a family unit and should be permitted in zones normally restricted to related individuals.

See: GROUP HOME; HOUSING FOR FAMILIES; *MOORE v. CITY OF EAST CLEVELAND, OHIO; VILLAGE OF BELLE TERRE v. BORAAS*

Faneuil Hall Marketplace

A renovated historic complex located adjacent to Boston's waterfront that was developed by the Rouse Company. It is comprised of Quincy Market, built in 1826 for warehouse and office use, and North and South Markets, built in 1824 for market use to relieve crowding at Faneuil Hall, a prerevolutionary public meeting area and market.

Today Quincy Market (whose renovation was completed in 1976) contains a large variety of restaurants, food stands and specialty shops, while North and South Markets (which were completed in 1977 and 1978, respectively) are filled with furniture, clothing and gift boutiques as well as additional restaurants. With more than 35,000 visitors passing through each day, the stone buildings have become a major tourist attraction, a lucrative source of revenue for the city and a catalyst for other revitalization projects. (See Fig. 14)

See: ADAPTIVE USE; ECONOMIC DEVELOPMENT; GHIRADELLI SQUARE; HISTORIC PRESERVATION; WATERFRONT REVITALIZATION

Farm Mortgage

A loan that is obtained by farmers in order to raise capital for their farm operation or to acquire additional farm property and is secured by their farm real estate.

Farm Pond

A small, man-made water body created for personal or farm use that is maintained by surface runoff and groundwater. Farm ponds, which average 0.25 to 2 acres (0.1 to

(a)

(b)

(c)

Fig. 14. Faneuil Hall Marketplace: (a) a late-19th century photo of Quincy Market and (b) as it appears today. A rendering of the rehabilitated marketplace (c) shows Quincy Market in the middle and North and South Markets to its left and right respectively. Credit: Courtesy of Faneuil Hall Marketplace

0.8 hectare) in size, with depths of 8 to 15 feet (2.4 to 4.5 meters), may be used for livestock water supply, fishing, emergency irrigation or recreational uses such as ice skating.
See: ARTIFICIAL WATER BODIES; EMBANKMENT POND; EXCAVATED POND

Farmers Home Administration (FmHA)

An agency within the U.S. Department of Agriculture that provides credit to rural residents, associations, municipalities and businesses that are unable to obtain conventional credit at reasonable rates and terms. FmHA finances a variety of programs, largely from three revolving funds: the Agricultural Credit Insurance Fund, the Rural Housing Insurance Fund and the Rural Development Insurance Fund. For farmers there are loan programs for operating capital, emergencies related to natural disasters, farm purchase and development, soil and water conservation, and conversion of land to outdoor recreation uses. For rural housing there are loans and grants for low- and moderate-income home ownership, housing rehabilitation or construction, rural rental housing, farm labor housing, self-help housing, and housing site acquisition and preparation. For rural communities there are loans and grants for water supply and waste disposal systems, community facilities, industrial development, watershed protection and flood prevention, and natural resource conservation. For American Indian tribes there are loans for land acquisition within tribal reservations. The FmHA also guarantees lenders against losses of up to 90 percent for loans to businesses and industries in rural areas with populations of no more than 50,000 and guarantees loans to alcohol fuel production facilities in both rural and nonrural areas.

The FmHA was created in 1946 as the successor to several New Deal agencies, including the Rural Rehabilitation Corporation, the Resettlement Administration and the Farm Security Administration. The Housing Act of 1949 placed all rural housing programs within FmHA, and through 1981 FmHA has participated in loans for the purchase, construction or rehabilitation of approximately 2 million housing units. The 1961 Consolidated Farmers Home Administration Act (Title III of PL 87-128) extended FmHA's ability to make loans to nonfarmers residing in rural areas.
See: COMMUNITY FACILITY LOAN; OFFICE OF COMMUNITY SERVICES (OCS); RESETTLEMENT ADMINISTRATION; RURAL HOUSING PROGRAMS; SECTION 502 FmHA HOUSING PROGRAM; SECTION 504 FmHA HOUSING PROGRAM; SECTIONS 514 AND 516 FmHA HOUSING PROGRAMS; SECTION 515 FmHA HOUSING PROGRAM

Farmland Protection

Measures taken by government to protect prime agricultural land from urbanization. Given a finite amount of highly productive farmland, protection, which can become

necessary where the opportunity costs of continued farming are high, encourages continued food production and open-space preservation. There are several alternative methods of farmland protection that have been utilized by federal, state and local governments. While none of the approaches is, by itself, totally effective, and in the United States extensive farmland is still being converted to urban uses annually (estimated at 3 million acres [1.2 million hectares] of rural land, about one-third of which is cropland), these techniques can protect a certain amount of agricultural land.

Over 40 states have some form of real property tax relief for agricultural land. In the past, farmland in the exurban fringe was frequently heavily taxed to finance nearby public sewers, water and other infrastructure, often forcing farmers to consider sale to developers. Tax relief exempts or reduces taxes, usually within designated agricultural districts, as long as the land remains in agricultural use. Federal estate taxes have been eased to help farmers retain family-owned farms, as have inheritance taxes in many states, and other federal and state tax incentives are available to aid in farmland preservation.

Land use controls, including zoning and subdivision regulations, have been utilized to restrict or prohibit development of agricultural land. Zoning—such as extreme large-lot zoning (150 acres [61 hectares] or more), impact zoning, creation of exclusive agricultural use zones or conditional use with conversion standards—directly controls the land use or size of development. Quarter-quarter zoning and sliding scale zoning allow the preservation of the speculative value of some of the land but require the continuation of farming on the remainder, preserving much of its productive capacity. Subdivision regulations may prevent development if off-site public facilities are not considered adequate. The sale or transfer of development rights is gaining in use, while landbanking is another preservation method.

Since the placement of roads and utilities has often encouraged the urbanization of farmland, the planning of public infrastructure improvements so as not to promote development is also a form of farmland protection. For example, a public sewer that would connect a small village to a central city's sewer system by crossing farmland would make public sanitary sewers available to the intervening area—one of the prime requisites for intense urban development. Circumferential highways and the interstate system had the side effect of dramatically improving access and allowing commuting from previously rural areas. The Farmland Protection Policy Act, passed in 1981, now requires federal agencies to assess the effects of their programs and to mitigate those that have a negative effect on farmland preservation.

In recent years a few states have taken action by establishing either state planning guidelines or requirements that protect some farmland from potential development. Two ways in which this may be accomplished are through establishment of zones for farm use—such as in Oregon,

Hawaii and Wisconsin—or by establishing agricultural preserves, as in California, where the state has oversight over development within a specified area. A statewide inventory of farmlands to serve as a base for assessing farmland loss over time is also being compiled in California.

To enable selection of agricultural land for preservation, the U.S. Soil Conservation Service has developed a new program that facilitates evaluation of agricultural land to determine the most valuable areas for agricultural purposes. Called LESA, which stands for Agricultural Land Evaluation and Site Assessment, it enables evaluation of numerous factors related to the land, the value of its production and its relationships to urbanized or urbanizing areas, as well as factors related to conversion of the land to nonagricultural use. The Soil Conservation Service's land capability classification system, which is based on the physical characteristics of the soil and climate, is a simpler approach that is widely used.

See: AGRICULTURAL DISTRICT; AGRICULTURAL LAND USE; CRITICAL AREAS; EXURBIA; FARMLAND PROTECTION POLICY ACT; FULL-VALUE ASSESSMENT; GROWTH MANAGEMENT; OPEN-SPACE PRESERVATION; TRANSFER OF DEVELOPMENT RIGHTS (TDR)

Farmland Protection Policy Act

This legislation which is Subtitle I of the Agriculture and Food Act of 1981 (PL 97-98), authorizes the secretary of agriculture to develop criteria for identifying the effects of federal programs on the conversion of farmland to nonagricultural uses. It also directs all units of the federal government to use the criteria established by the secretary of agriculture to identify and mitigate adverse effects of federal programs on the preservation of farmland. Compliance by federal agencies with state, municipal and private farmland protection policies, to the extent practicable, is also directed.

Other provisions of the Agriculture and Food Act create a Special Areas Conservation Program of financial assistance to land owners for soil, water and related conservation improvements in designated geographic areas. A matching grant program to local units of government through state soil conservation agencies is authorized for noncapital conservation activities, such as technical assistance, and a conservation loan program to agricultural producers is created. The act also authorizes a reservoir sedimentation reduction program to assist in testing methods for reducing sedimentation.

A Resource Conservation and Development Program consisting of technical and financial assistance to states, local governments and nonprofit organizations is also created. This program is designed to assist the operation and maintenance of a planning and implementation process to enable land conservation; define land uses that are compatible with conservation objectives; develop programs to enable use of natural resources; and improve the social,

economic and environmental conditions of rural areas. The program, which is applicable only to designated areas, may also fund capital projects.
See: FARMLAND PROTECTION; SOIL CONSERVATION SERVICE (SCS)

Fasano v. *Board of County Commissioners of Washington County* (264 Ore. 574, 507 P.2d 23 [1973])

A decision by the Supreme Court of Oregon involving action by the legislative body of Washington County to amend the county's zoning map by applying a floating zone zoning district to a tract of land.

The court found the type of action taken—a rezoning of a single parcel of land—to be an exercise of authority that was judicial in nature rather than legislative, and therefore subject to a greater degree of judicial review. Ordinarily, the person challenging the rezoning would have to prove that the rezoning was an arbitrary abuse of legislative authority. However, because of the judicial nature of the action, the court found that the Board of County Commissioners had the burden of proof; in order to sustain the rezoning, the board would have to show that the rezoning was in accordance with the comprehensive plan for the county.
See: FLOATING ZONE; REZONING

Fast-Food Restaurants

Restaurants that provide a small menu of low-priced pre-prepared foods that customers may consume on the premises or take with them. Fast-food restaurants rely on large volumes of customers who stay for short periods of time; they therefore locate on major arterial roads, at freeway interchanges and in shopping centers.

Often situated in their own small buildings, they may require larger parking lots than other drive-in facilities to accommodate people waiting for orders in addition to seated customers and staff. In densely populated downtown areas, however, they may not require parking, since they function as part of the commercial area.

Fast-food restaurants are viewed as problems in some municipalities because of their sometimes flamboyant architecture and potential nuisance aspects, such as littering and noise. To control their design and proliferation, many communities have imposed varying types of regulations. Some have also established regulations on how closely together they may be located, while others require that they be clustered in specified areas.
See: DRIVE-IN FACILITIES

Fast-Track Construction

A form of accelerated design and construction in which construction contracts are awarded, and construction is undertaken for parts of the project, before the entire project is designed. The traditional building procedure of programming, design, development of construction drawings and contracts, bidding and award of contracts, construction and acceptance of the completed project is followed. The procedure is divided, however, so that construction tasks that would normally be undertaken early in the construction process can proceed prior to completion of project design. As examples, site clearance and site preparation (development of water supply, sewerage and electrical sources) and even foundation work and superstructure contracts can be awarded before all design details have been approved.

Fast-track construction requires exceptionally efficient project management to ensure coordination of all contracts. It usually produces a project that is less costly than conventional construction projects, because the small contracts attract a greater number of bidders, resulting in lower bids.

Fault

A fracture of the Earth's crust along which there has been vertical, horizontal or oblique movement of adjacent masses of rock. A fault may run for only a few inches, or it may span a distance of hundreds of miles, as in the 600-mile (966-kilometer) long San Andreas Fault in California, which extends from the area of the Mojave Desert to north of San Francisco. Similarly, each fault movement between the two adjacent masses may result in a displacement, which can run from as little as 1 inch (2.54 centimeters) to 25 feet (7.6 meters).

If fault movements have been observed or recorded, a fault is considered active, and additional movements may occur at any time. The San Andreas Fault and many other faults in California are in this category. Passive, or inactive, faults are those without a recorded history of movement; while they are thought likely to remain static, their status can never be assured.

It may be difficult to locate some faults; although there are geologic indicators that help point to their presence, the fault may be deeply buried. Faults encountered during excavation or construction indicate the need for special precautions; any construction must be able to compensate for future movement should the fault become active.

There is a known close association between fault lines and earthquakes. Earthquakes are thought to be caused by a sudden movement or slippage along a fault. This underscores the importance of avoiding fault areas, even if thought inactive, for sensitive development such as dams or nuclear power plants.
See: EARTHQUAKE HAZARD MITIGATION; GEOLOGIC HAZARDS

Feasibility Study

1. A study of the possibility of implementing a particular project. Planners might examine the feasibility of a new civic building, a housing development, a shopping mall or a parking structure. Feasibility studies can also be used to assess the likelihood for success of a program being considered.

Many factors must be evaluated in these analyses, including the fiscal, legal, political and social aspects of project initiation and completion. Fiscal aspects, for example, include taxes that will be generated or lost; the extent of government subsidy or expenditure, if any, that might be required to support the project; and expenditures necessary for project construction or support facilities, such as sewers, water lines or police protection. Political aspects of a feasibility study are extremely important for certain kinds of projects, particularly those opposed by a segment of the community.

2. In real estate the term often refers to an analysis of the probable rate of return on money invested in a development. The study may be required by a lending institution as necessary support data prior to the granting of a loan commitment.
See: MARKET STUDY

Federal-Aid Highway Act of 1944

Federal legislation (PL 78-521) that authorized the construction of a National System of Interstate Highways of up to 40,000 miles (64,360 kilometers). The system was to connect the principal metropolitan cities, other cities and industrial centers; to serve the national defense; and to connect with routes of continental importance in Canada and Mexico. Because the system was envisioned at that time to be a well-coordinated network of federal-aid system routes, funding was not provided beyond that which was appropriated for the federal-aid primary, secondary and urban routes. The system is now largely complete but was developed and financed as a result of provisions of the Federal-Aid Highway Act of 1956.
See: FEDERAL-AID HIGHWAY ACT OF 1956; FEDERAL-AID PRIMARY AND SECONDARY SYSTEMS; FEDERAL-AID ROAD ACT OF 1916; INTERSTATE HIGHWAY SYSTEM

Federal-Aid Highway Act of 1956

Landmark legislation that authorized the largest road-building program in the history of the United States and created the Highway Trust Fund, the financial mechanism for funding the Interstate Highway System. While other federal highway aid for primary and secondary roads was on a 50 percent federal–50 percent state basis (or more recently a 75 percent federal basis), this act (PL 84-627) provided 90 percent federal financing for interstate highways. In addition to establishing a 13-year funding program for the interstate system, the act also authorized expenditures for 1957 and 1958 for federal primary and secondary roads and for other federal roads, such as those in national parks and forests.
See: FEDERAL-AID HIGHWAY ACT OF 1944; FEDERAL-AID PRIMARY AND SECONDARY SYSTEMS; HIGHWAY TRUST FUND; INTERSTATE HIGHWAY SYSTEM

Federal-Aid Highway Act of 1981

An act (PL 97-134) that authorizes large increases in expenditures for repair of the interstate highway system for fiscal years 1983 and 1984 and that limits eligibility for interstate highway construction projects. The legislation also expands the repair program for resurfacing, restoration and rehabilitation to include reconstruction and increases the federal matching share for these projects from 75 percent to 90 percent.

The construction funding limitation set by this act includes a maximum highway width of six lanes in rural areas and urban areas with populations of less than 400,000 and a maximum of eight lanes in urban areas with populations of 400,000 or more. High-occupancy vehicle lanes are also eligible for funding. Projects not eligible for funding under the construction allowances may be funded through the considerably smaller repair allowances.

See: FEDERAL-AID HIGHWAY ACT OF 1956; SURFACE TRANSPORTATION ASSISTANCE ACT OF 1982

Federal-Aid Primary and Secondary Systems

Federal-aid primary and secondary roads are highways that have been placed on a system of roads, adopted by each state, that entitles them to federal funding on a matching grant basis for construction, improvement and engineering costs. Federal-aid primary roads, now referred to by the Federal Highway Administration as consolidated primary, are classified by function and are located throughout the state. Secondary roads are only located in rural areas and in municipalities with a population under 5,000. Roads can be added to the system, within each classification, with state approval. The federal government provides a 75 percent match to state and local funding and allots these funds to the states annually. Each state then determines which projects will be funded.

See: FEDERAL-AID URBAN SYSTEM (FAUS); FUNCTIONAL ROAD CLASSIFICATION; INTERSTATE HIGHWAY SYSTEM; SURFACE TRANSPORTATION ASSISTANCE ACT OF 1982

Federal-Aid Road Act of 1916

An act that provided for grants to states on a matching basis for the purpose of constructing federal-aid primary routes. Prior to this legislation, federal roadway activity was primarily limited to research and education rather than construction. This act sought to improve the inadequate intercity road network that was in place at the time and to accommodate the rapid rise in automobile ownership.

See: FEDERAL-AID PRIMARY AND SECONDARY SYSTEMS

Federal-Aid Urban System (FAUS)

A federal grant program established by the Federal-Aid Highway Act of 1970 that provides matching grants for street, highway and mass transportation projects to urban areas with populations greater than 5,000. Projects eligible for funding are:

1. Improvements to streets and highways, such as widening, traffic signal improvements and intersection improvements.

2. Provision of preferential or exclusive lanes for high-occupancy vehicles (HOVs).

3. Ridepooling assistance, such as promotion and matching grants to vanpool operators.

4. Provision of parking facilities related to public transportation, such as park-and-ride lots and carpool staging areas.

5. Provision of pedestrian and bicycle facilities—including overpasses, underpasses, bike paths and automobile restricted zones—with related landscaping, street furniture and lighting.

6. Financing of public transportation capital improvements, such as the purchase of buses, construction or reconstruction of rail facilities, and construction of off-street loading facilities and bus shelters.

Projects must be included in Transportation Improvement Programs (TIPs) prepared by local governments and in the state's annual Statewide Federal-Aid Program, which is submitted to the Federal Highway Administration. Funding is allocated to the states on the basis of their percentage of the total United States urban population. A specified part of the funds must be used in areas having a population of 200,000 or more (referred to as attributable funds), and the remainder may be used in any area with a population of over 5,000 (referred to as nonattributable funds). Funds may be transferred from highway projects to mass transit projects under the program if local, state and federal governments approve. FAUS nonattributable funds may also be transferred to Federal-Aid Primary System project funds or vice-versa with local, state and federal approval. Funding is provided on the basis of 75 percent federal participation and 25 percent local participation.

See: AUTOMOBILE RESTRICTED ZONE (ARZ); BUS SHELTER; FEDERAL-AID PRIMARY AND SECONDARY SYSTEMS; PARK-AND-RIDE FACILITIES; RESERVED LANES; RIDEPOOLING; TRANSPORTATION IMPROVEMENT PROGRAM (TIP)

Federal Aviation Administration (FAA)

A division of the Department of Transportation with responsibility for fostering aviation safety, advancing civil aviation and a national system of airports, and achieving efficient use of navigable airspace.

Among the activities of the FAA of greatest interest to planners are its role in airport planning and its awarding of grants to public agencies for airport system planning, single-airport master planning and public airport development. The FAA also constructs and maintains visual and electronic aids to navigation and operates a network of airport traffic control towers, air route traffic control centers and flight service stations.

See: AIRCRAFT NAVIGATIONAL AIDS; AIRPORT NOISE; AIRPORT PLANNING; NOISE CONTROL ACT OF 1972

Federal Crime Insurance

A program, authorized by Title VI of the Housing and Urban Development Act of 1970, intended to enable property owners in areas subject to high crime rates to obtain insurance. Crime insurance may be issued against losses resulting from robbery, burglary, larceny and related crimes. It may include personal theft insurance; mercantile open stock, robbery and safe burglary insurance; storekeepers' or office burglary and robbery insurance; or business interruption insurance. It does not include automobile insurance or losses resulting from embezzlement.

Administered by the Federal Insurance Administration, direct insurance is available to property owners for properties in locations where statewide programs are not available or for which conventional insurance is available only at a prohibitive cost. The program is intended to prevent real estate disinvestment in these locations and to encourage continued economic activity that might not otherwise be feasible.

See: FEDERAL RIOT REINSURANCE; SECTION 223 (e) HOUSING PROGRAM

Federal Depository Libraries

A library that receives copies of a wide range of unclassified United States government publications that are designated for depository use by the superintendent of documents.

There are over 1,200 depository libraries in the United States, which may be public libraries, college or university libraries, or government libraries. Most of these receive specific groups of materials in categories that they select. An elite group of depository libraries, known as regional libraries, are required to receive all depository publications. The regional libraries are usually located at large state universities or state libraries. Depository libraries are an excellent source of planning information, including census data and the reports of many government agencies.

Federal Emergency Management Agency (FEMA)

A United States agency responsible for federal programs related to emergency and disaster mitigation and response. Through its six subagencies it administers and coordinates federal, state and local programs in the areas of hazard mitigation, preparedness planning, relief operations and recovery assistance.

The Federal Insurance Administration (FIA), one of the six agencies, administers the national flood insurance program and the crime insurance and riot reinsurance programs. The State and Local Programs and Support Directorate administers the president's disaster-relief program, the disaster-preparedness improvement grant program, and the earthquake and hurricane grant program. It also assists local civil defense programs by making grants available and providing technical aid.

The United States Fire Administration (USFA) administers programs designed to reduce loss of life and property damage resulting from fires, such as through grants and technical advice for municipal fire protection planning activities and the support of improvement and enforcement of fire-related codes and regulations. USFA also maintains the National Fire Data Center to collect, assess and disseminate data on fires. The National Preparedness Programs Directorate develops and implements plans and policies for peacetime and wartime emergencies, including coordination of civil emergency preparedness for nuclear attack, nuclear power plant accidents and nuclear weapons accidents.

Training programs in many areas of FEMA's work are provided to federal, state and local government personnel by the Training and Education Directorate, which operates the National Emergency Training Center (encompassing the Emergency Management Institute and the National Fire Academy) in Emmitsburg, Maryland. FEMA also publishes numerous booklets and produces films on its programs.

See: DISASTER PREPAREDNESS IMPROVEMENT GRANTS; EARTHQUAKE AND HURRICANE PREPAREDNESS PLANS; FEDERAL CRIME INSURANCE; FEDERAL RIOT REINSURANCE; NATIONAL FLOOD INSURANCE PROGRAM

Federal Farm Credit System

A system of borrower-owned banks and associations that make below-market rate loans available to rural families and farm-related businesses. The system consists of several types of cooperative banks, including the federal land banks, the federal intermediate credit banks and the banks for cooperatives, all of which are supervised by the Farm Credit Administration, an independent federal agency. There are 12 federal Farm Credit districts, in which a federal land bank, a federal cooperative bank and a federal bank for cooperatives are located. Initially capitalized by the federal government, the system is now owned by its users, and funds are raised by the sale of securities.

The federal land banks and/or bank associations make long-term loans on rural real estate and single-family housing. When a loan is granted, the borrower purchases stock in a federal land bank association, and the association purchases a like amount in the district federal land bank; the stock is retired when the loan is repaid. The federal intermediate credit banks make loans to and discount agricultural paper for production credit associations, state and national banks, and other organizations. Through these organizations, loans may be issued for agricultural purposes or for purchase or repair of housing or mobile homes. The banks for cooperatives make loans to associations of farmers, ranchers, or producers or harvesters of aquatic products.

See: RURAL HOUSING PROGRAMS

Federal Highway Administration (FHWA)

An agency within the Department of Transportation that administers the federal-aid highway program, including the interstate highway program and other highway-related programs, and is responsible for construction of roads in federal forests, national parks and Indian reservations.

The FHWA administers programs to increase highway and pedestrian safety and provides matching grants to states for specific highway safety programs. It also monitors and is responsible for the transportation of hazardous materials and motor carrier noise abatement.

See: DEPARTMENT OF TRANSPORTATION (DOT); FEDERAL-AID PRIMARY AND SECONDARY SYSTEMS; FEDERAL-AID URBAN SYSTEM (FAUS); INTERSTATE HIGHWAY SYSTEM

Federal Home Loan Bank System (FHLBS)

A federal system created to make a credit reserve permanently available to eligible institutions that are involved in home mortgage lending. Eligible members of the Federal Home Loan Banks are savings and loan institutions, building and loan and homestead associations, savings and cooperative banks, and insurance companies.

The FHLBS, which was created by legislation enacted in 1932, functions via 12 regional Federal Home Loan Banks, each of which has its own board of directors and its own capital stock owned by its member institutions. These regional banks provide advances (loans) to their members to supplement the flow of savings, aiding member savings institutions in meeting the demand for residential mortgages. This process helps to stabilize the housing industry and the residential mortgage market.

The Federal Home Loan Banks are supervised by the Federal Home Loan Bank Board (FHLBB), an independent agency within the executive branch of the United States government. The FHLBB is directed by a three-member board appointed by the president of the United States and is advised by the Federal Savings and Loan Advisory Council, an independent statutory body composed of elected and appointed members from the 12 regional banking areas. The FHLBB also supervises activities of the Federal Savings and Loan Insurance Corporation, which insures savings, and the Federal Home Loan Mortgage Corporation, which provides a secondary market for conventional mortgages.

See: FEDERAL HOME LOAN MORTGAGE CORPORATION (FHLMC); SECONDARY MORTGAGE MARKET

Federal Home Loan Mortgage Corporation (FHLMC)

An agency that makes a secondary mortgage market primarily for savings and loan associations. Also called "Freddie Mac" and "The Mortgage Corporation," it was established by Congress in 1970. FHLMC, which functions under the general control of the Federal Home Loan Bank System, concentrates on conventional mortgages and is the largest buyer and seller of these mortgages in the world.

When The Mortgage Corporation was created, the secondary market in conventional mortgages was relatively small. To increase the liquidity of conventional mortgages and permit mortgage funds to be redistributed within regions and to other regions, it created a standardized process that thrift institutions could easily use. To sell the mortgages it purchases, The Mortgage Corporation issues

mortgage participation certificates (PCs) and guaranteed mortgage certificates (GMCs); each type of instrument has its own secondary market.

When a savings and loan association wishes to sell some of its mortgages so that it can grant new mortgages, it will typically offer a "participation" package to The Mortgage Corporation. This might include a group of 8 or 10 mortgages, of which 85 percent of their face value is sold to The Mortgage Corporation, while the thrift institution retains 15 percent of the value of the loans and continues to service them. Home buyers are generally unaware that the sale has occurred, and the sale generally has no effect on their home ownership.

See: FEDERAL HOME LOAN BANK SYSTEM (FHLBS); SECONDARY MORTGAGE MARKET

Federal Housing Administration (FHA)

An agency established by the National Housing Act of 1934 to administer housing insurance programs created by that act. Its functions were transferred to the Department of Housing and Urban Development (HUD) in 1965. While the FHA no longer exists, the mortgage insurance programs still bear the name of the agency, and the director of housing programs within HUD has the title of Assistant Secretary for Housing/Federal Housing Commissioner.

The FHA functioned independently until 1939, when it became part of the Federal Loan Agency. In 1942 it was reinstituted as a division of the Federal Housing Agency, and in 1947 its functions were transferred to the Housing and Home Finance Agency.

See: FEDERAL HOUSING ADMINISTRATION (FHA) MORTGAGE INSURANCE

Federal Housing Administration (FHA) Mortgage Insurance

Government guarantees for mortgage loans that serve low- and moderate-income persons and are administered by the Federal Housing Administration (FHA). The National Housing Act of 1934 created the FHA to encourage mortgage lending by offering government insurance. The legislation related to single-family homes and home improvement and created a Mutual Mortgage Insurance Fund that was financed by a premium charged to the borrower that was to accumulate in the fund to pay for defaults on mortgages. FHA underwriting and fee requirements are charged to the borrower by the lending institutions. Part of the additional premium is retained by the bank as a service fee, and the FHA receives the remainder. The national underwriting and documentation standards of this program, such as requirements that the mortgages be amortized in equal monthly payments (rather than in lump sum repayments more common during the Depression) and that insured buildings meet minimum property standards established by the FHA, helped to reestablish the secondary mortgage market, although the federal insurance also played a role.

A major benefit of the FHA mortgage insurance has been the generally below-market interest rates charged on mortgages because of rates set by the FHA; in some cases subsidies further reduce the interest rate. The use of lower required down payments has also enabled many families to qualify for mortgages. Because of the federal insurance, borrowers in some inner city areas have been able to obtain financing that would otherwise have been unobtainable, either because of the type of project or because of its location. FHA mortgage insurance programs, however, also have limits on who may apply by virtue of maximum income and maximum insurable housing cost. As a result, in some parts of the country, the programs have been underutilized because of high prevailing housing prices. In addition, points may not be charged to the borrower but, when required, are imposed on the seller, making sales to FHA applicants less attractive.

While the basic premises of the initial FHA program have remained, a whole series of variations have been added, including insurance for multifamily housing, for subsidized housing, for housing in urban renewal areas, for condominiums and even for some types of medical facilities.

See: FEDERAL HOUSING ADMINISTRATION (FHA); SECONDARY MORTGAGE MARKET; SECTIONS 203 (b) and (i) HOUSING PROGRAMS; SECTION 207 HOUSING PROGRAM; SECTION 213 HOUSING PROGRAM; SECTION 221 (d) 2 HOUSING PROGRAM; SECTIONS 221 (d) 3 and 221 (d) 4 HOUSING PROGRAMS; SECTION 223(e) HOUSING PROGRAM; SECTION 223 (f) HOUSING PROGRAM; SECTION 231 HOUSING PROGRAM; SECTION 234 HOUSING PROGRAM; SECTION 235 HOUSING PROGRAM; SECTION 236 HOUSING PROGRAM; SECTION 237 HOUSING PROGRAM: SECTION 244 HOUSING PROGRAM; SECTION 245 HOUSING PROGRAM; SECTION 232 PROGRAM; SECTION 241 PROGRAM; SECTION 242 PROGRAM; VETERANS ADMINISTRATION (VA) MORTGAGE INSURANCE

Federal National Mortgage Association (FNMA)

A private corporation, commonly known as "Fannie Mae," that operates in the secondary mortgage market. It functions as a buyer of government-insured and government-guaranteed mortgages when mortgage money is scarce and sells them when demand for mortgages lessens. Since 1970 Fannie Mae has also purchased and sold conventional mortgages.

Created by Congress in 1938 to establish a secondary market in Federal Housing Administration (FHA) mortgages, the Federal National Mortgage Association's functions were expanded in 1954 to include activities that promoted an increased supply of mortgage money for special programs, such as low-income housing, in which the conventional secondary market was not participating. Although it was originally a government-owned corporation, its functions were separated in 1968 so that the special programs division became the Government National Mortgage Association (GNMA), which remained a government entity, while Fannie Mae became a private, for-profit corporation under Department of Housing and Urban Development (HUD) direction and regulation.

Fannie Mae sells its mortgage purchases to the capital markets via debentures and short-term discount notes. Because of the nature of its operation, in which mortgages are bought during periods of high interest rates and sold when interest rates drop and money becomes more plentiful, Fannie Mae is able to realize a profit on the resale of mortgages in its portfolio, as well as make money available for mortgage-granting purposes.

See: GOVERNMENT NATIONAL MORTGAGE ASSOCIATION (GNMA); HOUSING AND COMMUNITY DEVELOPMENT ACT OF 1980; SECONDARY MORTGAGE MARKET

Federal Nonnuclear Energy Research and Development Act of 1974

An act (PL 93-577) that establishes a 10-year, $20-billion program of research and development in nonnuclear sources of energy. The act requires that the Energy Research and Development Administration (ERDA—subsequently merged with the Department of Energy [DOE]) submit an annually revised comprehensive plan for energy research, development and demonstration offering solutions to the short-, middle- and long-term energy needs of the country and a program for implementing the recommendations in the plan.

The energy research program is to investigate and undertake demonstrations in diverse means of energy production, including solar, geothermal, oil shale, synthetic fuels, coal gasification and fuel cells. It is to emphasize energy conservation, environmental protection, development of renewable resources and analysis of water requirements of the new technologies. Other areas of research that were specified are use of waste (e.g., sewage, solid waste, agricultural waste and waste heat), materials recycling, improved design of auto and mass transit engines, and advanced urban and architectural design to improve energy efficiency. Incorporated into the act, for purposes of creating a single appropriation for all nonnuclear energy activities, are programs established by three related acts: the Solar Heating and Cooling Act of 1974 (PL 93-409); the Geothermal Energy Research, Development and Demonstration Act of 1974 (PL 93-410); and the Solar Energy Research, Development and Demonstration Act of 1974 (PL 93-473).

The Federal Nonnuclear Energy Research and Development Act authorizes federal assistance through such mechanisms as joint federal-industry cooperation; contractual agreements with corporations, consortia, universities and others; contracts for the construction and operation of federally owned facilities; guarantees of federal purchases or price guarantees for products produced by demonstration plants; federal loans to entities investigating new technologies; and incentives to inventors. The act also generally requires that the federal government retain the rights to technologies developed under the program.

See: DEPARTMENT OF ENERGY (DOE); ENERGY SECURITY ACT; RENEWABLE ENERGY SOURCES

Federal Railroad Administration (FRA)

An agency within the Department of Transportation responsible for policy development and research related to intercity rail transportation and for railroad safety. It also has responsibility for revitalization of rail passenger service in the northeast corridor of the United States, an area that encompasses railway trackage from Boston to Washington, D.C., and for operation of the Alaska Railroad. The FRA operates the 50–square mile (130–square kilometer) transportation test center near Pueblo, Colorado, where tests are conducted on advanced and conventional design rail and urban rapid transit vehicles.

See: URBAN MASS TRANSPORTATION ADMINISTRATION (UMTA)

Federal Register

A publication of the federal government of the United States that updates the *Code of Federal Regulations.* It prints federal agency rules; notices of proposed changes in rules, which often allow opportunities for public comment; and other executive branch legal documents, such as executive orders. Federal agencies use the *Federal Register* for legal notices, such as for hearings or investigations. The publication also includes listings of "Sunshine Act" meetings scheduled to be held, which are those meetings that are legally required to be open to the public.

The *Federal Register* is published each working day; it therefore constitutes one way for interested individuals to remain current on federal regulations and requirements.

See: GOVERNMENT IN THE SUNSHINE ACT OF 1976

Federal Riot Reinsurance

A federal mortgage reinsurance program, established by the Housing and Urban Development Act of 1968, designed to enable acquisition of mortgages in areas subject to riots or other civil disorders. The program, which was terminated by the Housing and Urban-Rural Recovery Act of 1983, reinsured insurance companies against losses and was intended to reduce redlining of ghetto areas.

See: FEDERAL CRIME INSURANCE; REDLINING

Federal Water Pollution Control Act Amendments of 1972

Federal legislation (PL 92-500) that strengthens restrictions on the discharge of pollutants into surface waters. Unlike past legislation, which allowed for different water quality standards for different areas depending on use, the 1972 amendments set a single national goal for all bodies of water—to make all waters swimmable and fishable by 1983 and to eliminate all water pollutant discharges by 1985. To reach this goal, the amendments require industry to utilize the "best practicable control technology currently available" by 1977 and the "best available technology economically achievable" by 1983. Municipal sewage treatment plants are required to eliminate 85 percent of their pollution (secondary treatment) by 1977 and, to the extent practicable, incorporate technology by 1983 that would eliminate the discharge of all pollutants.

The 1972 Water Pollution Control Act provides the basic framework for Environmental Protection Agency water quality activities. It also establishes a system of pollutant discharge permits and requires states to prepare and implement plans for waste treatment and water quality improvement. In addition, the law authorizes grants for water quality planning and construction of treatment plants and incorporates provisions of the Water Quality Improvement Act of 1970, which relate to oil and hazardous substance pollution.

Other provisions of the 1972 law include the requirement that industries pretreat sewage before discharging it into municipal sewer systems; that states classify the conditions of all publicly owned freshwater lakes and determine procedures to remedy the problems that are found; and that river basin planning be undertaken for all river basins in the country. The law, which is modified by the Clean Water Act of 1977, also authorizes numerous studies on water pollution control. Together with the 1977 act and later amendments, this legislation is now generally referred to as the Clean Water Act.

See: AREAWIDE WASTE TREATMENT MANAGEMENT PLANNING (SECTION 208); BEST MANAGEMENT PRACTICES (BMPs); BEST PRACTICABLE TECHNOLOGY (BPT); CLEAN WATER ACT OF 1977; MARINE PROTECTION, RESEARCH AND SANCTUARIES ACT OF 1972; MUNICIPAL WASTEWATER TREATMENT CONSTRUCTION GRANT AMENDMENTS OF 1981; NATIONAL POLLUTANT DISCHARGE ELIMINATION SYSTEM (NPDES); STATE WATER QUALITY MANAGEMENT PLAN (SECTION 303 [e]); WASTEWATER FACILITY PLANNING (SECTION 201); WATER QUALITY ACT OF 1965; WATER QUALITY IMPROVEMENT ACT OF 1970

Fee in Lieu of Dedication

A requirement found in subdivision regulations that states that cash payments will be required of a developer of a subdivision when appropriate land for public uses, such as parkland, is not available on the site. It has been a long-established procedure to require a developer to dedicate street and public utility rights-of-way necessary to serve a development. More gradually, requirements for open space and school land dedication are becoming accepted, particularly when there is supporting enabling legislation for such requirements. The site of a new development may not, however, contain any location suitable for a school or park.

Payment of a fee, upon municipal request, rather than actual dedication of land allows a community to acquire only those properties logically sited for park, playground or school use and allocates the burden equitably among new subdivisions. In order to impose this requirement, the municipal subdivision regulations should state the circumstances under which payment will be required rather than a dedication of land and contain a definite standard for the amount of land or the amount of any fees that will be required in lieu of land dedication. Although this practice has not always been found to be legal, other factors that can help to assure the legality of such a system include the existence of appropriate state enabling legislation, the establishment of a special fund earmarked for those purposes stated in the municipal regulations and a relationship between the demands generated by the new development and the fees required and facilities that are provided.

When this practice first began, it was common for municipalities to require the fair market value of the amount of land that would have been dedicated. It is now considered better procedure to set a fee related to the number of units that will be developed (or the number of expected residents), as this bears a more direct relationship to the needs of the development.
See: ASSOCIATED HOME BUILDERS OF GREATER EAST BAY, INC. v. *CITY OF WALNUT CREEK*; DEDICATION; EXACTION; OPEN-SPACE PRESERVATION; SUBDIVISION REGULATIONS

Fee Simple

Sometimes referred to as fee simple absolute or a fee estate, the term refers to the broadest, most extensive and unconditional estate in land that can be enjoyed. A fee simple estate is perpetual in duration (subject to the sovereign power of eminent domain) and may be conveyed by its owner either during his life or upon his death.

A fee simple estate includes all the lesser estates or interests that may be created in land, such as easements and life estates.

Feedback

A means of introducing new data into an activity that is based on reactions to that activity. Derived from computer terminology, the term is now often used to describe the way in which programs are modified as a result of experience in their operation. The term *feedback* may also describe opinions and statements made by the public that are then incorporated into a program.

Fence

A barrier erected around land to prevent trespassing, confine animals, create privacy or serve as screening. Depending upon their use, fences may be low or high, have visual openings or be fully enclosing. Fences of many materials are in use, with certain styles and designs particularly popular in some areas. Common forms are the wood picket, split rail and post rail; stone fences; and metal fences, such as the barbed wire and cyclone (metal mesh)

fence. Fences of living plants, such as evergreen or deciduous hedges or those of cactus, are widely used.
See: COMMUNITY CHARACTER; SCREENING; VISIBILITY CLEARANCE AT INTERSECTIONS

Fenestration

The arrangement, proportions and design of windows and doors in a building. Fenestration provides light, air and access to a building and also serves as a major design element in the streetscape.
See: SCALE OF DEVELOPMENT; STREETSCAPE

Ferry

A boat or ship that carries passengers and vehicles across relatively short spans of water. Ferry service has been largely replaced by bridges throughout the world but is still used extensively in resort areas and other low-density locations. The land component of ferry service usually requires a building to house waiting passengers and an area to contain waiting cars. Where cars are not transported, a parking lot may be necessary.
See: HYDROFOIL

Fertility Rate

The general fertility rate is the number of births that occur for each 1,000 women who are in the age group of 15 to 44 years old. Because the composition of a population (in terms of age and sex) has such a large effect upon the number of births that occur, the fertility rate was developed to help minimize the differences between populations for comparison purposes. It does this by focusing upon women in their childbearing years rather than the total population. It is possible to isolate aspects of the fertility rate, such as the marital fertility rate or age-specific fertility rates.
See: BIRTHRATE; DEMOGRAPHY; MORTALITY RATE; REPRODUCTION RATE

Fill

1. In grading, the amount of material that must be added to depressions or low-lying areas to achieve the contours specified in a grading plan. (See Fig. 19.)
2. Material—such as earth, rubble or rubbish—that has accumulated or is disposed of at a site and has the effect of raising the ground elevation, or that is deliberately added to a site to improve its suitability for construction. Fill has a wide variety of applications; it may, for example, be used to raise a depression in the landscape in road construction, to create new land area at a shoreline or to permit construction at the site of an abandoned quarry.

In much of Europe and many of the older cities in North America, building foundations lie upon layers of rubble that are the remains of earlier buildings. This has raised ground level in these cities a number of feet above the original ground surface. It is important to ascertain whether or not land has been filled prior to construction; although masonry rubble makes a good foundation, the remains of an old refuse dump, for example, can present problems because of methane gas buildup.

Fill has often been used to create buildable land from what were once tidal flats or marshlands. Significant amounts of the total land area of the Netherlands have been created in this manner. Many cities in the United States are also built partially on reclaimed land.
See: BORROW; CUT; GRADING; LAND RECLAMATION

Filtering

A theory that suggests that the housing requirements of lower-income groups are served by basic movements in the housing market. During a period of housing surplus, higher-income groups vacate existing housing for new or more desirable units, leaving their unit vacant (which theoretically drops in price because there is now a surplus of housing) for a family of lesser income. This series of moves percolates through the entire housing market until, at the lowest end of the market, substandard units are removed from the housing supply.

Filtering, also called the trickle-down theory, is sometimes used to justify the construction of more expensive housing as a means of improving housing opportunity for low-income groups. It is predicated, however, on the creation or existence of housing surpluses, which do not generally exist for extended time periods.
See: HOUSING; HOUSING CHOICE; HOUSING STOCK

Filtration

A process used in the treatment of water and sewage that enables the removal of suspended solids and colloids and the reduction of bacteria and other organisms. It is accomplished by passing water or effluent through a bed of sand (which in large water filtration plants may be several acres in size) or through pulverized coal or a mat of fibrous material. Common sewage treatment filters are intermittent sand filters and trickling filters, while pressure filtration is used for sludge dewatering.
See: DEWATERED SLUDGE; OXIDATION PROCESSES; SEWAGE TREATMENT; SUSPENDED SOLIDS (SS); WATER TREATMENT

Final Cover

The ultimate surface of a sanitary landfill (or one that is applied if the intermediate surface is going to be exposed to the elements for more than one year). Generally, final cover is applied in 6-inch (15.2-centimeter) units, which are each compacted until the cover depth is at least 2 feet (0.6 meter). Certain types of uses and characteristics of the soil may require greater cover thickness. The roots of trees and shrubs, for example, penetrate to a depth of more than 2 feet.

The final cover must be properly graded to facilitate the ultimate use of the sanitary landfill site and to prevent erosion and the ponding of water.
See: COVER MATERIAL; DAILY COVER; SANITARY LANDFILL

Final Plat

A finalized drawing showing the details of a proposed subdivision, which—upon receiving final approval—may be filed with appropriate authorities.

Much of the same information required to appear on the preliminary plat also appears on the final plat. Included on the final subdivision plat are the name and location of the subdivision, lot layout, lot numbers, setback lines, street lines, street layout and rights-of-way, and names of adjoining properties. It also contains enough engineering data so lines on the map may be reproduced on the ground, an accurate scale, locations of utility easements and deed restrictions.

Although the reviewing agency may request changes in the final plat, in practice it is common for it to be checked primarily for compliance with any conditions agreed upon for the preliminary plat. At the point in the subdivision review process when the final plat is submitted for approval, it is difficult and expensive for changes to be made, as the subdivision has already undergone extensive review.

As a final step, the legislative body of the municipality accepts any streets, open space or other facilities that are to be dedicated to the public. The plat is then filed and recorded in official records, usually at the county level, along with any other legal documents required for recording the subdivision. The officially filed plat provides a permanent legal record of all dedications and easements, and also serves as a simplified way of identifying lots within the subdivision—that is, they can be identified by subdivision name and lot number rather than metes and bounds.
See: PREAPPLICATION CONFERENCE; PRELIMINARY PLAT; SUBDIVISION REGULATIONS; SUBDIVISION REVIEW

Financial Guarantees for Improvements

Guarantees that all required improvements in a new development, such as roads and utilities, will be installed. Such a guarantee is aimed at protecting the municipality against developer defaults or other financial problems or unexpected costs that may prevent the developer from starting or completing necessary improvements.

Financial guarantees come in a number of forms. One type is the requirement that an escrow fund be established, to which the developer deposits funds that are held by a financial institution. Should the developer fail to complete the required improvements, the municipality may draw upon these funds for that purpose. Performance bonds are also in use, but communities sometimes find it difficult to collect from the bonding company. A third type of guarantee that has proved popular with municipalities is one provided by the lending institution financing the development. Not only does the financial institution have a vested interest in seeing the development properly completed but this type of guarantee does not require the developer to set sums of money aside as security.
See: PERFORMANCE BOND

Finding of No Significant Impact (FONSI)

A public document that sets forth the reasons why a proposed federal action or project will not have a significant impact on the environment. A finding of no significant impact is made following an environmental assessment and either includes or summarizes the assessment.

See: ENVIRONMENTAL ASSESSMENT; ENVIRONMENTAL IMPACT STATEMENT (EIS)

Finger Fill Canals

A form of shorefront development in which a shallow bay or estuary is dredged to create a series of narrow, deep canals, interspersed with narrow peninsulas of land made from the dredged material. This landform is used to create residential subdivisions in which every lot abuts or has access to a canal.

Although popular in the southern United States, where the climate permits year-round use of waterfront areas, this type of canal development has been severely criticized because of the effect the dredging and filling has on wetlands, water quality and coastal ecosystems. Activities such as the dredging of wetlands are now regulated by the Army Corps of Engineers and by other federal, state and local controls.

See: ARMY CORPS OF ENGINEERS' PERMIT PROGRAM

Finger Pattern

Regional growth in a form resembling a human hand, the fingers generally being considered the extensions of urbanization and the palm the main city center. Growth follows along major arterials, with subcenters (knuckles) along each finger. (See Fig. 24)

The finger pattern seems to occur most frequently where major features, such as a body of water or steep terrain, limit growth in some directions. The undevelopable areas—or designated greenbelt areas, in some cases—are the spaces between the fingers. Stockholm, Sweden is particularly well known for its long-range, regional finger pattern plan, featuring new towns as subcenters.

See: RADIAL PATTERN; SECTOR THEORY

Fire Department

A municipal agency responsible for fire fighting, maintenance of fire-fighting equipment and fire prevention programs. Departments may be all volunteer, partly paid or fully paid.

The majority of departments are at least partly volunteer, in that all or most of the fire fighters are employed in other occupations but leave their work and proceed to the fire when an alarm is sounded. Fully paid departments are usually found in heavily urbanized municipalities. Fire rating schedules of insurance companies, which are used to establish property fire insurance rates, generally divide municipalities into classes on the basis of the type of department they maintain as well as their record in fire fighting.

The local fire chief is usually an appointed deputy state fire marshal as well. His staff is responsible for supervising local fire prevention activities, such as building inspections to detect violations of the fire code and issuance of corrective orders. Fire marshals also investigate fires of suspicious origin. Fire department personnel generally assess community needs for additional fire equipment and new fire houses which are included in capital budget proposals. Master planning for fire prevention and control may also be undertaken in which assessments are made of fire-fighting resources and personnel, effectiveness of fire and building codes, short- and long-term prevention needs, and plans developed to meet these needs.

See: FIRE FLOW; FIRE STATION; PUBLIC SAFETY BUILDINGS

Fire Flow

The amount of water required by fire companies to provide fire protection services, measured in gallons per minute (gpm). Required fire flow varies with the population of a community, the existence of concentrated business or industrial areas, the height of residential buildings and the degree of residential congestion. Fire flow requirements, which often dictate the size and type of water supply system needed by a community, are set by the American Insurance Association.

See: FIRE DEPARTMENT; WATER SUPPLY SYSTEM

Fire Insurance Atlas

A series of maps, prepared primarily for the use of fire insurance underwriters, that contain useful information for planning purposes. They indicate the shape of a building and its location on the site, the number of stories and the type of materials used in construction, as well as the street address of the structure. They may be used for reference purposes or to help construct a large-scale map of a developed area.

Fire Ratings

Ratings that classify buildings as to their ability to resist fires according to standards that are incorporated into state and municipal building codes. Building codes use different classes of construction, which generally range from fire-resistive, with the most stringent requirements, to wood-frame construction, with the least stringent requirements. Fire ratings are usually given as the number of hours required for the effects of a fire (e.g., heat, flames) to cause structural elements to falter. Four hours is considered to be fire-resistive while shorter time periods connote lesser classes of protection.

Agencies that have produced model standards are the American Insurance Association (formerly the National Board of Fire Underwriters), which has developed the National Building Code (NBC), and the Building Officials and Code Administrators International Inc. (BOCA). Building materials are also tested and rated as to their fire-resistive qualities by evaluating agencies. These ratings are published in promotional information supplied by the manufacturers, for use by architects, engineers and building officials.

Two types of fire protection must be designed into buildings: life safety (e.g., fire escapes) and property protection (e.g., sprinklers). Building codes provide specific requirements for each of these in addition to the fire resistance requirements.
See: BUILDING CODE; FIRE-RESISTIVE CONSTRUCTION

Fire-Resistive Construction

Building construction that is rated by one of several fire rating systems as being capable of withstanding the effects of fire for a relatively long period of time. It is a type of construction in which walls, partitions, columns, floors and roof are noncombustible, with sufficient fire resistance to withstand the effects of a fire and prevent its spread from story to story. In buildings that are classified as fire-resistive, required fire resistance varies from four hours for exterior and interior bearing walls, columns, beams and trusses to one hour for nonbearing walls.
See: FIRE RATINGS

Fire Station

A building that houses a fire engine company and/or ladder company and its fire-fighting equipment. Fire station location is determined as part of a system of stations that serve an entire municipality. Depending upon the area's density of development, predominant building age, type of construction and type of land use, fire stations may be located a maximum distance of 0.75 mile to 3 miles (1.2 to 4.8 kilometers) from any point within their service area. Heavily industrialized areas, business and institutional districts, and areas where large groups of people assemble, such as theaters, schools, etc., should have fire stations that are spaced at the lower end of this range.

Fire station siting should be near intersections, where possible, to permit travel in several directions and provide adequate room for maneuvering fire vehicles and for parking for fire department personnel. Attractive building design that is compatible with surrounding land use and architectural styles is also desirable.
See: COMMUNITY FACILITY PLANNING; FIRE DEPARTMENT; FIRE FLOW; PUBLIC SAFETY BUILDINGS

Firebreak

A fire prevention or fire-fighting technique in which all flammable materials are removed from a strip of land. As a prevention technique, an area may be cleared of trees, or a road or natural feature, such as a river, may act as a firebreak. In fire fighting, trenches may be dug in the direction that the fire is heading and then a fire set on the fire side of the break to effectively widen it.
See: FOREST FIRE CONTROL

Fireproof Construction

Building construction that permits the building to withstand the effects of fire for a relatively long time period. Since it is not feasible to construct buildings that are completely fireproof, the term is gradually being replaced in building codes by the term *fire-resistive*. Generally, buildings that are known as fireproof have fire ratings consistent with the highest fire-resistive category.
See: FIRE RATINGS; FIRE-RESISTIVE CONSTRUCTION

First Refusal

Sometimes referred to as a right of first refusal, the term refers to the right to have the first opportunity to purchase property when it is put on the market for sale, or the right to match any other offer made for the property.

Municipalities sometimes seek to acquire this right with respect to land owned by a country club, so they can be assured of having the opportunity of preserving open space if the land is ever offered for sale.

A right of first refusal differs from an option to purchase in that an option to purchase may be exercised at any time during its term, at the election of the one holding the option. A right of first refusal is not triggered until the landowner puts the property on the market for sale, or receives a bona fide offer to purchase the property that he is willing to accept.
See: OPTION

Fiscal Impact Analysis

An analysis of the impact on a municipal budget of the cost of expanding municipal services to meet the needs of a proposed development. Fiscal impact analysis is often used by communities with growth management programs and may be undertaken by a developer at a municipality's request or by a planning department. This technique is also useful in evaluating land use alternatives and in capital program development.

Fiscal impact analysis is an expansion of cost-revenue techniques into the areas of municipal involvement that are less directly affected by a proposed project. As an example, while cost-revenue analysis will analyze the number of lanes that must be added to a street to accommodate traffic, fiscal impact analysis will also examine how many more policemen, firemen and garbage collectors will be necessary. The technique does not, however, analyze secondary impacts, such as the effect on the economy.

Methods of conducting fiscal impact analysis range from simple models applying available cost standards for the provision of municipal services (e.g., X dollars per acre of subdivision development) to more complex multidimensional models that attempt to apply detailed unit costs for each of the numerous aspects of municipal involvement, such as provision of sanitation services. The most successful studies are those using costs that are specific to the particular municipality. The six basic types of fiscal impact studies identified by a major Rutgers University study are the per capita multiplier, the case study method, the service standard method, the comparable city method, the proportional valuation method and the employment anticipation method, each of which calculates costs differently. Because of the wide range of techniques that may be used in conducting fiscal impact analysis, it is important that all assumptions, methodology and data sources used in a study be specified.

See: COST-BENEFIT ANALYSIS; COST-REVENUE ANALYSIS; FISCAL ZONING; GROWTH MANAGEMENT

Fiscal Year

A 12-month accounting period used by government or business, which may or may not match the calendar year. The United States federal fiscal year traditionally ran from July 1 to June 30 but in 1977 was changed to close on September 30 to facilitate the budgetary process. There are units of local government, however, that operate on a calendar year. In Britain the financial year for government runs from April 6 to April 5, while in Canada it begins on March 1.

Fiscal Zoning

Zoning in which a prime consideration is the amount of tax revenues that a development will yield as compared to the costs to the municipality of providing public services to the new development.

Under fiscal zoning the types of development that are often sought are industrial and commercial. Age-oriented developments that do not permit children under 18, and attract financially comfortable, middle-aged couples who require few governmental services are also popular. Because of the high cost of providing public education, single-family homes almost invariably cost the local government more than they provide in taxes, as they tend to produce larger populations of school-age children.

Fiscal zoning may sometimes be applied in a way that is actually fiscally irrational. Many communities that welcome single-family housing have rejected condominium developments featuring small housing units or apartment buildings, on the premise that they will receive insufficient tax revenues as compared to the expected number of schoolchildren the development will produce. Numerous studies have shown, however, that apartment buildings (particularly if they are high-rise) and small condominium units generate a fraction of the school population of single-family housing. Without a careful examination of the total costs of providing municipal services to a proposed development, analyses concerning projected tax revenues provide only a portion of the information that is necessary to evaluate a development's fiscal impact.

Fiscal zoning can also lead to a land use mix that is not compatible with viable long-term development patterns. An overemphasis, for example, on housing units that will not add children to the school-age population can lead to a steadily increasing median population age, a shortage of housing for workers with families, and a school-age population that declines so rapidly as to force school closings.

See: FISCAL IMPACT ANALYSIS; ZONING

Fixed-Rate Mortgage (FRM)

The traditional means by which the purchase of single-family homes has been financed in the United States. In a fixed-rate mortgage the interest rate does not change over the life of the mortgage. It has proved highly advantageous to homeowners who obtained mortgages prior to the greatly escalating interest rates of the 1970s and early 1980s.

Prior to 1983, fixed-rate mortgages were extremely difficult to obtain. Because of the recent interest rate volatility, which affects a bank's cost of money, banks have become less willing to grant fixed-rate mortgages. Since then, however, fixed-rate mortgages have been more readily available.

See: MORTGAGE; VARIABLE-RATE MORTGAGE (VRM)

Flex-Time

The use, by an employer, of an operating schedule within which the employee has the right to choose working hours. The hours may be decided on a permanent or day-to-day basis but usually include a core time, generally 9:30 to 12:30 and 2:00 to 3:30, during which all employees must be present. The concept can be expanded to flex-weeks and flex-months for businesses that have heavy and light business cycles.

This is a relatively new management tool, which many businesses find advantageous because it results in decreased absenteeism and lateness and, often, increased productivity and employee satisfaction. Transportation planners encourage flex-time to spread commuting peaks over longer periods, thus enabling more efficient use of the transportation system, cutting undesirable peak-hour congestion and decreasing the need for further capital investment to handle peak periods. The Canadian government has put the 35,000 federal employees in Ottawa on flex-time or staggered work hours, which has markedly improved rush hour transportation.

See: STAGGERED WORK HOURS; TRANSPORTATION SYSTEM MANAGEMENT (TSM)

Flexible Regulations

Regulations that set forth general standards, with specific implementation dependent upon the judgment of governmental officials or bodies. In land use regulation, there has been an increasing trend towards the use of flexible devices that have the potential of encouraging improved design and innovative approaches to land use problems. Among these types of devices are incentive zoning, planned unit development and floating zones.

Flexible controls were developed in response to the premise that not all land uses or aspects of design can be anticipated and set forth in advance in specific form. Instead, official municipal policies and guides to decision making are formulated, performance standards are frequently adopted, and negotiation with applicants often takes place. Flexible regulations may be contrasted to as-

of-right zoning, in which all aspects of development are predetermined.
See: AS-OF-RIGHT ZONING; NEGOTIATION

Floating Zone

A zoning district whose requirements are completely set forth in a municipal zoning ordinance but that is initially unmapped. It remains unmapped until application is made by a prospective developer and approval is granted by the municipality for the zone to be applied to a particular parcel of land, providing that the development meets all of the requirements described in the ordinance. Generally, mapping of this zone requires action by the legislative body of the municipality.

Floating zones may be designed to replace existing zoning or serve as an overlay to existing zoning, depending upon the purpose of the zone. Most commonly, they are designed to replace existing zoning and are used to accommodate large-scale developments, such as industrial parks or shopping centers. One example of the use of floating zones as an overlay is the application of historic district controls that do not supplant existing zoning concerning permitted uses.
See: FLEXIBLE REGULATIONS; *ROGERS* v. *VILLAGE OF TARRYTOWN*

Flood

A rise in the water level of a water body, or the rapid accumulation of water from runoff or other sources, so that land that is normally dry is temporarily inundated by water. Among the principal causes of floods on rivers and streams are heavy rainfall and the rapid thawing of large accumulations of snow and ice. Coastal flooding is caused primarily by various types of storms at sea, such as hurricanes and typhoons, or by seismic activities, such as underwater earthquakes. Additional causes of flooding include ice jams (which prevent water from flowing freely and form a natural dam), the rupture of glacial ice, the breakage of dams and various forms of landslides.

For the purpose of the National Flood Insurance Program, flooding is also defined to include mudslides connected with accumulations of water, and land subsidence along water bodies.
See: FLOOD CONTROL; FLOODPLAIN; FLOOD-PRONE LAND

Flood Control

Techniques for reducing the incidence of flooding and for minimizing damage when flooding does occur.

A wide variety of flood-control structures and methods have been developed to attempt to reduce or contain floodwaters. Included are floodwalls, levees and channel improvements, in which channel capacity is increased by widening, deepening, straightening or making the channel smoother. The use of reservoirs and dams to control floodwaters, in which some of the flood is impounded by the dam and then gradually released to reduce peak flooding, has been widely adopted. Land use controls, such as regu-

lation of floodplains and other flood-prone land, as well as land management practices that preserve the infiltration capacity of the soil, are also used in combination with other methods. Flood warning systems are often used on larger rivers and streams to reduce loss of life and property damage. On these larger streams, peak floodwaters usually occur some period of time after a rainstorm, allowing time to evacuate people, to move property and possessions vulnerable to water damage and possibly to construct temporary flood barriers.

At a local level a prime means by which flooding is controlled is through on-site detention of stormwater, which is then slowly released to maintain runoff rates at the level that existed before development took place. Communities participating in the National Flood Insurance Program must also appropriately manage their floodplains and other flood-prone areas.

Individuals may also take measures to protect their property against flood damage through appropriate design and construction or by alteration of buildings to make them more floodproof. One technique used is a design that elevates the lowest floor of a building above probable flooding levels. New buildings may be constructed or existing buildings altered to include such features as steel bulkheads that can cover windows and doors when flooding is probable, anchoring to prevent flotation and movement, elevation of electrical systems and their controls, sealing of all cracks and special coatings to reduce water seepage.
See: CHANNELIZATION; DAM; FLOOD; FLOODPLAIN MANAGEMENT; FLOOD-PRONE LAND; FLOODWALL; NATIONAL FLOOD INSURANCE PROGRAM; RESERVOIR; STORM DRAINAGE SYSTEM; STORM FREQUENCY

Flood Disaster Protection Act of 1973

An act (PL 93-234) that requires communities with areas determined to be "flood-prone" to participate in the National Flood Insurance Program in order to qualify for any federally assisted construction project in a flood-prone area. Participation also enables its residents to be eligible for federal or federally assisted loans that would finance construction or development in these areas or that use real estate in flood-prone areas as loan collateral. Other incentives to participation created by the act are eligibility of property owners to purchase flood insurance at a federally subsidized rate and the ability of the municipality and residents of its flood-prone areas to obtain disaster relief in the event of a flood. This legislation also adds coverage for shoreline areas that are undermined by waves and currents, making them eligible for flood insurance.

The act virtually prohibits federal participation directly or through federally supervised lending institutions such as banks or mortgage companies in construction projects or mortgage investments in the flood-prone areas of municipalities that do not participate in the program. As a result, the vast majority of communities subject to flooding have chosen to participate in the program. This legislation produced the first floodplain management efforts in many communities and enabled insurance of over $25 billion worth of property through 1980.

Amendments enacted in 1977 add a provision enabling owners of property located in a regulatory floodway to obtain a low-cost loan for the purpose of raising buildings on the property above the base flood level, while another provision permits the federal government to purchase a property that has been severely damaged by floods (at least three times within five years) for transfer to a state or local jurisdiction.
See: NATIONAL FLOOD INSURANCE ACT OF 1968; NATIONAL FLOOD INSURANCE PROGRAM

Flood Fringe

The part of a floodplain that lies beyond the delineated borders of a regulatory floodway. It may also be known as a floodway fringe.
See: FLOODPLAIN; NATIONAL FLOOD INSURANCE PROGRAM; REGULATORY FLOODWAY

Flood Hazard Boundary Map (FHBM)

A map, often based upon preliminary flood data, that outlines those approximate areas of a community considered to be flood-prone. This map is prepared for a community by the Federal Emergency Management Agency (FEMA), and is in effect during what is known as the "emergency phase" of a flood insurance program. During the emergency phase, all structures in a community within the flood-prone areas are eligible to receive a limited amount of subsidized flood insurance.
See: NATIONAL FLOOD INSURANCE PROGRAM

Flood Insurance Rate Map (FIRM)

A map that depicts in detail the boundaries and elevations of the 100-year and 500-year floodplains for a particular community as part of the National Flood Insurance Program. A FIRM, which is prepared following a detailed engineering study conducted by the Federal Emergency Management Agency (FEMA), divides the community into specific flood insurance risk zones for use in the regular phase of the flood insurance program. Under the regular phase, more comprehensive flood insurance coverage is available than may be obtained during the emergency phase of the program, but insurance rates are based upon the zones depicted on the FIRM.

Any community that is enrolled in the regular flood insurance program must use the flood elevations that appear on the FIRM as a basis for governing the elevation of new construction above certain flood levels.
See: FLOOD HAZARD BOUNDARY MAP (FHBM); NATIONAL FLOOD INSURANCE PROGRAM

Flood Record

Information concerning the incidence of past flooding, which is used in projecting future flood conditions. Flood record data may be available from a variety of local sources, including engineering or public works depart-

ments, soil and water conservation districts, planning or environmental management agencies, and the accounts of area newspapers. Various state agencies are an additional source of information, as are several federal agencies. The U.S. Geological Survey and the U.S. Department of Agriculture both publish data useful to determining past flooding patterns.
See: FLOOD CONTROL

Floodplain

For planning and engineering purposes, the term means the low and generally flat land areas adjoining a body of water that often floods or has the potential of flooding. Geologists define the term *floodplain* more specifically as consisting of the relatively smooth and flat land area adjacent to a river or stream, also known as an alluvial plain, that is still actively being formed by sediment deposited by the stream. This may be contrasted to a terrace, which is an abandoned floodplain at a higher elevation.

Because of the high probability of a floodplain's being flooded at periodic intervals, these lands are often controlled by some form of government regulation for the purposes of protecting public health and safety. Floodplain zoning is frequently imposed to limit the types of land uses that may be developed, and building codes may specify certain types of construction standards for floodplains. Waterfront parks are a frequent use of floodplain lands, as they sustain relatively little damage when flooding takes place. (See Fig. 15)
See: FLOOD CONTROL; FLOODPLAIN MANAGEMENT; FLOOD-PRONE LAND

Floodplain Management

The design and implementation of a cohesive program for the use and protection of floodplains, aimed at minimizing flood damage.

A major component is the development of a variety of municipal regulations that control the type, intensity and structural form of development that takes place within the floodplain. Regulatory measures, such as zoning ordinances, subdivision regulations, building codes, sanitary codes and special floodplain ordinances, may be used individually or in combination to prohibit incompatible uses and minimize hazards to the public. These uses include

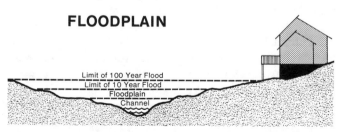

FLOODPLAIN

Limit of 100 Year Flood
Limit of 10 Year Flood
Floodplain
Channel

Fig. 15. Cross section of a floodplain indicating the normal level of the stream channel and the land areas at higher elevations that flood during storms of different frequencies.

those most likely to sustain heavy flood damage or to increase potential flooding damage, and those uses that can cause other public dangers if subjected to flooding, such as release of toxic substances or explosion.

Although certain agricultural uses, and open space uses, such as parkland or nature preserves, are often mentioned as appropriate uses of floodplain land, it may be possible to safely use floodplains as part of other types of development. As an example, an adjoining clustered residential development outside of the floodplain may reserve certain floodplain land as part of an open space requirement. Other municipal regulatory provisions for floodplains may be directed at such areas as prohibiting conventional septic systems, and requiring certain construction standards and provisions, such as bridge or culvert openings capable of passing flood debris and substantial flood discharges. Municipalities may also take steps to discourage development on floodplains through such measures as public information programs, warning signs, and the recording of flood hazard information on land records.

Another component of floodplain management is the planning of provisions for floodplains and other flood-prone areas that are already developed. Steps that may be taken include the construction of flood control projects or flood warning systems and requirements that buildings be floodproofed. Government agencies may also consider acquiring certain developed floodplain lands or less than fee interests in the land, particularly if development is located on the floodway.

See: FLOOD CONTROL; FLOODPLAIN; FLOOD-PRONE LAND; NATIONAL FLOOD INSURANCE PROGRAM

Flood-Prone Land

A land area that is frequently inundated by water. In the United States at least 50,000 square miles (130,000 square kilometers) of land are flood-prone, and many countries, such as the Netherlands, have a much higher proportion of land subject to flooding.

Because flood-prone areas often have many appealing features, they are frequently heavily populated and developed despite their propensity for flooding. Many flood-prone areas are valleys with fertile, flat land suitable for agriculture and residential and commercial development. In some countries these valleys were virtually the only suitable areas in which these activities could take place. In other instances the river itself attracted development because it served as a source of water and a means of transporting people and materials.

One response to protection of these flood-prone areas has been the development of a wide range of flood-control works, such as dams and floodwalls. Because such structures can never guarantee protection against flooding, and because development of flood-prone lands limits natural flood storage capability, various land use controls have been adopted in many communities to limit the types of uses that may be developed in areas of flood hazard. It is possible for residents of a flood-prone area officially iden-

tified by the Federal Insurance Administration to purchase government-subsidized flood insurance, providing that the community adopts floodplain management measures.

See: FLOOD; FLOOD CONTROL; FLOODPLAIN; FLOODPLAIN MANAGEMENT; NATIONAL FLOOD INSURANCE PROGRAM; REGULATORY FLOODWAY

Floodwall

A concrete wall built to protect an area endangered by floodwaters. Floodwalls are usually constructed along a length of a river or around developed areas where space is too restricted to build levees (wide embankments made of earth and sandbags).

See: DAM; DIKE; FLOOD CONTROL; SEAWALL

Floor Area Ratio (FAR)

The ratio between the amount of floor area permitted to be constructed on a building lot and the size of the lot. Floor area ratio is intended to regulate bulk while allowing a developer certain freedom to decide the height of a building and its placement on the lot.

An FAR of 2.0, for example, on a 40,000-square foot (3,700-square meter) lot would permit 80,000 square feet (7,400 square meters) of development. This floor area might be arranged as four 20,000-square foot stories occupying one-half of the lot area, ten 8,000-square foot stories occupying one-fifth of the lot or two 40,000-square foot stories using all of the lot. In practice, zoning regulations often combine the use of FAR with other regulations so that it may not be possible to build a structure occupying 100 percent of a lot or rising more than a certain height. Economic considerations also limit, to some extent, the number of possible combinations of height to building coverage that will be considered during the design process. (See Fig. 16)

See: FLEXIBLE REGULATIONS; HEIGHT CONTROLS; LOT COVERAGE; ZONING

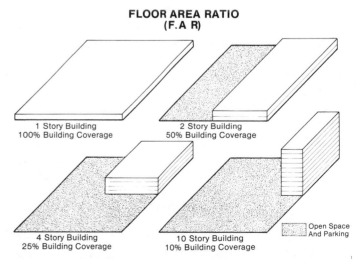

FLOOR AREA RATIO (F.A R)

1 Story Building
100% Building Coverage

2 Story Building
50% Building Coverage

4 Story Building
25% Building Coverage

10 Story Building
10% Building Coverage

Open Space And Parking

Fig. 16. A floor area ratio of 1:0 with different coverage restrictions yields buildings of differing height and configuration.

Floor Plan

A horizontal cross section of a building, as seen from above, taken at a height above the floor that enables maximum detail to be illustrated. It will show the location of outside and inside walls and their thicknesses, lengths and construction materials; all door and window openings in the walls; locations of stairs and elevators; the directions in which doors swing; and other data pertaining to built-in features and plumbing fixtures. It may also show ceiling fixtures and beams or joists that support the floor above, although they would not actually be visible from the perspective of a floor plan. A separate floor plan is usually drawn for each level of a building.(See Fig. 22)
See: SCHEMATIC DRAWING; WORKING DRAWINGS

Footing

That part of a building foundation that distributes the loads of bearing walls, piers or columns to the soil, rock or piles on which the structure rests. Footings, which are usually constructed of concrete, are designed in size, shape, construction and degree of reinforcement to spread the loads transmitted by the structure in relation to the supporting characteristics of the soil on which the structure will be located. The most common types are pedestal footings, spread footings, combined footings and wall footings.
See: BEARING WALL; CONCRETE; FOUNDATION; FROSTLINE; PIER

Force Main

Water supply lines and sewerage pipes whose contents are pumped to maintain a stated water pressure and to permit uphill flow. Force mains require a pumping station or stations that can deliver the necessary amount of pressure. They are used extensively in water supply systems; sewerage systems rely on them in pumping stations and where it is necessary to pump sewage to a higher elevation or over a hill, although this situation is avoided whenever possible.
See: GRAVITY FLOW; PUMPING STATION; SEWERAGE SYSTEM; WATER SUPPLY SYSTEM

Foreign Trade Zones

Designated areas where goods can be imported for processing, assembly or storage on a duty-free basis. Authorized by the Foreign Trade Zones Act of 1934, in which they were defined as "an isolated, enclosed or policed area, operated as a public utility," these zones can provide significant financial benefits to certain types of businesses and to the areas in which the zones are located.

No customs duty is paid when goods enter a foreign trade zone; it is only when they leave the zone and enter areas within U.S. Customs jurisdiction that duty payments are required. If the goods are exported directly out of the United States, no payments are necessary; it is as if they never entered U.S. territory. One aspect of the financial benefits of the zones is that goods that will remain in the United States can be processed so as to obtain the lowest duties and freight tariffs. This is designed to encourage the final processing of goods in the country of import rather than the country of export. As an example, the duty rate for constituent parts is sometimes higher than the rate imposed on the finished product, making it economical to import parts into the zone, assemble them, and ship a finished product out of the zone "onto U.S. soil."

As of mid-1983, there were 77 foreign trade zones in operation in the United States as well as an additional 18 subzones devoted to manufacturing, a substantial increase over the number of zones in operation in the 1970s. The zones, which are under the authority of the Foreign Trade Zones Board within the Department of Commerce, are in such diverse locations as Brooklyn, New York; New Orleans, Louisiana; Little Rock, Arkansas; Westmoreland County, Pennsylvania; Miami, Florida; and McAllen, Texas.

Foreign trade zones are often operated by a port authority or economic development agency, under grants of authority from the federal government. Typically, foreign trade zone operations are conducted in terminal warehouse–type facilities or industrial parks from which exports are monitored by U.S. Customs.

In connection with proposed enterprise-zone legislation, it has been recommended by the Reagan administration that those enterprise zones thought to be suitable be designated foreign trade zones as part of the federal incentives of the proposed enterprise zone program.
See: ECONOMIC DEVELOPMENT INCENTIVES; URBAN ENTERPRISE ZONES

Forest Fire Control

The prevention, detection and suppression of forest fires using a variety of techniques. Forest fires are responsible for the loss of many millions of acres of forest each year throughout the world.

Forest fires may be crown fires, burning across the tops of trees; surface fires, the most common type, feeding on vegetation and debris; or ground fires, sustained by underlying organic materials. Peak fire occurrence varies with climate and vegetation growth, but most regions have an identifiable fire season. In the northeastern United States, for example, it is the spring and fall, while in Canada almost all forest fires strike between May and August.

One focus of forest fire prevention activity is public education regarding the hazards of forest fire and the ease of starting a fire accidentally. Fires may also be prohibited in campgrounds and picnic areas when fire risk is high. This type of approach, which attempts to prevent ignition of the fire, is called risk reduction. Hazard reduction, the other approach, attempts to eliminate flammable material through such activities as prescribed burning. A substantial proportion of forest fires occurring in North America each year are of human origin; another major cause of such fires is lightning.

Lookout towers are still one of the main ways in which fires are detected, along with supplemental air patrols. New devices, such as infrared scanners, can even detect campfires from high altitudes. Increasingly, air transport is also being relied upon for fire fighting.

See: FIREBREAK; FORESTRY

Forest Service

An agency within the Department of Agriculture that is responsible for management of the 154 national forests and 19 national grasslands that comprise the National Forest System and for national programs in forestry, forest research and human resources programs related to forestry.

The Forest Service manages the 188 million acres (76 million hectares) under its authority under principles of multiple use and sustained yield, providing both recreational opportunities and valuable sources of timber. Basic research in aspects of forestry is another area of concern and is often undertaken in cooperation with state agricultural colleges.

A program of grants to state foresters for nonfederal forest lands is provided for state and local level forestry programs, including state forest resources planning, urban forestry assistance, and rural fire protection and control. The Forest Service also manages several Job Corps programs and related programs, such as the Youth Conservation Corps, that engage in forestry and conservation activities.

See: BUREAU OF LAND MANAGEMENT (BLM); FORESTRY; NATIONAL FOREST; SOIL CONSERVATION SERVICE (SCS)

Forestry

The management of forests and forest land to enable the most efficient use of their resources. Traditionally, the most significant function of forests has been the provision of timber. Other important functions that forests serve, however, are the provision of habitat for wildlife, the protection of watershed lands, the prevention of soil erosion and the reduction of runoff. In addition, forests provide valuable and highly scenic recreation areas.

The multiple-use policy of managing forests to enable many of these various functions to continue and exist within them has attracted increasing favor and is in operation in many forested areas of the United States. It has been the policy in national forests since 1960, when the Multiple-Use Sustained Yield Act was passed, that variety of use rather than the uses that would yield the greatest dollar return was most important.

Another common practice in forestry is sustained yield, in which the forest is managed so that continuous production of timber, forest products and forest services can be attained. This is achieved, in theory, by removing only a portion of the forest at any given time on a rotating basis. Because of the length of time that it takes many varieties

of trees to grow and the possibility of tree loss through natural causes such as fire, storms and tree disease, long-range planning must be flexible.

In the United States approximately 20 percent of the forest land is federally owned, while most of the remainder is in private hands.

See: CALIPER; CLEARCUTTING; FOREST FIRE CONTROL; TREE PRESERVATION ORDINANCE

Formula Grant

A type of intergovernmental grant, usually allocated by state, that is distributed on the basis of an established formula. The formula may take into account demographic data for a given jurisdiction as well as such other information as population density, persons with incomes below the poverty level, housing conditions or mileage of mass transit routes. The majority of available funds for a particular grant program (subject to the limitation of the total funding reserved for the state) is generally allocated to locations having the greatest need as measured by the particular formula. Funding is based upon approval of a noncompetitive application that indicates that funds will be used in compliance with the intent and requirements of the program. The funds may be given directly to the applying jurisdiction or pass through the state for distribution. Most of the block grant programs are formula grants.

See: BLOCK GRANT; ENTITLEMENT GRANT

Fossil Fuels

Naturally occurring organic fuels—such as coal, oil, natural gas and oil-bearing shale—formed from decaying plant and animal matter over millions of years.

In the United States there has been an increasing trend toward the use of coal because of its abundance. The United States possesses more than 25 percent of the world's coal reserves, and coal usage rose 8.6 percent from 1978 to 1979. By contrast, in that same time period, natural gas usage increased by 2.7 percent; petroleum consumption fell by 2.2 percent; and nuclear power usage declined by 7.7 percent. Other countries are also increasing their coal usage because of the high price of oil or the uncertainty regarding its availability.

Among the environmental effects caused by use of coal and other fossil fuels are the problems associated with strip mining; occurrence of acid rain; and increased concentration of atmospheric carbon dioxide, which causes a "greenhouse effect," trapping heat that can eventually raise global temperatures.

See: ACID RAIN; ELECTRIC POWER GENERATION AND TRANSMISSION; OFFSHORE DRILLING; OIL POLLUTION; OUTER CONTINENTAL SHELF (OCS); STRIP MINING; SYNTHETIC FUELS

Foundation

1. That portion of a building which rests on the earth. The design of a foundation is closely related to both the design and weight of the structure and the characteristics

of the subsoil; if structure design and soil characteristics are not both accommodated, the structure will settle unevenly.

Three forms of foundation are used in differing soil conditions to support structures of various weights. Foundations may be spread by the use of footings or foundation walls to distribute the load over the earth, so that the earth's safe weight-bearing capacity per square foot is not exceeded. Another method is to excavate to a lower soil stratum or to bedrock to find the necessary supporting characteristics. A third method is to drive piles (long shafts of wood or concrete) into the ground until they rest on bedrock or are sufficiently embedded to be able to carry the building load without sinking further. Footings are then built on top of the piles.

Walls that form foundations may be bearing walls, or they may enclose spaces between supporting columns. Depending on the building load and the soil conditions, foundation walls may require the additional support of footings.

2.   An organization, established by endowment, that usually supports specific causes and often makes grants to private and public projects in which the foundation has a particular interest.
See: BEARING WALL; FOOTING; FROSTLINE; GRANT APPLICATION; PIER; SOIL HORIZON; SOIL SURVEY

Fountains

A basin into which water flows naturally or by mechanical means. In ancient times fountains were strictly utilitarian in nature and were fed by a stream or well. As their principal purpose was provision of water to the public, they were generally centrally located and a focus of community activity.

During Greek and Roman times, fountains also became decorative and were frequently used in the courtyards of private residences. Complexity of fountain design greatly increased during the Italian baroque period and in the 17th century. Since that time fountains have continued to be popular but have generally been less elaborate in design and of a smaller scale.

Fountains are still considered to be a necessary part of the design of formal plazas because of their almost universal ability to attract large numbers of viewers and create a natural gathering place. Fountains also have the ability to soften urban noise levels in their vicinity by substituting the sound of flowing or trickling water, considered by many to be a welcome contrast to city noises. Two mid-20th-century fountains that have gained nationwide attention serve as focal points for urban activity but are vastly different in design. The multilevel fountain in Lovejoy Plaza in Portland, Oregon encourages climbing on parts that are not submerged, while the waterfall fountain in Paley Park in New York City encourages passive viewing and listening.
See: AMBIENCE; AMENITY; DEVELOPMENT FOCUS

Fred F. French Investing Company, Inc. v. City of New York (39 N.Y.2d 587, 350 N.E.2d 381; appeal dismissed 429 U.S. 990 [1976])

A decision by the New York Court of Appeals (the highest court in New York) holding that the rezoning of private parkland with development potential to public park use, thereby prohibiting all private economic use of the property, was an unconstitutional deprivation of property without due process.

New York City attempted to preserve the development rights taken by the rezoning by allowing the owner of the rezoned land, under specified conditions, to transfer the development rights severed from the land to certain parcels of land within a specified "receiving area." The court found that the creation of transferable development rights did not save the rezoning from being unconstitutional, since the utility and value of the new rights were uncertain and did not preserve the economic value of the development rights that had been lost through the rezoning.
See: PENN CENTRAL TRANSPORTATION COMPANY v. CITY OF NEW YORK; TAKING; TRANSFER OF DEVELOPMENT RIGHTS (TDR)

Freedom of Information Act

The Freedom of Information Acts of 1966 (PL 89-487) and 1974 (PL 93-502) require federal agencies and those who receive federal funds to make their records, information and annual reports available to the press and public. The 1974 act strengthens and clarifies the mandated requirements for agencies, including the extent of data to be made available and the time periods allowed for response to specific requests (generally ten days). Both the 1966 and 1974 acts exempt nine categories of materials from public disclosure, such as classified data, personnel matters, and items excluded by specific legislation. The Privacy Act of 1974 (PL 93-579) provides additional protection for information held in federal data banks concerning individuals.

The Freedom of Information Act has been used extensively by investigative journalists and lobbying organizations to obtain details of matters not usually released to the press.
See: GOVERNMENT IN THE SUNSHINE ACT OF 1976; PRIVACY

Freeway

An expressway with full control of access. Freeways constitute a very small percentage of the total road system but carry very high volumes of traffic. They are generally part of, or connect to, the interstate highway system.

Cross sections of typical freeways provide a right-of-way of 200 to 300 feet (61 to 91.4 meters); four to eight 12-foot (3.7-meter) moving lanes; shoulders at least 8 to 10 feet (2.4 to 3.0 meters) in width; service or frontage roads, or building setback lines at least 75 feet (22.9 meters) from the right-of-way; extensive landscaping; and a median of 8 to 60 feet (2.4 to 18.3 meters) in width. The road may be

depressed, at grade or elevated. A maximum grade of 3 percent and a design speed of 60 mph (96.5 kph) should be provided.
See: CONTROL OF ACCESS; EXPRESSWAY; INTERSTATE HIGHWAY SYSTEM

Freight Handling Facilities

Terminals that process goods. Such terminals vary in the type of freight handled, which may be bulk or packaged cargo, and in the transportation modes they serve. Freight handling facilities contain equipment that can load and unload the transporting vehicles; they differ from warehouses in that they store goods the minimum time necessary prior to shipment of the freight to its ultimate destination. Some freight handling operations also have warehouses connected with them for longer storage as well as business offices.

Freight handling facilities take many forms, such as railroad freight yards, containerized vessel loading at harbors, truck terminals, air freight and ship cargo loading. All require the ability to transfer cargo to trucks of various sizes for further shipment. They also require substantial land area with good highway transportation access and a location that can tolerate high levels of truck movement and noise as well as reduced air quality.
See: TRUCK TERMINALS; WAREHOUSE FACILITIES

Frequency Distribution

A means of classifying and depicting the distribution of a variable. Data are systematically assigned to groups or class intervals to make them more readily understandable and to allow additional statistical operations to be performed. Frequency distributions are then plotted graphically as a frequency distribution curve, in which the x-axis represents the class interval and the y-axis represents the frequency of occurrence.
See: NORMAL DISTRIBUTION

Freshwater Marsh

A wetland that may be found inland or near the coast and in which the water level varies according to rainfall and runoff. Freshwater marshes are fed from stream flow, groundwater, runoff, rain or a combination of these sources; typical vegetation consists of grasses, sedges or rushes such as water lilies, cattails and reeds. Plant growth in the marsh may be submerged under water, or it may rise above water level.
See: BOG; SALT MARSH; SWAMP; WETLANDS

Fringe Area

The area of transition between two different, dominant land patterns. In planning, the term is often used to describe the exurban area between city and country. It is also used for the transition area between a downtown and the surrounding neighborhood or between a stable residential neighborhood and a nearby commercial-industrial zone.

The term *fringe area* can also denote any zone between two different, recognizable characteristics, such as between areas of differing racial or ethnic composition or between areas of different market value.
See: EXURBIA; TRANSITIONAL LOT

Front-End Recovery

Methods by which recyclable waste materials—such as iron, aluminum, glass and paper—are separated from the remainder of urban waste prior to shredding, incineration or other means of waste processing. In contrast, back-end recovery refers to recovery of materials after some form of processing has taken place. Examples of back-end recovery are the retrieval of metals or glass after incineration or the recovery of organic materials through such methods as composting.
See: RECYCLING

Front Foot

A measurement of the extent to which real property abuts a public street, highway or other right-of-way. Each foot of frontage—the boundary of the property abutting the right-of-way—is equal to one front foot. Width is distinguished from front foot or frontage, in that width refers to the distance of a property between its side lines, and in the case of an irregular lot, this distance may vary at different distances from the front.

The extent of frontage is important for uses where visibility from a public right-of-way is important, as is the case with certain retail uses. The extent of a property's frontage, however, may not be an accurate indicator of a site's utility where the site lacks sufficient uniform depth to permit construction of a desired structure.
See: FRONTAGE

Front Lot Line

The line that serves as a boundary between a lot and the street. When a lot abuts more than one street, the zoning ordinance may specify that the building inspector shall designate the front lot line. Alternatively, the ordinance may give the property owner the right to select which street line shall be the front lot line, subject to certain provisions. This is instrumental in determining which of the other lot lines delineate the sides and rear of a property and, ultimately, which portions of the parcel become the front, rear and side yards. (See Fig. 50)
See: LOT LINE; YARD

Front Money

Cash needed at the outset of a development project to pay for such costs as feasibility studies, property options, appraisals, surveys, test borings, attorneys' fees and loan charges before financing is available.
See: SEED MONEY

Front Yard

The yard on an occupied building lot that lies between the front lot line and an imaginary line that is drawn across the lot at the point at which the building is closest to the front lot line. A front yard spans the full width of a building lot. On a corner lot both of the yards bordering the street may be considered to be front yards in many communities. (See Fig. 50)
See: CORNER LOT; FRONT LOT LINE; SETBACK; YARD; YARD REQUIREMENTS

Frontage

The extent to which a lot extends along a street. Zoning ordinances with frontage requirements may have more specific requirements that apply to corner lots, through lots, and lots that have adequate width throughout most of their length but that narrow near the street line. Property that abuts a body of water is described as having "water frontage."
See: FRONT FOOT; LOT; ZONING

Frostline

The maximum soil depth to which frost can penetrate. This figure varies widely with climate and may range from under 5 inches (12.7 centimeters) in many parts of the southern United States to 80 or 90 inches (203.2 to 228.6 centimeters) or more in the most northerly parts. The frostline may be expressed as an average depth over a number of winters, a figure for a single winter or the lowest recorded figure.

In construction it is necessary for footings to extend below the frostline so that they will not be affected by frost action and will remain steady. It is common for building codes to specify that footings reach at least 1 foot below the frostline for that particular area.

Permafrost, or ground that is always frozen, is found throughout much of Alaska and the Soviet Union as well as northern Canada. It presents special construction problems, since buildings or structures placed on permafrost can help to thaw it and may result in heaving of the earth as well as erosion. Special techniques have been developed for permafrost cnstruction, including the placement of structures on piles. The Alaska pipeline, the largest construction project ever attempted in permafrost conditions, included measures such as refrigeration of parts of the pipeline that went underground and elevation of the pipeline above the ground to avoid contact with permafrost.

Full-Value Assessment

The assessment of property at its market value. Full-value assessment—as opposed to fractional assessment, which is more common—is used in a few states to permit the tax burden to be divided fairly among the properties.

While full-value assessment was the original means of property assessment in the early 19th century when property taxation began, communities shifted to a system of assessment at a fraction of full value in the later part of the century. This occurred when states assumed responsibility for property taxation, assigning local assessors to value properties. In an attempt to reduce their towns' share of the state's tax burden, the assessors undervalued properties, whether on a systematic or a random basis, within each jurisdiction. Because of the lack of state supervision of the process until the middle of the 20th century, local autonomy permitted the development of poor-quality property valuation combined with the application of arbitrary assessment ratios, making determination of property tax equity almost impossible.

The return to full-value assessment, mandated by some states, is not easy, however. First, all properties must be reassessed so that current value is known. This process in itself is politically difficult because properties that have not been assessed in many years will probably have markedly higher values, causing their owners large tax increases. Second, when the tax rate is applied to the reassessed properties, some classes of properties that may have been assessed at lower assessment rates than others (typically single-family houses and small farms) will take on a larger percentage of the community's tax burden than they had prior to full-value assessment.

To ease transition to full-value assessment, legislative action may be taken to permit relief for certain classes of property. Measures that are used include a variety of tax reduction tools that may also be used for other purposes. Included are full or partial homestead exemptions or tax credits, circuit-breaker refunds or credits, and tax exemptions for a period of years. Another method, used in a number of agricultural states, is valuation of use value rather than market value, in which a capitalization rate is applied to the earnings from the property to determine its value rather than having the sales prices of comparable properties used. Deferred valuation (often called green acres) is another approach, in which farmlands in fringe areas may defer payment of property tax increases until the property is sold for another use. Other methods by which tax relief is granted are deferred taxation, in which residents (who are usually elderly) are permitted to pay the lower tax amount until they sell the house or die, and property classification, which permits certain property classes to pay a lower percentage of the tax burden. Used by many states, property classification is implemented by applying a factor that has been established by law to the property's full value, effectively lowering the property's assessed valuation. This method presents problems, however, because of difficulties in its administration and its common reduction of the municipal tax base where some categories are assessed at partial value and others at full value.
See: ASSESSED VALUATION; CIRCUIT BREAKER TAXES; TAX ABATEMENT; UNIFORM ASSESSMENT PROCEDURES

Functional Obsolescence

Used in connection with the cost approach to appraising the value of property, functional obsolescence, along with physical deterioration and economic obsolescence, is one of the three factors used to adjust the estimated replacement cost of a structure for depreciation.

Functional obsolescence is an impairment of desirability and usefulness brought about either by a defect in design, or by changes over time which have made some aspect of the structure or its design, materials or fixtures obsolete. An example of functional obsolescence that is curable is a residential building with out-of-date bathroom fixtures. The cost to cure is the cost to replace the existing fixtures with modern ones. Incurable functional obsolescence may include a building built to support the erection of additional stories at a future date, where the addition of new floors is no longer legal or desirable.
See: ADAPTIVE USE; APPRAISAL; APPRAISED VALUE; COST APPROACH APPRAISAL; WHITE ELEPHANT

Functional Road Classification

The establishment of a hierarchy of road classes that divides roads by purpose and design. Two primary classification systems are used, one for urban roads, the other for rural roads. Urban roads are classified as freeways, expressways, arterials, collectors and local roads. Rural roads are classified as interstate, primary, secondary and tertiary roads. Classification of roads by function is undertaken for administrative, planning, design and funding purposes.

The determination of classification is a combination of the function of the road, the control of access to abutting streets and/or land uses, the spacing of roads of a similar nature, the length of the road, and linkages or interchanges with other roads and with major land uses.
See: ARTERIAL ROAD; COLLECTOR STREET; EXPRESSWAY; FREEWAY; INTERSTATE HIGHWAY SYSTEM; LOCAL STREET; PARKWAY; PRIMARY ROAD; SECONDARY ROAD; TERTIARY ROAD

Future Land Use Requirements

The projected future land use needs of the various activities that occur within a given area. This concept incorporates both quantitative needs (the actual acreage required to accommodate each activity) and qualitative needs (the type and location of the land required).

Estimating future land use requirements is a major component of the land use plan. Future land needs can often be derived from various studies typically undertaken by planning offices concerning such factors as employment, population and income. For example, if employment in manufacturing has been growing and is expected to continue to grow, additional space will likely be needed to accommodate these expanding firms and to house new employees. While these studies can be used to give an approximation of future needs, more precise forecasting techniques must be employed to obtain specific estimates.
See: LAND USE PLAN

Future Transportation Modes

Most future forms of transportation will be faster and more comfortable than current modes, as well as more

Fig. 17.   A prototype of a tracked levitated train that rides on a cushion of air.
Credit: Courtesy of the U.S. Department of Transportation

efficient in their use of energy supplies and manpower. Transportation systems that have been proposed, are in various stages of study or have been temporarily dismissed as too costly are discussed below.

- *Rail:* Tracked air cushion vehicles that have sufficient pressure to raise them above the ground and those that use magnetic levitation (repelling magnetic forces) to raise them have been tested extensively. They are currently being used in the design of people movers and are considered applicable to intercity rail service. They must travel on a guideway and be propelled by electromagnetic forces between the vehicle and the guideway or by jet turbine-powered engines and can be expected to reach speeds of 300 mph (483 kph). Gravity vacuum transit (GVT), the use of pneumatic tubes for high-speed passenger rail service, is also being studied. (See Fig. 17)
- *Air:* Vertical and short takeoff and landing (VTOL and STOL) aircraft are being studied for eventual urban application.
- *Auto:* Automatic auto travel on freeways may be a possible mode of transportation. It would permit automatic entry to and exit from the highway and placement into the traffic stream by electronic devices and cables implanted in the roadway and in the car. Since cars would travel at more closely spaced intervals than at present, the system could increase the capacity of existing roadways. For urban use small electric cars with rechargeable batteries are being developed.
- *Freight:* Pneumatic tubes are considered applicable to freight distribution, particularly in urban areas. It is thought that it would be possible to package freight in capsules and ship the capsules to various destinations by underground pneumatic tubes or in tunnels with rails on which the capsules would run. This system, if implemented, could reduce the time that is lost in transporting goods through clogged urban streets.
- *Water:* Jet-propelled vessels that travel on a cushion of air, such as the hydrofoil, are expected to gain in use.

See: HIGH-SPEED RAIL TRANSPORTATION; HYDROFOIL; PEOPLE MOVER; PERSONAL RAPID TRANSIT; SHORT TAKEOFF AND LANDING (STOL); VERTICAL TAKEOFF AND LANDING (VTOL)

G

Galaxy Pattern

A regional or metropolitan land use pattern characterized by a number of urban centers that are relatively independent of each other, like stars of a galaxy. A galaxy pattern usually implies several centers of varying sizes separated by open space or low-density development that are dependent upon auto travel and an extensive highway system. The terms *variegated network* and *checker pattern* have also been used to describe this type of development. (See Fig. 24)
See: LAND USE PATTERN; MULTIPLE-NUCLEI THEORY; SATELLITE PATTERN

Garbage

The animal and vegetable wastes associated with food preparation and handling.
See: SOLID WASTE

Garden Apartment

A dwelling unit in a low-density apartment complex or building, generally located either in the suburbs or away from the central city. Garden apartment buildings usually have two to three stories and sometimes contain duplex apartments. In a suburban area, density often ranges from about 10 to 15 dwelling units per acre. Garden apartment complexes frequently are required to provide off-street parking, usually include common open-space areas and may include such amenities as tennis courts, swimming pools and clubhouses.
See: APARTMENT; HOUSING TYPE

Garden City

A type of town, described by Sir Ebenezer Howard in his writings, that is characterized by compact development and a large belt of open space encircling it. Howard envisioned his garden city as incorporating the best of both urban and rural life and saw it as an answer to the overcrowding and poor living conditions of the cities and the lack of urban amenities of the country.

Ideally, a garden city would be constructed on a limited land area, so as not to impinge upon the protected open space. It would be able to accommodate industrial and agricultural uses as well as residences for a maximum of 30,000 people on a tract of about 6,000 acres (2,400 hectares), of which only about 1,000 acres (400 hectares) would be developed. A civic and cultural complex—containing such facilities as a library, hospital and concert hall—would be placed at the precise center of the town, with avenues radiating from this point. Other rings would contain parks, shopping, residences and industry served by a railroad.

An important aspect of the proposal was the means by

which a garden city could be financed. Howard advocated ownership by a limited-dividend company in which shares would be sold. All excess profit would be used for community benefit, and the company would be able to regulate land use. In 1903 Howard successfully founded Letchworth, the first garden city, and Welwyn Garden City followed in 1919.

A number of early 20th century developments in the United States were also strongly influenced by the philosophies of Ebenezer Howard but tended to be predominantly residential. An early American garden suburb, Forest Hills Gardens in New York City (in the Borough of Queens), was sponsored by the Russell Sage Foundation and completed in 1913. Frederick Law Olmsted Jr. was responsible for site planning for the project (for which Grosvenor Atterbury was architect). It incorporated a central square, Tudor-style architecture and central park area that connected the residential blocks. Forest Hills Gardens immediately emerged as one of New York City's most select residential developments and commanded prices well above the reach of the working class.

Sunnyside Gardens, constructed during the years 1924–1928 (also in Queens) was another American version of a garden city, intended to be an experiment before the development of other larger projects. A joint endeavor of Clarence Stein, Henry Wright and Alexander Bing, it spanned 56 acres (22.7 hectares) and consisted of 1,202 housing units. It featured garden apartment buildings as well as single-family, two-family and three-family homes grouped around large interior garden areas and common greens. In addition, each home had its own small, private garden and the project was conveniently located a short train ride from Manhattan.

Sunnyside Gardens attracted the moderate income worker as planned and was a sufficient economic and design success to encourage the same team to try a project on a larger scale—Radburn, New Jersey. Although Radburn was initially conceived as an opportunity to create a full-fledged garden city, complete with greenbelt and places of work, it ultimately evolved as a garden suburb without greenbelt or industry.
See: GREENBELT TOWNS; HAMPSTEAD GARDEN SUBURB, ENGLAND; HOWARD, SIR EBENEZER; LETCHWORTH, ENGLAND; OSBORN, SIR FREDERICK JAMES; RADBURN, NEW JERSEY; STEIN, CLARENCE S.; UNWIN, SIR RAYMOND

GBF/DIME Files

Computerized census files of 277 Standard Metropolitan Statistical Areas (SMSAs) in the United States, used by the Bureau of the Census for coding addresses to be sent the 1980 questionnaires, and the responses to the questionnaires. Geographic Base File (GBF) refers to the name of the base map series first developed for use in the 1970 Census, because no standardized mapping existed for the entire country. Standardized maps were necessary for

census data enumeration because this was the first census administered largely by mail. Because the 1980 maps were prepared in anticipation of the census, they represent 1977 geography. Dual Independent Map Encoding (DIME) refers to the technique used to prepare the computer files (via node points and street segments) and check their accuracy.

GBF/DIME files show each street in straight-line segments. For each segment they indicate: street name and type—e.g., street or avenue; building number ranges on both sides of the street; the block number and census tract number on each side of the street; and the node numbers assigned to the segment. Latitude and longitude values are used to place nodes. Since areas that do not conform to any other municipal or census boundaries can be identified by use of the node points, e.g., groups of blocks that do not adhere to block group or census tract boundaries, the files permit the user to obtain data for any geographic area he wishes to define.

Municipalities have also found that the files produce computer maps that are useful as base maps for municipal information systems, police patrol scheduling, refuse collection routing, school bus pickup locations and schedules, and health planning studies. They are available from the Bureau of the Census, as are a number of related software packages.

For the 1990 Census, the Census Bureau expects to use a new geocoding system called TIGER (Topologically Integrated Geographic Encoding and Referencing System) which will integrate aspects of the GBF/DIME system, MARF (Master Area Reference File—tables that link a location hierarchically to its other designations), and new technology to enable better computer mapping for field operations and publication products.
See: GEOCODING; NODE

Geddes, Sir Patrick (1854–1932)

Born in Scotland and trained in biology and sociology, Geddes is considered one of the major contributors to the development of modern urban and regional planning. His academic career as a professor of botany in Scotland and as a sociology professor in London and India helped him to form a planning philosophy based upon the impact of people on their environment and the effect that environments have upon human population. He stressed the importance of considering social and economic factors whenever physical planning is contemplated and strongly advocated the use of data gathering surveys before planning was begun.

A major component of any survey, according to Geddes, was the impressions gained by the planner by visiting the site, as well as information gathered concerning the area's economy, geography and demography. He also advocated the importance of comprehensive planning within a regional context.

Geddes participated in major planning projects in Scot-

land, Israel and India. In addition, he published a number of works, such as *City Development* (1904) and *Cities in Evolution* (1915), which influenced the evolution of planning.
See: CONURBATION

General Obligation Bond

A government bond backed by the "full faith and credit" (primarily the taxing power) of the jurisdiction issuing it; essentially an unlimited claim on a community's tax base. Capital improvement projects such as municipal buildings or schools are often financed with this type of bond, although it may be used to finance any type of project. By contrast, bonds secured by the income of the projects that they finance, and possibly the facility as well, are called revenue bonds.
See: BOND; BOND RATINGS; DEBT LIMIT; MUNICIPAL BOND; REVENUE BOND

General Services Administration (GSA)

A federal agency that manages government property and records; federal acquisitions and dispositions; and other internal communications, transportation and storage systems. The agency, which is responsible for federal building construction, frequently consults with local planning agencies to coordinate plans and offers excess federal property at below market value to state and local governments and nonprofit agencies. The GSA also manages the National Archives and Records Service (NARS), which preserves records of value, such as presidential papers and legislative and regulatory documents. It also publishes laws as they are passed, the annual *United States Statutes at Large* and *United States Government Manual*, the *Federal Register*, the *Code of Federal Regulations* and presidential documents.
See: PROPERTY DISPOSITION

Gentrification

A process of social and economic change within an area of a city wherein generally young, affluent and well-educated individuals move into frequently substandard housing or industrial space in a decaying neighborhood and invest large amounts of money to rehabilitate their structures. This process inevitably causes rent and property value increases, forcing out former residents who may be elderly or lower-income families. As the image of the area improves, it also frequently results in a turnover in commercial property, with older neighborhood stores being replaced by expensive boutiques, as well as conversion of apartment buildings, warehouses and other commercial space to cooperative or condominium apartments.

The phenomenon escalated during the 1970s in cities where housing costs in desirable areas were too high for middle-income families who preferred to stay in the city rather than find housing in the suburbs. The solid structures and interesting architectural amenities of central city housing and industrial buildings in declining and de-pressed neighborhoods offered the alternative of sufficient space at a relatively reasonable cost.

Gentrification has been the subject of considerable controversy because, along with displacement and consequent neighborhood tension and unrest, it has brought significant benefits to many communities. In addition to attracting middle-income residents to decaying urban areas, it has been responsible for upgrading substandard housing and improving the municipal tax base. With these increased tax revenues, one option that communities can choose to protect longtime residents but still encourage improvements in the area is the subsidization of rent payments.
See: NEIGHBORHOOD PRESERVATION

Geocoding

The assigning of geographic codes or identifiers to data that are spatially distributed. Postal zip codes and telephone area codes are two examples of geocodes, which may be assigned manually or by computer. The GBF/DIME system, used by the U.S. Bureau of the Census, is an example of a software system that assigns geocodes to address ranges.

Geocoding, which has a broad range of uses in the planning profession, enables one set of data to be readily compared to another. In addition, it serves as input for more complex applications such as computer mapping or resource allocation. As an example, Hartford, Connecticut geocoded its voter registration files, which contain birthdates, to determine the number and location of elderly persons. This information was then used in planning the number and location of facilities needed to serve the elderly.
See: GBF/DIME FILES

Geodesic Dome

A form of dome in which a skeleton of triangular or polygonal facets, composed of light metal struts, distributes stress within the structure, eliminating the need for supporting arches or vaulting. The skeleton supports enclosing materials such as glass. It is the only form of dome that can be set on the ground as a complete structure. Designed by R. Buckminster Fuller, the geodesic dome's frame increases in strength in a logarithmic ratio to its dimensions, which implies that there is no limit to a geodesic dome's potential size. Fuller has suggested that they be employed as covers to entire cities to provide climate and environmental control and that they be used to enable the development of communities in hostile climates.
See: SKELETON FRAME CONSTRUCTION

Geological Survey (USGS)

A bureau of the Department of the Interior that performs a variety of functions related to the survey and investigation of the nation's lands and resources. These studies cover topography, geology, and mineral and water resources. Data collected are classified, published in reports, mapped in a variety of ways and disseminated to the public.

Established in 1879, the USGS consolidated four organizations that had been engaged in topographic and geologic mapping and the collection of data on public lands. In 1882 a general plan for the production of a standard series of topographic base maps was adopted to enable adequate mapping of natural resources. The mapping program has expanded to include other parts of the world, a wide variety of base map scales and maps that indicate locations of natural resources. Many of the data collected by the USGS are mapped, but before this stage is reached, the data may also be available in an advance or draft form. This material may be particularly useful for local mapping programs where new data are necessary. Other products made available are aerial photos, which form the basis of topographic mapping; orthophotoquads, aerial photos matched to form a standard USGS quadrangle format; and LANDSAT imagery, remotely sensed data collected by LANDSAT satellites.

The USGS publishes technical and scientific reports and maps, which are described in the monthly *New Publications of the Geological Survey,* and nontechnical publications, described in *Popular Publications of the United States Geological Survey.* A periodical, *Earthquake Information Bulletin,* is also available. USGS maps are available through the National Cartographic Information Center, the EROS Data Center and local distributors. The Hydrologic Information Unit and the Geologic Information Unit, both located at USGS headquarters in Reston, Virginia, answer questions about data availability on these respective matters. The USGS also has responsibilities with respect to review of environmental impact statements for projects that may have a water resource or geological impact.
See: DEPARTMENT OF THE INTERIOR; EARTH RESOURCES OBSERVATION SYSTEMS (EROS) PROGRAM; NATIONAL CARTOGRAPHIC INFORMATION CENTER (NCIC); USGS MAPS

Geologic Hazards

Geologic conditions of the subsurface or surface, either of natural origin or intensified by human activity, that pose a threat to life and property. Examples of geologic hazards are faults, volcanoes, landslides, earthquakes and land subsidence.

A clear understanding of the cause of geologic hazards, the extent to which they can be prevented or minimized, and the degree of hazard involved is essential to proper and careful planning and development. The use of all available geologic information, detailed environmental analysis of a proposed site, and special design and engineering techniques to counter unusual conditions can prevent casualties and minimize property damage.

The U.S. Geological Survey has developed a program in which it gives warnings of geologic-related hazards to pertinent government units and provides technical assistance.

In addition, the survey focuses on public information programs and long-range measures that can be taken to mitigate the hazard. Although prediction of geologic hazards is not yet a fully developed science, certain types of predictions can be made with accuracy, and research continues into the nature of these hazards.
See: EARTHQUAKE HAZARD MITIGATION; FAULT; LAND SUBSIDENCE; MASS WASTING

Geologic Map

Map showing the distribution and type of rock units, such as formations; their relationship to each other; and other physical features, such as fault lines. A cross section and contour lines are also commonly included, while the legend is generally arranged so that the youngest rock units appear at the top, the oldest at the bottom. The scale of geologic maps ranges considerably, depending upon their purpose.

Although they cannot replace detailed site investigation and engineering tests, geologic maps present many types of information useful to the planner. From these maps, for example, one may identify potentially productive agricultural lands; deposits of construction materials, such as gravel or limestone; or the depth of underground aquifers. Engineering features such as load-bearing capacity, difficulty of excavation and slope stability may also be deduced. Data concerning the area's geology will aid in the siting of sensitive development requiring careful site selection, such as power plants or sanitary landfills.

Geologic maps are available from a number of sources. In the United States they may be obtained from federal agencies—including the U.S. Geological Survey (USGS), the Army Corps of Engineers and the Bureau of Reclamation—as well as from various state agencies. Canada's Geological Survey and Britain's Institute of Geological Sciences are also useful map sources. The USGS publishes a wide variety of geologic and mineral resource surveys and maps. Maps are available for geologic, geophysical and geochemical data; for assessment of mineral resources; and for analysis of the distribution, quantity and quality of coal, gas, oil, uranium and geothermal resources. In addition, offshore geologic surveys assess these mineral resources.
See: REFERENCE MAPS

Geometric Design

Geometric design, or roadway geometrics, refers to the physical dimensions of a roadway and the degree to which its design accommodates the variables of vehicle operation, vehicle design and vehicle operator judgment. Good geometric design is intended to coordinate the effect of a variety of roadway characteristics on each other and on the vehicles and drivers using the road. These include vertical and horizontal alignment (the degree of vertical and horizontal curvature of the roadway surface or the difficulty of such curves); sight distance; roadway grades or steepness; superelevation, or road banking on curves;

pavement characteristics—e.g., slick or bumpy; roadway cross section (numbers and widths of lanes, shoulders, median); presence of interchanges; presence of lighting; and quality of traffic signs. Combined with these physical characteristics are factors of vehicle design, such as speeds at which the vehicle is designed to be operated and other vehicular characteristics, as well as human factors, such as human reaction time and human behavior and psychology.

The term *geometric design* is also used in connection with mass transit facility planning to refer to necessary rights-of-way, lane widths, vertical clearance, design speed, horizontal alignment, maximum grade and control of access for buses, trolleys and rapid transit.
See: CONTROL OF ACCESS; DESIGN HOUR VOLUME (DHV); GRADE; LANE WIDTH; SIGHT DISTANCE; TRAFFIC CONTROL DEVICES

Geothermal Energy

The naturally occurring heat in the Earth's interior that results from the radioactive decay of selected elements. It represents a large and primarily untapped source of energy, potentially available to many nations. In the United States, however, almost all of the known geothermal resources are in the western states, away from concentrations of population, making it more difficult to use these resources.

Geothermal energy sources may be grouped into four types: dry steam, which is most rare but most easily used; wet steam, which is more commonly found but more difficult to use; hot brine, readily found but presenting greater use difficulties; and hot rock, the most common and most difficult source to use. Dry steam fields were first developed in 1904 in Larderello, Italy, where a large-scale power plant is in operation; another large plant, known as the Geysers, is located north of San Francisco and supplies a significant percentage of that city's power. The Geysers is, however, the only dry steam resource that has currently been found in the United States that is not in a national park. Wet steam fields have been harnessed in New Zealand, Iceland, Mexico, Japan and the Soviet Union, but greater problems have been encountered in developing the other two types of geothermal energy sources.
See: ENERGY SECURITY ACT; RENEWABLE ENERGY SOURCES

Ghetto

An area, largely composed of one ethnic group, within which its inhabitants are compelled to live by law or because of social, economic or political pressure. The term is derived from the Getto area (iron foundry) of Venice, where Jews were required to live after 1517.

Modern ghettos are largely the result of social discrimination and poverty and, as a result, often have slum conditions. Except in those countries where government policies prescribe ghettos, most countries encourage the dispersal of population subgroups through such methods

as antidiscrimination legislation and policies related to government grant allocation.
See: AFFIRMATIVE FAIR HOUSING MARKETING; FAIR HOUSING LEGISLATION; REDLINING; SLUM; SOCIAL PLANNING

Ghiradelli Square

One of the best-known examples of adaptive use in the United States, in which a chocolate factory was converted into a complex of specialty shops and restaurants. One of San Francisco's earliest adaptive use projects, the popular complex was completed in 1968.

As a result of its success, many other projects of a similar nature have been developed or are underway throughout the United States. In addition, it has transformed its waterfront neighborhood by attracting tourism as well as many other new businesses, including The Cannery, another adaptive use commercial complex located in what used to be a canning factory.
See: ADAPTIVE USE; HISTORIC PRESERVATION; WATERFRONT REVITALIZATION

Glasphalt

A new type of road surface in which recycled glass is used as a pavement component. Although possibly more expensive than conventional pavement, it has the potential of providing a large market for waste glass, thus reducing the volume of solid waste requiring disposal. Tests have also indicated that glasphalt is easier to repair in cold weather than conventional aggregates.
See: CULLET; PAVEMENT; RECYCLING

Global Environmental Monitoring System (GEMS)

A system established in 1975 that coordinates ongoing international environmental monitoring activities, categorizes and stores data that are collected in data banks, and makes the data available for distribution. It does not conduct its own research or undertake monitoring. GEMS, which is operated under the auspices of the United Nations Environment Program (UNEP), maintains a center of operations at UNEP headquarters in Nairobi.

Major international environmental areas that GEMS actively monitors are the climate, the spread of pollutants across large distances, renewable resources, human health and the oceans. Current or recent research topics are a world glacier inventory, with data provided by research stations in 21 countries; a background atmospheric pollution monitoring network; acid rain; and soil degradation and desertification. Tropical forests and the health effects of toxic substances are also under study, and a regional seas program, aimed at monitoring and reducing marine pollution, is being conducted.
See: EARTHWATCH

Goal

The long-term ideal or end product that is desired. Goals are developed after systematic study helps to identify community needs that should be met. An example of a

goal might be the provision of a range of adequate and affordable housing for all components of the community's population. Goal formulation is an integral part of the planning process, helping to direct planning efforts and the allocation of community resources.
See: OBJECTIVE

Goldblatt v. *Town of Hempstead* (369 U.S. 590, 82 S.Ct. 987, 8 L.Ed.2d 130 [1962])

A decision by the United States Supreme Court upholding a local zoning ordinance that had the effect of requiring the termination of an existing lawfully conducted nonconforming use (sand mining and excavation at a quarry), which was located in a densely populated residential area.

The ordinance did not expressly proscribe any future excavation. Rather, it conditioned future operations on the issuance of a special permit and the correction of various conditions that were considered hazardous to public safety. One of the dissenting opinions in the case, however, pointed out that the cost of correcting these conditions was so high as to have the practical effect of forcing the quarry owner to terminate operations.

The Court followed the traditional rule that legislative action is presumed valid and is to be upheld if it can be supported on any rational basis. In this instance, the Court found the ordinance to be within the police power delegated to the Town of Hempstead to adopt legislation in furtherance of the public safety. This finding was made even though the effect of the ordinance was to require the property owner involved to terminate his profitable use of the property without offering him any compensation.
See: NONCONFORMING USE; TAKING

Golden v. *Planning Board of the Town of Ramapo* (30 N.Y.2d 359, 285 N.E.2d 291; appeal dismissed 409 U.S. 1003 [1972])

A decision by the New York Court of Appeals (the highest court in New York) sustaining the Town of Ramapo's right to enforce phased residential growth.

The town limited the right to develop land for residential purposes to those parcels that were serviced by a minimum number of municipal facilities. Under Ramapo's development plan, parcels were allocated points based on proximity to municipal facilities, roads, adequacy of drainage and other factors. Parcels could be developed only after they had been allocated a sufficient number of points. Under a series of capital budget plans, it was contemplated that all residentially zoned land would qualify for development on a phased basis over 18 years. However, a landowner could accelerate the date his parcel would be available for development by providing municipal facilities at his expense.

The court upheld the limitation on development as being within the scope of New York's zoning enabling legislation, relying in part on the town's uncontested assertion that the additional municipal facilities were necessary to

adequately serve the demand that would be created by additional development and that the development restrictions had a definite termination date.

With growth rates greatly reduced, Ramapo repealed its point system in 1983 as no longer being necessary.
See: ADEQUATE PUBLIC FACILITIES ORDINANCE; *CONSTRUCTION INDUSTRY ASS'N OF SONOMA COUNTY* v. *CITY OF PETALUMA*; GROWTH MANAGEMENT; PHASED DEVELOPMENT CONTROLS

Golf Course

The variety of facilities that permit the game of golf. The 18-hole course is the standard size, requiring between 100 and 160 acres (40 and 65 hectares) of land, with fairway distances that may range from 600 to 2,500 yards (549 to 2,286 meters). The fairways at any given course are designed for varying degrees of difficulty but may be easier at public courses to permit more players per day. The 9-hole course, which requires 60 to 90 acres (24 to 36 hectares), has essentially the same design as the 18-hole course but usually has fairways with 300- to 600-yard (274- to 549-meter) distances. The par 3 course, a relatively new design, is a 9-hole course that has very short fairways and greens on a small site but has the general appearance of a larger course. Suitable where large parcels of land are unavailable and particularly popular with the elderly, this type of course can be designed for a site of from 10 to 50 acres (4 to 20 hectares). All of these courses require the presence of a clubhouse—which generally contains managerial facilities, toilets, lockers and food services and is located near the first tee and the 9th and 18th greens—and a parking lot. A site that has uneven topography, good drainage and some wooded areas is desirable, and a watering system may be necessary.

Driving ranges, which permit golfers to practice long drives and require an area of about 300 × 30 yards (274 × 27 meters) or more, are often provided at 18-hole courses and in commercial areas. Putting greens, varying in size from 3,000 to 15,000 square feet (279 to 1,394 square meters), permit practice in putting and may also be located at large courses as well as on lawns in resort areas.

Because of the large amount of land they occupy, golf courses and related facilities conserve valuable open space and are often used as the focal point of new luxury housing developments. Upon their completion, sanitary landfills are sometimes able to be converted to golf courses, providing a means by which new golf courses may be created in densely developed areas.
See: COUNTRY CLUB

Gorieb v. *Fox* (274 U.S. 603, 47 S.Ct. 675, 71 L.Ed. 1228 [1927])

A decision by the United States Supreme Court upholding the principle that state and locally adopted zoning regulations that establish setback requirements and other development restrictions should not be overturned unless they are clearly arbitrary and unreasonable.

Government in the Sunshine Act of 1976

An act aimed at assuring public and media access to government agencies' meeting transcripts and minutes. This act (PL 94-409) establishes regulations requiring that federal agencies open meetings to the public unless the subject matter is one of 10 subjects listed as permissible grounds for closing a meeting, such as discussion of national defense or matters that might lead to premature financial speculation. Transcripts of closed meetings are to be kept and made available to the public, with confidential material deleted. Among the principal requirements of this legislation are the mandatory publication and posting of meeting dates, locations, subject matter and whether the meeting is to be open or closed. Many states have also adopted their own sunshine laws regarding meetings.
See: FREEDOM OF INFORMATION ACT

Government National Mortgage Association (GNMA)

A government corporation within the Department of Housing and Urban Development (HUD), also known as Ginnie Mae, that administers support programs in the secondary mortgage market for mortgages that are not of sufficient economic appeal to attract the private sector. The purpose of these programs is to add liquidity to the secondary mortgage market, thereby making more funds available for the initiation of new mortgages.

GNMA operates two primary programs. The Mortgage-Backed Securities (MBS) program guarantees the payment of principal and interest on securities based on pools of government-underwritten mortgages. The largest program operated by HUD, it guaranteed $135 billion in mortgage-backed securities between 1970 and 1982, helping to finance nearly 3.8 million home purchases. The mortgage purchase, or "tandem," program involves the purchase of mortgages for housing that either cannot readily be financed at normal market interest rates on the private market, such as for low-income families, or that counter declines in mortgage lending and housing construction. Some of GNMA's special assistance and emergency mortgage purchase functions, however, were repealed by the Housing and Urban-Rural Recovery Act of 1983.
See: FEDERAL NATIONAL MORTGAGE ASSOCIATION (FNMA); HOUSING AND COMMUNITY DEVELOPMENT AMENDMENTS OF 1978; SECONDARY MORTGAGE MARKET

Grade

1.   The existing elevation, or the established reference level of the ground, also known as grade level. The term "at grade" refers to roads or structures which are built on the ground, in contrast to the term "below grade" which describes construction partially or completely below ground.

2.   The proposed level of the ground after grading, also known as the finish (or finished) grade.

3.   The gradient, or percent of slope, of a road or railroad. Minimum grades are generally required to facilitate drainage, while the establishment of maximum grades permits ease of travel and the provision of necessary sight distance.
See: ELEVATION; GRADE SEPARATION; GRADING; SLOPE

Grade Crossing

1.   The intersection of two or more roadways of four or more legs at the same ground level.

2.   The intersection at grade level of a roadway with railway tracks. Also known as a railroad crossing, and as a level crossing in Britain, such intersections should be used only where there are low traffic volumes on the intersecting road and infrequent train movement. Higher volumes warrant grade separation for purposes of safety and maintenance of traffic flow.

Current practice is to replace grade crossings with grade-separated overpasses where physically and economically feasible.
See: AT-GRADE INTERSECTION; GRADE

Grade Requirements

Requirements appearing in subdivision regulations concerning the grade of the various streets and the way they relate to terrain within a proposed subdivision. Grade requirements are set forth in municipal ordinances to promote attractive, safe and functional development.

One type of requirement that is found sets forth a minimum and maximum permissible grade. Although these figures will vary by community, a typical minimum grade of about 0.5 percent is often found to permit adequate drainage. Maximum grades are generally allowed to be steeper on minor streets than on collectors or arterials. On a minor street, a maximum permitted grade might be approximately 10 percent to 12 percent; on a major or collector street, the permitted upper limit might be 5 percent to 7 percent. Without these limits, roads could be built that are too steep for safe access.

Another type of requirement may concern the length and radius of vertical curves that connect changes in grades. It may be required that they meet the approval of the municipal engineer so that safe sight distances are assured. Similarly, the regulations may recommend an avoidance of combinations of steep grades and curves and have special requirements concerning the elimination of obstructions to visibility if such a combination does occur.

One type of design standard often found in subdivision regulations concerns the relationship of the street plan to the original terrain of the development. A close conformation of the planned road network to the site's topography means less cut and fill (and lower site development costs for the developer) as well as less erosion and an appearance that more closely resembles the natural profile of the site. Another design standard may recommend that the road network be designed so as many of the building sites as possible are located at or above street grade.

Still another consideration is the utility network. Because the sewer system is located, whenever possible, in the street right-of-way, the streets should follow the topography in a way that allows the operation of a gravity-flow system.

See: GRADE; GRADING; SUBDIVISION REGULATIONS

Grade-Separated Interchange

An intersection of two or more roadways at which preference for through traffic is provided by use of bridge structures or tunnels, which permit traffic to flow unimpeded; traffic can move between the roads via ramps. Interchanges are classified by the number of intersecting legs, whether the ramps follow the natural direction of traffic and whether they are signalized or unsignalized.

The three principal forms of grade-separated interchanges are the cloverleaf, directional and diamond. Because it is necessary to provide ramps that slope gradually to the intersecting road for deceleration and traffic storage purposes, grade-separated interchanges consume large amounts of land, frequently in excess of 10 acres (4 hectares). (See Fig. 18)

See: CLOVERLEAF INTERCHANGE; DIAMOND INTERCHANGE; DIRECTIONAL INTERCHANGE; GRADE SEPARATION

Grade Separation

1. The use of one or more bridge structures to vertically separate two or more intersecting roadways, thereby permitting vehicles to cross other traffic without interference. Grade separation is employed when it is necessary to accommodate extremely high traffic volumes, to eliminate hazardous intersection conditions and as standard practice in the design of freeways.

2. The use of bridge structures to vertically separate different forms of transportation, permitting automobiles, pedestrians and railroads to each move without conflict.

3. The placement of opposing roadway lanes at different elevations to minimize the amount of cut and fill necessary for construction of the road.

See: PEDESTRIANIZATION

Grading

The movement and reshaping of earth to create new contours. Grading is undertaken for a variety of purposes, such as the proper replacement of soil removed during excavation with an optimum balance of cut and fill, or the rearrangement of soil to create functional surface and subsurface drainage patterns and minimize soil erosion. Grading is also used to reshape earth to obtain a desirable view or to avoid an undesirable one, to improve appearance or to permit the creation of a continuous plane of uniform width, as in the construction of roads. In agriculture it permits the creation of flat areas that are easy to irrigate,

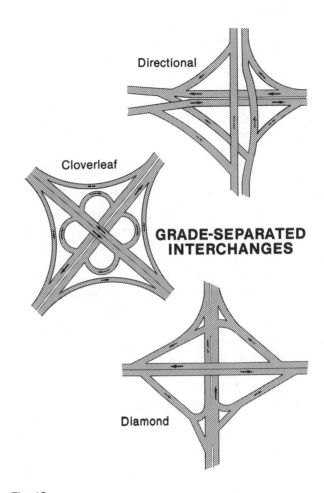

Directional

Cloverleaf

GRADE-SEPARATED INTERCHANGES

Diamond

Fig. 18.

dikes to hold rainfall or terraces to reduce washing of the soil from cultivated slopes.

Grading on construction sites may simply involve dispersal of surplus fill to the best advantage; in most cases, however, a grading plan is required. The grading plan indicates what the new contours of the land will be after completion of construction, showing areas that are to change in elevation and those that are to remain undisturbed. Contour levels are usually drawn at 1-foot, 2-foot or 5-foot intervals to show in detail the changes to be made in grade level, although more simple plans indicate spot elevations without contour lines. These spot elevations and contours are used on the construction site for the placement of stakes on which the proposed elevation is indicated, so that the land can be built up or cut down to the indicated level. The land area between stakes is smoothed to facilitate adequate drainage as well as for visual appeal. Critical elevations are also shown on the grading plan, such as the base of existing trees or stone walls to be saved and the height of the first floor of new or existing buildings. Existing utility lines and elevations of adjacent areas should also be shown. Where a site requires extensive grading, the site plan may require partial or total modification when the grading plan is completed.

Road design requires that grading create a smooth surface of stated width with proper vertical and horizontal curvature. Adjacent areas must provide drainage, be stabilized against erosion, provide access to property as necessary and be attractive. The grading plan is developed by drawing the centerline of the road, determining vertical curves and smoothing them to create a continuous route with grades within a desired range. The centerline of the road may then be moved to permit a decrease in grade and to minimize cut and fill operations. (See Fig. 19)
See: CUT; FILL; GRADE; GRADE REQUIREMENTS

Graduated-Payment Mortgage (GPM)

A mortgage designed for young, first-time home buyers with a good expectation of rising income. In the GPM, payments are initially lower than they would be under a standard mortgage amortization schedule. The payments rise gradually, eventually reaching a plateau that is higher than standard to compensate for the early subsidized years and to completely amortize the mortgage loan.

Unlike the variable-rate mortgage or the renegotiable-rate mortgage, the interest rate remains constant over the lifetime of the mortgage. The payment schedule is merely modified to match the expected income curve of a young but upwardly mobile home buyer.

GPM loans are available through banks on a commercial basis but are also sponsored by the Department of Housing and Urban Development (HUD). HUD insures GPM mortgages through Federal Housing Administration (FHA)-approved lenders. A choice of payment plans of varying duration and rate of increase is offered to qualified applicants who have not owned a home in the preceding three years. This program, and all other HUD single-family mortgage insurance programs, was exempted by Congress from state usury laws in 1979. Over 131,000 GPM mortgages were insured by HUD in that year, more than twice the volume of 1978. In 1983 HUD's GPM were extended to multifamily residential structures by the Housing and Urban-Rural Recovery Act.

Types of graduated-payment mortgages are also available in both Britain and Canada.
See: MORTGAGE; RENEGOTIABLE-RATE MORTGAGE (RRM); SECTION 245 HOUSING PROGRAM; VARIABLE-RATE MORTGAGE (VRM)

Graffiti

Words, phrases or other markings that are drawn, painted or in some other manner applied to the walls of buildings, sidewalks, trains or buses or to natural features such as rock outcroppings and trees. With the advent of spray paint and similar devices, the application of graffiti is no longer restricted to scratching and etching of public sculptures and buildings but has expanded to extensive painted areas.

Derived from the Italian term *graffito,* used by archaeologists to describe scribbling or writing on a wall, such as that found in Roman ruins, the practice has, in recent history, become synonymous with urban decay and is viewed as an indicator of breakdown in a social system unable to prevent the defacement and destruction of pub-

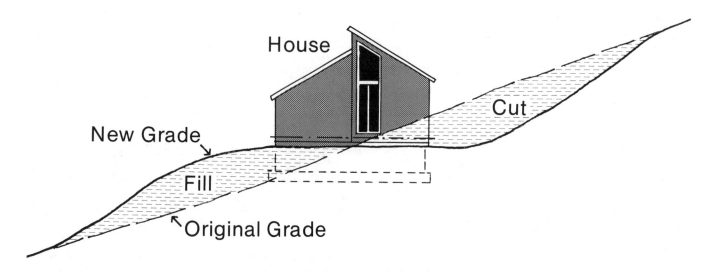

GRADING
For Building Construction

Fig. 19.   Grading to enable placement of a building can involve creation of a plateau by cutting into the hill at a higher elevation and filling at a lower elevation.

lic facilities. In addition, the practice represents a drain on municipal finances and manpower needed to repair damaged surfaces and to police locations particularly popular with graffiti artists, such as subway yards. The popularity of this activity has led to a new emphasis upon developing surfaces that are either unconducive to graffiti or easily cleaned.
See: BEHAVIORAL DESIGN; WALL ART

Grandfather Clause

A provision in a newly adopted law regulating certain conduct or activities that allows the regulated activity to continue as previously conducted or otherwise exempts it from compliance with the new law. As an example, a project begun before imposition of a state requirement that an environmental impact statement be prepared may be "grandfathered"—released from provisions requiring the statement.

A new zoning ordinance will typically contain a grandfather clause allowing all uses that are in existence on the date that the new ordinance takes effect but that do not comply with the ordinance to remain as legal nonconforming uses. Failure to grandfather existing uses could render the new ordinance vulnerable to constitutional challenge as a taking of property without due process. It is usually permissible, however, to require a landowner to phase out an existing nonconforming use over a number of years.
See: AMORTIZATION OF NONCONFORMING USES; NONCONFORMING USE

Grant Application

A formal request for funding that is made to a government agency, a foundation or a corporation. Many government agencies have their own application forms and extremely specific requirements that must be met in filing the grant application. The agency may also have a scoring system in which points are awarded based on the answers given to specific questions or based upon community characteristics and needs. Foundation and corporation grants may have no required format, but a proposal should be submitted that summarizes the qualifications of the organization, the need for the program, the way it will be operated, its budget and other sources of financial support.

In government grant programs, applications must be made for activities that the program is permitted to fund by its enabling legislation. Foundation proposals are more likely to be funded if the proposal is sent to those foundations that have expressed interest in the subject area. Foundations may also have guidelines that specify the types of activities they will fund—e.g., personnel but not construction. All grant applications should be clear and well thought out, worded as concisely as possible and submitted before the application deadline.

A basic source of information for available federal grants is the *Catalog of Federal Domestic Assistance. The*

Foundation Directory—which lists foundations and their addresses, financial data and the types of activities they fund—is also useful. Both references are available in many public libraries.
See: FOUNDATION; GRANT-IN-AID

Grant-in-Aid

An allocation of funds made by the federal government to state or local government, or by a state to a unit of local government, to be spent in accordance with specific regulations and standards.

There is a long tradition of support by the federal government for certain types of projects. Federal monies for road projects and for education were made available on a limited basis as early as the beginning of the 19th century. There was, however, a great increase in the use of grants in the 1930s and another surge of new grant activity in the 1960s.

Some areas in which the federal government conducts major grant programs are public assistance, public health, highways, education, housing and community development, and wastewater treatment. Few federal agencies do not conduct grant programs of some type. Some are sweeping in scope, such as the program that funded the nationwide system of interstate and defense highways, while others have more limited goals. All programs, however, serve as a means by which a proportion of the revenues collected from states and communities are redistributed and returned to state and municipal government. Grant-in-aid programs of various types are in use in countries other than the United States, including Britain and Canada, where grants are made to local authorities and to provinces, respectively.
See: BLOCK GRANT; CATEGORICAL GRANT; GRANT APPLICATION

Grantsmanship

The ability to obtain grants and subsidies for all types of purposes; a skill requiring an extensive knowledge of government agencies, foundations, programs and data sources.
See: GRANT APPLICATION; GRANT-IN-AID

Graphic Reproduction Processes

Nonprinting processes or printing processes by which maps and other graphic materials may be reproduced. The most widely used nonprinting processes include: direct contact positives, as used in diazo reproduction; direct contact negatives, such as blueprints; photostats; and xerography. Printing processes include letterpress and offset printing (lithography).

In general, nonprinting methods are most suitable when small quantities of copies are needed, as the unit reproduction cost is low but relatively constant. Printing methods are best suited to longer runs, as the unit cost of

printing each illustration or map decreases as the run becomes longer.
See: BLUEPRINT; DIAZO REPRODUCTION; PHOTOSTAT; REPRODUCIBLE; SEPIA INTERMEDIATE

Gravity Flow

The design of sewerage and water supply systems that rely upon the force of gravity whenever possible rather than upon the use of pumps, which are costly to build, maintain and operate. It is therefore necessary to place pipes at a specified minimum slope to allow flow at velocities that will prevent deposits that can clog the pipes. Maximum velocities are also established to prevent abrasion and excessive pressure.

Sewer pipes are designed to operate at one-half of their capacity during normal flow periods to allow for peak flows. Water pipes are generally designed to operate at full capacity, since a water supply system is predicated on the maintenance of an available specified water pressure level. While only minimum velocities are necessary to prevent sedimentation in water pipes, friction in the pipes reduces water pressure; increased pipe diameters are selected to compensate for this loss where the slope of the water mains cannot be increased.
See: FORCE MAIN; PUMPING STATION; SEWERAGE SYSTEM; WATER SUPPLY SYSTEM

Gravity Model

A mathematical model used in transportation planning to forecast trip distribution in state or regional transportation studies. Use of the model may be confined to one mode of transportation, such as roads, or include all transportation forms.

The model uses estimates of trips between any two zones, expressing the relationship of these trips as being inversely proportional to their spatial separation, called the friction factor. The friction factor may be related to travel time or distance. An exponent for trip purpose may also be applied. When all pairs of zones in a study area are evaluated, and estimates of travel demand between them for the design year are obtained, the need for improved transportation to selected zones can be determined.
See: TRIP DISTRIBUTION

Gray Area

1. Any area that is considered to be blighted or that has officially been designated as being blighted.
2. A colloquial term that refers to areas in Britain more formally described as "intermediate areas." This designation describes an area in which economic growth is still occurring, but at a rate much slower than is desirable. The word *intermediate* is used because these areas have growth rates slower than areas of strong economic growth but faster than areas in which little or no growth, or decline, is taking place.
See: BLIGHTED AREA

Great Lakes Water Quality Agreement of 1978

A treaty between the United States and Canada, expanding provisions of a similar 1972 treaty that requires the prevention of further pollution in the Great Lakes basin. The purpose of the agreement is to enable restoration and maintenance of the chemical, physical and biological integrity of the basin's waters.

The agreement established policies relating to cessation of pollution and mechanisms to study, report and control problems. The basic policies of the agreement are the elimination of the discharge of toxic substances, financial assistance for construction of public waste treatment plants, and the development and implementation of coordinated planning processes and best management practices to ensure control of all pollutant sources.
See: FEDERAL WATER POLLUTION CONTROL ACT AMENDMENTS OF 1972; INTERNATIONAL JOINT COMMISSION

Greenbelt

A band of open space protected from intense development, usually placed at an urban periphery to contain outward expansion. The greenbelt concept was originated in Great Britain in the 1930s as a wide ring encircling London, generally reserved for agriculture, recreation or other open-space use but allowing development on some parcels. The Greenbelt Act of 1938 was intended to preserve agricultural and open-space lands, and only later, in the Town and Country Planning Act of 1947, were greenbelts designed to limit metropolitan development. The term *greenbelt* has come to include any large contiguous open-space area that is preserved to provide amenities and influence metropolitan development.

In the United States there has been reluctance to provide the combination of financial support for land acquisition and legislative support for strict land use controls that enabled the concept to be implemented in Great Britain and Scandinavia. Critics of the concept point out that even the London greenbelt has suffered intrusions (greenbelts in other cities, including Tokyo, and in several developing nations have not been able to be preserved) and that large peripheral open spaces are both inaccessible and prone to criminal activity. Yet despite these difficulties, greenbelts are frequently favored as an urban design approach to limit growth and preserve open space, because they have been largely successful where strict controls have been applied. In the United States, greenbelts have been preserved around many of the new towns.
See: GROWTH MANAGEMENT; OPEN-SPACE PLANNING

Greenbelt Towns

Towns constructed under the sponsorship of the federal Resettlement Administration during the 1930s that incorporated some of the aspects of Britain's garden cities. Intended to serve as model planned communities, to provide housing for displaced farm families and to create employment during the Depression, these towns preserved large areas of open space as part of the community design. They more closely resembled garden surburbs, however, due to the lack of industry within the towns.

Four sites were selected for the construction of greenbelt towns: Greenbelt, Maryland; Greenhills, Ohio; Greendale, Wisconsin; and Greenbrook, New Jersey, which was never built. The three towns that were constructed were built on federally owned land, obtained through eminent domain, as suburbs of Washington, D.C., Cincinnati and Milwaukee. Greenbrook, New Jersey was never built because of the outcome of a lawsuit in which a U.S. Court of Appeals ruled that the federal government did not have the power to use eminent domain for such a program. The construction of these towns ended in 1938 when Congress stopped the resettlement project, and federal ownership of the towns terminated during the late 1940s and early 1950s. When the program ended, housing for 2,100 families had been built in the three towns.
See: GARDEN CITY; NEW TOWN; PLANNED COMMUNITY; RESETTLEMENT ADMINISTRATION

Gridiron Pattern

A development pattern in which land is divided into a latticelike plan, so that streets cross each other at right angles and rectangular-shaped blocks have relatively equal dimensions. The predominant land use pattern of the 19th century (when it was employed to expedite the sale of real estate), the gridiron pattern became the form of many city plans. As a rule, the plan was placed on the landscape without regard to topography, so that streets are sometimes exceptionally steep.

While its order permits easy orientation and efficient land division, a rigid system of cross streets is no longer considered to be an optimum land pattern because it frequently disregards natural features, is vulnerable to speeding traffic and is often aesthetically uninteresting. A variation in design, in which streets are interconnected in a relatively uniform pattern but are curved to fit topography, provides the advantages of a grid but allows a greater degree of environmental sensitivity. (See Fig. 24)
See: CURVILINEAR PATTERN; LAND USE PATTERN; RADIAL PATTERN

Grit Chamber

A device used in sewage treatment plants to remove grit, which consists of sand, gravel, silt, eggshells, seeds, coffee grounds and similar items. Grit has a tendency to clog pumps, form deposits in pipes, and cause mechanical problems. Grit that is removed must be washed to free it of organic matter and then disposed of, usually at a landfill site.
See: SCREENING; SEWAGE TREATMENT

Groin

A beach improvement structure built perpendicular to the shore for the purpose of interrupting sand movement, minimizing sand loss and helping to widen a particular beach section. The groin—constructed of wood, steel, concrete, rock or sand-filled bags—traps sand and prevents it, to some extent, from moving to another section of beach; this deprives the adjacent downdrift shore of sand. When additional parallel groins are constructed to protect adjacent beaches, the sand can be forced offshore entirely, depriving the entire shoreline of sand. Because of this, groins are most suitable when the downdrift beach is expendable.

One measure that is often taken in areas with parallel groins is to artificially add sand to the area between groins to provide a constant supply of sand to the downdrift shore. Permeable groins, constructed of latticework or the like, allow some of the sand to pass through and have a lesser impact than solid groins on adjacent beaches, shorter groins are also preferable to longer groins.
See: BEACH EROSION

Gross Floor Area

The sum of the area of all of a building's floors existing within its exterior walls. A municipal zoning ordinance may define gross floor area as extending to the outer surface of the exterior walls; in commercial leasing, however, gross floor area is measured to the inside finish of these walls.

Generally, elevator shafts, stairwells, hallways, balconies, porches and mezzanines are included in gross floor area calculations. Ordinances vary from community to community as to whether portions of the building such as basements, roof areas, attics, space used to house mechanical equipment and exterior stairways are included. Generally, interior parking or loading areas are excluded from all calculations of gross floor area.
See: FLOOR AREA RATIO (FAR); NET FLOOR AREA

Gross Rent

1. A figure that includes the contract rent as well as an amount paid for utilities.

2. A figure that expresses the total rental income derived from a property before expenses are deducted. It may be used to help arrive at an estimation of the value of an income property.
See: CONTRACT RENT; GROSS RENT MULTIPLIER

Gross Rent Multiplier

A quick method of arriving at some approximation of the market value of real estate generating an income. The annual gross rent of a building is multiplied by the gross rent multiplier, also called the gross income multiplier, to produce an estimate of value. This multiplier is derived from an analysis of comparable sales that show a more or less uniform relationship between gross rental income and sales price.

If, for example, an office building generates an annual income of $250,000, and other similar office buildings are valued at four times the gross income, then the building might be said to be worth approximately $1 million. Because of the formula approach involved in the use of the gross rent multiplier, the estimate of value it produces should be viewed only as a gross approximation. Factors that may detract from its precision include few available comparable properties to draw data from and features that are unique to the subject property. For these and other reasons, it is most effecive as a guideline only and should be used along with other, more accurate techniques of appraising real property.
See: GROSS RENT; INCOME APPROACH APPRAISAL

Ground Cover

Plant material grown in order to minimize soil erosion from both wind and water and for landscaping purposes.

Temporary cover, such as rye grass, may be used when soil will be left exposed for relatively short time periods, as on a construction site, or when the season makes it difficult to establish permanent cover; it should be able to grow rapidly.

Permanent cover is selected for its long-term suitability to the site and its soils, climate, its intended use, ease of maintenance, longevity and visual appeal. Very different selections would be made for a playground or other heavily trafficked area, where a durable type of grass would be chosen, versus a steep slope, where plants such as crown vetch or honeysuckle might be picked for their low maintenance requirements, long life and erosion control abilities. There are many more varieties of ground cover that can be selected in humid areas than in dry regions.

In agricultural areas cover crops—such as buckwheat, oats, rye and crimson clover—are often grown specifically for soil protection.
See: LANDSCAPING; SOIL EROSION CONTROL TECHNIQUES

Groundwater

Water that occupies the spaces in underground geological structures. The upper zone of groundwater is the water table, and the lower limit of groundwater is the zone in which the spaces between solid rock particles are few and downward movement is not possible.

Groundwater, also called subsurface water, is replenished by precipitation, seepage from surface water bodies and primary water that originates deep within the Earth as a byproduct of chemical and physical processes. It is desirable as a water supply source because of its steady availability, general purity, cold temperature and lack of sediment and is an especially important water resource in arid and semiarid areas. Among the many planning concerns that are related to groundwater are the potential of pollut-

ing the groundwater supply through such practices as waste disposal, the effects on the water supply of excessive groundwater withdrawal and the relationship between the stability of hillsides and groundwater conditions.
See: AQUIFER; ARTESIAN WELL; GROUNDWATER POLLUTION; INFILTRATION; WATER RESOURCES MANAGEMENT; WATER TABLE

Groundwater Pollution

Destruction of subsurface water supplies by contamination. The primary problem with pollution of groundwater resources is the slow velocity of the water, which means that once it is polluted it will remain polluted for many years.

Major sources of groundwater pollution include leaky sewers, septic tanks and cesspools, municipal and private sewage lagoons, and in coastal areas, saltwater intrusion. Since groundwater moves in relation to gravity, care must be taken in the siting of shallow wells on sloping ground so that a well is above septic tanks or other sources of contamination. Land use regulation and health department control over extraction of groundwater and the siting of disposal areas are planning tools that can aid in preventing groundwater pollution.
See: GROUNDWATER; INFILTRATION; RECHARGE; SALTWATER INTRUSION; SEWAGE TREATMENT; WATER RESOURCES MANAGEMENT

Group Home

A residential facility designed to accommodate a group of individuals, usually physically impaired or with emotional or social problems, in a noninstitutional, neighborhood setting. Often located in areas zoned for single-family homes, group homes are intended to serve as single housekeeping units, are usually licensed by a governmental entity and provide a supervised setting for approximately 5 to 25 individuals. Their residents receive a variety of health-related and social services through sponsoring public, voluntary nonprofit or proprietary agencies, which are subject to state and federal regulations.

As an outgrowth of a program of deinstitutionalization that evolved in the 1970s, the group home was developed as a means of allowing certain individuals to live semi-independently in a "normal" community environment. Early efforts to open group homes were, however, often unsuccessful due to community opposition. Among the problems encountered in siting and developing group homes have been a lack of citizen participation in the decision-making process and a lack of adequate regulatory standards. Community residents have often also expressed a fear of residents of such facilities or a fear of property devaluation. Recently, zoning ordinances have begun to deal with group homes on a more objective basis by incorporating standards that relate to occupancy, licensing, safety and conventional site plan requirements such as access and parking.
See: FAMILY; HALFWAY HOUSE

Growth Management

Implementation of government regulations that control the type, location, quality, scale, rate, sequence or timing of development. The prohibitions contained in a traditional zoning ordinance are a form of growth management, but the term implies a much greater involvement of local government in development decisions. Sophisticated growth management systems are closely tied to comprehensive land use plans and specific development policies. In communities that manage their growth, the usual belief that development brings progress is tempered by concerns about the fiscal and environmental impacts of growth and the loss of community character and scale. Critics of growth management techniques argue, however, that they can have exclusionary effects, increase development costs and interfere with normal market processes.

Methods of growth management include a variety of restraints, incentives and negotiating tools. Requirements for environmental impact and fiscal impact studies control the types and locations of development, as does permitting development only in urban service areas where full public services are available. Transferable development rights, by which an owner may sell or move his property's development potential to another lot, protect the land from which the rights are transferred. Environmentally sensitive areas—such as hillsides, flood-prone areas, wetlands and coastal zones—may be protected by prohibiting or severely restricting their development, while annexation and extraterritorial zoning powers protect outlying areas from premature development. Development quotas and development moratoriums control the rate of growth and permit timely installation of public utilities. Delay in processing requests for zoning permits is a more passive approach to slowing development.

Farmland preservation—including exclusive agricultural zones that prohibit housing development, preferential taxation of farmland and public purchase of development rights—permits the continued use of land for agricultural and open-space purposes, while public land ownership is the ultimate control over land use. Cluster development and planned unit development enable the protection of certain amounts of open space by encouraging development of the portions of a site most suitable for building, while environmentally sensitive lands and other valuable areas may be protected. Bonus density provisions encourage increased density but in a manner that advances municipal aesthetic goals.

See: ANNEXATION; CLUSTER DEVELOPMENT; *CONSTRUCTION INDUSTRY ASS'N OF SONOMA COUNTY* v. *CITY OF PETALUMA*; ENVIRONMENTAL IMPACT STATEMENT (EIS); ENVIRONMENTALLY SENSITIVE LANDS; EXTRATERRITORIAL ZONING; FARMLAND PROTECTION; FISCAL IMPACT ANALYSIS; *GOLDEN* v. *PLANNING BOARD OF THE TOWN OF RAMAPO*; INCENTIVE ZONING; LAND BANK; MORATORIUM; NO GROWTH; PHASED DEVELOPMENT CONTROLS; PLANNED UNIT DEVELOPMENT (PUD); PUBLIC LAND OWNERSHIP; TRANSFER OF DEVELOPMENT RIGHTS (TDR); ZERO POPULATION GROWTH (ZPG)

Growth Theory

Generalizations from studies of urban geography concerning the location of cities, city growth and land use patterns within cities and regions.

A city locates, at a central place, a transportation point or a site uniquely suited for a specialized function. The key to growth is basic industries that produce goods for sale outside the city. Through a multiplier effect, a basic economic activity generates other "spin-off" economic activities, and as a city's population reaches a threshold level, the market potential is big enough to add new economic activities. Other factors influencing city growth are the size of the hinterland, economies of scale, transportation, technology, resources and the availability of capital.

Growth within a city is determined by many functions and land uses. They cluster to maximize communication within an industry, to be near complementary functions or to avoid conflicts with incompatible land uses. According to the concentric zone theory, the city consists of a central business district (CBD), ringed by zones dominated by other uses. As the city grows, each zone expands outward into the next zone. According to the sector theory, each land use (particularly class-segregated residential areas) grows outward from the CBD in a radial pattern. The multiple-nuclei theory allows for a more complex spatial pattern. Growth patterns may also be influenced by social

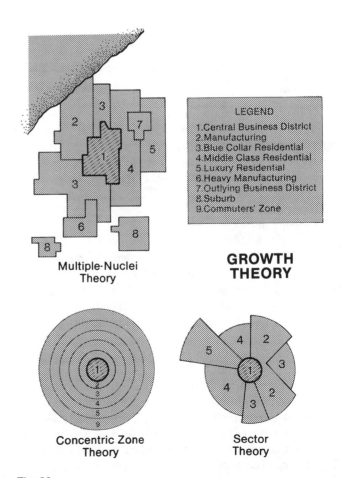

LEGEND
1. Central Business District
2. Manufacturing
3. Blue Collar Residential
4. Middle Class Residential
5. Luxury Residential
6. Heavy Manufacturing
7. Outlying Business District
8. Suburb
9. Commuters' Zone

Multiple-Nuclei Theory

GROWTH THEORY

Concentric Zone Theory

Sector Theory

Fig. 20.

values and the unique cultural or topographic features of a city. (See Fig. 20)
See: CENTRAL PLACE THEORY; CONCENTRIC ZONE THEORY; ECONOMIC BASE THEORY; MULTIPLE-NUCLEI THEORY; SECTOR THEORY; URBANIZATION

Guardrail

1.   A safety rail or handrail located on staircases and where pedestrians may require barriers to prevent accidents. Guardrails are also being installed in public places to assist the handicapped, in compliance with barrier-free site design standards.

2.   A safety rail at the side of a highway that is used to warn drivers of a steep drop in grade beyond the barrier and to restrain cars from driving over an embankment. A variety of metal guardrails mounted on metal posts and curved concrete barriers are commonly used because they can often deflect an errant vehicle and return it to the roadway. Metal guardrails are also used as barriers in parking lots.

See: ARCHITECTURAL AND TRANSPORTATION BARRIERS

Guidelines

General indications of the policies that a government agency endorses, as opposed to specific quantitative standards or regulations.

Guidelines are sometimes used in various municipal ordinances to provide information and guidance to those preparing development proposals. The proposal is then reviewed by the authorized government body for compliance with the guidelines as well as with other existing regulations and requirements. Guidelines may sometimes be found, for example, as part of planned unit development ordinances or historic district ordinances.

Although guidelines can encourage creative approaches to compliance with municipal regulations, they can also be sufficiently vague as to provide little basis for the decisions of review boards.
See: STANDARDS

H

Hadacheck v. *Sebastian* (239 U.S. 394 [1915])

An early decision of the United States Supreme Court upholding the right of municipalities to regulate land use through adoption of local land use control ordinances. The Court declined to find the ordinance an unconstitutional taking of private property, even though its effect was to reduce the value of previously made investments in real estate.

At the time, this case was thought by some to signal the Supreme Court's implicit approval of land use zoning and led to the adoption in 1916 by New York City of the first comprehensive zoning code in the United States.
See: NEW YORK CITY ZONING CODE

Halfway House

A facility designed to provide short-term, health-related care for individuals attempting to resume their life in society. While halfway houses were originally intended primarily to assist those with mental or emotional illnesses, the concept has in recent years been broadened to include assistance for individuals such as juvenile delinquents, parolees or those suffering from alcoholism or drug addiction.

A halfway house is intended to serve as a bridge between an institution, such as a hospital or jail, and the community, with an emphasis on development of social and job skills required to reenter the community as a fully functioning and independent citizen. Since the 1950s halfway houses have grown in number in reaction to an increased awareness of the psychological costs as well as the high financial costs of institutionalization and as a result of

growing emphasis on having patients maintain close community ties.
See: GROUP HOME

Hamlet

A rural or suburban area, more populated than surrounding areas, which may have a concentration of service stores, a post office and religious facilities. Hamlets are often identified by name but not by officially prescribed boundaries, since they are usually unincorporated areas within larger towns. A hamlet differs from a village in that a village is incorporated under state law and has official boundaries.
See: NEIGHBORHOOD; UNINCORPORATED AREA

Hampstead Garden Suburb, England

A planned residential development built in London in 1907 to accommodate residents of varying incomes and to provide a range of housing types within subway distance of central London. Planned by Barry Parker and Raymond Unwin, who were also responsible for Letchworth, Hampstead Garden Suburb attracted considerable attention. It incorporated innovative features, such as major open-space areas, culs-de-sac and the use of a hierarchical road system in which roadway design was more closely related to function. It rapidly inspired the construction of other garden suburbs throughout the world, such as Forest Hills Gardens in New York City, which was completed in 1913 and served as an American suburban model.
See: GARDEN CITY; LETCHWORTH, ENGLAND; UNWIN, SIR RAYMOND

Harbor

A sheltered portion of a large body of water that has been improved in order to protect vessels using it from the damaging effects of waves and currents. Natural harbors occur in a few places in the world, but the large majority are man-made through dredging, to provide sufficient depth for ships, and have been enclosed by breakwaters.

Harbors have been responsible for the growth and development of major cities throughout the world because shipping, historically the predominant commercial transportation mode, caused economic growth in adjacent areas.

See: BREAKWATER; PORT

Hardware

1. The physical equipment that is part of a computer system. Hardware is engaged in activities such as the input, processing, storage and output of data.
2. The metal accessories and fittings used in building construction, such as hinges or doorknobs.

See: DATA PROCESSING; SOFTWARE

Hartford Commission on a City Plan

The first officially formed, permanent municipal planning commission in the United States, created by the Connecticut Legislature in 1907. The city charter of Hartford was amended to establish a commission composed of the mayor, city engineer, presidents of the board of street commissioners and board of park commissioners, a board of aldermen member, a common council board member and two citizens who held no other municipal office.

The commission was authorized to prepare maps that indicated proposed locations for new public buildings and facilities—such as streets, parkways and parks—as well as proposed changes in location for certain existing facilities. The common council was also required to refer matters concerning public buildings, roads and open space to the commission before taking any action. Although the commission was not granted any significant authority over private land uses, it was permitted to establish building lines and also had jurisdiction concerning new streets in proposed subdivisions.

Similar planning boards were formed in other cities—such as Milwaukee (1908), and Chicago, Detroit and Baltimore (1909)—soon after the creation of the Hartford Commission.

Haussmann, Baron Georges-Eugene (1809–91)

Prefect of the Seine under the Emperor Napoleon III from 1853 to 1870. Haussmann was chiefly responsible for the design and construction of large-scale projects throughout Paris that transformed the appearance and functioning of the city. The straight, wide and tree-lined boulevards and avenues that cross Paris are the work of Haussmann, who attempted to improve the movement of traffic and make additional light and air available. He is also charged by many, however, with focusing unduly

upon security and with attempting to create an easily defensible Paris in which troop movements were facilitated in the event of urban unrest, sometimes at the expense of existing communities.

Among Haussmann's achievements are the creation of a circulation system for Paris as a whole that still exists today. He also created numerous parks and open spaces, modernized sewer and water facilities, and built the Opera of Paris as well as numerous civic projects throughout the city.

Hazardous Areas

Areas subject to dangerous natural phenomena such as earthquakes, landslides, rock slides, avalanches, forest fires and floods or to unplanned, hazardous consequences of certain man-made developments. Hazard mitigation techniques—which may include special construction requirements for development, prevention of development or other land use controls—are designed to be applied in these areas to protect inhabitants and to prevent destruction and economic loss.

See: CRITICAL AREAS; ENVIRONMENTALLY SENSITIVE LANDS; FLOOD-PRONE LAND; FOREST FIRE CONTROL; GEOLOGIC HAZARDS; HAZARDOUS WASTE; RADIATION HAZARD

Hazardous Waste

Those wastes that can cause or help to cause illness or death, or that, in the absence of proper management, represent a significant threat to either human health or the environment. Pursuant to the provisions of the Resource Conservation and Recovery Act of 1976, the U.S. Environmental Protection Agency (EPA) has developed a list of hazardous wastes based upon the criteria of ignitability, corrosivity, reactivity and toxicity.

EPA defines these characteristics as follows. Ignitable wastes are those posing a fire hazard during routine management. Corrosive wastes require special containers that they cannot corrode, or they must be separated from other wastes because of their potential for dissolving and spreading toxic contaminants. Reactive wastes have a tendency to react spontaneously, can be unstable to shock or heat, and tend to react vigorously with air or water, to generate toxic gases or to explode. Toxic wastes are those that when improperly managed can release sufficient quantities of toxicants as to pose substantial hazards to human health or the environment. Examples of hazardous wastes are toxic metals (e.g., mercury), explosives, pesticides, radioactive wastes, flammables and infectious materials.

Despite the large volumes of hazardous wastes generated each year, primarily by industry but also by such sources as hospitals and research facilities, it has been estimated by the EPA that only 10 percent of all hazardous wastes are disposed of properly. Instead, it is far more common for hazardous wastes to be illegally dumped or placed in unsecured landfills. Because of this, thousands of hazardous waste disposal sites are scattered across the

United States, some of which will be discovered only when they cause a health or environmental emergency.

A number of techniques involving various degrees of effectiveness and cost are available for managing and disposing of industrial wastes. An extremely desirable option is the development of industrial processes that produce smaller volumes of hazardous waste. Waste exchanges, in which industrial wastes from one industry are used as raw materials by another, are also gaining increased success, particularly in Europe, Canada and Israel. Hazardous wastes may also be processed in such a way as to recover energy or materials. In addition, hazardous wastes may be incinerated so that they become less hazardous or be subjected to chemical treatment (e.g., neutralization), physical treatment (e.g., sedimentation) or biological treatment (e.g., activated sludge treatment) to accomplish that same goal. Still another option is secure land disposal, in which separate cells are constructed for different types of hazardous waste. A variety of measures are also taken to prevent leaching to the groundwater supply.

Hazardous waste generation, transportation, storage and disposal in the United States is regulated by the Resource Conservation and Recovery Act of 1976 as amended. "Superfund" legislation was also passed in 1980 providing cleanup money for uncontrolled hazardous waste sites or spills or releases of toxic substances.
See: COMPREHENSIVE ENVIRONMENTAL RESPONSE, COMPENSATION AND LIABILITY ACT OF 1980 (CERCLA); INDUSTRIAL WASTE; LOVE CANAL; PESTICIDES; PHENOLS; POLYCHLORINATED BIPHENYLS (PCBs); POLYVINYL CHLORIDE (PVC); RADIOACTIVE WASTES; RESOURCE CONSERVATION AND RECOVERY ACT OF 1976 (RCRA); TOXIC SUBSTANCES

Headwater

The point of origin and upper reaches of a stream or river, usually located at the highest elevations of a water body.
See: RIVER BASIN

Headway

The time interval between two vehicles traveling on the same route in the same direction. Selection of headways is a fundamental part of planning for bus routes, mass transit and commuter rail service. Headways determine the hourly carrying capacity of a transit route, the capital and operating costs, and to an extent, the ability of the route to attract passengers. Frequent headways, although expensive, reduce waiting time at stops and are more attractive to people who have the option of using a private automobile.
See: BUS ROUTE PLANNING; MASS TRANSIT; SUBURBAN COMMUTER RAILWAY

Health Care System

A network of facilities providing a full range of health services in a variety of settings. At the primary level is the doctor's office, the outpatient clinic or the neighborhood health center. A new form of outpatient clinic is the health maintenance organization (HMO). Following care at the primary level, an individual may be referred to the secondary level of more specialized care provided in short-term acute care hospitals on an inpatient basis, in an emergency care facility or in the office of a specialist. The patient requiring very specialized care may be referred to a tertiary care facility, such as a regional medical center.

Beyond a short-term stay in a hospital, a patient may go to an extended care facility for a period of recuperation following an illness. For long-term care an individual may enter a nursing home, a term encompassing health-related or intermediate care, skilled nursing care, personal care and domiciliary care. Patients diagnosed as having a terminal illness may use a hospice. Individuals who can remain at home but require health services may receive home health care or can attend a day-care health facility. Environmental and occupational health services or health education may also be provided through the municipal health department.

The differentiation of appropiate levels at which diverse forms of health care are given is important for health planning purposes. Where federal or other government aid is given to health care facilities, specialization of function reduces costly overlap in facility development and equipment purchasing. Specialization also enables better patient care since personnel who perform functions repetitively become expert in their fields of operation.
See: ACUTE CARE HOSPITAL; DAY HEALTH CARE FACILITIES; HEALTH MAINTENANCE ORGANIZATION (HMO); HEALTH PLANNING; HOSPITAL PLANNING; INTERMEDIATE CARE FACILITIES (ICF); LONG-TERM CARE FACILITIES; MEDICAL BUILDING; NURSING HOME; SKILLED NURSING FACILITY (SNF)

Health Department

The city, county or state agency responsible for providing services related to public health.

The area of communicable disease control, in which most health departments have programs, is directly related to the planning of new public and private development. In this capacity, the health department grants permits for installation of septic systems, determines the adequacy of wastewater treatment and its effects on water supplies, tests water quality for drinking and swimming, and continually monitors these areas. It may also test air quality and operate air pollution control programs. Other areas in which health departments frequently have programs are maternal and child health care, public health nursing and emergency health services.

Most health departments maintain statistics on births, deaths, disease and air quality that can be obtained for analytical purposes.
See: HEALTH CARE SYSTEM; SANITARY CODE; SEPTIC SYSTEM; SEWERAGE SYSTEM; WATER SUPPLY SYSTEM

Health Maintenance Organization (HMO)

An organization that provides a comprehensive range of health care services to a contractually enrolled membership who prepay a fixed premium for these services, regardless of the nature or quantity used. An HMO integrates both inpatient and outpatient services and represents an alternative to the more traditional fee-for-service payment to physicians with a third-party insurance reimbursement. HMO programs are designed to encourage prevention of illness, with programs for early detection and treatment aimed at minimizing the likelihood of more serious health problems and their related high cost.

Largely as a result of their cost-containment features, the development of HMOs was listed as one of 10 priority concerns in the National Health Planning and Resources Development Act of 1974.

See: NATIONAL HEALTH PLANNING AND RESOURCES DEVELOPMENT ACT OF 1974

Health Planning

A discipline concerned with the provision, distribution and financing of health care resources to meet the needs of a population of a designated geographic area. In the context of a medical institution, health planning has an internal orientation focusing on development of new services or enhancement of existing ones.

Most recently health planning has become equated with the hierarchical system of regulatory agencies established under the National Health Planning and Resources Development Act of 1974. As a result of this legislation, health planning was transformed from what had been a largely voluntary effort involving independent facilities seeking to solve common problems into a highly regulated process carried out on a local, state and national level. Although the process is still concerned principally with proper allocation of health care resources, greater emphasis is placed on coordination of planning efforts among facilities within a predetermined service area and on cost containment related to preventing unnecessary expansion or duplication of services for a given population.

In Canada planning is coordinated among private and public hospitals, largely at the provincial level of government. In Britain, where all hospitals are government-owned, planning is the responsibility of a National Health Service, administered through regional and area health agencies.

See: ACUTE CARE HOSPITAL; ANNUAL IMPLEMENTATION PLAN (AIP); CATCHMENT AREA; CERTIFICATE OF NEED (CON); HEALTH CARE SYSTEM; HEALTH SYSTEMS AGENCY (HSA); HEALTH SYSTEMS PLAN (HSP); HOSPITAL BED NEEDS; HOSPITAL PLANNING; OCCUPANCY RATE

Health Systems Agency (HSA)

A local areawide planning body, established through enactment of the National Health Planning and Resources Development Act of 1974, for the purpose of analyzing the needs and conditions of a health service area, and developing a Health Systems Plan (HSP) and Annual Implementation Plans (AIP). Under this legislation, an HSA can be either a nonprofit or governmentally sponsored unit, and is responsible for recommending approval or disapproval of the use of federal funds for health related projects and services proposed by hospitals, nursing homes, and other health facilities. In particular, the approximately 200 HSAs in the United States are mandated to review health care in terms of accessibility, availability, continuity of care, cost, and quality of care.

An HSA is a community based organization insofar as each unit is governed by a regional board of directors which consists of local volunteers representing the consumers and providers of health care services. Through careful review of proposals for development or expansion of health care facilities or services, the HSA attempts to facilitate an equitable distribution of services and cost-effective use of facilities.

In Canada, where provincial governments are largely responsible for delivery of health care services, funds are allocated to local and regional authorities with monitoring usually provided by advisory boards and committees. In Britain, area health authorities, consisting largely of voluntary members, are also responsible for development of area plans which are, in turn, monitored by regional authorities responsible for allocation of health resources.

See: ANNUAL IMPLEMENTATION PLAN (AIP); CERTIFICATE OF NEED (CON); CONSUMER OF SERVICES; HEALTH SYSTEMS PLAN (HSP); NATIONAL HEALTH PLANNING AND RESOURCES DEVELOPMENT ACT OF 1974; PROVIDER OF SERVICES

Health Systems Plan (HSP)

A document containing a long-range statement of the goals of a health systems agency (HSA), based on a review and assessment of the existing and future needs of a delineated population and the resources available to deal with such needs. The HSP presents a list of broad strategic actions, which are to be implemented over a period of five years, aimed at the development of an efficient and economic health care system in a community.

The plan is concerned with the broad range of health care services, including acute hospital care, ambulatory care, emergency medical services, environmental and occupational health, home health care, long-term care, mental health, rehabilitation and health education. It is intended to serve the community as a framework for institutional or other planning and becomes the basis for development of the HSA's annual implementation plan. The HSP is intended to be the basis for statewide plans and for formulation of national health policy.

See: ANNUAL IMPLEMENTATION PLAN (AIP); HEALTH SYSTEMS AGENCY (HSA)

Heat Island

A condition found in urban areas in which temperatures are measurably higher than are temperatures in surrounding areas. In part, heat islands are formed because of the large numbers of heat generators that occur in close proximity to each other, such as automobiles, power plants and underground steam lines. Another factor is the large amount of pavement, which absorbs heat during the day and cools more slowly at night than does the soil of undeveloped areas, resulting in a large night temperature differential between urban areas and their surroundings.

In large cities, differences of as much as 10 degrees Celsius (18 degrees Fahrenheit) may be observed between the city and its surrounding area. Cities are typically foggier, have more cloud cover and more rain than adjoining areas. An air circulation system is generally also found in which warm air rising and spreading is replaced by cool air from the surrounding areas, sometimes forming a closed circulation system that is usually ended only by fairly strong winds. In the absence of these winds, pollutants can be trapped under what is known as a haze hood or dome, contributing to increased urban air pollution problems.
See: AIR POLLUTION; MICROCLIMATE

Heat Pump

A device that can heat and cool interior spaces with a high degree of energy efficiency, serving as both a heating and an air-conditioning system. Operating in a manner similar to that of a refrigerator, a heat pump (in its heating mode) uses a refrigerant to transfer heat from an area that is cooler to one that is warmer. The cycle can also be reversed in the summer, and heat pumps can function as air conditioners by transferring heat from the indoors to the outdoors.

Although heat pumps have been in existence since the 1920s, when a type of pump was first used in Scotland, they came into disfavor in the 1950s because the pumps of that era were mechanically unreliable. The greatly improved modern heat pump offers energy users the opportunity to reduce heating costs under appropriate conditions. They are most cost-effective when they are used throughout the year for both heating and cooling and when they are used in fairly mild climates. When winter temperatures typically fall below 25 degrees Fahrenheit (minus 4 Celsius), a backup heating system is necessary.
See: ENERGY CONSERVATION PLANNING

Heavy Industry

Industrial uses—such as the manufacture or processing of chemicals, cement or rubber products; stockyards; steel mills; or distilleries—that generally produce nuisances making them incompatible with most other land uses. These nuisances may be in the form of air pollutants; excessive noise, traffic, glare or vibrations; noxious odors; danger of explosion; or unsightly appearance. Municipalities may specify permitted uses or performance standards for their zoning districts that permit heavy industry and will usually exclude residential, commercial and often light industrial uses from such districts. Particularly offensive industries, such as slaughterhouses, may only be per-

mitted by special permit or may be excluded from the municipality.
See: FACTORY; FREIGHT HANDLING FACILITIES; INDUSTRIAL AREA; INDUSTRIAL SEWAGE; INDUSTRIAL WASTE; JUNKYARD; LIGHT INDUSTRY; PERFORMANCE STANDARDS

Hectare

A unit of land area in the metric system that is equal to 100 ares (10,000 square meters). One hectare is the equivalent of 2.471 acres; there are 258.998 hectares in a square mile.
See: ACRE

Height Controls

Regulations that specify the maximum permitted height for structures by zoning district or by geographic area. Generally, height is expressed in number of stories as well as in feet or meters, to prevent buildings from being constructed with lower than desirable ceilings so that extra stories may be built.

The way in which height is calculated varies by community and depends upon the way in which the regulations require that vertical distance be measured. The highest point of a building may be defined to exclude only the chimney, elevator penthouse and similar utility structures, or, for example, it may be considered to be the mean height between the eave and the ridge for all but flat or mansard roofs. Generally, vertical measurement begins at grade, which is considered to be the average level of the finished ground surface adjacent to the building's exterior walls. Special provisions are usually inserted, however, to cover the situation in which buildings are to be constructed on sloping property.

Height controls help to prevent the restriction of an adequate supply of light and air to adjacent structures, allow sunlight to reach the street in densely developed areas and encourage development that is harmonious in scale and compatible with existing development. Special height controls are also used to provide clearance in the vicinity of airports. Another goal of height development regulations is the protection of scenic views. In San Francisco, for example, where view protection is of great concern to the community, controls are in existence to protect significant views of the city and to emphasize its hilly profile.

In some municipal ordinances height controls have been replaced by floor area ratios (FAR), which set limits on the ratio of permitted development to the size of the lot. More often, however, ordinances contain both height limits and a permitted FAR.
See: AESTHETIC ZONING; AIRPORT ZONING; FLOOR AREA RATIO (FAR); ZONING

Heliport

A landing area for helicopters, which can be located on land, on a floating platform, on a building or on a ship's deck. The primary elements of a heliport are (1) the touchdown pad, a paved takeoff and landing surface; (2) the peripheral area, an obstacle-free zone surrounding the takeoff and landing area; (3) approach and departure paths, which are selected to provide the best lines of flight to and from takeoff and landing areas. These take into consideration winds; locations and heights of buildings and other objects; and environmental factors relating to noise, exhaust emissions and public safety. It is desirable that a heliport have two approach-departure paths separated by an angle of 90 degrees or more.

Heliports are classified in accordance with their use by the Federal Aviation Administration (FAA), based on function rather than ownership, as follows: class 1—private heliport, class 2—small public heliport and class 3—large public heliport, with successively larger facility requirements, such as heliport buildings and helicopter storage areas, as the function of the heliport broadens.
See: AIRPORT PLANNING; VERTICAL TAKEOFF AND LANDING (VTOL)

High-Rise Housing

An apartment building sufficiently tall as to usually require elevator service. Whether or not a building is considered to be high-rise is largely determined by comparison to prevalent building heights in that municipality or region. In some areas a building of about five stories is considered high-rise, while in other parts of the country the minimum would be substantially higher. Nonresidential development of a similar height may also be described as high-rise.
See: APARTMENT; HOUSING TYPE; LOW-RISE HOUSING; MID-RISE HOUSING

High-Speed Rail Transportation

New intercity trains that are capable of traveling over 100 miles per hour (161 kilometers per hour) and are used for regularly scheduled passenger service between major urban centers. High-speed rail has been put into service in several countries, both to improve ground transportation and to reduce air traffic. The electrically powered TGV trains in France, which were first put into operation in 1981, are capable of speeds of up to 238 miles per hour (380 kilometers per hour) but because they operate on reserved rights-of-way for only portions of their routes (as well as for safety reasons) they are restricted to a maximum speed of 163 miles per hour (260 kilometers per hour).

The Metroliner, which travels between Washington and New York, and the British APT (Advanced Passenger Train) are both electrically powered, automated systems capable of traveling at 160 miles per hour (251 kilometers per hour) but restricted to 110 miles per hour (177 kilometers per hour) and 125 miles per hour (201 kilometers per hour), respectively; the tracks they operate on are neither straight enough nor smooth enough to permit the higher speed. The Bullet Train in Japan is the most extensive system in the world; it carried an average of 344,000 passengers daily in 1981. The trains are electrically powered

by overhead wires, are automated and operate on their own right-of-way. In 1981 the system operated 270 trains a day at an average speed of 130 miles per hour (210 kilometers per hour). The Bullet Train has virtually replaced air travel between cities that are less than 220 miles (351 kilometers) apart (about a two-hour train trip). (See Fig. 21)
See: INTERCITY RAIL TRANSPORTATION

Highest and Best Use

Usually considered to be that use which most fully exploits a site's potential. It is the use that, at the time the property is being evaluated, is the most profitable likely use to which the property is put or may be put in the foreseeable future. The concept is often used in connection with the preparation of an appraisal for a site, when the goal of the appraisal is to estimate fair market value for purposes of sale or development.

The highest and best use of a site may change over time, along with existing zoning and other laws and the character of the surrounding area. When valuing an improved site, the improvements can only be considered as adding value to the site if they are consistent with the highest and best use of the land. For example, farm buildings on land whose highest and best use is for development as a regional shopping center cannot be considered as adding value to the land when the site as a whole is being valued at its highest and best use.
See: APPRAISAL; APPRAISED VALUE

Highway

A colloquial rather than a technical term that is used to describe roads, streets or freeways of varying sizes.

Highway Beautification Act of 1965

Legislation (PL 89-285) as amended, establishing a program of sign control and removal or screening of junkyards, dumps and sanitary landfills in noncommercial

Fig. 21.   A TGV high-speed train on its own right-of-way on the Paris-Southeast line. Underpasses were provided for livestock and wildlife crossings.
Credit: Courtesy of the French National Railroads (SNCF)

areas along the interstate and primary highway systems. Project grants, administered by the Federal Highway Administration (FHWA), are offered for 75 percent of the cost of control—e.g., sign removal or junkyard screening—and a 10 percent reduction in federal highway funding is imposed on states that do not participate in the program.

Provisions of the act require states to prevent construction of off-premises advertising signs within 660 feet (201 meters) of interstate and federal-aid primary highways in urban areas not zoned for commercial or industrial use (or where unzoned, not developed with industrial or commercial uses) and to the limits of visibility outside of urban areas in zones that are neither commercial nor industrial. Other requirements are that states remove nonconforming signs (off-premises signs already existing in these zones) and regulate the size, lighting and spacing of off-premises signs in commercial and industrial zones according to federal criteria. Provisions relating to junkyards, dumps and sanitary landfills require that those outside of industrial areas within 1,000 feet (305 meters) of interstate or primary highways be screened or removed.

One of the first pieces of environmental legislation passed in the United States, this act has been relatively unsuccessful in removal of nonconforming signs (46 percent removed through 1982) and screening or removal of junkyards (28 percent). The major problem is that the act imposed the requirement that states compensate owners for removal rather than permitting them to mandate removal via the police power. This requires the states to pay 25 percent of both the purchase and the removal costs, making the program very expensive when there are many signs or junkyards requiring removal.

Some states, including Maine, Alaska, Hawaii and Vermont, have successfully established their own, more stringent highway beautification programs, prohibiting off-premises signs in all zones adjacent to interstate and federal-aid primary highways. Certain other state initiatives to require amortization of billboards rather than state purchase have, however, been thwarted by the federal Highway Beautification Act.
See: BILLBOARD; DUMP; JUNKYARD; SANITARY LANDFILL; SIGN REGULATION

Highway Capacity Determinants

The amount of traffic that a road, or section of road, is capable of carrying in an hour is its capacity. Major roads have a calculated capacity, which is used for traffic assignment purposes and for determining the possibility of further loading because of unused capacity. Factors that determine the capacity of a road are the number and widths of lanes, presence of auxiliary lanes and shoulders, absence of obstructions, roadway geometrics, design speed, prevailing conditions, number and design of intersections, amount of land use accessibility and operational characteristics of the traffic on the road.

Capacity is calculated on the basis of a specific pre-vailing condition and will change if other prevailing conditions are substituted. Prevailing conditions are divided into three classes: prevailing roadway conditions (road structure), prevailing traffic conditions (nature of traffic and drivers) and ambient conditions (weather and time of day).
See: AUXILIARY LANES; CAPACITY; CAPACITY UNDER IDEAL CONDITIONS; GEOMETRIC DESIGN; LANE WIDTH; NETWORK ASSIGNMENT; SHOULDER

Highway Trust Fund

A fund that administers monies received from taxes on fuel, oil, rubber and vehicle parts and reserved largely for highway development and repair. Created by Title II of the Federal-Aid Highway Act of 1956, the Highway Trust Fund is administered by the Federal Highway Administration.

The massive funding available through the Highway Trust Fund (over $3 billion in 1981) has made possible 90 percent federal funding of most of the Interstate Highway System as well as funding for the federal-aid primary, secondary and urban system roads and the $2.5 billion renovation of the northeast corridor railroad system, a part of Amtrak. Since 1975 the Highway Trust Fund has supported bus purchases and rail transit in urban areas if localities choose to use their urban highway funds for those purposes. Since 1976 municipalities have been permitted to trade funding for nonessential segments of the interstate system for mass transit projects, and in 1983 a Mass Transit Account was added to the Highway Trust Fund to enable direct support for certain mass transit facilities.
See: FEDERAL-AID HIGHWAY ACT OF 1956; SURFACE TRANSPORTATION ASSISTANCE ACT OF 1982

Hiking Trail

Trails provided in parks of all sizes that are suitable for hiking or walking, depending upon their design. In general, trails are developed so that hikers can reach scenic views or other points of interest or can pass through areas of scenic quality or variety. They are generally planned so that several trails are linked, enabling a change of direction or a trip extension or curtailment.

A heavily used, short trail should be 10 feet (3 meters) wide, while a footpath may be 2 to 4 feet (0.6 meter to 1.2 meters) wide. Ideally, average grades of heavily used trails should be about 5 percent or less, while other trails may have grades as high as 15 percent. A parking area should be located at the beginning of popular trails, and picnic tables, grills and toilets may also be furnished in very heavily used areas.

Shelters for overnight camping may be provided at points along very long distance trails. For purposes of differentiation, trails may be labeled in terms of such categories as length, degree of difficulty, scenic features to which they provide access and special features (e.g., interpretive trail, braille trail). Typically, color markings or blazes are provided to help hikers follow a trail, and maps may be available at the trailhead.

See: BRAILLE TRAIL; BRIDLE PATH; PRIMITIVE REC-REATION AREA

Hillside Protection Ordinances

These ordinances, also known as slope conservation restrictions, regulate the development and alteration of hillsides, primarily for safety reasons related to the stability of the slope. In addition, the protection of slopes can help to minimize erosion and runoff, thereby protecting the water supply from runoff pollution, and can lessen the chances of downstream flooding. Hillsides are also a prominent part of the landscape; improper development can greatly damage community appearance.

Among the general principles recommended in hillside regulation are the conservation of vegetation for slope stability and control of runoff and erosion, and the minimization of grading and excavation. The preservation of distinctive natural and scenic features—such as ridge lines, vistas and hillcrests—is also important.

One of the approaches often taken in the regulation of hillside development involves slope-density provisions. They set a permissible development density based upon the average degree of slope for each parcel of land, with decreasing permitted densities as slope increases. Another method, soil overlay regulations, is used to set additional requirements for sewage disposal, grading or other types of development or land modification, based upon soil characteristics. A third method applies an overlay district to land that exceeds a designated slope. These requirements may also be supplemented by required minimum standards.

The development and enforcement of hillside regulations requires reliable data concerning soils, geology and hydrology. Supplemental controls—e.g., grading requirements—may also prove necessary to hillside protection.

See: MASS WASTING; ENVIRONMENTALLY SENSITIVE LANDS

Hills v. *Gautreaux* (425 U.S. 284 [1976])

A decision by the United States Supreme Court concerning the authority of federal courts to direct the Department of Housing and Urban Development (HUD) to engage in remedial efforts to correct past discriminatory housing practices that it had perpetuated.

The Court held that federal courts are empowered to require HUD to engage in remedial action over a metropolitan region extending beyond the boundaries of the City of Chicago, despite the fact that the prior violations that led to the need for remedial action were committed by HUD within Chicago's municipal boundaries. The Court found that the metropolitan area was the relevant housing market for minority citizens affected by HUD's past discriminatory practices.

Historic American Building Survey (HABS)

A branch of the Historic American Building Survey/Historic American Engineering Record whose purpose is the documentation of American building arts and architecture as well as endangered historic buildings. The HABS archives, comparable to those found in many European countries, are comprised of measured drawings, photographs and written records to ensure that information will always be available concerning all types of construction and buildings for all historic periods and regions of the country.

The criteria for selecting buildings to be recorded are architectural merit and historical association. Special priority is also given to historic buildings that are in danger of being altered or demolished.

HABS, which began its work in 1933, is a cooperative endeavor of the U.S. Department of the Interior, the American Institute of Architects and the Library of Congress. Its archives are available for public use through the Prints and Photographs Division of the Library of Congress. (See Fig. 22)

See: HISTORIC AMERICAN ENGINEERING RECORD (HAER); HISTORIC PRESERVATION; NATIONAL REGISTER OF HISTORIC PLACES

Historic American Engineering Record (HAER)

A branch of the Historic American Building Survey/Historic American Engineering Record whose purpose is the documentation of important American structures, such as dams or factories; technological networks, such as railroads; or industrial processes. Many of these technological achievements become endangered as they become obsolete or uneconomical; without HAER it is possible that no other record would remain of their existence.

In order to qualify for recording by HAER, a site or system is measured against the following criteria: its significance to the economic or industrial development of the nation or a smaller geographic area; its significance to engineering history; whether it was designed by a famous engineer, architect or craftsman; whether it is typical of certain early engineering or industrial structures; and whether it is the last remaining example or a representative example of its particular type.

HAER, established in 1969, operates under an agreement between the National Park Service, the American Society of Civil Engineers (ASCE) and the Library of Congress. Its collection—which consists of measured drawings, photographs, flowcharts, films of specific industrial processes, maps and reports—is available for public use at the Library of Congress.

See: HISTORIC AMERICAN BUILDING SURVEY (HABS); HISTORIC PRESERVATION; NATIONAL REGISTER OF HISTORIC PLACES

Historic District

An area that is related by historical events or themes, by visual continuity or character, or by some other special

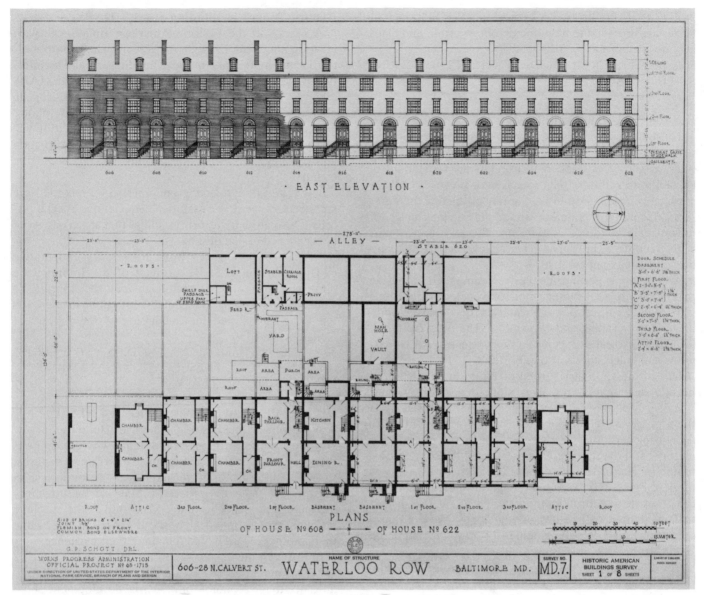

Fig. 22. Plans and an elevation of Waterloo Row, by architect Robert Mills, built in 1819 in Baltimore. Part of an eight-sheet draft by G.P. Schott done for the Historic American Buildings Survey. Waterloo Row was razed in 1970.
Credit: HABS, Library of Congress

feature that helps to give it a unique historic identity. Historic districts may be designated at a number of levels of government and given various types of official status or protection. At the federal level they may be designated as National Historic Landmarks or entered in the National Register of Historic Places. Many states have also passed enabling legislation allowing the enactment of historic preservation ordinances at the local level, and as a result, numerous municipalities have created historic districts under this authority or under their right to zone. When an area is designated a historic district, the architectural and historic quality of the district is more likely to be preserved, both because inappropriate physical changes may be prohibited and because the area receives increased attention and publicity. In addition, financial incentives to

rehabilitation may be available, such as federal investment tax credits or reduced local tax assessments.

In a municipally designated historic district, a variety of controls can be imposed. Among the things that might be regulated are alterations to existing buildings, demolitions, the design of new construction, street furniture, landscaping and lighting, but this varies considerably by community.

The edges or boundaries of historic districts are delineated in a variety of ways for regulatory purposes. Depending upon the nature of the district, they may be selected by historic factors, such as the original boundaries of a settlement or a planned community, or by visual factors, such as architectural character or topography. Other considerations that may play an important role in edge delineation

are physical boundaries, such as highways; major open spaces; rivers; or major land use changes.
See: HISTORIC DISTRICT ORDINANCE; HISTORIC PRESERVATION; HISTORIC REVIEW BOARD; LANDMARKS COMMISSION ORDINANCE

Historic District Ordinance

A type of municipal statute in which a specifically defined area is formally designated as a historic district and a review board established with the power to review and/or control such activities as proposed alterations, demolitions and new construction in that district. The entire physical setting of the district—including its open spaces, vistas and street furniture—is regulated by the ordinance to preserve its unique appearance and historic value.

The first official historic district was established in Charleston in 1931. Since that time districts have been created in a wide range of municipalities, either under the authority granted by specific statewide enabling legislation or by the use of the municipalities' right to zone.

Historic district controls are often imposed as an overlay to existing zoning, so that the boundaries of a historic district can be delineated by more logical criteria than existing zoning boundaries, which may be unrelated to historical or architectural unity. This practice also allows a historic area crossing various zoning districts to be regulated and protected.

Historic district ordinances are most often used by communities with a readily identifiable and relatively concentrated historic area. In contrast, landmarks commission ordinances enable the designation of individual structures throughout a municipality regardless of their proximity to each other.
See: HISTORIC DISTRICT; HISTORIC PRESERVATION; HISTORIC REVIEW BOARD; LANDMARKS COMMISSION ORDINANCE; MINIMUM MAINTENANCE STANDARDS

Historic Preservation

The process of identifying, evaluating, managing, conserving, maintaining and, when necessary, rehabilitating, stabilizing, restoring and reconstructing historic properties so that they are protected for the use of future generations. Other aspects of historic preservation include the documentation and recording of these properties, as well as their acquisition.

Historic preservation has been attracting increased attention because of the many contributions it can make to community well-being. Apart from preserving the character, appearance and identity of an area, it can provide such tangible economic benefits as increased tourism, additional housing stock or places of employment, increased tax base and improved neighborhood conditions. Rehabilitation of historic structures is often more cost-efficient than new construction.

To support the preservation of historic properties, many federal, state and local programs have been enacted, ranging from the establishment of the National Register of Historic Places to the enactment of preservation ordinances and the creation of local revolving funds. Significant federal tax advantages, enacted most recently in the Economic Recovery Tax Act of 1981, are also available for investment in the rehabilitation of older buildings and historically significant buildings.
See: ADAPTIVE USE; ADVISORY COUNCIL ON HISTORIC PRESERVATION; ARCHAEOLOGICAL SITE; BUILDING CODES FOR HISTORIC BUILDINGS; DEMOLITION BY NEGLECT; EMERGENCY REPAIR AND STABILIZATION; FACADE EASEMENT; FANEUIL HALL MARKETPLACE; GHIRADELLI SQUARE; HISTORIC AMERICAN BUILDING SURVEY (HABS); HISTORIC AMERICAN ENGINEERING RECORD (HAER); HISTORICAL SOCIETY; HISTORIC DISTRICT; HISTORIC DISTRICT ORDINANCE; HISTORIC PRESERVATION TAX INCENTIVES; HISTORIC RECOGNITION PROGRAMS; HISTORIC REVIEW BOARD; HISTORIC SURVEY; LANDMARK; LANDMARKS COMMISSION ORDINANCE; MINIMUM MAINTENANCE STANDARDS; NATIONAL HISTORIC LANDMARK; NATIONAL HISTORIC PRESERVATION ACT OF 1966; NATIONAL REGISTER OF HISTORIC PLACES; NATIONAL TRUST FOR HISTORIC PRESERVATION; PRESERVATION; PRESERVATION PLAN; RECONSTRUCTION; REHABILITATION; RESTORATION; REVOLVING FUND; SECRETARY OF THE INTERIOR'S STANDARDS FOR REHABILITATION; STATE HISTORIC PRESERVATION OFFICER (SHPO); TRANSFER OF DEVELOPMENT RIGHTS (TDR); VIEUX CARRE

Historic Preservation Tax Incentives

Tax benefits that encourage investment in the preservation and rehabilitation of historic buildings. Prior to the Tax Reform Act of 1976, the Internal Revenue Code not only offered little incentive to preserving historic buildings but contained disincentives because of the differing schedules of tax-deductible depreciation for new buildings as compared to older buildings. The Tax Reform Act, however, along with the Revenue Act of 1978 and the Economic Recovery Tax Act of 1981, opened a whole range of tax incentives to owners of historic property wishing to undertake rehabilitation projects. As an example, the Economic Recovery Tax Act of 1981 included provisions for a 25 percent investment tax credit in connection with certain qualified rehabilitation expenses of certified historic structures.

A wide range of state and local tax incentives and benefits are also available to historic property owners. For example, in some states assessments on historic property may be reduced to a level consistent with the degree to which their market value might be restricted by the provisions of a preservation ordinance. Assessments may also be held at a fixed level for a designated time period in exchange for rehabilitation. Another approach is the

granting of tax credits in exchange for the restoration of a building that is located in a historic district, is designated as a landmark or meets some other requirement.
See: ECONOMIC RECOVERY TAX ACT OF 1981; HISTORIC PRESERVATION; TAX ABATEMENT; TAX EQUITY AND FISCAL RESPONSIBILITY ACT OF 1982 (TEFRA)

Historic Recognition Programs

Programs in which buildings of historic significance are officially selected, designated or recognized in some way. Recognition programs may range from the National Register of Historic Places, which is nationwide in scope, to state historic registers or municipal listings of important historic buildings.

In some cases, such as the National Register of Historic Places, some degree of protection is afforded to a building because of its inclusion on this list. Municipalities may also use their recognition programs as a means of identifying the community's historic assets that are worthy of preservation. In other cases, recognition extends only to affixing markers or plaques upon buildings, an activity that has attracted controversy because some contend that it detracts from the buildings' appearance and historic authenticity.
See: HISTORIC DISTRICT; HISTORIC PRESERVATION; HISTORIC SURVEY; NATIONAL REGISTER OF HISTORIC PLACES

Historic Review Board

An officially designated municipal body with authority granted it by the provisions of a historic district ordinance, a landmarks commission ordinance or some other type of regulatory procedure aimed at protecting historic sites and structures. As of 1981, 850 municipalities in the United States had some type of preservation ordinance.

Among the powers often granted to such a review board are the right to review and/or regulate proposed alterations, the design of new construction in historic districts and the demolition of historic structures. Although municipal ordinances vary, many communities require that the board be composed of architects, historians, planners, realtors, attorneys, residents of the affected neighborhoods or other individuals possessing special skills.

In reviewing the appropriateness of new construction or alterations in an area regulated by a preservation ordinance, the review board generally considers such features as height, width, shape, gross volume, roof design, proportion and color. Pattern, materials, rhythm and general visual compatibility are also important. In addition, it examines the proposed use of architectural details and embellishment as well as the landscaping.
See: ARCHITECTURAL REVIEW BOARD; HISTORIC DISTRICT ORDINANCE; HISTORIC PRESERVATION; LANDMARKS COMMISSION ORDINANCE

Historic Sites Act of 1935

An act that expanded the scope of federal preservation activities and established a national preservation policy "to preserve for public use historic sites, buildings and objects of national significance for the inspiration and benefit of the people of the United States." In addition, it provided the authority for a program in which historic and cultural resources are identified and evaluated. Those determined to be of national significance become eligible for designation as National Historic Landmarks.
See: HISTORIC PRESERVATION; NATIONAL HISTORIC LANDMARK

Historic Survey

A means of systematically collecting data concerning historic structures and artifacts through field inspection and research.

Historic surveys are conducted at the federal level by agencies surveying the properties under their control. Other federal survey programs include the Historic American Building Survey/Historic American Engineering Record and the National Register of Historic Places. State agencies participate actively in conducting surveys as part of their participation in the National Register program; some states also have their own state registers of historic places. Lower levels of government also conduct surveys as part of their planning programs and often use the survey results as an aid to establishing policy, nominating properties to registers, establishing historic districts, designating landmarks or undertaking rehabilitation programs.

Information typically collected during a survey often includes the date of construction and architect, architectural type, building materials used, structural system, condition and surroundings of a building. Photographs and drawings may also be made and research conducted concerning its prior owners.
See: HISTORIC AMERICAN BUILDING SURVEY (HABS); HISTORIC AMERICAN ENGINEERING RECORD (HAER); HISTORIC PRESERVATION; NATIONAL REGISTER OF HISTORIC PLACES; PRESERVATION PLAN

Historical Society

A nonprofit group organized to preserve and protect the historic heritage of a community. Historical societies generally preserve community artifacts, books and genealogical records and often maintain a local museum that is open to the public. Many conduct systematic surveys of the buildings in their communities and help to complete survey forms for the National Register of Historic Places. Historical societies, too, may often acquire endangered buildings of historic value to prevent their demolition and may later sell these buildings to an appropriate buyer. Other historical society activities may include the operation of revolving funds and historic recognition programs and the holding of easements and restrictive covenants. A historical society usually differs from a landmarks commis-

sion or historic district commission in that it is not an officially appointed government commission authorized to administer a municipal preservation ordinance.
See: HISTORIC PRESERVATION; HISTORIC REVIEW BOARD

Hold Harmless

An amount of federal funding that is guaranteed for a stated amount of time to enable a community to make a gradual transition to a lower funding level. Funds are held harmless in a variety of situations. One example is the creation of a block grant program to replace several categorical grant programs in which the block grant funding will be lower than the total funding under all the previous grants. A change in the formula of a grant program that would yield a lower funding level to a community is another cause. Another basis on which a hold harmless amount is set is the availability of new census data that indicate a decline in variables included in a formula, such as population or housing units without plumbing, which places the community in a lower funding category.

The term derives from the concept of protecting a community from significant cuts in financial aid resulting from activities or events beyond its control.
See: BLOCK GRANT; CATEGORICAL GRANT

Home Equity Conversion

The process by which the equity in a home (i.e., the value of a home less any debts, such as a mortgage) is made available to homeowners while they retain occupancy. Home equity conversion programs are seen as potential solutions to the financial problems of the elderly homeowner with substantial capital invested in a home but with little income with which to pay housing expenses, such as property taxes or utility costs, or other basic living expenses.

Equity conversion programs, many still in their formative stages, may take a number of forms. In one version a nonprofit organization in Buffalo, New York, Home Equity Living Plan (HELP), pays for all taxes, insurance fees and repairs; takes care of maintenance; and offers monthly cash stipends. The amount of payment is based on a combination of the value of the home and the projected life expectancy of the owner(s). Upon the death of the elderly homeowner, HELP assumes title to the home, sells it and puts the proceeds back into the program. This demonstration project was instituted in 1981 with the aid of federal community development block grant funds.

Another form of home equity conversion, known as a reverse annuity mortgage (RAM), is also used. In this financing arrangement, which federally chartered savings and loan institutions and savings banks have been permitted to offer since 1979, a loan, secured by the value of the home, is made by the bank to the homeowner. The loan is then used to purchase an annuity from an insurance company, which provides the elderly homeowner with income. Upon the death of the borrower or the sale of the home, the lending institution is repaid. In a variation of the RAM, known as a reverse mortgage (also called a rising debt loan), an annuity is paid directly to the borrower by the lending institution. This type of loan becomes due after a specified time period. The homeowner may be able to extend the loan if the value of the home has increased sufficiently, but it is possible otherwise that the home may have to be sold at that time to repay the debt. Various forms of reverse annuity mortgage programs have been instituted in Marin County, California; Ohio; Maine; and New Jersey.

Additional types of home equity conversion include programs by which property tax payments may be deferred until the death of the elderly occupant and sale of the home (used in Oregon and California) and sale-leaseback. Several New Jersey communities also make long-term financing available to elderly homeowners to enable them to add a rental unit for an older person needing housing.
See: EQUITY; HOUSING FOR THE ELDERLY; MORTGAGE

Home Improvement

A modification to a residence or its surrounding land that adds value to the home. A home improvement may be distinguished from ordinary maintenance and repairs, which merely maintain the value of a home during its useful life. Examples of home improvements include finishing an attic or basement, adding a room to a home (e.g., by enclosing a porch) or remodeling a kitchen.

The extent to which an improvement will add dollar value to a home will depend upon the visibility of the improvement, its general desirability, the level of home improvements of the surrounding community and other factors.

Home Occupation

A type of limited commercial activity that is carried on within an individual's dwelling. Several approaches may be taken by municipalities attempting to define which home occupations are to be permitted and are least likely to have an adverse impact upon the residential neighborhood.

Many communities choose to define the characteristics that make a home occupation acceptable. Among the requirements frequently mentioned are: (1) that the occupation be clearly secondary to the use of the structure for dwelling purposes, (2) that the character and exterior of the structure remain unchanged, (3) that no stock or merchandise be kept on the premises and (4) that no manufacturing or commercial repair be done on the premises. Other restrictions may be imposed concerning the permitted number of employees not living on the premises, the amount of the home's square footage that may be used for the enterprise and required parking. Decisions are made on a case-by-case basis concerning the acceptability of a particular enterprise.

A second way of approaching the problem is the addition of examples of permitted and prohibited home occupations to a list of general performance criteria that the occupation must meet. The ordinance might specify, for example, that while individual tutoring and instruction are permitted, group instruction is prohibited. A third approach taken by municipalities is the detailed enumeration of permitted and prohibited home occupations without a specific discussion of desirable performance criteria. An obvious problem with this method is the likely omission of many types of home occupations from either the permitted or the prohibited list.

An increase in the number and variety of home businesses is one likely outcome of the continuing trend toward two-income families. This suggests the importance of modern and realistic regulations concerning the operation of home occupations.
See: ZONING

Home Rule

The concept of local government's exercising certain powers conferred by the state. Home rule enables local government to control certain functions, thereby providing greater government responsiveness to the citizen.

Home rule is granted by the state constitution and acts of the state legislature. Degree of home rule power generally varies with size and type of municipality (cities, towns and villages). The exercise of home rule within prescribed limits is usually carried out by adoption of local laws and ordinances; where a local law is adopted within the scope of the constitutional home rule grant, it has an equivalent legal status to that of a statute enacted by the state legislature. A home rule message is occasionally required to be sent to the state legislature notifying it of the municipality's actions.

Along with the benefits of home rule come burdens for financing activities subject to local control. This often leads to difficulty, since the local tax base may not be sufficient to support services at the desired level.
See: LOCAL GOVERNMENT; POLITICAL SUBDIVISION; PROPOSITION 13

Home Weatherization

Methods by which heat loss may be minimized in existing homes, thereby saving energy and reducing fuel bills. The major techniques used to reduce heat loss are the addition of insulation, caulking and weather stripping and the use of storm doors and windows. The cost of many of these improvements is rapidly repaid in terms of fuel savings.
See: ENERGY CONSERVATION PLANNING; THERMAL WINDOWS

Homeowners' Association

A nonprofit organization consisting of homeowners or owners of dwelling units such as condominiums. In the case of condominium development, the organization is normally called a condominium association. The function of a homeowners' association is the maintenance of common areas and other facilities and the provision of services to residents. Sometimes exterior home maintenance and repair are also undertaken.

Normally, a homeowners' association is organized by the project's developer, who records bylaws regulating the association, restrictions, covenants and easements. When the development is completed, he transfers control to the association, which becomes responsible for enforcement of these provisions.

Membership in a homeowners' association may be either automatic or elective. When automatic, the property owner is a voting member of the association by virtue of his ownership of property, is entitled to use all facilities and is obligated to pay an assessment to the association to defray operational expenses. When membership is elective or nonautomatic, the property owners may choose whether they wish to join and pay, often making collection of fees for the association difficult. Many associations also form as nonprofit corporations to provide for limited liability for their members and to allow ownership of the common property to be recorded in the name of the organization.
See: COMMON AREAS; CONDOMINIUM HOUSING; PLANNED UNIT DEVELOPMENT (PUD)

Homestead Act of 1862

A United States act that provided free land to any individual willing to live on it and cultivate it for a five-year period. The quarter sections (160 acres, or 65 hectares) that were offered lured thousands of new settlers each year to states such as Minnesota, Kansas, Nebraska and the Dakotas, helping to settle that part of the country. Although many failed to successfully complete the five-year residency (and thus gain full title) because of lack of capital or farming knowledge, almost 957,000 title applications were filed by 1890, and large numbers of successful farms were founded during that period in history.

Hospital Bed Needs

An estimate of the number of hospital beds required to serve a population of a defined geographic area. Methodologies are available for determining the demand for hospital beds for short- and long-term care and are a tool for comparing available resources to actual need.

In general, available methodologies all entail calculations using patient days (the total number of patients multiplied by the total number of days hospitalized), an average daily census and occupancy rates to develop a range of estimates. Bed needs are normally determined for major clinical services—including medical and surgical, pediatric

and obstetrical—and if required, estimates of short-term bed need may be prepared for various age and sex groupings of a population. For long-term bed needs, estimates are based on the size of the population that will be 65 years or older in a target year.
See: HEALTH PLANNING; HOSPITAL PLANNING; OCCUPANCY RATE

Hospital Planning

A proposal for a new hospital facility (e.g., a new hospital, a new wing, or purchase of major equipment) must follow a federally mandated planning review process, which results in the issuance of a certificate of need. To a large extent, the preliminary analysis required to justify a new facility will also provide a basis for decisions concerning location, building design and programs for the hospital, as well as the total number of beds and the relationship of the facility to other areawide providers of health care.

Conventional hospital design criteria and standards include the relationship of the proposed facility to surrounding land use, availability of utilities and public transportation, parking and the anticipated impact on the socioeconomic and environmental conditions of the neighborhood surrounding the proposed hospital. Availability of a large labor pool and an adequate supply of affordable housing for employees are also important factors.
See: ACUTE CARE HOSPITAL; CERTIFICATE OF NEED (CON); HEALTH CARE SYSTEM; HEALTH PLANNING; HOSPITAL BED NEEDS; OCCUPANCY RATE

Hot Line

A telephone line, often staffed by volunteers, that is used by some municipalities to enable quick responses to complaints or requests for assistance or to obtain public opinion. When complaints are received, matters are usually referred to pertinent agencies for action, while specialized hot lines, such as for street repairs, may be operated by the responding agency. When a hot line is used for polling purposes, responses to particular public issues serve as input to decision making.
See: CITIZEN PARTICIPATION TECHNIQUES; FEEDBACK

Hotel

A multistoried building containing many rooms for the accommodation of transients and usually providing a variety of rooms for dining, entertainment, exhibitions, and convention or sales activities as well as personal services for guests.

Hotels vary in style, accommodation quality and price according to the clientele they wish to attract and their locations. They range from elegant to marginal facilities, including a large middle ground composed of business and tourist hotels, inns, hostels and YMCAs. Other variations include boarding houses, which are private homes with rooms that are available to transients, and residential ho-

tels, which generally contain rooms or apartments with kitchen facilities rented on a weekly or monthly basis. Each urban area generally contains most of these hotel forms, so that the needs of diverse groups can be served.

Hotels have also become a focal point in planning for the renovation of urban centers, where they are employed to attract a core population to use surrounding urban facilities. They are also an important element of airport planning, providing rooms for passengers awaiting connections and corporate meeting facilities for large corporations that must periodically gather far-flung executives. Resort hotels are another form, in which the hotel is part of a large complex of recreational facilities, usually located in a scenic area and often constituting a major component of the area's economy.

Because hotels are generally located in commercial areas, planning for them involves the provision of substantial off-street parking and loading space. Sites selected should also be near scenic or cultural amenities and public transportation facilities.
See: MOTEL; OFF-STREET PARKING REQUIREMENTS; SINGLE-ROOM OCCUPANCY (SRO); TOURISM

House Connection

A sewer pipe that carries wastewater from a building to a lateral located in the street. The recommended minimum diameter of a house connection is 4 inches (10.2 centimeters).
See: LATERAL; SEWERAGE SYSTEM

Household Size

The number of persons residing in a particular dwelling unit with common housekeeping arrangements. As a result of the rapid growth of single-person and nontraditional households, average household size in the United States has been steadily declining. Average household size decreased from 3.11 persons per household in 1970 to 2.75 persons per household in 1980—a drop of 11.6 percent over the decade. This occurred during the same period in which the number of households increased by almost 27 percent, to a total of 80.4 million in 1980.

This trend has important implications for the housing market. A larger number of housing units are required to house the same total population as household size declines. This means that even in the absence of population growth, an increase in housing stock is necessary. In addition, smaller households usually require different styles and types of housing than families, making a certain proportion of the housing stock inappropriate for their needs without conversion of larger units into additional smaller housing units. Some communities are permitting the conversion of certain large old homes (some of which had become unmarketable) into apartments, which can also help to preserve historic structures.
See: FAMILY; HOUSEHOLD TYPE; HOUSING CHOICE; HOUSING STOCK; HOUSING TYPE; ILLEGAL CONVERSION

Household Type

The status of individuals comprising a household, which may range from conventional nuclear families to single-parent households or those composed of unattached individuals. Household type is significantly affected by social trends. For example, the number of traditional family households has declined in the United States, while the number of single-person and female-headed households has been consistently increasing. Household type is also related to life cycle, and as individuals pass through stages of life (e.g., marriage, family formation, empty nest), the type of housing unit required changes. It is desirable for the housing stock of a municipality to be sufficiently diversified so that it provides a range of housing opportunities suitable for various types of households.

See: AGE-ORIENTED COMMUNITY; EMPTY NESTERS; FAMILY; HOUSEHOLD SIZE; HOUSING CHOICE; HOUSING FOR FAMILIES; HOUSING FOR THE ELDERLY; HOUSING STOCK

Housing

Dwellings provided for residents of a community. Within the context of urban planning, housing, which occupies 40 percent of the total land area in an average community, is one of the primary elements of study and regulation. Its placement, design, density, quantity, cost, form of tenure and appurtenances are all matters of public policy.

In many urban communities the effort to eliminate blighted and deteriorating housing in the 19th and 20th centuries was the basis for the city planning movements that followed. The use of housing and sanitary codes as well as the establishment of zoning and subdivision regulations are firmly rooted in the intent to improve housing.

In spite of this regulation, housing in the United States is produced almost solely by private developers. The construction of housing and, in recent years, the expenditures for housing additions and alterations comprise a substantial segment of the economy. Public housing, which comprises only about 3 percent of the housing stock, is the only form of housing owned by a government entity. Government subsidies—such as housing allowances, tax credits, and mortgages and loans offered at below market rate interest—are among the incentives intended to induce housing production by the private sector and to enable low- and moderate-income persons to afford decent housing. In several western European countries, on the other hand, the federal government has built a substantial portion of the new housing stock, while in communist countries virtually all new housing is built by the government.

Planners produce housing plans that attempt to suggest solutions to imbalances in supply and demand. Other related issues that are studied include regional housing distribution, exclusionary practices, condominium and cooperative conversions, rent control and gentrification. Neighborhood revitalization, housing for the elderly and handicapped, mobile home developments, and urban homesteading and self-help projects are some of the other areas related to housing with which a planning agency may be involved.

Development of funding mechanisms to stimulate housing construction and improvement is another way in which planners participate in the provision of housing. The leveraging of government seed money and private capital, once used largely for commercial and industrial development, has now been extended to housing and has become a mechanism for its rehabilitation. The use of state or municipal tax-exempt bond issues to generate revenues for low- and moderate-income housing loans and mortgages has been successful in some cases, as in Chicago. Exactions from developers of nonresidential projects have been used successfully in San Francisco to help finance low- and moderate-income housing. In another approach, a proposal has been made in New York City for the development of a housing trust fund, to be funded by assessments on developments in conjunction with discretionary developer-requested zoning or permit actions that increase property value; developer contributions for floor area ratio bonuses permissible under the city's zoning resolution; and other sources. The fund would be used to make loans to nonprofit community development corporations for construction and rehabilitation of low- and moderate-income housing and, in certain cases, for housing assistance payments to households.

See: CONDOMINIUM HOUSING; COOPERATIVE HOUSING; DEPARTMENT OF HOUSING AND URBAN DEVELOPMENT (HUD); DWELLING UNIT; EXCLUSIONARY ZONING; FAIR SHARE; FEDERAL HOUSING ADMINISTRATION (FHA) MORTGAGE INSURANCE; GENTRIFICATION; HIGH-RISE HOUSING; HOUSEHOLD TYPE; HOUSING CHOICE; HOUSING CODE; HOUSING LOCATION; HOUSING PLAN; HOUSING STANDARDS; HOUSING STOCK; HOUSING SUBSIDY; HOUSING TENURE; HOUSING TYPE; INDUSTRIALIZED HOUSING; LOW-RISE HOUSING; MID-RISE HOUSING; MOBILE HOME; MULTIFAMILY HOUSING; OVERCROWDING; PUBLIC HOUSING; RENT CONTROL; RENTAL HOUSING; SINGLE-FAMILY HOUSING; SLUM; SQUATTER SETTLEMENTS; STATE HOUSING FINANCE AGENCIES; SUBURBAN GROWTH

Housing Act of 1949

Federal legislation (PL 81-171) that established a national program of slum clearance and community development and redevelopment (later called urban renewal); a policy of housing production and development of well-planned communities; and a farm housing program. The act also reauthorized low-rent public housing.

Title I of the act authorized loans and capital grants for redevelopment projects and established the parameters of the slum clearance program. The Declaration of National Housing Policy enunciated a goal of a "decent home and a suitable living environment for every American family." The policy also stipulated that governmental assistance would be used to stimulate the involvement of private enterprise in the production of housing and community renewal and that the goals of the program were the production of sound housing, the reduction of housing cost, an increase in the efficiency of residential construction through new methods and standardization of dimensions and assembly, and a high annual volume of residential construction.

The farm housing program authorized loans to farm owners for construction or repair of farm buildings. This act also authorized the decennial census of housing.

See: FARMERS HOME ADMINISTRATION (FmHA); NATIONAL HOUSING ACT; UNITED STATES HOUSING ACT OF 1937; URBAN RENEWAL

Housing Act of 1954

Federal legislation (PL 83-560) that established the Section 701 planning assistance grant program for smaller municipalities and changed the name of the slum clearance program to urban renewal. The requirement for a "workable program" as a basis for funding under the urban renewal and public housing programs was also imposed.

Other provisions of the act created Federal Housing Administration (FHA) mortgage programs for disaster victims, for housing in urban renewal areas and for relocation housing and rechartered the Federal National Mortgage Association.

See: COMPREHENSIVE PLANNING GRANTS (SECTION 701); HOUSING ACT OF 1949; HOUSING ACT OF 1959; NATIONAL HOUSING ACT

Housing Act of 1959

Federal legislation establishing the Section 202 program of housing for the elderly through a combination of Federal Housing Administration (FHA) mortgages and low-interest loans made directly to nonprofit sponsors. This act (PL 86-372) also authorized an FHA program for nursing homes and urban renewal relocation payments.

The Section 701 program was broadened by extension of planning grants for comprehensive planning to states, regional and metropolitan planning agencies, and large cities. Provisions were also included to enable expenditures for capital improvement programming, intergovernmental coordination and preparation of regulatory and administrative measures to support the comprehensive plan. In addition, states were encouraged to use local public agencies (established for urban renewal purposes) on a statewide basis to assist smaller communities, thereby expanding the state role in planning.

See: COMPREHENSIVE PLANNING GRANTS (SECTION 701); NATIONAL HOUSING ACT; SECTION 202 HOUSING PROGRAM; SECTION 232 PROGRAM

Housing Act of 1961

Federal legislation that established the Section 221 (d) 3 housing program, which authorized Federal Housing Administration (FHA) insurance for low-interest mortgages on moderate-income multifamily housing. The Sec-

tion 514 rural housing program for farm workers was also authorized.

Another significant provision of the act (PL 87-70) was the establishment of grants for open-space land acquisition to "help curb urban sprawl . . . encourage more economic and desirable urban development, and . . . provide necessary recreational, conservation and scenic areas. . . . " This legislation also extended federal community facility loan authorization, previously permitted for such projects as sewer and water facility development, to mass transit facilities.

See: NATIONAL HOUSING ACT; SECTIONS 221 (d) 3 AND 221 (d) 4 HOUSING PROGRAMS; SECTIONS 514 AND 516 FmHA HOUSING PROGRAMS

Housing Act of 1964

Omnibus legislation (PL 88-560) that authorized the Section 312 rehabilitation loan program and extended to the handicapped housing programs originally intended exclusively for the elderly. Other provisions increased grants under the Section 516 FmHA program to pay up to two-thirds of the development costs of housing for farm laborers; authorized training and fellowship programs for graduate education in city planning and urban and housing specialties; and expanded numerous provisions of other housing programs as well as funding for them. Another significant provision was the requirement that buildings in urban renewal areas be considered for rehabilitation before they could be approved for clearance and that municipalities institute housing code compliance programs in urban renewal areas to reduce the amount of clearance necessary.

See: NATIONAL HOUSING ACT; SECTIONS 514 AND 516 FmHA HOUSING PROGRAMS; SECTION 202 HOUSING PROGRAM; SECTION 312 HOUSING PROGRAM

Housing and Community Development Act of 1974

This act (PL 93-383) significantly changed the structure of federal assistance for both community development and housing. Several major types of categorical grants, including urban renewal and Model Cities, were replaced under Title I by the Community Development Block Grant Program. The act stipulated that locations within Standard Metropolitan Statistical Areas (SMSAs), including cities with populations over 50,000 and urban counties with a minimum population of 200,000, be entitled to automatic block grants according to a formula based on population, amount of overcrowded housing and poverty (weighted twice), as compared with average figures for other entitlement communities. Many communities were further entitled to a hold harmless funding level. Small communities and those in rural areas could also receive hold harmless funding if they had previously participated in an urban renewal, Model Cities, neighborhood redevelopment or code enforcement program, while others were permitted to apply for discretionary funds. All applicants were required to submit a housing assistance plan (HAP) and an application that discussed community needs and a program to meet the needs. Entitlement communities were also required to submit a three-year program of activities. Many of these provisions were subsequently amended by later legislation.

Title II created the Section 8 program and gave the bulk of federal support for the production of low-income housing to that program, although it also allocated additional funds for new public housing. The Section 8 program, which was originally described as a modified Section 23 program, gave the Department of Housing and Urban Development authority to build housing for low-income families by contracting directly with developers rather than using public housing authorities (PHAs) for this purpose, although PHAs were also permitted to be the contracting agencies. Via the Section 8 program, low-income households were permitted to find housing in the community of their choice subject to locating a unit able to meet Section 8 criteria.

This act also modified many existing programs, allowed Federal Housing Administration (FHA) coinsurance under the Section 244 housing program, instituted mobile home safety standards and initiated the federal urban homesteading program. It expanded eligibility for Farmers Home Administration assistance to rural communities with populations of up to 20,000 (the previous limit had been 10,000) and authorized a rural loan program for condominiums. The act also established the Secretary's Discretionary Fund in the Department of Housing and Urban Development and the National Institute of Building Sciences.

See: COMMUNITY DEVELOPMENT BLOCK GRANT (CDBG); FARMERS HOME ADMINISTRATION (FmHA); HOLD HARMLESS; HOUSING AND COMMUNITY DEVELOPMENT ACT OF 1977; NATIONAL INSTITUTE OF BUILDING SCIENCES (NIBS); SECRETARY'S DISCRETIONARY FUND; SECTION 8 HOUSING PROGRAM; SECTION 23 HOUSING PROGRAM; SECTION 244 HOUSING PROGRAM; URBAN HOMESTEADING

Housing and Community Development Act of 1977

Omnibus legislation (PL 95-128) modifying community development and housing programs and creating the Urban Development Action Grant (UDAG). UDAG was the most innovative aspect of the act, providing funding on a project-by-project basis, with decisions to award grants based significantly upon the ability to leverage private participation. The 1977 act also revises the Community Development Block Grant Program by modifying requirements of the Housing Assistance Plan (HAP); adjusts the entitlement formula by giving additional aid to northeastern and midwestern cities that had been losing population; broadens eligibility for economic development projects; and changes citizen participation requirements.

The rural housing program is expanded in the 1977 act to include provisions for the handicapped and for congregate housing for the elderly. The act also changes the title

of required biennial reports by the president of the United States from National Urban Growth Policy to National Urban Policy, reflecting changes in population trends and their effects in urban areas.

See: COMMUNITY DEVELOPMENT BLOCK GRANT (CDBG); COMMUNITY REINVESTMENT ACT OF 1977 (CRA); HOUSING AND COMMUNITY DEVELOPMENT ACT OF 1980; HOUSING AND COMMUNITY DEVELOPMENT AMENDMENTS OF 1978; HOUSING AND URBAN DEVELOPMENT ACT OF 1970; URBAN DEVELOPMENT ACTION GRANT (UDAG)

Housing and Community Development Act of 1980

An act (PL 96-399) that modifies requirements of the Urban Development Action Grant Program (UDAG) and makes energy conservation programs and studies eligible for funding under that program. It expands the urban county concept to include independent cities within counties and requires that properties either on the National Register of Historic Places or meeting requirements for inclusion in the register be identified and the effect of any proposed project on such property be noted. Another requirement imposed by this act is that effects of a UDAG project on historic buildings be reviewed by preservation agencies in a two-step program.

The 1980 act also allows the Federal National Mortgage Association (FNMA) to purchase home-improvement loans, expanding the secondary market in rehabilitation loans. In addition, the law authorized interstate compacts and agreements for the establishment of interstate or regional agencies for purposes of comprehensive planning and provided funding under the Section 701 Program for development of the comprehensive plans

See: HOUSING AND COMMUNITY DEVELOPMENT AMENDMENTS OF 1981; URBAN COUNTY

Housing and Community Development Amendments of 1978

Legislation (PL 95-557) that established the Neighborhood Reinvestment Corporation, the Livable Cities Program and the Neighborhood Self-Help Program and extended funds for major housing and community development programs. This legislation, which initiated flexible subsidies for FHA-insured multifamily projects in financial trouble, also permits the Department of Housing and Urban Development to insure rehabilitation loans made by financial institutions for one- to four-family residences and permits the Government National Mortgage Association (GNMA) to purchase these loans. The act also establishes a congregate program of meals and social services to the elderly and handicapped living in low-rent housing, to be supplied on a contractual basis by local providers.

See: HOUSING AND COMMUNITY DVELOPMENT ACT OF 1977; HOUSING AND COMMUNITY DEVELOPMENT AMENDMENTS OF 1979; LIVABLE CITIES; NEIGHBORHOOD REINVESTMENT CORPORATION (NRC); NEIGHBORHOOD SELF-HELP DEVELOPMENT ACT OF 1978

Housing and Community Development Amendments of 1979

Legislation (PL 96-153) that initiated the Pockets of Poverty program, funded community development activities and extended federal insurance programs relating to riots, crime and floods. Housing programs—including Section 8, public housing and rural housing programs—also received appropriations, and insurance ceilings were raised on many Federal Housing Administration (FHA) loans.
See: POCKETS OF POVERTY

Housing and Community Development Amendments of 1981

Part of the Omnibus Budget Reconciliation Act of 1981 (Title III, subtitle A of PL 97-35), in which many housing and community development programs are reauthorized. A substantial portion of the act is concerned with changes in the Community Development Block Grant Program (CDBG). Provisions of the act require applicants for CDBG grants to prepare a statement of their goals and proposed use of funds and to hold at least one public hearing on these matters, and they delete a requirement that nonentitlement communities prepare a housing assistance plan (HAP). The legislation, however, requires entitlement communities to include in their HAPs an estimate of the effect of projected employment opportunities and population on housing needs of low-income persons residing in or expected to reside in the community. Other provisions relating to the CDBG program require annual review of community programs by the Department of Housing and Urban Development for compliance with the primary objectives of the program, make community planning programs eligible for funding under the CDBG program to replace the 701 funding that had been ended and allow states to assume responsibility for the Small Cities program.

The legislation provides funds for construction or acquisition of subsidized housing (Section 8 and public housing), to be made available at a mix of 55 percent for new units and 45 percent for rehabilitated units; requires that new Section 8 units be of modest design; and permits Section 8 funds to be used, under specified conditions, for single-room occupancy dwellings and mobile homes. Another provision creates a procedure (to replace state laws) to be followed by HUD when foreclosing on Federal Housing Administration-insured or HUD-assisted multifamily properties.
See: COMMUNITY DEVELOPMENT BLOCK GRANT (CDBG); SECTION 8 HOUSING PROGRAM

Housing and Home Finance Agency (HHFA)

The United States federal agency responsible for administration of federal housing and urban renewal programs between 1947 and 1965. The agency was disbanded in 1965 when its functions were transferred to the Department of Housing and Urban Development. The Urban Renewal

Administration and the Community Facilities Administration, units of the HHFA, were also abolished at that time.
See: DEPARTMENT OF HOUSING AND URBAN DEVELOPMENT (HUD); FEDERAL HOUSING ADMINISTRATION (FHA)

Housing and Urban Development Act of 1965

Federal legislation that authorized direct rent subsidies, via payments on behalf of certain low-income tenants (generally elderly, handicapped or those displaced by urban renewal), for rental units in private nonprofit, limited dividend or cooperative housing approved for mortgage insurance under Section 221 (d) 3. The Section 23 low-rent public housing program was also authorized.

In addition, this act (PL 89-117) made rehabilitation grants available to homeowners in urban renewal areas and provided mortgage insurance for land development and grants for concentrated code enforcement programs. Grants for construction of basic water and sewer facilities and neighborhood facilities, such as for recreational or social purposes, were authorized, and the open-space acquisition program was extended to include grants for open-space development.
See: HOUSING ACT OF 1961; NATIONAL HOUSING ACT; SECTION 23 HOUSING PROGRAM; SECTIONS 221 (d) 3 AND 221 (d) 4 HOUSING PROGRAMS

Housing and Urban Development Act of 1968

Federal legislation (PL 90-448) that authorized several major new programs, including riot and flood insurance and new community development. Also created were programs to encourage home ownership by low-income families, including the Section 235 program and the Section 235 programs for cooperative and condominium housing, and the Section 236 housing program of mortgage interest reduction to enable rent reduction for lower-income families. In addition, a program of grants to municipalities to enable land acquisition for public facilities was also initiated.

Other areas addressed by the legislation were the regulation of interstate land sales, introduction of Federal Housing Administration (FHA) mortgage insurance for nonprofit hospitals and demonstration of the use of new technologies in the construction of lower-income housing, which was later named Operation Breakthrough. The Federal National Mortgage Association (FNMA) was divided into two agencies. FNMA became a private corporation under government direction, and the other agency created, named the Government National Mortgage Association, remained a government entity.
See: FEDERAL NATIONAL MORTGAGE ASSOCIATION (FNMA); FEDERAL RIOT REINSURANCE; GOVERNMENT NATIONAL MORTGAGE ASSOCIATION (GNMA); NATIONAL FLOOD INSURANCE PROGRAM; NATIONAL HOUSING ACT; NEW COMMUNITIES ACT OF 1968; SECTION 235 HOUSING PROGRAM; SECTION 236 HOUSING PROGRAM; SECTION 242 PROGRAM

Housing and Urban Development Act of 1970

Federal legislation that established the requirement that the president submit a report on urban growth to Congress every two years. Called the Urban Growth Policy, its principal purpose is to support proper growth and development of new communities and inner city areas and to recommend extensions and amendments of laws relating to housing and urban development.

Other provisions of the act (PL 91-609) authorized federal crime insurance, congregate facilities (such as dining and social rooms) in Section 202 housing for the elderly and public housing, and a demonstration housing allowance program. Provisions for new community development, first authorized in 1968, were extended.

See: FEDERAL CRIME INSURANCE; HOUSING AND COMMUNITY DEVELOPMENT ACT OF 1977; NATIONAL HOUSING ACT; SECTION 202 HOUSING PROGRAM; URBAN GROWTH AND NEW COMMUNITY DEVELOPMENT ACT OF 1970

Housing and Urban-Rural Recovery Act of 1983

Legislation (PL 98-181) that extends funding for numerous housing and community development programs and creates several new programs.

The Community Development Block Grant (CDBG) and Urban Development Action Grant (UDAG) programs are extended through 1986. The requirement that a percentage of CDBG funds be reserved for the Secretary's Discretionary Fund remains although a cap is placed on the amount. These programs must benefit low- and middle-income persons. A requirement for the CDBG program that recipient communities submit a statement certifying that at least 51 percent of funds will benefit these populations is imposed and the statement must also include short- and long-term program objectives. A new provision of the UDAG program permits communities having less than 50,000 in population to form consortia with neighboring low-population municipalities for purposes of applying for UDAG funds.

The Urban Homesteading program is funded through 1985 with required residence extended from 3 years to 5 years before ownership may be obtained, and a demonstration multifamily urban homesteading program is initiated. A minimum of 75 percent of residents of a multifamily homestead must be lower-income families. Also created is a demonstration neighborhood development program of grants to neighborhood development organizations of not more than $50,000 annually for programs that will create permanent jobs or establish businesses in the neighborhood; develop, rehabilitate or manage housing stock; develop delivery mechanisms for neighborhood services; or promulgate voluntary neighborhood improvement efforts. The program requires a competitive application to be judged on the basis of amount of economic distress, benefit to low- and moderate-income persons and participation and voluntary contributions by neighborhood residents and businesses, and funding must be matched by the neighborhood development organizations. Funding is also authorized to continue the Section 312 rehabilitation loan program in 1984 and for the Neighborhood Reinvestment Corporation for 1984 and 1985.

Section 8, Section 202 and Public Housing programs are continued but the Section 8 New Construction program is repealed. A demonstration housing voucher program is authorized, permitting approximately 15,000 very low income families to receive certificates to be used toward their rent, while Section 8 rental assistance is extended on a general basis to people living in single-room-occupancy dwellings (it had previously been permitted on a discretionary basis) and to the elderly and handicapped who live in shared housing arrangements. A demonstration child care program using CDBG funds is authorized for children residing in public housing, and the congregate housing service program of meals to elderly and handicapped residents of public housing is continued. Also authorized are a program to coordinate the housing programs conducted by the Department of Housing and Urban Development (HUD) and those conducted by the Department of Health and Human Services (HHS) for welfare recipients, and another program of grants to enable provision of emergency shelters and programs for the homeless.

A major new program to assist rental housing is authorized under Section 17, consisting of a moderate rehabilitation program with grants to localities based on the CDBG formula, and a new construction program based on a competitive application judged, among other things, on the basis of rental housing shortage severity, cost-effectiveness of proposed projects and the extent to which the project contributes to neighborhood development and mitigates displacement. Funds for the rehabilitation program are given on a 50 percent federal–50 percent local basis and must benefit lower-income families. This program may be undertaken only in neighborhoods where the median income does not exceed 80 percent of the area median income and may not cause the involuntary displacement of very low income families by those in a higher income bracket. The new construction program, which may also be used for substantial rehabilitation of buildings, requires that at least 20 percent of its units be occupied by persons with an income that does not exceed 80 percent of the median income of the area, and may not be converted to condominium or cooperative status for at least 20 years. The new housing voucher program is expected to be used in conjunction with this program. Localities receiving grants may administer them as grant or loan programs to developers.

The Housing and Urban-Rural Recovery Act of 1983 also reauthorizes and funds housing programs conducted by the Farmers Home Administration and authorizes a new rural housing preservation grant program in which localities may use grants to offer loans or grants to persons or organizations wishing to rehabilitate housing for low and very low income families and persons. The program, to be used in municipalities with populations of 10,000 or less, is eligible for owner or renter-occupied single-family or multifamily housing.

Federal Housing Administration (FHA) mortgage insurance programs are extended and modified and the requirement that FHA interest rates be set by law is rescinded. A demonstration mortgage reinsurance program is authorized that allows private mortgage insurance companies to reinsure FHA mortgages in an attempt to reduce federal risk and administrative costs. The Section 242 hospital insurance program is extended to public hospitals, and the Section 232 intermediate care facility program is extended to "board and care homes." The Section 245 graduated payment mortgage program is extended to multifamily housing. Three new FHA insured mortgage programs are created as well: Section 251 adjustable-rate single-family mortgages, Section 252 shared-appreciation mortgages for single-family housing and Section 253 shared-appreciation mortgages for multifamily housing.

Other programs reauthorized by this act are the federal flood insurance program and the crime insurance program, while the riot reinsurance program is terminated. Funding is authorized for the National Institute of Building Sciences, the Solar Energy and Energy Conservation Bank and the weatherization program conducted by the Department of Energy, and commitments are set for the Government National Mortgage Association's (GNMA) Mortgage-Backed Securities Program for 1984 and 1985. Special assistance and emergency mortgage purchase assistance functions of GNMA are repealed, however.
See: HOUSING AND COMMUNITY DEVELOPMENT AMENDMENTS OF 1981

Housing Assistance Plan (HAP)

A required housing plan, necessary for allocation of funds to communities under the federal Community Development Block Grant (CDBG) program.

In a HAP each entitlement community or urban county must present a statistical profile concerning the condition of its existing housing stock in terms of the number of standard and substandard units and the number of substandard units it has that are suitable for rehabilitation. It must also set forth the housing assistance needs of lower-income households and must do so by household type (i.e., elderly, small family and large family). For each of these types of households, the plan must specifically consider the needs of the very low income households, those households expected to be involuntarily displaced and those expected to reside in the community based upon such factors as planned employment. Other factors that must be taken into account include numbers of lower-income minority households and other lower-income groups with special housing needs, such as handicapped persons.

This profile is used to develop a three-year housing goal that considers the number of units to be assisted in terms of rehabilitation or new construction by tenure, and the number of lower-income households that would receive rental subsidies by type of household. General locations of proposed projects must be indicated. Once submitted, housing assistance plans are reviewed by the U.S. Department of Housing and Urban Development to ensure that all requirements are met.
See: COMMUNITY DEVELOPMENT BLOCK GRANT (CDBG); HOUSING AND COMMUNITY DEVELOPMENT AMENDMENTS OF 1981

Housing Authority

An official body, created under state law, that is eligible for federal support to provide decent, sanitary housing for low-income persons. Authorized by the Housing Act of 1937 (PL 73-479) as amended, these bodies are officially known as public housing authorities (PHAs) and are usually municipal, though some are countywide or statewide; the authority board members are appointed for fixed terms of office. By virtue of the required state enabling legislation to qualify for federal assistance, housing authorities have the legal ability to float bonds for the construction of public housing and are eligible to receive annual support from the Department of Housing and Urban Development (HUD).

The primary responsibility of most housing authorities is administration of the public housing program. Housing authorities also often manage state housing programs, Section 8 Moderate Rehabilitation programs and Section 8 Existing Housing programs.

Housing authorities generally have met their mandate to provide housing that the poor can afford, in part because they have independent boards that are not responsive to local political pressure. Because of their independence and their strong association with low-income housing, however, housing authorities are often viewed as a political liability, and some recent housing production programs, such as Section 8 New Construction, have avoided or reduced housing authority control and visibility. Housing authorities face another obstacle in that they are dependent upon the federal government for their operating, debt service and modernization funds as well as for the guidelines under which they function, making their ability to build and operate housing largely dependent upon the federal commitment.
See: PUBLIC HOUSING; SECTION 8 HOUSING PROGRAM

Housing Choice

The availability of different styles and types of housing in a variety of price ranges to various segments of a housing market. The primary factor influencing housing choice for a household is income, and lower-income households generally have a much more limited selection of housing and are forced to spend a larger proportion of their income on housing costs. Housing type, location, types of amenities and the nature of the community are all a matter of individual choice, within the constraints of income.

Vacancy rates may be considered to be one indication of the extent of available housing choice. Higher vacancy rates permit more mobility for housing consumers and facilitate movements within the housing market.

See: FILTERING; HOUSEHOLD SIZE; HOUSEHOLD TYPE; HOUSING LOCATION; HOUSING STOCK; HOUSING TENURE; HOUSING TYPE; REDLINING; VACANCY RATE

Housing Code

A code that stipulates the minimum sanitary, ventilation, safety and maintenance requirements for existing housing. Housing codes can also restrict the number of occupants per dwelling unit, require an adequate level of plumbing and heating, and prescribe the minimum space needed per occupant.

Although housing codes can help to upgrade existing housing, problems are often encountered in the proper enforcement as well as the adequacy of many municipal codes. The existence of local housing codes in the United States is largely a post-World War II phenomenon spurred by requirements of the urban renewal program.

See: BUILDING CODE; CODE ENFORCEMENT; SUBSTANDARD HOUSING

Housing Counseling

Information and advice on financial management, property maintenance, available housing programs, energy conservation and other matters related to housing that is available from local agencies providing this service. The U.S. Department of Housing and Urban Development (HUD) provides a free program for home buyers, homeowners and tenants of HUD-insured and assisted housing, in which approved local agencies offer counseling to low- and moderate-income families. Some of the agencies receive grants as partial reimbursement of their costs.

Housing for Families

Housing units of sufficient size for families, possessing amenities important to this group, such as play areas for children. Options for families in the American rental housing market are increasingly narrowed, particularly if the families are large, as the shortage of affordable rental housing encourages landlords to restrict tenancy to only those tenants who are considered most desirable. Landlords often equate children with increased maintenance costs and noise as well as occasional vandalism, and assuming they can rent their apartments without permitting children, would often prefer to do so. A University of Michigan survey conducted in 1980 discovered that 26 percent of rental properties had policies prohibiting families with children as compared to 17 percent with such a policy in 1974, indicating that this tendency is increasing. In reaction to this problem, many municipal ordinances prohibiting discrimination against families in rental housing have been passed recently. In 1982 the California Supreme Court ruled that a failure to rent to a family solely because the family contains children is in violation of that state's civil rights law.

Another aspect of the problem of providing housing for families is the growing popularity of age-restricted condominium and cooperative developments. For the developer the age-restricted housing development, oriented toward mature adults and senior citizens, represents a means of tapping a growing and relatively affluent segment of society that, because of prior home ownership, may not be materially affected by high mortgage rates. Many communities also encourage this type of development because the residents generally require many fewer and less costly public services than would families with children.

See: AGE-ORIENTED COMMUNITY; HOUSEHOLD SIZE; HOUSEHOLD TYPE; HOUSING CHOICE; HOUSING TYPE; OVERCROWDING; RENTAL HOUSING

Housing for the Elderly

Housing that is located and designed to meet the special needs and accommodate the changing living arrangements of an elderly population. In recognition of the economic, social and functional losses encountered by many older individuals, housing for the elderly represents an attempt to provide a physical environment conducive to maintenance of an independent life-style.

Development of housing for the elderly has evolved largely as a refinement of post-World War II government housing programs. In the United States the Section 202 direct loan program for builders of housing for this population has stimulated the bulk of units currently extant. Within the public housing program, congregate facilities may now be provided as well as a congregate meals program for the elderly and the Section 8 program has enabled other low income elderly to find suitable units. Certain home improvement loan programs also give preferential rates to the elderly, and permit funds to be used to make modifications to enable an elderly person to be more self-sufficient, e.g., for installing hand rails or reducing utility costs. Development of large-scale retirement communities has provided for the housing needs of the more affluent elderly.

In Canada, several provinces have made grants available for housing for the elderly, in some cases supplying up to one-third of capital costs. European countries and cities have provided public housing as well as a variety of production incentives including capital grants, interest and operating subsidies and loans and grants for building improvements. Housing allowances are also provided to enable the elderly to stay in housing that is escalating in cost.

Although much of what has been built in the last 25 years has consisted of medium- and high-rise structures, single-family homes, townhouses and low-rise apartments have also been constructed, containing from 100 to 800 units. For planning purposes, however, a range of 100 to 300 units per development is considered optimal to be able to support common services and facilities but still be able to integrate the development into the community fabric.

The type of housing to be provided, the type of common facilities and the relationship of private to public areas is largely determined by the level of independence of the population to be served. Housing can be arranged to maximize individual privacy, with only a community center for social interaction, or it can be designed to foster interaction at all levels of daily functioning. The location of the housing should take into consideration a number of factors, including proximity to neighborhood shopping and community facilities and accessibility to mass transit.

Site design should consider the amount of space required for parking and service areas and the types of outdoor space needed to accommodate recreational activities. In order to accommodate changing needs, common areas should be designed for flexibility of use. Within the units and public areas, special features for safety and comfort should include provisions for access by the handicapped or physically impaired, use of special surface materials to eliminate hazards and minimize cleaning, and some form of communication system to obtain assistance in times of crisis.

As housing needs of the elderly increase, programs are being developed to provide housing in unconventional ways. In Australia a "granny flat" program operated by the Ministry of Housing provides temporary factory-built housing that is located at the home of the elderly person's family. Also called "elder cottages" and "echo housing," these units can be provided in the form of mobile homes that are temporarily attached to an adult child's house. Although zoning laws in the United States generally prevent them, this form of housing for the elderly is permitted by special permit in Frederick County, Maryland and is being considered by other U.S. communities. Home-sharing, a program that is becoming increasingly more popular in the United States and is actively promoted by many nonprofit organizations serving the elderly, encourages the matching of persons with extra room in their homes with others seeking affordable housing. Either, or both, the "home provider" or "home seeker" may be elderly.
See: CONGREGATE HOUSING; HOME EQUITY CONVERSION; ILLEGAL CONVERSION; PLANNING FOR THE ELDERLY; RETIREMENT COMMUNITY

Housing Location
The proximity of housing to community facilities, most notably schools, public transportation, shopping areas and places of employment. The distance from these facilities is one gauge of housing value and may be a critical element in the choice of a housing site for a given population. As an example, housing for the elderly requires a location within a short distance of stores and mass transit.

There are no general proximity standards for housing. In densely urbanized areas, walking distance to shopping areas or employment may be highly prized, while in some suburban areas a short drive might be considered to be that equivalent. Location preferences within a community may also change over time as a result of many influences, including improvements to community facilities.

In the redevelopment of urban areas, emphasis is now placed on designs that permit walking and short transit

rides to reach most facilities. In new town development optimum distances from various facilities are established, and housing is located within these distances.
See: NEIGHBORHOOD UNIT CONCEPT; SCATTER-SITE HOUSING

Housing Plan
A policy guide to the role of government in stimulating the construction of housing by the private sector, regulating the development and maintenance of housing, and meeting those housing needs not addressed by the private sector. A housing plan is often an element of a comprehensive plan.

Most housing plans can be divided into three parts. The first part consists of an analysis of the housing market and an identification of present and future needs. Included in this analysis is an examination of the supply, condition and demand for housing; vacancy rates; replacement rates; the characteristics of the physical community and services that support housing; and the demographic and economic characteristics of the population. Also included is an evaluation of the availability and distribution of private financial resources that examines interest rates, credit policies and lending practices, and an assessment of the effect of government policies and regulations on housing. Emerging from this analysis is an identification of deficiencies in the market and an estimate of future housing needs.

The second section of the plan contains goals and objectives. Most plans contain general statements concerning public health and safety, protection of property values and elimination of substandard housing, as well as more specific goals relating to the amount and type of new construction and rehabilitation needed. The third section of the plan focuses on implementation. Since most housing is provided by the private sector, an emphasis is often placed on reducing construction and rehabilitation costs through such means as tax exemptions, grants, interest subsidies, tax-exempt bonds and low interest loans. Plans may also address such areas as capital spending to provide appropriate community infrastructure, and the effectiveness of land use controls and building regulations.
See: COMPREHENSIVE PLAN; HOUSING ASSISTANCE PLAN (HAP)

Housing Programs for Native Americans
Federal programs designed to assist in the improvement of housing conditions for Native Americans.

One program, authorized by the United States Housing Act of 1937 as amended by the Housing and Community Development Act of 1974, provides a variety of housing opportunities for low-income Indians and Alaska natives through Indian Housing Authorities (IHAs). IHAs build and operate rental housing in a manner similar to the operations of public housing authorities. In addition or instead, they may provide "mutual-help" home ownership projects, allowing the home buyer-occupant to contribute either the site, building materials, labor or cash and to provide monthly payments toward the purchase of the house as well as all maintenance. IHAs fund these projects through the sale of tax-exempt obligations and receive annual contributions from the Department of Housing and Urban Development (HUD) toward debt service and, for rental projects, toward maintenance costs, reserve funds and maintenance of low rents.

A program that is administered by the Bureau of Indian Affairs in the Department of the Interior, called the Indian Housing Improvement Program (HIP), provides grants for housing rehabilitation, construction when absolutely necessary and resident training programs in housing construction and maintenance. Authorized by the Snyder Act of 1921 (PL 67-85), it enables Indian tribes in remote locations or with few families to improve their housing conditions without forming an Indian Housing Authority, which is required for the HUD program. While these programs are specifically designed for low-income Native Americans, other housing programs administered by HUD, the Farmers Home Administration and the Federal Housing Administration either contain funding reserves for or are open to Native Americans.
See: RURAL HOUSING PROGRAMS

Housing Standards

Criteria that help to determine the adequacy of housing so that housing conditions may be assessed. Although often difficult to measure, among the standards frequently considered in evaluating housing adequacy are cost, condition, degree of crowding, availability of choice, neighborhood quality and accessibility to facilities and services.

Housing standards reflect the economic, cultural and social values of a population applied to its housing, and housing that may be considered substandard in Western nations is often acceptable in underdeveloped nations.
See: CODE ENFORCEMENT; HOUSING; HOUSING CHOICE; HOUSING CODE; HOUSING LOCATION; HOUSING TYPE; OVERCROWDING; SUBSTANDARD HOUSING

Housing Stock

The total supply of dwelling units in a given locality. The amount of housing stock continually changes through new construction, rehabilitation of uninhabited units, conversion of nonresidential properties and conversion of single-family homes into multifamily uses. At the same time, the housing stock is reduced through demolition, necessary because of deterioration, natural disasters, urban redevelopment, or highway or other public construction.

Housing stock may be categorized from a variety of perspectives and then analyzed in terms of that category. Housing type, housing tenure, housing cost, housing size and housing quality are different means of viewing the housing stock.
See: DEMOLITION; FILTERING; HOUSING; HOUSING CHOICE; HOUSING STANDARDS; HOUSING TENURE; HOUSING TYPE; ILLEGAL CONVERSION; SUBSTANDARD HOUSING; VACANCY RATE

Housing Subsidy

A supplement to household income designed to bring the cost of housing within the economic reach of lower-income groups. Housing subsidies are generally of two types: (1) those vested in a housing unit or (2) money paid to families or landlords by the government. Prior to the 1970s there was an emphasis in the United States on subsidies to housing units through construction of public housing and subsidized interest rates to nonprofit sponsors of low-income housing. In contrast, under the Section 8 program, which was authorized in 1974, families are given the difference between what it is determined that they can afford to pay for housing and fair market rentals.

Subsidies to individuals are portable. The thrust behind such a program is the integration of low-income groups into the mainstream of community life and a reliance upon landlords' receiving fair market rents to bring existing housing stock up to housing code standards. The cost to the government per family subsidized is much less than the cost of construction of new units. Subsidies to families do not, however, directly enlarge the stock of units available.

Housing Tenure

A term that describes whether a housing unit is owner-occupied or occupied by a renter.
See: HOUSING

Housing Type

The diversity of forms and arrangements that housing may take. One common means by which housing may be classified is by its physical structure, as in high-rise, low-rise, detached, cluster housing or row housing. Another way of categorizing housing type is by the number of dwelling units that are found within each structure, as in single-family housing, two-family dwellings or multifamily buildings.

Within each of these categories, further distinctions may be made. As examples, modern single-family homes may assume many styles and configurations, such as Cape Cod, split-level or ranch, while multifamily buildings may be garden apartments or high-rise and served by an elevator. Although condominiums and cooperatives are often thought of as a physical type of housing, they are actually ownership arrangements that may be found in a variety of physical forms.
See: HOUSING

Howard, Sir Ebenezer (1850–1928)

A self-trained British planner who founded the influential garden city movement. Although Ebenezer Howard supported himself for much of his life as a shorthand reporter, he became increasingly concerned with the problems of urban life and the overcrowding found in cities. In 1898 he published *To-morrow: A Peaceful Path to Real Reform* (later reissued as *Garden Cities of To-morrow*), in which he put forth the idea of the garden city as a solution to many planning and social problems.

As a result of the attention the book generated, Howard founded the Garden City Association in 1899 (which later became the Town and Country Planning Association) to help promote his theories. In 1903 he formed a limited-dividend company, First Garden City Ltd., and with the help of his supporters, successfully founded Letchworth, located north of London. A second planned community, Welwyn Garden City, was also begun in 1919. In each instance, Howard demonstrated the viability of his ideas and also developed a mechanism by which garden cities could be financed.

The examples set at Letchworth and Welwyn Garden City helped to secure passage of the New Towns Act of 1946. They also had a significant effect upon the evolution of planning in the United States, such as the later construction of the greenbelt towns by the Resettlement Administration.

Ebenezer Howard served as first president of the International Garden Cities and Town Planning Association, which subsequently became the International Federation for Housing and Planning. He was knighted in 1927, one year before his death.
See: GARDEN CITY; LETCHWORTH, ENGLAND; NEW TOWN; NEW TOWNS ACT 1946; OSBORN, SIR FREDERICK JAMES; WELWYN GARDEN CITY, ENGLAND

Human Scale

An aesthetic concept that is derived from the size of the human body as it relates to the architectural and natural environment. The term refers to objects or spaces that, to the individual observer, appear to be proportional to the dimensions of the human anatomy.

As a design tool, human dimensions have historically been considered a building block for the development of architectural space standards. Depending on the intent of the designer, these can be utilized to establish a sense of intimacy, as in a small courtyard, or by contrast, to establish a sense of drama or power, as in a monumental edifice.
See: SCALE OF DEVELOPMENT

Human Settlements

Locations where groups of people have established permanent residence, generally in connection with occupational pursuits. This may be contrasted with nomadic settlements and campsites, which are of a temporary nature.

Human settlements began when tribal groups developed rudimentary agricultural skills and started farming land. While simple farming communities are still common, and are prevalent in certain parts of the world, huge and highly complex communities with a myriad of physical and social problems have evolved. Planners study the range of settlement types that have occurred throughout history to understand the relationships of urban functions, and a science of these relationships, called ekistics, has been created.
See: EKISTICS

Hundred-Year Storm

A storm of an intensity that recurs, on the average, once every 100 years or that has a 1 percent chance of occurring in any given year, measured during a 24-hour time period.
See: BASE FLOOD; STORM DRAINAGE SYSTEM; STORM FREQUENCY

Hydroelectric Power

The conversion of the energy produced by falling water into electricity. This is usually accomplished, with the aid of turbine generators, by creating a large storage lake through dam construction. The amount of energy that can be produced is strongly influenced by "head," which is the distance that the water stored behind the dam falls before reaching the foot of the dam. A larger head means a greater energy potential.

Water power has been used in various forms since at least the 1st century B.C., when a horizontal waterwheel was developed. The use of water to generate electricity, however, dates back to the latter part of the 19th century. An early major installation was developed at Niagara Falls in 1895.

Because of the various problems associated with the production of power using oil- or nuclear-fueled plants, hydroelectric power is attracting renewed interest. In Quebec a $4 billion hydroelectric complex is under construction at James Bay in the Canadian subarctic. It is projected that by about the year 1990, Quebec will be producing 50 percent of its electricity using hydroelectric power.

Small, abandoned hydroelectric stations, particularly in the Northeast, are also being reopened as they gradually become economically feasible to operate. For example, Paterson, New Jersey received a license in 1981 to renovate and reopen a hydroelectric plant that had been closed for 67 years. Other reopenings have begun or been completed in New York, Connecticut and Massachusetts.

There are, however, a number of factors that tend to limit the development of hydroelectric power. Among these are the high cost of dam construction, the environmental problems associated with the damming of rivers and the shortage of suitable hydroelectric plant sites. In addition, peak water flow occurs in spring and late fall, when there is the lowest demand for electricity.
See: ELECTRIC POWER GENERATION AND TRANSMISSION; PUMPED STORAGE POWER SYSTEM; RENEWABLE ENERGY SOURCES; TIDAL POWER

Hydrofoil

A vehicle that travels on an air cushion above the water, powered by gas-turbine engines and driven by propellers. Hydrofoils are capable of traveling at speeds ranging from 25 to 75 knots and have been built in various configurations that can carry up to 260 passengers and 32 cars. Smaller vessels are used for transportation over marsh and flood areas as well as for recreation.

Hydrofoils—often called Hovercraft, a trade name—

have been used predominantly to provide ferry service across bodies of water between 3 and 25 miles wide. A ferry service across the English Channel has been in operation since the early 1970s and has largely replaced air ferry service and, to a lesser extent, conventional sea ferry service. Hydrofoil ferry service is also in use in Canada, the United States, Sweden, Italy and the Soviet Union.
See: FERRY

Hydrographic Survey

A survey of a body of water—such as an ocean, lake or stream—conducted to obtain data on its characteristics that may be used for navigation, engineering projects or other purposes. Particular attention is paid to such factors as tidal currents or fluctuation in water level, underwater relief, water depth, stream discharge and the characteristics of the adjoining shoreland.

Hydrologic Study

A systematic assessment of various aspects of the waters of a geographic area. Hydrologic studies may be con-ducted for such purposes as the quantitative evaluation of the water supplies of an area; soil conservation; flood control; the design of dams and reservoirs; and the determination of probable effects of proposed development and means of ameliorating these effects.

Among the types of measurements that may be made during the course of a hydrologic study are rate and amount of infiltration; intensity and volume of precipitation; extent of groundwater supplies; and presence of various chemicals in water supplies. The data may then be used, with the aid of models, to forecast probable future conditions.
See: WATER RESOURCES MANAGEMENT

Hypothesis Testing

A systematic statistical process that allows the validity of a hypothesis about a specific factor or event to be evaluated.
See: NULL HYPOTHESIS

I

Ice-Skating Rink

A flat ice surface that may be frozen by natural means or by mechanical techniques that can also maintain the ice in warmer weather.

Artificial rinks—provided in many shopping centers, multiple-use urban centers and municipal parks—have pipes placed beneath the surface of the ice that continually freeze the surface. Natural ice rinks are flat areas of ground, tennis courts, football fields, parking lots or other areas on which water is sprayed to a desired thickness and permitted to freeze. Ponds and lakes that freeze to a sufficient depth are also desirable for skating and are often monitored for ice thickness by recreation departments to ensure safety.

Skating rinks may be used for figure skating, hockey or curling. For hockey an area of 85 × 185 feet (26 × 56 meters) is necessary.

Illegal Conversion

The alteration of a residential or commercial building to a use or density not permitted by the zoning ordinance. The issue of illegal conversion has become a problem in many cities and suburban communities, as homeowners have added kitchens, bathrooms and separate entrances to single-family dwellings and created separate rental units. Although empty nesters with limited income and surplus living space are one group that often turns to the creation of illegal accessory apartments as a means of maintaining their home, other groups also find this practice expedient. For young couples, creation of an accessory apartment can allow them to afford home ownership. Single-parent families and those who travel extensively but don't wish to leave their homes unoccupied are also often motivated to create accessory apartments.

The illegal conversion of housing into use for two or more families can exert strain on municipal services, such as refuse collection and sewerage systems, while denying the municipality the property taxes to which it is entitled. On the positive side, however, the creation of accessory apartments offers a means of tapping surplus residential space that was going unused and expanding the housing stock of communities that are often suffering an acute housing shortage, particularly of rental units. Because of this and because of the prevalence of the practice, a number of communities have taken steps to legalize accessory apartments. In Babylon, New York legalization is operated as a special permit procedure, while in other communities, such as Westport, Connecticut, it is an option open only to homeowners and tenants over 62 years old.
See: CONVERSION; EMPTY NESTERS; HOUSEHOLD TYPE; HOUSING; HOUSING CHOICE; HOUSING FOR THE ELDERLY

Illuminated Sign

A sign that is artificially lighted. Illuminated signs may have direct illumination, such as light behind a translucent sign that illuminates it from the rear, or neon or other tubular lighting on its face. Flashing signs, with changing lighting or colors, are another form of direct illumination. Signs may also have indirect illumination—that is, artificial lighting projected from an external source, often arranged to prevent direct rays from projecting into surrounding areas.

Business signs vary in their use of lighting and are generally regulated by zoning requirements, sign regulations or design standards. Billboards usually have indirect lighting, as do most highway signs.
See: ADVERTISING SIGNS; DESIGN STANDARDS; SIGN REGULATION

Imhoff Tank

A two-compartment tank, used in the treatment of sewage, in which both sedimentation (primary treatment) and sludge digestion (secondary sludge treatment) can take place. Invented in Germany in 1904, the Imhoff tank is used in small treatment plants because it is compact and requires relatively little supervision. Larger plants must use separate sedimentation and sludge digestion tanks.

In an Imhoff tank, settleable solids collect in its upper compartment and then pass into the lower compartment, where anaerobic digestion occurs; sludge is then periodically removed from this digestion compartment.
See: PRIMARY TREATMENT; SECONDARY TREATMENT; SEDIMENTATION TANK; SLUDGE DIGESTION; SUSPENDED SOLIDS (SS)

Impact Sound

The sound arising from the collision of two masses. Impact sound, also known as impulsive sound, is characterized by a sudden onset and a short duration. Typical examples of this phenomenon are gunshots and sonic booms.

Generally considered to be of greater annoyance than a steady-state sound of a comparable level, an impact noise can startle those exposed to it. A variety of factors related to impact sound, such as the number of repetitions of the sound that occur, help to determine the extent to which hearing may be harmed.
See: NOISE POLLUTION; SONIC BOOM; STEADY-STATE SOUND

Impact Zoning

A fairly new type of zoning in which the emphasis is upon evaluating the potential adverse impact of a new development upon a community's environment, its public utility system and other community services, and its fiscal structure. In an impact zoning system, an ordinance generally defines the standards that must be met before the development can be approved in terms of these types of considerations. Each proposed development is then subjected to intensive analysis in terms of its projected impact upon the community as part of a standard review process.

Variations of this technique—which may be viewed as an extension of the performance standards approach to a wider range of community concerns, including fiscal concerns—are sometimes used by communities attempting to regulate and manage their rate of growth.
See: FISCAL IMPACT ANALYSIS; GROWTH MANAGEMENT; PERFORMANCE STANDARDS; ZONING

Impervious Surfaces

Surfaces such as concrete or asphalt-paved streets or parking lots that prevent rainfall from infiltrating the soil and can increase the amount of runoff dramatically. This has implications for the magnitude of urban flooding as well as for the pollution of water bodies.

As a partial solution to this problem, various types of permeable surfaces are being developed that can be used on less heavily traveled roadways, parking lots, sidewalks and driveways. Porous pavement, such as porous asphalt applied over a gravel base, can allow infiltration and reduce the need for drainage facilities. Although this type of pavement is still in the developmental stage because of a tendency to clog, it has future promise. There are, however, other porous surfaces, such as lattice concrete blocks, through which grass can grow. Gravel and crushed rock is a simple and inexpensive type of porous paving that may be suitable in a number of applications.
See: FLOOD CONTROL; PAVEMENT; RUNOFF

Impound

1. To collect and store water for such purposes as the generation of hydroelectric power, provision of drinking water or irrigation.
2. A reservoir or other water body used for water storage.
See: DAM; RESERVOIR

Improved Land

Raw land to which a water supply, a sewerage system, streets and other basic facilities have been added. The term is sometimes used, too, to describe land that has also been developed with structures; planners generally refer to such land, however, as "developed land."
See: IMPROVEMENTS; RAW LAND

Improvements

Permanent additions to real property that are designed to make the property more useful or to increase its value, such as buildings and paved driveways. On tax rolls the assessed value of improvements is frequently shown separately from that of land, making it possible to determine the relative value of each.

In Accordance with a Comprehensive Plan

A phrase taken from the Standard State Zoning Enabling Act of 1922, which provided that all zoning ordinances "shall be in accordance with a comprehensive plan." Following the example of this model act, many states included this provision when they passed their zoning enabling acts.

Despite the inclusion of this phrase, municipalities tended to ignore, for decades, any relationship between a zoning ordinance and a comprehensive planning process. The zoning ordinance, in effect, was thought of as the comprehensive plan. The courts tended to support this position as well, requiring only that an ordinance be applied comprehensively with internal consistency. Communities were not required to have a plan, nor did their zoning ordinance have to agree with the plan if one existed.

Relatively recently a movement has begun to require comprehensive plans that are based upon extensive study and analysis; in addition, zoning must be consistent with these plans. Contributing to this movement has been the development of flexible zoning controls, which can be abused in the absence of an official public policy governing land development, and the increased use of growth management programs, which again require the existence of comprehensive plans and programs. A number of states—including California, Florida, Oregon, Kentucky, Nebraska and Colorado—have adopted legislation that requires comprehensive planning.

See: COMPREHENSIVE PLAN; FLEXIBLE REGULATIONS; GROWTH MANAGEMENT; STANDARD STATE ZONING ENABLING ACT; ZONING

Incentive Zoning

Zoning ordinance provisions in which developers receive bonuses, typically permission to build at a higher density or higher floor area ratio, in exchange for offering certain types of amenities that the community considers important.

The types of public amenities encouraged by incentive zoning can vary markedly with individual community needs. In dense business districts public plazas, arcades, direct access to transportation terminals, indoor atriums, through-block passageways and urban parklets are often gained through incentive zoning. In residential areas bonuses may be given in exchange for the development of a specified number of subsidized low- or middle-income units within a private development or for the incorporation of certain design features, such as underground parking or protection of sensitive environmental features.

A zoning ordinance that seeks to make use of development incentives should include a system that clearly delineates the nature and amount of the permitted bonus for each type of amenity. Despite this, it is sometimes possible for a community to give away a great deal of additional development and not receive commensurate value in public amenities. For example, many questioned the value of the vast stretches of cement public plaza that sprang up in Manhattan's business districts as a result of incentive provisions in the New York City zoning ordinance. In exchange for these little-used and poorly designed plazas, buildings were allowed to be constructed that were disproportionately large and created undesirable concentrations of congestion. New ways of using incentive zoning, such as through the preservation of theaters in the Broadway theater district, as well as increased control of the additional development are being considered as a remedy to this problem.

Incentive zoning appears likely to become increasingly popular, particularly since it is perceived as a means of solving certain difficult-to-resolve community problems and obtaining public amenities that the municipality cannot afford to construct. The pioneering efforts of the first communities to use this technique have suggested many more applications of incentive zoning that can be used in the future.

See: FLEXIBLE REGULATIONS; NEGOTIATION; ZONING

Incineration

Controlled burning or oxidation of waste into gases and a residue that contains little or no combustible material. Incineration was initially tried in England in the 1870s and was first introduced into the United States in about 1885. It is an efficient means of reducing waste volume by about 80 percent to 90 percent and allows densely developed urban areas to make the most efficient use of the remaining capacity of their sanitary landfills. Increasingly, new municipal plants incorporate resource recovery, in which energy generated during the incineration process is captured and used for various purposes.

An inevitable problem associated with incineration is the generation of air pollution. Carbon monoxide, carbon dioxide, nitrogen oxides, hydrocarbons and particulates are among the end products of incineration. Because of federal air pollution control regulations, a variety of equipment—such as expansion chambers, fly ash collectors, wet scrubbers and electrostatic precipitators—is used to keep emissions at acceptable levels, sometimes at great expense.

Siting of central incineration plants that will serve a sizable population is usually a topic of controversy, as is generally the siting of any waste disposal facility. Any large facility and its surrounding road network must be able to accommodate the expected volume of truck traffic. Adequate space must also be available for the storage of any waste that cannot be processed immediately. Special incentives are sometimes offered by a larger regional agency to a municipality if it will agree to accept a central incineration plant. Payment in lieu of taxes is one type of incentive that can compensate a community for the loss of an industrial site and the inconveniences of accepting the incineration plant. Another lure that has been offered, where resource recovery systems are planned, is the promise of special energy rates on the power generated by the plant.

See: AIR POLLUTION; CODISPOSAL; RESOURCE RECOVERY; SANITARY LANDFILL; SOLID WASTE MANAGEMENT

Income Approach Appraisal

Together with the cost and market data approaches, one of the three basic approaches to appraising real estate.

The income approach arrives at an estimate of value by discounting to present value the anticipated future net income to be generated by a property over its remaining useful life. The first step in this approach is to estimate gross fair rental value based on current income of the property and comparable properties. The fair rental value of the property must be adjusted by taking an allowance for vacancy loss. Second, expenses of operating the property in the future must be estimated and subtracted from estimated gross rental value to arrive at an estimate of net income. In the third step, the remaining economic life of the improvement on the property must be estimated. This is the anticipated period that the property will generate the estimated fair rental value. Fourth, the appropriate capitalization rate must be chosen in order to discount the estimated future stream of net income to present value. The choice of an appropriate rate is critical, since small differences in the capitalization rate may produce large differences in estimated value. In addition, the rate must be chosen with consideration to allowing the property owner to recapture his investment in the improved portion of the real estate over its remaining useful life.

The income approach to value is most significant when income-producing property is being appraised, since prospective purchasers are most apt to evaluate such property based on its future income potential.

See: APPRAISAL; APPRAISED VALUE; CAPITALIZATION

Income Tax

A tax on the annual income and capital gains of individuals and businesses that, in the United States, accounts for over 80 percent of federal revenues and for a substantial percentage of state revenues. While the primary function of an income tax is to raise revenues, it has also been found to be an important tool in stabilizing economic fluctuations. In addition, in some countries an income tax has been used as a wealth transfer mechanism.

While the federal government's marginal rate of taxation is usually greatest, many states now impose their own income tax as well. Several hundred cities also levy an income tax on individuals, businesses and commuters to offset growing budgetary expenses; the City of Philadelphia was the first to do so, in 1939. State and local income taxes vary in the degree to which they are graduated and in what they tax—e.g., earned income; investment income, such as dividends and interest; and capital gains.

The effect of the local income tax on land use decisions was shown to be considerable during the 1960s and 1970s, when many northern industries moved to southern states with no income tax or to states with lower tax rates; cheaper labor, land and energy sources; and lower real estate taxes. These same pressures cause business and personal moves among localities within the same region with differing state or municipal income taxes.

See: PROPERTY TAX; SALES TAX

Incrementalism

A pragmatic theory of growth and change, derived from the field of public administration and developed in response to the frequent inability of long-term comprehen-sive planning to meet its objectives, that accepts the slow process of change as being most practical and desirable. Incrementalists believe that long-term comprehensive planning is neither possible nor realistic. Rather, planners should proceed cautiously, planning and implementing on a step-by-step basis and responding to issues only as they emerge.

While plans are typically implemented incrementally, most planners still generally believe that some type of comprehensive long-term plan is needed in order to provide a framework within which planning can take place. Such a long-term plan is based upon a serious consideration of goals and objectives and an evaluation of differing alternative courses of action.

See: COMPREHENSIVE PLAN

Incubator Building

1. A building that offers space at low rentals and is consequently attractive to small, newly formed businesses. Typically, labor-intensive manufacturers or businesses requiring only about 10,000 square feet (929 square meters) of space will locate in an incubator building until they are ready to expand. Many municipalities have used public funds to finance incubator buildings as a means of supporting the formation and survival of new business ventures. The city of Buffalo, for example, which built one of the first municipally sponsored incubator buildings, offers low rentals to a business for two years. In addition to low rents, municipalities often provide free business assistance to incubator tenants.

2. A building designed for the testing of new techniques of construction and operation.

See: ECONOMIC DEVELOPMENT; ECONOMIC DEVELOPMENT INCENTIVES

Independent Living for the Disabled

A program, conducted by the Office of the Special Advisor for the Handicapped in the Department of Housing and Urban Development, that is designed to prevent discrimination against physically and mentally disabled persons by assuring access to federally assisted housing.

Numerous studies have shown that the costs to both individuals and the government are much higher if the disabled are institutionalized than if they can live independently in residential units. While some federal housing programs require that a certain number of units be made available to the disabled, many do not have a minimum requirement. Under Section 504 of the Rehabilitation Act of 1973, discrimination against the disabled is prohibited.

See: PLANNING FOR THE DISABLED; SECTION 8 HOUSING PROGRAM

Indicator Species

A type of organism whose presence can help to provide information on prevalent environmental conditions in a particular ecosystem. Indicator species, usually plants or micro-organisms, are generally sensitive to certain types of environmental changes. A particular species may also be designated an indicator for the purposes of environmental studies because it lends itself to the type of study being conducted. Examples of indicator species are sea lettuce, which may indicate eutrophication when found growing in dense concentrations, and mosses, which frequently are indicative of acid soil.

Indirect Source

A facility that attracts or has the potential of attracting mobile sources of air pollution. Included in this category are buildings and structures, including parking structures; roads; and real property, including parking lots. Provisions are made in the Clean Air Act Amendments for including an indirect source review program, if a state desires, in its state implementation plan. In such a program, indirect air pollution sources would be reviewed on a case by case basis, and measures would be taken, when necessary, to prevent proposed new or modified indirect sources from attracting sufficient numbers of mobile sources as to prevent maintenance of national ambient air quality standards.

See: AIR POLLUTION; MOBILE SOURCE; STATE IMPLEMENTATION PLAN (SIP)

Indoor Recreation Center

A building in which a variety of recreational facilities and instructional opportunities are provided. Indoor recreation centers are generally sponsored by quasi-public agencies, such as YMCAs; by public agencies; and by locally established community groups. These facilities may be housed in permanent structures, public buildings or schools, where they are in operation after school hours. They frequently include a gymnasium, pool, meeting rooms and offices; often have programming in arts and crafts, physical fitness, personal skills and the performing arts; and may offer special lectures and events. Some also provide nursery school, day care and other special activities for children.

Principal planning requirements for an indoor recreation center include sufficient parking for all programs, outdoor lighting, drop-off areas protected from vehicular traffic and removal of architectural barriers.

See: COMMERCIAL INDOOR RECREATION FACILITIES; COMMUNITY CENTER; MULTISERVICE CENTER; RECREATION SYSTEM

Industrial Area

That part of a municipality that is zoned to permit certain types of industries, often specified as light industry, heavy industry or industrial park use.

Typically, residential uses and most other nonindustrial uses are prohibited in industrial districts, although commercial uses may be permitted. Light industry may sometimes be permitted in a district zoned for heavy industry, but heavy industry is usually not allowed in any other district. Types of industrial uses may be specified in a zoning ordinance, but the current trend is to set per-

formance standards for these areas and to exclude industries that do not meet them.

Industrial areas must be located near freeways and major arterial roads for truck access and require railroad sidings for some industries. Many older industrial areas were located near port facilities, near railroad freight yards or near necessary raw materials, so that industrial uses often still remain in these locations. Other areas have ceased to be used for industry, particularly those that once housed industries that now require one-story buildings for assembly line purposes. These have moved to outlying areas where land is cheap enough to permit this form of construction. Off-street loading areas are now an essential requirement; where not available, municipalities have had to ban on-street parking and even through traffic to permit truck access.

Many communities now require that industrial plants be subject to design review with respect to their site plans, landscaping, architecture and signs. They are also usually subject to a variety of environmental regulations related to such areas as air and water pollution, noise pollution and the disposal of wastes.

See: ECONOMIC DEVELOPMENT; FACTORY; FREIGHT HANDLING FACILITIES; HEAVY INDUSTRY; INDUSTRIAL PARK; INDUSTRIAL PLANT LOCATION; INDUSTRIAL WASTE; JUNKYARD; LIGHT INDUSTRY; OFF-STREET LOADING; OFF-STREET PARKING REQUIREMENTS; PERFORMANCE STANDARDS; TRUCK TERMINALS; WAREHOUSE FACILITIES; WATERFRONT REVITALIZATION

Industrial Development Agency (IDA)

A public benefit corporation with power to issue tax-exempt industrial revenue bonds on behalf of industrial and commercial enterprises. The property it owns is also exempt from local property taxes, but typically the enterprise on whose behalf the bond was issued makes a payment to the IDA in lieu of taxes, which is then dispersed to appropriate units of government or governmental departments. The issuance of industrial revenue bonds is subject to federal requirements that public hearings be held and approval be granted either by a referendum or by elected public officials.

Industrial development agencies, which can be created only by a state enabling act, may be either state, regional or local agencies and are found in almost every state. An IDA is governed by a board of directors, usually made up of representatives from both the public and private sectors appointed by the chief executive of the unit of government sponsoring the IDA.

See: ECONOMIC DEVELOPMENT; INDUSTRIAL REVENUE BONDS

Industrial Park

A planned industrial development on a tract of land that is generally 80 acres (32 hectares) or larger, containing an internal road network suitable for trucks and employee traffic and adequate utilities, including a sufficient water supply, sanitary and storm sewers, and electric and gas lines. Rail spurs to plant sites may also be provided.

Industrial parks must have convenient access to freeway interchanges, while access to a rail line or an airport is useful, and is important for some industries. The land must be capable of bearing industrial loads and should have good drainage and be separated from nonindustrial land uses to the degree necessary to protect these uses from the undesirable qualities of industrial development. Sites that are larger than 150 acres (61 hectares) are most suitable for very large plants.

Building sites may be sold or leased, and building sizes and designs may be subject to design standards. Building expansion space may also be controlled by the park's developer, who usually prepares the site design for the park. In general, industrial parks are designed with a wide buffer area, which may be 200 feet (61 meters), around them; the buffer may be landscaped and/or used partially for parking purposes. Individual buildings are also landscaped. Wide internal roads and off-street truck loading areas are required, both of which may be depressed so that truck floors are level with building floors. Train track spurs may also be depressed for this reason. Roads and rail lines within the park are planned so that they do not intersect, generally preventing the use of a site that is bisected by a rail line.

See: AIRPORT INDUSTRIAL PARK; CAMPUS OFFICE PARK; DESIGN STANDARDS; INDUSTRIAL AREA; INDUSTRIAL PLANT LOCATION; OFF-STREET LOADING; OFF-STREET PARKING REQUIREMENTS

Industrial Plant Location

The selection of a location for an industrial plant is determined by a variety of factors related to convenience, efficiency, cost and access. The most critical concerns are generally proximity to materials, access to major highways, proximity to consumer and supplier markets, availability of a suitable labor force and energy costs. Less critical but still important factors are wage rates, degree of unionization, tax rates, public policy and the nature of municipal requirements or incentives, cultural amenities and the quality of housing and schools. Once a general location has been selected, a specific site is chosen based upon criteria such as size of site, topography, land use regulations, site development costs, water supply, sewage disposal, and electric and gas service.

In the past 30 years, most industrial development has taken place in suburban locations, encouraged by a preference for one-story buildings with spacious loading facilities and superior highway access. Industrial parks have also become popular because they encourage operating efficiency and often have rail freight service or proximity to airports as well as good road access.

While most industrial plants continue to be constructed in suburban locations, urban sites can still be attractive to industry. In order to be competitive, they should offer benefits such as good public transit service, ready availability of a large labor force, and either large enough and attractively priced developable parcels or existing industrial buildings of good quality that can be renovated relatively inexpensively.

See: HOUSING LOCATION; INDUSTRIAL AREA; INDUSTRIAL PARK; OFFICE BUILDING LOCATION

Industrial Revenue Bonds

Tax-exempt bonds that are used by government to stimulate investment and employment and are issued by a state, county or local industrial development agency on behalf of a private firm. The capital raised through the bonds can be used to finance new construction, rehabilitation or expansion. The bond proceeds must be used for either land or fixed assets such as plant and equipment.

Industrial revenue bonds are not backed by the full faith and credit of the issuing municipality but rather are financed by rental payments that the firm makes on its new facility. The company is generally given a long-term lease, and rent payments are set at an amount that can cover both principal and interest payments on the bonds. Because the bonds are exempt from federal taxes, their interest rate is usually 60 percent to 70 percent of the prime lending rate. The bonds can be used to finance 100 percent of the cost of a project, but the Treasury Department specifies that they cannot be issued for more than $10,000,000. Bonds are rarely issued for less than $500,000, and the term of a bond is customarily 15 to 20 years.

Industrial revenue bonds, also known as industrial development bonds (IDB's) in use in 47 states, were first used during the Depression (in Mississippi in 1936) as a means of attracting industry to areas with high unemployment. Although the concept did not at first spread rapidly, by 1980 it was estimated that $8.4 billion in industrial revenue bonds were issued in that year. In addition, many of these federally subsidized bonds were used to finance the projects of large established firms.

In reaction to the drain on the treasury and the limited restrictions placed on the use of these bonds in many states, federal restrictive measures were adopted as part of the Tax Equity and Fiscal Responsibility Act of 1982 (TEFRA). TEFRA contains a requirement that public hearings be held and official approval granted by elected officials unless a public referendum has been held prior to issuance of the bonds. In addition, accelerated depreciation benefits are generally not available to a company to the extent that the property in question was financed using these tax-exempt bonds.

See: BOND; INDUSTRIAL DEVELOPMENT AGENCY (IDA)

Industrial Sewage

Wastewater produced by industrial processes that is either derived from the raw materials, such as food-processing wastes; from the products that are produced, such as oil from refineries; or from the substances used in manufacturing, such as catalysts. The amount and specific nature of industrial sewage must be known for effective operation of a municipal sewage treatment plant, since the biological or chemical constitution of the sewage can have an adverse effect on the plant's ability to treat it. Highly acid or alkaline discharges can also weaken the structure of some sewer pipe materials and other sewerage system components.

Industrial sewage can constitute a large proportion of a municipality's sanitary waste, depending upon the amount of industry and its particular requirements. Because of the volume and the deleterious effects that some industrial contaminants can have on the sewage treatment system and receiving waters, municipalities issue permits for industrial connections into municipal sewers only after considering the precise nature of the industrial discharge of a proposed plant. Despite this, illegal industrial connections to municipal sewerage systems are often made and are a major concern since they may be difficult to locate.

To control the amount or quality of industrial sewage, municipalities may require that industry pretreat its waste to remove certain contaminants, treat and completely dispose of its own waste or recycle its used water to reduce the volume of wastewater. Modern municipal sewage treatment plants frequently have a separate system for treating industrial sewage, which is brought to them by truck rather than discharged into sanitary sewers. After treatment, the industrial sewage is mixed with domestic wastewater in the main plant. Characteristics of industrial sewage may also be regulated by industrial performance standards incorporated into the municipal zoning ordinance.

See: HAZARDOUS WASTE; INDUSTRIAL WASTE; PERFORMANCE STANDARDS; PRETREATMENT; PRETREATMENT STANDARDS; RECEIVING WATERS; SANITARY SEWER; SEWAGE TREATMENT; TOXIC SUBSTANCES; WASTEWATER; WATER POLLUTION

Industrial Waste

The waste that results from industrial and manufacturing processes. Industrial wastes present special disposal problems because, according to U.S. Environmental Protection Agency (EPA) estimates, 10 percent to 15 percent of the industrial waste produced annually is hazardous. This amounts to approximately 51 million tons (46.4 million metric tons) of waste requiring special handling each year.

Industrial wastes have been shown to have undesirable effects upon air, land and water, depending upon the industrial process involved and the method of final disposal. Casual disposal practices in the past have led to problems such as the seepage of chemicals and radioactive wastes into public water systems and wells, as well as rivers and lakes. Federal regulations, generally administered by the EPA and state agencies, concerning emission of gaseous wastes and emission of pollutants into waterways now require the issuance of permits before discharges into water-

ways may be made and set emission limits on pollutants issuing from stacks. Municipalities may also set performance standards that further regulate industrial development. Industrial waste management should be considered at the time that new industry is locating in a community so that proper plans for waste disposal may be made.

Certain types of industrial wastes, although usually not hazardous wastes, can be recycled. This process is facilitated by industrial waste exchanges, organizations that help the discards of one industry reach another where the materials comprising the "waste" may be reused. First established in Europe in the early 1970s, where they are known as waste bourses, waste exchanges actually buy and sell these industrial wastes and identify new uses for which they may be sold. The net result is a decrease in the amount of waste requiring disposal and a savings of raw material and energy. As of 1981, 25 waste information exchanges were in operation in the U.S., the first of which was formed in St. Louis, Missouri in 1975. An additional nine waste exchanges were involved in buying, selling, reprocessing and identifying potential users.

See: HAZARDOUS WASTE; INDUSTRIAL SEWAGE; NATIONAL AMBIENT AIR QUALITY STANDARDS (NAAQS); NATIONAL POLLUTANT DISCHARGE ELIMINATION SYSTEM (NPDES); RECYCLING; SOLID WASTE; SOLID WASTE MANAGEMENT; TOXIC SUBSTANCES

Industrialized Housing

Housing constructed entirely or partly in a factory, in contrast to conventional construction, in which the majority of building parts are assembled by workers on the construction site. Industrialized housing construction, which may be used in combination with conventional construction techniques and new methods of on-site construction, requires conventional site preparation and building foundation construction. In addition, all of these techniques have been applied to nonresidential construction and have also received significant attention and use in underdeveloped countries, where they enable housing to be built rapidly and inexpensively. Most forms of industrialized housing, however, allow cost savings over conventional construction only when large numbers of dwelling units (usually over 300) are to be constructed.

Modular housing is a type of industrialized housing that is partially constructed in a factory and shipped to the site, often in room-sized sections. These may be lightweight, self-contained boxes, such as mobile homes or sectional homes, which can remain mobile or be permanently installed; or they may be heavyweight boxes (volumetric components), such as those used in Habitat '67 in Montreal. Heavyweight units are room-sized or smaller components, constructed of concrete, steel sandwich or fiber-reinforced plastic, which can be grouped horizontally or vertically to create single or multifamily housing. Much interior finishing is usually completed in the factory prior to shipping, and bathroom and kitchen units are usually fully equipped. Lightweight units are also referred to as manufactured housing.

In prefabricated housing, homes are precut and packaged for delivery to the construction site in kits consisting of raw materials such as lumber, brick and pipe. Often sold directly to the homeowner, who may provide some of the labor necessary for construction to further reduce costs, the various kit components are ready for assembly with little modification required.

Building systems, another industrial technique, uses factory-constructed panels, often large enough to constitute entire walls, partitions, floors or roofs, which are assembled at the site. The systems may either be open systems, in which special molds are made for large projects, or closed systems, in which components are interchangeable with those of other systems.

Framework, generally constructed of lightweight steel or lightweight concrete, manufactured in parts in a factory and shipped to the site for assembly, is known as structural frame. Building components—such as prefabricated walls, partitions and roofs—are usually attached to the framework on the construction site. (See Fig. 23)
See: CONSTRUCTION TECHNOLOGY: MOBILE HOME; MODULAR CONSTRUCTION

Inferential Statistics

Statistical methods that allow conclusions to be drawn about a total population or phenomenon based upon sample data. Inferential statistics, also known as inductive statistics, are based upon probability theory.
See: DESCRIPTIVE STATISTICS; HYPOTHESIS TESTING

(a)

(b)

(c)

(d)

Fig. 23.   Industrialized housing: (a) modular units under construction at the factory; (b) a room-sized unit being placed on top of lower housing level at the construction site; (c) a building system that uses prefabricated wall panels with factory-installed windows and insulation; (d) completed prefabricated duplex housing in Alexandria, Virginia.
Credit: Courtesy of the U.S. Department of Housing and Urban Development

Infill Development

Residential or nonresidential development that occurs on vacant sites scattered throughout the more intensely developed areas of municipalities. Generally, these sites are vacant because they were once considered of insufficient size for development, because an existing building located on the site was demolished or because there were other, more desirable sites for development. Despite the normally higher cost per dwelling unit or per square foot of building on these sites, as land becomes scarce, such development occurs because of market demand.

An extreme example of infill development has occurred in New York City, where sliver or needle buildings of at least 15 stories have been constructed on sites that are often no more than 20 feet (6 meters) wide. These sliver apartment buildings frequently are large enough for only a single apartment per floor or per every two floors. Despite the small floor area per story, however, Manhattan apartment values are high enough to make construction of these towers economically feasible. This has caused considerable controversy when proposals have been made to construct slivers on blocks consisting entirely of low-rise townhouses.

Infiltration

1. The process by which soil absorbs water percolating through it. This phenomenon allows soil to function as a reservoir that gradually releases water to aquifers and surface streams. The rate at which soil can absorb water, known as its infiltration capacity, is affected by the dryness of the soil and its other features, precipitation characteristics, temperatures, wind, ground cover, topography, amount of development and other factors.

2. The seepage of groundwater into sewer and water pipes through cracks and joints that are not tightly sealed. Large amounts of seepage into sanitary sewers can reduce a sewage treatment plant's capability to process sanitary sewage.
See: GROUNDWATER; INFILTRATION AND INFLOW (I&I) ANALYSIS; PERCOLATION; RUNOFF

Infiltration and Inflow (I&I) Analysis

An investigation of a sanitary sewerage system to determine the presence and amount of excessive groundwater infiltration and stormwater inflow. Infiltration is caused by groundwater seepage into pipes through cracks and joints. Inflow is stormwater runoff from roof and cellar drains that are connected, usually illegally, to the sanitary sewer (since stormwater runoff from buildings should be directed to storm sewers).

An I&I analysis is used to determine the locations of health hazards caused by backing up of sewage into homes, onto streets and into waterways and to enable an assessment of the effects of infiltration and inflow on the capacity and performance of pumping stations and sewage treatment plants. The analysis will aid in determining whether the most cost-effective solution is to repair the

sewers or to increase the capacity of the treatment plant. The I&I analysis is the first part of a Sewer System Evaluation Program required under the Water Pollution Control Program established by the Clean Water Act. The analysis customarily includes cost estimates for sewer system rehabilitation and a detailed plan for a Sewer System Evaluation Survey (the second part of the program) if excessive infiltration or inflow is found.
See: FEDERAL WATER POLLUTION CONTROL ACT AMENDMENTS OF 1972; INFILTRATION; SEWER SYSTEM EVALUATION SURVEY (SSES)

Information System

A centralized and generally computerized system of collecting, storing and disseminating data that may be easily retrieved and organized for analysis. Information systems, which were developed to serve the administrative needs of business and government, require periodic updating to maintain the accuracy of the data base.

Typically, a planning department will be one of a number of departments within a unit of government that provides input into and uses a municipal information system. Although some information will have little planning relevance, other information can be extremely useful, including that concerning such matters as assessed value, land use and land ownership by parcel; building permits; utilities; and public safety records. A planning agency may also develop its own data base to provide information on other subject areas of particular importance to that planning jurisdiction.

Information systems for planning began appearing in the 1960s, but early efforts proved disappointing in many cases. Excessive amounts of information were often collected without a clear view as to how it would be used, and difficulties were also encountered in keeping the data base current. Today, more limited systems are typically developed that concentrate on serving specific information needs. This can enable such planning functions as development of long-range plans and preparation of planning studies and grant applications to be carried out more easily. Information systems can also be used to provide data for various types of statistical analyses or development of models.
See: DECISION SUPPORT SYSTEMS (DSS)

Infrared Photography

The use of infrared film and optical systems in photographs. Because infrared film is sensitive to infrared radiation, certain types of aerial photograph features become visible that are not easily discernible when noninfrared film is used.

Infrared is particularly good at penetrating haze and at emphasizing water bodies. It is also frequently used in the analysis of vegetation, because it tends to make deciduous trees photograph in lighter tones than evergreens (which absorb more infrared radiation). Infrared may also be used in "color," known as false color film because the colors do not resemble those that the eye sees. Originally developed for military purposes, it enables healthy trees to be differentiated from those that are dying or under stress. It also helps to distinguish vegetation from soil or rock.

Infrared photography, which cannot detect heat, should be differentiated from infrared scanning equipment or imagery, which can. Infrared imagery has been found to be extremely useful in forest fire detection, in the mapping of fault lines, in locating minerals and geothermal energy sources and in detecting crop disease or damage from frost or heat.
See: AERIAL PHOTOGRAPHY; REMOTE SENSING

Injunction

A court order that either directs that some action be taken or that prohibits certain activity from being engaged in.

A municipality may seek an injunction against a landowner in the process of violating provisions of the zoning ordinance, requiring that the violations be eliminated and prohibiting any future violations.

In-Migration

The process of moving to a residence in a particular defined geographic area—e.g., a city or county—from an address outside that geographic area. In-migration to an area is also out-migration from the area of prior residence. In-migration may be distinguished from immigration, which involves moves into an area from outside of national boundaries.
See: DEMOGRAPHY; NET MIGRATION; OUT-MIGRATION

Inner City

A term that is often used to refer to older urban areas with a variety of urban problems. It has also been used more generally to contrast the central city with suburbs and outlying areas.

Inner city areas generally have a greater amount of poverty and urban decay than newer areas. By virtue of need, many planning programs and federally funded programs are concentrated in these areas to improve housing and community facilities and to increase economic opportunities.
See: COMMUNITY ACTION PROGRAM (CAP); COMMUNITY DEVELOPMENT BLOCK GRANT (CDBG); COMMUNITY DEVELOPMENT CORPORATION (CDC); MODEL CITIES PROGRAM; NEIGHBORHOOD PRESERVATION; SLUM; URBAN DEVELOPMENT ACTION GRANT (UDAG); URBAN PARK AND RECREATION RECOVERY PROGRAM (UPARR); URBAN RENEWAL

Input

1. Information that is fed into a computer.
2. The device or equipment that is used to feed information into a data processing system.
3. Data that an organization or agency receives from a variety of sources, particularly from the public. An example would be statements and comments made at public hearings.
See: CITIZEN PARTICIPATION; DATA PROCESSING

Input-Output Analysis

A technique for measuring interindustry linkages within a specific geographic entity, based upon the fundamental assumption that every economic activity is related to every other economic activity in a quantifiable manner.

These interindustry relationships are expressed in matrices or tables in which the basic structure of the table expresses the linkages in dollars. Horizontally, outputs for each sector of the economy are indicated by sales to the other sectors. Vertically, the table shows inputs or purchases made in one sector by all other sectors.

Input-output analysis establishes the relationship between the volume of specific inputs needed to produce a specific volume of outputs and can be used to show the effects a change in demand for a specific product will have on all the inputs needed to make that product—e.g., materials, labor. The theory also has recently been applied to the urban economy, where, in addition to examining interindustry linkages, the analysis can be used to compare the structure of one urban center to another.

Although input-output analysis is considered useful in studying the economy of larger regions or metropolitan areas, such an analysis is quite sophisticated and can be costly to undertake. Consequently, smaller areas have rarely conducted studies using this technique. In addition, the method analyzes interindustry linkages at a given point in time. With rapid technological developments, these linkages might change dramatically in only a few years.
See: ECONOMIC BASE ANALYSIS; ECONOMIC FORECASTING TECHNIQUES; URBAN ECONOMICS

Institute of Transportation Engineers (ITE)

An organization, formerly called the Institute of Traffic Engineers, designed to serve the needs of transportation engineers and professionals in related fields, and to aid in meeting human needs for mobility and safety. The 6,500 member organization, founded in 1930, helps to promote the professional growth of its members and to improve public awareness concerning various aspects of transportation through the research and educational programs it conducts.

International in scope, with members from more than seventy countries and branches in the United States, Canada, Britain, Israel, Australia, Brazil and India, it is governed by an International Board of Direction, assisted by staff in its Washington, D.C. headquarters. A Technical Council, which coordinates and organizes the activities of the many technical committees of the organization, helps to review, disseminate and publish a variety of technical reports and publications. Among the best known of the publications is the *Transportation and Traffic Engineering Handbook.*

Integrated Pest Management (IPM)

A means of controlling various forms of pest infestation through a combination of biological, cultural and chemical approaches. One important reason IPM has come into favor in recent years is the increasing numbers of insect strains that are resistant to at least one chemical pesticide. Additional reasons for the interest in IPM are the environmental contamination caused by many pesticides and the effects of pesticides on human health.

One important aspect of IPM is biological controls over pests. Among these types of controls are the development of crop types and livestock varieties able to resist pest infestation more effectively, the use of viruses that will attack only a particular species and the use of harmless predator species that will attack particular kinds of pests. Male insects may also be sterilized by radioactive exposure and then released to harmlessly attempt to breed with fertile females. Cultural controls include agricultural practices such as crop rotation, intercropping (in which different crop types are planted in alternate rows) and the use of trap crops, in which crops of little value are planted in close proximity to valuable crops to lure pests from the desirable crop.

Although insecticides and other pesticides are still used in integrated pest management, they are applied only when necessary and often in smaller amounts, as they are no longer the primary means of protection against pests. As an example, an IPM program aimed at protecting municipally owned shade trees in several California cities resulted in drastically reduced levels of insecticide use. In another instance new strains of early-maturing cotton introduced in Texas have enabled the production of this crop with reduced amounts of insecticide, fertilizer and irrigation water.
See: PESTICIDES; TOXIC SUBSTANCES

Interceptor Sewer

A sewer line that collects wastewater from trunk lines and conducts it to a sewage treatment plant.
See: SEWAGE TREATMENT PLANT; SEWERAGE SYSTEM; TRUNK SEWER

Intercity Rail Transportation

The movement of people or goods between urban centers by rail. Intercity rail passenger transportation has declined markedly in North America but is still a predominant intercity transportation mode in Europe and Asia. However, railroads are a major carrier of intercity freight in North America and abroad. They haul freight predominantly over long distances, while the trucking industry has become the dominant short-haul freight handling mode.

Introduction of high-speed passenger train service in Europe and Japan has kept the railroad lines competitive with air travel. In the United States the use of piggyback freight service (truck trailers that can be loaded onto railroad flatcars and transported as if they were railroad cars) has expedited rail shipment of goods, while the use of car-trains (trains that can carry automobiles as well as

passengers) and higher-speed intercity trains has increased passenger demand somewhat. Proposals for new high-speed passenger rail connections between major cities in a few rail corridors, such as Los Angeles—San Diego, as well as current railroad mergers that are enabling faster transcontinental freight service, cost reductions and greater profits for the railroad companies, also augur a better intercity rail position (vis-à-vis air and trucking) in the future.

In addition, the Railroad Revitalization and Regulatory Reform Act of 1976 requires that states undertake railroad planning as part of their overall tranportation and economic development planning. This assures consideration of the importance of rail links between municipalities prior to their proposed abandonment by railroad companies.
See: FUTURE TRANSPORTATION MODES; HIGH-SPEED RAIL TRANSPORTATION; PASSENGER RAILROAD REBUILDING ACT OF 1980; RAILROAD RIGHTS-OF-WAY

Interconnected Power Network

The coordination of separate power systems to form a large integrated system that offers increased reliability as well as economies of scale. Because of the existence of this interconnected system, utilities are able to buy power from each other, and no single utility has to maintain as large a required generation reserve as would otherwise be necessary.
See: ELECTRIC POWER GENERATION AND TRANSMISSION

Intergovernmental Agreement

A formal contract or informal understanding between two or more units of government concerning a policy matter or the way in which a function or service will be performed for their mutual benefit. Intergovernmental agreements may be made at the national, state or local level and may take place between governmental units at the same level or at different levels.

International or interstate agreements generally concern large-scale issues, such as waterways, ports or air pollution. At the local level it is common for communities to agree to share facilities—such as water supply systems, schools or fire departments—so that better equipment may be purchased or specialized personnel hired. In another type of intergovernmental agreement, a county can provide certain services for its cities, villages and towns on a contractual basis. In a third type of agreement, a number of communities might agree to subscribe to a policy concerning a particular issue.

Interim Zoning

Zoning that is applied on a temporary basis to a particular area and is used to halt or strictly limit development while new plans or regulations governing that area are formulated. The most common use of interim develop-

ment controls is in areas that have been recently annexed by a municipality.
See: ZONING

Interior Side Yard

A side yard that is either adjacent to another lot or that is located next to an alley, beyond which there is another lot.
See: LOT; SIDE YARD; YARD

Intermediate Care Facilities (ICF)

Residential facilities designed to provide continuous personal care for individuals who, as a result of mental or physical conditions, are in need of assistance in performing daily routines, including dressing and eating. Also referred to as a health-related facility (HRF), such establishments provide licensed nursing personnel who administer medication or treatments prescribed by a physician. Generally, ICFs are not intended to serve patients requiring continuous nursing supervision, as may be available in an acute care hospital or skilled nursing facility.

Although regulations vary among states, the majority of intermediate care facilities are required to provide for special nutritional needs of the patients and for regularly scheduled recreational activities. ICFs are eligible for federal reimbursement through Medicaid but not through Medicare.
See: ACUTE CARE HOSPITAL; NURSING HOME; SKILLED NURSING FACILITY (SNF)

Intermittent Stream

A water body that exists for most of the year but that dries up periodically during drought or stops flowing occasionally for other causes. Conversely, it can flood a drainage area during heavy storms. Most commonly, intermittent streams may be found in arid regions where the water table is much below the surface or in colder areas in which water is frozen during the winter months.

An intermittent stream may be distinguished from an ephemeral stream, which carries water only near periods of precipitation. A perennial stream stops flowing only under conditions of severe drought.
See: RIVER BASIN; WATER TABLE

Intermodal Terminal

A term used to describe a transfer station between two or more vehicular travel modes—e.g., a railroad station with bus connections and auto and taxi pickup areas. Technically, all traditional terminal facilities are intermodal in nature, in that they provide the ability to transfer from one mode of transportation to another. In modern usage, however, an intermodal terminal is one that facilitates movement between modes by providing ample areas for each of the modes, thereby encouraging and easing transfers. For example, a new railroad station might also include a bus terminal, a parking structure for all-day parking and a heliport on top, as well as traditional auto and taxi pickup areas.

Numerous retail concessions to provide services can also be included. Fees from concessions have been shown to yield 60 percent or more of the construction and operating costs of certain intermodal facilities. Intermodal terminals, too, are often built as a part of joint development projects.

In Britain an intermodal terminal is called a travel interchange.
See: JOINT DEVELOPMENT

International City Management Association (ICMA)

A professional and educational organization for government administrators, primarily the chief administrators of city or county government, or councils of government, and their assistants. Founded in 1914, ICMA is concerned with improving the quality of government by the use of professional managers; improving the competence of government administrators; and providing data, information and new techniques that can be applied to the operations of governments. ICMA, whose offices are in Washington, D.C., has members throughout the United States, Canada and Europe.

ICMA holds annual meetings and training seminars and provides assistance in job placement. Two subscription information services offered by the organization are the Management Information Service (MIS), in which information is provided on current managerial practice, and the Urban Data Service (UDS), which provides data on such topics as municipal salaries and municipal finances.

ICMA maintains an active publications program on such topics as finance, personnel, management, human services and planning, including the Municipal Management Series, usually known as the ICMA "green books." One such volume is *The Practice of Local Government Planning,* a well-known planning textbook. A *Municipal Year Book* is issued annually with a variety of articles and profiles on cities with populations of 10,000 or more. Publications that may be obtained with membership include the *ICMA Newsletter,* published biweekly; *Public Management,* a monthly magazine; several directories; and reports and newsletters on special topics.

International Conference of Building Officials (ICBO)

A nonprofit organization, established in 1922, whose main purposes include publication and dissemination of the *Uniform Building Code* and its related documents, research concerning building safety and educational programs for building officials. The organization also seeks to encourage uniformity in building regulations and to develop guidelines for the operation of building departments. Membership of ICBO consists primarily of local, regional and state governments; individuals active in code enforcement; architects; and trade associations.

ICBO publishes a new edition of the *Uniform Building Code,* a widely adopted international model code, every three years and issues supplements in intervening years. A number of other codes that are compatible with the *Uniform Building Code* are also sponsored or cosponsored by the organization. These include the *Uniform Mechanical Code, ICBO Plumbing Code, Uniform Housing Code, Uniform Sign Code, Uniform Code for the Abatement of Dangerous Buildings* and *Uniform Fire Code.* ICBO publishes a number of textbooks, manuals and reports, as well as a bimonthly magazine, *Building Standards.* The organization's headquarters are in Whittier, California.

International Council on Monuments and Sites (ICOMOS)

An international organization concerned with the study and preservation of historic structures throughout the world, and with attracting the interest of individuals in protecting the cultural and architectural heritage of their country. Founded in 1965, ICOMOS holds international symposia, disseminates information, and maintains a UNESCO/ICOMOS Documentation Centre in which pertinent literature and materials on architectural and historic preservation and restoration are filed and made available to the public. ICOMOS, whose headquarters are in Paris, France, is comprised of sixty national committees representing member countries from throughout the world as well as individual members. U.S./ICOMOS was formed in 1973 and is located in Washington, D.C.

International Federation for Housing and Planning (IFHP)

An international organization whose main interests are expanding the body of knowledge concerning housing, planning and allied fields and improving professional practice in these fields. Based in The Hague, The Netherlands, IFHP's members consist of governmental agencies at all levels, corporations, national associations, universities, research institutes and individuals engaged in some aspect of the fields of planning, housing and urban development.

IFHP, which was founded in 1913, has members in 65 countries. It holds annual conferences in various parts of the world, as well as seminars, training courses and study tours. It maintains a research library and has consultative status with several United Nations agencies. Publications include a *News Sheet,* issued seven times per year; special publications; and reports on conferences and seminars that are held.

International Joint Commission

An official bilateral organization of the United States and Canada that was established in 1911, pursuant to the Boundary Waters Treaty of 1909. Its purpose is to prevent disputes regarding the use of boundary waters; settle questions between the two countries involving rights, obligations or interests on the common border; and resolve other matters that arise. The regional office in Windsor, Ontario evaluates and encourages compliance with the Great Lakes Water Quality Agreement of 1978.
See: BOUNDARY WATERS TREATY OF 1909; GREAT LAKES WATER QUALITY AGREEMENT OF 1978

International Solar Energy Society (ISES)

A nonprofit, interdisciplinary organization concerned with encouraging research on solar energy and its applications, educating the public, and collecting and disseminating information. Among the interests of ISES are solar energy characteristics, heating and cooling using solar energy, photovoltaic processes and energy storage.

The organization puts out a number of publications and holds international conferences on solar energy in different countries. ISES, with headquarters in Melbourne, Australia, also has national sections in various parts of the world that are substantially autonomous and often have their own publications, conventions and workshops.

The American Solar Energy Society (ASES) was known until 1982 as the American Section of the International Solar Energy Society. ASES, which retains affiliation with ISES, has headquarters in Boulder, Colorado. It maintains a number of divisions, including Architecture and Construction, Passive Systems and Socioeconomics, and operates a reference library. In addition, ASES publishes various manuals and conference proceedings as well as several periodicals. It holds both an annual meeting and an annual conference on passive solar energy.

Interstate Highway System

The national system of interstate and defense highways was established under the Federal-Aid Highway Act of 1944 and the Federal-Aid Highway Act of 1956. It links the country's principal metropolitan areas and connects with routes of importance in Mexico and Canada. It comprises about 1 percent of the total United States highway mileage but carries close to its expected volume of 20 percent of the country's traffic. Funding for an interstate highway (given to the state that will build the road and within which the road is located) is supplied at the rate of 90 percent federal to 10 percent state matching funds.

As of 1981 there were 42,939 miles (69,089 kilometers) of road designated eligible for such funding, which includes new roads to be built as part of the system or improvements to existing roads to bring them up to the standards of the system. Certain toll roads are also considered to be part of the interstate system but are not eligible for interstate highway funding and are not included in the 42,939-mile figure. Federal funds for the interstate system had been authorized by Congress in the amount of $77.7 billion from 1956 through fiscal year 1982. The estimate of the cost to complete the system was an additional $53 billion.

Highways on the Interstate Highway System are initiated and designed locally, and their subsequent administration and maintenance remains a local function. The importance of the interstate system lies not only in the breadth of the highways constructed but also in the establishment of standards of highway construction and maintenance that have been implemented nationally.

In Canada the Trans-Canada Highway was constructed

as a joint venture by the federal and provincial governments. It is 4,796 miles (7,716 kilometers) long.

In Britain the system of motorways and trunk roads for through traffic is designed and financed entirely by the federal Department of the Environment under the authority of the secretaries of state for England, Wales and Scotland. Construction and maintenance is supervised by one of six federal Road Construction Units if the cost of the project is over £5 million; if below that figure, these functions are carried out by local authorities as agents for the central government. In 1979 the trunk road-motorway system had a total length of 9,613 miles (15,467 kilometers), with an additional 78 miles (126 kilometers) under construction.
See: FEDERAL-AID HIGHWAY ACT OF 1981; SURFACE TRANSPORTATION ASSISTANCE ACT OF 1982

Intertidal Zone

The area lying between the average high- and low-tide levels. Algae, mussels, barnacles, starfish, crabs, snails and other marine life and vegetation of this zone must be capable of withstanding temperature extremes, periodic submersion in saltwater, drying by sun and wind, or even freshwater immersion after storms.
See: COASTAL ZONE

Inverse Condemnation

A term that refers to two different, yet related, ways in which eminent domain power is formally invoked after a de facto taking has occurred.

Both cases start from a situation in which a landowner's property has been effectively taken by some governmental action (or by action of some nongovernmental entity that has been delegated the power to condemn property via eminent domain). This action could be continuous low-flying airplane overflights, trespass upon and development of private property, or enactment of confiscatory regulation.

In one case the landowner sues for just compensation on account of the taking, on the theory that his property has been inversely condemned by the government's action. In the other case the landowner sues to enjoin or invalidate the government's action (e.g., to stop any further airplane overflights), and the taking entity counterclaims for a decree of inverse condemnation (i.e., that it be allowed to acquire the property at issue through eminent domain) even though it did not proceed through the channels normally required in order to condemn property.

In either case, if a judgment of inverse condemnation is granted, the taking entity will acquire title to the property or interest it has sought, and the landowner will have his constitutional right to just compensation.
See: *BOOMER* v. *ATLANTIC CEMENT COMPANY*; CONDEMNATION; EMINENT DOMAIN; TAKING

Inversion

A phenomenon in which a cool air layer is trapped by a warm air layer above it, preventing the cool air from rising. This presents a special problem with respect to air pollution because, in the absence of winds, there is no way for the pollutants to disperse into the atmosphere. Major air pollution episodes have generally occurred at the time of inversions.
See: AIR POLLUTION; AIR POLLUTION EPISODE

Investment Tax Credit

An economic development incentive designed to encourage expansion, rehabilitation and construction of commercial and industrial facilities. Investors in certain depreciable property can apply a credit against the income tax of the government that offers the credit. These credits are usually based on the amount of the depreciable investment.

In the United States the federal government offers a tax credit of 10 percent of the investment made in depreciable property that has a useful life of at least five years. A 6 percent tax credit is available for property with a useful life of at least three years. More substantial tax credits are available for investment in older and historic buildings under the Economic Recovery Tax Act of 1981.

A number of state governments also offer tax credits. The size and nature of eligible activities varies considerably among states.
See: ECONOMIC DEVELOPMENT INCENTIVES; ECONOMIC RECOVERY TAX ACT OF 1981

Irrigation

Supplemental water applied to soil, above that provided by rainfall, to enable crops to grow or to increase crop production. Irrigation is an ancient practice, which dates as far back as 5000 B.C. in Egypt, when the Nile was used for that purpose. Mormon settlers introduced the first substantial irrigation project to the United States in 1847 in Utah.

Today there are over 50 million acres (20 million hectares) of irrigated land in the United States alone, mainly in the western states, and many times that land area worldwide. Among the many countries in which large-scale irrigation is practiced are Canada, India, Israel, China, Japan and the Soviet Union.

A number of irrigation methods are practiced: surface irrigation, subirrigation, sprinkler or overhead irrigation, and drip irrigation. Techniques have been developed making it possible to reuse irrigation water, minimizing water waste and agricultural pollution from pesticides and sediment. This can be done by collecting runoff from irrigated areas in ponds and then pumping the water to other fields needing irrigation. Irrigated areas should have a properly designed drainage system to help prevent accumulations of salt as well as waterlogging of the land.
See: AGRICULTURAL LAND USE; LAND RECLAMATION

J

James v. *Valtierra* (402 U.S. 137 [1971])

A decision by the United States Supreme Court upholding an amendment to the California state Constitution that provided that no publicly sponsored low-income housing project could be developed in a community unless the project was approved by referendum in a local election.

The case has been cited as embodying the proposition that exclusionary zoning cannot be attacked as violative of the United States Constitution merely because it results in economic (as distinguished from racial) discrimination.

See: CITY OF EASTLAKE v. *FOREST CITY ENTERPRISES, INC.*; EXCLUSIONARY ZONING; *STATE OF WASHINGTON ex. rel. SEATTLE TITLE TRUST COMPANY* v. *ROBERGE, SUPERINTENDENT OF BUILDING OF CITY OF SEATTLE*

Jetty

1.   A structure built at a tidal inlet to protect a harbor. A much larger version of a groin, a jetty also prevents the flow of sand into a channel and protects ships from waves and crosscurrents. When the channel is narrowed by the jetty, the increased current force reduces the buildup of sand and silt on the channel's bottom.

A jetty may be constructed of steel, concrete or rock and must be high enough to block the sand stream being transported by waves and current. As the sand is then prevented from traveling downstream, the shore that is downdrift from the inlet begins to erode. To prevent this, an arrangement is sometimes made to dredge the impounded sand at the updrift jetty and pump it to the eroding beaches. (See Fig. 9)

2.   In Britain a term used to refer to a wharf or pier.

See: BEACH EROSION; GROIN

Job Training Partnership Act of 1982

Legislation (PL 97-300) that transfers authority for job training or manpower programs for the economically disadvantaged from the federal government to the states and establishes the mechanisms by which they are to be implemented. This act authorizes a financially scaled-down version of the Comprehensive Employment and Training Program (CETA) to be operated under the oversight of each governor and state "job training coordinating council" and to be implemented by a "private industry council" in each service area established. Activities previously conducted under the CETA program and agencies that had conducted them are still eligible for funding, but individual activities must be authorized by a two-year job training plan drawn by the private industry council and approved by the state council and governor.

Activities that are eligible for funding under the act include training services for adults and youths, job search assistance, job counseling, remedial education, skill and on-the-job training, outreach, job development, preapprenticeship programs and supportive services to enable individuals to participate in the programs. Programs for summer employment for youths and employment and training assistance for dislocated workers are also authorized. Programs must also meet performance standards established by the secretary of labor.

Although the states are to take responsibility for a large part of the program, the federal government will retain authority for employment and training programs for Native Americans, migrant and seasonal farm workers, and veterans. It will also continue to manage the Job Corps programs that affect multistate areas, research and pilot projects, and development of data on occupational employment. The act also authorizes the development of a nationwide computerized job bank and job matching program and establishes a National Commission for Employment Policy to advise the president and Congress on national employment and training issues.

See: JOB TRAINING PLAN

Job Training Plan

A funding plan developed by a private industry council, often in conjunction with a local government, for job training activities to be undertaken during a two-year period within the council's designated service area. The private industry council is composed largely of representatives of local industry, labor unions and educational institutions, with a component of public sector officials. A prerequisite for funding under the Job Training Partnership Act of 1982, the job training plan describes the programs to be provided, their estimated cost and duration, procedures for selecting participants, procedures for selecting agencies to provide services, program goals, coordination of activities, and budget estimates for the following two years. The plan must give adequate public notice and be approved by the governor of the state.

Performance standards established by the secretary of labor are imposed on all activities. The governor is directed to provide technical assistance to programs that do not meet performance standard criteria after the first year. If after two years standards are still not met, the governor must intervene by either forming a new private industry council, prohibiting the use of a specific service agency, selecting an alternate service provider or using other means to assure performance.

See: JOB TRAINING PARTNERSHIP ACT OF 1982

Joint Development

The development of a transit facility and commercial project as a joint venture. Joint development is often initiated by public agencies for locations that are expected to become concentrations of activity because of the presence of a major transit facility, with developers being sought to propose generally large commercial complexes on top of or in connection with the transit facility. For urban areas that can support this level of economic activity, joint development is attractive to all parties. The government sets design criteria and gains revenue from what could otherwise be a financial liability, while the developer is absolved from site acquisition (since the public agency assembles the land) and obtains a site on which infrastructure is partially provided by the government.

Sites that are suitable for joint development include those where an existing downtown facility is expected to be improved or a major station of a new fixed-transit line. In the latter location a major housing complex may also be constructed. A regional bus terminal is another appropriate location. Public funding, often obtained from Urban Mass Transportation Administration (UMTA) grants, is used to leverage private development. The specific design, management of construction, and operating agreements must be negotiated based on the particular requirements of each project.
See: ECONOMIC DEVELOPMENT; JOINT VENTURE

Joint Venture

A partnership formed for the limited purpose of carrying out a development or commercial venture to which partners contribute their capital and skills. Unlike general partnerships, joint ventures, which are often formed for large development projects, are usually tied to a specific project and are of a more limited scope and duration.

Joint ventures are advantageous because they allow developers with limited capital to undertake more than one development project at a time. They also provide access to financing for undercapitalized firms and distribute the risk of a project among the various partners. In addition, joint ventures may take place between a real estate developer who has the expertise to conceive and manage a real estate venture but lacks the necessary capital and a business, such as an insurance company, that has access to capital but no expertise in development.

In the economic development process, joint ventures are often undertaken between the public sector and a private developer, with each bearing a share of development costs. Many recent waterfront development projects have been completed in this way.
See: DOWNTOWN REVITALIZATION; ECONOMIC DEVELOPMENT; ECONOMIC DEVELOPMENT INCENTIVES; JOINT DEVELOPMENT

Jones v. *Alfred H. Mayer* (392 U.S. 409 [1968])

A decision by the United States Supreme Court holding that the Civil Rights Act of 1866 prohibits all racially discriminatory housing practices, even those by private individuals.

The Court upheld the constitutionality of the statute, even though it affected actions by individuals not involving any state action or interstate activity. The Court found racial discrimination in housing to be a relic of slavery and the statute to be authorized by the 13th Amendment to the Constitution, which authorized Congress to adopt legislation implementing the proscription against slavery.

Journey to Work

A trip from home to place of work. Planners frequently make studies of the types of transportation used in journey-to-work trips to obtain data on the number of people who use various kinds of vehicles (commuter rail, subway, bus, taxi) or walk and the distance traveled between home and work. This information is used to suggest transportation improvements in local areas, in the form of recommendations for specific new bus routes, bus stops, changes in the frequency of transit service or ridepooling, as examples.

Three questions were asked in the 1980 United States Census of Population and Housing related to distance traveled to work; these concerned place of work, travel time and means of transportation. The results of these questions indicated that the national average travel time to work was 21.7 minutes. While 84.3 percent drove to work in a car, truck or van, 6.3 percent used public transportation, 5.5 percent walked to work, 1.6 percent used other transportation modes, and 2.2 percent worked at home.

Jug-Handle Turn

Also called a trumpet intersection, a jug-handle turn is a form of channelized and signalized intersection in which a storage lane is provided for left-turning vehicles at the right side of the roadway. Use of the lane, which is shaped like the handle of a jug, requires that vehicles exit to the right from the through lanes and turn to the left around an island to a traffic signal or stop sign. This maneuver will permit the cars to cross the through traffic perpendicular to it. Use of jug-handle turns is common on urban arterials for left and U-turns. On freeways they are often employed as part of grade-separated interchanges that direct traffic to toll booths. (See Fig. 5)
See: AT-GRADE INTERSECTION; GRADE-SEPARATED INTERCHANGE; RAMP

Junkyard

A piece of property, often without a building, employed for the storage and sale of used and frequently nonfunctioning merchandise. Many junkyards in the United States store and sell only automobile parts, so that the term is often synonymous with this use. A junkyard may, however, contain any form of junk—such as scrap paper, glass or metal—that is usually intended for resale.

Generally an outdoor use, these yards tend to be unsightly, dirty and noisy. Zoning ordinances usually restrict junkyards to heavy industrial areas or to commercial strips where automobile repair and sales are common uses.

Screening is also required by many ordinances. In addition, the Highway Beautification Act of 1965 required that junkyards within 1,000 feet (304.8 meters) of interstate highways and primary system roads be screened or removed; states not complying would suffer a 10 percent reduction in highway funding. The federal legislation also provided a 75 percent cost-sharing of the program.
See: SCREENING

Just Compensation

The constitutionally mandated compensation to which a property owner is entitled when his property is acquired by eminent domain. It is normally construed to mean the monetary equivalent of the property that was taken.

Where an owner's entire property is taken, just compensation will ordinarily be the fair market value of the property immediately before the taking. However, where only part of a property is taken, or where an easement over property is taken, just compensation may comprise a number of other elements in addition to the direct damages, which is the value of the property or interest taken. These other elements may include severance damages to the remainder parcel (those damages resulting from the division of one integral parcel into two separate parcels or property interests) and consequential damages to the remainder parcel (those damages resulting from the use to which the acquired property or interest is put by the taking authority).

If the owner and the condemning authority cannot agree on the amount of just compensation, the owner is entitled to have the amount determined by court after a trial or valuation proceeding.
See: CONDEMNATION; EMINENT DOMAIN

Just v. Marinette County, Wisconsin (56 Wis.2d 7, 201 N.W.2d 761 [1972])

A decision by the Supreme Court of Wisconsin upholding a locally adopted shoreland zoning ordinance that prohibited the filling of wetlands, other than on a limited basis.

The ordinance, adopted pursuant to state legislation requiring the adoption of regulations protecting shorelands and navigable waters, limited the use of wetlands to certain uses consistent with the use of land in its natural state and certain additional uses permitted only by a conditional use permit.

The court found the ordinance to be a proper exercise of police power, in that it limited the use and development of land to avoid damage to environmentally sensitive wetlands that were related to protection of water purity, navigability and fishing. The regulation did not amount to an unconstitutional taking of property without just compensation, since it did not interfere with the use of land in its natural, indigenous state but only limited its development and use in a way that could harm the public interest. In effect, the court found that a property owner did not have a constitutional right to change wetlands into commercially usable land at the expense of significant public interests entitled to protection.
See: WETLANDS

K

Kitimat, British Columbia

A Canadian new town that was developed when the Aluminum Company of Canada selected the site for an aluminum smelter. Located 400 miles (644 kilometers) north of Vancouver, this wilderness area was chosen because of attributes that included a potential for hydroelectric power and a suitable deep-water harbor. Clarence Stein served as chief planning consultant for the town, which was completed in 1954 and features residential areas sited on terraces.
See: COMPANY TOWN; NEW TOWN; STEIN, CLARENCE S.

L

Labor Force

All persons 16 years of age and over who are either employed, looking for a job or are in the armed forces. The labor force of a particular community consists of community residents who are actively employed or looking for employment either within or outside that community. Students, housewives, retired workers, institutionalized persons and seasonal workers counted during an off-season are not considered to be part of the labor force.

Since census statistics are all collected and tabulated based on place of residence, data on place of work that are included in the census for a particular area do not necessarily provide the total number of individuals who work in that area. Instead, the data represent only those individuals who both work and live in the area being tabulated. Thus, as an example, when looking at place of work data for a central business district within a standard metropolitan statistical (SMSA), no figures would be provided in the census for that area for individuals commuting to work from outside that particular SMSA.

As a result of an increase in the number of adult women and youth entering the labor force in the United States, the labor force has grown at a more rapid pace than the population. As of October 1983, the civilian labor force of the United States was 111,815,000. Employer-based rather than residence-based statistics are also available from the Department of Labor for payroll employment by industry, known as nonagricultural employment. In October 1983, nonagricultural employment in the United States was 91,073,000.

Ladder of Citizen Participation

A framework for analyzing the amount of control that citizens have in government policy decisions. Postulated by Sherry R. Arnstein, the ladder has eight steps of citizen involvement, ranging from nonparticipation to actual control. The concept has been influential in the development and analysis of citizen participation programs.

At the bottom of the ladder, rungs 1 and 2 are called manipulation (placing citizens on advisory panels) and therapy (distracting attention from basic problem causes and attempting to change reactions to problems), both of which she calls nonparticipation. Levels 3, 4 and 5, which she calls tokenism, are informing (notification of decisions made that affect a group), consultation (holding public hearings or attitude surveys) and placation (appointment to decision-making boards with advisory powers). Level 6 is partnership (authority shared by citizens and government), and level 7 is delegated power (final project approval), while level 8 is citizen control (total control). She terms the final three categories citizen power.
See: CITIZEN PARTICIPATION

Lagoon

1. A shallow body of water that is near, or connects with, a larger body of water or the sea. A sound, channel, pond or lake may also be considered to be a lagoon. Relatively small lagoons are frequently used as the design focal point for housing, hotel and recreational developments, often featuring marinas or beaches. Artificial lagoons may also be created to enable recreational waterfront development.

2. In the treatment of sewage sludge, lagoons are used to contain raw or digested sludge where it may be exposed to the air to permit sludge digestion, drying or disposal. Sludge can be left in a lagoon for long periods of time or permanently; when dried, it can be scraped up and disposed of. Sludge lagoons, which are shallow earth basins 4 to 5 feet (1.2 to 1.5 meters) deep, are frequently used at treatment plants, where they require large amounts of land adjacent to the plant.
See: DEWATERED SLUDGE; FINGER FILL CANALS; SEWERAGE SYSTEM; SLUDGE DIGESTION; SLUDGE DISPOSAL

Lake Country Estates Inc. v. *Tahoe Regional Planning Agency* (440 U.S. 391 [1979])

A decision by the United States Supreme Court concerning whether local governments and their officials could be held liable to property owners for zoning actions that violate the constitutional rights of property owners.

The Court, expanding on its 1978 decision of *Monell* v. *Department of Social Services of New York* by applying the decision in a land use context, held that a regional planning agency was not entitled to the sovereign immunity guaranteed to states. The agency could therefore be held liable for damages to a property owner in the event that land use restrictions adopted by the agency were found to have violated the property owner's constitutional rights under the 5th and 14th Amendments to the United States Constitution.

The Court went on to rule that the individual members of the planning agency were immune from damage liability under Section 1983 (the section of the Civil Rights Act of 1871 under which the property owner had brought suit) so long as the agency members had acted in their legislative capacity. However, the Court suggested that individual agency members could lose their immunity if it were found that they personally profited from the unconstitutional land use restrictions imposed upon other property owners.
See: MONELL v. DEPARTMENT OF SOCIAL SERVICES OF NEW YORK

Land and Water Conservation Fund (LAWCON)

A fund administered by the National Park Service that provides matching grants to states for planning, acquisition and development of outdoor recreation and conservation areas and also finances federal open-space land acquisitions. The revenues for LAWCON, which was created by the Land and Water Conservation Fund Act of 1964 (PL 88-578), are derived from entry fees at federal recreation areas, federal motor boat fuel taxes and proceeds from the sale of surplus federal land. Sixty percent of the funds distributed annually are reserved for states, while 40 percent are set aside for federal use. Participating states are required to prepare a statewide outdoor recreation plan before funding may be obtained. State agencies are responsible for local project selection, but projects must comply with the state plan and meet standards for regional significance and proximity to urban areas.
See: STATEWIDE COMPREHENSIVE OUTDOOR RECREATION PLAN (SCORP)

Land Assembly

The process of acquiring and combining land parcels that adjoin in order to form one large development site.

This process, also called assemblage, is often characterized by great secrecy as the assembler attempts to purchase options to each of the parcels needed without paying greatly inflated prices. To expedite development and improve urban areas, government agencies may sometimes aid in land assembly when a formal commitment has been made by a developer to build a project considered beneficial to the community.

See: OPTION

Land Bank

Undeveloped land purchased and held by government for future use. A land bank is part of a program to hold land in reserve for unspecified future public uses, to control the location or pace of development, or to capture any increase in the value of the land.

Proponents of land banking say that it can avoid sprawl, prevent land speculation and make possible orderly, planned development in accordance with a public plan. Opponents cite the high cost of purchasing land and removing it from tax rolls as well as possible legal complications. In the United States, under the power of eminent domain, government may condemn land for a specific public use, but it is unclear whether this authority may be extended to achieve general planning goals.

Land banking has been used extensively in Alberta and Saskatchewan, Canada under Canada's National Housing Act, which provides federal financial assistance for municipal or provincial land assembly projects via the Central Mortgage and Housing Corporation. In Alberta the provincial government has been most active and has imposed strict planning controls on development on government land banks. In Saskatchewan, cities have been primarily responsible but have not imposed special controls and use the land banks to permit development when considered appropriate. Large-scale land banking has also been used extensively in Sweden, but it remains virtually untested in the United States, where there is a strong tradition of private land ownership, and zoning is the primary method of development control.

Land donated to a public agency and land acquired for the future expansion of a specific public facility may also be considered to be land banks. In declining cities widespread property abandonment may create a land bank by default. As the city assumes title to tax-delinquent real estate, large parcels may be assembled and held for redevelopment.

See: GROWTH MANAGEMENT; OPEN-SPACE PRESERVATION

Land Endowment

A gift of land to a government body, a foundation or a public charity. The land may be given to enable construction of a building or other necessary facility or to provide open space.

Because the land is a gift, donors frequently put restrictions on its use. In some cases, this has placed obstacles to a change of use that may be appropriate because of chang-

ing conditions in the surrounding area, such as development of a portion of a nature preserve for a playfield when surrounding density increases. In other cases, the restrictions have helped to prevent modifications explicitly in opposition to the wishes of the donor, such as sale of land donated as a wildlife sanctuary for shopping center development. A donor may also require a life estate.

See: CHARITABLE CONTRIBUTION OF REAL ESTATE; PROPERTY ACQUISITION; RESTRICTIVE COVENANT

Land Management

The practice of guiding the development or preservation of land to achieve the greatest long-term benefits. This concept encompasses the requirements of the existing population, the probable needs of future generations, and the preservation of the natural environment.

See: CARRYING CAPACITY; COASTAL AREA PLANNING; COMPREHENSIVE PLAN; CRITICAL AREAS; ENVIRONMENTALLY SENSITIVE LANDS; FARMLAND PROTECTION; FLOODPLAIN MANAGEMENT; FORESTRY; GROWTH MANAGEMENT; LAND RECLAMATION; LAND USE; LAND USE CONTROLS; OPEN-SPACE PRESERVATION; RANGELAND MANAGEMENT

Land Reclamation

1. Altering land so that it is capable of accommodating development or more intensive development. This may be accomplished by bringing water to arid or semiarid lands through the construction of such structures as dams, canals and aqueducts. This type of reclamation has been practiced extensively in the western United States, Israel and Egypt.

In contrast, wetlands may be drained and filled to provide additional land areas suitable for construction. In the Netherlands newly created land, or polders, is carefully managed through a series of dikes, dams and pumps that maintain a delicate balance between land and sea. Waterfront property has also been created in many parts of Florida.

Problems have been associated with both of these forms of land reclamation. In the United States irrigation of arid land for the purpose of agriculture has been charged with being wasteful of valuable water resources, as there are more suitable agricultural lands where water could be better utilized. Irrigation has also been associated with salinization and excessive withdrawal of groundwater supplies. Drainage and filling of wetlands has also met with numerous criticisms, as wetlands fulfill many important functions, such as maintenance of an area's ecosystem, flood control and shoreline stabilization. Dredging, filling and other activities in most wetlands are strictly controlled in the United States by the Army Corps of Engineers.

2. Return of land that has been disturbed by mining activities to productive use. Reclamation procedures include addition of topsoil, return of vegetative cover, planting of trees and restoration of landforms.

See: ARMY CORPS OF ENGINEERS' PERMIT PROGRAM; IRRIGATION; SANITARY LANDFILL; STRIP MINING; WETLANDS

Land Subsidence

The downward movement or collapse of the earth's surface. It is generally caused by the removal of supporting materials from beneath the earth—as in the mining of coal, salt, gold or other substances—or by the extraction of fluids, such as water or oil. The potential for this condition must be investigated at the time a site is considered for development, so that necessary precautions may be taken.

Subsidence due to mining activities occurs most often when abandoned mine workings are left at fairly shallow depths underground. Portions of Pennsylvania and the midlands of England are examples of coal mining regions with many old mine workings. When construction takes place in these areas, a number of procedures may be used to try to identify the extent of the mine, to change the construction site if necessary or to design a structure that can adjust to the expected amount of settlement. Techniques have also been developed for backfilling or refilling the mined-out underground areas with solid materials, so that a solid support foundation is provided. This is done either under hydraulic pressure or by pneumatic injection when the use of water can increase the danger of subsidence.

Subsidence caused by pumping fluids from the ground can occur whenever fluid removal is accompanied by certain geologic conditions, such as a prevalence of clays and silts. In Mexico City the pumping of water has resulted in the dramatic settling of numerous buildings. Many parts of Arizona, Texas and California have also had subsidence problems due to water removal, while portions of Italy's Po Delta have been sinking as a result of methane gas extraction. When subsidence caused by fluid removal is severe, it may be countered by injecting fluids back into the ground under pressure.
See: GEOLOGIC HAZARDS

Land Use

The various ways in which land may be employed or occupied. Planners compile, classify, study and analyze land use data for many purposes, including the identification of trends, the forecasting of space and infrastructure requirements, the provision of adequate land area for necessary types of land use, and the development or revision of comprehensive plans and land use regulations.
See: LAND USE CLASSIFICATION SYSTEM; LAND USE CONTROLS; LAND USE DETERMINANTS; LAND USE MAP; LAND USE PATTERN; LAND USE PLAN; LAND USE SURVEY

Land Use Buffer

A land use that creates a spatial, visual and/or psychological separation between two other land use types, such as a commercial or open-space area between residential and industrial areas. Land uses that create nuisances—such as fumes, traffic or noise—particularly require land use buffering.
See: BUFFER ZONE; LAND USE

Land Use Classification System

A means by which specific land uses may be grouped into meaningful categories for different types of analysis and assigned codes that facilitate the use of computerized data bases. This type of classification allows a detailed examination of land development patterns and activities; computerization also permits aggregation of the data in a variety of ways so that the data may be examined from a number of perspectives. There is no single standardized land use code in the United States, although a number of other countries do have standardized codes. Most United States land classification systems bear a close resemblance, however, to the Standard Industrial Classification (SIC) system of the Office of Management and Budget.

One common code, the federal *Standard Land Use Coding Manual,* which was derived from the SIC system and completed in 1965, provides 9 major categories, such as residential, manufacturing and undeveloped land. These 9 one-digit categories are further refined into 67 two-digit categories, 294 three-digit categories and 772 four-digit categories of increasing specificity. There is also a one-digit auxiliary code that describes functions that are separate from but linked to the main operation, such as automobile parking. A retail grocery store (code 5410) may have its own parking lot (auxiliary category 5), for example, which is auxiliary to the store. The combined code would then become 5410-5.

Generally, it is recommended that the entire four digits be recorded, because even if this level of detail is not necessary for a small community, it can allow comparisons across a region. The community can elect to use the two- or three-digit level for most purposes while maintaining records based upon the complete code for possible future use.
See: STANDARD INDUSTRIAL CLASSIFICATION (SIC) SYSTEM

Land Use Controls

Those devices by which government may exercise its police power authority to regulate the use of land. The principal types of land use controls that are employed today are zoning (of which there are many types and forms), subdivision regulations and the official map.
See: OFFICIAL MAP; POLICE POWER; SUBDIVISION REGULATIONS; ZONING

Land Use Determinants

Natural and human factors that influence the location of specific land uses.

The human environment is a significant determinant of land use. Development is influenced by accessibility, traffic volume and proximity to complementary, compatible and incompatible land uses. Development also responds to local market conditions and patterns of population and employment growth. In addition, land use is affected by the availability of basic services such as roads, utilities, sewers, schools, parks, public transportation, and fire and police protection.

Consumer tastes and the reputation of an area are cultural determinants of land use. Institutional factors that affect land use decisions include legal and political constraints, such as land use regulations, private covenants and environmental regulations; government policies, such as subsidies for development and tax policy that encourages or discourages certain types of construction; public works projects; the economic system; and land ownership patterns.

Development potential is limited in environmentally sensitive areas, such as floodplains, faults, wetlands and steep hillsides. Other natural factors, such as topography and soil conditions, affect the cost and intensity of development. Natural resources—such as waterfront location, dramatic views or mineral resources—can increase the desirability of a site for particular uses but may also be associated with strict land use controls.
See: CENTRAL PLACE THEORY; GROWTH THEORY; LAND USE CONTROLS; LAND USE PATTERN

Land Use Intensity Standards (LUI)

A comprehensive system used to calculate and regulate the intensity at which land can be developed, intended to replace conventional height, bulk and density requirements and to permit greater flexibility in planned residential developments, apartment buildings and townhouses.

The basic control device is a scale of land use intensity ratings that correlates land area, floor area, open space, and recreation space, as well as car storage space. This scale is designed to restrict intensities while at the same time encouraging amenities such as pedestrian open space and unusual building configurations. For a community to adopt this system, it must establish LUI districts for its residentially zoned land and incorporate definitions and rules into its zoning ordinance relating to these controls. Different ratings that correspond to each district determine the maximum LUI allowable for that district.

This system was adopted by the Federal Housing Administration in the mid-1960s and was designed to be applicable to a wide range of situations, from low-density suburbs to high-density central city sites. Although a number of communities have used it for planned developments, relatively few have adopted the LUI system in place of conventional regulatory devices.
See: ZONING

Land Use Map

A map that depicts selected categories of land use in a geographic area as well as other major features, such as political boundaries, transportation arteries and water bodies.

The number of categories presented may vary considerably, depending upon the size of the planning area, the map scale that is selected, the degree of homogeneity of land use, the type of land use survey data available, the intended use of the map and the available budget. The simplest type of land use map may be printed in black and white, using various patterns to distinguish land use categories and differentiate residential uses, commercial uses, industrial uses, public uses and vacant land. A more complex system is often required, however, in which various housing densities or types are distinguished as well as types of business, public and institutional uses.

Increasingly, color is being employed in land use maps because of its superior ability to convey information, particularly when numerous land use categories are involved. When maps are prepared in color, a conventional color code is generally used. Various graphic displays of land use may also be produced by computer printout when a land use survey has been coded for computer processing.
See: COLOR CODE; LAND USE; LAND USE CLASSIFICATION SYSTEM; LAND USE PLAN; LAND USE SURVEY

Land Use Pattern

The generalized spatial distribution of development. The land use pattern is a general description of how land is occupied or utilized and how land uses tend to cluster. The names given to the various patterns connote the predominant physical pattern created by local streets and building locations in a developed area, by major arterials and highways or by relative population densities in a metropolitan area, and the spatial relationships among municipalities within a regional area. (See Fig. 24)
See: AXIAL GROWTH; CEREMONIAL AXIS PLAN; CIRCUMFERENTIAL PLAN; CURVILINEAR PATTERN; DIRECTIONAL GROWTH; DISPERSION PATTERN; FINGER PATTERN; GALAXY PATTERN; GRIDIRON PATTERN; GROWTH THEORY; LAND USE, RADIAL PATTERN; RING PATTERN; SATELLITE PATTERN

Land Use Plan

A generalized scheme or proposal regarding how land should logically be used and where growth and renewal should occur. The land use plan, often one element of a comprehensive plan, is frequently developed concurrently with other closely related documents, such as transportation plans, environmental plans and community facility plans.

A land use plan estimates future land use requirements, examines alternative ways in which the built environment can be structured to meet probable requirements and attempts to assure that land will be used for appropriate purposes. Land use plans often contain some or all of the following components: a statement of goals and objectives; a discussion of existing conditions, often accompanied by a land use map; a summary of both the qualitative and quantitative future land use requirements; plan alternatives; recommendations concerning the most appropriate alternative; and means of implementing the recommended plan.

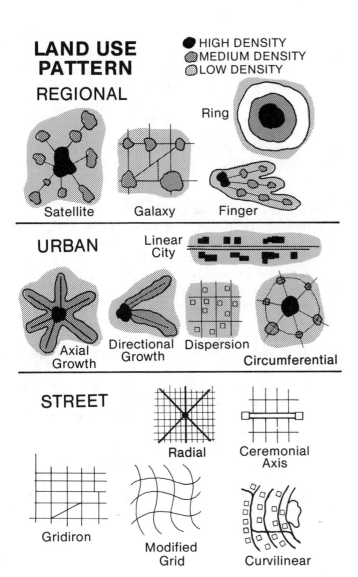

LAND USE PATTERN

● HIGH DENSITY
◍ MEDIUM DENSITY
◯ LOW DENSITY

REGIONAL

Ring

Satellite   Galaxy   Finger

URBAN

Linear City

Axial Growth   Directional Growth   Dispersion   Circumferential

STREET

Radial   Ceremonial Axis

Gridiron   Modified Grid   Curvilinear

Fig. 24.

In developing a land use plan, a planning area is defined, and various basic studies are conducted. The studies may examine such subjects as population, employment, housing needs, environmental concerns and needs, and areas experiencing development pressures. Estimates of future land use requirements are made, and various means of distributing and locating these land use requirements are developed. Within this process, attempts are made to achieve a balance between the needs of the various components of the community and to take into consideration existing land use, the physical characteristics of the land, economic conditions and other necessary factors.

Although land use plans are often intended to cover a 20- to 25-year time span, shorter-range land use plans, sometimes called land development plans, may also be prepared to aid in implementing the longer-range plan and to address issues that develop over time.
See: COMPREHENSIVE PLAN; FUTURE LAND USE REQUIREMENTS; LAND USE MAP; LAND USE SURVEY

Land Use Survey

A comprehensive inventory of the way in which land is used in a planning area.

A survey may be conducted in a variety of ways, ranging from windshield checks by automobile in sparsely populated areas to door-to-door surveys on foot in densely developed areas. It may also be possible to use community records, such as those of the assessor's office, as the basis for a land use survey if the records are kept current; field checks may then be limited to "spot checks" and to resolving data gaps or ambiguities in the records. Aerial photographs are also a valuable information resource.

There are two basic ways in which survey information may be recorded: on base maps or on standardized forms that are keyed to maps so that a particular parcel may be identified. The annotated map approach is chosen more often in smaller communities, where the data will likely be stored in map form. The standardized form is more frequently used in larger urban areas, where the survey will become part of a computerized data base. When this approach is chosen, standardized notations are used by all survey participants, and the forms that are filled out in the field are designed so that they may be readily coded.

Information collected during a land use survey may be presented by map and/or by a series of tables. Tables often show the number of acres and the proportion of developed land in the planning area devoted to each land use category that has been enumerated.
See: INFORMATION SYSTEM; LAND USE CLASSIFICATION SYSTEM; LAND USE MAP; LAND USE PLAN; WINDSHIELD SURVEY

Land Value Tax

A form of real property taxation in which only land is taxed and in which buildings and other improvements are exempted. A modified version of this taxation system, in which land is heavily taxed while improvements are taxed at a lower rate, instead of the predominant form of property tax, in which improvements are usually taxed at a higher rate, is also used. Also called a site value tax, land value taxation, in one form or another, is used in parts of western Canada, Australia and British Commonwealth countries in East and Central Africa. It is also used successfully in Pittsburgh, Pennsylvania and a few other localities in the United States.

Those who favor this form of taxation argue that it avoids any discouraging effect on building, makes the holding of vacant property for speculative purposes undesirable and can effectively capture increases in land values. It is also thought that the land value tax can encourage better use of scarce land and inner city rehabilitation because building improvements are not taxed. Its detractors argue, however, that buildings require municipal services and that taxation on the land alone cannot yield adequate revenue to provide these services.
See: BETTERMENT TAX; PROPERTY TAX

Land Write-down

The reduction in the offering price of land to less than its fair market value, used as a subsidy technique by public agencies to attract private capital.

In urban redevelopment projects, public agencies purchase blighted properties, remove the structures and then sell the land, sometimes at less than its appraised value, as an inducement to redevelopment. A public agency may also write down the cost of land in order to dispose of surplus properties or properties acquired through tax foreclosure. In these cases, the cost of the write-down is the difference between what the agency could have received and what it actually received.
See: ECONOMIC DEVELOPMENT INCENTIVES; SUBSIDY

Landform

One of the naturally formed and distinctive physical features and configurations that comprise the Earth's surface. Mountains are examples of landforms, as are valleys, plains and plateaus. Erosion by water, wind and ice, as well as weathering and other forces of nature, help to shape these physical features and continue to slowly change them. Landforms, in turn, influence their immediate environment and affect such crucial factors as the availability of water and exposure to sunlight. The study of the nature and origin of landforms is known as geomorphology.

Landing Strip

A small airport with a runway generally capable of accommodating aircraft having a maximum gross weight of 12,500 pounds (5,670 kilograms). The runway area will be graded but not necessarily paved, and service buildings may or may not be available. Landing strips are the principal airport facilities of rural and outlying areas. In many towns in the northern provinces of Canada, they are the only investment in intercity transportation; there are no roads connecting many towns.
See: AIRPORT PLANNING

Landlocked

A parcel of land owned by one person that has no access to a public road or right-of-way, except over land belonging to others.

If the landlocked piece had ever been held in common ownership with any of the adjoining parcels having access to a public road, a court may grant the owner of the landlocked parcel an easement of access to the public road over the land formerly held in common. This easement is sometimes called an easement by implication, on the theory that when the landlocked parcel was created, it must have been the intent to provide for access to a public road. The easement may be called an easement by necessity, since its creation is supported by public policy, which disfavors creation of parcels of land that are not capable of being used.
See: ACCESS; EASEMENT

Landmark

1.   A historic or architecturally significant structure that has been officially designated by a government ordinance that often affords it some degree of protection.

2.   A man-made or natural object that helps to mark the boundaries of land.

3.   A prominent feature of the landscape or a man-made structure that serves as a guide.
See: HISTORIC PRESERVATION; LANDMARKS COMMISSION ORDINANCE; NATIONAL HISTORIC LANDMARK

Landmarks Commission Ordinance

A type of municipal statute that controls designated historic landmarks throughout a municipality. The landmarks commission ordinance generally differs from a historic district ordinance in that it provides the authority to designate and regulate individual historic landmarks that may be scattered geographically. The landmarks ordinance also usually contains a mechanism for nominating and establishing additional historic sites, structures and districts. Formal landmark designations are usually made by the legislative body.

A landmarks commission is established by the ordinance, whose authority may include the right to regulate proposed exterior changes or to delay demolition of a designated landmark. The landmarks commission also serves as an advisory resource to the legislative body, may assist property owners with design problems, and may often be placed in charge of the community's historic survey.
See: HISTORIC DISTRICT ORDINANCE; HISTORIC PRESERVATION; HISTORIC REVIEW BOARD; LANDMARK; MINIMUM MAINTENANCE STANDARDS

LANDSAT

A satellite program designed to collect data on the natural resources of the earth on a continuing basis. The program began in 1972 with the launching of the first Earth Resources Technology Satellite (ERTS), the original name for LANDSAT. LANDSAT 2 (ERTS B) was launched in 1975, LANDSAT 3 in 1978 and LANDSAT 4 in 1982. Although initially run by the National Aeronautics and Space Administration, the program is now operated by the National Oceanic and Atmospheric Administration.

The first three LANDSATs, no longer in orbit, circled the earth in an orbit 570 miles (917 kilometers) high and completely covered the earth's surface every 18 days. They relied for remote sensing primarily on a multispectral scanner (MSS) that covers a strip of land below the satellite in different spectral bands. Each band helped to show particular qualities of the terrain, such as distribution of land and water, topographic detail or tonal contrast (a good indicator of land use type).

LANDSAT 4 also carries a multispectral scanner, but in addition is equipped with an improved type of sensor system known as a thematic mapper. This device is capable of sensing light in seven different spectral bands and of assigning a number from 0 to 256 to the sensed light based on degree of gray. Images are transmitted with much greater clarity than was possible with earlier LANDSATs, and the features of areas less than 1/6 of an acre (0.067 hectares) in size can be detected as compared with the 1.2 acres (0.48 hectares) previous LANDSATs were capable of distinguishing.

LANDSAT 4, which has an orbit that is 430 miles (692 kilometers) high, covers each point on earth every 16 days as compared with the 18 days of earlier satellites. It has, however, been encountering equipment failures and is now expected to stop operating sooner than had been planned. The next LANDSAT may be launched ahead of schedule to preserve continuity of transmission, while LANDSAT 4 is expected to be diverted to an orbit where it may later be fixed or recovered by the space shuttle.

LANDSAT data are transmitted to ground stations throughout the world and subsequently made available to the public in a variety of forms. The satellite information is being used for an increasingly wide range of applications related to planning. As examples, LANDSAT information may become the basis for a regional land use inventory, as was done in the Portland, Oregon, area, or it may be used to monitor air pollution. Mapping and analysis of flood-prone areas has been accomplished with the help of LANDSAT, as has the management of agricultural lands, rangelands and forests. Satellite data may also be used in exploration for mineral resources and fossil fuels and monitoring of coastal erosion. Many types of maps may readily be produced, highlighting vegetation, land use, wetlands or other characteristics. Because LANDSAT data are frequently updated, it is possible to closely monitor changes in development and in the environment.

Proposals have been made by the Reagan administration to sell LANDSAT satellites and weather satellites to private industry. Necessary data would then be purchased by government from private contractors. In reaction to these proposals, Congress passed a measure in June 1983 (which was part of legislation providing National Aeronautics and Space Administration funding in fiscal year 1984) forbidding such a sale unless congressional approval is granted. (See Fig. 25)

See: EARTH RESOURCES OBSERVATION SYSTEMS (EROS) PROGRAM; EARTH RESOURCES TECHNOLOGY SATELLITE (ERTS); REMOTE SENSING

Landscape Architecture

The art and science of reshaping land for practical or aesthetic purposes. Landscape architecture generally comprises the redesign of a site to accommodate specific land uses, buildings and structures, and the selection and placement of landscape features such as trees, other plantings and ponds. In the design of a project, moreover, the landscape architect might also design structures, street furniture and signage.

An ancient art, modern landscape architecture is directly descended from 18th-century English garden design. Landscape architects today are generally the princi-

pal designers of parks and other planned open areas, but they are also employed by architects and planners to design areas around buildings for purposes of aesthetics, screening, energy savings and wind control.

Various styles have developed since man began altering landscapes. The ancient Egyptians had formal symmetrical gardens, while the Babylonians and Persians had more varied environments, ranging from enclosed game reserves to terraced areas with hanging gardens. Greek and early Roman gardens turned inward to the atria of houses where water fountains were located and trees and foliage were often frescoed on the walls. Late Roman gardens at private villas expanded the use of fountains by bringing the garden outside the house. Islamic gardens, which were brought to Europe by Arab invasions as far north as Spain, were characterized by numerous pools of water and colonnaded courtyards similar to those of the Greeks but color was added by an abundance of flowers and the use of blue tiles at the base of the pools to reflect the sky.

Medieval gardens were characterized by trick apparatus, such as mechanical trees with birds that flapped their wings and sang, located in enclosed courts. Renaissance gardens, however, were the first to evoke the large formal park environment that persisted until the middle of the 18th century. The Italians of the Renaissance period used water on a large scale in park design. In the most famous case (the Villa d'Este near Rome), they channeled a river that runs down the steep slope on which the gardens are located to operate a wide variety and number of fountains. They also added the use of vistas, statuary, garden structures and axial relationships among park elements. The French took these principles to extremes, most notably at Versailles where its landscape architect André LeNôtre provided many of the elements of this style on a grand scale. Topiary, which became popular in Holland was also added to this general design. A major reversal from formality to naturalness was brought about in England in the middle of the 18th century under the influence of William Kent and later Lancelot "Capability" Brown, who advocated placement of trees in natural clumps, removal of structures, and meandering paths.

Oriental garden design, with roots in religious philosophy, emphasizes a succession of distinct sensations evoked by natural elements such as rocks, trees and ponds, that are placed to emulate a small-scale version of the larger world. Increased trade brought the use of some of these elements to England as early as the mid-18th century and its use in western landscape architecture persists, generally in small garden areas of larger parks.

Fredrick Law Olmsted, who coined the term landscape architecture, is credited with development of the art in the United States. In his designs for numerous parks he placed emphasis on the English natural style but incorporated more formal environments in small areas.

See: AESTHETICS; ARCHITECTURE; LANDSCAPING; OLMSTED, FREDERICK LAW; OPEN-SPACE PLANNING; SITE DESIGN; STREET FURNITURE; URBAN DESIGN; URBAN PLANNING

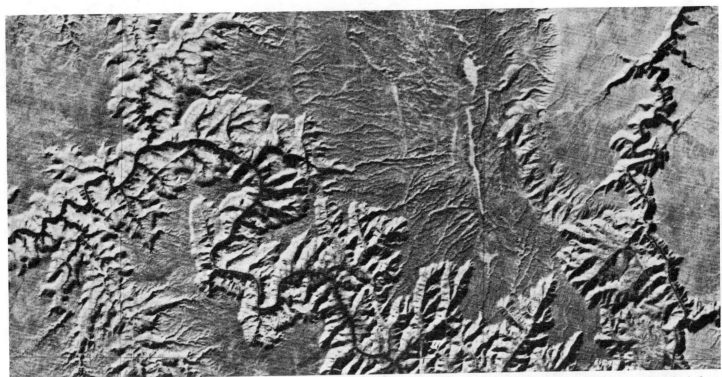

Fig. 25.   LANDSAT image of part of the Grand Canyon in Arizona (scale 1:500,000). This is a composite of multispectral bands 4, 6 and 7 which emphasizes information about vegetation, land and water contrast and water with high sediment content. Band 5 (not shown) would emphasize cultural features such as buildings and roads.
Credit: U.S. Geological Survey, EROS Data Center

Landscaping

The art or practice of arranging plant materials—including ground cover, shrubs and trees—along with other natural or man-made elements, such as rocks and fencing, as a means of enhancing some portion of the built or natural environment. Landscaping serves as an architectural element by creating visual changes in texture, adds color to the man-made environment and is used to soften spaces or surfaces that appear cold and unwelcoming. Plantings can be used to screen objects or land uses that are undesirable or unsightly, buffer incompatible uses and create privacy and shade. In large developments landscaping is conceived as a total pattern: Homogeneous plant materials or planting patterns are used to delineate important areas; lines of trees, to define major street axes; and clumps of planting, to mark focal points. The designer will also include landscaping in plazas and enclosed malls to divide spaces and add color.

Landscaping of large paved areas, such as parking lots and streets, is of concern to the planner since these areas can be extremely unattractive in the absence of trees and shrubs. Zoning ordinances or municipal reviewing agencies may require that a minimum percentage of a parking area be landscaped as well as screened.

See: DECIDUOUS TREES; EVERGREENS; GROUND COVER; LANDSCAPE ARCHITECTURE; SCREENING; SHADE TREE COMMISSION; STREET BEAUTIFICATION

Lane Width

The selection of width of roadway lanes depends upon several factors: available right-of-way, topography, unavoidable obstructions, expected traffic flow, requirements for parking and budget. Given these constraints, it is recommended that wherever possible, through-travel lanes be 12 feet (3.7 meters) in width. Experience has shown that economizing by building narrower lanes results in lower road capacity than anticipated, as well as reduced safety and comfort. Lane widths of 13 to 14 feet (4.0 to 4.3 meters) have been found useful on high-speed, two-lane rural roads but, if wider, cause drivers to create a third lane.

Determination of appropriate width requires an analysis of the clearances that vehicles require between each other and with objects along the road. Generally, vehicles require 2.5 feet (76.2 centimeters) between parallel vehicles but move more comfortably where they are at least 6 feet (1.8 meters) apart. Roads that carry large numbers of trucks and buses warrant 12-foot (3.7-meter) lanes, since the size of the larger vehicles reduces perceived distance between vehicles. Obstructions such as light poles, bridge abutments, retaining walls or parked cars, when closer than 6 feet (1.8 meters) to a travel lane, can reduce effective lane width by up to 28 percent.

See: AUXILIARY LANES; HIGHWAY CAPACITY DETERMINANTS; SHOULDER

Large-Lot Zoning

Zoning in which the minimum permitted lot size for construction of a residence is at least 1 acre (0.4 hectare). In some communities minimum required lot sizes may be as large as 5 or 10 acres or even more.

This practice, also known as acreage zoning, has frequently been labeled a form of exclusionary zoning, in that it prevents anyone unable to afford a large parcel of land from owning a home. The courts have generally viewed the practice of large-lot zoning with disfavor in recent years, unless it can be shown that this zoning is necessary for the general welfare of the public. Factors that might tend, however, to make this practice more acceptable in certain cases might include exceptionally rugged terrain; other critical environmental factors, such as a shortage of water; and an adequate supply of a variety of housing types in other portions of the community or throughout the region.

See: EXCLUSIONARY ZONING; FARMLAND PROTECTION; ZONING

Lateral

1. A small-diameter sewer pipe that houses and businesses connect into and that conducts wastewater to a sewer main. Laterals are located in every street that is served by a sewerage system.

The minimum-sized pipe most states require for laterals is 8 inches (20.3 centimeters) in diameter to allow small objects to flow through. This size is large enough to serve most single-family residential development.

2. A term sometimes used to refer to water pipes serving local streets to differentiate them from the larger water mains.

See: HOUSE CONNECTION; SEWER MAIN; SEWERAGE SYSTEM; WATER SUPPLY SYSTEM

Leachate

A solution that forms when water seeping through a sanitary landfill absorbs suspended and dissolved solid matter as well as bacteria. If the leachate percolates down to mix with groundwater, it can pollute the water supply.

The amount of leachate produced by a landfill depends upon soil composition, permeability, the topography of the site, hydrology and the type of waste found at the landfill. Although landfills are thought to produce less contamination over time, they can continue to produce leachate many years after they have been completed.

Landfills may be designed so that the spread of leachate from the site can be controlled to some extent. Among the methods used are impermeable linings placed beneath a landfill, which lower the rate of infiltration, and diversion and recovery of leachate by using wells or drain tiles located for that purpose so that the leachate may be disposed of separately.

See: GROUNDWATER POLLUTION; SANITARY LANDFILL

Leapfrog Development

A pattern of growth in which vacant parcels adjacent to existing development are bypassed and land farther out developed instead. Leapfrog development generally occurs as developers choose to build on less expensive, more removed parcels.

Considered part of a sprawl pattern, leapfrog development uses excessive amounts of land and requires extra utility extensions. The utility costs of leapfrogging, if borne by the development without government subsidy, would often exceed the land cost differential of building closer in. Tight control of utility extensions as well as land use controls can help to limit leapfrog development.

See: GROWTH MANAGEMENT; SPRAWL

Le Corbusier (1887–1965)

A Swiss architect and city planner (born Charles Edouard Jeanneret) who strongly influenced the practice of modern architecture and urban design throughout the world. He was a painter and sculptor as well, with many of his designs being characterized by sculptural elements and innovative uses of concrete and other building materials. He also developed many theories of importance to planning and architecture, including one in which design is related to the scale of the human body.

Largely self-taught, Le Corbusier traveled through Europe from 1907 to 1911 studying various techniques, including the use of reinforced concrete. He began living and working in Paris and in 1920 helped to found a review of architecture and city planning known as *L'esprit nouveau*. Two years later he opened a studio with Piere Jeanneret, his cousin, with whom he maintained a partnership until 1940. During these years he tackled a wide range of architecture and planning projects, some of which were never built but still attracted great attention because of their innovative concepts.

Among the features he incorporated into his designs were open floor plans, lack of ornamentation, support pillars that created usable areas beneath a building and roof terrace/gardens that were integrated with living areas. He also envisioned a city (the Ville Contemporaine) in 1922 in which skyscrapers containing offices were set amid open spaces and surrounded by a ring of apartment house development that incorporated gardens and parks. An extensive greenbelt was to separate this development from industrial areas. Among the projects he designed during this era were the Swiss Dormitory at the Cite Universitaire in Paris (1931–32), the Ministry of Education and Health in Rio de Janeiro (1936) and master plans for Algiers and Buenos Aires.

Post-World War II projects for which he is famous include the Chapel Notre Dame-du-Haut at Ronchamp (1950–55), the National Museum of Western Art in Tokyo (1960) and Harvard University's Carpenter Visual Center (1964). He also won renown for his design for the Indian capital city of Chandigarh, which gained worldwide attention. In addition, Le Corbusier was the author of numerous articles and books.

Legal Notice

Notice to the public mandated by federal, state or municipal law, generally required before certain types of action may be taken. It is usually necessary for the notice to appear in one or more publications, such as a local newspaper, a set period of time before the action or event—e.g., a public hearing. It may also have to be posted in designated locations and/or mailed to specific concerned parties, such as the owner of property that is the subject of a hearing. Proof must usually be obtained that the legal notice was given as required.

See: PUBLIC HEARING

Leisure Opportunities

Chances to participate in recreational pursuits. Recreation planning today endeavors to provide a broad range of leisure opportunities by expanding program types, hours of operation and forms of recreational facilities. Increasing leisure opportunities are also being offered by libraries, museums, universities, public and private schools, and religious institutions.

See: LEISURE SERVICES

Leisure Services

A diverse range of alternative activities provided for time not occupied by employment or required functions. Programs may be offered for many population groups and include adult education, physical fitness classes, cultural activities and competitive sports activities.

Planning for many recreational and cultural facilities now includes the provision of leisure services as a means of drawing attendance or expanding the functions that the facilities serve. Special events programming for public parks, lecture series at museums, and open rehearsals of theater or concert productions are among the wide variety of activities being offered.

See: CULTURAL RESOURCES PLANNING; RECREATION FACILITIES; RECREATION PLANNING; RECREATION SYSTEM

L'Enfant, Major Pierre Charles (1754–1825)

A French engineer, architect and planner responsible for the plan for Washington, D.C. A volunteer officer in the American revolutionary army, L'Enfant received a commission to survey what was to become the District of Columbia and was subsequently hired by George Washington to prepare a plan for the district.

When completed, his plan for the new capital city focused on the Capitol Building and the home of the president (later called the White House). A gridiron street pattern was created, with diagonal streets (such as Pennsylvania Avenue) superimposed upon the grid. His plan also called for large areas of public open space and smaller open-space areas at the intersections of radial streets for the location of fountains and monuments.

L'Enfant was dismissed in 1792 over conflicts with the commissioners of the city, but much of his plan was eventually followed in the development of Washington, D.C.

Letchworth, England

The first garden city in Britain, which began to be developed in 1903. Letchworth was built by a company, First Garden City Ltd., founded by Ebenezer Howard for the purpose of putting his ideas into practice.

Located in Hertfordshire, about 35 miles (56.3 kilometers) north of London, Letchworth was created to be a self-supporting community with its own industrial employment base and was built according to the master plan prepared for it by Raymond Unwin and Barry Parker. The plan called for an ultimate population of no more than 35,000, with most of the land retained for open space. One of the most prominent features of Letchworth is the greenbelt that surrounds it and is used for permanent open space. Industry is also separated from residential uses, and extensive landscaping is employed throughout the city.

Letchworth, which has been widely imitated, helped to form the foundation for the eventual adoption of a new towns policy in Britain.

See: GARDEN CITY; HOWARD, SIR EBENEZER; NEW TOWNS ACT, 1946; UNWIN, SIR RAYMOND; WELWYN GARDEN CITY, ENGLAND

Level of Service (LOS)

The quality of conditions afforded to a driver or passenger on a particular facility. Most often applied to roads, level of service analysis can also be applied to public transit, rail and air traffic. The Transportation Research Board has defined the factors involved in roadway level of service as: (1) speed or travel time, (2) traffic interruptions or restrictions, (3) freedom to maneuver, (4) safety, (5) driving comfort and convenience, and (6) cost of operating the vehicle. In the absence of quantifiable means of analysis for most of the above factors, two factors are used to determine a specific level of service: speed or travel time and the ratio of traffic volume to the capacity of the road.

Six levels of service have been established by the Transportation Research Board in its 1965 *Highway Capacity Manual* to describe the conditions on any link of a highway, street or intersection; they are designated A through F, with A representing the most favorable driving conditions.

- *Level A.* Low volumes of traffic flow freely at high speeds with little restriction on maneuverability.
- *Level B.* Traffic volumes associated with those of rural highways flow at a stable rate and at high speeds but are somewhat restricted by other traffic on the road.
- *Level C.* Higher traffic volumes associated with those of urban roads flow at a stable rate but at satisfactory lower operating speeds.
- *Level D.* High traffic volumes approach an unstable traffic flow, which can cause substantial drops in operating speeds, freedom of maneuverability, comfort and convenience.
- *Level E.* Traffic volumes at or near highway capacity operate at lower speeds than Level D.
- *Level F.* Traffic volumes below capacity exhibit

forced flow, low speeds and stoppages. This is essentially a peak-hour phenomenon, with the road serving as a storage area for parts of the peak period.

Level of service was formerly called practical capacity.

Leverage

1. The ability to increase the rate of return on an investment through the use of borrowed money. This can be done when the debt service on the borrowed funds and any applicable operating expenses are less than the cash flow generated by the investment. Real estate acquisitions are often leveraged; for example, if the property is purchased with a 20 percent cash investment, the owner still benefits from the appreciation in value and income generated by 100 percent of the property. The larger the percentage of the purchase price that the mortgage represents, the larger the potential rate of return on equity, providing that the rate of return on the total investment in the property (cash invested and loan incurred) remains higher than the interest rate on the borrowed funds. Of course, leveraging also increases the potential loss on an unprofitable investment.

2. Sometimes used to describe the additional amount of private investment that a certain amount of government investment can generate. It is common with programs such as community development or those related to economic development for a public expenditure of $1 million to leverage $6 million worth of private investment. Commercial or housing rehabilitation may be used as an example of how this can occur.

If government programs are used to provide a number of tangible examples in particular neighborhoods of how deteriorated housing or commercial structures may be improved, it often spurs subsequent private investment. Sometimes the model buildings selected are of sufficient significance to the neighborhood that their improvement alone uplifts the area and makes it a more attractive investment for private capital. In addition, many government programs feature partial grants, guaranteed loans or loans in which the interest rates are partially subsidized. Each of these types of programs has the potential of luring private investment totaling many times the amount of the government investment. For example, subsidizing the interest rate on a rehabilitation loan to bring the rate down to 5 percent will cost a government program a given amount per loan. But because the low-interest money becomes available, many more property owners will be encouraged to improve their property and to spend substantially more than the cost of the interest rate subsidy.

Levittown

Three large suburban communities built after World War II near New York City and Philadelphia characterized by compact houses and a homogeneous population of young families; the term *Levittown* became synonymous in the United States with prototypical suburban development. The first Levittown was established in 1947 in Nassau County, New York, where Levitt and Sons Inc. built 15,000 identical houses. Construction was begun on the second Levittown in 1951 in Bucks County, Pennsylvania, and the third was established in Willingboro, New Jersey in 1955.

Sold at low prices, often to returning veterans, the Levitt houses were built on a concrete slab using precut materials. Levitt was the first to build suburban tract housing on a mass-production basis and the first to include appliances with the house. In addition to the houses, stores, playgrounds, swimming pools and a community hall were also provided, and land was set aside for schools and parks. Houses in the Levittowns were built in neighborhood groupings with a school and a park at the center of each, a plan not used in subdivisions prior to these developments.

See: NEW TOWN; SUBURBAN GROWTH

Library

A public, quasi-public or private collection of books, periodicals and maps. While specialized libraries—such as university, medical and engineering society libraries—are regional in nature, public libraries have more general collections and thus tend to serve neighborhoods in close proximity. Public library systems are frequently organized by the size and depth of their book collections, with central or main libraries having the most extensive collections and branch libraries having smaller selections.

Libraries should be easily accessible, located on a collector or arterial street, and convenient to public transportation. Since they frequently function, in part, as community centers, they should also be located near other community facilities, such as a commercial area or park, and contain meeting space. Off-street parking should also be provided in lower-density areas.

See: ARCHITECTURAL AND TRANSPORTATION BARRIERS; COMMUNITY FACILITY PLANNING; FEDERAL DEPOSITORY LIBRARIES

Licensing of Planners

A means of registering planners and granting permission for them to practice. In the United States there is no nationwide licensing system for planners, although the American Institute of Certified Planners does certify planners who have passed its exam and who meet its eligibility requirements. This certification is not necessary, however, in order to practice planning, although it is becoming more common as a prerequisite for certain types of employment.

New Jersey is the only state that requires planners to obtain a license, by meeting eligibility requirements and passing a written exam. To do consulting work for a governmental unit, the principal of the firm must be licensed, and no unlicensed planner may sign a plan. Michigan certifies planners, but certification is not required in order to practice; the state is currently considering substituting a required license. Several other states, including Colorado and California, are also considering instituting a licensing system.

See: AMERICAN INSTITUTE OF CERTIFIED PLANNERS (AICP); CODE OF ETHICS AND PROFESSIONAL CONDUCT

Light Industry

Industrial uses that, generally, do not have offensive characteristics and can be conducted entirely within enclosed buildings. These may include: industrial processes, such as printing; manufacturing of products from component parts; food packaging; warehousing; or automotive sales and service.

See: FACTORY; HEAVY INDUSTRY; INDUSTRIAL AREA; PERFORMANCE STANDARDS; WAREHOUSE FACILITIES

Light Table

A table with a top made of heavy glass that is illuminated from below. Light tables make it easier to trace details from one or more maps onto an overlying sheet of plastic or tracing paper.

Limited-Dividend Housing Company

A housing development and management company that agrees to a limit on profits and dividends to investors in exchange for government subsidy or insurance. First created in New York state in 1926 as a result of the state's Limited-Dividend Housing Companies law, such companies became widespread from the 1950s on, tied to Federal Housing Administration (FHA) mortgage insurance and Department of Housing and Urban Development (HUD) rental subsidy programs, such as the Section 221(d)3, Section 236 and Section 8 housing programs.

The limited-dividend housing concept holds that provision of government subsidy or mortgage insurance for a project substantially reduces the risk taken by developers and investors, so that they are entitled to a more limited profit or dividend. While typically restricted to a 6 percent profit, and monitored extensively by HUD, limited-dividend housing can be profitable. As an example, builder's fees are an additional permissible profit under some programs. In addition, the rapid depreciation of low-income housing projects is permitted under federal tax laws. The value of the depreciation can be used to offset taxes due on other income and is often syndicated to a partnership of investors primarily interested in such tax shelter. Limited-dividend housing companies have proved an effective device for developing low- and moderate-income housing.

Linear City

A metropolitan development plan based on a single spine road that serves as the principal transportation route. All development is located adjacent to the spine and is accessible by transport along the route. A proposal made in 1882 by the Spanish architect Don Arturo Soria y Mata envisioned a city that could grow indefinitely in two directions but would be surrounded by countryside. (See Fig. 24)

See: AXIAL GROWTH; FINGER PATTERN; RADIAL PATTERN

Linear Open Space

Open land with a linear form, such as a 30-foot (9-meter) wide strip that is several miles long, that takes this form because it is part of another linear land use. Sometimes called corridor open spaces because they follow the corridor of a highway or river, they may include the rights-of-way of highways, utilities, abandoned railroads and aqueducts. Linear parks along the banks of water bodies are common to many municipalities, serving as extremely important elements of park planning and civic design. It is the narrower, less traditional linear area, however, that is usually referred to as linear open space.

These open areas of rights-of-way are already, to some extent, preserved as open space by virtue of their primary functions. Because they are also often located near concentrations of population, recreation planners in recent years have sought to use them for outdoor recreation as well. The uses most often proposed are for development as a bikeway or acquisition of public access for hiking.

See: RAILROAD RIGHTS-OF-WAY

Line Functions

Functions directly related to the production or delivery of a product or service. Within government, the departments of transportation, sanitation, social services and health are examples of agencies that perform line functions, while community development or economic development departments are sometimes also considered to be line agencies.

See: STAFF FUNCTIONS

Line-Item Budget

A budget format used in most municipalities in which departmental financial requests for such items as salaries, supplies, travel, equipment and rent are specified in great detail. No indication is made of what functions the personnel will be serving or what the purchased items will be used for, although a general description of the agency's activities may be shown. In small local governments or school districts, where department activities are well defined and discrete, this form of budget may be adequate, in that it gives a general idea of the functional purposes of the proposed expenditures. Unlike other budgets, however, it gives no indication of the appropriate level of expenditure, whether the cost is as low as possible or whether sufficient units of work will be performed.

See: BUDGET; PERFORMANCE BUDGET; PROGRAM BUDGET; ZERO-BASE BUDGET (ZBB)

Line Source

A source of air pollution that has a linear configuration. As an example, a congested freeway is a more or less continuous linear source of air pollution generated by the automobiles moving along it.

See: AIR POLLUTION; AREA SOURCE; POINT SOURCE

Linkage

A term used in planning to describe the complex, but necessary coordination of the many federal, state and local agencies and programs that are often involved in major planning or development projects.

Litter

Waste that is discarded improperly and often found strewn along streets, highways and in vacant lots. Litter is not only extremely unsightly but is also responsible for health and safety problems, such as tire blowouts and resulting accidents. Ultimate collection of litter and cleanup of littered areas is also much more expensive than standard waste collection.

Two alternative approaches to the control of litter are bottle bills and the litter tax. Bottle bills mandate a deposit collected by retailers on beverage containers, increasing the likelihood that the containers will be returned for the refund rather than improperly discarded. Litter taxes, in existence in a number of states, are imposed upon manufacturers who produce products likely to be littered. The resulting fund is used to help clean up the litter and for public education on litter control. However, the litter tax is thought to do little to prevent littering.

See: BOTTLE BILL; SOLID WASTE MANAGEMENT

Little City Halls

Small municipal government offices located within communities in order to decentralize some municipal functions or to act as liaisons between communities and centralized government personnel.

The function of little city halls, which have been established in a few large cities, is to provide a direct link to affected communities for official monitoring of local reactions to services and to enable services to be provided more efficiently at a community level. They are an attempt to coordinate services in order to effectively address local problems and to offer visible proof of government concern for local needs.

See: CITIZEN PARTICIPATION; DECENTRALIZATION; MULTISERVICE CENTER

Livable Cities

A program, authorized by the Housing and Community Development Amendments of 1978 but never funded, that was designed to stimulate art and cultural and historic projects in urban communities. The program was also intended to create employment, primarily for low- and moderate-income residents of neighborhoods requiring revitalization.

Local Authority

A British term that refers to the elected body (the county, district or borough council or the Corporation of the City of London) that provides or supervises services to a local or regional area. England, Wales and Scotland have a two-tier system of local government in which the upper tier consists of a metropolitan or nonmetropolitan county and the lower tier consists of districts, several of which comprise one county. Northern Ireland has a one-tier system of districts. The greater London area (governed by the Greater London Council) differs from the rest of Britain in that it is divided into 32 boroughs and the City of London instead of districts. Local authorities are responsible for public health, highways, police, education, housing, environmental health, social services, traffic administration, planning, fire services, libraries and property tax collection and generally have a staff of professionals to provide these services.

Planning functions are divided between the county and district councils. County councils are responsible for strategic planning—i.e., structure plans, development plans governing the preparation of local plans and certain classes of development proposals—and for traffic, transportation and highway functions (except trunk roads, which are a national government function). District councils are responsible for local plans and make decisions concerning most applications for planning permission and matters of development control. They also maintain minor urban roads, provide some municipal parking structures, may run local bus services and are responsible for housing. In addition, district councils act as the local water authority's agent for sewerage functions. Provision of parks and recreational facilities, museums, and refuse collection and disposal are undertaken by counties and districts.

See: CITY COUNCIL; NATIONAL LAND USE POLICY

Local Government

Levels of government below the state level that derive their powers from the state charter or state laws. The structure of local government varies because of a number of factors, including individual state requirements, size of municipal population and governmental functions that local levels have traditionally performed since colonial days. Local initiative in the adoption of home rule powers is generally reflected in the locality's charter. The principal levels of local government in the United States are described below.

County. The principal subdivision of the state. Its functions often include budget development and tax levy; maintenance of the courts and public records; provision of welfare programs; law enforcement; school administration; electoral functions; and provision of a variety of facilities and services such as secondary roads and bridges, airports, health programs, libraries, public utilities, parks and recreation, and transportation. The state of Louisiana has parishes, and Alaska has boroughs, which serve these functions, but the states of Connecticut and Rhode Island have no similar level of government. The county level of government was derived from the English shire during the colonial period.

Township and town. Subdivisions of counties that traditionally administer local roads, parks, public safety, libraries and, in some states, schools. While heavily urbanized towns, in many cases, have responsibilities similar to cities, towns are increasingly relinquishing many of their functions to the county. In the six New England states, however, the town is the principal level of local government, which traditionally handles the functions performed by counties and cities in other states. The town and township forms of government were derived during the colonial period from the English parish as it was constituted at that time.

City. A municipal corporation of a minimum population specified by state law, which usually contains a larger population than other incorporated areas within the state. It functions under a charter granted by the state that is the basis for its governmental form and operation. Cities traditionally have a greater degree of independence from state rule than do other levels of local government. They also provide many or all of the services offered by counties, as well as other services that are necessary for a more urbanized population. The city and village form were derived during the United States colonial period from the English borough of that time.

Village. An incorporated urbanized area with less authority and a simpler government structure than a city. States generally place stricter limitations on the types of functions that villages may perform and on their taxing and borrowing powers. In some states, municipalities with the same structure and functions as villages are called towns or boroughs.

See: CITY COUNCIL; CITY MANAGER; COUNCIL OF GOVERNMENT (COG); COUNTY EXECUTIVE; HAMLET; HOME RULE; LOCAL AUTHORITY; MAYOR; POLITICAL SUBDIVISION; SCHOOL DISTRICT; SPECIAL DISTRICT; TOWN SUPERVISOR; UNINCORPORATED AREA

Local Street

A road that primarily provides access to abutting property. It typically has low traffic volumes and low speeds. The primary land-access system, local streets constitute approximately 60 percent to 80 percent of the mileage of the total urban road system. Traffic from local streets is funneled into the collector street system; through traffic on the local street system is discouraged.

Typical cross sections provide a 50-foot (15.2-meter) right-of-way; pavement width of 36 feet (11.0 meters), which would include two 10-foot (3.0-meter) moving lanes and two 8-foot (2.4-meter) parking lanes; and sidewalks at least 4 feet (1.2 meters) wide with curbs and gutters. A maximum grade of 6 percent and a design speed of 25 mph (40 kph) should be provided. A local street should be designed to carry no more than 1,500 vehicular trips per day, and substantially less where community values dictate elimination of traffic.

In recent years, many municipalities have experimented with local street closings in selected locations where only vehicles destined for housing on that street are permitted to enter. The closed streets, sometimes called woonerfs (translated "living yard"), were first used in Delft, Holland where, in addition to traffic reduction, other street amenities are added. They may include street furniture,

bicycle racks, plantings and play equipment. To keep vehicle speeds low, speed-reduction bumps, bollards (posts), chicanes (S-curves) and marked parking spaces are added so that vehicles have to slow down to maneuver around them. (See Fig. 43)

Loft Housing

A dwelling unit created in what was originally unpartitioned commercial or manufacturing space. Occupants of loft housing typically purchase or rent unfinished space that may or may not include bathroom or kitchen facilities or interior walls. Loft housing may be leased as an apartment or purchased as a cooperative or condominium.

Consumer interest in loft housing is a by-product of the general renewed interest in central cities. In New York City the first occupants of loft housing were artists who moved into commercial and industrial districts to take advantage of the low rents, high ceilings and open living areas. In many instances, the existence of a dwelling unit in the midst of commercial space was an illegal conversion, and whatever improvement the tenant made to the dwelling unit was at his own risk. Now, renting and owning large open housing areas has become fashionable, and in New York City the cost of loft housing has risen dramatically. To prevent a further loss of manufacturing jobs through the conversion of industrial space to housing use, the city adopted new zoning regulations for lofts and procedures by which loft residents, as of a certain date, could apply for grandfather exemptions from these regulations.

See: ADAPTIVE USE; GENTRIFICATION

Long-Term Care Facilities

Facilities designed, equipped and staffed to provide maintenance and often restorative services to individuals, most often elderly, who are chronically ill or disabled. Included are boarding houses, personal care facilities, nursing homes, hospices and day health care programs. Long-term care institutions differ from extended care facilities, which are designed to provide skilled nursing care only during the recuperative phase of an illness. A recent innovation in the area of long-term care is the hospice, a facility specifically designed to provide care for patients diagnosed as terminally ill.

Emphasis is also being placed on day health care and home health care services, which assist an individual in maintaining an independent life-style for as long as possible as an alternative to institutionalization. Although this approach has only recently received attention in the United States, government policy in both Canada and Britain has encouraged home health services as an alternative to long-term care for many years.

See: INTERMEDIATE CARE FACILITIES (ICF); NURSING HOME; SKILLED NURSING FACILITY (SNF)

Loretto v. *Teleprompter Manhattan CATV Corp.* 458 U.S. 419, 102 S. Ct. 3164 [1982])

A decision by the United States Supreme Court that

established a "per se" taking rule for statutes that authorize a permanent physical occupation of a landowner's property.

The Court distinguished taking claims based upon physical intrusions from taking claims based upon other types of regulatory activity. For claims of the latter category, the Court announced it would continue to evaluate such claims only in the context of a multifactor analysis that considered the economic impact of the regulation on the property owner, the extent to which the regulation created potential damage to the investment in the property and the character of the governmental action. However, where government purported to authorize a permanent physical invasion of private property (in *Loretto*, the intrusion consisted of running cable television transmission facilities by cable TV companies through privately owned apartment buildings), the Court held that such action in itself constituted a taking, without any need for engaging in a multifactor analysis.
See: PENN CENTRAL TRANSPORTATION COMPANY v. CITY OF NEW YORK; TAKING

Los Angeles County Regional Planning Commission

The first county planning board in the United States. It was established in 1922, two years after the formation of the City of Los Angeles planning commission, in reaction to the many planning problems facing Los Angeles that were regional in scope.

Among these concerns were periodic flooding and runoff, which originated in the hills outside of Los Angeles but greatly affected the city, and pollution of the water supply because of the lack of sewers in developed communities lying at higher elevations than Los Angeles. Other problems included control of the fires that were prevalent in the area's dry hills, provision of parks and beaches for the region, zoning and subdivision control in unincorporated and undeveloped areas, waste disposal and provision of an adequate transportation network.
See: LOS ANGELES ZONING ORDINANCE

Los Angeles Zoning Ordinance

A new concept in land use regulation, pioneered in the United States in 1909 by the City of Los Angeles, which used zoning on large undeveloped land areas to guide future development patterns. The city's ordinance established seven industrial districts and zoned most of the remainder of the municipality for residential use, although certain businesses were permitted in these residential areas.
See: LOS ANGELES COUNTY REGIONAL PLANNING COMMISSION

Lot

An area of land with defined boundaries that is designated in official assessor's records as being one parcel and is employed or will be employed for one principal use, together with its accessory buildings and uses.

In order to be considered suitable for development under zoning regulations, a lot must be able to fulfill the stated requirements for its zoning district. Many zoning ordinances have special requirements and provisions for specific types of lots, such as corner lots or those of an irregular shape. (See Fig. 26)
See: CORNER LOT; DEEP LOT; FRONT LOT LINE; FRONTAGE; LARGE-LOT ZONING; LOT COVERAGE; LOT DEPTH; LOT LINE; LOT WIDTH; MINIMUM LOT SIZE; REAR LOT LINE; SIDE LOT LINE; TRANSITIONAL LOT; ZERO LOT-LINE DEVELOPMENT; ZONING

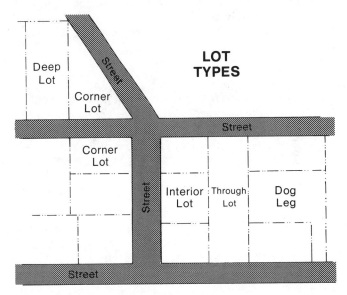

Fig. 26.

Lot-by-Lot Development

A common development approach in which each building lot is considered to be a complete unit of development in terms of lot design and compliance with all appropriate land use regulations. This approach may be contrasted to newer techniques, such as planned unit development or cluster development, in which a large parcel of land with a number of structures is planned, designed and reviewed as a unit for compliance with zoning.
See: CLUSTER DEVELOPMENT; PLANNED UNIT DEVELOPMENT (PUD); ZONING

Lot Coverage

The proportion of the surface of a lot that is covered by buildings or that the municipal ordinance permits to be covered by buildings. This figure is typically stated as a percentage of the lot area, so that if a lot measures 10,000 square feet (900 square meters) and coverage is set at 20 percent, a maximum of 2,000 square feet (180 square meters) of lot area may be covered. Coverage requirements are generally intended to preserve open space, limit the intensity of development and, in some cases, limit the amount of impermeable surface that may be created.

Some ordinances exclude accessory structures from cov-

erage requirements, while others specifically exclude buildings or structures if they are located completely below ground. Usually uncovered porches and terraces are not counted as part of lot coverage. Still other ordinances make a distinction between building coverage and gross land coverage, which includes paved surfaces as well as structures.
See: FLOOR AREA RATIO (FAR); IMPERVIOUS SURFACES; LOT; ZONING

Lot Depth

The distance between the front lot line and the rear lot line, often measured from the midpoint of each line. Excessive lot depth in relation to width can result in design and development problems. (See Fig. 50)
See: DEEP LOT

Lot Line

A property line that bounds a plot of ground described as a lot in municipal records. Lot lines are located at the front, rear and sides of lots and may separate a lot from public property, from roadways or from other lots.
See: FRONT LOT LINE; LOT; REAR LOT LINE; SIDE LOT LINE

Lot Width

The distance that can be measured between a lot's side lot lines at right angles to the depth of the lot. A municipal ordinance may require that the measurement be made at the minimum required building setback line or at a point midway between the front lot line and the rear lot line. (See Fig. 50)
See: FRONT FOOT; FRONTAGE

Love Canal

An area in Niagara Falls, New York that has become symbolic of the problems caused by indiscriminate dumping of toxic wastes. Love Canal, an abandoned waterway, was used for the dumping of chemical wastes for a period of years in the 1940s and 1950s. The site was eventually filled and sold, and a school and tracts of housing were constructed. The chemicals gradually spread to the basements, backyards and swimming pools of these homes, and by the late 1970s unusual rates of illness, spontaneous abortions and congenital malformations had been observed.

In 1978 the state of New York declared an emergency and evacuated individuals living within a block and a half

of the canal; these homes were subsequently demolished. In 1980 a declaration of emergency was issued by President Jimmy Carter, and most of those living up to about six blocks from the canal were evacuated.

In 1982 a federal study was released indicating that although the initial area evacuated was still unsafe, the area farther from the canal that was evacuated in 1980 was habitable. It was planned that those homes would be sold by the state after additional cleanup took place.

In September 1983 , however, the U.S. Environmental Protection Agency (EPA) found leakage of chemicals beyond the location where a containment wall for the chemicals was proposed to be built. As a result, new studies must be conducted at the site in order to determine how best to contain and clean up the chemical wastes. A clay cap is currently being constructed to cover the canal, but other measures are necessary for the dioxin-contaminated creeks and storm sewers of the area and the recently discovered migration of chemicals. Ultimately, the decision about the area's habitability will be made by New York State and the Federal Center for Disease Control.

The discovery of Love Canal and other similar abandoned dumping grounds for hazardous substances throughout the country helped to bring about the passage of the Comprehensive Environmental Response, Compensation and Liability Act of 1980 (CERCLA). This legislation created a $1.6 billion "superfund" to finance the cleanup of hazardous substances that have been spilled or dumped.
See: HAZARDOUS WASTE; TOXIC SUBSTANCES

Low-Rise Housing

A residential building that generally contains no more than two or three stories. Garden apartments and townhouses are examples of this type of development. Nonresidential development of a similar height may also be described as low-rise, such as one-story buildings in shopping centers.
See: GARDEN APARTMENT; HIGH-RISE HOUSING; HOUSING TYPE; MID-RISE HOUSING

Luxury Housing

Housing specifically designed for occupancy by upper-income groups. Luxury housing usually includes more living space and a larger variety of options and amenities than housing designed for middle- or lower-income groups.
See: FILTERING; HOUSING TYPE

M

Magnetic Separation

A process by which magnetic metals may be separated from the solid waste stream so that they can be recovered and reused. Sale of the recovered metal can help to fi-

nance a portion of the cost of solid waste disposal and decrease the volume of waste requiring ultimate disposal.

Magnetic separators are generally of the drum magnet type or the overhead belt magnet type and may be placed

at one or more of a number of different points in a resource-recovery process. Shredding also helps in the reclamation of magnetic metals. Magnetic separation must take place before incineration or any treatment involving burning, or the materials lose much of their market value.
See: FRONT-END RECOVERY; RECYCLING; SHREDDING

Main Street

Historically, a main avenue for commercial and office activity that served as a center of town life. In the development of most American cities, a "main street" was typically the focus of community growth, with small stores, professional offices and service activities all clustered along one avenue for reasons of convenience as well as economic interdependence.

In many cases the impetus for growth of the main street was the arrival of the railroad. Towns developed at depot locations, and as they grew, the main street became the nucleus of the downtown area of the city. More recently, in the post-World War II period, the main street was undermined as a viable economic or social entity largely as a result of suburbanization, the related growth of shopping centers and malls, and a heightened dependence on the auto.

Despite the loss of its significance as the central shopping area, the concept of the main street as an old-fashioned, small-scale shopping, service and entertainment area is being preserved in most small-town business district rehabilitation plans.
See: CENTRAL BUSINESS DISTRICT (CBD); DOWNTOWN REVITALIZATION; STREET BEAUTIFICATION; STREETSCAPE

Management By Objectives (MBO)

An approach to government and corporate policy formulation and implementation in which organizational objectives are developed by high ranking management, refined at lower management levels by development of targets and plans, and subsequently agreed upon by all management groups. This form of management is often used as a basis for budget development and planning of department activities.

Management by objectives is also used as an approach to administration, by permitting all members of an organization or department to participate in setting organizational and individual goals. Theoretically, they all know why the goals have been established, the expected rate of progress and how their individual assignments are integrated with those of others. MBO requires a mutual commitment by staff and management to attain established goals.
See: PROGRAM BUDGET; ZERO-BASE BUDGET (ZBB)

Mandatory Referral

The requirement that a proposed action or development proposal be submitted to a planning agency for review. The procedure may be established by federal, state or local law and operates in a variety of ways. One type of mandatory referral requires that all departments, as well as the legislative body within a particular municipality, submit proposed projects, such as a new police station, to the planning department so that the planning agency can comment upon the relationship of the project to the community's comprehensive plan. Another variation of the mandatory referral mandates submission of certain zoning or development proposals at the city, village or town level to the county planning department for its comments.

The purpose of this process is the coordination of individual government activities and expenditures with overall development plans. The planning agency should have at its disposal background information and data that can be used to support any recommendation it makes. In its review of zoning and development decisions at the local level, the county or regional agency has the advantage of information it receives from many communities, so that a broader view may be taken of the potential impact of a project.

Man-Hours

The number of hours required for a task to be completed by one person with the required skills, even if numerous persons with varying degrees of skill actually undertake the work. Estimates of the amount of time required for completion of any labor-intensive project or study are often made on the basis of required man-hours so that staff can be properly assigned to various phases of the project.

Manhole

A covered opening in the ground that permits access to an underground structure or facility—such as sewer or water pipes; septic tanks; or electric, gas or telephone conduits—so that they may be repaired and cleaned.

Manholes are located at varying intervals, depending upon maintenance requirements. For pipes and conduits street intersections are commonly used as manhole locations, as they permit access to several elements that join in the beds of the intersecting streets, such as pipes of differing size. Additional locations may be necessary if the distance between intersections is great. The use of too many manholes is discouraged, however, since they can weaken the pavement and have a tendency to leak in heavy storms, causing flooding of underground chambers or stormwater infiltration of sanitary sewers.

Map Scale

A description of the relationship between the size of objects or physical features on a map and their size in life. Three formats are commonly used to represent scale; frequently more than one of these formats may be used on a particular map.

The representative fraction (RF) expresses the map scale in proportion form—e.g., 1 : 63,360 or 1/63,360. This indicates that one map unit is equal to 63,360 units on the ground. This same scale may be expressed in words as 1 inch equals 1 mile (there being 63,360 inches in a mile); this is called the verbal scale. A third way of depicting map scale is the graphic approach, in which a line of a given length indicates a particular scale; in this case a 1-inch line would equal 1 mile. The graphic scale might also include parallel scales representing feet and kilometers. An advantage of the graphic approach is that in enlargement or reduction of the map, the scale is still accurate.

In general, maps that cover large areas and have scales such as 1 : 100,000 or 1 : 500,000 are known as small-scale maps; specific land areas or properties are too small to be differentiated or for any detail to be observed clearly. Large-scale maps—e.g., 1 : 25,000—cover much smaller areas and allow much greater detail to be observed for specific land areas. Selection of a proper scale for a map depends upon the size of the study area, the proposed use for the map, the detail required and the desired size of the final product.

Mapped Street

A street that appears on the official map of a municipality but has not yet necessarily been developed. Many state enabling acts do not allow building permits to be issued for property lacking access to an improved mapped street. In a number of states, streets that appear on subdivision plats that are properly approved by municipal law automatically become part of the official map. If a community has no official map, it is usually required that the property have access to an existing state, county or municipal street or highway before a building permit may be issued.
See: OFFICIAL MAP; PAPER STREET

Marginal Land

Land that has a minimal economic value because it is inaccessible, has topographic features that prevent its use or development, or has a climate that restricts its use.

Marina

A shorefront development that provides pleasure boat mooring, launching, fueling, repair and on-shore service facilities. Generally designed to serve boats of various sizes, marinas are usually constructed of wood or metal docks that are either mounted on piers, anchored or of the floating variety. The mooring areas, called slips, are perpendicular to the docks and may be provided with catwalks between the slips, to facilitate access to boats. A breakwater is often necessary to protect the marina from wave action.

Landside development at private marinas will generally include provisions for fueling; launching by hoist, derrick or ramp; and at larger marinas, boat repair and storage. Other facilities that may also be provided are toilets and showers, electrical connections for boats, boat and food supplies, a restaurant, hotel accommodations and a boat

sales area. Marinas in public parks, however, are often essentially mooring facilities. Parking is needed at all facilities.

Marinas are popular in resort areas and areas that have warm climates for most of the year. Boaters enjoy having their boats moored near their homes, and since marinas are often attractive, they are frequently designed as a focal point of residential or resort development. In planning for a marina, an assessment of the number of potential boaters and the sizes of their boats is necessary. The facility's impact on local land use must also be assessed, as well as its environmental impact, particularly with respect to the ecology of the water body and the effect on nearby beach areas.

On small lakefronts, boathouses and small docks may serve the same purpose that marinas serve on larger water bodies and often accommodate rowboats, paddle boats, canoes and their storage.
See: BOAT LAUNCH RAMP; COASTAL AREA PLANNING; MOORING FACILITIES

Marine Protection, Research and Sanctuaries Act of 1972

Federal legislation (PL 92-532) that establishes a permit system to regulate the disposal of wastes by ocean dumping from other than land-based outfalls. Permits, which are issued by the Environmental Protection Agency (EPA) and the Army Corps of Engineers, designate the type and amount of material to be dumped, the location where it may be dumped, an expiration date and other special requirements. The act also sets standards for EPA permit regulations for the transportation of materials and their disposal into the ocean.

Use of deep sea dumping locations, rather than those located on the continental shelf, is encouraged, and civil and criminal penalties for violations are set. Ocean dumping of radioactive wastes and chemical, biological and radiological warfare materials is prohibited by this legislation. The act also authorizes the designation of marine sanctuaries as far seaward as the outer edge of the continental shelf.
See: FEDERAL WATER POLLUTION CONTROL ACT AMENDMENTS OF 1972; OCEAN DUMPING

Market Data Approach Appraisal

Together with the cost and income approaches, one of the three basic approaches to valuing real estate.

The fundamental principle behind this approach is that the value of a property may be viewed as what it would sell for in a transaction between a willing and knowledgeable buyer and a willing and knowledgeable seller, neither acting under any compulsion. The method employed is that of comparing the property being valued with comparable properties that have recently sold or are currently on the market.

The first step in this approach is to find comparable properties with the same highest and best use for which current sales data are available. Next, the comparable sale is examined to discern whether it was a free market, arm's-length transaction reflective of fair market value (that is, a transaction between knowledgeable unrelated parties, neither acting under any compulsion). Third, each comparable sale is compared with the subject property being appraised, and the comparable sales price is adjusted for perceived differences between the comparable and the subject, such as location, time, plot configuration, the improvements on the property and other characteristics. Last, an opinion of value is drawn, based on the values indicated by each of the adjusted comparable sales.

The market data approach is often considered the most generally applicable and widely used valuation approach, since it can be used for improved and unimproved property as well as for commercial, industrial or residential property. The principal limiting factor in the use of this approach is the existence of comparable sales. For properties that are considered single-use specialty properties that do not have a market, use of the market data approach may be impossible.
See: APPRAISAL; APPRAISED VALUE

Market Demand

A term borrowed from market research that, when used by planners, refers to the needs and wants of local constituents for a particular project or program. A determination of the amount of market demand is often made by surveying the affected population.

Planners may wish to assess market demand as the basis for new community facility planning, so that facilities can be adequately sized, or as the basis for deciding whether certain programs should be instituted. Conversely, as the basis for capital project approval, sufficient demand should be a determining factor. Market demand may also be studied by a community development or economic development department seeking to bolster a downtown area in order to determine what improvements are desirable or necessary. In addition, developers typically study market demand and use this information in order to select a site for their development that will enable the project to be a commercial success.
See: MARKET STUDY

Market Study

A study conducted to determine whether or not there is demand for a particular development on a particular site and to assess the nature of the competing markets. This information is used by developers to determine potential sales or rental volumes and the scale of development that the market can absorb and to evaluate financial aspects of the project.

There are many ways in which market studies can be used by planners. For example, a planning project aimed at downtown revitalization may focus, among other things, upon potential demand for types of uses the downtown currently lacks and whether existing buildings can

accommodate these uses. If a market study indicated strong demand, this information would be presented to lending institutions, developers and existing merchants.

Planners are also interested in the market from which new development expects to draw customers. A new shopping center could, for example, rely upon drawing patrons of an existing shopping center in that community or from its downtown. If there is no evidence of additional demand, the net communitywide impact of the new shopping center could be adverse.
See: FEASIBILITY STUDY

Market Value

Generally considered to be the price that a property would bring if sold on the open market. More precisely, market value is sometimes defined as the highest price that a property would bring if exposed for sale on the open market, allowing a reasonable time to find a willing buyer, where both buyer and seller are informed about the property and are knowledgeable about all potential uses. Neither buyer nor seller must be under any undue compulsion to act.
See: APPRAISAL; APPRAISED VALUE

Mass Transit

Transportation for people (as opposed to goods) on a fixed-route and fixed-schedule basis, generally on conveyances such as buses, rapid transit vehicles and commuter rail facilities. Intercity bus and rail service is generally not referred to as mass transit.

Mass transit, in most cases, is operated by municipal transportation departments or authorities that manage often diverse transit modes in a coordinated manner, and that may also supervise privately operated transit services. Municipal takeovers of completely private systems of transportation ensued following the requirement of the Urban Mass Transportation Act of 1964 (which offered funding for capital construction of mass transit facilities and for their planning) that the systems be government-managed to receive funding. Federal funding was initiated because of a recognition of an imbalance in federal expenditures for the relatively wealthy (i.e., those with private automobiles who receive benefits from massive highway construction programs), as opposed to the poor and otherwise transportation disadvantaged (the elderly and handicapped) who were forced to use mass transportation. New-facility construction, bus purchases and service improvements were undertaken to better serve this population and, it was also hoped, to induce drivers to leave their cars for the new, more attractive and cheaper public transportation. Revitalization of many urban areas by construction of fixed-route lines and other facilities was also envisioned.

The 1980 census reported that 6.1 million people commuted to work on mass transit and 81.4 million used private cars. In addition, car ownership is increasing steadily while mass transit ridership is increasing only slightly.

These factors have led to a reevaluation of public transit funding programs, reducing emphasis on capital construction and shifting to encouragement of solutions to the problems that mass transit has not solved, i.e., lowering transportation costs for the poor, providing service for the elderly and handicapped and increasing security, cleanliness, maintenance and comfort. Proposals often revolve around new pricing strategies, such as increased fares for commuters to offset reduced fares on subways, and paratransit to provide better service for the infirm and others in locations where fixed-route, fixed-schedule service is not cost-effective, such as in most suburbs. It is expected that in the future mass transit capital projects will principally involve replacement and rehabilitation rather than new construction.

Trolleys (now called rapid light rail) and subways (rail rapid transit) were the first forms of mass transit to serve densely populated cities. Their development from the 1880s on provided an important part of the urban infrastructure, aiding in the development of an expanded labor force and an extended area from which to draw clientele. Buses began to replace trolleys in the 1920s and constituted the predominant form of transportation until the post–World War II period. The steady growth in car ownership, from the time the automobile was introduced, greatly increased during the 1920s and 1930s. But in those years the car was used primarily for recreation. It was in the post–World War II era that it became competition to mass transit for general transportation purposes.

During the 1960s, efforts to counter the trend toward reliance on the auto concentrated on development of new forms of mass transportation that were faster, automated, less noisy and, later, less energy consumptive. Monorails, people movers and computerized rail rapid transit, such as the San Francisco Bay Area Rapid Transit (BART), were developed. The TRANSBUS, developed by the Urban Mass Transportation Administration, offered special features for the handicapped, such as kneeling steps that lowered to become wheelchair elevators. Personal rapid transit, a rapid transit system that would offer automobile-sized vehicles for individual or group use on a rail-type infrastructure, was offered as a possible alternative combining aspects of the auto with those of the people mover. But these have not been built and only a few of the other systems have been built or are planned. (MARTA in Atlanta is an automated rail rapid transit system, and a few locations are planning to develop downtown people movers.) Instead, major emphasis has been placed on improvements to buses, their scheduling and support facilities, e.g., bus shelters, maps, etc. Some consideration has also been given to use of the trolley, which is popular in Europe, largely to reduce pollution and conserve gasoline, and transportation system management has been emphasized to enable the existing infrastructure to work more efficiently, thereby reducing the need for costly capital improvements. Another system in use, like that in southeastern Virginia served by the Tidewater Trans-

portation District Commission, involves the separation of policy development and transportation management from facility operation. This approach to service delivery permits the use of various transit means (e.g., fixed-route, express service, vanpools, private commuter buses, shared-ride taxi service and special services for the disabled) that are operated by a variety of public and private providers.

See: BUS ROUTE PLANNING; COMMUTATION; DEMAND-RESPONSIVE TRANSPORTATION (DRT); PEOPLE MOVER; SUBURBAN COMMUTER RAILWAY; SUBWAY; TRANSPORTATION PLANNING; TRANSPORTATION SYSTEM MANAGEMENT (TSM); TROLLEY

Mass Wasting

A term that describes the movement of rock and earth materials downslope, either slowly or at great speed, under the influence of gravity. In mountainous regions mass wasting can be a major environmental hazard, resulting in extensive property damage as well as loss of life. Damage is often caused not only directly by the sliding, flowing or falling earth, rock or mud but indirectly by the waves generated when these materials fall into fiords or lakes. Many types of natural phenomena and human activity can cause mass movement, including earthquakes, erosion of slopes, excavation, mining or undercutting, saturation of the soil or disturbance of the natural vegetation.

Among the slowest forms of movement is soil creep, which occurs on almost all moderately steep, soil-covered slopes and can indicate a potentially dangerous condition. This very slow downslope movement can be detected by a telltale lean of telephone poles, fence posts and the like and is generally caused by such factors as the wetting and drying of soil, heating and cooling, the burrowing activities of animals or root growth.

Earthflow is a slow flow of water-saturated earth and is common on steep slopes after heavy rainfalls. Within a few hours extensive property damage can occur, and roads can be blocked, but because of the slow speed of the earthflow, there are rarely fatalities.

Mudflow—also known as mudspate, mud avalanche and mudstream—is a faster movement of mud and water down a channel, stream course or canyon that occurs when masses of loose sediment on steep slopes are subjected to heavy rainfall or rapid thawing. The mudflow is capable of carrying large rocks and boulders with it.

Landslides are the sudden and rapid downward motion of large masses of rock and debris and are a relatively common occurrence. Rockslides are the rapid sliding of masses of newly detached bedrock along a fault plane or rock fracture. They can and do occur wherever there are steep mountain slopes, such as those found in Switzerland, Norway or the Canadian Rockies, and development in valleys bordered by these steep mountains is often in danger. Rockfalls are similar to rockslides, but the rock masses free-fall through the air.

Mass wasting occurs almost everywhere that significant

slopes are found. In the United States various types of slides and flows are particularly prevalent in portions of the California and Oregon coast and in segments of the Allegheny, Ozark, Olympic and Rocky mountains. Many parts of Canada are also plagued by this problem.

Prevention and control of damage from mass wasting can be accomplished in a number of ways. The examination of stereoscopic aerial photographs often reveals the presence of old landslides not generally visible from the ground, allowing these slopes to be measured and analyzed for stability prior to development. Many of the California slope failures have been found to have occurred on ancient landslide sites. Site inspection can also reveal signs of movement. Structures built subsequent to the institution of rigorous ordinances—which require geologic investigation, proper soil compaction and grading, and other measures—have fared better in the slide-prone areas surrounding Los Angeles.

Although some types of slides and flows are caused purely by natural phenomena, such as heavy rainfall or earthquakes, human activity has been traced to many of these disasters. The Portugese Bend landslide in the Palos Verdes Hills of Los Angeles is thought to have been caused by heavy infiltration of water from cesspools and lawn watering; similarly, large-scale slides in the Thompson River Valley in British Columbia were probably caused by irrigation. Proper drainage can be an effective means of slide control through special piping systems as well as methods that prevent infiltration. In the past, many slides have been caused by excavation and mining; geologic studies can permit excavation to be avoided in areas where it can contribute to slope failure. Finally, a variety of engineering techniques have been developed that are aimed at protecting existing development on slide-prone slopes.

See: GEOLOGIC HAZARDS; HILLSIDE PROTECTION ORDINANCES

Matching Funds

Funds that must be provided by a unit of government or an organization, usually representing a fixed share of the cost of a project, as a condition for receiving additional money from another unit of government or an organization. Matching requirements may be in effect between two levels of government, between a unit of government and an organization, or between two organizations.

For example, the federal government might have a program funding economic development ventures in which it pays 75 percent of the cost of eligible activities, providing that the remaining 25 percent of the project cost is paid for by those seeking the grant. Often it is permitted that the nonfederal share be paid for through in-kind contributions such as personnel and office space. It is more common for a grant program to require some form of matching participation by the grant recipient than for it to pay for the total cost of a project.

See: GRANT-IN-AID

Mature City

A city that has already reached its greatest level of population and economic activity. While history has shown that many cities reach a point of maturity and then remain stable or decline, much city planning until the 1970s was based on the premise of continued growth. It is now perceived that many American metropolitan areas, particularly in the Northeast and Midwest, are mature cities and that future planning must be based on maintenance or controlled shrinkage rather than expanding growth.

In a mature city there is greater need for improvement of aging public infrastructure and economic base redevelopment. In addition to population decline, there is usually change in the age structure, ethnic mix and income levels of the population, requiring expanded social service programming. These changes also frequently result in a lower tax base along with higher municipal costs, often causing financial difficulty for the municipality.

See: MUNICIPAL SERVICES; POPULATION DECLINE; PUBLIC INFRASTRUCTURE

Mayor

The elected chief executive of a city or village who, in most municipalities, is a part-time official. The mayor may be either chief administrator, as in the strong mayor-council form of government, or largely a ceremonial figure, as in the weak mayor-council, mayor-city manager or commission forms of government.

In more than half of all municipalities with mayors that have populations of 5,000 or more, the mayor possesses a veto power over city council actions, which, in turn, may be overridden by a two-thirds vote of the council. In all municipalities the mayor is empowered to make recommendations to the council.

See: CITY MANAGER; COMMISSION FORM OF GOVERNMENT; COUNTY EXECUTIVE; MAYOR-COUNCIL FORM OF GOVERNMENT; TOWN SUPERVISOR

Mayor-Council Form of Government

The form of municipal government in which an elected chief executive presides over an elected legislative body called a council. The mayor-council type of government takes several forms, the most common being the weak mayor-council and the strong mayor-council.

The weak mayor-council form is distinguished by the narrowly defined powers of the mayor. Although the mayor exercises general administrative powers, committees of the council exercise strict control over his actions, including budget appropriations. The mayor's personnel appointments and removals are also subject to council review. This form of government may also employ a city manager to handle administrative functions.

The strong mayor-council form provides the mayor with the most power, including responsibility for the preparation and administration of the budget, the power to appoint department heads without council approval and often some form of veto over legislative actions taken by the council.

See: CITY COUNCIL; CITY MANAGER; COMMISSION FORM OF GOVERNMENT; COUNCIL-MANAGER FORM OF GOVERNMENT

Mean

An arithmetic average obtained by adding together the sum of the values and dividing by the number of values. At the mean the sum of deviations from the mean is equal to zero. If the mean in a distribution is higher or lower than the median, the distribution is skewed.

See: MEASURES OF CENTRAL TENDENCY; MEDIAN; MODE; SKEWNESS

Measures of Central Tendency

Statistical measurements that help to describe the nature of a group of data by assigning one number to represent the entire group. The number that is selected represents the point in a frequency distribution where values or scores tend to be concentrated. Common measures of central tendency are the mean (or arithmetic average), median and mode.

Measures of central tendency are often used by planners to enable a comparison of related data, such as the median income of families in various communities.

See: FREQUENCY DISTRIBUTION; MEAN; MEASURES OF DISPERSION; MEDIAN; MODE

Measures of Dispersion

Measures showing the amount of spread or scatter of a group of values from a central point in a distribution, such as from the mean. They help to provide additional information concerning the nature of the distribution by indicating the extent of difference among the observations in the distribution. For example, although the mean single-family home value of two communities may be an identical $80,000, one community may have houses ranging widely in value from $20,000 to $600,000, while the other community may have houses ranging from only $65,000 to $90,000. Dispersion is measured by range, interquartile range, mean deviation, or most commonly, standard deviation or variance.

See: MEASURES OF CENTRAL TENDENCY; STANDARD DEVIATION; VARIANCE

Median

1. The portion of a road that separates traffic lanes in opposing directions or separates express and local traffic in the same direction. Its functions are to prevent encroachment from opposing traffic and to provide a stopping area for emergencies, storage for left- and U-turning vehicles, moderation of headlight glare, separation of fast-moving and slow traffic, and islands for pedestrian safety. Wide medians are a convenient location for future roadway expansion and provide space for landscaping, for drainage

and for snow storage. When located on wide roadways, medians also facilitate the use of reversible traffic lanes.

Medians vary in width from a traffic stripe to a wide green space in open areas and may be either elevated, depressed or level. Traffic barriers are often constructed within the median, as are traffic signs and signals, storage lanes and turning areas.

Median barriers are used principally to prevent head-on collisions. While they reduce accident severity, they often increase the accident rate, because the perceived road width is narrower, and because vehicles often collide with the barriers.

Medians that are 25 feet (7.6 meters) wide, or more, generally reduce traffic noise and driving tension and eliminate headlight glare. A median of 10 feet (3.0 meters) is sufficient for vegetative planting, and a 60-foot (18.3-meter) width permits a parklike environment.

2. The value that appears at the midpoint of a distribution and divides the distribution in half. If there are 51 annual family incomes, the 26th income would be the median, with 25 incomes less than that figure and 25 incomes higher.

See: ARTERIAL ROAD; AUXILIARY LANES; EXPRESSWAY; FREEWAY; GUARDRAIL; LANE WIDTH; MEAN; MEASURES OF CENTRAL TENDENCY; MODE; REVERSIBLE LANES

Medical Building

A building designed for the provision of various types of health care and associated uses, such as pharmacies. Medical buildings are generally analogous to office buildings in their physical requirements. In some cases, however, zoning ordinances permit medical buildings to locate in designated residential areas in which other office buildings are not permitted.

Principal required design features are the elimination of architectural barriers in front of and within the building and provision of adequate parking and patient drop-off areas. Screening of parking areas may also be necessary because of the round-the-clock nature of this use.

See: HEALTH CARE SYSTEM; OFFICE DEVELOPMENT; OFF-STREET PARKING REQUIREMENTS

Megalopolis

The combination of several metropolitan areas into one enormous urbanized area. The term *megalopolis,* taken from the name of an ancient Greek city, was first used by Jean Gottman in 1961 to describe the geographic area between Portsmouth, Maine and Norfolk, Virginia. In his opinion, the various cities and metropolitan areas in the northeastern United States had grown together to form one virtually continuous urban corridor. Other such megalopolises include San Diego to Los Angeles, California; Gary, Indiana to Milwaukee, Wisconsin (the Great Lakes megalopolis); the Ruhr Valley in West Germany; and Tokyo to Osaka, Japan.

The term *megalopolis* indicates more than just a very

large urban area; it denotes the blending together of what had once been distinct regions and the loss of farmland and open space between cities in an entire region. The gradual development of a megalopolis introduces new complications in intermunicipal relationships relating to development in close proximity to other municipalities, requirements for improved transportation in intervening areas and the need for land conservation measures to protect remaining large open-space areas from development. The recognition of this development trend is an opportunity to control it through metropolitan, regional or national growth policy.

See: AGGLOMERATION; METROPOLITAN AREA; NATIONAL LAND USE POLICY; REGIONAL PLANNING

Megastructure

As originally proposed by Le Corbusier in his Fort l'Empereur project of 1931, megastructures were a futuristic approach to city building in which a city-sized framework was to be constructed to house all of the functions and land uses commonly found in a complex society. It was thought that prefabricated boxes, in either single or multiple units, could be designed to fit into spaces in the framework in predesigned patterns and could also be moved to other locations in the framework by detaching utility connections and reattaching them in the new location. This proposal is partly responsible for the development of prefabricated housing as it is known today.

The use of a single, super-sized framework to construct large development projects of a more conventional design, such as universities and town and civic centers, was also taken from original megastructure principles. As an example, the design of a large university—which would normally have numerous buildings for its various departments as well as athletic and administrative functions—would be built within, above and below one huge framework, which would also have open-space areas, parking, bookstores and cafeterias. Because of their size and the diversity of uses within these structures, they retained the name *megastructure*.

The town center in the Scottish new town of Cumbernauld is considered to be the most complete megastructure that has been built because of the large variety of land uses that are combined within one structure. Megastructure projects, however, are no longer considered to be as practical as they were once envisioned to be because their costs were found to be excessive except where land values are extremely high or land is difficult to assemble.

See: JOINT DEVELOPMENT; MIXED-USE DEVELOPMENT (MXD)

Mesotrophic Lake

A lake that is changing from the oligotrophic stage, characterized by clear waters and low levels of nutrients to the eutrophic stage, which has high levels of nutrients, extensive plant growth and murky waters.

See: EUTROPHICATION; OLIGOTROPHIC LAKE

Meter-Controlled Parking

The use of mechanical time-measuring devices to collect revenue at public parking spaces and to limit permissible parking time. Provision of parking meters in public parking areas and on business streets is a principal method used by municipalities to recoup their capital and operating costs for parking lots or structures. Meters can also control the amount of time that a parker will be allowed by limiting the amount of time on the meter—e.g., providing one-hour meters in shopping areas to encourage turnover.

New computerized parking meters are being introduced in public parking lots in northern Europe. These can be programmed for various permissible time periods, can monitor six or more vehicles at a time and can inform a central policing station of a violation.

Metes and Bounds

A method of describing land so that a particular piece of property may be uniquely and specifically identified. A readily definable starting point is selected, such as a monument—e.g., a tree, stream or marker—or the intersection of two streets, and then the land boundaries are followed using measured distances, compass bearings and the location of monuments. An accurate description must trace the entire boundary back to the starting point. In general, if there is a conflict between the measured distances and the measured spacing of the monuments, the conflict is resolved in favor of the monuments.

Metes and bounds are commonly recorded in the legal description of property that is found on deeds, particularly in urban areas. It is a more precise and reliable means of identifying property than street address, subdivision block and lot, or tax bill descriptions and may sometimes be used in conjunction with other forms of legal description.

See: SURVEY

Metromedia, Inc. v. *City of San Diego* (453 U.S. 490, 101 S. Ct. 2882, 69 L.Ed.2d 800 [1981])

A decision by the United States Supreme Court striking down a municipal ordinance regulating signs and billboards on First Amendment constitutional grounds.

The decision is significant for planning purposes, in that the Court expressly acknowledged that municipal aesthetics, one of the goals sought to be furthered by the ordinance, was a substantial government interest, sufficient to justify application of the police power to regulate advertising. However, because the ordinance in question was not neutral as to the content of permissible billboard advertising—commercial billboards were favored over those with noncommercial messages—the Court held that free speech rights were violated.

See: SIGN REGULATION

Metropolitan Area

The densely populated region surrounding a city that is tied to it by economic and social factors. Most metropolitan areas are identified by one central city, though some are polynucleated. Economic ties are most often used to define a metropolitan area, particularly the region within which people commute daily to work. Other factors that define the metropolitan region include market delineations, such as newspaper circulation; image items, such as rooting for sports teams; and use of regional facilities, such as airports. The U.S. Census Bureau uses and defines the phrase *Metropolitan Statistical Area* primarily in terms of population and journey-to-work data.

Metropolitan areas frequently cross municipal, county and even state political boundaries. Some planning issues, such as transportation and air pollution, can therefore only be realistically managed on a metropolitan area basis. While metropolitan area governments are commonplace around the world, only a few locations in the United States—including Indianapolis, Indiana; Dade County, Florida; and Minneapolis-St. Paul, Minnesota—have a strong metropolitan area government.

See: CONURBATION; COUNCIL OF GOVERNMENT (COG); METROPOLITAN STATISTICAL AREA (MSA); REGIONAL PLANNING

Metropolitan Statistical Area (MSA)

An area, defined for statistical reporting by federal agencies, that closely resembles the definition of a standard metropolitan statistical area (SMSA) but is less liberal in its inclusion of outlying counties. Outlying counties are included in an MSA only if they meet standards on commuting to the MSA and development density.

MSAs with a population of at least 1 million are termed primary metropolitan statistical areas (PMSAs) if they meet requirements concerning commuting and percentage of urbanized development, while those not meeting these requirements are termed level A MSAs. Those with lesser populations are called level B (250,000 to 1 million), level C (100,000 to 250,000) and level D (less than 100,000) MSAs. Two or more adjacent MSAs are called a consolidated metropolitan statistical area (CMSA) if their total population is 1 million, there is substantial commuting between them, they are within the same urbanized area, and the urbanized area constitutes at least 60 percent of the total area.

In 1983, the MSA and CMSA replaced the SMSA and standard consolidated statistical area (SCSA) for census data reporting. While the MSA is closely comparable to the SMSA, the CMSA is very different from the SCSA. SCSA requirements specified that at least one of the component cities have a population of 1 million and that the urbanized area be 75 percent of the total area.

See: CENSUS; STANDARD CONSOLIDATED STATISTICAL AREA (SCSA); STANDARD METROPOLITAN STATISTICAL AREA (SMSA); URBANIZED AREA (UA)

Microclimate

The climate of a small area such as a community, a portion of a community or a building site. It is normally described in terms of temperature, wind speed, amount of

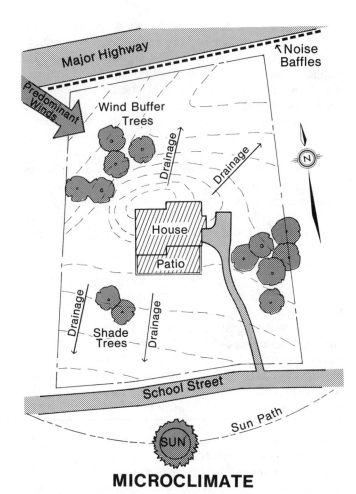

MICROCLIMATE

Fig. 27. Microclimate is created by the elements and natural and cultural features on and near a site. Buffers provided by trees on this site reduce effects of wind and late day sun. Noise baffles are necessary to reduce traffic noise.

sunlight or other environmental conditions that characterize it. Because any large site may contain many microclimates due to variations in slope, cover or orientation, standard meteorological data do not normally reflect existing conditions.

In planning, the characteristics of the microclimate are of prime importance to a site planner, who must be able to recognize climatic variations and use this information as a basis for design and siting decisions. An experienced designer should be able to take advantage of favorable characteristics to maximize access to light, air and other features of the site. Similarly, avoidance of other portions of the site can help to avoid unnecessary energy consumption. (See Fig. 27)

See: CLIMATIC CONDITIONS; ENERGY-EFFICIENT LAND USE PRACTICES

Microwave Radiation

A type of electromagnetic wave that lies in the spectrum between the longest infrared waves and conventional radio waves. Interest in this type of wave began as a result of the use of radar during World War II, and many modern applications for microwave technology have been developed in recent years. Microwaves are used extensively for many purposes, including a number of manufacturing processes; home ovens; communication systems, such as television and telephone; and tracking the orbits of spacecraft. Microwaves have also been suggested as a future means by which energy collected by solar power satellites could be transmitted to Earth.

A land use issue involved in microwave transmission for communication purposes is the use of repeaters or amplifiers that are sited in such a way as to accommodate a straight line of travel for the beam. This is usually achieved through the use of towers and location of microwave equipment on hilltops, making it quite visible.

An additional issue is the question of microwave safety. Extensive studies have been conducted concerning the potential biological effects of microwave radiation. Although microwave ovens are considered safe when used properly because they do not leak radiation, workers involved in activities in which they are exposed to substantial microwave radiation may be subject to some degree of risk. Because of this, standards are in effect in a number of countries—including the United States, Britain, Canada, Sweden and the USSR—for maximum occupational exposure to this type of radiation.
See: TELEPHONE SYSTEM

Microzoning

Zoning with an unusual degree of detail that is applied to a small area requiring special regulation, such as the area surrounding a transportation terminal. In microzoning it is possible for different land use categories to be assigned to the portions of buildings fronting on the street versus the rear of the buildings and to different floors of each building. Varying floor area ratios may also be used in microzoning as well as special incentives for the accomplishment of certain types of design goals and the provision of public amenities.
See: FLOOR AREA RATIO (FAR); INCENTIVE ZONING; SPOT ZONING; VERTICAL ZONING

Mid-Rise Housing

A residential building that generally contains approximately three to seven stories, although this standard may vary by geographic area. Nonresidential development of a similar height may also be described as mid-rise.
See: HIGH-RISE HOUSING; HOUSING TYPE; LOW-RISE HOUSING

Minimum Lot Size

A zoning ordinance provision that specifies the minimum size that a building lot must be for a building to be constructed legally at that site.

Although minimum lot sizes may be used in any type of zoning district, they are used extensively in residential districts, where lot size is the prime distinguishing factor between single-family residential districts. In urban areas

minimum lot sizes in the most dense residential districts may be as small as 2,500 square feet (232 square meters) or less. Conversely, some communities in suburban areas may have districts where the minimum lot size may be 5 or 10 acres (2 or 4 hectares) or even more. Many communities will have a range of residential districts with a commensurate range of minimum lot sizes. Other zoning requirements concerning minimum frontage, yards and setback will be proportionate to the required minimum lot size.
See: EXCLUSIONARY ZONING; LARGE-LOT ZONING; ZONING

Minimum Maintenance Standards

Requirements that specify that an owner of a designated historic landmark or a property located in a historic district must maintain the property and keep it in good repair. This type of provision is sometimes found in preservation ordinances to prevent demolition by neglect. In the City of New Orleans ordinance that regulates the historic Vieux Carre, owners are notified if their properties have specific defects and fined if they do not correct these deficiencies.
See: DEMOLITION BY NEGLECT; HISTORIC PRESERVATION; VIEUX CARRE

Minimum Residential Floor Area Requirements

Requirements that specify the minimum number of square feet of floor area that a dwelling unit or house must have. These requirements are often found in municipal housing codes, where they are intended to promote public health through the prevention of overcrowding. A number of government and nonprofit agencies have also published recommended minimum standards by family size.

The use of high minimum floor area requirements in zoning ordinances, however, has increasingly met with opposition as a form of exclusionary zoning and a means of unnecessarily raising housing cost. Some zoning ordinances may contain provisions requiring large apartment or house size or requiring features such as a minimum of three bathrooms for three bedroom units and defend these practices as a means of preserving community character or protecting property values.

In a 1979 Supreme Court of New Jersey case, *Home Builders League of S. Jersey* v. *Township of Berlin,* the court found zoning ordinances requiring minimum residential floor areas that were unrelated to the number of occupants to be invalid. It was found that such ordinances not only serve no valid public purpose but actually run counter to the promotion of the general welfare by supporting economic segregation through an increase in local housing costs. The court did emphasize, however, that minimum floor area requirements that are tied to the number of occupants are a valid subject for zoning ordinance control.
See: EXCLUSIONARY ZONING; LARGE-LOT ZONING; MINIMUM LOT SIZE; OVERCROWDING; ZONING

Minor Civil Division (MCD)

A term used by the Bureau of the Census to describe political and administrative subdivisions of counties, which are called townships or towns in most states. MCDs are used for census purposes in 30 states, while census county divisions (CCDs) are used in the remaining 20 states. CCDs, subdivisions of counties that follow relatively permanent natural or man-made boundaries, are used where MCD boundaries are unstable or are not meaningful.
See: CENSUS; POLITICAL SUBDIVISION

Minor Subdivision

A land subdivision in which relatively few lots are proposed. Many communities set four or five as the maximum number of lots permitted for a subdivision to be considered a minor subdivision. It may also be required that no new streets be created and that no extension of municipal facilities be involved for a development to receive minor subdivision status. An additional requirement may be that the proposed subdivision not interfere with the future development of any portion of the parcel remaining undeveloped; it also should not be in conflict with the municipal master plan, official map or zoning ordinance.

When a subdivision receives official minor subdivision status, it is generally subject to a significantly streamlined review process, and far fewer requirements must be met. The types of general data that may be required on a minor subdivision plat application may be limited to copies of pertinent deeds and covenants, a survey of property boundary lines, evidence of compliance with public health requirements and a basic plat map.
See: SUBDIVISION; SUBDIVISION REGULATIONS; SUBDIVISION REVIEW

Mixed-Use Development (MXD)

A project in which a variety of complementary land uses are planned and constructed in one coordinated development. Typical mixed-use projects have office towers, street-level retail areas or malls, parking structures, and a subway and/or bus station at their base. Some have a hotel, theater or park as well.

A mixed-use project—such as Rockefeller Center in New York City, Charles Center in Baltimore, Peachtree Center in Atlanta or Renaissance Center in Detroit—is built as a megastructure that encompasses several square blocks. All buildings are connected at the base of the structure by interior and exterior arcades and parking areas, so that movement from place to place within the development is possible without leaving the structure. While costly, these developments generally become major urban and tourist attractions that often spur an upgrading of surrounding areas.

In suburban shopping mall design, mixed-use development is occasionally being added in the form of movie theaters, ice-skating rinks or office space, either within the center itself or in another on-site location.
See: MEGASTRUCTURE; MIXED-USE ZONING; PLANNED UNIT DEVELOPMENT (PUD)

Mixed-Use Zoning

Zoning regulations that authorize a variety of land uses to be located within one development. Although planned unit developments also allow some degree of land use mix, typically the nonresidential uses are accessory to the residential uses. Mixed-use zoning has become common for large downtown projects in which a complementary array of land uses—such as offices, retail development and residences—are integrated within one development or structure.
See: MIXED-USE DEVELOPMENT (MXD); PLANNED UNIT DEVELOPMENT (PUD); VERTICAL ZONING; ZONING

Mobile Home

A portable housing unit consisting of a chassis that sits on axles and wheels. It is transported to a housing site, sometimes in sections, where it is attached to utility lines and frequently placed on a foundation. Often, its axles and wheels are removed and it remains permanently at that site, in contrast to the much more mobile recreational vehicle or motor home, which is not designed for long-term habitation.

Although when first introduced mobile homes were 8 feet (2.4 meters) by 30 feet (9 meters), 10-, 12- and 14-foot (3-meter, 3.6-meter and 4.2-meter) wide units are now available. Doublewide units, often measuring 24 feet (7.2 meters) by 60 feet (18 meters), are currently popular. These homes contain 1,440 square feet (130 square meters) of living space, which is considered comparable to the average size of 1,550 square feet (140 square meters) for conventionally built homes. Also, mobile homes today are often built to simulate the design of traditional homes, with pitched, shingled roofs and siding. Considerably less expensive than conventional single-family homes, they can be purchased completely outfitted with appliances and furniture and are usually financed through loans resembling those made for automobile purchase. Mobile homes, which are generally taxed as personal rather than real property, represented 21 percent of total single-family housing production in the United States in 1980.

Although mobile homes are sometimes viewed as being unsafe, energy-intensive and of flimsy construction as a result of past practices, all mobile homes built after June 15, 1976 have come under the jurisdiction of the Manufactured Homes Construction and Safety Standards Act of 1974. Under this act the U.S. Department of Housing and Urban Development sets quality and safety standards, approves state inspection agencies and provides for inspection at plant sites.

In many cases, mobile homes have been prohibited

restricted to mobile home parks or permitted only in a very small area of a community. Recently, however, a number of states, including California and Florida, have provided for nondiscriminatory practice with respect to manufactured housing, specifying usually that the manufactured units have the appearance of conventional single-family homes.

See: HOUSING TYPE; INDUSTRIALIZED HOUSING; MOBILE HOME PARK; RECREATIONAL VEHICLES (RV)

Mobile Home Park

Property that is divided into sites for rent or purchase by owners of mobile homes and is to be used for the permanent parking of the homes. In the past mobile home parks were owned and operated by a management team that provided utilities, trash collection and community facilities and maintained landscaping in return for rental fees. However, there are presently appearing in the United States mobile home condominiums, which operate in a manner similar to apartment condominiums. Mobile home parks must sometimes meet licensing requirements and comply with various regulations in order to stay in operation.

Most mobile home parks able to offer a range of community facilities and services have at least 20 acres (8 hectares) and contain at least 100 to 150 housing units. Individual lot size should be at least 2,800 square feet (260 square meters) for single-width units and at least 4,500 square feet (418 square meters) for doublewide units. Generally, the unit should not occupy more than one-third of the total square footage of the lot. A well-designed mobile home park will have direct vehicular access from major highways and a properly laid out minor road network of no more than moderate grade. At least 10 percent of the total park area should be devoted to open space and community facilities, with the scope and nature of the facilities to be determined by the rental or ownership structure of the park. Off-street parking for residents and visitors should be incorporated into the park design.

See: HOUSING TYPE; MOBILE HOME

Mobile Source

A source of air pollution capable of movement, a major category of air polluters regulated by the Clean Air Act Amendments of 1970 and 1977. Examples of mobile sources are motor vehicles, aircraft and ships.

Mobile sources are often the single largest producers of air pollution in industrialized countries. As a result, many air pollution control laws and regulations have been directed at motor vehicles. One way in which reduced air pollution has been achieved is through the requirement that new automobiles be able to meet specified emission standards for hydrocarbons, carbon monoxide and nitrogen oxide. Among the approaches taken to comply with these standards are improved engine design; fuel modifi-

cation, such as the use of unleaded gasoline; and the use of catalytic converters. Other provisions set standards for trucks, buses and motorcycles.

The 1977 Clean Air Act Amendments require the implementation of automobile inspection and maintenance programs by those states with regions that were unable to meet carbon monoxide or ozone standards by 1982. The intent of these programs is to identify vehicles requiring repairs that will help to reduce their emission levels. In addition, the 1977 legislation requires coordination between the U.S. Environmental Protection Agency and the U.S. Department of Transportation with regard to air quality and transportation planning.

One traditional planning response to the need for reduction of mobile source air pollution has been the development of policies, programs and services aimed at decreasing reliance upon the automobile. Improved mass transit service, incentives for ridepooling and park and ride, and innovative transit systems are among the approaches currently in use. Land use policies may also be formulated that stress more concentrated development patterns for which transit service may readily be provided, as well as increased mixed-use development, which can help to decrease the amount of necessary commutation.

See: AIR POLLUTION; STATE IMPLEMENTATION PLAN (SIP); STATIONARY SOURCE

Modal Split

A study, used for transportation planning purposes, of the number of people in a given population who use each of the various modes of transportation available to them and an estimate of their future transportation choices. This information is expressed in the form of number of trips by mode type—e.g., private auto, subway, commuter rail, bus. Models used to predict modal split analyze trip length and trip cost for each possible choice between zones and frequently include factors for trip safety, comfort or discomfort, convenience of mode, socioeconomic characteristics of riders and trip purpose. In calculating these factors, trip length is defined as the time from door to door by each available mode and includes walking, transfer and waiting time as well as actual travel time. Trip cost is calculated as the total fare, if public transit is used, or the cost of fuel, tolls and parking if private auto is the mode. These models divide the population into captive transit riders (those who do not own private vehicles) and choice transit riders (those who do).

Estimates of future transportation choices must be based on specific criteria and assumptions concerning travel conditions (e.g., improved subway service), future economic factors (e.g., high oil prices) and social factors (e.g., high crime rate) in order to predict change in mode use. Improvements—such as new transit lines, increase in the speed of commuter railroads, provision of parking areas or reduced bus fares for certain population groups—will affect estimation results. Modal split should be esti-

mated for peak travel periods, during which public transit receives its greatest use and road congestion is greatest.
See: NETWORK ASSIGNMENT; TRANSIT FARE SUBSIDIES; TRANSPORTATION PLANNING

Mode

The value that appears most often in a particular distribution.
See: MEAN; MEASURES OF CENTRAL TENDENCY; MEDIAN

Model

A systematic attempt to depict a segment of the real world, either as it exists or as it ideally should exist. A model can take a physical form, as in the case of architectural or engineering models, be mathematical in nature (as in simulation models) or take other diverse forms, such as computer programs, laws, regulations or maps.

Models may be used for many purposes related to urban and regional planning. One common example is the predictive model, which is used to illustrate the relationships that are found in data and the patterns they tend to form over time. These models are often depicted as a series of equations, in which data from the past and present are used to predict or describe probable future circumstances. Such models may be linear, in that data from the past are simply extended into the future via a straight line, or they may be more complex and take into account multiple independent variables or assume a nonlinear form.

Optimizing models are used to attempt to provide optimal answers to problems in which particular constraints are imposed, such as environmental limitations or fiscal shortages. Queuing models are used to devise solutions to the problem of people or entities waiting on line for a service or result, as in cars waiting at intersections or toll booths and planes waiting to land, so as to provide an improved level of service.
See: ARCHITECTURAL MODEL; DECISION SUPPORT SYSTEMS (DSS); SIMULATION; SYSTEMS ANALYSIS

Model Cities Program

An early program of the U.S. Department of Housing and Urban Development that gave federal grants directly to citizens' organizations in low-income urban neighborhoods to plan and operate programs designed to meet local needs in housing, education, health and other areas. The Model Cities Program, which was authorized by the Demonstration Cities and Metropolitan Development Act of 1966, was active from 1966 to 1974, when it was absorbed by the Community Development Block Grant Program.

Residents of a Model Cities district would form a City Demonstration Agency to identify the neighborhood's needs, set priorities, and plan and administer programs. Federal funds were provided directly to the citizens' group, bypassing the local government. This was the first federal program to emphasize neighborhood-level planning and mandate citizen participation in all phases of planning and implementation.

Model Cities was criticized for the ineffectiveness and poor financial controls of the local programs, and local government officials resented the independence of the City Demonstration Agencies. But Model Cities successfully trained neighborhood residents in community organizing techniques and also encouraged citizens' groups to expect to have a voice in the development and administration of programs designed to improve their neighborhoods.
See: CITIZEN PARTICIPATION; COMMUNITY DEVELOPMENT BLOCK GRANT (CDBG); NEIGHBORHOOD PLANNING

Model Legislation

Legislation prepared by a sponsoring organization, usually a nonprofit professional group or a government agency, as a means of demonstrating an improved way in which certain activities may be conducted. The zoning and city planning enabling acts that the Department of Commerce put forth in the 1920s are an early example of model planning legislation. Most states eventually adopted these enabling statutes, helping to define many aspects of planning and zoning. A more recent example is the American Law Institute's *A Model Land Development Code,* issued in 1975.

Model ordinances are often made available to local planning agencies to assist them in drafting their own versions. It is particularly useful to be able to obtain models for new types of land use regulation for which few good examples are available.
See: AMERICAN LAW INSTITUTE MODEL LAND DEVELOPMENT CODE; STANDARD CITY PLANNING ENABLING ACT; STANDARD STATE ZONING ENABLING ACT

Modular Construction

The use of a standard dimension in the design of structures to enable the economical production of building elements that can reduce construction costs. A key to the industrial production of buildings, adoption of a modular size implies that all building dimensions will be a multiple or a simple fraction of that size and that individual building elements, including associated joints between structural members, will also be a multiple of the module. The availability of standard stock sizes of building components, which are manufactured according to adopted modular dimensions, tends to cause modular construction to some degree even when modular construction is not necessarily intended.

In North America a module of 4 inches has been adopted. A standard dimension of 10 centimeters (which is close to the North American (4-inch module) has been adopted by a number of European countries (Belgium, Britain, Denmark, France, Germany, Italy, the Netherlands, Norway, Poland, the Soviet Union and Sweden).
See: INDUSTRIALIZED HOUSING

Monell v. Department of Social Services of New York (436 U.S. 658 [1978])

A decision by the United States Supreme Court concerning whether municipalities could be held liable for damages under a section of the Civil Rights Act of 1871 (now known as Section 1983) that allows individuals to sue for monetary damages against any person who, apparently acting under law, deprives another of his constitutional rights. The Court held that local governments could be sued under Section 1983 for monetary damages resulting from these unconstitutional acts.

While not a land use case, the decision opened the possibility of a municipality's being sued for damages by a landowner alleging that a particular zoning ordinance constituted a taking of his property without due process or just compensation.

See: LAKE COUNTRY ESTATES INC. v. *TAHOE REGIONAL PLANNING AGENCY*

Monorail

1. A railway that runs on a single rail with trains suspended from above or supported from below. Trains of a monorail have a single set of wheels and are electrically powered by conventional motors. Monorails have been built as a form of transportation in Tokyo, as well as in amusement parks, and as airport transportation. They are a slow form of rail transportation and have been largely superseded by more advanced technology, such as the people mover.

2. A name sometimes used for single-guideway people movers.

See: FUTURE TRANSPORTATION MODES; PEOPLE MOVER

Moore v. City of East Cleveland, Ohio (431 U.S. 494, 97 S.Ct. 1932, 52 L.Ed.2d 571 [1977])

A decision by the United States Supreme Court holding unconstitutional a zoning ordinance that prohibited members of an extended family unit from living together in a single residential dwelling unit.

The Court was able to distinguish this case from its decision in *Village of Belle Terre* v. *Boraas* by noting that in *Belle Terre,* which upheld a zoning ordinance restricting occupancy of a single dwelling unit to persons related by "blood, adoption or marriage," the effect of the ordinance was to protect and promote the family unit. In contrast, the East Cleveland ordinance interfered with family values by dictating which members of a family group could choose to live together. In effect, the Court held that it was unconstitutional for zoning laws to differentiate among relatives of varying degrees of consanguinity.

See: FAMILY; *VILLAGE OF BELLE TERRE* v. *BORAAS*

Mooring Facilities

Provisions for boat mooring on water bodies and at public and private shorefront areas. In locations where boating is popular, moorings allow boaters to leave their boats for periods of time for land-based activities. Moorings may be provided in the form of slips at marinas, posts along seawalls or bulkheads where boats can be tied, or at buoys offshore. Mooring facilities differ from marinas in that boat launching, fueling and servicing are generally not provided, but like marinas, they must be protected from waves, wind and the wakes of other boats, and their effects on the local water body must be assessed.

See: BOAT LAUNCH RAMP; MARINA

Moped

A motor-powered vehicle with two wheels, handlebars and pedals; an engine under 50 cubic centimeters in size and under 1.5 horsepower; a single-speed transmission; and an automatic clutch. A moped gets from 100 to 200 miles per gallon (42.5 to 85 kilometers per liter) of gasoline, has a design speed of no more than 25 to 30 mph (40 to 48 kph) on level ground and can also be pedaled. Used extensively in Europe since the 1950s, the moped is becoming increasingly popular in the United States because of its usefulness for short local trips, its fuel efficiency and its low purchase price. In most European countries both a driver's license and a vehicle registration are required to operate a moped. In the United States these requirements vary from state to state, as do regulations that control the sizes of mopeds permitted on public roads.

Although there are concerns about the safety of mopeds in the context of American traffic patterns because of their low silhouettes and low speeds, they are seen to have potential for use as urban transportation.

See: OFF-ROAD VEHICLE (ORV)

Moratorium

1. A temporary prohibition on new construction. Typically, a moratorium is imposed by government as a response to rapid growth that threatens to exhaust the capacity of the water or sewer system or that is inadequately controlled by local land use regulations. The form of the moratorium may be a refusal to issue new building permits or zoning approvals, a prohibition of new water or sewer connections, or a combination of these techniques.

If the moratorium is imposed for environmental reasons, there is usually a provision for its expiration when needed facilities, such as a new sewage treatment plant or a new reservoir, become available. If inadequate land use planning or land use controls are the justification, the moratorium generally stays in effect while a master plan is being formulated and ends when a new zoning ordinance goes into effect. Frequently, a moratorium is only partial, with interim development controls that permit limited development, particularly in hardship cases.

2. Any officially authorized delay period, such as a moratorium on debt payment.

See: GROWTH MANAGEMENT

Morbidity Rate

The incidence of illness, or of a specific illness, in a given population per 1,000 or 100,000 people for a defined time

period. Many different measures of morbidity are made to examine factors such as the duration of illness or the severity of illness. Morbidity statistics are used in the planning, location and administration of health care facilities, as well as for disease and epidemic control.
See: DEMOGRAPHY; MORTALITY RATE

Mortality Rate

The mortality, or death, rate, representing the number of deaths for a given population, may be calculated or described in varying ways. The crude death rate, which is the total number of annual deaths in a particular geographic area per 1,000 people, is the most common measure. Rates may also be calculated on a monthly rather than an annual basis. Specific death rates are used to study the mortality patterns of particular segments of the population by age group, sex, race or other characteristics. Mortality figures may also be calculated by cause of death.
See: BIRTHRATE; DEMOGRAPHY; FERTILITY RATE; MORBIDITY RATE; REPRODUCTION RATE

Mortgage

An instrument by which real property is used as collateral security for the payment of a debt. The borrower is known as the mortgagor, while the lender is the mortgagee.

In the United States, state practice varies as to whether the mortgagee actually holds title to the property or holds a lien on it. States that have the lien form of arrangement are called lien states. States in which legal title is actually in the name of the mortgagee are called title states. Mortgages, like deeds, are recorded in public records, usually at a municipal office building or courthouse, to protect the mortgagee's interest in the property.

Typically, single-family homes are bought with the help of mortgages, so that prevailing mortgage interest rates and other mortgage terms have a great influence on the housing market. A fairly standard arrangement through much of the 1970s was a required down payment of about 20 percent to 30 percent of the purchase price. The lending institution would then offer a mortgage on the remaining 70 percent to 80 percent of the purchase price for a term of 10 to 30 years, after appraising the property and scrutinizing the financial situation of the prospective borrower. Banks liked to see a steady monthly income that was four times the amount of the monthly mortgage payment plus real estate taxes. Mortgages could be obtained at an interest rate of 9 percent or 10 percent in many parts of the country in the late 1970s.

By 1980, because of a combination of factors—including inflation, changes in lending laws and the lessening attractiveness of bank deposits—mortgage rates in some areas had risen as high as 18 percent for single-family homes and higher for cooperatives and condominiums, resulting in a severe disruption of the residential resale market. Many first-time homebuyers found it extremely difficult to meet the downpayment requirements and still be able to handle carrying charges that often exceeded $1,000 per month. At the same time, older families were often forced to keep homes too large for their current needs.

These factors gave rise to the development of many new forms of mortgage financing in the late 1970s and early 1980s, such as the shared-appreciation mortgage and the graduated-payment mortgage. As of 1981 it seemed likely that the traditional fixed-rate mortgage, which had helped to finance most American homes since the Depression, would become increasingly rare. However, with the introduction of money market accounts and other accounts attractive to depositors that bring new flows of cash to banks, a large increase in fixed-rate mortgage lending occurred during the first quarter of 1983 as compared to the last quarter of 1982. At the same time, other forms of mortgage financing declined somewhat, although this decline is likely to reverse if at a later date fixed-rate mortgages again become unavailable.

Alternative forms of mortgage financing of a number of types are also available in other countries. In Britain, for example, other financing techniques exist, particularly for first-time buyers and those with lower or moderate incomes. An option mortgage approach allows the borrower to trade the tax deduction he would normally receive on his mortgage interest payments for a subsidy, which has the effect of reducing the rate of interest on the mortgage loan. The mortgage loan, under this program, may also be for up to 100 percent of the value of the house, provided it does not exceed a set amount. Under the Home Purchase and Housing Corporation Guarantee Act of 1978, first-time home buyers with savings can be given a tax-free cash bonus on these savings, which they receive when they purchase their home, as well as a loan on which no interest is owed for five years. The loan is then repaid over the remaining term of the mortgage. A form of the graduated-payment mortgage as well as shared-appreciation systems are also found in Britain.
See: AMORTIZATION; BALLOON MORTGAGE; BLANKET MORTGAGE; CONVENTIONAL MORTGAGE; FARM MORTGAGE; FIXED-RATE MORTGAGE (FRM); GRADUATED-PAYMENT MORTGAGE (GPM); HOME EQUITY CONVERSION; PURCHASE-MONEY MORTGAGE; RENEGOTIABLE-RATE MORTGAGE (RRM); SHARED-APPRECIATION MORTGAGE (SAM); VARIABLE-RATE MORTGAGE (VRM); WRAPAROUND MORTGAGE

Moses, Robert (1888–1981)

An American public official who substantially shaped the development of New York state and its land use patterns during his many years of public service.

He served as head of the New York state park system for nearly four decades, commencing in 1924, and was simultaneously New York City park commissioner from 1933 to 1959. During that same time period, he also held numerous other powerful positions, including the post of New York City's construction coordinator and head of the State Power Commission.

With the extensive network of resources at his disposal, Moses acquired vast amounts of parkland for New York state and built 13 bridges, a large portion of New York City's highway network, many famous parks, public housing and cultural facilities. Among the many projects in which Robert Moses was involved are Jones Beach State Park, Adirondack Park, Lincoln Center for the Performing Arts, the United Nations, Shea Stadium and the Co-op City Housing Development. He was also responsible for the development of the Verrazano-Narrows Bridge, the Triborough Bridge, the Throgs Neck Bridge, the Henry Hudson Parkway and most other highways, bridges and tunnels built in the New York metropolitan area during his long reign.

In his efforts to build this wide array of projects, Moses, known as "the master builder," used a broad range of methods, including drafting the enabling legislation that granted him his powers and obtaining widespread support from the press. Not surprisingly, however, Moses stirred considerable controversy and was the focus of much criticism during portions of his career. He believed in getting the job done by whatever means necessary, and his projects, which were often grand in scale, involved large commitments of funding and extensive relocation to make way for highways, parks and bridges. By focusing his efforts intensively upon the development of automobile-oriented facilities, he also helped to ensure increased automobile use and suburban development in New York.

Ultimately, as times changed, it became impossible for Robert Moses to continue to carry out projects as he had in the past. For example, a favorite Moses project, a bridge that would span Long Island Sound and link Westchester County with Long Island, was never built due to massive public opposition. He relinquished his New York City positions in 1959 in order to head the New York World's Fair of 1964–65 and lost the majority of his state positions in 1962. His vision of New York was, however, largely fulfilled and helped to serve as a model for American urban development for many years.

Motel

A hotel for automobile travelers, generally located in a commercial area along an arterial, on a scenic tourist route or in a resort area. Often low-rise buildings, motels are characterized by large parking lots situated to provide convenient room access.

Large motel chains have stylized this form of hotel to include ample landscaping and dining facilities; they usually also have a swimming pool and may sometimes contain meeting rooms. Larger facilities may have a resortlike quality and contain many of the same features as hotels. Low-budget versions generally provide only rooms, relying on neighboring restaurants and amenities as support facilities. In Europe country inns still generally serve the function that motels serve in the United States and Canada.

See: HOTEL; OFF-STREET PARKING REQUIREMENTS; TOURISM

Motor Vehicle Registration

The registration and licensing of motor vehicles by state agencies, which can provide useful data for a variety of purposes. Because it is mandatory that vehicles be registered and current addresses supplied, and because these data are largely computerized, a data base exists that can be readily adapted to particular uses. For example, total number of vehicles registered in a particular county is an indicator of vehicle use and availability. As the data are generally available on an annual basis, trends from year to year can be observed. Planners studying use patterns at a particular facility, such as a shopping center or a park, can record the license plate numbers of the parked vehicles. Through arrangements with the motor vehicle bureau, a printout can be obtained that lists the community or county of origin so that a user profile may be prepared.

Multifamily Housing

A multiple-dwelling building, generally described as having three or more housing units. Multifamily housing usually has a common heating and hot water system for the entire building, but water, gas and electrical use may be metered separately for each unit. In a multifamily structure each unit may have access to common hallways, stairs and elevators, or in a low-rise building, each may have individual access to a street or common courtyard.

The Department of Housing and Urban Development (HUD) defines the term as applying to dwellings having three or more units, differentiating it from one- and two-family housing for purposes of enforcement of mandatory construction standards (called minimum property standards) that differ for the two classes. The standards are imposed on all federally assisted housing, but efforts are currently being made to persuade HUD to discontinue their use to permit more innovative design and use of materials. Many Federal Housing Administration (FHA) programs are specifically designed for multifamily housing, but for these programs a multifamily building is defined as having a minimum of four or five units, depending upon the program.

See: SINGLE-FAMILY HOUSING

Multilevel Development

An approach to site development that either takes advantage of changes in slope or uses artificial means to create variations among levels of activities. Unless purely a function of topographic variation, multilevel development is often a result of a need to separate conflicting activities, such as auto and pedestrian circulation in a shopping area. It can also be employed for more efficient space utilization in a densely developed area.

Aside from its functional advantages, variation in level is also a common means of creating architectural interest and a sense of vitality, because it offers the visual excitement associated with different levels as well as many opportunities to vary the character of spaces. Although it is more expensive than a standard one-level approach, these advantages are often thought to be worth the additional

costs. Most downtown redevelopment plans now include a major multilevel complex that serves as a focal point for the design.
See: MIXED-USE DEVELOPMENT (MXD)

Multiple-Nuclei Theory

A theory of urban growth based upon a pattern of a number of urban centers rather than one central business district. The multiple-nuclei theory was first conceived by R.D. McKenzie and more fully developed by Chauncy D. Harris and Edward L. Ullman in the 1940s. The terms *conurbation* and *variegated network* have also been applied to such polynucleated metropolitan areas.

The multiple-nuclei theory describes those cities that have grown to encompass, though not obliterate, villages and smaller cities. Many cities also develop more than one nucleus, sometimes induced by a large hospital, office complex or college campus. This theory also accommodates newer cities, where private automobile travel is more prevalent than mass transit radiating from a single center. Los Angeles and Houston are examples of multiple-nucleated metropolitan areas. (See Fig. 20)
See: CONURBATION; GROWTH THEORY

Multiservice Center

A building within which a variety of social services are made available to residents of a neighborhood. From a municipal standpoint, advantages include coordinated service delivery and reduced capital and operating costs for agencies sharing a facility. Although building type and size will vary, the basic services provided in most centers are similar, ranging from traditional services such as education, recreation and counseling to more extensive programs that provide health care, drug treatment, legal aid, and youth and senior citizen services. A center may also have an ombudsman or liaison between the community and city hall.

Multiservice centers are best located in a focus of neighborhood activity well served by mass transit for ease of access. Association with an established community facility, such as a church or civic hall, can help establish roots in a neighborhood and act as a catalyst for attracting membership and can also make use of what might otherwise be an underutilized facility.
See: COMMUNITY CENTER; LITTLE CITY HALLS

Multivariate Analysis

A set of statistical techniques involving two or more independent variables. Univariate analysis, by contrast, involves the impact of one independent variable (called the *x* variable in mathematical terms) on one dependent variable (the *y* variable). A univariate equation in its simplest form would be expressed as:

$$Y = a + bX + E,$$ where E represents statistical error.

A multivariate equation would be written mathematically as:

$$Y = a + b_1 X_1 + b_2 X_2 \ldots b_n X_n + E$$

Multivariate analysis techniques include various types of regression and correlation measures used to draw inferences and derive mathematical constructs describing the relationships between those variables. As an example, a very simplistic univariate regression analysis to predict family consumption expenditure based on family size would be of limited usefulness. A more complex multivariate analysis that takes into account such factors as income, age of head of household, cost of consumer items in that geographic area and family size would be a far better predictor of expenditures.
See: REGRESSION ANALYSIS

Mumford, Lewis (1895–   )

American writer, sociologist and teacher who approaches his many works on urban planning and architecture from a humanistic and ecological viewpoint. Strongly influenced by the work of Sir Patrick Geddes, Mumford began his career by systematically surveying the New York City region. Through his early writings in many periodicals, he became known to prominent planning figures of the time, such as Clarence Stein, and took part in the Regional Planning Association of America and the New York State Commission of Housing and Regional Planning. He served as an associate editor of *The Dial* and in 1932 began writing a column for *The New Yorker* on architecture.

Among Mumford's many books are *The Culture of Cities* (1938), *The City in History* (1961) and *The Urban Prospect* (1968). He also served on the faculties of Stanford University, the University of Pennsylvania, the Massachusetts Institute of Technology and Wesleyan University in Connecticut. In 1957 he received the gold medal of the Royal Town Planning Institute of Great Britain, and in 1961 he received the royal gold medal of the Royal Institute of British Architects.
See: GEDDES, SIR PATRICK

Municipal Bond

A bond that is issued by state government or by a unit of local government—such as a city, town, village or county—as opposed to the federal government or a corporation. Municipal bonds may be sold for a wide range of purposes, including the financing of roads, parks, schools, water and sewer facilities, environmental projects and public housing.

Revenue bonds, general obligation bonds, special assessment bonds and tax anticipation notes are all types of municipal bonds; they differ, among other ways, in the manner in which payment is guaranteed. Whereas the taxing power of the municipality backs a general obligation bond, a revenue bond is repaid from the funds generated by one or more specific facilities. Special obligation bonds are the obligation of those who benefit from the particular improvement rather than the community at large. Tax anticipation notes are backed by taxes scheduled to be collected.

A particular feature of municipal bonds is that their interest is exempt from federal taxation. In addition, taxes are often not levied by state or local government on their own securities, although taxes are often charged on those issued by another state. Although municipal bonds generally sell at lower yields than comparable taxable bonds, their tax-exempt status may make them attractive to those in high tax brackets.

See: BOND; BOND RATINGS; GENERAL OBLIGATION BOND; REVENUE BOND; TAX ANTICIPATION NOTE

Municipal Clerk

The city, town or village clerk is an elected municipal officer who functions as an official record keeper and often serves as secretary to the legislative body. The clerk frequently issues licenses and permits, is sometimes charged with managing elections and in some communities may also function as a municipal manager and may have a policymaking role. Depending upon the size of the municipality, the clerk may either function alone on a part-time or full-time basis or have a staff.

Municipal Corporation

The basic form of local self-government in the United States, a municipal corporation is a political body organized pursuant to state law consisting of the inhabitants of a designated area.

A municipal corporation is often referred to as a creature of the state, since all of its powers are derived from and subordinate to the power of the state creating the municipality. To the extent authorized by state law and the municipality's charter, granted by the state, a municipal corporation may tax, spend, borrow, exercise the police power and the power of eminent domain, and otherwise regulate its inhabitants and the land within its borders.

A municipal corporation may only be created by an act of the state's legislative body, but it may be created with or without the consent of the inhabitants of the area to be incorporated.

Depending upon their size, the degree of self-government conferred by the state and the nomenclature adopted by the state, municipal corporations may be designated as cities, boroughs, towns, townships or villages.

See: LOCAL GOVERNMENT

Municipal Parking Facilities

Parking lots and structures that are built and operated by a municipality to supplement curb parking and commercial parking facilities. Municipal parking facilities are generally located in commercial areas and at transportation terminals and are often built in connection with major civic center or mixed-use development. They are usually metered, while tickets are used in some municipal parking structures. In densely developed areas an hourly-rate scale that increases in cost with the length of stay may be imposed to encourage frequent parking space turnover.

In general, municipalities build parking lots or structures when parking demand dictates its necessity, as at an airport, and when required off-street parking and commercial parking facilities cannot meet the demand. When located at transportation nodes or in shopping areas, parking facilities may be built by the municipality but franchised to commercial concerns that operate them and pay a percentage of their income to the municipality. In large cities the recent trend is toward reducing parking availability to encourage carpooling and use of public transit.

See: AUTO DISINCENTIVES; COMMERCIAL PARKING FACILITIES; METER-CONTROLLED PARKING; OFF-SITE IMPROVEMENTS

Municipal Services

The functions performed by municipal government that provide for the general well-being of those who live or work in the community. Water supply, sewerage, garbage collection, public transportation facilities, street maintenance, police and fire protection, public health services, hospitals, parks and recreation programs, public welfare programs, housing programs and libraries are among the types of municipal services that can be provided.

More municipal services are generally available in larger communities, but the extent to which services are provided is usually closely related to both the wealth of the community and the willingness of its residents to pay for nonessential municipal services, such as libraries or swimming pools. The level of facility maintenance is also dependent on the tax base and may become deficient in communities experiencing tax base decline.

Municipalities frequently use their ability to provide services as a guide to determining whether new development should be permitted or encouraged. As a tool of growth management, a development's fiscal impact is sometimes determined and is then used as a basis for project approval. A municipality with a superior transportation network or abundant water supply, for example, might also use these attributes as a basis for encouraging economic development. The availability of a wide range of municipal services, in addition, is often a major determinant of business location.

See: ECONOMIC DEVELOPMENT; FISCAL IMPACT ANALYSIS; GROWTH MANAGEMENT; PUBLIC INFRASTRUCTURE

Municipal Treasurer

The chief financial officer of a municipality, who is responsible for receiving all municipal revenue (including that from taxes and licenses) and for the proper deposit of these funds. He also raises and disburses funds necessary to conduct municipal business, generally acting on authority granted by the legislature and with the approval of the legal department. The municipal treasurer may be elected by the public or appointed by the chief elected official or legislative body. In some municipalities using an appointive system, the person who holds this post is called the commissioner or director of finance, or the comptroller;

some large cities have both a finance commissioner and a comptroller and divide the functions of this position.
See: BUDGET DIRECTOR

Municipal Waste

The residential and commercial solid waste that a municipality generates.
See: SOLID WASTE

Municipal Wastewater Treatment Construction Grant Amendments of 1981

Legislation that reauthorizes the grant program for sewage treatment plant construction and related sewerage established by the Water Pollution Control Act Amendments of 1972 but reduces the scope of projects it will fund, the amount of the annual authorizations and the federal share of costs. The major thrust of the act (PL 97-117) is to remove federal funding for excess capacity in sewage treatment plants after October 1, 1984, thereby withdrawing support for growing communities that are planning for future population growth when building treatment works. It is the intent of Congress that the federal government only pay for the existing population. In addition, the federal cost share is reduced from 75 percent to 55 percent as of that date, but projects begun prior to that time are grandfathered.

This legislation limits federal funding to construction of sewage treatment facilities that provide at least secondary treatment, new interceptor sewers and correction of infiltration and inflow into sewers. Further, it redefines secondary treatment to include oxidation ponds, lagoons, ditches and trickling filters if their effectiveness can be demonstrated. Other provisions of the act create a special authorization for funding for the correction of combined sewer overflows into marine bays and estuaries, allow the governor of a state to use up to 20 percent of his state's annual allotment under this act for discretionary projects not otherwise funded and continue the program of increased funding for use of innovative and alternative technologies. The law also directs the Environmental Protection Agency to reserve funds for state water quality management planning in the annual amount of $100,000 per state to be used to study such issues as cost-effective methods for reducing point and nonpoint source pollution and specifies that states must have adopted new water quality standards within three years of the adoption of this act in order to continue receiving federal funding. The latter requirement is intended to force states to reevaluate their standards to see if they are still supportable.
See: CLEAN WATER ACT OF 1977; INFILTRATION AND INFLOW (I AND I) ANALYSIS; WASTEWATER FACILITY PLANNING (SECTION 201)

Munn v. *Illinois* (94 U.S. 113 [1877])

A decision by the United States Supreme Court that paved the way for future government regulation of private development by implying the validity of locally adopted development control ordinances in existence at that time.

N

National Ambient Air Quality Standards (NAAQS)

Standards promulgated by the U.S. Environmental Protection Agency (EPA) for specified air pollutants, pursuant to the provisions of the Clean Air Act Amendments of 1970. National ambient air quality standards are currently in effect for those pollutants for which criteria documents have been published: total suspended particulates (TSP), sulfur dioxide (SO_2), carbon monoxide (CO), nitrogen dioxide (NO_2), ozone (O_3), hydrocarbons (HC) and lead (Pb). Because of this, the substances are known as "criteria" pollutants.

Both primary and secondary standards are set. Primary standards are those thought necessary for the protection of the public health, including those members of the population most vulnerable to the effects of air pollution, such as infants or asthma victims. Secondary standards are intended to protect other aspects of human welfare, such as vegetation, wildlife, building materials, etc. Provisions of the Clean Air Act Amendments of 1977 require that NAAQS criteria be reviewed every five years.
See: AIR POLLUTION; AIR QUALITY CRITERIA

National Association of County Planning Directors (NACPD)

An organization, with headquarters in Washington, D.C., whose membership consists primarily of the chief planning executives of county, city-county or multicounty agencies. Other planners interested in the purposes of NACPD may apply for non-voting membership.

An affiliate of the National Association of Counties (NACo), the organization was founded in 1965 to facilitate information exchange among county planning directors, local elected officials and the federal government. NACPD is also concerned with improving county planning practice, serving as an information resource concerning federal programs and guidelines, and highlighting local planning programs within counties. NACPD meetings and conferences are scheduled to coincide with national NACo meetings.

National Association of Development Organizations (NADO)

An organization, founded in 1967, whose purpose is to promote and support the economic development of rural areas. Membership consists of multicounty planning and development organizations, government agencies, businesses, educational institutions and individuals. NADO activities include the formulation of a legislative program, the dissemination of information to its members concerning relevant government programs, provision of technical assistance and presentation of awards. The organization, with offices in Washington, D.C., publishes *NADO News* weekly as well as an annual report.

National Association of Home Builders of the United States (NAHB)

A Washington, D.C.-based trade association founded in 1942 whose members consist of residential and commercial builders, developers, planners, architects, utility companies, financial institutions and others with an interest in the building industry.

NAHB, which has over 100,000 members, actively lobbies for the housing industry at the federal, state and local level. It conducts basic research on a broad variety of topics related to building—including housing economics, energy, construction techniques and development of open-space communities—and maintains an extensive reference library. In addition, many workshops and seminars are offered to its members and their employees, including specialized courses such as the Registered Apartment Manager program. Services to its members include management and marketing aids; information on legislation and regulations; advice and information on such issues as zoning, flood insurance and construction safety; and access to a computerized legal information system. Members may also serve on committees devoted to such topics as condominiums, rural housing, federally assisted housing, mortgage finance, sensible growth, or energy and the environment.

NAHB publications include *Builder,* a weekly newsletter, and *Builder Magazine,* published monthly. Additional specialized publications are available by subscription, including *Economic News Notes, Econometric Model* and *Legislative Report.* Many additional books and technical publications are issued by NAHB on construction, land development, energy, environment, management and related topics.

National Association of Housing and Redevelopment Officials (NAHRO)

A Washington, D.C.-based organization, founded in 1933, consisting of public agencies and individuals involved in community development programs, provision and administration of public housing, housing rehabilitation and neighborhood conservation. NAHRO provides input to the formulation of national public policy concerning housing and community revitalization and assists in drafting legislation.

NAHRO operates a housing management certification program and other training programs, conferences and technical workshops on a variety of topics. It also conducts an information service, maintains a technical library and publishes a number of technical publications, policy papers, manuals and handbooks. NAHRO periodicals are the *Journal of Housing,* published 11 times per year, and *NAHRO Monitor,* published semimonthly.

National Association of Realtors® (NAR®)

An association with over 685,000 members actively involved in the sale, management and appraisal of real estate. NAR®, which is comprised of 50 state and 1,848 local real estate boards, was founded in 1908. In 1916 it began using the term *Realtor®,* which is a registered trademark. This designation may be used only by those real estate brokers that are members of state and local NAR® boards. Sales staff may apply for the designation of "Realtor®-Associate."

NAR®, whose offices are in Chicago, promulgates a code of professional standards to which its members must agree to adhere. Among the activities of the organization are research, operation of educational programs, community service projects and annual conferences. The organization also operates an extensive real estate reference library and issues a number of publications. Numerous national organizations in related areas of real estate are affiliated with NAR®.

National Cartographic Information Center (NCIC)

A division of the U.S. Geological Survey intended to serve as the primary source of cartographic and geographic information for the public. The NCIC offers a wide range of maps for purchase and will also provide information concerning maps that may be acquired from other government agencies or from private organizations.

In addition, the NCIC, which maintains regional offices, provides a range of research and information services. As an example, it can trace the path of a long since dismantled railroad line or help to find early aerial photographs of a particular geographic area.

See: GEOLOGICAL SURVEY (USGS); USGS MAPS

National Council for Urban Economic Development (CUED)

An organization, founded in 1966, whose members consist of persons in the public and private sectors actively involved in economic development. The Washington, D.C.-based organization keeps its members informed on such subjects as new techniques and trends in the field and new legislation and programs through its various publications: *Urban Economic Developments,* a monthly newsletter; *Legislative Reports*; and *Economic Development Commentary*. It also publishes a variety of special reports, catalogs and handbooks on a wide range of subjects related to economic development.

An information service is available to provide answers to all types of problems related to the technical aspects of economic development or to federal programs and legislation. In addition, a Community Advisory Service can also make available a visiting team of CUED members to help assess and make recommendations concerning economic development problems. Conferences, workshops and intensive training institutes are also conducted.

National Energy Act of 1978

An act consisting of five separate pieces of legislation that covers a broad spectrum of energy-related issues.

The Public Utility Regulatory Policies Act (PL 95-617) requires state utility commissions and nonregulated electric companies to consider implementing rate structure revisions that could save energy, such as seasonal rates and reduced rates for energy use in off-peak hours.

The Energy Tax Act (PL 95-618) provides tax credits of up to $300, representing 15 percent of the cost of installing energy-saving improvements such as insulation or storm windows. A credit of up to $2,200 is also authorized for homeowners installing solar, wind or geothermal energy equipment in their primary residence. A "gas guzzler" tax is imposed on cars of model year 1980 and later that are inefficient users of fuel.

The National Energy Conservation Policy Act (PL 95-619) requires utilities to provide their customers with information concerning energy-saving measures and to provide energy audits and arrange financing for implementing recommended conservation measures. It also authorizes "weatherization" grants for low-income families and grants to schools and hospitals so that they can take steps to improve their energy savings.

The Powerplant and Industrial Fuel Use Act (PL 95-620) requires new electric power plants and major fuel-burning facilities to be able to burn coal or some fuel other than gas or oil and prohibits them from relying upon oil or natural gas as their major source of energy. Existing plants, in general, may not use natural gas after January 1, 1990. Listed in the act are a variety of circumstances under which exemptions from these requirements can be granted.

The Natural Gas Policy Act (PL 95-621) provides for gradual decontrol of the price of new natural gas. Effective January 1, 1985, federal price controls would be removed entirely.
See: ENERGY CONSERVATION PLANNING; ENERGY SECURITY ACT

National Environmental Health Association (NEHA)

A nonprofit organization for professionals, educators and students in the field of environmental health. Among the purposes of NEHA, which was founded in 1939, are the dissemination of information and the formulation of policy on environmental health issues.

NEHA holds an annual conference, maintains a reference library and offers participation in a number of specialized sections, such as the air, land and water section and the environmental management section. The organization, which is located in Denver, Colorado, also publishes the bimonthly *Journal of Environmental Health* and educational materials, such as a series of learning modules. Modules are currently available on such topics as water quality, effects and measurements of common air pollutants, environmental noise and industrial emission control.

National Environmental Policy Act of 1969 (NEPA)

Federal legislation (PL 91-190) that establishes a national environmental policy and requires that the president submit to Congress an annual report on environmental quality. It also establishes the Council on Environmental Quality (CEQ) and requires environmental impact statements (EISs) for federally funded, licensed or sponsored projects.

Formulated primarily as a policy document, NEPA's purpose is to promote coordination within the federal government and in the use of federal funds, with respect to reduction of environmental damage. As the basis for this policy, NEPA stipulates that adverse environmental effects of a proposed project be evaluated and mitigated and that alternatives to the project be studied.

In numerous states—including California, New York and Minnesota—state environmental policy acts have been adopted, patterned on the federal law.
See: COUNCIL ON ENVIRONMENTAL QUALITY (CEQ); ENVIRONMENTAL IMPACT STATEMENT (EIS)

National Environmental Satellite, Data and Information Service (NESDIS)

A part of the National Oceanic and Atmospheric Administration (NOAA), founded in December 1982. It replaces two previous federal services, the National Earth Satellite Service (NESS) and the Environmental Data and Information Service (EDIS).

NESDIS is intended to integrate the development and use of civilian satellite-based environmental remote sensing systems with the acquisition, management and dissemination of global environmental data. These data are used throughout the world by business, government, scientists, engineers and the public at large. NESDIS is also responsible for environmental data and information management. The large amounts of data NOAA collects concerning the oceans, atmosphere, Earth and space as well as additional data gathered by other agencies, organizations and individuals in the United States and abroad are, once they have served their original purpose, eventually channeled to NESDIS national data centers, where they are made part of the national environmental data base.

Four centers are currently operated: the National Climate Data Center (NCDC), the National Geophysical Data Center (NGDC), the National Oceanographic Data Center (NODC), and the Assessment and Information Services Center. A variety of products and information services may be obtained from these centers.
See: LANDSAT; NATIONAL OCEANIC AND ATMOSPHERIC ADMINISTRATION (NOAA)

National Flood Insurance Act of 1968

This act, Title XIII of the Housing and Urban Development Act of 1968 (PL 90-448), and subsequent amendments to it, authorizes a program of subsidized personal and property insurance for property owners within "flood-prone" areas of eligible communities. Flood insurance is provided by premiums paid by property owners to a pool of underwriters that are supervised by the Federal Insurance Administration. Communities become eligible by implementing floodplain management controls that limit and regulate development in flood-prone areas. The program established by this act is intended to substitute flood insurance for expensive disaster-relief measures that are required when development occurs in inappropriate locations or does not adhere to appropriate standards.

Amendments to the act, enacted in 1969, created an interim program that is effective until necessary floodway and floodplain mapping is completed. The amendments also add provisions for areas subject to mudslides, making them eligible for flood insurance. The 1973 act mandates participation in the program to qualify for disaster assistance and other federal programs.
See: FLOOD DISASTER PROTECTION ACT OF 1973; NATIONAL FLOOD INSURANCE PROGRAM

National Flood Insurance Program

A program established by the National Flood Insurance Act of 1968 that provides federally subsidized flood insurance to residents of participating flood-prone communities. The program was created in response to increased flood losses and the disaster-relief measures they have required, the lack of privately available flood insurance, and the widespread mismanagement and development of floodplains in the United States. In return for the availability of subsidized flood insurance, however, communities are required to adopt and enforce floodplain management measures.

Under this program, which is administered by the Federal Insurance Administration (FIA) within the Federal Emergency Management Agency (FEMA), the federal government is charged with tentatively identifying flood-prone communities, publishing maps indicating the location of all flood-prone areas and providing communities with copies of the maps, known as flood hazard boundary maps (FHBM). Upon receipt of these maps, a community has the option of challenging its flood-prone designation and proving it is not flood-prone or applying for the initial

phase of the flood insurance program, known as the emergency program.

In the emergency program a limited amount of flood insurance may be obtained by community residents, providing that the community adopts specified minimum floodplain management standards. Essentially, the community must, at this time, require building permits for all proposed construction or development and review the applications with regard to risk from flooding. Additional requirements must also be met for the community's flood-prone areas with regard to anchoring, proper construction materials, proper drainage in new subdivisions and siting and design of new or replacement water and sanitary sewer systems.

Communities become eligible for the regular phase of the flood insurance program after the completion of a detailed field survey by the federal government. At this time, additional amounts of flood insurance coverage become available, and a flood insurance rate map (FIRM) is issued, which specifies the actuarial rate for each building site. To qualify for participation in the regular program, a community is required to take steps to ensure that new construction and substantial improvements are elevated above the base flood level or are floodproofed. Additional requirements must be met concerning floodways or coastal high-hazard areas.

When the National Flood Insurance Program was first introduced, relatively few eligible communities participated. Subsequent amendments have, however, imposed strict penalties for nonparticipation. If a community is identified by the federal government as containing areas of special flood hazard, no federal financial assistance for acquisition or construction may be approved for these flood-prone areas unless the community participates in the flood insurance program. In addition, banks, savings and loan associations and other similar institutions subject to federal regulation, supervision or insurance are prohibited from making, increasing, extending or renewing loans secured by improved real estate that is located in an area of special flood hazard unless the community participates in the National Flood Insurance Program.
See: BASE FLOOD; FLOOD DISASTER PROTECTION ACT OF 1973; FLOOD FRINGE; FLOOD HAZARD BOUNDARY MAP (FHBM); FLOOD INSURANCE RATE MAP (FIRM); FLOODPLAIN; FLOODPLAIN MANAGEMENT; NATIONAL FLOOD INSURANCE ACT OF 1968; REGULATORY FLOODWAY

National Forest

A land area that provides recreational opportunities, wildlife habitat, watershed protection and natural resource materials such as timber and minerals. As of 1982, 191 million acres (77.3 million hectares) of land were in United States Forest Service management; there were 155 national forests and 19 national grasslands.

National forests and grasslands must be assessed every 10 years and a program prepared recommending a policy of management and administration for these lands. National policy stresses multiple use of forest lands, with a balance between competing uses. Inevitably, as the value of resources such as timber rises, conflicts occur between competing interests. Among the issues that continue to spark debate are the proportion of national forest lands that should be placed in the National Wilderness Preservation System and allowed to remain roadless, the rate at which timber should be allowed to be harvested and the size of areas that can be clear-cut.

In Britain the Forestry Commission maintains more than 2 million acres (800,000 hectares) of forest land, primarily for timber production. It operates seven forest parks on 600,000 acres (240,000 hectares) in England, Scotland and Wales that are open for public recreation.
See: CLEARCUTTING; FOREST SERVICE; FORESTRY; NATIONAL WILDERNESS PRESERVATION SYSTEM

National Foundation on the Arts and the Humanities

A United States federal agency composed of the National Endowment for the Arts, National Endowment for the Humanities and the Federal Council on the Arts and the Humanities.

The National Endowment for the Arts awards grants to individuals, to state and regional arts agencies, and to nonprofit organizations that represent the highest quality in the arts. The National Endowment for the Humanities awards grants to individuals and groups or institutions—such as universities, museums, libraries and public television stations—for the study of such subjects as literature, history and archeology and for the study and application of the humanities to the environment. Grants are also made to local organizations to encourage public discussion on local policy issues. The Federal Council on the Arts and the Humanities coordinates the activities of the two endowments and related programs of other federal agencies.

In Canada the Canada Council awards grants for the arts to individuals and organizations. Grants are available in categories that include architecture and arts administration as well as visual and performing arts, music, creative writing and other areas.
See: COMMUNITY ARTS COUNCILS; CULTURAL RESOURCES PLANNING; STATE ARTS AGENCIES

National Health Planning and Resources Development Act of 1974

A comprehensive system of national, state and area planning agencies established under P.L. 93-641 to provide a mechanism for coordinating local plans for health care delivery as a basis for the development of state and national health and hospital plans. In turn, statements of state and national needs, goals and priorities are intended to serve as guidelines for health planning by area agencies.

On the national level funding is provided for a National Council on Health Planning and Development, which advises the secretary of the Department of Health and Human Services on guidelines for health planning. On the

state level funding is authorized for state Health Planning and Development Agencies, which are responsible for development of an annual State Health Plan based on Health Systems Plans developed by the areawide Health Systems Agencies. The act also requires that each state develop a certificate of need (CON) review program as part of a comprehensive attempt to deal with rapidly escalating expenditures in the medical care service sector. Amendments enacted in 1979 (P.L. 96-79) extended the planning program and introduced new priorities and review criteria aimed at strengthening competition in the health care industry.
See: CERTIFICATE OF NEED (CON); HEALTH SYSTEMS AGENCY (HSA); HEALTH SYSTEMS PLAN (HSP)

National Historic Areas

Those units of the National Park System that are primarily associated with historic events, activities or persons that are of prominence in the history of the United States. A wide range of nomenclature related to the variety of enabling legislation and the size of the historic areas is applied to these sites. The system includes designations related to military history—such as *national battlefield* (10 as of 1982), *national battlefield park* (3), *national battlefield site* (1) and *national military park* (10)—as well as *national monument* (78, but some are designated for natural resource rather than historic values), *national historical park* (26) and *national memorial* (23). The most common designation applied by Congress in recent years has been *national historic site,* of which there were 62 as of 1982.

These historic park system units, which are more prevalent than protected natural areas, are generally preserved or restored to reflect the period during which they were most historically significant. Examples of national historic areas include Independence National Historic Park in Philadelphia, which preserves structures associated with the founding of the United States, and Mount Rushmore National Memorial in South Dakota.
See: HISTORIC PRESERVATION; NATIONAL HISTORIC LANDMARK; NATIONAL PARK SYSTEM

National Historic Landmark

A property formally designated by the secretary of the interior as having national historic significance. The Historic Sites Act of 1935 initially provided the secretary of the interior with authority to identify and evaluate these nationally significant historic sites, beginning the National Historic Landmarks Program. The program was subsequently specifically authorized by the 1980 amendments to the National Historic Preservation Act.

All National Historic Landmarks appear in the National Register of Historic Places and are afforded the benefits of such a listing. Pursuant to the National Historic Preservation Act Amendments of 1980, however, owner consent is required before a privately owned property may be designated a National Historic Landmark. As of 1982, there were 1,574 National Historic Landmarks, including Mon-

ticello (the home of Thomas Jefferson) and Walden Pond (the site of the cabin of Henry David Thoreau).
See: HISTORIC PRESERVATION; HISTORIC SITES ACT OF 1935; NATIONAL REGISTER OF HISTORIC PLACES

National Historic Preservation Act Amendments of 1980

Legislation (PL 96-515) that effected a number of changes, some primarily legal or procedural, in the national historic preservation program of the United States. It incorporated into law many of the requirements of Executive Order 11593 (1971), "Protection and Enhancement of the Cultural Environment," by providing that federal agencies properly locate, inventory and manage the historic properties under their jurisdiction. They are directed to nominate those properties to the National Register of Historic Places when applicable, exercise caution concerning their care, and maintain and use them whenever possible. The National Historic Landmarks program is also specifically authorized by the 1980 amendments.

Several changes were also made concerning the National Register of Historic Places. The amendments require that the owner give consent before a property may be listed on the National Register and that a mechanism be established by the states by which qualified units of local government are allowed to take part in nominating properties to the National Register. States must allocate at least 10 percent of the historic preservation funds they receive from the federal government for distribution to certified local government units. States are also given more flexibility in using their federal matching funds.
See: HISTORIC PRESERVATION; NATIONAL HISTORIC PRESERVATION ACT OF 1966; NATIONAL REGISTER OF HISTORIC PLACES

National Historic Preservation Act of 1966

An act (PL 89-665) that established many of the nation's ongoing historic preservation programs. It expanded the National Register of Historic Places to include districts, sites and structures of statewide and local importance; previously, official recognition was given only to nationally significant properties within the National Park System or to National Historic Landmarks. In addition, it created a program in which matching grants were given to the states for their historic preservation programs, including conducting surveys, drafting state historic preservation plans and preserving historic properties. Matching grants were also made to the National Trust for Historic Preservation to enable it to continue carrying out its programs.

The National Historic Preservation Act of 1966 also created the federal Advisory Council on Historic Preservation.
See: ADVISORY COUNCIL ON HISTORIC PRESERVATION; HISTORIC PRESERVATION; NATIONAL HISTORIC PRESERVATION ACT AMENDMENTS OF 1980; NATIONAL REGISTER OF HISTORIC PLACES

National Housing Act

Legislation adopted in 1934 that created federal mechanisms for increasing the housing supply for low- and moderate-income persons.

One major provision of the act (PL 73-479) was the establishment of the Federal Housing Administration (FHA) for the purpose of insuring home mortgages and administering sales of its insured mortgages to National Mortgage Associations. The legislation set ceilings on the insurable amount of a property, the interest rate and the FHA premium for mortgage processing, as well as minimum standards for loan approval. It also established an insurance program for property improvement loans. The FHA was authorized to charter National Mortgage Associations having a minimum capital stock of $5 million to provide a secondary mortgage market that would increase the availability of mortgage funds. The act also created the Federal Savings and Loan Insurance Corporation (FSLIC) to insure accounts in savings and loan associations.

The initial legislation in the field of housing, it has been amended frequently through subsequent housing and community development acts. In general, FHA insurance programs are attributed to Title II or other titles of the National Housing Act, even if authorized by later legislation; loan insurance programs, such as home improvement, are attributed to Title I; and government-administered secondary mortgage corporations are attributed to Title III.
See: FEDERAL HOUSING ADMINISTRATION (FHA); UNITED STATES HOUSING ACT OF 1937

National Housing Act Amendments of 1941 and 1942

Wartime legislation (PL 77-24) that in 1941 established Defense Housing Insurance and a Defense Housing Insurance Fund to stimulate construction of one- to four-family housing in designated areas. In 1942 legislation was enacted (PL 77-559) that changed the program's name to War Housing Insurance and added a new section (Section 608) to provide insurance for construction of rental housing for defense industry workers.
See: NATIONAL HOUSING ACT

National Housing Conference (NHC)

An organization dedicated to working for better housing and improved housing programs in the United States. Its members consist of housing authorities, developers, tenants, bankers, unions, government officials, senior citizens and others with an interest in housing. NHC was founded in 1931 as the National Public Housing Conference but changed its name in 1949 to reflect a broader interest. NHC provides information to the public through its monthly newsletter and periodic reports and bulletins. In addition, it holds housing forums on topics of interest as well as an annual housing convention. The organization is located in Washington, D.C.

National Housing Rehabilitation Association (NHRA)

An organization consisting of developers, contractors, property managers, finance professionals, public agencies involved in housing rehabilitation and those in related fields concerned with multifamily housing rehabilitation, historic preservation and adaptive reuse. Among the interests of NHRA, founded in 1970, are new financing, design or construction techniques for rehabilitation; government programs and actions with potential impact on housing rehabilitation; and new business opportunities in rehabilitation.

NHRA, which is located in Washington, D.C., maintains committees on legislative issues, Department of Housing and Urban Development (HUD) affairs, tax matters, educational programs, design and construction, and historic preservation. It publishes a newsletter, *Recycling Real Estate,* six times per year and holds an annual meeting and several information forums each year.

National Institute of Building Sciences (NIBS)

A nonprofit organization that was created by the Housing and Community Development Act of 1974 to study and provide advice on matters related to building technology, standards, regulation and other technical aspects of the building sciences. A consultative council is composed of private trade, professional and labor organizations; private and public standards, code and testing bodies; public regulatory agencies; and consumer groups. Its function is to provide input to the organization and, through established divisions, to present the position of the building and housing industries on matters that require study and the manner in which they should be studied. Contracts are awarded to specific testing or construction corporations to study specified subjects. Operating funds are obtained primarily from an annual federal appropriation, with additional revenues derived from contracts, grants and fees paid by members of the consultative council.

Studies produced by NIBS have covered topics such as building energy efficiency, the reduction of duplication and conflict in codes and regulations, and guidelines for rehabilitating buildings. Through its four divisions (Codes, Standards and Regulations; Technology; Information Systems; and Land Use), it plans to study topics as diverse as cost savings in land use development, performance criteria suitable for use by building departments and evaluation of new building materials and systems. NIBS currently has four consultative councils in individual states as well as its primary consultative council. The Building Seismic Safety Council (BSSC), an additional independent body that functions under the auspices of NIBS, studies earthquake hazard mitigation regulations for buildings. NIBS publications on some of its studies and related work as well as a periodical, *Building Sciences,* are available from its offices in Washington, D.C.

National Land Use Policy

National legislation that, in general, defines policies on development, housing, employment, transportation, energy and other land use matters and may offer incentives or disincentives to development in designated places. National land use policy is based on the concept that the national settlement pattern and related issues of economic efficiency, public service costs, amenities of living and environmental protection are appropriate matters for national policy. It is typically concerned with the need to prevent overpopulation of certain urbanized areas or population depletion of certain rural areas or to counter trends related to urban decay. Many countries (particularly in Europe) have introduced either directives or incentives to channel growth to locations that will benefit from new growth and will protect other sensitive areas from development.

National land use policy has been formulated in different ways in different countries. In Britain, for example, beginning with the New Towns Act, 1946 and the 1947 Town and Country Planning Act, a policy of new town development coupled with growth constraints around existing urban conurbations directed new growth to designated areas and instituted a system of national control of development based on locally developed long-term plans. More recently, however, economic decline throughout Britain has caused the reversal of certain policies, requiring greater emphasis on depressed urban areas and protection of historically significant areas. Local authorities are also assuming more control over these activities.

In Sweden the 1947 Building and Planning Act directed that national policy objectives be established and that municipalities prepare detailed development plans to control postwar development. Today a three-tiered system of government—national, county and municipal—must review plans, with each level having responsibility for certain aspects of development. Municipalities are largely dependent on federal funding for all activities but are able to sway planning decisions in many cases. The National Physical Plan, developed in 1972, designated environmentally sensitive areas and established guidelines for development in undeveloped and historically important areas. This plan has been successful in preventing the destruction of natural areas and controlling land speculation.

National land use legislation in the United States has been introduced in the form of a national urban policy but has never received legislative approval. Instead, federal legislation is directed at various aspects of the way in which land is used and developed, such as laws related to community development, air and water pollution, and surface mining reclamation. Via mandated actions that prevent natural resource degradation and financial funding incentives to produce certain forms of development in designated locations, federal legislation controls many diverse forms of land use development.

See: LOCAL AUTHORITY; NEW TOWNS ACT, 1946

National Mass Transportation Act of 1974

An act (PL 93-503) that provided funding for improved mass transportation in urbanized areas. Apportioned on a formula basis related to total population and population density, funding for fiscal years 1975 to 1980 was permitted to cover up to 80 percent of capital costs, an increase from 66⅔ percent authorized in 1964, and up to 50 percent of operating costs, a new provision. Funding for demonstration fare-free urban transportation programs was also authorized.

The National Mass Transportation Act marked the beginning of federal recognition of the need for analysis of the social and environmental effects of mass transportation projects by requiring that a continuing comprehensive transportation planning process be carried on and that adverse economic, social and environmental effects of projects be fully considered and minimized or eliminated. These requirements are still in effect.
See: SURFACE TRANSPORTATION ACT OF 1978; URBAN MASS TRANSPORTATION ACT OF 1964

National Monument

A monument focused upon a particular archaeologic, historic or scientific feature of national significance. It is generally smaller and less diverse than a national park, containing only sufficient land to protect its main feature. As of 1982 there were 78 national monuments in the National Park System. Well-known examples include the Statue of Liberty, the Washington Monument, Death Valley and Devils Tower.
See: NATIONAL PARK; NATIONAL PARK SYSTEM

National Oceanic and Atmospheric Administration (NOAA)

An agency within the Department of Commerce with responsibility for charting of the world's oceans, management and conservation of ocean resources, and analysis and prediction of atmospheric conditions, including those of the sun and in space.

NOAA collects and disseminates a wide variety of data on the environment via a national environmental satellite system and through a system of meteorological, oceanographic, geodetic and seismological data centers. It also conducts research on methods that may provide alternatives to ocean dumping and develops policies in the areas of ocean mining and energy. NOAA, in addition, is responsible for the administration of grants to states for coastal zone management plans and programs. Other activities include preparing nautical and aeronautical charts as well as precise geodetic surveys, conducting experiments in weather modification and protecting marine mammals.

The National Weather Service, the National Ocean Survey, the National Marine Fisheries Service and the National Environmental Satellite, Data and Information Service are among the subsidiary agencies of NOAA.
See: NATIONAL ENVIRONMENTAL SATELLITE, DATA AND INFORMATION SERVICE (NESDIS)

National Park

Parks in the United States receive this designation because they cover large and diverse land areas of outstanding natural quality. Each national park exemplifies the particular types of scenic and natural values it represents. As of 1982 there were 48 national parks with over 46 million acres (18.6 million hectares). Among the best-known national parks in the United States are the Grand Canyon, Yellowstone and Yosemite.

Canada is also well-known for its high-quality and diverse national parks. The 28 national parks in Canada, as of 1978, were located throughout the country, ranging from Terra Nova in Newfoundland to Auyuittuq inside the Arctic Circle.

National parks offer excellent opportunities to engage in such activities as sightseeing, hiking, camping, boating and fishing. Because of these attractions, overly large numbers of visitors are often found in concentrated areas. Visitor volume as well as traffic congestion has led to environmental degradation in some of the national parks; as a result, resource management plans are being formulated for national park system units to control these problems.
See: NATIONAL PARK SYSTEM; YELLOWSTONE NATIONAL PARK

National Park Service

An agency within the Department of the Interior that is responsible for the National Park System. The service develops the units within the system and manages the parks and related visitor facilities.

In 1981 the Park Service assumed responsibility for administration of a number of programs that had previously been conducted by the Heritage Conservation and Recreation Service (an agency that was in existence from 1978 to 1981). These include: state programs of the Land and Water Conservation Fund; the Nationwide Outdoor Recreation Plan and state comprehensive outdoor recreation planning; the Urban Park and Recreation Recovery Program; technical services for parks and recreation; planning for the National Wild and Scenic Rivers System and the National Trails System; the National Register of Historic Places; historic preservation; the Historic American Building Survey and the Historic American Engineering Record.
See: HISTORIC AMERICAN BUILDING SURVEY (HABS); LAND AND WATER CONSERVATION FUND (LAWCON); NATIONAL PARK SYSTEM; NATIONAL REGISTER OF HISTORIC PLACES; NATIONAL WILD AND SCENIC RIVERS SYSTEM; STATEWIDE COMPREHENSIVE OUTDOOR RECREATION PLAN (SCORP); URBAN PARK AND RECREATION RECOVERY PROGRAM (UPARR)

2

58 *National Park System*

National Park System

The National Park System of the United States contained, as of January 1, 1982, over 79 million acres (32 million hectares) of land of outstanding natural, scenic and historic value. The system, which is comprised of 333 separate areas, is divided into such categories as national parks, monuments, recreation areas, seashores and historic sites.

The system was gradually expanded after the establishment of Yellowstone National Park in 1872, mostly with land carved from federal land holdings in the western United States. Additions to the National Park System generally require congressional approval. Other programs concentrate on the management and protection of more specialized uses and may be operated on National Park System lands or other government land. The National Wilderness Preservation System, the National Wild and Scenic Rivers System, the National Trail System and the National Wildlife Refuge System are examples of these programs.

As of 1980 Canada's National Park System encompassed 1.3 percent of that country's large land area. Parks Canada shares responsibility with the United States for the operation of areas along Canada's border, such as Glacier National Park and Roosevelt Campobello International Park.

See: NATIONAL FOREST; NATIONAL HISTORIC AREAS; NATIONAL MONUMENT; NATIONAL PARK; NATIONAL PARK SERVICE; NATIONAL PARKWAY; NATIONAL RECREATION AREA; NATIONAL SEASHORE; NATIONAL URBAN RECREATION AREA; NATIONAL WILD AND SCENIC RIVERS SYSTEM; NATIONAL WILDERNESS PRESERVATION SYSTEM; YELLOWSTONE NATIONAL PARK

National Parks and Recreation Act of 1978

A major piece of legislation (PL 95-625) that expanded the national park system and directed increased federal funding for acquisition and maintenance of recreation facilities and open spaces. It created the Urban Park and Recreation Recovery Program, the Pinelands National Reserve in New Jersey and the Santa Monica Mountain National Recreation Area in California. It also expanded the network of federal park and open-space facilities by additions to national parks, national forests, national wildlife refuges, national wild and scenic rivers, the national trail system and national historic sites. Some of these additions were controversial, such as the authorization to preserve areas that had been sought for logging in California.

See: NATIONAL PARK SYSTEM; URBAN PARK AND RECREATION RECOVERY PROGRAM (UPARR)

National Parkway

A scenic road situated in a parklike setting. Designed for lower travel speeds, it may run through another unit of the National Park System or on land specifically set aside for parkway use. As of 1979 approximately 160,000 acres (64,000 hectares) of land were devoted to four national

parkways, including the Blue Ridge Parkway, the first ever constructed, which follows the Blue Ridge Mountains from Virginia to North Carolina.

See: NATIONAL PARK SYSTEM; SCENIC ROAD

National Planning Board

A board created in 1933 within the Public Works Administration to assist the secretary of the interior in choosing and scheduling the many federal public works projects being launched at the time. Charles W. Eliot II was chosen to be its executive director. The board's major activities included research; encouragement of state, regional and municipal planning; and coordination of planning activities at the federal level.

As a result of the National Planning Board's offer to assist states if they, in turn, would create state planning boards and planning programs, almost all states had such state boards in operation within a few years. In addition, many states began to develop long-range construction programs and engage in other long-term planning efforts. The National Planning Board was renamed several times and was finally terminated by Congress in 1943.

National Pollutant Discharge Elimination System (NPDES)

A licensing system for effluent discharge, established by Section 402 of the Federal Water Pollution Control Act Amendments of 1972. No industrial facility, public sewage treatment plant or other point source may discharge into any waterway in the United States without obtaining an NPDES permit. Permits are issued by the Environmental Protection Agency (EPA), except where EPA has delegated this authority to a state agency. The term of a permit is limited to 5 years.

Each permit specifies conditions under which the discharge is allowed, sets limits on its quantity and establishes a schedule for compliance with state pollution standards. EPA has strong enforcement authority—for example, if a municipal sewage system fails to meet the conditions of its permit, EPA may prohibit new sewer hookups.

See: AREAWIDE WASTE TREATMENT MANAGEMENT PLANNING (SECTION 208); ENVIRONMENTAL PROTECTION AGENCY (EPA); FEDERAL WATER POLLUTION CONTROL ACT AMENDMENTS OF 1972; WATER POLLUTION

National Recreation and Park Association (NRPA)

A 16,000 member organization, located in Alexandria, Virginia, dedicated to promoting the availability of high quality recreational and leisure opportunities as well as to maintaining parks and recreational sites. Its membership consists of recreation and park practitioners and managers, citizens, educators and students. Although founded in 1965, NRPA was created by the merger of a number of organizations established much earlier, such as the American Institute of Park Executives (1898) and the National Recreation Association (1906).

Among its activities are providing continuing education programs for professionals in the field; accrediting universities and colleges offering curricula in park and recreation studies; and conducting research and disseminating the findings on such topics as safety standards for playgrounds. An extensive library is maintained by the organization. It also publishes a monthly magazine, *Parks & Recreation,* as well as other publications including the *Journal of Leisure Research.*

National Recreation Area

Each national recreation area was originally part of a dam construction project and focused upon the reservoir that was created—e.g., Coulee Dam National Recreation Area. The concept has been broadened since that time to include other land and water areas suitable for recreational use, including recreation areas in major urban centers. Some of the areas are managed by the Forest Service and are not a part of the National Park System.
See: FOREST SERVICE; NATIONAL PARK SYSTEM; NATIONAL URBAN RECREATION AREA

National Register of Historic Places

An official listing of the most significant historic and cultural resources in the United States. Although at one time the National Register consisted only of national historic landmarks or nationally significant properties within the National Park System, as a result of the National Historic Preservation Act of 1966, statewide or local significance is a sufficient basis for nomination to the National Register. As of September 30, 1982, there were 25,487 properties listed in the National Register of Historic Places.

National Register proposals often originate at the local level as a result of municipal surveys or other preservation activities. Official nominations to the National Register are, however, made by the state historic preservation officer, unless the state lacks an officially approved preservation program, in which case nominations may be made by individuals or local governments. At the federal level the keeper of the National Register certifies that the nomination conforms to designated criteria before the secretary of the interior approves and signs the new register entry.

The National Register serves a variety of functions related to the identification and protection of historic properties. It acts as an official guide that various levels of government as well as private citizens may use in planning programs for properties worthy of protection. Under Section 106 of the National Historic Preservation Act, the Advisory Council on Historic Preservation must be allowed to comment upon any case in which federal, federally assisted or federally licensed activities will affect properties listed in the National Register. A variety of federal income tax benefits are extended to the owners of properties listed in the National Register for substantial rehabilitation of these properties. In addition, federal grants and insured loans are sometimes available to prop-

erty owners for the rehabilitation and protection of their National Register properties. There are, however, certain disincentives to demolition of historic properties listed in the National Register; these deterrents were first instituted in 1976 and later, partially repealed by the Economic Recovery Tax Act of 1981.

As a result of the 1980 amendments to the National Historic Preservation Act, a property owner is allowed to object to the inclusion of his property in the National Register, and the property will not be added until the owner gives his permission. This is also the case if the majority of the property owners in a historic district object to National Register listing.
See: ADVISORY COUNCIL ON HISTORIC PRESERVATION; HISTORIC AMERICAN BUILDING SURVEY (HABS); HISTORIC AMERICAN ENGINEERING RECORD (HAER); HISTORIC PRESERVATION; HISTORIC PRESERVATION TAX INCENTIVES; HISTORIC SURVEY; NATIONAL HISTORIC LANDMARK; NATIONAL HISTORIC PRESERVATION ACT AMENDMENTS OF 1980; NATIONAL HISTORIC PRESERVATION ACT OF 1966

National Seashore

A unit of the National Park System intended to protect coastal shoreline areas as well as off-shore islands. A national seashore designation helps to preserve a stretch of coastal land from development while making this land available for recreational use. As of 1982 there were 11 national seashores, covering approximately 601,840 acres (243,556 hectares). They include Cape Cod, Fire Island and Cape Hatteras on the Atlantic Coast; Padre Island on the Gulf Coast; and Point Reyes on the Pacific. There are also 4 national lakeshores, all located on the Great Lakes.

As a result of a comprehensive study of the coastal resources of England and Wales conducted by the Countryside Commission, a program is underway in those countries to designate and protect heritage coasts that have outstanding scenic value. Working jointly with local authorities, the Countryside Commission had protected 33 heritage coasts by 1980, totaling 620 miles (998 kilometers). In addition, the National Trust, a private organization, operates a project in Britain called Enterprise Neptune, through which 400 miles (644 kilometers) of coastline have been protected.
See: COASTAL AREA PLANNING; NATIONAL PARK SYSTEM

National System of Airports

A system of civil (nonmilitary) and joint use (military/civil) airports within the United States and its territories, considered necessary to provide facilities that can meet the needs of air carriers (commercial airlines) and general aviation (all other nonmilitary aircraft operations). Established by the National Airport System Plan (NASP), it is part of the Federal-Aid Airport Program called ADAP (Airport Development Aid Program). It is authorized by

Section 3 of the Federal Airport Act of 1970 and Section 3 of the Federal Airport Act of 1946.

The plan is prepared annually by the Federal Aviation Administration (FAA) with the aid of the states and submitted to Congress by the secretary of transportation. It requires that an airport be owned by a public agency and be included in the plan to be eligible for federal aid.
See: AIRPORT CLASSIFICATION

National Trust for Historic Preservation

A private, nonprofit organization chartered by Congress to engage in a wide variety of programs aimed at preserving the architectural and historical heritage of the United States. The National Trust—supported by membership dues, federal grants and private contributions—acts as a national clearinghouse on preservation activities, provides information and advice, maintains a comprehensive reference library and owns a variety of historic properties, some of which are operated as museums.

The National Trust, which was founded in 1949, also makes funding available for local projects, such as the establishment of a revolving fund. In addition, it has an ongoing program under which it purchases endangered historic properties of national significance and then looks for appropriate buyers for the properties. The National Trust publishes numerous books and periodicals including *Preservation News,* a monthly newsletter, *Conserve Neighborhoods,* a newsletter issued 6 times a year, and *Historic Preservation,* a bimonthly magazine. National Trust headquarters are located in Washington, D.C., but regional offices are also maintained.
See: HISTORIC PRESERVATION; NATIONAL HISTORIC PRESERVATION ACT OF 1966

National Urban Recreation Area

Not a formal federal designation, this term describes those national recreation areas that are located in urban areas. The creation of Gateway in the New York-New Jersey metropolitan area and Golden Gate in San Francisco in 1972 marked the establishment of a new federal policy of bringing recreation areas to city dwellers.

Gateway National Recreation Area has four sections, located in New Jersey and in three New York City boroughs (Brooklyn, Queens and Staten Island). It offers bathing beaches, numerous recreational facilities and a large wildlife refuge that may be reached by subway.

Golden Gate National Recreation Area wraps around the northern and western borders of San Francisco and includes features as diverse as the remains of Alcatraz prison and a maritime museum.

An additional urban park, Cuyahoga Valley National Recreation Area, located between Cleveland and Akron, Ohio, was authorized in 1974 and established in 1975. It includes still rural areas of the Cuyahoga River Valley as well as features of historic interest, such as the Ohio and Erie Canal System.
See: NATIONAL PARK SYSTEM; NATIONAL RECREATION AREA

National Urban Recreation Study

A study, published in 1978 by the Heritage Conservation and Recreation Service and the National Park Service, of the needs, problems and opportunities associated with urban recreation.

The primary findings of the study indicated that there are insufficient urban recreation opportunities because of a lack of funding for local recreation activities and facilities, among other reasons. A national urban recreation policy was cited as being necessary to guide local recreation and park planning and to provide federal support. Options proposed for meeting urban recreation needs emphasized an increased role for the federal government in providing funding and technical assistance to urban areas. The study also encouraged a better utilization of volunteers and local and state resources for recreation planning, programming and operations.
See: NATIONAL PARK SERVICE; NATIONAL PARKS AND RECREATION ACT OF 1978; RECREATION PLANNING; RECREATION SYSTEM; URBAN PARK AND RECREATION RECOVERY PROGRAM (UPARR)

National Wild and Scenic Rivers System

A system of rivers intended to be preserved in a free-flowing state for public use. Created by the Wild and Scenic Rivers Act of 1968 (PL 90-542), this system is intended to protect rivers of outstanding quality from pollution and inappropriate development. In order to be considered for designation, a river or portion of a river must be free-flowing, have excellent water quality and have outstanding scenic, recreational, geologic, fish and wildlife, historic or cultural values or features.

Three different types of river classifications are made, ranked according to degree of accessibility. Wild rivers are those that show few traces of civilization and are mostly inaccessible, except by trail. Scenic rivers are primarily undeveloped but may be reached by road in certain places. Recreational rivers may be reached by road or railroad and are more developed. Rivers may be added to the system by Congress (in the case of federally managed components) or by the actions of state legislatures (in which case, the Secretary of the Interior may name the river or river segment to the system, providing an acceptable river management plan has been prepared).

As of 1981 segments of 54 rivers, totaling over 6,915 miles (11,129 kilometers), had been officially designated. Inventories are conducted to identify additional rivers that could merit inclusion in this system.
See: NATIONAL PARK SYSTEM

National Wilderness Preservation System

A system established by the Wilderness Act of 1964 to ensure that certain lands in federal ownership would be allowed to retain their wilderness character without signs of human intervention. In wilderness areas no permanent roads or motor vehicles are permitted, and no structures may be built, although hiking and sometimes primitive camping and horseback riding are permitted. Congress must approve the addition of any federal lands to the Wilderness System, which totaled 79.8 million acres (32.3 million hectares) as of December 1, 1982.

From 1977 to 1979 the Forest Service conducted a Roadless Area Review and Evaluation Process, known as RARE II, to identify additional wild areas in national forests and grasslands that should be protected. As a result of this study, it was recommended by the Carter Administration that 15.4 million acres (6.23 million hectares) be added to the system. In addition, further study was recommended for 10.8 million roadless acres (4.4 million hectares), and 36.2 million roadless acres (14.6 million hectares) were made available for multiple use management.

Subsequently, various laws were enacted that formally added substantial land areas to the National Wilderness Perservation System. In 1980, for example, 2.2 million acres (0.89 million hectares) in central Idaho, known as the River of No Return Wilderness, were formally designated. Other wilderness areas were designated in Colorado, Louisiana, Missouri, New Mexico, South Carolina and South Dakota, and additional areas were under consideration. Large land areas in Alaska (56 million acres or 22.7 million hectares) were also named as wilderness by the Alaska National Interest Lands Conservation Act (PL 96-487), which became law in 1980.

Parks Canada has developed a type of zoning system for Canadian national parks, based upon the need certain park areas have for protection. In special preservation areas with rare or unusual features, motorized access and man-made facilities are prohibited. In wilderness areas user visits are controlled, and only primitive facilities are provided; motor vehicles are also prohibited.
See: NATIONAL FOREST; NATIONAL PARK SYSTEM

Natural Cooling

Space cooling in which an emphasis is placed upon design techniques that help cool indoor areas as well as other alternatives to energy-intensive air conditioning.

Shading of south-facing windows with awnings, overhangs and vegetation is one simple natural cooling method, as is the maximum use of ventilation. Ventilation may be encouraged by appropriate window orientation, size, type and location to maximize desirable airflow patterns. Evaporative cooling systems can work effectively in hot, dry climates by the use of rooftop sprinkler systems, in which water is sprinkled upon the roof and allowed to evaporate, while rooftop ponds may also be used for cooling.
See: ARCHITECTURAL DESIGN FOR ENERGY CONSERVATION; EARTH-COVERED BUILDING; PASSIVE SOLAR ENERGY SYSTEM; SOLAR ENERGY; THERMAL MASS

Natural Increase

Natural increase is the difference between the number of births and the number of deaths that occur. It is, along with net migration, a major component of change in a population. It may be a positive figure or a negative figure (if deaths outnumber births).
See: DEMOGRAPHY; NET MIGRATION

Nature Conservancy, The

1. A national organization, based in Arlington, Virginia, that promotes the preservation of ecological diversity by protecting ecologically significant natural areas. In 1983 The Nature Conservancy owned and provided stewardship for approximately 700 nature preserves, which it had acquired through either gift or purchase. Since its founding in 1951, it has undertaken 3,170 preservation projects in the 50 states, Latin America, the Caribbean and Canada, often in conjunction with local government, totalling in excess of 2.1 million acres (0.9 million hectares). It maintains chapters in 31 states and publishes a newsletter, *The Nature Conservancy News,* six times a year.

2. The Nature Conservancy Council is an official British agency that establishes, maintains and manages national nature reserves. It also undertakes research and is the official advisory agency to the government on conservation matters.
See: NATURE PRESERVE

Nature Preserve

An area, also known as a nature reserve, where the natural environment is protected for purposes of conservation and study. Varying in size from relatively small holdings of several acres to several million acres, as in the national parks, a preserve is generally managed to protect it from natural or man-made destruction. Nature preserves also serve as wildlife refuges and aid in conserving forests and watershed land, but they differ from certain other forms of land reservations in that they are intended to remain substantially protected from human activities. In contrast, state and national forests, as examples, may be managed for timber or other natural resource production.

Most nature preserves are open, at least in part, to limited public use, such as hiking on designated trails. Educational programs may be provided, as well as an interpretive building or museum. Some areas, however, are so fragile that only very occasional intrusion is possible, requiring that permits for access be issued to qualified individuals or that access be allowed only under direct supervision.
See: NATIONAL WILDERNESS PRESERVATION SYSTEM

Nectow v. *City of Cambridge* (277 U.S. 183, 48 S. Ct. 447, 72 L.Ed. 842 [1928])

A decision by the United States Supreme Court clarifying one aspect of the landmark decision of *Village of Euclid* v. *Ambler Realty Co.* by holding that zoning restrictions may not be imposed with respect to a specific parcel of land if, in terms of that parcel, they do not bear a substantial relation to the public health, safety, morals or general welfare.

The Court held that an ordinance that rendered a landowner's property of little practical or economic use without promoting the general welfare was an unconstitutional taking of property without due process, in violation of the 14th Amendment.

See: POLICE POWER; *VILLAGE OF EUCLID* v. *AMBLER REALTY CO.*

Negative Easement

An easement in which one party has the right to prohibit the other party from using or otherwise enjoying his property. In a negative easement the owner of the easement (in the case of an easement in gross) or the owner of the dominant estate (in the case of an easement appurtenant) has the right to prohibit the owner of the servient estate from using his property in ways that otherwise would be within the lawful right of a landowner. For example, an easement of light and air prevents the owner of the servient estate from building on his property in a manner that would interfere with the light and air of the dominant estate.

See: AFFIRMATIVE EASEMENT; EASEMENT

Negotiation

A process aimed at reaching an agreement between two or more parties. In planning, negotiation most commonly takes place between a developer and various public officials concerning a particular development proposal. Negotiation takes place because municipal ordinances generally cannot detail every aspect of a development that will require approval and instead leave some of the approval process to the discretion of municipal officials. In addition, many newer forms of zoning, such as incentive zoning, encourage a negotiation process. In incentive zoning, for example, additional public amenities are provided by the developer in exchange for the right to build additional stories or to build at greater densities.

Common topics for negotiation include the general design and layout of the development, the final appearance of the development, the improvements that the development will require and the responsibility for paying for these improvements. The negotiation process is facilitated and is better able to promote the mutual interests of the public and the private developer if there are specific development standards and procedures guiding the process that serve as a framework within which discussions and decision making can take place.

Another common application of negotiation occurs when a unit of government seeks to purchase real property for a municipal purpose and attempts to obtain the best possible price and conditions of purchase.

See: FLEXIBLE REGULATIONS

Neighborhood

An identifiable geographic area within the larger urban area; it is the residents' perceptions of landmarks, boundaries, institutions and each other that create a neighborhood. Neighborhoods provide a sense of place within cities, and the social interaction and attitudes within neighborhoods are one of the building blocks of urban life. Unlike the neighborhood unit concept based on elementary school service areas, real neighborhoods vary enormously in size and character; they may have over 100,000 persons with commercial and industrial areas or consist of a residential area of only a few hundred people.

Neighborhoods are viewed by planners as a manageable unit in which to study and solve problems, while neighborhood civic groups have become a foundation of citizen participation in planning matters.

See: CITIZEN PARTICIPATION; COMMUNITY; COMMUNITY CONTROL; NEIGHBORHOOD BUSINESS STREET; NEIGHBORHOOD CHANGE; NEIGHBORHOOD IDENTITY; NEIGHBORHOOD PARK; NEIGHBORHOOD PLANNING; NEIGHBORHOOD PRESERVATION; NEIGHBORHOOD SCHOOL; NEIGHBORHOOD SHOPPING CENTER; NEIGHBORHOOD STATISTICS PROGRAM; NEIGHBORHOOD UNIT CONCEPT; NEIGHBORHOOD ZONING PARTICIPATION

Neighborhood Business Street

A collector or arterial street in a residential area on which stores that serve the local population are located. Stores in these areas generally sell convenience goods and provide services—e.g., banks and hairdressers—but may also sell clothing and specialty items. On-street parking is most common, although some communities are now providing small, off-street metered parking lots. In heavily urbanized areas neighborhood business streets may extend for 5 miles (8 kilometers) or more, although they frequently serve only the population that is within a five-minute walk or drive.

Main business thoroughfares, which are usually arterials, differ from neighborhood business streets in that they accommodate larger stores—e.g., automobile or appliance sales—that have a wider service area. These thoroughfares will frequently have local office development and drive-in facilities as well, and may also have some light industry.

See: NEIGHBORHOOD SHOPPING CENTER

Neighborhood Change

A term that describes changes in the character of a neighborhood unit, primarily in cities, over varying periods of time. Whereas the term is most frequently used to describe a change from a stable, usually white, middle-class area to an economically declining area with a higher concentration of minorities, older adults and the poor, it has also been used more recently to refer to areas undergoing revitalization, with a higher-income population moving in. In either case, a change in socioeconomic composition is usually accompanied by either a decline or an improvement in the quality of public services and a deterioration or an upgrading of the physical infrastructure of the neighborhood.

Recent analysis of neighborhood change has suggested the importance of neighborhood image, as depicted in the media or by word of mouth, in influencing the market forces that contribute to neighborhood change.

See: BLOCKBUSTING; GENTRIFICATION; NEIGHBOR-HOOD PRESERVATION; REDLINING; TIPPING POINT

Neighborhood Housing Services (NHS)

A program of grants and technical assistance by the Neighborhood Reinvestment Corporation (NRC) to a private nonprofit corporation that is attempting to bring about reinvestment in one or more low- or moderate-income blighted or declining neighborhoods. The program, which was operating in 127 cities in 1982, involves systematic housing inspections; increased public investment, such as for infrastructure; increased private lending; greater investment by residents, such as in the form of home improvements; and a revolving loan fund to make loans available at flexible rates and terms to homeowners not meeting private lending criteria. Operating funds are provided by local investors such as banks and corporations.

Neighborhood Housing Services of America Inc. (NHSA), a nonprofit tax-exempt corporation, has been established to provide a secondary market for NHS revolving fund loans, enabling the NHS program to replenish its loan funds. Neighborhood Reinvestment Corporation grants provide NHSA with capital and operating funds.

See: NEIGHBORHOOD REINVESTMENT CORPORATION (NRC)

Neighborhood Identity

An image, or quality of recognition, associated with a residential enclave or neighborhood unit. Traditionally, neighborhood identity refers to the image associated with a residential area having commonly recognized physical boundaries and a reasonably homogeneous population. The identity of the neighborhood derives from the particular physical qualities of the area and the unique cultural qualities of the population, the most notable examples being the Chinatowns of several big cities. The numerous neighborhoods within municipalities and their different identities contribute to the varied characters of communities.

From a physical standpoint, identity may refer strictly to such properties as the boundaries; building types; infrastructure (as represented by major streets and transit lines); focal points, such as a town square; special features, such as fountains; or unique facilities. Beyond the physical characteristics, however, is a sociocultural identity related to traditions or common activities and life-styles, which

may differ sharply among neighborhoods. In urban design and social planning, the establishment of a neighborhood identity is used as a means of generating a sense of community and civic pride.

See: AMBIENCE; COMMUNITY CHARACTER; NEIGH-BORHOOD UNIT CONCEPT; SENSE OF PLACE

Neighborhood Park

A pedestrian-oriented park located at the approximate center of a neighborhood, designed to serve one or more of the recreational needs of a neighborhood population of about 5,000. Typically ranging in size from 2 to 20 acres (0.8 hectare to 8.0 hectares), they may be landscaped areas designed for passive recreation or contain a broad range of recreational facilities, such as play equipment, playfields, athletic courts, a recreation building and a swimming pool. The facilities provided are a function of community requirements in a specific location and other facilities available elsewhere.

In recent analyses of park use, it has been found that larger parks are frequently grossly underutilized, often because of fear of crime. To prevent the potential waste of a large capital investment, and to place recreation facilities closer to more people, some communities have switched from the provision of one central neighborhood park to numerous smaller parks dispersed throughout a neighborhood. Some suburban communities have found, however, that smaller parks have less attendance and greater vandalism, largely because backyard play equipment is prevalent. In these locations attendance is greater at parks with pools and tennis courts.

See: COMMUNITY PARK; PLAYGROUND

Neighborhood Planning

Development of plans and strategies for neighborhood improvement or revitalization. Undertaken by officially designated neighborhood planning boards, nonprofit neighborhood development organizations, civic groups or a municipal planning department, neighborhood planning activities may range from relatively direct problem solving, such as petitioning the city for a traffic light where accidents have occurred, to comprehensive neighborhood planning. The latter might involve a study of all facets of neighborhood activity, followed by recommendations concerning necessary improvements to its infrastructure and to the way in which municipal services are made available to the neighborhood. In some cases, neighborhood planning efforts have evolved into neighborhood development activities, a logical step to implementing planning recommendations.

Neighborhood planning, which creates a forum for discussion of neighborhood issues, is considered the most practical level for effective improvements in the areas of housing, economic development, health and crime prevention. The process of planning often creates a strong local citizen body within the neighborhood that increases its political strength and frequently results in increased municipal and private investment as well. Some cities created elaborate neighborhood planning organizations in the 1970s, largely as the result of required citizen participation programs, but in recent years many municipal programs have been cut because of financial constraints. Community organizations, often in the form of community development corporations, now appear to be assuming a more influential role in neighborhood planning, while neighborhood planning boards have been created in some jurisdictions to oversee ongoing planning matters.

See: COMMUNITY DEVELOPMENT CORPORATION (CDC); DECENTRALIZATION; NEIGHBORHOOD; NEIGHBORHOOD REINVESTMENT CORPORATION (NRC); NEIGHBORHOOD ZONING PARTICIPATION; URBAN PLANNING

Neighborhood Preservation

The stabilization of the economic, physical and social forces within a neighborhood to maintain its viability and desirability as a place of residence and employment. The focus of neighborhood preservation is largely a social one that is targeted toward the conservation of existing human and physical resources as a means of maintaining a stable population and averting neighborhood deterioration.

From the standpoint of combatting inner-city decline, the neighborhood unit is viewed as a manageable size for attacking such large-scale, citywide problems as economic decline, crime and pollution. Neighborhood preservation activities usually include improved social services programs, rehabilitation of existing housing stock, reinvestment in public facilities and stimulation of commercial and industrial development.

Federal, state and local agencies provide funds for neighborhood self-help projects and seed money to attract private investment in commercial development. Many municipalities also select target neighborhoods, where various forms of government assistance will be concentrated, in an effort to reverse a trend toward neighborhood decline.

See: BLOCKBUSTING; COMMUNITY DEVELOPMENT CORPORATION (CDC); ECONOMIC DEVELOPMENT; MULTISERVICE CENTER; NEIGHBORHOOD CHANGE; NEIGHBORHOOD UNIT CONCEPT; REDLINING; TARGET AREA

Neighborhood Reinvestment Corporation (NRC)

A federally sponsored public corporation, based in Washington, D.C., that finances programs designed to organize community involvement in neighborhood revitalization. Its services include technical assistance, training programs, seed money grants and periodic program evaluation. NRC is the successor to the Urban Reinvestment Task Force, which was a demonstration program authorized in 1974 to study housing and community rehabilitation projects. NRC's board of directors is composed of: the Chairman of the Federal Home Loan Bank Board; the Secretary of Housing and Urban Development; a member of the Board of Governors of the Federal Reserve System; the Chairman of the Federal Deposit Insurance Corporation; the Comptroller of the Currency; and the Administrator of the National Credit Union Administration.

The NRC conducts several programs concerned with reinvestment in declining neighborhoods. Neighborhood Housing Services, for low-or moderate-income neighborhoods, was operating in 171 neighborhoods in 127 cities in 1982. Newer programs, such as the Apartment Improvement Program (AIP) and the Owner Built Housing Program, are being expanded. The apartment program is an attempt to rehabilitate financially and physically troubled privately owned and conventionally financed apartment buildings. The owner program is designed to stimulate single-family housing development by neighborhood residents, using conventional financing.

See: NEIGHBORHOOD HOUSING SERVICES (NHS)

Neighborhood School

An elementary school located at the center of population of a neighborhood and near other community facilities that serves, along with its playground, as a neighborhood focal point. Ideally, all children should be able to walk to the neighborhood school, but in more sparsely developed areas, school buses are usually necessary.

Current educational philosophy suggests that neighborhood schools be small, as are the British infant schools, with student populations of around 300. School economics, however, often requires that they have as many as 1,200 students, while an average size is 800.

See: NEIGHBORHOOD PARK; NEIGHBORHOOD UNIT CONCEPT; SCHOOL LAND REQUIREMENTS; SCHOOL SERVICE AREAS

Neighborhood Self-Help Development Act of 1978

Federal legislation that, under Title VII of the Housing and Community Development Amendments of 1978, established a program of grants to nonprofit neighborhood organizations to support housing, community and economic development projects. Each project that was funded was required to both benefit and actively involve residents of a low- or moderate-income neighborhood by including a self-help component, in which residents volunteered their time or financial resources. The program was terminated in 1982.

See: SELF-HELP HOUSING

Neighborhood Shopping Center

A unified development of retail stores located on a 3- to 10-acre (1.2- to 4-hectare) tract of land, usually containing 30,000 to 100,000 square feet (2,787 to 9,290 square meters) of leasable floor space. A neighborhood shopping center, which is designed to serve a population of 2,500 to 40,000, offers the convenience goods and personal services usually available near home and is therefore designed in a configuration that permits easy access, ample parking for short stays and quick recognition of stores that provide desired merchandise. A straight row of stores or an L-shaped or U-shaped design, with parking in front of the building, is most often used. A large supermarket is frequently the prime tenant.

While pedestrian areas may be restricted to sidewalks in front of stores, newer developments are adding awnings and small playgrounds and are paying increased attention to shopping center appearance. All of these features tend to keep shoppers at the center for longer periods of time, thereby encouraging unanticipated purchases. Mini-marts, in which all stores are accommodated within one building of usually 3,000 to 5,000 square feet (278 to 465 square meters), are another form of neighborhood shopping center.
See: NEIGHBORHOOD BUSINESS STREET; SHOPPING CENTER DESIGN; STRIP DEVELOPMENT

Neighborhood Statistics Program

Socioeconomic profiles of participating neighborhoods prepared by the Bureau of the Census using 1980 Census data. The profiles contain information on age, employment, income, shelter costs and other 100-percent and sample data.
See: CENSUS

Neighborhood Strategy Area (NSA)

An area targeted by local government for comprehensive neighborhood revitalization activities under the Community Development Block Grant (CDBG) program or the Section 8 housing program. NSAs, which are no longer requirements of these programs, reflect federal policy of the late 1970s encouraging the concentrated targeting of limited housing and community development resources rather than the dispersal of CDBG funds throughout a city. A city designated its NSAs as part of a three-year comprehensive plan for upgrading the NSAs through housing rehabilitation, public services and physical improvements or for concentrated development of Section 8 Substantial Rehabilitation Units.
See: COMMUNITY DEVELOPMENT BLOCK GRANT (CDBG); SECTION 8 HOUSING PROGRAM; TARGET AREA

Neighborhood Unit Concept

The optimum size and arrangement of a neighborhood that was postulated by Clarence Perry in 1929 in the *Regional Survey of New York and Its Environs.* The concept, which has become the building block of cities, has been used widely in the United States and in various forms has served as the blueprint for post-World War II suburbs and influenced new town planning.

The concept calls for a residential area containing about 5,000 persons, the optimum size to be served by an elementary school in 1929. The neighborhood unit is residentially oriented, with single-family homes occupying most of the land area and 10 percent of the land reserved for parks and open space. An elementary school and other

community facilities are located at the center of the neighborhood. Perry suggested that the size of a neighborhood should be 160 acres (64.8 hectares), with a density of 10 dwelling units per acre, and that children should not have to walk more than 0.5 mile (0.8 kilometer) to school.

In the neighborhood unit concept, major arterial roads denote the perimeter of the neighborhood, with minor arterials connecting to residential areas and the community facility core. Commercial facilities and community facilities that serve more than one neighborhood are located at the periphery of the neighborhoods at the intersections of major arterials. Multifamily structures are used as a buffer and are located on busy streets between the commercial center and single-family areas.
See: NEIGHBORHOOD; NEW TOWN; *REGIONAL PLAN OF NEW YORK AND ITS ENVIRONS*

Neighborhood Zoning Participation

Formal neighborhood involvement in the zoning process at one of a number of levels. One type of procedure to encourage neighborhood participation is administrative decentralization, in which field offices of the central organization are established throughout a community to administer zoning matters and answer public inquiries, although no neighborhood advisory body is created. In another, more common, system a neighborhood board is officially formed with advisory power concerning a number of areas, including zoning. Generally, the board is responsible for such matters as the review or development of plans for its area and making comments and recommendations concerning zoning matters. Communities that have implemented this system include Portland, Oregon; Birmingham, Alabama; and New York City.

Although neighborhood zoning authorities do not usually have any decision-making power, it is often required that matters be referred to them. It has also been proposed in some communities that additional power, such as the right to approve minor zoning variances, be delegated to neighborhood bodies.
See: DECENTRALIZATION; LITTLE CITY HALLS; NEIGHBORHOOD; NEIGHBORHOOD PLANNING; ZONING

Net Acre

The amount of land that is developable after land that is required for roads or other dedicatory purposes, such as a municipal park, is subtracted from the total acreage. As an example, if a 10-acre (4-hectare) site is to be subdivided into lots for single-family housing, the site would have 10 gross acres but perhaps only 7 net usable acres (3 hectares).
See: BUILDABLE AREA

Net Floor Area

The total floor area of a structure minus the square footage devoted to elevator shafts, stairwells, interior space used for parking or loading, equipment and utility

rooms, and most basement areas. Net floor area is often equivalent to about 85 percent of the gross floor area.
See: FLOOR AREA RATIO (FAR); GROSS FLOOR AREA; ZONING

Net Migration

The difference between in-migration and out-migration. If more in-migration than out-migration has occurred, the balance of the two figures is termed net in-migration; if the reverse is true, it is called net out-migration.

In population projection net migration may be approximated by comparing individual age groups for two separate censuses. If the population from each age group in the earlier census—e.g., 1970—is aged forward 10 years to 1980 (after appropriate survival rates have been applied), an estimate is obtained of population trends without the effects of migration. If the actual 1980 Census data by age group are then compared to the 1970 Census population that has been aged to 1980, the difference between these figures may be assumed to represent net migration approximately.

In making current population estimates, net migration is often derived by comparing elementary school enrollment data with the number of students that might be expected based on the most recent census and subsequent data on new births. After survival rates are applied, net migration is assumed to be the difference between the actual elementary school population and the theoretical population. This is converted to a migration rate and then adjusted to include the entire population.
See: COHORT SURVIVAL METHOD; CURRENT POPULATION ESTIMATES; DEMOGRAPHY; IN-MIGRATION; OUT-MIGRATION

Network Assignment

A study employed in transportation planning to predict the use of sections of a future transit or highway system by allocating estimates of the numbers of passengers or vehicles that might be expected to use various segments of the system. Estimates are made of future trips and traffic volume and are then assigned to segments of the system. These traffic assignments permit determination of potential loading on proposed transit or highway improvements and the effect of these improvements on the rest of the network.

Models used to assign vehicles assume that traffic originates and terminates at central points of zones called centroids. Street intersections and highway interchanges are called nodes, and connecting segments between nodes are known as links. Traffic volumes are assigned to each link, and volumes between centroids can be determined for each link in a system. Assignments are made in terms of two-way daily traffic. Assignment of traffic on roads generally presumes that a driver will select a route that takes the least time. Problems in estimating are compounded by the possible selection of routes to avoid tolls and the po-

tential of reduced speed on high-speed roads when traffic assignments from all routes under study are made to the same road.

Mass transit assignment uses a similar technique, substituting transit stations or stops for nodes. Assignment of passengers becomes complex when a variety of transit modes are available between two zones in high density urban areas. The assumption of shortest travel time or lowest cost is often inaccurate here, where safety and comfort may have higher prevailing values. British transportation studies generally assign a much higher percentage of trips to public transit than do North American studies because of markedly lower levels of car ownership.
See: MODAL SPLIT; NODE; TRANSPORTATION PLANNING

New Communities Act of 1968

Legislation that authorized the U.S. Department of Housing and Urban Development (HUD) to issue loan guarantees for private developers of large-scale new communities. Authorized by Title IV of the Housing and Urban Development Act of 1968, the act enabled HUD to guarantee obligations of up to $50 million per project for land acquisition and site improvements. It also authorized HUD to make supplemental grants to state and local governments, intended to cover the local share required by federal matching grant programs for water, sewer and open-space projects. This act was superseded by the Urban Growth and New Community Development Act of 1970.
See: URBAN GROWTH AND NEW COMMUNITY DEVELOPMENT ACT OF 1970

New Law Tenement

A tenement constructed under the New York Tenement House Law of 1901. This law was passed to remedy the insufficiency of light and air, fire danger, lack of sanitary facilities and overcrowding that were prevalent at the turn of the century and were documented in a comprehensive study conducted by the Tenement House Commission. Considered to be the most stringent housing law of its time, it was widely copied by other cities throughout the United States that were concerned with housing reform.

Among its provisions, it provided greater access to light and air, required that buildings taller than 60 feet (18 meters) be fireproof, provided for running water and toilets in each apartment and prohibited any room (other than the bathroom) from being smaller than 70 square feet (6.3 square meters). In addition, it prohibited new construction, alterations or conversions without a permit. The permit was issued only after detailed inspection of the plans, and no occupation was permitted until the premises had been inspected. It also provided for the establishment of a permanent Tenement House Department to ensure that the provisions of the law would be enforced.
See: OLD LAW TENEMENT

New Source Performance Standards (NSPS)

1. Limitations set by the Environmental Protection Agency (EPA) on the discharge of industrial sewage directly into navigable waterways or the ocean if the construction of the industrial plant was begun after publication of proposed regulations. Performance standards reflect the greatest degree of pollutant reduction that EPA determines to be achievable through application of the best available demonstrated control technology, processes, operating methods or other alternatives. Where practicable, the standard may specify no discharge of pollutants.

Performance standards are established and reviewed annually for classes of pollutants as 1-day and 30-day average discharge limitations.

2. Limitations on the emission of allowable air pollutants for different types of new or expanding stationary sources. Under the Clean Air Amendments of 1970, the Environmental Protection Agency (EPA) is directed to set emissions limitations, such as for plants and factories on an industry-by-industry basis, to be used as guidelines by states in establishing specific limits for individual plants. State standards must be at least as stringent as EPA standards.

See: CLEAN AIR AMENDMENTS OF 1970; EMISSION STANDARD; FEDERAL WATER POLLUTION CONTROL ACT AMENDMENTS OF 1972; INDUSTRIAL SEWAGE; PRETREATMENT STANDARDS

New Town

A planned, self-contained community of sufficient size to support a mixture of housing, work places and services. While the term can refer to any planned community, it is particularly used for those that are part of a planned form of metropolitan growth.

New towns are communities that are planned from inception (as opposed to agglomeration), with specific limits to eventual growth. They are intended to provide a beneficial mixture of different types of housing, recreational facilities, social programs, transportation systems, commercial establishments and varied employment opportunities. Different-sized new towns have been proposed and built, but a community designed for 50,000 to 100,000 persons is generally believed to be necessary for self-sufficiency.

While planned communities date back to antiquity, the new town concept related to regional growth was originated in England by Ebenezer Howard near the beginning of this century. Howard proposed a number of satellite garden cities a distance from London and eventually built 2 such communities. The concept was implemented on a large scale by the New Towns Act of 1946. More than 30 new communities have actually been built housing over 1.6 million people throughout Great Britain.

Many other nations—notably France, Finland and Sweden—have constructed complete and aesthetically pleasing new communities. In the United States early attempts at new town construction included Radburn, New Jersey and the greenbelt towns constructed by the Resettlement Administration. Since the 1960s there have been several privately developed successful new communities, most notably the Rouse Corporation's Columbia, Maryland; Reston, Virginia; and the Irvine Ranch in California. The Housing and Urban Development Acts of 1968 and 1970 provided loan guarantees for new communities but resulted in more financial failures than successes because building costs far exceeded original estimates. The new town, however, represents an influential and constructive urban planning concept, offering the potential of planned communities that effectively provide housing, jobs and services while also helping to manage metropolitan growth.

See: COLUMBIA, MARYLAND; COMPANY TOWN; GREENBELT TOWNS; HOWARD, SIR EBENEZER; KITI-MAT, BRITISH COLUMBIA; NEW COMMUNITIES ACT OF 1968; NEW TOWNS ACT, 1946; PLANNED COMMUNITY; RADBURN, NEW JERSEY; RESTON, VIRGINIA

New-Town-in-Town

A planned community within the boundaries of a major city. The new-town-in-town concept calls for large-scale residential, commercial, recreational and sometimes light industrial development on vacant urban land. Most projects, however, are large housing developments with supporting commercial and cultural facilities that are more accurately described as new neighborhoods than new towns.

The concept of new-towns-in-town has been promoted by planners as a tool for the revitalization of large vacant areas of major cities that have a strong economic potential. The Urban Growth and New Community Development Act of 1970 supported the new-town-in-town project of Cedar-Riverside on an urban renewal site near the University of Minnesota in downtown Minneapolis, where 1,300 housing units were built. Another major project, Roosevelt Island in New York City, was developed by the Urban Development Corporation with 2,200 housing units plus shops and parks. Neither of these projects, however, has reached its originally projected size. Battery Park City, which is being constructed on landfill in the Hudson River, is expected to be more successful because of its proximity to New York City's financial district and its more even residential and commercial land use mixture. (See Fig. 28)

See: NEW TOWN; URBAN DEVELOPMENT CORPORATION (UDC); URBAN GROWTH AND NEW COMMUNITY DEVELOPMENT ACT OF 1970

New Towns Act, 1946

British legislation that empowered the minister of town and country planning or the secretary of state for Scotland, after consulting with pertinent local authorities, to designate any area of land as the site of a proposed new town and to appoint a public development corporation to de-

Fig. 28.   Roosevelt Island, New York City, a new-town-in-town created on an island in the East River that affords views of Manhattan to residents of these buildings.
Credit: Courtesy of the U.S. Department of Housing and Urban Development

velop it under his supervision. The act specified that an existing town or village could become the nucleus of the proposed new town and that a target population be determined before planning could begin. The legislation was based on proposals made in the Greater London Plan of 1944, which recommended a deconcentration of the population of the London conurbation.

A New Towns Committee, formed to select locations and set planning requirements for the new towns, established physical, social and economic directives for them, many of which have been exported to new towns in other countries. Among the requirements were an optimum population of 30,000 to 50,000; a balanced social composition; groupings into neighborhoods; a peripheral greenbelt; facilities for commerce and industry; a variety of housing types for diverse needs of the population; recreational facilities, ranging from parks to theaters; and control of outdoor signs. Thirty-two new towns were built under authority of this act between 1947 and 1970, most surrounding an existing village nucleus. The development corporations are now gradually being dissolved.
See: COUNTY OF LONDON PLAN

New York City Zoning Code

The first comprehensive zoning ordinance in the United States, adopted in 1916. It combined the regulation of such elements as land use, building height and the size of yards in a single ordinance and imposed these controls throughout the city. It also introduced the use of detailed zoning maps, which showed the locations and boundaries of each zoning district.

The ordinance was adopted in response to growing concern about regulating the height of skyscrapers and preventing the incursion of factories into fashionable midtown Manhattan shopping areas. In the haste to develop and adopt an ordinance, however, it was done without first developing a long-term comprehensive plan. Instead, the ordinance focused upon withstanding legal challenges rather than upon logically regulating and accommodating future land use requirements or the new development that would be necessary.

Because it appeared to be thorough, New York City's zoning ordinance, including some of its less logical aspects, was widely copied in the United States. This perpetuated a tradition, for many years, of developing and adopting zon-

ing ordinances in the absence of a comprehensive plan or as a substitute for such a plan.
See: HADACHECK v. SEBASTIAN; IN ACCORDANCE WITH A COMPREHENSIVE PLAN

New York State Commission of Housing and Regional Planning

A commission, formed in 1923 and chaired by Clarence S. Stein, that issued the first state planning report in 1926. The report, which recommended that a public housing subsidy program be formed, led to the passage of legislation in New York in 1926 authorizing the first such program. It created a state housing board authorized to grant partial tax exemptions to limited-dividend housing corporations, provided that they built housing that did not exceed specified rents and was available for people of lower incomes.
See: STEIN, CLARENCE S.

No Growth

1. A descriptive term for state or local government policies that severely limit development. "No-growth" policies and programs emerged in the 1970s in rapidly growing and environmentally attractive areas, such as California, Colorado, Florida and Oregon. No-growth policies may not completely halt development, but these strict limitations on growth contrast sharply with the progrowth boosterism that once prevailed in most areas. The need to protect critical areas, an increased sensitivity to the costs of growth in terms of provision of municipal services and facilities, and a desire to preserve small-town character contributed to the emergence of these programs.

Critics charge that no-growth policies are exclusionary, restricting population mobility and discriminating against outsiders and the poor. In the early 1980s, however, the decline in development that was affecting much of the country as a result of an economic recession began to affect most of the high-growth areas that had adopted these policies. As a result, no growth programs essentially became mechanisms for growth management.

2. A condition in which a municipality or region ceases to grow in population, generally caused by economic stability or decline.
See: GROWTH MANAGEMENT; MATURE CITY; ZERO POPULATION GROWTH (ZPG)

Node

1. Point on a map where a street or special feature, such as a river, intersects with another street or special feature, comes to an end or changes direction. Computerized geographic files, such as the GBF/DIME system used by the U.S. Bureau of the Census, codify data on a map by two sets of information, node points and lines (streets), which when connected form enclosed areas. An entire map can be derived from a series of interrelated nodes and lines. In highway and mass transit planning, estimates of trips between specified nodes, such as intersections, are used to plan facilities and schedules.

2. A hub or center of activity where two or more systems intersect. For example, transportation nodes are points where several transportation systems converge. Pennsylvania Station in New York City is a major transportation node, since commuter rail service, long-distance rail service and subway lines all meet there. Most cities developed around transportation nodes. The growth of Chicago, for example, is largely attributed to the intersection of the railroad with Lake Michigan.
See: GBF/DIME FILES; NETWORK ASSIGNMENT

Noise Control Act of 1972

Legislation that authorizes establishment of federal noise emission standards and regulations for purposes of noise control. Under the act (PL 92-574), the Environmental Protection Agency (EPA) is directed to develop noise emission standards for equipment used in construction and transportation, for motors and engines, and for electrical and electronic products, and manufacturers are required to warrant that new products conform to the federal regulations. EPA is also directed to evaluate airport and aircraft noise, while the Federal Aviation Administration is directed to set or amend standards for measurement, control and abatement of aircraft noise and sonic boom, after consultation with EPA.

The act also directs all federal agencies to help control noise and authorizes them to establish noise-control regulations, which are coordinated by EPA. As a result of these requirements, many projects constructed with federal assistance now include provisions for noise reduction, such as transportation projects for which noise barriers are installed and use of transportation equipment that emits less noise.
See: AIRPORT NOISE; NOISE POLLUTION; QUIET COMMUNITIES ACT OF 1978

Noise Pollution

Unwanted sounds that have an adverse physiological and psychological effect on humans.

Although it is relatively difficult to determine the long-range effects of noise pollution, numerous studies have shown a relationship between noise and hearing loss and impairment, sleep disturbances, interference with speech communication, anxiety and fatigue. The U.S. Environmental Protection Agency has estimated that approximately 20 to 25 million people in the United States are exposed to noise levels sufficient to affect their hearing ability, and approximately 102 million individuals are exposed to noise levels sufficient to interfere with daily activities.

The major sources of noise pollution are aircraft operations, ground vehicular traffic, construction and heavy equipment. Aircraft operations produce the most intense noise, but vehicular traffic is the most prevalent noise source.

Noise may be controlled at its source, at the path of transmission and at the receiver's or user's end. The making of quieter engines controls noise at the source; the placing of baffles or mufflers controls noise at the transmission path; and the installation of insulation or landscaping controls it at the receiver's end. Until very recently, most attempts to control noise focused only on regulating it at the source. As an example, the Noise Control Act of 1972 encourages the use of quieter engines or machines by setting emission levels for the major noise sources. The Quiet Communities Act of 1978 does, however, encourage communities to take a more comprehensive and integrated approach toward reducing noise pollution.

To date, the most comprehensive approach to noise pollution control has been in the area of aircraft operations. By requiring quieter planes, controlling flight paths, restricting landing hours and carefully planning the location and design of airports, communities have employed an integrated approach to the problem of aircraft noise. Similar approaches may be necessary to successfully regulate noise from other sources.
See: AIRPORT NOISE; AMBIENT NOISE; DECIBEL; EACH COMMUNITY HELPS OTHERS (ECHO); IMPACT SOUND; SONIC BOOM; STEADY-STATE SOUND

Nonattainment Area

Any area that exceeds the national ambient air quality standards for any air pollutant. Pursuant to Clean Air Act provisions, states with air quality control regions in this category must comply with a variety of federal regulations, including a requirement that permits be issued before new or modified major stationary sources can be constructed or operated. These new facilities may not be built unless the state has adopted a plan adequate to attain national air quality standards and unless the company is prepared to install equipment necessary to meet the lowest achievable emission rate. In addition, the act provides that the new facilities may not be built unless the amount of pollution from existing facilities is reduced to a greater degree than the amount of pollution that will be generated by the new facility.

Existing stationary source polluters in a nonattainment area are required to retrofit their facilities with, at a minimum, reasonably available control technology (RACT). States with pollution problems particularly related to oxidants and carbon monoxide are given until the end of 1987 to attain national standards. In turn, they must include in their state implementation plans an analysis of alternate sites for new major pollution sources, adopt motor vehicle inspection programs and develop means of improving public transportation.
See: AIR POLLUTION; ATTAINMENT AREA; MOBILE SOURCE; STATIONARY SOURCE

Nonconforming Lot

A lot that does not now conform to the requirements of the zoning district in which it is located but that prior to enactment or amendment of the zoning ordinance did meet community requirements. Another term for this type of lot is a substandard lot of record. A lot may be non-conforming with respect to total lot area; any of its dimensions, such as width; or some other characteristic of the lot. Zoning ordinances generally allow the lot to remain in use under this circumstance, although if several nonconforming lots are held by the same owner and adjoin, the lot lines may be required to be redrawn.

Nonconforming lots may also be created through condemnation. This can occur when a government agency takes part of the owner's property, such as for a road widening, leaving the owner with a lot that now in some way does not comply with the zoning ordinance.
See: AMORTIZATION OF NONCONFORMING USES; NONCONFORMING STRUCTURE; NONCONFORMING USE; ZONING

Nonconforming Structure

A structure that does not now conform to the requirements of the zoning district in which it is located but that did meet all requirements prior to adoption or amendment of the municipal ordinance. A building or structure may be nonconforming with respect to coverage, floor area ratio, height, yard dimensions or a variety of other characteristics.

In general, zoning ordinances do not prohibit the continuing use of nonconforming structures but often prevent them from being expanded or enlarged. In addition, in the case of significant destruction of the structure by fire or other cause, the owner may in some communities be prohibited from reconstructing it.
See: AMORTIZATION OF NONCONFORMING USES; NONCONFORMING LOT; NONCONFORMING USE; ZONING

Nonconforming Use

A land use that does not now conform to the requirements of the zoning district in which it is located but that met municipal requirements prior to adoption or amendment of the zoning ordinance. An example of a nonconforming use is a retail store located in a district zoned exclusively for residential use or a gasoline station in a commercial zone in which such stations are prohibited.

Generally, if a nonconforming use is abandoned for a time period specified in the municipal zoning ordinance, that use may not be resumed at a later date, and any future use of the property must be in compliance with the ordinance. Similarly, if a property owner changes to a conforming or more closely conforming use of the property, he will not be allowed to revert to the original nonconforming use allowed on the property. In addition, nonconforming uses cannot be expanded or enlarged.
See: AMORTIZATION OF NONCONFORMING USES; NONCONFORMING LOT; NONCONFORMING STRUCTURE; ZONING

Nondegradation Clause

Provisions aimed at preventing air quality from deteriorating in clean air areas with air quality exceeding the national ambient air quality standards. Prevention of sig-

nificant deterioration (PSD) rules are incorporated in the Clean Air Act Amendments of 1977. They set different requirements for three separate categories of regions, of which Class I, encompassing many units of the National Park System, is the most restrictive.
See: AIR POLLUTION

Nonpoint Source

One or more of the various diffuse discharges, such as runoff, that contribute to water pollution. Although several definitions of this phenomenon are in use, it is usually considered to include water pollution deriving from agriculture, silviculture, mining, irrigation return flows, urban runoff, runoff from construction sites, hydrologic modification, solid waste disposal practices and individual (rather than municipal) sewage disposal facilities, such as septic systems.

In urban areas urban runoff is a major cause of water pollution, affecting over half the river basins in the United States. In rural areas agricultural runoff represents the primary threat to water quality, distributing a wide variety of pollutants to water bodies.

Relatively little progress has been made in controlling nonpoint source pollution (as compared to point source pollution) because the causes are so diverse. In addition, the existing water pollution control legislation does not give the Environmental Protection Agency (EPA) authority to regulate most forms of nonpoint pollution sources, as this is not considered within the realm of federal jurisdiction.

Best management practices (BMPs) have been developed, however, as part of the Water Quality Management Program that is conducted pursuant to Section 208 of the Federal Water Pollution Control Act Amendments of 1972 as amended. BMPs identify and recommend particular procedures and techniques that can aid in reducing nonpoint source pollution. As an example, changes in farming practices can reduce agricultural runoff and its resulting pollution, and changes in the storage, handling and application of deicing chemicals used on roadways in the winter can lessen this form of pollution. In addition, a number of states have passed or are proposing programs in which they partially subsidize expenses necessary to controlling nonpoint source pollution. As an example, in Illinois farmers have been compensated for using soil tilling methods that lessen soil erosion. A number of prototype programs have also been conducted with the support of the U.S. Department of Agriculture and EPA aimed at providing answers to common nonpoint source pollution problems.
See: AGRICULTURAL POLLUTION; BEST MANAGEMENT PRACTICES (BMPs); CLEARCUTTING; IRRIGATION; POINT SOURCE; SANITARY LANDFILL; SEPTIC SYSTEM; URBAN RUNOFF; WATER POLLUTION

Nonrecourse Loan

A loan or other monetary obligation, such as a mortgage, for which no one is personally liable. A nonrecourse loan typically is secured by specific collateral. In the event

the borrower defaults in paying the loan, the lender's sole remedy is to foreclose upon the collateral; the lender has no recourse against the borrower if the collateral is not sufficient to repay the debt.

Nonrecourse financing frequently occurs in real estate transactions. In part, this is because real estate is generally considered to be a relatively safe form of collateral for a lender to loan against; its value is relatively nonvolatile and can be readily ascertained by comparison with other properties or by examining the income it produces. There also exists a well-established, secure and reliable method for obtaining a lien against real estate by means of recording a mortgage against the property.

Nonresident Park User

One who attends a municipal, regional or state park but is a resident of another political jurisdiction. At parks for which entrance or use fees are charged, nonresidents may be charged a higher fee than residents so that use by nonresidents will be discouraged, total attendance can be kept at manageable levels and/or residents can be rewarded for their tax support or tolerance of the facility.

At municipal parks that have received federal funding through programs administered by the National Park Service, higher nonresident fees are permitted as long as the National Park Service considers them to be "reasonable," but entrance may not be denied to nonresidents. At facilities built by the Army Corps of Engineers, however, differential fees are not permitted. These policies have caused some jurisdictions to avoid federal assistance for construction of park facilities, such as beaches, that they wish to restrict entirely to local residents.
See: USER CHARGES

Nonwhite

1. A term used in the 1960 U.S. Census of Population to categorize persons who described themselves as other than white in response to the race question on the census form. Nonwhite included Negro, American Indian, Japanese, Chinese, Filipino, Hawaiian, part Hawaiian, Aleut, Eskimo and a residual category of all other races.

While the term has not been used in a decennial census since 1960, many planners still use it for ease of reference when reporting data for aggregations of racial groups. Since one or another nonwhite ethnic group frequently predominates over other nonwhite groups in an area by total population count, a reference to the nonwhite population in that area may essentially refer to the predominant population subgroup.

The question on race in the 1980 Cenus has been expanded, offering a choice among the following: white; black or Negro; Japanese, Chinese; Filipino; Korean; Vietnamese; Indian (American); Asian Indian; Hawaiian; Guamanian; Samoan; Eskimo; Aleut; and other, to be specified. Substantial data are available for these subgroups.

2. A person who is not Caucasian.
See: CENSUS

Normal Distribution

A type of frequency distribution that when drawn forms a completely symmetrical and bell-shaped curve. In a normal curve the mean, median and mode are all equal.

The normal distribution has the property of having a constant proportion of the cases or area of the curve within one unit of standard deviation from the mean in either direction. Thus, 34.13 percent of all cases will fall between the mean and $+1$ standard deviation unit, and 34.13 percent of all cases will fall between the mean and -1 standard deviation unit. In other words, in a normal distribution approximately two-thirds of the cases (68.26 percent) will fall within one standard deviation unit of the mean. In addition, 95.44 percent of all cases will fall within two standard deviation units of the mean, and 99.74 percent within three standard deviation units.

See: FREQUENCY DISTRIBUTION; SKEWNESS; STANDARD DEVIATION

Nuclear Energy

Energy that is created by nuclear fission or nuclear fusion. Currently, all commercial nuclear power plants involved in electricity production use nuclear fission, which is the splitting of the nuclei of heavyweight atoms. The first large-scale nuclear power plant was opened in England at Calder Hall in 1956. Since that time nuclear power plants have been built throughout the world. In the United States, as of late 1983, there were 79 nuclear plants licensed for full power operations and an additional 3 plants licensed for fuel loading and low power testing; these plants were located in 28 states. Approximately 50 additional nuclear power plants were under construction. Nuclear power plants provide roughly 12 percent of total U. S. electric power.

Despite the fact that fission reactions are capable of producing large amounts of energy with very little fuel, as compared to power plants using fossil fuels, there are unique problems associated with nuclear power plants. The danger of nuclear accidents, nuclear reactor safety and disposal of the nuclear wastes produced during plant operation are among the concerns that have led to the development of a rigorous plant licensing procedure. One key area is the siting of proposed nuclear plants, and numerous studies are required to evaluate a site and the region's geology, hydrology, likelihood of earthquake, population concentrations and trends, and land uses. Other regulations set standards for design, construction, operation and maintenance of power plants.

Despite these precautions, the worst nuclear power plant accident in United States history occurred on March 28, 1979 at the Three Mile Island plant near Allentown, Pennsylvania. A presidential commission established to investigate the accident concluded that there were serious deficiencies in the regulation and management of nuclear power that were industrywide rather than limited to that specific facility, such as inadequate Nuclear Regulatory Commission (NRC) standards for power plant operator training.

As a result of Three Mile Island, much greater attention has been focused on emergency planning in connection with nuclear power plants. A Nuclear Safety Oversight Committee was formed by the President in 1980 to monitor progress being made by the NRC, other federal agencies, states and utilities in elevating the safety level of power plants. The Federal Emergency Management Agency (FEMA) was also charged with responsibility for offsite planning and emergency response in connection with power plant accidents, and for determining whether or not adequate planning is taking place at the state or local level. The NRC depends on FEMA findings in determining if a plant should be licensed.

Perhaps the most controversial aspect of emergency planning has been the issue of evacuation of the surrounding population in the event of a power plant emergency. This is particularly a problem when plants are located in areas of relatively dense population or when road networks near the plant are inadequate. A number of the nation's nuclear power plants are operating without approved emergency evacuation plans. In several instances, when a plan has been developed local governments have refused to approve the plans because of their real or perceived inadequacies, or they have refused to take part in practice drills. Several states have enacted legislation requiring fees from companies operating nuclear plants to fund emergency planning.

See: COOLING TOWER; ELECTRIC POWER GENERATION AND TRANSMISSION; NUCLEAR REGULATORY COMMISSION (NRC); RADIATION HAZARD; RADIATION STANDARDS; RADIOACTIVE WASTES

Nuclear Regulatory Commission (NRC)

A United States federal agency that licenses and regulates the uses of nuclear energy. Among its responsibilities are the licensing of the construction and operation of nuclear reactors and the transport and disposal of nuclear materials.

Issues related to siting and operation of nuclear power plants and nuclear waste disposal areas are major concerns of many local governments. Public concern about possible nuclear accidents and environmental contamination has made it extremely difficult to find locations for these land uses, even in relatively remote areas once thought suitable for them. NRC systematically reviews data on the operations of nuclear plants, which are also subject to stringent review prior to and during construction, and inspects NRC-licensed activities. In addition, resident inspectors are located at most nuclear reactor sites.

See: ENVIRONMENTAL PROTECTION AGENCY (EPA)

Nuclear Waste Policy Act of 1982

Legislation (PL 97-425) that creates a federal program of development of disposal sites for high-level radioactive waste and spent nuclear fuel from civilian nuclear power plants. High-level wastes are radioactive liquids that are by-products of nuclear fuel reprocessing. Spent nuclear fuel is not classified as a waste because it still contains minerals that can be extracted.

The growing quantities of spent fuel that are currently stored in pools of water at power plant sites will exceed current storage capacity by the late 1980s. The program established by this act requires the development of two permanent repositories for spent fuel and high-level radioactive wastes, the temporary storage of spent fuel from civilian reactors at federally owned nuclear facilities and a study of the need for monitored retrievable storage facilities, where wastes and spent fuel can be kept for future reprocessing or final disposal. Deposits in these facilities would become property of the federal government.

Provisions of the act prescribe the site selection process, require federal coordination with states and Indian tribes on site selection and permit a state or Indian tribe to reject a nuclear waste facility within its borders. Other provisions establish a Nuclear Waste Fund to pay for facility construction and operation (to be supported by fees collected from utility companies) and an Office of Civilian Radioactive Waste Management in the Department of Energy to administer the program. The act requires that the first permanent site be designated by 1987 and the second by 1990.
See: OCEAN DUMPING; RADIOACTIVE WASTES

Nuisance

An activity consisting of an unlawful or unreasonable use of property by an individual that causes injury or damage to another or to the public in general. Common examples of phenomena generally considered to constitute nuisances include excessive noise, odor, smoke or vibration.

Nuisances are classified as public or private. A public nuisance is one that affects an indefinite number of persons or the public at large. A private nuisance refers to unlawful conduct that particularly injures a specific person or his property. Of course, a nuisance may be both public and private.

The remedy for a public nuisance includes a summons leading to a fine, or an order to cease and desist from continuing the nuisance, or both. Remedies for a private nuisance include legal actions for damages, or injunctions against maintaining the nuisance, or both.

Nuisance law constitutes both a basis and a rationale for zoning. One purpose of separating uses by zones or conditioning certain uses on the issuance of a special permit is to reduce circumstances under which normal activity by one user (e.g., heavy industrial) will interfere with the rights of neighboring land owners to employ their property for another use (e.g., residential).
See: BOOMER v. *ATLANTIC CEMENT COMPANY*

Null Hypothesis

A hypothesis, formulated for research and statistical purposes, that states that there is no difference between

situations or groups with respect to the particular variable that is the subject of investigation. In contrast to the null hypothesis, an alternative or research hypothesis is also formulated, which states positively that a difference does exist. The null hypothesis is designated as H_0, while the alternative hypothesis is usually labeled H_1.

Examples of the two types of hypothesis are as follows:

H_0 There is no difference between the quality of wastewater that has received secondary treatment and the quality of wastewater that has not received this treatment.

H_1 A difference exists between the quality of wastewater that has received secondary treatment and the quality of wastewater that has not received this treatment.

The researcher hopes to indirectly prove the alternative hypothesis by rejecting the null hypothesis after statistical tests are performed. The null hypothesis may not, however, be proved to be true in a technical sense. Rather, the investigation may fail to provide information necessary to reject the null hypothesis.
See: TYPE I ERROR; TYPE II ERROR

Nursery School

A small school facility for preschool children. Often located in small buildings or private houses, in rented space in churches or in multifamily buildings, nursery schools require a small outdoor fenced area for play equipment.

Although in the United States nursery schools are frequently commercial ventures, they are usually permitted in residential districts, but they may be regulated by special permit. In planned communities, and elsewhere if possible, it is desirable to locate nursery schools within a 0.25-mile (0.4-kilometer) radius of most housing and preferably in a location that can be reached without crossing a street when walking. Off-street parking is desirable for staff and parents who are dropping children off, and a safe passenger loading area is necessary on busy streets.
See: DAY-CARE CENTER

Nursing Home

A residential facility designed to provide a range of personal and medical care services to chronically ill or disabled individuals. The term, which applies to a wide spectrum of institutions classified by the level of care provided, includes skilled nursing, health-related, personal care and domiciliary care facilities.

Whereas domiciliary care facilities are intended primarily to provide only room and board, with some assistance in daily routines, most nursing homes provide varying degrees of nursing care, ranging from administration of medication through intensive care services. The vast majority of such facilities are proprietary and must meet some form of minimal state code or licensing requirements.

In the design of nursing homes, it is important to establish an environment that allows residents to maintain as active and independent a life-style as possible. To accomplish this, spaces should be designed to encourage interaction with other residents and to accommodate community activities. To minimize feelings of abandonment and isolation related to institutionalization, nursing home design should also integrate the facility into the life of the community.

See: INTERMEDIATE CARE FACILITIES (ICF); LONG-TERM CARE FACILITIES; SKILLED NURSING FACILITY (SNF)

O

Objective

A specific target that must be met as an intermediate step in achieving a long-term goal. Each goal generally has more than one objective that fulfills specific aspects of the goal. If the goal, for example, is to increase the range and quality of housing in a community, an objective might be the addition of 200 units of multifamily housing in the next three years. Objectives should be defined in a manner that allows progress toward the ultimate goal to be measured.
See: GOAL

Occupancy Rate

The ratio of actual patient days to the maximum possible number of patient days in a health care facility, as determined by bed capacity, during any given period of time. Also referred to as percentage of occupancy or utilization rate, the occupancy rate, along with the number of beds, length of stay and discharge rate, is considered an indication of the need for health care services. Occupancy rates are also used as a means of comparing the performance of the hospital systems of different countries. National guidelines for health planning, in addition, have prescribed minimum occupancy standards, which when tied to Medicare and Medicaid reimbursement rates, provide a mechanism for decreasing or eliminating excess bed capacity, which contributes to the high cost of hospital care.
See: HEALTH PLANNING; HOSPITAL BED NEEDS

Ocean Dumping

The disposal of sewage sludge, dredged material, industrial wastes, radioactive wastes or other material at sea. The absence of suitable sites on land for disposal of these materials has necessitated this practice, but lack of knowledge about long-term effects on the ocean ecosystem has raised sufficient concern to cause numerous countries to set limits on ocean dumping.

The 1972 Convention on the Prevention of Marine Pollution by Dumping of Wastes and Other Matter (London Ocean Dumping Convention), which 39 nations had either formally agreed to or agreed to in principle by 1979, regulates the types of materials that may be dumped. It requires a permit for dumping and special authorization for hazardous materials disposal and prohibits ocean disposal of high-level radioactive wastes. In the United States the Marine Protection, Research and Sanctuaries Act of 1972 implements requirements of the convention by requiring that the Environmental Protection Agency (EPA) and the United States Army Corps of Engineers administer permit systems to control ocean dumping. Permits must be issued for all materials, the Army Corps of Engineers supervising those for dredged material subject to EPA review (EPA analyzes it to determine whether the dredged material has been contaminated by toxic substances, bacteria and viruses, and organic chemicals and investigates the proposed dumping site). According to the law, permits are issued only if it is determined that dumping will not harm the marine environment or public health. The 1980 reauthorization of the Marine Protection Act (PL 96-572) required that dumping of sewage sludge and industrial wastes be ended by December 31, 1981. An amendment in 1981 (PL 97-16), however, authorized additional funds for EPA to study sites that would be appropriate for continued dumping. This action recognized the difficulty that large cities were having in finding land disposal sites for the large increases in sewage sludge generated by mandated requirements for secondary sewage treatment.

Low-level radioactive waste disposal is permitted by the London Convention under international supervision and control. Isolation and containment of wastes at a minimum seabed depth of 4,000 meters is recommended by the International Atomic Energy Agency (IAEA). However, a two-year moratorium on the dumping of low-level radioactive wastes was instituted in the United States in 1982.
See: HAZARDOUS WASTE; INDUSTRIAL WASTE; SLUDGE DISPOSAL; SPOIL; TOXIC SUBSTANCES

Ocean Thermal Energy Conversion (OTEC)

A means of producing energy in which the differences in temperature between the sun-warmed water at the ocean's surface and the cold water lying deep below the surface are exploited. In a floating OTEC plant at sea, a fluid, such as ammonia, would be vaporized by the warm water, used to drive a turbine and then condensed by the cold underlying water to complete the cycle. Power would have to be transmitted through submerged cables or used to produce energy-intensive products on-site that could then be transported.

OTEC is technologically possible and is now in the developmental stage. It is most feasible in areas receiving maximum sunlight as well as having cold, deep water from polar ice cap melt, such as the southeastern coast of the United States. Two key questions that are under investigation are the ultimate costs of producing OTEC power and the potential environmental effects of this process.

See: RENEWABLE ENERGY SOURCES

Off-Road Vehicles (ORV)

Vehicles designed for use on varied terrain as well as, or instead of, on roads. Included in this class are the snowmobile, which has skis; the trail bike, moped and motorbike; the dune buggy; the all-terrain vehicle (ATV), which has tractor treads; and the air-cushion vehicle (ACV), for use on land or water. The more common forms are the motorcycle and four-wheel drive automobile.

Off-road vehicles can provide valuable transportation potential for specialized situations but have caused problems when used for recreation because they come into conflict with many other types of recreation. Excessive noise and serious damage to hiking trails, vegetation, and fish and wildlife are among the problems associated with ORV use.

See: MOPED

Off-Site Improvements

Improvements, such as the widening of adjacent streets, that a developer may be required to make on land located outside of a proposed subdivision or other proposed development as a condition of receiving development approval. The legality of this practice varies with state and situation and may be dependent upon the existence of enabling legislation authorizing payments for specific types of off-site improvements.

Certain types of off-site improvements may also be provided voluntarily by a developer in order to enhance the marketability and attractiveness of his development. He might, for example, decide to improve adjacent roads or provide additional off-site parking, even if not required to do so, if he thought it beneficial to his project.

See: EXACTION; SUBDIVISION REGULATIONS; ZONING

Off-Site Parking

The provision of off-street parking spaces on a site other than the one being developed. Some zoning ordinances permit required off-street parking to be provided on another lot within a specified distance or even in another zoning district in which the principal use would not be permitted. Application of this concept allows the developer some creativity in the provision of parking spaces.

Permission to provide parking off the site also encourages participation by a developer in the development of public parking lots or structures where the developer provides his requisite number of spaces as part of the total structure and bears the cost of that portion of the development.

See: OFF-STREET PARKING

Off-Street Loading

Berths at which trucks may receive and deposit cargo without disrupting the flow of traffic. Most modern zoning ordinances contain minimum off-street loading requirements for all land uses likely to need these facilities, such as industrial and commercial uses, hotels, schools and hospitals, and public buildings. The zoning ordinance will usually specify, by land use type, the dimensions required of each berth, a gross floor area at which a first loading berth is required and a gross floor area at which a second and subsequent berths must be provided. Absent such requirements, loading and unloading of cargo can significantly interfere with traffic flow and give rise to other effects incompatible with surrounding land uses.

In older downtown areas, developed before the advent of loading requirements, there is often insufficient land available to provide adequate off-street loading areas. When this situation exists, it is desirable to control and regulate on-street loading through practices such as designated loading zones, time limits and the use of off-peak hours during which loading and unloading can take place.

See: OFF-STREET PARKING; TRUCK TERMINALS; ZONING

Off-Street Parking

Parking spaces provided in parking lots, parking structures and private driveways. Zoning ordinances typically require that off-street parking spaces be made available for certain types of land uses; requirements may vary by zoning district. The minimum number of off-street parking spaces required within a development is often made proportional to some factor (e.g., square footage, number of dwelling units) that will determine the intensity of use of the development. Placement on the site, or within a building, may also be specified in a zoning ordinance or the subdivision regulations. In addition, the location of spaces may be subject to review by the planning board or the building inspector.

Demand for parking varies according to the nature of the land use, the availability of public transportation, income levels and public policy on the availability of on-street and off-street public parking spaces. Provision of sufficient off-street parking space is often an inducement to rental or sale of a development.

See: OFF-STREET PARKING REQUIREMENTS; PARKING LOT DESIGN; PARKING RATIO

Off-Street Parking Requirements

Zoning ordinance requirements that relate to the provision of off-street parking spaces in conjunction with land use development. The specific requirements for each zoning district and for most types of land use are generally shown in the schedule of zoning district regulations, if one is provided, or the text of the zoning ordinance. Shown below are examples of the wide range of parking requirements found in different zoning ordinances. Requirements can vary markedly within and between communities, based upon the availability of public transit and the likelihood that it will be used.

Where units other than area (i.e., other than square feet or square meters) are used in the following table, a multiplier is included in the ratio for other persons who are likely to use the facility.

See: OFF-STREET PARKING; PARKING RATIO

Off-Street Parking Requirements

Land use	Unit	Number of required parking spaces
		(range found in selected zoning ordinances)
Residential		
Single-family	Dwelling unit	1–3
Multifamily	Dwelling unit	0.5–3
Retail	1,000 sq. ft. (92.9 sq. m) of gross floor area	1.5–6
Shopping center	1,000 sq. ft. (92.9 sq. m) of gross floor area	1.5–8
Office	1,000 sq. ft. (92.9 sq. m) of gross floor area	2–10
Industrial	Employee	0.33–1
Theater	Seat	0.08–0.5
Restaurant	Seats and employees	0.2–0.5/seat + 0.2–0.5/employee
Hotel, motel	Rooms and employees	0.5/guest room +0.5/employee– 1/guest room +1/employee
	+ 1,000 sq. ft. (92.9 sq. m) of public space	1.5–10
Hospital	Bed	0.25–3.4
Church	Seat	0.1–0.5
College, university	Students and Staff	0.15–0.95/ student + 0.5–0.9/staff member

Office Building Location

The location of an office building is determined by a number of factors. The availability of a suitable labor force, transportation, tax levels, wage rates and utility rates all play a role in the decision-making process. Traditionally, however, the need to be near financial institutions, law firms and certain ancillary services, such as printers, restaurants and hotels, played a key role in determining the location of an office building and often resulted in the clustering of office buildings within the central business district. The need for certain related businesses to be near each other and the importance of personal communication reinforced these locational patterns.

In recent years more office buildings are being con-

structed in suburban locations, often in large, campuslike settings. The growing attractiveness of suburban locations is attributable to the shift of the white-collar population to the suburbs; the improvements in telecommunications, reducing the need for personal contact; the desire for large, sprawling complexes; and the relatively low cost of land. For office buildings located in the suburbs, highway access and proximity to an airport are important considerations in determining location, while an adequate labor force and a sufficient supply of affordable housing for clerical and lower-level staff must be readily available.

See: CENTRAL BUSINESS DISTRICT (CBD); HOUSING LOCATION; INDUSTRIAL PLANT LOCATION; OFFICE DEVELOPMENT

Office Development

The construction of office buildings as real estate ventures or to house operations of sponsoring companies. Office development takes several forms: high-density, high-quality construction for central business and commercial district locations; low-density, high-quality construction for suburban office park locations; and lower-quality construction for smaller-scale real estate purposes in lower-rent urban commercial areas, strip commercial areas and neighborhood business areas.

High-quality office buildings with architectural interest have strong impacts on surrounding areas, generally setting a pattern for social dynamics at the street level in urban areas. These types of buildings, often the work of well-known architects, can also help to suggest a design pattern that the area should follow. Because of these abilities, zoning ordinances frequently require or award innovative street-level design that encourages public use, as well as designs that help to preserve open space in suburban areas.

In older urban areas adaptive use of older buildings for office development has been found both profitable and attractive. Development of office condominiums, in which space is owned rather than rented, is another new trend in office development.

See: ADAPTIVE USE; CAMPUS OFFICE PARK; CONFERENCE CENTER; CORPORATE TRAINING CENTER; EXECUTIVE HEADQUARTERS; INCENTIVE ZONING; OFFICE BUILDING LOCATION

Office of Community Services (OCS)

An operating agency within the Department of Health and Human Services that is responsible for administration of the Community Services block grant and discretionary grant programs authorized by the Omnibus Reconciliation Act of 1981 (PL 97-35). Functions, such as the Community Action Program, formerly administered by the Community Services Administration (which has been abolished) are being closed out by the OCS.

The Division of Block Grants administers a program intended to ameliorate causes of poverty in communities and Indian tribes. Block grants are provided to localities on a formula basis for programs such as those that assist the poor in securing meaningful employment, education and housing, or achieving self-sufficiency. The Division of Discretionary Grants administers grants, loans, contracts or jointly financed cooperative arrangements for a variety of programs. Funding is available for ongoing programs that assist private, locally initiated community development programs in obtaining employment and business development opportunities for persons of low income, and operating programs for seasonal and farm workers and low-income youth. The division also administers Rural Development Loan Fund loans and guarantees, and technical assistance and training programs in rural housing and community facility development.

See: COMMUNITY ACTION PROGRAM (CAP); COMMUNITY SERVICES BLOCK GRANT; DEPARTMENT OF HEALTH AND HUMAN SERVICES (HHS); FARMERS HOME ADMINISTRATION (FmHA)

Office of Human Development Services (HDS)

A federal agency within the Department of Health and Human Services (HHS) that administers human services programs for a variety of population groups via several operating agencies with specialized clientele.

The Administration on Aging (AOA) is the principal agency designated to carry out provisions of the Older Americans Act of 1965. The chief policymaking body on aging within HHS, it develops programs for the aged, conducts training programs and promotes community-based systems of comprehensive social services for the elderly.

The Administration for Children, Youth and Families (ACYF) administers programs related to quality of life improvement for this population, such as services that promote sound child development and day care.

The Administration for Native Americans (ANA) has responsibility for developing HHS policy on the social and economic development of Native Americans and administers a grant program to provide funding for a wide range of projects.

The Administration on Developmental Disabilities (ADD) administers grant programs related to the removal of physical, mental, social and environmental barriers encountered by the disabled. The grant program also funds development of comprehensive state plans for treatment and services for the developmentally disabled and administration of interdisciplinary programs that benefit this population. ADD has primary responsibility for formulating HHS policy on matters affecting the disabled.

See: DEPARTMENT OF HEALTH AND HUMAN SERVICES (HHS)

Official Map

A document that indicates the location of future streets, highways or public facilities—such as parks, drainage systems or reservoirs—along with existing streets and facilities. It is adopted by a municipal legislature, pursuant to state enabling legislation, and is intended to inform the public of specific future government acquisition so that those areas that are not already developed remain in that state until government acquisition can be effected. Generally, building permits are not issued for structures on those areas designated for future improvement, such as the bed of a mapped street. The official map is usually coordinated with a capital improvement program for project financing. In addition, the official map is intended to serve as a guide in the design of subdivisions, so that streets and open space may be properly located and subdivision regulations may be properly administered.

Development of an official map requires careful and precise mapping and property delineation best attained with coordination between municipal departments. Sometimes confused with the zoning map or the comprehensive plan, it may be differentiated from either of those documents. Unlike the zoning map, it does not assign zoning categories or regulations to property; it is also not a general representation of long-term community development goals and objectives, as is the comprehensive plan, but functions in a shorter time range and addresses only specific public facilities.

See: LAND USE CONTROLS; MAPPED STREET; PAPER STREET

Offshore Airports

With increased air traffic, many airports are reaching their capacities and have no land on which to expand. Offshore sites, in some cases, appear to represent a cost-effective alternative to a new land-based site as well as a solution to the problem of noise impact. The major difficulties of using offshore sites are lack of access to the airport, high cost, environmental damage to the water body and frequency of fog.

Several methods of construction have been considered: landfill, which can provide an extension to an existing airport; dikes and polders, which can be used to create an offshore island on land below sea level; piles or caissons, which can provide a bridge structure that supports the airport; and floating islands.

Because the cost of offshore development is so high, it has been proposed that other uses that can take advantage of the offshore environment be induced to locate there and share in the cost. Among the kinds of development that have been suggested are water desalination plants, refineries and tank farms, power plants and cruise ship ports.

Offshore Drilling

The use of sophisticated mobile drilling platforms for the extraction of oil and gas from beneath the sea. Despite the expense, dangers and environmental risks of offshore drilling, offshore exploration for petroleum and gas has increased rapidly because of rising fuel prices and demand for fuel. The first offshore well was drilled off the Louisiana coast in 1945. Since that time numerous sites throughout the world have been explored for their potential, including the three coasts of the continental United States, portions of coastal Alaska, the North Sea, the English Channel and the Southeast Asian seas.

New proposals for offshore drilling often generate considerable controversy. One concern is the effect that spilled or escaping oil can have upon the marine ecosystem as well as on the coastal beaches, affecting communities both aesthetically and economically. Some of the most promising areas for offshore oil are also located amid centers of intense commercial fishing activity, such as Kachemak Bay in Alaska or George's Bank off the coast of Massachusetts. Another potential area of conflict is the effect on a community of absorbing all of the rapid development and the necessary facilities required onshore, such as refineries or distribution and storage centers, when an offshore strike is made.

See: COASTAL ZONE MANAGEMENT IMPROVEMENT ACT OF 1980; FOSSIL FUELS; GROWTH MANAGEMENT; OIL POLLUTION; OUTER CONTINENTAL SHELF (OCS)

Oil Pollution

Pollution of coastal waters, coastlines, beaches and land areas by oil that is either massively spilled or gradually leaked. Because of the increasing demand for oil and the long distances that oil is transported, oil pollution is a persistent problem.

Major oil spills may occur because of oil well blowouts, tanker collisions or accidents, or pipeline ruptures. As an example, on August 6, 1983 the Spanish tanker *Castillo de Bellver,* carrying 1.7 million barrels of oil, caught fire and split in two near the southern tip of Africa. The worst major oil well blowout took place in the Gulf of Mexico in June 1979, resulting in the spillage of 3 million barrels over a seven-month time span. Oil well spills of even greater potential damage are currently taking place in the Persian Gulf as a result of Iranian wells that have been damaged during the course of the multiyear war with Iraq. Multiple oil well blowouts have occurred in various offshore fields, making the spills difficult to contain and clean up.

Although far less dramatic, the many smaller discharges of oil that occur daily may have a greater long-term effect on the environment. As oil is drilled and transported, it is continually leaked on both land and sea. This occurs when the oil is transferred—e.g., from terminal to tanker or from refinery to pipeline; it may also occur when oil is discharged as a tanker cleans its tanks, pumps its bilge or deballasts. Deballasting and tank washing account for a larger volume of oil pollution than do oil spills. In addition, there are other smaller sources of pollution, such as gasoline stations washing their premises.

Among the short-term effects of oil pollution are massive bird kills, kills or pollution of shellfish, and the economic and social costs of ruined coastal resort areas and coastal land. The long-term effects of oil pollution on the environment are still unknown.

Oil pollution can be combatted by improved cleanup procedures and by the prevention and containment of oil spills and leakage. Methods such as mechanical removal,

absorbents, dispersants and burning of the oil have had varying degrees of success. Most crucial is the containment of the spill when it first begins. Waters where oil spills are thought likely are constantly monitored so that the spills may be rapidly contained.

Accidental dispersement of oil may be lessened by new standards for international oil tankers adopted at the International Conference on Tanker Safety and Pollution Prevention held in 1978. These standards require segregated ballast (which keeps oil separate from ballast water) and crude oil washing (which reduces oil discharges that occur when cargo tanks are washed) in all new crude tankers over 20,000 deadweight tons. Other standards agreed upon are aimed at reducing the likehood of collision.

See: CLEAN WATER ACT OF 1977; OFFSHORE DRILLING; WATER QUALITY IMPROVEMENT ACT OF 1970

Old Law Tenement

Those tenements built in New York City under the New York Tenement House Law of 1879, which amended an 1867 law. This law sought to improve tenement living conditions by prohibiting land coverage greater than 65 percent of a lot, unless it was a corner lot. It provided for dumbbell type buildings, in which windows opened onto narrow air shafts. Each room was required to have a 12-square foot (1.1-square meter) window, and every occupant was provided with a minimum of 600 cubic feet (17 cubic meters) of air space. In addition, each floor was required to have two toilets that could be reached from the building's hallway.

See: NEW LAW TENEMENT

Older Americans Act of 1965

This act (PL 89-73), as amended, provides federal aid to community programs serving senior citizens. Grants are given to commissions on aging of states and localities (or other acceptable agencies) for a range of activities, including nutrition programs, senior volunteer or community service employment programs, and multipurpose senior center operation. Also funded are in-home services; employment and antidiscrimination programs; legal services; and community services, such as transportation, outreach and referral. Grants range from 50 percent to 90 percent of program cost, depending upon type.

Funds are distributed to states on a formula basis by the Office of Human Development Services (HDS) and are given to social service agencies operating community-based programs under state supervision. To be eligible, localities must have an acceptable community plan for services for the aging that coordinates volunteer, private and local government efforts and is approved as consistent with the state plan. This, in turn, must be approved by the federal Administration on Aging, an agency within HDS. Funds for development of plans are provided on a 75 percent federal matching basis.

See: HOUSING FOR THE ELDERLY; OFFICE OF HUMAN DEVELOPMENT SERVICES (HDS); PLANNING FOR THE ELDERLY

Oligotrophic Lake

A lake characterized by a low level of nutrients and large amounts of dissolved oxygen in its deeper waters. Oligotrophic lakes, in contrast to eutrophic lakes, are generally deep, have clear cold water, and have scant plant or algal growth. Fish species commonly found in oligotrophic lakes are such valuable coldwater species as lake trout, in contrast to the rough fish, such as sunfish and perch, found in eutrophic lakes.

See: EUTROPHICATION

Olmsted, Frederick Law (1822–1903)

Noted for the many public parks of outstanding quality that he designed, Olmsted is considered the "father of landscape architecture" and was responsible for the development of the concept to replace the older and narrower discipline of landscape gardening.

He and Calvert Vaux, a young British architect, won the opportunity to design New York City's Central Park in a major competition held in 1857. Olmsted was made architect-in-chief of this early attempt to combine art with nature in a large-scale public park. Major innovations in Central Park's design included the concept of grade separation and the use of the overpass, now standard techniques.

As a result of the attention that Central Park received, Olmsted was commissioned to develop many of the other major parks of that era in the United States. Olmsted-designed parks include Riverside and Morningside parks in Manhattan; Prospect Park in Brooklyn; Washington and Jackson parks in Chicago; Mount Royal Park in Montreal; the Back Bay Fens of Boston; Belle Isle Park in Detroit; and Golden Gate Park in San Francisco. Other major Olmsted projects were the design of the grounds at the Capitol in Washington, D.C. and Stanford University at Palo Alto, California.

Olmsted was the first commissioner of Yosemite National Park and designed plans that led to New York state's decision to preserve the scenic setting of the Niagara Falls. In one of his last projects, Olmsted was selected to be in charge of landscape design at the World's Columbian Exposition in Chicago in 1893, an event that greatly influenced the direction of planning in the United States.

Olmsted's son, Frederick Law Olmsted Jr., was involved in many planning projects, including the design for Forest Hills Gardens (an early garden suburb in New York City), and helped to found the American City Planning Institute.

See: CENTRAL PARK; LANDSCAPE ARCHITECTURE; WORLD'S COLUMBIAN EXPOSITION

1 Percent for Art Law

State and municipal requirements that 1 percent of the budget for a new public building be allocated for public art, to be placed around or within the development. Many government and private projects have adopted this figure as a standard even without legislative action.

See: PUBLIC ART

Open Burning

Fires that are allowed to burn at municipal dumps in order to reduce waste volumes. As municipalities close dumps (no longer considered an acceptable means of waste disposal) or replace them with upgraded sanitary landfill operations, they must first extinguish these fires. This difficult task is often accomplished through excavation and transfer of the burning waste into thinner layers.

See: DUMP; SANITARY LANDFILL

Open Space

Land that is either undeveloped or is relatively free of buildings and other structures. Open space is usually thought of as public parks and playgrounds; in its broadest definition, however, it includes all land that acts as a contrast to the man-made environment. Generally included in the broader definition of open space are relatively permanent land uses, such as reservoir lands; utility rights-of-way; cemeteries; institutional and government-owned land developed at a very low density; and private golf, tennis and beach clubs. Other relatively undeveloped areas—such as estates, farmland and privately owned land held for speculative purposes—may also be categorized as open space for some purposes, particularly if they are expected to remain undeveloped for an extended period of time. In densely developed areas office parks and low-density suburban housing may sometimes be included in open-space calculations because of the contrast they provide and because the undeveloped areas around the buildings generally cannot be further developed.

Planners view open space as a positive attribute, not merely the absence of development. Open space performs a number of valuable functions in both urban and less intensively developed areas. In urban areas it provides additional light and air and offers welcome visual relief as well as opportunities for recreation. In suburban and rural areas, it preserves ecologically important natural environments, helps to shape urban form and limit urban growth, and acts as a land bank for future development.

See: LINEAR OPEN SPACE; OPEN-SPACE PLAN; OPEN-SPACE PLANNING; OPEN-SPACE PRESERVATION; OPEN-SPACE RATIO

Open-Space Plan

A guide to the amount, location and quality of land intended to be preserved in an undeveloped or relatively undeveloped state. Open-space plans, which are often elements of the municipal comprehensive plan, may be combined with the parks and recreation element or be developed as an independent element.

The focus of an open-space plan differs somewhat from a parks and recreation plan in its broader examinations of the many purposes and components of open space, of which recreation and parkland are but one part. Other functions of open space include the shaping of urban form through the use of devices such as greenbelts and the protection of important environmental resources for reasons such as aesthetics, public safety, ecology and economic value. Open space also serves to preserve land for future development and for land uses requiring large open land areas, such as airports.

As a result of the far-ranging consequences of adequate amounts of appropriately located open space, open-space plans often consider such topics as growth management, long-term economic development and protection of the public from natural disasters, such as flooding, that may be averted by appropriate management of open space.

See: COMPREHENSIVE PLAN; OPEN SPACE; OPEN-SPACE PLANNING; PARKS AND RECREATION PLAN

Open-Space Planning

The delineation of open-space areas for a municipality or other study area as an element of comprehensive planning. Depending upon the range of uses that are envisioned for open space, open-space planning may consist of studies on parks and recreation, environmental protection, open-space preservation or the use of open space as a device for shaping urban form.

In past years open-space planning consisted largely of parkland acquisition, often pursued in relation to population. While parkland is still being acquired, the emphasis is now on preserving ecologically important or scenic sites, as well as those sites in strategic locations that are threatened with development.

Another important element of open-space planning is the development of planning and legal tools that can help to assure the continuation of open-space uses. Study of new applications for land use controls, conservation and scenic easements, and other land-conserving development tools, such as cluster development and transfer of development rights, has yielded some of the most effective methods of land conservation. Development of public relations that emphasizes community interest in stewardship may also be effective.

See: FARMLAND PROTECTION; OPEN SPACE; OPEN-SPACE PLAN; OPEN-SPACE PRESERVATION; OPEN-SPACE RATIO; RECREATION PLANNING

Open-Space Preservation

The retention and maintenance of land in an open condition. Open space is preserved by a variety of voluntary and/or government-imposed methods. A property owner may retain his land as open space or contribute all of his land, or an interest in it, to a government or charity. If permitted by the municipality, he may build a cluster development in which specific land areas are preserved or develop his land using a conventional pattern, reserving a portion of the land for donation to the municipality as

open space. Alternatively, the landowner is often permitted to pay a fee to enable land acquisition elsewhere. A property owner can also transfer development rights to another property or sell them if a municipal program authorizing this activity is in effect.

Governments may offer tax incentives, such as agricultural district designation, for retaining land in an open state. Land use controls are also employed to preserve small quantities of land—e.g., setback, coverage and buffer strip requirements. Floodplain zoning and other controls that protect natural areas, such as hillsides, may also be imposed. Governments may also establish greenbelts and land banks and, where permanent preservation is desired, may purchase land or conservation easements. Large land areas that require preservation for ecological, economic and/or scenic purposes may be officially designated as preservation areas, such as the 5.7-million-acre (2.3-million-hectare) Adirondack Forest Preserve in New York state, and have special controls imposed on development within the areas.

See: CLUSTER DEVELOPMENT; CONSERVATION EASEMENT; FARMLAND PROTECTION; FEE IN LIEU OF DEDICATION; GREENBELT; LAND BANK; NATURE PRESERVE; OPEN SPACE; OPEN-SPACE PLANNING; STEWARDSHIP; TRANSFER OF DEVELOPMENT RIGHTS (TDR)

Open-Space Ratio

1. The ratio of the area of a parcel of land that has no buildings or other specified improvements to the area that is covered by buildings, or the percentage of the total land area that has no buildings. An open-space ratio is a measure of land use intensity that may be prescribed by zoning.

This ratio is used by municipalities to describe the desired amount of space to be preserved for specified areas. Its usefulness as a tool for open-space preservation, however, depends upon whether improvements, such as paved parking areas and tennis courts, are permitted in required open-space areas and the amount of the open-space area that they are permitted to constitute.

2. The number of public park acres per 1,000 population in a municipality. Until the 1970s open-space planning consisted largely of parkland acquisition and development for parks of various classifications. Ratios were established in an attempt to provide sufficient facilities and were adhered to in some jurisdictions, with land acquisition made as the population increased. In recent years municipal finances and increasing private recreation opportunities have caused these ratios to be used largely as guidelines in planning. Ratios of specific types of recreation facilities to population, such as tennis courts per 1,000 people, are also used as guidelines for planning purposes.

See: LAND USE INTENSITY STANDARDS (LUI); LOT COVERAGE; OPEN SPACE; PARK AND OPEN-SPACE CLASSIFICATION

Operating Budget

A plan of expected revenues and expenditures for programs and agency operations that is usually adopted annually for the forthcoming fiscal year. Some operating budgets also include capital expenditures, particularly if the municipality does not adopt an annual capital budget.

See: BUDGET; CAPITAL BUDGET

Option

The right to purchase, sell or lease a specific piece of real property for a stated price and within a given time period. Options are frequently used by land developers in property acquisition and the assemblage of larger parcels. As an example, if a developer were uncertain as to whether he would be able to acquire each of the contiguous parcels he needed for a large project, he might purchase options rather than buy the parcels to lessen the risk of failing to obtain all the land he needed.

Investors also make use of options in speculative ventures. For example, options might be acquired on land that a speculator expects to rise in value within a specific time period, perhaps because he predicts that development of a certain type will occur nearby. If proved right, he exercises the option, purchases the property at the agreed-upon price and then resells it at a potentially large profit. If wrong, he has lost the price of the option, usually a relatively small amount.

Government agencies often obtain rights of first refusal on land they may wish to acquire at a later date for such purposes as parkland. This differs from an option agreement in that the land is not available until the owner decides to sell it. In addition, if the owner receives a legitimate offer from another party, the holder of the right of first refusal must be prepared to match that offer.

See: FIRST REFUSAL

Ordinance

A law, rule or regulation issued by the governing body of a local municipality under legal authority granted by the state. Ordinances are limited to the area over which the local governing body has jurisdiction and govern matters not already covered by state or federal law. Commonly adopted ordinances concern zoning and public safety. The term is also used to describe certain state and federal enactments.

Ordinance of 1785

Ordinance adopted by the Continental Congress of the United States to facilitate the survey and sale of lands in the public domain so that the national debt could be lessened. It established a system that imposed a gridiron pattern upon most land west of the Appalachians and provided that land was to be sold for at least $1.00 per acre. Certain sections were also reserved for public schools, national government use and veterans of the Revolutionary War.

This ordinance had a significant impact upon land settlement patterns in the United States as well as upon early city planning practice. The gridiron pattern it imposed upon much of the United States still remains, and it encouraged the development of gridiron street systems, using section lines as the logical location for roads in rural areas.

See: GRIDIRON PATTERN; TOWNSHIP AND RANGE SURVEY SYSTEM

Origin-Destination (O-D) Study

A transportation planning study used to determine predominant travel patterns in a given area. An origin-destination study provides data on the directions that people wish to travel, indications of where people stop between their origin and destination, the type of vehicle or mode of transportation used for travel, the time of day during which they travel and the purpose of the trip. This information is basic to making decisions on the location of new roads or transit routes or the expansion of existing ones, on the location of roadway interchanges or transit stops, and on the geometric design of roadways. Results of O-D studies are used as input to network assignment and modal split studies.

The procedure used to undertake an O-D study is to establish a cordon line around an area and to study trips as they relate to it by sampling techniques.

Data collected are generally displayed on desire-line diagrams or maps, which indicate the volume of riders and drivers who desire to go between various points, regardless of route or mode. (See Fig. 29)

See: CORDON AND SCREENLINE COUNTS; DESIRE LINE; TRAFFIC COUNTS

Osborn, Sir Frederic James (1885–1978)

British author, urban planner and advocate of new town construction. Self-educated, he began his career with a London housing society and in 1912 was appointed to manage a cottage-building society in Letchworth, where he stayed until 1917. During this period he became deeply interested in the concept of the garden city and as a result helped to form a group, the National Garden Cities Committee, along with Ebenezer Howard and others. He wrote *New Towns After the War* (1913) for this group, which advocated the dispersal of the population to new towns surrounded by greenbelts as a remedy for urban ills. In 1919 Osborn was appointed estate manager of Welwyn Garden City, a position he held until 1936. He subsequently held a number of posts in which he helped to further the concept of new towns, including many key positions with the Garden Cities Association, later renamed the Town and Country Planning Association (TCPA). He also served as adviser to the minister of works and buildings and was an officer for the International Federation of Housing and Planning (IFHP). Ultimately, Osborn's continuous efforts in lecturing, writing and otherwise publicizing the benefits of population dispersal and new town construction helped lead to

ORIGIN-DESTINATION (O-D) STUDY

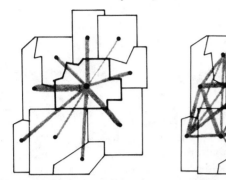
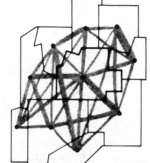

Central Business District-Internal Trips

Internal-Internal Trips

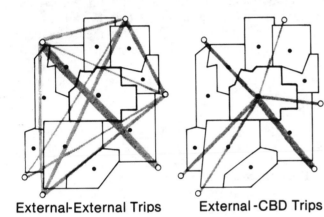

External-External Trips

External-CBD Trips

Fig. 29.   Lines represent traffic volume between nodes but do not necessarily represent routes taken.

the passage of the New Towns Act, 1946. This act has had a lasting effect upon international planning practice and policy.

Osborn wrote many other articles and books in which he put forth his views on planning. He was knighted in 1956 and received the silver medal of the American Society of Planning Officials in 1960 and the gold medal of the Royal Town Planning Institute in 1963.

See: HOWARD, SIR EBENEZER; LETCHWORTH, ENGLAND; NEW TOWNS ACT, 1946; TOWN AND COUNTRY PLANNING ASSOCIATION (TCPA); WELWYN GARDEN CITY, ENGLAND

Out-Migration

The process of moving from a particular defined geographic area to an address outside that area. If the new address is outside of national borders, the move may be distinguished from out-migration and called emigration.

See: DEMOGRAPHY; IN-MIGRATION; NET MIGRATION

Outdoor Lighting

Illumination of outdoor areas to provide nighttime visibility and security. Lighting fixtures should be provided in areas that are heavily used by pedestrians and vehicles and in areas that would otherwise be dangerous, such as stairways. Good lighting is also necessary to deter crime and to provide a sense of security.

Lighting fixture location depends upon the area to be illuminated and the intensity and distribution of light provided by the fixtures; fixture types and heights can generally be selected to suit particular requirements. Recommended lighting levels for various locations are published by the Illuminating Engineering Society and by various government agencies. In general, overhead lighting provides better economy and light distribution than low-level lamps.

See: DEFENSIBLE SPACE; OUTDOOR LIGHTING TYPES

Outdoor Lighting Types

Outdoor lighting fixtures are available for use at varying heights, in numerous styles and with a variety of lamp types for reasons of economy of electricity, variation in wattage and life span, and aesthetics.

High-intensity types—such as mercury vapor, metal halide and high-pressure sodium—are generally used on tall posts to light extended areas, such as large recreational, commercial and industrial areas, highways and parking areas; while incandescent and fluorescent lamps are frequently used for lower-intensity mall and walkway lighting. Post heights vary from 2 to 3 feet (0.6 to 0.9 meters), for use along walkways, to 10 to 15 feet (3.1 to 4.6 meters), common to shopping malls. Most roadway lights are mounted 30 to 50 feet (9 to 15 meters) above the road, while major developments—e.g., a sports complex—might use 100-foot (31-meter) posts to illuminate large parking lots. Underground or ground-level flood or spotlights are used to highlight building facades, sculptures, fountains and trees for visual interest.

Fixture placement should permit light patterns to overlap at a height of 7 feet (2.1 meters) to permit people to be illuminated. Where low walkway lighting is provided, additional peripheral illumination should sufficently expose surrounding areas.

See: OUTDOOR LIGHTING

Outdoor Recreation

Leisure-time activities that take place outside of enclosed structures. Today the distinction between indoor and outdoor facilities has been blurred, as many previously outdoor activities (e.g., tennis) are now available indoors, and some bubble structures even allow a facility to go from indoors to outdoors with the seasons.

Most of the traditional recreation facilities provided by park departments have been for outdoor recreation, stemming from the 19th-century public park movement, which suggested the need for areas where people could find fresh air in densely developed cities. Recreation planning, until the 1960s, was almost totally involved with the provision of outdoor recreation facilities.

See: RECREATION FACILITIES

Outdoor Seating

Benches, parapets, retaining walls, staircases and movable chairs that are provided to permit public seating in outdoor areas. Outdoor seating is essentially a recreational facility provided to permit people to rest and observe their surroundings and other people.

Typically, permanently mounted benches are provided in parks of all sizes and in shopping areas with sufficient space. Modern office building developments frequently provide plazas where fountains, sculptures, steps and landscaped spaces are used as seating in good weather. Movable chairs are available in some public parks, notably in London, and in a few areas adjacent to public institutions, providing the opportunity to locate in a comfortable spot. Most indoor shopping malls also provide public seating in central areas.

Provision of outdoor seating is often directly related to the amount of use that a park or other facility will receive. It is also conducive to drawing people to common areas in residential settings for socialization purposes and to deterring criminal activity. In addition, the locations and arrangements of benches may dictate how, and how often, they are used.

See: DEFENSIBLE SPACE; PEDESTRIAN IMPROVEMENTS; PERSONAL SPACE

Outer Continental Shelf (OCS)

An offshore area rich in oil, gas and other mineral resources that was defined in the Outer Continental Shelf Lands Act of 1953 as that land lying between the outer edge of each coastal state's boundary, which ranged from 3 to 10.5 miles (4.8 to 16.9 kilometers) offshore, and the edge of the continental shelf, sometimes as far as 150 miles (241.5 kilometers) from shore. The federal government retained control of the mineral rights to that land and established a leasing system for oil and gas drilling based upon competitive bidding. It also relinquished to the states, at that time, the mineral rights of the land, known as the submerged land, lying between the low-tide mark and the state boundary.

The first major revision of that legislation occurred when the Outer Continental Shelf Land Act Amendments of 1978 were passed. The revision required a comprehensive five-year proposed leasing schedule and gave the states, concerned about their resort and fishing industries, greater input into federal leasing decisions.

It has been estimated that 60 percent of the undiscovered gas and oil of the United States may lie in the OCS. However, a number of the leases let through the 1970s in areas thought promising, such as the Gulf of Alaska, proved disappointing, suggesting a possible error in the magnitude of the earlier predictions. In an effort to increase the production of gas and oil, leases on many more acres of land will be offered in the future. Because of water depth and weather conditions that are often severe, only new technology makes exploration in some of these areas possible.

See: BUREAU OF LAND MANAGEMENT (BLM); OFFSHORE DRILLING; OIL POLLUTION

Outfall

A structure designed to conduct treated or untreated wastewater or other water discharges to a specific location in a receiving water body. One type of outfall uses an interceptor-sized pipe located in a seawall along the shore, from which effluent is allowed to enter the stream below the low-water level. In a second kind of outfall, an extended pipe is carried into deep water, and finger-shaped diffusers are used to disperse effluent or sludge from a treatment plant. Diffusers are useful in helping to dilute effluent, since they spread its release over an extended area, where it can mix with the receiving waters.

Since many municipalities have drinking water intakes downstream from sewage plant outfalls, the siting of outfalls requires careful analysis and study. Their location can also have a significant effect on recreation areas and fisheries.

See: EFFLUENT; RECEIVING WATERS; SEWAGE TREATMENT; SLUDGE DISPOSAL

Outreach

A social planning tool in which a concentrated effort is made to identify various needs of a particular population and to find a means of meeting those needs through delivery of financial, health, housing, social or other types of services. Frequently the target group of an outreach project, which is usually operated at a community level, is a disadvantaged, homebound or otherwise isolated segment of society that is unaware of the existence of programs designed to assist them or unable to take advantage of various government or private programs.

As a means of locating these individuals, several approaches are used, including direct contact (in person or by phone); advertising in various media, such as newspapers or radio; and sponsorship of community activities, such as health or nutrition fairs, group discussions or lectures. Following contact and the establishment of a relationship with clients in one outreach program, clients' needs in other areas can often be determined and other appropriate outreach assistance obtained.

Federal funding, although limited, has most often been available for outreach activities in the areas of nutrition and health programs for the elderly and housing for the disadvantaged.

See: SOCIAL SERVICES PLANNING

Overall Economic Development Program (OEDP)

An assessment of a community's economic needs and the actions necessary to stimulate economic development. An OEDP was, at one time, a requirement for financial assistance from Economic Development Administration (EDA) programs as authorized by the Public Works and Economic Development Act of 1965. Agencies applying for funds are still encouraged to prepare OEDPs.

In addition to providing a historic overview and an assessment of past development efforts, an OEDP analyzes current economic development activities conducted by every agency and organization, designates economically distressed areas and states the overall economic development strategy for these areas. Economic needs, development potentials and constraints, and a realistic program for implementation are also included in an OEDP, which should be updated and revised frequently.

The OEDP was to be supplemented by the Comprehensive Economic Development Strategy (CEDS) after 1978, but this course was never imposed because of sharp cutbacks in EDA funding in 1981. The more sophisticated economic development agencies, however, generally produce both an OEDP and a CEDS as the basis for investment of municipal funds in economic development projects.

See: COMPREHENSIVE ECONOMIC DEVELOPMENT STRATEGY (CEDS); ECONOMIC DEVELOPMENT ADMINISTRATION (EDA)

Overcrowding

A condition in which people have an inadequate amount of living space, usually measured by the number of people per room residing in a dwelling unit. The Bureau of the Census considers more than 1.01 persons per room to represent an overcrowded housing unit and 1.51 persons per room or more to be a severely overcrowded housing unit.

Overcrowding in the United States has been steadily declining because of such factors as smaller family size, smaller size of households and migration to the suburbs. Young families who have not reached complete size and nonwhite households are among the groups most likely to be living in overcrowded housing units. Crowding is also more common in renter- than owner-occupied units, which is partially a factor of the smaller size of rental units. A major motivational consideration in household moves, overcrowding reduces privacy for family members and adds stress to the household structure. The extent to which living conditions are perceived to be crowded, however, varies considerably among countries and cultures.

See: HOUSING STANDARDS; PERSONAL SPACE; SUBSTANDARD HOUSING

Overlay District

An additional level of zoning requirements that is superimposed upon existing zoning in specified areas shown on the zoning map. Any existing or new development within the overlay district must then comply with the requirements of the underlying zone as well as with the generally more restrictive requirements of the overlay zone.

Overlay zones are most commonly used when an area requires special protection or has a special problem. Ex-

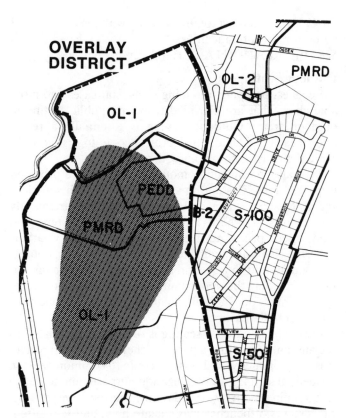

Fig. 30. Part of a zoning map indicating the locations where certain overlay regulations are in effect in addition to the regulations of the underlying zoning districts.

amples of situations in which overlay zones might be used include areas of special scenic or historic interest or areas in which physical conditions, such as steep hillsides or floodplains, dictate special care. (See Fig. 30)
See: ZONING; ZONING DISTRICT

Oxidation Pond

A relatively shallow earthen basin generally used in secondary sewage treatment to permit stabilization of primary effluent. Oxidation ponds hold settled effluent for a period of days to permit algae to form and feed on carbon dioxide and other waste products produced by the decomposition of organic matter. Also called stabilization ponds, they are used extensively by small communities because of low construction and operating costs and their ability to remove from 40 percent to 70 percent of the biochemical oxygen demand (BOD). They are also frequently used to treat industrial sewage and mixtures of industrial and domestic sewage.

A similar method, called an oxidation ditch, invented in the Netherlands in the 1950s, combines the appearance of the oxidation pond with the principles of the activated sludge process by continuously aerating raw or treated wastewater. This process can remove 90 percent to 97 percent of the BOD.
See: BIOCHEMICAL OXYGEN DEMAND (BOD); OXIDATION PROCESSES; SEDIMENTATION TANK; SEWAGE TREATMENT

Oxidation Processes

Aerobic sewage treatment processes that encourage the biological growth of organisms in wastewater. This aids in removing suspended or colloidal solids or those in solution, so that the organic content of wastewater is reduced. Oxidation processes work by providing a supply of oxygen to settled wastewater, thereby creating aerobic conditions and exposing the wastewater to a population of microorganisms that feed on the organic matter in the sewage. This encourages growth of the microorganisms, which enables their separation from the remaining effluent.

Oxidation processes are generally used during secondary sewage treatment, but they may also be employed as primary or tertiary processes, depending upon the other operations performed by the treatment plant. The three types of oxidation processes are filtration, aeration (including the activated sludge process) and the use of oxidation ponds.

See: ACTIVATED SLUDGE PROCESS; AERATION; FILTRATION; OXIDATION POND; SETTLING TANK; SEWAGE TREATMENT

P

Package Treatment Plant

A prefabricated sewage treatment plant intended for use by a residential development or a small town without industrial sewage. Delivered to the site in one or more units and readily assembled, package plants are generally designed to provide secondary treatment of wastes and, with proper supervision, are as effective as custom-built plants.

Package treatment plants may also be used to supplement treatment in a large sewerage system by pretreating some of the wastes, as does the plant in Golden Gate Park in San Francisco, or they may be used by a municipality to treat septage removed from septic tanks. Use for treatment of industrial sewage containing primarily organic substances, such as food wastes, may also be possible.

See: SEPTIC SYSTEM; SEWAGE TREATMENT

Packaging

The process of securing the necessary commitments and approvals required before development can begin. Financing, site selection, zoning approval, obtaining sewer connections and road access, and generating public support are all part of the packaging process.

Paper Street

A street that appears on the official map of a community but has never been built. Most state enabling acts do not allow building permits to be issued until the street has been improved according to municipal requirements.

See: MAPPED STREET; OFFICIAL MAP

Parapet

1. A low wall or similar barrier, usually supported only at its base, designed to protect the edge of a roof, bridge, staircase or other structure.

2. That part of a wall entirely above the roof of a building.

See: GUARDRAIL

Paratransit

A general term for the local public transportation modes that provide service using conventional transit vehicles but on innovative operation plans, in contrast to fixed-route and fixed-schedule mass transit. Included in this term are jitney services, demand-responsive services and ridepooling. Paratransit services are being instituted both to supplement conventional modes and to provide public transportation in low-density areas where conventional modes are not cost-effective.

Jitneys (small buses or vans) travel on regular routes and may have a regular schedule or wait to be filled at designated locations, thereby providing very frequent service but at low capital cost. Demand-responsive service includes taxicabs and dial-a-ride operations. Ridepooling includes car, van and buspooling.

See: DEMAND-RESPONSIVE TRANSPORTATION (DRT); DIAL-A-RIDE; RIDEPOOLING

Park and Open-Space Classification

A system of categorizing parks and public lands based upon their size, use and service area. Classification systems usually include the following park and open-space categories: neighborhood, community, citywide and regional. Home-oriented areas, such as backyards, are also included in some classification systems.

Open-space ratios have traditionally been used to establish numbers of parks and park acreage, while the type of facilities placed within a particular park relates to its location within a community—e.g., playgrounds are usually placed in a neighborhood park or picnic grounds in a regional park. Park size is usually a function of the area a park is intended to serve, with the largest parks providing recreation for the largest geographic areas.

See: CITYWIDE PARK; COMMUNITY PARK; NATIONAL PARK SYSTEM; NEIGHBORHOOD PARK; OPEN-SPACE PLANNING; OPEN-SPACE RATIO; PLAYGROUND; RECREATION PLANNING; REGIONAL PARK; STATE PARK

Park-and-Ride Facilities

Also known as intercept parking facilities, these are parking lots or structures, located at rail stations or along bus routes, designed to encourage transfer from the private auto to mass transit for commutation to the city center. Parking lots at suburban commuter railroad stations have been heavily used since the 1950s, which saw the advent of the two-car family. A more recent application of this concept is the provision of park-and-ride lots in fringe areas along freeways leading to the city center. These can provide both express bus service and an opportunity for ridepooling.

Park-and-ride facilities are growing in both number and variety of applications because of observed successes and because demonstration funding has been available from the Urban Mass Transportation Administration (UMTA). Federal involvement began in 1968 with the National Highway Urban Fringe Parking Program.
See: AUTO DISINCENTIVES; RIDEPOOLING

Parking Lot

An area for off-street parking provided at ground level. It is the most common form of off-street parking that is found in low- and medium-density residential, commercial and industrial development and at airports. In Britain parking lots are called car parks.

Parking lots may be privately owned and operated, publicly owned but privately operated as a concession, or publicly owned and operated.
See: PARKING LOT DESIGN; PARKING STRUCTURE

Parking Lot Design

Parking lots are designed for efficiency in the use of space or efficiency in the ease of parking, but not necessarily both. The decision about which is to be satisfied is based on knowledge of whether predominant parking is long-term (e.g., all day) or short-term (e.g., one-half hour) and whether the lot is to allow self-parking or attendant parking. For example, if predominant parking is short-term self-parking, design should encourage quick in-and-out movement by providing wide parking spaces and aisles for easy maneuvering. A configuration that will allow this will provide fewer parking spaces than one with narrower dimensions.

The following general rules should be adhered to:

1.   Parking lot entrances and exits should be located away from busy pedestrian areas and busy intersections.

2.   Traffic conflict within the lot should be minimized by providing a one-way circulation pattern with left-turning movements (right-turning in Britain), although a two-way pattern will be acceptable where 90-degree parking and wide aisles are provided.

3.   An attempt should be made to maximize the number of parking spaces for a given set of requirements by placing a row of parking spaces around the perimeter of the site, placing aisles and rows of parking parallel to the long dimension of the site and placing a row of parking on each side of the aisle.

4.   Where self-parking is provided, car stalls should be a minimum of 8.5 feet (2.6 meters) wide for long-term parking and 9.0 feet (2.7 meters) wide for short-term parking. Car stalls at supermarkets or other locations where large packages are handled should be 9.5 to 10.0 feet (2.9 to 3.1 meters) in width. A stall length of 18.5 feet (5.6 meters) is considered sufficient for most American cars. Stalls with smaller dimensions for compact cars may be provided. Where attendant parking is provided, stalls can be as narrow as 8.0 feet (2.4 meters).

5.   Aisle widths will depend on the angle of parking and the width of the car stalls to be provided. Parking at 90 degrees requires the widest aisles, 25 to 28 feet (7.6 to 8.5 meters) but will permit placement of the greatest number of spaces. Parking at a 45-degree angle requires only 11- to 13-foot (3.4- to 4.0-meter) aisles but provides the fewest parking spaces. Parking at a 75-degree angle requires 22- to 25-foot (6.7- to 7.6-meter) aisles and at 60 degrees, 15- to 18-foot (4.6- to 5.5-meter) aisles. As the parking angle decreases, the number of parking spaces that can be located on the lot decreases and the ease of access increases.

6.   Parking lot surfaces should be graded to allow for drainage; a 1 percent grade is recommended for asphalt surfaces and a 0.5 percent grade for concrete surfaces. Use of a porous pavement may also be considered.

7.   Lighting should be provided in such a way that it does not disturb adjacent residential areas.

8.   Trees and shrubs should be selected to withstand fumes and pavement heat and should be placed so that they will not be damaged by cars or obstruct sight distance at entrances and exits.
See: COMPACT CAR PARKING; IMPERVIOUS SURFACES; LANDSCAPING

Parking Ratio

The relation of the number of off-street parking spaces to specific land uses, used by planners to determine the number of parking spaces needed to accommodate demand.
See: OFF-STREET PARKING; OFF-STREET PARKING REQUIREMENTS

Parking Structure

A multilevel building that is designed for the purpose of providing parking stalls for automobiles. Parking structures may be single-purpose buildings, used exclusively for parking, or multipurpose—that is, part of another land use or combination of land uses. Where they are located beneath other uses, their use of space is usually less efficient than single-purpose parking structures, since the placement of columns that support the upper floors often interferes with the layout of parking stalls and aisles.

Parking structures vary in the number of floors they have according to the cost and availability of land. The cost of building parking structures varies with the number of floors, the cost of land and the method of construction. Permanent construction is the most costly but appears to have the longest useful life. Prefabricated systems are cheaper but more suitable where parking is a temporary use of the site. Architectural input in the design of the bulk, shape and facades of parking structures may enhance their appearance and their relationship to surrounding development.

See: PARKING LOT

Parking Study

An inventory of existing parking spaces and their use, for the purpose of assessing additional parking needs. Parking studies are undertaken to determine both deficiencies in the total number of spaces and the time span for which parkers use the spaces. This information is used to establish programs that can provide better utilization of existing parking spaces consistent with local requirements and offers a basis for recommendations concerning the need for additional parking facilities.

Elements of a parking study include: (1) an inventory of total parking supply within a delineated area, including parking spaces in adjacent areas if they serve the primary area; (2) analysis of specific problems—e.g., employee parking in shopping center lots that are reserved for shoppers; (3) a study of parking duration and turnover at each of the locations under study. A parking study might also analyze the distances that people are willing to walk from their cars to their destinations; long-term parkers are generally willing to walk farther than short-term parkers.

Parkland Leasing

1. The leasing of public parkland to permit the construction and operation of a publicly desirable facility by private individuals or a club.

By granting a lease for a particular type of facility on a particular site, municipal parks agencies are frequently able to provide an expensive facility—such as a tennis club, swimming pool complex or summer theater—that would not otherwise be possible because of constraints on capital spending. In addition, the municipality may dictate design and operating standards and fee schedules, and will usually obtain a percentage of the facility's gross income that it can use to offset operating costs of other facilities. At the end of the contract period, the municipality will either take possession of the facility or may elect to have the lessee remove it.

2. The granting of leases on public parkland to individuals and corporations for such purposes as mining, grazing and timber production.

See: CONCESSIONAIRE

Parks and Recreation Department

The government department responsible for the administration of park areas and recreation programs and facilities that are within the jurisdiction of that particular unit of government. These functions may also be performed by separate parks departments and recreation departments.

Parks and recreation departments are frequently governed by a citizen board, which sets policy and oversees activities, while a professional director or commissioner directs the staff and departmental operations. Since park facilities are an important part of the municipal plan, the parks department usually participates in open-space planning activities and helps coordinate applications for open-space grants.

See: OPEN-SPACE PLANNING; RECREATION PLANNING

Parks and Recreation Plan

A guide to public policy and private decisions concerning the range, quality and location of parks and recreation facilities and programs, generally prepared jointly by the planning and parks/recreation department. Such a plan, which is usually long-range and policy-oriented, is often an element of the municipal comprehensive plan.

Typically, a parks and recreation plan contains a description of existing conditions; an inventory and analysis of existing facilities, land and programs; and an analysis of current user patterns and degree of user satisfaction. Special problems, such as accommodating the handicapped or large numbers of nonresident users, are also considered. Ultimately, particular needs and deficiencies as well as alternative ways of achieving municipal goals and objectives are articulated. The plan also generally contains a discussion of the means of implementation, including actions that must be taken and financing strategies.

See: COMPREHENSIVE PLAN; OPEN-SPACE PLAN; OPEN-SPACE PLANNING; RECREATION PLANNING

Parkway

An expressway for noncommercial traffic, with full or partial control of access, usually located within a park or in a parklike setting. The Bronx River Parkway in Westchester County, New York was the first of its kind. Originally designed as a pleasure drive route in 1906, it became a commuting route leading north from New York City by the time it was opened in 1923.

The provision in the early parkways of green open-space borders, grade separation of intersecting roads, separation of pedestrian and vehicular areas, and grade separation of opposing lanes where natural grades were different became the precursors of modern expressway design.

See: CONTROL OF ACCESS; EXPRESSWAY; GRADE SEPARATION

Particulates

A general term describing finely divided particles, whether liquid or solid, that can be suspended in gas or air. Examples of particulates are dust, smoke, mist, fumes and fog.

Particulates derive from both natural processes and human activities. Among the largest sources of natural particulate emission are volcanic eruptions, forest fires, ocean spray and soil erosion by wind. Man-made emissions of particulates derive from such sources as waste dumps, industrial processes and motor vehicles.

National ambient air quality standards (NAAQS) have been in effect for total suspended particulates (TSP) for a number of years in the United States. Control measures taken to decrease TSP emissions, such as prohibitions on the open burning of solid waste and the installation of appropriate equipment at industrial plants, are thought likely to have been responsible for the substantial drop in man-made TSP emissions recorded during the period 1970 to 1980. Most parts of the United States have already attained NAAQS for TSPs or are expected to be able to attain the standard in the foreseeable future.
See: AIR POLLUTION; AIR POLLUTION CONTROL; DUST; NATIONAL AMBIENT AIR QUALITY STANDARDS (NAAQS); SMOG; SMOKE; STACK

Partners for Livable Places (PLP)

A national civic organization consisting of nonprofit organizations, municipalities, government agencies, corporations, foundations and individuals concerned with all aspects of the livability of communities and improving the quality of the built and natural environments. A particular goal of PLP is encouraging civic leadership in creating livable communities.

Founded in 1977, Partners sponsors conferences, national meetings, and local workshops and conferences, and conducts research and information exchange projects in a number of broad subject areas. One such topic, The Economics of Amenity, is a long-term technical assistance program intended to demonstrate the role urban amenities, such as open space or good design, play in influencing the economy of an area by affecting such factors as business location decisions. Other programs include The New Civics, concerned with new management, legal, political and financial skills; Livable Communities, in which information is collected, categorized and stored concerning successful community projects; and Learning from Europe, in which the most innovative and successful approaches to such topics as urban waterfront development or management of open spaces are studied.

Partners, whose offices are in Washington, D.C., has recently begun operating a new information system, Partnerships Dataline, USA, in cooperation with the Citizens Forum on Self-Government/National Municipal League. PLP publishes *PLACE,* a monthly magazine; *Livability Digest,* a quarterly; and *Livability,* a semi-annual newsletter, as well as a number of books and reports.

Party Wall

A wall, usually built on a dividing line between plots of land, which is intended or adapted for joint use as an exterior supporting wall of the buildings on each lot. The party wall is generally owned subject to an express or implied cross-easement, which gives each party the right to use it and the mutual responsibility for its maintenance. The wall may also be built entirely on one property and held in one ownership.
See: COMMON WALL

Passenger Railroad Rebuilding Act of 1980

Legislation (PL 96-254) that amends the Railroad Revitalization and Regulatory Reform Act of 1976 (PL 94-210) by increasing funding for improvement of the northeast corridor railroad system from $1.75 billion to $2.5 billion and requiring its completion by the end of 1985. The act changes the emphasis of the northeast corridor program from trip time reduction to an increase in ridership and reliability but authorizes studies relating to the removal of impediments to development of high-speed intercity service.

Other studies authorized include those related to improvement of other high-speed rail corridors, such as the Los Angeles-San Diego corridor, and the improvement of service on other corridors that have the greatest potential either to attract riders, to reduce energy consumption or to provide cost-effective passenger service. The secretary of transportation is also directed to consult with the secretaries of housing and urban development and commerce on the best use of federal assistance, made available by these departments, for public and private redevelopment projects in the vicinity of urban rail stations on the northeast corridor.

Passive Recreation

Pleasurable activities that involve relative inactivity, such as sitting, strolling, card playing and family picnics. Opportunities for passive recreation are provided in a variety of settings, ranging from traditional parks to vest-pocket parks and outdoor plazas. Whenever possible these facilities should be designed to encourage use by diverse population groups.
See: ACTIVE RECREATION

Passive Solar Energy System

A solar energy system in which the basic building components are used to collect energy and mechanical equipment is kept to a minimum. Instead of using equipment to transfer solar-heated fluid to an area where it is needed, a passive system relies on natural convection, conduction or radiation of heat.

Also called a direct system, a passive solar system uses such techniques as extensive areas of south-facing glass to admit heat and thermal storage areas, such as stone or brick walls or floors, to store heat. Additional insulation, nighttime shutters for windows and other glazed surfaces, and extra glazing are also frequently used. One way in which existing homes may be retrofitted for a passive solar system is by the addition of an appropriately sited attached greenhouse, which can be used to collect heat.

See: ACTIVE SOLAR ENERGY SYSTEM; ARCHITECTURAL DESIGN FOR ENERGY CONSERVATION; EARTH-COVERED BUILDING; ENERGY CONSERVATION PLANNING; NATURAL COOLING; SOLAR ACCESS; SOLAR ENERGY; SUN-TEMPERED BUILDING; THERMAL MASS; THERMAL WINDOWS

Pavement

A man-made surface, placed on the ground, that facilitates passage. Pavements are provided for streets, sidewalks, parking lots, bikepaths, airport runways and other specialized areas. Their design structure is dependent upon the volume of traffic and the static (weight) and dynamic (force) loads the pavement is expected to carry. It is likely that each of the functions above would require pavements of differing cross sections. The life of a pavement will be determined by the number and thicknesses of base layers and their composition, the strength of the earth subgrade below the road, the amount and type of traffic, the amount of freezing and thawing, and the type and thickness of the top course. The selection of a particular pavement type is often determined by local experience with respect to wear and maintenance of similar pavements.

There are two predominant pavement types: flexible pavements and rigid pavements. Flexible pavements are composed of aggregates and bituminous material (asphalt and tar products) that, when combined, form a strong, compact, waterproof mass. Types of flexible pavements include surface treatments, penetration-macadams, road mixes and plant mixes. Surface treatments consist of the application of a liquid bituminous material over an aggregate base. Penetration-macadam consists of firmly compacted successive layers of consecutively smaller, sharp, angular stones, which are consolidated by rollers, after which each layer is sprayed with a bituminous binder. Road mixes (combined on site) and plant mixes (combined at the plant), both of which are known as asphalt concrete, consist of a top layer of bituminous material mixed with aggregate that is layered over a prepared base of crushed stone. Special flexible pavements are commonly used for playgrounds, where additional materials—such as cork, sponge or rubber—may be mixed with asphalt for extra resiliency around play equipment.

Rigid pavements are concrete pavements. Where heavy loads are expected, steel reinforcement may be added for additional strength and to prevent cracking. Prestressed concrete has been used in runway design to handle the heavy loads imposed by landing aircraft and to reduce the thickness of concrete that would be necessary without reinforcement. Concrete may also be used as a base layer for flexible pavements.

Another type of pavement—gravel mixed with clay, lime or iron oxide placed on top of a graded roadbed—is used in rural areas and on paths as an inexpensive form of pavement suitable for very low traffic volumes. Brick and cobblestone paving were early forms of road pavement and are still in use in many parts of Europe.

See: AGGREGATE; CONCRETE; GLASPHALT; IMPERVIOUS SURFACES; PAVERS; PRESTRESSED CONCRETE; REINFORCED CONCRETE; SIDEWALK

Pavers

Blocks or tiles, formed from quarry stone or other natural or man-made materials, that are used for the decorative pavement of sidewalks, streets and pedestrian areas. The numerous materials available for use as pavers include the natural stones, such as slate, quartzite, sandstone, granite, marble and flagstone; brick in a wide variety of colors and finishes; concrete and asphalt blocks and tiles; wood paving block; clay tile; and rubble stone block.

The tiles or blocks are laid in many patterns and are used in combination with concrete and asphalt paved surfaces, and with each other, to create interesting patterns or to emphasize paths, such as crosswalks. Pedestrians have complained that some of the decorative pavers are too slippery in wet weather and that their many joints can cause falls, suggesting that the specific materials and their configurations must be selected with consideration of the effect of weather conditions and the types of people—e.g., elderly—who will use them. Care should also be taken to select materials that can support the expected volume of traffic.

See: PAVEMENT

Pay-As-You-Go Financing

The practice of paying for capital improvements as the costs are incurred rather than deferring payment through long-term bond financing. In this approach a certain amount of municipal revenue can be deposited each year to a fund set aside for larger capital works, while smaller projects may be completed annually.

The advantages of pay-as-you-go usually cited are a savings in interest payments, a reduced cost burden to future generations and a smaller burden of fixed debt should there be a period of economic uncertainty.

A major disadvantage is a built-in inflexibility to the system: Funds will accumulate at a given rate but a community might have a number of urgent or unexpected capital needs that cannot be met by the fund. Under a strict pay-as-you-go policy, these projects would have to be delayed, even if matching funds that will not be available at a later date are available to assist in payment.

Inflation is also an argument against pay-as-you-go, as long-term financing allows a project to be paid for with cheaper dollars than would be required of a cash outlay at the time of construction. When construction costs are rising rapidly, the project may cost a community much more than it saves in interest if it wants to accumulate the entire cost of a project in its fund.

See: CAPITAL IMPROVEMENT PROGRAM (CIP)

Peak-Demand Period

The time when the greatest demand for service is placed upon a utility or other system serving a community. The term may refer to a variety of functions, such as the provision of electric power or water. Peak demand, which tends to vary seasonally or by time of day, exerts a much larger drain upon a system than the normal hourly average. Domestic water demand, for example, tends to escalate during the early morning and evening, while large requirements are placed upon electric power production during the hottest summer days. Planning for the provision of these utilities requires that the size, duration and frequency of peak-period demand be carefully assessed.

Peak-Hour Traffic Volume

The largest amount of traffic that is generated during hourly periods of the day or year. Traffic counts indicate differences in hourly, weekday-weekend and seasonal volume and can be arrayed to show the number of hours that exhibited the highest volumes. Knowledge of peak-hour volumes is basic to determination of available roadway capacity and is therefore fundamental to urban planning and transportation proposals.

For transportation studies weekday morning and evening peak commuting hours are most critical, since they must be provided for by road or transit improvements that can accommodate the demand. Evening peaks are often higher and of longer duration than morning peaks, because the population that has accumulated in the urban center over the course of the day is generally much greater than the morning peak population. Traffic volumes measured near specific types of facilities, such as theaters or amusement parks during their peak-use hours, indicate their impact on the transport network.

The peak hour has volume peaks within itself, which must be studied to determine the higher rates of traffic flow that exist over short periods. Failure to do so may result in an erroneous choice of design hour volume on new roads or road sections to be improved. Peak 5-minute (phf_5), 6-minute (phf_6) or 15-minute (phf_{15}) flows indicate periods within the peak hour that exceed the average for the peak hour.
See: AVERAGE ANNUAL DAILY TRAFFIC (AADT); DESIGN HOUR VOLUME (DHV); FLEX-TIME; HIGHWAY CAPACITY DETERMINANTS; TRAFFIC COUNTS

Pedestrian Improvements

The range of elements employed in design to improve or otherwise enhance the experience of the pedestrian in a streetscape, plaza or other pedestrian environment.

In addition to proper design allowing for separation of pedestrian and auto circulation and adequate widths for walkways, improvements include the provision of street furniture, pedestrian-scale lighting and clear directional or informational signage. Other improvements used are landscaping for visual and environmental advantage, a variety of surface materials for visual and perceptual interest, and the introduction of color in the form of street graphics, flags or sculpture for vitality. For access by the disabled, curb cuts and ramps are a vital element.
See: OUTDOOR LIGHTING; PAVERS; PEDESTRIANIZATION; STREET FURNITURE; STREET GRAPHICS

Pedestrianization

Encouragement of walking by the provision of facilities that induce pedestrian use and by the curtailment of automobile use. Pedestrian plans vary in their scope, but all are designed to make movement on foot attractive and comfortable and to reduce dependence on motorized vehicles for short trips. Growth in the use of private automobiles brought increased traffic congestion to central cities, leading to the subsequent decay of many central business districts because of their replacement by more accessible suburban shopping centers. Urban revitalization plans now recognize the chief attraction of these shopping centers (pedestrian space free of conflict with cars, and convenient parking) and are attempting to duplicate them downtown.

Pedestrian areas include new shopping mall complexes and pedestrian areas created from city streets, either on a permanent or a temporary basis. Permanent pedestrian areas include shopping malls, which prohibit vehicles, and transit malls created from city streets, which have some provision for mass transit within them and which prohibit auto use. Temporary pedestrian areas are usually provided by closing streets for short periods of time or for special events.

Street improvements that do not prohibit the auto but may reduce the traffic capacity of the street have also been shown to encourage pedestrian use. Examples of these include widened sidewalks; provision of frequent crosswalks and curb cuts for carriages and wheelchairs; sensing crosswalk signals, which give longer crossing times when necessary; improved street furniture and outdoor lighting; and improved landscaping. Covered walkways or arcades are also popular in areas with extreme weather conditions. Accelerating, or moving, walkways may also have application in pedestrian areas. Plans for pedestrianization generally also call for improved mass transit and/or provision of parking structures or parking lots within a five-minute walk from the pedestrian area.

In planning the development of new towns and suburban areas, pedestrian pathways, or pedways, are often included to provide formal pedestrian access to open-space areas. These paths are frequently placed in the interior of the development, far from vehicular access, providing a protected, and usually attractive, pedestrian route. The development of Radburn, New Jersey provided the model for these separate pedestrian ways. The pedway concept is considered to have possibilities for application to urban areas in the form of underground tunnels that connect buildings and have retail areas, as in Houston and Philadelphia, or elevated pedestrian bridges that connect buildings, as in Minneapolis, and are increasingly being included in plans for new downtown building developments.

See: ACCELERATING WALKWAY; AUTOMOBILE RESTRICTED ZONE (ARZ); DOWNTOWN REVITALIZATION; RADBURN, NEW JERSEY; SHOPPING MALL; STREET FURNITURE; TRANSIT MALL

Penn Central Transportation Company v. City of New York (438 U.S. 104, 98 S.Ct. 2646 [1978])

A decision by the United States Supreme Court upholding the validity of New York City's landmarks preservation ordinance.

The Court held that the ordinance, which prevented the owner of Grand Central Terminal from building on air rights above the terminal, did not constitute a taking of property, requiring just compensation. The owner was permitted to transfer development rights to a number of sites in the vicinity of the terminal (several owned by the owner of the terminal), at least some of which were found suitable for construction of office buildings.

In reaching its conclusion, the Court relied on findings that included: that the landmark designation did not interfere with the existing use of the terminal; that the existing use of the terminal was affording its owner a reasonable return on its investment; and that the right to transfer the development potential of the air rights above the terminal constituted an economically valuable right. The Court noted that while the transferable development rights may not have constituted just compensation within the constitutional sense if a taking of property had been found, the rights could be considered by the Court in determining whether the effect of the ordinance on the terminal resulted in a taking.

Of particular significance for landmarks preservation ordinances—which, in contrast to zoning ordinances, can apply to individual properties rather than to neighborhoods or districts—the Court found that the mere fact that landmarks ordinances apply to individual properties does not make them unlawful, discriminatory or unconstitutional takings of property.

See: FRED F. FRENCH INVESTING COMPANY INC. v. CITY OF NEW YORK; HISTORIC PRESERVATION; TAKING; TRANSFER OF DEVELOPMENT RIGHTS (TDR)

Pennsylvania Coal Co. v. Mahon (260 U.S. 393, 43 S.Ct. 158, 67 L.Ed. 322 [1922])

A decision by the United States Supreme Court holding unconstitutional a statute of the Commonwealth of Pennsylvania that prohibited the subsurface mining of coal under private property where the right to mine had been reserved by a prior owner of the property at the time he conveyed the surface rights to the land.

The Court found that the right to mine coal was an estate in land and that the broad prohibition on this activity whenever the owner of the surface of the land was not the same as the owner of the subsurface rights destroyed any economic utility of the subsurface rights. The Court concluded that the statute went beyond regulation and constituted a taking of property that required just compensation.

See: TAKING

People Mover

People movers, or automated guideway transit (AGT) systems, are fully automated transit systems located on narrow guideways 20 feet (6.1 meters) or more above the street, which are being built in several central business district areas in the United States and Japan to augment surface mass transit. People mover manufacturers provide a variety of vehicle sizes that can be employed, carrying from as few as 15 people to 75 or more, with provisions for coupling cars together. The cars are narrow and lightweight, traveling on rubber tires or air cushions or are magnetically levitated. Most are operated on a single-car basis on very short headways to minimize waiting time.

Downtown people movers (DPM) have been used successfully at airports, amusement parks and universities. Their application to urban areas, which require longer system lengths, is being supported through Urban Mass Transportation Administration (UMTA) grants to cities that have agreed to build them; grants are also made for research in design and performance.

DPMs, which are quieter than rail lines and have lower capital and operating costs, generally employ concrete guideways that are inexpensive to construct and maintain. They are usually narrow in cross section—e.g., a one-way width of 12 to 15 feet (3.7 to 4.6 meters), permitting their placement either in the middle or at the side of a street. Vehicles can operate on, or be suspended from, the guideway, depending on the system used; all people movers can operate without drivers, are electrically powered and can accommodate large passenger volumes for short distances. The cities of Los Angeles, Detroit, Miami and St. Paul all have people mover projects approximately 3 miles (4.8 kilometers) long in various stages of planning. (See Fig. 31)

See: FUTURE TRANSPORTATION MODES; PERSONAL RAPID TRANSIT

People v. Stover (12 N.Y.2d 462, 191 NE.2d 272, 240 N.Y.S.2d 734 [1963])

A decision by the New York Court of Appeals (the highest court of New York) holding that a zoning ordinance adopted to further a community's aesthetic goals is valid. The court found that zoning legislation designed to promote aesthetics is a valid and permissible exercise of the police power.

A secondary issue in the case was whether the ordinance in question—which prohibited the erection of clotheslines in front or side yards without a special permit—could be constitutionally applied against a property owner who

Fig. 31.   People movers at Orlando (Florida) International Airport transport passengers to or from outlying boarding-deplaning gates and the main terminal building. This automated guideway transit system, developed by Westinghouse Electric Corporation, can transport 32,000 passengers per hour for the 1½-minute trip between buildings, traveling at 28 miles per hour (45 kilometers per hour). Credit: Courtesy of the Greater Orlando Aviation Authority

claimed that the ordinance constituted an infringement of his freedom of speech. The property owner claimed that his violation of the ordinance was intended as a protest against local taxing policies.

The court held the application of this ordinance to the property owner did not violate his First Amendment "free speech" rights, since there was no necessary relationship between the ordinance and the dissemination of ideas or opinions.
See: AESTHETICS; POLICE POWER

Per Capita

A term used in planning and budgeting that refers to the average amount of expenditure, income, or specified commodity or activity for each individual within a given population. Per capita income figures are an indicator of the relative wealth of a community, while per capita expenditure figures might describe the extent of government spending. Any commodity or activity being studied—such

as number of automobiles, trips to the beach or water consumption—can be analyzed on a per capita basis.

Per capita figures are often used for comparative purposes to enable the comparison of data from one year to another or to permit contrast between expenditures, income or wealth from one political jurisdiction to another. They are also used as the basis of design for municipal facilities that are sized according to average use levels, such as water supply and sewerage system components.
See: MUNICIPAL SERVICES

Percolation

Downward movement of water through rock or soil interstices. Determining the rate at which water can percolate is useful to planners in assessing soil drainage and in providing for on-site sewage disposal through septic systems.
See: GROUNDWATER; INFILTRATION; PERCOLATION (PERK) TEST; SEPTIC SYSTEM

Percolation (PERK) Test

A test used to evaluate the capacity of soil to absorb liquid. It is usually performed in connection with the proposed installation of septic tanks, injection wells for sewage treatment plants or other kinds of development to help avoid pollution of groundwater and health hazards related to seepage.

Local regulations generally require that experienced personnel, usually attached to health departments, perform this test. There are various means of conducting a percolation test in the field; generally, a measured pit or a number of specifically sized test holes are dug and are then filled with water. The soil is made completely wet to simulate soil conditions during wet seasons, and then the holes or pits are refilled to a specific depth. After a waiting period, measurements are made of the rate at which the water has dropped.

The percolation rate is the number of inches that the water level drops per hour or the time it takes for the water level to fall 1 inch, depending upon the method used. If the rate is within the permissible range, residential septic fields may be permitted; a certain number of square feet of disposal field per bedroom may be required for each dwelling unit.

See: PERCOLATION; RURAL SANITATION; SEPTIC FIELD

Performance Bond

A bond posted by a contractor or subcontractor that contains the guarantee of a surety that a specific project will be completed and meet any standards or specifications that have been agreed upon. Performance bonds may be required by municipalities to ensure the installation of any necessary improvements that are the developer's responsibility.

Generally, the performance bond provides that should the contractor fail to meet his obligations and complete the project, the surety company will either complete the work or pay damages up to the bond's limit. When all the work has been satisfactorily completed, the bond is terminated. Normally a labor and materials bond is combined with the performance bond to guarantee payment of all claims for labor and materials that may have been previously contracted.

Because bonds can be expensive for the developer, and because it is sometimes difficult for the community to collect what is owed it by the bond company, municipalities often require alternative forms of financial guarantees.

See: FINANCIAL GUARANTEES FOR IMPROVEMENTS

Performance Budget

A budget format in which funds to be allocated are shown in relation to activities to be performed. Its main application is as a tool to encourage production of more units of work, thereby lowering per-unit cost, but it does not necessarily increase quality of performance. The performance budget differs from the program budget, its successor in development, by not necessarily relating work units to a program or to program goals.

In performance budgeting, work goals (as opposed to program goals) are specifically enumerated by estimating how many units of work will be done during the year, such as how many social service cases will be processed or how many units of housing rehabilitated. In a program budget the goals for these activities might be an increase in employment in construction jobs for unskilled and unemployed teenagers. The federal government and many municipalities present appropriation requests for many administrative units in a combined program budget and performance budget, thereby combining favorable aspects of both budget forms.

See: PROGRAM BUDGET

Performance Standards

General criteria that are set to ensure that a particular structure, type of land use or development will be able to meet certain minimum standards or that its effects on the community will not exceed set limits. Performance standards differ from specification standards in that they are designed to provide a desired result or performance without specifying exactly what must be done to achieve this result. As an example, a performance-oriented building code might require a set degree of structural strength from a building component without specifying what construction materials must be used to provide this degree of strength.

Performance standards in zoning ordinances are often applied to industrial land uses. Rather than attempting to inclusively list all industries permitted in various light and heavy industrial zones, a set of standards is drawn governing noise, vibration, smoke, odor, heat, glare, fire hazard, traffic generation, etc. Those industries that are able to perform within the limits prescribed by the ordinance are then permitted. In the case of some performance criteria (particularly those concerning air and water pollution), federal or state regulations are enforced, and local requirements may primarily be addressed at the areas for which no other regulations, or inadequate ones, exist.

Effective use of performance standards is dependent upon a municipality's possessing the technical ability and the often costly equipment necessary to measure performance. Without the ability to quantify the amount of noise a particular industrial facility is making, for example, sound limits enumerated in decibels in the municipal ordinance cannot be enforced. Because of this, smaller communities often tend to rely on specification standards rather than performance standards.

See: SPECIFICATION STANDARDS; VALUE ENGINEERING (VE); ZONING

Performance Zoning

A type of land use control whose main purpose is the protection of important environmental features while encouraging the development of a diversity of housing types. First implemented in Bucks County, Pennsylvania in the early 1970s, the system controls development intensity through standards concerning required minimum open space, maximum impervious surface coverage and maximum density. In addition, other controls are imposed based upon the prevalent problems in an area. In the Bucks County system, no development, filling or encroachment is permitted on floodplains, alluvial soils, wetlands, streams, lakes or ponds. Other requirements limit development on areas of steep slopes, natural retention areas, prime agricultural soils, and forests.

Once the pertinent environmental features of a site are mapped and measured, calculations are performed to determine the number of dwelling units permitted on that site (or the permitted maximum floor area ratio, in the case of nonresidential development), as well as the permitted coverage by impervious surfaces and open-space requirements. After these requirements are met, any type of housing may be constructed on the portion of the site designated as buildable, provided that it not exceed a specified density, serving as an incentive to the construction of housing of a broader price range than is often found. Clustering provisions also allow the same development intensity on the buildable portion of the site as would have been permitted on the entire site under standard zoning regulations.

Performance zoning has been gaining in popularity and is now in use, or proposed for use, in 26 communities in Bucks County as well as a number of other communities, including Kettering, Ohio; Largo, Florida; San Antonio, Texas; and Lake County, Illinois. The system may be adapted to the particular needs of a community by, for example, applying the system to all zoning districts or limiting its use to certain types of development or certain districts.
See: ENVIRONMENTALLY SENSITIVE LANDS; ZONING

Permissible Use

A land use that, assuming it can meet all necessary requirements, may be allowed in a particular zoning district. Included in those land uses that are permissible are all permitted uses as well as those allowed only by special permit or by some other special review procedure.
See: PERMITTED USE; SPECIAL-USE PERMIT; ZONING

Permit

Written authorization, granted by a governmental agency, that allows an individual or organization to undertake some activity. In the absence of the permit, the activity may not legally take place. Types of permits often encountered by planners are the building permit, the special-use permit and the zoning permit.
See: BUILDING PERMIT; SPECIAL-USE PERMIT; ZONING PERMIT

Permitted Use

A type of land use that is authorized by right for a particular zoning district, assuming only that it meets standard development criteria concerning such factors as height and bulk. By contrast, some land uses, such as special-permit uses, are approved only on a case-by-case basis and must meet specified conditions.
See: AS-OF-RIGHT ZONING; PERMISSIBLE USE

Personal Rapid Transit

A proposed form of extensive people mover that would permit the vehicles on it to take passengers nonstop from an origin station to a destination station. Vehicles would be very small, seating two to four passengers, and would operate automatically. The system would be electrically powered and computer-operated.

The object is to increase the capacity of existing transportation corridors without increasing highway lanes necessary for that purpose. Personal rapid transit could provide this extra capacity in one lane of existing corridors while offering some of the ambience of the private automobile. (See Fig. 32)
See: CORRIDOR STUDY; PEOPLE MOVER

Personal Space

The physical envelope, or dimension of space, surrounding an individual, within which another person's presence is perceived as an intrusion. Personal space travels with the individual and varies with the situation as well as the person. For example, most Americans find 4 to 7 feet (1.2 to 2.1 meters) a comfortable distance for business conversations but need less space for social conversations.

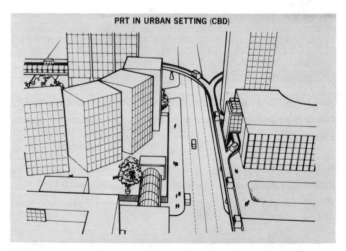

Fig. 32.   An artist's conception of a personal rapid-transit system in a downtown commercial area. It is pictured as an elevated structure constructed over sidewalks and the existing street system.

Credit: Courtesy of the U.S. Department of Transportation

Persons of different cultural backgrounds perceive their personal space needs differently; Mediterranean people traditionally prefer to be closer for communication as compared with northern Europeans, who require more space.

The provision of adequate personal space avoids feelings of crowding and is an important design factor in the habitability of homes and the efficiency of offices. The manner and degree to which people use plazas, streets and other public places has recently been shown (in studies by William Whyte) to depend, in part, upon appropriate provisions for personal space in seating areas, meeting places and walking areas. The arrangements of furniture and work spaces as well as building design help to determine available personal space and consequently the degree to which people feel comfortable.

See: BEHAVIORAL DESIGN; ENVIRONMENTAL PSYCHOLOGY; OVERCROWDING; PRIVACY; TERRITORIALITY

Perspective Rendering

A graphic presentation of a building, civil engineering project, cityscape or landscape that shows it as if seen in three dimensions. Perspective renderings are drawn by mechanically projecting two-dimensional plans, elevations or cross sections to a third dimension by established procedures and are finished in many artists' mediums, such as pencil, ink, tempera and watercolor. Also known as perspective projection, these drawings are done in one-point, two-point and three-point perspectives, depending upon their intended use.

See: ARCHITECTURAL ILLUSTRATION; CROSS SECTION; ELEVATION; FLOOR PLAN; PROJECTION DRAWING

Pesticides

Substances used to destroy plants or animals that pose a threat to human activities, such as agriculture, or to general well-being. Pesticides are commonly categorized by the control function they are intended to serve—e.g., insecticides are used to kill insects, defoliants to strip trees of their leaves and rodenticides to destroy rodents.

The use of pesticides greatly accelerated after World War II as such effective compounds as DDT (useful in combatting disease-bearing mosquitoes) and 2,4-D (a herbicide) were introduced. Pesticides help to perform such useful functions as the control of diseases, such as malaria, bubonic plague and typhus; the protection of numerous agricultural crops; and the preservation of forests. Many of the same features that make pesticides valuable in pest control, however, can also make certain pesticides dangerous to human health and to the environment in general.

DDT, aldrin, dieldrin, endrin and heptachlor are often singled out by environmental scientists as being particularly hazardous because, in addition to being highly toxic, they tend to persist for long periods of time and become concentrated as they move through the links of the food chain. These pesticides are also extremely mobile and are readily transported to ecosystems great distances away. In addition, these types of chlorinated hydrocarbons are capable of killing nontarget species that may have been helping to control the undesirable pest population. One further problem is the development of pest strains that are resistant to pesticides after long-term use of a pesticide.

As a result of the problems associated with these types of pesticides, DDT was banned for use in the United States by the Environmental Protection Agency in 1972 for all except emergency situations. Aldrin and dieldrin, implicated as possible causes of cancer and birth defects, were banned in 1974, and use of chlordane and heptachlor was suspended in 1975. Despite these bans, significant levels of DDT and other banned pesticides are still found throughout the environment in various portions of the food chain.

To minimize the hazards associated with pesticides, new approaches to pest management are being explored that combine the use of biological and natural controls, such as the use of pest-resistant crops and species-specific viruses, with traditional chemical pesticides.

See: INTEGRATED PEST MANAGEMENT (IPM); TOXIC SUBSTANCES

Phased Development Controls

Development regulations that govern the sequence and timing of construction. Traditional zoning ordinances designate and regulate permitted land uses, but phased development controls add to this a time dimension.

Permission to subdivide land or build housing may be contingent on the availability of sewers, water, roads, and other public services and facilities. In the simplest case, development is prohibited in areas that lack sewers or some other basic public service. In more sophisticated systems a combination of services must be available before development is permitted. Usually, the developer may, at his own expense, supply services that are lacking. The number of building permits issued may be subject to a quota, with preference given to proposals that meet public goals by providing good design, open space, public amenities or low-cost housing. Some uses, such as nonresidential development or housing for the elderly, may be exempt from the controls.

Phased development controls can slow growth to allow municipalities to budget expenditures for expansion of municipal services to developing areas over a longer time period. Slower growth prevents the overburdening of existing facilities while new facilities are being constructed. Phasing can also encourage growth near existing built-up areas, helping to prevent sprawl.

Ramapo, New York and Petaluma, California were two communities often cited as among the best-known examples of phased development controls in the United States in the 1970s. Ramapo used a point system that was tied to a capital improvement program. Petaluma held an annual competition to select housing development proposals to fill the year's quota for various locations and housing

types. In 1983, however, with growth rates dramatically decreased, Ramapo repealed its point system as no longer serving a purpose. One key concern was the extent to which the system might be preventing economic growth in the town. Petaluma still maintains a quota (although a somewhat higher figure) on the number of dwelling units that may be built each year, but in recent years development applications have been below that quota. In addition, developments of less than 15 units have been exempted from the quota.
See: CONSTRUCTION INDUSTRY ASS'N OF SONOMA COUNTY v. CITY OF PETALUMA; GOLDEN v. PLANNING BOARD OF THE TOWN OF RAMAPO; GROWTH MANAGEMENT

Phenols

A class of organic compounds commonly derived from coal tar, members of which can be toxic to human and aquatic life. In lower concentrations, phenols can also be responsible for lowering water quality by imparting unpleasant tastes and odors.

Phenols are widely used in industrial applications, such as for production of pesticides, pharmaceuticals, tanning agents, resins and dyes. As a result, they have gradually been discovered in many water bodies.
See: TOXIC SUBSTANCES; WATER POLLUTION

Photogrammetry

The use of photographs to supply accurate measurements for surveying and for making maps. The photographs may be taken from ground level (terrestrial photogrammetry) or, more commonly, from the air.

Terrestrial photogrammetry was developed by a French engineer in the mid-19th century and first used in North America in mountainous western Canada in 1886. At ground levels camera stations are carefully selected to form specific geometric patterns, which are used for control purposes.

In aerial photogrammetry, flight strips are flown in which each path overlaps the other by about 60 percent. Side overlap of about 10 percent to 15 percent is also necessary. This overlap provides the basis for stereoscopic imagery, allows better orientation and minimizes the number of control points (positions carefully marked on the ground and on the photos to serve as reference points) that are required. Flight altitude varies with mapping need, particularly related to the desired contour intervals, and may range up to about 25,000 feet (7,620 meters).

The resulting photographs are used in a variety of ways in map preparation. In one common procedure pairs of adjacent overlapping photographs can be placed in a stereoplotting system. This instrument uses visible control points for orientation in order to plot the outlines of features, such as roads, as well as to plot contour lines.
See: AERIAL PHOTOGRAPHIC APPLICATIONS; AERIAL PHOTOGRAPHY; PLANIMETRIC MAP; TOPOGRAPHIC MAP

Photostat™

A trade name for a type of photographic copying (photocopying) in which an original is photographed and wet-developed on sensitized paper. A prism in the lens allows a right-reading image (that is, from left to right) to be made directly. The machine is capable of enlarging copies to varying degrees.
See: GRAPHIC REPRODUCTION PROCESSES

Physical Deterioration

The extent to which improvements on real property have suffered from decay and wear and tear. Physical deterioration, along with functional obsolescence and economic obsolescence, is one of the three forms of depreciation considered in real estate appraisal.

Physical deterioration may be further classified as either curable or incurable. Curable deterioration may be remedied by expending reasonable sums of money for deferred maintenance expenses such as exterior painting or a new roof. The amount expended is known as the "cost to cure" the defect. Curable deterioration also includes the concept of a major building component that is partially worn out and will need replacement or repair at a future date. Incurable deterioration involves building components not readily correctible or impractical to repair or replace.

Preventing and reversing the physical deterioration of residential and commercial areas is frequently a major planning concern. Numerous programs are directed at this activity, ranging from major federal grant programs to code enforcement at the local level.
See: APPRAISAL; COST APPROACH APPRAISAL; REHABILITATION

Physical Life

The expected life span of a properly maintained building. This estimate may be based on evidence obtained concerning other similar buildings or a detailed physical inspection of the structure by a qualified individual.
See: USEFUL LIFE

Physical Planning

Traditionally the primary focus of planners and planning agencies, physical planning is concerned with land use issues as they affect the implementation of particular goals and objectives. Physical planners tend to focus on the spatial composition of a community and are often involved in developing a comprehensive plan that visualizes the community in the future and estimates future land requirements for various land use categories and types of community facilities. Many other types of plans may also be prepared, such as plans for a central business district, for an institution or for a recreational facility.

Physical planners may also be involved in developing zoning ordinances, subdivision regulations and other land use controls. On a project basis physical planning involves such issues as site selection, building design and site design.

In the 1960s and 1970s, planners broadened their range of activities to include a much greater emphasis on social, economic and environmental issues. This occurred partially in reaction to the failure of certain planning and physical redevelopment projects that gave insufficient weight to social, psychological and economic factors. While physical planning remains an important planning component, it now typically takes place in the context of a consideration of these additional concerns.
See: COMPREHENSIVE PLAN; SOCIAL PLANNING

Picnic Area

A place equipped with such facilities as picnic tables, trash baskets and outdoor grills or that is otherwise designated as an area appropriate for picnicking. Areas designed for large numbers of people may also have a picnic shelter for cover in the event of sudden rainfall. Many urban parks permit picnicking but provide no special facilities for this activity.

Except in extreme climates, picnicking is one of the most popular forms of outdoor recreation. It is available to persons of all ages and physical conditions and is one of the least expensive recreation facilities that can be offered. In planning picnic areas, sites should be selected with scenic views or near other recreational facilities, such as softball fields or boating, while tables should be provided in both sunny and shady locations. Separate facilities for large groups may also be desirable. Other improvements necessary in areas designed for large numbers of people are a potable water supply, toilets and parking areas.

Pier

1. A reinforced concrete column that supports the weight of a large building. Unlike piles, piers are not driven into the ground; rather, they are usually cast in predrilled holes or sunk into position and used when suitable bearing strata are located far below ground. They may reach depths of 100 feet (30 meters) or more.
2. A vertical support for large structures, such as bridge spans or arches.
3. A type of dock that projects from shore and is designed to enable ships to load passengers and cargo. Consisting of a platform—which may be made of steel, concrete or timber—and a supporting system of piles, the pier may have an open deck or accommodate sheds, structures or special equipment for cargo handling. The clear area between piers is known as a slip. Piers may also be designed to accommodate recreational needs, such as boating or fishing.

Pile-supported piers and floating docks are considered superior to solid-fill structures from an environmental perspective because they cause less disruption to the water flow along the coast. It is also preferable, when possible, to construct them so that they reach deep water, where boats can dock, to minimize dredging requirements.

Various regulations have been adopted by the Corps of Engineers and state and local governments limiting the extent to which piers can encroach upon coastal waters because of possible interference with navigation. Environmental requirements may also be established regulating pier design and construction.
See: COASTAL AREA PLANNING; DREDGING; HARBOR; PORT; WHARF

Pipeline

A network of pipe, along with any necessary pumping equipment, valves and other machinery required to convey fluids or gas through the pipe. Pipelines are used to transport a wide variety of substances, such as petroleum, natural gas, pulverized coal, steam, water, sewage, chemicals and refined products. Pipelines may be constructed of a variety of materials, including steel, iron, concrete, plastics and copper and are of either the pressure or the nonpressure type. Pressure lines, such as long-distance petroleum lines, are those in which either pumps are used to move materials along, or large changes in elevations, such as are found when elevated towers are used, generate pressure. Nonpressure lines, found in sewer lines, rely on gentle gravity flow. All pipelines must be able to resist leaking, and pressure lines must also be able to withstand a specified degree of pressure.

Pipelines are an energy-efficient means of transporting fluids and are widely used. The Alaska Pipeline, which transports oil from fields on the North Slope to Valdez, an ice-free port, is a recent example of major pipeline construction.
See: FOSSIL FUELS; FROSTLINE

Plan Implementation

The process of translating the comprehensive plan or any other community plan into action which, ideally, begins at the start of plan development. A broad spectrum of tools and mechanisms are available to aid in plan implementation although many of these mechanisms were not developed specifically for that purpose.

A major and direct means of implementing plans are the use of land use controls such as subdivision regulations, zoning ordinances and official maps. Other police power regulatory activities, such as the use of building codes, housing codes, special purpose ordinances (e.g., floodplain ordinances, sign control ordinances) and sanitary codes also are intrinsically involved in plan implementation.

The use of eminent domain to take land needed for public purposes by paying just compensation is a standard, but expensive and often controversial, means of implementing certain aspects of plans. It is most often used for such activities as acquisition of road or utility rights-of-way or land necessary for public facilities.

Another broad group of tools are related to the financial activities of government. These activities include the imposition of income tax, real property tax, sales tax and special tax assessments, and the use of various types of preferential tax incentives. The development and use of long-term public improvement programs and capital budgets to guide expenditures may also be placed in this group. The formation of special districts and public authorities may, in addition, be used to accomplish certain goals, such as the development of utility systems or public housing.

A final category of mechanisms that may be considered in plan implementation are those that concern the interactions within government and between government and the public at large. Public involvement and participation in the development of the plan from its earliest beginnings, as well as participation of all officials who will be involved in any aspect of plan implementation, are essential. Additional implementation activities in this category include the public information activities that the planning office offers and the formation of advisory groups.

See: BUILDING CODE; CAPITAL IMPROVEMENT PROGRAM (CIP); CITIZEN PARTICIPATION TECHNIQUES; COMPREHENSIVE PLAN; EMINENT DOMAIN; HOUSING CODE; OFFICIAL MAP; SANITARY CODE; SUBDIVISION REGULATIONS; TAX ABATEMENT; ZONING

Plan Preparation

The process of formulating a plan designed to guide development or some aspect of a community's development. Communities may undertake this process voluntarily, with the initiative taken by government, citizen groups or joint public-private efforts. Alternatively, communities may be required to develop plans by federal or state mandates, sometimes linked to the availability of funding for other endeavors.

Plan preparation is usually the responsibility of the planning staff. The staff may undertake all of the work, be aided by other departments, or be aided by consultants. In small communities, consultants may be retained to prepare the entire plan. In addition to the planning staff, the officials who will use the plan and the public affected by the plan are given opportunities to participate in the various stages of plan development. Most units of government hold formal hearings at various stages in the process as well as informal discussions with various civic and business organizations. Other means used to involve the public include advisory organizations, information meetings and presentations on television and radio.

Ultimately, it is considered important for the plan to be adopted by the appropriate government body, thereby indicating that it formally supports the document and endorses the concepts it contains.

See: COMPREHENSIVE PLAN; PLAN IMPLEMENTATION

Planimeter

A device that allows land area to be calculated from a map, even if the parcel is of an irregular shape. The planimeter consists of a weighted leg, which remains stationary, fastened to a leg with a calibrated wheel and scale, which is used to trace the outline of the area. Trac-

ing is done in a clockwise direction. To increase accuracy, the area is often traced more than once, and the calibrated reading is then divided by the number of times the area was traced. The accuracy of the planimeter estimate may also be checked by comparison, for example, with parcels of land of known size or by the use of grids drawn to a particular scale.

Planimetric Map

A map in which features are depicted horizontally without regard to differences in elevation. Roads, municipal boundaries, water bodies, railroads, etc., are all accurately represented, but information concerning the topography is not included. In contrast, topographic maps indicate land elevations, usually by means of contour lines. Planimetric maps might be used instead of topographic maps when topography is unimportant and more space is required for annotation—e.g., in the case of road maps. They are also often used as base maps in conjunction with a set of overlays, one of which might be a separate topographic overlay. (See Fig. 33)

See: BASE MAP; TOPOGRAPHIC MAP

Planned Community

A community that is the result of an overall design rather than the agglomeration of unrelated development. Planned communities have been built throughout history, often based on a philosophic or political concept. They range from small religiously oriented communities (such as Oneida, New York) to major cities (such as Brasilia, Brazil) and new towns (such as Tapiola, Finland). What each shares is a comprehensive plan rather than incremental, individual growth decisions.

At a smaller scale, large housing developments by one builder are frequently termed planned communities, since all facilities are planned, and often built, at the same time. Planned unit developments and retirement communities are also usually planned communities.

See: AGGLOMERATION; NEW TOWN; PLANNED UNIT DEVELOPMENT (PUD)

Planned Unit Development (PUD)

A type of development characterized by comprehensive planning for the project as a whole, clustering of structures to preserve usable open space and other natural features, a mixture of housing types and sometimes a variety of nonresidential uses as well. The advantages of PUDs over lot-by-lot development include additional flexibility in project design and the preparation of a unified site plan that can make the best use of the land.

PUDs may vary markedly in size, covering only a few acres or many hundreds of acres. In some communities increased overall gross densities are permitted in PUDs, and density bonuses are awarded for amenities such as provision of a variety of housing types, provision of housing units of various sizes, open-space reservation or excellence in design and landscaping. Not all communities per-

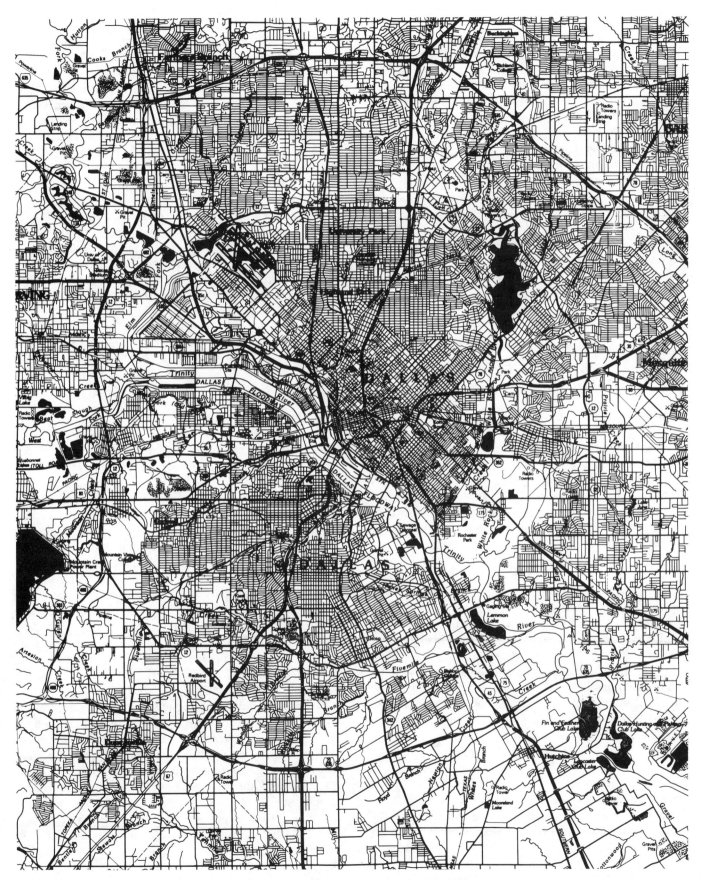

Fig. 33. A section of a planimetric base map of Dallas County, Texas. Street pattern, water bodies
and major cultural features are shown.
Credit: U.S. Geological Survey

mit density increases, however, and some may only allow clustering of buildings for design flexibility. Mixed land uses in PUDs are permitted in a majority of communities, but the nonresidential uses are most often restricted to uses accessory to the residential aspects of the development or those primarily required because of the need generated by the PUD, such as retail stores.

Planned unit development regulations may be written as separate zoning districts or treated as a special-permit use. The administration of a planned unit development typically requires a considerable exercise of discretion on the part of the reviewing body in reviewing site plans, as extremely detailed development standards are generally not included in PUD regulations to preserve maximum design flexibility. Negotiation is also a fundamental part of the review process, particularly where density bonuses may be granted. Because of this, successful administration of PUD regulations usually requires the aid of a professional planning staff.

See: CHENEY v. *VILLAGE 2 AT NEW HOPE, INC.* CLUSTER DEVELOPMENT; FLEXIBLE REGULATIONS; INCENTIVE ZONING; LOT-BY-LOT DEVELOPMENT; MIXED-USE ZONING; NEGOTIATION; SITE PLAN REVIEW; SUBDIVISION REGULATIONS

Planning Area

1. The territory for which a particular planning agency has official planning responsibility, based upon state enabling legislation, local ordinance or other legal authority.

2. The specific geographic area, also called the study area, selected as being pertinent to the study of a particular problem. The boundaries of the area are drawn to include those features—such as centers of employment, major transportation corridors or watersheds—that are necessary to an analysis of the defined problem. For example, a study of the problems associated with a particular airport would have to define a much larger planning area than that encompassed within the airport boundaries to allow consideration of noise and safety in the surrounding community, access to the airport and the possibilities of expansion.

It is desirable to define planning areas, when possible, so that maximum data will be available from standardized sources. Defining planning areas to coincide with county, municipal or SMSA boundaries, for example, will expedite the use of certain types of census data.

See: CATCHMENT AREA; TARGET AREA

Planning Commission

An appointed board of laymen that, depending upon government organization, either has direct control over certain city planning functions or has an advisory or policy-making role. The wide use of the planning commission in local government stems from the Standard City Planning Enabling Act of 1928, which supported the planning commission form. A planning commission may also be known as a planning board.

The independent planning commission, found in many

smaller communities, generally has responsibility for a number of activities. It usually has jurisdiction over subdivision review and approval and is often closely involved in developing or revising the comprehensive plan, as well as in evaluating proposed developments for compatibility with the plan. The commission is generally consulted on proposed zoning amendments, capital improvements and other planning-related matters, and may also be involved in such activities as site plan review. In addition, it may have a professional staff that is responsible to the commission and works under its direction. In an alternative organizational structure, the planning commission serves as one component of a two-part planning administration in which a body of laymen plays an advisory role to the professional planning department. In this form the department may act independently of the commission but seek the commission's advice on policy matters, or it may use the commission as an intermediary to carry its message to the chief executive or to the public.

Planning commission members are usually appointed for overlapping terms by the chief executive or municipal council; ex officio membership, such as council members or other department heads, may also be specified.

See: CITIZEN BOARD; PLANNING DEPARTMENT

Planning Department

A government agency generally responsible for long-range and short-range land use planning; land use development management, including the administration of zoning and subdivision regulations; coordination of various projects; and coordination among different departments and different units of government. Other major functions include policy analysis, capital program preparation and review, project planning, research and community development planning. Although a planning department performs both staff and line functions, it is most often considered to be a staff department. In this capacity it frequently functions as an adviser to the chief executive or legislature and to other government departments. The planning department also advises the planning board on matters delegated to that board and supervises consultants hired to perform certain aspects of its work.

The planning department is headed by a planning director or commissioner and frequently has an organization in which special divisions are assigned areas of the department's work. The divisions generally relate to local needs and practice, while new divisions may be created periodically to manage major government grant programs. Large planning departments often have divisions specializing in community development; housing; long-range or policy planning; research and statistical analysis; project planning and capital program development; and local land use management, including zoning and subdivision and site plan administration and review. Specialized areas with which planning departments are usually concerned include open-space and school planning, environmental management, historic preservation, central business district planning and neighborhood redevelopment. Very small departments may have only a single planner, who, with the aid of support staff, must accommodate a community's most important planning needs.

The planning department also provides services to the public, such as technical advice or assistance in interpretation of land use regulations and access to a planning library. In addition, a variety of ordinances, maps, published studies on specialized topics, and educational and audiovisual materials are usually made available. Through its citizen participation programs, including public meetings and hearings, as well as regular appearances by professional personnel at meetings of civic organizations, the planning department provides public information on land use policies and programs and elicits public input.

A planning department's success depends upon the influence it can bring to bear on matters before it. Its authority in these matters derives from its competence in producing carefully prepared analytic studies, the application of its advice to problems that have been successfully resolved, the reasonableness of its proposals and its ability to communicate its findings and proposed policies to gain support. A planning department usually has a wide forum in which to present its views because of the diverse roles it plays and the various bodies it serves—e.g., legislative, planning board, capital projects review committee. In some communities, where the planning department also functions as an advisory agency to the zoning board of appeals, another level of land use control influence may be exercised.

See: COMMUNITY DEVELOPMENT DEPARTMENT; ECONOMIC DEVELOPMENT DEPARTMENT; PLAN IMPLEMENTATION; PLAN PREPARATION; PLANNING COMMISSION; PLANNING DIRECTOR

Planning Director

The chief administrator and, to an extent, the unofficial policymaker of a planning department or planning agency, who is the department's spokesman and is responsible for work allocation and supervision within the department. The planning director, usually a professional planner, is an appointed official serving at the pleasure of the chief executive or the planning commission.

As the chief expert on planning matters, who presents professional studies and reports to elected officials and to the public, the planning director plays a direct role in the establishment of the importance of the planning function and of the planning department within municipal and regional government. His personal effectiveness in convincing politicians, government officials, developers and the public of the need for certain planning measures is often the key to assuring the implementation of department recommendations.

See: PLANNING DEPARTMENT

Planning Education

Formal education intended to provide training for planning careers. The first academic department in city planning was established by the University of London in 1902.

In that same year Harvard offered the first course in planning in the United States and in 1922 established the first planning department in America. In 1941 only 7 United States schools offered graduate degrees in planning in programs emphasizing the physical aspects of planning. By 1981, however, over 100 schools in the United States and Canada offered planning degrees, and the range of courses and specialties offered had greatly expanded. Sixty-eight of these schools offered programs officially recognized by the American Planning Association (APA) based on criteria developed by the American Institute of Certified Planners, APA's affiliate organization for professional planners.

While some schools do offer undergraduate degrees in planning, graduate programs are more common. Although initially most applicants to planning programs had undergraduate degrees in architecture, civil engineering or landscape architecture, a wide range of backgrounds is now acceptable, reflecting the much greater emphasis given to the social, economic and environmental aspects of planning.

See: AMERICAN PLANNING ASSOCIATION (APA)

Planning Federation

An association of local government planning professionals and nonprofessionals, organized at the state, regional or county government level. Planning federations serve to inform their constituents about current planning matters, particularly as they relate to state or local activities, and to educate members of lay boards, such as planning board and zoning board of appeal members, regarding current planning practice.

Large and active planning federations—such as the statewide organizations in New York, New Jersey, Massachusetts and Minnesota—produce periodicals, hold seminars and may give awards for excellence in planning administration. In New Jersey the federation is closely linked with the planning program at Rutgers University, while other federations may ally themselves with the American Planning Association (APA), as in Minnesota, or be independent bodies. Another arrangement, used by the Westchester County Municipal Planning Federation in New York, consists of administration by the county planning department, assisted by a board composed of municipal planners, officials and planning board members.

Planning for the Disabled

The design and development of a barrier-free environment for the physically impaired. Planning for the disabled focuses on the modification or alteration of facilities normally accessible to unimpaired individuals, by removing obstructions to the blind, crippled or otherwise handicapped individual. It also involves the development of parallel systems or facilities where existing ones defy modification and outreach programs to encourage participation of disabled persons in community activities.

Commonly modified building elements include stairs, which are replaced by or used with ramps; and plumbing

fixtures, elevator panels and other controls, most of which are lowered for the wheelchair-bound and altered to be legible to the blind. Standards for these modifications have been developed by federal, state and local agencies in conjunction with architectural and transportation barrier removal programs. More subtle modifications may also include provision of nonslip surfaces, sidewalk curb cuts and reserved parking spaces. The development of dial-a-ride systems is a parallel approach to public transportation that helps to give the disabled person increased mobility.
See: ARCHITECTURAL AND TRANSPORTATION BARRIERS; BRAILLE TRAIL; DIAL-A-RIDE; INDEPENDENT LIVING FOR THE DISABLED; OUTREACH

Planning for the Elderly

Activities aimed at identifying the special problems and requirements of the elderly and devising solutions to enable these needs to be met. Planning for the elderly may be undertaken as an adjunct to planning for various facilities, such as parks and transportation facilities, or in a broader context in which plans are developed for overall needs.

When undertaken as part of other activities, the main concern is with design elements that increase physical safety or enable an elderly person to use the facility. In the broader sense, planning for the elderly is concerned with the provision of diverse programs to encourage continued self-sufficiency. These programs may include home food and health programs, employment and legal services, assistance in obtaining or maintaining housing, recreation and transportation programs, and provision of community centers.

To apply for funding for such programs under provisions of the Older Americans Act, communities and states must prepare a plan for services for the aging that coordinates the efforts of all agencies (volunteer, private and government) that conduct programs designed for this population. In addition, offices for the aging usually act as advocates for the aging in community matters and may undertake studies of problems of the aging that provide a basis for development of new programs.
See: ARCHITECTURAL AND TRANSPORTATION BARRIERS; CONGREGATE HOUSING; HOUSING FOR THE ELDERLY; OLDER AMERICANS ACT OF 1965; RETIREMENT COMMUNITY; TRANSIT FARE SUBSIDIES

Planning-Programming-Budgeting System (PPBS)

A complex system of evaluation of program objectives as a basis for establishment of a budget, used to link planning and budgeting operations. PPBS requires that all program objectives be clearly understood and that all alternative programs to reach those objectives as well as direct and indirect costs and benefits of each alternative be evaluated. PPBS also requires annual development of multi-year programs and financial plans that anticipate project development in the near future and program delivery that may occur many years later.

Earlier forms of PPBS were developed by private industry in the 1940s and 1950s, adopted by the Department of Defense in 1961 and applied to the entire federal government by President Lyndon Johnson in 1965. A large-scale effort to introduce the use of PPBS to state and local governments was made in 1967 but was largely a failure. Since that time, PPBS has been regarded by most governments as a good idea that is too cumbersome for general use. Although it has been used successfully by some municipalities and by universities and school districts, it has largely been abandoned by the federal government.

The program budget, which was an outgrowth of PPBS and is less complex to undertake, has largely replaced PPBS in communities that want to connect the planning and budgetary functions. Other important by-products of earlier experiments with PPBS are an emphasis on cost-benefit studies, which have been applied to a large extent throughout government, and an increasing emphasis upon citizen participation in policy development.
See: BUDGET; DIRECT AND INDIRECT BENEFITS; DIRECT AND INDIRECT COSTS; PROGRAM BUDGET; ZERO-BASE BUDGET (ZBB)

Play Street

A public street that is officially closed for certain hours of the day or certain days of the week to provide space for outdoor recreation. Used largely in inner city areas without sufficient or nearby public parks or playgrounds, such street closings allow the streets to function as play areas free of interference from traffic. Periodic closings of certain park drives and parkways to permit bicycling is an extension of this concept that has become popular.

Provision of play streets is a quick and inexpensive way in which recreation areas can be made available. It is a particularly useful technique where permanent open space cannot be reserved for financial or other reasons.
See: PLAYLOT; VEST-POCKET PARK

Playground

The primary location for outdoor play for children from the ages of approximately 5 to 14. Generally containing play equipment—such as climbers, swings, a balance beam, a horizontal ladder or more modern creative play equipment—they may also contain areas for court or field games and a playlot for younger children.

The playground has for many years been the focus of park planning at the neighborhood level, designed to serve as the source of recreation closest to home. Since traditional guidelines call for a 6- to 8-acre (2.4- to 3.2-hectare) site, 0.25 to 0.5 mile (0.4 to 0.8 kilometer) from home, the playground has often been placed adjacent to the elementary school and planned in conjunction with it. In older areas, however, where space for such a complex is not available, playgrounds are provided on sites of all sizes and may contain only one feature of the ideal playground, such as play equipment. An area of approximately 6,000 to

7,000 square feet (557 to 650 square meters) is adequate play space for about 50 children.

See: ADVENTURE PLAYGROUND; ATHLETIC COURTS; ATHLETIC FIELDS; CREATIVE PLAY AREAS; NEIGHBORHOOD PARK; PLAYGROUND DESIGN; PLAYLOT

Playground Design

Selection and placement of play apparatus and appurtenances to provide an environment conducive to children's play. The principal concerns in playground design are safety, variety of activity, aesthetic appeal, durability and ease of maintenance.

The creative play area, which involves the use of a large variety of component parts generally available from catalogs in combination with permanently placed mounds and structures, is the playground form employed in most development today. In this form, virtually all playgrounds can be different, can fit into a stated budget and can be appealing to children. However, while use of the components in a linked system is most supportive of imaginative play, use of the components without linking may be no more interesting to children than conventional play equipment.

Fencing and single entrances to playgrounds are considered best for control of access, while use of synthetic paving materials, other "soft" pavements, sand or turf are advisable for safety around play equipment. Benches should be provided, particularly in spots suitable for supervision of children, but away from entrance areas to prevent clogging them. A shelter, toilets, an equipment storage building and water fountains are desirable, as are areas of shade and sun.

Where athletic courts and playfields are to be available on the same site, they should be placed sufficiently apart from each other and from areas designed for younger children. This will allow adequate space for each function and should prevent participants of one activity from being forced to cross the path of another. When possible, sites should be selected that do not require extensive grading and that have existing features, natural or man-made, that can be used in the design of the park.

See: CREATIVE PLAY AREAS; OUTDOOR SEATING; PAVEMENT; PLAYGROUND

Playlot

An enclosed area of a park that contains play apparatus designed for preschool children. Playlots often contain the traditional swings, slides, climbing apparatus, sandbox, small merry-go-round or animal sculptures that young children particularly enjoy but may also have more creative play equipment or a spray pool.

While playlots, also called totlots, are typically provided at parks of most sizes, they may also be located on individual sites near housing developments, where they are ideally sited 300 to 400 feet (91 to 122 meters) from entrances to the units. An area of 2,000 to 4,000 square feet (186 to 372 square meters) will accommodate 30 to 50 children.

Shaded and grassed areas may also be provided for group activities or running games.

See: CREATIVE PLAY AREAS; PLAYGROUND; VEST-POCKET PARK

Plaza

An open space, generally found in an urban environment, that serves as a point of assembly, as a physical link between buildings and as a stage for the display of sculpture. As a component of architectural design, a plaza, which is usually paved, is considered a principal means of articulating space, whether as a common element in a group of buildings or as a break in a line of buildings.

Plazas vary greatly in size, in the type of materials used and in the character or ambience generated. Historically, plazas were formal in design, often forming part of a grand plan encompassing wide avenues, monuments and elaborate architectural structures. In recent years plazas have become recognized as a more vital element of urban design and as an amenity for the public. Zoning ordinances often include incentives to developers to include a plaza or some form of open space in heavily developed areas.

See: AMENITY; INCENTIVE ZONING; TOWN SQUARE

Plottage

The concept that two or more contiguous undeveloped parcels of land held by one owner usually have a greater value than the sum of the value of the individual parcels if they were in separate ownership. The additional value is considered to be a result of the greater flexibility and increased marketability possible with the larger parcel. Plottage is often considered in real estate appraisal practice and in eminent domain proceedings where a judgment of fair market value must be reached.

See: APPRAISAL; EMINENT DOMAIN

Plume

The visible emission that issues from a stack. The dispersal of a plume into the atmosphere is governed by many factors including the height and width of the stack it issues from, ambient temperature, atmospheric stability, wind speed, and the temperature and exiting velocity of the gas.

See: AIR POLLUTION; STACK

Pneumatic Structure

Buildings made of flexible membranes—composed of cloth, rubber or synthetic materials—that are supported by air pressure or gas. Very large structures may have the additional support of a wire frame. The more than 250,000 shapes that can be created are determined by the shapes of the individual membranes and, if they are used, by the wire supports.

Pneumatic structures in simple bubble form are often used for temporary buildings, such as seasonal covered tennis courts and swimming pools. They have been used, as well, as formwork in the construction of concrete houses, where the pneumatic structure is covered with concrete and then removed, leaving a concrete shell in 90 minutes.

Pockets of Poverty

Areas of otherwise financially healthy municipalities that have a substantial number of residents with incomes below the federal poverty level.

The Housing and Community Development Act of 1979 established a "pockets of poverty" program, in which municipalities can use Urban Development Action Grants (UDAG) for these areas. As defined in that program, at least 70 percent of the residents of a pocket of poverty are required to have incomes of less than 80 percent of the local average, and at least 30 percent are required to have incomes that are 30 percent below the federal poverty level. In municipalities or urban counties of 50,000 or greater population, a pocket of poverty is required to contain the lesser of either 10 percent of the total population or 10,000 people, while in smaller municipalities they need to have 2,500 people or 10 percent of the population, whichever is greater.

A pockets of poverty program is used in municipalities that have only one or a few pockets of poverty, as opposed to other communities that have numerous areas that meet the criteria and that are certified as UDAG communities.
See: POVERTY LEVEL; URBAN DEVELOPMENT ACTION GRANT (UDAG)

Point Source

1.   An individual and distinct conduit—such as a pipe, culvert or ditch—through which water pollution can reach a waterway. Sewage treatment effluent is a typical example of point source pollution. Since more diffuse sources of pollution may eventually reach pipes or ditches and enter the waterway, as a practical matter point sources are usually defined as consisting of industrial discharges, discharges from sewage treatment plants and overflows from combined storm and sanitary sewers.

Measurable progress has occurred in recent years in controlling point source water pollution in the United States as a result of federal legislation that supports the construction and improvement of municipal sewage treatment plants and procedures aimed at regulating pollution discharges, such as the National Pollutant Discharge Elimination System (NPDES).

2.   An individual and distinct stationary source of air pollution, such as an exhaust stack. For purposes of implementing the Clean Air Act, this term is defined more specifically in the Code of Federal Regulations in terms of stationary sources emitting more than a specified amount of a particular pollutant, sometimes based on the population density of the area. Additional stationary sources, such as certain chemical processes or metallurgical industries, are automatically considered to be point sources, regardless of the quantity of their emissions.
See: AIR POLLUTION; NATIONAL POLLUTANT DISCHARGE ELIMINATION SYSTEM (NPDES); NONPOINT SOURCE; WATER POLLUTION

Pointing

1.   A term used in masonry construction for the process of filling mortar joints (mortar layers between stones or bricks) that have been raked—that is, cleaned of mortar for a short distance back of the face to permit further finishing. The mortar is kept back from the face of the stone to a depth of about 0.75 inch (1.9 cm) to enable the placement of a special mortar to make a tighter and more attractive joint.

2.   The material used for the final filling of mortar joints. As buildings age the pointing often deteriorates, requiring that it be reapplied to ensure watertightness between masonry elements.

Points

Money paid to a lending institution in connection with a loan, either as a service charge or as an additional interest charge. The term is most commonly associated with mortgage loans, with one point equal to 1 percent of the loan.

The points are paid at the time the loan is made so that, for example, if 2 points are being charged the lender gives the borrower 100 percent of the loan amount and the borrower pays 2 percent of the loan amount to the lender. The borrower must repay the entire loan amount; the 2 percent point payment is not deducted from the principal amount of the loan.

Points allow lenders to receive a competitive rate of return on mortgage loans when interest rate ceilings are in effect. In the case of Federal Housing Administration (FHA) or Veterans Administration (VA) insured mortgages, the buyer of the home may not be charged points, but the seller is permitted to pay them.

Police Department

The municipal department responsible for maintaining order, enforcing state laws and local ordinances, regulating traffic and investigating crimes. Most police forces also have record-keeping units from which records of local criminal activity can be obtained for use in social and criminal justice planning. Traffic accident data are also maintained and made available, and in some smaller communities the police department will review proposed new development for its relationship to traffic patterns and public safety. For administrative convenience the police department of large cities is divided into police precincts; where data of a local nature are required, they can often be obtained for the specific precinct under study.
See: ACCIDENT RATES; CRIMINAL JUSTICE PLANNING; PUBLIC SAFETY BUILDINGS; UNIFORM CRIME REPORTS

Police Power

The inherent authority reserved to the states in the 10th Amendment to the United States Constitution to adopt laws for the purpose of promoting or protecting the public health, safety, morals or welfare. The police power may be delegated to or conferred upon local governments through enabling legislation.

The police power includes the right to regulate land use through zoning, health, environmental and related legislation; to license engineers, architects, real estate brokers and other professionals; to tax and collect taxes; and to adopt laws regulating real estate and commercial transactions.

In the exercise of its police power, the state may take various actions that directly and indirectly affect the value of private property positively or, without any compensation to the property owner, negatively. Through zoning and related regulations, local governments may directly reduce the value of private property. However, the police power does not include the power of eminent domain; if the state wishes to acquire private property, it is constitutionally required to do so in accordance with due process of law and to provide just compensation to the property owner. Thus, if a regulation adopted pursuant to the police power unreasonably interferes with the use or enjoyment of private property, it may be found to constitute a taking and therefore be unconstitutional.

See: BUILDING CODE; *CONSTRUCTION INDUSTRY ASS'N OF SONOMA COUNTY* v. *CITY OF PETALUMA; PEOPLE* v. *STOVER*; PUBLIC PURPOSE; SUBDIVISION REGULATIONS; TAKING; *VILLAGE OF BELLE TERRE* v. *BORAAS;* ZONING

Policy Development

The process of selecting from alternative courses of action to arrive at a choice consistent with a set of defined goals and objectives. As an example, a community objective of revitalizing the commercial center may be achieved by a policy that emphasizes incentives and subsidies, by one that emphasizes regulations and code enforcement or by one combining these approaches. Policy development is the process of deciding which of the alternatives to adopt.

Policy development involves analyzing the potential impact of each alternative and obtaining input from a broad range of governmental officials, community groups and citizens. Because the selection of one policy over another is often controversial, it is extremely important that during the development phase an attempt be made to secure a broad-based consensus for the preferred policy.

See: POLICY STATEMENT

Policy Statement

A statement describing the general philosophy that motivated a particular course of action or that guided or will guide decision making. With respect to government, policy statements may be found in such documents as legislation, reports, comprehensive plans or regulations.

See: POLICY DEVELOPMENT

Political Subdivision

1. A portion of a state with specified boundaries that serves to perform activities delegated to it by the state and has been granted limited powers of self-government by the state. The political subdivisions of a state (the various levels of local government) include counties, cities, towns and villages.

2. The Census Bureau categorizes political subdivisions as states, counties, minor civil divisions (towns and townships) and places (incorporated cities, towns, villages and boroughs).

See: HAMLET; HOME RULE; LOCAL GOVERNMENT; MINOR CIVIL DIVISION (MCD)

Pollutant Standard Index (PSI)

A standard index that allows air quality in various parts of the United States to be compared on a uniform basis. The PSI, established by provisions of the Clean Air Act Amendments of 1977, translates data concerning five major air pollutants (sulfur dioxide, nitrogen dioxide, carbon monoxide, ozone and total suspended particulates) into a single number representing air quality.

On this scale, which ranges from 0–500, a rating of 0–49 is good, 50–99 is moderate, 100–199 is unhealthful, 200–299 is very unhealthful, and a rating of 300 or more is described as hazardous. A rating of 250, for example, would mean that a warning would be issued to elderly persons and those with heart and lung diseases to stay indoors and to decrease their amount of physical activity. The PSI is widely used by those state and local agencies that monitor air pollution levels, and is also reported by news media to provide notice to those individuals needing to take special precautions as a result of air pollution levels.

See: AIR POLLUTION

Pollution

The alteration of any part of the environment to the extent that it becomes hazardous or potentially hazardous to human, plant or animal life, or to the extent that the environment becomes impaired or is made less desirable. Although, in its broadest sense, a pollutant is simply anything that causes pollution, the term *pollutant* often refers to a man-made substance or to a substance introduced in significant concentrations to a particular location by human activity.

See: AGRICULTURAL POLLUTION; AIR POLLUTION; CONTAMINANT; INDUSTRIAL WASTE; NOISE POLLUTION; PESTICIDES; RADIOACTIVE WASTES; SOLID WASTE; THERMAL POLLUTION; TOXIC SUBSTANCES; WASTEWATER; WATER POLLUTION

Polychlorinated Biphenyls (PCBs)

A class of toxic industrial chemicals that have been used in the manufacture of a wide variety of products, ranging from plastics to the insulating fluids used in electrical transformers. PCBs are attracting attention and concern because they are capable of causing environmental contamination for long periods of time and tend to concentrate at the higher ends of the food chain.

The presence of PCBs in many water bodies has led to

restrictions on commercial fishing in some locations, resulting in the loss of considerable revenues to the fishing industry. Bans on or warnings against the consumption of certain types of fish have also been put into effect in a number of states, including Connecticut, Michigan and New York.

It was specifically mandated by Congress in the Toxic Substances Control Act of 1976 that the manufacture, processing, use and disposal of PCBs be controlled. Currently, efforts are being made to develop safe means of destroying waste materials containing high concentrations of PCBs through such methods as high-temperature incineration and chemical destruction processes.

See: TOXIC SUBSTANCES; TOXIC SUBSTANCES CONTROL ACT OF 1976 (TSCA)

Polyvinyl Chloride (PVC)

A commonly used plastic that emits hydrochloric acid when burned and is found in a wide range of domestic articles, such as furniture and clothing. The Environmental Protection Agency has designated PVC as a hazardous air pollutant, and standards have been established limiting emissions that result from its manufacture.

See: AIR POLLUTION; EMISSION STANDARD

Population Characteristics

Facts concerning a community's population, which are necessary for many planning purposes. Among the characteristics that are of greatest interest to planners are the size of the population, age distribution, spatial distribution, income patterns and information concerning household formation and size. Other useful information concerns racial and ethnic composition, educational characteristics and employment patterns.

These facts not only are necessary background for comprehensive planning but provide an immediate frame of reference for specific planning problems. Household size, for example, and the type of household—e.g., single adults or elderly—have important implications for present and future housing demands and needs. Income patterns also provide data on housing needs as well as an indication of the types of community facilities that might be required. Occupation and employment patterns help to determine the types of commuting facilities that might be necessary and have a major impact upon the decisions of employers to locate their businesses in a community.

Data concerning population characteristics are often necessary in completing grant applications and required government forms.

See: AGE STRUCTURE; CURRENT POPULATION ESTIMATES; DEMOGRAPHY; POPULATION DISTRIBUTION; POPULATION PROJECTION

Population Decline

A reduction in the number of inhabitants of a neighborhood, city or region. Population decline usually occurs because of a lowered birthrate, a lack of economic opportunity or changes in business technology prompting large-scale worker layoffs that cause net out-migration. Population decline may also be caused by housing obsolescence, fear of crime, changing public tastes or a combination of these phenomena. In rural areas population decline may occur when young people are attracted by job opportunities or the wider range of activities available in the city.

Within metropolitan areas in the United States, population decline has occurred in many central cities, reflecting a desire for low-density housing and the movement of residents, jobs, retail activity and business investment to the suburbs and exurbs. Under these circumstances, population decline may be associated with subsequent central city housing abandonment and reduced numbers of individuals in the central city who are in middle-income brackets.

See: POPULATION MOBILITY; SUBURBAN GROWTH; ZERO POPULATION GROWTH (ZPG)

Population Distribution

The spatial distribution of population is a major factor in determining the location of most types of community facilities and land uses. These uses, in turn, are likely to influence future population distribution.

One means of viewing population distribution concerns place of residence. Residential distribution may be analyzed for geographic areas of varying size, such as state, county or town, by means of past census data and current estimates. This will provide information on the current distribution and the ways in which distribution patterns are changing, indicating future trends. The daytime distributions, greatly influenced by place of work, may be obtained partially or indirectly from census data; other sources include the data produced in origin and destination studies and special studies or surveys.

Population distribution is often depicted graphically. Dot maps, in which each dot represents a specific number of people are common. Circles of varying sizes may also be used to represent the population of an entire community on a small-scale map.

See: DEMOGRAPHY; DENSITY; POPULATION CHARACTERISTICS; POPULATION PROJECTION

Population Mobility

The ability of people to migrate to another region or to shift residence within a region for such reasons as improved climate, economic opportunity or social factors. Population mobility may involve the overall population, such as the movement to the sunbelt that has been occurring, or a specific subgroup, such as the movement of an ethnic group from a central city neighborhood to a suburban community.

See: BOOMTOWN; NO GROWTH; SUBURBAN GROWTH; SUNBELT

Population Projection

A prediction concerning the future that is made expressly contingent upon stated assumptions. Technically, it differs from a forecast, which predicts future events without these expressed assumptions. Planners sometimes, however, use these terms interchangeably.

Population projection is essential to almost all aspects of planning. It provides a framework for the formation of a comprehensive plan and for long-range planning by indicating what the future population of an area might reasonably be expected to be. In addition, it enables daily decision making affecting future plans and resource commitments to take place. The planning of schools, sewage treatment plants, transit systems and recreation facilities, for example, requires reasonably accurate projections to permit future needs to be satisfied without an overcommitment of public funds.

Although accuracy can never be assured, it is more likely that projections for large areas, such as nations or states, will be accurate than will those prepared for small areas.
See: COHORT SURVIVAL METHOD; CURRENT POPULATION ESTIMATES; POPULATION PROJECTION METHODS

Population Projection Methods

There are a number of ways in which the projection of population for communities may be conducted.

The simplest means of looking at future population is through an approach in which past trends are assumed to continue in the future. An arithmetic projection assumes a constant amount of population change each year; if drawn on graph paper, the result is a straight line. A geometric projection assumes a constant rate of change; this also appears as a straight line if plotted on semilogarithmic graph paper. Neither of these methods is particularly satisfactory because of their single-minded emphasis upon past growth patterns. More complex mathematical techniques —like the method of least squares, multiple regression or the logistic curve—are also used in projections.

Ratio methods of projection use projections that have been prepared for larger geographic areas—e.g., a state. Calculations are made to determine the proportion of the projected population that the geographic subdivision can expect.

Economic variables may also be used in making projections. This approach assumes that economic advantages, such as good job availability, will have a significant impact upon future migration. One way of using this method could be based upon prior employment projections or other economic analyses for a particular area.

The cohort survival method is often selected by planning agencies. Although, like any projection, it can prove to be inaccurate, it has the advantage of examining the components of population change (births, deaths and migration) separately.
See: COHORT SURVIVAL METHOD; CURRENT POPULATION ESTIMATES; POPULATION PROJECTION

Port

A natural or man-made harbor where ships can load, unload or anchor. Ports usually provide docking facilities as well as a variety of services for ships, including repair and maintenance, towage, fueling, warehousing, stevedoring and replenishment of ship's provisions. These services may be provided by a port authority, by independent contractors or by the shipping companies.

Docking facilities for freight carriers and ocean liners require considerable land support facilities. For freight and passenger loading and unloading, and temporary storage, 20 acres (8.1 hectares) of land and/or dock area per berth has been suggested as optimal. It is also common that a large land area surrounding port facilities be devoted to commercial uses related to port activities. Modern ports must also be able to accommodate containerized shipping, which is the placement of cargo into truck trailer-sized containers and the subsequent placement of the containers onto specially equipped ships. This advance in the shipment of freight enables quick ship loading and unloading and therefore faster turnaround time for these vessels.

Offshore port improvements are now required to a greater extent to accommodate super-sized ships. Channel dredging, larger turning basins and more complex systems of navigational aids and traffic control are necessary for these larger ships.
See: HARBOR; PIER; WHARF

Port Authority

A special district created to build and maintain port facilities. The most notable example is that of the Port Authority of New York and New Jersey, which was formed in 1921 by a compact between the two states. Within an area comprising about 1,500 square miles (3,885 square kilometers), it is responsible for port facilities, interstate bridges, tunnels, bus and truck terminals, and airports.
See: PORT; SPECIAL DISTRICT

Potable Water

Water fit for human consumption. Among the measures of potability are absence of human, animal or bacterial contamination; degree of mineralization; and salt concentration.
See: DESALINATION; GROUNDWATER; SALTWATER INTRUSION; WATER QUALITY CRITERIA; WATER SAMPLING; WATER TREATMENT

Poverty Level

A term used to designate an income level necessary to support a minimum acceptable standard of living in a particular area or country.

In the United States the Office of Management and Budget defines the poverty level as a function of family size. In 1981, for example, the poverty level in the United States was $8,450 for a nonfarm family of four and $7,190 for an equivalent farm family. Data from the 1980 U.S. Census, when compared with poverty-level figures, indicated that there were 25.2 million persons below the poverty level based on 1979 income.

See: GHETTO; POCKETS OF POVERTY; SLUM; SOCIAL SERVICES PLANNING; SOCIAL STRATIFICATION; URBAN INDICATORS

Preapplication Conference

A meeting held between a prospective developer and municipal officials (generally professional planners) at a point early in the planning and design process and before formal application has been made for subdivision approval or approval of a zoning application.

The intent of the preapplication conference is a mutually beneficial exchange of information between all concerned parties. The prospective applicant learns about relevant municipal plans, community goals and development regulations that will apply to the project. In turn, the municipality is likely to be able to influence the project's design, as this early stage is the least costly time for the developer to alter or adjust design concepts.

Other topics that may be discussed at a preapplication conference include available data concerning the site, availability of utilities and municipal services, and relevant off-site considerations. The municipality will be able to make sure that the applicant understands what steps are involved in securing project approval, which can help to avoid future costly delays. The developer may also be given an informal opinion on how the project will be viewed in the formal review process, based upon how it seems to conform, at this stage, to municipal plans and ordinances.

In a smaller municipality the entire preapplication review may be able to be completed in one meeting. In larger communities the information presented by the developer at the preliminary meeting is customarily circulated to appropriate agencies—e.g., public works and health—for informal review and comment. These comments are then presented to the applicant at a later meeting and are sometimes able to prevent major design or development errors from occurring. When a major obstacle to the development is found at this stage, it is also possible for the developer to drop the project before a substantial commitment of funds has been made.

See: NEGOTIATION; SKETCH PLAN; SUBDIVISION REVIEW

Precast Concrete

Concrete that has been formed into various construction components, either in a factory or near a construction site, prior to being placed in a structure. It differs from poured-in-place concrete, which is cast in forms in the position it will occupy in a finished structure. Precast elements may be unreinforced, reinforced or prestressed and include floor and roof slabs; walls and partitions; joists, beams, girders and columns; and arches, rigid frames and domes.

Precasting is advantageous because it permits mass production of concrete units, facilitates quality control and allows the use of higher-strength concrete than can be mixed on the construction site. Complex thin-shell structures, which would be costly if cast in place, may become more economical when precast.

See: CONCRETE; PRESTRESSED CONCRETE; REINFORCED CONCRETE

Preliminary Plat

A map or series of maps showing the layout of a proposed subdivision, which is submitted for the review and approval of a municipal agency, usually the planning commission.

A prospective subdivider is expected to present in the preliminary plat a carefully designed and drawn-to-scale subdivision plan. It should include such features as lot layout and approximate dimensions and area of each lot; road layout; topographic features, including contour lines; drainage details; property boundaries; and other facilities or structures proposed for the site. The municipality may also require a locational sketch, the designation of any land to be deeded for public recreation, and plans and specifications for any road construction or new utilities that will be needed. Despite the level of detail required for a preliminary plat, however, the drawings need not be finalized, as they must be for the final plat.

In reviewing a preliminary plat, a planning board, with the help of its planning staff, will be checking the subdivision for compliance with subdivision regulations, zoning regulations and the municipal comprehensive plan. Particular points of interest will be the size and arrangement of the lots and the road network; the relationship of the subdivision design to the natural features and topography of the site; planned access points; and proposed facilities for drainage, sewage and water supply.

The degree of detail required in a preliminary subdivision plat represents a substantial commitment of capital in terms of the costs of land acquisition or options and the legal, surveying, engineering, planning and architectural fees. Because of this, usually preliminary plat maps are no longer the first opportunity a municipality has to see a new development proposal. Instead, the preapplication conference, a two-way exchange of information, and the preliminary sketch plan are used as an earlier and less expensive way in which the basic concepts for a subdivision may be shaped. The preliminary plat should then reflect these concepts. (See Fig. 34)

See: FINAL PLAT; PREAPPLICATION CONFERENCE; SKETCH PLAN; SUBDIVISION REGULATIONS; SUBDIVISION REVIEW

Prescriptive Easement

The acquisition of an easement over property by means of the continued use of the property for a period of time prescribed by statute. The use must be open, inconsistent with the claims of others and under a claim that the use is lawful. However, unlike the case of adverse possession, where possession must be exclusive, the use of property subject to the prescriptive easement need not be exclusive, nor must it prohibit use by the owner of the property.

See: ADVERSE POSSESSION; EASEMENT

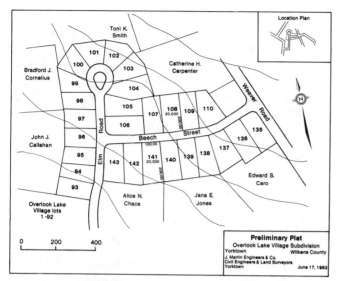

Fig. 34. A preliminary plat of a proposed subdivision of land into single building lots.

Preservation

The process of encouraging the useful existence of structures for as long as is feasible, through practices such as stabilization and preventive maintenance. The term may also be used to apply to many other planning-related areas, such as neighborhood preservation or preservation of the economic base of a community.
See: HISTORIC PRESERVATION; NEIGHBORHOOD PRESERVATION

Preservation Plan

A document that identifies historic resources worth conserving and discusses means by which this may be accomplished. Preservation plans may vary in content but often include a community history, a description of the community and the results of a survey of historic resources with discussion of their relative importance. They also contain desired community goals and objectives with respect to preservation, and a range of options that may be exercised to achieve these goals. Among these options are the adoption of ordinances, the establishment of regulatory commissions, the use of easements and the amendment of existing municipal policies and codes to make them more compatible with historic preservation.

A preservation plan may be a separate document or an element of the municipal comprehensive plan.
See: COMPREHENSIVE PLAN; HISTORIC PRESERVATION

Prestressed Concrete

Concrete into which high-strength steel wires or cables or high-strength alloy steel bars (all of which are called tendons) have been placed prior to pouring of the concrete and that have been tensioned by hydraulic jacks to a required tensile strength. Concrete that is tensioned after the concrete is poured is called posttensioned concrete.

Generally precast, both prestressed and posttensioned concrete are similar to reinforced concrete but are more expensive. They are usually used only when a higher tensile strength is required than can be obtained with reinforced concrete. Prestressed and posttensioned elements are used extensively in bridge design, domes and airport runways.
See: CONCRETE; PRECAST CONCRETE; REINFORCED CONCRETE

Pretreatment

Processes used in wastewater treatment to remove material such as grease and scum prior to primary sedimentation to enable more effective treatment. Pretreatment is used at municipal sewage treatment plants in the treatment of domestic sewage and at private treatment plants associated with industry and food handling. It may include the use of skimming tanks, grease traps, preaeration tanks or flocculation tanks.

The term may also be used to refer to any form of sewage treatment that may be required to remove impurities or reduce the volume of industrial sewage prior to discharge to the municipal sewerage system.
See: DOMESTIC SEWAGE; INDUSTRIAL SEWAGE; PRETREATMENT STANDARDS; SEDIMENTATION TANK; SEWAGE TREATMENT

Pretreatment Standards

Standards established by the Environmental Protection Agency (EPA) for pretreatment of industrial sewage prior to its discharge into a public sewer system. Substances are classified into categories, and daily and monthly average limitations are established and reviewed annually for each category. Pretreatment standards for existing sources (PSES) and new sources (PSNS) may differ.
See: FEDERAL WATER POLLUTION CONTROL ACT AMENDMENTS OF 1972; INDUSTRIAL SEWAGE; NEW SOURCE PERFORMANCE STANDARDS (NSPS); PRETREATMENT

Primary Road

Primary roads are rural highways that, as a system, provide an integrated network serving travel corridors of statewide or interstate importance, connect all major population centers and carry high volumes of traffic. While they are not usually controlled-access routes, access to adjacent land is typically limited to facilitate traffic movement. Primary roads constitute about 17 percent of the rural road system.

The Federal Highway Administration uses the term *rural arterial system* for primary roads and divides them into two classes: rural major arterial and rural minor arterial. Rural major arterials connect population centers of 25,000 or more people to each other. Rural minor arterials serve smaller cities and towns and may terminate at resort areas. The latter carry volumes somewhat lower than those of major arterials but higher than those of secondary roads.
See: ARTERIAL ROAD; FUNCTIONAL ROAD CLASSIFICATION; SECONDARY ROAD

Primary Treatment

The most common form of sewage treatment, in which up to 60 percent of the suspended solids and up to 40 percent of the organic matter in wastewater can be removed. Primary treatment generally involves a screening process for removal of coarse solids; grit removal; primary sedimentation, in which effluent and sludge are separated and floating solids skimmed; and chlorination of the effluent.
See: SECONDARY TREATMENT; SEWAGE TREATMENT; TERTIARY TREATMENT

Primitive Recreation Area

A natural environment where only a few recreational activities, such as hiking, backpacking, primitive camping and canoeing are permitted. Fishing and hunting may also be allowed at certain times of the year, and wilderness skills, such as survival techniques, may be taught. In many national, state and regional parks where the land is left in its natural state, only these forms of recreation may be consistent with the maintenance of the area's ecology. In remote regions, such locations may be known as wilderness areas.
See: NATIONAL WILDERNESS PRESERVATION SYSTEM; NATURE PRESERVE

Principal Use

The primary purpose or use of a parcel of land or a structure or structures. A retail store is, for example, a principal use in a commercial retail district; a house is a principal use in a residential district. By contrast, a storage facility might be considered an accessory use to the retail store, while a garage or toolshed would be an accessory use to the house. Accessory uses are not usually permitted in the zoning district unless they are serving a particular principal use, and it is sometimes forbidden to construct an accessory use until the principal use is built, to ensure that it will be constructed.
See: ACCESSORY BUILDING; ACCESSORY USE; ZONING

Priorities

The relative order of importance assigned to various community needs. The establishment of priorities helps to define community goals and objectives, the order in which capital projects will be funded, the types of government programs that are operated or given preference, and the ways in which revenue is spent.

Privacy

1. The physical seclusion of one party from the view or scrutiny of others. Assuring privacy is an aspect of habitability most often associated with residential architecture. Psychologists have identified several different types and levels of home privacy needs associated with families and individuals as well as needs in work places. Privacy may include total protection from view or from intrusions such as noises, or it may involve conveying a sense of privacy through less than totally isolating techniques, such as partial screening and differences in grade levels. Zoning regulations often call for privacy fencing or screening to restrict views of heavily used areas, such as commercial facilities, from nearby residential properties.

2. The protection of data regarding one party from the scrutiny of others. The Bureau of the Census, as an example, protects the privacy of individual census returns by making only aggregated information public.
See: BEHAVIORAL DESIGN; PERSONAL SPACE; SCREENING; TERRITORIALITY

Private Mortgage Insurance

Insurance for mortgage lenders in the case of default on mortgage loans. Private mortgage insurance existed as early as 1885, but the industry was essentially eliminated by bankruptcies during the bank holidays of 1933. In 1957 private mortgage insurance was again instituted by the Mortgage Guarantee Insurance Company (MGIC) of Milwaukee, Wisconsin, which remains the largest of the 15 existing firms. Private mortgage insurance is accepted for trading in the secondary mortgage market, and its availability has allowed greater flexibility in loan underwriting.

For a fee paid for by the mortgagee, private mortgage insurers are able to provide insurance with very liberal eligibility limits, such as property price or income of mortgagee. They are also able to respond more quickly than the Federal Housing Administration (FHA) and to be more flexible in underwriting criteria, particularly with respect to down payment ratios. Private mortgage insurance is available for income properties as well as for residential properties.

Unlike the FHA in most cases, private mortgage insurers often insure only the "top" 20 percent of a loan, which is the portion of the loan carrying the greatest risk. This means that if there is a default on the loan, the private mortgage insurer is responsible for only 20 percent of the loan amount, while the value of the property, even with default-related costs, is relied on to provide at least 80 percent of the mortgage loan amount.
See: FEDERAL HOUSING ADMINISTRATION (FHA) MORTGAGE INSURANCE; SECONDARY MORTGAGE MARKET; VETERANS ADMINISTRATION (VA) MORTGAGE INSURANCE

Private Road

A street constructed as a land access road that may or may not conform to local subdivision or land development codes and has not been offered, or has not been accepted, as a public street. It may be built to serve residential, commercial or industrial land use. The road is constructed by a private owner or owners for either private or public use and is maintained by the owners.
See: DEDICATION; DRIVEWAY; MAPPED STREET

Program Budget

A budget that lists programs to be undertaken and the funding allotted to each program by function. A program budget may be contrasted with the more standard line-item budget, which lists allocations for supplies, personnel, etc., for each department. In the preparation of a program budget, policy objectives of potential and existing governmental programs are studied, alternatives to these programs are considered, and the costs and benefits of the programs are analyzed. The program budget is an outgrowth of the planning-programming-budgeting system (PPBS), which sought a more comprehensive analysis of all program possibilities.

Use of a program budget forces municipal agencies to analyze their goals and objectives, but the difficulty in defining program objectives is also one of its main limitations. The program budget enables the amalgamation of parts of the same program that are the responsibility of different departments, so that total program costs and benefits can be calculated and overlap removed; the projection of program costs for future years is shown as well. Some program budgets also indicate performance criteria to aid in quantifying proposed accomplishments. Program budgeting is now often associated with management by objectives (MBO), in which programs are developed in conjunction with the staff responsible for them.

See: BUDGET; LINE-ITEM BUDGET; MANAGEMENT BY OBJECTIVES (MBO); PERFORMANCE BUDGET; PLANNING-PROGRAMMING-BUDGETING SYSTEM (PPBS)

Program Evaluation and Review Technique (PERT)

A planning and control device that can reduce production time and/or cost by designing a work process that is efficiently organized. It uses a linear programming model to show the interrelated network of activities involved in a project so that time and cost estimates, and adjustments, can be made. PERT permits estimation of scheduled completion dates, and resource and manpower allocations in coordination with those dates, as well as determination of critical problems requiring special attention. First used by the U.S. Navy's Special Projects Office in the Polaris missile project in 1958, it is now most often used in scheduling projects for which no precedents exist—hence its use in planning, research and development.

Computation of time estimates involves determination of three estimates for each activity (optimistic, most likely and pessimistic) and the path through the network that takes the longest time to be completed, known as the critical path. Through this process it is possible to determine where slack time is permissible and where attempts should be made to shorten required time spans.

The network model is expressed in the form of a PERT chart, which shows circles for each completed activity (events) and arrows pointing to and from the circles that represent the duration of the activities. Numerous activities within a project are generally undertaken concurrently.

See: CRITICAL PATH METHOD (CPM)

Projection Drawing

Drawings of objects that show several facets in one view. They may give the appearance of three dimensions but are drawn so that the shape and size of the object are correctly scaled in some or all of its dimensions, in contrast to the completely distorted dimensions of perspective drawing.

Projection drawing uses mechanical methods to project an image of an object or structure from a plan and/or elevation to a multisided figure. The methods of projection are known as orthographic projection, axonometric projection and oblique projection. Projection drawings are frequently found on working drawings, where they illustrate details of construction.

See: PERSPECTIVE RENDERING; WORKING DRAWINGS

Property Acquisition

The purchase of land and/or buildings or their receipt as gifts. Property acquisitions are generally accomplished by contract, after negotiation concerning the price of the property. In government acquisitions, however, if agreement cannot be reached, the government may resort to condemnation, in which the government takes the land and the courts determine the appropriate price.

When land is purchased by government either for open space or for a future facility, other forms of acquisition may be used. These include sale and leaseback, in which the former owner may lease and use the property for a specified number of years; lease-purchase, in which the government leases the property and acquires it over a period of years by paying a stipulated amount per year; or life estate, in which the former owner who has sold the land to a government may use it for the duration of his lifetime. The selection of a particular form of acquisition depends upon the immediacy of need for the property and availability of funds.

Besides the purchase of land, municipal governments frequently obtain land from higher units of government or acquire real estate as gifts from the public. Because acceptance of property entails future costs for the recipient, offers may be refused.

Selection of property to be acquired is generally preceded by studies of alternative sites and their ability to support the intended use, as well as comparisons of the costs of acquisition and development of the respective properties.

See: APPRAISED VALUE; ARM'S-LENGTH TRANSACTION; CHARITABLE CONTRIBUTION OF REAL ESTATE; CONDEMNATION; COUNTY RECORDS; PROPERTY DISPOSITION; SALE-LEASEBACK; STEWARDSHIP

Property Disposition

The sale of land and/or buildings or their donation as gifts. Records of property sales are generally available for public use at county land record offices.

Unlike private property sold on the open market, government property dispositions are often accomplished by first offering sites to lower government levels, sometimes free of charge or at nominal cost. If not accepted, the property is put up for bid at public auction and sold to the highest bidder. An upset price is frequently established to prevent the property from being sold below an acceptable amount.

See: PROPERTY ACQUISITION; SALE-LEASEBACK; UPSET PRICE

Property Numbering System

A uniform numbering system adopted to make it easier to locate property in a community. It may be necessary because large new developments are being built or because the previous system has become unworkable. A property numbering system begins from some central reference point, such as the center of the business district.

In general, any system should assign numbers consecutively and uniformly based upon street frontage. Numbers assigned to one side of the street (usually the north and east sides) should be even, while those on the opposite side are odd. The system must also allow new buildings and new streets to be properly numbered.

See: STREET NAMING SYSTEM

Property Tax

A tax levied annually on the value of real property (consisting of both land and structural improvements) and, in some localities, upon personal property such as business and farm equipment, commercial inventories, automobiles, jewelry or securities. Property taxes are the main source of income for most local governments in the United States, Canada, Britain (where they are called rates) and other British Commonwealth countries. The tax is imposed upon the value of property without regard to the personal circumstances of the owner and therefore constitutes a legal municipal claim against the property.

In urban planning the property tax is of concern because of its potential effects upon land use and the economy. As an example, when municipalities within the same state, and particularly within the same region, tax at differing levels, businesses may be attracted to the municipalities with the lower rates. Similarly, since some states tax only real property as opposed to personal property, there is an inducement for certain businesses to relocate to those states, particularly when their tax rates are low and when a variety of cost increases make an existing location untenable. These business relocations have large impacts, both positive and negative, upon local economies. In addition, they often cause land development pressure in places that may be unsuitable for, or poorly equipped to deal with, such relocations because of a lack of necessary municipal infrastructure. Property tax rate increases are another form of land development inducement, particularly where farms and large estates must pay taxes related to their land use development potential rather than their present use. These properties may often be sold or subdivided in the absence of taxing policies related to preservation of their present use.

Another planning problem associated with the property tax is the difficulty of its collection in declining neighborhoods and the pressure it imposes on landlords to abandon distressed properties. The relationship of the property tax to the support of the public school system is yet another area of concern to planners. The majority of a school district's revenues are derived from property taxes. Where the tax base of a community is small or declining, expenditures for education may be grossly different among neighboring municipalities, leading to an undue emphasis upon the need to attract ratables.

Because of inequities in property tax administration, attempts have recently been made to standardize tax assessment procedures. These procedures are established at the municipal level and vary from community to community.

See: ABANDONMENT; AGRICULTURAL DISTRICT; ASSESSED VALUATION; ASSESSMENT RATIO; BETTERMENT TAX; CERTIORARI; CIRCUIT BREAKER TAXES; EQUALIZATION RATE; FISCAL ZONING; GROWTH MANAGEMENT; IMPROVEMENTS; LAND VALUE TAX; RATABLES; TAX ABATEMENT; TAX ASSESSMENT ROLL; TAX-EXEMPT PROPERTY; TAX MAP; TAX RATE; UNIFORM ASSESSMENT PROCEDURES

Proposition 13

The Jarvis-Gann Property Tax Initiative, which was approved by the voters of California and put into effect on July 1, 1978. The initiative, commonly known as Proposition 13, placed a 1 percent property tax ceiling on municipalities and limited local control over other revenue sources, severely reducing available funds for municipal programs. Proposition 13 and Proposition 2½ in Massachusetts are the two major tax limitation measures that have been imposed by state governments on local municipalities. In Massachusetts a 2.5 percent property tax limitation was imposed, but municipalities may override the limit upon local initiative.

The immediate effect of the property tax reduction in California was a $7 billion annual drop in local government revenues, but because the state has been willing to distribute surplus revenues to municipalities, the net loss has been considerably reduced. To recoup most of the lost revenue, municipalities have raised other municipal fees such as for facility use, licenses and permits, fines and service charges.

The major effect of tax limitation measures on planning, however, relates to the ability of a municipality to construct capital projects, which is generally no longer possible via general obligation bonds because of the tax ceiling.

Instead, local governments are required to create special districts, where this is possible, or to use revenue bonds or leaseback arrangements. The cost of development is also rising in California since municipalities are unable to make many infrastructure improvements that they once made in conjunction with major developments, requiring that developers pay for more off-site improvements. Since property taxes are no longer sufficient to pay for the increased municipal costs that result from development—such as sanitation, police and fire protection—municipalities now carefully evaluate the fiscal impact of projects, and of housing developments in particular.

While both the state and federal governments gained increased revenues as a result of Proposition 13 (by reduced income tax deductions for local taxes), future state surpluses and their continued donation to municipalities are uncertain. The more profound issues, however, are the limitation of home rule powers, the need to depend on intergovernmental aid for revenue and the potential long-term effects of these actions.
See: HOME RULE

Provider of Services

A person who receives, directly or through an immediate family member, more than one-fifth of his income from health-related employment, or who is otherwise employed in the health field, as defined in the National Health Planning and Resources Development Act of 1974 and amendments. Providers of services and consumers of services were defined by the act as the two constituencies that were to be represented on the boards of directors of health systems agencies (HSAs). The act requires that from 40 percent to 49 percent of the membership of HSA boards be composed of providers of services.
See: CONSUMER OF SERVICES; HEALTH SYSTEMS AGENCY (HSA); NATIONAL HEALTH PLANNING AND RESOURCES DEVELOPMENT ACT OF 1974

Public Art

Works of art that are placed so that they may be viewed by large numbers of people in the course of their activities. Sculpture, monuments and murals are the traditional forms, while paintings, woven hangings, photography and wall art are emerging as popular new mediums for enhancing the appearance of public places.

Since ancient times, it has been traditional to prominently place large works of art so they could be readily seen and act as a focal point for community activity. Public art is evident in all large-scale planning projects to this day for the same reasons. A more recent phenomenon, however, is the use of public art in conjunction with the design of individual public and corporate buildings, brought about, in part, by the need to decorate the austere architecture that has evolved since the 1950s. Public art has also become more popular because of the need for special design treatments for the many large plaza areas whose development has been encouraged by zoning incentives. In these plazas, which are often devoid of appealing features, public art has increasingly helped to fill a literal void.
See: DEVELOPMENT FOCUS; FOUNTAINS; INCENTIVE ZONING; 1 PERCENT FOR ART LAW; WALL ART

Public Buildings

Buildings that are financed largely by public funding and are available for public use, as distinguished from buildings that are government-financed but are intended for private use—e.g., public housing.

Public buildings are traditionally designed so that they are recognizable as public buildings and often feature high ceilings, rotundas and the use of relatively indestructible construction materials. Perpetuation of a public building image dates from ancient times and is desirable, since it imparts a sense of importance to the buildings and their surroundings and tends to create a distinctive community character. The use of large amounts of artwork in public buildings is a current design trend intended to enhance their appearance. Adaptive use of significant old public buildings, such as city halls and firehouses, is also becoming widespread and is important for the preservation of community character.

Because they are built by government agencies, buildings of higher governmental units are usually legally exempt from local zoning requirements, although, by custom, they often comply with municipal regulations. Where they do not comply, care should be taken to ensure that the buildings harmonize with their surroundings.
See: ADAPTIVE USE; ARCHITECTURAL AND TRANSPORTATION BARRIERS; CEREMONIAL AXIS PLAN; CIVIC CENTER; COMMUNITY FACILITY PLANNING; 1 PERCENT FOR ART LAW

Public Easement

An easement granting members of the public a right to make some specified use of the servient estate. Examples include pedestrian and vehicular rights-of-way, water-access easements and easements to use hiking trails. Public easements may be acquired by eminent domain, by prescription or by donation by the property owner.
See: CONSERVATION EASEMENT; EASEMENT

Public Health, Safety and Welfare

Public purposes that are legally sufficient to support the exercise by the state of its police power. Public welfare has been construed to include such important interests as political and social order, morals, economic welfare, aesthetics, recreation, public convenience and promotion of commerce.
See: POLICE POWER; PUBLIC PURPOSE

Public Hearing

A hearing employed by a legislative or administrative body as part of the process by which legislation or regulations are adopted or other decisions are made.

Administrative agencies are often required by statute to

hold public hearings prior to adopting new regulations. Depending upon the circumstances, interested members of the public may comment upon the proposed regulations either by way of oral testimony given before the administrative body or by a written submission to be included as part of the record of the hearing.

Congress often holds hearings prior to the enactment of new laws; the record of these hearings then forms a source of legislative history, aiding in the interpretation of the laws.

Public hearings are conducted for a variety of other purposes related to the activities of government, such as for selection of the corridor for a major transportation route or development of a major grant application for which public participation is required.

See: LEGAL NOTICE

Public Housing

Housing for low- and moderate-income persons provided by public housing authorities authorized by federal and state law. In the United States experimentation with public housing began early in the New Deal, and the Housing Act of 1937 instituted public housing nationwide. Built largely for low-income families, it is intended to provide decent, sanitary and safe housing at modest cost. Public housing is financed by tax-exempt bonds issued by a public housing authority (PHA) and supported by an annual assistance contract with the Department of Housing and Urban Development and rental paid by residents. Some states added their own programs, often for moderate-income families, to supplement federally supported programs.

Public housing, which was built directly for PHAs (often as part of urban renewal projects), developed rapidly after World War II but soon encountered difficulties. While a variety of housing design types were used—including high-rise, medium-rise and garden apartments—the public began to associate public housing with the large-scale, high-rise and high-density projects found in many urban areas. Since public housing projects were available to all low-income families by statute and policy, many public housing projects accepted a greater percentage of minority residents and maladjusted families than was representative of the community as a whole, since these were the populations having difficulty finding housing in the open market. Management and maintenance, funded by rents determined in relation to tenants' incomes and by limited federal operating assistance, were frequently inadequate. Public housing often came to be viewed as housing of last resort, and because of this stigma, normal municipal services (including police protection) were provided at insufficient levels. The Pruitt-Igoe project in St. Louis, part of which was demolished because of design problems related to height and density as well as serious crime problems, came to symbolize the troubled state of public housing.

Starting in the mid-1960s, efforts were made to improve public housing. A modernization program administered by HUD provides funds for significant rehabilitation of public housing projects. Some PHAs had already begun their own security forces, and efforts to improve management have included greater tenant participation. Turnkey development was authorized primarily to reduce construction costs (which had been high for public housing in part due to federal regulations). Turnkey, along with Section 23 Leased Public Housing; the experimental Operation Breakthrough program, which encouraged use of innovative construction techniques; and a program that permits PHAs to purchase existing housing, resulted in greater private developer participation in public housing and an increased variety of housing. In addition, current federal design standards for development of public housing projects (called minimum property standards) permit only low-rise construction for family housing except in very dense cities. In 1982 there were over 1,300,000 public housing units nationwide, about 2 percent of the housing stock of the United States, including heavy concentrations in major cities. In recent years, however, new public housing has been limited to relatively small numbers of units, often for the elderly, due to local concerns as well as national budget constraints.

In Britain, by contrast, council housing (housing constructed by local authorities and largely populated by laborers and unemployed persons, including the elderly) consisted of nearly 7,000,000 units in 1981 and comprised about one-third of the total housing stock. It has been government policy since 1980 to encourage the tenants of these units to purchase them. A discount on the market value of each unit of from 33 percent to 50 percent is offered to public sector tenants who have occupied their homes or apartments for at least three years; they may also be eligible for a mortgage from the local authority to enable the purchase. Problems related to crime and poor construction have required the demolition of some council housing, as in the United States.

See: HOUSING AUTHORITY; LOCAL AUTHORITY; SECTION 8 HOUSING PROGRAM; SECTION 23 HOUSING PROGRAM; TURNKEY PROJECT; UNITED STATES HOUSING ACT OF 1937

Public Information

1. A term describing the reports, materials and tools that a planning agency prepares and makes available for public use. It includes information that is distributed, such as reports and newsletters, as well as materials that are presented, such as displays, models, films and exhibits. Agencies generally also have resources on premises—such as a library collection and map, picture and ordinance files—that are available for use by the public.

2. That information in government possession which is subject to Freedom of Information Act (or state equivalent) request, as opposed to that information which the government is not required, or is not permitted, to make available.

See: FREEDOM OF INFORMATION ACT

Public Infrastructure

The services and facilities provided by a level of government. In urban planning, the term refers primarily to physical facilities, such as sewers, roads, subways and schools. In social planning, infrastructure describes the structure of public services that are made available, such as health services and social service programs.
See: MUNICIPAL SERVICES

Public Land Ownership

Government ownership of land to advance public goals. By purchasing land, the government gains more control over its use than through zoning regulations but must pay for this right in three ways: the cost of acquiring the land, of holding it and paying maintenance costs, and of removing it from the tax rolls.

The government may buy land for a specific public use (e.g., construction of a building), to prevent it from being developed (e.g., for use as a nature preserve) or to develop it for private use according to a public plan (e.g., for middle-income housing). Public land ownership in the form of a land bank can be used to control the pace, location and type of development or to prevent premature development, sprawl and land speculation. It may also be used to implement public policy, such as a land use plan.

Public land banking has been used on a large scale as a planning tool in Alberta and Saskatchewan, Canada; Sweden; and Israel. In Stockholm, for example, publicly owned land is held until urban services are available and is then leased to developers.
See: LAND BANK

Public Purpose

A purpose that is legally sufficient to support the exercise by a government of its police power. That is, a public purpose is one reasonably related to the promotion of the health, safety, morals or welfare of the community at large or all the inhabitants of a political subdivision, not merely for the welfare of a specific individual or a small class of persons. Virtually all exercises of governmental authority related to planning or zoning have their foundation in the furtherance of a public purpose.
See: POLICE POWER; PUBLIC HEALTH, SAFETY AND WELFARE; PUBLIC USE

Public Record

1. Records that units of government are required by law to produce or maintain in furtherance of their legal obligations or governmental responsibilities. These records may only be considered public if they are generally made available for public inspection at governmental offices—e.g., the offices of the county clerk—or if the governmental unit maintaining the record must permit it to be inspected by a private citizen who makes a request under an applicable state or federal freedom of information act.

2. Records of legal transactions or events that are maintained for the purpose of creating a system for the resolution of conflicting interests in real estate or personal property. Such records include registers of deeds, mortgages, liens against personal property and judicial judgments entered against a party to a lawsuit.
See: COUNTY RECORDS; FREEDOM OF INFORMATION ACT

Public Safety Buildings

Police stations, fire stations, civil defense and emergency control centers, police investigative laboratories, fire training and police training facilities, jails and penitentiaries. These facilities have differing requirements, from a planning perspective, in that some are located on numerous sites throughout the municipality and must be easily accessible, while others serve the entire community or region and may require seclusion.

Police and fire stations are located throughout a municipality on the basis of population distribution, crime rates and possible fire incidence; these and emergency control centers are essential components of community facility planning. The other facilities are built as the need arises, so that planning for them may be limited to feasibility studies and site selection.

Training and investigative facilities may have a centralized location for easy access or be located on a suburban site that provides more space and seclusion. Small jails are usually built in conjunction with court facilities, but larger jails and penitentiaries require more remote locations that provide sufficient security and space.
See: COMMUNITY FACILITY PLANNING; CRIMINAL JUSTICE PLANNING; FIRE STATION

Public Use

The requirement that private property may be taken only for a public use is, together with the requirement of just compensation, the principal constitutional limitation upon the exercise of the power of eminent domain.

A public use has come to be formally defined to include any use that enables a governmental authority to carry out its functions and to preserve or promote public health, safety and welfare. It also includes takings (where permitted) by a nonpublic body (e.g., public utilities, common carriers) that are required to enable it to serve the public.

It has been asserted that eminent domain comes close to violating the public use prescription during the course of urban renewal programs, where land in blighted areas has been condemned and then sold to private developers for private purposes. In those cases, the public use limitation has been considered satisfied by noting that elimination of slums and blighted areas furthers a public purpose.
See: CONDEMNATION; EMINENT DOMAIN

Public Utilities Plan

A set of recommendations and priorities to ensure that utility improvements, including both construction of new facilities and upgrading of existing facilities, are consistent with local and regional development policies.

A public utilities plan is generally developed jointly by the planning and public works departments, and focuses on those utilities deemed so essential that they are either owned or strictly regulated by the government, such as water, gas, electrical and sewerage systems. Most plans contain an inventory of existing facilities by utility, generally depicted in a series of maps. The age, condition and capacity of each utility is also usually provided. This information is used to determine the adequacy of each utility, and is analyzed with respect to projected population and employment, projected ultimate service area and probable required levels of service to determine future needs, including rehabilitation and expansion requirements. In addition, the plan should address new or probable future requirements of federal or state agencies concerning the level of service that must be provided or standards that must be achieved, to ensure that any deadlines that are imposed can be met.

Emerging from this analysis is a plan for improvement and expansion of the systems. Because resources are scarce, most plans prioritize these needs based on the goals and objectives of the particular unit of government. Included in the plan may be policy recommendations concerning management and efficiency levels of the systems and a section on financing options.

Traditionally, communities prepared public utility plans to ensure coordination between population growth, new development and the location of utilities. Today, however, many municipalities are most concerned with the deterioration of their existing utilities and, consequently, stress rehabilitation and replacement, and the development of innovative ways to finance these improvements.
See: COMPREHENSIVE PLAN

Public Works and Development Facilities Program

Grants to assist in the construction of public facilities that will initiate or encourage long-term economic growth in designated "redevelopment areas" or "economic development centers" as established by the Public Works and Economic Development Act of 1965. Funding is available from the Economic Development Administration for construction of facilities—such as access roads to industrial parks, port facilities, water and sewer systems, railroad sidings, public tourism facilities or vocational schools—provided the facilities also further the objectives of the Economic Opportunity Act of 1964.

Grants of up to 80 percent are made for projects in redevelopment areas; these areas may also be eligible for an additional 10 percent for public works projects. In other areas 50 percent grants may be available, while long-term, low-interest loans are also sometimes made to enable the community to finance its matching share.
See: ECONOMIC DEVELOPMENT ADMINISTRATION (EDA)

Public Works and Economic Development Act of 1965

An act (PL 89-136) that established federal support for economic development planning, implementation and related public works activities in economically depressed areas. Grants on a 50 percent matching basis as well as loans (in some cases without interest) and loan guarantees were provided to eligible "redevelopment areas," and a revolving fund was established to pay for these activities. Technical assistance was also made available to these areas. The act prescribed qualifications for designation as a redevelopment area (relating to amount of unemployment, median income, underdevelopment and area population) and required that the area submit an overall economic development program (OEDP). Also included were provisions for the establishment of economic development districts (to permit economic development planning on a broader scale) and economic development centers (areas larger than redevelopment areas, where economic development might alleviate conditions in redevelopment areas), which would also be eligible for federal assistance. In addition, the act established regional action planning commissions.

Amendments to this legislation, adopted in 1974, increased funding for planning efforts related to the mandated overall economic development program to 80 percent and required that they be related to a state economic plan. The amendments also financed job opportunity programs and created a disaster-recovery program related to redevelopment of the economy of disaster areas. Amendments adopted in 1976 were aimed at combatting a recession and included substantial public works funds. This legislation was repealed in 1981, but some of the programs received continued funding through other authority.
See: ECONOMIC DEVELOPMENT ADMINISTRATION (EDA); ECONOMIC DEVELOPMENT DISTRICT (EDD); OVERALL ECONOMIC DEVELOPMENT PROGRAM (OEDP); REGIONAL PLANNING COMMISSION

Public Works Department

The local government agency responsible for the provision and maintenance of part or all of the physical infrastructure that is operated by a municipality. Public works departments are traditionally responsible for public roads, public buildings and public utilities such as water supply, sewerage and solid waste handling. They may sometimes also be responsible for airports, port facilities, and municipal gas and electric utility operation. Planning for these facilities is usually undertaken by the public works department in conjunction with the planning department.

Public works departments are usually headed either by a single commissioner, typically a civil engineer, or by a board. The department head or a delegated staff engineer is generally recognized by the state as the "municipal engineer" responsible for road and bridge closings when a hazard is detected.

Pumped Storage Power System

A method of producing hydroelectric power in which water is pumped to a storage reservoir at a higher elevation during off-peak hours, when there is surplus power, and then released to provide additional energy during peak hours, when it is most needed. Reversible turbines are used both to pump the water and to generate the electricity when the water is later released.

Although this type of system can actually consume more energy than it produces, it can help to avoid the construction of additional power plants that might be needed for peak-load periods. It is especially useful when employed in conjunction with a nuclear plant that generates a constant output of electricity throughout the day. One controversial aspect of pumped storage systems is the effect upon the storage reservoir's appearance and its ability to support recreational use. At various times of day, large mud flats could be exposed, which would be unsightly and also prevent such activities as swimming and boating. (See Fig. 35)
See: ELECTRIC POWER GENERATION AND TRANSMISSION; HYDROELECTRIC POWER

Pumping Station

Part of a water supply or sewerage system at which water or sewage is pumped to a higher elevation.

Pumping stations are used in a water supply system either to provide service across a hilly area that cannot be served by a gravity supply or to increase water pressure in the pipes. Main pumping stations are located as near as possible to the middle of the distribution system to obtain the greatest hydraulic advantage. Auxiliary or booster sta-

tions are frequently used in fringe areas of overextended distribution systems to increase water pressure or to supply water to elevated tanks. Sewage pumping stations are used, predominantly, to lift sewage over a ridge so that it may then flow by gravity, to lift sewage out of a hollow that is lower than the surrounding sewer lines or to pump sewage from a basement that is below the sewer line. They are also used at treatment plants to lift treated waste.

In locating pumping stations, sites should be selected that will protect the water supply from potential disasters, allow for expansion and be compatible with surrounding land use. Sites that facilitate underground placement are frequently chosen.
See: FORCE MAIN; GRAVITY FLOW

Purchase-Money Mortgage

A mortgage that the seller receives from the buyer to serve as a portion of the payment for purchased property when the seller agrees to help finance the sale.
See: MORTGAGE

Pyrolysis

The decomposition of waste by heat in the absence of oxygen or in an atmosphere where the presence of oxygen is strictly controlled. As a result of this process, combustible gases or liquids are produced that, in theory, could be transported or stored and marketed as fuel.

The practical application of pyrolysis to resource recovery is still in the developmental stage, but pilot plants have been constructed in Baltimore, San Diego County and Redwood City, California, as well as in Luxembourg.
See: RESOURCE RECOVERY

Q

Quiet Communities Act of 1978

Legislation that authorizes a variety of programs to be conducted by the Environmental Protection Agency (EPA) relating to research, information and technical aid to promote noise control. This act (PL 95-609) also provides for a program of grants to states, regional planning agencies and local governments for identification of noise problems and development of programs and evaluation of methods to control noise.

EPA is directed to provide technical assistance to local governments, including development of model noise control legislation and the purchase of monitoring equipment to be lent to municipalities. The legislation also directs the Federal Aviation Administration (FAA) to respond to EPA within 90 days of promulgation of proposed aircraft noise regulations in an effort to obtain its compliance with requirements of the Noise Control Act of 1972. Fines of up to $10,000 per day for issuance of products by manufac-

turers that violate EPA noise emission standards are authorized as well.
See: EACH COMMUNITY HELPS OTHERS (ECHO); NOISE CONTROL ACT OF 1972; NOISE POLLUTION

Quiet Enjoyment

The right of an owner or lessee of real estate to use the property free of interference from others or claims of others.

The concept is most often used in connection with real estate leases, which generally contain the landlord's covenant that the tenant is entitled to the quiet enjoyment of the leased premises. In a lease these words normally would mean that the tenant has the right to occupy and use the leased premises free from interference or disturbance by the landlord, a former or future tenant, a holder of a mortgage on the property or any other person.

R

Racket Sports

A group of court games played with a racket and a ball that includes tennis and squash and their variations. Most may be played either indoors or out on a paved surface, while some, such as tennis, may also be played on a clay or grass surface.

Tennis has been the most widely played of these activities, with facilities provided in many urban parks and at most resorts. It requires a large court, which is 78 feet (23.8 meters) long and 27 feet (8.2 meters) wide for singles play or 36 feet (11 meters) wide for doubles play, plus an additional 20 to 40 feet (6 to 12 meters) outside the court. When more than one court is provided, they are generally located in banks for ease of supervision and maintenance and economy of space and are laid out in a north-south direction, if possible. Each court or group of courts is surrounded by a chain link fence. In the 1970s, when tennis was enjoying extraordinary popularity, private tennis clubs emerged to handle the boom. These clubs have, to some extent, reduced the need for public courts and in many places are provided in public parks on a concession basis. In some places overbuilding of racket sports facilities has necessitated their adaptive use for other activities, such as exercise programs.

Badminton courts, which may be laid out in the same manner as tennis courts, are smaller, requiring a length of 44 feet (13.4 meters) and a width of 17 feet (5.2 meters) for singles or 20 feet (6.1 meters) for doubles, plus an additional 5 feet (1.5 meters) on all sides. Paddle tennis courts have very similar dimensions, a 50-foot (15.2-meter) length and a 20-foot (6.1-meter) width, but require a little more space around them (10 feet [3 meters] at the ends and 8 feet [2.4 meters] at the sides).

Deck or platform tennis is a relatively new version, in which the court is placed on a wooden deck surrounded by a chain link fence, with required overall dimensions of 30 feet (9.1 meters) by 60 feet (18.2 meters). It can be built almost anywhere, because it is elevated above the ground, and is very popular during cold winter months because its construction allows snow to be swept through spaces between the wood boards.

Official racketball courts are 40 feet (12.2 meters) long and 20 feet (6.1 meters) wide, with front and side walls that are 20 feet (6.1 meters) high and a rear wall that is 12 feet (3.7 meters) high. This size court is also the official size for four-wall handball and paddleball. A North American singles squash court requires a 32-foot (9.8-meter) length and 18.5-foot (5.6-meter) width, with a front wall height of 16 feet (4.9 meters) and a rear wall height of 6.5 feet (2 meters). The International (English) size court is 2.5 feet (0.8 meter) wider. All of these courts, however, are most often located at indoor recreation centers and at private clubs. Paddleball and racketball are also often played at handball courts provided in many urban parks.
See: ATHLETIC COURTS

Radburn, New Jersey

A planned community in Fairlawn, New Jersey that was designed by Clarence Stein and Henry Wright in 1928. One of the earliest efforts to create a model new town, Radburn had a substantial influence upon land development in the United States and the design of Swedish and British new towns.

Radburn's design used the superblock concept, in which large areas of common open space are preserved. Homes bound this common area, and pedestrian walkways link segments of the community and are separated from main roadways so that it is not necessary to cross streets. Fast-moving traffic is also channeled to feeder roads, while houses are accessible from culs-de-sac, although they front on landscaped areas.

Radburn is composed of a mixture of housing types as well as a commercial center, community center, school and recreation areas. It was originally intended to house 30,000 people and contain a wider variety of land uses. Development was halted by the Depression, however, after the completion of two superblocks on a 149-acre (60.3-hectare) parcel accommodating approximately 3,000 persons.
See: GARDEN CITY; GREENBELT TOWNS; NEW TOWN; STEIN, CLARENCE S.

Radial Pattern

A land pattern, also known as an axial pattern, in which streets radiate from central nodes like spokes of a wheel. Several arterial roads begin at a major focal point, such as a government building or park, and proceed outward, often intersecting with other nodes.

Radial patterns have been superimposed on several major cities. Washington, D.C. (designed by Pierre L'Enfant), London (designed by Christopher Wren) and Paris (designed by Baron Haussmann) each have some radial boulevards of ceremonial dimensions. Cities with this form, although visually interesting, have many intersections where three or more roads cross, often making them difficult to administer from a traffic engineering standpoint. Where central nodes become overcongested, it may be necessary to provide a circumferential road for alternative routing. (See Fig. 24)
See: AXIAL GROWTH; LAND USE PATTERN

Radiation Hazard

The hazard caused by the emission of particles and rays by materials that are radioactive. Although it is well known that large radiation doses, such as might be received from a nuclear weapon, are capable of causing rapid death, low-level radiation exposure has been linked to increased rates of cancer, chromosome damage and an acceleration of the aging process.

Radiation exposure is cumulative in effect, and some experts contend that there is no minimum level below which radiation definitely ceases to have any negative effects on human beings. One source of concern is the accumulation of such radioactive contaminants as strontium-90 in the food chain. The average person in the United States is exposed to approximately 200 millirems of radiation annually from background radiation, medical exposure, global fallout and the use of nuclear power.
See: NUCLEAR ENERGY; RADIATION STANDARDS; RADIOACTIVE WASTES

Radiation Standards

Standards set by the federal government that regulate the transportation of materials that are radioactive and set permissible limits for exposure to radioactive substances. Standards are in effect for the emission of radiation from all sources, as it affects human beings and the environment, as well as specifically for individual nuclear plants.
See: NUCLEAR ENERGY; RADIATION HAZARD; RADIOACTIVE WASTES

Radioactive Wastes

Wastes that are the by-products of nuclear reactor operation and also result from a variety of other activities, such as industry, medical research or military operations. The expected increase in the use of nuclear power, the potential dangers of radiation and the long half-lives (the time it takes for radioactive materials to decay by 50 percent) of many radioactive substances make the management of radioactive wastes a difficult endeavor.

Suitable long-term storage facilities for these wastes should be isolated for the foreseeable future, secure, geologically and seismically stable, and protected from natural disasters such as hurricanes. It should also be possible to transport wastes to such sites without having to convey them through heavily populated areas. One of the options that has been considered for storage is burial in long-stable geologic formations, such as abandoned salt mines or unfractured granite.

In 1982 the Nuclear Waste Policy Act was passed in response to the growing quantities of high-level radioactive waste requiring disposal. The law requires the establishment of federal radioactive waste repositories.
See: HAZARDOUS WASTE; NUCLEAR ENERGY; RADIATION HAZARD; RADIATION STANDARDS

Railroad Rights-of-Way

The real property used for the operation of railroads. The reduction in demand for railroad services for a variety of reasons has caused rail lines in North America and Britain to cease service on numerous routes, leaving unused railroad tracks and rights-of-way. In many communities they are being converted to other uses, such as highways, bikeways and recreational trails.

The Railroad Reorganization and Regulatory Reform Act of 1976 (PL 94-210) contains a number of provisions that direct the Department of Transportation and the Interstate Commerce Commission on matters relating to rail line abandonment. Among these, it directs the Department of Transportation to analyze the potential for conversion of rights-of-way to alternate uses and to preserve railroad tracks and other rail properties in areas in which fossil fuel deposits or agricultural production are located, where railroads may potentially serve these industries. The demonstration Rails to Trails program, also authorized by this act, gave federal assistance to local governments for acquisition of abandoned railroad rights-of-way for recreation purposes.

Railway Yard

A large uncovered area where railroad and rapid-transit trains are stored, cleaned and repaired and cars are matched and connected. An engine shed or roundhouse, for the repair and servicing of locomotives, and shops for car repair are often located within the yard. Freight yards may also have warehouse facilities associated with them.

Ramp

1. A roadway that connects two or more intersecting or parallel roadways, so that traffic from one may merge with traffic on the other. Types of ramps include: diagonal; loop; semidirect and direct connections; and cloverleaf, which includes a loop and an outer connection.

2. An inclined floor used to provide vehicular and pedestrian access to upper floors of a building or different elevations of a complex of buildings. Ramps are frequently used in garages, shopping centers and other multilevel developments. They are becoming a standard design element in public places to provide for the needs of the handicapped.
See: ARCHITECTURAL AND TRANSPORTATION BARRIERS; PLANNING FOR THE DISABLED

Random Sample

A type of sampling technique used in conducting research, in which each member of the population or universe under consideration has an equal chance of being selected. In addition, every possible combination of members of the population has an equal chance of being chosen.

Common means by which random samples are selected are with the aid of random number tables or by drawing lots. In general, a prerequisite to selecting a random sample is a listing of all of the members of that population being sampled, called a sampling frame. In the type of practical research usually conducted for urban planning purposes, these types of lists, such as the names of all people over 60 in a particular state, do not exist or contain

omissions or duplications. If a sampling frame is judged to be sufficiently inadequate, a researcher has the options of attempting to compile a complete list or using other sampling methods.
See: SAMPLING

Rangeland Management

The preservation and improvement of land suitable for grazing. Rangeland management encompasses erosion control and soil retention, maintenance or betterment of scrub or other ground cover used for forage fire control and improvement of water supply, as well as stocking rate for grazing animals. As a result of land management practices that are used to preserve rangeland, the general public receives such benefits as reduced downstream siltation and improved flood control.
See: FARMLAND PROTECTION; LAND MANAGEMENT

Ratables

Properties yielding large tax payments to a municipality and requiring relatively few municipal services. The term is derived from the British terms *rates* (a local tax levied on property) and *ratable* (which means taxable).

Properties often referred to as ratables are large corporate office buildings, office parks and shopping centers, because they do not require schools, parks or social programs for their employees, provide private garbage collection, and often finance desirable physical improvements or contribute to municipal projects such as parking structures. These types of properties are actively sought by many municipalities to offset municipal budget increases.
See: TAX BASE

Raw Land

Land, also called unimproved land, that is vacant and lacking utilities, interior streets or any other type of improvement or development.
See: IMPROVED LAND

Real Estate Atlas

A set of maps, usually derived from tax maps, that show municipal boundaries; lot sizes, shapes and dimensions; street names and dimensions; tax assessor's section, block and lot numbers; and subdivision name and lot numbers, if applicable. Real estate atlases, generally compiled commercially, present tax map data in one or more convenient volumes that may be purchased. The atlases are updated frequently and the property lines kept reasonably up to date. They allow instant access to data that might otherwise only be available by visiting the assessor's office in a number of communities and then copying the information from each office's tax maps.
See: REFERENCE MAPS; TAX MAP

Real Property

Sometimes used synonymously with the term *real estate*, real property refers to land, what lies below or is permanently affixed to the surface of the land and the air rights above the land's surface.

Among the interests in real property that may be enumerated are a fee simple interest, a leasehold interest, a life estate, a mortgage, an easement and a condominium interest. Personal property may be distinguished from real property in that personal property includes property that is either movable or intangible (for example, a share of stock or a debt).

The distinction between real property and personal property is often critical. For example, transactions involving real property and personal property are subject to different rules regarding the need for the transaction to be in writing and the need for a document evidencing the transaction—e.g., a deed—to be recorded. (Conveyances of real property must be in writing and are ordinarily recorded.) The rules for obtaining a mortgage on real property and a lien on personal property are different, and tax laws often treat real property and personal property differently.

Rear Lot Line

Generally considered to be the line that is opposite from the front lot line and also farthest in distance from the front lot line. Zoning ordinances sometimes contain special provisions for defining rear lot lines on lots that are irregularly shaped or triangular in shape. (See Fig. 50)
See: LOT; LOT LINE

Rear Yard

A yard that extends across the entire width of a lot containing a building and is located between the rear lot line and a parallel line running through the point of the building closest to the rear lot line. The municipal zoning ordinance may require that the rear yard remain unoccupied, or it may permit accessory buildings to be located in the yard. (See Fig. 50)
See: REAR LOT LINE; YARD

Receiving Waters

The water bodies to which sewage effluent and other liquid wastes are discharged. Discharges into the receiving body must be treated sufficiently, prior to release, so as not to degrade the water quality of that body.
See: EFFLUENT; NATIONAL POLLUTANT DISCHARGE ELIMINATION SYSTEM (NPDES); OUTFALL; WATER QUALITY STANDARDS

Recharge

Addition of water to the groundwater supply, either through infiltration of precipitation or through downward seepage from surface water bodies. The rate at which aquifers are recharged varies greatly with soil characteristics and can be significantly affected by paving or otherwise altering land surfaces.

Artificial recharge methods have been developed to add water to groundwater supplies that have been seriously

depleted or are in danger of suffering pollution from salt water. As an example, stormwater may be impounded and used for recharge purposes. Other methods use treated sewage effluent or recycle water used for air conditioning to induce recharge.
See: AQUIFER; GROUNDWATER; GROUNDWATER POLLUTION; INFILTRATION; SALTWATER INTRUSION; WATER TABLE

Reconstruction

The process of completely recreating a structure that once existed. Approximately 50 percent of the buildings at Colonial Williamsburg in Virginia are reconstructions, built after extensive research and archaeological excavation. As a result of the Williamsburg development, many workers were trained in building crafts that were becoming extinct. Reconstruction is, however, the most drastic (and most controversial) of preservation activities because it involves considerable speculation as to what the buildings being created actually looked like.
See: ALTERATION; HISTORIC PRESERVATION; PRESERVATION; REHABILITATION; RESTORATION

Recreation Facilities

Any physical setting explicitly used for leisure-time pleasurable activities.
See: RECREATION PLANNING; RECREATION SYSTEM

Recreation Planning

The process of relating space and facilities to existing and proposed recreational programs. Recreation planning traditionally focused on the amount, location and design of recreational facilities and placed a particular emphasis on parks. Recently, there has been increased emphasis on the entire recreational system, including indoor and outdoor facilities, private and publicly operated facilities, and programmatic concepts such as available staff, instruction and organization.

Recent trends in park and recreation use indicate changes in patterns that reflect increasing private sector involvement and diminished interest in conventional park development. Recreation planning is therefore increasingly concentrating on the development of new recreation forms, such as creative play areas, and on integrating programs and facilities with cultural resources, such as presentations of symphony concerts in parks. Because of budget constraints, coordination with private clubs and quasi-public agencies that also offer recreational opportunities has been pursued, while multiple use of nonrecreational facilities, such as swimming in reservoirs, has been suggested to reduce capital development costs.

Standards, such as open-space ratios, were once used to determine community needs, but newer methods concentrate on user preferences, measures of effectiveness, carrying capacity and other innovative techniques. Use of park classifications is still popular to establish a hierarchy of park types related to population size and service area, but the definitions of park categories are changing because of local preferences and financial constraints. (See Fig. 35)
See: LEISURE OPPORTUNITIES; NATIONAL URBAN RECREATION STUDY; NONRESIDENT PARK USER; OPEN-SPACE PLANNING; OPEN-SPACE RATIO; PARK AND OPEN-SPACE CLASSIFICATION; PARKLAND LEASING; PARKS AND RECREATION PLAN; RECREATION SYSTEM; SELF-SUPPORTING RECREATIONAL FACILITIES

Recreation System

The combination of facilities and programs that provide a range of community recreational opportunities. The recreation system includes the entire gamut of recreational facilities and open spaces, whether active or passive, that are school-owned, public, quasi-public and private. The system also includes the programs, staff and volunteer committees that run the programs. The recreation system thus includes everything from the nature walk and vest-pocket park to the commercial bowling alley and Little League.
See: RECREATION FACILITIES; RECREATION PLANNING

Recreational Vehicles (RV)

Motorized vehicles that include a cabin for living accommodations and are commonly used for recreational travel and touring. Vehicles included in this category come in several forms; travel trailers, tent trailers and camping trailers, all of which must be towed by a car; and truck campers, motor homes and camper vans, all of which have the motor within the body of the vehicle.

Recreational vehicles have become popular with families in North America and Europe because they provide an

Fig. 35. Recreation planning provided multiple use of the Blenheim-Gilboa Pumped Storage Power Project in upstate New York. Boating and fishing are permitted on the lower reservoir (the powerhouse is in the background), while an adjacent state park built in conjunction with the power project provides swimming pools and other recreation facilities.
Credit: Courtesy of the New York Power Authority

inexpensive place to live while on vacation. Because of their popularity, park planning and road design in resort areas may provide adequate space for RV maneuvering and parking, as well as camping facilities where a demand is likely and where RVs can be accommodated without unduly compromising scenic and environmental qualities.

Recycling

The process by which materials in the waste stream are reused to create useful products. Recycling of waste is doubly advantageous because it decreases the quantity of waste requiring disposal while it encourages the conservation of resources.

Recycling may be conducted at various levels. The simplest and most conserving type is the reuse of an article, such as the washing and refilling of a returnable bottle. A second level of recycling consists of the reuse of a material for a product of similar quality, such as the use of waste newspaper to produce newsprint. Still other levels use a waste product to produce a product of lower quality (such as the use of waste glass to produce fiberglass insulation) or use a material to produce a completely different kind of product (such as the composting of waste to produce fertilizer). Finally, materials may be reused strictly for their thermal value, as in the incineration of waste for energy production.

As of 1978 there were more than 3,000 independent recycling centers operating in the United States. Despite this, it has been estimated that only about 7 percent of all municipal solid waste was recycled in that year. Several factors have contributed toward preventing the growth of recycling as rapidly as might otherwise be expected. In some cases, it has been difficult to obtain steady markets for the materials that are collected. The market is still very limited, for example, for recycled glass or cullet. Prices have also traditionally been fairly low.

It is likely, however, that recycling will continue to increase, particularly with respect to certain materials. Energy costs have made it profitable to produce aluminum from recycled materials, resulting in much higher prices being offered for used aluminum cans. This, in turn, has stimulated the collection of aluminum for resale. Increased recycling of paper is also expected to continue, as it has been demonstrated that the production of newsprint from recycled newspaper can be accomplished economically, at energy savings and with decreased pollution.
See: BOTTLE BILL; CULLET; FRONT-END RECOVERY; GLASPHALT; MAGNETIC SEPARATION; RESOURCE RECOVERY; SOLID WASTE MANAGEMENT; SOURCE SEPARATION

Red Tides

The discoloration of coastal waters by high concentrations of types of ocean plankton that can be toxic to marine life and to humans consuming affected fish. It is not known precisely what causes red tides—also called red sea or red water—to occur, although it is thought to be related in some way to eutrophication.

Red tides have been known since early history (the Red Sea is thought to have been named for this phenomenon), but their occurrence may be accelerating. Although few red tides were observed, for example, on the Florida coast prior to 1942, they became common after the population of the area grew rapidly. In the laboratory one type of red-tide organism prevalent in the North Atlantic was caused to bloom, or grow to many times its normal concentration, by light, nutrients, warm water temperatures and lowered salinities.

Many types of these plankton can cause symptoms in humans, ranging from eye and respiratory tract irritation as a result of airborne exposure, to death, in the most extreme cases, following consumption of poisoned shellfish. They are also capable of causing large fish kills. Monitoring programs have been developed in parts of Canada and the United States to provide an early warning of the presence of red-tide toxins.
See: EUTROPHICATION

Redlining

The refusal of a lending institution to grant mortgages on properties in certain neighborhoods, generally those located in older sections of the inner city or those with a higher minority population. Decisions to deny mortgages are frequently based on a perception by the lender, often unfounded, of a greater risk or lesser yield than can be found elsewhere.

Redlining often leads to disinvestment by the private sector, which may initiate or accelerate the decline of an area. The term is allegedly derived from the practice of drawing a red line on a map around neighborhoods in which mortgages would not be granted. In response to the problem, a number of federal antiredlining regulations have been adopted, including parts of the Home Mortgage Disclosure Act, the Equal Credit Opportunity Act, the Fair Housing Act and the Community Reinvestment Act. In most cases, these regulations require public disclosure of the locations of property on which mortgage loans are being made as a means of identifying the institutions that may be practicing redlining.

Another type of redlining involves a refusal by insurance companies to write policies in areas with a high incidence of arson, a violation of state insurance department rules.
See: BLOCKBUSTING

Reference Maps

Maps of varying types that contain information useful for planning studies or for compiling other special-purpose maps. Planning agencies use maps obtained from a wide range of sources, including tax departments, state and municipal engineering and highway departments, historical societies and many federal agencies, such as the Geologi-

cal Survey. Planning departments also produce reference maps that are compiled, printed and distributed for public use. Additional maps are available from commercial sources.
See: FIRE INSURANCE ATLAS; GEOLOGIC MAP; REAL ESTATE ATLAS; SOIL MAP; TAX MAP; TOPOGRAPHIC MAP; USGS MAPS; VEGETATION MAP

Referendum

1. A public vote on a budgetary matter, required by most states when a proposed expenditure on a particular project exceeds a maximum amount stipulated by law. The referendum asks for public approval of the issuance of bonds or the expenditure of funds for a specific purpose.

2. A public vote required by law on any matter.
See: MUNICIPAL SERVICES

Reforestation

The reestablishment of forest growth by seeding or planting nursery stock on land on which a forest once stood. It may be necessary because of fire or because the land has not naturally restocked with the desired tree species. Reforestation may be differentiated from afforestation, which is the conversion of nonforested land to forest.

Forest planting programs are usually conducted to provide a continuing supply of lumber and wood products. Trees may also be planted, however, as part of watershed protection programs or in land reclamation.
See: FOREST FIRE CONTROL; FORESTRY

Refuse-Derived Fuel (RDF)

Solid waste that is mechanically processed, through procedures such as milling and screening, so that it is converted to a fuel that may be burned in standard utility and industrial boilers as well as incinerators. Noncombustible or hard-to-burn materials are generally removed, and the remaining solid waste fraction is converted to small particles for ease of burning.

A number of types of refuse-derived fuel may be produced, depending upon the type of system in which the RDF will be used. Fluff RDF is processed to a particle size of 0.25 inch to 2 inches (0.64 centimeter to 5.08 centimeters) and is designed to be burned in suspension-fired boilers as a coal supplement. This process was demonstrated successfully in St. Louis, where the Union Electric Company became the first investor-owned utility in the United States to use fluff RDF in its boilers. Other types of RDF being tried elsewhere are densified RDF, dust RDF and wet RDF.

One advantage of RDF, which has approximately half the heating value of coal, is that it is transportable and may be used in standard boilers. Because it is subject to spontaneous combustion and is extremely flammable, however, it is usually not transported for long distances. RDF plants are in operation in such diversified locations as Ames, Iowa; Baltimore County, Maryland; East Bridgewater,

Massachusetts; Milwaukee; Chicago; and Monroe County, New York.
See: RESOURCE RECOVERY; SHREDDING; SOLID WASTE MANAGEMENT

Regional Park

A term used in defining a hierarchy of park sizes, service areas and facilities that usually describes a large public park or preserve that is natural resource-oriented and serves a metropolitan area. Often 500 acres (202 hectares) or larger, a regional park provides extensive areas for passive recreation and may also have regional recreational facilities that complement urban resources—e.g., a lake for swimming and boating, beach facilities or a ski area.

The designation of a park as regional, however, is often a political rather than a practical matter. Where parklands are administered by a regional or state agency or park district, they can usually be classified as regional, but when administered by a county or city agency, they may be restricted for the use of local residents, even though they fit the physical description of a regional facility. In addition, there are numerous parks, preserves and cultural facilities of smaller size—e.g., botanical gardens—that serve as regional resources. Use of the term is therefore often a matter of local definition.
See: NONRESIDENT PARK USER; PRIMITIVE RECREATION AREA

Regional Plan Association (RPA)

The oldest private metropolitan planning organization in the United States, founded in 1922 by the Russell Sage Foundation as the Committee on the Regional Plan of New York and Its Environs. Incorporated in 1929, it is supported by individual members, businesses, municipalities and counties, government agencies, civic groups and foundations.

RPA, which is located in New York City, conducts research and education programs and endeavors to find means of improving the physical, economic, environmental and social conditions of the region, which includes portions of New York, New Jersey and Connecticut. In 1968, after 10 years of work, RPA issued a draft *Second Regional Plan* and a number of related supplements for specific geographic areas, intended to help shape the region's growth to the year 2000. RPA periodically issues various reports and publications.
See: REGIONAL PLAN OF NEW YORK AND ITS ENVIRONS

Regional Plan of New York and Its Environs

A major plan for the New York City region, released in 1929, that covered an area of approximately 5,500 square miles (14,245 square kilometers) and over 500 incorporated communities. The preparation of the plan was financed by the Russell Sage Foundation, and the work was undertaken under the direction of Thomas Adams.

The Regional Plan of New York and Its Environs was a landmark, in that it used extensive amounts of information on subjects such as the economy of the region, demography, transportation, recreation and neighborhoods as a basis for the plan's development. It also recognized that implementation of the plan depended upon the individual actions of the numerous governmental entities in the planning region, so an emphasis was placed upon cooperation with municipal officials to achieve a workable plan.

The Regional Plan Association (RPA) was founded in 1929 as a successor organization to the Committee on the Regional Plan of New York and Its Environs to help guide regional development in the directions of the newly released plan.

See: NEIGHBORHOOD UNIT CONCEPT; REGIONAL PLAN ASSOCIATION (RPA)

Regional Planning

Comprehensive planning for a region, as defined by natural boundaries (such as a river basin) or political boundaries (such as a state or county), or for a metropolitan area (two or more municipalities with common interests and concerns).

Regional planning was first undertaken as a means of directing growth around major urban centers, as in the 1909 Chicago Plan. At the county level, planning undertaken for Los Angeles in 1922 endeavored to solve problems related to water resources and recreational facilities. At the state level, regional planning was used to stimulate economic development by planning major highways. Regional planning in England in the 1940s had a major impact on subsequent regional planning practice throughout the world. In the Greater London Plan of 1944, a system of new towns was proposed to be built in the countryside to reduce population pressures in the London area and to limit population growth in London.

Major river basin planning in the United States began with the creation in 1933 of the federally owned Tennessee Valley Authority (TVA), which was authorized to undertake water resource projects, including development of hydroelectric, and now nuclear, facilities. The development of projects by the TVA has enabled major economic development of the area. A similar approach was taken with the establishment of the Appalachian Regional Commission in 1965 to stimulate economic, physical and social development in the 13-state Appalachian region in the middle eastern section of the United States. A federal-state agency, it performs activities related to highway development, creation of jobs, provision of health care facilities and development of community facilities for the 397 counties within its boundaries.

In more recent years regional planning has been either mandated or encouraged in various categorical programs supported by federal funding. Regional transportation planning was required for funding of certain highway and mass transit programs and was the catalyst for the establishment of regional planning agencies in many metropolitan areas. Coastal zone planning is now also undertaken by some areas on an interstate basis and councils of government have been established in many areas to review applications for federal funding and to manage regional problems.

Regional planning is the basis for the work of special assessment districts, such as sewer and park districts. It has also been used as the basis for comprehensive municipal planning, as in the Minneapolis-St. Paul area, where a generalized land use district system is established for use by area communities. The districts, which divide land into urbanized areas, urbanizing areas, areas approved for future development and protected areas, aid in protecting farmland and environmentally sensitive lands, and suggest appropriate locations for development. In Oregon regional planning is required for the establishment of urban boundary lines, while regional planning for housing on a fair share basis is required in New Jersey. In Canada several provinces mandate that planning be undertaken at the regional level.

See: REGIONAL PLANNING COMMISSION; RIVER BASIN COMMISSION; STATE PLANNING; TENNESSEE VALLEY AUTHORITY (TVA); URBAN PLANNING

Regional Planning Commission

A planning agency established by state, multistate or federal action to plan for one or more land uses. Regional planning commissions function in a variety of ways. At the metropolitan level they may be created to manage one function, such as to implement a federal program in transportation planning. The range of activities, however, may be considerably greater, as in the case of Minneapolis-St. Paul, Minnesota. There the Twin Cities Metropolitan Council oversees all land use activities and has the authority to review and approve the comprehensive plans of independent functional agencies, boards and commissions, including the Metropolitan Transit Commission, the Metropolitan Airports Commission and the Metropolitan Waste Control Commission. It also reviews the mandated comprehensive plans of municipalities and counties, examines applications for federal and state aid and prepares a development guide for the metropolitan region designating growth and conservation areas and public facility locations with which municipal and county plans must conform. A similar arrangement exists in the Toronto metropolitan area and has been instituted in other metropolitan regions of Ontario.

Within a state single-purpose and multipurpose regional planning commissions exist in locations other than metropolitan areas. Examples of this are the regional planning districts in Florida, which prepare comprehensive plans and oversee local land development having a regional impact; the District Environmental Commissions in Vermont, which issue development permits based on state guidelines to proposed developments that are over specified dimensions or that are on sites higher than 2,500 feet (762 meters) above sea level; or the Meadowlands Development Commission in New Jersey, formed to develop the Hackensack meadowlands.

Multistate commissions are formed for similar purposes, such as the now-defunct Tri-State Regional Planning Commission (whose planning area included parts of New York, New Jersey and Connecticut), which was originally formed as the Tri-State Transportation Commission, or the eight Regional Action Planning Commissions formed for economic development purposes under authority of the Public Works and Economic Development Act of 1965. These agencies lost their federal funding in 1981. River basin commissions are another type of multistate regional planning commission, while the Appalachian Regional Commission, a federal agency, plans for a larger area than most regional commissions.

See: REGIONAL PLANNING; TENNESSEE VALLEY AUTHORITY (TVA)

Regional Shopping Center

A unified development of retail stores located on a tract of land often 40 acres (16 hectares) in size or larger. Regional shopping centers usually contain in excess of 400,000 square feet (37,160 square meters) of leasable floor space. In suburban areas they may have interior roads and parking surrounding the buildings, while in urban areas they will have parking structures. They generally have one or more major department store branches and 50 or more smaller shops providing the widest selection of merchandise outside of the central business district of major cities. Super-regional shopping centers will have three or more department stores. Generally designed as shopping malls, they may have an additional concentration of service facilities, such as movie theaters, offices or a supermarket at another location on the site.

Since such shopping centers are intended to serve a population of over 100,000 within a radius of from 4 to 15 miles (6 to 24 kilometers), locations are often selected near freeway interchanges so that they are visible to large numbers of people and have good access. While some regional centers have direct access from a freeway, most have access from an arterial road that either crosses or parallels a freeway. Traffic exiting from the freeway and entering the shopping center, however, often creates major traffic jams. The best site is one surrounded by arterial streets, about 0.5 mile (0.8 kilometer) or more from the freeway exit, but entrances to shopping centers should never be less than 1,000 feet (305 meters) from an exit. In urban areas good public transit access is also essential.

Sites for regional shopping centers are chosen on the basis of their visibility and market potential as well as the relative lack of comparable sites zoned (or potentially zonable) for that use. Where they do not compete with an established central business district, regional shopping centers provide both a valuable community service and considerable tax revenues. Municipalities may ask developers to design facilities to accommodate civic functions so that new public meeting areas are made available to the community. In addition, they may require off-site improvements, such as road widening.

See: SHOPPING CENTER DESIGN; SHOPPING CENTER PARKING

Regional Tax Base Sharing (TBS)

The distribution of property tax revenues to two or more municipalities although the property being taxed is wholly within only one of the municipalities.

Revenues may be shared in this manner by two different methods currently in use. In the first an agreement is made by the municipalities with respect to a particular development, such as an industrial park or shopping center, that will receive services or labor from the various participating municipalities. The communities jointly agree to a formal arrangement concerning provision of specific services and infrastructure in exchange for specific percentages of the revenue. In the second method a state statute is adopted providing that property taxes obtained from existing industrial and commercial properties continue to go to the municipality in which they are located. A proportion of the revenues from new development, however, must be put into a pool for distribution by formula to all the other municipalities within the established regional TBS area. This procedure is in use in Minnesota and New Jersey.

Tax base sharing is a recent attempt to equalize fiscal disparities between neighboring municipalities in light of the recognition of their mutual support, and its use is increasingly being considered. It is one way of providing partial compensation to neighboring communities for the impacts they suffer as a result of adjoining development, such as the air pollution that may result from industrial uses. In some instances, TBS may also obviate the need to compete for ratables.

See: PROPERTY TAX; RATABLES; REGIONAL PLANNING; SPECIAL DISTRICT

Regional/Urban Design Assistance Team (R/UDAT)

A program of the American Institute of Architects (AIA) instituted in 1967 that provides design and problem-solving assistance on urban design matters through an interdisciplinary team. Any community may request a R/UDAT through its local AIA chapter, providing that it is willing to sponsor the design team by paying its members' travel and living expenses. The community and the AIA sponsor must also provide background data, define the problem they want studied and provide support services. As an additional service, the AIA has also created a Preservation/Reuse Assistance Team (P/RAT), specializing in historic preservation and adaptive reuse.

See: AMERICAN INSTITUTE OF ARCHITECTS (AIA)

Regression Analysis

A statistical technique designed to use data about past performance to predict or make a forecast of future performance. Linear regression is a relatively simple technique that involves data expressed as pairs of variables, usually denoted as an independent variable (X) and a dependent variable (Y). A simple example from water resources planning is the correlation of the number of tons of some toxic effluent, the independent variable, with some statistical measure of water quality, the dependent variable.

A scatter diagram, the plotting of the X and Y values in a regression, provides a meaningful way of visualizing the variables in the regression. A line can be drawn representing the best fit of scatter points. That line can then, in theory, be extended to predict future relationships between the two variables to answer such questions as the impact of decreased toxic sewage wastes on overall water quality at some future point in time. The correlation coefficient measures the closeness of the relationship between the two variables. The higher the correlation coefficient, the better the predictive value of the regression analysis.

As with all statistical techniques, care should be exercised in using regression relationships as a predictive tool. In general, however, the higher the correlation between two variables (the tighter the scatter diagram points around the "line of best fit"), the better the regression will explain the relationships between the two variables.
See: CORRELATION; MULTIVARIATE ANALYSIS; VARIANCE

Regulatory Floodway

The portion of a hundred-year floodplain consisting of a river channel or other watercourse and any adjacent land area required by federal, state or local requirements to remain open and unobstructed. A regulatory floodway must be able to allow a hundred-year flood to discharge without raising water surface elevations by more than a specified height. The boundaries of floodways are designated on floodplain maps by floodway encroachment lines.
See: FLOOD FRINGE; FLOODPLAIN; NATIONAL FLOOD INSURANCE PROGRAM

Rehabilitation

The process of performing repairs and modifying structures, when necessary, to enable them to become or to remain usable. Rehabilitation has been widely used as part of a strategy to conserve neighborhoods, public facilities and business districts, as well as to avoid the demolition of historic structures. It has also provided a means by which many substandard buildings have been preserved for continued residential use or adapted for residential use, often at substantial savings over the cost of new construction.

Expenditures for rehabilitation have been encouraged by a variety of federal legislation, including the Economic Recovery Tax Act of 1981, in which investment tax credit is given for rehabilitation of commercial and industrial buildings 20 years old or older and for rehabilitation of certified historical structures. In order to ensure that the historic properties of the structures are not destroyed, rehabilitation must comply with Department of Interior standards.
See: ADAPTIVE USE; ECONOMIC RECOVERY TAX ACT OF 1981; HISTORIC PRESERVATION; PRESERVATION; RECONSTRUCTION; RESTORATION; SECRETARY OF THE INTERIOR'S STANDARDS FOR REHABILITATION

Reinforced Concrete

Concrete into which steel bars or steel mesh has been embedded before the concrete is poured into a form. The steel is added to give tensional (ability to stretch) strength. Reinforcement is also used in columns to reduce the cross section necessary for a particular load, as steel has greater compressive (weight-supporting) strength than an equal volume of concrete.

Reinforced concrete is used in building and civil engineering projects in piles, columns, beams and girders, concrete slabs, concrete framing, walls, rigid frames, arches, domes, shell structures, roads and runways.
See: CONCRETE; PRECAST CONCRETE; PRESTRESSED CONCRETE

Relief

The difference in elevation between parts of the Earth's surface.
See: CONTOUR LINES; TOPOGRAPHIC MAP; TOPOGRAPHY

Relocation

1. The forced movement of people, businesses, organizations and buildings from a site by government agencies to clear the way for an alternate use of the land. In American planning terminology, relocation became synonymous with the urban renewal and highway construction projects of the 1950s and 1960s but occurs less commonly today. Relocation can disrupt neighborhoods and may be especially disturbing for extended families, who often cannot be housed near each other; the elderly, who have long-standing neighborhood ties; and small businesses, which rely on goodwill established over many years. In addition, relocation often leads to increased housing and business costs for those relocated after alternative housing and business locations are secured.

2. The movement of a building to a new site, often to avoid its demolition. Historic buildings may be moved to museum-type settings, or older homes may be purchased inexpensively and moved to more desirable surroundings.
See: HISTORIC PRESERVATION; URBAN RENEWAL

Remote Sensing

The collection and analysis of information about physical features by relying upon the detection of electromagnetic energy. Remote sensing may be used to differentiate types of natural resources or land surfaces by detecting patterns of spectral reflectance, known as signatures, that are characteristic of a particular type of natural resource. The range of applications of remote sensing is extremely broad. Planning departments, for example, can use remote sensing for environmental inventories, pollution control, land use classification and many types of mapping.

Aerial photography is the best-known form of remote sensing and has been in existence the longest. Cameras using standard film can, however, only sense a small portion of the electromagnetic spectrum. Many other types of sensors that focus upon different portions of the spectrum are available.

Thermal scanners, which can detect heat, have numerous planning applications. Multispectral scanners used in LANDSAT employ a series of detectors, each of which scans a particular frequency. They record this information by photoelectric means and make digital records that can be stored on magnetic tape or transmitted and then converted to a photograph, if desired.

Microwave sensors, which may be passive or active (radar), come in many forms. One type of system, known as side-looking radar (SLAR), has attracted attention because of its ability to penetrate cloud cover and to show fine differences in terrain. Over-the-horizon (OTH) radar, which operates outside of the microwave portion of the spectrum, is gradually being used in nonmilitary applications.

It is expected that new uses will continue to be found for remote sensing and that sensing techniques will undergo further refinement.
See: AERIAL PHOTOGRAPHY; INFRARED PHOTOGRAPHY; LANDSAT

Renegotiable-Rate Mortgage (RRM)

A recently developed type of mortgage in which the interest rates are renegotiated on a periodic basis, usually every 3 to 5 years, based upon standard economic indexes. Generally, the mortgage is for a term of 30 years, and the interest rate is not permitted to rise or fall more than 5 percentage points over the life of the mortgage. It also may not increase by more than 2 ½ percentage points in a 5-year period. This type of mortgage, also known as a rollover mortgage, helps the lending institution protect itself against rising interest rates.
See: MORTGAGE

Renewable Energy Sources

Those energy sources whose supply can be or is being continually replenished. Among those types of energy that may be considered "renewable" are solar energy, wind power, geothermal power, hydropower, biomass energy, tidal power and breeder nuclear energy reactors.

Many of the renewable energy sources in use or in development today are simply larger and more technologically advanced versions of long-established energy production techniques, such as the windmill. But the fluctuating costs of petroleum and natural gas, the political problems associated with the importation of oil and the environmental problems encountered in using fossil fuel and nuclear power have caused these techniques to be reexamined in light of current situations and costs. Renewable energy sources vary markedly in the degree to which they are geographically available, cost-effective and environmentally safe. In those instances where they are already economically feasible, efficient and safe, however, the use of renewable energy sources is steadily growing.
See: ACTIVE SOLAR ENERGY SYSTEM; BIOMASS ENERGY; GEOTHERMAL ENERGY; HYDROELECTRIC POWER; OCEAN THERMAL ENERGY CONVERSION (OTEC); PASSIVE SOLAR ENERGY SYSTEM; RENEWABLE RESOURCE; SOLAR ENERGY; TIDAL POWER; WIND POWER; WOOD FUEL

Renewable Resource

A resource that can naturally replace itself or that can be regenerated through human intervention within a reasonable time period. Trees and other plants, air and water are all renewable resources. Water replaces itself through rainfall; new trees can be planted if they are cut or destroyed. A nonrenewable resource is of a finite quantity and irreplaceable except over very long time periods. Oil is a nonrenewable resource, as are most minerals.
See: RENEWABLE ENERGY SOURCES

Rent Control

Use of the police power to control aspects of the landlord-tenant relationship, including the regulation of maximum legal rents, the right of a tenant to continued occupancy of his apartment and a landlord's right to evict a tenant or to convert rental housing to cooperative or condominium status.

Rent control is generally imposed as a reaction to housing shortages that threaten to drive the cost of rental housing beyond the means of low- and moderate-income people. Unlike in many European countries, there was never widespread rent control in the United States except for a limited period after World War I and during World War II. After the Second World War, housing controls were continued in New York City and were gradually adopted by other cities and municipalities facing housing shortages. One estimate made in the mid-1970s indicated that approximately one-eighth of all rental units in the United States were subject to rent control in some manner, with many of these units located in New York and the great majority in the corridor between Boston and Washington, D.C. In contrast, many European countries have had rent control for decades, employed as part of comprehensive housing policies adopted by these countries.

The effects of rent control on the existing housing stock and the wisdom of employing rent control as a permanent part of a comprehensive housing policy have been matters of considerable debate. One point that is frequently made is that rent control contributes to the reduction in the supply of new rental housing for low- and moderate-income persons. This is particularly true in the United States, where subsidized housing constitutes a relatively small proportion of total housing construction. This occurs because controls encourage the shift of investment to owner-occupied dwellings and other forms of investment. Rent control can have an adverse effect upon the maintenance and repair of controlled housing stock, since the owner's return on his investment is not necessarily related to the quality of repair of his building. Rent control has also been charged with contributing to the trend toward converting existing rental housing to cooperative and condominium housing, thereby further diminishing the supply of rental housing. Finally, rent control has been accused of being an inequitable and inefficient response to problems caused by a housing shortage; apartments are controlled without regard to the ability of the tenants involved to pay a fair market rental.

There has been some movement on both sides of the Atlantic to deemphasize rent control, either by eliminating controls for new or existing housing or by lessening the degree of control.

See: RENTAL HOUSING

Rental Housing

Housing that is occupied by a tenant, who makes periodic rent payments to a property owner or landlord. The 1980 Census indicates that over 28 million households, just over one-third of the nation's total, rent their homes, with the proportion higher in large cities and along the coasts. Rental housing serves the young, the old, the poor and those who do not choose to tie up their resources in ownership.

Since the 1970s there has been concern about the decrease of available rental housing in many locations and the substantial decline in the construction of rental housing. Increased land and construction costs, when combined with increased financial costs, often make it more economically rewarding to develop housing in a form that can be sold rather than rented—enabling the developer to obtain an immediate return on his investment. In addition, rental housing in some locations is rapidly being converted to a condominium or cooperative form of ownership. Where it is in effect, rent control is also believed to have caused the conversion of some rental buildings to cooperative or condominium status and to have substantially decreased builder interest in new rental development.

A variety of programs has been instituted over the course of many years to promote the development of rental housing. Low-income rental housing has been built with massive federal support through public housing and Section 8 programs. Federal Housing Administration (FHA) mortgage insurance programs have had some impact, and property tax abatement programs have been attempted in some communities. Title VI of the Housing and Community Development Act of 1980, moreover, states that federally insured lending institutions should be discouraged from lending funds for condominium or coop-

erative conversions where there would be adverse impacts on housing opportunities for low- and moderate-income and elderly and handicapped tenants. Despite these efforts, the development of rental housing and the continued provision of varied housing opportunities is becoming increasingly more difficult in certain locations, particularly for persons of low and moderate income.

See: HOUSING; LIMITED-DIVIDEND HOUSING COMPANY; PUBLIC HOUSING; RENT CONTROL; STATE HOUSING FINANCE AGENCIES

Replacement Cost

A term used in real estate appraisal to describe the cost of replacing a building with a structure that is a functional equivalent, although not an exact replica in terms of design or materials.

See: COST APPROACH APPRAISAL; REPRODUCTION COST

Reproducible

A map or other type of graphic display from which copies may be made by a contact process, such as diazo or blueprinting. The graphic art being reproduced must be on transparent or translucent materials.

See: GRAPHIC REPRODUCTION PROCESSES

Reproduction Cost

A term used in real estate appraisal to describe the cost of constructing a replica of an existing building in which the exact materials or very similar materials are used. It can sometimes be difficult to estimate reproduction cost because of changes in construction methods or because certain types of materials or craftsmanship are no longer available.

The most common means of calculating this cost is through comparative methods, which use unit cost construction figures of similar buildings and apply these figures to the dimensions of the building for which cost is being estimated. Two other methods of calculating reproduction cost are the quantity survey method (in which all materials and the hours of labor required are enumerated separately) and the unit-in-place method (in which unit prices are obtained for a building element already constructed—e.g., price per square foot of brick wall).

See: CONSTRUCTION COST DATA; COST APPROACH APPRAISAL; REPLACEMENT COST

Reproduction Rate

A measure of the extent to which a population group can replace itself through births. Generally, this rate is concerned with the number of females who will be born rather than the total number of children. Both gross and net reproduction rates may be calculated. Gross reproduction rate represents the number of daughters that a particular cohort of women (i.e., those born in the same year) will have, from the beginning through the end of their childbearing years. It assumes that all females survive

through that period. Net reproduction rate measures the degree to which a group of female infants can be expected to replace themselves when mortality rates and age-specific fertility rates are factored in.
See: BIRTHRATE; DEMOGRAPHY; FERTILITY RATE

Request for Proposal (RFP)

An invitation to selected consultants to make a proposal to a unit of government or corporation regarding their approach to studying or designing a requested service. A standard method for soliciting a variety of study approaches and obtaining consultant cost estimates for undertaking a project, RFPs are often used as a basis for consultant selection. When writing an RFP, it is necessary to be as specific as possible concerning the details of the work to be performed to enable proposals to be directly responsive to the request.
See: CONSULTANTS

Reserved Lanes

Lanes within a street or limited-access highway that are limited to use by high-occupancy vehicles (HOVs). These lanes, either permanently established for such vehicles or so designated for peak-use periods (as by use of movable barriers), permit HOVs to travel at greater speeds than regular traffic during peak travel hours.

Most common are bus lanes, for exclusive use by buses between 4 p.m. and 7 p.m. Lanes for automobiles carrying more than two or three passengers have been employed on bridges, tunnels and expressways in the Atlanta, Chicago, New York, San Francisco and Washington, D.C. areas.

Where permanent bus lanes (busways) are established for a substantial distance, bus stations have been provided along the route. These require a separate loading lane in each direction, out of the through-travel bus lane. Bus routes of this nature are usually constructed in roadway medians, which are sufficiently wide to permit them. (See Fig. 36)
See: BUS LOADING AREA

Fig. 36. Reserved bus lanes.
Credit: Courtesy of the U.S. Department of Transportation

Reservoir

Artificial or natural water body designed to hold water for public supplies for varying time periods. Aside from storage functions, reservoirs are also used for such purposes as recreation, hydroelectric power and irrigation. Typically, modern reservoirs serve more than one function.

The site and size of reservoirs differ with the role they play in a water supply system. Large reservoirs may sometimes be located hundreds of miles from urban areas and are designed to store water for long intervals to help prevent flooding during high-flow periods. In turn, they cushion the supply system by releasing water during periods of low flow and drought. Reservoirs that are part of a distribution system are usually located near water treatment plants and are used to regulate the flow of water into the system and provide enough water to meet peak demands, such as for fire fighting.

The effectiveness of a reservoir can be destroyed by an accumulation of sediment at its bottom, which reduces its storage capacity. Because of the expense of removing the sediments, reserve capacity is often designed into the system. Seepage and evaporation are also potential sources of water loss.
See: AQUEDUCT; DAM; WATER CONSERVATION; WATER SUPPLY SYSTEM

Resettlement Administration

A federal agency in the U.S. Department of Agriculture that was created in 1935 by the Emergency Relief Appropriations Act and headed by Rexford G. Tugwell. The Suburban Resettlement Division of the agency was responsible for the construction of three greenbelt towns in Maryland, Ohio and Wisconsin that served as model garden suburbs. The agency was abolished in 1938.
See: GREENBELT TOWNS; WORKS PROGRESS ADMINISTRATION (WPA)

Residue

The end product of solid waste handling after gases, liquids or certain solids have been removed. Incinerator residue consists of the solid materials that remain after incineration.
See: SOLID WASTE

Resort Area

A region in which the attraction of substantial numbers of tourists is a primary economic activity. Resort areas generally have an outstanding feature or attraction, such as Florida's sunshine and beaches, Nevada's gambling and Colorado's mountainous scenery and ski slopes. While most major cities attract tourists, resort areas are economically dependent upon massive short-term tourism, requiring a preponderance of hotels, restaurants, and recreational and entertainment facilities.

Resort areas must accommodate vast numbers of visitors, usually for only a portion of the year, as they often have a weather-dependent season. Providing adequate local roads and services, such as police and emergency health care for tourists, can be a substantial burden on the relatively small number of permanent residents. Atlantic City is an interesting example of a resort community that is now using gambling as a year-round tourist attraction to spur rejuvenation after its original seasonal attraction as a beach resort waned. Some resort areas—such as Michigan's Upper Peninsula and Hilton Head Island, South Carolina—have maintained their natural amenities as their primary attraction and are also second-home areas. The city of Miami, which originated and grew as a classic resort community, has now matured and is no longer primarily a resort area, while its neighbor Miami Beach still is.

See: SECOND-HOME AREA; TOURISM

Resource Allocation

1. The allotment by municipalities of available funding to specific areas or types of projects that have a demonstrated need and priority. In this sense, communities may use cost-benefit analyses and sophisticated budgeting methodologies to determine funding priorities and may pinpoint neighborhoods that require a concentration of projects and programs to stabilize them and to prevent or reverse deterioration.

2. The allotment of funds for regional economic development programs that are designed to aid areas in building an economic base or in recovering from major economic decline. This form of resource allocation is used extensively in eastern European countries.

See: TARGET AREA

Resource Conservation and Recovery Act of 1976 (RCRA)

An act (PL 94-580) that authorizes federal assistance for solid waste management, emphasizing resource recovery and conservation as goals. Assistance is made available to state and regional agencies for regional solid waste management programs, which the act requires as a prerequisite for funding, thereby creating incentives for local governments to join regional programs. Assistance also includes financing of full-scale demonstration resource-recovery facilities; funding on a formula basis for such programs as solid waste management, resource recovery, resource conservation and hazardous waste management; and special funding for rural communities.

This act resulted in the establishment of a variety of demonstration facilities and resource-recovery programs, many of which were successful, and directed the secretary of commerce to study markets for recycled materials. It also required that all open dumps be discontinued or upgraded to sanitary landfills within five years and generally expanded the federal role in a traditionally local field.

In addition, RCRA initiated federal participation in the hazardous waste management issue by requiring that the U.S. Environmental Protection Agency develop regulations for hazardous waste programs and offer financial assistance for program development. It also authorizes fines for violations and pursuit of court injunctions to control a hazardous waste that endangers public health or the environment.

See: HAZARDOUS WASTE; RESOURCE RECOVERY; RESOURCE RECOVERY ACT OF 1970; SOLID WASTE DISPOSAL ACT AMENDMENTS OF 1980; SOLID WASTE MANAGEMENT

Resource Recovery

The recovery of materials, and particularly energy, from solid waste. Although a relatively new development in the United States, the recovery of energy from wastes has been widely practiced in Europe for many years because of such factors as the smaller amount of land available for landfill and the higher costs of alternative energy sources. In 1977 Denmark was transforming 60 percent of all its waste to energy, while the Netherlands and Sweden were converting 30 percent of their waste. By contrast, in that same year the United States had only converted 1 percent of its municipal wastes to energy.

There has been, however, a noticeable acceleration in interest in resource recovery in the United States. The success of various systems in European use, increasing scarcity of suitable landfill sites and rising energy costs have caused municipalities and private concerns across the country to consider the construction of resource-recovery systems. Although only 20 plants were in operation in 1977, an additional 10 were under construction, 30 had completed the advanced planning stages, and 70 additional plants were in earlier planning stages.

The most common types of energy-recovery systems are the waterwall incinerator, which generates steam; the modular incinerator (suitable in small communities), in which small package units use boilers to capture waste heat; and the production of solid fuel directly from refuse, known as refuse-derived fuel (RDF). Pyrolysis, another form of resource recovery, is in an earlier stage of development.

Most successful resource-recovery projects pay close attention to prospective markets for the energy that will be produced and use this as a guide to selecting an appropriate system and locating the system.

See: PYROLYSIS; RECYCLING; REFUSE-DERIVED FUEL (RDF); SOLID WASTE MANAGEMENT; WATERWALL INCINERATION

Resource Recovery Act of 1970

Legislation that emphasized the need for resource recycling. It provided federal assistance, in the form of grants-in-aid of up to 75 percent, for the planning and development of demonstration projects for improved solid waste disposal facilities or resource recovery facilities. Funding was also provided for surveys of solid waste disposal problems, preparation of solid waste disposal plans, and pilot projects for handling abandoned vehicles. In addition, the act (PL 91-512) called for a study of federal hazardous waste disposal sites, encouraged regional cooperation, and shifted responsibility for solid waste management on the federal level to the Environmental Protection Agency.

This act was largely superseded by the more extensive and detailed requirements of the Resource Conservation and Recovery Act of 1976.

See: RESOURCE CONSERVATION AND RECOVERY ACT OF 1976 (RCRA)

Reston, Virginia

A new town in Fairfax County, founded in 1962 and located 18 miles (29 kilometers) west of Washington, D.C. It is sited on 7,400 acres (2,995 hectares), with a population of over 35,000 in 1981 and a projected population upon completion in the 1990s of approximately 65,000 to 70,000.

Designed to be a self-contained community, Reston combines a diversity of housing types with office and industrial uses, commercial centers and a wide variety of community facilities. As of 1981 there were over 12,000 jobs in Reston and almost 3 million square feet (278,700 square meters) of office and industrial development, including the U.S. Geological Survey National Center.

Residential development is grouped in clusters, often focusing upon a man-made lake. The first such village center opened in 1965 at Lake Anne and includes townhouses, high- and low-rise apartments, shops and professional offices. Other centers focus upon lower-density development. Overall, approximately 17 percent is detached single-family housing, 35 percent is in townhouse development, 42 percent in low-rise apartments, 3 percent in high-rise apartments and 3 percent in patio homes. Two senior citizen housing complexes are also completed.

Open space and recreation are a major aspect of Reston. Almost 700 acres (283 hectares) of preserved open space, a network of pedestrian and bicycle paths, and a nature center are included within the community. (See Fig. 37)

See: COLUMBIA, MARYLAND; NEW TOWN; PLANNED COMMUNITY

Restoration

The process of adding or removing components of a structure or any built environment so as to authentically recreate its appearance at an earlier time period. Usually conducted so that a structure or area may be returned to its original architecture, this process often requires considerable research as well as expense. It is frequently undertaken for museum or public viewing purposes but may also take place as part of a strategy to improve the economic vitality of a business district, to attract tourism or to improve community appearance.

A problem that has been encountered is the overuse of "restoration," so that many attractive additions and changes made over the course of a building's or an area's history are removed in order to return it to its earliest form. To counter this, some preservation organizations

(a)

(b)

Fig. 37. Reston, Virginia; (a) aerial view of Reston showing housing clusters separated by wooded areas. Lake Anne Village, a focal point of Reston, is in the upper left portion of the photograph; (b) a view of Lake Anne Village.
Credit: Courtesy of the U.S. Department of Housing and Urban Development. Photograph (b) by David Valdez

have established a policy of preserving a building in its latest form in order to show its historical evolution. Another practice that is frowned upon is the "return" of a building or an area to an era that predates its construction, known as "earlying up."

See: ADAPTIVE USE; ALTERATION; HISTORIC PRESERVATION; PRESERVATION; RECONSTRUCTION; REHABILITATION

Restricted Development Areas (RDA)

Environmentally sensitive and hazardous areas in the provinces of Ontario and Alberta, Canada, on which land use controls are imposed to prevent their degradation. These are locations specified by provincial legislation within which development may be restricted or prohibited. There is no requirement that the government purchase the land or pay compensation to the owner. In the Yukon and Northwest Territories, land management

zones are designated for sensitive areas, wherein most construction, earth moving and extractive operations, such as mining, are controlled by permit, as is the use of vehicles weighing in excess of 5 tons (4.5 metric tons) anywhere within these zones.
See: CRITICAL AREAS

Restrictive Covenant

In real estate practice the term refers to provisions placed in a deed or other instrument of conveyance that restrict or limit the use of the property being conveyed. The restrictions, sometimes referred to as "private zoning," may require that the land, or certain portions of the land, remain undeveloped; they may prohibit the erection of certain types of structures on the land; or they may limit the uses to which the land may be devoted. The developer of a subdivision may incorporate restrictive covenants in all deeds as a means of controlling future development and the character of the community.

A restrictive covenant may be drafted to run with the land and bind all subsequent transferees, or it may provide that the restriction will expire upon the passing of a certain date or the occurrence of some event specified in the restrictive covenant.

Restrictive covenants may be terminated by agreement between the owners of the parcels burdened and benefited by the restriction, by acquiescence in repeated violations of the restrictions or by merger of the burdened and benefited parcels. However, certain restrictive covenants that are illegal or against public policy, such as those providing for racial discrimination, will not be enforced. In addition, because public policy favors the free and unencumbered use of property, any ambiguities in the restriction will generally be strictly construed against those seeking to enforce it.
See: EASEMENT; SOLAR EASEMENTS AND COVENANTS

Retaining Wall

A wall whose function is to support loose materials, most commonly a bank of earth. The retaining wall may be constructed of concrete, stone or wood and must be built so that it cannot overturn or be moved on its base under the pressure of the materials it is supporting.

There are a number of types of retaining walls, including gravity, semigravity, cantilever, counterfort and crib walls. Among the ways in which they differ is in the degree of reinforcement they need, the type and amount of materials they require, and their suitability for different situations. An important consideration is the nature and characteristics of the earth to be retained, since this helps to determine the magnitude of the load that a retaining wall has to support. Drainage is important and may be provided through weep holes in the wall at periodic intervals or by a continuous back drain. The base of the wall must also extend below the frostline so that it will remain stable.

Retention Basin

A pond or reservoir designed as part of a storm drainage system to accept excess runoff and hold it for long-term storage. A retention basin serves a purpose similar to that of a detention basin but differs in the time frame over which water is stored. Retention basins may also sometimes serve a dual purpose and be used for water-based recreation.
See: DETENTION BASIN; FLOOD CONTROL; RUNOFF; STORM DRAINAGE SYSTEM

Retirement Community

An age-oriented, residential community planned for and occupied predominantly by persons who have retired from their occupations. The number of retirement communities has grown rapidly in recent years, particularly in sunbelt states such as Florida and Arizona. Retirement communities, as distinct from housing for the elderly, offer a community environment specifically designed for their elderly residents, often featuring community centers with varied programs as well as commercial and health facilities.

In order to provide a range of services, retirement communities are often large. Some—such as Sun City, Arizona and the Century Villages in Florida—have over 10,000 units, although most are smaller, with 1,000 to 3,000 units being more common. Residence is usually restricted to those over a specific age, ranging from 55 to 65. Condominium ownership is most popular among retirement communities, although rentals and other types of ownership are also utilized. The residential units are designed specifically for one or two elderly persons. Typically they feature one-bedroom, two-bedroom or efficiency units. A common design uses garden apartment-type structures, but high-rise elevator buildings are sometimes used, as are one- or two-bedroom houses. Often units are located around a central feature, such as a golf course or pool.

Retirement communities provide a life-style that avoids major home maintenance responsibilities while offering much companionship, security and recreational opportunity; however, they have also been criticized as ghettos for the elderly. In some cases, developers have not provided all of the services that were promised. Retirement communities can also place a heavy burden on local health facilities, mass transit and some social services, but the residents, usually on fixed incomes, are often reluctant to support tax increases, especially for services that do not benefit them.
See: AGE-ORIENTED COMMUNITY; HOUSING FOR THE ELDERLY; SECOND-HOME AREA

Retrofitting

The process of providing an existing building, facility or machine with new components, parts or improvements that were developed or perfected at a later time. Frequent planning applications of retrofitting are the conversion of heating or hot water systems for solar power or the addition of pollution control equipment to industrial plants. The term is derived from the phrase retroactive refit.

Revenue Bond

Government bonds issued for the purpose of financing a revenue-producing facility. The proceeds of the facility are then used to pay principal and interest requirements on the debt; the debt may also be secured by the property or facility itself. Typical projects financed with revenue bonds are water and sewer systems, toll roads, bridges and transit systems, but revenue bonds have been used to finance facilities ranging from swimming pools and boat basins to parking lots and auditoriums.

Revenue bonds became much more widely accepted after the Depression of the 1930s, although they have been in existence since about 1900. Factors contributing to their acceptance were the decline in value of assessed real property, and thus in borrowing power of local government; a public resistance to incurring new debt; and a need for public works projects. A major feature of revenue bond financing is that the courts have generally found constitutional debt limitations to be inapplicable to this type of financing, which makes it attractive to communities approaching their legal debt limit. Use of revenue bonds continues to grow, representing an increasing proportion of the total municipal debt burden each year. The cost of borrowing money, however, is often higher for revenue bonds than for other types of bonding supported by the taxing power of the municipality.

The definition of revenue bond has been expanded in recent years to sometimes include other types of debt obligations not subject to constitutional debt limits, such as bonds payable from non–property tax revenues.
See: BOND; BOND RATINGS; GENERAL OBLIGATION BOND; MUNICIPAL BOND

Revenue Sharing

A program established by the State and Local Fiscal Assistance Act of 1972 (PL 92-512), as amended by the State and Local Fiscal Assistance Amendments of 1976 (PL 94-488), that directs the transfer of a portion of federal income tax revenues directly to state and local governments.

This is an entitlement program, with no application required. Only minimal financial reporting, public hearing, prevailing wage and civil rights restrictions are imposed on recipients. States are required to maintain their standard level of assistance to local governments but may use revenue sharing funds either for new programs or to stabilize or reduce taxes.

Congress periodically passes legislation that establishes the total amount of revenue sharing funds for each of the next several years. These funds are then distributed among recipients according to a complex series of formulas. The basic formula allocates payments according to population, per capita income and tax effort (the ratio of state and local revenues to personal income). A second formula uses the same three factors, as well as urbanized population and state income tax revenues. Funds are allocated to states based on whichever formula is more favorable to each state. A state's allocation is split so that one-third is paid to the state government and two-thirds is paid to local governments.
See: ENTITLEMENT GRANT

Reversible Lanes

Roadway lanes that can be reversed in direction to alleviate traffic congestion during peak travel periods. This system provides that one or more lanes are used for traffic in one direction for part of the day and for traffic in the opposite direction for the remainder of the day. It provides more lanes of movement for the heavier direction of traffic flow, increasing capacity without requiring the construction of additional lanes.

Applications of this method have included lane reversals on arterials, freeways, bridges and tunnels, as well as reversals of all lanes to a single direction on some major two-way streets during peak periods.
See: RESERVED LANES

Reversion Clause

1. A requirement in some communities that unless certain activities occur within a specified period of time following the granting of a rezoning or a special-use permit, the property will return to its prior zoning category or the permit will lapse. Required activities depend upon the community and may range from applying for or receiving a building permit to actively pursuing construction. Communities use this device to prevent applications' being made for purely speculative purposes when no development is actually intended by the applicant. To prevent legal challenges based upon procedure, municipalities returning a property to its prior zoning classification should follow proper zoning amendment procedures.

2. A requirement that real estate be returned to the ownership of the grantor or the grantor's heirs because a condition stipulated in the deed, which provides for such reversion, was not complied with. It is quite common, for example, for land to be donated to a municipality exclusively for park use. If the land fails to be used for a park or park use is terminated at a later date, the land should, according to the terms of the deed, revert to the original owner. It is essential for municipal officials to be aware of any deed restrictions applying to municipally owned land (including land donated many years ago), especially if a change in land use is contemplated.
See: DEED; LAND ENDOWMENT; REZONING; SPECIAL-USE PERMIT; ZONING

Revetment

A facing or reinforcement of stone, concrete or the like to protect earth or sand from wave or water action. It is

used along a stream to protect the banks from stream erosion. At a beach it may be placed along the slope face of a dune or bluff to protect it from wave action. A revetment can accomplish this with less of an undesirable impact upon the beach than a vertical wall would cause, because it is more effective at dissipating wave energy.
See: BANK PROTECTION; BEACH EROSION; RIPRAP

Revolving Fund

Capital that is initially raised or made available for specific projects and then used and reused. A revolving fund is usually replenished by the proceeds of sale or the income produced by the projects that were previously financed.

Although revolving funds are used for many purposes, the use of such funds for projects related to historic preservation has attracted substantial interest recently. A fund is used to purchase and rehabilitate a historic property and is then replenished through the sale of the property or by borrowing against the property with a mortgage that is paid for with rental income. Restrictive covenants obligating the purchaser to maintain the property and restricting alterations may be incorporated into the property's deed at the time it is sold to ensure its preservation by subsequent owners.

Revolving funds, first used for historic preservation in the late 1950s by the Historic Charleston Foundation, have been used successfully by local groups to save endangered historic properties, to conserve or improve declining or deteriorated neighborhoods, and to revive commercial areas. Generally, once a number of carefully selected buildings are restored, the remainder of the neighborhood becomes more attractive to private capital. Among the municipalities in which revolving funds for preservation purposes are operating or have operated are Savannah, Georgia; Pittsburgh, Pennsylvania; Galveston, Texas (where the fund is applied to commercial areas); Baltimore, Maryland; and Denver, Colorado.
See: HISTORIC PRESERVATION

Rezoning

A modification of, or an amendment to, the zoning ordinance. A number of types of actions may be considered to be rezonings.

The first type of rezoning is a thorough overhaul of the entire ordinance, including both the text of the ordinance and the zoning map. Such comprehensive revisions are undertaken based upon a reexamination of community needs; difficulties that have been encountered in using and enforcing the existing ordinance; emerging techniques and trends; and other factors, such as zoning litigation that affects the principles on which the ordinance is based. Ideally, comprehensive zoning ordinance revisions should be scheduled on a regular basis; in practice, however, many communities undertake comprehensive revisions only rarely.

A second type of rezoning consists of changes made to a portion of the zoning text. Such a change might be required by an oversight or deficiency that is discovered, an attempt to accommodate a land use that has been ignored or an inconsistency that is found. Changing community needs might also dictate a modification of the requirements and conditions of a particular zone. Examples of this type of rezoning include a change in a zoning ordinance definition or an addition of a permitted land use in a particular zone.

A third type of rezoning consists of a zoning map change for one or more parcels of land. This type of change should be based upon the municipal comprehensive plan and should not be granted for an incompatible land use.

Most types of rezonings are acted upon by the legislative body of the community involved. Planning staff and commissions are generally consulted and involved in fact finding, ordinance drafting and the making of recommendations prior to a final decision by the legislative body.
See: COMPREHENSIVE PLAN; *FASANO* v. *BOARD OF COUNTY COMMISSIONERS OF WASHINGTON COUNTY;* SPOT ZONING; ZONING; ZONING ADMINISTRATION; ZONING MAP; ZONING ORDINANCE

Ridepooling

The use of a private vehicle by more than one person or the use of a group-owned or corporate-owned vehicle by more than one person, usually for commutation purposes. The term encompasses the familiar carpool, which uses a private auto; the vanpool, which uses an eight- or nine-passenger van, often purchased for ridesharing by a group of people or a company; and the buspool or subscription bus service, which uses a purchased or rented bus to make trips to the central city or to an outlying business location on a regular basis. These are considered to be high-occupancy vehicles, entitled to special handling in traffic-congestion situations. Government agencies encourage them by using preferential toll and parking rates as inducements and using reserved lanes to reduce peak-period congestion. The 1980 U.S. Census reported that 19,075,929 people traveled to work in car, truck and vanpools.

Ridepooling arrangements are often made within companies, but transportation brokers are increasingly being employed. These are intermediaries between those who would be willing to ridepool and those who have vehicles that could be made available for the purpose, usually auto companies. The broker, usually an independent nonprofit corporation, will arrange for the vehicle with the auto dealer, provide insurance and establish rates for riders, and then find the riders.
See: COMMUTATION; RESERVED LANES

Right-of-Way (R-O-W)

The strip of land reserved for a linear transit element (i.e., roads, railroads, fixed-route mass transit or bikeways) or utility elements (i.e., high-tension lines, gas and oil pipelines, aqueducts and sewer lines).

For roads all highway elements—including roadway pavement, median, shoulders and border areas—are provided within the right-of-way. Right-of-way widths vary from 50 feet (15 meters) in urban areas to 350 feet (107 meters) for freeways in rural areas.

Utility rights-of-way vary in width from 20 feet (6 meters) to several hundred feet but may lend themselves to multiple use because power lines may be submerged or elevated. In some cases, the right-of-way may be limited to an easement across the property of others and may not be visible in any way.

Current practice encourages the multiple use of rights-of-way to maximize public benefit and to detract from the negative aspects of certain types of facilities. For example, placement of public or private buildings or parks on air rights is common in city centers through which depressed roadways pass.
See: RIGHT-OF-WAY ACQUISITION

Right-Of-Way Acquisition

The purchase of land to provide a linear path on which a road, transit line or utility line will be constructed. Acquisition of land for right-of-way purposes is a complex undertaking. Planning skills are necessary for selection of a route that is minimally disruptive to existing communities and is environmentally compatible and attractive. Selection of cross section design for specific areas can be varied for different segments—e.g., narrower median in very dense areas—thereby allowing the preservation of specific sites or neighborhoods or their enhancement by provision of parks or public areas in conjunction with development of the road, transit line or utility line. Specific engineering designs for the proposed facility are needed in order to permit identification of properties that will have to be acquired.

Land acquisition for roadway rights-of-way involves from 5 percent to 50 percent of the total project cost. Costs are specific to locale and depend on population density, prevailing real estate values and availability of public lands held in reserve. Land acquisition for all modes of transportation is costly, time-consuming and a source of community conflict. Because of the disruption in land use caused by such acquisition and subsequent construction, it is important that all land, including that to be reserved for future use, be acquired at the commencement of the project. Detailed design of the ultimate facility will generally be sufficient to substantiate to the courts the necessity for taking land beyond that which is immediately required, should condemnation become necessary.

Because a right-of-way is of considerable length, it can cause numerous acquisition problems. Often-posed problems are the need for partial acquisition of properties and the potential removal of access, or landlocking, of the part of a property not taken (often referred to as the remainder parcel). Partial acquisition can be compensated for, but the damages attributable to the severance of a single piece of property are often difficult to assess. Landlocking, however, may require the acquisition of an entire piece of property if no access can be found for it.
See: PROPERTY ACQUISITION; RIGHT-OF-WAY (R-O-W); TAKING

Ring Pattern

A land use pattern for metropolitan development based upon several concentric rings, with each ring containing a higher density of development than the next outer ring. The term *ring* was used by Patrick Abercrombie and J.R. Forshaw in their landmark 1943 County of London study, which was the basis for greenbelt and new town legislation.

A related variation of the term *ring* refers to a development pattern totally focused on the circumference, with the center preserved as open space. In this sense, it is similar to a circumferential plan. (See Fig. 24)
See: CIRCUMFERENTIAL PLAN; CONCENTRIC ZONE THEORY; COUNTY OF LONDON PLAN; GREENBELT; LAND USE PATTERN

Ringelmann Chart

A chart used to make subjective field evaluations of the smoke being emitted by stacks and other sources. It consists of a series of diagrams, formed by black horizontal and vertical lines of successive concentration, that represent the shades of gray of various smoke densities. On this 0–5 scale, 0 is perfectly white, while at the other extreme 5 is dense, black smoke. The charts may be used in various air pollution control monitoring and enforcement activities, such as prohibiting smoke emission of a density that exceeds a particular Ringelmann number.
See: AIR POLLUTION

Riparian Rights

The rights of an owner of land bordering or transversed by a natural watercourse to use and enjoy the water and the land under the water. These include rights to fish, swim, use water for irrigation or domestic purposes, build piers or wharves, or use the running water to create power. Where a river or stream is navigable, all rights of a riparian owner are subject to the public's right to navigate over the waterway.

The riparian owner's fee ownership rights to the land bordering the waterway generally end at the high-water mark, although he may use the land between the low- and high-water marks. For nonnavigable waterways, the riparian owner may own the land beneath the river or stream, generally up to the midpoint of the waterway.

A riparian owner's rights to a waterway generally include the right to prevent diversion or misuse by upstream owners; he, in turn, is subject to a similar obligation to owners downstream from him.
See: ACCRETION; ARMY CORPS OF ENGINEERS' PERMIT PROGRAM; AVULSION

Riprap

1. A means of protecting an earth surface with a facing of rock. Riprapping may be used to protect stream banks, earthen dams or areas that have been cut leaving an exposed earth slope. In stream bank protection, if the stones are placed too smoothly, it may add to the velocity of the current and increase downstream erosion. As a result, the stones are often dumped in an irregular pattern, and a mixture of concrete fragments and irregular stones may be used.

2. Term also used to describe a foundation, wall or bulkhead built of loosely thrown together stone with no particular pattern.
See: BANK PROTECTION; REVETMENT

River Basin

A drainage area for a river that is separated from other drainage basins by a divide. Although a river basin may include a number of political subdivisions, it forms a cohesive unit for water resource planning purposes and for undertaking projects such a flood control, irrigation, channel improvement, dams and reservoirs.
See: DRAINAGE BASIN; FLOOD CONTROL; RIVER BASIN COMMISSION; WATER RESOURCES MANAGEMENT

River Basin Commission

A planning agency that develops water resource and land use plans for one or more river basins. Often operated by a board composed of representatives of the numerous jurisdictions that lie within the river basin, the commission prepares a comprehensive plan for water and related land development, recommends and establishes priorities for water resource development projects, undertakes studies related to water resources planning and coordinates plans and goals of all jurisdictions and public works agencies, such as the Army Corps of Engineers, that may be involved.

In the United States river basin commissions have been established for both single-basin and multibasin regions. Most of the multibasin commissions, which were established under Title II of the Water Resources Planning Act (PL 89-80) to develop comprehensive plans for basins crossing state lines, lost federal funding in 1981 and are attempting to reorganize under local authority. Certain of the single-basin commissions, such as the Delaware and the Susquehanna, established under other legislation, continue to receive federal appropriations as well as sizable appropriations from member states. In Canada these bodies are called river basin boards and function largely under provincial jurisdiction.
See: RIVER BASIN; TENNESSEE VALLEY AUTHORITY (TVA); WATER RESOURCES COUNCIL (WRC); WATER RESOURCES MANAGEMENT

River Engineering

The process by which engineering methods are used to control the water flows of rivers and streams to enable improved flood control, water supply, navigation, irrigation and power generation. River engineering projects of major scope have been carried out throughout the world, aimed at stabilizing and improving natural channels using techniques such as the deflection of currents to reduce erosion at a particular location. Other standard techniques include dredging of river channels to maintain navigable depth; armoring of banks to enable them to resist erosion; and the construction of flood-control works such as diversion channels and reservoirs.
See: ARMY CORPS OF ENGINEERS; BANK PROTECTION; BREAKWATER; CHANNELIZATION; DAM; DIKE; DREDGING; FLOOD CONTROL; FLOODWALL; JETTY; RESERVOIR

Rock Outcrop

Bedrock that is visible at the Earth's surface. Although it can present problems in development, it may also be incorporated into site design so that its natural visual appeal is highlighted. Provisions for the protection of visually prominent outcrops may be included in hillside protection ordinances.
See: BEDROCK; HILLSIDE PROTECTION ORDINANCES

Rodgers v. Village of Tarrytown (302 N.Y. 115, 96 N.E. 2d 731 [1951])

A decision by the New York Court of Appeals (New York's highest court) upholding the validity of the floating zone concept as adopted and applied by the Village of Tarrytown.

The court distinguished the permissible floating zone technique from unlawful spot zoning. In both cases, the court found, a small plot may be singled out from neighboring plots and uniquely affected, and in both cases the result may be to create, in the center of a large zone, small areas or districts devoted to a different use. However, if the ordinance is adopted and applied pursuant to a comprehensive plan for the general welfare of the community, it may be upheld as a floating zone. In contrast, if the ordinance is adopted and applied for the benefit of individual property owners without reference to the community's comprehensive plan, then it is improper spot zoning.
See: FLOATING ZONE; SPOT ZONING

Rolling Stock

The vehicles used to carry passengers by a railroad or transit line or to carry freight by a motor carrier. It is a measure of the size of the company or system. A count of railroad rolling stock includes passenger and freight cars and locomotives. Counts of transit stock include subway or trolley cars, buses, paratransit vehicles or taxis.

Rotary

An intersection of two or more roadways at which traffic merges into and emerges from a one-way roadway around a central area. Rotaries, also called traffic circles in the United States, are called roundabouts in Britain.

The design of a rotary requires that the central area be approximately round; its diameter depends on the design speed of the rotary and the distance between the roadways that radiate from it.

Rotaries were once common in highway design in the United States but are now rarely used because the amount of weaving necessary to negotiate them is considered unsafe. Rotaries of all sizes have been used successfully in Britain and still remain an important element in intersection design. During the 1920s and 1930s, rotaries were used extensively in the United States in residential areas to maintain low traffic speeds and add visual interest. (See Fig. 5)
See: AT-GRADE INTERSECTION

Rowhouse

A residential building, constructed as a single-family residence, that shares a common wall and occasionally a common roof with another similar building. Today rowhouses are often referred to by the more modern term *townhouse*. In the past, however, rowhouse development was typical of the less dense sections of central cities and did not necessarily indicate the type of unified development built by a single builder that exists today. Many of these older buildings in central city locations have been converted to multifamily use.
See: HOUSING TYPE; TOWNHOUSE

Royal Architectural Institute of Canada (RAIC)

A professional organization whose aims include the encouragement of excellence in architectural practice and service to the public. The RAIC, established in 1907, maintains its headquarters in Ottawa, Ontario. As of 1982, there were 3,500 members, associates, students and affiliates of the RAIC.

Royal Institute of British Architects (RIBA)

A professional organization for architects, founded in 1834 and located in London, England. RIBA's purposes include promotion of excellence in architecture, conservation of the built environment and elevation of public knowledge and awareness of both the architectural and natural environment.

The institute, which has approximately 27,000 members, undertakes a large range of activities. It promulgates a code of professional conduct, recognizes schools of architecture and maintains the British Architectural Library and Drawings Collection. It also serves as a liaison with architectural professionals from other countries, collects data related to architecture and promotes architectural research. Many additional activities take place at the regional and chapter level. Regular publications of the RIBA include *Transactions,* published twice yearly, and the *RIBA Journal,* published monthly, but a number of other specialized publications are available.

Royal Town Planning Institute (RTPI)

An organization of professional town planners with headquarters in London, England. Founded in 1914 and incorporated by royal charter, RTPI's interests include the advancement of the field of planning, demonstration of high standards of proficiency and integrity by its membership, and professional planning education.

Two basic classes of corporate (professional) membership are available: fellowship (FRTPI) and membership (MRTPI) in the institute. Individuals holding either of these classes of membership may refer to themselves as a "Chartered Town Planner." To attain corporate membership it is necessary either to have completed a recognized course of study in planning or to have passed a comprehensive examination. In addition, two years of planning work experience and a student membership period are required. Fellowship requires at least five years of planning experience and a minimum age of 30. RTPI has about 12,000 members, of which approximately 6,500 have corporate status, with the remainder in such categories as student member or honorary member.

Among the activities of RTPI are promulgating a code of professional conduct, conducting meetings and conferences, operating an information service and performing liaison activities with other planning-related organizations. It sponsors an annual Town and Country Planning Summer School and maintains a library. Regular publications of RTPI are *The Planner,* issued every two months, and *RTPI News,* a monthly newsletter. Other publications are available on various aspects of planning practice and issues in planning.

Runoff

That portion of precipitation which rejoins surface water bodies either directly or indirectly. It includes water that flows over the ground to reach surface water bodies as well as water that slowly infiltrates through the surface of the soil and eventually reaches surface water supplies. Generation of runoff can be significantly affected by modifications of the Earth's surface. Deforestation, removal of vegetation or addition of pavement can all affect the amount and timing of the storm runoff that is generated by lowering infiltration capacity in an area.

An understanding of runoff processes aids the planner in site analysis and design, in assessing the consequences of potential development and in devising methods of minimizing the impact of development. It is becoming common in the United States for municipalities to require that when new development takes place, procedures be undertaken to assure that the rate of runoff not exceed that which existed before the development took place. This may be accomplished by a variety of methods, such as the use of detention basins.

It is possible to estimate storm runoff volumes by using standard methods that take such factors as land use, soil characteristics, topography and vegetative cover into account. Municipalities usually specify procedures they wish

followed in calculating probable runoff after development and thus for determining the volume and type of facilities required to detain the runoff. These methods are usually some version of the rational runoff formula.
See: RUNOFF CALCULATIONS; RUNOFF EROSION; STORM DRAINAGE SYSTEM; URBAN RUNOFF

Runoff Calculations

Computations used to estimate storm runoff volumes, which are commonly used in planning and designing such facilities as storm sewers.

A frequently used method for estimating peak runoff rates is the rational runoff formula, which is best suited to urban catchment areas that are smaller than 200 acres (81 hectares), although it is often used for areas of as much as 1 square mile (2.6 square kilometers). This method is expressed by the formula $Q = CIA$, in which Q equals the quantity of runoff in cubic feet per second.

C equals the average runoff coefficient. This figure is a function of such variables as soil characteristics, vegetation and topography. Typical rational runoff coefficients are available in published tables. As an example, concrete walks and streets have a coefficient of 0.80 to 0.95 because they are highly impervious. Conversely, flat lawns with sandy soil have a coefficient of 0.05 to 0.10. Typical downtown business districts often have coefficients ranging from 0.70 to 0.95, while single family residential areas usually have coefficients ranging from 0.30 to 0.50.

I equals rainfall intensity in inches per hour. This figure may be estimated by using the formula $I = \dfrac{K}{t + b}$, in which t is equal to the elapsed time since the storm began, and K and b are constants that are a function of storm frequency and geographic portion of the United States (K and b may be obtained from standard published tables).

The final variable, A, is equal to the size of the total drainage area being evaluated, expressed in acres.
See: RUNOFF

Runoff Erosion

Erosion caused by the flow of water over land surfaces. Generally, three different types of runoff erosion are identified: sheet erosion, rill erosion and gully erosion.

The beginning stage in runoff erosion is removal of plant cover, followed by rain striking the unprotected soil surface and moving soil particles into new positions. This particle movement helps to seal natural openings in the soil, which normally permit water to infiltrate, causing water to flow across its surface.

Sheet erosion occurs primarily on plowed farmland and is characterized by removal of layers of soil in a more or less uniform fashion across the fields. Because it takes place gradually and evenly, it may not be noticed for some time. The loss of these surface layers or topsoil may, over a period of time, significantly affect soil fertility.

Sheet erosion may progress into rill erosion when land is steeply sloped and there are heavy volumes of runoff.

Rills, or narrow channels or trenches, are formed by rivulets of water running across the field. Significant soil loss can occur from rill erosion, but the condition may be improved and the rills eliminated with normal tilling procedures.

Gully erosion may develop from unchecked rill erosion when particular rills attract large and repeated volumes of runoff. If no counteractions are taken, the rill may develop into a steep-sided, eroding waterway. It is highly desirable to avoid this condition through early preventive action, as the control of gully erosion and the elimination of existing gullies is expensive and difficult.
See: RUNOFF; SOIL EROSION; SOIL EROSION CONTROL TECHNIQUES; SOIL EROSION FACTORS

Rural Development Act of 1972

This act (PL 92-419), with its subsequent amendments, provides federal financial support for rural development projects including water supply systems, sewer systems and sewage treatment facilities, and industrial development. Grants of up to 50 percent of project costs are made for comprehensive rural development plans and for some specific types of projects, such as pollution control or solid waste and water management. Loans and loan insurance are available for a wider range of public- and private-capital projects and operating costs, such as business development. Other programs authorized include those for development of water supplies, fire protection, technical assistance in rural development, and a land inventory and monitoring program. The Agricultural Credit Insurance Fund and the Rural Development Insurance Fund function as revolving funds that support the programs.

An additional provision of this act authorizes the Federal Housing Administration to guarantee certain rural housing loans even if the applicants cannot obtain conventional credit.
See: COMMUNITY ECONOMIC DEVELOPMENT ACT OF 1981: COMMUNITY FACILITY LOAN: EMPLOYMENT AND TRAINING ADMINISTRATION (ETA); RURAL DEVELOPMENT POLICY ACT OF 1980

Rural Development Policy Act of 1980

Legislation (PL 96-355) that amends the Rural Development Act of 1972 by encouraging establishment of a national rural development policy. It authorizes the secretary of agriculture to develop a comprehensive rural development strategy based on the needs, goals, plans and recommendations of local communities, states and regions and requires this strategy to be updated annually. The objective of the act is to maximize coordination of federal programs affecting rural areas.
See: RURAL DEVELOPMENT ACT OF 1972

Rural Electrification Administration (REA)

An agency within the Department of Agriculture that assists in the financing of rural electric and telephone systems. Utilities may obtain REA loans, guarantees of loans or approval of security arrangements that permit them to obtain private financing. The Rural Electrification and Telephone Revolving Fund (RETRF), established in 1973, provides funding for REA loans.

Rural Housing Programs

Loans for farmers and others living in rural areas, aimed at providing decent, affordable housing and removing safety and health hazards. The federal government has long been active in rural housing, initially to assist farmers and later to extend aid to others residing in rural areas.

The bulk of rural housing programs are administered by the Farmers Home Administration (FmHA) and are available to farmers, ranchers, other rural residents, developers and nonprofit agencies. FmHA programs include loans and grants for home ownership, housing rehabilitation, rural rental housing and housing for migrant farm workers. Relatively low interest farm mortgage loans are available through the Federal Farm Credit System, and the Federal Housing Administration (FHA) 203 (i) program provides mortgage insurance for one- to four-family nonfarm housing in rural areas. Some Department of Housing and Urban Development programs are targeted to serve rural areas, while the Veterans Administration mortgage program is also available to these areas.
See: FARMERS HOME ADMINISTRATION (FmHA); FEDERAL FARM CREDIT SYSTEM; HOUSING PROGRAMS FOR NATIVE AMERICANS; RURAL PLANNING

Rural Planning

The application of planning techniques to one or more of the diverse concerns of rural areas, which may be undertaken by town, village and county government. Rural areas consist of farmland, countryside, forested lands and more urbanized places. The Farmers Home Administration, as an example, includes municipalities with up to 20,000 residents as rural areas that are entitled to aid via its programs. Rural communities share many of the same planning interests as urban areas, in that they must be concerned with provision and maintenance of community facilities, housing, roads and public transportation, as well as land management, economic development and operation of human resources programs. Although the scale of the problems may differ, many of the same analytic, administrative and regulatory techniques found in urban areas may be used.

Rural areas do, however, have a number of special planning concerns not encountered in more urbanized communities, or of lesser scale in urbanized areas, such as provision of electrification to remote areas and housing for farm laborers. Other areas of concern may include surface mining reclamation, soil erosion control or tourism, while in some states rural planning emphasizes farmland protection; control of second home development; management of scarce resources, such as water; or control of boomtown development, perhaps related to extraction of natural resources. Implementation of state environmental controls is another aspect of rural planning.

Planners working in rural areas often have small staffs, necessitating their reliance on officials of other government agencies for certain aspects of their work. Typically, the district conservationist of the U.S. Soil Conservation Service and the local agricultural extension agent provide advice on matters related to use of land, while the local building inspector and the health department may study specific aspects of proposals as they relate to state and local land use regulations.
See: AGRICULTURAL POLLUTION; COUNTY PLANNING; FARMLAND PROTECTION; FORESTRY; RANGELAND MANAGEMENT; RURAL HOUSING PROGRAMS; RURAL SANITATION; SOIL EROSION; URBAN PLANNING; WILDLIFE MANAGEMENT

Rural Sanitation

Procedures used in areas of low population density to protect the public health through such measures as proper disposal of sewage and solid waste, and protection and purification of drinking water supplies. For example, sparse population frequently makes typical urban sanitation systems, such as sewage treatment plants, prohibitively expensive. Instead, rural areas often rely upon individual septic systems which, when properly located, constructed and maintained, provide a safe means of disposing of sewage.
See: DUMP; SANITARY LANDFILL; SEPTIC SYSTEM; WELL

S

Safe Drinking Water Act

Legislation enacted in 1974 that authorizes the federal government to set national quality standards for public drinking water and to establish treatment requirements. Prior federal legislation covered bacteriological contamination and water testing frequency, but this act represents the first federal regulatory control over chemical and radiological pollutants in drinking water. In addition to authorizing the establishment of contamination standards, the act (PL 93-523) directs the Environmental Protection

Agency (EPA) to set standards concerning taste, odor and appearance. These standards are to be enforced by the states, under EPA supervision. The act requires water utilities to inform the public if they violate EPA standards, and it also gives EPA authority over drinking water emergencies, including control of the distribution of treatment chemicals such as chlorine.

Other provisions include authorization to establish regulations for state programs in which fluid is injected into wells to increase subsurface water supplies, grants to states to initiate enforcement programs and grants for demonstration water supply projects. Guaranteed loans for small public water systems and a survey of rural drinking water supply, quantity and quality were also authorized.
See: WATER TREATMENT

Sale-Leaseback

A financing technique sometimes used by government and other nonprofit institutions. In one form of sale-leaseback, a tax-exempt organization, most often a unit of government, sells one of its buildings or other facilities to a private investor or investment group (but retains ownership of the underlying land) and then leases that facility back on a long-term lease. The government unit gains immediate income from the sale, which may be used to finance rehabilitation, construction or other municipal projects, while the investors receive a substantial tax shelter for an already occupied building and usually are not responsible for operating or maintenance expenses. A clause is generally included in the lease that gives the municipality the right to buy back the building at the end of the lease period or to renew the lease. Problems sometimes mentioned in connection with this technique, however, include public opposition to such sales or legal restrictions concerning this type of procedure.

The city of Oakland, California recently used sale-leaseback to sell and then lease back the Oakland Museum. At the end of 30 years, the city, which retained title to the land, may repurchase the museum for its fair market value. The money raised through this procedure will be used to improve a theater complex. Other cities have used, or are considering using, this technique with other municipal buildings, their utility systems or their transit equipment.

Sale-leaseback may also be used in another way by government and nonprofit groups, for such purposes as preservation of open space. A piece of land considered important for its long-term open-space value may be purchased by a government agency and simultaneously leased back to the seller for a stipulated time period. Eventually, the land is used for park or other open-space purposes.

In a variation of the sale-leaseback technique, known as lease-purchase, public facilities are built by private enterprise and then leased to the unit of government. When the lease period is over, the title is conveyed to the unit of government, as the rental will have been set at an amount sufficient to pay for the project cost as well as interest.
See: CAPITAL IMPROVEMENT PROGRAM (CIP); PROPERTY ACQUISITION; PROPERTY DISPOSITION

Sales Tax

A tax on the consumption of certain goods and services that supplies a large proportion of state revenues and is increasingly being used to supplement municipal revenues.

Statewide sales taxes are widely used, and municipalities in some states are also permitted to add and collect an additional percentage or impose their own sales tax if no state tax exists. In states where only cities are permitted to impose sales taxes, surrounding unincorporated areas frequently attract new commercial development, such as shopping centers, seeking to avoid the increased tax burden. Similarly, communities with a lower sales tax may experience more rapid commercial development than those with much higher rates, requiring income potential from sales tax to be weighed against other factors.

Sales tax is considered to be regressive, in that people of varying incomes pay an equal percentage of tax on the cost of purchases. A sales tax is relatively easy for municipalities to impose, however, in contrast to raising the property tax or imposing an income tax, since the tax is collected in small amounts.
See: INCOME TAX; PROPERTY TAX

Salt Marsh

Those wetlands characterized by periodic inundation of tidal waters and the presence of salt-tolerant vegetation. Salt marshes are particularly prevalent on the east coast of North America, where they are found from Nova Scotia to Florida, but are also fairly common in northern Europe, Australia and New Zealand.

Salt marshes serve as nurseries for many types of fish and shellfish, and are an important waterfowl habitat. They are also efficient trappers of sediment, helping to reduce the need for dredging in nearby waters, and can serve as buffers to coastal storms, helping to protect development farther inland. Common types of vegetation found in the salt marsh are spike grass, sea lavendar, arrow grass, seaside plantain, gerardia and aster. In areas with larger amounts of fresh water, species such as cattail, reed grass and sedges are found.
See: ESTUARY; WETLANDS

Saltwater Intrusion

Invasion of salt water into groundwater. This usually occurs in coastal areas in which excessive pumping of well water lowers a water table. The reduction in the amount of fresh water in an aquifer lowers pressure in the freshwater zone, disrupting the normal balance that exists between fresh and saline water and allowing saltwater encroachment into freshwater supplies.

Saltwater intrusion is a common problem in developed coastal areas, islands and peninsulas throughout the world. Once saltwater intrusion begins to occur, the chief options open to a community are reduced dependence on local groundwater supplies and the use of artificial recharge methods, in which water is injected into an aquifer to prevent the salt water from moving farther inland.
See: AQUIFER; GROUNDWATER; RECHARGE; WATER RESOURCES MANAGEMENT; WATER TABLE; WELL

Sampling

1. A means of obtaining information from a sample of the population that accurately reflects the population as a whole.

In the context of sample surveys, a population consists of all individuals, objects, etc., that have a specific definable characteristic (e.g., homeowners residing in a municipality, persons over 60 years of age, maple trees of a particular size). Adequate sample size is a function of many variables, including the degree of precision the research requires. The accuracy of the sample may be assessed by comparing known facts about the entire population to the characteristics of the sample.

A variety of sampling techniques are available, including random sampling, systematic sampling, stratified sampling and cluster sampling.

2. The process of procuring and examining representative samples of air, water, soil, etc. to assess their characteristics and quality.
See: CLUSTER SAMPLE; RANDOM SAMPLE; STRATIFIED SAMPLE; SURVEY RESEARCH; SYSTEMATIC SAMPLE

San Francisco Plan

A plan prepared in 1906 by Daniel Burnham, along with Edward H. Bennett, for the Association for the Improvement and Adornment of San Francisco. Burnham's first attempt at planning for all of the land within the boundaries of a major American city, it applied the principles he developed earlier in planning for the World's Columbian Exposition and Washington, D.C.

The plan called for the reservation of large areas of open space, parkways, a civic complex linked by boulevards, a system of radial roadways, an outer highway belt and a subway system. It also suggested methods of locating industry based upon prevailing wind patterns, to minimize the impact of smoke generated by factories, and recommended the location of major streets at the borders of residential areas so that through traffic in residential areas would be minimized.

Many of the features of the plan became standard planning practice in that era. Little of the San Francisco plan was ever implemented, however, because of the San Fran-

cisco earthquake and fire in 1906, which encouraged rapid rebuilding at a time when the plan was still little known.
See: BURNHAM, DANIEL; CITY BEAUTIFUL MOVEMENT

Sanitary Code

Regulations that control matters broadly related to public health. A sanitary code is usually promulgated at the state level, but lower levels of government may then enact sanitary regulations and provisions, providing that they are not inconsistent with the state code. Although content may vary widely by state, among the areas that may be covered in a sanitary code are the qualifications of health care personnel and of those individuals who operate facilities that affect the public health, such as sewage or water treatment facilities. The operations of food service establishments, water supply, sewerage, sanitation of habitable buildings, water quality at swimming pools and beaches, application of pesticides and air pollution control are other common sanitary code topics.

Sanitary code enforcement is closely related to a number of planning activities. As an example, proposed subdivisions may have to comply with code provisions with respect to the intended methods of providing drinking water, sewer facilities and drainage. New home sites in unsewered areas may also be subjected to a review process to ensure adequacy of the septic systems and/or wells.

Sanitary Engineering

A specialized field of civil engineering that includes the areas of water supply engineering; sewerage system engineering; solid waste systems engineering; environmental engineering; sanitation of living, work and recreational areas; food-handling mechanisms; rodent and insect control; and control of exposure to radiation.
See: ENVIRONMENTAL ENGINEERING; SOLID WASTE MANAGEMENT; WASTEWATER MANAGEMENT; WATER SUPPLY ENGINEERING

Sanitary Landfill

A method of solid waste disposal in which waste is spread in layers, compacted to reduce its volume and then covered each day with earth or another inert material. Although properly run landfills are free of rodents, smokeless and have little odor, they are often confused with dumps, which are an unsatisfactory means of waste disposal and are being phased out across the United States. Experimented with throughout the early part of the century in the United States and Europe, sanitary landfills were first used in England (where the method is called "controlled tipping") in 1912.

In selecting a site for a sanitary landfill, many different factors must be considered. It should have adequate space for the projected amount of refuse requiring disposal as well as road access capable of accommodating truck traffic and should not be so far from the collection points as to

SANITARY LANDFILL

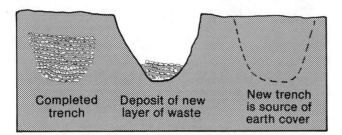

Fig. 38.   A cross section of a landfill site showing a trench that has been completey filled with final cover placed on top, a trench that is being filled and an area reserved for future sanitary landfill from which cover material can be taken.

greatly increase the overall disposal cost. It should, of course, be appropriately sited with regard to surrounding land uses, have community support and approval, preferably have suitable cover material available on the site and be environmentally suitable for refuse disposal. Among the important environmental considerations are the selection of a site in which topographic and soil characteristics will help to minimize infiltration of surface water and the avoidance of flood-prone sites or sites with high water tables to minimize leaching and water supply contamination.

A final use for the site should be considered when the site is being selected, to ensure its ultimate suitability for that use. The generation of gases, such as methane, and the settling that can occur for a prolonged period of time make completed landfills more suitable for low-density nonresidential and open-space type development. Among the common uses made of completed landfill sites are athletic fields, parks, golf courses, airport extensions and ski slopes.

In recent years escalating land values and shortages of appropriate undeveloped land near populated areas have made it difficult to acquire new sanitary landfill sites and expensive to purchase the sites when they can be found. New technology is increasingly being relied upon to prolong the life of existing landfill sites and to minimize the amount of additional land that is needed. Among the technologies being used are shredding and baling of refuse, recycling, codisposal and various types of resource-recovery plants. (See Fig. 38)
See: BALING; CODISPOSAL; COVER MATERIAL; DAILY COVER; DUMP; FINAL COVER; LEACHATE; RECYCLING; RESOURCE RECOVERY; SHREDDING; SOLID WASTE MANAGEMENT

Sanitary Sewer

A sewerage system designed to receive and carry waste-water from homes, businesses and industry. A sanitary system is not intended to accept stormwater runoff, al-

though its design does allow for a calculated amount of groundwater infiltration.
See: INFILTRATION; SEWERAGE SYSTEM; STORM SEWER; WASTEWATER

Satellite Pattern

A regional land use pattern characterized by the presence of discrete outlying subcenter communities separate from, but related to, the urban core. Satellite communities, which are located around a central city but at some distance from it, serve as bedroom communities, use cultural facilities, or are otherwise economically tied to or dependent upon the central city. Satellite communities may also serve as second-home or resort areas for the central city. A satellite pattern is distinguished from sprawl by the presence of open space or very low density development between communities. (See Fig. 24)
See: GALAXY PATTERN; LAND USE PATTERN; MULTIPLE-NUCLEI THEORY; SPRAWL

Scale of Development

A design term that describes the size of a project as it relates to its surrounding environment.

It is generally considered desirable to relate the scale of development of one building or space to another so that it may harmonize with an existing area or, by virtue of contrast, contribute in a positive way to the visual and aesthetic appeal of a physical setting. In the absence of appropriate scale, a development may appear incongruous or "out of scale" in comparison to its surroundings, as could be the case with a skyscraper surrounded by low-rise residential development. In another context, however, the same building might be considered to be architecturally distinctive and correctly scaled.
See: HUMAN SCALE

Scatter-Site Housing

A type of subsidized housing developed in the mid-1960s in the United States. In scatter-site housing, projects are kept small so that they do not overwhelm a neighborhood, or subsidized housing units are leased in buildings that include a mix of economic groups. Viewed as an alternative to large-scale public housing projects, scatter-site housing was also an attempt to locate public housing tenants near expanding job opportunities outside central city locations. A major problem that this program faced was opposition by the communities selected as sites for new scatter-site housing projects.
See: PUBLIC HOUSING

Scenario Writing

The creation of a chain of events that will take a particular problem from its current position to a point in the future via different routes. A scenario might, for example, show the alternatives to be followed given different funding levels; the effects caused by the actions of other programs, agencies or levels of government; the varying levels of private or voluntary input; or the changes in attendance or use because of varying improvements or charges. A scenario might be freely developed in an hour or two or require use of a complex computerized model to include the variables being analyzed.

Scenario writing is a process that is used in business management but is applicable to planning activities such as goal formulation and the development of alternative courses of action. It is thought that its use in the early stages of planning can help to broaden the range of possibilities that will be considered and to clarify organizational responsibilities.
See: DELPHI PROCESS

Scenic Easement

A type of conservation easement intended to restrict or preclude action (e.g., development or alteration of the land) by a landowner that would interfere with a scenic view intended to be preserved. Scenic easements are generally acquired along public rights-of-way or over land adjoining public property.

Scenic easements may also be affirmative in nature. One example is the right acquired by a state to plant and maintain a green buffer zone on land adjoining a highway.
See: CONSERVATION EASEMENT; EASEMENT

Scenic Overlook

An area at the side of a road from which one can observe a scenic vista. Scenic overlooks are often provided along roads and highways that pass through scenic areas, to permit parking and observation of views. These overlooks, which usually accommodate 10 or more cars, reduce the need for viewers to slow down, thereby slowing traffic, and also provide rest areas. Picnicking and toilet facilities may also be placed in these locations.

If the site is not a natural overlook, periodic tree thinning may be required to prevent view obstruction, while scenic easements may be necessary to protect some views.
See: SCENIC EASEMENT; SCENIC ROAD; VIEW PROTECTION REGULATIONS; VISTA

Scenic Road

A general term for a highway that passes areas of natural beauty or cultural value and is therefore designated as a "scenic road" by a public or private organization. A scenic designation helps to promote tourism and publicizes the unique qualities of an area.
See: NATIONAL PARKWAY

Schad v. *Borough of Mount Ephraim* (452 U.S. 61, 101 S.Ct. 2176, 62 L.Ed.2d 671 [1981])

The Borough of Mount Ephraim, New Jersey applied its zoning ordinance, construed to prohibit commercial live entertainment throughout the borough, to prohibit live nude dancing in an adult bookstore. The United States

Supreme Court held the ordinance, as so construed, to be unconstitutional. The Court acknowledged the usual presumption of validity of municipal zoning ordinances, so long as they are rationally related to a legitimate state interest. However, since this ordinance, as applied, impinged upon the right to free expression protected by the First Amendment, the Court held that different standards apply—the governmental interest furthered by the ordinance must be substantial, and it must be furthered in the way that intrudes least on activity protected by the First Amendment.
See: YOUNG v. AMERICAN MINI THEATRES

Schedule of District Regulations

A portion of the zoning ordinance that includes, in chart form, most of the permitted activities and important provisions for each zoning district. Typically, a zoning schedule will include land uses permitted by right and by special permit, uses that are specifically prohibited and standards for minimum lot area, height, yards, coverage, etc. The schedule may also contain other requirements of the zone, such as those regarding parking.

Generally, schedules of district regulations make zoning ordinances easier to use and more readable. It is always necessary, however, for the ordinance user to check references made in the schedule to portions of the text and to read any other descriptions or requirements concerning a zone that are found in the text, so that a complete understanding of the pertinent regulations is gained.
See: ZONING; ZONING ORDINANCE

Schematic Drawing

A sketch or drawing, usually to scale, of a proposed structure in its early design stages. Schematics generally show principal floor plans and elevations; a perspective drawing may also be provided to enable a client who is not proficient in reading drawings to review the schematics. Schematics are often drawn on tracing paper so that different floor plans can readily be compared by placing one over the other.
See: ELEVATION; FLOOR PLAN; PERSPECTIVE RENDERING; WORKING DRAWINGS

School District

A school authority, usually independent of municipal or state control, that among other things, sets the school tax levy, engages and discharges teachers, and establishes educational policy. The school district chooses a school superintendent, who administers the school system. School district consolidation, which has recently been occurring with much greater frequency, has sharply reduced the number of districts; while there were 127,000 school districts in the United States in 1932, there were only 15,929 by 1979. Consolidation allows a more efficient use of funds, and larger school districts are better able to provide a variety of educational facilities and services.

Cities often have a school system administered by a school board rather than school districts. Various state statutes may also authorize school administration by county educational systems, by township administration and, in New England, by town school committees.
See: SCHOOL PLANNING; SPECIAL DISTRICT

School Enrollment Projections

Population estimates of school age children. These are used by planners to estimate school facility requirements and service areas as the basis for school planning, building programs and staffing.

A variety of sources are employed to make projections. The cohort survival method is frequently used to project population by age group in the municipality by aging children from one grade level to the next. These figures may then be adjusted to reflect enrollment by modifying them based upon changes in the birthrate; past enrollment trends for public and private schools; building trends within the school service areas and their expected student yields; and changes in the land use pattern, such as gentrification of industrial areas. Determination of first-grade enrollment is often made by analyzing ratios of births in the municipality compared to first-grade enrollment figures six years later.
See: COHORT SURVIVAL METHOD; SCHOOL PLANNING; SCHOOL SERVICE AREAS

School Land Requirements

School site selection involves the choice of properties that are large enough to permit construction of a school along with the varied recreational, athletic and parking facilities that are normally part of the building program.

Recommended standards for each school level are given in ranges because school sizes, topography of the land and program requirements vary. Elementary school sites should generally contain at least 7 acres (3 hectares) but rarely need more than 18 acres (7 hectares). Junior high school sites vary in size from 18 to 32 acres (7 to 13 hectares) and senior high school sites from 32 to 50 acres (13 to 20 hectares). In heavily urbanized areas, however, smaller sites are generally provided.
See: SCHOOL PLANNING

School Planning

Decisions concerning the number of schools that are needed, their location and design, and the programs and facilities that should be available in them. School planning is undertaken by analysis of population and development trends to ascertain changes and the evaluation of existing school facilities to determine required improvements. School planners are frequently educators in administrative positions, but some larger school systems employ urban planners.

School planning issues most closely related to urban planning are a determination of appropriate school sites and sizes, on the basis of demographic analysis, and site design. In communities with declining school enrollments, planners help to assess which schools should be closed and to find alternate uses for these buildings.
See: EDUCATIONAL PARK; NEIGHBORHOOD SCHOOL; NURSERY SCHOOL; SCHOOL ENROLLMENT PROJECTIONS; SCHOOL LAND REQUIREMENTS; SCHOOL SERVICE AREAS; SURPLUS SCHOOLS

School Recreational Facilities

Generally active recreation facilities provided by an educational system or institution. They often include playing fields, running tracks, gymnasiums, stadiums, swimming pools and children's play equipment. These same facilities are frequently made available for use by the community during nonschool hours and are part of the recreation system.
See: ACTIVE RECREATION; RECREATION FACILITIES; RECREATION SYSTEM

School Service Areas

The land area or population that a school is expected to serve. When schools are built, they are located at the approximate center of the population they are to serve so that most children will be able to walk to school. Exceptions are less dense suburban areas and rural areas, where most children are bused. Guidelines for school service areas recommend that elementary schools serve one average-size neighborhood, or a radius of 0.25 to 0.5 mile (0.4 to 0.8 kilometer) and a total population of from 1,500 to 7,000. Junior high school service areas should have a radius of 0.5 to 0.75 mile (0.8 kilometer to 1.2 kilometers) and include a population of 10,000 to 20,000 or approximately two to three neighborhoods. A population of 14,000 to 34,000 is desirable for a high school, with a service area ranging from a 0.75- to a 1-mile (1.2- to 1.6-kilometer) radius, which is roughly equivalent to five or more neighborhoods.

As populations change around the schools, the school service area is redistricted so that classrooms will remain filled or will not become overcrowded. When this happens, children may be required to travel farther to school.
See: NEIGHBORHOOD SCHOOL; SCHOOL PLANNING

Scoping

The process of determining the range of actions, alternatives and impacts to be considered in an environmental impact statement (EIS). According to the regulations for implementing the National Environmental Policy Act, at least three types of actions, three alternatives and three impacts must be considered.

Actions that are either connected or closely related and actions that when viewed with other proposed actions have cumulative impacts should be discussed in the same impact statement. Actions that are similar, such as in terms of location or timing, may be discussed in one statement when the most accurate analysis can be performed in this manner. Alternatives that must be considered include a "no action" alternative, other reasonable courses of action and mitigating measures. Direct, indirect and cumulative impacts must also be considered.

The scope of an environmental impact statement is developed in a series of meetings conducted by the agency primarily responsible for preparing the EIS, known as the lead agency, with the participation of affected federal, state and local agencies and other interested persons. In addition to identifying significant issues and eliminating those that are not significant, the allocation of assignments among the agencies and the timing of the various steps of the analysis may be determined during these sessions.
See: ENVIRONMENTAL IMPACT STATEMENT (EIS)

Screening

1. The use of landscape planting, fences or other structures to obscure vision of an unsightly or undesirable land use, to prevent outdoor lighting from intruding on neighboring property or to create privacy. It is also used to modify climatic conditions by reducing the effects of high winds or by blocking strong sunlight in hot climates.

Densely planted evergreens or other thick foliage, solid or closely woven fences, stone walls or the placement of a building so that light or unsightly development are not visible can both improve the aesthetic quality of an area and reduce the effect of the natural or man-made nuisance. Zoning ordinances frequently include screening requirements for certain types of land uses, such as junkyards, or for land uses that may be incompatible with adjoining properties when located on the border of a different zoning district, such as parking lots adjacent to residential development.

2. The first step in the treatment of wastewater, in which coarse solids are removed to prevent damage to pumps and other equipment. The procedure consists of the passage of the wastewater through bar racks (parallel bars) or fine screens (wire mesh or perforated plates). After this process, the materials that have been intercepted are removed and disposed of either by grinding and then returning them to the treatment process, by hauling to a landfill site, by incineration or by burial on the treatment plant site.

3. Bar racks or other devices that are used at water supply intakes to prevent debris or other large objects from entering the pipes. Some are electrically charged to keep fish away.
See: CLIMATIC CONDITIONS; COMMINUTION; FENCE; LANDSCAPING; SEWAGE TREATMENT; ZONING

Seawall

A massive solid wall at the shoreline that is designed to protect the shore, prevent inland flooding, hold fill in place on its earthward side and elevate development above flood levels. Engineered to withstand direct wave impact, seawalls are more effective in protecting shorefront development than in protecting beaches. They are thought, in fact, to have a role in accelerating beach erosion where beaches adjoin seawalls, as the force of the waves is directed downward onto the beach after striking the wall. (See Fig. 9)
See: BEACH EROSION; BULKHEAD

Second-Home Area

An attractive area in which well-to-do families purchase weekend or vacation retreats. Second-home areas develop because of amenities such as beautiful countryside, beaches or skiing. Unlike most residential development, daily commute to employment is not required for weekend or vacation homes, although reasonable access, usually by auto but sometimes by plane, is necessary. Examples of second-home areas include sections of Cape Cod, Massachusetts; Lake Tahoe, in California and Nevada; and Aspen, Colorado. Second homes, which sometimes become retirement homes, can range from modest cabins to luxury condominiums and villas.

In developing second-home areas, it is important that the qualities that first attracted interest, particularly natural features, be maintained. Typical attractions that may bring large numbers of short-term tourists are often not compatible with second-home development unless they are well removed from residential sections.
See: RESORT AREA; TIMESHARING

Secondary Mortgage Market

The market in which institutions that grant mortgage loans—such as commercial banks, savings banks and mortgage companies—are able to sell portions of their mortgage loan portfolios to investors, government agencies and other institutions. This contrasts with the primary mortgage market, where the mortgage is initiated between the borrower and the lender.

The purpose of the secondary mortgage market is to assure liquidity in the mortgage market and to provide an adequate supply of mortgage money. The secondary market serves this purpose by bringing into contact mortgage initiators, such as banks and other lending institutions, with those wishing to invest in pools of mortgages. The result is a flow of additional money that is available for new mortgages. Money is also injected into the mortgage market in periods of tight financing.

The Federal National Mortgage Association (FNMA), a private corporation, and three government organizations—the Government National Mortgage Association (GNMA), the Federal Home Loan Mortgage Corporation (FHLMC) and the Federal Home Loan Bank System (FHLBS)—are involved in the functioning of the secondary mortgage market.
See: FEDERAL HOME LOAN BANK SYSTEM (FHLBS); FEDERAL HOME LOAN MORTGAGE CORPORATION (FHLMC); FEDERAL NATIONAL MORTGAGE ASSOCIATION (FNMA); GOVERNMENT NATIONAL MORTGAGE ASSOCIATION (GNMA)

Secondary Road

A rural collector road that provides access to a primary road or a freeway and connects small communities to each other. Secondary roads generally serve an intracounty function. Trip lengths and travel speeds are lower than on primary roads, and access to abutting land is provided. Secondary roads constitute about 10 percent of the rural road system. Also called the rural collector system, secondary roads can be classified as major collectors and minor collectors, indicating different traffic volumes.
See: COLLECTOR STREET; PRIMARY ROAD

Secondary Treatment

The biological treatment of wastewater, generally by use of oxidation processes and sludge digestion after the wastewater has undergone sedimentation. Secondary treatment of this type can remove 80 percent to 90 percent of the suspended solids and organic matter present in the wastewater. Septic tanks and Imhoff tanks are also considered to be secondary treatment facilities, since they provide for the biological treatment of sludge.

Worldwide environmental problems related to pollution of receiving waters have caused many countries to consider the need for upgrading primary treatment plants to provide secondary treatment. In the United States the upgrading of municipal plants is mandatory where primary treatment is not sufficient to protect the water quality of receiving waters. For purposes of the sewage treatment plant construction program in the United States, secondary treatment is defined as the removal of a minimum of 85 percent of suspended solids and organic matter as well as removal of minimum levels of many chemicals.
See: FEDERAL WATER POLLUTION CONTROL ACT AMENDMENTS OF 1972; IMHOFF TANK; MUNICIPAL WASTEWATER TREATMENT CONSTRUCTION GRANT AMENDMENTS OF 1981; PRIMARY TREATMENT; SEPTIC TANK; SEWAGE TREATMENT; TERTIARY TREATMENT

Secretary of the Interior's Standards for Rehabilitation

Standards promulgated by the Department of the Interior to ensure that the significant historical and architectural features of historic structures are protected during the course of rehabilitation. These standards, designed to allow a property owner flexibility in making repairs or alterations, must be adhered to in order for an owner of historic property to qualify for federal tax benefits available for the rehabilitation of such properties. Guidelines are also available to aid in the application of the standards.
See: ECONOMIC RECOVERY TAX ACT OF 1981; HISTORIC PRESERVATION; REHABILITATION

Secretary's Discretionary Fund

A fund administered by the Department of Housing and Urban Development that is used to implement some of the programs authorized by Title I of the Housing and Community Development Act of 1974 as amended in 1981. The fund provides Community Development Block Grant (CDBG) funds for areas not eligible under the entitlement or Small Cities Program—e.g., Guam and the Virgin Islands. Funding for technical assistance to states, municipal governments, Indian tribes and areawide planning organizations is made available, while in previous years appropriations were also made for special projects requested by states and municipal governments. Funding is appropriated annually.
See: DEPARTMENT OF HOUSING AND URBAN DEVELOPMENT (HUD)

Section 8 Housing Program

A low- and moderate-income rental subsidy program that was added to the Housing Act of 1937 by the Housing and Community Development Act of 1974. Tenants pay a percentage of their income (25 percent to 30 percent), and the Department of Housing and Urban Development (HUD) makes up the difference between what the tenant pays and an established fair market rent (FMR). From 1977 through 1983 Section 8 was the major subsidized housing production program in the United States.

Section 8 New Construction, which is no longer funded except for housing for the elderly (the Section 202 program), was an aspect of the program in which a developer secured a contractual Section 8 commitment for a specified number of units and time period (20 to 30 years). That Section 8 contract could be utilized to obtain the necessary financing for construction from banks, the state housing finance agency or mortgage-backed bonds. Section 8 projects that were managed by the developer (who rented units to Section 8 eligible tenants) were sometimes insured by the Federal Housing Administration.

Section 8 Substantial Rehabilitation, which was similar in operation to Section 8 New Construction, provided for acquisition and "gut" rehabilitation of existing structures to HUD minimum property standards. Costs for substantial rehabilitation under this Section 8 program were comparable to the costs of new construction. In Section 8 Moderate Rehabilitation, which is still funded, buildings are improved to a less demanding standard. Contracts are usually for 15 years and are intended for basically sound structures in need of some repair. Often administered by local public housing authorities, the Moderate Rehabilitation Program provides a lower level of rent subsidy (lower fair market rents) than New Construction or Substantial Rehabilitation, but tenants still pay the same proportion of income. Under the Section 8 Existing Housing Program, which is also often administered by local public housing authorities, tenants may use a Section 8 eligibility certificate to secure existing apartments meeting minimum standards. This program has the lowest subsidy level of the Section 8 programs.

A major advantage of the Section 8 program has been

the flexibility available to developers and tenants within program guidelines. It has enabled the construction of certain outstanding projects and allowed tenants to attempt to find their own housing in neighborhoods of their choice. But as interest rates rose in the late 1970s, costs to subsidize the mortgage interest rates over the 30-year contract period grew dramatically.

The Housing and Urban-Rural Recovery Act of 1983 repealed authority for the Section 8 New Construction and Substantial Rehabilitation Programs, but amended eligibility requirements for Existing Housing Program units to permit residents of single-room occupancy dwellings and elderly persons in shared housing facilities to obtain Section 8 authorizations. The 1983 act also instituted two new housing programs thought to be potential replacements for the Section 8 Program: a rental housing program and a housing voucher program. A housing appropriations act that had been passed earlier in 1983 authorized a modest continuation of the Moderate Rehabilitation Program and the issuance of 35,000 certificates for the Existing Housing Program.

See: HOUSING AND COMMUNITY DEVELOPMENT AMENDMENTS OF 1981; HOUSING AND URBAN-RURAL RECOVERY ACT OF 1983

Section 9 Block Grant Program

A formula block grant program distributed to municipalities for mass transportation capital and operating purposes. Authorized by the Surface Transportation Assistance Act of 1982, the program is administered by the Urban Mass Transportation Administration.

Funding is provided at 80 percent for all capital projects—including planning, acquisition and construction—and at 50 percent for operation, but a stipulated amount of capital funding can be traded for operating funds. An applicant must submit a "program of projects," which serves as the principal element of the application. The program of projects lists projects that are realistically expected to be funded under the block grant program, giving a description of each and noting that its inclusion in the list has been subject to public comment. All projects listed must also appear in the annual element of the transportation improvement program.

Annual appropriations are distributed on the basis of a formula relating to population. Municipalities with populations of more than 200,000 receive 88 percent of the appropriation, distributed among them according to population, population density and bus and/or fixed guideway revenue miles and fixed guideway route miles. Municipalities with 50,000 to 200,000 people receive 9 percent of the funding on the basis of population and density, while non-urbanized areas receive 3 percent of the funding, distributed on the basis of population alone.

See: SURFACE TRANSPORTATION ASSISTANCE ACT OF 1982; URBAN MASS TRANSPORTATION ADMINISTRATION (UMTA)

Section 23 Housing Program

A housing program that allowed public housing authorities to lease low-income public housing rather than build and operate their own. The cost of the new or existing housing beyond the rent paid by the tenants (25 percent of their income) was covered by an annual assistance contract with the Department of Housing and Urban Development. Section 23, which was added to the United States Housing Act of 1937 by the Housing and Urban Development Act of 1965, was innovative in allowing the private builder and developer to participate in public housing. The Section 23 program had produced over 72,000 housing units as of 1977, when it was superseded by the Section 8 housing program, with which it had operated concurrently since 1975.

See: HOUSING AUTHORITY; PUBLIC HOUSING; SECTION 8 HOUSING PROGRAM

Section 202 Housing Program

A program authorized by the Housing Act of 1959 (PL 86-372) that gives direct construction and mortgage loans to private nonprofit sponsors of rental or cooperative housing for elderly or handicapped persons. Funds are generally made available at below market interest rates set by the Federal Housing Administration. A minimum of 20 percent of the units must receive Section 8 rent supplements, although in some cases all units do.

The Section 202 program has proved to be a highly successful one, and there is often strong competition for available funding. Approximately 150,000 units have been built under the program since its inception. Part of Section 202's local appeal is that it is limited to those over 62 years of age or the physically handicapped. Another aspect is that, as a direct loan program, Section 202 approval virtually assures a project's completion, because it is a complete financing package that covers construction, mortgage and rent supplements. The 202 program was one of the few housing finance programs to be funded, though at a reduced level, into the 1980s.

See: SECTION 8 HOUSING PROGRAM

Sections 203 (b) and (i) Housing Programs

The primary Federal Housing Administration (FHA) program for insuring mortgage loans for one- to four-family homes, authorized by Sections 203 (b) and (i) of the National Housing Act of 1934. Section 203 (b) allows the Federal Housing Administration to insure commercial lenders against losses on home mortgage loans. Section 203 (i) extends the program to outlying areas e.g., Guam and the Virgin Islands. The provision of FHA insurance, for up to 97 percent of the property value to a maximum loan amount, reduces risk to the lender and allows for lower down payments, while the FHA-established interest rate is generally lower than conventional mortgage rates.

The FHA program was widely successful in the 1950s and 1960s, enabling many people to purchase homes with reduced down payments. As of 1980 the Section 203 program had insured approximately 11 million residential units. The program was especially strong in new suburban developments, leading to some criticism that the underwriting standards tended to support suburban rather than inner city housing.

The use of the 203 program has declined in recent years, due principally to the ceilings that have been set on home costs (especially a problem in some parts of the country, such as California), and lengthy approval processes.
See: FEDERAL HOUSING ADMINISTRATION (FHA) MORTGAGE INSURANCE

Section 207 Housing Program

A program that provides Federal Housing Administration (FHA) mortgage insurance for a broad range of multifamily rental housing types and for mobile home courts. Authorized by Section 207 of the National Housing Act of 1934, the program insures loans made by lending institutions to private developers of projects with five or more units and does not place an income ceiling on tenants. This program had insured the construction or rehabilitation of nearly 300,000 multifamily units and the development of nearly 65,000 mobile home spaces throughout the nation as of 1981.
See: FEDERAL HOUSING ADMINISTRATION (FHA) MORTGAGE INSURANCE; MOBILE HOME PARK; MULTIFAMILY HOUSING

Section 213 Housing Program

A program that provides Federal Housing Administration (FHA) mortgage insurance for cooperative housing. This section of the National Housing Act, which was created by Section 114 of the Housing Act of 1950 (PL 81-475), makes FHA insurance available for nonprofit cooperatives of five or more units, whether for new construction, rehabilitation or refinancing of existing housing stock.
See: COOPERATIVE HOUSING; FEDERAL HOUSING ADMINISTRATION (FHA) MORTGAGE INSURANCE

Section 221(d)2 Housing Program

A program that provides Federal Housing Administration (FHA) mortgage insurance on one- to four-family owner-occupied housing for low- and moderate-income families. This program is authorized by Section 221(d)2 of the National Housing Act, added by Section 123 of the Housing Act of 1954 as amended. The Section 221(d)2 housing program was particularly active throughout the 1960s, when it was used to assist families displaced by urban renewal to purchase, rehabilitate or build homes; it still offers special terms for displaced households. It provides insurance, within specified mortgage limits, relatively quickly and with more flexible underwriting standards and fewer fees than other FHA programs. More than 900,000 housing units were insured under this program through 1981.

See: FEDERAL HOUSING ADMINISTRATION (FHA) MORTGAGE INSURANCE; SECTIONS 203(b) AND (i) HOUSING PROGRAMS

Sections 221 (d) 3 and 221 (d) 4 Housing Programs

Programs that provide mortgage insurance for low- and moderate-income and displaced families in multifamily rental or cooperative housing. These programs were added to the National Housing Act of 1934 by the Housing Act of 1954 (PL 83-560). Section 221 (d) 3 provides insurance for 100 percent of the project cost for nonprofit, limited-dividend and cooperative mortgagors and 90 percent insurance to profit-motivated borrowers. Section 221 (d) 4 provides 90 percent insurance to profit-motivated borrowers for moderate-income projects. At one time, Section 221 (d) 3 nonprofit projects could obtain financing even further below market rate interest as well as rent supplements for low-income families, but the Department of Housing and Urban Development stopped making these subsidies available in the late 1970s. The mortgage insurance alone is a limited inducement, because the interest rates are generally not low enough to permit economically feasible projects.

Some of the projects built under Sections 221 (d) 3 and 4 now face financial difficulties, often due to increases in the cost of fuel, utilities and other items and the limited ability of lower-income tenants to pay required rent increases. Section 8 rent supplements are used to aid eligible low-income families.
See: FEDERAL HOUSING ADMINISTRATION (FHA) MORTGAGE INSURANCE; SECTION 8 HOUSING PROGRAM

Section 223 (e) Housing Program

Section 223 (e) of the National Housing Act, as added by Section 103 (a) of the Housing and Urban Development Act of 1968, provides for Federal Housing Administration (FHA) mortgage insurance for single-family or multifamily homes within declining, but still viable, older urban areas. Insurance is made available for home purchase, rehabilitation or infill-type new construction. Underwriting standards were relaxed under this program, but properties still must be an "acceptable risk." Section 223 (e) was developed partly in response to criticism that FHA programs had helped to build the suburbs and have thereby contributed to urban decline. It had insured over 183,000 units as of the end of 1981.
See: FEDERAL HOUSING ADMINISTRATION (FHA) MORTGAGE INSURANCE; SECTIONS 203 (b) and (i) HOUSING PROGRAMS

Section 223 (f) Housing Program

A program that provides Federal Housing Administration (FHA) mortgage insurance for the purchase or refinancing of existing multifamily rental housing with five or more units. Section 223 (f), which was added to the National Housing Act of 1934 by the Housing and Community Development Act of 1974 (PL 93-383), has largely been used for projects that receive some form of federal subsidy. It has been of benefit in circumstances where the purchase or refinance of conventionally financed projects with the lower-interest FHA mortgage has enabled the property owner to reduce debt service and consequently maintain rent levels within the means of low- or moderate-income tenants.

See: FEDERAL HOUSING ADMINISTRATION (FHA) MORTGAGE INSURANCE

Section 231 Housing Program

A program authorizing Federal Housing Administration (FHA) mortgage insurance for construction or rehabilitation of rental housing for the elderly or handicapped that was added to the National Housing Act of 1934 by Section 201 of the Housing Act of 1959. Section 231 insurance is available to private developers, nonprofit sponsors and government agencies and had insured mortgages covering approximately 65,000 dwelling units as of 1980. By the late 1970s inflation and interest rates had made most rental housing difficult to finance, even with FHA insurance. As a result, the Department of Housing and Urban Development placed more emphasis on the Section 202 program, which provides rent subsidies as well as insured mortgages.

See: FEDERAL HOUSING ADMINISTRATION (FHA) MORTGAGE INSURANCE; SECTION 202 HOUSING PROGRAM

Section 232 Program

A program that provides Federal Housing Administration (FHA) mortgage insurance for construction or renovation of nursing homes, as authorized by the Housing Act of 1959 (PL 86-372), added to the National Housing Act of 1934 as Section 232. The Section 232 program insures mortgages of facilities that meet state skilled nursing care requirements as well as intermediate care facilities in states licensing this level of care and may be used by either nonprofit or profit-motivated developers. The 232 program had insured nearly 150,000 nursing home beds as of 1980, thereby contributing to the availability of these facilities in many communities. In 1983 this program was extended to board and care homes.

See: FEDERAL HOUSING ADMINISTRATION (FHA) MORTGAGE INSURANCE; NURSING HOME; SECTION 242 PROGRAM

Section 234 Housing Program

A program authorized by Section 234 of the National Housing Act, added by the Housing Act of 1961 as amended, that provides Federal Housing Administration (FHA) mortgage insurance for condominium mortgages. The program is available to purchasers of condominium units or to condominium developers for construction or major rehabilitation of buildings with four or more units.

Section 234 has been successful in states such as Florida where the condominium form of ownership is popular.

See: FEDERAL HOUSING ADMINISTRATION (FHA) MORTGAGE INSURANCE; SECTION 213 HOUSING PROGRAM

Section 235 Housing Program

A program in which mortgage insurance and interest subsidies for low- and moderate-income home buyers were provided pursuant to Section 101 of the Housing and Urban Development Act of 1968 (PL 90-448), added to the National Housing Act of 1934 as Section 235. Prior to 1976 interest rates were as low as 5 percent, but after that date they were higher, although still below the market rate. Purchase of existing homes was also permitted prior to 1976, but after that date funding was limited to those that were newly constructed or substantially rehabilitated.

Despite the fact that by the early 1980s only funding left over from prior years was still available, the Section 235 program is noteworthy because, within specified income limits, it supported home ownership for moderate-income families, who were expected to pay only 20 percent of their adjusted income and make a minimum down payment of 3 percent. However, mortgage limits for the homes were set relatively low, and the homes, which were often built by developers to meet the specific requirements of the Section 235 program, were in some cases criticized for being too cheaply constructed.

See: FEDERAL HOUSING ADMINISTRATION (FHA) MORTGAGE INSURANCE

Section 236 Housing Program

A major federal mortgage insurance and interest subsidy program that was available to sponsors of rental and cooperative multifamily housing for lower-income families during the late 1960s and early 1970s. The reduced interest rate, sometimes as low as 1 percent, was the initial subsidy. Additional subsidies covered the increasing difference between operating costs and rentals to enable low-income tenants to pay no more than 25 percent of their income for rent. Later the management of many of these units was transferred to the Section 8 housing program, the successor rental subsidy program.

Section 236, which was added to the National Housing Act by Section 201 of the Housing and Urban Development Act of 1968, was available to nonprofit, limited-dividend and cooperative organizations, as well as to private builders who were preparing turnkey projects for such organizations. Under the 236 program, not all tenants were required to be low-income; unsubsidized, market rate tenants were also permitted, making it an attractive program to sponsors. Over 460,000 units were built under the Section 236 program, and although funding authorizations have ended, the units built under the program continue to benefit from the mortgage insurance provisions. Very low income households in existing Section 236 housing now receive subsidies via either Section 8 or Section

101 "deep subsidies," which provide rent supplements for this population.
See: FEDERAL HOUSING ADMINISTRATION (FHA) MORTGAGE INSURANCE; SECTION 8 HOUSING PROGRAM

Section 237 Housing Program

A program, authorized by Section 237 of the National Housing Act as added by Section 102 of the Housing and Urban Development Act of 1968, that provides Federal Housing Administration (FHA) mortgage insurance and home ownership counseling for special credit-risk low- and moderate-income families. Section 237 is intended for families (often residing in inner cities) who, despite marginal income levels, are able to meet special underwriting standards, thus enabling them to achieve home ownership. The program has had limited use (slightly over 5,200 units through 1981), in part because of low mortgage limit amounts.
See: FEDERAL HOUSING ADMINISTRATION (FHA) MORTGAGE INSURANCE; HOUSING COUNSELING; SECTION 235 HOUSING PROGRAM

Section 241 Program

This program, which is authorized by Section 241 of the National Housing Act as added by Section 307 of the Housing and Urban Development Act of 1968, provides Federal Housing Administration (FHA) insurance for loans made by private lending institutions for improvements to apartment buildings, nursing homes or medical facilities. The 241 program has been reserved for improvements to projects that originally received FHA mortgages, although the program is not legally restricted to such projects. Improvements that are commonly insured under the 241 program include energy-saving modifications and improvements in fire-safety equipment.
See: FEDERAL HOUSING ADMINISTRATION (FHA) MORTGAGE INSURANCE

Section 242 Program

A program authorized by Section 242 of the National Housing Act of 1934 in which Federal Housing Administration (FHA) mortgage insurance is made available for the construction or rehabilitation of hospitals. Section 242 provides mortgage insurance for proprietary and nonprofit hospitals that meet state certification requirements. The 242 program had been used to insure mortgages covering over 42,000 hospital beds throughout the nation as of 1980. In 1983 this program was extended to public hospitals.
See: FEDERAL HOUSING ADMINISTRATION (FHA) MORTGAGE INSURANCE; HEALTH CARE SYSTEM; SECTION 232 PROGRAM

Section 244 Housing Program

A program that allows other lenders to coinsure mortgages along with the Federal Housing Administration (FHA) to provide speedier processing of mortgage insurance applications. Under Section 244, which was added to the National Housing Act by Section 307 of the Housing and Community Development Act of 1974, the lender expedites processing by underwriting the loan directly, without certain FHA reviews, and coinsures a minimum of 20 percent of its value. The lender also assumes responsibility for its portion of the risk of the loan and receives a portion of the FHA premium fee. The borrower still has a fully insured loan and pays the same insurance premium, but receives faster processing and improved loan servicing.

Under Section 244 approved private lending institutions may coinsure mortgage loans for buildings containing one to four housing units, and state housing finance agencies may coinsure multifamily rental projects.
See: FEDERAL HOUSING ADMINISTRATION (FHA) MORTGAGE INSURANCE; PRIVATE MORTGAGE INSURANCE; STATE HOUSING FINANCE AGENCIES

Section 245 Housing Program

Federal Housing Administration (FHA) mortgage insurance for graduated-payment mortgages offered under authority of Section 245 of the National Housing Act (as added by Section 308 of the Housing and Community Development Act of 1974). This program is designed to encourage early home ownership for families who expect their incomes to rise substantially but who are unable to meet high mortgage payments initially. Graduated-payment mortgages have monthly payments that increase periodically; the borrower qualifies at the lowest initial payment, with increased income projected to cover the later, higher payments. In 1983, the 245 program was broadened to permit purchasers of multifamily structures to obtain mortgage insurance. The Section 245 program had insured almost 295,000 units through 1981.
See: FEDERAL HOUSING ADMINISTRATION (FHA) MORTGAGE INSURANCE; GRADUATED-PAYMENT MORTGAGE (GPM)

Section 312 Housing Program

A program authorized by Section 312 of the Housing Act of 1964 (PL 88-560) providing building rehabilitation loans to be used within geographic areas receiving certain types of federal assistance, such as Community Development Block Grant target areas, urban renewal areas and code enforcement areas. Section 312 makes available low-interest loans that have been used for the most part for residential buildings but may also be used for mixed-use and commercial structures. The emphasis is on serving moderate-income individuals who can repay the low-interest loan but could not afford normal bank rates.

The 312 program has been widely utilized and was one of the earliest federal rehabilitation programs. As interest rates rose in the late 1970s, however, the cost of providing loans at a substantially reduced interest rate greatly increased, and by the 1980s the 312 program was being curtailed.

Section 502 FmHA Housing Program

This program, established by Section 502 of the Housing Act of 1949 as amended by the Consolidated Farmers Home Administration Act of 1961 (PL 87-128), provides below-market rate mortgage loans to low- and moderate-income families for construction, purchase, rehabilitation or weatherization of single-family homes in rural areas. Additional subsidies are given for lower-income families who must pay more than 20 percent of their income for housing, a way in which the FmHA 502 program to some degree parallels the Federal Housing Administration (FHA) 235 program. The 502 mutual self-help program is available to groups of 6 to 8 families wishing to construct their own housing with the same credit conditions as the basic 502 program.

FmHA loans are provided directly to applicants (except for the weatherization loans, which are available from a Rural Electrification Administration-financed utility company), usually after evidence that conventional financing is not available. The FmHA 502 program and the companion 504 repair program involved more than 1.6 million housing units through 1981.
See: FARMERS HOME ADMINISTRATION (FmHA); RURAL HOUSING PROGRAMS; SECTION 235 HOUSING PROGRAM; SECTION 504 FmHA HOUSING PROGRAM; SELF-HELP HOUSING

Section 504 FmHA Housing Program

A program that provides loans of up to $7,500 to low-income rural residents for home repairs, as per Section 504 of the Housing Act of 1949. Applicants must be able to pay back the 1 percent interest loans but generally do not have sufficient income to qualify for the Section 502 FmHA Housing Program. Combined loans and grants are made available to very low income applicants over 62 years of age. Repairs that are permissible under this program must remove safety and health hazards.
See: FARMERS HOME ADMINISTRATION (FmHA); RURAL HOUSING PROGRAMS; SECTION 502 FmHA HOUSING PROGRAM

Sections 514 and 516 FmHA Housing Programs

The Section 514 program provides low-interest loans for the construction or rehabilitation of residences for farm workers; the Section 516 program provides grants for the same purpose. Established by Sections 514 and 516 of the Housing Act of 1949, as amended by the 1961 Farmers Home Administration Consolidation Act (PL 87-128), it makes both loans and grants available. Grants are made only to nonprofit agencies and are given in cases where even extremely low interest loans cannot be repaid and there is a serious need for housing. Loans are made primarily to nonprofit agencies or regional organizations but

are sometimes made to private parties when no appropriate organization or agency is available. Between 1961 and 1981 these programs provided over $280 million for improved living conditions for farm workers.
See: FARMERS HOME ADMINISTRATION (FmHA); RURAL HOUSING PROGRAMS

Section 515 FmHA Housing Program

This program, established by Section 515 of the Housing Act of 1949 and amended by the Consolidated Farmers Home Administration Act of 1961 (PL 87-128), provides low-interest loans for multifamily rental or cooperative housing in rural areas. The Farmers Home Administration acts as a lender of last resort, providing low-interest loans for the construction or major rehabilitation of rental housing or cooperative housing available to those with low or moderate incomes or over 62. It also makes loans for congregate housing for the elderly. These loans are available to public, nonprofit and private entities that are unable to obtain conventional credit on terms and conditions they can meet.

The rural rental housing program has been active throughout the United States and is a significant housing production program to which more than $5 billion had been committed between 1961 and 1981. The 515 program has also been used in urban fringe areas meeting technical requirements as rural and as a financing source in conjunction with the Section 8 program.
See: FARMERS HOME ADMINISTRATION (FmHA)

Sector Analysis

A technique used to analyze an urban economy that focuses on individual sectors of the economy, such as manufacturing and retail trade. Sector analysis, also called component analysis, is useful in describing past trends in a sector as well as in predicting future trends. Generally, employment levels and sales volumes in each sector are compared to similar data in another locale or to similar data within one locale over several time intervals.

Sector analysis is a relatively simple technique that uses information that is readily available, such as the publications of the Bureau of the Census. One advantage of performing a sector analysis rather than certain other types of analysis is that the sector analysis provides detailed information on each economic sector, whereas many other techniques provide only aggregate information. For greater accuracy and depth, the method may also be combined with shift-share analysis or other analytic techniques.
See: ECONOMIC BASE ANALYSIS; ECONOMIC FORECASTING TECHNIQUES; SHIFT-SHARE ANALYSIS; URBAN ECONOMICS

Sector Theory

A theory of urban growth based upon a pattern of pie-shaped wedges (sectors) located along major transportation routes radiating from the city's center. Sector theory, as proposed by Homer Hoyt in 1939, held that the location of high-income sectors was a key determinant of city development.

Hoyt postulated that high-income neighborhoods were categorized by ease of access, natural amenities and the location of community leaders' residences. There was a gradient of housing costs in all directions from high-income areas, with middle-income neighborhoods located as close as possible to the most desirable areas. Commercial facilities, stores and offices also tended to follow the location of high-income areas. All neighborhoods, particularly the key high-income areas, tended to grow outward toward the open space surrounding the city. Hoyt noted that as close-in developments became less desirable, new growth was located farther out, but in the same sector. (See Fig. 20)
See: GROWTH THEORY

Sedimentation

1. The practice in wastewater treatment of using gravity to settle out the solid particles in wastewater.
2. The process by which particles are separated from their parent material, settle out of suspension and are transported, through the forces of erosion. The particles, or sediments, tend to collect in certain areas, particularly in water bodies, causing damage, pollution or the need for expensive maintenance. For example, sediment accumulation in reservoirs diminishes storage capacity and increases the cost of filtering and treating drinking water, while sedimentation of harbors and navigation channels leads to the need for dredging. Farmland, farm crops and fish breeding grounds can be damaged by sediment. Flooding is also increased because of clogged stream channels and flood-prevention reservoirs.

Studies have demonstrated a clear correlation between the alteration of the natural state of land, through activities such as farming and construction, and the rate of sedimentation. Simple and relatively inexpensive soil conservation measures can reduce sedimentation, but other measures—such as sediment basins, which detain runoff and trap sediment—may also be necessary.
See: BANK PROTECTION; SEDIMENTATION TANK; SILT; SOIL EROSION CONTROL TECHNIQUES

Sedimentation Tank

Part of a sewage treatment plant that is designed to remove settleable solids from wastewater and to reduce its nonsettleable solids content by skimming those that rise to the top. Primary sedimentation tanks may be designed as the main form of treatment where only primary treatment is to be undertaken or as a preliminary step where secondary treatment is to be undertaken. Sedimentation tanks have also been used as stormwater detention tanks for combined or storm sewers, where they serve, during overflow periods, to remove a proportion of the organic solids that would otherwise be discharged to receiving waters.

Wastewater is detained in a sedimentation tank for one to two hours, providing a period during which solids can settle. After settling, the material at the bottom of the tank (sludge) is separated from the remaining wastewater. When a skimming arm (known as a clarifier) is placed at the top of the tank, scum and floating solids can also be removed. When efficiently operated, sedimentation tanks can remove 50 percent to 60 percent of the suspended solids and 25 percent to 40 percent of the biochemical oxygen demand (BOD).
See: BIOCHEMICAL OXYGEN DEMAND (BOD); SETTLING TANK; SEWAGE TREATMENT; SLUDGE; SUSPENDED SOLIDS (SS)

Seed Money

Like front money, seed money is the capital needed to begin a development project. The term is more often used, however, to describe start-up money provided by the government rather than by equity investors.

The Department of Housing and Urban Development, for example, provides interest-free seed money loans to nonprofit sponsors of certain low- and moderate-income housing developments. The seed money may be used to pay for up to 80 percent of typical preliminary development costs such as surveys, market analyses, site engineering studies, site acquisition and loan application fees.
See: FRONT MONEY

Self-Help Housing

Housing built by groups of individuals for their own use, often with technical assistance or financial aid from government agencies. Self-help programs are generally designed to stimulate construction or rehabilitation of sound housing for low-income persons, usually in decaying inner city neighborhoods or in rural, underdeveloped areas.

Urban self-help programs usually relate to rehabilitation of existing housing stock and are often conducted under the aegis of a neighborhood development agency. Rural self-help housing, however, may consist of the construction of substantial amounts of new housing, as in the successful program conducted by the government of Puerto Rico that enabled the construction of 37,800 houses in 396 rural communities between 1950 and 1970. The small houses, of government design and made of reinforced concrete, were generally constructed by the pooled labor of 30 to 50 families. The government provided free technical aid as well as a loan for the purchase of building materials and purchased the materials at a reduced cost.

The Farmers Home Administration currently administers two self-help housing programs. One offers grants to qualified organizations that will give technical assistance to low-income rural families; the other is a program of loans for site acquisition and the construction of the housing by groups of six to eight families.
See: NEIGHBORHOOD SELF-HELP DEVELOPMENT ACT OF 1978; SECTION 502 FmHA HOUSING PROGRAM; SWEAT EQUITY

Self-Supporting Recreational Facilities

Recreation facilities that generate sufficient revenue to meet or exceed the facilities' operating expenses and sometimes their capital expenses as well. Swimming pools, golf courses and horseback riding stables are examples of facilities that generally charge fees for their use, which, in some cases, are sufficient to meet these expenses. Fees are rarely charged for playgrounds or playfields, although in some communities fees for other facilities are raised to cover the expenses of free parks.

In the United States it has become common for governments to require that there be a user fee for many recreational facilities to cover costs and in some cases to enable the facility to be built. Because government agencies often feel that they cannot generate sufficient revenue with government management and staffing (since these costs may be higher for government than for the private sector), they frequently utilize concessions or leases for facility construction and operation, or for operation alone, and receive a percentage of the gross revenues.

See: CONCESSIONAIRE; PARKLAND LEASING; USER CHARGES

Sense of Place

The quality of a location that makes it readily recognizable as being unique and different from other locations. Any location that is different from its surroundings can be said to have a sense of place, as can unique natural formations such as the Grand Canyon.

In urban design the creation of a sense of place is desirable to enable people to orient themselves to a unique area, such as to Times Square in New York City, or to enable identification with a visual quality, such as with the half-timbered cottages of small British towns. In new housing developments and shopping malls, the creation of a sense of place is employed to establish a unique ambience and to attract the attention of potential buyers or shoppers.

See: AMBIENCE; COMMUNITY CHARACTER; NEIGHBORHOOD IDENTITY

Sensitivity Analysis

The study of how the values in an optimal solution to a model vary given changes in the underlying assumptions. Since a model is a hypothetical construct or an abstraction, the underlying relationships may be subject to considerable debate. Sensitivity analysis guides the need for empirical (observed) investigation by pointing out what variables are most critical—i.e., have the potential of producing the greatest change in result for any given change or changes in assumed value. The most sensitive variables are those requiring more investigation if the model is to be used as a tool to test alternate formulations.

Government and land use decision making operates in a dynamic environment in which constant changes occur in such factors as land value, labor costs and unemployment levels. If a computer model is used to support manage-ment decision making, the changes in key variables over time are critical input that must be factored into the model. Sensitivity analysis measures the ways in which these changes affect the optimal solution to the model.

See: MODEL; SIMULATION; SYSTEMS ANALYSIS

Sepia Intermediate

A type of diazo positive print on translucent paper. It is useful for many types of applications because it may be modified or revised and then reproduced, while the original remains intact. All copies are the same size as the original. Sepia intermediates are often made in reverse (a mirror image), as that allows better quality reproductions to be made; the resulting prints are right-reading (read from left to right).

See: GRAPHIC REPRODUCTION PROCESSES

Septic Field

The secondary phase of a septic system, in which effluent from a septic tank, now a semiclarified liquid, is released to a disposal system for distribution to the soil, where it will be aerobically oxidized and decontaminated.

Three forms of effluent disposal are used, depending upon soil conditions and topography. Leaching cesspools release the effluent to the soil from one or more basins, called cesspools. This system requires the least amount of land but cannot be used in semi-impervious or impervious soils. Subsoil disposal beds are porous drainage lines (drainage tiles), laid in patterns suitable for the soil type and topography, that allow the effluent to drain to the surrounding soil. A single-family home with one to four residents would require a minimum of 150 feet (45.7 meters) of 4-inch (10-centimeter) drainage tile in a soil with a medium absorption rate for effective disposal of effluent. Sand filters are used for impervious soils, where a drainage system is laid in a sand bed and a collection line located at the far end to retrieve the effluent after it has been oxidized. It is then taken elsewhere for disposal. All three effluent-disposal systems require an effluent sewer to bring the effluent to the septic field from the septic tank and a distribution box to control the flow of effluent to various parts of the distribution system.

See: OXIDATION PROCESSES; PERCOLATION (PERK) TEST; SEPTIC SYSTEM; SEPTIC TANK

Septic System

A sewage treatment and disposal system used in both rural and suburban areas where development is widely spaced, soil conditions are suitable, and sewers are not available. Septic systems are used for individual residences or groups of homes, as well as for schools, hospitals, summer camps, trailer parks, parks, restaurants and motels.

The system consists of a house sewer line connecting to a septic tank, where the raw sewage is anaerobically treated and sludge is stored, and a septic field, which distributes the effluent through an extended area of soil, where it is aerobically oxidized. The system may also have a grease trap, which collects grease, particularly from kitchen sewers, before the wastewater enters the septic tank, and a sludge pit, which can serve as the sludge-storage facility so that the sludge can be removed without interfering with the operation of the septic tank. Sludge that is removed from the septic tank (also referred to as septage) may be taken to a sewage treatment plant for further treatment or disposed of through conventional sludge-disposal methods.

Septic system design must be approved by the health department based on the results of percolation tests throughout the septic field, which indicate whether the soil can adequately absorb the effluent that is produced. The health department may also monitor installation and operation of the system to ensure that the system will not contaminate water supplies. Overly dense development that relies upon septic systems can overtax the capacity of the soil to process effluent and result in toxic elements in the sewage seeping into the groundwater. When conditions near this point, it is common for municipalities to require all new subdivisions or other large developments to provide on-site sewage treatment plants until a municipal sewerage system or sewage treatment plant is completed or extended. Soil limitations, on the other hand, are now used in some communities as a limiting factor on growth and as a basis for large-lot zoning. (See Fig. 39)
See: GROWTH MANAGEMENT; OXIDATION PROCESSES; PACKAGE TREATMENT PLANT; PERCOLATION (PERK) TEST; SEPTIC FIELD; SEPTIC TANK; SLUDGE DIGESTION; SLUDGE DISPOSAL; WATER POLLUTION

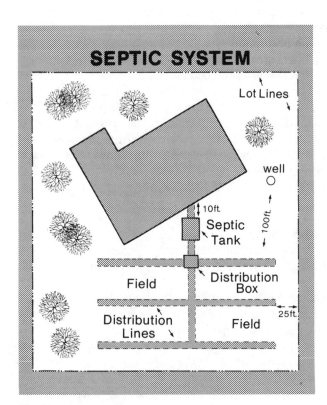

Fig. 39.

Septic Tank

An underground, on-site sewage treatment facility designed to anaerobically treat raw sewage generated by a single residence or other small development and store the sludge that is produced.

The size of a septic tank is predicated on the number of persons who use the building it serves or, if a residence, upon the number of bedrooms. For a residential facility, a capacity that will allow a 24-hour detention period for raw sewage is mandatory to permit adequate sedimentation; for larger developments a somewhat shorter detention period is used. The septic tank should also have sufficient capacity to store sludge for two to three years, unless a separate sludge pit is provided, to permit sludge digestion before it is removed for disposal.
See: SEDIMENTATION TANK; SEPTIC SYSTEM; SLUDGE DIGESTION

Service Stations

Gasoline filling stations, many of which provide automotive repair services in addition to selling petroleum products. They are generally restricted to commercial and industrial districts, with a principal concern being convenient access and egress that do not cause traffic delays or sight distance problems. Newer stations often have facades that blend with neighborhood appearance and landscaping.
See: DRIVE-IN FACILITIES

Setback

Depending upon the municipality involved, setback may be considered to be the required distance between the front of a structure and the front lot line or the required distance between the structure and each of the lot lines. Setback requirements may be either included in municipal zoning regulations or established by covenants that are found in deeds, or occasionally they are specified in building codes. In modern usage setback has essentially the same meaning as the term *yard.*
See: YARD; YARD REQUIREMENTS; ZONING

Settlement House Movement

A phenomenon in which neighborhood-based agencies or community centers are established in disadvantaged areas and help to institute programs and services that will generally improve life in that neighborhood. Settlement houses view an entire neighborhood rather than a particular age, ethnic or racial group as their constituency and work with community residents to provide a variety of activities as well as needed community facilities.

The first settlement, Toynbee Hall, was founded by Samuel Augustus Barrett in east London in 1884. The concept was brought to the United States in 1886 by Stanton Coit, who founded Neighborhood Guild, which subsequently became University Settlement, on New York City's Lower East Side. Another early settlement house pioneer was Jane Addams, who helped to found Hull House in Chicago in 1889.

Settlement houses played a major role in the United States in assisting new immigrants in adjusting to the country and receiving education and health care. The movement has also spread to many other countries, including Canada, Denmark, the Netherlands and Sweden. In 1926 an International Federation of Settlements was formed, which maintains observers at the United Nations.
See: SOCIAL SERVICES PLANNING

Settling Tank

1. In sewage treatment a settling tank (also called a sedimentation tank or a clarifier) is a tank in which wastewater that has been aerated in the activated sludge process or in the trickling filter process is allowed to settle so that the liquid and solid components can separate. In the activated sludge process the tank is equipped with a return pipe so that some of the sludge can be sent back to the aeration tank.

2. In water treatment settling tanks are used to permit floc (masses of solids) to settle after the water has been chemically treated. They are often referred to as coagulation or settling basins or as clarifiers if they are equipped to continuously scrape the collected floc.
See: ACTIVATED SLUDGE PROCESS; AERATION; SEDIMENTATION TANK; SEWAGE TREATMENT; WATER TREATMENT

Sewage Treatment

The removal or treatment of objectionable substances in wastewater to reduce the hazards they represent to health and the environment. Sewage treatment is a cumulative process of mechanical operations followed by biological or chemical processes.

First, coarse solids, debris, grease and oils are removed by screens and grit-removal facilities. Finer suspended solids are removed next by sedimentation, filtration or precipitation. Dissolved organic matter and colloidal matter are then removed or treated by biological or chemical processes, and the remaining bacteria are disinfected by chlorination. Depending upon the types of operations used and the degree to which the wastewater is cleaned, the treatment is called primary, secondary or tertiary.

Sewage treatment yields two end products: a liquid, called effluent, and a semisolid, called sludge. The sludge may require additional drying to prepare it for disposal. (See Fig. 40)
See: ACTIVATED SLUDGE PROCESS; AERATION; BIOCHEMICAL OXYGEN DEMAND (BOD); CHLORINATION; EFFLUENT; FEDERAL WATER POLLUTION CONTROL ACT AMENDMENTS OF 1972; FILTRATION; GRIT CHAMBER; IMHOFF TANK; OXIDATION PROCESSES; PRETREATMENT; PRIMARY TREATMENT; SCREENING; SECONDARY TREATMENT; SEDIMENTATION TANK; SETTLING TANK; SEWAGE TREATMENT PLANT; SLUDGE; SUSPENDED SOLIDS (SS); TERTIARY TREATMENT; WASTEWATER; WATER POLLUTION

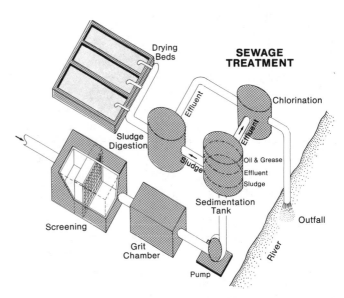

Fig. 40. A variety of sewage treatment processes separates solids from liquids and reduces biological and toxic content.

Sewage Treatment Plant

A structure in which wastewater is treated and its resulting products prepared for disposal. Sewage treatment plants are located adjacent to bodies of water to permit disposal of effluent and may require large land areas to accommodate numerous treatment and storage tanks or to allow for expansion. These requirements often make a plant hard to site, since its presence is usually considered to be a nuisance by residents of the surrounding area, although it may have relatively inoffensive characteristics. New plants are frequently planned so that part of the site is developed as a park, either by providing a deck over the plant or by using available open space around it thereby making the use more palatable to neighbors. Plants with covered tanks may also reduce nuisance characteristics.

One sewage treatment plant may serve numerous drainage areas or sewage districts, requiring that it have sufficient capacity to accommodate diversified land uses and increased development in outlying areas or in undeveloped pockets of land. It must also be able to handle expected peak sewage flows and changes in life-style, such as the proliferation of kitchen garbage disposals, that may affect sewage production. Because treatment plants are extremely expensive to build and often require many years of planning and construction before they can be used, they are planned for a 25- to 50-year life expectancy.
See: OUTFALL; PACKAGE TREATMENT PLANT; SEWAGE TREATMENT; SEWERAGE SYSTEM

Sewer Capacity

The maximum amount of wastewater that a sewer pipe can hold. For sanitary sewers the capacity is expressed as a certain number of gallons per capita per day (gcd). As a rule, lateral sewers are designed to accommodate 400 gcd, while sewer mains and trunk lines, which are larger in diameter and receive sewage from a wider area over a more extended time period, have a capacity of 250 gcd. Although the accepted average production of domestic sewage is 100 gcd, the higher capacity figures are used to allow for seasonal variations in water use.

Sewer systems are planned for a designated time period, which may be 25 to 50 years in the future, although laterals are usually designed to reach capacity sooner. It is therefore necessary to make detailed design year population and density projections for the areas surrounding sewer lines, so that the different types of sewer lines can be adequately sized.

For storm sewers, sewer line capacity is determined by rainfall intensity and frequency, by the area and shape of the drainage basin, by the slope of the land and by the amount of impervious ground cover. Storm sewer design is often based on the assumption that the sewer system will occasionally exceed capacity and result in infrequent flooding. However, in heavily urbanized areas where flooding could cause extensive damage, storm sewer systems are designed to accommodate the most severe storms.

See: BYPASS; COMBINED SEWER; IMPERVIOUS SURFACES; SEWERAGE SYSTEM; SEWERED POPULATION; STORM SEWER

Sewer Main

A large-diameter sewer pipe that collects wastewater from laterals and delivers it to a trunk sewer. The numerous sewer mains that may be located in a community are sited in valleys that are tributary to the principal valley of a drainage basin. The terms *sewer main* and *branch sewer* are often used interchangeably.

See: LATERAL; SEWERAGE SYSTEM; TRUNK SEWER

Sewer System Evaluation Survey (SSES)

A study that determines the specific site at which infiltration and/or inflow are entering a sewerage system so that detailed cost estimates for repair can be made. It requires physical inspection of the sewer pipes in which excessive infiltration and inflow problems have been determined by the use of smoke and dye-water testing, intensive flow monitoring, cleaning and television inspection. The SSES is the second part of a sewer system evaluation process.

See: INFILTRATION AND INFLOW (I&I) ANALYSIS

Sewerage System

The processes and equipment used to collect, treat and dispose of wastewater. Sewerage systems vary according to the size and distribution of a given population and the nature of the wastewater—i.e., the percentages of domestic, industrial and storm wastes. Other factors affecting sewerage system design relate to the desired degree of treatment, environmental requirements concerning the receiving waters and disposition of solids, and the amount of money available for the construction of system components. Sewerage systems, which are individually designed to meet the specific requirements of each location, were introduced in London in the 1840s as a result of cholera epidemics that could be traced to the contamination of drinking water by sewage.

The typical sewerage system uses sewer pipes of differing diameters to conduct the sewage from its source through a network of laterals, mains, trunk lines and interceptors to pumping stations (where necessary) and finally to a treatment plant. At the treatment plant solids are removed, and the liquid effluent and more solid sludge are treated and disposed of separately. Where separate sanitary and storm sewer systems are present, stormwater is generally discharged from the sewers directly to a receiving water body without being treated at a sewage treatment plant.

The initial step in design of a collection system is the preparation of a map showing the entire drainage area in which the sewerage system will be located. This serves as a base for calculation of wastewater production, and is necessary for the determination of pipe sizes and the location of all sewer lines so that they run in a continuously downhill direction in the beds of streets to facilitate drainage. Trunk lines are placed first by starting at the outlet for the drainage area (usually the lowest elevation) and moving uphill in a route that climbs at a minimum slope. Mains and then laterals are designed in the same manner, each connecting into the larger sewer line. Each type of line is routed so that it ends at the upper edge, or ridge, of the drainage area to enable all wastewater entering it to flow

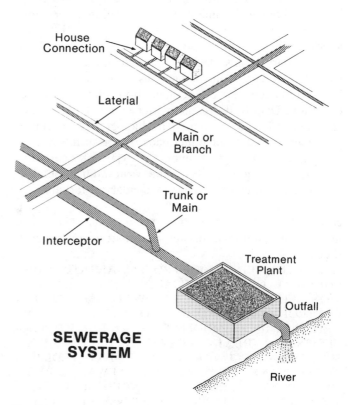

Fig. 41.

downward. Sewage treatment plants are located adjacent to a body of water that is capable of biologically handling the effluent produced, sometimes requiring that the wastewater be pumped over a hill to reach it. Sludge-disposal methods and/or sites are selected to coordinate with treatment plant design. Rural locations rely on septic systems to treat sewage but may provide disposal facilities for the solids removed from septic tanks.

Planning for an entire sewerage system, a new main or trunk, or a treatment plant relies on basic planning studies of population growth, density and movement, economic development, environmental management, topography and established policies on future land use. Since sewer lines are a major part of an urban infrastructure, they can cause development to occur along their path or discourage it by their absence, requiring that sewer line and treatment plant locations and capacities be coordinated with long-term community planning. Communities sometimes use sewer system design, capacities and proposed extensions to control the type and pace of development. (See Fig. 41)
See: BYPASS; CATCH BASIN; COMBINED SEWER; DOMESTIC SEWAGE; DRAINAGE BASIN; EFFLUENT; FORCE MAIN; GRAVITY FLOW; GROWTH MANAGEMENT; HOUSE CONNECTION; INDUSTRIAL SEWAGE; INFILTRATION AND INFLOW (I&I) ANALYSIS; INTERCEPTOR SEWER; LATERAL; MANHOLE; OUTFALL; PACKAGE TREATMENT PLANT; PUMPING STATION; RECEIVING WATERS; SANITARY SEWER; SEPTIC SYSTEM; SEWAGE TREATMENT PLANT; SEWER CAPACITY; SEWER MAIN; SEWER SYSTEM EVALUATION SURVEY (SSES); SEWERED POPULATION; SLUDGE DISPOSAL; STORM SEWER; TRUNK SEWER; WASTEWATER; WASTEWATER MANAGEMENT

Sewered Population

The extent of a geographic area that is served by sewers. The term is used for comparative purposes to differentiate the number or percentage of households, businesses or persons served by sewers from those that are not.

The term *served by sewers* means that sewers are provided in the street and are available for house connections or lateral connections. Therefore, the term *sewered population* does not indicate the actual number or percentage of households with sewer connections but rather those eligible to be connected, unless local health codes make connection mandatory.
See: SEWERAGE SYSTEM

Shade Tree Commission

An official municipal body, usually consisting of three to five appointed unpaid members, that is authorized to establish rules and regulations regarding the planting, removal or trimming of trees and shrubs on public thoroughfares. Where authorized, shade tree commissions may also design street tree-planting plans and supervise their implementation and may also have authority over trees in other public places. Basic to most programs of shade tree commissions are inventories of street trees and recommen-

dations for protective mechanisms against harm induced by development or abuse.
See: DECIDUOUS TREES; EVERGREENS; LANDSCAPING; STREET BEAUTIFICATION

Shadow Pattern

The composite shadow shape that will be cast by a structure or an object over a particular time period. Analysis of shadow patterns is important for the effective use of solar energy because the greater the degree to which collectors are shaded, the less the heat that can be generated by a solar energy system. This type of analysis is also performed for other planning purposes, such as assessing the shadows that a proposed tall building would cast over a park or in providing shade in hot climates.

Generally, it is most useful for solar energy application to analyze winter shadow patterns, as they are longer because of the sun's position in the sky. This assures year-round protection of solar access. Planners may use a variety of techniques to approximate the shadow of any proposed structure or vegetation. For example, standardized tables are available that give the shadow length of a one-foot pole for different latitudes, directions and percentage slopes on December 21. Templates may also be created for a proposed development (providing that there is relatively flat terrain) that show the shadow pattern of each building. They may then be placed in different combinations on a base map so that the total shading effect can be assessed.
See: SKYSPACE; SOLAR ACCESS; SOLAR ENERGY

Shared-Appreciation Mortgage (SAM)

A mortgage loan made at a below-market interest rate in exchange for a percentage of the appreciation of the property upon its resale. The loan might be made, for example, at a rate one-third less than prevailing rates, for an agreement that the borrower will give the lender one-third of any future gain on the home.

This type of mortgage, also known as an equity-participation mortgage, has many appealing features for first-time home buyers and for households with insufficient income to qualify for a conventional mortgage, as the lowered interest rates allow them to become homeowners and to make reduced monthly payments. Although they have to trade away a portion of the potential future profit, they are able to enjoy the tax and other benefits of home ownership and retain some of the profit available in a rising real estate market.

Negative aspects of a SAM include the fact that in periods when real property values are rapidly increasing, the SAM borrower might ultimately have to pay the lender a much larger amount, in total, for the mortgage when the profits from the sale are calculated. This mortgage type might also create a disincentive to capital improvements, depending upon how such improvements are factored into the determination of the profits when the property is sold.
See: MORTGAGE

Shelter Belt

Long windbreaks stretching over large land areas, composed of strategically planted trees and shrubs, whose purpose is to protect farmlands and to reduce wind erosion. Shelter belts help to reduce topsoil loss, particularly in arid or semiarid areas or when land is not covered by plant material.

Much early experience with shelter belts was reported in the Soviet Union, where they were put into use in the early 19th century. The wide-scale use of this technique began in North America after the drought of 1934 converted a substantial portion of the Great Plains into a dust bowl. Lands being cultivated were left unprotected when the drought began; the crops died; and the strong prairie winds carried prairie soil as far away as New York and Washington.

A proposal was made to create shelter belts within a 100-mile (161-kilometer) wide zone extending across the plains from the Texas Panhandle to the Canadian border. Over a seven-year period, from 1935 to 1942, shelter belts consisting of over 200 million trees and shrubs were planted across 30,000 farms. These belts, along with the introduction of improved agricultural practices, have helped greatly to improve conditions. The Netherlands, France, Denmark and China also have shelter belt programs.
See: WINDBREAK

Shift-Share Analysis

An expansion of economic base analysis, traditionally used to measure growth in an area's basic industries. A fairly simple technique that uses readily available data, the method is based upon the relationship of a metropolitan area to the larger area of which it is a part and uses data extending over a period of time to determine this relationship. It is used primarily to determine whether a community is becoming more or less competitive as a location for a specific industry. Shift-share analysis can also be used to predict future economic performance.

In this method an employment change in a particular industry is identified as coming from one of three sources. The first source, known as the "growth effect," attributes growth in a particular industry to overall growth in the regional or national economy. The second source, "industry mix effect," attributes growth in an industry to regional or national growth trends in that industry. The third source, the "local effect," attributes employment changes to local conditions and is used to determine whether a location is suitable for a particular industry. As an example, the change over time of employment in a particular industry in a city may be compared either to overall growth in employment or to growth in that industry. The local effect in each case is the difference between actual growth and growth that would have been expected to occur based solely on either of the first two growth sources.
See: ECONOMIC FORECASTING TECHNIQUES; URBAN ECONOMICS

Shopping Center Design

The size, number of stores and arrangement of buildings, parking and landscaping on a site intended for development as a shopping center. Shopping center design is dependent upon the number and types of anchor stores and the area from which the developer expects to draw customers. Those that cater to a local area are smaller and have a more exposed plan providing easy access to one store, whereas larger centers draw shoppers from a wide area. In the more extensive shopping center, the customer is expected to wander and visit many stores.

The major neighborhood shopping center plans are the strip center (a straight row of stores) and the L-shaped and U-shaped centers. The shopping mall is the predominant form used for regional shopping centers. New shopping center forms that have developed in recent years are the vertical shopping mall, popular in dense urban areas, and the superstore (called hyper-marches in Europe). Superstores contain 60,000 to 150,000 square feet (5,574 to 13,935 square meters) of floor area and offer all the items one might find in a shopping center but in a warehouse atmosphere under one roof.
See: ANCHOR STORE; COMMUNITY SHOPPING CENTER; NEIGHBORHOOD SHOPPING CENTER; REGIONAL SHOPPING CENTER; SHOPPING CENTER PARKING; SHOPPING MALL

Shopping Center Parking

Shopping center design is predicated on ample parking and a relatively short walk to a desired store. As a result, for grade-level parking, the most successful site arrangement provides access drives at the outer periphery of the site and adjacent to the buildings, with transverse drives where necessary. Parking stalls are often arranged at 90-degree angles to the buildings and within 350 feet (107 meters) of them where possible, but in some regions parking at an angle is popular. Regional and community shopping centers usually locate parking around the buildings or in parking structures, while neighborhood shopping centers and strip development usually have parking spaces in front of and to the sides of buildings. Truck delivery areas are generally located away from parking areas at the sides or rear of buildings or sometimes beneath the buildings in regional shopping centers.

The ratio of necessary parking spaces to gross leasable floor area (GLA) in regional and community shopping centers is now generally accepted as between 1.6:1 and 2:1, which translates to a parking index of 4 to 5 spaces per 1,000 square feet (93 square meters) of GLA, although earlier requirements were as high as 3:1 (7.5 spaces per 1000 square feet of GLA). Because they are smaller, however, neighborhood shopping centers require a higher ratio of parking spaces to floor area (about 3:1) to accommodate peak-hour shopping. The specific amount for a particular development is related to the shape of the site, whether parking is provided in structures and the specific requirements of stores in the complex.

Landscaping of open parking areas is necessary to relieve the monotony of stretches of asphalt, as well as to provide shaded areas. Current practice at larger shopping centers is to provide a 20- to 30-foot (6- to 9-meter) wide planted strip around the periphery of the site and planted strips between rows of cars.

See: PARKING LOT DESIGN; SHOPPING CENTER DESIGN

Shopping Mall

A shopping center design that places retail buildings in a linear pattern on two sides of a wide pedestrian walk and that may be open to the air or fully enclosed. The most common design for regional and community shopping centers, it is particularly successful in encouraging pedestrian traffic through the length of a mall when department stores are placed at opposite ends and smaller stores are placed along its length.

Width of the mall area is generally at least 50 feet (15 meters) to permit landscaping and seating and to prevent crowding. It may, however, be narrower in enclosed malls where stores have large, open entrances or wider at points to permit public gatherings, civic activities or promotional campaigns—activities that shopping malls are increasingly providing. Many of the newer malls are enclosed multi-level buildings, but most are one story in height except for anchor stores. Another new mall design, called the cluster plan, places several smaller buildings around courts, encouraging the shopper to meander from one court to another. Sometimes more attractive than the conventional mall, it is less successful from the retailer's viewpoint since shoppers are not forced to pass every store.

See: ANCHOR LEASE; ANCHOR STORE; COMMUNITY SHOPPING CENTER; REGIONAL SHOPPING CENTER; TRANSIT MALL

Short Takeoff and Landing (STOL)

Aircraft of a normal configuration that are capable of ascending and descending at steep angles, so they can land and take off from runways considerably shorter than those of conventional size. STOL aircraft may one day be used as major intercity carriers, capable of cruising at speeds comparable to those of conventional aircraft. Takeoff and landing speeds would be slower, however, increasing the safety of that part of the trip. Use for freight shipping is also contemplated. Since currently operating STOL aircraft require runways only 1,500 to 2,000 feet long (458 to 610 meters) as compared with conventional runways, which are usually in excess of 2,500 feet (762 meters), STOL ports can be located closer to downtown areas than conventional airports.

See: AIRPORT PLANNING; VERTICAL TAKEOFF AND LANDING (VTOL)

Shoulder

An area at the side of a road, between the through-traffic pavement and the curb or the roadway border, designed to accommodate a standing vehicle. Shoulders permit the maintenance of traffic capacity and, in some cases, increase the effective width of traffic lanes. Continuous shoulders of a minimum of 8 to 10 feet (2.4 to 3.0 meters) in width are recommended for all limited-access roadways; 12 feet (3.7 meters) in width is recommended where there is heavy truck use. Where this is not feasible, turnout bays spaced 1,000 to 1,500 feet (305 to 457 meters) apart will reduce potential congestion and hazard caused by disabled vehicles. On ramps a 4-foot (1.2-meter) shoulder may be sufficient to permit traffic to move around a stopped vehicle if the moving lane is at least 12 feet (3.7 meters) wide.

See: HIGHWAY CAPACITY DETERMINANTS; LANE WIDTH

Shredding

A means of reducing the volume of solid waste by grinding it into small pieces. The technique is often combined with baling. Shredded refuse has little odor and does not attract rodents and insects. In addition, it decomposes faster than refuse that has not been shredded and creates only a minimal fire hazard. Although not an inexpensive process, shredding (sometimes termed milling or grinding) offers a means of stretching the capacity of a landfill and making the landfill operation less intrusive to the surrounding community.

See: BALING; SANITARY LANDFILL; WASTE REDUCTION

Side Lot Line

Zoning ordinances take a number of different approaches to defining a side lot line. Some municipalities consider it to be any lot line that is not the front lot line or the rear lot line. Another way in which it is defined is as a line that extends from the front to the rear lot line and separates a lot from an adjacent lot that faces on the same street. Still a third approach is to consider a side lot line to be any lot line that connects with the end of a front lot line, usually at an angle of at least 30 degrees. (See Fig. 50)

See: LOT LINE

Side Yard

A yard located between a side lot line and a line parallel to that side lot line passing through the portion of the building that is closest to that lot line. Generally, a side yard extends from the front yard to the rear yard. If there is no front or rear yard, then the front or rear lot line is used as the appropriate boundary. (See Fig. 50)

See: CORNER LOT; FRONT YARD; REAR YARD; SIDE LOT LINE; YARD

Sidewalk

A paved path at the side of a road provided for pedestrian use, called a footway or pavement in Britain. In recent years sidewalks have become a serious design consideration as the result of studies that indicated that walking patterns in business districts are related to traffic signals and crowding. As a result of zoning changes that permit greater building height where buildings have greater setbacks, sidewalks are being widened in business areas, providing substantially more pedestrian space and comfort.

While many subdivision ordinances require that sidewalks be built, residents of older subdivisions without sidewalks often do not want them, suggesting that they have an urbanizing effect.

See: BIKEWAY; CURB; PAVEMENT; PAVERS; PEDESTRIAN IMPROVEMENTS; PEDESTRIANIZATION; PERSONAL SPACE; STREET BEHAVIOR

Sidewalk Cafe

A restaurant with tables located on the sidewalk in front of its premises. Having originated in Mediterranean countries, where the warm climate made outdoor dining more comfortable than indoor dining, sidewalk cafes are now popular in urban areas in most countries that have a temperate climate for at least part of the year.

Where downtowns are being improved, plans often prescribe wide sidewalks to accommodate and encourage this use. In older cities, however, where sidewalks are narrow, sidewalk cafes often encroach on pedestrian space. This can be a particular problem when restaurant owners provide winter enclosures for outdoor tables. Cities frequently allow this use only by special permit, to control the extent and location of both outdoor cafes and the enclosed variety.

The popularity of outdoor dining, in general, has been extended to restaurants of all sizes in both rural and urban areas on outdoor patios and boardwalks, as well as in front of restaurants. Resorts, shopping centers, college campuses and multipurpose developments of all kinds provide space for this amenity.

Sight Distance

The distance along a road within which a driver of a vehicle can clearly see the level of the road or obstructions to it. It is governed by the vertical and horizontal alignments of the road, roadside planting, building obstructions and available light. Three categories have been established for computation purposes in highway engineering and design: stopping sight distance, passing sight distance and intersection sight distance.

Stopping sight distance is the distance necessary to safely stop a vehicle traveling at the roadway design speed after the driver spots an obstruction in the lane in which it is traveling.

Passing sight distance is the distance necessary for a vehicle on a two- or three-lane road to overtake another vehicle and return to the right lane without interfering with the speed of an oncoming vehicle.

Intersection sight distance is the distance necessary to see the signals at an approaching intersection. Where "stop" or "yield" signs are used, intersection sight distance is sufficient clearance to see and react to an ap-

proaching vehicle on the intersecting road and an additional second to change speed to avoid collision.

See: GEOMETRIC DESIGN

Sign Regulation

Usually contained in the zoning ordinance, sign regulations are most often concerned with size, location on the structure, height and other such characteristics as lettering size, color, lighting and design of signs. Signs that flash or move are often prohibited, and billboards are also controlled.

The degree of sign regulation varies among zoning districts. For example, very strict controls are usually in force in residential districts, where signs may be limited to notices that homes are for sale or small name placards for permitted home occupations, such as a doctor's office. Historic districts may also have special requirements concerning the size, and particularly the design, of signs. Less restrictive requirements are usually in effect in commercial districts, although in some central business districts and commercial areas, signage is treated as an essential unifying design element and must be of a specific style. Signs that are nonconforming with respect to municipal regulations are often required to be removed after an amortization period of appropriate duration.

The regulation of signs is now widely accepted as a proper function of government; regulation may even be based on purely aesthetic grounds. However, this was not true three or four decades ago. In the early part of the 20th century, in the few cases in which sign control regulations were upheld by the courts, the rationale was nearly always based upon police power purposes related to public health and safety rather than to aesthetics. Typical, and rather farfetched, reasoning of the time was that billboards could legitimately be banned because they offered hiding places for criminals and for illicit sexual activity. Gradually links were made between aesthetics and other public considerations, such as economic welfare, until now, sign regulations are increasingly being upheld on aesthetic grounds alone.

In recent years courts have dealt more strictly with off-premises signs than on-premises signs and, in some cases, have upheld regulations totally banning off-premises outdoor advertising. Political advertising and posters are generally treated more liberally because of their importance to the political process and the free speech implications that are involved.

See: ADVERTISING SIGNS; AESTHETIC ZONING; AESTHETICS; AMORTIZATION OF NONCONFORMING USES; BILLBOARD; ILLUMINATED SIGN; *METROMEDIA, INC.* v. *CITY OF SAN DIEGO*

Silt

1. Fine particles of soil that are grouped between clay and sand in texture. In the United States Department of Agriculture system, silt is defined as particles ranging in size from 0.002 to 0.05 millimeter in diameter. The larger

sand particles range from 0.05 millimeter to 2.0 millimeters, and the smaller clay particles are less than 0.002 millimeter in diameter.

2. Soils that are composed of at least 80 percent silt and less than 12 percent clay.
See: SEDIMENTATION; SOIL CLASSIFICATION

Simulation

Use of operations research and computer modeling techniques to create a model representing a theoretical abstraction of a real world system. In its simplest applications, engineering wind tunnels and architectural scale models are simulations. The term is now more commonly used, however, to describe a body of sophisticated computer techniques for predicting the behavior of complex systems, such as the transportation system of an entire metropolitan area.

Computer simulation techniques were originally developed for military applications because of the obvious impracticality of "practicing" many military maneuvers. Among the many areas for which simulation is currently in use are economics, traffic and transportation systems, housing, industry and scientific research. As an example, the U.S. Department of Transportation funded several metropolitan transportation simulation studies in the 1970s in which a city would be broken into traffic zones based upon population or neighborhood nodes. Boundaries and size of the zones were based on population density, street patterns and travel origin-destination pairs. Nodes were connected in alternative ways to simulate the transportation network, and time and costs to move along the various commonly traveled routes were calculated using different combinations of mass transit and auto routes. The resulting models were used to calculate the costs, benefits and impact of alternative scenarios of road and mass transit capital improvements.

Simulation can be useful in providing an abstract computational device by which to test the impact of alternative development strategies, the significance of alternative assumptions, the complex interrelationships between variables and the sensitivity of the recommended solutions to changes in the underlying assumptions. Major simulation efforts have, however, often proved to be both complex and expensive undertakings and are frequently a source of controversy, particularly with respect to the validity of the underlying assumptions.
See: MODEL; SIMULATION GAMES

Simulation Games

Mechanisms to test mutual dependencies and conflicting interests and to enable participants to obtain a greater understanding of a particular subject area through role playing within the context of a specified set of rules and requirements. Simulation games, also known as operational games, are frequently used as educational devices in universities and for military and management training. They provide insight into the process of real-life decision making by requiring players to follow sets of rules and to operate within prescribed resource and economic limitations.

Games are usually iterative—players or teams representing different actors or participants take turns; each player's move is in large part influenced and constrained by the actions of the previous players. Although a game may span several hours, it typically simulates a more extended time period.

The simplest type of game is one in which two persons play, and one player can win only what the other loses (known as a zero-sum game). A variety of significantly more complicated large-scale games have been developed in the area of land planning in which many players participate, often in teams, to take part in simulations of real-life processes. One well-known planning game is CLUG (Community Land Use Game), in which players buy land and develop industry, commercial centers and residential areas while they contend with transportation access and cost, utility service, taxes, municipal finance and natural disasters. Other planning games that have been developed include APEX, Metropolis, CITY I, REGION and SIMSOC.

Within the context of planning, simulation games are thought to be most useful in sensitizing individuals to the dilemmas encountered by others in planning and developing the built environment. As an example, citizens may assume the role of, or attempt to solve the problems routinely encountered by, the planning director or chief elected official. Games are thought, however, to be of relatively little use as actual analytic or predictive tools.
See: SIMULATION

Single-Family Housing

A housing unit intended for occupancy by one family. Typically, a single-family residence has its own heating and hot water facilities and direct street access. It is considered to be a single-family detached unit if it is a freestanding structure.

Traditionally the lowest-density residential use, it is the most prevalent housing type in the United States. The drastic rise in the price of single-family housing along with high mortgage rates has, however, priced the conventional single-family detached home beyond the income range of many families. As an alternative, many younger families are turning to a variety of structural alternatives, such as townhouses, and to various ownership alternatives, such as cooperatives and condominiums, both for their frequently lower cost and for their lesser maintenance requirements. As of the 1980 census, there were 53,943,425 detached single-family homes in the United States and an additional 3,530,964 attached single-family homes out of a total housing stock of 88,411,263 units.
See: ATTACHED HOUSING; CONDOMINIMUM HOUSING; COOPERATIVE HOUSING; DETACHED HOUSING; HOUSING CHOICE; HOUSING TENURE; HOUSING TYPE; MULTIFAMILY HOUSING; TOWNHOUSE

Single-Room Occupancy (SRO)

A housing type, found most often in large cities, consisting of small housing units, usually with kitchenettes or cooking facilities and shared bathrooms. Census statistics for housing units without private plumbing facilities are an indicator of the number of SROs in a census tract.

The residents of SROs are primarily transients, the elderly or welfare recipients, and tenancy in a building containing SROs changes frequently. Living conditions in single-room occupancy units are often substandard, but the number of SROs has been declining as buildings have been demolished or converted to luxury or middle-income use, as has been occurring extensively in New York City. This, in turn, creates a new problem, as former SRO occupants are rendered homeless unless suitable replacement housing is found.

Site Design

The arrangement of buildings, structures, lot lines, roads, utilities and plantings on a particular piece of property (site). Site design takes place, to varying degrees, regardless of the size of the property being developed.

Site design involves a thorough analysis of site characteristics, such as topography, vegetation, geology, wind direction, views, climate, hydrology and soil characteristics. Existing improvements, such as roads and utilities, are also assessed. Physical improvements are then placed so that they comply with zoning, subdivision and other municipal regulations and so that natural elements can be used in an effective manner. Economy of construction is another important consideration in site design. A grading plan may be a necessary design component.

An increasingly important element of site planning is the protection of the environment from adverse effects of the proposed project, necessitating careful analysis of the project's impact on that site and on its surroundings. Environmental aspects that must be addressed are prevention of flooding, soil erosion and water pollution. Other aspects of site design relate to design of traffic and pedestrian circulation systems, safe ingress and egress, placement of utilities, view protection, landscaping and screening, outdoor lighting and design for solar access or wind control.

See: ARCHITECTURAL CONTROLS; BUILDING ORIENTATION; CIRCULATION PATTERN; DESIGN POPULATION; ENVIRONMENTAL ANALYSIS; FLOOD CONTROL; GRADING; LANDSCAPING; MICROCLIMATE; SITE ORIENTATION; SITE PLAN; SOIL EROSION CONTROL TECHNIQUES; SOLAR ACCESS; WIND CONTROL

Site Orientation

The predominant direction in which a piece of land faces. As an example, a hilly property can be said to be facing south. Site orientation can also be described in terms of scenic vistas that are visible from it, such as water views. Property that is oriented toward a scenic view or that allows a building to stay warmer in winter and cooler in summer will usually have a higher market value and greater design potential than a lot without these features.
See: BUILDING ORIENTATION; SOLAR ACCESS

Site Plan

An accurately scaled development plan that illustrates the existing conditions on a land parcel as well as depicting details of a proposed development. Among the features generally required on a site plan are the property boundaries and lot lines; major features of the landscape, such as topography, wetlands, significantly sized trees, other important vegetation and rock outcrops; and proposed street and utility networks, as well as planned access points.

The location of all proposed structures, parking lot design and number of spaces, sidewalks and areas designated for open space are also shown. Additional features that are usually required include the proposed landscape design, lighting and use of screening. (See Fig. 42)
See: SITE PLAN REVIEW; ZONING

Site Plan Review

A procedure in which proposed site plans are reviewed for compliance with all requirements of the zoning ordinance, municipal site plan regulations and any other appropriate municipal ordinances. The official reviewing body is most often the municipal planning commission, assisted by its staff, but depending upon state enabling legislation and municipal preference, may be another official body, such as the zoning board of appeals.

Among the aspects scrutinized during the site plan review are the bulk, height, design and arrangement of all structures on the site and the relationship of these structures to the site's environmental features and to surrounding land uses. All provisions for vehicular and pedestrian circulation and vehicular parking and loading are reviewed, as well as the adequacy of landscaping, screening and lighting. Another area of concern during site plan review is the adequacy of proposed sewer and water facilities and the impact of the development upon these and other municipal facilities. Provisions for soil conservation, proper drainage and minimization of runoff are also reviewed, and the plan is checked to ensure that public safety and emergency vehicles can gain ready access to any portion of the development in the event of fire or another hazard.

Site plan review provisions are important because they allow a depth of review to be given to projects where no subdivision review is required that is similar to the review for projects that are subject to subdivision approval. This is particularly essential when major residential, commercial and industrial developments are involved.
See: SITE PLAN; SUBDIVISION REVIEW; ZONING

Skeleton Frame Construction

A form of construction in which a frame is built that supports the weight of the walls, floors and roof of a build-

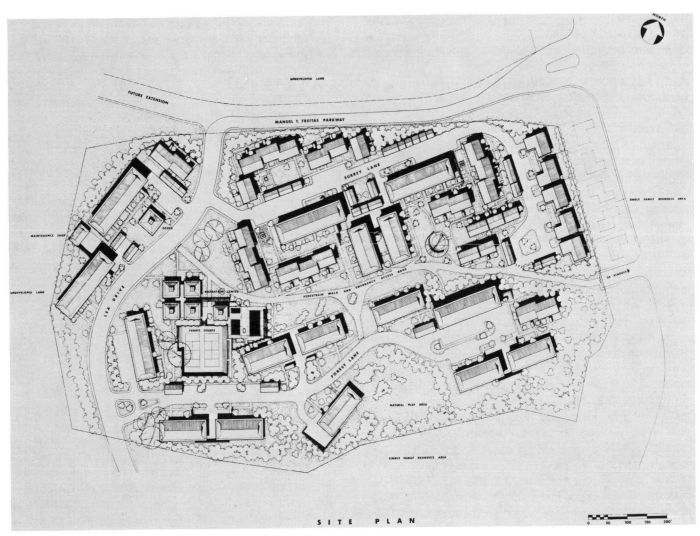

Fig. 42.   Site plan of a proposed residential development.
Credit: Courtesy of the U.S. Department of Housing and Urban Development

ing. Columns (called exterior or wall columns) are placed along the building line, while interior columns are set at required intervals within the body of the building. A framework formed by the columns, and the girders that stretch horizontally between the columns, carries the walls at each story level; beams that rest on the girders carry the floor and roof loads. Since the walls serve only to enclose the structure and carry no loads, they can be thin and made of a non-weight-bearing material, such as glass.
See: BEARING WALL

Sketch Plan

A rough plan of a proposed subdivision or other development proposal that is used early in the planning process as the basis for discussion and negotiation. Also known as a concept or outline plan, a sketch plan for a subdivision is usually developed prior to the preapplication conference so that basic concepts concerning the proposed subdivision layout may be informally reviewed by the planning staff or commission. Changes are far more easily made at this

stage of the subdivision design and review process than at any other time.

In other types of development proposals, sketch plans may also be used to demonstrate preliminary ideas and concepts and to elicit comment from municipal officials and citizens.
See: NEGOTIATION; PREAPPLICATION CONFERENCE; SCHEMATIC DRAWING; SITE PLAN; SUBDIVISION REVIEW

Skewness

A term used to describe a frequency distribution curve that is not symmetrical, as opposed to a normal distribution curve, which is symmetrical. If the longer tail of the distribution curve is toward the right, where the higher scores are found, the distribution is said to be positively skewed. In the opposite case, the distribution is negatively skewed.

In a skewed distribution the mean and median are not equal. Because the mean is influenced by extreme values while the median is not, calculation of these measures of central tendency will indicate the direction of the skew. Generally, in a positively skewed distribution, the mean is greater than the median.

See: FREQUENCY DISTRIBUTION; MEASURES OF CENTRAL TENDENCY; NORMAL DISTRIBUTION

Ski Area

An area of a mountain that, at a minimum, has been cleared of trees, boulders and large stones to permit snow accumulation for skiing, and that also provides tows to propel skiers to the top of the slope, a base lodge and a parking area. Ideally, the site should be able to collect a minimum of 60 inches (1.5 meters) of snow annually and should permit 80 to 85 skiing days a year. Slopes should be designed so that they are a minimum of 100 feet (30 meters) wide and face east or northeast if possible. Grades of less than 20 percent are necessary for beginners, 20 to 35 percent for intermediate skiers and over 35 percent for experts.

Ski areas are generally of three types. (1) The resort area, generally located on a mountain with a large vertical fall, has multiple slopes of varying difficulty, numerous tows and lifts, snowmaking equipment where necessary, a ski school, a large base lodge with cafeteria and ski equipment rental facilities, and hotel accommodations in the near vicinity. Some areas also provide facilities for ski jumping or tobogganing. Many larger ski areas are located in state parks or forests. (2) The day-use facility, with relatively few slopes and tows and a minimal base lodge with toilets and snack bar, caters to those wishing to ski near home or for just a few hours, and is often located in a municipal park. (3) Many ski areas today also provide trails for cross-country skiing and a number of areas specialize in this form. Cross-country trails, which are generally placed on flatter terrain than downhill trails, are cut in a variety of widths and lengths, and warming facilities are provided at appropriate intervals. In areas where skiing is popular, all three of these forms may be available.

The dependence on snowmaking equipment at large ski areas has become a matter of concern to planners in recent years, primarily because of the noise the machinery creates and, in some places, because of the large amount of water it uses. In some communities, where the ski slope is near a large population concentration, the hours of snowmaking have been severely restricted.

See: RESORT AREA

Skilled Nursing Facility (SNF)

An inpatient facility designed for individuals requiring intensive nursing care services on a daily basis. Generally, such facilities are intended to accommodate patients suffering from a chronic disease or requiring convalescence over a prolonged period of time. Medical care and treatment are administered on doctor's orders, and skilled rehabilitation services are available. Although regulations vary among states, SNFs are normally required to provide for special nutritional needs of patients and for regularly scheduled recreational activities. Skilled nursing facilities are eligible for federal reimbursement through both Medicare and Medicaid.

See: ACUTE CARE HOSPITAL; INTERMEDIATE CARE FACILITIES (ICF); NURSING HOME

Skyline

The outline of a group of buildings against the sky. Normally the term refers to a concentrated group of structures in a major urban center that creates a characteristic profile, as in the New York City skyline. The term, however, also refers to the outline created by buildings situated on a distinctive topography, such as the seven hills of Rome. The changing nature of a skyline is also a generally accepted indicator of both the growth and the dynamic nature of a city, with height and bold architectural forms serving as distinguishing features.

Until the advent of skyscrapers, skylines were historically characterized by the towers and spires of religious edifices, with many older sections of European cities still retaining a reasonably level horizon, punctuated solely by church towers. Proposals for skyscraper development have caused debate in many European municipalities because of the potential damage to the skyline.

Another issue confronting urban designers is the appearance of skylines consisting of rows of boxlike glass towers that contribute to an anonymous profile and a skyline that lacks distinction. Recent zoning ordinances and design standards for specialized areas have attempted to encourage variation in height and style, as a means of restoring diversity to city skylines.

Skyspace

The area of sky to the south of a solar collector that must not be obstructed if the collector is to be able to function efficiently. Required skyspace is a function of latitude as well as proposed use for a collector. Solar systems that will be used to produce hot water all year, for example, require that the skyspace boundary be defined by the lowest winter and highest summer sun angle. If used for space heating only during the heating season, a lower skyspace boundary may be used for spring, summer and fall.

See: BULK PLANE; SHADOW PATTERN; SOLAR ACCESS; SOLAR COLLECTOR

Slope

The inclination of the ground from the horizontal. It may be calculated from topographic maps by measuring the number of feet of horizontal distance between two points, then reading the elevations of the two points from the contour lines and determining the change in elevation. When the change in elevation is divided by the horizontal distance, a decimal results that, when multiplied by 100, yields the average percentage of slope between two points.

For example,

$$\frac{100 \text{ feet (elevation)}}{1,000 \text{ feet (distance)}} = 0.10$$

Engineers generally express slope in degrees. A 100 percent slope, for example, represents an equivalent ratio of vertical distance to horizontal distance (rise to run), which may be expressed as 1:1 or 45 degrees. In the preceding example, the 10 percent slope is equal to 5.8 degrees.

Slope analysis is important because it helps to determine suitable land uses and identifies potential environmental hazards, such as erosion, and safety hazards, such as slopes susceptible to sliding. The steeper the slope, the more expensive construction becomes and the more difficult it may be to provide a safe access road, sewers and proper drainage and to stabilize the soil. Completely flat ground, on the other hand, is difficult to drain. Generally speaking, slopes over about 10 percent may be considered to be steep, and roads should preferably not exceed that limit. Lawns cannot be mowed on slopes in excess of 25 percent.
See: CONTOUR LINES; HILLSIDE PROTECTION ORDINANCES; MASS WASTING; TOPOGRAPHIC MAP

Sludge

1. The semisolid end product of sewage treatment that is formed by the processes of filtration, sedimentation and/ or biological treatment. It has a high water volume and a high organic content and may also have a high inorganic content, making it a concentrated pollutant that is difficult to dispose of.

The characteristics of sludge vary depending upon the type of processing to which it has been subjected, its origin and its age. It may have an offensive odor, contain a quantity of gases that are gradually or quickly released, and have a temperature high enough to support combustion. Raw sludge consists of the solids removed during primary treatment, leaving a putrescible, decomposing substance, while digested sludge has been subjected to a biological process, such as anaerobic digestion, in which decomposition of organic matter is stabilized. Most sludge contains less than 10 percent solids. Since sludge must be pumped from treatment tanks to trucks, barges or drying beds, this concentration is considered to be the maximum that will permit this form of conveyance. Sludge that has been dried will contain between 40 percent and 90 percent solids.

2. The suspended solids removed during water supply treatment, as a result of sedimentation and coagulation processes, that are returned to a water body.
See: DEWATERED SLUDGE; SEWAGE TREATMENT; SLUDGE DIGESTION; SLUDGE DISPOSAL; SLUDGE INCINERATION; WATER TREATMENT

Sludge Digestion

The stabilization of sewage sludge so that its biochemical oxygen demand (BOD) is reduced to an environ-mentally acceptable level. Sludge digestion occurs naturally when sludge is left to decompose for a substantial amount of time, but in secondary sewage treatment mechanical equipment is used to speed the decomposition. Sludge digestion processes can remove 75 percent or more of the BOD, depending upon the amount of time the sludge is detained.

In anaerobic digestion (which occurs in the absence of oxygen), complex organic substances in the sludge are broken down by biochemical processes that require continuous mixing of the sludge within an established range of temperatures. Sludge must be detained in digestors for 10 to 30 days or longer to permit it to decompose to an acceptable state. Anaerobic digestion will reduce odor and volume and produce sufficient gases to operate elements of a treatment plant, such as generators that produce electricity for the plant.

Aerobic digestion is generally used in small treatment plants and is less common because of higher operating costs associated with the required supply of oxygen. It also does not produce methane, a useful power source for large plants, as a by-product of digestion.
See: BIOCHEMICAL OXYGEN DEMAND (BOD); LAGOON; SECONDARY TREATMENT; SLUDGE

Sludge Disposal

The ultimate disposition of sewage sludge. Sludge is disposed of primarily on land, but ocean dumping of digested sludge has been practiced for many years by a number of coastal cities in the United States, Britain and Germany, although the practice is gradually being phased out.

Disposal on land can take several forms. Raw or digested sludge may be placed in earth lagoons for drying or indefinite storage, or it can be disposed of in landfill sites. Stabilized sludge can be dumped in an abandoned quarry or mine, while wet digested sludge can be spread over farmlands and plowed under to condition the soil and improve its moisture retentiveness, a practice used extensively in Europe. It can also be dried, ground, fortified with nitrogen and bagged for sale as a fertilizer. Recent studies indicate, however, that heavy metals and toxic substances in sludge, resulting from industrial sewage and the proliferation of complicated organic and inorganic compounds, can contaminate crops and soil and seep into groundwater. Its use is therefore no longer recommended for food crops or grazing areas, where the toxic elements could enter the food chain.

More recently cities such as Philadelphia have been trucking industrially contaminated sludge to strip-mining areas, where it can be mixed with the soil that has been removed for later replacement in mined areas. Since the soil above coal beds has a high metal content, the nutrients in the sludge actually improve the soil quality and encourage trees and vegetation to grow.

Incineration and wet oxidation processes are used to

substantially reduce sludge volume by converting it to ash, which is then generally disposed of at a sanitary landfill.
See: CODISPOSAL; DEWATERED SLUDGE; LAGOON; OCEAN DUMPING; OXIDATION PROCESSES; SANITARY LANDFILL; SLUDGE; SLUDGE INCINERATION

Sludge Incineration

Processes used in the treatment of sewage sludge to reduce its organic content and volume. Incineration can be undertaken for sludge that contains 30 percent or more solids. No supplementary fuel is necessary (except for start-up and control of temperature) because heat is emitted naturally while the sludge decomposes. Sludge can be combined with solid waste or incinerated alone; when burned alone, it is useful to incinerate it as raw sludge, which generates more heat energy than digested sludge.

Several different systems for incineration of sludge are used. Ash, the end product of each procedure, is usually buried at a landfill site, although other alternatives are being studied. In some systems the gases that are emitted are used as an additional source of power.
See: CODISPOSAL; DEWATERED SLUDGE; SLUDGE; SLUDGE DISPOSAL; ZIMMERMAN PROCESS (ZIMPRO)

Slum

An area that has substandard, squalid and overcrowded conditions and that is usually characterized by a high crime rate.

Slums are sometimes a product of rapid urbanization, such as those that developed during the industrial revolution and those resulting from urbanization in underdeveloped countries. In such cases, urbanized areas developed without sufficient utilities and open spaces to support the needs of the dense populations that inhabit them. Slums also develop, however, where these basic facilities are provided. In these situations, the causes of slum formation are more subtle and less controllable, and it has been postulated that they are related to social disorganization, to societal inequities and to the inability of certain subgroups to adjust to urbanized areas.

Urban planning has traditionally reacted to this phenomenon largely via modification of the physical setting through capital improvements, housing renovation and redevelopment programs, although increasing social emphasis has led to the development of programs such as urban homesteading and the concentration of many types of support services in slum areas.
See: DEPRESSED AREA; INNER CITY; REDLINING; SLUM CLEARANCE; URBAN HOMESTEADING

Slum Clearance

The demolition of concentrations of blighted, substandard structures. Many early urban renewal efforts in the 1950s and the 1960s focused on the removal of dilapidated buildings that did not meet health codes and were considered to be unfit for human habitation. The intent of these efforts was to eliminate overcrowded, deteriorating tene-

ments; provide public housing; and promote economic redevelopment. By the late 1960s, however, slum clearance had developed a negative image because of the extent to which it uprooted ethnic neighborhoods, dislocated residents and businesses, and led to the demolition of historic structures. It became evident that while unsafe buildings should be removed, a more sensitive, site-specific solution than wholesale clearance was needed.
See: BLIGHTED AREA; REHABILITATION; SUBSTANDARD HOUSING; URBAN RENEWAL

Small Business Administration (SBA)

A United States government agency with responsibility for aiding and protecting the interests of small businesses. It ensures that such concerns receive a fair portion of government contracts and sales of government property, makes loans to small businesses and to victims of disasters or riots, and regulates and makes loans to small business investment companies.

The SBA provides financial assistance in the form of loans to small business concerns to help them finance plant construction or expansion, acquire equipment or supplies, and obtain working capital. Loans are made to victims of floods, riots, civil disorders and natural disasters for repair or replacement of homes, businesses or other property. Loans are also available to handicapped individuals, businesses employing the handicapped and small businesses located in areas with high proportions of unemployed or low-income individuals, among several other categories. The pollution control financing program offers 100 percent guarantees of loans, leases or contracts related to financing of pollution control equipment. Programs are also conducted to encourage minority and women-owned businesses.
See: CERTIFIED DEVELOPMENT COMPANY; SMALL BUSINESS INVESTMENT COMPANY (SBIC)

Small Business Investment Company (SBIC)

A private corporation or partnership that is licensed by the Small Business Administration (SBA) under the Small Business Investment Act of 1958, as amended, to provide long-term loans and equity capital to qualifying small businesses. The intent of the program is to obtain maximum private-sector participation in making venture capital available, with an emphasis placed on funding those small business concerns developing new processes, products and markets.

SBICs vary widely in size, from fairly small groups of local investors to publicly traded companies or subsidiaries of larger corporations. Typically, they seek investments in which they have an opportunity to obtain equity participation in the growth of the small business. As an example, an SBIC may obtain warrants in exchange for a loan to a small business that allow the SBIC to purchase common stock at an attractive price for a particular time period.

An SBIC may issue SBA-guaranteed debentures that are sold to the Federal Financing Bank (a federal entity that coordinates federal agency borrowing and sells and purchases those obligations that are guaranteed or issued by federal agencies). In addition, SBICs often provide management and consulting services to the small businesses they are financing. Generally, the small business investment company is not permitted to invest more than 20 percent of its capital in any one small business or to take control of the business. It must also have qualified management and meet minimum capital requirements.

An additional specialized program is operated under the authority of Section 301 (d) of the Small Business Investment Act of 1958, as amended. SBICs that are formed according to the provisions of this section, known as Section 301 (d) licensees or 301 (d) SBICs, serve as a source of long-term financing, equity capital and management assistance to owners of small businesses who are economically or socially disadvantaged.
See: CERTIFIED DEVELOPMENT COMPANY; COMMUNITY DEVELOPMENT CORPORATION (CDC); ECONOMIC DEVELOPMENT; SMALL BUSINESS ADMINISTRATION (SBA)

Small Cities Program

A component of the Community Development Block Grant Program that offers funding for rural areas and small communities located in metropolitan areas. Unlike large cities and urban counties, which receive entitlement funding directly according to a formula, Small Cities applicants compete for the balance of funds, which are allocated on a formula basis to the states.

In 1981 federal legislation gave states the option of administering the Small Cities Program or letting the Department of Housing and Urban Development remain as the administrator. States that choose to run the program receive a Small Cities formula grant—which they, in turn, allocate—but must contribute an additional 10 percent to the funding, perform community development planning and provide localities with technical assistance.
See: COMMUNITY DEVELOPMENT BLOCK GRANT (CDBG)

Small Towns Institute (STI)

A nonprofit organization comprised of planners, businessmen, researchers, citizens and organizations concerned with the problems of small communities in the United States and Canada. STI, which is located in Ellensburg, Washington, maintains a Small Towns Resources Center, from which information is available concerning a wide variety of subject areas, including comprehensive planning, historic preservation, economic development, housing, rural development and sanitation. Resource books on special community problems and a bimonthly magazine, *Small Town,* are published by STI.

Smog

A term originally coined in the early 20th century to describe a combination of smoke and fog in reaction to the type of air pollution that plagued many British cities. The term has subsequently come to be used to describe other types of air pollution typical of urban areas that may be unrelated to smoke and/or fog.

Smog is often characterized as being of one of two types. Sulfurous smog is typical of European cities and of the eastern United States and derives from sulfur oxides. It is worsened by dampness and significant amounts of suspended particulates. Concentrations of sulfur dioxide can cause respiratory difficulties. Photochemical smog, however, typically attracts greater attention. The type for which Los Angeles is infamous, it is caused by automobile exhausts and other emissions undergoing photochemical reaction in the atmosphere. Usually unrelated to either smoke or fog, photochemical smog is responsible for health problems, such as eye irritation and respiratory ailments; plant damage; and reduced visibility.
See: AIR POLLUTION

Smoke

A gaseous suspension consisting of finely divided solid or liquid particles, generally produced by the incomplete combustion of a fuel, such as coal.
See: AIR POLLUTION; PARTICULATES; STACK

Social Planning

The study of the social welfare of groups in a society and the development of policies and programs to promote improvement of their situations. Social planning's main goals involve such areas as alleviating poverty and racial discrimination and improving the standard of living, while the functional areas in which it operates are generally housing, health, education, employment, crime prevention and public assistance.

The provision of programs is generally referred to as social services planning or human services planning. Other aspects—such as establishment of social policies (e.g., use of housing allowances rather than provision of public housing), advocacy planning that supports locally initiated proposals, and citizen participation—are more accurately termed social planning. Since the 1970s, in addition, analysis of the social aspects of major new projects has been part of the evaluation of the feasibility of certain federally supported projects, such as the location of a transportation corridor, and planning proposals for neighborhood improvement now also concern themselves with the problems of persons and businesses who might be displaced if gentrification were to occur.

At a different level social planning connotes major changes in the manner in which society functions, such as changes in the distribution of wealth. In the United States major social changes were undertaken in the form of economic programs developed in the 1930s that created savings systems and unemployment compensation that could prevent poverty for a substantial segment of the population. The success of these programs in reducing poverty spurred many more societal programs, such as the public housing program, as well as additional programs at the state and local government levels. Government support for industrial automation, as in Japan, or a reduced work week are other forms of social planning.

See: ADVOCACY PLANNING; COMMUNITY ACTION PROGRAM (CAP); COMMUNITY SERVICES BLOCK GRANT; CRIMINAL JUSTICE PLANNING; HEALTH PLANNING; MODEL CITIES PROGRAM; POVERTY LEVEL; PUBLIC HOUSING; RECREATION PLANNING; SCHOOL PLANNING; SOCIAL SERVICES PLANNING; WORKS PROGRESS ADMINISTRATION (WPA)

Social Services Planning

The determination of need for specific social services and the development of methodologies for their delivery. Social services planning is practiced by government and private agencies that are responsible for program delivery and for preventive care. Planning departments may also perform aspects of social services planning, usually to assist line agencies.

In its most common form, social services planning involves determination of recipient groups eligible for available funds and outreach to encourage their application for aid. Eligibility may be determined by use of prescribed requirements, as for federal programs, or by development of a profile of those expected to benefit most from a program. Determination of populations that meet eligibility requirements and their locations is accomplished by use of census data; social indicators, such as crime reports or health statistics; or case files of another social service program geared to the same population.

More sophisticated levels of social services planning may involve policy development; program planning and management, including determination of cost-effectiveness and performance evaluation; or development of an information system as a data base. Coordination of diverse programs provided by numerous organizations is necessary for comprehensive social services planning, while projection of major changes in social service needs, caused by technological changes such as advancements in medical treatment, is necessary to determine future programs.

See: CATCHMENT AREA; HEALTH PLANNING; MULTISERVICE CENTER; NEIGHBORHOOD CHANGE; OUTREACH; PLANNING FOR THE DISABLED; PLANNING FOR THE ELDERLY; SOCIAL PLANNING; TRANSIT FARE SUBSIDIES; URBAN INDICATORS

Social Stratification

The class, status and power structures of a society. Those who are at the bottom of the social order are often unable to obtain the basic needs of that society, such as adequate housing, employment and health care.

Social planning and legislation at the federal level in the United States has been responsible for ameliorating some of the effects of social stratification. Federal housing programs for construction and rent subsidy have aided in the provision of housing to those in low- and moderate-income groups, while programs related to job training and education have aided economic advancement. Social service and food programs have, to some extent, prevented extreme poverty and malnutrition. In addition, public health and insurance programs for the elderly and the poor are responsible in part for better health care for these groups.

See: SOCIAL PLANNING; SOCIAL SERVICES PLANNING

Social Structure

The complex variety and patterns of roles and statuses that define an individual's behavior and relations to others and that, collectively, define a society's hierarchical relationships and behavioral roles. The matrix of an individual's relationships depends upon population characteristics such as age, sex, race and religion; educational achievement; economic status; and environmental and cultural settings.

Social structure analysis is a means of identifying subsections of the community, their relationships and their problems and is particularly useful in planning studies related to design of public areas, such as parks, that are intended for use by diverse populations. Analysis of population characteristics to ascertain trends that might affect planning—such as greater numbers of elderly persons and two-income childless households, fewer children and declining family size—is basic to long-term planning. Social impact analysis, an outgrowth of environmental impact analysis, is a means by which the effects of a proposed project on the residents of the surrounding area may be anticipated, so that changes designed to alleviate potentially damaging social consequences can be suggested.

See: DEFENSIBLE SPACE; SOCIAL PLANNING; SOCIAL STRATIFICATION; URBAN SOCIOLOGY

Society of Real Estate Appraisers (SREA)

A professional organization of real estate appraisers and analysts. Founded in 1935, SREA has over 18,000 members from numerous chapters in the United States, Canada and the Caribbean. Three different membership classifications are available, depending upon professional experience and training: Senior Real Estate Analyst (SREA), Senior Real Property Appraiser (SRPA), and Senior Residential Appraiser (SRA).

Among the activities of SREA, which is located in Chicago, are an extensive series of courses, seminars and workshops in appraisal training, the promulgation of standards of professional practice and conduct, and liaison with governmental agencies. Regular publications of the organization include *The Real Estate Appraiser,* a quarterly journal; *Appraisal Briefs,* a weekly newsletter; an annual directory of membership; and an annual directory of government and corporate appraisal officers. A number of books and appraisal guides are also available.

Software

The programs, routines and other nonhardware elements that enable a computer system to operate. System software assists in the general operation of the computer and the performance of standardized tasks, while application software is designed to fulfill a particular function.
See: DATA PROCESSING; HARDWARE

Soil and Water Resources Conservation Act of 1977

Federal legislation (PL 95-192) that authorizes the Soil Conservation Service (SCS) to conduct a national appraisal of soil, water and related resources, including fish and wildlife habitats, and to develop a detailed statement of policy regarding soil and water conservation activities of the Department of Agriculture.

The SCS is also authorized to conduct a soil and water conservation program in cooperation with soil conservation districts and state and national agencies and organizations. The program includes analysis of existing resources, government programs and private programs as well as evaluation of alternative methods for conservation and their relative costs and benefits.
See: SOIL CONSERVATION SERVICE (SCS)

Soil Association

A group of soils that have been defined and that occur together in a characteristic pattern in particular geographic areas. Soil associations are generally used as the mapping unit on small-scale or generalized soil maps where individual soils are not delineated.
See: SOIL CLASSIFICATION; SOIL MAP; SOIL SURVEY

Soil Classification

A number of different methods have been developed for grouping and categorizing the thousands of soils in existence. Each system emphasizes different characteristics and serves somewhat different purposes.

The United States Department of Agriculture developed a classification system in the 1930s (subsequently modified a number of times) that takes into account both the chemical and physical properties of soil and that may be used for either cultivated or virgin soil. This system classifies soils into the categories of order, suborder, great group, subgroup, family and series. There are 10 groupings of orders and progressively more divisions in each subsequent category. Planners and engineers generally find the soil series the most useful classification because of the detail of description found at this level.

Engineers have developed additional systems for their work that stress the physical properties and performance capabilities of soils, such as permeability, volume change, plasticity and elasticity. The American Association of State Highway and Transportation Officials (AASHTO) stresses load-bearing ability in its classification system and groups soils accordingly. The soils with the best capability to carry loads, such as well-graded gravel mixtures or predominantly coarse sands, are given ratings of A-1; the worst bearing capacities are found among the clay soils.

The Unified Classification System, which was originally developed for the Army Corps of Engineers, divides soils into the three general categories of coarse-grained soils, such as gravel or sandy soil; fine-grained soils, such as silts and clays; or organic soils, such as peat. Within these groups further subdivisions, such as well-graded gravel or silty sands, are established; general observations may be made from these categories concerning factors such as compressibility, permeability when compacted, workability as a construction material and relative desirability for uses such as roadways and foundations.

There are also a number of simple tests by which soils may be generally identified in the field.
See: SOIL ASSOCIATION; SOIL HORIZON; SOIL PROFILE; SOIL SERIES; SOIL SURVEY; SOIL TYPE

Soil Compaction

A means of increasing soil density by the use of machinery or equipment that strikes it, causes the soil to vibrate, rolls the soil or loads it with weight. It is one of the methods by which soil conditions for foundations may be improved by the rearranging, addition or removal of soil particles.

Compaction of soil or artificial fill can help to reduce settlement, decrease permeability and increase strength and stability. Degree of compaction is dependent upon both the water content of the soil and the compaction effort. A laboratory test, known as a compaction test, may be performed to arrive at the most appropriate moisture level.

Soil compaction is often used in the construction of highways and roads, structures, parking lots and dams to prevent settlement at a later date.

Soil Conservation

The practice of preventing or minimizing soil deterioration from erosion, loss of soil structure, loss of organic matter or loss of plant nutrients.

The history of United States settlement is one of free land available for the claiming, encouraging land to be used up and abandoned and new land to be claimed. The unfamiliarity of European settlers with the terrain, soil, crops and climate of North America also led to soil conservation problems. Other factors contributing to soil mismanagement were the abuse of prairie lands and the availability of public rangelands for overgrazing.

As a result of these and other factors, major government efforts to combat soil deterioration began in the United States early in the 20th century. A series of erosion experiment stations were opened in 1930, and the Soil Erosion Service, a temporary agency, was established in 1933. With the creation in 1935 of its successor, the Soil

Conservation Service, major soil conservation programs were begun that continue today.

See: SHELTER BELT; SOIL CONSERVATION SERVICE (SCS); SOIL EROSION; SOIL EROSION CONTROL TECHNIQUES; SOIL EROSION FACTORS

Soil Conservation District

A local organization, usually formed at the county level, through which both federal and state agencies provide assistance to municipalities and landowners. Empowered by state legislation, the soil conservation districts came into being in 1936, when the Department of Agriculture decided that this was the mechanism through which the Soil Conservation Service would serve community needs.

Typically a district is managed by a board or committee, which usually has five members. The board may be elected or appointed, and a minimum number of the board members must often be farmers. As the scope of interest of the districts broadened to include flooding and other related problems, most states modified their enabling legislation to allow the name to be changed to soil and water conservation districts.

Conservation districts typically have the power to conduct surveys, investigations and research; to carry out preventive and control measures; and to develop comprehensive plans for the conservation of soil and water resources. Depending upon state legislation, they may also make available machinery, seeds and fertilizer and act as agents for the United States in connection with the construction, acquisition, operation and maintenance of soil conservation, water management, flood prevention or sediment damage prevention projects.

See: SOIL CONSERVATION SERVICE (SCS)

Soil Conservation Service (SCS)

An agency within the Department of Agriculture that produces numerous studies that are useful in land planning and analysis and makes recommendations on land conservation and pollution abatement. It also administers several conservation programs.

The SCS provides technical assistance on conservation techniques to individuals and communities through local soil and water districts. It also conducts local soil surveys and has responsibility for the National Cooperative Soil Survey, which is carried out in cooperation with state agricultural experiment stations and state and federal agencies. SCS inventories and monitors the conditions of soil and water, as well as trends in land use, and publishes maps indicating the locations of important farmlands. These studies are used by all levels of government for analytic purposes.

The SCS undertakes river basin surveys in cooperation with other federal agencies for purposes of water resource planning and floodplain management and undertakes investigations and surveys for small watershed projects at the request of local organizations. It cooperates on improvements to reduce erosion, floodwater and sediment damage; to conserve, utilize and dispose of water; and to reduce flooding. It also has responsibility for carrying out emergency watershed protection.

Under the Great Plains Conservation Program, the SCS administers a program designed to promote greater agricultural stability and conservation in designated counties in the 10 Great Plains states by participating in a cost sharing of conservation practices with farmers and ranchers. The SCS also has responsibility for administration of the rural abandoned mine program, in which grants of between 25 percent and 100 percent are made to reclaim lands that have been mined for coal. Under the Surface Mining Control and Reclamation Act of 1977, it is responsible for identifying prime farmland within areas proposed for surface mining, providing technical assistance to mine operators on land reclamation, and reviewing and commenting both on permits that involve prime farmland and on state reclamation plans. Another program, resource conservation and development in multiple-county areas, is accomplished by assistance to municipalities for projects such as erosion control, farm irrigation, water-based recreation, fish and wildlife facilities, and long-range planning.

See: FARMERS HOME ADMINISTRATION (FmHA); FARMLAND PROTECTION; FARMLAND PROTECTION POLICY ACT; SOIL AND WATER RESOURCES CONSERVATION ACT OF 1977; SOIL CONSERVATION DISTRICT

Soil Erosion

The process by which soil particles are weathered and broken down and then transported by wind and water. Some degree of erosion is inevitable; this type of erosion, called geologic or natural erosion, is part of the larger pattern in which natural forces carve and sculpt the surface of the Earth. Accelerated erosion, on the other hand, occurs when human activities, such as agriculture or construction, increase the pace of erosion so that it occurs at a rate much faster than soils can be formed.

Soil erosion not only directly affects agricultural productivity, reducing crop yields significantly; it is also a major source of pollution of rivers and streams. Any type of activity that removes plant cover from the soil causes a marked increase in the rate of erosion.

Farmland, particularly where conservation practices are not in effect, ranks high as a land use with substantial soil erosion potential, while forestland produces little erosion. The extensive deforestation that took place much earlier in history throughout the Mediterranean is directly related to the severe soil erosion found all through the hillsides of Italy, Greece, Turkey and Lebanon. It is only in some of the valley bottoms, where much of the productive soil has accumulated, that the prime agricultural land is located. Soil erosion hazard in the United States is especially high along the Missouri and Mississippi Rivers. The intensely grazed or cultivated portions of the Southwest and the rolling hills of Virginia and Tennessee are also quite erosion-prone.

See: RUNOFF EROSION; SOIL CONSERVATION; SOIL EROSION CONTROL TECHNIQUES

Soil Erosion Control Techniques

A number of land management practices are available for reducing soil erosion. They usually concentrate upon retaining some form of cover on the land and preventing water from concentrating and running directly downhill. Soil erosion control techniques may be classified as vegetative, such as planting of ground cover, or mechanical, such as terracing. Selection of land uses suitable to the topography and soils found on the site as well as proper site design and layout are basic to soil erosion control. Specific applications of these techniques have been developed for farming and construction—two major sources of soil erosion and sediment pollution.

Contouring, crop rotation, strip-cropping, stubble mulching, minimum tillage, terracing and the planting of cover crops are all used on agricultural lands. Contouring describes the plowing and planting of sloping fields across the hill following natural contour lines rather than up and down the slope. Use of this practice greatly slows the rate of runoff downhill, thereby enabling more rainfall to infiltrate the soil and preventing valuable soil from being washed away. Crop rotation, which is often combined with strip-cropping, stresses the planting of different types of crops—such as legumes, grasses and cotton—in a rotating cycle to maintain and improve soil productivity.

Strip-cropping uses alternating rows of close-growing plants and clean-cultivated crops, such as corn, to arrest erosion caused by wind or runoff. In stubble mulching, crop residues are left on the ground rather than plowed under or burned to help retain soil moisture and improve soil quality. *Minimum tillage farming* is a general term describing various techniques in which plowing is usually not done prior to planting but in which seeding, fertilizing and the application of pesticides, if any, occur simultaneously.

Many management techniques can reduce soil erosion that originates at construction sites. For example, certain sensitive stages of construction are sometimes scheduled for the portions of the year when erosion hazard is least. Other useful measures include the installation of permanent structures and sediment basins, if necessary, at an early stage in the process. Similarly, only those areas in which construction is scheduled to begin should be cleared and graded. Proper use of construction equipment can also reduce erosion hazard; for example, the creation of deep wheel tracks moving up and down slopes can accelerate erosion.

Among the mechanical measures used to reduce erosion on construction sites are controlled use of grading; the construction of subsurface drains to prevent accumulation of groundwater or to lower a high water table; or the construction of diversions, consisting of channels and ridges running cross-slope, which divert runoff above critical slopes. Outlets, such as grassed waterways, channel water from diversions, parking lots and roadways. Sediment basins detain runoff as well as trap sediment. Berms, storm sewers, and stream channel and bank stabilization may also be necessary.

Vegetative measures may be used to reduce soil erosion during construction and to permanently stabilize the site after construction. Mulches, such as small-grain straw or hay, can be used to protect slopes until the weather permits seeding and help establish cover in difficult spots. Fibrous materials, such as jute or cotton or paper netting, can be used to hold mulch in place, while fiberglass matting also has a variety of uses in erosion control. Rapid-growing temporary cover crops can be used for periods of a few months or longer to protect cleared areas from erosion.

See: BANK PROTECTION; GROUND COVER; SHELTER BELT; SOIL EROSION; SOIL EROSION FACTORS; TERRACE; WINDBREAK

Soil Erosion Factors

The extent to which soil is subject to erosion is generally a function of the soil composition; other physical factors, such as climate; and land management practices.

Soil composition characteristics—such as the amount of sand, silt or clay found in a particular soil—influence the ease with which soil particles may be separated from the soil body and transported. Dry, structureless sands, such as those found in coastal areas, are particularly susceptible to the strong coastal winds. The light organic fen soils of England also are readily transported by winds because of their low weight. Silt and clay particles are readily carried by water, while sand particles, although easily detached, are large enough to resist movement by water unless the water is moving rapidly on a steep slope or rainfall is intense.

Slope greatly increases the rate of soil erosion, as does rainfall. It has been shown that heavy rainfall can have a much greater influence on erosion than the total amount of precipitation, which may be partially in the form of mist or light rain. Because of this, Britain, where rain tends to fall lightly, is subject to much less rain-induced erosion than is the United States. Tropical areas are troubled by a combination of heavy rainfall concentrated within several months of the year and a dry period during which plant cover dies, leaving the soil more exposed for the next rainy season.

Land management practices greatly influence the extent to which soil erosion occurs. Farmlands on which the soil is allowed to remain bare or that are hilly but not cultivated on the contour suffer extensive erosion losses. Overgrazing, resulting in the loss of natural range cover, also

leads to increased erosion, as can certain forestry and construction practices.
See: SOIL CONSERVATION; SOIL EROSION; SOIL EROSION CONTROL TECHNIQUES

Soil Horizon

The distinctive layers or zones of soil, running approximately parallel to the ground, which are differentiated from the layers above and below by their physical characteristics. Generally, the layers are identified as the A, B and C horizons. The A horizon, the uppermost layer, is the horizon of maximum organic activity and contains substantial amounts of humus. It is also known as the zone of leaching, because water-soluble materials are leached through this horizon. The B horizon is known as the horizon of accumulation, because suspended materials from the A horizon tend to be concentrated here. It generally is rich in iron and aluminum in temperate climates and often contains a high proportion of clay. The C horizon, the source of the overlying soil, is the layer in which unconsolidated parent material, such as windblown silt, alluvium or glacial material, may be found.

Below the C layer is consolidated bedrock, which is sometimes designated as the R or D layer. Other subdivisions of the horizons have been made as well, differing somewhat by country according to usage. An area above the A horizon is sometimes labeled O, or O_1 and O_2, or H and describes the loose leaves and organic debris on the Earth's surface that are still unaltered. Numbers have also been added to the A and B layers to further describe the gradations of these horizons. Letters are also sometimes used following the numbers in the B horizon to further describe materials that accumulate.
See: SOIL PROFILE

Soil Map

A map that shows the distribution and location of the soils in an area. Soil maps may be prepared in several ways: They may be detailed, large-scale soil survey maps compiled through extensive field investigation; they may be generalized—i.e., made by combining preexisting soil survey maps; or they may be schematic and prepared through sampling at varying intervals or by remote sensing.

The scale of soil maps varies widely, depending upon the map's proposed use. A map intended for site planning in an area in which intensive development is planned would be prepared at a large scale to enable the identification and interpretation of fairly small, homogeneous areas of soil. At the other extreme, macro-intensity soil maps are made at scales ranging up to 1:1,000,000 to provide a broad overview of the kind and distribution of soils in large areas such as states, river basins or countries.

Most often, phases (significant characteristics with implications for soil management) of soil series are the categories depicted on soil maps. Generally, phases are related to such factors as slope, erodibility or the presence of rock,

resulting in a description such as "very stony." If it is not possible to clearly delineate separate soils series, a soil complex may be mapped in which the word *complex* follows the soil name or else a hyphen separates the names of the series, as in Fayette-Dubuque silt loam. If it is not considered worthwhile to differentiate the soils because their characteristics are so similar, a conjunction rather than a hyphen is used, as in Alden and Sun. Descriptions are also found on soil maps for miscellaneous land areas that have been extensively altered through grading, filling, paving, etc. Typical labels for this category are "urban land" or "made land."

Interpretive maps may be prepared from soil maps to enable the limitations of the soil for particular uses to be more readily visualized. For example, a map may be colored to illustrate limitations on septic tank usage, with red generally representing severe soil limitations; yellow, moderate limitations; and green, slight or no limitations.
See: REFERENCE MAPS; SOIL CLASSIFICATION; SOIL SERIES; SOIL SURVEY

Soil Profile

A vertical cross section depicting the various soil horizons of a particular area or spot.
See: SOIL HORIZON

Soil Series

Soils with similar soil profiles, in terms of their characteristics and arrangements, but different surface soil texture. This important unit of soil classification is assigned a name that is derived from the location at which the series was first identified. Examples of soil series names are Stockbridge, Merrimac, Potsdam and Charlton; each series represents a specific combination of soil characteristics unique to that series.
See: SOIL CLASSIFICATION; SOIL HORIZON; SOIL MAP; SOIL PROFILE; SOIL SURVEY

Soil Survey

A detailed and systematic inspection of soils, both in the field and in the laboratory, in order to analyze and describe their characteristics, classify them, map their boundaries and interpret their adaptability to various types of agricultural and urban uses.

County soil surveys, prepared by the United States Soil Conservation Service, are widely available and, along with accompanying survey maps, provide many types of useful information, including depth to bedrock; depth to the water table; permeability; slope; content of sand, silt and clay; erodibility; load-bearing capacity; and runoff potential. Land use planning and development are facilitated by the use of soil surveys for such tasks as determining the most appropriate uses for land areas, locating and regulating floodplains, administering zoning ordinances and subdivision regulations, choosing suitable landscaping and identifying potential conservation problems and resources. Soil surveys also contain data that are useful to engineers and developers in site selection, route selection for roads and utility lines, and construction of all types of residential and nonresidential structures and facilities.

In conjunction with the soil survey, the Soil Conservation Service also prepares land capability survey maps, aimed at evaluating the suitability of land for agricultural use. Eight classifications are made, ranging from class 1 lands, which are flat or nearly flat and suitable for all types of agricultural use, to class 8, which should only be considered for watershed, recreation or wildlife habitat use. Classes 2, 3 and 4 can be cultivated to varying degrees if proper soil conservation measures are instituted. Classes 5, 6 and 7 are primarily suited to grazing or forestry.
See: SOIL CLASSIFICATION; SOIL MAP

Soil Type

A subgroup of a soil series based upon the surface layer texture of the soil. Adams sand is an example of a soil type within the Adams soil series.
See: SOIL CLASSIFICATION; SOIL MAP; SOIL SERIES; SOIL SURVEY

Solar Access

Availability of direct sunlight so that it is possible to use solar collectors and solar energy systems for a given project. Effective use of solar energy requires access to a threshold amount of energy for a specified number of hours per day, making the protection of solar access desirable for any community or individual wishing to support or use solar energy now or in the future.

Various levels of solar access may be protected, depending upon the type of solar energy use being encouraged. Rooftop protection is most suited to active solar systems (although some passive systems are possible) and is usually best in high-density areas, while south wall solar access is ideal for either active or passive systems. South lot protection is well suited to passive use and offers the opportunity of using greenhouses and solaria. Detached collector protection is primarily suited to active systems and is used when other systems are not practical. It is easiest to protect rooftop solar access and most difficult to protect access at ground level, because the lower locations are more vulnerable to shading.
See: ACTIVE SOLAR ENERGY SYSTEM; ENERGY CONSERVATION PLANNING; PASSIVE SOLAR ENERGY SYSTEM; SOLAR ACCESS DESIGN TECHNIQUES; SOLAR COLLECTOR; SOLAR EASEMENTS AND COVENANTS; SOLAR ENERGY

Solar Access Design Techniques

Techniques related to factors such as site selection, site design (including the orientation of streets and buildings) and landscaping that can improve solar access opportunities for a development.

An important consideration in solar access design is the probable use pattern at the site. A long heating or cooling season, for example, will influence energy use. Preliminary site analysis and planning should also include a careful evaluation of topography and other features of the site; potential obstructions to solar access, such as tall trees or other objects; and special features of the site that can influence energy conservation, such as prevailing wind direction or location of water bodies. In general, south-facing slopes have the shortest shadows and receive the most intense solar rays, making them optimal for solar access.

In laying out a development in which solar access is to be maximized, it is best for streets to be oriented in an east/west direction. This facilitates the siting of buildings with their longest dimensions oriented east/west, which exposes more wall and roof area to winter sunlight but still offers protection against summer sun. Even in warmer climates, this orientation is most appropriate, because it allows for maximum shading and protection from the afternoon sun. Any solar collector should, however, be oriented in a direction that is roughly southerly. Solar access can also be improved by zero lot-line development, in which buildings are sited abutting the north lot line to allow additional yard area south of the building that the owner may use to prevent restriction of his sunlight. Accessory structures and fences should also be placed where they will not block the building's southern exposure.

Useful landscaping principles to follow in maximizing solar access include an analysis of the mature height and canopy breadth of any proposed planting, locating the new trees beyond a roughly 50-degree arc located south of any proposed or existing solar collector, and locating only low plantings in close proximity to collectors.
See: SHADOW PATTERN; SKYSPACE; SOLAR ACCESS; SOLAR EASEMENTS AND COVENANTS; ZERO LOT-LINE DEVELOPMENT

Solar Cell

A device that can absorb solar energy and convert it directly into electricity. Also known as photovoltaic cells, the cells are usually made from silicon crystals and consist of two crystal layers with wires between them.

Each solar cell can produce only a small amount of electricity, often requiring that many cells be connected to produce a panel of solar cells. Photovoltaic panels are used as the prime power source for satellites, such as SKYLAB, and for the provision of power in remote areas where use of lower-cost energy alternatives is not possible. Currently, the chief obstacle to wider use of solar cells is their high cost; however, research is underway to develop cells that can deliver higher performance at an economically viable cost.
See: SOLAR ENERGY

Solar Collector

A device used to capture solar energy and convert it into heat, which is generally necessary for the operation of an active solar energy system. A variety of solar collectors are in use at this time.

The most prevalent and least expensive type is the flat-plate collector, which consists of a glass cover plate, an absorber plate made of a good heat-conducting material that is painted black and a series of tubes through which is pumped a fluid that absorbs heat. Concentrated collectors focus solar energy and reach higher temperatures than the flat-plate type. Evacuated-tube collectors use a vacuum to minimize heat loss and are very efficient and able to reach high temperatures. The type of collector selected will be a function of available sunshine, prevailing temperatures and the temperature required to make a system operate.

Solar collectors may be mounted on rooftops, on adjacent structures, on the ground or on the south wall of a structure. It is possible to mount collectors so that they are less visible by placing them behind parapets (if appropriate to the building's design) or by placing them out of the street-level sight line. Berms may be used to conceal ground-level or wall-mounted collectors. Alternatively, the collector may be stressed as an architectural component of the structure.

See: ACTIVE SOLAR ENERGY SYSTEM; DETACHED SOLAR COLLECTOR; ENERGY SHARING; SOLAR ACCESS; SOLAR ACCESS DESIGN TECHNIQUES; SOLAR ENERGY

Solar Easements and Covenants

Two types of private agreements that may be implemented between owners of property for the protection of solar access.

A solar covenant involves an undertaking by one person to refrain from activities that would restrict the use of solar collectors by another person. It might, for example, limit structures or vegetation that could cast shadows that extend a certain distance beyond the parcel's boundaries. Further specifications might also be included as to the times of day that these shadows would be restricted. Solar covenants may be mutual (each person covenanting in favor of the other), may apply to all parcels within a particular development and may be incorporated in documents (e.g., deeds) that are recorded in public land offices.

A solar easement is a negative easement restricting activities on the parcel burdened by the easement that can limit solar access to the parcel in whose favor the easement runs. A solar skyspace boundary is defined in order to protect solar access, and structures and vegetation are prohibited that can cast shadows upon any solar collector's skyspace. Existing property law generally permits the drafting of solar easements, but some states have laws specifying the precise requirements that solar access easements must meet.

See: EASEMENT; NEGATIVE EASEMENT; RESTRICTIVE COVENANT; SKYSPACE; SOLAR ACCESS; SOLAR ENERGY

Solar Energy

The electromagnetic radiation that the sun emits. This large source of energy reaching Earth is responsible for almost all other forms of fuel, as it underlies plant growth, wind, tides and other aspects of the environment. Among the advantages of the direct use of solar energy are its virtually inexhaustible supply and its abundance. The primary disadvantage is the cost of constructing facilities or architectural elements capable of most efficiently storing and using the sun's energy, as well as the lack of available solar energy at night and the diminished energy on cloudy days.

Solar energy may be harnessed directly for space heating, cooling, hot water or the production of electricity. It has been estimated that 88,000 residences in the United States were equipped with solar installations of some type as of 1978, and the number continues to grow. Solar energy may also be used in industrial processes. A food-processing plant in Oregon, for example, built 12,000 square feet (1,080 square meters) of solar collectors that track the sun and uses solar energy to generate steam.

See: ACTIVE SOLAR ENERGY SYSTEM; ANGLE OF INCIDENCE; DETACHED SOLAR COLLECTOR; ENERGY CONSERVATION PLANNING; ENERGY SHARING; PASSIVE SOLAR ENERGY SYSTEM; RENEWABLE ENERGY SOURCES; SHADOW PATTERN; SKYSPACE; SOLAR ACCESS; SOLAR ACCESS DESIGN TECHNIQUES; SOLAR COLLECTOR; SOLAR EASEMENTS AND COVENANTS; SOLAR POWER SATELLITE; SUN-TEMPERED BUILDING; SURFACE-TO-VOLUME RATIO; THERMAL MASS

Solar Energy and Energy Conservation Bank

A bank that provides subsidized loans and grants for energy conservation and solar energy improvements in residential and commercial buildings. Established in 1980 by Title V of the Energy Security Act, the bank is also authorized to establish a secondary market in these loans. Authorized through 1987, the bank has the same powers as those of the Government National Mortgage Association, and its board of directors is chaired by the secretary of housing and urban development. An Energy Conservation Advisory Committee and a Solar Energy Advisory Committee advise the bank on these respective functional areas.

Subsidies are made available via loans from local financial institutions that agree to provide below market level interest rates on a loan or to reduce the principal on the loan. These banks receive payment from the Energy Bank, with stipulations on maximum amounts that may be loaned. Loan amounts depend upon the income of the applicant and the type of structure to be improved, with lower-income individuals receiving greater subsidies. As an example, a person whose income is 80 percent of the area's median would receive 50 percent of conservation improvement costs, up to $1,250 for a single-family building or up to $3,500 for a building with four dwelling units. Persons with incomes ranging between 120 percent and 150 percent of the area's median, however, can only receive 20 percent of the costs. Larger multifamily and commercial buildings are eligible for 20 percent of conservation improvement costs up to established maximums. Subsidies for solar energy improvements are given at a higher percentage of costs, up to maximum established amounts.

A secondary market function enables the Energy Bank to repurchase the loans made in accordance with Title V of the Energy Security Act as well as mortgages secured by newly constructed one- to four-family homes having solar energy systems. This function permits local banks to make more money available for energy conservation and solar energy installations.

See: GOVERNMENT NATIONAL MORTGAGE ASSOCIATION (GNMA)

Solar Energy Research Institute (SERI)

A contractor-operated, government-owned laboratory, located in Golden, Colorado, that functions as a national center for federally sponsored research on solar energy and its development. SERI was established pursuant to the provisions of the Solar Energy Research, Development and Demonstration Act of 1974 and opened in 1977. Research is concentrated primarily in the areas of photovoltaics, wind energy, thermal energy, alcohol fuels, biomass energy, energy storage, and active and passive solar heating and cooling. SERI also manages the Solar Energy Information Data Bank, a nationwide network of technical organizations.

Solar Power Satellite

A proposed power system in which a satellite would orbit the Earth and use solar cells to generate electricity, which would be transmitted to Earth as a microwave beam. A central receiving station on Earth would receive this beam and convert it to usable energy. This system is expected to be extremely expensive to develop and is thought likely to be economically feasible in the future only if implemented on a very large scale.

See: RENEWABLE ENERGY SOURCES; SOLAR CELL; SOLAR ENERGY

Solid Waste

Nonliquid materials that have been discarded. *Solid waste* (synonymous with *refuse*) is a broad term that includes a number of subcategories. It may be classified by point of origin (such as agricultural waste, industrial waste, domestic waste or construction waste) or by the kind of waste involved (such as rubbish, ashes, garbage, special waste or abandoned automobiles).

See: DOMESTIC WASTE; GARBAGE; HAZARDOUS WASTE; INDUSTRIAL WASTE; LITTER; MUNICIPAL WASTE; SOLID WASTE GENERATION; SOLID WASTE MANAGEMENT

Solid Waste Disposal Act

Legislation that initiated federal funding of programs to improve solid waste disposal. The act (PL 89-272), passed in 1965, authorized grants of up to 50 percent to states

and interstate agencies for studies of solid waste disposal problems and development of solid waste disposal plans. Grants to public and private agencies and individuals for research, training, demonstration and facility construction were also authorized.

See: RESOURCE RECOVERY ACT OF 1970

Solid Waste Disposal Act Amendments of 1980

Federal legislation (PL 96-482) that reauthorizes provisions of the Resource Conservation and Recovery Act of 1976 (RCRA); transfers authority for coal mining wastes to the secretary of the interior, to be administered under authority of the Surface Mining and Reclamation Act of 1977; and establishes an Interagency Coordinating Committee on RCRA activities to coordinate programs of the Environmental Protection Agency (EPA), the Department of Energy, the Department of Commerce and other agencies. A National Advisory Commission on Resource Conservation and Recovery is also established in the executive branch for a limited time period, to report on the status of resource conservation and recovery programs and improvements that can be made.

Provisions of the act authorize funds for mandatory state inventories of dumps at which hazardous wastes have been stored and for the relocation of toxic dumps of up to 65 acres (26 hectares) in size located above aquifers. The act also gives EPA power for emergency cleanup of dumps that may present an imminent threat to health or the environment and authorizes criminal penalties consisting of fines or imprisonment for disposal of hazardous wastes in a blatantly negligent manner.

See: RESOURCE CONSERVATION AND RECOVERY ACT OF 1976 (RCRA)

Solid Waste Generation

Although not increasing as rapidly as it once did, the rate at which solid waste is generated still continues to rise. During the years 1970 to 1978, municipal waste loads increased at a rate of approximately 2 percent a year compared to an average annual increase of 5 percent in the decade 1960 to 1970. Average individual waste generation per person was 3.85 pounds (1.73 kilograms) per day in the United States in 1978.

The U.S. Environmental Protection Agency projects continued increases in municipal waste loads. Although total municipal waste in the United States was estimated at 154 million tons (140 million metric tons) for 1978, the projected figure for 1990 is 200 million tons (182 million metric tons). Industrial waste generation also continues to grow and totaled approximately 378 million tons (344 million metric tons) in 1977.

See: INDUSTRIAL WASTE; MUNICIPAL WASTE; SOLID WASTE MANAGEMENT; WASTE REDUCTION

Solid Waste Management

The systematic procedures by which solid waste is collected, processed and disposed of. Increasingly, the recycling of waste materials and the recovery of energy from the processing of waste are also being incorporated into waste management.

Collection of solid waste, generally a municipal responsibility, involves decisions concerning the frequency of pickup and the location from which waste will be collected (e.g., backyard, curbside). In addition, a municipality may require that newspapers or other recyclable materials be separated from other waste, necessitating multiple collection trips or collection equipment that has divided compartments to hold the various materials. Each decision concerning type and frequency of collection affects total disposal costs. A community may also choose to allow individual collection vehicles to transport the waste directly to the disposal site, or may have them bring the refuse to a transfer station where waste from a number of vehicles is combined for additional transporting in larger vehicles.

Although sanitary landfills are used by most communities for either disposal of solid waste or the residues remaining after other processes have been used, increased interest is developing in resource recovery systems, in which energy is recovered during the disposal process. Recycling of materials such as glass, aluminum or paper, is also becoming more common as is the use of processes that help to extend the useful life of sanitary landfills, such as shredding and baling.

One of the most significant roles the planner plays in solid waste management is in the selection of appropriate sites for facilities such as landfills, transfer stations and resource-recovery plants. Planners are also closely involved in the redevelopment and reuse of sanitary landfill sites when the landfills reach their capacity.

See: BALING; CODISPOSAL; COMPOSTING; DUMP; HAZARDOUS WASTE; INCINERATION; RECYCLING; REFUSE-DERIVED FUEL (RDF); RESOURCE RECOVERY; SANITARY LANDFILL; SHREDDING; SOLID WASTE; SOLID WASTE GENERATION; TRANSFER STATION; WASTE REDUCTION

Sonic Boom

A loud, explosive-sounding noise created by aircraft traveling at speeds in excess of the speed of sound (supersonic flight). The noise, heard on the ground, is caused by shock waves that are generated only at supersonic speeds. The shock waves are produced continuously during supersonic flight, and sonic booms may be audible at any time that the waves reach the ground rather than only when the aircraft first passes the speed of sound, as is commonly thought. Factors affecting the extent to which sonic booms may be heard include aircraft speed, altitude and route, which are all controllable, as well as meteorological conditions, air turbulence at ground level and topography.

Special Federal Aviation Administration noise regulations are in effect for supersonic aircraft to limit their potential noise impact. Since 1973, civilian aircraft that can fly at supersonic speeds have generally not been permitted to operate at speeds of more than Mach 1 (above which sonic booms may be generated) anywhere in the United States. Since 1978, planes arriving at or departing from an airport in the United States have been prohibited from doing so in a manner that would cause a sonic boom to reach the surface anywhere in the United States. The military has also established operating areas and procedures that govern military aircraft that can fly supersonically.

See: NOISE POLLUTION

Sound-Level Meter

An electronic instrument, designed for field use, that is employed to measure sound level. A sound-level meter is composed of a microphone, an amplifier and an output meter that is calibrated to read sound levels in decibels.

Sound-level meters also contain three or four scales or filters that are either A-,B-,C- or D-weighted. The A scale is the one most commonly used to measure neighborhood noise or noise in the work place, because it responds to sound much the way the human ear does. The other scales are used to measure sounds of very high or low frequencies.

See: A-WEIGHTED SOUND LEVEL; DECIBEL; NOISE POLLUTION

Source Separation

The separation of recyclable waste materials—such as paper, glass and metal—at their point of origin. Municipal collection programs may involve either collection at curbside by the municipality or operation of recycling centers to which the materials are brought.

One advantage of source separation is a decrease in the volume of solid waste requiring disposal, since recycling is facilitated. In addition, materials that are separated at their source are less contaminated and command higher prices. It is also relatively simple to institute a source-separation program, requiring only a modest capital investment for a storage facility for the separated wastes and possibly for specialized collection vehicles that are compartmentalized.

Source separation has been gaining steadily in popularity. By 1978, 40 municipalities had collection programs using the entire range of recyclable materials, while an additional 196 municipalities had newspaper collection programs. Many private companies also separate paper from the rest of their daily waste stream and market it.

Community cooperation is crucial to the success of source-separation programs, and very different results have been obtained in different communities. Municipal ordinances mandating separation are sometimes adopted as well, making source separation a regular component of the community's solid waste disposal system.

See: RECYCLING; RESOURCE RECOVERY; SOLID WASTE MANAGEMENT

***Southern Burlington County NAACP v. *Township of*
Mt. Laurel (67 N.J. 151, 336 A.2d 713 [1975])**

A decision by the New Jersey Supreme Court holding
that a developing municipality had a duty to provide opportunities through its land use regulations for the construction of low- and moderate-income housing. The court
held that the municipality's obligation extends at least to
its "fair share" of the present and prospective regional
need for such housing.

In 1983 the New Jersey Supreme Court reexamined the
issues raised by its *Mt. Laurel* decision. In a case bearing
the same name (92 N.J. 158, 456 A.2d 390 [1983]), the
court reaffirmed its prior decision and attempted to establish interpretative guidelines and administrative machinery to facilitate the implementation of its *Mt. Laurel* decision by lower courts.

See: EXCLUSIONARY ZONING; FAIR SHARE

Special District

A unit of metropolitan government, sometimes called
an authority, established to perform one or more specialized functions. Special districts are commonly formed to
provide water, sewer or transportation facilities and parks,
to facilitate fire protection or to provide soil and water
conservation services and may comprise a small area of
a municipality or cross municipal or state boundaries.
School districts are often considered to be special districts
but are thought of as units of local government by political
scientists.

The special district, created by state law and generally
subject to referendum, often has a small governing board
with its own taxing and borrowing powers and may also
have the power of eminent domain. Special districts are
formed to enable the construction and financing of a facility over an area with many political subdivisions and to
evade constitutional taxation and borrowing restrictions
on local units of government. They also serve to equalize a
tax burden over a wide area and to remove a particular
problem from local political control.

See: DEBT LIMIT; PORT AUTHORITY; SCHOOL DIS-
TRICT

Special-Use Permit

A permit granted by the appropriate municipal body,
often the zoning board of appeals, for a land use identified
in the zoning ordinance as requiring this permit. Traditionally, special-permit uses are those that have strong
potential to conflict with surrounding uses if not appropriately sited within a given zoning district; thus, such uses
are subjected to a thorough review procedure and must
meet certain conditions. Among the types of land uses
frequently identified as requiring a special permit are hospitals, gasoline stations and funeral homes.

A land use requiring a special permit in a particular
zoning district must follow a specific application and re-

view procedure set forth in the zoning ordinance. The
reviewing body will then determine whether the applicant
can meet designated zoning ordinance conditions for a
special-permit use and will set any additional conditions it
believes to be reasonable and necessary for the protection
of the neighborhood. Only when all conditions are or can
be met will the permit be granted.

Although special permits are sometimes thought to be a
type of variance, this is not the case. A special-permit use
is specifically identified as being permissible in a given
zone, providing it can meet specified standards and conditions. A variance, on the other hand, is an exception to the
zoning ordinance that is granted to relieve a specific hardship created by the application of the ordinance.

Special-use permits are referred to by a wide variety
of names, including conditional-use permits and special-
exception permits; the land use involved may be known as
a conditional use, a special use or a special-exception use.
See: ZONING; ZONING BOARD OF APPEALS; ZONING
VARIANCE

Special Zoning District

A zoning district that is created to meet the needs of an
area experiencing special problems or that is designed to
accommodate special needs. Special districts are formed
to minimize certain types of land use conflicts, to protect
sensitive areas and to contain offensive land uses.

In contrast to a standard commercial or industrial zoning district, which might be mapped in a number of locations in a municipality, a special district is much narrower
in terms of purpose and is customized to respond to a
particular problem. Examples of special districts are a university zone aimed at easing the impact of a large educational institution upon the surrounding community and a
historic district designed to protect historically and architecturally significant structures. Other types of special districts include adult entertainment zones, which regulate
sex-related businesses; hotel/motel districts; and hospital
districts.

An unlimited number of special zoning districts may be
created, and many larger cities list a wide range of these
districts in their municipal ordinances. When creating a
special district, however, a municipality must clearly state
the purpose of the district, and this purpose should be an
appropriate area of police power concern.
See: ADULT ENTERTAINMENT ZONE; AIRPORT ZON-
ING; HISTORIC DISTRICT; SPECIAL DISTRICT; ZON-
ING; ZONING DISTRICT

Specification Standards

A type of standards in which precise requirements are
specifically enumerated concerning permitted types of development, the standards the development must meet or
the methods of construction that must be adhered to. For
example, as applied to an industrial district, a specification
standard approach would list permitted and prohibited

types of industrial use. By contrast, a performance standard approach applied to this district would define the conditions that an industrial use would have to meet in order to be permitted. A proposed industrial use would, for example, be limited as to the amount of noise, smoke, vibration, etc., it could emit, but should it be able to meet those standards, it would be permitted in the district.

Specification standards are more confining than performance standards and are sometimes overly restrictive, in that they can prohibit uses that would be able to meet performance standards. However, they are more commonly used because of the ease with which they can be administered.
See: PERFORMANCE STANDARDS

Spoil

1.   The waste materials produced as a result of mining activities. The spoil that results from strip mining has been altered both chemically and physically by the mining activity, often making it difficult to establish new vegetative cover. Consisting primarily of rock fragments with small amounts of soil, the spoil may be devoid of nutrients essential for plant growth, have a high acidity content or have toxic concentrations of such elements as manganese.

New procedures in which land reclamation is conducted simultaneously with the surface mining process can help to minimize the problems associated with spoil.

2.   Materials that have been dredged from water bodies. Dredging that is related to activities such as channel and harbor maintenance and underwater mining produces a sizable volume of spoil, which must be disposed of properly. Traditionally, substantial proportions of dredged spoil were dumped directly into the water or used to fill wetlands. Changing federal and state regulations on wetlands and concern about the estuarine environment have stimulated a search for sounder means of spoil disposal.

Spoil can be disposed of with fewer adverse effects if it is placed in deep ocean waters rather than in estuarine waters. Land disposal of spoil is increasingly encouraged when appropriate sites, such as existing spoil banks where wetlands have already been filled, are available. Pipeline transport of spoil to inland locations is also being explored. It is estimated that approximately one-third of all dredged spoil is polluted by sewage sludge, petrochemicals or other contaminants, and these polluted spoils require special handling and treatment.
See: DREDGING; OCEAN DUMPING; STRIP MINING; SURFACE MINING CONTROL AND RECLAMATION ACT OF 1977

Sponsor

1.   Housing terminology that describes a nonprofit organization that initiates the development of a low- or moderate-income housing project. Community groups, religious organizations and public housing agencies are typical sponsors.

To stimulate the production of multifamily housing by sponsors, the Department of Housing and Urban Development offers free advice and technical assistance. An interest-free loan program for Section 202 housing for the elderly and handicapped is also available to private nonprofit sponsors. The loans, which are made from a revolving loan fund, can be used to cover 80 percent of the costs of preliminary development, including site acquisition, market analyses, architectural and engineering fees, and application and loan commitment fees.

2.   An individual or organization that financially supports or otherwise lends its influence to a community activity or public project.
See: SECTION 202 HOUSING PROGRAM

Spot Zoning

The assignment of a zoning classification different from the surrounding zoning classifications to a relatively small land parcel. The term is usually employed when the use classification is intended to benefit a particular property owner and is incompatible with the surrounding area. When this occurs, and the zoning is also in violation of the community's comprehensive plan, the zoning action may be subject to invalidation by reason of its not being in furtherance of the general welfare and therefore beyond the proper scope of the police power.

There are circumstances in which spot zoning may be applied appropriately. Many of the new flexible zoning techniques (such as floating zones) or special zoning districts (such as historic districts) are in a sense spot zones, in that they are applied to a small, selectively picked area. The courts are likely to support these techniques, however, when they are clearly in accordance with the municipal comprehensive plan and are helping to achieve a public benefit. This, rather than the size of the area being zoned, differentiates legal from illegal spot zoning.
See: FLEXIBLE REGULATIONS; *ROGERS* v. *VILLAGE OF TARRYTOWN;* SPECIAL ZONING DISTRICT

Sprawl

The uncontrolled growth of urban development into previously rural areas. Sprawl usually refers to a mixture of land uses occurring in an unplanned pattern; it is generally identified with the outward suburban growth of cities that occurred after World War II. The popularity of the single-family, suburban subdivision and the greater use of automobiles on improved roadway systems were key contributors to this form of development. Other factors related to urban sprawl included the extension of municipal utilities (i.e., sewer and water systems); changes in industrial building design favoring one-story structures near highways over older inner city multistory buildings; and government programs, such as Federal Housing Administration and Veterans Administration mortgages, that supported suburban growth.

Urban sprawl has been strongly criticized as an unattractive and inefficient use of land and resources, causing excessive infrastructure costs related to extending utilities to remote areas. It has also been accused of eliminating environmentally important open space while leapfrogging developable parcels. Suburban jurisdictions were often administratively unprepared for growth pressures and have suffered costly long-term effects of poor growth control, such as undersized utility systems that now need replacement. Sprawl has also been accused of debilitating central cities by helping outlying developments, such as shopping centers, compete with downtowns for the same market.

Zoning and subdivision regulations are most frequently used to prevent or control sprawl, but capital programming and environmental regulations also tend to limit sprawling development patterns. The greenbelt concept, in which a greenbelt encircles a city and helps to prevent sprawl, has been utilized in Britain, while planned developments and, on a larger scale, new towns are considered alternatives to sprawl.

See: GROWTH MANAGEMENT; LAND USE PATTERN; LEAPFROG DEVELOPMENT; STRIP DEVELOPMENT; SUBURBAN GROWTH; URBANIZATION

Squatter Settlements

Groups of shelters erected by persons who are illegally occupying public or private land. Squatter settlements are often characterized by makeshift dwellings without plumbing or water supply that are constructed in violation of building and development codes. They are a common form of housing in developing countries and in frontier areas, such as the Yukon Territory of Canada, and are also found in many inner city areas.

Conditions in a squatter settlement are generally slumlike, unhygienic and a fire hazard. Yet in some cities—such as Maracaibo, Venezuela and Ankara, Turkey—almost half of the population consists of squatters. Countries that have such large volumes of squatters usually are unable to provide housing for this population through conventional methods, such as in government-constructed or subsidized housing, and do not have programs by which squatters may be dispersed to other areas.

Squatter settlements are usually a haphazard arrangement of buildings, but some are planned, to an extent, with uniform lot sizes. Commercial enterprises also operate within squatter settlements without legal rights to the property. Where settlements are of a permanent nature, homes are sold and rented without deeds or contracts.

Squatters in some older cities also settle in abandoned buildings, which they may attempt to partially rehabilitate to make them habitable.

See: ADVERSE POSSESSION; HOUSING

Stack

A vertical structure—such as a chimney, duct or flue—intended to permit the gaseous products resulting from combustion to disperse into the atmosphere. Stacks may vary greatly in size, from the fireplace chimneys of residences to electric utility stacks that may be in excess of 800 feet (244 meters) in height. Stacks are designed to allow pollutants to reach a sufficient height before they are released to enable them to be diluted to an acceptable level and dispersed in the atmosphere in order to reduce ground-level concentrations.

Although the use of tall smokestacks can help to improve ambient air quality levels on a local basis, they are also thought responsible for the long-range transport of air pollution to other regions and for exacerbating the problem of acid rain. As a result, the U.S. Environmental Protection Agency (EPA) is permitted to disapprove a state implementation plan if sources in that state are going to help lead to national ambient air quality standard violations elsewhere. EPA was also directed by the Clean Air Act Amendments of 1977 to propose regulations that would specify what "good engineering practice" is with regard to stack height.

See: ACID RAIN; AIR POLLUTION; PLUME

Stadium Facilities

Structures that provide seating from which sports events can be viewed as well as necessary support facilities. Stadiums may enclose the field on which the sport is played, as in professional baseball and football stadiums, or be located adjacent to the field, as at a racetrack. Stadiums may also be enclosed for year-round use.

Stadium sizes are determined on the basis of either estimated attendance at sporting events of the team to be accommodated or the typical attendance found at other similar types of facilities. A large range of sizes and types may be found. Small facilities, such as a high school football stadium for 400 people, may consist only of bleachers surrounded by a permanent wall. In contrast, a major regional facility, such as the Giants Stadium in the New Jersey Meadowlands, accommodates almost 77,000 people, while the Meadowlands Racetrack has a capacity of 41,000. Parking for 24,000 cars and 400 buses is also provided for the Meadowlands complex.

In recent years many jurisdictions have considered the construction of a major stadium as a stimulus for economic development, as an inducement for other recreational and tourism development, as a means of generating employment opportunities or as a way to retain or gain a major sports team. Some have been successful in gaining revenue and/or other secondary economic benefits, but others have found that the huge costs create debt rather than income.

In evaluating the stadium's likelihood for success in generating a profit, there are several factors related to projected attendance that must be considered. The nature of the game to be played, the specific team in residence and factors related to attendance at such a game, such as how far people are willing to travel, must be clearly set forth. Competition from other stadiums within a reasonable distance of the proposed facility is a crucial element, while the effect of local weather conditions might also be a determining factor. Other serious considerations are operating costs and income based on projected charges and on

other events that might be attracted to the facility. The accessibility of the site to roads, parking and mass transit as well as the availability and cost of necessary utilities must also be assessed.
See: ECONOMIC DEVELOPMENT

Staff Functions

Functions that assist other persons or departments within an organization in delivering goods or services. Because staff functions are generally those in which planning, analysis, budgeting and other assistance and advice are given, planning departments are usually categorized as staff agencies.
See: LINE FUNCTIONS

Staggered Work Hours

The adoption of work schedules by business and government that allow employees of various firms or departments to arrive and leave work at different hours, to reduce rush hour traffic congestion. All employees within a firm or department work on the same schedule—e.g., 8:00 to 4:00. The alteration in arrival and departure hours by numerous firms serves to lessen the peaking effect and tends to extend the peak period in duration but holds volume to a more efficient and manageable level. The federal government has been using staggered hours in its Washington, D.C. offices since the 1940s.
See: FLEX-TIME; TRANSPORTATION SYSTEM MANAGEMENT (TSM)

Standard City Planning Enabling Act

A model enabling act issued by the U.S. Department of Commerce in 1928. Secretary of Commerce Herbert Hoover appointed a number of well-known planners of the time—including Edward M. Bassett, Alfred Bettman and Frederick Law Olmsted Jr.—to the committee that drafted the act.

The model act, which was widely copied and adopted, stressed the importance of a city planning commission and of a comprehensive plan. It also recommended that the zoning commission powers be transferred to the planning commission and that the planning commission, rather than the legislative body, be in charge of any planning department staff. The effects of these and other recommendations upon current planning practice are still readily visible.

Despite its wide appeal to states considering the adoption of planning enabling legislation, there were many flaws in the model act. For example, it suggested that the content of a comprehensive plan should be concerned with streets, other public grounds, public buildings, public utilities and zoning. The only mention of the fact that there are many other topics a comprehensive plan might consider appears in a footnote. It also included a statement that many states interpreted as support for publication and

adoption of portions of a plan independent of each other, thus seeming to encourage piecemeal planning.
See: BETTMAN, ALFRED; ENABLING ACT; OLMSTED, FREDERICK LAW; STANDARD STATE ZONING ENABLING ACT

Standard Consolidated Statistical Area (SCSA)

Two or more Standard Metropolitan Statistical Areas (SMSAs) that meet established criteria of urban character, social and economic integration, and contiguity of urbanized areas. In addition, at least one of the SMSAs must have a population of 1,000,000 or more. The Census Bureau has established 17 SCSAs for data reporting purposes, including New York-Newark-Jersey City, Miami-Fort Lauderdale and Seattle-Tacoma.

After 1982 this term will no longer be used for census reporting purposes but will be replaced by the Consolidated Metropolitan Statistical Area (CMSA), where appropriate.
See: CENSUS; METROPOLITAN STATISTICAL AREA (MSA); STANDARD METROPOLITAN STATISTICAL AREA (SMSA); URBANIZED AREA (UA)

Standard Deviation

A commonly used measure of the dispersion of a distribution; it is often represented by the lowercase letter sigma (σ), although s or SD may also be used. It is calculated by subtracting each value in a distribution from the mean for the distribution and then squaring each of the resulting numbers to eliminate plus or minus signs. The arithmetic mean of these squared values is obtained and the square root of this mean calculated to arrive at the standard deviation.

Standard deviation is considered a useful measure because it allows a comparison between different distributions and also allows a particular value within a distribution to be analyzed in the context of the distribution. In addition, the standard deviation has various applications in inferential statistics. The standard deviation of a distribution is equivalent to the square root of the variance.
See: INFERENTIAL STATISTICS; MEASURES OF DISPERSION; VARIANCE

Standard Industrial Classification (SIC) System

A code developed for the Office of Management and Budget that classifies all types of activities and commerce, with an emphasis upon industrial uses, and assigns to each a specific code number. The SIC is intended to standardize data collection by federal agencies, particularly with respect to economic and industrial data, and is also used by many state and local governments and independent research organizations.

Ten major categories are used in this system to describe agriculture and forestry; mining and construction; manufacturing; transportation, warehousing, communications and utilities; wholesale and retail trade; finance, insurance and real estate; service-related enterprises, including education and the arts; and government. Each major category is assigned a one-digit number, with two one-digit numbers reserved for manufacturing and the service sector. The categories are then further divided into two-, three- and four-digit classifications, with each additional digit adding detail to the classification. Agencies select the degree of detail they require by choosing the number of digits they will use.

Many types of land use classification systems are modeled upon the SIC approach.
See: LAND USE CLASSIFICATION SYSTEM

Standard Metropolitan Statistical Area (SMSA)

A large population nucleus and adjacent counties having a high degree of economic and social integration with that nucleus, as represented by population size, commuting ties and metropolitan character. Data were tabulated for SMSAs by the Bureau of the Census, which defines an SMSA as either: (1) a city with a population of at least 50,000 within its corporate limits or (2) an urbanized area, as defined by the Census Bureau, with a population of at least 50,000 and a total SMSA population of at least 100,000. In addition, entire counties (or towns in New England) are included as part of the SMSA even though only portions of them may be within the urbanized area.

SMSAs have one or more central cities, up to a maximum of three, except for the Nassau-Suffolk, New York SMSA, which has no central city; SMSAs often cross state lines as well. In the 1980 Census extensive data were tabulated for 323 SMSAs. Since SMSAs include entire counties, historical comparability is possible, but the census user must determine which counties were included, since they change from census to census. In 1983, the SMSA was replaced by the *Metropolitan Statistical Area* (MSA) for census data reporting.

The Census of Canada uses the designation *Census Metropolitan Area* (CMA) to describe a similar area. A CMA is the main labor market of a continuous built-up area having a population of 100,000 or more, while a Census Agglomeration (CA) has a population ranging between 10,000 and 99,999. In 1981 there were 24 CMAs and 88 CAs.
See: CENSUS; CENSUS HISTORICAL COMPARABILITY; METROPOLITAN AREA; METROPOLITAN STATISTICAL AREA (MSA); STANDARD CONSOLIDATED STATISTICAL AREA (SCSA); URBANIZED AREA (UA)

Standard State Zoning Enabling Act

A model act issued by the U.S. Department of Commerce in 1922 that had a substantial influence upon state enabling legislation concerning zoning. The act was prepared by a committee appointed by Herbert Hoover, then secretary of commerce. The committee chairman was Edward M. Bassett.

The model act promulgated the concept of zoning that "shall be in accordance with a comprehensive plan" but did not specifically define the nature or content of a comprehensive plan. Although it led to confusion for many years regarding the proper relationship between zoning and comprehensive planning, the act helped significantly to further the concept of municipal zoning within a framework of proper state authorization.
See: ENABLING ACT; IN ACCORDANCE WITH A COMPREHENSIVE PLAN; STANDARD CITY PLANNING ENABLING ACT

Standards

1. Rules or measurements establishing a minimum level of quality or quantity that should or must be complied with or satisfied. Standards are used for a wide array of purposes in planning, ranging from the way in which facilities should be built to the amount of pollution a particular facility may emit.

2. In a zoning ordinance, standards usually apply to the physical design requirements, such as required setback and height, rather than the type of permitted uses.
See: DESIGN STANDARDS; LAND USE INTENSITY STANDARDS (LUI); PERFORMANCE STANDARDS; SPECIFICATION STANDARDS

State Arts Agencies

Agencies at the state level that dispense state funds and some federal funds for creative and performing arts projects. They are administered by a commission of citizens active in the arts who make decisions concerning grant applications and by a director who oversees the activities of sections of the agency responsible for specific arts categories, such as music, literature and visual arts. In some Canadian provinces similar activities are undertaken by the Ministries of Culture.

In issuing grants state agencies tend to allocate funds to areas on a per capita basis, while still attempting to emphasize arts programs for which there are more qualified applicants. Grants are made on the basis of an evaluation of the merits of an application, funding availability and, usually, a requirement that the applicant be able to provide some proportion of the funding necessary for the project on a matching basis. Grants may also be made to operate community arts councils or to supply funds that such arts councils can allocate locally.
See: COMMUNITY ARTS COUNCILS; NATIONAL FOUNDATION ON THE ARTS AND THE HUMANITIES

State Historic Preservation Officer (SHPO)

The state official appointed by the governor to direct that state's historic preservation program in accordance with the National Historic Preservation Act. Among the responsibilities of an SHPO are: the administration of federal assistance programs for historic preservation within the state, the comprehensive statewide historic inventory, the state's National Register of Historic Places activities,

and development and implementation of a state preservation plan. The SHPO is also charged with assisting and cooperating with other levels of government in a variety of preservation-related activities. A state historic preservation officer is often head of the state historical commission or holds some other post such as director of the state's parks and recreation or natural resources department.
See: HISTORIC PRESERVATION; NATIONAL HISTORIC PRESERVATION ACT OF 1966; NATIONAL REGISTER OF HISTORIC PLACES

State Housing Finance Agencies

Quasi-public agencies created by individual states to assist in providing housing for low- and moderate-income persons. In 1982, 46 states had state housing finance agencies (SHFAs).

SHFAs raise money for housing by issuing bonds, which are usually exempt from federal and state income taxes. These funds are then used to provide mortgage loans at lower rates than are available from conventional financing sources. They have been a source of mortgage financing for both single-family and multifamily housing, and many Section 8 rental apartment developments were built with SHFA financing. SHFAs also provide seed money for nonprofit developers or act as developers themselves. Some SHFAs act as a secondary mortgage market, purchasing mortgages from lenders or making loans to lenders, while a few SHFAs have their own mortgage insurance programs.
See: HOUSING

State Implementation Plan (SIP)

A plan required by the Clean Air Amendments of 1970 in which each state must describe the measures that it will take to meet, maintain and enforce national ambient air quality standards (NAAQS) for each air quality control region partially or totally within its boundaries.

In order to comply with the requirements of the U.S. Environmental Protection Agency (EPA), a plan must provide for the attainment of each primary standard as expeditiously as practicable and, where secondary standards are applicable, for the attainment of the secondary standard within a reasonable time frame. A plan must also include emission limitation and compliance schedules, as well as other such control measures necessary to attaining NAAQS.

Although states are free to develop the most appropriate control measures for their circumstances, acceptable measures include economic incentives, such as taxes; an indirect-source review program; staggered work hours; and various land use controls. A wide range of transportation controls may also be invoked, including gasoline rationing, tolls, parking restrictions, preferential bus or ridepool lanes, motor vehicle inspection and general improvement of the transportation system.

Plans must be amended periodically to comply with ad-

ditional or modified NAAQS, to rectify deficiencies EPA finds and to reflect new ideas or technology.
See: AIR POLLUTION; AIR QUALITY CONTROL REGION (AQCR); CLEAN AIR AMENDMENTS OF 1970; EMISSION STANDARD; INDIRECT SOURCE; NATIONAL AMBIENT AIR QUALITY STANDARDS (NAAQS)

State of Washington ex. rel. Seattle Title Trust Company v. *Roberge, Superintendent of Building of City of Seattle* (278 U.S. 116 [1928])

A decision by the United States Supreme Court invalidating a municipal ordinance that would have permitted a philanthropic home for children or the elderly to be established in a residential district only upon approval by the owners of two-thirds of the land within 400 feet of the proposed use.

The Court found the ordinance to constitute an impermissible delegation of the municipality's authority to other property owners, since these property owners could arbitrarily prevent the use of land for the philanthropic purpose and were not required to act in accordance with any standard established by the municipality.
See: JAMES v. VALTIERRA

State Park

A park, preserve, forest, beach or other natural area, or a significant historic or archeological site that is purchased and/or managed by a state government. State parks vary in type from small historic buildings on their surrounding land to vast wilderness areas or fully developed beach areas spanning miles of coastline.

In general, states attempt to preserve areas of scenic, economic, ecological or historic importance and to provide recreation opportunities at sites that can accommodate large numbers of people. In addition, they usually attempt to provide recreation facilities in the larger parks that are consistent with their natural environments and that complement facilities provided in local areas. Typical activities are hiking, fishing, camping and picnicking. A recent extension of the state park concept is that of the Adirondack Forest Preserve in New York, in which the state owns part of the preserve but has established control over development in the area that it does not own, thereby protecting the ecological and economic value of the entire area.
See: NATIONAL PARK; OPEN-SPACE PRESERVATION; PRIMITIVE RECREATION AREA; REGIONAL PARK

State Planning

Planning programs conducted by state planning agencies. States generally engage in planning for the development of state facilities, statewide coordination of federal programs and regulation of one or more land use issues on a statewide basis. In addition, other means by which states plan may include selection of locations within which the state will have development oversight; state directives guiding municipal, regional or county planning; or development of state land use policy, to which municipalities are directed to conform.

State facilities typically include roads, parks, courthouses, penitentiaries, mental hospitals and colleges, and planners normally engage in planning activities related to them. Where federal funding must pass through the state for allocation by the state or review of plans by the governor, as occurs in senior citizen or job training programs, or when a state plan is required, such as for water quality management, state planning agencies (or planners in other departments) undertake or review plans and proposals. In addition, statewide programs controlling various aspects of pollution or environmental assessment of proposed projects, in which a planning component is involved, are prevalent.

More direct control of land use, however, is obtained when the state owns sizable properties that it will use for conservation or development. State parks and forests, which are publicly owned, are managed for recreation and natural resource production. The extension of this approach, used in the Adirondack State Park in New York, involves control of development and natural resource production in a defined area outside of the park that is in private ownership. Another approach, taken by Arizona, was to place 575,000 acres (232,700 hectares) of state-owned land on the market for sale or lease but to permit only development conforming to state policy for specific areas. Plans for this land are proposed by developers and are accepted subject to state and local government review. A third approach, used in California, is the establishment of a defined area within which the state will have development oversight. This has been used to protect environmentally sensitive areas and farmland. In Canada land banking has been used by the provincial governments of Saskatchewan and Alberta to control growth and to stabilize land prices around the cities of Saskatoon, Red Deer and Edmonton.

Directives that municipalities adopt comprehensive plans have been adopted in the United States by such states as Florida, California and Oregon, as well as by several Canadian provinces, including New Brunswick and Ontario. In Oregon, for example, the directives require that the municipal plans adhere to state development goals that have the force of law and that cities and counties jointly establish urban growth boundaries (UGB). All agricultural land outside UGBs that is not specifically designated for nonfarm uses must be zoned for exclusive farm use (EFU). In Florida municipal regulations must agree with municipal master plans, and if municipalities or the counties they are in do not promulgate plans, the state may do it for them. In Florida, however, once municipal plans are adopted, all development—public, private and state—must conform with the plans. In the Canadian provinces municipal comprehensive plans must conform with comprehensive plans adopted by regional planning bodies,

and in many cases, municipal bylaws must conform with municipal and regional plans.

A few states, such as Oregon and Vermont, have enacted state land use policies to act as a guide for municipal comprehensive planning and/or as a means of directing state investment in capital infrastructure. Hawaii, however, has the most comprehensive state system. There the State Land Use Commission has apportioned the state's land area into four types of zoning districts: urban, agricultural, rural and conservation. In urban districts the counties may institute their own land use regulations that further define permitted land use, and development is under the control of both the county and the state. The State Land Use Commission controls all development in agricultural and rural zones, while the State Department of Land and Natural Resources is responsible for land use control in conservation districts. State planning in Hawaii was initiated in 1961 and has been a model for state planning initiatives in a number of other states.

See: NATIONAL LAND USE POLICY; REGIONAL PLANNING

State Water Quality Management Plan (Section 303 [e])

A water quality improvement plan required by Section 303 (e) of the Clean Water Act. The act requires states to undertake a continuous planning process (CPP) that will result in the implementation of effluent limitations and compliance schedules to achieve state water quality standards in all intrastate waters. Planning for interstate waters, which is not specified in the act, is traditionally undertaken by all the states that border the waterway. In these cases, each state may plan for its part of the waterway, or the plans may be coordinated.

The plan must identify waters (called water quality limited segments) where established limitations are not stringent enough to meet the state standards, and the state must establish and allocate total maximum daily pollution loads for these waters. This loading must include thermal levels and take seasonal variation into account. The plan must also incorporate river basin plans and areawide waste treatment management plans, and list and prioritize needed waste treatment projects.

See: AREAWIDE WASTE TREATMENT MANAGEMENT PLANNING (SECTION 208); CLEAN WATER ACT OF 1977; WATER QUALITY STANDARDS

Statement of Intent

1. A description of the purposes and objectives of a zoning ordinance or of a particular type of district within a zoning ordinance. A statement of intent helps illustrate the relationship of the zoning ordinance to the comprehensive plan and highlights what the municipality wishes to accomplish through the ordinance. A statement preceding a particular district helps to clarify the intention of the legislative body in adopting that district and serves as an interpretive aid.

Legal challenges concerning particular zoning districts often result in close scrutiny by the court of the statement of intent so that the court may construe the intended purpose of the zoning ordinance and determine if a proper public purpose is involved.

2.   A description of the purposes and objectives of any type of legislation or study that is placed at its beginning and helps the reader to understand its context.
See: ZONING

Statewide Comprehensive Outdoor Recreation Plan (SCORP)

A plan required of each state, every five years, to qualify for funding under the Land and Water Conservation Act of 1967. The plan generally includes a description of factors influencing outdoor recreation, such as climate, location, topography and extent of population and urbanization; a list of federal and state agencies that are and will be responsible for administering and funding parks and recreation areas; and an inventory of existing publicly and privately owned recreation areas. Also required is an estimate of usership for various common outdoor recreation activities in the state; a statement of recreation needs of the state and local governments; a statement of recreation needs of special populations—e.g., the handicapped; and a description of proposed activities for the next five-year planning period, such as land acquisition and park development, which will provide more outdoor recreational opportunities. Emphasis is placed on preservation of areas of environmental significance, such as scenic rivers and forests, which provide multiuse opportunities for recreation. This program is administered by the National Park Service.
See: OPEN-SPACE PLANNING; OPEN-SPACE PRESERVATION; OUTDOOR RECREATION; RECREATION FACILITIES; RECREATION PLANNING; RECREATION SYSTEM

Stationary Source

A producer of air pollution that remains in a fixed position—such as a power plant, an incinerator or an industrial plant—as compared to mobile sources, such as automobiles.
See: AIR POLLUTION; AIR POLLUTION CONTROL; MOBILE SOURCE; NONATTAINMENT AREA; POINT SOURCE

Steady-State Sound

A sound with a noise level that remains relatively constant over time. A sound is considered to be a steady-state sound when the fluctuation, as measured on a sound-level meter, is less than 6 decibels. The sound coming from an air-conditioning unit is an example of a steady-state sound.
See: IMPACT SOUND; NOISE POLLUTION

Stein, Clarence S. (1882–1975)

An American architect and town planner who designed many classic communities in the United States and whose works have had a significant worldwide impact. Although trained as an architect, Stein became increasingly interested in the planning of communities and the provision of housing for the working class. Influenced by the projects and writings of Ebenezer Howard, Patrick Geddes, Raymond Unwin and Frederick Law Olmsted, Stein designed the first American versions of the garden city.

His designs are characterized by superblocks in which large areas of common open space are preserved in the center, the use of footpaths and overpasses to separate pedestrian from vehicular traffic and the siting of homes on traffic-free culs-de-sac. Among the projects he designed with Henry C. Wright were Sunnyside Gardens in New York City in 1926; Radburn, New Jersey in 1928; and Chatham Village in Pittsburgh. In addition, he acted as consultant during the planning of Greenbelt, Maryland; Greendale, Wisconsin; Greenhills, Ohio and Baldwin Hills Village in Los Angeles and was chief consultant in 1951 for the development of the Canadian new town of Kitimat.

Stein was also active in other aspects of planning. He chaired the New York State Commission of Housing and Regional Planning, which issued the nation's first state planning report, and helped to found the Regional Planning Association of America in 1923. He was awarded the gold medal of the American Institute of Architects in 1956, the distinguished service award of the American Institute of Planners in 1958 and the Ebenezer Howard Memorial Medal in 1960. *Toward New Towns for America*, in which Stein discussed many of his projects, was published in 1950.
See: GEDDES, SIR PATRICK; GREENBELT TOWNS; HOWARD, SIR EBENEZER; KITIMAT, BRITISH COLUMBIA; NEW YORK STATE COMMISSION OF HOUSING AND REGIONAL PLANNING; OLMSTED, FREDERICK LAW; RADBURN, NEW JERSEY; UNWIN, SIR RAYMOND

Stereo Viewing of Aerial Photographs

The technique of viewing aerial photographs so that they appear to have a third dimension, allowing contours and terrain to be visualized. To achieve this effect, it is necessary to have a pair of overlapping aerial photos with the same image appearing on each photo; the two photos are known as a stereopair or stereoscopic pair.

They should be lined up so that a particular image on each photo is superimposed. The photographs are then separated until the images are about 2.25 inches (5.7 centimeters) apart. A stereoscope, an instrument with two magnifying lenses mounted in a frame on a stand, is then placed above the photographs, which are aligned in the direction of flight, with shadows oriented toward the viewer. With minor adjustment of the stereoscope and the photographs, it is possible to view the images in three dimensions.
See: AERIAL PHOTO INTERPRETATION; AERIAL PHOTOGRAPHY

Stewardship

1. The care of land to preserve its natural amenities. Land is often donated to organizations such as The Nature Conservancy for this purpose, but one may be the steward of one's own land.

2. The preservation of open space through the efforts of property owners without expenditure of government funds for acquisition. Such a program was first recommended in 1965 by the Open Space Action Committee for the New York metropolitan area in an attempt to protect valuable open-space areas from growing development pressures. A stewardship program may be accomplished in one of several ways to ensure continued open-space use of the land. Donation of all or part of the land to a park authority or conservation organization is one popular method, while donation of a scenic or conservation easement allows the owner continued use and removes pressures for development. Creation of deed restrictions on types of development, tree cutting or mining is a third way that the current land use can be perpetuated. For a land owner who wants to sell land for development, he may select a buyer who will design a cluster development that preserves part of the land.
See: CHARITABLE CONTRIBUTION OF REAL ESTATE; CLUSTER DEVELOPMENT; CONSERVATION EASEMENT; LAND ENDOWMENT; NATURE CONSERVANCY; SCENIC EASEMENT

Storm Drainage System

A system designed to channel and accommodate stormwater during periods of precipitation. Drainage systems serve to minimize flood damage, prevent stormwaters from undermining the foundations of all types of structures, stabilize slopes and protect against mudslides.

In areas of very low density development, natural surface drainage may be adequate to channel stormwater safely to streams, lakes and other water bodies. Minimal pavement, significant planted areas, proper grading and such drainage facilities as culverts and ditches are among the measures sometimes used to avoid construction of expensive underground storm sewers.

Typically, however, a storm drainage system consists of the drainage surface; groups of gutters, ditches and culverts; and underground storm sewers that may be constructed of vitrified clay or concrete and are reached, for service and maintenance purposes, by means of manholes. The drainage surface must have a minimum slope to encourage the flow of water at a reasonable rate. Gutters and ditches serve to channel stormwater and direct it to sewer pipes or stormwater detention areas.

A series of studies is conducted prior to design and construction of a storm drainage system for a site. In addition to analyses of topography and soil characteristics, existing natural drainage channels must be assessed and estimates prepared of the probable volumes of stormwater runoff that would be produced by storms of varying frequencies.
See: FLOOD CONTROL; RUNOFF; RUNOFF CALCULATIONS; STORM FREQUENCY; STORM SEWER

Storm Frequency

Either the possibility that a given storm will equal or exceed a certain amount of precipitation in a particular time period or the average time period that might be expected to elapse before a storm of a given magnitude occurs again.

Storm frequency is used in the planning and design of a wide variety of structures and facilities, such as storm sewers and flood-control dams. A decision is made concerning the level of storm that the public should be protected against in terms of probable flooding damage, and a calculation is made concerning the cost of achieving a particular level of protection against the costs of sustaining the flood damage.

A wide variety of information related to precipitation is available from the National Weather Service, which maintains local offices.
See: FLOOD CONTROL; HUNDRED-YEAR STORM; RUNOFF; STORM SEWER

Storm Sewer

A sewerage system designed to collect stormwater runoff from streets and roofs. Sewerage systems built since the advent of large-scale sewage treatment provide separate storm and sanitary sewers to enable the economic construction of treatment plants of sufficient capacity to handle sanitary sewage but not stormwater runoff. It is felt that the extreme dilution of organic materials and suspended solids in stormwater reduces its need for treatment prior to its release to receiving waters.

Storm sewer pipes are generally much larger than those of sanitary sewers, since they must be capable of handling large quantities of water in relatively short time periods. Pipe sizes are determined by analysis of storm frequency, rainfall rates, expected surface runoff and the value of property to be protected. In most downtown areas storm systems are engineered for a 25-year design storm, while other areas are usually designed for a 1- to 10-year design storm frequency.
See: COMBINED SEWER; RUNOFF; SANITARY SEWER; SEWERAGE SYSTEM; STORM FREQUENCY; SUSPENDED SOLIDS (SS)

Straight-Line Depreciation

A common method of depreciation, for tax purposes, of the cost of income-producing property. It assumes that the property is reduced in value by a constant amount during each year of its useful life. If, for example, a structure is purchased or constructed for $50,000 (the land it rests on is not depreciable) and its useful life is 25 years, the owner would be permitted to deduct $2,000 a year for tax purposes.

This method may be used whether the property was purchased new or used, providing that additional useful life remains, and whether or not it is mortgaged. The same principles apply to all depreciable assets, whether they are buildings or machinery.
See: ACCELERATED DEPRECIATION; USEFUL LIFE

Stratified Sample

A means of sampling in which a population is divided into groups that are homogeneous with respect to a particular variable or variables—e.g., females or females over 18. Samples are then selected from within the groups with the aid of random or systematic sampling techniques. This technique is used in an attempt to provide greater accuracy in sampling.
See: SAMPLING

Street Beautification

The improvement of the appearance of urban streetscapes as a municipal program or by a citizen beautification committee formed for this purpose. Often directed at central business district revitalization, fund raising from private and corporate sources has enabled many successful projects to be undertaken, generally in conjunction with municipal programs or authorities.

Typical improvements have included planting of street trees and landscaping and provision of small parks, fountains, outdoor seating areas, sidewalk benches, planters and attractive wastebaskets. As an example, the White Plains Beautification Foundation Inc. in White Plains, New York, a suburban city in the New York metropolitan area, completed more than 60 such projects for the $450,000 that it raised from private sources between 1965 and 1982. Included were trees, thousands of flower bulbs and a carillon. All projects were approved by city agencies and donated to the city, while foundation members continue to help with maintenance.
See: AESTHETICS; CIVIC GROUPS; LANDSCAPING; MAIN STREET; PEDESTRIAN IMPROVEMENTS; PUBLIC ART; SHADE TREE COMMISSION; STREETSCAPE

Street Behavior

The style and tone of interaction in a public setting. Street behavior includes the demeanor and attitude of an individual or group as they see or pass strangers, as well as the play, banter, mutual watching and human contact that are typical of high-density urban life. Communities frequently project codes of street behavior that must be planned for in designing public areas, such as the communal street life of an ethnic area or the more rigid code of sidewalk use expected in a higher-income housing area.
See: DEFENSIBLE SPACE; PERSONAL SPACE; TERRITORIALITY

Street Furniture

Elements of the streetscape, whether freestanding or fixed, generally associated with amenities for pedestrians, that occupy a place on the sidewalk, on a plaza or in another type of pedestrian zone. Normally included in the category of street furniture are benches or other forms of seating, planters, kiosks, signage, graphic displays such as maps, lighting fixtures, shelters and waste disposal containers.

In urban design, consideration of street furniture and coordination of styles of seating, lighting and related items with the character of existing or proposed architecture is considered important to the development of an aesthetically appealing environment. Placement and design of street furniture is a major component of many downtown improvement programs in which an effort is being made to make the business district more attractive and functional.
See: DOWNTOWN REVITALIZATION; PEDESTRIAN IMPROVEMENTS; STREETSCAPE

Street Graphics

Any form of lettering, diagram or symbol used on private and public signs to convey information or offer goods and services. Street and plaza names, building names or inscriptions, directional signage or symbols, signposts, kiosks or other information signs, and pavement markings are all examples of street graphics. If properly coordinated with surrounding architecture of the buildings and street furniture, street graphics can add vitality to the environment and reduce the visual chaos that can frequently be a part of the cityscape.

Regardless of their intent, graphics should be appropriate in terms of character and scale and should also be organized and legible for successful communication of a message. With basic design in place, stylization, color and lighting can be used to create a dramatic effect or highlight an architectural feature.
See: ADVERTISING SIGNS; BILLBOARD; PEDESTRIAN IMPROVEMENTS

Street Naming System

A comprehensive system used to assign names to municipal streets. A uniform street naming system helps people locate addresses and avoids the confusion of name duplication. A good system also prohibits names that sound quite similar and establishes policies concerning streets that run for long distances, change directions or are not continuous.

Methods are available that make it easier to locate any given address in the community. One common device assigns a meaning to the suffixes that follow street names. Traditionally, all streets run east-west, while avenues run north-south. Other designations, such as *boulevard*, may be reserved for wide thoroughfares; *drive* or *lane* for minor streets; and *court* or *place* for a cul-de-sac or permanent dead-end street.

An alternative method is to assign names based upon a theme, such as tree names or presidents; streets may also be named in alphabetical order. In another approach a velopment. High traffic volume is a key factor in causing strip development, encouraging a diversity of commercial uses, but ironically, strip development tends to hinder the very traffic that created it by reducing the road's ability to carry through traffic. Traffic congestion associated with strip development has required major improvements to arterial systems and has often been the basis for the location of interstate highways, frequently in parallel routes.

In recent years zoning regulations have been structured to avoid strip development, with commercial development focused at intersections or in major shopping malls. Another alternative to strip development is the placement of residential development along arterials with fenced-in rear yards abutting the street, sometimes referred to as back-lotting.
See: ARTERIAL ROAD; DRIVE-IN FACILITIES; NEIGHBORHOOD BUSINESS STREET

Strip Mining

A method of mining coal or other minerals by removing the overlying soil and rock, known as overburden, and extracting the mineral. Also known as surface mining or open-pit mining, it increased greatly in popularity after the development of large power shovels. It is widely used in portions of Europe and the United States.

Strip mining is an economical means of mining coal deposits at shallow depths; it is also safer for mine workers than underground mining. In addition, a high percentage of the coal can be recovered from the deposits.

The major problem associated with strip mining is the restoration of the mined land after mineral extraction; unrestored land presents a scarred and wastelandlike appearance. Among the other environmental problems of strip mining are potential landslides and mudflows because of unstable spoil banks, acid water drainage polluting neighboring water bodies and aquifers, and soil erosion. A number of ways of reclaiming this land have been developed. For example, topsoil may be stockpiled. After the mining is completed, the spoil can be reshaped into suitable landforms and the soil reapplied so that vegetation can be made to regrow; this has been accomplished successfully in England, Germany and the United States. Methods have also been developed in which reclamation occurs while mining is taking place, minimizing siltation and acid water formation.
See: LAND RECLAMATION; SLUDGE DISPOSAL; SPOIL; SURFACE MINING CONTROL AND RECLAMATION ACT OF 1977

Structure

Something that is constructed and is either located on the ground or is attached to an object on the ground. Buildings are structures, as are toolsheds, permanent signs, swimming pools and sometimes, for zoning purposes, mobile homes. Simple paving and surfacing is not considered to be a structure.
See: BUILDING

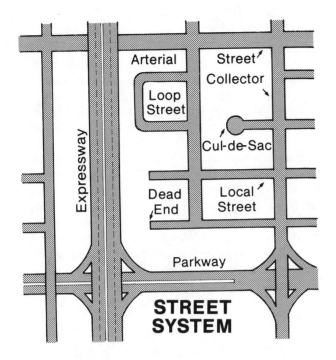

Fig. 43. Streets of differing width and control of access perform different traffic functions.

community is divided into quadrants and a suffix, such as *northwest,* assigned to the name.
See: PROPERTY NUMBERING SYSTEM

Streetscape

A design term referring to all the elements that normally constitute the physical makeup of a street or avenue and that, as a group, delineate its character. As opposed to a landscape of natural features, a streetscape normally includes building frontage, street paving and furniture, street tree planting, lighting and signage.

Within the context of urban design, the coordination and articulation of these elements becomes part of a total design effort to define a particular architectural style and to lend a particular ambience to a street.
See: HUMAN SCALE; URBAN DESIGN

Strip Development

Intense, largely commercial development along a length of arterial roadway, which can include offices and multifamily housing as well as retail uses. Strip development generally occurs along both sides of a road and, unlike planned shopping centers, may extend for miles.

Many zoning ordinances, particularly those prepared from the 1930s through the 1960s, tried to manage the problem of rapidly increasing traffic on arterials by zoning the abutting land "commercial" or "multifamily residential." The resulting strip development, with its plethora of signs and parking lots, has become an aesthetically displeasing but typical characteristic of American urban de-

Fig. 44. A conventional subdivision of single-family houses on lots of approximately the same size.
Credit: Courtesy of the U.S. Department of Housing and Urban Development

Subdivision

1. The process of dividing a larger land area into smaller building lots. When a number of lots are involved, street networks, utilities, open-space areas and other necessary facilities are laid out at the same time.

Generally, land subdivision takes place so that the original owner of the property may divide it into a number of parcels, each of which constitutes a legal building lot under local subdivision and zoning regulations. If, for example, a landowner holds 50 acres (20.2 hectares) of land zoned for 1-acre residential use, he must limit development to one residence until the property has been legally subdivided into an appropriate number of building lots.

Subdivision regulations generally govern most land subdivision when more than a minimum number of lots is being created (the minimum varies from two lots to as many as five) or when the construction of a new street is involved. Some states have special provisions exempting land from the definition of "subdivision"—for example, if agricultural land is being divided into large agricultural parcels.

2. An area of land that has been subdivided. (See Fig. 44)
See: ABORTIVE OR PREMATURE SUBDIVISION; MINOR SUBDIVISION; SUBDIVISION REGULATIONS; SUBDIVISION REVIEW

Subdivision Regulations

Municipal ordinances that govern the division of land into smaller building lots and the subsequent development of the land.

Subdivision regulations are intended to facilitate the orderly conversion of vacant land to developed land and to ensure that the new developments are compatible with surrounding development. One typical area controlled by subdivision regulations is the provision of utilities and new streets and their relationship to the existing utility and

street networks as well as to any future planned streets or facilities. Subdivision regulations also govern site design, including the layout of the street system, the length and width of streets and blocks, the location of each lot, and the location and design of open space and recreational facilities. Other areas that may be governed by subdivision regulations are landscaping requirements, floodplain requirements, the adequacy of parking facilities and the provision of sidewalks and street lighting.

Regulations also typically specify the amount of and manner in which land is to be dedicated to the local government for necessary public purposes, such as open space, as well as the payment of fees in lieu of parkland dedication. Regulations may sometimes specify payments toward the construction of major municipal facilities, such as new sewage treatment plants, as well. In addition, subdivision regulations contain detailed procedures governing the entire subdivision process, including the manner in which application may be made to subdivide, the method by which subdivision review is conducted and the payment of fees.

The particular content of municipal subdivision regulations can vary significantly from state to state and community to community. In some cases subdivision regulations contain requirements that, in another community, would appear in a different set of regulations, such as the zoning ordinance. In Houston, for example, where there is no zoning ordinance, the subdivision regulations contain certain requirements that are traditionally found in zoning ordinances, such as minimum lot size.
See: ABORTIVE OR PREMATURE SUBDIVISION; EXACTION; FEE IN LIEU OF DEDICATION; FINAL PLAT; FINANCIAL GUARANTEES FOR IMPROVEMENTS; MINOR SUBDIVISION; NEGOTIATION; PREAPPLICATION CONFERENCE; PRELIMINARY PLAT; SKETCH PLAN; SUBDIVISION; SUBDIVISION REVIEW; VISIBILITY CLEARANCE AT INTERSECTIONS; ZONING

Subdivision Review

The process by which a proposed subdivision is scrutinized for compliance with all municipal regulations and in which its design and its relationship to the surrounding neighborhood and to the community are studied.

Most typical subdivision regulations specify a series of steps the developer must take prior to receiving approval for a subdivision. An initial preapplication conference at which a sketch plan may be presented is followed by submission of the preliminary subdivision plat and then the final plat. During these steps a review process is initiated and coordinated by planning staff or planning consultants or, where no professional assistance is available, by the planning commission or the legislative body.

The review process includes study by the planning staff or planning commission as well as the solicitation of comments from appropriate municipal agencies and outside agencies and groups. Municipal agencies that should be contacted and given an opportunity to review the subdivision plat (when a community has these agencies) include the following: public works or the municipal engineer, the traffic engineer, water and sewer, parks and recreation, public safety and finance. Other agencies and organizations that are often given an opportunity to comment on the proposed subdivision are the affected school district, the telephone and power companies, and any sewer or water district or other special district in which the project may be located.

Various state and county laws may also dictate a mandatory referral of the proposed subdivision to the county planning department, the county health department, the state highway department or other state agencies, such as the department of state or agencies concerned with environmental quality.
See: FINAL PLAT; NEGOTIATION; PREAPPLICATION CONFERENCE; PRELIMINARY PLAT; SKETCH PLAN; SUBDIVISION; SUBDIVISION REGULATIONS

Subsidy

A grant or loan at below-market interest rates made by government to a person, company or other unit of government for an undertaking that is considered to be in the public interest.

Subsidies are generally granted for economic or social purposes, such as to aid ailing industries or to boost new industries. They may be in the form of direct cash grants, or they may be more indirect, with the subsidy being used to reduce the costs of the goods or services being purchased. Public housing, food stamps and tax abatements are all examples of indirect subsidies. Although they tend to be costlier than direct cash grants, indirect subsidies are more easily hidden and can, therefore, often be more acceptable politically. Other types of subsidies include the reduction of interest rates, guaranteed or insured mortgages or loans, or the sale or leasing of government properties at less than market value.
See: GRANT-IN-AID; HOUSING SUBSIDY

Substandard Housing

Housing possessing defects that cannot be repaired in the course of normal maintenance. Substandard housing typically includes some or all of the following conditions: nonexistent or faulty indoor plumbing, shared or deteriorating kitchen facilities, leaking roofs, missing stairs, broken plaster and inadequate heating systems.

Accurate data for the tabulation of the number of substandard housing units in a locality are usually not readily available. The Bureau of the Census has attempted to provide this information in the past with little success. In 1950 the Census defined substandard housing as units that were lacking complete plumbing or were dilapidated. In 1960 the Census used enumerators to evaluate the number of housing units in a census tract that were either sound, deteriorating or dilapidated, but spot-checks of the enumerators' surveys disclosed wide differences in perceptions of housing condition. Subsequently, the delineation

of housing condition was dropped from the 1970 and 1980 Censuses, although data are shown concerning lack of plumbing and overcrowding.
See: CODE ENFORCEMENT; HOUSING CODE; HOUSING STANDARDS; ILLEGAL CONVERSION; OVERCROWDING

Suburb

A municipality located outside the boundaries of a major central city but within the metropolitan area. Once pictured as essentially middle-class bedroom communities whose wage-earning members commuted to work in the central city, many suburbs have gained diversity, including industrial and commercial employers, office parks, multifamily housing and a range of services.

As suburbs matured, some became complete communities, sharing attributes and problems with central cities, while others remained bedroom communities. There has been suburban development in Europe and elsewhere, but not to the same extent as in the United States. The 1980 U.S. Census shows, for the most part, continued population decline in central cities and increases in suburbs, verifying that the suburbs have become an overwhelmingly important part of metropolitan regions.
See: BEDROOM COMMUNITY; COMMUTATION; LEVITTOWN; MATURE CITY; METROPOLITAN AREA; SUBURBAN GROWTH

Suburban Commuter Railway

A railway that serves a limited area near a central city. Commuter railways operate their own rolling stock on main line rail tracks but serve local stations not usually on intercity routes. Electrification of suburban lines is generally being pursued as a means of noise reduction and to increase service without dependence on the availability of additional locomotive engines. Commuter trains travel at an average peak-hour speed of 35 miles per hour (56 kilometers per hour); however, the Lindenwold high-speed line from Philadelphia to southern New Jersey travels at speeds up to 75 miles per hour (121 kilometers per hour). Train cars usually provide comfortable seating for about 100 passengers and a small amount of space for standing passengers.

Commuter railways are common throughout the United States; their construction early in the 20th century is considered responsible for the suburban development that took place at that time.
See: MASS TRANSIT

Suburban Growth

A form of metropolitan area development and evolution often closely tied to available transportation modes. While the areas outside cities were at one time viewed as provincial, as in Europe, an easy commute by rail or highway helped make the suburban single-family home attractive to families. Industry preferred the space necessary for single-story plants near highways; and shopping centers, located at major intersections, thrived. Some government programs—including highway construction, public utility support and mortgage subsidies—also helped to spur suburban growth. The suburb was no longer provincial but a successful competitor to the city that spawned it.

The availability of relatively inexpensive housing spurred the growth of suburbs, while the continued inability of cities to deal with urban problems drove large segments of the middle class to the new outlying communities, which were often pictured as idyllic. Suburbs have continued to be built, and many older suburbs have matured. While typical early development resulted in a sprawl pattern and strip development, newer suburbs are often built as planned communities and newer commercial areas as shopping centers.

Some planners today still feel that growth of suburban areas is temporary and that future growth will be in the city as it is improved. Others predict continued suburban growth but at a slower rate that will reflect a lowered birthrate and economic constraints.

See: BEDROOM COMMUNITY; COMMUTATION; LAND USE PATTERN; MATURE CITY; METROPOLITAN AREA; PLANNED COMMUNITY; SPRAWL; SUBURB

Subway

1.   A rapid-transit rail system that is grade-separated and designed to serve large passenger volumes. Subways of various lengths and route complexities have been built in cities throughout the world. Older systems run on steel wheels and rails, while some newer systems use rubber tires and concrete. Most are electrically powered by a third rail. Systems in densely populated areas are commonly built underground; they may, however, operate above ground on elevated tracks in lower-density areas. Subway systems currently in design and construction, as well as those built recently, are computerized, reducing manpower necessary to operate them. Because of the high capital cost of rapid-transit systems, new subways are proposed only for very densely populated areas, where they will be certain to attract riders in large volumes. Less costly transportation modes, such as trolleys and buses, act as feeders from lower-density areas to the subway system.

Subway systems are most effective when stations are placed a considerable distance apart. This spacing permits the street transportation system, consisting of buses and taxis, to handle the short-distance trips and increases the subway's operating speed. Where parking in the central business district is discouraged, it is advantageous to provide long-term parking lots adjacent to some of the transit stations. Subway cars, which have 50 seats on the average, are usually designed with more room for standees than for seated passengers because of the high-volume, on-off nature of rapid-transit systems.

2.   A subway is an underground pedestrian pathway in Britain.

See: MASS TRANSIT

Summary Tape Files (STF)

Magnetic computer tapes produced by the Bureau of the Census that contain the majority of data derived from the *1980 Census of Population and Housing.* The set of five tapes provides data on a much broader range of subject categories and geographic areas than the printed census reports. The files also contain extensive cross-tabulations for data for the various census geographic areas, such as counties and census tracts.

See: CENSUS; CENSUS REPORTS

Summer Camp

Traditionally, a group of rustic cabins in a natural environment where children spend their summers. At present, however, the term requires the broader definition of a location away from home where children, adults, the elderly or the handicapped may spend several weeks or more in outdoor and other group activities in all seasons. Camps may be located at sites specifically designed for them or in nontraditional spaces that are available for the time period—e.g., college dormitories.

The change reflects the growth of the concept of summer camping from being place-oriented to being activity-oriented. While rustic summer camps for children are still very popular, so are rustic camps for adults, seniors and the handicapped. Luxury camps that offer such activities as scuba diving or tennis lessons as well as educational camps that feature activities like computer programming are also increasing in number. Summer camping is a major recreational industry, but recreation departments generally also provide programs for groups not served by other organizations.

Sites that are most appropriate for summer camping are often in resort areas or low-density areas with large amounts of open space. They may or may not be permanently developed for camping but usually have some recreational facilities, such as a lake or swimming pool, on the property and can adequately accommodate the population group for whom the camping program is designed. Day camps require relatively little space and are often housed in school buildings with substantial recreational facilities or on relatively undeveloped suburban sites.

Sunbelt

An area often considered to be a crescent-shaped portion of the southern and western United States extending from North Carolina to California. While there is no single definition of the sunbelt, modern usage often defines it as that land area below the 37th parallel.

With its mild climate, modern cities and recreational opportunities, the sunbelt has seen major population growth in recent decades, often at the expense of older industrial cities in the Northeast and the Great Lakes area. Large-scale sunbelt growth began in the 1950s with military installations and the weapons industry; with the development of air conditioning, the warm climate attracted high-technology industries. Low taxes and wages and the availability of nonunionized labor were additional reasons why the southern United States became attractive to industry. By 1982, however, indicators showed a decline in the rapid growth trend because increasing costs and tightening labor markets in portions of the sunbelt made other areas more competitive again.

Sun-Tempered Building

A building that is oriented toward the south in order to capture maximum solar heat in cold weather. In a sun-tempered building, the major glazed surfaces (windows and glass doors) as well as the length of the building will face south, but a variety of shading devices, overhangs and landscaping techniques are employed to prevent excessive summer heat buildup.
See: PASSIVE SOLAR ENERGY SYSTEM; SOLAR ENERGY

Superblock

A residential site-planning concept in which the central area of a block is reserved for pedestrian walks and amenities and is surrounded by housing; access and parking are located on the periphery. Compared to conventional city blocks, superblocks are substantially larger and turned inside out, with the focus of activities on the vehicle-free interior space rather than on the streetscape. The interior open space provides recreation facilities and other amenities as well as pedestrian passage that is safe from vehicles.

Superblocks, connected by pedestrian links, have been a part of both British and American new town planning. The superblock concept has also been applied to redevelopment, where one or more city streets are closed to traffic and converted into central open space; a well-known example was designed by I.M. Pei for the Bedford-Stuyvesant Restoration Corporation in New York. The superblock concept has also provided important amenities in suburban locations and cities with row houses or townhouses. When used insensitively, however, particularly in high-density development, superblocks can disrupt urban street life and may become security problems. (See Fig. 45)

Surface Mining Control and Reclamation Act of 1977

Landmark legislation on the control of strip mining of coal. The act (PL 95-87) establishes performance standards for environmental protection and site reclamation to be met at all major surface mining operations and provides for joint enforcement by the states and the federal government. The act also authorizes the protection of lands considered unsuitable for strip mining and establishes an Abandoned Mine Reclamation Fund, to be supported by fees from mined coal and sales of reclaimed land, to enable the reclamation of abandoned surface and deep mines. The Office of Surface Mining Reclamation and Enforcement in the Department of the Interior is created to administer the program.

The Surface Mining Control and Reclamation Act, which establishes a supervisory system that includes issuance of permits (on the basis of filed and approved reclamation plans), requires performance bonds, federal or state inspections of operations, and fees for violations and is intended to prevent the worst abuses that have already scarred much of the Appalachian coal region. The act does not, however, establish regulations for the surface mining of other minerals, such as copper.
See: LAND RECLAMATION; STRIP MINING

Surface-to-Volume Ratio

A figure that expresses the relationship between exposed building surface and occupied volume. This ratio, which helps to indicate the degree to which a building is exposed to climatic conditions, may be used to assess various architectural designs for their energy-conserving potential.
See: ARCHITECTURAL DESIGN FOR ENERGY CONSERVATION; ENERGY CONSERVATION PLANNING

Surface Transportation Act of 1978

Legislation (PL 95-599) that provided funds to encourage the completion of the Interstate Highway System. It also required filing of environmental impact statements for all interstate roadway segments by 1983 and obligation of funds by 1986 for every segment to be included in the system. Another provision of this act was that interstate highway funds could be traded by a state or locality for mass transit assistance at an 85 percent federal share, a greater amount than the standard 80 percent for mass transit facilities funded under other proposals. Other features of the act included funding for an interstate highway repair program, a bridge rehabilitation program, ridepooling programs, bikeway construction and highway safety programs.

Major authorizations for mass transit facilities were also included. A reconstructed discretionary grant program was established for mass transit projects that involve major investments of federal funds. Funding from this program was directed partly to reconstruction and improvement of existing mass transit facilities, partly for urban development projects involving transit facilities and partly for projects along the northeast rail corridor. Funds were also earmarked for studies on innovative transit services.

In addition, funding for several formula grant programs was authorized by this legislation. These included the basic formula grant, the second-tier program (for the largest cities), the bus capital grant program, and a commuter rail and fixed guideway grant program. The act also required that in all areas with populations of at least 50,000, a transportation system management (TSM) program be carried on as part of a transportation improvement program (TIP).
See: NATIONAL MASS TRANSPORTATION ACT OF 1974; SURFACE TRANSPORTATION ASSISTANCE ACT OF 1982

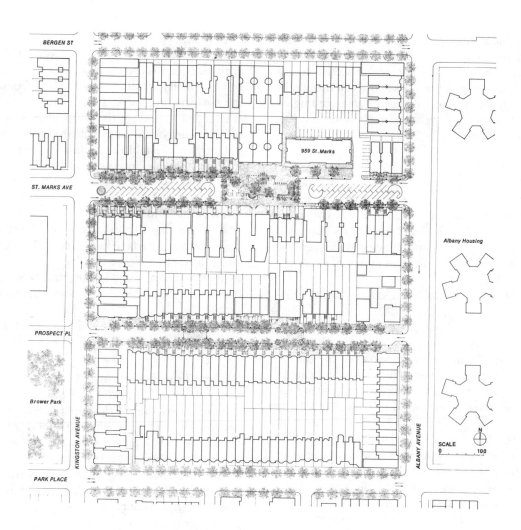

Fig. 45.   A superblock created from city streets in the Bedford-Stuyvesant section of Brooklyn, New York (I.M. Pei & Partners, architects; M. Paul Friedberg & Partners, landscape architects; Travers Associates, traffic consultants). (a) Plan of three city blocks of housing and the streets between them that became the superblock. St. Marks Ave. (above center block) became a park and two parking lots. Prospect Place (below center block) became a limited-access street with special paving to slow speed of vehicles. To the right of this superblock is a typical superblock created for public housing. (b) The park in St. Marks Ave. (c) Prospect Place with planters, new paving and new lighting.
Credit: Courtesy of I.M. Pei & Partners. Photographs by George Cserna

Surface Transportation Assistance Act of 1982

Legislation (PL 97-424) authorizing funding for federal-aid highways for fiscal years 1983 to 1986 and for interstate highways for fiscal years 1984 to 1990, based on the passage of a 5-cents-a-gallon increase in the federal excise tax on motor fuel purchases. This legislation is also notable for its emphasis on highway and bridge rehabilitation projects, pursuit of completion of the interstate highway system and establishment of a Mass Transit Account in the Highway Trust Fund to receive one-fifth of the 5-cent tax increase, with the remainder going to the Highway Trust Fund.

Title I of the act, the Highway Improvement Act of 1982, includes the continuation of the ability to remove planned but unbuilt segments from the interstate system for purposes of transfer of funds to other segments or mass transit but excludes those segments designated after March 7, 1978. The act also includes the requirement that a minimum of 40 percent of all highway allocations be spent on 4R projects (resurfacing, restoring, rehabilitating and reconstructing) for existing roads and permits the secretary of transportation to allocate monies from a discretionary fund for construction of very high cost road segments or for 4R projects. Cost-share provisions of the act offer an increase in the federal share from 75 percent to 90 percent for 4R projects on the interstate system if federal-aid primary funds are traded for this purpose, thereby encouraging this transfer. Ridepool, bicycle and pedestrian facilities on the interstate system are funded at 100 percent, an increase from the standard 90 percent interstate share. Funding at 95 percent, a 20 percent increase, is provided for certain primary system projects in economic growth centers, for access to lakes and for priority primary routes. Expenditure of funds for certain other project types is authorized, including fringe and corridor parking facilities and ramps to parking structures where high-occupancy vehicle lanes lead directly to them, as for implementation of an automobile restricted zone.

Major funding for bridge rehabilitation and replacement is also authorized. Considered one of the most important programs of this act because of nationwide problems relating to bridge deterioration, it is also a labor-intensive program that is expected to generate significant employment. The act also permits tandem-trailer trucks to use the interstate highways and authorizes certain studies and demonstration projects.

Title II, the Highway Safety Act of 1982, authorizes funding for elimination of highway hazards and other safety programs for fiscal years 1983 to 1986.

Title III, the Federal Public Transportation Act of 1982, revises the federal approach to public transportation assistance and authorizes funding for fiscal years 1983 to 1986. Under it a new block grant program for urbanized areas is created that can fund capital construction, planning for capital projects, acquisition, maintenance and operating expenses of public transportation systems. Capital construction is permitted at an 80 percent federal matching share, and operating expenses receive a 50 percent match. Maximum operating amounts are also set, but capital funds may be transferred to operating funds if one-third of the allocation, above a stipulated level, is surrendered to the secretary of transportation for discretionary purposes. Funding is provided annually on a formula basis, with large communities that have extensive bus and rail ridership receiving the biggest percentage of the annual allocation. Title III also extends the discretionary grant program for funding of extremely costly capital projects, such as fixed-guideway systems and other transit projects, for which the block grant is insufficient.

See: FEDERAL-AID HIGHWAY ACT OF 1981; SECTION 9 BLOCK GRANT PROGRAM; SURFACE TRANSPORTATION ACT OF 1978; URBAN MASS TRANSPORTATION ADMINISTRATION DISCRETIONARY GRANT PROGRAMS

Surface Water

In its most broad meaning, the term describes all waters on the Earth's surface, including its oceans. The term is, however, often used much more narrowly to mean the water that is found in stream channels. It is sometimes also expanded from this narrow definition to include lakes, reservoirs, wetlands, and the water in glaciers and ice sheets, in contrast to subsurface water, such as groundwater.

See: GROUNDWATER; RUNOFF; STORM DRAINAGE SYSTEM

Surplus Schools

School buildings that have been closed because of reduced school enrollments caused by population and/or birthrate decline. School boards will close schools to consolidate services and reduce costs, usually selecting those that are the oldest or in need of the most repair and those in neighborhoods with the smallest school-age population.

Because of the large number of school buildings that have been declared surplus, and their frequent architectural significance, extensive effort has been made to market them for new uses. Many have been converted to civic buildings, community centers and apartment houses.

See: ADAPTIVE USE; NEIGHBORHOOD SCHOOL; SCHOOL PLANNING

Survey

1. The process by which particular features or characteristics are carefully examined or researched to provide information on which planning and decision making may be based. Surveys may be made of soil, shopping behavior, attitudes, housing condition, transportation or almost any other subject.

2. The delineation of precise land boundaries for a variety of purposes, including mapping, preparation of accurate legal property descriptions or subdivision of

property. There are also numerous types of specific surveys, such as a route survey or a construction survey.

3. The document or map that results when surveying procedures are followed. Surveys generally include all property boundaries and their dimensions, as well as the location of structures, particular physical features, roads or driveways, easements and encroachments.
See: LAND USE SURVEY; METES AND BOUNDS; SOIL SURVEY; SURVEY RESEARCH

Survey Research

A means of obtaining information from the public through such techniques as telephone or personal interviews or mailed questionnaires. Survey research has a wide variety of planning applications, ranging from obtaining public opinion concerning a particular issue to help determine policy, to assessing the effectiveness of an existing program. Many major government studies, including components of the decennial census, are based upon sample survey techniques.

Self-administered questionnaires, used when a survey is mailed or being administered to a group, are more economical but do not allow the opportunity for respondents to ask questions and clarify problem areas. Generally, self-administered questionnaires are kept short and when mailed, postage-paid envelopes are enclosed to encourage a response. Personal or telephone interviews do allow opportunities for clarification and also achieve an improved response rate, but are more costly and more subject to the effects of interviewer bias.

Questionnaires may be precoded to facilitate data tabulation. As an example, numbered answer codes may be used that correspond to various choices and are entered in appropriate columns at the margin of the questionnaire.
See: SAMPLING

Suspended Solids (SS)

Solids in water and sewage that are about 1 micron (μ) in size or larger but smaller than coarse solids and grit. Suspended solids, which contain organic and inorganic materials, are composed of settleable and nonsettleable solids. When the liquid is placed in a nonagitated container, settleable solids will settle to the bottom within two hours; in wastewater the ratio of settleable solids to sludge, produced by sedimentation during primary treatment, is approximately equal. The nonsettleable solids can be removed by biological or chemical coagulation (secondary treatment).
See: GRIT CHAMBER; PRIMARY TREATMENT; SCREENING; SECONDARY TREATMENT; SEDIMENTATION TANK

Swale

An open channel designed to carry runoff during periods of precipitation. A swale is often dug in lieu of placement of a pipeline in rural or suburban areas because of its lower cost and compatibility with the landscape.
See: FLOOD CONTROL; RUNOFF; STORM DRAINAGE SYSTEM

Swamp

A wet, low-lying area that, unlike a marsh, often supports an extensive number of woody plants, such as trees and shrubs. It may also be dry in the summer, although it is submerged in water in the winter and spring. Examples of sizable swamps are the Dismal Swamp, which covers portions of Virginia and North Carolina, and the Florida Everglades. Predominant tree types in swamps include the northern white cedar, black ash, red maple, black gum, willow, alder, water oak and bald cypress.
See: BOG; FRESHWATER MARSH; SALT MARSH; WETLANDS

Sweat Equity

An investment of labor and effort in the rehabilitation of a structure, generally for residential occupancy. Unlike conventional owner's equity, represented by an investment of capital in a building, sweat equity usually consists of the time and materials required to renovate a structure and make it livable, often without a traditional monetary commitment in the form of a down payment and mortgage.

Conceived of as a means of encouraging home ownership for low- and middle-income families in declining or abandoned neighborhoods, the concept of sweat equity has been successfully employed in a number of American cities, such as New York and Baltimore, where homesteading movements have helped to revitalize inner city residential areas. Similar efforts have also been employed in renewal of commercial areas through rehabilitation of abandoned shops.
See: URBAN HOMESTEADING

Swimming Pools

One of the most popular recreational facilities, swimming pools are important components in the design of private clubs, hotels and motels, many housing developments and public recreation and education systems. They may be built as indoor or outdoor pools or have enclosures that permit them to be used either way. While private and indoor pools may be small—e.g., 20 × 40 feet (6.1 × 12.2 meters), providing sufficient space only for recreational swimming—public pools are usually large enough for competitions. Competitive swimming lengths of 25 yards (22.9 meters) and 50 meters may be provided in regional swimming pools, while only the shorter distance may be accommodated in neighborhood pools. A public pool width of 45 feet (13.7 meters) is common.

Pools are also designed in many shapes and depths. Rectangular pools or variations, such as an L or T shape, best accommodate competitions. Irregular and freeform shapes, however, may be more suitable for residential or resort installations. Separate children's pools and diving pools may be provided, or either may be combined as an area of one larger pool. A spray and/or wading area for toddlers may also be included. Between 75 percent and 85 percent of the pool should have a maximum depth of 5 feet (1.5 meters) for the great majority of swimmers; a depth of 4 feet (1.2 meters) is the minimum required for competitions.

For outdoor pools the deck space provided around the pool should, at minimum, equal the area of the pool and ideally be three to four times its area. Studies have shown that as few as one-quarter to one-third of those in attendance use a pool at one time, so that a large deck area will permit much greater pool use. For competitive pools, diving boards of 1 and 3 meters are necessary, while some pools also have 5-meter or higher diving platforms. Other water-related activities that are popular are water slides of varying widths and wave-making equipment.

Pools should be sited so that they will receive sunlight for the entire day but will be blocked from prevailing winds that may chill bathers. Trees should not be located next to the pool, since leaves and insects that may fall will be a nuisance. A bathhouse and parking area of sufficient size should be provided, as well as night lighting and fencing of the entire area.
See: BEACH FACILITIES

Synthetic Fuels

Those fuels that must be manufactured. The term generally refers to fuels derived from fossil fuels such as coal, oil shale and tar sands. Synthetic fuels ("synfuels") unlike the fuels from which they are derived, are generally in liquid or gaseous form and can thus be readily transported by pipeline and more easily stored. Synthetic liquid fuels can also be used to power motor vehicles. Other reasons for interest in synfuels are the large supplies of available coal worldwide and widely fluctuating crude oil prices.

Among the types of synthetic fuels that can be produced are low-Btu gas (a natural gas substitute made by combining coal, air and steam) and a liquid fuel produced by heating coal in the absence of oxygen. Oil shale may be crushed and heated to produce a synthetic crude oil, and tar sands may be processed to produce both synthetic crude oil and gas.

A number of problems are associated with the production of synthetic fuels, including the high cost of constructing large-scale conversion plants and the increased strip mining that would be necessary to supply synthetic fuel production plants. In addition, large quantities of water are needed for most synthetic fuel plants, and much of the coal being considered for synthetic fuel production is in arid areas, putting synthetic fuel production in competition with agricultural and industrial uses that also require

water. A government-sponsored United States Synthetic Fuels Corporation was created in 1980 to assist in the establishment of a synthetic fuels industry.
See: ENERGY SECURITY ACT; FOSSIL FUELS

System

A group of physical entities, ideas or principles that are interrelated in some way.
See: SYSTEMS ANALYSIS

Systematic Sample

A sampling technique similar to the random sample, in which a starting point on a list is chosen at random and then each subsequent selection from the list is made based on a constant numerical interval whose size is a function of the size of the desired sample and the population. This technique can produce a biased sample if the list is ordered in some specific way that can have a bearing on the characteristic being sampled.
See: SAMPLING

Systems Analysis

The study of complex problems by splitting them into their component parts and applying various analytic tools with a view toward furthering optimal performance of the interrelated systems. Modern systems analysis can trace its roots to the large body of military research undertaken during World War II. Systems approaches were also used extensively by the defense and aerospace industries in the 1960s. As a result of this intensive use of the process, applications to planning and government were developed, particularly in transportation planning but also in such areas as provision of health care, budgeting, social services, management of wastes and housing. Other applications—such as PPBS (Planning Programming Budgeting System), PERT (Program Evaluation and Review Technique) and CPM (Critical Path Method)—were also developed during the postwar years.

Systems analysis, which usually depends upon models and simulation techniques, is generally undertaken with the aid of computers because of the complexity of the problems that are analyzed. It begins with the formulation of a problem and its division into small but identifiable subsystems, which may be described with the aid of models. Various analytic techniques are then used to evaluate the efficiency of operation of the system, and computer simulation may be used to experiment with alternatives. Finally, the best alternatives are selected. After an attempt is made to implement portions of the recommended system, further refinements are made to suggest future courses of action.
See: DECISION SUPPORT SYSTEMS (DSS); MODEL; SIMULATION; SIMULATION GAMES

T

Taking

A governmental action by which the government either acquires property or an interest in property from a private owner or otherwise substantially diminishes the value of property or substantially deprives the owner of the use and enjoyment of his property.

A taking normally results from the exercise of eminent domain power. The "taking issue" refers to the question of when governmental regulation adopted as an exercise of the police power so severely interferes with the private owner's use and enjoyment as to constitute a taking for constitutional purposes. At stake is the right to compensation—if a regulation is upheld as a valid exercise of the police power, no compensation need be provided; where a regulation is found to result in a taking of property, the constitution mandates that if the regulation is to stand, just compensation must be paid.

See: AGINS v. CITY OF TIBURON; ASSOCIATED HOME BUILDERS OF GREATER EAST BAY, INC. v. CITY OF WALNUT CREEK; COMPENSABLE REGULATIONS; CONFISCATORY REGULATION; EMINENT DOMAIN; *GOLDBLATT v. TOWN OF HEMPSTEAD;* INVERSE CONDEMNATION; *PENN CENTRAL TRANSPORTATION COMPANY v. CITY OF NEW YORK; PENNSYLVANIA COAL CO. v. MAHON;* POLICE POWER; *WINDFALLS AND WIPEOUTS*

Target Area

One or more geographic areas within a municipality or other planning area chosen to receive a concentration of certain types of funding or other assistance. One reason that target areas are selected is to concentrate the commitment of resources within those areas or sites considered most promising in terms of attaining certain community goals and objectives. As an example, an area considered to have good potential for industrial development may be one of a few select sites targeted to receive funding for sewer, drainage and road improvements in a particular year. Another example of targeting occurs when a particular need exists, as when a community has areas in which the housing stock is rapidly deteriorating. Such areas may be targeted for code enforcement and rehabilitation loans and grants in order to halt this negative trend.

See: PLANNING AREA

Task Force

A group that is formed for the purpose of investigating a particular issue or problem and then reporting on its findings. Task force members are usually selected for their experience in and knowledge about the area being studied. The term derives from military usage, where it described a temporary consolidation of units under one commander for a particular mission.

See: BLUE-RIBBON COMMISSION

Tax Abatement

A partial or total tax exemption for a particular building or project for a specified number of years, aimed at providing indirect financial assistance to an individual in order to gain a public benefit. Tax abatement is a government tool that can be used to encourage objectives—such as construction of middle-income housing, commercial development in a declining area or historic preservation—without the use of additional public funds.

The form that the abatement takes is often tailored to a specific project unless it is used widely within a municipality. It may consist of a total exemption or reduced assessments for a specified period, a gradual increase or phase-in to the appropriate tax level over a period of years, or taxes based on the property's preimprovement status for a specified time period.

See: ECONOMIC DEVELOPMENT INCENTIVES; LIMITED-DIVIDEND HOUSING COMPANY; TAX-EXEMPT PROPERTY

Tax Anticipation Note

A form of short-term borrowing to enable municipalities to meet current operating expenses that are due before anticipated tax revenues are forthcoming. The notes are retired upon collection of the outstanding tax monies.

The need for tax anticipation notes derives from the typical pattern of constant expenditure requirements most municipalities have over the year for such expenses as payroll, while income is often collected at discrete intervals during the year. This occurs, for example, when local property taxes are not collected until the fiscal year is well underway. This has often been the case in areas with an agricultural economic base, where the fall harvest is a major source of income for taxpayers. Many other factors can contribute to a temporary shortage of cash, even though the community operates within a balanced budget when the fiscal year is viewed as a whole.

Another term used for this practice is *revenue anticipation borrowing.*

See: MUNICIPAL BOND

Tax Assessment Roll

The list of properties within a municipality that are subject to property taxation. The assessment roll is retained for reference purposes by the local tax department or commission, the assessor and the county tax department. The tax roll indicates a property's assessed value, often listed separately for land and improvements, as well as showing properties that receive partial tax exemptions and sometimes those that are tax-exempt. In addition, for any particular piece of property, the tax roll usually lists the name and mailing address of the owner(s), the property's tax block and lot designation (or other similar designation), and the size of the property and may sometimes contain a land use classification code.

See: ASSESSED VALUATION; IMPROVEMENTS; LAND USE CLASSIFICATION SYSTEM; PROPERTY TAX; TAX MAP

Tax Base

The total value of real property within a municipality or other taxing district on which it can levy a property tax. The assessment base is the total assessed value of real property within the boundaries of the taxing district. Both terms are used to describe a community's relative wealth.

The tax or assessment base is estimated or calculated annually in most municipalities, so that the municipality can determine the tax rate necessary to yield sufficient revenue to cover its proposed expenditures. A marked drop in the tax base often signifies a declining economy, while an increase may indicate a growing economy or the effects of inflation on property value.

See: PROPERTY TAX; TAX RATE

Tax Department

A local government department that maintains the tax assessment roll and tax maps and that may be headed by the municipal tax assessor. The municipal tax department keeps tax records up to date by posting assessments made by the assessor and maps new parcels of land as they are carved from previous parcels. A county-level tax department, however, may simply retain these records for use in setting a county tax rate, providing one convenient location where the public may view the tax records of many municipalities.

Current tax information is a useful tool for planners in investigating land use. It enables the pattern of property ownership in a defined area to be determined and aids in the estimation of property values.

See: ASSESSOR; TAX ASSESSMENT ROLL; TAX MAP

Tax Equity and Fiscal Responsibility Act of 1982 (TEFRA)

An act (PL 97-248) that makes many modifications in the Internal Revenue Code, among which are changes affecting historic tax incentives granted in the Economic Recovery Tax Act of 1981 (ERTA).

TEFRA reduces somewhat the tax benefits available in connection with the rehabilitation of certified historic structures. The Economic Recovery Tax Act of 1981 included provisions for a 25 percent investment tax credit in connection with certain qualified rehabilitation expenses of certified historic structures. TEFRA retains the tax credit but adds a new requirement that the tax basis of the certified historic structure used for calculating income tax depreciation deductions be reduced by one-half of the 25 percent tax credit. Under this new limitation, of the total qualified rehabilitation expenses, only 87.5 percent can be depreciated for income tax purposes, instead of the full 100 percent of expenses as originally adopted under ERTA.

Even after taking TEFRA changes into account, however, qualified rehabilitation of certified historic structures continues to receive more favorable tax treatment than other qualified rehabilitation. For buildings at least 30 and 40 years old, tax credits of 15 percent and 20 percent, respectively, of qualified rehabilitation expenditures are available. However, in such cases the full amount of the tax credit (and not just one-half of the credit, as with certified historic structures) must be subtracted from the tax basis.

TEFRA also contains provisions that limit the use of tax-exempt industrial revenue bonds, also known as industrial development bonds (IDBs). It contains a requirement that public hearings be held and official approval be granted by elected officials unless a public referendum has been held prior to issuance of the bonds. Previously these bonds were often issued by a separate agency without such requirements. In addition, accelerated depreciation benefits are generally not available to a company to the extent that the property in question was financed using these tax exempt bonds.

Other provisions of TEFRA provide for additional taxes on such items as airplane passenger tickets to raise revenues for the Airport and Airway Trust Fund and authorize expenditures from this fund for airport development, noise-abatement projects and air traffic control facilities and equipment. Controls set by Congress in 1980 on the use of tax-free mortgage subsidy bonds were also relaxed by TEFRA effective July 1, 1982.

See: ECONOMIC RECOVERY TAX ACT OF 1981; HISTORIC PRESERVATION TAX INCENTIVES; INDUSTRIAL REVENUE BONDS

Tax-Exempt Property

Property on which a property tax is not levied. When additional properties are excluded from taxation, they add to the large body of property already granted tax-exempt status. This creates a reduced tax base and can consequently require imposition of a higher tax rate on taxable property. In deciding to grant tax-exempt status, five issues are generally considered by states and municipalities: (1) Who is the owner? (2) What is the use of the property? (3) Who occupies the property? (4) Are there private gains? and (5) Does the property generate profits?

Most public property is tax-exempt because of constitutional limitations or because taxing would not yield any net tax return. Public buildings, schools, parks and institutions comprise a large percentage of tax-exempt property. Some government projects, however, pay a fee in lieu of taxes.

Property used for religious, philanthropic, educational or benevolent purposes also receives tax-exempt status in most states. It is argued that these are not profit-making functions and that they are often functions that the state would otherwise have to perform. While there are arguments against providing tax exemption to religious institutions because of the doctrine regarding separation of church and state, most jurisdictions believe that religious, charitable and educational facilities should be encouraged because they improve the quality of life. Some states have challenged the tax-exempt status of benevolent societies because of questions regarding their charitable activities. In Britain public, agricultural and public utility property is either partially or fully tax-exempt, but charitable properties pay up to one-half of the imposed rates.

See: CIRCUIT BREAKER TAXES; ELEEMOSYNARY USES; PROPERTY TAX; TAX ABATEMENT

Tax-Increment Financing

A means of financing redevelopment projects in which an area is improved with the proceeds of a bond issue slated to be repaid by the additional taxes the new development is expected to generate. If, for example, it is considered feasible to redevelop a downtown area, a district is established in the downtown, and the tax revenues that district generates are computed. After redevelopment has been completed using the funds generated by the sale of tax-increment bonds, the increased tax revenue of the district, or the increment above the previously established tax level, is used to service the bonds. Upon retirement of the bonds, all taxes from the district become part of the community's normal tax base.

Because tax-increment financing requires that tax monies be used to retire the bond rather than be added to general municipal revenues, state enabling legislation is necessary to authorize use of this financing technique. It has been employed successfully in a number of states, particularly California.

Tax Map

A map prepared and maintained for property tax purposes that shows the location, boundaries, size and dimensions of land parcels in relation to their surroundings. Each parcel is assigned a number or code that links it to the tax rolls. These rolls contain a listing of the parcels and information such as the owner's name, assessed value of the property and any improvements, taxes paid and taxing jurisdictions—e.g., water district. They may also contain a code that indicates the use classification of the improvements.

Tax maps and rolls are extremely helpful in conducting land use research. The linked names on the tax rolls show ownership of the parcels, often useful when ownership patterns are important or when property acquisition is being considered. Data in the tax rolls on the assessment of land and buildings also indicate whether the property is developed and, if so, give an indication of the value of the improvements. Tax maps can also serve as the basis for base maps for a small area being studied if it is known that the maps are updated as changes occur in property lines.

See: REAL ESTATE ATLAS; REFERENCE MAPS

Tax Rate

A levy on real property, usually expressed as a percentage of the assessed value or in mills ($.001) or dollars per $100 or per $1,000 of assessed value. Tax rates are determined by local taxing jurisdictions based on their annual revenue requirements and are generally limited by state statute. In many countries the tax rate is set only by the town, city or county government. In the United States, however, the rate may be determined by two or more levels of government, such as the town, the school district, other special districts or the county.

Although property tax rates of various communities are frequently compared to determine relative tax burdens, they must first be applied to the municipal assessment ratio to make them comparable; for example, a tax rate of 5.5 percent multiplied by an assessment ratio of 30 percent to 40 percent yields an effective tax rate of 1.7 percent to 2.2 percent.

See: ASSESSED VALUATION; ASSESSMENT RATIO; PROPERTY TAX; TAX BASE

Tax Structure

The variety of forms of taxation imposed by a government to generate necessary revenues and the percentage of that revenue that each tax comprises or is expected to comprise. The tax structure is usually indicated in the budget of a unit of government. Typically, local governments rely heavily upon the property tax and, to a much lesser extent, upon the sales tax and income tax.

See: INCOME TAX; PROPERTY TAX; SALES TAX

Telephone System

The mechanical and electrical devices that transmit speech by electrical current. The telephone system has three basic components: the transmitter, which converts sound to electrical impulses; the transmission system; and the receiver, which converts electrical impulses back to sound.

Of most interest to the planner is the transmission system, consisting of a network of wire, radio and satellite communications. Wire transmission may consist of open wire located on poles, or it may consist of multipair cables or coaxial cables, which may be suspended from poles, buried directly in the ground, placed in underground conduits or used as submarine cable for underwater crossings. In developed areas telephone cable is increasingly being placed underground. When located on poles, telephone wires generally share poles with electrical lines.

When microwave transmission is used, microwave towers spaced about 30 miles (48 kilometers) apart must be constructed so that they are at least 50 feet (15 meters) taller than intervening hills to avoid obstructing the micro-

waves. The tall towers required in microwave transmission as well as the uncertainty over the long-term effects of microwave use are persistent problems associated with the use of microwave transmission. Where possible, sites for microwave towers should be away from residential or other populated areas.
See: CABLE TELEVISION; ELECTRIC TRANSMISSION LINE; UNDERGROUNDING OF UTILITIES; UTILITY EASEMENT

Tennessee Valley Authority (TVA)

A United States federal agency created in 1933 to plan and develop the resources of the drainage basin of the Tennessee River. This river basin covers 40,000 square miles (103,600 square kilometers) and lies in parts of seven states: Alabama, Georgia, Kentucky, Mississippi, North Carolina, Tennessee and Virginia.

Among the broad range of activities that the TVA is empowered to engage in are flood control, navigation improvements, power generation, reforestation and development of recreation areas. Since its creation, the TVA has built an extensive water control system that has prevented major flood damage in this area. A 650-mile (1,046-kilometer) long, 9-foot (2.7-meter) deep channel has also been constructed to facilitate navigation, substantially increasing shipping along the river. Through its network of multipurpose dams and power plants, TVA became a major producer of electric power, and numerous recreation areas were also created.

This experiment in regional planning and economic development has helped planning efforts in other river basins across the country and has gained worldwide attention.
See: REGIONAL PLANNING; RIVER BASIN; RIVER BASIN COMMISSION

Terrace

1. A flat, relatively flat or rolling area constructed on the contour of a slope that is designed to minimize runoff and erosion or to allow cultivation on a hillside.

2. An area of fairly level ground formed by natural processes that is bounded on one side by an ascending slope and on the other by a descending slope. Streams, for example, may form terraces when they cut through alluvial deposits (stream deposits of silt, sand, clay and gravel). The ocean may also form terraces by building up or cutting back cliffs through the action of waves on the shore.

3. A term often used to describe an outdoor balcony.
See: SOIL EROSION CONTROL TECHNIQUES

Territoriality

The need to identify and protect from intrusion a fixed geographic area, which usually surrounds the home. Anthropologists have demonstrated that humans, like many animals, need a secure home area. The street gang concept of "turf" is perhaps the most vivid example of urban territoriality; people often consider their block, street, neighborhood or town as their territory and feel entitled to protect that area and determine its future.
See: DEFENSIBLE SPACE; ENVIRONMENTAL PSYCHOLOGY; PERSONAL SPACE; PRIVACY; STREET BEHAVIOR

Tertiary Road

A rural local road that principally provides access to abutting properties. These roads constitute about 71 percent of the rural system. They funnel traffic to secondary and primary roads and serve local purposes—e.g., residence to store.
See: LOCAL STREET; PRIMARY ROAD; SECONDARY ROAD

Tertiary Treatment

Often referred to as advanced waste treatment, it is a form of sewage treatment, generally imposed after secondary treatment, in which organic pollutants and suspended solids in the effluent are further reduced. The quantities of inorganic ions, such as nitrates and phosphates, which stimulate algae and aquatic growth, and complex organic compounds are also diminished.

Tertiary treatment may be required to protect very small receiving bodies of water or reservoirs, to remove certain industrial pollutants or to obtain water suitable for specialized uses. The type of treatment will depend upon the specific pollutants that the effluent contains and the intended use for the end product. With sufficient treatment, sewage subjected to tertiary treatment may be used as a supplementary source of water by mixing it with conventional water supplies. Some of the tertiary processes can also be used for treatment both of raw sewage and of effluent from primary treatment.
See: EFFLUENT; PRIMARY TREATMENT; SECONDARY TREATMENT; SEWAGE TREATMENT

Theaters

Generally free-standing buildings designed for performances of plays, music, dance or motion pictures. Important cultural amenities of communities of all sizes, theaters are generally located in commercial areas with good transportation access and sufficient off-street parking space.

Very large theaters that attract world and nationally famous companies, theater districts and complexes of theaters are often magnets for supporting commercial development, such as restaurants, hotels, rehearsal studios and stage-production supply companies. They draw national and even international attendance and are an important economic base. College campuses that offer major theater facilities may also attract regional audiences. Movie theater complexes, either in converted old moviehouses or in new shopping center locations, provide a local magnet and encourage some support facilities, such as restaurants. Outdoor amphitheaters and outdoor theaters in ancient ruins also act as regional facilities because of their unique ambience. Many municipal main streets have at least one movie theater that becomes a weekend center of activity.

In heavily urbanized areas theater buildings have become a target for development of their valuable air rights. In many cases theaters have been replaced by office buildings, although the theaters have sometimes been rebuilt at the base of the new buildings. While some theaters do not have architectural significance, many older ones do. When such theaters are threatened with sale by their owners, interested local groups have been active in obtaining funding for their rehabilitation and continued use.
See: AIR RIGHTS; AMPHITHEATER

Thermal Mass

A material that is capable of absorbing and storing the sun's energy during the day and releasing it at night or on cloudy days during the winter. Construction materials that are often selected when thermal mass is required are masonry, concrete, rock and adobe. Thermal mass can also help cool an area in summer by absorbing the coolness of the night and later releasing it.
See: PASSIVE SOLAR ENERGY SYSTEM; SOLAR ENERGY

Thermal Pollution

A phenomenon in which the temperature of a body of water is raised, either through natural or human causes, to the point where it adversely affects some aspect of the aquatic environment. The most common cause of thermal pollution is the operation of electrical power plants, in which cold water is often used to condense steam so that it may return to the boiler as water. Steel and chemical plants are also common users of water as a coolant.

Thermal pollution is disruptive to fish life in a variety of ways. Each fish species has a temperature range necessary for its survival, and temperatures in excess of this range can result in immediate fish kills. In addition to causing direct mortality, higher temperatures can disrupt fish reproduction, reduce the amounts of available dissolved oxygen and help to hinder fish migration.

Thermal pollution can also foster the growth of the sometimes toxic blue-green algae, which is not a desirable food source for most aquatic animals and can adversely affect water quality. Many smaller aquatic organisms are killed either by movement through an industrial plant's condensers or by the chemicals used to keep the coolant pipes clear. In order to minimize the effects of thermal pollution, cooling towers or cooling ponds are sometimes used to absorb waste heat.

Although heated water discharged back into its natural environment often causes environmental problems, several beneficial uses for the warmed coolant water have been found. In cold-weather areas, the heated water may be used to provide an area free of ice in which waterfowl may spend the winter. Experiments have also been conducted in which warmed water produced by an industrial

plant was used to prevent frost damage to fruit trees. Experiments in aquaculture are also being conducted in which certain warm-water fish species are raised in heated waters. Carp are being raised this way in Russia, while this method is being considered as a means of increasing lobster production in the state of Maine.
See: AQUACULTURE; COOLING TOWER; ELECTRIC POWER GENERATION AND TRANSMISSION

Thermal Windows

Windows that can help to reduce winter heat loss and summer heat gain. It has been estimated that about one-fourth of all energy expended in the United States for space heating and cooling of commercial buildings and residences is wasted as a result of heat transfer through windows. As fuel costs rise, increased attention is being paid to this phenomenon.

Storm windows are a standard method of preventing winter heat loss, but more sophisticated windows have been developed to accommodate passive solar energy designs. A bead window, for example, in which styrofoam beads are sandwiched between two sheets of glass or plastic, may be emptied of beads when heat gain is desired and filled with beads via a pump and blower system to prevent heat loss overnight. Insulated shutters are a simpler means of adjusting heat gain and loss. A heat mirror, a new device in which a thin coating of special material is applied to glass, allows sunlight to enter but prevents heat from escaping. This may be combined with an optical shutter, a gel-like substance placed between glass layers that reflects light when temperatures reach a certain level, helping to prevent summer heat gain.
See: ENERGY CONSERVATION PLANNING; HOME WEATHERIZATION; PASSIVE SOLAR ENERGY SYSTEM; SOLAR ENERGY

Through Lot

A lot that has frontage upon two streets that are parallel or nearly parallel at that point. Through lots are also known as double-frontage lots. (See Fig. 26)
See: LOT

Tidal Power

Electric power generated by using the incoming and outgoing tidal flow to power a hydraulic turbine which, in turn, drives a generator. Tidal power has been in use since the 11th century, but it is only relatively recently that large-scale tidal plants have been constructed because of the costs involved and the necessary site requirements.

Tidal power plants require a large difference in sea level between high and low tide, known as tidal range, as well as a bay or inlet capable of being economically enclosed with a dam or dike. Limited numbers of sites throughout the world meet these requirements, but where they do exist, sizable energy potential is present. Currently, two tidal power plants are in operation: one at La Rance in Brittany, and one experimental plant in the Soviet Union. A

prototype plant is also scheduled for completion in 1983 in Nova Scotia's Bay of Fundy, which is thought to have the largest tidal range in the world. If the demonstration is successful, it is hoped that one day three-fourth's of Nova Scotia's power can be generated by this means. Few potential sites exist in the United States, but the one most often considered as a plant site is the Maine side of Passamaquoddy Bay on the Canadian border.
See: ELECTRIC POWER GENERATION AND TRANSMISSION; RENEWABLE ENERGY SOURCES

Timesharing

1.   Purchase of the ownership of or the right to use real property or other property for a designated portion of each year. The concept, which first became popular in Europe, is used primarily in attractive vacation areas, where timeshares in condominiums, hotel rooms, yachts and other accommodations are acquired for portions of the year. Typically, these areas offer a special attraction, such as proximity to a major ski area or the beach, as well as tennis courts, swimming pools and other recreational facilities.

Timesharing, sometimes known as interval ownership, varies in its form and procedures. One form involves acquiring actual ownership of the unit, which may be sold or leased. This may involve ownership of a specific time slot (e.g., the first week in July), the right to reserve a time slot during the year or the opportunity to alternate the time of year of the vacation. Alternatively, the buyer may purchase the right to use the premises, which expires after an agreed-upon number of years.

Among the advantages of timeshares are acquisition of a fixed-price vacation accommodation with appreciation potential, freedom from maintenance or rental responsibilities during the portion of the year not in residence and standard prorated real estate tax deductions. The rapid proliferation of timesharing has, however, necessitated the adoption of laws specifically to regulate this practice, such as those found in California, Hawaii, New Hampshire and Virginia.

2.   The use of a computer system by multiple users at the same time working on disparate problems. The rapidity with which the computer operates enables it to accommodate the various users in sequence, although it seems as if they are being served simultaneously.

T-Intersection

A three-leg, at-grade intersection where one of the intersecting legs is perpendicular to the others. (See Fig. 5)
See: AT-GRADE INTERSECTION

Tipping Point

The point at which enough members of a particular ethnic or racial group move into a neighborhood so that members of other groups will no longer buy or rent housing in that area. While tipping points are tied to numerous factors relating to the desirability of the housing and con-

cern about one's investment, an influx of minority group residents sufficient to comprise 25 percent to 45 percent of the neighborhood's population is often sufficient to tip the balance leading to a segregated neighborhood.
See: AFFIRMATIVE FAIR HOUSING MARKETING; BLOCKBUSTING

Title I Housing Program

1.   Federal Housing Administration (FHA) loan insurance for building-improvement loans, authorized by Section 2, Title I of the National Housing Act of 1934 as amended. Insurance on loans, within specified limits, is available to finance major and minor improvements, alterations and repairs of homes, apartments, apartment buildings and nonresidential structures, whether owned or leased, as well as new construction for agricultural or nonresidential purposes. The loan insurance makes the cost of these home-improvement loans, the interest rate for which is set by the FHA, generally cheaper than conventional loans. In addition, specific provisions were added in 1974 concerning loan insurance for rehabilitation of residential buildings on the National Register of Historic Places.

2.   A program that provides FHA loan insurance for purchase or rehabilitation of mobile homes as authorized by Section 2, Title I of the National Housing Act of 1934. Despite the fact that mobile home loans have historically been treated as automobile loans and been offered at higher interest rates than home mortgages, the program has been successful in encouraging the financing of mobile homes because of the loan insurance and the somewhat lower FHA loan interest rate.
See: FEDERAL HOUSING ADMINISTRATION (FHA) MORTGAGE INSURANCE; MOBILE HOME; SECTION 207 HOUSING PROGRAM

Toll Road

A highway, bridge or tunnel on which fees are charged to repay the debt incurred in its construction and to finance its maintenance. Bonds to finance construction costs are often issued by state governments or special authorities established to build and operate a facility. The toll collected is to be used in repayment of these bonds.

Tolls have been charged for the use of public roads since ancient times, but their popularity with modern road builders stems from the post–World War II road-building era, during which highway design became vastly more sophisticated than in prior years. The advanced design required more funding than could be obtained from standard capital financing, and the extremely heavy use of the new roads indicated that drivers would be willing to bear the cost of the improved designs. The use of toll roads is popular in both the United States and Europe.

Topographic Map

A map that represents the configuration of a land area and also provides detailed information on many types of natural and man-made features. Topographic maps are generally prepared on a large enough scale so that relief, exact elevations above sea level, the size and shape of landforms, and the locations of physical features—such as streams, rivers, lakes, vegetation, etc.—are all identifiable. Cultural features—such as roads, parks and municipal boundaries— are also generally included.

A skilled reader of a topographic map is able to see an approximation of the land area in its three dimensions rather than as a flat surface. Not only will the major land features, such as mountains and valleys, be apparent, but related information—such as drainage patterns, slope steepness and configuration, and general suitability of land for development—can also be identified or deduced from the data on these maps.

Topographic maps are widely used by planners for numerous purposes, including site planning and development; regional planning; natural resource planning; analysis of potential locations for roads, parks or many other types of facilities; or as base or reference maps. Virtually all other professionals involved in land use—such as engineers, geologists, surveyors and architects—have uses for topographic maps.

Many maps are prepared by government agencies, such as the United States Geological Survey, Canada's Topographic Survey or Britain's Ordnance Survey. Others are prepared by state or municipal agencies or consultants, particularly if detailed data are needed for small areas. (See Fig. 48)
See: CONTOUR LINES; GEOLOGICAL SURVEY (USGS); RELIEF; USGS MAPS

Topography

A term that describes the collective physical features of a geographic area. Topography is sometimes also described more narrowly as consisting of surface relief.

A major determinant of development patterns, topography strongly influences the design of site plans. Such factors as slope, surface features, drainage patterns and impressive views are all taken into account during the design process, and modern flexible development techniques, such as cluster development, are intended in part to allow development to conform more naturally to topographic constraints and advantages. On a larger scale, topography has played a significant role in the physical form of cities and towns as well as their location. As an example, river valleys have always been attractive to human settlement because of their level terrain and proximity to a river, which served as both a source of water and a means of transportation.
See: RELIEF; SLOPE; TOPOGRAPHIC MAP; USGS MAPS

Tourism

The sector of an area's economy associated with attracting and serving people who visit the area for both pleasure and business purposes. Tourism supports a wide range of businesses offering goods and services to visitors.

Because many communities have suffered a decline in manufacturing, the traditional base of their economy, they have tried to make up for this loss with an increase in tourism. As a result, the attraction of tourists has become a major thrust of many economic development programs. In order to do this, many communities have financed substantial development projects oriented toward capturing this market, such as large waterfront developments, historic preservation projects, sports and entertainment facilities, and convention centers.

Tourism benefits an area in many ways and generates income that multiplies through the local economy. For example, tourism contributes directly to increased tax revenues through increased sales tax collections. It also produces income indirectly, through the generation of additional business, resulting in increased taxable income and enhancement of property values, leading to additional real estate tax collections. In addition, tourism increases local employment, particularly in the labor-intensive service industries, and helps to support the retail district of a community.
See: CHAMBER OF COMMERCE; CONVENTION CENTER

Town and Country Planning Association (TCPA)

An organization originally founded as the Garden City Association by Ebenezer Howard to promote the concept of garden cities. Today this London, England-based organization is more broadly concerned with the diverse aspects of planning and with helping the public to understand the principles of planning, but special interests include the decentralization of crowded urban areas and the formation of new towns.

TCPA provides a planning information service, holds conferences and operates study tours and a reference library. Its publications are *Town and Country Planning* and *Bulletin of Environmental Education,* both published monthly; *Planning Bulletin,* published weekly; and *Planning Bulletin Europe,* published every two months.
See: HOWARD, SIR EBENEZER

Town Square

An outdoor space—enclosed by major civic, cultural and commercial structures—that traditionally formed the core of a downtown area and functioned as the center of activity for a community. In many parts of the world, town squares have generally served as public gathering places. In England, however, the town square was most often surrounded by townhouses and its use restricted to their residents.

In the United States and Canada today, with the exception of collegiate squares and modern-day plazas, town square functions have largely been replaced by downtown shopping and office districts. In many other countries, however, town squares remain an important part of the urban structure. Generally paved and heavily used as a

meeting place and center of merchant activity, the town square is usually the location of a public market.
See: PLAZA

Town Supervisor

The elected chief executive of a town or township, called a trustee in several states. The supervisor has responsibility for administering town government, except where an appointed town manager has been delegated this responsibility. He generally presides over the town board, also serves on the county board in some states, and may serve as municipal tax assessor.

Supervisors in populous suburban towns have gained significant prestige and power in recent years because of the growing number of services these towns are providing and because of their increasing urbanization, while supervisors in more rural areas have turned over many responsibilities to county government.
See: CITY MANAGER; COUNTY BOARD; COUNTY EXECUTIVE; LOCAL GOVERNMENT; MAYOR

Townhouse

An attached dwelling, designed for residence by a single family or household, that shares a party or common wall and occasionally a single roof with at least one other similar residence. Townhouses today usually have more than one story within the dwelling and are frequently grouped with other residences of similar architectural design, often in planned unit developments or cluster developments. Townhouses and the land they rest upon are usually individually owned, but in the case of townhouse condominium development, a frequent arrangement, the townhouse dweller will own a proportional interest in the common areas of the development.

Originally, the term *townhouse* referred to a home in a city owned by someone with a primary residence in another location. It has now become a more modern way of referring to a rowhouse.
See: CLUSTER DEVELOPMENT; HOUSING TYPE; PLANNED UNIT DEVELOPMENT (PUD); ROWHOUSE

Township and Range Survey System

A system, established by Congress in the Ordinance of 1785, that divides and describes large portions of the land area of the United States lying north and west of the Ohio River. Known also as the congressional survey, rectangular survey method or government survey method, it apportions land into squares known as townships, with 6 miles (9.7 kilometers) to a side, and then subdivides townships into sections equal to 1 square mile, or 640 acres (259 hectares), a common unit of farm measurement. Further subdivisions are also made into half-sections, quarter-sections and quarter-quarters (40 acres, or 16 hectares). The system is based upon principal meridians (lines running north and south) and base lines (which run east and

west). Vertical rows of townships, known as ranges, were measured from either side of the principal meridians.

Congress specified this orderly and regular system of land division to counter the irregular patterns that had prevailed in the eastern states during the colonial period. It has had a very substantial effect upon land development patterns, ownership of agricultural land and the establishment of governmental districts in the areas in which it is in effect. (See Fig. 46)
See: ORDINANCE OF 1785

Toxic Substances

Those chemical substances that can cause harm to humans or the environment through various types of exposure. Toxic substances can cause immediate deleterious effects (acute toxicity) or long-term effects (chronic toxicity). Environmental toxicity refers to a circumstance in which a substance generally affects some aspect of the environment.

A variety of federal statutes are aimed at controlling various aspects of toxic substances, including their development and manufacture, their use and their disposal. Among these are the Toxic Substances Control Act; the Occupational Safety and Health Act; the Resource Conservation and Recovery Act; the Insecticide, Fungicide and Rodenticide Act; and the Clean Water and Clean Air Acts. Another act—the Comprehensive Environmental

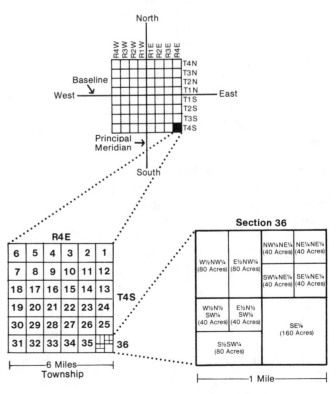

Fig. 46. The division of land into ranges, townships and sections was specified by Congress for many states lying north and west of the Ohio River.

Response, Compensation and Liability Act of 1980—is directed at protecting the public from toxic waste exposure by providing funding to help clean up or contain releases of hazardous substances or abandoned hazardous waste dumping sites.
See: HAZARDOUS WASTE

Toxic Substances Control Act of 1976 (TSCA)

A law (PL 94-469) that regulates many aspects of the testing, production and distribution of chemical substances in order to minimize unreasonable risks to human health and the environment due to exposure to toxic chemicals.

The act requires that all chemicals slated for commercial production be screened and tested prior to manufacture and that the U.S. Environmental Protection Agency be notified before production and be provided with test data. If EPA finds that there is insufficient information concerning the safety of the chemical, it can choose from a wide range of regulatory options, including requiring special labeling, limiting production or use, or banning use of the substance.

The act also authorizes EPA to control existing chemicals if they are thought to pose unreasonable risks. In addition, EPA is specifically required to regulate any chemical posing significant risks of birth defects, gene mutation or cancer. EPA was also directed by the act to develop and maintain a complete list of all chemicals subject to TSCA (the act exempts a number of substances, including food additives, drugs and nuclear materials from its provisions).

The act specifically bans the manufacturing, processing and distribution of PCBs. Other well-known chemicals that have come under new controls as a result of TSCA are asbestos; chlorofluorocarbons (CFC), which are used as spray can propellants; and dioxins.
See: HAZARDOUS WASTE; POLYCHLORINATED BIPHENYLS (PCBs); TOXIC SUBSTANCES

Track and Field Facilities

Coordinated athletic facilities that accommodate track events, such as sprints and high hurdles, as well as field events, such as the discus throw.

The running track is a recreational facility that is usually provided at high school and college athletic facilities but is also being included in some municipal and resort facilities. Generally built as a 0.25 mile (402-meter) track with an end radius of between 100 and 125 feet (30 and 38 meters), it requires an overall space of about 600×300 feet (183×91 meters) plus areas outside for spectators. Facilities for field events—such as jumping pits or areas for shotput, javelin, hammer and discus throw—are generally placed within the track. Where bleachers are provided, as at a high school, the track is sometimes designed with a football field in its interior so that the bleachers can double for both events.
See: ATHLETIC FIELDS

Traffic Control Devices

Traffic signs, signals, road marking and road bumps, which are used by traffic engineers to display regulations, to warn of potential hazards, to guide traffic, to segregate streams of traffic and to control vehicle speed. Efficiency of a road system is obtained by these devices, which permit competing users of a road system to use the system at the same time. Traffic control devices, singly or in combination, can also markedly change travel patterns and volumes. For example, signalization (placement of traffic signals) at intersections requires complex analysis of traffic movements and of the effects of the traffic signals on carrying capacity in order to permit the intersection to function optimally.

Placement of sign and traffic signal standards and the aesthetic impact of large or highly illuminated signs occasionally pose problems for planners. When the design or placement of a specific device is flexible, consideration should be given to reduction in size or lighting. Landscape screening can also be employed to protect adjacent land use. Control devices and road bumps can be used productively to reduce traffic volume and speed in residential areas, where land access and pedestrian safety are the principal functions of the street system.

Traffic Counts

An enumeration of vehicular movements taken at specific points of a road system. Counts are taken to show hourly volume and directional flow and—when taken for seven-day, monthly or annual periods—will indicate the average daily traffic (ADT), average annual daily traffic (AADT) and seasonal variation in use. Traffic counts are used by planners as a basic scale of comparison indicating the relative importance of various links in a road system.

A count on a specific road is an indicator of unused capacity in that road, inefficiency in the road system and the road's comparative safety. When performed on a systemwide basis, traffic counts are taken as sample counts on several of each type of road in the system—i.e., expressway, arterial, collector and local street. Counts are usually taken by mechanical recorders. Personal counting is necessary, however, at intersections, using hand-operated counters or tally sheets to obtain the numbers of turning movements in each direction, since mechanical counters are unable to differentiate between vehicles turning and those traveling straight through. Personal counts are also taken of trucks, buses and taxis for specific purposes.
See: AVERAGE ANNUAL DAILY TRAFFIC (AADT); PEAK-HOUR TRAFFIC VOLUME

Traffic Flow

The speed, volume and concentration of vehicles on a roadway. Its fundamental variables are vehicles per hour, vehicles per mile and the speed of traffic as determined by the mean speed of vehicles traveling over a given length of road (space mean speed) and the mean speed of vehicles passing a point during a given time interval (time mean speed).

Vehicles traveling on roadways are affected by a variety of prevailing conditions, which include roadway geometrics, sight distance, widths of lanes and shoulders and nearness to obstructions, entrances and exits, traffic controls, design speed, tolls, merging movements and other vehicles. The degree to which these conditions infringe on drivers causes variation in the flow of a stream of traffic. Knowledge of traffic flow characteristics for specific links in a road system is an important input to network assignment models and is useful in analyzing and evaluating geometric design and traffic control devices.

See: GEOMETRIC DESIGN; LANE WIDTH; NETWORK ASSIGNMENT; SHOULDER; SIGHT DISTANCE; TRAFFIC CONTROL DEVICES

Traffic Generator

A term used most often when describing a facility that draws large numbers of vehicles or pedestrians. Studies are undertaken by developers of proposed facilities to determine requirements for on-site circulation and parking, as well as to determine the site's accessibility by public roads and transit. Local planning and traffic agencies frequently undertake similar studies to enable a determination of road and parking capacity needed to accommodate such a facility. The specific areas that are addressed in these studies are the peak periods during which traffic will be generated; the amount and type of traffic—e.g., trucks expected; and the site improvements a developer would be required to make to enable the public street or transit system to function properly.

See: HIGHWAY CAPACITY DETERMINANTS; OFF-STREET PARKING; PEAK-HOUR TRAFFIC VOLUME; TRIP GENERATION

Train Terminal

The first and last stop of a passenger or freight train, which serves as the center of a regional area or as a location where several lines meet. Passenger terminals are generally located in central business districts (CBDs) and are large buildings that contain ticket sales booths; waiting areas; passenger facilities, including small shops; and transfer points to other transportation modes. They often contain 10 or more platforms for simultaneous train loading and accommodate both intercity and suburban rail lines. Train stations, which are generally located in CBDs of municipalities along the route between terminals, are usually smaller and have fewer platforms, depending upon the population they serve and whether intercity trains make stops. Freight terminals are large railway yards located in industrial districts.

Planning for passenger terminal districts should provide for a variety of facilities important to travelers, including access to a majority of intracity transportation modes, long-term parking areas (where space is available), and hotels and restaurants. Encouragement of office development in the vicinity is also a logical use, particularly where large numbers of workers commute by train.

Many passenger terminals and stations were built in the late 19th century, when use of the railroads was reaching its peak, and they often are architecturally important buildings. They are frequently sought after, however, as sites for office building development, either on air rights above them or as a replacement, incorporating train terminal uses at the basement levels of the proposed buildings. Alternatively, many train stations and terminals have been adapted to new uses, such as restaurants and retail facilities, which also provide space for passenger facilities.

See: ADAPTIVE USE; AIR RIGHTS; HIGH-SPEED RAIL TRANSPORTATION; HISTORIC PRESERVATION; INTERMODAL TERMINAL; *PENN CENTRAL TRANSPORTATION COMPANY* v. *CITY OF NEW YORK;* RAILWAY YARD; SUBURBAN COMMUTER RAILWAY

Transfer of Development Rights (TDR)

A land management device by which the development potential of one piece of property is severed from that property and transferred elsewhere. The concept views the right to develop property as a part of the bundle of rights comprising land ownership that may be transferred to others, leaving the property owner with all remaining rights of ownership.

TDR is used most commonly to protect historic sites, environmentally sensitive areas or key open-space parcels. Ideally, TDR attempts to mitigate the economic burden of requiring a single property owner to bear the cost of preserving a particular site or landmark structure without incurring the public cost of acquiring (by purchase or eminent domain) a conservation easement or similar interest in the property. However, the use of TDR as a constitutional means of limiting or restricting development has been subject to mixed judicial acceptance.

With TDR the police power, rather than the power of eminent domain, is used to restrict development. The property owner whose development rights have been restricted is compensated by being allowed to transfer those rights to other parcels he may own in a designated receiving area. Alternatively, he may sell those rights to other owners of property in the receiving area, but in such a case, the viability of the TDR program depends upon the salability of the rights to be transferred.

TDR programs have been proposed or adopted in a variety of areas of the United States, including the cities of New York and Chicago and several smaller New York state communities. (See Fig. 47)

See: FRED F. FRENCH INVESTING COMPANY, INC. v. *CITY OF NEW YORK; PENN CENTRAL TRANSPORTATION COMPANY* v. *CITY OF NEW YORK*

Transfer Station

A facility that serves as an intermediate destination for solid waste. At the transfer station waste delivered by smaller collection vehicles is compacted to reduce its vol-

**TRANSFER
OF DEVELOPMENT RIGHTS
(TDR)**

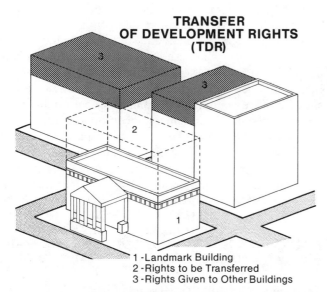

1 - Landmark Building
2 - Rights to be Transferred
3 - Rights Given to Other Buildings

Fig. 47. Transfer of development rights is being utilized in some locations to protect historic buildings by permitting their owners to sell unused-development rights for use within a specified area.

ume, aggregated and then transported in much larger vehicles to waste disposal plants or sanitary landfills.

Transfer stations are used when there are substantial distances between collection points and the solid waste disposal facility in order to reduce transportation costs and prolong the life of collection vehicles. The most significant problem that planners face in relation to transfer stations is finding an appropriate location for this type of facility. A site must be located where surrounding land uses are not adversely affected, where the expected volume of truck traffic can be accommodated and for which community approval can be secured.
See: RESOURCE RECOVERY; SANITARY LANDFILL; SOLID WASTE MANAGEMENT

Transit Fare Subsidies

Discounts on public transit fares for the elderly and disabled. Fare subsidies are offered by municipalities so that these groups are not prevented from using transportation because of high costs. Fare subsidies are also made available to children who must use public transit to go to school.

Usually valid only during nonrush hours, these subsidies encourage mobility of these relatively immobile groups while producing some revenue during time periods in which the system is underutilized. Discounts on entrance fees for parks and cultural facilities are offered for the same reasons.
See: PLANNING FOR THE DISABLED; PLANNING FOR THE ELDERLY

Transit Mall

A street that has been improved for pedestrian use but retains a roadway that is reserved for transit vehicles. A

transit mall is a type of shopping mall that prohibits vehicular use except mass transit, such as regular bus routes; transit mall jitneys; or fare-free buses, which provide access along the length of the mall. Delivery vehicles that must serve the stores along the mall are also permitted but may be limited to certain hours of the day. Taxis and bicycles are allowed in some transit malls as well.
See: PEDESTRIAN IMPROVEMENTS; PEDESTRIANIZATION; SHOPPING MALL

Transitional Lot

A lot bordering upon land that is in another zoning district. The "transitional lot" classification is used when the municipality has established a set of regulations aimed specifically at ameliorating difficulties that can occur at the boundaries of two zoning districts.

Transitional yards are sometimes required on transitional lots where a more intensive land use abuts a less intensive use. The transitional yard requirements replace standard yard requirements for that district to ensure that an adequate buffer zone is provided.
See: BUFFER ZONE; TRANSITIONAL USES; ZONING

Transitional Uses

Land uses that help to ease the transition between neighboring land uses where zoning districts of different permitted intensities abut. Potentially incompatible uses may be located backing upon each other or have additional required rear yard area between them. Comprehensive screening and/or fencing requirements are also used to encourage smoother land use transitions.
See: BUFFER ZONE; TRANSITIONAL LOT; ZONING

Transportation Department

The government agency responsible for the provision, operation and maintenance of public transportation facilities—e.g., buses and subways. For financing purposes these activities are undertaken by an authority rather than by a municipal department in some communities.

Transportation departments frequently have administrative commissioners who oversee department operations, as well as citizen boards that set policy. Department activities usually include development of service routes and schedules, application for federal grants and the purchase of transportation equipment. Road and highway design and maintenance may also be within a transportation department's jurisdiction, although these functions are frequently the responsibility of a public works department or a separate highway department.

Transportation planning may also be undertaken by the transportation department, but it is usually coordinated with planning department and regional planning agency activities.

Transportation Engineering

An umbrella term for all systemwide planning and analysis for transportation facilities. It is the level of civil engineering at which transportation policy is developed.

Within this branch of engineering are highway geometric design engineering, road traffic engineering, transit engineering, railroad civil engineering, transportation terminal engineering, transportation operations and maintenance engineering, and transportation vehicle engineering.

See: CIVIL ENGINEERING; TRANSPORTATION SYSTEM MANAGEMENT (TSM)

Transportation Improvement Program (TIP)

A detailed and prioritized list of proposed mass transit capital projects that is prepared annually by municipalities as the basis for funding allocations by the Urban Mass Transportation Administration. TIP is designed to enable implementation of short-term (five-year) transportation programs that are part of a municipality's Transit Development Program (TDP) or other form of transportation plan. TDP is a more narrative version of TIP, which also includes management and financial details. The Program of Projects (POP), now required for funding under the Section 9 program, is generally presented as part of TIP.

Both TIP and TDP were necessary for funding under the Urban Mass Transportation Act of 1964 but requirements for TDP have been rescinded. An ongoing transportation planning process is still required, however. This may be in the form of a TDP or in an alternate form and must be certified by the local municipality as an approved transportation plan.

Transportation Plan

An element of a comprehensive plan that indicates a community's street and mass transit network as of a future date. Based on an extensive analysis of circulation requirements related to proposed land use and community values, the transportation plan should show street classification; bus and rapid transit routes; rail lines; airports; principal terminals; and other significant improvements, such as busways and parking facilities.

See: COMPREHENSIVE PLAN; LAND USE PLAN; TRANSPORTATION PLANNING; TRANSPORTATION SYSTEM MANAGEMENT (TSM)

Transportation Planning

The development of plans for the orderly and efficient movement of people and goods through the establishment of goals and objectives, the analysis of existing patterns of movement and system conditions, the development of models to test proposed improvements and the development of alternative plans of action. Transportation planning is an integral part of land use planning and must be evaluated in connection with land use plans.

Transportation planning starts with the establishment of community goals and objectives to be met by the process. Forecasts of economic activity and land use conditions for future years must be made to provide a framework for alternative transportation plans. Data collection and analysis are necessary to identify a current base level of activity. Current population, land use, travel patterns, patterns of economic activity, the current transportation network (highway, mass transit, rail), pertinent local ordinances and policy, and available financing must all be studied. Where planning is undertaken for a large area, travel-demand models are employed to observe large-scale changes over projected time periods. Models for trip generation and trip distribution, mode choice or modal split, and traffic assignment and parking are typically employed. Analysis of specialized elements—such as freight handling, harbors and airport activity—must be included to determine their impact on the overall system.

Specific proposals for road improvements or other changes in the transportation system are made on the basis of these analyses. Alternative plans are often developed to offer a choice to the public and to provide a choice related to financing and other variables.

Many communities in the United States have largely completed construction of their transportation systems. In those communities the emphasis is on improving the quality of service while reducing public cost. To accomplish this, transportation system management is stressed as a means of making more efficient use of existing facilities. In municipalities where federal funds for mass transit are necessary, the development of a Transportation Improvement Program (a prioritized list of capital projects) is required.

See: TRANSPORTATION SYSTEM MANAGEMENT (TSM)

Transportation Research Board (TRB)

A unit of the National Research Council whose purpose is the advancement of knowledge concerning transportation systems. The TRB, which operates under the authority of the National Academy of Sciences, is a private, nonprofit organization that was established in 1920 as the Advisory Board on Highway Research. In 1924 it became the Highway Research Board, and in 1974 it received its current name, reflecting a broader interest in all modes of transportation. Among its range of interests is planning and design, construction, operation and financing of transportation systems.

The TRB, which is located in Washington, D.C., performs a wide variety of functions. It undertakes, monitors and administers research projects; coordinates committees and task forces; conducts conferences and workshops; and responds to inquiries from highway and transportation departments and others working in the transportation field. In addition, a number of computerized data storage and retrieval services are operated by the TRB to provide information on ongoing projects as well as article and report abstracts. Information is international in scope, provided by federal and state agencies in the United States as well as the International Road Federation and the International Road Research Documentation Network. The following services are available: the Highway Research Information

Service (HRIS), the Railroad Research Information Service (RRIS), the Maritime Research Information Service (MRIS), the Air Transportation Research Information Service (ATRIS) and the Highway Safety Literature (HSL) Service. Under development is an Urban Mass Transportation Research Information Service (UMTRIS). The TRB also issues many publications in general and specialized areas of transportation.

Transportation System Management (TSM)

A new form of transportation planning in which all transportation modes and systems are coordinated to obtain maximum efficiency and effectiveness. This approach is taken prior to recommending costly capital improvements for any of the individual modes. Based on a recognition that urban transportation systems are nearly complete in many urbanized areas, and that expansion of these systems is limited by financial resources and by often adverse community reactions, the transportation system management approach recommends improvements in the use of existing facilities. TSM is now a required prerequisite for federal transportation assistance and represents an attempt by the federal government to create a balance between highways and mass transit.

Typical TSM approach recommendations are: (1) those that deal with preferential facilities for high-occupancy vehicles (HOV), such as reserved lanes, preferential parking, auto disincentives, ridepooling proposals and ramp metering; (2) bus service improvements, such as express bus operations, improved scheduling and the provision of park-and-ride facilities; (3) road improvements—e.g., intersection channelization and widening and traffic signal improvements; and (4) preferential areas for nonmotorized traffic, such as facilities that provide pedestrian separation, automobile restricted zones (ARZ) and bikepaths.
See: AUTO DISINCENTIVES; AUTOMOBILE RESTRICTED ZONE (ARZ); BIKEWAY; FLEX-TIME; PARK-AND-RIDE FACILITIES; RESERVED LANES; REVERSIBLE LANES; RIDEPOOLING; STAGGERED WORK HOURS; TRANSPORTATION PLANNING

Tree Preservation Ordinance

A tree preservation ordinance regulates the cutting of mature trees of specific caliper on private property, and also specifies standards for protecting trees from damage from such sources as adjacent construction or grading. It may be applied on a community-wide basis, or specific zones may be established, generally in low density residential areas. Their basis are the many environmental and aesthetic benefits that trees provide including: protection of soil and watersheds; provision of wildlife habitat; buffering of noise and air pollution; and climate moderation.

Some types of tree preservation ordinances require that site plans for new developments locate all trees on the site of a designated size, and indicate which trees would be removed, which would be preserved, and state how the trees to be preserved will be protected during the construc-

tion. The plans are then reviewed before this may take place. In some communities, regulations may protect any tree in the community above a certain significant size, or any tree of a rare species, or trees that are serving a valuable purpose. Clearwater, Florida, for example, forbids the removal of mangrove trees, without a permit, if the trees, which help to prevent coastal erosion, are located within a specified distance of the shoreline.

In Britain local planning authorities can protect trees or woodlands through tree-preservation orders as well as require the planting of trees. If a "preserved tree" dies or is removed, the landowner may be required to replace it.
See: SHADE TREE COMMISSION

Trip

A journey between two points—e.g., home to office. Trip purposes, distances, durations, travel modes and frequency are studied by transportation planners to provide a data base for planning.
See: TRANSPORTATION PLANNING

Trip Distribution

The measure of the number of vehicles or passenger movements that are or will be made between zones. This measure is calculated by use of one of several models, all of which are based on the theory that a trip that originates in a given origin zone will find an attraction to a specific destination zone. Each model calculates the probabilities differently. Results of trip distribution studies show the distribution of all trips from one zone to every other zone.

The gravity model, the most common method of predicting travel movements, is relatively simple to use and is considered reliable. Other models used to predict trip distribution are the intervening opportunities model, the competing opportunities model, the Fratar growth-factor method and a linear programming approach.
See: GRAVITY MODEL; TRIP GENERATION

Trip Generation

The measure of the number of trips that originate or end at a specific facility or zone, for the purpose of determining demand on the road and transit systems and demand for parking facilities. For planning purposes trips are analyzed by type of land use, socioeconomic characteristics of the population, trip functions, time of day, travel mode, trip frequency and trip duration.

Trip generation estimates for a single program or facility will typically predict the number of trips that it will produce on the basis of observed rates at existing facilities that are as identical to it as possible. Citywide or systemwide analysis will project demographic counts and land use patterns to a future date as a basis for estimating trips between zones. Trip generation models are generally applied to known travel data, obtained by various types of traffic-counting studies, to estimate future trips.

Studies of trip generation in American and Canadian cities of different sizes have shown that individuals in

lower-density communities generally make more vehicular trips per day than those in higher-density communities. These observations are attributed to increased car ownership, greater dependence on the automobile, availability of parking space and relative unavailability of mass transit alternatives. Conversely, pedestrian trip rates and mass transit trip rates increase with greater population density.
See: CORDON AND SCREENLINE COUNTS; ORIGIN-DESTINATION (O-D) STUDY; PARKING STUDY; TRAFFIC COUNTS; TRAFFIC GENERATOR; TRIP

Trolley

A mass transit vehicle similar in appearance to a small train car that travels by rail over a fixed route and is powered by electricity supplied by overhead wires. A trolley, also called a streetcar or a tramway, is classified as rapid light rail transit (RLT).

Popular in many European cities since their introduction, trolleys are gaining increasing attention in North America as a replacement for buses because they are cheaper to operate, cause less air pollution and can carry more passengers. Trolleys, on their own right-of-way, are seen as a means by which large volumes of passengers can be handled at a cost considerably lower than that of a subway system. Proposals in various cities provide for lengths of trolley routes in tunnels, in the center mall of a freeway or on separate routes parallel to existing streets, as well as within streets.

Articulated vehicles (two cars attached by a flexible connection) are employed in many European cities to provide additional carrying capacity. In England the railbus, a trolley vehicle that has a railroad chassis and a bus body and is capable of operating on its steel wheels or on a set of rubber tires, is being tested for possible wide application. The railbus can run interchangeably as a trolley or a bus for various segments of its routes.
See: MASS TRANSIT

Truck Terminals

1. Buildings in which truck freight is transferred from collection vehicles to distribution vehicles or to freight haulers, and vice versa. Truck terminal buildings are usually located in central city industrial areas at the centers of package express routes, mail distribution areas and trucking areas. New and auxiliary terminals, however, are increasingly locating in industrial parks, which are ideally suited for heavy truck access. These buildings must provide facilities and space to accommodate a variety of truck types, as well as room for trucks to maneuver to permit efficient truck arrivals and departures. Warehouse space is often provided in or near the terminal.

2. Parking lots in which double trailer trucks are separated and a cab attached to each vehicle. These are usually located near freeway interchanges, outside of densely populated areas that prohibit double vehicles.

3. Parking lots for the storage and servicing of trucks.
See: FREIGHT HANDLING FACILITIES; INDUSTRIAL PARK; WAREHOUSE FACILITIES

Trunk Sewer

A large-diameter sewer pipe that collects wastewater from sewer mains and delivers it to an interceptor sewer, sewage treatment plant or outfall. Trunk lines are usually located in valleys at the base of the drainage basin that the sewer system serves. A sewerage system will have relatively few trunk sewers, because each trunk is sized to collect the large volume of wastewater produced by an entire catchment basin or drainage basin. In some classifications of sewer size, trunks are referred to as mains and mains are called branch sewers.
See: INTERCEPTOR SEWER; OUTFALL; SEWAGE TREATMENT PLANT; SEWER MAIN; SEWERAGE SYSTEM

Tunnel

An underground passageway that is produced by excavation and built for transportation or utility transmission purposes. Tunnels are constructed under bodies of water, through mountains and under populated areas to bypass more congested or circuitous routes and as a means of grade separation. In densely urbanized areas almost all utilities are tunneled under streets, and in some cities, as in Montreal, vast underground pedestrian networks connect stores, buildings and subway stations.

Turbidity

The existence of suspended materials in water or particles in air that cause cloudiness in the medium. Turbidity in water may be caused by a variety of factors, including dredging and runoff. Although suspended materials tend to settle to the bottom of a water body, they can be resuspended by rains, winds or passing boats. Degree of turbidity can also be affected by season and environment.

Turbidity controls the degree to which sunlight can reach aquatic vegetation and permit normal plant growth, a basic link in the food chain. Turbidity is also detrimental to the quality of drinking water and usually requires removal by water treatment processes.

Turnkey Project

1. A public housing project that is constructed by a private developer for a public housing agency. Developers are invited to submit proposals to the agency initiating the project, and the best proposal (or in some states the lowest bid) is selected to be built by the developer on the condition that the public agency will purchase it upon completion. Depending upon local requirements, either the developer or the municipality will supply the site. The name implies that the public agency need simply turn the key in the door of its new building without actually constructing it.

Developed in 1968, it has been a successful program, enabling cost reduction and relative ease of construction management. The principles of turnkey development have also been used in the construction of other types of municipal projects.

2. A term applied to a development that, upon prior agreement, is built by a developer and sold to another entity. Developers who specialize in this form of construction are known as turnkey developers.
See: PUBLIC HOUSING; SALE-LEASEBACK

Type I Error

A type I, or alpha, error is one in which the null hypothesis is rejected although it is true. For example, if the null hypothesis is that there is no difference in air pollution levels when cars are equipped with air pollution control devices, a type I error consists of incorrectly rejecting this hypothesis. Generally, the odds of making a type I error decrease as the level of significance (a cutoff point at which a researcher determines that nonchance factors are at work) decreases. This, however, increases the odds of making a type II error.
See: NULL HYPOTHESIS; TYPE II ERROR

Type II Error

A type II, or beta, error is one in which there is a failure to reject the null hypothesis although it is false. Generally, lowering the level of significance increases the probability of making a type II error.
See: NULL HYPOTHESIS; TYPE I ERROR

U

ULI—The Urban Land Institute

A nonprofit research and educational organization, founded in 1936, whose principal interest is quality land use planning and development. ULI members and associates consist of a wide range of participants in the field of land use, including developers, planners, architects, public officials, officers of financial institutions, lawyers, academicians and real estate professionals.

ULI maintains a reference library and information service at its Washington, D.C. headquarters and conducts research on a broad variety of topics related to land and development with the aid of its interdisciplinary staff. ULI has an extensive publications program through which it produces books; handbooks, including the *Community Builders' Handbook* series; case studies; and technical reports. A popular publication is its *Project Reference File* (PRF), which provides complete data on significant development projects of varying types. Data offered include site plans; photographs; project statistics; land use controls used; planning, architectural and engineering features; and marketing features. Regular monthly periodicals published by ULI are *Urban Land, Environmental Comment* and *Land Use Digest*. A Panel Advisory Service is also operated, in which panels consisting of ULI members will donate their time to aid local sponsors—such as planning commissions, economic development organizations or private developers—requesting assistance.

Undergrounding of Utilities

The placement of electric and telephone cables in underground trenches or ducts rather than on poles above the ground. In many urban and suburban areas, utility undergrounding is required by local legislation, largely for aesthetic reasons, although an underground location also protects them from the weather.

In areas that have previously been served by aboveground wires, burial of cables is an expensive undertaking, which usually proceeds slowly in conjunction with the construction of new subdivisions or other development. Here the expense may be borne jointly by the utility company and the developer.

In urban areas, where utility wires generally follow the street pattern, lines may be placed in the beds of the streets or under sidewalks or, less commonly, may run along rear property lines.
See: ELECTRIC TRANSMISSION LINE; TELEPHONE SYSTEM

Uniform Assessment Procedures

Proposed reforms of property assessment procedures that reduce a municipality's authority in the establishment of assessment ratios for tax purposes.

Full-value assessment is currently accepted as the most equitable approach to assessment, since when all properties are assessed at their full market value, assessment ratios may be eliminated entirely. The classified property tax—in which properties are assessed at market value but are grouped to permit either special assessment ratios, special tax rates or special in lieu taxes—is used to some extent in many states. With the classified property tax, the state rather than the municipality sets the discount received by a class of property. Equalization rates, imposed on total municipal assessed valuation where fractional assessment is practiced, yield a truer picture of the municipality's property values in comparison with other municipalities, enabling the state to more equitably distribute state aid.

Other ways that assessment administration may be improved include an increased use of professional assessors, better systems for recording property improvements and tax mapping, computerization of assessment data and

comprehensive reappraisals of property throughout a taxing district.
See: ASSESSED VALUATION; ASSESSMENT RATIO; EQUALIZATION RATE; FULL-VALUE ASSESSMENT

Uniform Crime Reports

Annual publications of the Federal Bureau of Investigation that report crime incidence and other related data for over 15,000 United States municipalities. The reports are useful for comparative purposes, as social indicators and in criminal justice planning.
See: CRIMINAL JUSTICE PLANNING; URBAN INDICATORS

Unincorporated Area

A geographic area to which certain powers are assigned by state law; included in this classification are counties, townships or towns, school districts, special districts and, in some states, boroughs. Unincorporated areas are quasi-corporations, since the state charter often grants them powers similar to those of some incorporated municipalities.

The boundaries of unincorporated areas are adopted by the state and are primarily intended to permit state services to be handled locally. Municipal corporations (predominantly cities and villages) are created at the request of local residents and have a larger measure of self-government, although the distinctions between the powers of municipal corporations and those of unincorporated areas are disappearing.
See: LOCAL GOVERNMENT; MUNICIPAL CORPORATION; POLITICAL SUBDIVISION

United States Housing Act of 1937

Legislation that established federal policy with respect to provision of "decent, safe, and sanitary dwellings for families of low income" and that authorized the public housing program and created the United States Housing Authority (USHA) to administer the program. This act (PL 75-412), which has formed the basis of federal public housing programs since that time, authorized the USHA to make loans and grants to local housing authorities to assist in the development, acquisition or administration of low-rent housing or slum clearance projects. Contributions to local public housing agencies were also authorized to enable them to continue providing housing at a low rent.
See: HOUSING AUTHORITY; NATIONAL HOUSING ACT; PUBLIC HOUSING

Universities

Generally regarded as an asset to a community, universities, colleges, specialized research institutes and community colleges have a complicated and unique relationship with municipalities. They are major employers, consumers of services and goods provided by local commerce and providers of educational and cultural resources. Con-

versely, they usually pay few taxes and may make large demands on the public infrastructure in the form of public transportation, road and traffic improvements, community revitalization, housing code enforcement and police protection. Except for small-scale development on the campus itself, planning for universities is often a joint effort of campus planners and community planners.

Siting of new universities usually takes place in one of two ways. In one case a large suburban site may be chosen on which a nucleus of college buildings is located, with a large land reserve for expansion and sports facilities. Alternatively, a large urban building can be converted to educational use although new construction may take place in urban areas.

Declining university enrollment related to population decline in the age group of traditional college attendance has forced many institutions of higher learning to seek student bodies with wide age ranges and educational goals. To accomplish this they must cater to the requirements of these groups by providing an expanded range of degree options and evening and weekend classes. In spite of this, many smaller colleges have closed.

Unwin, Sir Raymond (1863–1940)

A British architect and town planner who, along with Barry Parker, was responsible for the design of Letchworth, the first garden city. This development, a practical application of the theories of Ebenezer Howard, had a marked impact upon the evolution of town planning. Another significant development, Hampstead Garden Suburb, was also designed by Unwin and Parker.

Unwin held a number of important government positions in which he was able to influence the formulation of policy. He served as chief town planning inspector under the Local Government Board, was director of housing for the Ministry of Munitions (1916–18) and was chief architect for the Ministry of Health, whose *Housing Manual* he prepared in 1918.

From 1931 to 1933 Unwin served as president of the Royal Institute of British Architects (whose gold medal he received in 1937); he also taught at both Birmingham University (1911–14) and Columbia University (1936–40). He was knighted for his accomplishments in 1932.
See: HAMPSTEAD GARDEN SUBURB, ENGLAND; HOWARD, SIR EBENEZER; LETCHWORTH, ENGLAND

Unzoned Areas

1. Municipalities that have not adopted zoning regulations. Houston, Texas is the best known of those municipalities in the United States that have elected not to adopt a zoning ordinance or other form of zoning regulation to control land development. It relies instead on subdivision regulations to control subdivision layout, lot size and building setbacks from the street; a private street ordinance, which essentially extends subdivision controls to private multifamily housing developments; and deed restrictions established by developers in subdivisions to en-

sure continued use as single-family dwellings (these are estimated to cover two-thirds of the city). Capital improvements, a major thoroughfare and freeway plan, a generalized land use plan to induce development to locate where the city government would like it to and market demand for developable sites are also depended upon. In 1982 a municipal ordinance was adopted that controls building setbacks and block lengths in areas where these aspects of development were not previously controlled.

2.   Parts of municipalities that have not been included in any zoning district. Zoning ordinances sometimes leave unzoned those major land uses that are considered to be of a permanent nature or that have a useful life beyond the period for which the zoning ordinance is expected to have effect. Such land uses include public parks and buildings and other major public gathering places. Should their current use be threatened, a zoning designation for the area may be adopted to control future use of the site.
See: SUBDIVISION REGULATIONS; ZONING; ZONING DISTRICT

Upset Price

The lowest permissible sales price for a property. An upset price, also known as a minimum price, may be established by the courts in a foreclosure proceeding prior to public auction of property. Property owners may also set the lowest price they find acceptable, as when a government agency disposes of surplus property through auction or an individual offers a home for sale through a real estate broker.

Upzoning

1.   A zoning classification change for a parcel of land to a category that permits more intensive development. Examples of upzoning are changes from single-family to multifamily development or from residential to commercial development. The opposite of upzoning is downzoning.

2.   A zoning classification change to a zoning category permitting less intensive development. Although not the accepted meaning of the term as evolved from usage by the courts and professional planners, it is often used by the general public and news media.
See: DOWNZONING; HIGHEST AND BEST USE; ZONING

Urban and Regional Information Systems Association (URISA)

An organization concerned with the effective use of information systems and computers to aid public officials in making informed decisions. URISA, which was founded in 1963, derives its membership from elected and appointed government officials; professionals involved in such fields as planning, community development, systems analysis, municipal finance, assessment, public safety and engineering; government organizations; students and academicians; and representatives of the computer industry.

URISA activities include an annual conference; workshops and seminars on new technological developments; and publication of a bimonthly newsletter, the proceedings of the annual conference and professional papers. Special-interest groups have formed within URISA to concentrate on particular topics, such as geoprocessing, remote sensing, social indicators and the decennial census. URISA, which is located in Bethesda, Maryland, maintains local sections throughout the United States and Canada.

Urban County

A county that is eligible to receive funding under the Community Development Block Grant (CDBG) program as an entitlement municipality. To qualify for this designation, it must have a minimum population of 200,000 located outside of entitlement cities and be authorized by state law to conduct housing and community development programs in its unincorporated municipalities.

An urban county enters into cooperation agreements with those of its municipalities that elect to participate in the program. This agreement authorizes the county to undertake or to assist in the undertaking of essential community development and housing activities. Cities with populations of less than 50,000 may elect to participate in the Urban County program for a three-year period, or alternatively, they may apply for grants under the Small Cities Program.
See: COMMUNITY DEVELOPMENT BLOCK GRANT (CDBG); SMALL CITIES PROGRAM

Urban Cultural Park

An area of an older city that is designated for preservation and improvement of significant historic sites. A relatively new concept, it is an attempt to leverage private investment in culturally important areas by offering municipal or state seed money on a matching basis. It is expected that the result of such reinvestment will encourage tourism, create jobs, preserve historically valuable buildings and generally renew an area.
See: HISTORIC PRESERVATION

Urban Design

A process of design that treats the development of the built environment in a comprehensive manner as a means of achieving a unified, functionally efficient and aesthetically appealing physical setting.

In its simplest form, the term can refer to the development of a plan that coordinates building design with the design of other elements of the streetscape, including paving, landscaping and street furniture. In its more complex form, urban design may refer to a process in which a number of individuals—including designers, public officials and citizens—work with and coordinate the multitude of aesthetic, technical, financial and other forces that shape the environment. In either case, the goal of the process is to develop an overall plan that treats an area as a system of spaces, structures and inhabitants rather than as a series of unrelated buildings and streets.

See: BUILT ENVIRONMENT; DESIGN CONTINUITY; SENSE OF PLACE; STREETSCAPE; URBAN PLANNING

Urban Development Action Grant (UDAG)

A federal program authorized by Section 119 of the Housing and Community Development Act of 1977 that provides grants to support economic and neighborhood development projects in distressed urban areas. Eligible project categories are commercial (retail, office, hotel, etc.), industrial (warehouse or manufacturing) and neighborhood (including housing construction and rehabilitation).

UDAG projects must alleviate physical or economic distress, create jobs, increase the local tax base and attract private investment. Projects are required to have a leveraging ratio (the number of dollars of private investment generated by each dollar of the UDAG grant) of at least 2.5, while the average ratio of all projects to date is 6. Also required are a firm private financial commitment and assurances that the project would not be undertaken without the grant. UDAG proposals are evaluated by the Department of Housing and Urban Development on a competitive basis.

See: HOUSING AND COMMUNITY DEVELOPMENT ACT OF 1980

Urban Development Corporation (UDC)

A public corporation, established by New York state in 1968, that was intended to redevelop substandard areas of the state and build housing for low- and moderate-income families. To accomplish this, it was authorized to override local zoning and building laws, to condemn and acquire land, and to undertake development. By 1975, when its poor financial situation forced a reorientation of its objectives, it had undertaken 116 housing projects containing almost 33,000 dwelling units, including Roosevelt Island in New York City, and had begun construction of the new towns of Radisson, near Syracuse, and Audubon, near Buffalo. Thirty nonresidential projects were also underway.

UDC's power to override local zoning made it almost omnipotent, but in 1973 this authority was withdrawn by the legislature as a result of a bitter controversy over development of low-income housing in Westchester, a suburban county on New York City's northern border. Because of this setback and the major financial difficulties that led to the removal of its authority to issue tax-exempt bonds, UDC's mission was converted in the late 1970s to stimulating economic development. In this role it is responsible for developments such as the New York Convention Center, restoration of the historic Schermerhorn Row buildings in the South Street Seaport preservation project, participation in the Battery Park City development and the redevelopment of the 42nd Street area, all in New York City, as well as the Carrier Dome Stadium in Syracuse.

Numerous projects related to preservation of jobs and commercial revitalization, such as development of industrial parks and shopping malls, have also been undertaken in depressed areas throughout the state.

Urban Economics

The study of the system of production, consumption and distribution within an urban area and surrounding areas, to the degree that they are dependent on the urban area. Based on theories of regional economics, the techniques used to analyze an urban economy are also applicable to a regional or national economy. In fact, because of the difficulty in obtaining reliable data for smaller areas, these techniques are often more easily used on a regional level.

Two conceptual approaches are generally used to study an urban economy. The first views the economic structure of a city as intrinsically related to the economic structure of the region and nation. A city's economic position is a direct function of the share of regional and national goods produced by that city, and economic growth occurs when a city increases its share. Regional approaches focus on spatial linkages, on the interdependence of the city with the region and nation, and on the interdependence among various industries. Input-output analysis is an example of a regionally oriented approach.

The second approach is an urban-centered orientation. This orientation focuses on goods produced within a city that are consumed outside the city and views the economic structure of a city as a function of its export or basic activities. Economic base analysis is an example of an urban-centered approach.

Urban Enterprise Zones

A special designation granted to selected geographic areas on the basis of economic need. In an enterprise zone, business activities are encouraged by the removal or relaxation of many types of government controls as well as through financial incentives such as tax abatement. The enterprise-zone approach is envisioned as a kind of "free market" successor to earlier federal programs, such as urban renewal and Model Cities, that were aimed at improving conditions in specific distressed areas with large inflows of federal aid. In contrast, enterprise zones rely on the response of the marketplace to the various incentives that are offered in the zones.

Enterprise zones were first developed and used in Britain as a means of rejuvenating derelict areas, such as areas of abandoned docks and mines or factories that had become obsolete. In 1980, 11 zones averaging 250 acres (100 hectares) in size were designated for a ten-year experimental period (subject to renewal). In these zones, abatement of local property taxes and land development taxes is offered as well as incentives for capital investment and reduced planning controls.

In the United States, federal enterprise zone legislation has been introduced several times but has yet to gain approval. The most recent version of the administration bill, the proposed Enterprise Zone Employment and Development Act of 1983, provides for the nomination by state and local government of potential enterprise zones eligible for federal incentives. The Secretary of the Department of Housing and Urban Development would have the authority to designate as many as 75 zones from among the applications during a three-year period. Potential areas include over two thousand cities, rural areas and Indian reservations with eligibility based on criteria related to unemployment, poverty and decline in population. A major aspect of the selection process would focus on the extent that state and local government incentives would be granted, and the degree to which government burdens on development would be reduced. Those zones selected would be eligible for federal incentives for a period of up to 20 years as well as a 4-year period during which the program would be phased out.

Federal incentives available within an enterprise zone would include tax credits for capital investments in personal property; for rehabilitation or construction of commercial, industrial or rental housing structures; for payroll to employees above that paid in the year before zone designation; and for wages paid to disadvantaged workers. In addition, employees within a zone would be eligible for tax credits. Other incentives would include, if appropriate, the elimination of certain capital gains taxes, foreign trade zone designation and availability of industrial revenue bonds, even if this program is discontinued outside of enterprise zones. State and local units of government are also permitted to request relief from specific federal regulations hindering business activity, with the exception of minimum wage or civil rights laws, or those laws designed to protect public safety or the environment.

A number of states have already passed their own enterprise-zone legislation so that they may begin state programs at this time or be prepared to offer state incentives at such a time as federal enterprise zone legislation may be enacted. Among these states are Connecticut, Florida, Indiana, Louisiana, Maryland and Ohio. As an example, Connecticut, the first state to pass state enterprise zone legislation, offers such incentives as venture capital loans, tax credits, tax assessment freezes and grants for newly created jobs.
See: FOREIGN TRADE ZONES

Urban Growth and New Community Development Act of 1970

Legislation that, under Title VII of the Housing and Urban Development Act of 1970, authorized the Department of Housing and Urban Development (HUD) to provide loan guarantees and other assistance to public and private developers of four types of new communities: (1) satellite or suburban new communities within existing metropolitan areas, as an alternative to sprawl; (2) new-towns-in-town, located within existing central cities; (3) small town growth centers to be expanded into new communities; and (4) free-standing, self-sufficient new towns far from existing metropolitan areas. The goal was to encourage the development of well-planned, diversified and economically sound new communities.

The act authorized loan guarantees to secure a developer's obligations for land acquisition, site development and public facilities, as well as supplementary grants to cover the local matching funds necessary to obtain federal open space, sewer and water grants. Under the act, 11 new communities received loan guarantees, ranging from $5 million to the statutory limit of $50 million.

Between this act and its precursor, the New Communities Act of 1968, a total of 13 new communities received loan guarantees totaling almost $300 million. By 1975 enough projects were in financial difficulty for HUD to cease accepting new applications. Of the 13 projects, 12 went into default. By 1982 HUD had acquired 9 projects, of which it resold 7, and it was seeking new developers for the remainder. HUD is expected to phase out its involvement in new communities by 1984.

The financial problems were due partly to economic conditions (the 1973–75 recession and high interest rates), but other reasons included the large initial investment necessary for land, infrastructure and public facilities and the long wait until revenues from property sales cover these front-end costs. HUD accepted developers' overly optimistic financial projections, and it did not require developers to invest sufficient cash equity. Other problems were the lack of state and local government assistance, weak political support at the federal level and inadequate planning.

Despite financial problems, portions of six new communities were built at Park Forest South, Illinois; St. Charles Communities, Maryland; Cedar-Riverside, Minnesota; Jonathan, Minnesota; Riverton, New York; and The Woodlands, Texas.
See: COMMUNITY DEVELOPMENT BLOCK GRANT (CDBG); NEW COMMUNITIES ACT OF 1968; NEW TOWN

Urban Homesteading

An approach to the revitalization of urban areas whereby an individual is given an opportunity to become the owner of an abandoned or foreclosed property in return for a commitment to repair, occupy and maintain this property.

Originally conceived as a means of divesting government foreclosed properties while stabilizing or revitalizing decaying inner city neighborhoods through private home ownership, the idea was first implemented by several U.S. cities in the early 1970s. In 1974 the Department of Housing and Urban Development (HUD) included a homesteading program in the Housing and Community Development Act, which now provides local governments with funds to purchase vacant single-family properties from HUD, the Veterans Administration and the Farmers Home Administration. To participate in the program a municipality must apply to HUD and indicate defined homesteading areas. Upon program approval, vacant properties are transferred to the local jurisdiction which sells them for a nominal sum to individuals or families called "homesteaders." Homesteaders, who must be selected by the municipality on an equitable basis, are required to use the housing as their principal residences for at least 5 years and must bring it up to local code standards within 18 months. The homesteader is permitted to do the work himself or use contractors. When all conditions are met the homesteader receives full title to the property. A 1982 account of program activity indicated that since 1974, programs had been approved for 107 localities and that 6,233 formerly HUD-held properties had been transferred to 82 of the municipalities. In 1983 a demonstration multifamily urban homesteading program was initiated.

Historically, urban homesteading is rooted in the program created by the Homestead Act of 1862, in which individuals were offered 160 acres of frontier land in return for investing the time and resources necessary to make the land productive.
See: NEIGHBORHOOD PRESERVATION; SELF-HELP HOUSING; SWEAT EQUITY

Urban Indicators

Types of quantitative data that provide insight into the quality of life of an area. They may be used to compare two different communities or areas or to compare the same community in different years. Indicators can be particularly useful in measuring degrees of progress toward a defined community goal or objective.

Several types of urban indicators may be identified and are used for different purposes. Social indicators generally consider the state of the entire community as a whole and focus upon factors related to broad areas such as health, income, education, housing and public safety. Examples of social indicators are crime rates, median family income, families below the poverty level, percentage of high school graduates, infant mortality rates and number of substandard housing units. Social indicators are widely used in human services and health planning.

Impact indicators attempt to examine a particular program or plan more closely to see how well it is working. For example, an analysis of the effectiveness of a school district might focus upon measures of student performance and motivation, measures of teacher performance and attitudes, and the way in which the community perceives school district performance.

Performance indicators measure the volume of service rather than the quality of the service delivered. Number of inspections made, employees trained or housing units rehabilitated would be examples of this type of indicator. They are often used in connection with budget preparation or evaluation to monitor the costs of particular services.

Urban indicators are still in the early stages of development; although it is relatively simple to measure amount of output, quality or effectiveness is far more difficult to assess.

Urban Institute (UI)

An independent, nonprofit research and educational organization that conducts studies concerning the social and economic problems of urban areas. Another area of concern is the impact of government policies on urban communities and their populations. The Urban Institute provides information and research findings to aid government officials in their decision-making and formulation of policy, and to assist others concerned with government policy and its effects.

Research findings are made available to the public in a variety of books, reports and papers. A *Policy and Research Report* highlighting recent research findings and activities is published quarterly. The organization was founded in 1968 and is located in Washington, D.C.

Urban Mass Transportation Act of 1964

An act (PL 88-365), upon which all subsequent mass transportation legislation has been based, that provided federal support for mass transportation and rail systems. Funds were first administered by the Department of Housing and Urban Development and later by the Urban Mass Transportation Administration.

Grants were made available for two-thirds of the cost of capital projects (now 80 percent), including construction of rail lines, acquisition of rolling stock (trains and buses), right-of-way acquisition and station development. The act also extended indefinitely a $50 million fund for low-interest loans to metropolitan agencies for construction of mass transportation facilities. Transportation demonstration projects, previously authorized under the Housing Act of 1961, were continued and expanded under this act, and funding for research and development projects was also included.

Requirements are still in effect limiting this funding to government agencies and mandating that there be a coordinated transportation plan and an adequate relocation program for persons displaced by the construction projects. To accomplish this and enable a coordinated transit system, many jurisdictions created regional transportation authorities that often took over troubled private bus and rail companies or acted as pass-through agencies.
See: NATIONAL MASS TRANSPORTATION ACT OF 1974; TRANSPORTATION IMPROVEMENT PROGRAM (TIP); URBAN MASS TRANSPORTATION ADMINISTRATION (UMTA)

Urban Mass Transportation Administration (UMTA)

An agency within the Department of Transportation that administers federal programs related to mass transportation. Its purview includes assistance in the development of improved transportation facilities, encouragement of areawide urban mass transportation systems where they are cost-effective and assistance in the financing of transit systems.

UMTA offers a variety of grants and loans. If a unified or officially coordinated transportation system plan is in effect, formula grants are available for capital and operating costs. Projects must be programmed in a Transportation Improvement Program and in a Program of Projects that have been endorsed by the metropolitan planning agency and submitted to UMTA for approval. Discretionary grants of 75 percent or 80 percent for new projects and discretionary loans for capital project development or land acquisition are also available.

UMTA also funds research, development and demonstration projects and offers training grants.

See: SECTION 9 BLOCK GRANT PROGRAM; SURFACE TRANSPORTATION ASSISTANCE ACT OF 1982; URBAN MASS TRANSPORTATION ACT OF 1964; URBAN MASS TRANSPORTATION ADMINISTRATION DISCRETIONARY GRANT PROGRAMS

Urban Mass Transportation Administration Discretionary Grant Programs

Grant programs for extremely expensive transit projects that are administered by the Urban Mass Transportation Administration. Funding for the programs is from the Mass Transit Account of the Highway Trust Fund and is based on competitive application. Projects, such as construction of a fixed guideway system or major transit system rehabilitation, typically require funding beyond that received from block grants and are logical candidates for discretionary grants. Depending upon the program for which funds are requested, the federal cost share will be 75 percent or 80 percent.

The newest of these programs—the Section 3 Discretionary Grant, authorized by the Surface Transportation Assistance Act of 1982—emphasizes labor-intensive projects, construction or production of which can be begun within the shortest possible time.

See: HIGHWAY TRUST FUND; URBAN MASS TRANSPORTATION ADMINISTRATION (UMTA)

Urban Park and Recreation Recovery Program (UPARR)

A three-part federal program, created by the Urban Park and Recreation Recovery Act of 1978 (PL 95-625), that provides funds on a competitive basis for plans for the rehabilitation of recreation facility systems in inner city areas, and for the repair, rehabilitation and innovative management of the park facilities.

Recovery Action Program grants are given on a 50 percent federal-50 percent local matching basis for planning activities, while Rehabilitation grants and Innovation grants provide a 70 percent federal share.

See: NATIONAL URBAN RECREATION STUDY

Urban Planning

A process, also called city planning or town planning, that involves planning for the diverse elements that comprise an urbanized area, including its physical infrastructure, environment, housing and transportation, and management of land use and urban growth. The urban planning function is generally carried out by government and is implemented through such means as exercise of the police power (e.g., zoning, subdivision regulation and other land use and development regulations) and the power of eminent domain. Urban planning may also be undertaken by private action, as when a new town is designed.

The profession of urban planning, as practiced today, developed from social and land use reform movements that began in the latter part of the 19th century, although city planning in one form or another has existed at various times for much of the world's recorded history. In the 19th century recognition of poor living conditions in slum housing led to legislation that mandated more healthful design. One example is New York City's tenement house laws. At about the same time, interest developed in providing wholesome open space in the form of urban parks and recreation areas and in improving social conditions through the settlement house movement. The World's Columbian Exposition, held in Chicago in 1893, instructed society that formal planning and well-designed architecture produce both aesthetically pleasing and physically and economically functional areas. The development of zoning, in the late 19th and early 20th century, to control the placement of incompatible land uses signaled the institution of an increasingly more complex and comprehensive series of controls on the use of land and the siting of buildings and other improvements. The concept of planning for local areas expanded to planning for entire cities, for counties and for regional areas, as their interdependence was recognized, and the concept of comprehensive planning evolved from the need to integrate plans for the diverse elements of a city that inevitably have an effect on each other.

Urban planning has since expanded in scope to include concerns that are closely related to the well-being of urbanized areas. These include economic development; environmental management, such as management of solid waste disposal and air quality; social planning; preservation of historic resources and other important community assets; transportation planning; urban design; and school planning. The need for financial resources management to enable improvement of urban areas has led to the involvement of planners in capital program planning and capital budget development as well as the evaluation of proposals with respect to their feasibility, costs and benefits, and impact on the physical operation and financial condition of the municipality. Citizen involvement in the planning process, mandated by certain federal programs, has resulted in the widespread development of citizen participation programs that encourage public involvement in all stages of planning.

Concern with overpopulation of certain areas motivated development of growth management as a planning tool, while the need to stimulate growth in other locations has prompted the development of a range of specialized organizations and financial tools, including housing finance agencies, industrial development agencies, and various tax incentives and financing strategies. Having gone from an initial focus on a localized area to a broader focus on the city as a whole, the region or the creation of an entire new town, the planning profession has now returned to focus on improving localized areas, such as neighborhoods. The targeting of funds to improve relatively small areas has become a major planning tool of the 1980s.

Today urban planning in most western countries concentrates on the rehabilitation of urban places, the stimulation of housing construction, the improvement of mass transit, management of the urban environment, and the development or improvement of municipal infrastructure. Another recent concern is the integration of the elderly and handicapped into the day-to-day functioning of the city by promoting physical improvements to structures and transportation modes that permit the elderly or handicapped to move freely. The use of energy-efficient systems in the design of buildings and developments is another current issue.

See: COMPREHENSIVE PLAN; COUNTY PLANNING; CRIMINAL JUSTICE PLANNING; ECONOMIC DEVELOPMENT; ENERGY CONSERVATION PLANNING; GROWTH MANAGEMENT; HEALTH PLANNING; HOUSING; NATIONAL LAND USE POLICY; NEIGHBORHOOD PLANNING; OPEN-SPACE PLANNING; RECREATION PLANNING; REGIONAL PLANNING; RURAL PLANNING; SCHOOL PLANNING; SOCIAL PLANNING; SOCIAL SERVICES PLANNING; TRANSPORTATION PLANNING; URBAN DESIGN

Urban Renewal

A federal program for central city slum clearance and redevelopment, active from 1949 to 1974.

Under the original legislation authorized by Title I of the Housing Act of 1949, urban renewal was intended to improve housing conditions, and project sites had to be redeveloped for residential purposes. At that time urban renewal consisted only of demolition by an Urban Renewal Agency for subsequent redevelopment. In the Housing Act of 1954, the program was broadened to add neighborhood conservation and rehabilitation projects and to permit 10 percent of available funds to be used for projects that would ultimately be nonresidential after renewal. The percentage of funds available for nonresidential projects was increased by legislative amendments to 20 percent in 1959 and to 30 percent in 1961, reflecting a shift from housing to economic development.

Participating cities were required to adopt a comprehensive plan, known as a workable program or community renewal program. Based on the plan, the local government would designate an area as blighted, and the local public agency (LPA) would acquire the property through eminent domain. The LPA would assemble land, demolish the buildings and sell parcels to redevelopers for less than the city's costs. This difference, known as a "write-down," would be covered by federal grants.

Urban renewal was successful in replacing slums with new large-scale development—including offices, stores, industry, housing, colleges and hospitals—but accomplished this goal at the cost of a net loss of housing. In addition, most of the housing built was too expensive for the original residents, and many displacees received minimal relocation assistance, subsequently moving to nearby slums not affected by urban renewal.

See: BERMAN v. *PARKER;* BLIGHTED AREA; RELOCATION

Urban Runoff

Runoff that originates in densely developed areas. Urban runoff presents particular problems that are not present or are not as severe in suburban and rural areas. This is a result of the proportion of the earth's surface in an urban area that has been paved or rendered impervious, and the number and type of pollutants that are found.

The infiltration capacity of an area declines as the soil surface is covered by pavement, resulting in increased storm runoff that must be accommodated by storm drainage systems that may not be adequate to this task. Other related problems are increased flood and erosion damage, additional maintenance necessary for stream channels and reduced groundwater recharge. Urban runoff is also a chief cause of lowered water quality in urban areas. Among the many types of pollutants urban runoff accumulates are suspended solids; toxic substances (including heavy metals); bacteria; nutrients; asbestos; oil, grease and salt from city streets; construction materials and litter.

One important method that is in use to control the deleterious effects of urban runoff is on-site detention of stormwater, which is then gradually released to reduce flooding problems. This may be accomplished through excavated or natural basins, through rooftop storage areas, through parking lot storage, or through underground tanks. Increased infiltration may also be accomplished with the use of porous pavements (widely used in Europe) which reduce runoff. A variety of practices related to street cleaning, application of salt to roadways, construction management, etc. can be implemented to reduce pollution deriving from urban runoff.

See: BEST MANAGEMENT PRACTICES (BMPs); DETENTION BASIN; IMPERVIOUS SURFACES; NONPOINT SOURCE; RETENTION BASIN; RUNOFF; STORM DRAINAGE SYSTEM

Urban Service Area

An area within which local government services, facilities and utilities are provided. Depending upon the service or facility, the area may be coterminous with municipal boundaries or may cover a lesser or greater area. As an example, sewers may be provided to only part of a municipality; water supply may be available to areas beyond the municipal boundaries; and police service may be available anywhere within the municipality.

Since many services and facilities transcend or are un-

related to municipal boundary lines, special districts are frequently formed to administer them.
See: SPECIAL DISTRICT

Urban Sociology

The study of behavior and interrelationships in urban areas that provides basic information on how people with different backgrounds react to urban life.

Urban sociology is generally considered to have developed from two sources: the physical analysis of the "Chicago school" in the 1920s and 1930s, and the muckrakers and early social workers who popularized the plight of the working classes and the poor. The Chicago school, a group of urban theorists working with Robert Park at the University of Chicago, developed theories of urban life, such as the concentric zone theory, that related human factors to spatial forms.

These divergent sources still influence the study of life in urban areas. Urban designers attempt to analyze behavioral attributes via spatial relationships, while social planners analyze social and organizational interrelationships.
See: GROWTH THEORY; LAND USE PATTERN; SOCIAL PLANNING; SOCIAL SERVICES PLANNING; SOCIAL STRATIFICATION; SOCIAL STRUCTURE

Urban Wildlife Research Center (UWRC)

A nonprofit educational and scientific organization concerned with protecting urban wildlife and its habitat. UWRC, founded in 1973, develops techniques by which planners, developers, government agencies, homeowners and other concerned individuals and organizations can help to establish and maintain favorable conditions for wildlife. The organization, which is located in Columbia, Maryland, conducts research on a variety of topics, such as the implications of human activities for wildlife and maintenance of wildlife habitat, and planning and management techniques for new and existing development.

UWRC provides a number of services to its membership, including a quarterly publication, *Urban Wildlife News,* and various environmental programs. Recent major manuals and guides written by UWRC include *Planning for Wildlife in Cities and Suburbs, Planning for Urban Fishing and Waterfront Recreation,* and *Wildlife Considerations in Planning and Managing Highway Corridors.*

Urbanization

The change of a rural area into one with city characteristics. Urbanization can refer both to the outward expansion of a city and to a regional or even national shift from an agrarian to an urban society.

Urbanization includes changes in land use—such as homes, stores, factories and roads replacing farms and open spaces—as well as changes in the economic base from farming or other primary economic activity to commerce and industry. The traditional rural society and political system are also replaced by a more urban structure. Urbanization is a major, wide-sweeping pattern of change

based on economic and often technological factors. While it may be possible to plan for and modify the pattern of urbanization and mitigate severe dislocations, the forces resulting in urbanization are difficult to reverse.
See: EXURBIA; GROWTH MANAGEMENT; LAND USE PATTERN; MEGALOPOLIS; SPRAWL; URBAN PLANNING

Urbanized Area (UA)

1. A statistical standard used by the Bureau of the Census and other federal agencies that describes an area containing a minimum of 50,000 persons at a density of at least 1,000 persons per square mile (386 persons per square kilometer) but including some less densely populated areas within corporate limits.

2. An area that has a higher population density and a greater mixture of land use types than surrounding areas.
See: CENSUS; URBANIZATION

Use Variance

A variance that allows land to be used for a purpose not normally permitted in that zoning district.

The classic standard that is employed in determining whether a use variance is merited is a determination that the landowner would suffer unnecessary hardship absent the variance. The test enumerated by the New York State Court of Appeals in the 1939 case of *Otto* v. *Steinhilber* has been accepted in many other states as a reasonable definition of unnecessary hardship. In this case, it was decided that for a property owner to prove unnecessary hardship, the record must show: (1) that the land cannot yield a reasonable return if used only for one of the uses permitted in that zone, (2) that the owner's problem is caused by circumstances unique to that property rather than general neighborhood conditions and (3) that the use for which a variance is requested would not alter the essential neighborhood character.

Use variances have caused considerable controversy, as they provide a means by which an appointed body can, in effect, rezone a particular property, a function supposedly reserved for legislative action. Because of this, the validity of use variances is not recognized by the courts of several states, and state zoning enabling legislation sometimes prohibits the granting of use variances.
See: AREA VARIANCE; ZONING VARIANCE

Useful Life

The length of time over which a real estate improvement or other asset is likely to remain an economically feasible investment. Also known as economic life, the concept is often used in connection with the time period over which a property may be depreciated for tax purposes. Properties with shorter useful lives, as determined by standards and guidelines acceptable to the Internal Revenue Service, are entitled to larger percentage annual deductions. The actual useful life of a building, however, may be considerably longer or shorter than standards established by the IRS because of intrinsic or external factors.

The implementation of the accelerated cost recovery system method of depreciation by the Economic Recovery Tax Act of 1981 makes a determination of useful life unnecessary in many circumstances.
See: DEPRECIATION; PHYSICAL LIFE

User Charges

A means of generating governmental revenue in which individuals pay charges for those goods and services that benefit them directly. Types of services for which user charges are often levied are roads and bridges, sewage disposal, water supply, transit, recreational facilities, housing, auxiliary educational services and cultural facilities. An example of a user charge would be an admission fee to a municipal swimming pool.

The use of user charges has grown significantly since the 1940s and has come to represent a significant proportion of state and local government revenue.

USGS Maps

A wide variety of topographic maps, as well as many other types of maps for special purposes, provided by the U.S. Geological Survey.

Most topographic mapping in the United States is produced at the 1:24,000 scale, commonly called the 7.5-minute quadrangle because it covers 7.5 minutes of latitude and 7.5 minutes of longitude. At this scale, in which 1 inch equals 2,000 feet (1 centimeter equals 240 meters), detailed information is presented concerning the natural and man-made environment. As a result, the 7.5-minute quadrangle is extremely useful for many types of planning assignments and is also used as the basis for preparing maps of other scales. As of 1981, 7.5-minute coverage was available for 16 states in their entirety and for more than 77 percent of the coterminous United States.

An intermediate-scale map series is available for applications in which larger land areas must be depicted on one map. The USGS produces 1:50,000 and 1:100,000 maps to fulfill this function, usually using either the 15-minute or 30- by 60-minute format. This series provides multiple feature-separation drawings so that maps may be obtained with different layers of content. Intermediate-scale coverage is currently available for roughly 65 percent of the coterminous United States.

The largest scale at which complete topographic coverage is available for the entire United States is 1:250,000, in which 1 inch equals approximately 4 miles and 1 centimeter equals 2.5 kilometers. This map series, with quad-rangles that usually contain 2 degrees of longitude and 1 degree of latitude, is widely used by federal and state agencies and by the USGS in the preparation of state base maps, geological maps and special-purpose maps. Land use and land cover data, obtained primarily from high-altitude photography and satellite imagery, are also now being mapped at this scale.

A standard color code is used on most USGS topographic maps to differentiate the type of information that appears. In general, black designates cultural features and names; blue indicates water features and names; red indicates urban areas, highway classifications and U.S. land survey lines; and green depicts wooded areas, orchards and vineyards. In addition, brown is used to show topographic features and purple to show unverified data. Color separates may be obtained for each color that appears on USGS topographic maps.

Many other types of maps are prepared by the USGS in addition to standard topographic maps. For example, a special series for coastal area planning is being prepared that combines topography with bathymetry of the ocean floor. A variety of geologic, geochemical, geophysical and hydrologic maps are prepared as well. (See Fig. 48)
See: GEOLOGICAL SURVEY (USGS); LANDSAT; NATIONAL CARTOGRAPHIC INFORMATION CENTER (NCIC); TOPOGRAPHIC MAP

Utility Easement

An easement acquired by a utility for the location of transmission lines, pipelines and other utility facilities. Utilities that acquire easements include electric, gas and telephone companies as well as public utilities such as water supply and sewer departments. Utility easements are usually linear in shape and may be located at ground level, above ground (as in the case of electric transmission lines) or below ground (e.g., gas pipelines).

Because these facilities can extend for great distances and, once constructed, generally need relatively little maintenance, acquisition of an easement is often preferred because it permits sufficient access but is less costly than acquiring a fee interest in land.

Recent studies in the use of linear open space for bicycling, walking and riding have shown that utility easements are potentially suitable for these purposes. Abandoned utility rights-of-way—e.g., old aqueducts—and those with buried utility equipment are usually most appropriate.
See: EASEMENT; LINEAR OPEN SPACE; UNDERGROUNDING OF UTILITIES

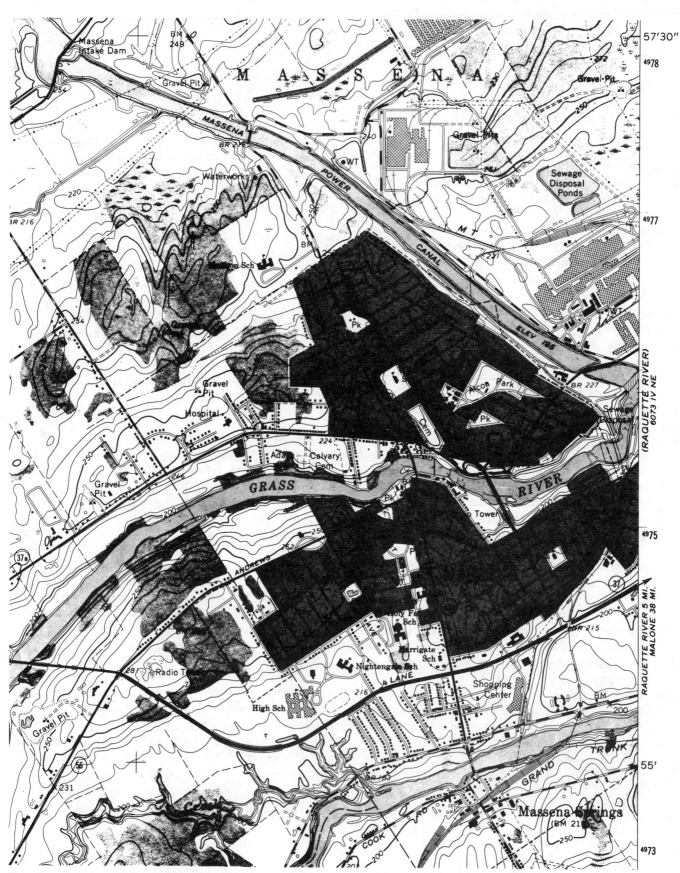

Fig. 48.   Part of a USGS 1:24,000-scale, 7.5-minute series topographic base map.
Credit: U.S. Geological Survey

V

Vacancy Rate

The ratio between the number of housing units that are vacant at a given time and the total housing stock or the number of units in a particular area being surveyed.

Units may be vacant for a variety of reasons; for example they may be used seasonally, used on an intermittent basis or rented but still unoccupied. For this reason, both gross and actual or available vacancy rates may be calculated, where the gross vacancy rate includes every housing unit unoccupied for any reason and the actual vacancy rate counts only those units that are not seasonal and are actually available for sale or rent.

Vacancy rates are an excellent indication of the degree to which a variety of housing choice is available. The lower the vacancy rate, the more difficult it becomes to relocate within a community to the type of housing that is desired. Since low vacancy rates generally indicate a shortage of housing, the cost of housing tends to rise until additional units are built. In a sound housing market, low vacancy rates act as a stimulus to the production of housing.
See: HOUSING; HOUSING CHOICE; ILLEGAL CONVERSION; OVERCROWDING

Vacant Land

Land that is unused, which may be improved or in its raw state. Vacant land, particularly when it is adjacent to developed land, can have a blighting effect on its surroundings. While it has the potential of serving as open space, lack of maintenance frequently causes it to become overgrown or to be used as a site for littering and dumping.

To counteract these problems, municipalities have found it beneficial to encourage interim uses—such as parking lots, vest-pocket parks or community gardens—on these vacant parcels. Another approach is to securely fence the land to keep out intruders. Any improvement of a privately owned site requires the permission of the owner, and any public use requires insurance.
See: COMMUNITY GARDEN; IMPROVED LAND; INFILL DEVELOPMENT; RAW LAND; VEST-POCKET PARK

Value Engineering (VE)

A procedure used in structural design that involves the systematic application of recognized techniques to identify a product or service, establish its monetary value and provide it at the lowest cost. Increasingly mandated by federal legislation and in building contracts, value engineering is concerned with finding products or services that have the necessary performance, maintenance, reliability, aesthetic and other qualities required in specific instances at the most reasonable price. As a result, the procedure is conducive to use of new methodologies and technologies.

Variable

A characteristic that may assume different numeric values or be assigned to different groups. Income and age of housing stock are examples of continuous variables, while housing type is a categorical variable. In contrast, the value of a constant, such as the amount of surface area defined to be an acre, is always the same.

Independent variables are those that cause changes in or affect the dependent variable. In controlled social experiments independent variables are manipulated so that the resulting effect upon the dependent variable can be observed, recorded and analyzed. In studies of transit use related to special discount fare programs, for example, the effect that varying fares (the independent variable) has upon ridership levels (the dependent variable) may be recorded and studied.

Variable-Rate Mortgage (VRM)

A mortgage in which the contract interest rate can be adjusted in accordance with prevailing economic conditions. It may be moved upward or downward as such indicators as the prime rate change. If interest rates increase, the monthly payment may be altered, or the term of the loan may be extended so that the monthly payments remain constant.
See: FIXED-RATE MORTGAGE (FRM); MORTGAGE; RENEGOTIABLE-RATE MORTGAGE (RRM)

Variance

The square of the standard deviation generally represented by σ^2 (the Greek letter *sigma* squared) or s^2. This measure of dispersion is calculated by individually subtracting from the mean of a frequency distribution each value in the distribution and then squaring each of the individual results. The arithmetic mean of the sum of these figures is calculated to arrive at the variance.

If the variance is zero, then every observation in the distribution will have the same value—the mean value. The larger the variance, the more the cases tend to differ from each other.
See: MEASURES OF DISPERSION; STANDARD DEVIATION; ZONING VARIANCE

Vegetation Map

A pictorial depiction of the location and type of plant materials that appear in a given land area. Vegetation maps may be prepared for parcels that will undergo development to aid in site planning, where the caliper and type of individual trees above a specified size and existing plant cover may be indicated. Maps are also used for much larger areas, as when the U.S. Forest Service prepares classifications for major forest areas. In addition to field inspection, information concerning the vegetation of an area may be obtained from such sources as U.S. Geologi-

cal Survey maps, standard aerial photographs and more sophisticated forms of remote sensing, such as the use of infrared film.
See: INFRARED PHOTOGRAPHY; USGS MAPS

Vertical Takeoff and Landing (VTOL)

Aircraft (including conventional helicopters) capable of vertical liftoff and landing in areas that are only slightly larger than the aircraft. Not yet refined for commercial passenger and freight use, experimental military VTOL aircraft have reached supersonic speeds while retaining the ability to take off and land at very slow speeds. A reported safety factor in the use of VTOL aircraft is the elimination of conventional takeoffs and landings, the source of many accidents.

The further refinement of this technology has important implications for planning, since VTOL airports can be located on small sites available even in urban centers. They eliminate the need for long, costly runways, which take large amounts of land, and do not require as restrictive a clear zone as conventional airports. The roof of an intermodal terminal may be adapted for use as a VTOL airport.
See: AIRPORT PLANNING; CLEAR ZONE; INTERMODAL TERMINAL; SHORT TAKEOFF AND LANDING (STOL)

Vertical Zoning

A type of zoning in which different land uses are permitted on various levels of a particular building. A common use of vertical zoning, also known as stratified zoning, is the reservation of the ground floor or lowest floors of a building for retail use. This may be done in central business districts in order to preserve retail continuity at the street level and encourage browsing and pedestrian movement. The upper floors of the building are then commonly used for office or residential purposes.
See: CUMULATIVE ZONING; EXCLUSIVE-USE ZONING; MICROZONING; MIXED-USE ZONING; ZONING

Vested Right

A right that has accrued and become fixed to a point where it is not subject to loss by subsequent events and may not be denied by governmental authority without compensating the owner of the right. A vested right is a right that has acquired the status of property, enjoying the constitutional protection that it may not be taken away, except in accordance with due process and by providing just compensation.

In general, a landowner does not have a vested right in the existence of a particular zoning ordinance. However, once development of a property has begun, a right accrues to complete construction and use the property as permitted at the time development commenced, regardless of whether the zoning designation of the parcel changes. The amount of development that must occur before a right

becomes vested varies among jurisdictions between application for a building permit, commencement of site improvements or commencement of actual building construction. Once the particular vesting point of a jurisdiction is reached, however, a developer is entitled to complete and use his property as a legal nonconforming use if zoning regulations change.
See: NONCONFORMING USE

Vest-Pocket Park

A very small site in a developed area that is used for recreation. The idea of the vest-pocket park developed from innovative use of vacant lots in inner city areas in the 1960s and 1970s, when, with supervision, local residents cleared the lots and built play equipment from scrap materials. Lack of funding for maintenance prevented most of these parks from becoming neighborhood fixtures, but the concept of the very small urban park remains a useful tool for provision of open space and recreational opportunities. Today, some communities provide several vest-pocket parks instead of one neighborhood park.

Vest-pocket parks are now usually formally conceived and developed. They may contain play equipment, seating, landscaping and quiet games areas if designed for a varied population, or they may be developed as a specialized facility. Paley Park, a vest-pocket park in midtown Manhattan, has only movable seating and trees, but its waterfall fountain makes it one of the most popular spots in that part of the city.
See: NEIGHBORHOOD PARK; PLAYLOT; VACANT LAND

Veterans Administration (VA) Mortgage Insurance

Insured, guaranteed and direct mortgage loans for veterans, one of several benefits granted by the Servicemen's Readjustment Act of 1944 as amended. Under this act the VA is authorized to guarantee or insure a percentage of a mortgage loan, up to a maximum figure, for eligible veterans. Direct loans are given in some rural areas where the other forms of financing are not available. While the allowable interest rate, the percentage insured and the maximum amount guaranteed all change periodically, the basic structure of the program remains the same. Because a percentage of the loan is guaranteed or insured by the federal government, the lender's risk is reduced. Unlike almost any other mortgage insurance program, there is no premium or fee for VA insurance and no required down payment.

VA mortgage insurance has in many ways been successful. The program succeeded in stimulating the post–World War II housing boom and helped millions of former servicemen to purchase homes; since it encouraged home ownership, the program was most aggressively marketed by mortgage bankers, often in association with suburban tract developers. The VA program was significant in help-

ing to standardize loan documentation, a required step in creating the secondary mortgage market. The success of the program also served as a model for the rebirth of the private mortgage insurance industry after the war.
See: FEDERAL HOUSING ADMINISTRATION (FHA) MORTGAGE INSURANCE; SECONDARY MORTGAGE MARKET

Veterinary Hospital

A building in which medical care is given to animals. Veterinary hospitals are usually restricted to commercially or industrially zoned areas because of the nuisance characteristics associated with animal noise and traffic volume. Although they are generally fully enclosed, when they are situated in an area that allows industry outdoor runs may be permitted, since animal noise may not be a disturbing factor.

Animal pounds, where stray animals are kept or destroyed, and animal neutering facilities, both of which may require relatively larger sites, are similarly restricted in location. All veterinary facilities, in addition, are regulated by the department of health.

Vieux Carre

The French Quarter of New Orleans, designated as a historic district in 1937 following an amendment to the constitution of the state of Louisiana. The second oldest historic district in the United States (Charleston was the first, in 1931), it spans about 260 acres (105 hectares) and was also named a National Historic Landmark.

Because of the importance of the Vieux Carre to the New Orleans economy as a result of the tourism it attracts, and because of the development pressures it experiences, stringent controls and procedures have been adopted by the Vieux Carre Commission. These include review at different points in the design process and frequent inspection of the district by building inspectors hired for that purpose to guard against deterioration or unauthorized alterations. Policies have also been established concerning such areas as lighting, awnings, paint colors, tree planting and roofing materials.

Extensive litigation has taken place concerning the regulation of the Vieux Carre that has influenced the development of preservation case law in the United States.
See: HISTORIC DISTRICT ORDINANCE; HISTORIC PRESERVATION; LANDMARKS COMMISSION ORDINANCE

View Protection Regulations

Regulations that control development so that scenic vistas may be preserved. Usually imposed as height limitations in zoning ordinances, they may affect a specified area surrounding a visual focal point, such as a public monument, or permit building height to be greater as distance from a scenic focus increases.
See: AESTHETIC ZONING; HEIGHT CONTROLS; VISTA

Village of Arlington Heights v. Metropolitan Housing Development Corporation (429 U.S. 252, 50 L.Ed.2d 450, 97 S.Ct. 555 [1977])

A decision by the United States Supreme Court involving a suburban municipality's rejection of a property owner's petition to rezone a parcel of land so that it could be developed for low- and moderate-income multifamily housing.

The Court refused to find the municipality's action unconstitutional because of the absence of proof that the decision not to rezone was motivated by racially discriminatory intent or purpose. The Court decided that the fact that the municipality's action might have a racially disproportionate impact was not sufficient reason to find the action unconstitutional.
See: EXCLUSIONARY ZONING

Village of Belle Terre v. Boraas (416 U.S. 1, 94 S.Ct. 1536, 39 L.Ed.2d 797 [1974])

A decision by the United States Supreme Court concerning the constitutionality of a zoning ordinance that limited occupancy of residences to either a single family (persons related by blood, adoption or marriage) or not more than two unrelated persons living together as a single housekeeping unit.

The Court held that the ordinance did not violate any constitutional rights of the owner or the occupants (six university students) of the residence whose use was being challenged under the zoning ordinance. The Court further held that the ordinance was within the police power delegated to the Village of Belle Terre, since promotion of "family values" is a valid police power goal of zoning.
See: EXCLUSIONARY ZONING; FAMILY; *MOORE* v. *CITY OF EAST CLEVELAND, OHIO;* POLICE POWER

Village of Euclid v. Ambler Realty Co. (272 U.S. 365, 47 S.Ct. 114, 71 L.Ed. 303 [1926])

A decision by the United States Supreme Court upholding the constitutionality of the zoning ordinance adopted by the Village of Euclid, Ohio.

The decision is considered a landmark in the zoning field, because it established the validity, as a general principle, of a comprehensive zoning ordinance that went beyond regulation of land uses merely to avoid nuisances or dangerous conditions. The Court upheld the ordinance as a lawful exercise by the municipality of delegated police power, against the petitioning landowner's claim that the ordinance represented a deprivation of property without due process. In this case, the landowner alleged that the effect of the ordinance was to reduce the value of his property by 67 percent to 75 percent.

The form of zoning ordinance approved in this case has come to be known as "Euclidean zoning." This term refers to an ordinance that establishes a series of use districts in which each successive district permits uses expressly designated for that district as well as all uses permitted in each of the preceding, less intensive use districts. Thus, in the most intensive use district (e.g., heavy industrial), all uses permitted in any other use district established by the ordinance are permitted.

The Euclidean zoning model is often depicted as a triangle or pyramid, with the least intensive permitted use district (e.g., residential) at the top, and each consecutive layer representing the next more intensive use district.
See: CUMULATIVE ZONING; EUCLIDEAN ZONING; EXCLUSIVE-USE ZONING

Visibility Clearance at Intersections

A space that is set aside on a corner lot in which all visual obstructions, such as structures and plantings, that can prevent visibility and thus be a hazard to traffic and pedestrian safety are prohibited. A typical height limit, in the roughly triangular wedge that is defined by the local ordinance, might be 3 feet (0.9 meter) above the center line of the street. Regulations concerning visibility clearance may appear in zoning ordinances and subdivision regulations. The area that must be kept clear is known as the visibility triangle, corner clearance or corner cutoff.
See: SUBDIVISION REGULATIONS; ZONING

Vista

1. A view to or from a particular point with a characteristic emphasis on length, as along a corridor or down an avenue, and with some sense of narrow enclosure, as through a canyon or between rows of trees. As with a plaza or courtyard, a vista is considered to be a type of space that may be shaped by the urban designer. Designers may choose to vary its character, as in a formal or informal garden plan, or to use it to lend dramatic impact to a building that acts as a terminal element, as in urban design.

More recently, emphasis in community design has been placed on visual resource management (VRM), the management of the scenic qualities of an area, through such techniques as preservation of vistas. VRM is mandated for certain federal lands by the requirement that scenic vistas be protected or enhanced through proper siting of buildings and landscaping and placement of utilities underground.

2. Volunteers in Service to America (VISTA) is a U.S. government corporation established by Congress in 1964. Its function is to provide opportunities for Americans to work with locally sponsored projects designed to eliminate poverty and poverty-related social and environmental problems. VISTA volunteers act as resource coordinators in many fields, including architecture and city planning, and train community participants to manage their own programs.
See: URBAN DESIGN; VIEW PROTECTION REGULATIONS

W

Wall Art

Large-scale paintings on the sides of buildings that generally use the entire wall as if it were a canvas. This technique was started in urban areas by artists who felt that they could brighten dismal areas that were created by dark, blank walls of old buildings. Among the techniques used in wall art are brightly colored artworks, the use of stark designs, scenes depicting community life, or trompe l'oeil windows and ivy to make the building surface more attractive. An outgrowth of mural painting, billboard art and supergraphics, wall art has become a common addition to the public art of urban areas, particularly near open areas and parking lots. These paintings are being used, in addition, to create interesting surfaces on certain public buildings to discourage graffiti. (See Fig. 49)
See: BILLBOARD; GRAFFITI; PUBLIC ART

Warehouse Facilities

Industrial buildings used for the storage of merchandise, components or raw materials. Warehouses may be used for short-term storage in production and marketing, in which case they are often called distribution centers, or for long-term custody storage. They are built in connection with manufacturing, freight handling and retailing and may be operated as public facilities, storing the goods of many firms, or private facilities (known as captive warehouses), handling only the goods of the firm that built them. Tank farms for the storage of liquids as well as silos and elevators for the storage of bulk products are also forms of warehouses.

Usually constructed with high ceilings and open floor plans, warehouses are designed to permit flexibility in the use of space. The design has made older warehouses popular for conversion to other uses, such as artists' studios and housing. Most modern warehouses are designed as single-story buildings, but in very large facilities this layout causes excessive travel within the structure. Depending upon the method of stacking used, most warehouses have at least 20-foot (6.1-meter) ceilings, and in some Western European installations they have ceilings as high as 102 feet (31 meters). In general, buildings that are long and narrow are more costly to construct and operate than those more evenly dimensioned. Warehouse sites within a given area are usually selected by determining locations that most effectively reduce transportation costs.

(a)

(b)

Fig. 49. Two building walls in New York City: (a) a vertical painting with a sculptural quality by Tania; (b) a trompe l'oeil painting by Richard Haas on the side of an old loft building. The Haas painting repeats the architectural detail of the front of the building. This photo, which was taken while the work was in progress, shows an area of the building (at its upper left) that was not yet completed.
Credit: Public Art Fund, New York. Photograph (a) by Joel Witkin. Photograph (b) by Donna Svennevik.

Warehouse facilities require good off-street loading areas capable of accommodating the number and sizes of trucks and packages that are expected. While some facilities provide many loading berths, security and temperature-control requirements may dictate fewer areas with automated handling to increase loading efficiency. Indoor loading of trucks and railcars is also increasingly popular. Off-street parking for employees may be necessary (with long-term warehouses generally employing fewer people than other types), and a railroad siding may also be required. Zoning ordinances generally restrict warehouses to general business and industrial areas or to industrial parks.

Mini-warehouses, designed for storage of personal goods, are rented for periods of time to individuals and small businesses. They are a new form of warehouse, in which either a standard warehouse is subdivided into room-size cubicles or rows of garagelike structures are built within a fenced area for access by car. While most often restricted to industrial areas, some municipalities permit them in commercial districts.
See: FREIGHT HANDLING FACILITIES; INDUSTRIAL PARK; LOFT HOUSING; TRUCK TERMINALS

Warth v. *Seldin* (422 U.S. 490, 95 S.Ct. 2197 [1975])

A decision by the United States Supreme Court that narrowly limited the persons who have standing to challenge local zoning regulations on the grounds that the regulations are exclusionary. To have standing (i.e., a right to challenge the ordinance), a person must be able to show specific concrete facts demonstrating that he has been damaged by the ordinance and would benefit by the court's intervention.

The decision is only directly applicable to challenges to zoning ordinances that allegedly violate federal law (i.e., federal statutes or the United States Constitution). It does not directly apply to claims based on violations of state law (e.g., that an ordinance is an improper exercise of delegated police power).
See: EXCLUSIONARY ZONING

Waste Reduction

At least three different approaches may be taken singly or in combination to reduce the amount of solid waste that a community must dispose of, helping the community to conserve resources, energy and landfill capacity.

In one approach, the emphasis is placed upon the production and purchase of products that are durable and easy to repair when they do break so that they need not be thrown away. Elimination of excess packaging also reduces the size of the waste stream without denying the consumer the actual product.

Another tactic concerns the recycling of certain waste products, such as paper, aluminum cans, scrap metal and bottles. Recycling could allow the reuse of a significant proportion of solid waste while providing energy savings and, in some cases, savings on the costs of materials for manufacturers.

A third way in which the volume, although not the amount, of waste is reduced is by actually compressing it into bales or grinding it into small pieces. These practices, known as volume reduction, can extend the life of a sanitary landfill.

See: BALING; RECYCLING; SHREDDING; SOLID WASTE MANAGEMENT

Wastewater

Wastewater, commonly called sewage, consists of three categories of liquid wastes: 1) those conducted away from all except industrial uses—known as sanitary, or domestic sewage; 2) those produced by industrial processes—known as industrial sewage; and 3) surface water, groundwater and stormwater that flow directly into or infiltrate sewers—known as storm sewage.

See: DOMESTIC SEWAGE; INDUSTRIAL SEWAGE; STORM DRAINAGE SYSTEM; WASTEWATER MANAGEMENT

Wastewater Facility Planning (Section 201)

The process of planning, constructing and upgrading sewage treatment plants and sewer facilities. Funding for this process is authorized by Sections 201 and 202 of the Clean Water Act. Grants are available for up to 75 percent of the cost of construction for sewerage and secondary sewage treatment until October 1984; after that date grants for new projects will be given at 55 percent funding. The project must be consistent with the areawide waste treatment management plan; the sewer system discharging into the plant must not have excessive infiltration; and alternative waste management techniques must be studied. Each plant is required to apply secondary treatment and at a later date must incorporate, to the extent practicable, technology that would provide for the reclaiming or recycling of water or that would otherwise eliminate the discharge of pollutants.

See: AREAWIDE WASTE TREATMENT MANAGEMENT PLANNING (SECTION 208); INFILTRATION AND INFLOW (I&I) ANALYSIS; MUNICIPAL WASTEWATER TREATMENT CONSTRUCTION GRANT AMENDMENTS OF 1981

Wastewater Management

The development of suitable systems of wastewater monitoring, treatment and disposal that adequately protect the population and the environment. Also called sewerage system engineering, it involves the selection and design of an appropriate form of sewage collection and treatment based on population size, population density and soil conditions of an area, as well as determination of the appropriateness of using septic systems or sewers and sewage treatment plants for specific sites. Other aspects of wastewater management are the analysis of industrial sewage and its treatment requirements, the selection of methods of disposal for sewage effluent and sludge, and the ongoing operation and monitoring of all elements of the wastewater disposal system.

See: ENVIRONMENTAL ENGINEERING; SEWERAGE SYSTEM

Water Conservation

Programs and procedures to reduce the amount of water consumed by households, industry and agriculture. Water is considered a renewable resource because supplies are continually replenished through precipitation, but much of the world's rainfall is returned to the atmosphere through the joint processes of evaporation and transpiration in plants. In addition, while most of the Earth's surface is covered with water, 97.3 percent of this water is seawater which, untreated, is not fit for human consumption or for most industrial uses. Freshwater resources may also be located far from populated areas, causing large population centers to draw water from distant sources through complex and expensive distribution systems.

An additional issue in water conservation is the large increase in water consumption in industrialized nations, which has risen geometrically rather than in proportion to population increase. New industrial processes, such as nuclear plants, require water for cooling; irrigation in arid regions also uses large quantities of water. Although much of the water used for industrial processes is returned to the hydrologic cycle, over 60 percent of the water used for irrigation is lost. Water table levels are also receding in many areas of the United States.

To counter these problems, a range of water conservation practices and technology is developing. These include improved management of runoff, reduction of evaporation in reservoirs by reducing shallow water areas and using water surface coating materials, and the use of brackish and recycled water for industrial purposes. Recycled water is also being used for groundwater recharge, while desalination techniques continue to evolve, enabling increased usage of salt water. In addition, public education to reduce consumption is leading to an increased citizen awareness; and the use of conservation devices, such as water flow restrictors in shower heads, helps to reduce demands upon the water supply.

See: DESALINATION; GROUNDWATER; POTABLE WATER; RECHARGE; RUNOFF; TERTIARY TREATMENT; WATER CONSUMPTION; WATER SUPPLY SYSTEM

Water Consumption

Amount of per capita water usage. This information is necessary for the planning and design of water supply and treatment systems. Typically, water utilized by households is considered nonconsumptive water use because it is returned to the hydrologic cycle, although some of it has been polluted, while much of the water used for irrigation and many industrial purposes may be lost to the cycle.

Water usage in the United States varies with time of day, day of the week and season of the year. Usage is frequently higher during the summer, when air conditioners and swimming pools are in use and lawns are maintained. Water consumption also varies with type of residential community and may be influenced by factors such as amount of industry, type of commercial operations and range of housing type. European countries typically use less water per capita than the United States. For American residential communities, figures range between 100 and 200 gallons (378 and 756 liters) per day per capita.

See: WATER CONSERVATION; WATER SUPPLY SYSTEM

Water Distribution System

A means of transporting water to its diverse consumers throughout a community. The system is generally composed of transmission mains, lateral mains, pipes that serve individual buildings, fire hydrants and distribution reservoirs. Pumping stations may also be required to maintain adequate pressure throughout the system and to facilitate gravity flow.

Transmission or feeder mains transmit water to a network of lateral mains, generally placed under streets. The favored design consists of a gridiron system that allows each portion of the system to receive water from multiple sources. Not only does this minimize the risk of leaving an area or customer without a water supply, but it can also provide more water for emergencies. The alternative design, considered less efficient, is known as a dead-end system, in which branches of diminishing size lead from the larger mains. Besides providing for no alternative water supply should a problem arise, the water can also develop an unpleasant taste and odor as it stagnates in the many end points in this type of system.

Fire hydrants, another part of the system, are used for fire emergencies and connect downward with the water main running under the street. Distribution reservoirs serve to store water for emergencies and provide a supplementary water source for periods of high usage. They may take the form of elevated tanks, ground storage reservoirs or standpipes.

Individual structures rely upon pipes constructed of copper, iron or plastic to convey water from the main in the street. Many communities meter the water used and bill the user based on quantity metered.

See: FIRE FLOW; PUMPING STATION; WATER SUPPLY ENGINEERING; WATER SUPPLY SYSTEM; WATER TOWER

Water Pollution

Impairment of the quality of water through the introduction of chemical, physical or biological substances; changes in water temperature; or other means. Despite the importance of a pure water supply to the public health, safety and welfare, the numerous sources and types of water pollution make protection and improvement of water quality exceedingly complex.

Among the many sources of water pollution are malfunctioning, inadequate or poorly designed sewage treatment plants; sanitary and industrial landfills; improperly sited or operated septic systems; discharge of industrial effluents; runoff from agricultural lands, urban areas and construction sites; mining activities, both on land and at sea; and irrigation. The types of pollutants that may be introduced include organic wastes, bacteria, chemicals, toxic wastes, sediments, plant nutrients and radioactive materials. The result of the various forms of contamination associated with these activities may range from human exposure to toxic chemicals to accelerated decay of surface water bodies through eutrophication.

Water quality data collected and analyzed by the federal government suggest that surface water body quality has generally stopped deteriorating, probably due to the efforts to control point sources of pollution, such as sewage treatment plants and industry. Studies also indicate, however, that groundwater supplies are not as pure as had once been thought, particularly with respect to toxic chemicals. In order to attempt to continue improving the quality of surface water bodies and to halt the deterioration of groundwater, a network of legislation and programs exists on the federal, state and local levels, although it does not cover each type of water pollution situation.

Major federal legislation related to water pollution and water quality problems includes the Federal Water Pollution Control Act and its amendments; the Safe Drinking Water Act; the Resource Conservation and Recovery Act; the Toxic Substances Control Act; the Surface Mining Control and Reclamation Act; and the Comprehensive Environmental Response, Compensation and Liability Act. States participate in improving water quality through such mechanisms as groundwater contamination laws, preparation of Water Quality Management Plans and administration of National Pollutant Discharge Elimination System permits where the U.S. Environmental Protection Agency has approved such a program. Municipalities participate by such mechanisms as regulation of the siting and construction of septic systems; proper siting and operation of sanitary landfills; and proper design, operation and maintenance of sewage treatment plants.

See: ACID RAIN; AGRICULTURAL POLLUTION; ALGAL BLOOM; COLIFORM BACTERIA; DOMESTIC SEWAGE; EUTROPHICATION; FEDERAL WATER POLLUTION CONTROL ACT AMENDMENTS OF 1972; GROUNDWATER POLLUTION; LEACHATE; MARINE PROTECTION, RESEARCH AND SANCTUARIES ACT OF 1972; NATIONAL POLLUTANT DISCHARGE ELIMINATION SYSTEM (NPDES); NONPOINT SOURCE; OIL POLLUTION; POINT SOURCE; RUNOFF; SALTWATER INTRUSION; SEPTIC SYSTEM; SEWAGE TREATMENT; SOIL EROSION; THERMAL POLLUTION; WASTEWATER MANAGEMENT; WATER QUALITY CRITERIA; WATER QUALITY STANDARDS; WATER RESOURCES MANAGEMENT

Water Pollution Control Federation (WPCF)

An organization whose chief concerns are the development of information concerning wastewater and its collection, treatment and disposal and making this information available to professionals in the field and to the general public. WPCF, which was established in 1928 and currently has more than 30,000 members, consists of autonomous associations throughout the world that have formed a federation for the purpose of achieving their common goals. Member associations are located throughout the United States and Canada, and in Australia, Brazil, Finland, India, Israel, Italy, Japan, Korea, Mexico, the Netherlands, New Zealand, Norway, South Africa, Spain, Sweden, Switzerland and the United Kingdom.

Among the activities of WPCF are conferences, seminars and workshops; development of policy and position papers; analyses of legislation; development of training materials and programs; and presentation of awards for achievement in the field. WPCF has an extensive publications program, through which it issues manuals of practice, other technical publications and training programs. The *Journal of the Water Pollution Control Federation, Highlights* (a newsletter) and *Deeds and Data* (which conveys information on pollution control facilities) are all published monthly. The federation's headquarters are in Washington, D.C.

Water Quality Act of 1965

Federal legislation (PL 89-234) that required states to designate segments of waterways for specific uses (such as swimming or industry), to set water quality standards appropriate for those uses and to adopt a plan for implementation and enforcement of the standards. The first major legislation intended to prevent pollution from occurring, the act authorized the federal government to set standards for interstate watercourses if states failed to do so. The intention of the act, which was based on the concept that a waterway can assimilate a limited quantity of waste, was to allocate the waste-load capacity among polluters. However, pollution, which is measured as a concentration in the waterway, varies with distance from the source, and the testing zone was not clearly defined.

Federal enforcement was authorized only when pollution had interstate effects or when a state requested federal intervention for an intrastate problem, and enforcement procedures were cumbersome and generally ineffective. This act, which was superseded by the Federal Water Pollution Control Act Amendments of 1972, also increased funding for construction of public sewage treatment plants, which had been previously authorized in the Water Pollution Control Acts of 1956 and 1961.
See: FEDERAL WATER POLLUTION CONTROL ACT AMENDMENTS OF 1972

Water Quality Criteria

Estimates of the maximum level of a pollutant that can be present in a body of water and still permit a particular water use to be safely conducted.

The U.S. Environmental Protection Agency (EPA) publishes its own set of water quality criteria on an ongoing basis for the guidance of states developing water quality standards. The EPA's criteria for various pollutants consist of quantitative guidelines and additional data concerning the effects that various pollutants are thought to have on human health and aquatic life. The EPA criteria are not binding on the states. Only those criteria formally adopted by states in their water quality standards are official.
See: WATER QUALITY STANDARDS

Water Quality Improvement Act of 1970

Legislation that regulates the discharge of oil and hazardous substances into navigable waters. For oil spills the act (PL 91-224) requires notification of federal authorities and gives the federal government the authority to clean up the spill and bill the offender for the cost. Prior legislation, the Clean Water Restoration Act of 1966 (PL 89-753), had required a ship owner to pay for cleanup only if the oil spill was caused by the deliberate acts or willful negligence of his crew. The 1966 act was repealed by the 1970 act, which, with few exceptions, made the owner responsible regardless of the cause. The 1970 act also establishes spill-prevention equipment requirements for ships and facilities handling oil.

For hazardous substance spills the act requires notification of federal authorities and provides for federal cleanup, but there is no requirement for spill-prevention equipment. Each of these provisions is incorporated into the 1972 amendments to the Federal Water Pollution Control Act.

Other provisions of the act include demonstration programs to reduce pollution of watersheds by mining operations and to control pollution in the Great Lakes. Control of untreated sewage discharge from vessels is authorized, and all federal agencies are directed to comply with requirements of the act. Applicants for federal licenses or permits to construct facilities that might potentially cause pollution are required to obtain a state certification that the facility will not violate water quality standards.

Title II of the act, the Environmental Quality Improvement Act of 1970, created the office of Environmental Quality to serve as staff to the Council on Environmental Quality.
See: COUNCIL ON ENVIRONMENTAL QUALITY (CEQ); FEDERAL WATER POLLUTION CONTROL ACT AMENDMENTS OF 1972; OIL POLLUTION

Water Quality Standards

A state management plan, required in the United States under the Clean Water Act, for surface bodies of water within a state. The purpose of water quality standards is the reduction of water pollution and the prevention of degradation of unpolluted waters. State water quality standards must be submitted to and judged acceptable by the U.S. Environmental Protection Agency.

Water quality standards consist primarily of a designation of the uses for which the water body requires protection (e.g., public water supply, recreation) and a set of criteria that specify the limits that will be set on concentrations of various pollutants to enable designated uses to continue. A policy of antidegradation is required, in which each state agrees to maintain and protect use levels that have already been attained—e.g., if a water body is safely swimmable, it must be maintained at a safe water quality level for swimming. Each state must also institute a surveillance system to ensure that standards are followed.

Two primary means by which water quality standards are enforced is through the National Pollutant Discharge Elimination System permit, for point sources of pollution, and the best management practices, adopted for nonpoint sources.

See: BEST MANAGEMENT PRACTICES (BMPs); NATIONAL POLLUTANT DISCHARGE ELIMINATION SYSTEM (NPDES); WATER QUALITY CRITERIA

Water Resources Council (WRC)

A United States federal agency within the executive branch that monitored water supplies and coordinated federal water supply programs from 1965 to 1982. Composed of six department and agency heads, it supervised the river basin commissions and a grant program to states for water resources planning and served as the primary federal liaison with state and regional water resource planning agencies. Funding for the WRC was terminated at the end of 1982, and its programs were also ended at the time.

WRC guidelines, published in a 1973 document called "Principles and Standards," set forth two equal national objectives: national economic development (NED) and environmental quality (EQ). Member agencies, in developing project proposals, were required to formulate alternative NED and EQ plans and evaluate their potential impacts. Later amendments emphasized water conservation and the formulation of a primarily nonstructural plan as one of the alternatives. The "Principles and Standards" are still in use by water agencies.

See: RIVER BASIN COMMISSION

Water Resources Management

The development of plans and programs for the use, protection and distribution of water resources, such as groundwater, rivers and streams. Included in the concept of water resources management are water conservation, development of new supplies of potable water, flood control and the use of water for such purposes as industry and agriculture. Scenic and historic values of natural waterways and the operation of fisheries are other concerns.

Intrinsic to the management of water resources is an attempt to accommodate the often conflicting needs of society for water. As an example, in a given area, a water body may be needed or used for drinking water, irrigation and industrial purposes. Other water bodies may be a focus of conflict concerning fishing and power generation. A key concern is always preservation of the purity and supply of drinking water for the protection of public health

and welfare. However, society's other basic needs for food, energy, transportation and manufactured products, as well as population pressures in certain areas of limited water supply, make the management of water resources a difficult task.

A network of federal, state and local government agencies exists to regulate and monitor different aspects of water resources and their use and control. Many federal programs and procedures are in effect that seek to control such areas as flooding, improvement of river navigation, hydroelectric power generation, sewage treatment, location of septic tanks, discharge of industrial effluents, disposal of toxic wastes and disposal of solid wastes.

Other solutions to the problems of water resources management seek to use technological improvements, such as more sophisticated desalination systems, improved design of wastewater treatment plants or recycling of water in industrial use. Land use controls and growth management strategies may also be employed in areas where water supplies cannot accommodate rapid population growth.

See: AQUACULTURE; ARTIFICIAL WATER BODIES; COASTAL AREA PLANNING; DESALINATION; FLOOD CONTROL; FLOODPLAIN MANAGEMENT; HYDROELECTRIC POWER; IRRIGATION; LAND RECLAMATION; RIVER BASIN COMMISSION; RIVER ENGINEERING; RUNOFF; SAFE DRINKING WATER ACT; SALTWATER INTRUSION; WATER CONSERVATION; WATER CONSUMPTION; WATER POLLUTION; WATER SUPPLY SYSTEM; WATERSHED; WETLANDS

Water Sampling

Procedures used to test water for impurities, primarily to determine whether the water is free of bacteriologic entities, such as coliform bacteria, that cause certain waterborne diseases. Under standards promulgated by the federal government in the Safe Drinking Water Act, municipal waterworks must draw frequent water specimens and subject them to a series of tests. Some of the primary factors dictating the number, type and frequency of required procedures are the size of the population served and the water source. Standards also exist for the sites chosen for drawing samples. In addition, different requirements are in effect for water that is used for recreational purposes rather than for human consumption.

See: BIOCHEMICAL OXYGEN DEMAND (BOD); COLIFORM BACTERIA; WATER QUALITY CRITERIA; WATER QUALITY STANDARDS

Water Supply Engineering

The section of civil engineering that directs the design, construction and maintenance of water supply systems. A water supply engineer is involved with the development of an adequate water supply, its purity, and its transmission and distribution.

The design of a water supply system for a municipality depends on the scope of demand for water, which can fluctuate hourly, daily and seasonally. In many communities water supply system requirements are determined

by the amount of water needed for fire protection services, which place a peak demand on the system in a short time span, while facilities necessary for water treatment are determined by the quality of the water supply.
See: FIRE FLOW; WATER CONSUMPTION; WATER DISTRIBUTION SYSTEM; WATER SUPPLY SYSTEM; WATER TREATMENT

Water Supply System

A utility system designed to carry water from a source to its diverse consumers. Such a system often consists of one or more water sources, a means of transporting water from the source to a water treatment plant, the plant itself and a distribution system for transporting water to individual consumers.

Sources of water supply for municipal systems derive from groundwater (e.g., wells), surface water (e.g., lakes, rivers and impounding reservoirs) or a combination of these sources. Rainwater may also be collected in areas with water shortages. Providing sufficient water for a populated area may be relatively simple, as when adequate supplies are located in the immediate vicinity, or it may require an extensive network of impoundments located a substantial distance from the area to be supplied, as is the case with New York City and Los Angeles.

Aqueducts, also called transmission mains, are used to transmit water from source to treatment plant. They may take the form of canals, tunnels or pipelines, depending upon climate, distance, size and scope of the system, and surface relief and may be designed to function as gravity-flow systems or, less commonly, force systems.

A variety of chemical and physical treatment methods are used to assure that safe drinking water is made available. The passage of the Safe Drinking Water Act of 1974 placed the responsibility for setting primary drinking water standards and maximum contamination levels with the U.S. Environmental Protection Agency. This made it necessary for some communities to revise their established means of treatment.

The distribution system consists of a network of transmission mains, lateral mains, small pipes leading to individual homes, fire hydrants and distribution reservoirs. Proper design of the system is essential to assure an adequate supply of water at both periods of normal usage and peak-demand periods.
See: AQUEDUCT; FORCE MAIN; GRAVITY FLOW; PUMPING STATION; RESERVOIR; WATER DISTRIBUTION SYSTEM; WATER SUPPLY ENGINEERING; WATER TOWER; WATER TREATMENT; WELL

Water Table

The upper limit of the zone in which the soil is fully saturated. The surface of the water table generally rises and falls with the contours of the land above it. In theory, the water table of an area is approximately the same as the water level of area wells.

Water table levels vary with the seasons, recede during periods of drought and may also be depleted by pumping

wells. Water stores are replenished through seepage from surface bodies of water and infiltration of rain or melted snow into the ground.
See: GROUNDWATER; INFILTRATION; RECHARGE

Water Tower

A water storage reservoir elevated on a steel structure or a tall cylindrical standpipe. Water towers are used to produce enough pressure to ensure a uniform flow of water during periods of increased demand.
See: RESERVOIR; WATER DISTRIBUTION SYSTEM

Water Treatment

Processes designed to remove harmful substances from water and make it palatable and safe for human consumption. The number and type of processes necessary in water treatment are closely related to the quality of the water source. Federal regulations promulgated under the Safe Drinking Water Act, known as National Interim Primary Drinking Water Regulations (NIPDWR), went into effect in 1977 and control the maximum permitted contaminant levels (MCLs) for more than 20 chemicals or organisms in community water systems. Thus, communities must provide a level of treatment that is adequate to meet these standards for microbiological contaminants, turbidity and chemical-radiological contaminants. Among the most common water treatment processes used are sedimentation, coagulation, filtration, disinfection, softening and aeration.

Sedimentation takes place in reservoirs or in settling basins during long-term storage of water. In sedimentation silt, clay and other sediments drop to the bottom of the reservoir or basin. In coagulation chemicals are added to water to form a floc, to which undesirable particles (e.g., bacteria, pollutants) adhere, which then settles to the bottom of the basin. Filtration is used to reduce suspended solids, bacterial content and the presence of other undesirable organisms. Often used in the United States are rapid sand filters, in which water flows over sand filter beds at rapid speed, usually by gravity but sometimes through pumping.

Disinfection to remove remaining pathogenic organisms is most commonly accomplished with chlorine, although ultraviolet light and ozone are sometimes used. Chlorine may be applied prior to filtration, after filtration or at both points in the treatment process, when necessary. Water softening may be performed in areas with high concentrations of calcium and magnesium salts. This process is used to prevent scale from forming in boilers and to minimize other problems and expenses caused by hard water, such as difficulty in doing laundry. Aeration consists of intermingling air and water by a variety of methods, such as bubbling air through water. It is performed in order to remove hydrogen sulfide, carbon dioxide and various unpleasant tastes and odors.
See: CHLORINATION; DESALINATION; FILTRATION; SEDIMENTATION; SETTLING TANK; TURBIDITY; WATER SUPPLY SYSTEM

Waterfront Revitalization

Reclamation and redevelopment of blighted waterfront areas, usually for commercial, residential and/or park uses. During the 19th century, when shipping and railroads were the primary freight transport modes, industry and the railroad lines located in port areas and along the water's edge, cutting it off from public use. The decay of these areas as a result of shifts in manufacturing and transport requirements has created an opportunity for redevelopment that allows both public access and renewed economic gains. Many cities—such as Boston, San Francisco and Baltimore in the United States and Toronto and Vancouver in Canada—have undertaken massive waterfront revitalization projects in which commercial development, in combination with waterfront access, has become a major tourist attraction.

Numerous cities have waterfront projects of varying sizes that are designed to bring renewed use and economic development to blighted areas and to take advantage of newly cleaned waterways. Projects of this nature have been undertaken with a mixture of private funds, community development block grant funds, urban development action grants, economic development grants and Urban Park and Recreation Recovery Program grants. These funding sources have been used to leverage additional private development. Many problems characteristic of waterfront development often can occur, however. Building along a navigable waterway, for example, frequently requires government permits from many more agencies than other development. Soil conditions in waterfront areas may also make development more difficult and more costly.
See: COMMUNITY DEVELOPMENT BLOCK GRANT (CDBG); ECONOMIC DEVELOPMENT; FANEUIL HALL MARKETPLACE; GHIRADELLI SQUARE; URBAN DEVELOPMENT ACTION GRANT (UDAG); URBAN PARK AND RECREATION RECOVERY PROGRAM (UPARR)

Watershed

1. Synonomous in American usage with the term *drainage basin*, thus encompassing a land area that can vary greatly in size.

2. Defined in certain other countries as the divide between drainage basins. In the United States this concept is expressed by the term *drainage divide*.
See: CATCHMENT BASIN; DRAINAGE BASIN; GROUNDWATER

Waterwall Incineration

A type of resource-recovery system in which water-filled pipes lining the sides of a specially designed incinerator recover the heat that is generated by the burning of solid waste. The resulting hot water may be used to make steam, which can, in turn, be used to generate electricity, provide heat or power industrial operations.

Widely used in Europe since the 1950s, the first waterwall incinerator in the United States was built at the U.S. Naval Station in Norfolk, Virginia and opened in 1967.

Waterwall incinerators are now in operation in Chicago; Harrisburg; Nashville; Norfolk; Portsmouth, Virginia; and Saugus, Massachusetts. The Saugus plant, which opened in 1976, is capable of processing 1,200 tons (1,089 metric tons) of waste per day, serves 12 different communities and sells its steam to General Electric.
See: INCINERATION; RESOURCE RECOVERY

Welch v. *Swasey* (214 U.S. 91, 29 S.Ct. 567, 53 L.Ed. 923 [1909])

An early decision by the United States Supreme Court recognizing the power of local government to regulate the development of land. The Court upheld a measure that regulated building heights by district in certain residential areas in Boston.

Well

An underground excavation for removing water, other fluids or gases from the earth. In addition, wells are used for underground storage.

In use since early history, water wells are still frequently employed as a water source, particularly in rural areas, and are common sources of water for irrigation. Initially, wells were dug that relied on extracting water from the upper surface of the water table. Dug wells, which may be up to 50 feet (15 meters) deep and range in diameter from about 3 to 20 feet (0.9 meter to 6 meters), are most often designed for personal or farm use. Because they are easily polluted by septic systems, cesspools and the like, they need to be located on higher ground than these potential polluting sources and an adequate distance away.

Today drilled wells are most common because they can be completed more quickly and can operate more efficiently. As of 1980 there were approximately 11 million individual drilled water wells and 2 million individual dug wells in the United States. Generally, drilled wells range from about 4 to 24 inches (10 to 61 centimeters) in diameter and are equipped with steel or wrought iron casing that is sealed to prevent surface water from entering. Like dug wells, they rely upon pumps of varying types to raise the water, depending upon the depth of the well. Drilled wells may range to 1,000 feet (300 meters) in depth or more and generally offer a better quality and more dependable water supply than the dug well.
See: AQUIFER; GROUNDWATER; OFFSHORE DRILLING; POTABLE WATER; WATER SUPPLY SYSTEM

Welwyn Garden City, England

A garden city, similar in concept to Letchworth, built in Hertfordshire about 20 miles (32.2 kilometers) from London under the leadership of Ebenezer Howard. In a second attempt to convince the public of the legitimacy of his views, Howard purchased the land for Welwyn in 1919 and formed the company to build it in 1920. It was planned by Louis de Soissons, who also designed many of its buildings.

Welwyn Garden City, after overcoming initial financial difficulties, was widely acclaimed for its design and archi-

tectural control. After the passage of the New Towns Act of 1946, which it helped to bring about, Welwyn was taken over and administered by a development corporation.
See: GARDEN CITY; HOWARD, SIR EBENEZER; LETCHWORTH, ENGLAND; NEW TOWNS ACT, 1946; OSBORN, SIR FREDERICK JAMES

Wet Scrubber

A type of air pollution control device that may be used for the removal of either particulates or gases. Wet scrubbers remove pollutants by bubbling waste gas through a liquid or spraying atomized liquid droplets through the gas. The droplets trap the pollutants, which are, in the case of particulates, then gathered on various types of collecting surfaces.

Many variations of the scrubber are in use to achieve different levels of collection efficiency. Certain types of scrubbers are also able to remove pollutant gases by absorption. Wet scrubbers, unlike certain other air pollution control equipment, are able to accommodate hot gases and sticky particulates and liquids.
See: AIR POLLUTION; AIR POLLUTION CONTROL

Wetlands

A term for land areas that are sufficiently saturated by surface water or groundwater as to be generally able to support vegetation or aquatic life requiring saturated soil conditions for at least part of the year. Examples of types of wetlands include swamps, marshes, bogs, sloughs, potholes and similar areas.

At one time, wetlands were considered to be useless acreage until drained for farmland or development, and federal policy encouraged the reclamation of wetlands. It is now recognized, however, that they perform a number of extremely important functions when left in their natural state. Among these functions are the storage of stormwaters, helping to avert flood damage, and the recharging of groundwater by holding runoff until it can percolate downward. Wetlands are also capable of filtering out pollutants and preventing them from entering the water supply. In addition, wetlands serve as important wildlife and waterfowl habitats and, in coastal areas, function as nurseries for a large number of fish and shellfish species and provide natural protection against storm waves. They also serve as scenic and recreational resources and sources of natural materials such as peat, timber and grasses.

Although their value is now evident, wetlands have gradually been disappearing throughout the world as a result of such activities as the construction of housing, marinas and roads; drainage to create farmland; flooding as part of reservoir development; and dumping of dredged materials and solid waste. To halt the trend toward destruction of wetlands, a variety of federal, state and local actions have been taken.

One traditional and effective technique of wetlands preservation is government acquisition as part of a national park or nature preserve. As an example, Everglades National Park in southern Florida and Big Thicket National Preserve in Texas contain large areas of wetlands. Financial incentives, such as preferential tax treatment or rental fees, are another means of preserving wetlands. As an example, the Water Bank Program, operated by the Agricultural Stabilization and Conservation Service of the U.S. Department of Agriculture, has been in existence since 1970. It provides for annual payments for 10-year periods to persons preserving and improving wetlands on their property in areas important to migratory waterfowl nesting and breeding.

A third approach to wetlands preservation is the adoption of protective regulations. At the federal level the Army Corps of Engineers operates a permit program that controls dredging, filling and similar activities in wetlands. Wetlands protection laws have been enacted by states to control development, often requiring the issuance of permits before development may take place. Some states have also adopted shoreland management acts, which affect the development of tidal wetlands.

Another tactic is the restriction of government activities that can detrimentally affect wetlands. As an example, pursuant to the provisions of federal Executive Order 11990—"Protection of Wetlands," issued on May 24, 1977— federal agencies are directed to provide leadership in protecting wetlands through such means as avoiding construction or avoiding providing assistance for construction located in wetlands unless "there is no practicable alternative to such construction." Practicable measures must also be taken to reduce damage to the wetlands that may result from new construction. An additional Executive Order, "Floodplain Management" (number 11988, May 24, 1977), provides a measure of additional control over wetlands, as a substantial number of the wetlands in the United States are on floodplains. In addition, the Coastal Barrier Resources Act (enacted in 1982) prohibits most federal investment in the development of coastal barrier islands, many of which contain substantial wetlands areas.
See: ARMY CORPS OF ENGINEERS' PERMIT PROGRAM; BOG; ESTUARY; FLOODPLAIN MANAGEMENT; FRESHWATER MARSH; *JUST* v. *MARINETTE COUNTY, WISCONSIN;* LAND RECLAMATION; SALT MARSH; SWAMP

Wharf

A structure built parallel to the shore, used to load passengers and cargo on and off ships. It is generally of open construction and surrounded by water, with a passageway connecting it to land, although the seaward side is usually the only part of the wharf at which ships are berthed. A quay wall is a simple form of wharf that serves as both a retaining wall for shorefront protection and a docking facility.
See: HARBOR; PIER; PORT

White Elephant

A property that represents a substantial capital investment but for which there is little or no use in its present form. When the term is applied to a property designed to produce income, a white elephant would cost more to operate than it would return in gross revenue. Circumstances that would contribute to this status include changes in popular custom, socioeconomic factors and obsolescence. Examples of white elephants are homes too large to be practical as modern residences and resort hotels in areas no longer considered attractive for vacationing.

One approach to certain white elephants is adaptive use, in which they are converted to new uses. As an example, a large home may often be successfully converted to apartment or office space, and outmoded industrial plants can frequently be transformed to residential or commercial uses.
See: ADAPTIVE USE; ECONOMIC OBSOLESCENCE; FUNCTIONAL OBSOLESCENCE

Wildlife Management

The maintenance and improvement of species and their natural habitats. Wildlife management concerns ecological systems and the preservation of environmental balance and species variety. The provision of food, cover and water is an integral part of management, as is the use of mitigating measures where wildlife is affected by development. Removal of predatory animals from developed areas and farmland is another topic of concern.

Most developed environments can accommodate birds and small mammals, while other animals that do not cause nuisances are also considered to be desirable and may increase property values. Any planning for large-scale development should assess potential damage to existing wildlife and devise ways in which it can be minimized. Projects can often reduce negative impacts by providing land reserves, through clustering or planned unit development, that protect significant wildlife habitats.
See: ENDANGERED SPECIES; FORESTRY; WILDLIFE REFUGE

Wildlife Refuge

A land area that is reserved for the purpose of providing a habitat for wild animals. Depending upon the requirements of the animals to be protected, the refuge may have thousands of acres or may be relatively small, and both the animals and their environment may be managed to assure a sufficient food supply.

The U.S. Fish and Wildlife Service within the Department of the Interior manages 410 National Wildlife Refuges and 89 National Fish Hatcheries. It is responsible for wild birds, endangered species, some marine mammals, inland sport fisheries and certain research activities, and its facilities also permit some forms of recreation. Most states and many municipalities also maintain wildlife refuges.
See: ENDANGERED SPECIES; NATURE PRESERVE; PRIMITIVE RECREATION AREA; WILDLIFE MANAGEMENT; ZOO

Wind Control

The regulation of the direction and velocities of airflows through design and engineering practices. Most frequently, wind-control efforts are intended to minimize potential negative impacts associated with airflows moving at excessive velocities. A combination of topographic changes (such as earth berms), plantings (such as windbreaks) and architectural elements (including wind baffles) are employed for this purpose.
See: CLIMATIC CONDITIONS; SHELTER BELT; WIND TUNNEL EFFECT; WINDBREAK

Wind Power

The harnessing of air currents across the surface of the Earth for the production of power. Wind power has a number of advantages over many other means of energy production because it is free, abundant and can produce power without pollution. Its main disadvantage is its variable nature, which often requires the construction of a storage system.

The use of wind power in sailing ships and windmills has been common for many centuries; the Netherlands became the most industrialized 17th-century nation by harnessing the wind. A recent development, however, is the use of wind power on a major scale, which is generally considered most feasible in regions characterized by high wind velocity of a fairly consistent direction. In 1980 near Palm Springs, California, the first stage of a proposed "windfarm" was put into operation. The Southern California Edison Company produces enough power with three 82-foot (25-meter) long wooden blades to supply electricity to 1,000 homes. The largest windmill ever built, standing 350 feet (106.7 meters) tall and having a 300-foot (91.4-meter) blade, was also completed in 1980 at Goldendale, Washington and connected to the regional power grid.
See: ENERGY SECURITY ACT; RENEWABLE ENERGY SOURCES

Wind Tunnel Effect

A condition created by the placement of buildings in an urban setting in which the velocity of an airflow is magnified to create an effect similar to that produced in a wind tunnel. Uncomfortably high winds often result when a row of skyscrapers and low-rise buildings combine to deflect airflows in such a manner as to funnel currents at much higher than normal velocities.

As a means of understanding the complexity of air movements between groups of buildings, designers and engineers will frequently construct an air tunnel in which a scale model of a proposed project is tested, using simu-

lated airflows at controlled velocities. The assemblage of data by trained personnel along with observation of air movement will generally permit design revisions capable of resolving or minimizing potential problems.
See: WIND CONTROL

Windbreak

A barrier, which may be of living trees and shrubs or constructed of various materials, that provides protection against the wind. It may be designed to protect a home, cultivated fields or orchards. In addition to providing shelter from wind, a windbreak may also provide protection against dust storms and snowstorms.

Strategically planted groups of trees have the ability to reduce wind velocity 50 percent in a downwind direction for a distance of 10 to 20 times the height of the trees. Windbreaks may also be designed to deflect wind from the area needing protection. Although evergreens are most effective for wind control on a year-round basis, deciduous trees perform very well in summer. The design of an effective windbreak depends upon many variables; such factors as tree species, ease of penetration by wind, height and width, and orientation to the prevailing winds can produce quite different results.
See: MICROCLIMATE; SHELTER BELT; WIND TUNNEL EFFECT

Windfalls and Wipeouts

A substantial financial benefit enjoyed (windfall) or loss suffered (wipeout) by a property owner as a result of public action. Examples include adoption of a zoning ordinance, which could add to or subtract from the value of property by affecting its development potential, or construction of public facilities, such as highways or airports. Attempts have been made to develop regulations that ameliorate the windfall or wipeout impact of public action. At this time, however, relatively little progress has been made in this area in the United States.

Britain has, however, addressed the issue of windfalls to landowners through the adoption of a development land tax that taxes increases in the development value of land. The object of the tax is to recapture increases in the development value of land that were conferred by the community.
See: BETTERMENT TAX; COMPENSABLE REGULATIONS; TRANSFER OF DEVELOPMENT RIGHTS (TDR)

Windrowing

A method used in composting in which waste is sorted and shredded and then placed in long piles that are occasionally turned to encourage aeration. A more efficient and much faster method of windrowing, called modified windrowing, blows forced air in controlled amounts through the waste material and uses periodic turning and shredding.

Windshield Survey

A field inspection or survey conducted from an automobile, used in compiling or verifying land use survey data. This technique allows efficient and inexpensive coverage of low-density areas, particularly if there is a driver and one or more recorder/observers.
See: LAND USE SURVEY

Wisconsin Planning Enabling Act of 1909

Legislation passed in 1909 by the state of Wisconsin permitting cities to form planning commissions and to prepare plans. The first state enabling act of its kind in the United States, it also granted subdivision review authority to planning commissions, including the right to review subdivisions outside of municipal boundaries.

Wood Fuel

The use of wood for the production of heat and power. Volatile fuel oil prices as well as the ready availability of wood in many parts of North America are leading to the increased use of wood stoves and furnaces for space heating. In addition to the 7 percent of United States homes using wood at least partially for heat, industry and utility companies are also expressing an increased interest in wood fuel, both in the United States and abroad. For example, Burlington, Vermont is planning to construct a 50 megawatt wood-powered generator that will provide electricity for 20,000 people. The city plans to fuel the unit, when possible, with wastewood, sawmill residues and deteriorated railroad ties. Michigan and Hawaii utility companies are also investing in wood-burning generators.

Although relatively inexpensive in areas of plentiful wood, wood fuel can cause major concentrations of air pollution. Deforestation may also result from rising demand for wood; this has been occurring at a rapid rate in the world's poorer countries.
See: RENEWABLE ENERGY SOURCES

Working Drawings

All of the drawings that are necessary for a contractor to erect a structure. A set of working drawings (also called a set of plans) is composed of plans, elevations, cross sections, details and notes that assist in the interpretation of the drawings. Large buildings frequently require separate sets of plans for the structural framing; for mechanical systems; for electrical work; for plumbing; and for heating, ventilating and air conditioning (HVAC).

Working drawings are used in conjunction with an accompanying set of specifications in the form of a book (often referred to as "specs"), which covers all of the features not shown on the drawings, such as quality and quantity of materials and the methods to be used in construction.
See: CROSS SECTION; ELEVATION; FLOOR PLAN; SCHEMATIC DRAWING; SITE PLAN

Works Progress Administration (WPA)

A United States federal agency that was created in 1935 to provide employment for the many unemployed persons of the Depression era. Renamed the Work Projects Administration in 1939, this agency had a particular impact upon the appearance and functioning of American communities.

During the agency's existence, approximately 8.5 million workers were employed, and many were assigned to public works projects, such as the construction of roads, bridges, airports and recreation facilities. Approximately 125,000 buildings were also constructed under this program. Artists were employed by the WPA as well, and thousands of murals and sculptures were prepared for American municipalities. The agency was disbanded in 1943, when wartime activities provided increased opportunities for employment.

World's Columbian Exposition

A world's fair held in Chicago in 1893 that significantly affected the course of urban planning in the United States. The fair, which was electrically illuminated, celebrated the 400th anniversary of the discovery of America by Christopher Columbus. Known as the "White City" because of its gleaming white classic-style buildings, the fair utilized the talents of some of America's most prominent designers. Frederick Law Olmsted Sr. selected the fair's location in Chicago and served as consulting landscape architect; Daniel Burnham and John Root were selected to be consulting architects and chose the architects who designed the fair's main buildings; and Augustus Saint-Gaudens provided advice concerning the design of statues and fountains.

The exposition, when completed, served as a model for the design and construction of a large-scale, visually pleasing project built according to the requirements of a detailed overall plan. It so impressed the many visitors who attended the exposition by its contrast to the typical industrial city of that time that it helped to stimulate urban planning projects across the country.
See: BURNHAM, DANIEL; CITY BEAUTIFUL MOVEMENT; OLMSTED, FREDERICK LAW

Wraparound Mortgage

A method of refinancing a mortgage in which a new lender assumes payment of the existing mortgage and advances an additional sum of money as well, at a higher interest rate than the original mortgage. The new mortgage is, in effect, "wrapped around" the original one, and the higher interest rate applies to the original money borrowed as well as to the new mortgage. In contrast, interest rates negotiated for a second mortgage have no applicability to the first mortgage.

This technique, which was first used in Canada in the 1930s, offers the lender a chance to earn a yield on the entire sum of money, including the original mortgage, when only the additional sums of money have actually been advanced. A borrower would tend to seek wraparound financing when he cannot or does not wish to prepay his first mortgage and cannot get acceptable refinancing terms with the first lender. The wraparound financing technique might be acceptable to an alternative lending source in circumstances where a second mortgage would not be acceptable; for example, because of the potentially higher yield and greater control that a wraparound mortgagee can obtain.
See: MORTGAGE

Wright, Frank Lloyd (1867–1959)

Distinguished American architect whose work had a profound effect upon 20th-century architects, planners and landscape architects. A principle upon which his designs were based was that of harmony between the buildings he designed and their natural surroundings, and this can be seen in many of his projects. He designed large numbers of residences during his career but also undertook a variety of other projects.

After working with Louis Sullivan, he established his own architectural practice in 1893 and proceeded to become a guiding force behind the "Prairie School" of architecture, which used mass-produced materials to create comfortable, roomy and modestly priced homes. A number of other architectural achievements rapidly followed, including a building for the Larkin Company in Buffalo, New York (1904), in which he incorporated mechanical ventilation, fireproofing and surfaces designed to absorb sound with an attractive work environment, and the Imperial Hotel in Tokyo (1916–22), which withstood the earthquake of 1923.

Wright was also interested in the development of communities and designed plans and models for ideal towns, such as Broadacre City (1930), which placed an emphasis on low-density development. He also developed at about this time the concept of the flat-roofed Usonian home, which could be built economically. Many of these homes, which contained numerous innovative features, were constructed.

Among the most famous of his projects constructed in the latter part of his career are Fallingwater (1936), a vacation home near Pittsburgh, Pennsylvania, built over a waterfall; Taliesin West (1938), in Scottsdale, Arizona, which was his winter home; the Johnson Wax Company administration building (1939), in Racine, Wisconsin; and New York City's Guggenheim Museum, which was completed in 1959.

Wright wrote many books during his career, including *An Organic Architecture* (1939) and *An American Architecture* (1955).

Y

Yard

1. An area of an occupied lot, intended to be set aside for open space, that is located between a lot line and the building or buildings on the lot. A yard may be located between the front, side or rear of a building and the lot line that is nearest to that portion of the building. Measurements are made from the point of the building closet to the lot line. (See Fig. 50)

2. A unit of linear measurement equal to 3 feet, 36 inches or 0.9144 meters.

See: FRONT YARD; INTERIOR SIDE YARD; LOT LINE; REAR YARD; SETBACK; SIDE YARD; YARD PROJECTIONS; YARD REQUIREMENTS; ZONING

Yard Projections

Portions of a structure that project into the required yard of a building lot and are generally partially exempt from the provisions of the zoning ordinance concerning yard requirements. Structural features—such as steps, eaves, bay windows and uncovered porches—are usually allowed to extend several feet into required yards.

See: YARD; YARD REQUIREMENTS; ZONING

Yard Requirements

The yard area that the municipal zoning ordinance requires to be set aside in the front, rear or side of a building lot. Zoning ordinance requirements vary as to whether any construction or encroachment may take place in required yards, but many ordinances permit limited encroachment, such as for fences.

Zoning ordinances generally contain yard requirements to ensure an adequate amount of open space and greenery, privacy and light and to provide a buffer between adjoining lots. They also help to contain fires that may start and provide access for fire-fighting equipment. As vacant land becomes more scarce and the price of land and development increases, variations in traditional yard requirements are being experimented with to see if the functions that yards are thought to provide can be accomplished through other design techniques.

See: CLUSTER DEVELOPMENT; PLANNED UNIT DEVELOPMENT (PUD); YARD; YARD PROJECTIONS; ZERO LOT-LINE DEVELOPMENT; ZONING

Yellowstone National Park

The first national park ever created. It served as a world model for the protection of outstanding natural land areas and helped to establish a tradition of national government ownership and management of these areas. Created in 1872 and spanning over 2,220,000 acres (898,400 hectares), Yellowstone is located in portions of three states: Wyoming, Montana and Idaho. Its vast area includes diverse terrain and natural features, ranging from mountains, dense forests, waterfalls and lakes to thermal phenomena such as geysers, hot springs and mud volcanoes.

See: NATIONAL PARK; NATIONAL PARK SYSTEM

Y-Intersection

A three-leg, at-grade intersection at which three roads converge in the form of the letter Y. Each leg enters the intersection at a different angle. A branch intersection, a form of Y-intersection, is one that looks like a Y but instead is the intersection of two roads at less than a 90-degree angle where one road ends at the intersection.

Y-intersections are not considered to be as safe as other forms of intersections from a traffic engineering standpoint. In building or modifying Y or branch intersections, current practice is to change the angle at which one or more of the intersecting legs approaches the intersection, causing it to become perpendicular to the other road or roads—i.e., to convert the Y to a T-intersection. (See Fig. 5)

See: AT-GRADE INTERSECTION; T-INTERSECTION

Young v. American Mini Theatres **(427 U.S. 50 [1976])**

A decision by the United States Supreme Court that upheld a city zoning ordinance intended to restrict the placement of "sexually oriented" businesses. The Court upheld a requirement that prohibited the establishment of

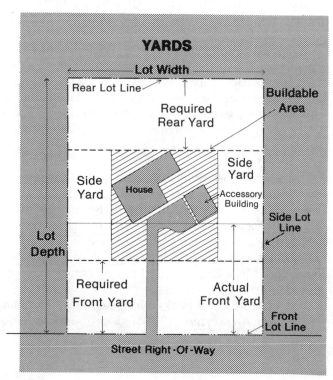

Fig. 50.

more than two adult-type uses within 1,000 feet against claims that the ordinance constituted a restraint on freedom of speech in violation of the First Amendment to the Constitution.

From a zoning perspective, the decision is significant, in that it reaffirms the validity of zoning for the purpose of controlling the aesthetic and sociological development of a community.

See: ADULT ENTERTAINMENT ZONE; *SCHAD* v. *BOROUGH OF MOUNT EPHRAIM*

Z

Zahn v. Board of Public Works of City of Los Angeles (274 U.S. 325 [1927])

An early zoning decision by the United States Supreme Court upholding the principle that a locally adopted zoning ordinance is presumed to be valid. The Court would not substitute its judgment for that of the local legislative body adopting the ordinance unless the ordinance and its effect on property were clearly arbitrary or unreasonable.

See: VILLAGE OF EUCLID v. *AMBLER REALTY CO.*

Zero-Base Budget (ZBB)

A budget format that treats each project or cost as if it were new, even though it may have received funding in the past. Its purpose is to seek new or less costly means of accomplishing agency goals, to eliminate unsuccessful programs and to introduce new programs in a cost-effective manner. The concept of zero-base is best described as starting each budget year without any programs and then adding only those programs whose worth can be demonstrated, up to an agreed-upon funding ceiling.

The process of budget development requires that each department or agency identify its organizational structure; senior management; decision units (subunits within the management structure responsible for implementing programs); and objectives of the decision units, which must, of course, agree with the goals and objectives of the department. Decision packages must then be developed by analyzing program alternatives and developing several funding levels for the best alternatives. The decision packages are then ranked by higher-level management, and a budget submission is proposed.

Zero-base budgeting was developed by the U.S. Department of Agriculture in the 1970s but abandoned a few years later; in 1977 its use was instituted for all federal departments. Because zero-base budgeting is an extremely time-consuming process, it has had mixed success in most applications.

See: BUDGET

Zero Lot-Line Development

Development in which a building is permitted to be placed abutting one or more of the property's lot lines. This can have the effect of providing a larger area of contiguous open space on the lot, if permitted development density and lot coverage remain unchanged, and can allow increased design flexibility. For example, zero lot-line regulations may be used to provide large common areas of open space or to improve solar access by protecting the area south of a solar collector. Zero lot-line development is generally permitted only in specific approved circumstances, such as in planned unit developments. (See Fig. 51)

See: LOT LINE; PLANNED UNIT DEVELOPMENT (PUD); SOLAR ACCESS DESIGN TECHNIQUES; ZONING

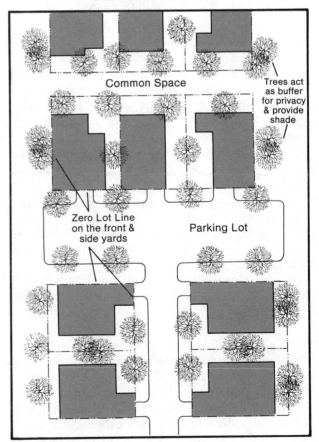

ZERO LOT LINE DEVELOPMENT

Fig. 51.

Zero Population Growth (ZPG)

1. The stabilization of the size of the human population through reduction of the birthrate until population growth ceases. The number of births would then equal the number of deaths for any time period. In theory, ZPG could be achieved by voluntary birth control, government incentives for small families or government restrictions on reproduction. Within a given municipality, however, ZPG often takes place without government intervention through a combination of lowered birthrate and increased out-migration or lack of in-migration.

Advocates of ZPG view overpopulation as a serious threat to long-term human survival, leading to physical and psychological overcrowding, social breakdown, and food and resource shortages. They argue that ZPG would improve the standard of living by reducing competition for limited resources. Opponents point out that ZPG would increase the average age of the population and could change consumer demand, the economy and the existing social structure. They link ZPG to the exclusionary aspects of no-growth policies and also argue that ZPG could cause zero economic growth (ZEG), a cessation of growth in the gross national product.

2. An organization, headquartered in Washington, D.C., dedicated to the achievement of ZPG. Zero Population Growth Inc. also supports ecologically sound land use planning and conservation of energy and nonrenewable resources.

See: NO GROWTH; POPULATION DECLINE

Zimmerman Process (Zimpro)

A wet oxidation process used in the treatment of sewage sludge in which its biochemical oxygen demand (BOD) and volume are reduced. Developed in Norway for treatment of pulp mill wastes, it is now used in the secondary treatment of sludge after removal from the primary settling tank and for sludge dewatering. The process enables efficient handling for sludge-disposal purposes, since the sludge is either dried or reduced to ash and is largely sterilized and deodorized.

Compressed air is mixed with ground sludge, heated and then pressurized in a reactor. The end products are a mixture of gases, liquid, and ash or dewatered sludge. The process can remove 80 percent to 90 percent of the BOD under high pressure.

See: BIOCHEMICAL OXYGEN DEMAND (BOD); DEWATERED SLUDGE; SLUDGE DISPOSAL; SLUDGE INCINERATION

Zoning

An exercise of the police power in which utilization and development of privately owned land is regulated through the division of a community into various districts and the specification of permitted and/or prohibited uses for each district. Zoning also controls numerous aspects of development within each district, such as intensity of development, height and bulk of development, required lot sizes, required yard sizes and parking requirements.

Modern zoning, which is by far the most common means of controlling land development in the United States, traces its origins to land use controls employed in the latter part of the 19th century in Europe, particularly in Germany. New York City is credited with adopting the first comprehensive zoning ordinance in the United States in 1916, but more limited efforts had been made earlier in various cities to control nuisances, limit height and otherwise regulate aspects of development. In 1926 the United States Supreme Court first upheld zoning as a constitutional use of the police power in *Village of Euclid* v. *Ambler Realty Co.*

At first, zoning was intended primarily to protect residential areas from intrusion by commercial or industrial uses. As such, zoning ordinances were often organized in a cumulative manner, in which the most "desirable" land uses, which were permitted in residential districts, were also permitted in the less desirable commercial or industrial zones. Similarly, commercial uses were also permitted in industrial zones, considered to be at the bottom of the land use pyramid. As zoning evolved, changes were introduced in many communities in which zones were created specifically to foster certain types of land uses. Another major change in zoning that may be perceived over time was the substantial refinement of zoning categories and a large increase in the number of use classifications that could be found.

Relatively recent trends in zoning include the use of zoning to achieve aesthetic goals and preserve historic buildings and sites, the increasing use of performance rather than specification standards and the generally more common use of flexible land development controls.

See: AESTHETIC ZONING; AIRPORT ZONING; AS-OF-RIGHT ZONING; BULK REGULATIONS; CONFISCATORY REGULATION; CONTRACT ZONING; CUMULATIVE ZONING; DEVELOPMENT ORDINANCE; DOWNZONING; ENVIRONMENTALLY SENSITIVE LANDS; EUCLIDEAN ZONING; EXCLUSIONARY ZONING; EXCLUSIVE-USE ZONING; FISCAL ZONING; FLEXIBLE REGULATIONS; FLOATING ZONE; HEIGHT CONTROLS; HISTORIC DISTRICT ORDINANCE; IMPACT ZONING; IN ACCORDANCE WITH A COMPREHENSIVE PLAN; INCENTIVE ZONING; INTERIM ZONING; LAND USE CONTROLS; LAND USE INTENSITY STANDARDS (LUI); LARGE-LOT ZONING; MICROZONING; MIXED-USE ZONING; PERFORMANCE ZONING; PHASED DEVELOPMENT CONTROLS; POLICE POWER; REZONING; SIGN REGULATION; SPECIAL ZONING DISTRICT; SPECIFICATION STANDARDS; SPOT ZONING; SUBDIVISION REGULATIONS; UNZONED AREAS; VERTICAL ZONING; VIEW PROTECTION REGULATIONS; ZONING ADMINISTRATION; ZONING BOARD OF APPEALS; ZONING DISTRICT; ZONING HEARING EXAMINER; ZONING MAP; ZONING ORDINANCE; ZONING PERMIT; ZONING VARIANCE

Zoning Administration

Governmental activity that involves the day-to-day enforcement of the zoning ordinance, the operations of an appeals body and the amendment of the zoning ordinance and zoning map.

The zoning enforcement officer examines requests for building permits for compliance with the zoning ordinance, issues zoning permits, makes inspections of property and issues certificates of occupancy when the buildings are properly completed and in compliance with municipal zoning and other regulations. Other functions include processing applications for variances and special permits, disseminating information concerning the municipal zoning ordinance, conducting inspections for zoning violations and maintaining zoning records. Most often, the responsibility for enforcing the zoning ordinance is assigned to the building inspector, as his functions generally include the processing of all building permit applications. An alternate approach (because of the complexity of some municipal zoning ordinances) is to make the planning department responsible for zoning administration. Still a third way of handling zoning enforcement, generally found only in larger communities, is the establishment of the office of zoning administrator. The zoning administrator and staff handle all aspects of zoning administration, serve the appeals body and, in some cases, are empowered to grant minor variances.

One of the main functions of the appeals body, usually called the zoning board of appeals or zoning board of adjustment, is to hear appeals that are made concerning decisions of the enforcement officer. This group also makes decisions concerning the granting of relief from the provisions of the zoning ordinance through the issuance of variances and makes decisions concerning the issuance of special permits.

A third aspect of zoning administration is the processing of changes in the zoning ordinance and map—that is, rezoning. This function generally involves the participation of the planning staff, the planning commission, the public and the local legislative body.

See: BUILDING INSPECTOR; REZONING; ZONING; ZONING BOARD OF APPEALS; ZONING HEARING EXAMINER; ZONING PERMIT; ZONING VARIANCE

Zoning Board of Appeals

A quasi-judicial municipal board, also known as a zoning board of adjustment. It hears appeals from property owners in matters related to the disapproval of building permits by the local zoning officer (usually the building inspector), grants variances as relief from hardship caused by strict adherence to zoning ordinance requirements and grants special permits where it is so empowered. In its administration of these responsibilities, the board must endeavor to preserve the intent of the zoning ordinance.

The zoning board generally has three broad areas of jurisdiction. First, it serves as the interpreter of the zoning ordinance and zoning map when appeals are made from a building inspector's decision. Another area of jurisdiction relates to requests for variances, which are automatically directed to the zoning board for its decision. It may grant area variances based on the inability to develop a property in strict accordance with zoning requirements, but zoning boards are often prohibited from granting use variances, which may be regarded as a legislative prerogative. Requests for special permits are also usually directed to the zoning board, although in some communities special permit applications are handled by the planning board.

When matters are brought before the board of appeals, a public hearing is held after legally required public notice is given. The zoning board subsequently decides upon the merits of the case and issues its findings as a formal opinion of the board, which includes the reasons for the decision that has been made. The board must keep adequate records of its hearings in sufficient detail to be suitable for use in cases that are appealed to a court. Such appeals may be undertaken by the applicant if denied approval, by a neighboring municipality angered by a special permit or variance approval for property near its border or by a citizen group opposed to the granting of an approval.

The zoning board is usually composed of five citizen members who are appointed for overlapping terms by the chief elected official or legislative body. In some communities one of the members may also be a member of the planning board. Although in most cases zoning board members volunteer their time, in some communities they receive nominal compensation.

The zoning board may have a staff or official counsel, be advised by the planning department or rely on the opinions of its members. The lack of professional advice in many jurisdictions, however, is the main failing of many zoning boards of appeals, causing opinions that are not adequately founded in fact or based on due process. Municipalities that provide professional assistance to the appeals board or that substitute a zoning hearing examiner for the board often have a better record of court decisions in their favor than those that rely solely on the board of appeals.

See: SPECIAL-USE PERMIT; ZONING; ZONING ADMINISTRATION; ZONING HEARING EXAMINER; ZONING VARIANCE

Zoning District

A portion of a community that is officially delineated on the zoning map and is subject to a particular set of land use requirements set forth in the zoning ordinance. These requirements, which are uniform throughout the district, control permitted uses as well as intensity of development and arrangement of buildings on the land. Typically, each zoning district will be assigned a descriptive title, such as R-1A residential (meaning a residential district with a required minimum lot size of 1 acre) or LI (light industrial).

All sections of the community located in a particular

zoning district will be permitted the same range of land uses, the same maximum height and the same maximum coverage. Depending on the size of a community and the complexity of its development patterns, a municipality may have only a few or as many as 50 or more zoning districts.

See: ZONING; ZONING MAP; ZONING ORDINANCE; ZONING VARIANCE

Zoning Hearing Examiner

A governmental official who is empowered to hold quasijudicial public hearings on zoning matters, such as applications for variances or special permits; take evidence; and either make recommendations concerning the application or make a decision on the application. In addition to special permits and variances, the jurisdiction of the zoning hearing examiner may include rezonings, zoning enforcement, sign variances and applications for planned unit developments. The actual range of responsibility varies considerably from community to community.

Modeled upon the federal administrative process, the use of zoning hearing examiners is intended to contribute a degree of professionalism to the administration of zoning that some feel may be lacking when complex problems are entrusted entirely to lay bodies. In addition, establishment of such an office helps to give planning commissions more time to devote to long-range planning problems and legislative bodies additional time to devote to their most pressing responsibilities, since many or all of the zoning functions normally under the jurisdiction of the zoning board of appeals, planning commission or legislative body are placed under the jurisdiction of the hearing examiner. Applicants are also usually able to receive a swifter response to their applications.

Typically, an application is made to the planning department and then forwarded to the zoning hearing examiner, who sets a hearing date and notifies all concerned parties and nearby property owners. After a public hearing (which is generally conducted according to due process requirements), the examiner either makes a written decision or submits a written recommendation to the decision-making body with responsibility for the type of application being made. The examiner's report generally includes findings as well as the rationale upon which the decision or recommendation is based. When the hearing examiner is the decision maker, appeals are usually made to the legislative body.

Maryland was the first state in which the position of zoning hearing examiner was established; Anne Arundel County instituted this practice in 1965. As of 1980 zoning hearing examiners were being used in 10 states in such diverse communities and counties as Los Angeles; Wheeling, West Virginia; Portland, Oregon; Niagara County, New York; and Tampa, Florida.

See: ZONING; ZONING ADMINISTRATION; ZONING BOARD OF APPEALS

Zoning Map

A map or set of maps that indicates the boundaries of zoning districts. A zoning ordinance consists of the zoning map or maps, the text of the ordinance and a schedule of district regulations, if one is used. The zoning map links the provisions of the zoning ordinance text to specific parcels of land in a community and enables the zoning district classification of any property to be identified.

See: SCHEDULE OF DISTRICT REGULATIONS; ZONING; ZONING DISTRICT; ZONING ORDINANCE

Zoning Ordinance

The official document that sets forth the zoning regulations and zoning districts that are applicable in a community. A zoning ordinance consists of the zoning text (which describes all regulations, standards and procedures and defines the terms that are used) and a zoning map or maps (which delineate the location of all zoning districts). A schedule of district regulations, in which various requirements are listed and summarized, may also be included.

The zoning ordinance is one of the major types of land use controls available for the regulation of development.

See: LAND USE CONTROLS; SCHEDULE OF DISTRICT REGULATIONS; ZONING; ZONING MAP

Zoning Permit

An official statement by the zoning officer that a proposed development or use of property is in accordance with zoning ordinance requirements or has been able to comply with all required conditions for a special permit or variance. The zoning permit, sometimes called a certificate of compliance, may be included as part of the building permit.

See: BUILDING PERMIT; CERTIFICATE OF OCCUPANCY (CO); PERMIT; ZONING; ZONING ORDINANCE

Zoning Variance

A waiver from compliance with a specific provision of the zoning ordinance granted to a particular property owner because of the practical difficulties or unnecessary hardship that would be imposed upon him by the strict application of that provision of the ordinance. The granting of variances traditionally is the responsibility of the zoning board of appeals.

Variances were developed as a relief mechanism because of the difficulties of applying to an entire community land use requirements that would be equitable in all cases. If, for example, a cliff abutting a residential lot makes it impossible for a property owner to provide the required rear yard, without a variance he would be unable to legally construct a house on his property. The variance is intended to assist in precisely this type of situation—that is, where the property owner would be denied reasonable use of his property without the granting of a variance. An improper reason for granting a variance, on the other hand, is that the owner could use his land more profitably if one were granted. Variances are properly granted to an applicant only when he suffers from a unique hardship or difficulty rather than from a condition that applies to an entire neighborhood. When neighborhoodwide conditions exist, they are most appropriately handled through zoning amendments, in which all property owners suffering the same problem are treated equitably.

Another requirement that applies to the granting of a variance is that the hardship may not be self-imposed. The variance application must also request relief from the provisions of the zoning ordinance rather than from some other requirement or mechanism, such as a deed restriction. In addition, the zoning board must also be certain that granting the variance does not run counter to the public interest and that neighboring properties will not be harmed significantly by this action.

Zoning variances have been granted so liberally in some communities as to distort the entire framework of the zoning ordinance and comprehensive plan. A number of reasons help to account for this. Zoning ordinances often give little guidance or few meaningful standards concerning the proper situations in which a zoning variance may be granted. The zoning board members may also have been appointed more for their local prominence or political service than for any practical experience or professional skills that they can bring to the board. In addition, zoning boards are not always assigned both legal and professional planning assistance to help them in their deliberations and to be present at meetings and hearings. Many individuals are also encouraged by municipal officials to apply for a zoning variance when they do not have an appropriate case for a variance (but do have a good argument for a zoning amendment) because it is so much simpler procedurally and politically to receive a variance. Despite problems encountered in the granting of zoning variances,

however, when properly administered they have served and can continue to serve a legitimate function.

See: AREA VARIANCE; USE VARIANCE; ZONING; ZONING ADMINISTRATION; ZONING BOARD OF APPEALS; ZONING HEARING EXAMINER

Zoo

An open-space reserve, also called a zoological park, in which animals are kept for display purposes, research and conservation. Three different approaches are currently most prevalent in modern zoos. In the first approach undomesticated animals are kept in cages or in naturalistic enclosures so that visitors to the zoo may view them safely from a variety of vantage points. In a second technique animals are permitted to roam freely, and people are restricted to private vehicles, enclosed monorails, buses or enclosed walks. A third approach is the specialized children's zoo, in which children may mingle with domesticated and other small animals. Some zoos combine two or more of these exhibit types by assigning them to different portions of the zoo. Aquariums, in which aquatic life is displayed, may also be considered a form of zoo. In addition to animal displays, most zoos are now integrating educational programs and recreational activities in the form of aerial, train or animal rides and animal shows, making them popular for recreational outings.

Zoos of every size are regional facilities, while some specialized or particularly well-known facilities may draw attendance nationally. As such, they have requirements for substantial amounts of parking space, good access from major highways and service by public transit. Larger facilities may generate considerable employment and economic activity.

See: WILDLIFE REFUGE

List of Acronyms

AADT *See:* **AVERAGE ANNUAL DAILY TRAFFIC (AADT)**

ACIR *See:* **ADVISORY COMMISSION ON INTER-GOVERNMENTAL RELATIONS (ACIR)**

ACPI *See:* **AMERICAN CITY PLANNING INSTITUTE (ACPI)**

AEDC *See:* **AMERICAN ECONOMIC DEVELOP-MENT COUNCIL (AEDC)**

AHPA *See:* **AMERICAN HEALTH PLANNING ASSO-CIATION (AHPA)**

AIA *See:* **AMERICAN INSTITUTE OF ARCHITECTS (AIA)**

AICP *See:* **AMERICAN INSTITUTE OF CERTIFIED PLANNERS (AICP)**

AIP *See:* **AMERICAN INSTITUTE OF PLANNERS (AIP)**

AIP *See:* **ANNUAL IMPLEMENTATION PLAN (AIP)**

AIREA *See:* **AMERICAN INSTITUTE OF REAL ES-TATE APPRAISERS (AIREA)**

ALI Code *See:* **AMERICAN LAW INSTITUTE MODEL LAND DEVELOPMENT CODE**

APA *See:* **AMERICAN PLANNING ASSOCIATION (APA)**

APCA *See:* **AIR POLLUTION CONTROL ASSOCI-ATION (APCA)**

AQCR *See:* **AIR QUALITY CONTROL REGION (AQCR)**

ASAE *See:* **AMERICAN SOCIETY OF AGRICUL-TURAL ENGINEERS (ASAE)**

ASCE *See:* **AMERICAN SOCIETY OF CIVIL EN-GINEERS (ASCE)**

ASCP *See:* **AMERICAN SOCIETY OF CONSULTING PLANNERS (ASCP)**

ASLA *See:* **AMERICAN SOCIETY OF LANDSCAPE ARCHITECTS (ASLA)**

ASPA *See:* **AMERICAN SOCIETY FOR PUBLIC AD-MINISTRATION (ASPA)**

ASPO *See:* **AMERICAN SOCIETY OF PLANNING OF-FICIALS (ASPO)**

BLM *See:* **BUREAU OF LAND MANAGEMENT (BLM)**

BLS *See:* **BUREAU OF LABOR STATISTICS (BLS)**

BMPs *See:* **BEST MANAGEMENT PRACTICES (BMPs)**

BOCA *See:* **BUILDING OFFICIALS AND CODE AD-MINISTRATORS INTERNATIONAL (BOCA)**

BOD *See:* **BIOCHEMICAL OXYGEN DEMAND (BOD)**

BPT *See:* **BEST PRACTICABLE TECHNOLOGY (BPT)**

CAC *See:* **CONSERVATION ADVISORY COUNCIL (CAC)**

CAP *See:* **COMMUNITY ACTION PROGRAM (CAP)**

CBD *See:* **CENTRAL BUSINESS DISTRICT (CBD)**

CDBG *See:* **COMMUNITY DEVELOPMENT BLOCK GRANT (CDBG)**

CDC *See:* **COMMUNITY DEVELOPMENT COR-PORATION (CDC)**

CEDS *See:* **COMPREHENSIVE ECONOMIC DEVEL-OPMENT STRATEGY (CEDS)**

CEQ *See:* **COUNCIL ON ENVIRONMENTAL QUAL-ITY (CEQ)**

CERCLA *See:* **COMPREHENSIVE ENVIRONMEN-TAL RESPONSE, COMPENSATION AND LIABIL-ITY ACT OF 1980 (CERCLA)**

CETA *See* **COMPREHENSIVE EMPLOYMENT AND TRAINING ACT OF 1973 (CETA)**

CFDA *See:* **CATALOG OF FEDERAL DOMESTIC AS-SISTANCE (CFDA)**

CFSG/NML *See:* **CITIZENS FORUM ON SELF-GOVERNMENT/NATIONAL MUNICIPAL LEAGUE**

CIP *See:* CANADIAN INSTITUTE OF PLANNERS (CIP)

CIP *See:* CAPITAL IMPROVEMENT PROGRAM (CIP)

CIUL *See:* COUNCIL FOR INTERNATIONAL URBAN LIAISON (CIUL)

CO *See:* CERTIFICATE OF OCCUPANCY (CO)

COG *See:* COUNCIL OF GOVERNMENT (COG)

CON *See:* CERTIFICATE OF NEED (CON)

CPL *See:* COUNCIL OF PLANNING LIBRARIANS (CPL)

CPM *See:* CRITICAL PATH METHOD (CPM)

CRA *See:* COMMUNITY REINVESTMENT ACT OF 1977 (CRA)

CSA *See:* COMMUNITY SERVICES ADMINISTRATION (CSA)

CSPA *See:* COUNCIL OF STATE PLANNING AGENCIES (CSPA)

CT *See:* CENSUS TRACT (CT)

CUED *See:* NATIONAL COUNCIL FOR URBAN ECONOMIC DEVELOPMENT (CUED)

CZMA *See:* COASTAL ZONE MANAGEMENT ACT OF 1972 (CZMA)

dB *See:* DECIBEL

DHV *See:* DESIGN HOUR VOLUME (DHV)

DOE *See:* DEPARTMENT OF ENERGY (DOE)

DOT *See:* DEPARTMENT OF TRANSPORTATION (DOT)

DRT *See:* DEMAND-RESPONSIVE TRANSPORTATION (DRT)

DSS *See:* DECISION SUPPORT SYSTEMS (DSS)

ECHO *See:* EACH COMMUNITY HELPS OTHERS (ECHO)

ED *See:* ENUMERATION DISTRICT (ED)

EDA *See:* ECONOMIC DEVELOPMENT ADMINISTRATION (EDA)

EDD *See:* ECONOMIC DEVELOPMENT DISTRICT (EDD)

EIS *See:* ENVIRONMENTAL IMPACT STATEMENT (EIS)

EPA *See:* ENVIRONMENTAL PROTECTION AGENCY (EPA)

EROS *See:* EARTH RESOURCES OBSERVATION SYSTEMS (EROS) PROGRAM

ERTS *See:* EARTH RESOURCES TECHNOLOGY SATELLITE (ERTS)

ESP *See:* ELECTROSTATIC PRECIPITATOR (ESP)

ETA *See:* EMPLOYMENT AND TRAINING ADMINISTRATION (ETA)

FAA *See:* FEDERAL AVIATION ADMINISTRATION (FAA)

Fannie Mae *See:* FEDERAL NATIONAL MORTGAGE ASSOCIATION (FNMA)

FAR *See:* FLOOR AREA RATIO (FAR)

FAUS *See:* FEDERAL-AID URBAN SYSTEM (FAUS)

FEMA *See:* FEDERAL EMERGENCY MANAGEMENT AGENCY (FEMA)

FHA *See:* FEDERAL HOUSING ADMINISTRATION (FHA)

FHA Mortgage Insurance *See:* FEDERAL HOUSING ADMINISTRATION (FHA) MORTGAGE INSURANCE

FHBM *See:* FLOOD HAZARD BOUNDARY MAP (FHBM)

FHLBS *See:* FEDERAL HOME LOAN BANK SYSTEM (FHLBS)

FHLMC *See:* FEDERAL HOME LOAN MORTGAGE CORPORATION (FHLMC)

FHWA *See:* FEDERAL HIGHWAY ADMINISTRATION (FHWA)

FIRM *See:* FLOOD INSURANCE RATE MAP (FIRM)

FmHA *See:* FARMERS HOME ADMINISTRATION (FmHA)

FNMA   *See:* FEDERAL NATIONAL MORTGAGE AS-SOCIATION (FNMA)

FONSI   *See:* FINDING OF NO SIGNIFICANT IMPACT (FONSI)

FRA   *See:* FEDERAL RAILROAD ADMINISTRATION (FRA)

Freddie Mac   *See:* FEDERAL HOME LOAN MORT-GAGE CORPORATION (FHLMC)

FRM   *See:* FIXED-RATE MORTGAGE (FRM)

GEMS   *See:* GLOBAL ENVIRONMENTAL MON-ITORING SYSTEM (GEMS)

Ginnie Mae   *See:* GOVERNMENT NATIONAL MORT-GAGE ASSOCIATION (GNMA)

GNMA   *See:* GOVERNMENT NATIONAL MORT-GAGE ASSOCIATION (GNMA)

GPM   *See:* GRADUATED-PAYMENT MORTGAGE (GPM)

GSA   *See:* GENERAL SERVICES ADMINISTRATION (GSA)

HABS   *See:* HISTORIC AMERICAN BUILDING SUR-VEY (HABS)

HAER   *See:* HISTORIC AMERICAN ENGINEERING RECORD

HAP   *See:* HOUSING ASSISTANCE PLAN (HAP)

HDS   *See:* OFFICE OF HUMAN DEVELOPMENT SER-VICES (HDS)

HHFA   *See:* HOUSING AND HOME FINANCE AGENCY (HHFA)

HHS   *See:* DEPARTMENT OF HEALTH AND HUMAN SERVICES (HHS)

HMO   *See:* HEALTH MAINTENANCE ORGANIZA-TION (HMO)

HSA   *See:* HEALTH SYSTEMS AGENCY (HSA)

HSP   *See:* HEALTH SYSTEMS PLAN (HSP)

HUD   *See:* DEPARTMENT OF HOUSING AND URBAN DEVELOPMENT (HUD)

HYDROPOWER   *See:* HYDROELECTRIC POWER

ICBO   *See:* INTERNATIONAL CONFERENCE OF BUILDING OFFICIALS (ICBO)

ICF   *See:* INTERMEDIATE CARE FACILITIES (ICF)

ICMA   *See:* INTERNATIONAL CITY MANAGEMENT ASSOCIATION (ICMA)

ICOMOS   *See:* INTERNATIONAL COUNCIL ON MONUMENTS AND SITES (ICOMOS)

IDA   *See:* INDUSTRIAL DEVELOPMENT AGENCY (IDA)

IFHP   *See:* INTERNATIONAL FEDERATION FOR HOUSING AND PLANNING (IFHP)

IMPULSIVE SOUND   *See:* IMPACT SOUND

IPM   *See:* INTEGRATED PEST MANAGEMENT (IPM)

ISES   *See:* INTERNATIONAL SOLAR ENERGY SOCI-ETY (ISES)

ITC   *See:* INVESTMENT TAX CREDIT

ITE   *See:* INSTITUTE OF TRANSPORTATION EN-GINEERS (ITE)

LAWCON   *See:* LAND AND WATER CONSERVATION FUND (LAWCON)

LOS   *See:* LEVEL OF SERVICE (LOS)

LUI   *See:* LAND USE INTENSITY STANDARDS (LUI)

MBO   *See:* MANAGEMENT BY OBJECTIVES (MBO)

MCD   *See:* MINOR CIVIL DIVISION (MCD)

MSA   *See:* METROPOLITAN STATISTICAL AREA (MSA)

MXD   *See:* MIXED-USE DEVELOPMENT (MXD)

NAAQS   *See:* NATIONAL AMBIENT AIR QUALITY STANDARDS (NAAQS)

NACPD   *See:* NATIONAL ASSOCIATION OF COUNTY PLANNING DIRECTORS (NACPD)

NADO   *See:* NATIONAL ASSOCIATION OF DEVEL-OPMENT ORGANIZATIONS (NADO)

NAHB   *See:* NATIONAL ASSOCIATION OF HOME BUILDERS OF THE UNITED STATES (NAHB)

NAHRO *See:* NATIONAL ASSOCIATION OF HOUSING AND REDEVELOPMENT OFFICIALS (NAHRO)

NAR® *See:* NATIONAL ASSOCIATION OF REALTORS® (NAR®)

NCIC *See:* NATIONAL CARTOGRAPHIC INFORMATION CENTER (NCIC)

NEHA *See:* NATIONAL ENVIRONMENTAL HEALTH ASSOCIATION (NEHA)

NEPA *See:* NATIONAL ENVIRONMENTAL POLICY ACT OF 1969 (NEPA)

NESDIS *See:* NATIONAL ENVIRONMENTAL SATELLITE, DATA AND INFORMATION SERVICE (NESDIS)

NHC *See:* NATIONAL HOUSING CONFERENCE (NHC)

NHRA *See:* NATIONAL HOUSING REHABILITATION ASSOCIATION (NHRA)

NHS *See:* NEIGHBORHOOD HOUSING SERVICES (NHS)

NIBS *See:* NATIONAL INSTITUTE OF BUILDING SCIENCES (NIBS)

NOAA *See:* NATIONAL OCEANIC AND ATMOSPHERIC ADMINISTRATION (NOAA)

NPDES *See:* NATIONAL POLLUTANT DISCHARGE ELIMINATION SYSTEM (NPDES)

NRC *See:* NEIGHBORHOOD REINVESTMENT CORPORATION (NRC)

NRC *See:* NUCLEAR REGULATORY COMMISSION (NRC)

NRPA *See:* NATIONAL RECREATION AND PARK ASSOCIATION (NRPA)

NSA *See:* NEIGHBORHOOD STRATEGY AREA (NSA)

NSPS *See:* NEW SOURCE PERFORMANCE STANDARDS (NSPS)

OCS *See:* OFFICE OF COMMUNITY SERVICES (OCS)

OCS *See:* OUTER CONTINENTAL SHELF (OCS)

O-D Study *See:* ORIGIN-DESTINATION (O-D) STUDY

OEDP *See:* OVERALL ECONOMIC DEVELOPMENT PROGRAM (OEDP)

ORV *See:* OFF-ROAD VEHICLES

OTEC *See:* OCEAN THERMAL ENERGY CONVERSION (OTEC)

PCBs *See:* POLYCHLORINATED BIPHENYLS (PCBs)

Perk Test *See:* PERCOLATION (PERK) TEST

PERT *See:* PROGRAM EVALUATION AND REVIEW TECHNIQUE (PERT)

PLP *See:* PARTNERS FOR LIVABLE PLACES (PLP)

PPBS *See:* PLANNING-PROGRAMMING-BUDGETING SYSTEM (PPBS)

PSI *See:* POLLUTANT STANDARD INDEX (PSI)

PUD *See:* PLANNED UNIT DEVELOPMENT (PUD)

PVC *See:* POLYVINYL CHLORIDE (PVC)

RAIC *See:* ROYAL ARCHITECTURAL INSTITUTE OF CANADA (RAIC)

RCRA *See:* RESOURCE CONSERVATION AND RECOVERY ACT OF 1976 (RCRA)

RDA *See:* RESTRICTED DEVELOPMENT AREAS (RDA)

RDF *See:* REFUSE-DERIVED FUEL (RDF)

REA *See:* RURAL ELECTRIFICATION ADMINISTRATION (REA)

RFP *See:* REQUEST FOR PROPOSAL (RFP)

RIBA *See:* ROYAL INSTITUTE OF BRITISH ARCHITECTS (RIBA)

R-O-W *See:* RIGHT-OF-WAY (R-O-W)

RPA *See:* REGIONAL PLAN ASSOCIATION (RPA)

RRM *See:* RENEGOTIABLE-RATE MORTGAGE (RRM)

RTPI *See:* ROYAL TOWN PLANNING INSTITUTE (RTPI)

R/UDAT *See:* REGIONAL/URBAN DESIGN ASSISTANCE TEAM (R/UDAT)

RV   *See:* RECREATIONAL VEHICLES (RV)

SAM   *See:* SHARED-APPRECIATION MORTGAGE (SAM)

SBA   *See:* SMALL BUSINESS ADMINISTRATION (SBA)

SBIC   *See:* SMALL BUSINESS INVESTMENT COMPANY (SBIC)

SCORP   *See:* STATEWIDE COMPREHENSIVE OUTDOOR RECREATION PLAN (SCORP)

SCS   *See:* SOIL CONSERVATION SERVICE (SCS)

SCSA   *See:* STANDARD CONSOLIDATED STATISTICAL AREA (SCSA)

Section 201   *See:* WASTEWATER FACILITY PLANNING (SECTION 201)

Section 303(e)   *See:* STATE WATER QUALITY MANAGEMENT PLAN (SECTION 303[e])

Section 701   *See:* COMPREHENSIVE PLANNING GRANTS (SECTION 701)

SERI   *See:* SOLAR ENERGY RESEARCH INSTITUTE (SERI)

SHPO   *See:* STATE HISTORIC PRESERVATION OFFICER (SHPO)

SIC Code   *See:* STANDARD INDUSTRIAL CLASSIFICATION (SIC) SYSTEM

SIP   *See:* STATE IMPLEMENTATION PLAN (SIP)

SMSA   *See:* STANDARD METROPOLITAN STATISTICAL AREA (SMSA)

SNF   *see:* SKILLED NURSING FACILITY (SNF)

SREA   *See:* SOCIETY OF REAL ESTATE APPRAISERS (SREA)

SRO   *See:* SINGLE-ROOM OCCUPANCY (SRO)

SS   *See:* SUSPENDED SOLIDS (SS)

SSES   *See:* SEWER SYSTEM EVALUATION SURVEY (SSES)

STF   *See:* SUMMARY TAPE FILES (STF)

STI   *See:* SMALL TOWNS INSTITUTE (STI)

STOL   *See:* SHORT TAKEOFF AND LANDING (STOL)

TBS   *See:* REGIONAL TAX BASE SHARING (TBS)

TCPA   *See:* TOWN AND COUNTRY PLANNING ASSOCIATION (TCPA)

TDR   *See:* TRANSFER OF DEVELOPMENT RIGHTS (TDR)

TEFRA   *See:* TAX EQUITY AND FISCAL RESPONSIBILITY ACT OF 1982 (TEFRA)

TIP   *See:* TRANSPORTATION IMPROVEMENT PROGRAM (TIP)

TRB   *See:* TRANSPORTATION RESEARCH BOARD (TRB)

TSCA   *See:* TOXIC SUBSTANCES CONTROL ACT OF 1976 (TSCA)

TSM   *See:* TRANSPORTATION SYSTEM MANAGEMENT (TSM)

TVA   *See:* TENNESSEE VALLEY AUTHORITY (TVA)

UA   *See:* URBANIZED AREA (UA)

UDAG   *See:* URBAN DEVELOPMENT ACTION GRANT (UDAG)

UDC   *See:* URBAN DEVELOPMENT CORPORATION (UDC)

UI   *See:* URBAN INSTITUTE (UI)

UMTA   *See:* URBAN MASS TRANSPORTATION ADMINISTRATION (UMTA)

UPARR   *See:* URBAN PARK AND RECREATION RECOVERY PROGRAM (UPARR)

URISA   *See:* URBAN AND REGIONAL INFORMATION SYSTEMS ASSOCIATION (URISA)

USGS   *See:* GEOLOGICAL SURVEY (USGS)

UWRC   *See:* URBAN WILDLIFE RESEARCH CENTER (UWRC)

VE   *See:* VALUE ENGINEERING (VE)

VRM   *See:* VARIABLE-RATE MORTGAGE (VRM)

VTOL   *See:* VERTICAL TAKEOFF AND LANDING (VTOL)

WPA   *See:* **WORKS PROGRESS ADMINISTRATION (WPA)**

WPCF   *See:* **WATER POLLUTION CONTROL FEDERATION (WPCF)**

WRC   *See:* **WATER RESOURCES COUNCIL (WRC)**

ZBB   *See:* **ZERO-BASE BUDGET (ZBB)**

ZIMPRO   *See:* **ZIMMERMAN PROCESS (ZIMPRO)**

ZPG   *See:* **ZERO POPULATION GROWTH (ZPG)**

INDEX

ENERGY AND POWER

Architectural Design for Energy
  Conservation
Biomass Energy
Codisposal
Conservation and Renewable Energy
  Inquiry and Referral Service
Dam
Department of Energy (DOE)
Energy Audit
Energy Conservation and Production
  Act
Energy Conservation Planning
Energy-Efficient Land Use Practices
Energy Security Act
Energy Supply and Environmental
  Coordination Act of 1974
Federal Nonnuclear Energy Research
  and Development Act of 1974
Fossil Fuels
Geothermal Energy
Heat Pump
Home Weatherization
Microclimate
National Energy Act of 1978
Ocean Thermal Energy Conversion
  (OTEC)
Offshore Drilling
Outer Continental Shelf (OCS)
Pipeline
Pyrolysis
Refuse-Derived Fuel (RDF)
Renewable Energy Sources
Surface-to-Volume Ratio
Synthetic Fuels
Waterwall Incineration
Wood Fuel

See also—ELECTRIC
POWER; NUCLEAR
ENERGY; SOLAR ENERGY;
WIND

ENTERPRISE ZONES—*See* URBAN
AREA, PLANNING AND
RENEWAL

ENVIRONMENTAL
PROTECTION

American Society of Agricultural
  Engineers (ASAE)
Comprehensive Environmental
  Response, Compensation and
  Liability Act of 1980 (CERCLA)
Council on Environmental Quality
  (CEQ)
Critical Areas
Earthwatch
Energy Supply and Environmental
  Coordination Act of 1974
Environmental Analysis
Environmental Assessment
Environmental Engineering

Environmental Impact Statement
  (EIS)
Environmental Management
Environmental Mediation
Environmental Protection Agency
  (EPA)
Environmentally Sensitive Lands
Finding of No Significant Impact
  (FONSI)
Global Environmental Monitoring
  System (GEMS)
National Environmental Health
  Association (NEHA)
National Environmental Policy Act of
  1969 (NEPA)
National Environmental Satellite,
  Data and Information Service
  (NESDIS)
Scoping

See also—CONSERVATION;
ENDANGERED SPECIES;
NATURAL RESOURCES;
POLLUTION;
WILDERNESS
PRESERVATION

ENVIRONMENTAL
PSYCHOLOGY

Behavioral Design
Defensible Space
Environmental Psychology
Partners for Livable Places (PLP)
Personal Space
Privacy
Street Behavior
Territoriality

EQUAL HOUSING
OPPORTUNITY

Affirmative Fair Housing Marketing
Blockbusting
Fair Housing Legislation
Fair Share
Ghetto
Hills v. Gautreaux (1976)
James v. Valtierra (1971)
Jones v. Alfred H. Mayer (1968)
Restrictive Covenant
*Southern Burlington County NAACP
  v. Township of Mt. Laurel* (1975)
Tipping Point
*Village of Arlington Heights v.
  Metropolitan Housing
  Development Corporation* (1977)

EROSION

Bank Protection
Beach Erosion
Best Management Practices (BMPs)
Bulkhead
Groin
Jetty

Revetment
Riprap
Runoff Erosion
Seawall
Shelter Belt
Soil Conservation
Soil Erosion
Soil Erosion Control Techniques
Soil Erosion Factors
Terrace

EXCAVATION

Borrow
Cut
Excavated Pond
Excavation
Frostline

EXCLUSIONARY ZONING

Berenson v. Town of New Castle
  (1975)
*City of Memphis et al. v. N.T. Greene
  et al.* (1981)
*Construction Industry Ass'n of
  Sonoma County v. City of
  Petaluma* (1976)
Exclusionary Zoning
Fair Share
James v. Valtierra (1971)
Large-Lot Zoning
Minimum Residential Floor Area
  Requirements
*Southern Burlington County NAACP
  v. Township of Mt. Laurel* (1975)
*Village of Arlington Heights v.
  Metropolitan Housing
  Development Corporation* (1977)
Village of Belle Terre v. Boraas (1974)
Warth v. Seldin (1975)

EXPROPRIATION—*See*
EMINENT DOMAIN

FAIR HOUSING
LEGISLATION—*See* EQUAL
HOUSING OPPORTUNITY

FAMILY

Empty Nesters
Family
Household Type
Housing for Families
Moore v. City of East Cleveland, Ohio
  (1977)
Single-Family Housing
Village of Belle Terre v. Boraas (1974)

FARMLAND—*See*
AGRICULTURE; RURAL
AREAS

James v. Valtierra (1971)
Jones v. Alfred H. Mayer (1968)
Just v. Marinette County, Wisconsin (1972)
Lake Country Estates Inc. v. Tahoe Regional Planning Agency (1979)
Loretto v. Teleprompter Manhattan CATV Corp (1982)
Metromedia, Inc. v. City of San Diego (1981)
Monell v. Department of Social Services of New York (1978)
Moore v. City of East Cleveland, Ohio (1977)
Munn v. Illinois (1877)
Nectow v. City of Cambridge (1928)
Penn Central Transportation Company v. City of New York (1978)
Pennsylvania Coal Co. v. Mahon (1922)
People v. Stover (1963)
Rodgers v. Village of Tarrytown (1951)
Schad v. Borough of Mount Ephraim (1981)
Southern Burlington County NAACP v. Township of Mt. Laurel (1975)
State of Washington ex. rel. Seattle Title Trust Company v. Roberge, Superintendent of Building of City of Seattle (1928)
Village of Arlington Heights v. Metropolitan Housing Development Corporation (1977)
Village of Belle Terre v. Boraas (1974)
Village of Euclid v. Ambler Realty Co. (1926)
Warth v. Seldin (1975)
Welch v. Swasey (1909)
Young v. American MiniTheatres (1976)
Zahn v. Board of Public Works of City of Los Angeles (1927)

LEGAL PROCEEDINGS

Amicus Curiae
Certiorari
Class Action
Common Law
Injunction
Legal Notice
Public Hearing
Referendum

See also—CRIME

LEGISLATION

American Law Institute Model Land Development Code
Model Legislation

See also—Names of acts under appropriate subject headings

LEISURE, VACATION AND RETIREMENT FACILITIES

Country Club
Campground
Leisure Opportunities
Recreational Vehicles (RV)
Resort Area
Retirement Community
Second-Home Area
Sunbelt
Timesharing

See also—AGE-RELATED PLANNING AND APPLICATION; ARTS AND CULTURE PROGRAMS AND PLANNING; BOATS AND BOATING; PARKS AND RECREATION FACILITIES; THEATERS; TOURISM

LIBRARIES

Council of Planning Librarians (CPL)
Federal Despository Libraries
Library

LIGHTING—*See* OUTDOOR LIGHTING

LIGHT PLANE

Bulk Plane

LOANS—*See* CREDIT; FEDERAL AID; MORTGAGES

LOCAL DEVELOPMENT CORPORATION (LDC)

Community Development Corporation (CDC)

LOS ANGELES

Los Angeles County Regional Planning Commission
Los Angeles Zoning Ordinance

LOT

Corner Lot
Deep Lot
Front Lot Line
Frontage
Large-Lot Zoning
Lot-by-Lot Development
Lot Coverage
Lot Depth
Lot Line

Lot Width
Minimum Lot Size
Nonconforming Lot
Rear Lot Line
Side Lot Line
Through Lot
Transitional Lot
Visibility Clearance at Intersections
Zero Lot-Line Development

See also—YARD

LOW-INCOME HOUSING—*See* EQUAL HOUSING OPPORTUNITY; HOUSING

LOW-RISE HOUSING—*See* APARTMENTS; ATTACHED HOUSING

MAPS AND MAPPING

Aerial Photo Interpretation
Aerial Photographic Applications
Base Map
Cartography
Census Display Maps
Color Code
Computer Graphics
Contour Lines
Digital Cartography
Fire Insurance Atlas
Flood Hazard Boundary Map (FHBM)
Flood Insurance Rate Map (FIRM)
GBF/DIME Files
Geologic Map
Land Use Controls
Land Use Map
Light Table
Map Scale
Mapped Street
National Cartographic Information Center (NCIC)
Nodes
Official Map
Paper Street
Photogrammetry
Planimetric Map
Preliminary Plat
Real Estate Atlas
Reference Maps
Reproducible
Soil Map
Tax Map
Topographic Map
USGS Maps
Vegetation Map
Zoning Map

MARINE LIFE—*See* AQUACULTURE

OUTDOOR LIGHTING

OWNERS, ABSENTEE—*See* PROPERTY: Absentee Owner

PARIS, FRANCE

PARKING

PARKS AND RECREATION FACILITIES

See also—BEACHES; BOATS AND BOATING; LEISURE, VACATION AND RETIREMENT FACILITIES; WILDERNESS PRESERVATION

PAVEMENT

PEDESTRIANS

Accelerating Walkway
Alley
Amenity
Automobile Restricted Zone (ARZ)
Circulation Pattern
Crosswalk
Curb
Federal-Aid Urban System (FAUS)
Guardrail
Outdoor Seating
Pedestrianization
Sidewalk Cafe
Street Furniture

PERMIT

Building Permit
Permit
Special-Use Permit
Zoning Permit

PESTICIDES

Integrated Pest Management (IPM)
Pesticides
Phenols

PETROLEUM—*See* OIL

PHOTOGRAPHY—*See* AERIAL PHOTOGRAPHY

PHYSICALLY DISABLED— *See* HANDICAPPED FACILITIES

PLANNED COMMUNITY— *See* GARDEN CITIES AND GREENBELTS; NEW TOWN

PLANNING

Active Recreation
Adequate Public Facilities Ordinance
Advocacy Planning
Aerial Photo Interpretation
Age Structure
Airport Planning
Alteration
Alternative Plans
American Institute of Certified
    Planners (AICP)
American Institute of Planners (AIP)
American Planning Association (APA)
American Society of Consulting
    Planners (ASCP)
American Society of Planning Officials
    (ASPO)
Built Environment
Canadian Institute of Planners (CIP)
Capital Improvement Program (CIP)
Cheney v. Village 2 at New Hope, Inc.
    (1968)
Circumferential Plan

Code of Ethics and Professional
    Conduct
Community Development Department
Community Facility Planning
Comprehensive Plan
Comprehensive Planning Grants
    (Section 701)
Consultants
Council of Planning Librarians (CPL)
Council of State Planning Agencies
    (CSPA)
County Planning
Criminal Justice Planning
Feasibility Study
Goal
In Accordance with a Comprehensive
    Plan
Incrementalism
International Federation for Housing
    and Planning (IFHP)
L'Enfant, Major Pierre Charles
    (1754-1825)
Licensing of Planners
Linkage
Livable Cities
Local Authority
Los Angeles County Regional
    Planning Commission
Mandatory Referral
Man-Hours
Market Demand
Market Study
National Association of County
    Planning Directors (NACPD)
National Planning Board
Neighborhood Planning
New York State Commission of
    Housing and Regional Planning
Objective
Per Capita
Physical Planning
Plan Implementation
Plan Preparation
Planned Community
Planned Unit Development (PUD)
Planning Area
Planning Commission
Planning Department
Planning Director
Planning Education
Planning Federation
Planning for the Disabled
Planning for the Elderly
Planning-Programming-Budgeting
    System (PPBS)
Program Evaluation and Review
    Technique (PERT)
Public Information
Recreation Planning
Regional Plan Association (RPA)
Regional Plan of New York and Its
    Environs
Regional Planning
Regional Planning Commission
Rural Planning
Scenario Writing
School Planning

Simulation Games
Social Planning
Social Services Planning
State Planning
Target Area
Task Force
Transportation Plan
Transportation Planning
Wisconsin Planning Enabling Act of
    1909

See also—AESTHETICS;
AGE-RELATED PLANNING
AND APPLICATION;
GARDEN CITIES AND
GREENBELTS; HUMAN
SETTLEMENTS; LAND
USE; NEW TOWNS;
TOWNS AND TOWN
PLANNING; URBAN AREA,
PLANNING AND
RENEWAL

PLAYGROUNDS

Adventure Playground
Creative Play Areas
Play Street
Playground
Playground Design
Playlot

PLAZA

Amenity
Plaza
Public Art

POLLUTION

Acid Rain
Agricultural Pollution
Air Pollution
Air Pollution Control
Air Pollution Control Association
    (APCA)
Air Pollution Episode
Air Pollution Filter
Air Quality Control Region (AQCR)
Air Quality Criteria
Ambient Air
Area Source
Areawide Waste Treatment
    Management Planning (Section
    208)
Attainment Area
Best Management Practices (BMPs)
Best Practicable Technology (BPT)
Clean Air Act Amendments of 1977
Clean Air Amendments of 1970
Clean Water Act of 1977
Coliform Bacteria
Contaminant
Cyclone Collector
Dust

Public Infrastructure
Public Safety Buildings
Public Works and Development
  Facilities Program
Public Works and Economic
  Development Act of 1965
Public Works Department
Settlement House Movement
Social Planning
Social Services Planning
Urban Service Area
User Charges
Works Progress Administration
  (WPA)

See also—HEALTH CARE
SYSTEMS AND
HOSPITALS; LIBRARIES;
PARKS AND RECREATION
FACILITIES;
PLAYGROUNDS;
SCHOOLS

PUBLIC HEARING

Legal Notice
Public Hearing
Zoning Hearing Examiner

PUBLIC LAND
OWNERSHIP

Abortive or Premature Subdivision
Bureau of Land Management (BLM)
Charitable Contribution of Real
  Estate
Dedication
Department of the Interior
Eminent Domain
Excess Condemnation
General Services Administration
  (GSA)
Just Compensation
Land Bank
Land Endowment
Ordinance of 1785
Public Land Ownership
Public Use

See also—OPEN SPACE;
PARKS AND RECREATION
FACILITIES; TAKING;
WILDERNESS
PRESERVATION

PUBLIC PURPOSE

Police Power
Public Health, Safety and Welfare
Public Purpose

PYRAMIDAL ZONING

Cumulative Zoning

RAILROADS

Federal Railroad Administration
  (FRA)
High-Speed Rail Transportation
Intercity Rail Transportation
Monorail
Passenger Railroad Rebuilding Act of
  1980
Railroad Rights-of-Way
Railway Yard
Suburban Commuter Railway
Train Terminal

RAPID TRANSIT

Subways

REAL ESTATE

American Institute of Real Estate
  Appraisers (AIREA)
Arms-Length Transaction
Bid
Charitable Contribution of Real
  Estate
Conveyance
County Records
Feasibility Study
National Association of Realtors®
  (NAR®)
Quiet Enjoyment
Society of Real Estate Appraisers
  (SREA)

RECLAMATION

Fill
Surface Mining Control and
  Reclamation Act of 1977

See also—SOIL

RECORDS

County Records
Public Record

RECREATION—*See* PARKS
AND RECREATION
FACILITIES; types of
Recreation, e.g., Theaters

RECREATIONAL
VEHICLES (RV)—*See*
OFF-ROAD VEHICLES
(ORV)

RECYCLING

Activated Sludge Process
Adaptive Use
Bottle Bill
Composting
Cullet

Front-End Recovery
Glasphalt
Industrial Waste
Magnetic Separation
Recycling
Resource Recovery
Resource Recovery Act of 1970
Solid Waste Management
Source Separation
Waste Reduction

REFERRAL AND REVIEW

A-95 Review
Executive Order 12372
Mandatory Referral

RELIGIOUS INSTITUTIONS

Church Uses

RENTS AND RENTALS

Contract Rent
Gross Rent
Gross Rent Multiplier
Rent Control
Rental Housing
Section 8 Housing Program
Section 23 Housing Program

See also—APARTMENTS

REPRODUCTION PROCESS

Diazo Reproduction
Graphic Reproduction Processes
Photostat™
Sepia Intermediate

RESEARCH—*See*
INFORMATION SYSTEMS,
SURVEYS AND RESEARCH

RESTAURANTS

Drive-In Facilities
Fast-Food Restaurants
Sidewalk Cafe

RETIREMENT—*See*
LEISURE, VACATION AND
RETIREMENT FACILITIES;
OLDER PEOPLE

RIGHT OF FIRST REFUSAL

First Refusal

RIGHT-OF-WAY

Right-of-Way (R-O-W)
Right-of-Way Acquisition

See also—EASEMENT

Department of Transportation
   (DOT)
Desire Line
Dial-A-Ride
Energy Supply and Environmental
   Coordination Act of 1974
Federal-Aid Urban System (FAUS)
Federal Railroad Administration
   (FRA)
Flex-Time
Future Transportation Modes
Geometric Design
Gravity Model
Headway
Institute of Transportation
   Engineers (ITE)
Intermodal Terminal
Joint Development
Journey to Work
Mass Transit
Modal Split
Monorail
National Mass Transportation Act
   of 1974
Network Assignment
Nodes
Origin-Destination (O-D) Study
Paratransit
People Mover
Personal Rapid Transit
Ridepooling
Rolling Stock
Staggered Work Hours
Subway
Surface Transportation Act of 1978
Surface Transportation Assistance Act
   of 1982
Transit Fare Subsidies
Transit Mall
Transportation Department
Transportation Engineering
Transportation Improvement Program
   (TIP)
Transportation Plan
Transportation Planning
Transportation Research Board (TRB)
Transportation System Management
   (TSM)
Trip
Trip Distribution
Trip Generation
Trolley
Urban Mass Transportation Act of
   1964
Urban Mass Transportation
   Administration (UMTA)
Urban Mass Transportation
   Administration Discretionary
   Grant Programs

See also—AUTOMOBILE
USE; BUSES; HIGHWAYS
AND ROADS; RAILROADS

TREES—*See* FORESTRY
AND TREES

TRICKLE-DOWN THEORY

Filtering

TRUCKS

Off-Street Loading
Truck Terminals

TUNNEL—*See* BRIDGE
AND TUNNEL

TWO-FAMILY HOUSE—*See*
DUPLEX HOUSING

UNIMPROVED LAND

Raw Land

**UNINCORPORATED
AREAS**

Hamlet

**UNIVERSITIES AND
COLLEGES**

College Town
Universities

UNPLANNED GROWTH

Agglomeration
Axial Growth

**URBAN AREA, PLANNING
AND RENEWAL**

Amenity
American City Planning Institute
   (ACPI)
American Institute of Planners (AIP)
American Planning Association
   (APA)
American Society of Planning
   Officials (ASPO)
Annexation
Axial Growth
Berman v. Parker (1954)
Bettman, Alfred (1873-1945)
Blighted Area
Burnham, Daniel (1846-1912)
Central Business District (CBD)
Central Business District Plan
Central Place Theory
Ceremonial Axis Plan
Chicago Plan (1909)
Cincinnati Comprehensive Plan
Circumferential Plan
City Beautiful Movement
Concentration of Activity
Conurbation
County of London Plan (1943)
Demonstration Cities and
   Metropolitan Development Act of
   1966

Department of Housing and Urban
   Development (HUD)
Design Fit
Downtown Revitalization
Finger Pattern
Geddes, Sir Patrick (1854-1932)
Gentrification
Gridiron Pattern
Hartford Commission on a City Plan
Haussmann, Baron Georges-Eugene
   (1809-91)
Housing Act of 1949
Housing Act of 1954
Housing Act of 1964
Housing and Community
   Development Act of 1974
Housing and Home Finance Agency
   (HHFA)
Housing and Urban Development Act
   of 1965
Housing and Urban Development Act
   of 1968
Housing and Urban-Rural Recovery
   Act of 1983
Housing Assistance Plan (HAP)
Le Corbusier (1887-1965)
L'Enfant, Major Pierre Charles
   (1754-1825)
Linear City
Livable Cities
Mature City
Megastructure
Model Cities Program
Mumford, Lewis (1895-   )
National Association of Housing and
   Redevelopment Officials (NAHRO)
National Council for Urban Economic
   Development (CUED)
Pneumatic Structure
Radial Pattern
Regional/Urban Design Assistance
   Team (R/UDAT)
Relocation
San Francisco Plan
Section 221 (d)2 Housing Program
Section 221 (d)3 and 221 (d)4
   Housing Programs
Section 223 (d) Housing Program
Section 312 Housing Program
Sector Analysis
Sector Theory
Skyline
Sprawl
Standard City Planning Enabling Act
Standard Consolidated Statistical
   Area (SCSA)
Superblock
Urban County
Urban Cultural Park
Urban Design
Urban Development Action Grant
   (UDAG)
Urban Economics
Urban Enterprise Zones
Urban Growth and New Community
   Development Act of 1970
Urban Homesteading